1949-2009
和谐水电
生机无限

2009年4月2日，中共中央政治局委员、新疆维吾尔自治区党委书记王乐泉视察新疆波波娜水电站工程

2009年6月9日，全国人大常委会副委员长严隽琪到吉林哈达山水利枢纽工地视察

2009年2月16日，水利部部长陈雷视察重庆观音洞水库工程

2009年8月9日，国家发展改革委副主任、国家能源局局长张国宝视察拉西瓦水电站

三峡泄洪

公伯峡水电站工程荣获2009年度国家优质工程金质奖

泰安抽水蓄能电站荣获2009年度中国建筑工程鲁班奖

金盆水利枢纽工程荣获2009年度中国建筑工程鲁班奖

紫坪铺水利枢纽大坝工程荣获2009年国际堆石坝里程碑工程特别奖

小浪底水利枢纽工程荣获中国水利工程优质（大禹）奖

洪家渡水电站工程荣获第八届中国土木工程詹天佑奖

拉西瓦水电站大坝

2009年5月18日，拉西瓦水电站首批机组投产庆典

龙滩水库

龙滩水电站地下厂房

2009年12月11日，溪洛渡水电站右岸电站首台18号机组（77万kW）基础环吊装就位

溪洛渡水电站工程上游全景图

小湾水电站工程

2009年5月28日，小湾水电站首台机组（70万kW）转子吊装成功

瀑布沟水电站一期蓄水至790m高程

向家坝水电站全景图

2009年5月2日，瀑布沟水电站首台发电机组6号机组转子成功吊装就位

构皮滩水电站

董箐水电站

大化水电站扩建工程水轮机组整体吊装

2009年5月21日，滩坑水电站最后一台机组（20万kW）转子吊装就位

仙居抽水蓄能电站下水库

宜兴抽水蓄能电站上水库

2009年5月19日，惠州抽水蓄能电站首台机组（30万kW）投产发电

桐柏抽水蓄能电站上水库

张家口风光储输示范项目鸟瞰效果图

江苏东台风电场

内蒙古洪格尔风电场一期工程

吉林长岭风电场一期、二期工程

2009年12月2日，南水北调中线丹江口大坝右岸土石坝加高全部达到设计高程

吉林哈达山水利枢纽

伊朗塔里干水利枢纽工程荣获2009年度中国建筑工程鲁班奖

苏丹麦洛维水利枢纽工程

全国2009年装机容量

万kW

项目 / 地域	总装机容量	水电	火电	核电	风电
中国大陆	87 409.72	19 629.02	65 107.63	907.82	1759.94
中国台湾	(3970.20)	(454.00)	(2463.00)	(514.40)	(34.69)
合计	91 379.92	20 083.02	67 570.63	1422.22	1794.63

注：1. 总装机容量数中还包括太阳能、潮汐、柴油等其他能源发电装机容量。
2. 未含香港、澳门数据。

全国2009年装机容量结构图

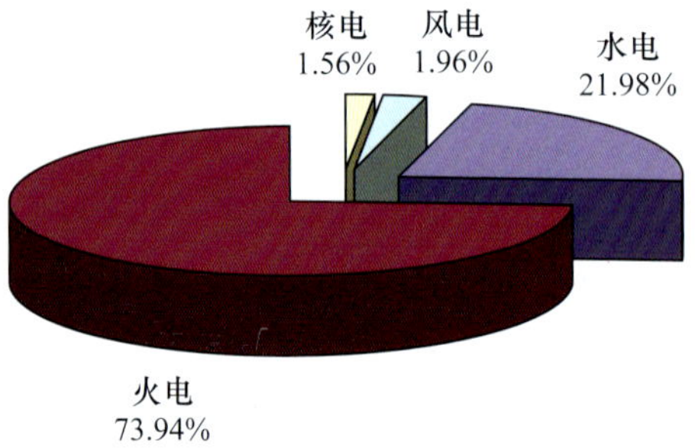

全国2009年年发电量

亿 kW・h

项目 / 地域	总发电量	水电	火电	核电	风电
中国大陆	36 811.86	5716.82	30 116.87	700.50	276.15
中国台湾	(2002.00)	(77.41)	(1307.00)	(392.60)	(6.00)
合计	38 813.86	5794.23	31 423.87	1093.10	282.15

注：1. 总发电量数据还包括其他能源发电量。
2. 未含香港、澳门数据。

全国2009年年发电量结构图

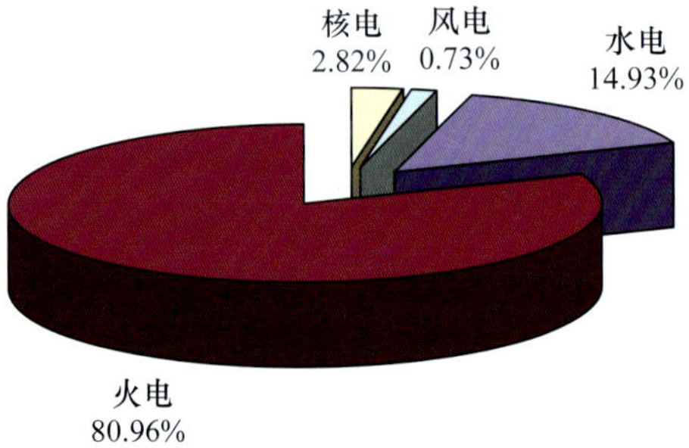

资料来源：中国大陆资料来源于中国电力企业联合会。中国台湾资料沿用2008年数据。

全国历年水电装机容量增长情况表

万kW

年份	中国大陆	中国台湾	全国合计	新增装机容量	年份	中国大陆	中国台湾	全国合计	新增装机容量
1949	36.0	18.0	54		1980	2031.8	138.6	2170	120.2
1950	36.2	22.1	58	4.3	1981	2193.3	138.7	2332	161.6
1951	37.8	(24.0)	(62)	(3.5)	1982	2295.9	138.7	2435	102.6
1952	38.5	(27.0)	(66)	(3.7)	1983	2416.5	143.1	2560	125.0
1953	53.0	(30.0)	(83)	(17.5)	1984	2560.0	148.0	2708	148.4
1954	60.6	33.0	94	10.6	1985	2641.5	248.9	2890	182.4
1955	69.5	(34.0)	(104)	(9.9)	1986	2754.2	256.4	3011	120.2
1956	91.4	(36.0)	(127)	(23.9)	1987	3019.3	255.8	3275	264.5
1957	101.9	(38.0)	(140)	(12.5)	1988	3269.8	255.8	3526	250.5
1958	121.6	(40.0)	(162)	(21.7)	1989	3458.3	256.2	3715	188.9
1959	162.0	(42.0)	(204)	(42.4)	1990	3604.6	256.2	3861	146.3
1960	194.1	44.8	239	34.9	1991	3788.3	256.2	4045	183.7
1961	233.3	(47.0)	(280)	(41.4)	1992	4068.1	257.7	4326	281.3
1962	237.9	53.8	292	11.4	1993	4489.3	257.7	4747	421.2
1963	243.0	(56.0)	(299)	(7.3)	1994	4906.1	364.8	5271	523.9
1964	268.3	(59.0)	(327)	(28.3)	1995	5218.4	418.3	5637	365.8
1965	302.0	62.8	365	37.5	1996	5557.8	428.8	5987	349.9
1966	363.8	(65.0)	(429)	(64.0)	1997	5972.6	428.8	6401	414.8
1967	383.9	(67.0)	(451)	(22.1)	1998	6506.5	442.2	6949	547.3
1968	438.8	(70.0)	(509)	(57.9)	1999	7297.1	442.2	7739	790.6
1969	505.3	72.2	578	68.7	2000	7935.2	442.2	8377	638.1
1970	623.5	90.1	714	136.1	2001	8300.6	442.2	8743	365.4
1971	780.4	(96.0)	(876)	(162.8)	2002	8607.4	451.1	9059	315.7
1972	870.0	113.1	983	106.7	2003	9489.6	451.1	9941	882.2
1973	1029.9	113.2	1143	159.9	2004	10 524.2	451.0	10 975	1034.5
1974	1181.7	136.5	1318	175.2	2005	11 738.8	451.0	12 190	1214.6
1975	1342.8	136.5	1479	161.1	2006	13 029.2	451.2	13 480.4	1290.4
1976	1465.5	136.5	1602	122.7	2007	14 823.2	452.0	15 275.2	1794.6
1977	1576.5	136.5	1713	111.0	2008	17 260.4	454.0	17 714.4	2439.2
1978	1727.7	139.2	1867	153.9	2009	19 629.0	(454.0)	20 083.0	2368.6
1979	1911.0	139.2	2050	183.3					

资料来源：2008年及以前的资料来源于《中国水力发电年鉴》第十三卷；2009年中国大陆资料来源于中国电力企业联合会；2009年中国台湾数据沿用上年数据。

注：（ ）内数据表示缺当年资料，用上、下数插补得出或沿用上年数据。

全国历年水电年发电量增长情况表

亿kW·h

年份	中国大陆	中国台湾	全国合计	年增率（%）	年份	中国大陆	中国台湾	全国合计	年增率（%）
1949	12.0	6.0	18		1980	582.1	29.3	611	11.8
1950	13.2	9.7	23	27.2	1981	655.5	47.9	703	15.1
1951	14.9	(10.0)	(25)	(8.7)	1982	744.0	47.8	792	12.6
1952	18.3	(12.0)	(30)	(21.7)	1983	863.6	49.9	913	15.4
1953	25.5	(14.0)	(40)	(30.4)	1984	867.8	44.3	912	−0.2
1954	32.0	15.6	48	20.5	1985	923.7	69.3	993	8.9
1955	34.0	(16.6)	(51)	(6.3)	1986	944.8	74.2	1019	2.6
1956	47.1	(17.0)	(64)	(26.7)	1987	1002.3	71.2	1073	5.3
1957	48.2	(18.0)	(66)	(3.3)	1988	1091.8	61.5	1153	7.4
1958	41.1	(19.0)	(60)	(−9.2)	1989	1184.5	66.8	1251	8.5
1959	43.6	(20.0)	(64)	(5.8)	1990	1263.5	81.9	1345	7.5
1960	74.1	20.6	95	48.9	1991	1248.4	55.1	1303	−3.1
1961	74.1	(21.1)	(95)	(0.5)	1992	1314.7	83.5	1398	7.3
1962	90.4	21.6	112	17.6	1993	1516.0	67.2	1583	13.2
1963	86.9	(23.0)	(110)	(−1.9)	1994	1667.9	88.9	1757	11.0
1964	106.0	(24.0)	(130)	(18.3)	1995	1867.7	88.8	1956	11.4
1965	104.1	24.4	129	−1.2	1996	1869.2	90.4	1960	0.2
1966	126.2	(25.0)	(151)	(17.7)	1997	1945.6	95.7	2041	4.2
1967	131.4	(27.0)	(158)	(4.8)	1998	2043.0	106.1	2149	5.3
1968	115.0	(28.0)	(143)	(−9.7)	1999	2129.3	89.4	2219	3.2
1969	160.1	30.5	191	33.3	2000	2431.3	78.5	2510	13.0
1970	204.6	26.4	231	21.2	2001	2611.1	82.3	2693	7.3
1971	250.6	(30.0)	(281)	(21.5)	2002	2745.7	57.9	2804	4.1
1972	288.2	34.2	322	14.9	2003	2813.3	64.3	2878	2.6
1973	389.0	34.0	423	31.2	2004	3309.9	59.7	3370	17.1
1974	414.4	47.1	461	9.1	2005	3964.0	59.7	4024	19.4
1975	476.3	52.6	529	14.6	2006	4147.7	80.0	4227.7	5.1
1976	456.4	42.8	499	−5.6	2007	4714.0	87.0	4801.0	13.6
1977	476.5	40.2	517	3.5	2008	5655.5	77.4	5732.9	19.4
1978	446.3	49.7	496	−4.0	2009	5716.8	(77.4)	5794.2	1.1
1979	501.2	45.7	547	10.3					

资料来源：2008年及以前的资料来源于《中国水力发电年鉴》第十三卷；2009年中国大陆资料来源于中国电力企业联合会；2009年中国台湾数据沿用上年数据。

注：（ ）内数据表示缺当年资料，用上、下数插补得出或沿用上年数据。

2009

中国水力发电年鉴

李锐

第十四卷

中国水力发电工程学会 主办
中国水力发电年鉴编辑部 编纂

中国电力出版社

二〇一〇年·北京

图书在版编目（CIP）数据

中国水力发电年鉴．第14卷，2009/中国水力发电工程学会编．—北京：中国电力出版社，2010.12
ISBN 978-7-5123-1215-9

Ⅰ.①中… Ⅱ.①中… Ⅲ.①水利电力工业-中国-2009-年鉴 Ⅳ.①F426.61-54

中国版本图书馆CIP数据核字（2010）第249899号

中国电力出版社出版、发行
（北京三里河路6号 100044 http：//www.cepp.com.cn）
北京盛通印刷股份有限公司印刷
各地新华书店经售
*
2010年12月第一版 2010年12月北京第一次印刷
787毫米×1092毫米 16开本 40.75印张 1337千字 12插页
定价 **298.00** 元

《中国水力发电年鉴》第十四卷

编 纂 委 员 会

陈广志	陈念水	李　军	李　毅	李小湄
李开海	李庆云	李向阳	沈清华	邹　君
杨　军	杨　薇	杨惠芬	余小波	余圣刚
张　纲	张　建	张文俊	张玉惠	张海泉
郑丽英	郑桂斌	郑淑芬	荆新爱	赵　欣
赵英林	钟共清	郭惠民	郭善成	高　菁
唐　兰	唐　勇	唐奇志	徐　芳	徐　洁
符志平	章义发	韩　冰	程　平	蒋志清
谢兴发	曾　浩	曾德安	蔡声芸	檀雅华

《中国水力发电年鉴》第十四卷
编辑出版工作人员

主　　编	邴凤山
副 主 编	黄景湖　王东棣　蔡明昌　常兆堂 毛亚杰　李　新　任景怀
技术编辑	王　玉　胡丹蓉　雷定演　孙　卓 兰海钰　李　明
终　　审	杨元峰
复　　审	杨伟国
责任编辑	安小丹　姜　萍　韩世韬　孙建英
美术设计	杨晓东
版式设计	张秋雁
责任校对	刘振英　郝军燕　闫秀英
出版印刷	蔺义舟

编　辑　说　明

（一）《中国水力发电年鉴》属专业性行业年鉴，主要面向全国水电行业从事规划、勘测、设计、施工、科研、咨询、建设管理、设备制造、生产运行、院校教育的工程技术人员、师生和各级有关领导与专家。

（二）本卷年鉴的资料时段为2009年，按序排列为第十四卷。框架结构由篇目、栏目、条目三个层次组成，共编列18个篇目、52个栏目、453个条目。每个篇目均以隔页列出，栏目、条目名称分别用通栏、双栏并铺以不同的网底印出，以示醒目。

（三）本卷年鉴的编辑工作，以邓小平理论和“三个代表”重要思想为指导，贯彻落实科学发展观，按照国家“在保护环境和做好移民工作的前提下积极开发水电”的方针，力求全面、真实地反映2009年度我国水电行业各方面所取得的成就和技术进步，做到“大事不漏、小事不上”，更好地服务于水电行业。

（四）本卷年鉴的框架结构保持相对稳定，编列的篇目为水电专业最基本的专题内容。2009年，适值新中国成立60周年，本卷年鉴在特载篇目中专门编辑了“新中国水电60年”栏目，用以纪念新中国水电建设发展的光辉历程。鉴于风力发电在新能源开发中占有重要地位，近年来有不少水电开发、建设部门已经积极涉入，本卷年鉴中仍然在“水能及风能开发”篇目中开列“风能开发”栏目，用以反映风电建设、发展的现状和前景。

（五）本年鉴实行文责自负，各条目的内容、数据、插图等均由撰稿人核对无误并由单位有关部门审定、核实。

（六）本卷年鉴编辑实行主编负责制。主编负责总体框架结构设计、征询意见、组稿与初审等工作；各篇目的编辑负责稿件的征集、修改、编排、整理。

“特载”篇目由邴凤山、蔡明昌编辑；“大中型水电工程”、“水工设计”、“人物、机构与学术团体”、“统计资料”、“大事记”篇目由黄景湖编辑；“工程勘测”、“土建施工”、“水电建设管理”、“环境保护与水库移民”、“水电工程综合效益”篇目由王东棣编辑；“机电及金属结构”、“国际合作与技术交流”、“技术标准和科技图书”、“水电站生产运行”篇目由常兆堂编辑；“水能及风能开发”、“科学研究与技术创新”、“农村水电及电气化”篇目由蔡明昌编辑；另外，英文目录由张晶晶翻译。

（七）《中国水力发电年鉴》始终坚持政治的严肃性，资料的准确性，内容的全面性、科学性、实用性和连续性，对历史负责，对后人负责。编辑过程中力求资料翔实、语言规范、文字精练。但由于水平所限，不妥、疏漏甚至错误之处在所难免，敬请广大读者批评指正。

联系地址：北京市西城区白广路二条1号中国水力发电工程学会《中国水力发电年鉴》编辑部，邮编：100761。

《中国水力发电年鉴》主编

郦凤山

2010.11

篇　　目

1. 特载
2. 水能及风能开发
3. 大中型水电工程
4. 工程勘测
5. 水工设计
6. 土建施工
7. 机电及金属结构
8. 科学研究与技术创新
9. 国际合作与技术交流
10. 技术标准和科技图书
11. 水电建设管理
12. 水电站生产运行
13. 环境保护与水库移民
14. 水电工程综合效益
15. 农村水电及电气化
16. 人物、机构与学术团体
17. 统计资料
18. 大事记

目　　录

编辑说明

1　特　　载

重要文件 …… 3
中共中央办公厅、国务院办公厅关于开展工程建设领域突出问题专项治理工作的意见 …… 3
关于印发《关于组织开展工程建设领域突出问题排查工作的意见》的通知 …… 5
规划环境影响评价条例 …… 7
国务院关于淮河流域防洪规划的批复 …… 10
国家发展改革委关于做好2009年电力运行工作的通知 …… 10
国家发展改革委关于完善境外投资项目管理有关问题的通知 …… 12
国家发展改革委关于加强中央预算内投资项目概算调整管理的通知 …… 13
国家发展改革委、国家电监会关于2008年7～12月可再生能源电价补贴和配额交易方案的通知 …… 13
国家发展改革委、财政部、水利部关于中央直属和跨省水利工程水资源费征收标准及有关问题的通知 …… 14
国家发展改革委关于完善风力发电上网电价政策的通知 …… 15
国家发展改革委、水利部关于加强小水电代燃料和水电农村电气化建设与管理的通知 …… 15
国家发展改革委办公厅关于2009年注册咨询工程师（投资）注册申报有关事项的通知 …… 16
国家发展改革委关于调整华北电网电价的通知 …… 18
国家发展改革委关于调整东北电网电价的通知 …… 19
国家发展改革委关于调整西北电网电价的通知 …… 20
国家发展改革委关于调整华东电网电价的通知 …… 21
国家发展改革委关于调整华中电网电价的通知 …… 21
国家发展改革委关于调整南方电网电价的通知 …… 22
国家发展改革委、国家电监会关于2009年1～6月可再生能源电价补贴和配额交易方案的通知 …… 23
财政部关于加强大中型水库库区基金征收管理有关问题的通知 …… 24
财政部关于征收跨省际大中型水库库区基金有关问题的通知 …… 24
财政部、国家税务总局关于再生资源增值税退税政策若干问题的通知 …… 27
水利建设市场主体信用信息管理暂行办法 …… 27
水利建设市场主体不良行为记录公告暂行办法 …… 29
供电监管办法 …… 30
水利部、国家工商行政管理总局、国家安全生产监督管理总局、国家电力监管委员会关于加强小水电站安全监管工作的通知 …… 33

领导讲话 …… 36
胡锦涛在第64届联大讲话强调加紧研发新能源和可再生能源 …… 36
国务院副总理李克强在全国能源工作座谈会上强调保能源供给推进结构调整和产业升级 …… 37
国家发展改革委副主任、国家能源局局长张国宝在水电可持续发展中心成立大会上的讲话 …… 37
水利部部长陈雷在全国农村水电工作会议上的讲话 …… 41
水利部副部长胡四一在全国小水电代燃料

工程建设现场会上的讲话（摘要） …… 46

新中国水电60年 …… 48

新中国60年水电发展的历程 …… 48

新中国60年水电建设体制的变革 …… 53

新中国60年水电科技国家级攻关项目 …… 56

新中国60年水电科技取得的主要成就 …… 56

六十“而立”的中国水电 …… 59

中国坝工技术走在世界前列 …… 60

中国大型水电机组制造瓶颈已彻底打破 …… 63

特高电压输电构筑中国电力高速公路（摘要） …… 65

新中国60年小水电波澜壮阔的发展历程 …… 67

专家论坛 …… 70

水电要为减排作更多的贡献 …… 70

叫停电站折射中国水电开发困局 …… 73

破解发展难题　有序开发水电 …… 77

从全国能源工作会议透视我国能源发展新情况 …… 78

中国如何避免水电惨案 …… 80

央企工作 …… 83

国家电网公司2009年工作情况 …… 83

中国长江三峡集团公司2009年工作情况 …… 86

中国水利水电建设集团公司2009年工作情况 …… 88

中国水电工程顾问集团公司2009年工作情况 …… 91

中国葛洲坝集团公司2009年工作情况 …… 94

2 水能及风能开发

流域规划与开发 …… 99

金沙江中游河段水电开发建设总体规划 …… 99

湖南省湘资沅澧“四水”干流水电开发方案 …… 101

西藏玉曲河流域水电开发规划 …… 102

新疆阿克苏库玛拉克河流域和台兰河流域水电开发情况 …… 102

四川绰斯甲河流域水电开发情况 …… 103

四川东义河流域水电开发及规划 …… 104

柳江梯级规划 …… 105

功果桥水电站水能利用综述 …… 111

贵州省芙蓉江沙阡水电站规划调整 …… 112

风能开发 …… 112

我国的风能资源与风力发电 …… 112

上海市海上风电场工程规划简介 …… 115

江苏省海上风电场工程规划工作简介 …… 118

江苏响水近海2MW试验风机项目实施情况 …… 119

江苏东台20万kW风电场介绍 …… 120

中水珠江规划勘测设计有限公司风电技术发展情况 …… 122

中水珠江规划勘测设计有限公司参与的几个风电项目简介 …… 123

中国水电顾问集团华东勘测设计研究院获批成立“华东海上风电省级高新技术企业研究开发中心” …… 124

3 大中型水电工程

常规水电工程 …… 129

三峡工程2009年建设情况 …… 129

溪洛渡水电站工程2009年建设情况 …… 130

向家坝水电站工程2009年建设情况 …… 132

拉西瓦水电站工程2009年建设情况 …… 134

积石峡水电站工程2009年建设情况 …… 134

瀑布沟水电站工程2009年建设情况 …… 135

深溪沟水电站工程2009年建设情况 …… 135

大岗山水电站工程2009年建设情况 …… 136

亭子口水利枢纽工程 …… 136

藏木水电站工程 …… 137

银盘水电站工程建设情况 …… 139

彭水水电站工程尾工建设情况 …… 140

潘口水电站工程简介及建设情况 …… 141

龙口水利枢纽工程2009年建设情况 …… 142

马鹿塘水电站二期工程建设情况 …… 144

蜀河水电站工程2009年建设情况 …… 145

苗家坝水电站工程建设情况 …… 146

万家口子水电站工程建设情况 …………………… 147
汉江崔家营航电枢纽工程 ……………………… 147
安江水电站 …………………………………… 148
浯溪水电站 …………………………………… 148
湘祁水电站 …………………………………… 149
白竹洲水电站 ………………………………… 149
铁川桥水电站 ………………………………… 149
巴山水电站建成发电 ………………………… 150
大化水电站扩建工程 ………………………… 150
中国水利水电建设集团公司投资的 7 个水电站 2009 年建设情况……………………… 151
中国国电集团公司在新疆、江西和云南的几个水电站 2009 年建设情况……………… 152
国电大渡河流域水电开发有限公司前期项目 2009 年筹建情况………………………… 153
四川一些水电站建设情况 …………………… 153
四川几个水电项目前期工作情况 …………… 155
贵州几个水电站建设情况 …………………… 156
云南几个水电站建设情况 …………………… 157
青海、新疆等地 7 个水电站开工建设 ……… 158
乐滩水电站工程简介 ………………………… 159
乐滩水电站老厂房利用改造情况 …………… 160
下只恩水电站建设情况简介 ………………… 160
河口水电站工程建设有关情况 ……………… 161
橙子沟水电站发电引水隧洞 C 标段工程建设简况 ……………………………………… 162
抽水蓄能工程 ……………………………… 163
蒲石河抽水蓄能电站 2009 年工程建设进展情况 ……………………………………… 163
仙居抽水蓄能电站 …………………………… 165
黑麋峰抽水蓄能电站工程 2009 年建设情况 ……………………………………………… 166
白莲河抽水蓄能电站工程 2009 年建设情况 ……………………………………………… 167
南水北调工程 ……………………………… 168
南水北调有关工程建设情况 ………………… 168

4 工程勘测

工程地质勘察与评价…………………………… 173
潘口水电站工程地质勘察与评价 …………… 173
西龙池抽水蓄能电站利用深厚覆盖层建坝工程地质研究 ……………………………………… 175
张河湾抽水蓄能电站上水库软弱夹层特性 … 176
琅琊山抽水蓄能电站上水库岩溶渗漏特征 … 177
瑯琊山抽水蓄能电站地下厂房蚀变岩工程地质特性 ……………………………………… 177
金沙江鲁地拉水电站麦叉拉沟内滑坡稳定性分析 ……………………………………… 178
溧阳抽水蓄能电站输水发电系统主要工程地质特征与评价 ……………………………… 180
红花水电站工程地质条件及评价 …………… 181
工程地质问题处理 ………………………… 183
龙开口水电站右岸变形体工程地质勘察评价及处理 ……………………………………… 183
锦屏二级水电站引水隧洞高地应力围岩破坏及其控制 …………………………………… 184
喜河水电站右导墙高陡边坡基础抗滑处理 … 186
岩溶通道涌水堵漏新技术 …………………… 188
台江水电站挡水建筑物基础处理 …………… 189
红花水电站工程地质问题的处理 …………… 190
勘测技术与设备 …………………………… 191
物探数据计算解译系统及规范化成图 ……… 191
地质雷达在西龙池抽水蓄能电站岩溶地层探测中的应用 ……………………………… 193
AutoMeas 自动测量技术在控制测量中的应用 ……………………………………………… 194
红花水电站勘测中新技术新方法的应用 …… 195

5 水工设计

大坝设计 …………………………………… 199
锦屏二级水电站拦河闸坝设计 ……………… 199
宜兴抽水蓄能电站下水库大坝设计 ………… 200
江边水电站闸坝工程设计 …………………… 202

向家坝水电站高水头大单宽流量底流消能技术研究 …… 203
混凝土面板堆石坝潜没式混凝土高趾墙设计 …… 205
张河湾抽水蓄能电站上水库沥青混凝土防渗设计 …… 207
响水涧抽水蓄能电站上水库设计 …… 208
景洪水电站左岸坝肩锚拉板设计及防渗设计 …… 209
戛洒江一级水电站坝基冲积层利用研究 …… 212
土石坝抗滑稳定分析的分项系数设计法使用简介 …… 213
地下工程设计 …… 216
小湾水电站超大型圆筒尾水调压井设计 …… 216
锦屏二级水电站地下厂房开挖支护动态设计 …… 218
响水涧工程地下厂房的优化调整设计 …… 220
糯租水电站厂区防渗设计 …… 221
岩壁吊车梁在地下洞室大范围Ⅳ～Ⅴ类围岩中的应用 …… 222
枢纽布置设计 …… 223
江苏宜兴抽水蓄能电站设计特点 …… 223
巴山水电站枢纽布置设计 …… 225
石虎塘航电枢纽工程设计简介 …… 226
官帽舟水电站枢纽布置设计 …… 227
红花水电站枢纽布置及建筑物优化设计 …… 228
导流建筑物设计 …… 229
向家坝水电站截流设计与施工 …… 229
巴山水电站大坝施工导流设计 …… 231
天花板水电站导流隧洞设计 …… 233
锦屏二级水电站进水口纵向围堰的设计与实施 …… 234

6 土建施工

大坝与围堰施工 …… 239
河口水电站基坑大体积黏土岩开挖施工 …… 239
河口水电站贯流式机组坝段施工技术 …… 240
莲麓一级水电站主体工程混凝土防渗墙施工 …… 241
锦屏二级水电站复杂地层围堰基础塑性混凝土防渗墙快速施工技术 …… 244
地下工程施工 …… 246
锦屏辅助洞工程施工 …… 246
思林水电站导流洞工程施工 …… 248
橙子沟水电站施工支洞塌方处理 …… 249
斜井施工的测量控制 …… 250
安全监测科技手段在南水北调东线穿黄隧洞工程安全管理中的应用 …… 252
截流 …… 253
锦屏二级水电站高水力学指标窄戗堤截流方案关键技术研究与实施 …… 253
毛尔盖水电站大坝枢纽工程截流与度汛施工 …… 256
钢筋石笼土石围堰在中小型水电站导截流工程中的应用 …… 257
其他 …… 260
柔性防护网系统在拉西瓦右岸高边坡防护的应用 …… 260
土锚杆在土质边坡处理中的应用 …… 261
砂浆加钢丝网截水沟在工程中的应用 …… 263
混凝土摩擦桩在复杂地质桥梁基础处理中的应用 …… 264
钢纤维混凝土的耐久性 …… 265
船坞沉箱围堰基床升浆技术研究及在青岛船坞围堰工程的应用 …… 266
玻璃钢管道施工技术 …… 268

7 机电及金属结构

水电机组及辅机 …… 273
拉西瓦水电站水轮机主要参数选择设计 …… 273
金川水电站水轮机主要参数选择 …… 275
景洪电站水轮发电机组转子组装 …… 277
彭水水电站 ALSTOM 机组水轮机接力器

安装调整 …………………………………… 279
彭水水电站水轮机埋件吊装技术 ……… 280
水轮机金属蜗壳安装施工技术 ………… 282
三峡水轮发电机组的国产化及创新 …… 284
中国水利水电第四工程局有限公司 2009 年
机电安装取得好成绩 …………………… 286
运用知识经济观念指导水机设计优化 … 286
电液同步控制筒形阀水电机组在多泥沙
水电站的应用 …………………………… 289
电气 ………………………………………… 290
小湾电站 700MW 水轮发电机组励磁系
统研制与应用 …………………………… 290
长江三峡水利枢纽船闸安全监测自动化
系统开工建设 …………………………… 292
拉西瓦水电站安全稳定控制工程 ……… 293
瀑布沟水电站送出安全稳定控制系统 … 294
新型数据采集装置在宜兴抽水蓄能电站
成功试用 …………………………………… 295
瑞丽江一级水电站跨国联网电气主接线
设计 ………………………………………… 296
抽水蓄能机组定子线棒嵌入施工工艺研究 … 297
亭子口水利枢纽左岸供水系统工程自控
设计 ………………………………………… 300
金属结构 …………………………………… 301
景洪升船机承船厢对接系统设计 ……… 301
小湾放空底孔平面链轮闸门制造关键
技术研究 …………………………………… 302
滩坑水电站泄洪洞工作弧门设计 ……… 304
红花水电站金属结构设计 ……………… 306
韩国潮汐电站钢闸门防腐蚀方案研究 … 308
超声波衍射时差法技术在瀑布沟水电站
蜗壳焊缝质量检测中的应用 …………… 309

8 科学研究与技术创新

水电科学研究 …………………………… 315
水利水电工程风险及其应对技术的研究 …… 315
丹江口重力坝加高裂缝处理研究 ……… 317
溪洛渡大坝孔口和预应力闸墩应力分析
与配筋设计研究 ………………………… 319
核安全级（1E 级）GFD 系列固定型铅酸蓄
电池组支架抗震计算分析 ……………… 321
白鹤滩水电站和桐柏抽水蓄能电站建设
运行对经济社会拉动效应研究 ………… 321
区域水资源系统供水短缺风险分析及经
济损失评估研究 ………………………… 322
吉沙水电站厂房后山坡三维有限元分析
研究 ………………………………………… 322
高陡崩塌边坡稳定性分析及 BQD 置入式
中空锚杆加固治理技术研究 …………… 323
混凝土高拱坝震害预警与对策系统研究 …… 323
300m 级高混凝土面板堆石坝可行性研究…… 323
近海风电场海上测风与试验研究 ……… 324
2009～2015 年全国小水电代燃料工程
规划调研与编制 ………………………… 325
黄河水利科学研究院科研项目进展情况 …… 325
泄洪洞内气泡运动的图像测量方法研究 …… 327
南京水利科学研究院 2009 科研工作情况…… 329
黄河水利科学研究院 2009 年科研工作
情况 ………………………………………… 330
中国水利水电建设集团公司科技工作
情况 ………………………………………… 332
中国水电顾问集团贵阳勘测设计研究院
2009 年科技工作简况 …………………… 332
太阳能电源点的合理开发 ……………… 332
水电技术创新 …………………………… 334
三峡右岸电站计算机监控系统研制开发 …… 334
小湾拱坝极限承载力及变形稳定分析
与评价 ……………………………………… 335
景洪水电站水力浮动式升船机整体模型
试验研究 …………………………………… 336
三峡梯调监控系统升级完善 …………… 337
湖南凤滩水电厂扩机工程计算机监控系统
研制开发 …………………………………… 337
葛洲坝水电厂二次设备 GPS 统一对时系统
改造 ………………………………………… 337
三峡左岸电站 WEB 生产实时信息发布系统
升级 ………………………………………… 338
车载式液压驱动泵装置研制 …………… 338
碧口大坝震后补强加固处理 …………… 339
不吊转子对 45MW 水轮发电机定子槽内进行
探查的方法研究与实践 ………………… 339
百龙滩水电厂重锤下坠防护方案研究 … 340
大化水电厂 2 号机协联曲线分析与校验 …… 340
乐滩水电厂汛期水位动态控制研究 …… 341
可调式密封盖在水轮发电机油槽上的
应用 ………………………………………… 341

微功耗无线网在线防误操作系统在那兰水电厂的应用 …… 342
黑启动试验方案首次在云南中型水电厂成功应用 …… 342
梨园水电站可能最大洪水研究 …… 342
云南省低热微膨胀水泥研发及其在水电工程中的应用 …… 344
工程地球物理层析成像技术的研究和应用 … 345
特大型深水软弱地基群桩基础施工成套技术研究 …… 346
国产化计算机监控系统在龙滩水电站的研制应用 …… 347
电气主接线可靠性定量分析研究及完全4/3断路器接线在龙滩水电站的应用 …… 347
中国水利水电第三工程局有限公司2009年科技工作情况 …… 347
中国水利水电第八工程局有限公司2009年科技工作情况 …… 348
获奖项目简介 …… 350
中华人民共和国水力资源复查成果（2003年） …… 350
特大型人工砂石系统研究与应用 …… 351
唐家山堰塞湖应急除险工程技术研究及实践 …… 352
水布垭高面板堆石坝施工关键技术研究与实践 …… 352
糯扎渡水电站截流和高土石围堰快速施工技术研究和应用 …… 353
水电站厂房和机电系统三维可视化协同设计研究与工程应用 …… 353
巨型水轮机转轮工地制造 …… 354
双曲薄拱坝快速施工技术研究与实践 …… 354
水利水电与电网气象综合监测系统 …… 355
大荷载、高扬程固定卷扬式启闭机研制 …… 355
变顶高尾水隧洞施工技术研究 …… 356
沅水流域梯级水库调度系统开发与应用研究 …… 357
《碾压式土石坝设计规范》(DL/T 5395—2007) …… 357
大花水狭窄河谷高碾压混凝土拱坝筑坝技术研究 …… 358
钢筋混凝土面板堆石坝坝身溢洪道关键技术研究及应用 …… 358
大坝安全实时监测和预警系统 …… 359
陡倾角薄层灰岩及大规模蚀变岩支护技术在地下洞室群中的研究应用 …… 360
水轮发电机组励磁大功率整流自冷散热系统 …… 361
瀑布沟水电站砾石土心墙料筛分输送系统的应用研究 …… 361
龙滩水电站大法坪砂石系统关键技术研究与应用 …… 362
新老混凝土结合界面密合剂 …… 362
高黏结高渗进在役混凝土复合增强材料的研究 …… 363
碾压式沥青混凝土面板防渗技术研究 …… 364
岩石与水耦合理论及其应用 …… 364
57MW超大型灯泡贯流式水轮发电机组安装技术研究 …… 365
大型渠道混凝土快速衬砌施工技术研究 …… 365
基于节能的水电厂监控软件 …… 366
《水电水利工程环境保护设计规范》(DL/T 5402—2007) …… 366
大掺量磨细矿渣混凝土关键技术研究与应用 …… 367
碾压混凝土外掺MgO筑坝技术研究与应用 …… 367
河谷边坡稳定性演化机理与调控方法 …… 368
高混凝土坝结构安全与优化理论及工程应用 …… 368
南京水利科学研究院2009年度科研项目获奖情况 …… 369
黄河水利科学研究院2009年度科技成果获奖情况 …… 369
中国水电顾问集团华东勘测设计研究院2008、2009年科技成果获奖情况 …… 370
中国水电顾问集团昆明勘测设计研究院2009年获奖情况 …… 370
中水珠江规划勘测设计有限公司2009年度获奖成果 …… 371
专利项目简介 …… 371
无源零开断的自动灭磁装置及方法 …… 371
无伸缩节坝后式引水压力钢管的结构 …… 372
水电站尾水管检修闸门翻板式锁定装置 …… 372
水力浮动式升船机运行对接控制装置 …… 374
高性能混凝土抗裂性能组合式评价装置 …… 374
地震波CT成像压电陶瓷串状检波器 …… 375
黄河水利科学研究院获四项国家专利 …… 375
中国水电顾问集团华东勘测设计研究院2009年获得专利情况 …… 376
中国水利水电第五工程局有限公司2009年度获得专利情况 …… 377

中国水利水电第八工程局有限公司 2009 年获得专利情况 …… 377

9 国际合作与技术交流

国际技术交流 …… 381
国际大坝委员会第 77 届年会和第 23 届大会简况 …… 381
第一届堆石坝国际研讨会在成都召开 …… 382
"气候变化对大坝的挑战"国际研讨会暨中日韩大坝委员会第六次学术交流会 …… 383
农村水电国际交流与合作 …… 384
武汉大学 2009 年水利水电国际合作与交流情况 …… 384
黄河水利科学研究院 2009 年国际学术交流情况 …… 385
对外经营与国外工程 …… 385
中国水利水电建设集团公司 2009 年国际经营情况 …… 385
越南广治水电站机电设备成套项目 …… 388
越南 SeSan4 水电站机电设备成套项目简介 …… 388
哈萨克斯坦玛依纳水电站设计简介 …… 389
几个中国投资或承包的国外水电工程建设情况 …… 390
中国水电工程顾问集团公司与缅甸联邦电力一部签署瑙帕与曼栋水电站开发谅解备忘录 …… 390
湄公河干流大坝战略环境评价（SEA）合作初步会议在昆明召开 …… 391

10 技术标准和科技图书

标准化工作管理 …… 395
2009 年电力标准化管理情况 …… 395
我国电力企业标准化工作开展情况 …… 396
2009 年农村水电技术标准制修订情况 …… 396
中国水电顾问集团贵阳勘测设计研究院标准化工作开展情况 …… 397
泰山抽水蓄能电站 2009 年标准化建设工作情况 …… 398
技术标准的制修订情况 …… 399
2009 年国家标准化管理委员会批准的电力国家标准计划项目 …… 399
2009 年住房和城乡建设部批准的电力工程建设国家标准计划项目 …… 399
2009 年国家能源局批准的电力行业标准计划项目（水电、电气部分） …… 401
2009 年电力标准英文版翻译计划项目 …… 408
电力行业标准《水电水利工程预应力锚索施工规范》（送审稿）通过审查 …… 408
《水电站气垫式调压室设计规范》送审稿通过审查 …… 409
新颁标准 …… 409
2009 年国家标准化管理委员会发布的电力国家标准 …… 409
2009 年国家能源局发布的电力行业标准（水电、电气部分） …… 410
2009 年水利标准完成情况 …… 413
科技图书出版 …… 414
中国电力出版社有限公司 2009 年出版的水电新书 …… 414
《中国小水电 60 年》出版发行 …… 415

11 水电建设管理

工程管理 …… 419
中国大唐集团公司水电工程建设管理综述 …… 419
缅甸太平江一级水电站项目建设管理 …… 421
江边水电站施工期的风险评估咨询 …… 422

琅琊山抽水蓄能电站项目监理档案的质量审核 …… 423
思林水电站导流洞工程施工监理 …… 425
缅甸瑞丽江一级水电站的开发建设模式 …… 426
水利水电建设项目的后评价 …… 427
对铁川桥水电站工程总承包的初步认识 …… 430
龙滩水电工程信息化管理体系 …… 430
企业管理 …… 432
中国长江电力股份有限公司 2009 年经营情况 …… 432
中国水利水电建设集团公司的企业经营管理 …… 434
黄河上游水电开发有限责任公司 2009 年经营管理情况 …… 435
龙滩水电开发有限公司 2009 年经营情况 …… 436
华能澜沧江水电有限公司开展融资租赁 …… 438
国网新源控股有限公司 2009 年工作情况 …… 439
黄河万家寨水利枢纽有限公司 2009 年经营管理情况 …… 440
国电陕西水电开发有限公司 2009 年经营管理情况 …… 441
国电海南大广坝发电有限公司 2009 年经营管理情况 …… 442
国电新疆艾比湖流域开发有限公司 2009 年经营管理情况 …… 443
新型水电厂培训仿真系统在二滩水电站成功应用 …… 444
中国水利水电第三工程局有限公司信息系统安全建设 …… 445

12 水电站生产运行

电力生产及管理 …… 449
中国长江电力股份有限公司 2009 年电力生产情况 …… 449
黄河上游水电开发有限责任公司所属大中型水电站 2009 年生产管理情况 …… 450
龙滩水电站 2009 年生产运行情况 …… 452
江苏宜兴抽水蓄能电站 2009 年运行及管理情况 …… 454
山东泰山抽水蓄能电站 2009 年运行及管理情况 …… 455
万家寨水利枢纽 2009 年生产运行情况 …… 456
乐滩水电厂 2009 年生产运行情况 …… 457
国电万安水力发电厂 2009 年生产运行情况 …… 458
国电四川南桠河流域水电开发有限公司生产运行有关情况 …… 459
龙羊峡电站开展推进无人值班运行专题调研 …… 460
国电长源老渡口水电有限公司的生产管理 …… 461
技术改造 …… 462
三峡发输电安全稳定控制系统改造工程 …… 462
二滩水电站送出安全稳定控制系统改造工程 …… 463
二滩水电站川电东送安控装置技术改造 …… 464
泰山抽水蓄能电站 2 号机组水导油槽盖板改造 …… 465
龚嘴水电站机组增容改造情况 …… 466
凤滩水电厂 2 号机组尾水锥管改造土建施工工艺 …… 467
水情预报与调度 …… 468
三峡水库洪水预报方案设计 …… 468
南瑞通用实时洪水预报系统设计与开发 …… 469
2008 年三峡入库洪水特点与预报效果评价 …… 470
南瑞通用实时洪水预报系统在三峡 2009 年洪水预报中的应用情况 …… 471
基于洪水地区组成的梯级水库群防洪控制水位研究 …… 472
碧口水库水情测报系统改造情况 …… 474
乌江流域梯级水库远程集中调度与水电站群安全经济运行 …… 475
华光潭梯级水电站的水库优化调度问题 …… 476
大坝安全管理 …… 477
2009 年水电站大坝安全监管工作概况 …… 477
2009 年水电站大坝安全注册情况 …… 478
2009 年水电站大坝安全定期检查工作进展情况 …… 478
2009 年水电站大坝安全信息化建设进展情况 …… 479
2009 年水电站大坝安全监测管理简况 …… 479
2009 年水电站大坝缺陷消除和补强加固工作情况 …… 479
强化大坝安全培训，夯实大坝安全管理的

基础 …………………………………………… 480
2009 年水电工程安全鉴定情况 ……………… 480
大坝安全管理与对丰满病坝的处理意见 …………………………………………… 482
参数查询在大坝安全信息系统中的应用 …… 483
乐滩大坝安全管理 …………………………… 484
大坝安全监测与分析 ……………………… 485
南瑞大坝安全信息管理系统使用 PocketPC 实现人工观测数据的自动化处理 ……………… 485
新型大坝安全监测系统在八盘峡水电站成功试用 …………………………………………… 486
二滩大坝安全监测系统技术改造 …………… 486
乐滩水电站大坝安全自动化监测系统试运行自评价 ………………………………………… 487
水电站高精度外部变形监测网 ……………… 488
我国大型水电工程的安全监测有关情况 …………………………………………… 490
大坝安全实时监控和预警系统的开发及应用 ………………………………………… 492
三板溪混凝土面板坝面板破损原因分析 …… 493
云鹏水电站大坝渗流安全监测资料分析 …… 494
陈村拱坝下游面 105m 高程水平向裂缝长期分析研究情况 ………………………………… 495
上标水电站压力钢管的安全监控系统 ……… 497
大坝维修 …………………………………… 499
混凝土防渗灌浆技术及在丰满电站降渗工程的应用 ………………………………………… 499
碧口水电站汶川地震受损修复情况 ………… 500
葛洲坝三江防淤堤护坡破损原因分析及加固措施研究 ……………………………………… 500
安康水电站表孔消力池底板破坏原因分析及补强加固处理 ………………………………… 501
鲁布革水电站发耐滑坡综合治理实施 ……… 503
葛洲坝二江弧门工作模态测试 ……………… 504

13　环境保护与水库移民

环境保护 …………………………………… 509
三峡水库开县消落区综合治理与保护规划 … 509
澜沧江水电开发与生态环境保护 …………… 510
向家坝水电站工程环境保护实施情况 ……… 512
金沙江白鹤滩水电站“三通一平”水土保持工作 …………………………………………… 513
锦屏二级水电站弃渣场防护 ………………… 515
光照水电站进水口分层取水工程 …………… 516
贵州北盘江水电开发两生态保护项目简介 … 516
滩坑水电站工程水土保持设计、监理和监测工作 ………………………………………… 517
桐柏抽水蓄能电站水土保持设施验收 ……… 520
周公宅水库水土保持工程设计 ……………… 521
龙开口水电站开展施工期环境保护与水土保持监理工作 ……………………………………… 523
多自然型河流建设措施的初探 ……………… 525
黄河上游已建梯级电站的水环境累积效应 … 527
龙滩水电工程库区水土保持治理 …………… 529
移民工程 …………………………………… 530
龙滩水电站库区移民实行淹没耕地长期补偿 …………………………………………… 530
现行水电工程移民人口界定方法的合理性 … 532
水电工程移民综合监理工作程序与方法研究 …………………………………………… 535
乐滩水电站 2009 年移民安置工作简况……… 536

14　水电工程综合效益

我国水电的经济效益和社会效益显著 ……… 541
沅水梯级开发综合效益显著 ………………… 543
清江梯级枢纽工程的综合效益 ……………… 545
新安江水电站建成 50 年来对钱塘江水量调节的贡献 ……………………………………… 547
棉花滩水电站的综合效益 …………………… 548
贵州农村水电惠及山区百姓 ………………… 549
猫跳河梯级建设对贵州经济社会发展的促进作用 …………………………………………… 550
我国 2009 年批准的清洁发展机制水电项目为世界每年减排温室气体 723 万余吨 …… 553

15 农村水电及电气化

农村水电建设 …… 557
小水电点亮中国农村 …… 557
2009年农村水电发展综述 …… 559
水电农村电气化建设 …… 561
小水电代燃料工程建设 …… 561
农村水电管理 …… 563
水能资源管理 …… 563
农村水电行业安全监管 …… 564

16 人物、机构与学术团体

人物 …… 569
中国科学院院士王光谦 …… 569
中国工程院院士张建云 …… 569
中国工程院院士钟登华 …… 570
机构 …… 570
水电建设单位情况一览表 …… 570
水电设计单位情况一览表 …… 571
水利设计单位情况一览表 …… 572
水利水电施工单位情况一览表 …… 573
华北水利水电学院简况 …… 575
学术团体 …… 576
中国水力发电工程学会2009年工作情况 …… 576
中国水力发电工程学会分支机构情况表 …… 578
各省、市、自治区水力发电工程学会组织情况表 …… 580
中国大坝协会2009年工作情况 …… 584
中国水利学会2009年工作情况 …… 587

17 统计资料

2009年全国水电增长情况表 …… 591
2009年全国电源工程建设项目投资完成情况表 …… 592
2009年水电施工企业完成产值及工程量表 …… 592
2009年全国农村水电年末装机及发电量情况表 …… 593
2009年全国大中型水电厂生产运行情况表 …… 594
2009年全国电力统计基本数据一览表 …… 598

18 大事记

CONTENTS

Chapter 1 Specials

1) Important Documents

Suggestions on the outstanding special undertaken problems in the field of engineering construction of CPC Central Committee and State Council

Circular on the issuance of "Advice on organizing outstanding troubleshooting work in the field of engineering construction"

Planning Environmental Impact Assessment Ordinance

State Council's approval on the Huai river basin flood control planning

Circular of State Development and Reform Commission on "Doing well in power operation work in 2009"

Circular of National Development and Reform Commission on "Improving project management issues related to overseas investment"

Circular of National Development and Reform Commission on "Strengthening budget adjustments administration of the inner central budget for investment projects"

Circular of National Development and Reform Commission and State Power Regulatory Commission on "The renewable energy price subsidies and quota trading program in July to December, 2008"

Circular of National Development and Reform Commission, Ministry of Finance and Ministry of Water Resources on "Water fee collection standards and related issues of the directly under the central government and inter-provincial water conservancy resources"

Circular of National Development and Reform Commission on "Improving the net power price policy of wind power generation"

Circular of National Development and Reform Commission and Ministry of Water Resources on "Strengthening the construction and management of fuel replaced by small hydropower and the rural electrification"

Circular of Office of the National Development and Reform Commission on "Registered consulting engineer (investment) report issues"

Notice of National Development and Reform Commission on the price adjustments in North China Power Grid

Notice of National Development and Reform Commission on the price adjustments in Northeast Power Grid

Notice of National Development and Reform Commission on the price adjustments in Northwest Power Grid

Notice of National Development and Reform Commission on the price adjustments in East China Power Grid

Notice of National Development and Reform Commission on the price adjustments in Central China Power Grid

Notice of National Development and Reform Commission on the price adjustments in Southern China Power Grid

Circular of National Development and Reform Commission, State Electricity Regulatory Commission on "The renewable energy price subsidies and quota trading program in January to June, 2009"

Circular of Ministry of Finance on "Enhancing the fund collection management issues of medium-sized reservoir"

Circular of Ministry of Finance on "Collection for the inter-provincial fund issues of medium-sized reservoir"

Circular of Ministry of Finance and the State Administration of Taxation on "VAT rebate policy on renewable resources, etc."

Interim Measures on the main credit information management of water construction market

Interim Measures on the notice of misconduct records of water construction market

Power supply monitoring and control measures

Circular of Ministry of Water Resources, State Administration for Industry, the State Administration of Production Safety Supervision and Management and State Electricity Regulatory Commission on "Strengthening the safety supervision of small hydropower stations"

2) Speeches of the Leaders

Hu Jintao's speech emphasizing to intensify the development of new energy and renewable energy at the 64th session of the General Assembly

Vice Premier Li Keqiang stressed the energy supply security to promote structural adjustment and industrial upgrading on the national energy forum

Speech of the deputy director of National Development and Reform Commission and the secretary of the National Energy Bureau Zhang Guobao at the sustainable hydropower development center established conference

Speech of Chen Lei, the Minister of Water Resources at rural electrification meeting

Speech of Hu Siyi, the vice minister of Water Resources in the national Small Hydropower replacing fuel project site (Abstract)

3) 60 Years of New China Hydropower

The 60 years' history of hydropower development in new China

The 60 years' structural reform of hydropower construction in new China

Hydropower projects included in the national scientific research

The 60 years' main achievements of hydropower technology in new China

The 60 years' construction fruits of China hydropower

The dam construction technology of China is at the leading position of the world

Bottlenecks in China's large hydropower generating units manufacturing have been completely broken

UHV transmission builds the highway of China Power (Abstract)

The 60 years' magnificent development of small hydropower of in new China

4) Expert Forum

Hydropower should make more contribution to emission reduction

Halting the station reflects the difficulties of China's hydropower development

Solve development problems and develop the hydropower orderly

Perspective the new situation of China's energy development from the national energy conference

How to avoid water tragedy in China-Inspiration from the Sayang tragedy of Russia

5) The Work of Central Enterprises

The work of State Grid Corporation in 2009

The work of China Three Gorges Corporation in 2009

The work of Sinohydro Corporation in 2009

The work of Hydrochina Corporation in 2009

The work of China Ge Zhouba (Group) Corporation in 2009

Chapter 2 Exploitation of Hydro and Wind Power

1) Planning and Development of River Basin

Major plan of hydropower development for the middle reaches of Jinsha River

Programme of hydropower development for Yuan Li Xiang Zi four rivers in Hunan province

Hydropower development planning of Tibet Yuqu river

Hydropower development of Akesukumalake and Tailan river in Xinjiang province

Hydropower development of Chuosijia river in Sichuan province

Hydropower development and planning of Dongyi river in Sichuan province

Cascade planning of Liujiang

Summary of Gongguoqiao hydropower station's water using

Planning and adjustment of Shaqian hydropower station based in Furongjiang of Guizhou province

2) Development of Wind Power

Wind resources and wind power generation of China

Introduction of offshore wind farm project planning in Shanghai

Introduction of offshore wind farm project planning in Jiangsu province

Implementation status of Offshore 2MW pilot wind turbine project in Xiangshui, Jiangsu province

Introduction of 200 000 kW wind power farm in dongtai, Jiangsu province

The development of wind power technology of China Water Resources Pearl River Planning Surveying and Designing Co., Ltd.

Introduction of several wind power projects of China Water Resources Pearl River Planning Surveying and Designing Co., Ltd.

China Hydropower Engineering Consulting Group East China Investigation and Design Institute is approved the establishment of 'East China maritime wind power of high-tech enterprises research and development centers of the provincial level'

Chapter 3 Big and Medium-Sized Hydropower Project

1) Conventional Hydropower Project

Construction situation of Three Gorges project in 2009

Construction situation of Xiluodu hydropower station in 2009

Construction situation of XiangJiaba hydropower station in 2009

Construction situation of Laxiwa hydropower station in 2009

Construction situation of Jishixia hydropower station in 2009

Construction situation of Pubugou hydropower station in 2009

Construction situation of Shenxigou hydropower station in 2009

Construction situation of Dagangshan hydropower station in 2009

Construction situation of Tingzikou Water Control Project

Construction situation of Zangmu hydropower station

Construction situation of Yinpan hydropower Project

Last construction work of Pengshui hydro-

power project
Introduction and construction situation of Pankou hydropower project
Construction situation of Longkou Water Control Project in 2009
The phase II construction work of Malutang hydropower station
Construction situation of Shuhe hydropower station in 2009
Construction situation of Miaojiaba hydropower station
Construction situation of Wanjiakouzi hydropower station
Hanjiang Cuijiaying Navigation Project
Anjiang hydropower station
Wuxi hydropower station
Xiangqi hydropower station
Baizhuozhou hydropower station
Tiechuanqiao hydropower station
Bashan hydropower station was established and began to generate power
Project extension of Dahua hydropower station
Seven hydropower construction work in 2009 invested by Sinohydro Corporation
Construction situation of several hydropowers in Xinjiang, Jiangxi and Yunnan province invested by China Guodian Corporation
Pre-project preparation status of Guodian Daduhe Hydropower Development Co., Ltd. in 2009
Construction situation of a number of hydropower stations in Sichuan province
Preliminary works of several hydropower projects in Sichuan province
Construction situation of several hydropower stations in Guizhou province
Construction situation of several hydropower stations in Yunnan province
Eight hydropower stations were under construction in Qinghai, Xinjiang province etc.
Hydropower project overview of Letan hydropower station
Rebuilding and reuse of the old plant of Letan hydropower station
Construction situation of Xiazhi'en hydropower station
Construction situation of Hekou hydropower station
Construction situation of C section of power tunnel project of Chengzigou hydropower station
2) Pumped Storage Project
Project progress of Pushihe pumped storage station in 2009
Xianju pumped storage station
Construction status of Heimifeng pumped storage station in 2009
Construction status of Bailianhe pumped storage station in 2009
3) South-to-North Water Diversion Project
Construction status of South-to-North water diversion project

Chapter 4 Engineering Investigation

1) Engineering Geological Exploration and Evaluation
Geological exploration and evaluation of Pankou hydropower station
Geological study of Xilongchi pumped storage station making use of overburden dam project
Soft interlayer of properties of reservoir of Zhanghewan pumped storage station
Characteristics of karst seepage of the reservoir of Langyashan pumped storage station
Geological characteristics of underground plants altered rock project
Stability analysis of Maichala ditch landslide of iang Ludila hydropower station

in Jinsha river
Major geological features and evaluation of Water transmission and power generation system of Liyang pumped storage station
Geological conditions and evaluation of Honghua hydropower station

2) Solutions of Engineering Geological Problems

Geological survey evaluation and treatment of the right bank deformed engineering of Longkaikou hydropower station
Diversion tunnel and the control of high stress surrounding rock mass and its control of Jinping-Ⅱ hydropower station
Basic anti-sliding treatment of the right guide wall high and steep slope of Xihe hydropower station
New technology of plugging in gushing water in karst channel
Foundation treatment of retaining buildings of Taijiang hydropower station
Treatment of engineering geological problems of Honghua hydropower station

3) Surveying Technology and Equipment

Geophysical data calculation & interpretation systems and standardized mapping
GPR application in the detection of karst formations of Xilongchi pumped storage station
Application of AutoMeas automatic measurement technology in the control measurement
Application of new technologies and new methods in the investigation of Honghua hydropower station

Chapter 5 Hydraulic Design

1) Dam Design

Sluice dam design of Jinping-Ⅱ hydropower station
Lower Reservoir dam design of Yixing pumped storage station
Dam engineering of Jiangbian hydropower station
Energy dissipation technology study on high head and large unit discharge flow of Xiangjiaba hydropower station
Submerged concrete high retaining wall design of concrete face rockfill dam
Asphalt concrete seepage design of the upper reservoir of Zhanghewan pumped storage station
Design of the upper reservoir of Xiangshuijian pumped storage station
Left abutment anchor board design and seepage control design of Jinghong hydropower station
Use of foundation alluvium of Gasajiang-Ⅰ hydropower station
User guide of the partial coefficient design of dam anti-sliding stability analysis

2) Design of Underground Engineering

Large cylindrical tail water surge tank design of Xiaowan hydropower station
Underground plant dynamic design excavation of Jinping-Ⅱ hydropower station
Optimal adjustment design of underground house of Xiangshuijian program
Seepage design of Nuozu hydropower station
Application of crane beam in a wide range of Ⅳ～Ⅴ class of underground rock

3) Pivot Layout Design

Design features of Yixing pumped storage station in Jiangsu province
Pivot layout design of Bashan hydropower station
Shihutang navigation and power complex preview
Pivot layout design of Guanmaozhou hydropower station
Pivot layout and building optimization of Honghua hydropower station

4) Design of Diversion Structures

Closure design and construction of Xiangjiaba hydropower station

Dam construction diversion design of Bashan hydropower station

Diversion tunnel design of Tianhuaban hydropower station

Longitudinal cofferdam intake design and implementation of Jinping-Ⅱ hydropower station

Chapter 6 Civil Construction

1) Construction of Dam and Cofferdam

Excavation and construction of foundation rock mass clay pit of Hekou hydropower station

Technology of tubular turbine dam construction of Hekou hydropower station

Concrete seepage wall of the main body construction of Lianlu-Ⅰ hydropower station

Rapid construction technology of complex formation based on plastic concrete cutoff wall cofferdam of Jinping-Ⅱ hydropower station

2) Underground Project Construction

Construction of Jinping auxiliary tunnel project

Construction of diversion tunnel of Silin hydropower station

Treatment of branch tunnel collapse construction of Chengzigou hydropower station

Measurement and control of shaft construction

Application of scientific and technological secure monitoring means in the safe management of the east line of South to North Yellow River tunnel project

3) Closure

Key technology research and implementation of mechanical index of narrow high-water dike closure scheme of Jinping-Ⅱ hydropower station

Dam closure and the flood control project construction of Maoergai hydropower station

Application of cofferdam reinforced gabion in diversion and closure project of small and medium-sized hydropower stations

4) Others

Application of flexible protection system in slope protection of right bank of Laxiwa hydropower station

Application of earth bolt in soil slope treatment

Application of drainage ditches mortar and steel mesh in the project

Application of concrete file in complicated geological bridge basic treatment

Durability of steel fiber reinforced concrete

Dock caisson cofferdam Foundation Bed prepacked research and its application in Qingdao dock cofferdam program

Construction technology of FRP pipe

Chapter 7 Mechanical and metal structure

1) Hydroelectric Units and Auxiliary Equipment

Main parameters of turbine design of Laxiwa hydropower station

The main parameters chosen of Jinchuan hydropower station turbine

Turbine generator unit's rotor assembly of Jinghong hydropower station

Installation adjustment of ALSTOM unit turbine servomotor of Pengshui hydropower station

Lifting technology of hydraulic turbines embedded parts of Pengshui hydropower station

Installation technology of turbine metal spiral

Domestication and innovation of Three Gorges hydro-generating unit

Good results of mechanical and electrical installation achieved in 2009 of Sinohydro Engineering Bureau 4 Co. , Ltd.

Using knowledge-based economy guiding hydraulic design optimization.

Application of cylinder valves electro-hydraulic synchronous control and hydraulic unit in sediment-laden hydropower station

2) Electricity

Development and application of 700MW hydro exciting system of Xiaowan hydropower station

Yangtze River Three Gorges lock safety monitoring automation system being under construction

Stability control project of Laxiwa hydropower station

Submitting stability control system of Pubugou hydropower station

Successful trial of new data acquisition device in Yixing pumped storage station

Transnational networking of main electric wiring design of Ruilijiang- I hydropower station

Study on pumped storage unit stator embedded technology

Left bank water supply self-controlled system engineering design of Tingzikou water control

3) Metal Structue

Ship Carrier docking system design of Jinghong hydropower station

Key technology of bottom sprocket plane making gate shorting of Xiaowan hydropower station

Spillway radial gate design of Tankeng hydropower station

Metal structure design of Honghua hydropower station

Steel gate anti-corrosion scheme of South Korea tidal station

Application of ultrasonic flight diffraction technique in detection of spiral weld quality of Pubugou hydropower station

Chapter 8 Scientific Research and Technological Innovation

1) Hydropower Research

Study on risk and countermeasures of hydropower and water resources

Study on treatment of Danjiangkou heightening gravity crack dam

Study on stress analysis and reinforcement design of orifice and prestressed pier of Xiluodu dam

Calculation and analysis of nuclear safety (1E-level) GFD series of fixed-type lead-acid batteries' seismic support

The pulling effect on the economy and society of the construction and operation of Baihetan hydropower station and Tongbai pumped storage station

Risk analysis and assessment of economic loss of the water supply shortage of regional water resources system

Three-dimensional finite element analysis of the Jisha hillside powerhouse

Study on stability analysis of steep slope and collapse into hollow bolt BQD reinforcement technology

Damage warning of concrete arch dam and countermeasure system study

Feasibility study on 300m high level concrete faced rockfill dam

Experimental study of wind offshore wind

farm at sea
Planning investigation and preparation of national small hydropower replacing fuel project in 2009～2015
Research progresses of Yellow River Institute of Hydraulic Research
Study on image measurement method of discharge inside bubble motion
Research work of Nanjing Hydraulic Research Institute in 2009
Research work of Yellow River Institute of Hydraulic Research in 2009
Technology work of Sinohydro Corporation
Research work of Hydro-China Guiyang Engineering Corporation in 2009
Rational development of solar power points

2) Innovation of Hydropower Technology

Research and development of power station computer monitoring system of the right bank of Three Gorges
Analysis and evaluation on ultimate bearing capacity of Xiaowan arch dam and its deformation stability
The overall model test of Jinghong hydraulic floating ship lift
Upgrade and improvement of the monitoring system of THREE GORGES CASCADED DISPATCH
Research and development of Hunan Fengtan hydropower plant expansion project computer monitoring system
The secondary device GPS system unification reform of Gezhouba hydropower plant
Upgrade of WEB production real-time information distribution system of Three Gorges left bank hydropower station
Study on truck-mounted hydraulic drive pump
Treatment after the earthquake reinforcement of Bikou dam
Research and practice of detection of not suspended rotor on 45MW turbine generator stator slot
Hammer fallen protection scheme of Bailongtan hydropower plant
Unit 2 connected curve analysis and verification of Dahua hydropower plant
Dynamic control of water level in flood season of Letan hydropower plant
Application of adjustable closures in turbine generator tank
Application of Micro-power wireless network online operating error prevention system in Nalan hydropower plant
The first successful application of Black Start Test program in Yunnan medium-sized hydropower plant
Probable maximum flood study of Liyuan hydropower station in the middle reaches of Jinshajiang
Low heat expansive cement R & D and its application in hydropower projects of Yunnan province
Research and application of engineering geophysical tomography technology
Foundation construction of complete sets technology of ultra-large group of soft soil deep pile
The reliability and quantitative analysis of main electrical wiring and its application in complete 4/3 breaker in Longtan hydropower station
Application and research of domesticated computer monitoring system of the giant hydropower station in Longtan hydropower station
Research work of Sinohydro Engineering Bureau 3 Co., Ltd. in 2009
Research work of Sinohydro Engineering Bureau 8 Co., Ltd. in 2009

3) Awarded Projects

Review results of water resources of PRC (2003)
Research and application of ultra-large artificial gravel system
Research and practice of emergency elimi-

nated danger engineering technology of TangJiangshan Yanse lake
Research and practice of the key construction technology of high CFRD of Shuibuya
Research and application of rapid construction technology of the closure and high cofferdam of Nuozhadu hydropower station
Study and engineering application of hydropower plant electrical and mechanical three-dimensional visualization of collaborative design
Site manufacturing of the giant turbine runner
Study and practice of rapid construction technology of double-curvature masonry arch dam
Water and weather power grid monitoring system
Development of heavy load and high-lift fixed hoist winch
Construction technology study of ceiling height changes tailrace tunnel
Development and application of the Yuanshui cascade reservoir system
"Rolled earth dam design standard" (SD/T 5395—2007)
High RCC arch dam construction technology of Dahuashui narrow valley
Application and key technologies of reinforced concrete-faced rockfill dam spillway
Real-time dam safety monitoring and early warning systems
Study and application of thin limestone and mass steep altered rock support technology in underground caverns
Hydro-generating unit excitation power rectifier self-cold and cooling system
Application of sieving conveyor system of gravel soil core material in Pubugou hydropower station
Key technology research and application of Dafaping aggregate system of Longtan hydropower station
The seal of new and old concrete mixture
Study on high infiltrated and high bond existing composite concrete reinforcement material
Impervious rolled asphalt concrete panel seepage technology
Theory and applications of rocks and water coupling
Installation technology study on 57MW ultra-large bulb tubular units
Construction technology study on quick lining of large concrete channels
Monitoring software of hydropower plants based on energy conservation
"Environmental design of hydropower" (DL/T 5402—2007)
Research and application of key technologies of amount of ground slag concrete
Research and application of MgO-RCC dam
Valley slope stability evolution mechanisms and control methods
The structural safety, optimization theory and engineering application of high concrete dam
Awarded projects of Nanjing Hydraulic Research Institute in 2009
Awarded projects of Yellow River Institute of Hydraulic Research in 2009
Science and technology achievements awards of Hydro-china Corporation East China Investigation and Design Institute
Awarded projects of Hydro-china Kunming Investigation and Design Institute in 2009
Awarded projects of China Water Resources Pearl River Planning Surveying & Designing Co., Ltd. in 2009
4) Patent Project Introduction
"Automatic zero-breaking passive excitation device and method" won the national invention patent

Introduction of practical new patents "No expansion joint dam toe penstock diversion structure"
Introduction of practical new patents "Tube maintenance gate turn plate locking device of hydropower station"
Introduction of practical new patents "Hydraulic floating lift ship operation docking control device"
Introduction of practical new patents "Combined Evaluation Device of crack resistance of high performance concrete"
Introduction of practical new patents "CT imaging of seismic wave detector clusters of piezoelectric ceramic"
Yellow River Institute of Hydraulic Research won four national patents
Patent cases of Hydro-china Corporation East China Investigation and Design Institute in 2009
Patent cases of Sinohydro Engineering Bureau 5 Co., Ltd. in 2009
Patent cases of Sinohydro Engineering Bureau 8 Co., Ltd. in 2009

Chapter 9 International Cooperation and Technology Exchange

1) International Technology Exchange
Brief of the 77th annual meeting of International commission on large dams and the 23rd sessions of general assembly
The first international rockfill dam symposium was held in Chengdu
The challenges of climate change on dam international symposium and the 6th academic symposium of China, Japan and South Korea committee on large dams
International exchanges and cooperation in rural hydropower
International cooperation and exchange of hydropower and water resource situation of Wuhan University
International cooperation and exchange of hydropower and water resource situation of Yellow River Water Resources Research Institute
2) International Business and Overseas Projects
International business of Sinohydro Corporation in 2009
Complete sets of mechanical and electrical equipment project of Vietnam Guangzhi hydropower station
Introduction of complete sets of mechanical and electrical equipment project of Vietnam SeSan4 hydropower station
Design introduction of Kazakhstan Mayina hydropower station
Construction state of several foreign hydropower projects invested or contracted by China
China Hydropower Engineering Consulting Corporation and the first Union of Myanmar signed the development and the understanding memorandum of Naopa and Mandong hydropower station
Mekong River dam strategic preliminary meeting of environmental assessment (SEA) cooperation was held in Kunming

Chapter 10 Technical Norms and Technological Book

1) Standardization Management
Standardized management of electricity in 2009
Implementation situation of standardization of power enterprises work in China
Revision situation of technical standards of rural hydropower technology
Implementation situation of standardization

of Hydro-china Corporation Guiyang Investigation and Design Institute
Standardization work of Taishan pumped storage station in 2009

2) Technical Standards Making and Amendment

Approval of national standards for electricity projects by National Standardization Management Committee in 2009
Approval of national standards of power engineering construction projects by the Ministry of Housing and Urban in 2009
Approval of the power industry standard project by National Energy Bureau in 2009
Translation projects of power standardization of English version in 2009
Power industry standard "For construction standard of hydropower and water conservancy prestressed cable (draft) " passed the censor
Standard "Air cushion surge chamber of hydropower station (draft)" passed the censor

3) Issue of New Standards

National power standards issued by State Committee for Standardization in 2009
National power standards issued by National Energy Bureau in 2009
Completion situation of water resources standards in 2009

4) Publishing of Technological Books

Hydropower book published by China Electric Power Press Co., Ltd. in 2009
The book "60 years of small hydropower in China" was published

Chapter 11 Management of Hydropower Construction

1) Management of Projects

Summary of construction management of hydropower project by China Datang Group Corporation
Project construction management of Burma Peace River 1st class hydropower station
The risk assessment consulting during the construction of Jiangbian hydropower station
The quality audit of project supervision files of Langyashan pumped storage station
Diversion tunnel construction supervision of Silin hydropower station
Development and construction model of Burma Ruili River 1st class hydropower station
Post-evaluation of water resource and hydropower construction projects
Preliminary knowledge of general contract to Tiechuanqiao hydropower station
Information management system of Longtan hydropower project

2) Management of Enterprises

Enterprise management of China Yangtze Power Co., Ltd. in 2009
Enterprise management of Sinohydro Corporation
Enterprise management of Yellow River Hydropower Development Co., Ltd.
Enterprise management of Longtan Hydropower Development Co., Ltd.
Huaneng Lancang River Hydropower Co., Ltd. carrying out financial leasing
Work situation of State Grid Xinyuan Holdings Limited in 2009
Operation and management state of Yellow River Wanjiazhai Water Limited in 2009
Operation and management state of Guodian Shanxi Hydropower Development Co., Ltd. in 2009
Operation and management state of Guodian Hainan Daguangba Generation Co., Ltd. in 2009
Operation and management state of Guodian Xinjiang Aibi Lake Basin Develop-

ment Co., Ltd. in 2009
New power plant training simulator system successful applied to the Ertan hydropower station
Information system security construction of Sinohydro Engineering Bureau 3 Co., Ltd.

Chapter 12 Production and Operation of Hydropower Stations

1) Power Generation and Management
Hydropower generation of China Yangtze Power Co., Ltd. in 2009
Production and management of Huanghe Hydropower Development Co., Ltd. owned large and medium-sized hydropower station in 2009
Production and operation of Longtan hydropower station in 2009
Operation and management of Jiangsu Yixing pumped storage station in 2009
Operation and management of Shandong Taishan pumped storage station in 2009
Production and operation of Wanjiazhai water control in 2009
Production and operation of Letan hydropower plant in 2009
Production and operation of Guodian Wan'an hydroelectric power plant in 2009
Production and operation of Guodian Sichuan Nanyahe Basin Water Development Co., Ltd.
Longyangxia hydropower station carrying out to promote the special investigations and studies of unattended operation
Production and management of Guodian Changyuan Laodukou Hydropower Co., Ltd.
2) Technology Update
Reconstruction project of Three Gorges power generation and transmission stability and safety control system
Reconstruction project of Ertan power submit stability and safety control system
Security and control device modification of Ertan hydropower station Sichuan to east power project
The water guide oil pot cover transformation of Taishan pumped storage power station unit 2
Rehabilitation unit case of Gongzui hydropower station
Civil construction technology of Fengtan hydropower plant unit 2 tail water reconstruction
3) Hydrologic Forecasting and Scheduling
Design of the Three Gorges reservoir flood forecasting
Real-time flood forecasting system design and development of Nari General
Characteristics of the Three Gorges reservoir flood of 2008 and the forecast Evaluation
Real-time flood forecasting system design and development of Nari General applied to flood forecasting of Three Gorges in 2009
Cascade reservoir flood control water level study based on flood area
Reconstruction of Bikou hydrological forecasting system
Remote centralized scheduling and safe economic operation of hydropower stations in Wujiang river cascade reservoirs
Optimal scheduling problem of reservoir in Huaguangtan cascade hydropower stations
4) Dam Safety Management
Overview of dam safety monitoring in 2009
Dam safety registration state in 2009
Progress of dam safety regular inspection in 2009
Progress of information construction of hy-

dropower dam safety in 2009
Brief introduction of monitoring and management of hydropower dam safety in 2009
Defect elimination of hydropower dam and reinforcement work in 2009
Strengthening the dam safety training, reinforcing the foundation of dam safety management
Safety appraisal situation of hydropower project in 2009
Dam safety management and opinions on the Fengman "disease dam"
Application of parameter query in the dam safety information system
Safety management of Letan dam

5) Dam Safety Monitoring and Analysis

Nari dam safety information management system using PocketPC to achieve automated processing by human observational data
Successful trial of new dam safety monitoring system in Bapanshui hydropower station
Reconstruction of Ertan dam safety monitoring system
Self-assessment test run of automatic monitoring system of dam safety of Letan hydropower station
High-precision external deformation monitoring grid of hydropower station
Safety monitoring situation of large hydropower projects in China
Real-time dam safety monitoring and the development and application of early warning system
Sanbanxi panel damage causes of CFRD
Safety monitoring analysis of dam seepage of Yunpeng hydropower station
Long-term analysis of Chencun 105m downstream surface of dam elevation horizontal cracks
Safety monitoring system of penstock of Shangbiao hydropower station

6) Dam Maintenance

Concrete impervious grouting technology and its application in infiltration reduction project of Fengman hydropower station
Repair of Wenchuan earthquake damage in Bikou hydropower station
Gezhouba Sanjiang silting damage causes of slope protection and reinforcement measure study
Spillway stilling cause analysis and reinforcement treatment of Ankang hydropower station
Comprehensive management implementation of resistant to landslide of Lubuge hydropower station
Arc gate work mode test of Gezhouba Erjiang

Chapter 13 Environment Protection and Resettlement of Reservoir Area Residents

1) Environment Protection

Comprehensive management and protection plan of Kaixian drawdown area of Three Gorges reservoir
Hydropower development and environment protection of Lancang River
Implementation of environmental protection of Xiangjiaba hydropower station project
Soil and water conservation of the "three open and one level" of Jinsha river Baihetan hydropower station
Java disposal Areas Protection of Jinping-Ⅱ hydropower station
Stratified water from the intake projects of Guangzhao hydropower station
Hydropower development of two eco-conservation project of Guizhou Beipanjiang

Soil and water conservation design, supervision and monitoring of Tankeng hydropower station project
Acceptance of soil and water conservation of Tongbai pumped storage station
Soil and water conservation engineering of Zhougongzhai reservoir
Longkaikou hydropower station carrying out the supervision work of the environmental protection and water conservation during the construction period
Study on more natural type of river-building measures
Water environment cumulative effect of cascade hydropower stations have been built in the upstream of Yellow River
Soil and water conservation in Longtan hydropower project reservoir area

2) Resettlement of Residents

Implementation of long-term compensation for the submerged land of the residents in Longtan hydropower project reservoir area
The reasonability of the definition method of the current hydropower project immigrant population
Program and method study of comprehensive supervision of hydropower project immigration
Resettlement briefing of Letan hydropower station in 2009

Chapter 14 Comprehensive Benefits of Hydropower Projects

Significant effect of economic and social benefits of hydropower in China
Comprehensive benefits of cascade development for Yuanshui
Comprehensive benefits of cascade water control project of Qingjiang
The contribution of Xin' anjiang hydropower station built for 50 years to the water regulation of Qiantang River
Comprehensive benefits of Mianhuatan hydropower station
Guizhou rural hydropower benefits to the mountain people
The promoting role of Maotiaohe Guizhou cascade construction to the economic and social development
The CDM hydro projects approved in 2009 reducing 7.23 million tons of greenhouse gas emission for the world

Chapter 15 Rural Hydropower and Electrification

1) Rural Hydropower Construction

Small hydropower lit rural China
Review of rural hydropower development in 2009
Electrification construction of hydropower in rural area
Construction of small hydropower instead of fuel

2) Rural Hydropower Management

Water resources management
Safety supervision of rural hydropower industry

Chapter 16 People, Agencies and Academic Groups

1) Prominent Figures

Wang Guangqian, Academician of Chinese Academy of Sciences
Zhang Jianyun, Academician of Chinese Academy of Engineering
Zhong Denghua, Academician of Chinese

Academy of Engineering

2) Agencies

List of hydropower construction corporation

List of hydropower designing corporation

List of water resource designing corporation

List of water resource hydropower construction corporation

Briefing of North China University of Water Resource and Electric Power

3) Academic Groups

Work state of China Society for Hydropower Engineering in 2009

Table of branches of China Society for Hydropower Engineering

Table of organization of provinces, municipalities and autonomous regions of Society for Hydropower Engineering

Work state of Chinese National Committee on Large Dams in 2009

Work state of Chinese Hydraulic Engineering Society in 2009

Chapter 17 Statistic Materials

National hydropower growth table in 2009

Completing table of national power construction project investment in 2009

Output value and engineering scale table of hydropower construction enterprises in 2009

Installed capacity and power generation table of national rural hydropower in 2009

Operation and production statistical table of the national large and medium hydropower station in 2009

List of the basic data of national power in 2009

Chapter 18 Big Events

彩色插页目录

2009年4月2日，中共中央政治局委员、新疆维吾尔自治区党委书记王乐泉视察新疆波波娜水电站工程

2009年6月9日，全国人大常委会副委员长严隽琪到吉林哈达山水利枢纽工地视察

2009年2月16日，水利部部长陈雷视察重庆观音洞水库工程

2009年8月9日，国家发展改革委副主任、国家能源局局长张国宝视察拉西瓦水电站

三峡泄洪

公伯峡水电站工程荣获2009年度国家优质工程金质奖

泰安抽水蓄能电站荣获2009年度中国建筑工程鲁班奖

金盆水利枢纽工程荣获2009年度中国建筑工程鲁班奖

紫坪铺水利枢纽大坝工程荣获2009年国际堆石坝里程碑工程特别奖

小浪底水利枢纽工程荣获中国水利工程优质(大禹)奖

洪家渡水电站工程荣获第八届中国土木工程詹天佑奖

拉西瓦水电站大坝

2009年5月18日，拉西瓦水电站首批机组投产庆典

龙滩水库

龙滩水电站地下厂房

2009年12月11日，溪洛渡水电站右岸电站首台18号机组（77万kW）基础环吊装就位

溪洛渡水电站工程上游全景图

小湾水电站工程

2009年5月28日，小湾水电站首台机组（70万kW）转子吊装成功

向家坝水电站全景图

瀑布沟水电站一期蓄水至790m高程

2009年5月2日，瀑布沟水电站首台发电机组6号机组转子成功吊装就位

构皮滩水电站

董箐水电站

大化水电站扩建工程水轮机组整体吊装

2009年5月21日，滩坑水电站最后一台机组（20万kW）转子吊装就位

仙居抽水蓄能电站下水库

宜兴抽水蓄能电站上水库

2009年5月19日，惠州抽水蓄能电站首台机组（30万kW）投产发电

桐柏抽水蓄能电站上水库

张家口风光储输示范项目鸟瞰效果图

江苏东台风电场

内蒙古洪格尔风电场一期工程

吉林长岭风电场一期、二期工程

2009年12月2日，南水北调中线丹江口大坝右岸土石坝加高全部达到设计高程

吉林哈达山水利枢纽

伊朗塔里干水利枢纽工程荣获2009年度中国建筑工程鲁班奖

苏丹麦洛维水利枢纽工程

全国2009年装机容量

全国2009年装机容量结构图

全国2009年年发电量

全国2009年年发电量结构图

全国历年水电年装机容量增长情况表

全国历年水电年发电量增长情况表

中國水力發電年鉴

1

特　　载

重　要　文　件

中共中央办公厅、国务院办公厅关于开展工程建设领域突出问题专项治理工作的意见

经党中央、国务院同意，2009年7月9日中共中央办公厅、国务院办公厅以中办发［2009］27号文，印发《关于开展工程建设领域突出问题专项治理工作的意见》的通知。意见内容全文如下：

为认真贯彻落实《中共中央关于印发〈建立健全惩治和预防腐败体系2008～2012年工作规划〉的通知》（中发［2008］9号）的有关要求，规范工程建设领域市场交易行为和领导干部从政行为，维护社会主义市场经济秩序，促进反腐倡廉建设，现就开展工程建设领域突出问题专项治理工作提出如下意见。

一、治理工作的重要性和紧迫性

近年来，各地区各部门采取有效措施，认真治理工程建设领域中存在的问题，工程建设市场不断健全，监管体制日益完善，钱权交易、商业贿赂等腐败现象滋生蔓延的势头得到了一定程度的遏制。但是，必须清醒地看到，我国工程建设领域依然存在许多突出问题。一是一些领导干部利用职权插手干预工程建设，索贿受贿；二是一些部门违法违规决策上马项目和审批规划，违法违规审批和出让土地，擅自改变土地用途、提高建筑容积率；三是一些招标人和投标人规避招标、虚假招标，围标串标，转包和违法分包；四是一些招标代理机构违规操作，有的专家评标不公正；五是一些单位在工程建设过程中违规征地拆迁、损害群众利益、破坏生态环境、质量和安全责任不落实；六是一些地方违背科学决策、民主决策的原则，乱上项目，存在劳民伤财的“形象工程”、脱离实际的“政绩工程”和威胁人民生命财产安全的“豆腐渣”工程。上述这些问题严重损害公共利益，影响党群干群关系，破坏社会主义市场经济秩序，妨碍科学发展和社会和谐稳定，人民群众反映强烈。为此，中央决定，用2年左右的时间，集中开展工程建设领域突出问题专项治理工作。

各地区各部门要充分认识开展工程建设领域突出问题专项治理工作的重要性和紧迫性，切实采取措施，加大治理力度，维护公平竞争的市场原则，推动以完善惩治和预防腐败体系为重点的反腐倡廉建设深入开展，促进工程建设项目高效、安全、廉洁运行，保证中央关于扩大内需促进经济平稳较快发展政策措施的贯彻落实，维护人民群众的根本利益，促进科学发展，保持社会和谐稳定。

二、治理工作的总体要求、主要任务和阶段性目标

（一）总体要求

高举中国特色社会主义伟大旗帜，以邓小平理论和“三个代表”重要思想为指导，深入贯彻落实科学发展观，全面贯彻落实党的十七大精神，紧紧围绕扩大内需、加快发展方式转变和结构调整、深化重点领域和关键环节改革、改善民生、促进和谐等任务，以政府投资和使用国有资金的项目为重点，以改革创新、科学务实的精神，坚持围绕中心、统筹协调，标本兼治、惩防并举，坚持集中治理与加强日常监管相结合，着力解决工程建设领域存在的突出问题，切实维护人民群众的根本利益，为经济社会又好又快发展提供坚强保证。

（二）主要任务

进一步规范招标投标活动，促进招标投标市场健康发展；进一步落实经营性土地使用权和矿业权招标拍卖挂牌出让制度，规范市场交易行为；进一步推进决策和规划管理工作公开透明，确保规划和项目审批依法实施；进一步加强监督管理，确保行政行为、市场行为更加规范；进一步深化有关体制机制制度改革，建立规范的工程建设市场体系；进一步落实工程建设质量和安全责任制，确保建设安全。

（三）阶段性目标

工程建设领域市场交易活动依法透明运行，统一规范的工程建设有形市场建立健全，互联互通的诚信体系初步建立，法律法规制度比较完善，相关改革不断深化，工程建设健康有序发展的长效机制基本形成，领导干部违法违规插手干预工程建设的行为受到严肃查处，腐败现象易发多发的势头得到进一步遏制。

三、治理工作的重点和主要措施

（一）认真进行排查，找准突出问题

深入开展自查。各地区各有关部门要对照有关法

律法规和政策规定，认真查找项目决策、城乡规划审批、项目核准、土地审批和出让、环境评价、勘察设计和工程招标投标、征地拆迁、物资采购、资金拨付和使用、施工监理、工程质量、工程建设实施等重点部位和关键环节存在的突出问题。要紧密结合实际，认真开展自查，摸清存在问题的底数，掌握涉及问题单位和人员的基本情况。

深刻分析原因。针对发现的问题和隐患，从主观认识、法规制度、权力制约、行政监管、市场环境等方面，分析产生的根源，查找存在的漏洞和薄弱环节，提出改进的措施和办法，明确治理工作的目标和责任要求，增强治理工作的科学性、预见性和实效性。

严肃自查纪律。对不认真自查的地方和部门，要加强督导；对拒不自查、掩盖问题或弄虚作假的，要严肃处理。对自查出的违纪问题，要根据情节轻重、影响大小等作出处理。对虽有问题但能主动认识和纠正的，可以按照有关规定从轻、减轻或免予处分。各地区各部门要将自查情况书面报告中央治理工程建设领域突出问题工作领导小组。领导小组适时对自查情况进行重点检查。

（二）加大监管力度，增强监管效果

突出监管重点。着重加强项目建设程序的监管，严格执行投资项目审批、核准、备案管理程序，规范项目决策，科学确定项目规模、工程造价和标准，认真落实开工报告制度、施工许可证制度和安全生产许可证制度，确保工程项目审批和建设依法合规、公开透明运行。着重加强对招标投标活动的监管，规范招标方式确定、招标文件编制、资格审查、标段划分、评标定标、招标代理等行为，改进和完善评标办法，确保招标投标活动公开、公平、公正。着重加强土地、矿产供应及开发利用情况的监管，完善土地及矿业权审批、供应、使用等管理的综合监管平台。着重加强控制性详细规划制定和实施监管，严格控制性详细规划的制定和修改程序。着重加强项目建设实施过程监管，严格依法征地拆迁，坚持合理工期、合理标价、合理标段，严格合同订立和履约，规范设计变更，科学组织施工，加强资金管理，控制建设成本，禁止转包和违法分包。着重加强工程质量与安全监管，落实工程质量和安全生产领导责任制，进一步完善质量与安全管理法规制度，明确质量标准，细化安全措施，强化施工监理，防止重、特大质量与安全事故的发生。

落实监管职责。各级政府要加强对工程建设项目全过程的监管，认真履行对政府投资项目的立项审批、项目管理、资金使用和实施效果等方面的职责。发展改革、工业和信息化、财政、国土资源、环境保护、住房城乡建设、安全监管等有关部门要依照有关法律法规，认真履行对项目决策、资金安排和管理、土地及矿业权审批和出让、节能评估审查、环境影响评价、城乡规划审批、安全生产等环节的行政管理职责。发展改革、工业和信息化、住房城乡建设、交通运输、铁道、水利、电监等部门要按照职责分工，重点做好对工程建设项目的监管。财政、审计部门要重点做好对政府投资项目资金和国有企业投资项目资金的监管，确保资金规范、高效、安全、廉洁使用。对因监管不力、行政不作为和乱作为以及行政过失等失职渎职行为造成重大损失的，要严肃追究责任单位领导和有关人员的责任。

创新监管方式。充分发挥招标投标部际联席会议机制作用，健全招标投标行政监督机制。建立健全相关制度，加强对招标投标从业机构和人员的规范管理。加大工程建设项目行政执法力度。组织实施对政府重大投资项目的跟踪审计。积极推进项目标准化、精细化、规范化和扁平化管理。发挥工程监理机构的专业监督作用，加强工程建设质量和安全生产的过程监管。推行管理骨干基本固定、劳务用工相对灵活、职责明确、高效运作的劳务管理模式。充分发挥新闻媒体的作用，加强对工程建设领域的舆论监督和社会监督。

（三）深化体制改革，创新机制制度

加快改革步伐。加强重大项目决策管理，推行专家评议和论证制度、公示和责任追究制度。发布招标投标法实施条例，抓紧研究起草政府投资条例、建筑市场管理条例。继续做好《标准施工招标资格预审文件》、《标准施工招标文件》贯彻实施工作，加快编制完成行业标准文件，实现招标投标规则统一。不断深化国库集中支付制度改革，加强工程项目政府采购管理。科学编制、严格实施土地利用总体规划，严格土地用途管制，严格土地使用权、矿业权出让审批管理。制定控制性详细规划编制审批管理办法，规范自由裁量权行使。严格执行国家有关法律法规，提高法律法规的执行力和落实度。

加强市场建设。按照政府建立、规范管理、公共服务、公平交易的原则，坚持政事分开、政企分开，打破地区封锁和行业垄断，整合和利用好各类有形建筑和建设市场资源，建立健全统一规范的工程建设有形市场，为工程交易提供场所，为交易各方提供服务，为信息发布提供平台，为政府监管提供条件。按规定必须招标的工程建设项目要实行统一进场、集中交易、行业监管、行政监察。建立健全统一规范的土地、矿业权等要素市场，大力推进土地市场、矿业权市场建设，探索显化土地使用权和矿业权转让市场的有效形式，规范土地使用权和矿业权市场交易行为。

充分利用网络技术等现代科技手段，积极推行电子化招标投标。加强评标专家库管理，提高专家的职业道德水平。制定全国统一的评标专家分类标准和专家管理办法。加强中介组织管理，严格土地使用权、矿业权价格评估的监管，规范招标代理行为。

健全诚信体系。完善工程建设领域信誉评价、项目考核、合同履约、黑名单等市场信用记录，整合有关部门和行业信用信息资源，建立综合性数据库。充分利用各种信息平台，逐步形成全国互联互通的工程建设领域诚信体系，实现全行业诚信信息共建共享，并将相关信用信息纳入全国统一的企业和个人征信系统。建立健全失信惩戒制度和守信激励制度，严格市场准入。

（四）加大办案力度，坚决惩治腐败

严肃查处违纪违法案件。要坚决查办工程建设领域的腐败案件，发现一起，查处一起，绝不姑息。重点查办国家工作人员特别是领导干部利用职权插手干预城乡规划审批、招标投标、土地审批和出让以牟取私利甚至索贿受贿的大案要案。严厉查处违法违规审批立项，规避和虚假招标，非法批地，低价出让土地，擅自变更规划和设计、改变土地用途和提高容积率，严重侵害群众利益等违纪违法案件。坚决查处在工程项目规划、立项审批中因违反决策程序或决策失误而造成重大损失或恶劣影响的案件。依法查处生产安全责任事故，严肃追究有关领导人的责任。既要坚决惩处受贿行为，又要严厉惩处行贿行为。坚决杜绝瞒案不报、压案不查的行为。

积极拓宽案源渠道。充分发挥各级纪检监察、司法、审计等机关和部门信访举报系统的作用，形成有效的举报投诉网络，健全举报投诉处理机制。注重在审计、财政监察、项目稽查、执法监察、专项检查、案件调查和新闻媒体报道中发现案件线索，深挖工程质量问题和安全事故背后的腐败问题。

健全办案协调机制。各级纪检监察机关、司法机关、审计部门和金融机构等要加强协作配合，完善情况通报、案件线索移送、案件协查、信息共享机制，形成查办案件的合力。对涉嫌犯罪案件，要及时移送司法机关依法查处。充分发挥查办案件的治本功能，深入剖析大案要案，严肃开展警示教育，认真查找体制机制制度方面存在的缺陷和漏洞，做到查处一起案件，教育一批干部，完善一套制度。

四、加强对治理工作的组织领导

成立中央治理工程建设领域突出问题工作领导小组，由中央纪委牵头，最高人民检察院、国家发展改革委、工业和信息化部、公安部、监察部、财政部、国土资源部、环境保护部、住房城乡建设部、交通运输部、铁道部、水利部、中国人民银行、审计署、国务院国资委、工商总局、安全监管总局、国务院法制办、电监会等为成员单位。领导小组下设办公室，承担日常工作。各地区各有关部门要切实加强领导，把治理工作作为一项重要任务列入工作日程，认真完成职责范围内的任务。各职能部门主要领导同志负总责，确定1名领导同志具体负责，落实责任分工。各级纪检监察机关要加强组织协调，会同有关部门作出总体部署，搞好任务分解，推动工作落实。各有关部门要及时沟通情况，加强协作配合，形成工作合力。

各地区各有关部门要结合实际，制定贯彻落实本意见的具体方案，确定治理重点，明确目标任务、工作进度、方式方法和时间要求。要深入排查问题、认真进行整改，完善体制机制制度，分阶段、有步骤地落实好专项治理工作的各项任务。中央治理工程建设领域突出问题工作领导小组适时组织对各地区各有关部门工作进展情况进行抽查。

各地区各有关部门要将专项治理工作与深入学习实践科学发展观活动相结合，着力解决影响和制约科学发展的突出问题以及党员干部党性党风党纪方面群众反映强烈的突出问题。要将专项治理工作与治理商业贿赂工作相结合，依法查处工程建设领域的商业贿赂案件，进一步规范市场秩序，维护公平竞争。要将专项治理工作与推进政务公开相结合，利用政府门户网站建立工程建设项目信息平台，向社会公示项目建设相关信息，明确审批流程，及时公布审批结果，实行行政审批电子监察。要将专项治理工作与纠正损害群众利益的不正之风相结合，大力加强部门和行业作风建设，着力解决工程建设领域侵害群众利益的突出问题。

各地区各有关部门要加强监督检查，开展分类指导，督促工作落实。要加强调查研究，注意解决苗头性、倾向性问题，总结经验，推动工作。对组织领导不到位、方法措施不得力、治理效果不明显的地方、部门和单位要提出整改要求，重点督查，限期整改，确保治理工作达到预期目标。

关于印发《关于组织开展工程建设领域突出问题排查工作的意见》的通知

中治工发［2009］12号

各省、自治区、直辖市治理工程建设领域突出问题工作领导小组，新疆生产建设兵团治理工程建设领域突出问题工作领导小组，中央和国家机关各部门：

《关于组织开展工程建设领域突出问题排查工作的意见》已经中央治理工程建设领域突出问题工作领导小组同意。现印发你们，请结合实际，认真贯彻执行。

排查问题是开展专项治理工作的重要步骤和基础。排查工作开展得好坏，直接关系整个专项治理工作的成效。各地区各有关部门要按照本意见的要求，以高度负责的态度，精心组织，求真务实，确保排查工作取得实效。

二〇〇九年十月二十八日

关于组织开展工程建设领域突出问题排查工作的意见

为贯彻落实《关于开展工程建设领域突出问题专项治理工作的意见》，按照《工程建设领域突出问题专项治理工作实施方案》的部署，现就组织开展工程建设领域突出问题排查工作提出如下意见。

一、排查的范围和重点

（一）排查范围。以政府投资和使用国有资金的项目为重点，对 2008 年以来立项、在建和竣工的建设项目进行排查。地方各级专项治理工作领导小组组织对本地区负责建设的项目开展排查；其中，县级对总投资额在 500 万元以上、市级对总投资额在 3000 万元以上、省级对总投资额在 5000 万元以上的项目进行重点排查。中央有关部门和国务院国资委分别负责组织对总投资额在 5000 万元以上，本部门（含直属单位）组织实施的建设项目和中央企业投资的建设项目进行排查。对于其他投资项目（非政府投资和未使用国有资金的项目），总投资额在 3000 万元以上的，也要对核准、备案、用地、规划、环评、质量、安全生产等情况进行排查。各地区各部门可以结合实际，进一步细化排查的范围和规模。

（二）排查重点。重点对以下问题进行排查：

1. 工程建设项目决策是否依法合规，是否存在违规审批、擅自调整投资计划、未批先建、决策失误造成重大损失等问题；

2. 土地使用权和矿业权管理是否规范，经营性用地和工业用地招标拍卖挂牌出让制度是否落实，是否存在非法批地、低价出让土地以及违法违规审批和出让探矿权、采矿权等问题；

3. 规划许可是否规范，程序是否合法，是否存在违规变更规划和改变土地用途等问题；

4. 招标投标活动是否规范，是否存在规避招标、虚假招标、围标串标、评标不公、监管不力等问题；

5. 工程建设实施和工程质量的管理是否严格，是否存在转包和违法分包、擅自改变项目建设规模和内容、施工监理不到位、工程质量低劣、安全生产领导责任制不落实等问题；

6. 物资采购和资金管理是否规范，是否存在物资采购监管薄弱、违规使用资金以及工程严重超概算等问题；

7. 工程建设项目信息是否公开透明，招标投标违法行为公告制度是否建立并得到落实；

8. 有关投诉和举报是否得到及时受理，工程建设领域违纪违法案件是否及时得到严肃查处。

各地区各部门在认真查找上述重点问题的同时，可以结合实际，确定排查重点。

二、排查的主要环节

（一）找准突出问题。各地区各部门和项目建设单位要对照有关法律法规和政策规定，认真查找工程建设关键环节和重点部位存在的突出问题，摸清存在问题的底数。

（二）深刻分析原因。针对发现的问题，从制度建设、主观思想、权力制约和监督、行政监管、市场环境等方面，分析原因、查找漏洞，提出有针对性的治理措施和要求，为建立健全防治工程建设领域突出问题长效机制奠定基础。

（三）分类做出处理。依据有关法律法规和政策规定，对排查出的问题区分不同情况进行认真处理。对一般违规问题，要及时纠正，认真整改；对严重违纪违法问题，要立案查处；涉嫌犯罪的，要及时移送司法机关依法处理。带有共性的问题要从加强制度建设的层面，研究和采取治本之策。

三、排查的时间和方式

排查工作自 2009 年 10 月开始，至 2010 年 3 月结束，分为自查自纠和重点抽查两种方式。

（一）自查自纠。项目建设单位对本单位负责建设的项目进行自查自纠，政府有关部门对履行项目审批、核准、备案和监管职责的情况进行自查自纠。各地区各部门要按照中央治理工程建设领域突出问题工作领导小组成员单位制定的重点环节治理工作指导意见所明确的自查标准，梳理自查项目，细化自查内容，认真开展自查自纠。

（二）重点抽查。各地区各部门要按照“谁建设，谁负责；谁主管，谁负责”的原则，认真做好抽查督导工作。地方各级专项治理工作领导小组要统一组织相关部门，对本地区负责建设的项目进行重点抽查；中央有关部门和中央企业要对本部门（含直属单位）组织实施的建设项目和本企业投资的建设项目进行重点抽查。负有工程建设项目审批监管职责的部门，要对本系统开展自查自纠的情况进行重点抽查。各地区各部门要认真研究确定抽查的范围和比例，点面结合深入开展排查工作。中央专项治理工作领导小组将适时组织力量，对部分重点项目的自查自纠情况进行抽查。

排查工作结束后，各地区各部门要在本地区、本系统逐级上报排查工作情况的基础上，对项目排查情况和履行审批监管职责的排查情况进行认真分析总结。2010 年 3 月底前，各省（区、市）和新疆生产建设兵团专项治理工作领导小组和中央有关部门将排查工作总结报中央专项治理工作领导小组。

四、工作要求

（一）严格工作责任。各地区各部门要高度重视排查工作，采取有效措施，确保全面排查不留死角、严格检查不走过场。要结合实际，对本地区本部门排查工作的时间进度、工作步骤和工作方式等做出具体安排，细化工作内容。要实行严格的工作责任制，明确有关领导和经办人员的责任，建立工作台账，严肃认真地填报排查工作统计表，并由单位领导负责任地签署意见。对自查不认真、填报不实，在重点抽查中发现问题的，要对有关单位的领导实施严格的问责。

（二）严肃工作纪律。各地区各部门要真抓实干、求真务实，按照规定的范围和标准，彻底清查，找准问题，认真整改。要把监督检查作为推动排查工作落实的重要手段，加强对自查自纠情况的重点抽查和督查，一级抓一级，层层抓落实。要严肃工作纪律，对主动认识和纠正问题的，可以按照有关规定从轻从宽处理；对排查工作中走过场的，要给予通报批评并责令“补课”；对拒不自查、掩盖问题或弄虚作假、拒不纠正、压案不查的，要严肃追究直接责任人和有关领导的责任。

（三）加强协同配合。各地区各部门要从大局出发，树立全局观念，加强协调配合和沟通联系，形成整体合力。在排查工作中既要确保监督检查到位，又要避免多头检查、重复检查。对于中央和地方联合投资的项目要加强协调，明确责任主体，认真开展排查。要做好专项治理工作与中央扩大内需促进经济增长政策落实情况监督检查工作的衔接，对中央检查组负责检查的中央新增投资扩大内需项目，在本次排查中不再重复安排检查。

（四）加强政策研究。各地区各部门对排查出来的问题要认真研究分析，区分不同情况，准确分类定性，明确处理的政策界限，正确适用法律和纪律，努力取得良好的政治、社会和法纪效果。要把排查工作与制度建设结合起来，要坚持边排查、边规范，以查促改、以查促建。排查工作中遇到的重大问题，要及时向上级专项治理工作领导小组请示报告。

规划环境影响评价条例

《规划环境影响评价条例》于 2009 年 8 月 17 日以国务院令第 559 号公布，自 2009 年 10 月 1 日起施行。全文如下：

规划环境影响评价条例

第一章　总　　则

第一条　为了加强对规划的环境影响评价工作，提高规划的科学性，从源头预防环境污染和生态破坏，促进经济、社会和环境的全面协调可持续发展，根据《中华人民共和国环境影响评价法》，制定本条例。

第二条　国务院有关部门、设区的市级以上地方人民政府及其有关部门，对其组织编制的土地利用的有关规划和区域、流域、海域的建设、开发利用规划（以下称综合性规划），以及工业、农业、畜牧业、林业、能源、水利、交通、城市建设、旅游、自然资源开发的有关专项规划（以下称专项规划），应当进行环境影响评价。

依照本条第一款规定应当进行环境影响评价的规划的具体范围，由国务院环境保护主管部门会同国务院有关部门拟订，报国务院批准后执行。

第三条　对规划进行环境影响评价，应当遵循客观、公开、公正的原则。

第四条　国家建立规划环境影响评价信息共享制度。

县级以上人民政府及其有关部门应当对规划环境影响评价所需资料实行信息共享。

第五条　规划环境影响评价所需的费用应当按照预算管理的规定纳入财政预算，严格支出管理，接受审计监督。

第六条　任何单位和个人对违反本条例规定的行为或者对规划实施过程中产生的重大不良环境影响，有权向规划审批机关、规划编制机关或者环境保护主管部门举报。有关部门接到举报后，应当依法调查处理。

第二章　评　　价

第七条　规划编制机关应当在规划编制过程中对规划组织进行环境影响评价。

第八条　对规划进行环境影响评价，应当分析、预测和评估以下内容：

（一）规划实施可能对相关区域、流域、海域生态系统产生的整体影响；

（二）规划实施可能对环境和人群健康产生的长远影响；

（三）规划实施的经济效益、社会效益与环境效益之间以及当前利益与长远利益之间的关系。

第九条 对规划进行环境影响评价，应当遵守有关环境保护标准以及环境影响评价技术导则和技术规范。

规划环境影响评价技术导则由国务院环境保护主管部门会同国务院有关部门制定；规划环境影响评价技术规范由国务院有关部门根据规划环境影响评价技术导则制定，并抄送国务院环境保护主管部门备案。

第十条 编制综合性规划，应当根据规划实施后可能对环境造成的影响，编写环境影响篇章或者说明。

编制专项规划，应当在规划草案报送审批前编制环境影响报告书。编制专项规划中的指导性规划，应当依照本条第一款规定编写环境影响篇章或者说明。

本条第二款所称指导性规划是指以发展战略为主要内容的专项规划。

第十一条 环境影响篇章或者说明应当包括下列内容：

（一）规划实施对环境可能造成影响的分析、预测和评估。主要包括资源环境承载能力分析、不良环境影响的分析和预测以及与相关规划的环境协调性分析。

（二）预防或者减轻不良环境影响的对策和措施。主要包括预防或者减轻不良环境影响的政策、管理或者技术等措施。

环境影响报告书除包括上述内容外，还应当包括环境影响评价结论。主要包括规划草案的环境合理性和可行性，预防或者减轻不良环境影响的对策和措施的合理性和有效性，以及规划草案的调整建议。

第十二条 环境影响篇章或者说明、环境影响报告书（以下称环境影响评价文件），由规划编制机关编制或者组织规划环境影响评价技术机构编制。规划编制机关应当对环境影响评价文件的质量负责。

第十三条 规划编制机关对可能造成不良环境影响并直接涉及公众环境权益的专项规划，应当在规划草案报送审批前，采取调查问卷、座谈会、论证会、听证会等形式，公开征求有关单位、专家和公众对环境影响报告书的意见。但是，依法需要保密的除外。

有关单位、专家和公众的意见与环境影响评价结论有重大分歧的，规划编制机关应当采取论证会、听证会等形式进一步论证。

规划编制机关应当在报送审查的环境影响报告书中附具对公众意见采纳与不采纳情况及其理由的说明。

第十四条 对已经批准的规划在实施范围、适用期限、规模、结构和布局等方面进行重大调整或者修订的，规划编制机关应当依照本条例的规定重新或者补充进行环境影响评价。

第三章 审 查

第十五条 规划编制机关在报送审批综合性规划草案和专项规划中的指导性规划草案时，应当将环境影响篇章或者说明作为规划草案的组成部分一并报送规划审批机关。未编写环境影响篇章或者说明的，规划审批机关应当要求其补充；未补充的，规划审批机关不予审批。

第十六条 规划编制机关在报送审批专项规划草案时，应当将环境影响报告书一并附送规划审批机关审查；未附送环境影响报告书的，规划审批机关应当要求其补充；未补充的，规划审批机关不予审批。

第十七条 设区的市级以上人民政府审批的专项规划，在审批前由其环境保护主管部门召集有关部门代表和专家组成审查小组，对环境影响报告书进行审查。审查小组应当提交书面审查意见。

省级以上人民政府有关部门审批的专项规划，其环境影响报告书的审查办法，由国务院环境保护主管部门会同国务院有关部门制定。

第十八条 审查小组的专家应当从依法设立的专家库内相关专业的专家名单中随机抽取。但是，参与环境影响报告书编制的专家，不得作为该环境影响报告书审查小组的成员。

审查小组中专家人数不得少于审查小组总人数的1/2；少于1/2的，审查小组的审查意见无效。

第十九条 审查小组的成员应当客观、公正、独立地对环境影响报告书提出书面审查意见，规划审批机关、规划编制机关、审查小组的召集部门不得干预。

审查意见应当包括下列内容：

（一）基础资料、数据的真实性；

（二）评价方法的适当性；

（三）环境影响分析、预测和评估的可靠性；

（四）预防或者减轻不良环境影响的对策和措施的合理性和有效性；

（五）公众意见采纳与不采纳情况及其理由的说明的合理性；

（六）环境影响评价结论的科学性。

审查意见应当经审查小组四分之三以上成员签字同意。审查小组成员有不同意见的，应当如实记录和反映。

第二十条 有下列情形之一的，审查小组应当提出对环境影响报告书进行修改并重新审查的意见：

（一）基础资料、数据失实的；

（二）评价方法选择不当的；

（三）对不良环境影响的分析、预测和评估不准确、不深入，需要进一步论证的；

（四）预防或者减轻不良环境影响的对策和措施存在严重缺陷的；

（五）环境影响评价结论不明确、不合理或者错误的；

（六）未附具对公众意见采纳与不采纳情况及其理由的说明，或者不采纳公众意见的理由明显不合理的；

（七）内容存在其他重大缺陷或者遗漏的。

第二十一条 有下列情形之一的，审查小组应当提出不予通过环境影响报告书的意见：

（一）依据现有知识水平和技术条件，对规划实施可能产生的不良环境影响的程度或者范围不能做出科学判断的；

（二）规划实施可能造成重大不良环境影响，并且无法提出切实可行的预防或者减轻对策和措施的。

第二十二条 规划审批机关在审批专项规划草案时，应当将环境影响报告书结论以及审查意见作为决策的重要依据。

规划审批机关对环境影响报告书结论以及审查意见不予采纳的，应当逐项就不予采纳的理由做出书面说明，并存档备查。有关单位、专家和公众可以申请查阅；但是，依法需要保密的除外。

第二十三条 已经进行环境影响评价的规划包含具体建设项目的，规划的环境影响评价结论应当作为建设项目环境影响评价的重要依据，建设项目环境影响评价的内容可以根据规划环境影响评价的分析论证情况予以简化。

第四章 跟踪评价

第二十四条 对环境有重大影响的规划实施后，规划编制机关应当及时组织规划环境影响的跟踪评价，将评价结果报告规划审批机关，并通报环境保护等有关部门。

第二十五条 规划环境影响的跟踪评价应当包括下列内容：

（一）规划实施后实际产生的环境影响与环境影响评价文件预测可能产生的环境影响之间的比较分析和评估；

（二）规划实施中所采取的预防或者减轻不良环境影响的对策和措施有效性的分析和评估；

（三）公众对规划实施所产生的环境影响的意见；

（四）跟踪评价的结论。

第二十六条 规划编制机关对规划环境影响进行跟踪评价，应当采取调查问卷、现场走访、座谈会等形式征求有关单位、专家和公众的意见。

第二十七条 规划实施过程中产生重大不良环境影响的，规划编制机关应当及时提出改进措施，向规划审批机关报告，并通报环境保护等有关部门。

第二十八条 环境保护主管部门发现规划实施过程中产生重大不良环境影响的，应当及时进行核查。经核查属实的，向规划审批机关提出采取改进措施或者修订规划的建议。

第二十九条 规划审批机关在接到规划编制机关的报告或者环境保护主管部门的建议后，应当及时组织论证，并根据论证结果采取改进措施或者对规划进行修订。

第三十条 规划实施区域的重点污染物排放总量超过国家或者地方规定的总量控制指标的，应当暂停审批该规划实施区域内新增该重点污染物排放总量的建设项目的环境影响评价文件。

第五章 法律责任

第三十一条 规划编制机关在组织环境影响评价时弄虚作假或者有失职行为，造成环境影响评价严重失实的，对直接负责的主管人员和其他直接责任人员，依法给予处分。

第三十二条 规划审批机关有下列行为之一的，对直接负责的主管人员和其他直接责任人员，依法给予处分：

（一）对依法应当编写而未编写环境影响篇章或者说明的综合性规划草案和专项规划中的指导性规划草案，予以批准的；

（二）对依法应当附送而未附送环境影响报告书的专项规划草案，或者对环境影响报告书未经审查小组审查的专项规划草案，予以批准的。

第三十三条 审查小组的召集部门在组织环境影响报告书审查时弄虚作假或者滥用职权，造成环境影响评价严重失实的，对直接负责的主管人员和其他直接责任人员，依法给予处分。

审查小组的专家在环境影响报告书审查中弄虚作假或者有失职行为，造成环境影响评价严重失实的，由设立专家库的环境保护主管部门取消其入选专家库的资格并予以公告；审查小组的部门代表有上述行为的，依法给予处分。

第三十四条 规划环境影响评价技术机构弄虚作假或者有失职行为，造成环境影响评价文件严重失实的，由国务院环境保护主管部门予以通报，处所收费用1倍以上3倍以下的罚款；构成犯罪的，依法追究刑事责任。

第六章　附　　则

第三十五条　省、自治区、直辖市人民政府可以根据本地的实际情况，要求本行政区域内的县级人民政府对其组织编制的规划进行环境影响评价。具体办法由省、自治区、直辖市参照《中华人民共和国环境影响评价法》和本条例的规定制定。

第三十六条　本条例自2009年10月1日起施行。

国务院关于淮河流域防洪规划的批复

国务院2009年3月26日以国函［2009］37号文对水利部《关于审批淮河流域防洪规划的请示》（水规计［2009］134号）批复如下：

一、原则同意《淮河流域防洪规划》（以下简称《规划》），请你们认真组织实施。力争到2015年，淮河干流上游防洪标准达到10年一遇以上，中游淮北大堤防洪保护区和沿淮重要工矿城市的防洪标准达到100年一遇，洪泽湖及下游防洪保护区的防洪标准达到100年一遇以上；沂沭泗河中下游主要防洪保护区的防洪标准达到50年一遇；跨省骨干支流防洪标准达到10～20年一遇；山东半岛主要河道防洪标准达到10～30年一遇；重要城市基本达到规定的防洪标准；重要易涝洼地排涝标准达到3～5年一遇，里下河地区排涝标准达到5～10年一遇。到2025年，建成较为完善的防洪排涝减灾体系，与流域经济社会发展状况相适应。

二、《规划》的实施，要遵循“蓄泄兼筹”的治淮方针，坚持全面规划、统筹兼顾、标本兼治、综合治理的原则，正确处理好防洪排涝与水资源综合开发利用和生态环境保护的关系，进一步巩固和扩大洪水出路，加强洪水管理和科学调度，逐步完善由水库、河道堤防、行蓄洪区、调蓄湖泊等工程措施和防洪管理措施相结合的综合防洪排涝减灾体系，全面提高淮河流域防御洪涝灾害的能力。

三、加强防洪骨干工程建设，继续推进淮河综合治理。在全面完成治淮19项骨干工程的基础上，重点安排行蓄洪区调整、安全建设和渐进式移民试点，改善行蓄洪区内群众生产生活条件；加强堤防达标与河道治理工程建设，提高防洪排涝能力；实施重点平原洼地排涝治理，改变涝灾损失严重的局面；加快实施病险水库除险加固，确保水库安全运行；加强城市防洪和海堤工程建设，不断完善重点城市防洪体系，完善城市防御超标准洪水预案；继续实施山丘区水土保持和兴建干支流控制性工程；推进防洪管理体系建设。

四、认真做好规划建设项目前期工作，按照基本建设程序报批。为加快治淮工程建设，除新建的水库工程外，对《规划》确定的其他建设项目原则上可直接编制可行性研究报告和初步设计报告报批。对防洪工程建设要严格实行项目法人责任制、招标投标制、工程监理制和合同管理制，认真组织，加强监督检查，确保工程质量。

五、加强防洪管理，提高洪水风险管理水平。严格按标准建设堤防，不得超过《规划》确定的标准；河道上的建设项目，必须实行洪水影响评价制度，任何工程建设均不得超越治导线；加强行蓄洪区管理，妥善处理区内群众正常生产生活与防洪运用的关系，保证行蓄洪区及时、安全、有效运用。地方各级人民政府及相关单位要加强防洪排涝设施的管理与维护，确保工程正常运行。淮河流域管理机构要切实履行规划、管理、监督、协调、指导的职责，加强流域防汛抗旱的统一管理和调度，加快流域防汛指挥系统建设，全面落实防洪法的配套法规和防洪管理措施，抓紧研究制订骨干水库联合调度运用方案。各类工程在汛期必须服从流域防洪调度。

《规划》的实施，对保障淮河流域人民群众生命财产安全，促进经济社会又好又快发展，构建社会主义和谐社会，具有十分重要的意义。各有关地区和部门要加强领导，密切配合，精心组织实施，确保淮河流域防洪安全。

国家发展改革委关于做好2009年电力运行工作的通知

为应对国际金融危机，保持国内经济平稳较快发展，各地电力运行主管部门和电力企业要根据中央经济工作会议、全国发展改革会议部署和要求，进一步加强电力运行调节，及时解决运行中的各种矛盾和问题，为经济平稳较快发展提供良好的电力保障环境，国家发展改革委于2009年2月26日以发改运行［2009］568号文要求做好2009年电力运行工作，通知如下：

一、围绕经济运行走势，加强电力运行监测分析

用电需求变化是经济运行走势的“晴雨表”。在

目前国际金融危机影响仍在延续、经济增速下滑尚未得到根本扭转的形势下，加强电力运行监测分析对判断经济形势和增强宏观调控的预见性、针对性尤为重要。

（一）各地电力运行主管部门要结合现有月度分析制度，重点加强本地区电力运行尤其是需求变化情况的监测分析，对用电增幅下降较大或回升较慢的行业摸清原因，加强趋势预测。

（二）国家电网公司和南方电网公司要加强本营业区内电力需求变化的监测，对新增用电报装和用户报停、减容的情况进行统计分析，做好供需形势预测，及时向政府有关部门提出建议。

（三）中央发电企业要加强本企业生产运营情况监测分析。

（四）各地电力运行主管部门、各电力企业要将本单位的月度监测分析报告，报我委经济运行调节局。

二、针对电力供大于求，强化生产运行调节

受用电增幅下滑的影响，今年将是近十年来电力供需形势较为宽松的一年，全国大部分地区供大于求，发电设备利用率进一步下降。为此，各地电力运行主管部门和电力企业要强化综合协调，采取有效措施，及时解决运行中出现的各种矛盾和问题。

（一）统筹安排好发电生产。各地电力运行主管部门要按照保障电网安全、服务于保持经济平稳较快增长、兼顾效率和公平的原则，做好发电生产的统筹组织和协调工作。

开展节能发电调度试点的省，要按照有关要求，结合本省实际，认真落实各项措施，不断完善试点方案，尤其是要会同有关方面妥善解决小机组减发后的有关问题。每季度末将试点工作的进展情况报送我委经济运行调节局。未开展试点的地区，要全面推行差别电量计划。在年度计划安排上，要全额安排可再生能源并网发电项目的上网电量；优先安排大型水电、核电、热电联产、资源综合利用机组发电；低污染、高效燃煤发电机组的年利用小时数应明显高于高污染、低效机组的年利用小时数，燃煤发电机组中容量、参数接近的要保持利用小时数基本相同。在实际运行中，要以保障电网安全为前提，加强对执行情况的监督检查，及时组织公布电力生产调度信息，及时化解厂网矛盾；要按照交易各方自主协商确定交易电量和交易价格的原则，会同有关方面制定完善清洁、高效机组替代中小火电机组的实施办法，并做好组织实施，推动节能减排，缓解发电企业经营压力，维护职工队伍稳定。同时，要维护担负调峰任务的中小机组顶峰发电能力不受影响，确保电网安全和夏季大负荷期间电力供需平衡。

（二）做好跨省区电能交易。国家电网公司、南方电网公司要积极配合我委做好跨省区电能交易工作，及时公布年度、季度和月度交易安排。各地电力运行主管部门要会同有关方面做好本地区电力、电量的平衡预测，按照有利于促进节能减排和电能资源优化配置的原则，统筹制定本地区年度区内发电和外来电或外送电的方案；要组织电网、发电和电力用户代表定期召开信息披露会，通报本地区经济运行和电力供需形势，公布电力、电量交易情况，预测电力供需走势；要会同有关方面加强对交易电力、电量、价格的监管，防止市场保护，防止过度交易，严禁虚假交易，促进电能交易规范有序进行。电力供应相对宽松的地区，外购电也应根据具体情况，适当参与本地电网调峰。

三、继续加强电力需求侧管理

针对电力供求矛盾缓解后有可能放松需求侧管理的倾向，各地要继续加强电力需求侧管理，充分发挥其在提高能效和强化有序用电方面的积极作用。

（一）积极推进提高电能效率。正在进行需求侧项目试点的江苏、广东省，要按照工作进度安排，积极推进相关工作。开展需求侧管理工作较早的河北、上海、北京、山西、湖南等省（市），要充分运用国家关于节能减排的经济激励政策，进一步完善工作机制，围绕当前企业结构调整的有利时机，推动本地区项目的开展，降低用电成本，提高企业竞争能力和经济效益。其他地区也要研究建立工作机制，做好培育市场中介服务组织、建立专家队伍、加强资源潜力调查和统计分析、推广先进适用技术和产品等基础性工作，为开展电力需求侧管理工作创造良好的环境。

（二）推动移峰填谷。各地电力运行主管部门、电网企业要继续推进电力负荷管理系统的建设和运行，加快蓄冷、蓄热项目建设，鼓励热电冷三联供项目并网运行，促进用电负荷移峰填谷，保障电网安全。

（三）完善有序用电方案。各地电力运行主管部门要继续会同有关方面研究制定不同负荷水平下的有序用电方案，重点做好节假日和“两会”、迎峰度夏、迎峰度冬特别是建国六十周年庆祝活动期间的用电保障，确保居民生活、医院、学校、铁路、交通枢纽、供水供热、广播、电信、金融机构、农业生产、石油天然气生产输送等涉及公众利益和国家安全的重要用户用电不受影响，全力保障全社会各行业对电力的需求，促进经济平稳较快增长。

四、细化落实电力应急措施和方案

各地电力运行主管部门要组织有关企业、相关部

门继续做好煤电油运应急预案、大面积停电事故应急预案，加强演练，增强可操作性。督促电网企业落实移动发电设备，督促广播电视、通信、铁路、交通枢纽、供水、能源生产供应、政府机关、金融机构、医院等重要用户落实自备保安电源，督促学校、商场、宾馆等人员聚集场所配备应急照明设施。继续跟踪火电厂煤炭库存情况，对可能导致大量缺煤停机、影响电力供应的趋势性、苗头性问题及早协调和反映。电网企业要加强输电线路防覆冰、除冰等技术、装备的研发和应用，加强与气象部门的沟通、会商，切实做好低温雨雪冰冻灾害的预防；对电煤库存低于警戒线的电厂，要按照以煤定电的原则安排发电生产。

五、组织换发《供电营业许可证》

根据《电力法》有关规定，我委2006年组织各地换发了《供电营业许可证》。鉴于近几年供电营业区划分方面出现较多的新情况、新问题，为保证供电营业许可工作正常开展，保障电力供应正常秩序，今年我委将组织换发新的《供电营业许可证》，具体事项另行通知。各省级电力运行主管部门负责本地区供电营业区划分管理和证书的换发、颁发工作，要力争年内完成，并对上次证书换发工作进行总结，分析存在的问题，提出相关政策建议。

国家发展改革委关于完善境外投资项目管理有关问题的通知

近年来，在国家关于实施“走出去”战略的统一部署下，我国企业对外投资发展较快，特别是大型境外收购和竞标项目明显增加。为适应新形势发展的需要，促进我国对外投资健康有序发展，国家发展改革委依据《境外投资项目核准暂行管理办法》（国家发展改革委第21号令），于2009年6月8日以发改外资［2009］1479号发文，就完善境外投资项目管理有关问题通知如下：

一、本通知所涉及境外投资项目，是指《政府核准的投资项目目录》规定由国家发展改革委核准或由国家发展改革委审核后报国务院核准的下列项目：

（一）境外收购项目，即国内企业直接或通过在境外设立的子公司或控股公司以协议、要约等方式收购境外企业全部或者部分股权、资产或其他权益的项目。

（二）境外竞标项目，即国内企业直接或通过在境外设立的子公司或控股公司参与境外公开或不公开的竞争性招标，以投资获得境外企业全部或者部分股权、资产或其他权益的项目。

上述项目以外的境外投资项目，仍按《境外投资项目核准暂行管理办法》的具体规定执行。

二、国内企业开展境外收购和竞标项目，要遵守国家法律法规、产业政策和境外投资管理规定，结合国家战略规划、企业发展战略和自身实力，在充分进行前期论证和尽职调查的基础上，科学决策，并且综合考虑各方面复杂因素，制定完善的工作方案和计划，稳步实施，有效防范投资风险。

三、有关企业在项目对外开展实质性工作之前，即境外收购项目在对外签署约束性协议、提出约束性报价及向对方国家（地区）政府审查部门提出申请之前，境外竞标项目在对外正式投标之前，应向国家发展改革委报送项目信息报告，并抄报国务院行业管理部门。

四、项目信息报告应说明投资主体基本情况、项目投资背景情况、收购或竞标目标情况、对外工作和尽职调查情况、收购或竞标的基本方案和时间安排等。项目信息报告的格式见附件一，可在国家发展改革委网站（www. ndrc. gov. cn）“外资利用”栏目下载。

五、中央管理企业可直接向国家发展改革委报送项目信息报告并抄报国务院行业管理部门，地方企业通过省级发展改革部门报送项目信息报告。

已有境外投资项目经国家核准的地方企业，可直接向国家发展改革委报送项目信息报告并抄报国务院行业管理部门，同时抄报省级发展改革部门。

六、国家发展改革委收到项目信息报告后，对于报告内容符合第四条要求的项目，在7个工作日内向报送单位出具确认函（格式见附件二），并抄送有关部门和机构；对于报告内容不符合第四条要求的项目，将及时通知报送单位补充和完善。

七、如果发现项目存在明显的重大不利因素，国家发展改革委将在确认函中作出特别备注，进行风险提示。

对于此类项目，国家发展改革委在项目核准时将严格审查，有关企业和金融机构应慎重决策。

八、确认函将标明一定的有效期。有关企业可在有效期内对外开展实质性工作，如在此期间未能完成，应根据情况办理确认函延期，或者重新报送项目信息报告。

九、确认函是有关企业向国家发展改革委报送项目申请报告的必备附件。

十、有关企业在对外完成实质性工作以及项目必要前期工作后，应按照《境外投资项目核准暂行管理办法》的规定向国家发展改革委报送项目申请报告，履行境外投资项目核准手续。

十一、对于违反本通知规定的国内企业，国家发展改革委将予以批评或通报批评，并责令纠正；对于性质严重、给国家和企业利益造成严重损害的，国家发展改革委将会同有关部门依法进行处罚，并追究有关领导和责任人的责任。

十二、国内金融机构要认真执行国家境外投资项目管理的有关规定，在进行充分风险评估和合规性审查的基础上，为国内企业境外投资项目提供金融支持，不得向违规项目发放贷款。

十三、各地方发展改革部门、各中央企业要认真贯彻国家境外投资管理的各项规定，指导有关企业扎实开展对外投资工作，提高对外投资的科学性和效益，有效维护对外投资秩序，促进我国对外投资稳步有序健康发展。

附件：一、境外收购或竞标项目信息报告（格式）（略）

二、境外收购或竞标项目信息报告确认函（格式）（略）

国家发展改革委关于加强中央预算内投资项目概算调整管理的通知

为严格执行财经纪律，加强和规范中央预算内投资项目概算管理，国家发展改革委于2009年6月15日以发改投资［2009］1550号发文，就概算调整管理有关事项通知如下：

一、依现行规定由国家发展改革委核定批准初步设计概算的中央预算内投资项目，在建设过程中由于价格上涨、政策调整、地质条件发生重大变化等原因导致原批复概算不能满足工程实际需要的，应向国家发展改革委申请调整概算。

二、申请调整概算时，应提交以下材料：

（一）原初步设计文件及初步设计批复文件；

（二）由具备相应资质单位编制的调整概算书，调整概算与原批复概算对比表，并分类定量说明调整概算的原因、依据和计算方法；

（三）与调整概算有关的招标及合同文件，包括变更洽商部分；

（四）调整概算所需的其他材料。

三、申请调整概算的项目，凡概算调增幅度超过原批复概算10％及以上的，国家发展改革委原则上先商请审计机关进行审计，待审计结束后，再视具体情况进行概算调整。

四、对于申请调整概算的项目，国家发展改革委将按照静态控制、动态管理的原则，区别不可抗因素和人为因素对概算调整的内容和原因进行审查。对于使用基本预备费可以解决问题的项目，不予调整概算。对于确需调整概算的项目，须经国家发展改革委组织专家评审后方予核定批准。

五、对由于价格上涨、政策调整等不可抗因素造成调整概算超过原批复概算的，经核定后予以调整。调增的价差不作为计取其他费用的基数。

六、对由于勘察、设计、施工、设备材料供应、监理单位过失造成调整概算超过原批复概算的，根据违约责任扣减有关责任单位的费用，超出的投资不作为计取其他费用的基数。对过失情节严重的责任单位，建议相关资质管理部门依法给予处罚并公告。

七、对由于项目单位管理不善、失职渎职，擅自扩大规模、提高标准、增加建设内容，故意漏项和报小建大等造成调整概算超过原批复概算的，将给予通报批评。对于超概算严重、性质恶劣的，将向国务院报告并追究项目单位的法律责任。

八、上述规定自本通知发布之日起执行。

国家发展改革委、国家电监会关于2008年7～12月可再生能源电价补贴和配额交易方案的通知

国家发展改革委、国家电监会根据《可再生能源发电价格和费用分摊管理试行办法》（发改价格［2006］7号）和《可再生能源电价附加收入调配暂行办法》（发改价格［2007］44号），于2009年6月17日以发改价格［2009］1581号发文，就2008年7～12月可再生能源电价附加调配、补贴等有关事项通知如下：

一、电价附加补贴的项目和金额

可再生能源电价附加资金补贴范围为2008年7～12月可再生能源发电项目上网电价高于当地脱硫燃煤机组标杆上网电价的部分、公共可再生能源独立电力系统运行维护费用、可再生能源发电项目接网费用。对纳入补贴范围内的秸秆直燃发电项目继续按上网电量给予临时电价补贴，补贴标准为每千瓦时0.1元。

具体补贴项目和金额见附件一、二、三、四。

二、电价附加配额交易

对收取的可再生能源电价附加不足以支付本省可再生能源电价附加补贴的省级电网企业，按照短缺资金金额颁发同等额度的可再生能源电价附加配额证，

以配额交易方式实现可再生能源电价附加资金调配。2008年7～12月电价附加配额交易方案见附件五。

配额卖方向买方出售配额证，配额买方应在收到配额证后10个工作日内，按额度将款项汇入卖方账户，完成交易。

三、电费结算

（一）可再生能源发电项目上网电价在当地脱硫燃煤机组标杆上网电价以内的部分，由当地省级电网负担；高出部分，通过本次电价附加补贴解决。由当地省级电网负担的部分，分为2008年7～8月和9～12月两段，分别使用7月1日和8月20日调整后的当地脱硫燃煤机组标杆价与发电企业结算。

（二）2008年7～12月电价附加有结余的省级电网企业，应在本通知下发之日起10个工作日内，对可再生能源发电项目结清2008年下半年电费（含接网费用补贴）。2008年7～12月电价附加存在资金缺口的山东、新疆等11个地区的电网企业，应在配额交易完成10个工作日内，对可再生能源发电项目结清2008年下半年电费（含接网费用补贴）。

（三）对2008年7～12月公共可再生能源独立电力系统的电价附加补贴，按本通知附件三所列的项目和金额，由所在省（区）的价格主管部门会同省级电网企业负责组织实施。

（四）本次配额交易完成后，电价附加有结余的省级电网企业，对已纳入补贴范围内的可再生能源发电项目按月结算电费，高于当地脱硫燃煤机组标杆上网电价的部分从电价附加中支付。

（五）各省级电网企业对可再生能源电价附加继续单独记账，余缺逐期滚存。

四、加强监管

未经许可，各地不得随意挪用可再生能源电价附加资金。个别省使用附加资金对省内不符合补贴规定的项目进行补贴的，要立即停止，并追回补贴资金。

各省（区、市）政府价格主管部门和各区域、城市电力监管机构要加强对可再生能源电价附加征收、配额交易、电费和补贴结算行为的监管，坚决纠正和查处违反本通知规定的电费结算行为，确保可再生能源电价附加补贴按时足额到位。

附件：一、2008年7～12月可再生能源发电项目补贴表（略）

二、2008年7～12月秸秆直燃项目临时电价补贴表（略）

三、2008年7～12月公共可再生能源独立电力系统补贴表（略）

四、2008年7～12月可再生能源发电接网工程补贴表（略）

五、2008年7～12月可再生能源电价附加配额交易方案（略）

国家发展改革委、财政部、水利部关于中央直属和跨省水利工程水资源费征收标准及有关问题的通知

为推进水价改革，促进水资源节约和保护，国家发展改革委、财政部、水利部根据《取水许可和水资源费征收管理条例》（国务院令第460号）有关规定，于2009年7月6日以发改价格［2009］1779号发文，就中央直属和跨省、自治区、直辖市水利工程的水资源费征收标准及有关问题通知如下：

一、制定水资源费征收标准的基本原则：

（一）促进水资源的合理开发、利用、节约和保护；

（二）与水资源条件和经济社会发展水平相适应，并充分考虑不同产业和行业的差别；

（三）保持同类性质用水水资源费征收标准的统一性，维护公平的市场环境。

二、由流域管理机构审批取水的中央直属和跨省、自治区、直辖市水利工程的水资源费征收标准，由国家发展改革委会同财政部、水利部制定和调整。

其他水利工程的水资源费征收标准，由省、自治区、直辖市价格主管部门会同同级财政、水行政主管部门制定和调整，报本级人民政府批准，并报国家发展改革委、财政部、水利部备案。

三、由流域管理机构审批取水的中央直属和跨省、自治区、直辖市水利工程的水资源费征收标准为：

（一）供农业生产用水暂免征收水资源费。

（二）供非农业用水（不含供水力发电用水）暂按取水口所在地现行标准执行。

（三）水力发电用水为每千瓦时0.3～0.8分钱，其中：取水口所在地省、自治区、直辖市制定的同类水力发电用水水资源费征收标准低于每千瓦时0.3分钱的，按0.3分钱执行；高于0.8分钱的，按0.8分钱执行；在0.3～0.8分钱之间的，维持不变。抽水蓄能发电用水暂免征收水资源费。

四、中央直属和跨省、自治区、直辖市水利工程单位（企业）缴纳的水资源费计入生产成本。

五、各地不得越权出台涉及中央直属和跨省、自治区、直辖市水电企业的新的行政事业性收费项目。

六、中央直属和跨省、自治区、直辖市水利工程

名录，由水利部商国家发展改革委、财政部确定并公布。

七、上述规定自2009年9月1日起执行。

国家发展改革委关于完善风力发电上网电价政策的通知

国家发展改革委为规范风电价格管理，促进风力发电产业健康持续发展，依据《中华人民共和国可再生能源法》，决定进一步完善《可再生能源发电价格和费用分摊管理试行办法》（发改价格［2006］7号）有关规定，于2009年7月20日以发改价格［2009］1906号文，就完善风力发电上网电价政策有关事项通知如下：

一、规范风电价格管理

（一）分资源区制定陆上风电标杆上网电价。按风能资源状况和工程建设条件，决定将全国分为四类风能资源区，相应制定风电标杆上网电价。具体标准见附件。

今后新建陆上风电项目，包括沿海地区多年平均大潮高潮线以上的潮上滩涂地区和有固定居民的海岛地区，统一执行所在风能资源区的风电标杆上网电价。跨省区边界的同一风电场原则上执行同一上网电价，价格标准按较高的风电标杆上网电价执行。

（二）海上风电项目上网电价，今后将根据建设进程，由国务院价格主管部门另行制定。

（三）省级投资及能源主管部门核准的风电项目，要向国家发展改革委、国家能源局备案。

二、继续实行风电价格费用分摊制度

风电上网电价在当地脱硫燃煤机组标杆上网电价以内的部分，由当地省级电网负担；高出部分，通过全国征收的可再生能源电价附加分摊解决。脱硫燃煤机组标杆上网电价调整后，风电上网电价中由当地电网负担的部分要相应调整。

三、有关要求

（一）上述规定自2009年8月1日起实行。2009年8月1日之前核准的风电项目，上网电价仍按原有规定执行。

（二）各风力发电企业和电网企业必须真实、完整地记载和保存风电项目上网交易电量、价格和补贴金额等资料，接受有关部门监督检查。各级价格主管部门要加强对风电上网电价执行和电价附加补贴结算的监管，确保风电上网电价政策执行到位。

附件：全国风力发电标杆上网电价表（略）

国家发展改革委、水利部关于加强小水电代燃料和水电农村电气化建设与管理的通知

发改农经［2009］1937号

有关省、自治区、直辖市、新疆生产建设兵团发展改革委、水利（水务）厅（局）：

为继续推进我国农村水电建设，国家从2009年第四批扩大内需中央预算内投资中安排3亿元用于水电农村电气化项目建设，安排3亿元用于小水电代燃料项目建设，项目投资计划已以《国家发展改革委、水利部关于下达农村小水电项目2009年第四批扩大内需中央预算内投资计划的通知》（发改投资［2009］1734号）下达。为做好项目实施工作，切实加强项目管理，现就有关事项通知如下：

一、认真做好项目前期工作

小水电代燃料工程和水电农村电气化工程是中央补助投资的地方项目，其前期工作程序按照《中央预算内投资补助和贴息项目管理暂行办法》（国家发展改革委第31号令）、《国家发展改革委关于改进和完善中央补助地方投资项目管理的通知》（发改投资［2009］1242号）有关规定执行。各地要严格按照国家批准的有关专项规划选择建设项目。小水电代燃料工程和水电农村电气化工程可行性研究报告由地方水行政主管部门提出审查意见后，由地方发展改革部门审批；初步设计报告由地方水行政主管部门审批。实施方案由县级水行政主管部门负责组织编制并会同发展改革部门上报，由省级水行政主管部门会同发展改革部门组织对实施方案进行审查和批复，报水利部备案，批复后的实施方案作为项目验收的依据。小水电代燃料工程主要建设内容包括代燃料电站建设和项目区建设，项目区范围应以行政村为单元，按照就近供电的原则合理确定；水电农村电气化建设主要内容是农村水电站建设。项目的建设内容要在项目实施方案中予以明确。

二、加强工程建设管理

小水电代燃料和水电农村电气化项目建设要严格实行项目法人责任制、招标投标制、建设监理制和合同管理制。要建立健全工程质量管理和监督机制，严

格执行各项制度，确保工程质量和安全。要采取有效措施，防止水土流失，保护生态环境。要大力推进技术进步，代燃料电站及配套变电站要实现无人值班、少人值守，统一标准标识，统一管理制度，把小水电代燃料和水电农村电气化项目建设成环境友好、社会和谐的农村水能资源开发利用典范。各地要安排资金用于小水电代燃料和水电农村电气化项目的前期工作、人员培训和监督检查等工作。

三、进一步完善有关体制机制

要按照保证代燃料电站长期稳定运行的要求，建立和完善管理体制。建立健全国家投资出资人制度，明确代燃料电站的所有权、经营权和使用权，实现所有者、经营者和使用者权利和义务的统一。按照“国家补助、企业运作、农民受益、协会监督”的要求，建立和完善运行机制。要成立县级小水电代燃料领导小组，切实加强组织和领导。组建以代燃料户为主体的代燃料用户协会，对代燃料电站的建设、运营、供电，代燃料户用电和禁止砍伐森林等进行监督管理。项目法人、代燃料用户和有关各方要签订相关协议，落实责任、明确权利、承担义务，确保代燃料工程长期稳定发挥效益。

就近直接供电是降低小水电代燃料电价的有效办法，有关部门和电网企业应积极支持代燃料电站就近直接供电，不具备直接供电条件的可借网供电，按成本核定过网费。将代燃料电价列入电价目录，按程序核准代燃料电价，并保持相对稳定。要最大限度地降低代燃料到户电价，使农民得到实惠，生态得到保护。

水电农村电气化项目建设要探索国有投资的有效管理模式，通过壮大农村集体经济，改善农村基础设施，建立让农民直接受益的新机制。加强对中央补助投资形成资产的监管，明确和落实资产监管的主体和职责，确保国有资产的安全、有效利用和保值增值。

四、加强资金筹措和计划管理

小水电代燃料项目建设资金由地方负责落实，中央给予补助，中央补助投资占项目总投资的比例，西部地区和享受西部政策地区 45%左右，中部地区38%左右，东部地区 15%左右。各地要积极争取各级财政对小水电代燃料工程的支持，省级安排的投资，西部地区和享受西部政策地区应不低于总投资的10%，中部地区不低于 15%，东部地区不低于 25%。项目法人要多渠道筹集资金，积极争取金融机构的支持和国家政策性贷款。要认真执行国家关于中央预算内资金管理的有关规定，严格专户专账管理，不得滞留、挤占和挪用。

水电农村电气化项目建设采取政府引导、市场运作、社会参与的方式，也要多渠道筹集资金。中央投资实行定额补助，地方应按照不低于中央投资规模的比例支持水电农村电气化项目建设，地方资金应与中央安排的资金同步到位。

小水电代燃料和水电农村电气化项目年度投资建议计划应由省级发展改革部门和水行政主管部门审查后联合报送国家发展改革委和水利部。省级发展改革部门会同省级水行政主管部门根据国家发展改革委和水利部下达的投资计划联合下达具体项目投资计划。项目投资计划一经下达，必须严格执行。因特殊情况需要变更，涉及项目调整、建设地点、建设规模等重大变动的，须报原审批单位批准，其他一般性变更，须报原审批单位备案。

五、加强项目监督检查和验收

省级水行政主管部门和发展改革部门负责本行政区域内小水电代燃料和水电农村电气化建设项目的监督和检查。检查重点是建设程序、工程质量和进度、资金筹措和使用、管理体制和机制，以及实施方案所确定目标任务的完成情况。

各地要按照项目验收有关标准和规定，认真做好竣工验收工作。项目完成后，由项目所在县级水行政主管部门和发展改革部门进行初步验收，并提出验收申请。省级水行政主管部门和发展改革部门联合进行验收，验收报告报水利部和国家发展改革委备案。水利部会同国家发展改革委对全国小水电代燃料和水电农村电气化项目的实施进行督查。

小水电代燃料和水电农村电气化建设工作涉及多部门、多方面，各地要高度重视，加强领导，精心组织，有效实施，确保小水电代燃料和水电农村电气化建设任务的顺利完成。

国家发展改革委　水利部
二〇〇九年七月二十三日

国家发展改革委办公厅关于2009年注册咨询工程师（投资）注册申报有关事项的通知

根据《注册咨询工程师（投资）注册管理办法（试行）》（发改投资［2005］983 号，以下简称 983 号文）的规定，国家发展和改革委员会办公厅于2009 年 7 月 24 日以发改办投资［2009］1580 号文，将 2009 年注册咨询工程师（投资）注册工作的有关事项通知如下：

一、总体要求

注册申请人应根据983号文及本通知的规定和要求，认真准备注册申请材料，保证申请材料的真实、准确和完整。

二、注册类别和申请人范围

（一）初始注册：2003～2009年合法取得注册咨询工程师（投资）执业资格证书，尚未初始注册的；注册有效期已过，未参加继续注册的；准予预初始注册后，执业单位经过认定未取得工程咨询单位资格的。

（二）变更注册：已获得注册证，要求变更注册的。变更注册包括变更执业单位、变更专业。工程咨询单位发生分立、合并、兼并、改制、转让等情况，应首先申请办理注册咨询工程师（投资）执业单位的变更注册，再重新申请工程咨询单位资格。

（三）继续注册：2006年获得初始注册，注册有效期将于2010年1月到期，要求继续注册的。

（四）注销注册：已获得注册证，应予注销注册的。

三、申请材料

申请材料分为电子文件和文本文件两部分。申请人应登录《注册咨询工程师（投资）注册管理系统》（http：//www.cnaec.com.cn，以下简称注册管理系统），根据申请的注册类别，在线填写相应的申请内容，上传相应的证明材料扫描件，并通过注册管理系统打印文本申请材料，在规定时间内报送初审机构。具体内容如下：

（一）初始注册：包括初始注册申请表、人员证明材料和业绩证明材料三部分，分别装订成册。

1. 初始注册申请表

（1）行政许可事项申请表（封面）；

（2）承诺书；

（3）基本情况；

（4）工作简历；

（5）相应专业的工程咨询业绩。

2. 人员证明材料

（1）正在生效的执业单位企业法人营业执照或事业单位法人证书；

（2）执业单位的工程咨询资格证书（正本）复印件（注册在拟新申请工程咨询资格的单位无需提供）；

（3）执业资格证书（编号页、照片及签章页）、身份证、毕业证书和职称证书复印件。其中，2003年通过考核认定方式取得执业资格证书的，还需提交注册咨询工程师（投资）认定合格人员培训班结业证书的复印件；

（4）执业单位出具的正在生效的一年以上申请人被任命文件（或聘用合同）复印件和申请人的职业道德证明；

（5）企业法人执业单位为申请人缴纳的社会养老保险证明材料，内容包括：参保单位名称及公章、交费人员姓名及社会保险号、社保部门有效印章；事业法人执业单位需提交申请人的人事证明材料（必须由上级主管单位的人事部门出具并加盖公章）。如果申请人是事业法人执业单位聘用的事业编制以外的专业技术人员，还需提交执业单位为其缴纳的社会养老保险证明材料；

（6）近期正面免冠2寸彩色证件照片2张（尺寸要求：宽3.6cm×高5.0cm）。

3. 业绩证明材料

（1）业绩范围：按照管理权限，已经获得相关部门批准的作为主持人或主要参加人完成的发展规划（专题研究报告）、项目建议书（预可行性研究报告）、可行性研究报告、项目申请报告、资金申请报告、项目评估报告、项目后评价报告。

（2）业绩数量要求（必须同时满足下列条件中的2类）：

1）发展规划（专题研究报告）不少于2项（按照《国务院关于加强国民经济和社会发展规划编制工作的若干意见》（国发［2005］33号）的规定，国民经济和社会发展规划按行政层级分为国家级规划、省（区、市）级规划、市县级规划；按对象和功能类别分为总体规划、专项规划、区域规划。申请人所提供的编制行业规划和特大型企业集团中长期发展建设规划的业绩可视同为规划业绩）；

2）项目建议书（预可行性研究报告）不少于3项；

3）可行性研究报告、项目申请报告或资金申请报告不少于2项；

4）项目评估报告不少于5项（包括对规划、项目建议书、项目可行性研究报告、项目申请报告、资金申请报告、初步设计的评估咨询以及项目概预决算审查等）；

5）项目后评价报告（规划和项目的后评价）不少于5项。

（3）业绩材料要求：应包括业绩文本原件封面页、署名页、目录页的复印件，相关部门批复文件的复印件或由委托单位（委托人）出具的有效证明。每项业绩的证明材料应排列在一起。

（二）变更注册

1. 变更执业单位：包括变更注册（单位）申请表和人员证明材料两部分，分别装订成册。

（1）变更注册（单位）申请表：

1）行政许可事项申请表（封面）；

2）承诺书；

3）变更注册申请表（单位变更）；

4）备案登记表（跨初审机构变更需提供）。

（2）人员证明材料：

1）新执业单位的正在生效的企业法人营业执照或事业单位法人证书复印件；

2）新执业单位的工程咨询资格证书（正本）复印件（注册在拟新申请工程咨询资格的单位无需提供）；

3）《中华人民共和国注册咨询工程师（投资）注册咨询工程师（投资）注册证书》及复印件；

4）新执业单位出具的正在生效的一年以上申请人被任命文件（聘用合同）复印件；

5）新执业单位为申请人缴纳的社会养老保险证明材料（具体要求与初始注册要求相同）；

6）申请人与原执业单位的解聘证明。

2. 变更注册专业：包括变更注册（专业）申请表、人员证明材料和业绩证明材料三部分，分别装订成册。

（1）变更注册（专业）申请表：

1）行政许可事项申请表（封面）；

2）承诺书；

3）变更注册申请表（专业变更）；

4）相应专业的工程咨询业绩。

（2）人员证明材料：

1）《中华人民共和国注册咨询工程师（投资）注册咨询工程师（投资）注册证书》及复印件，职称证书复印件；

2）学制在一年以上的与新申请专业相关的专业培训、学历或学位证明；

3）执业单位为申请人缴纳的社会养老保险证明材料（具体要求与初始注册要求相同）。

（3）业绩证明材料：具体要求与初始注册要求相同。

（三）继续注册：包括继续注册申请表和人员证明材料两部分。因注册咨询工程师（投资）继续教育工作尚未开展，申请人在向初审机构提交申请材料时，不需提交继续教育学时证明。

1. 继续注册申请表：包括封面、承诺书和继续注册申请。

2. 人员证明材料：

（1）《中华人民共和国注册咨询工程师（投资）注册咨询工程师（投资）注册证书》及复印件；

（2）正在生效的执业单位企业法人营业执照或事业单位法人证书复印件；

（3）执业单位的工程咨询资格证书（正本）复印件；

（4）执业单位出具的正在生效的一年以上申请人被任命文件（聘用合同）复印件和申请人的职业道德证明；

（5）执业单位为申请人缴纳的社会养老保险证明材料（具体要求与初始注册要求相同）。

（四）注销注册：

1. 注销注册申请表：包括封面及基本情况两部分；

2.《中华人民共和国注册咨询工程师（投资）注册咨询工程师（投资）注册证书》及复印件。

四、注意事项

（一）申请人必须填写承诺书并签字，承诺对申请材料及内容的真实性、准确性和完整性负责，并承担相应法律责任。

（二）电子文件填写和上传原件的扫描件均需注册管理系统在线完成，相关证明材料均需上传原件的扫描件。

（三）上报申请材料一律用 A4 复印纸打印，以非活页方式装订。

（四）上报申请材料应按照要求格式填写（一式一份），在申请材料封面上加盖执业单位公章后装入档案袋。在注册管理系统中打印档案袋封面并粘贴在档案袋正面。

（五）申请材料应严格按照规定的顺序装订，不能擅自调整。

（六）业绩证明复印件的装订顺序必须与业绩表中的业绩排列顺序一致。

（七）除本通知要求的内容外，申请单位不需要在申请材料中附加其他材料。

五、申报时间和程序要求

注册申请人应在 2009 年 9 月 24 日之前向初审机构报送申请材料。申请材料不齐全或者不符合规定形式的，初审机构应在 5 个工作日内一次告知申请单位需要补正的全部内容。初审机构应在 2009 年 10 月 30 日前将申请人的申请材料和初审意见统一报送国家发展改革委。

六、国家发展改革委将组织专家评审，按规定程序向社会公告准予注册的注册咨询工程师（投资）人员名单并颁发注册证书。

国家发展改革委关于调整华北电网电价的通知

为疏导电价矛盾，完善电价结构，促进可再生能源发展，国家发展改革委经商国家电监会、国家能源局，决定适当调整电价水平。2009 年 11 月 18 日以发改价格［2009］2919 号文就调整华北电网电价有关事项通知如下：

一、调整发电企业上网电价

（一）为合理反映燃煤电厂投资、煤价、煤耗等情况变化，将山西省统调燃煤机组标杆上网电价每千瓦时上调 1 分钱。山西省神头第一发电厂、漳泽电厂执行标杆上网电价，山西太一发电、太原第一热电厂、太原第二热电厂上网电价每千瓦时提高 1.7 分钱。同时，适当提高部分电价偏低、亏损严重电厂的上网电价，逐步与标杆电价填平补齐。

（二）山西、内蒙古西部电网向京津唐电网送电价格分别提高到每千瓦时 0.334 4 元和 0.349 元；山西电网向河北南部电网送电价格每千瓦时提高 1 分钱。山西省以点对网方式向京津唐电网送电的电厂送电价格提高到每千瓦时 0.348 元。陕西府谷电厂向河北南网送电价格核定为每千瓦时 0.326 8 元。

（三）为促进水电站库区和移民安置区经济社会发展，缓解水电企业亏损严重、更新改造资金不足等问题，适当提高部分水电企业的上网电价。北京华电密云水电厂、京西水电厂容量电价分别调整为每月每千瓦 36 元和 20 元。河北省华电混合蓄能水电有限公司、大唐王快水力发电厂、大唐岳城水电站、潘家口水力发电厂 1 号机组上网电价每千瓦时提高 5 分钱。

（四）北京京丰燃气发电有限责任公司、华润协鑫（北京）热电有限公司、北京太阳宫燃气热电有限公司、华电（北京）热电有限公司、北京正东电子动力集团有限公司燃气发电机组上网临时结算电价调整为每千瓦时 0.528 元。

有关电厂调整后的上网电价水平见附件一。

二、理顺发电企业上网电价与销售电价关系。2008 年 8 月全国火力发电企业上网电价提高影响电网企业增加的购电成本，通过调整销售电价予以疏导。

三、根据可再生能源发展需要，按照《可再生能源法》和《可再生能源发电价格和费用分摊管理试行办法》（发改价格［2006］7 号）有关规定，将可再生能源电价附加标准提高到每千瓦时 0.4 分钱。

四、各省（区、市）销售电价每千瓦时提高 0.2 分钱，暂用于解决电网企业“一户一表”改造投资还本付息等问题。

五、适当提高电网销售电价。有关省（区、市）销售电价平均提价标准每千瓦时分别为：北京市 3.97 分钱、天津市 3.35 分钱、河北北部地区 3 分钱、河北南部地区 2.99 分钱、山东省 3.28 分钱、山西省 3.88 分钱、内蒙古西部地区 2.4 分钱。各类用户调价后具体电价标准见附件二～附件八。

六、进一步优化销售电价结构。同意北京市商业、非居民照明、非工业、普通工业用电价格合并为一般工商业电价类别，山西省实行城乡各类用电同价，内蒙古西部地区商业、非工业和普通工业、非居民照明用电价格合并为一般工商业电价类别。

七、在保持销售电价总水平基本稳定的前提下，将河北南网高峰和低谷时段的电价浮动比例分别调整为 44.5％和 40％，将尖峰时段电价上浮比例和“蓄冷蓄热”设备低谷时段电价下浮比例均调整为 50％。

八、以上电价调整自 2009 年 11 月 20 日起执行。其中，电力用户 11 月 20 日后的用电量，可按对应抄表周期内日平均用电量乘以应执行调整后电价的天数确定。

九、各地价格主管部门要精心组织，周密安排，做好宣传解释工作，确保本通知规定的各项措施及时得到贯彻落实。执行中如有问题，请及时报告我委。

附件：一、华北电网部分电厂上网电价表（略）
二、北京市电网销售电价表（略）
三、天津市电网销售电价表（略）
四、河北北部电网销售电价表（略）
五、河北南部电网销售电价表（略）
六、山东省电网销售电价表（略）
七、山西省电网销售电价表（略）
八、内蒙古西部电网销售电价表（略）

国家发展改革委关于调整东北电网电价的通知

为疏导电价矛盾，完善电价结构，促进可再生能源发展，国家发展改革委经商国家电监会、国家能源局，决定适当调整电价水平。2009 年 11 月 18 日以发改价格［2009］2920 号文就调整东北电网电价有关事项通知如下：

一、调整发电企业上网电价

（一）为合理反映燃煤电厂投资、煤价、煤耗等情况变化，辽宁省统调燃煤机组标杆上网电价每千瓦时下调 0.38 分钱，现行上网电价高于标杆电价的统调机组，按上述标准同步下调。

（二）黑龙江、吉林、内蒙古东部地区燃煤机组脱硫加价标准由每千瓦时 1.5 分钱调整为 1.3 分钱，燃煤机组脱硫标杆电价保持不变。

（三）黑龙江燃煤机组向辽宁送电价格每千瓦时提高 0.5 分钱。内蒙古东部地区通辽发电总厂、元宝山电厂 1 号、2 号机组向辽宁、吉林送电价格每千瓦时提高 1 分钱。内蒙古东部地区新增跨省交易电量输电价格按每千瓦时2分钱执行。

（四）尼尔基水电站上网电价每千瓦时提高3分钱。松江河发电厂新投产机组上网电量结算电价暂按东北各省（区）燃煤机组脱硫标杆电价执行。

二、理顺发电企业上网电价与销售电价关系。2008年8月全国火力发电企业上网电价提高影响电网企业增加的购电成本，通过调整销售电价予以疏导。

三、根据可再生能源发展需要，按照《可再生能源法》和《可再生能源发电价格和费用分摊管理试行办法》（发改价格［2006］7号）有关规定，将可再生能源电价附加标准提高到每千瓦时0.4分钱。

四、将各省（区）销售电价每千瓦时提高0.2分钱，暂用于解决电网企业"一户一表"改造投资还本付息等问题。

五、为逐步完善跨省跨区电网输电价格机制，此次辽宁省、吉林省、黑龙江省、内蒙古东部地区提高的销售电价中每千瓦时含东北电网公司输电价格0.1分钱。

六、适当提高电网销售电价。各省（区）销售电价平均提价标准每千瓦时分别为：辽宁省2.8分钱、吉林省2.8分钱、黑龙江省2.5分钱、内蒙古东部地区2.6分钱。各类用户调价后具体电价标准见附件一～附件四。

七、进一步优化销售电价结构。吉林省、黑龙江省和内蒙古东部地区商业、非居民照明与非普工业用电价格合并为"一般工商业及其他"电价类别。"一般工商业及其他"用电执行峰谷分时电价等需求侧电价管理制度。

八、同意内蒙古东部地区实行城乡居民生活用电同价。黑龙江省实行城乡农业生产用电同价，两年内实现其他类别用电同价。

九、以上电价调整自2009年11月20日起执行。其中，电力用户11月20日后的用电量，可按对应抄表周期内日平均用电量乘以应执行调整后电价的天数确定。

十、各地价格主管部门要精心组织，周密安排，做好宣传解释工作，确保本通知规定的各项措施及时得到贯彻落实。执行中如有问题，请及时报告我委。

附件：一、辽宁省电网销售电价表（略）
二、吉林省电网销售电价表（略）
三、黑龙江省电网销售电价表（略）
四、内蒙古东部电网销售电价表（略）

国家发展改革委关于调整西北电网电价的通知

为疏导电价矛盾，完善电价结构，促进可再生能源发展，国家发展改革委经商国家电监会、国家能源局，决定适当调整电价水平。2009年11月18日以发改价格［2009］2921号文就调整西北电网电价有关事项通知如下：

一、调整发电企业上网电价

（一）为合理反映燃煤电厂投资、煤价、煤耗等情况变化，适当调整统调燃煤机组标杆上网电价水平。陕西、甘肃、青海省燃煤机组标杆上网电价每千瓦时分别上调1.2分钱、0.5分钱和1.5分钱。同时，适当提高部分电价偏低、亏损严重电厂的上网电价，逐步与标杆电价填平补齐。

（二）为促进水电站库区和移民安置区经济社会发展，缓解水电企业亏损严重、更新改造资金不足等问题，适当提高部分水电企业的上网电价。将陕西石泉发电有限公司、二郎坝、喜河水电站上网电价提高到每千瓦时0.303元。青海省龙羊峡水电站上网电价提高到每千瓦时0.163元，其他大中型水电站上网电价每千瓦时提高0.3分钱，小水电上网电价每千瓦时提高0.2分钱。

（三）由于水电项目开发的政策环境变化较大，新建水电暂停执行我委核定的水电标杆电价。青海省拉西瓦水电站上网电价暂按每千瓦时0.23元执行。

（四）核定宁夏哈纳斯天然气热电厂上网临时结算电价为每千瓦时0.505 8元。甘肃省国投白银捡财塘、大唐景泰风电场上网电价按中标价格执行。

有关电厂调整后的上网电价水平见附件一。

二、理顺发电企业上网电价与销售电价关系。2008年8月全国火力发电企业上网电价提高影响电网企业增加的购电成本，通过调整销售电价予以疏导。

三、根据可再生能源发展需要，按照《可再生能源法》和《可再生能源发电价格和费用分摊管理试行办法》（发改价格［2006］7号）有关规定，将可再生能源电价附加标准提高到每千瓦时0.4分钱。

四、各省（区）销售电价每千瓦时提高0.2分钱，暂用于解决电网企业"一户一表"改造投资还本付息等问题。

五、为逐步完善跨省跨区电网输电价格机制，此次陕西省、甘肃省、青海省、宁夏自治区提高的销售电价中每千瓦时含西北电网公司输电价格0.08分钱。

六、适当提高电网销售电价。有关省（区）销售电价平均提价标准每千瓦时分别为：陕西省3.67分钱、甘肃省2.01分钱、青海省2.02分钱、宁夏自治区2.23分钱。各类用户调价后具体电价标准见附件二～附件五。

七、进一步优化销售电价结构。同意陕西省、青海省商业、非普工业和非居民用电价格合并为一般工商业电价类别。

八、以上电价调整自2009年11月20日起执行。其中，电力用户11月20日后的用电量，可按对应抄表周期内日平均用电量乘以应执行调整后电价的天数确定。

九、各地价格主管部门要精心组织，周密安排，做好宣传解释工作，确保本通知规定的各项措施及时得到贯彻落实。执行中如有问题，请及时报告我委。

附件：一、西北电网部分电厂上网电价表（略）
　　　二、陕西省电网销售电价表（略）
　　　三、甘肃省电网销售电价表（略）
　　　四、青海省电网销售电价表（略）
　　　五、宁夏自治区电网销售电价表（略）

国家发展改革委关于调整华东电网电价的通知

为疏导电价矛盾，完善电价结构，促进可再生能源发展，国家发展改革委经商国家电监会、国家能源局，决定适当调整电价水平。2009年11月18日以发改价格［2009］2924号文就调整华东电网电价有关事项通知如下：

一、调整发电企业上网电价

（一）为合理反映燃煤电厂投资、煤价、煤耗等情况变化，适当调整燃煤机组标杆上网电价水平。上海市、浙江省、江苏省、福建省统调燃煤机组标杆上网电价每千瓦时分别下调0.50分钱、0.87分钱、0.58分钱、0.80分钱。上海市、浙江省、江苏省、福建省现行上网电价高于标杆电价的机组，按上述标准同步下调。

（二）为促进水电站库区和移民安置区经济社会发展，缓解水电企业亏损严重、更新改造资金不足等问题，适当提高部分水电企业的上网电价。

（三）华东电网公司联络线口子统销电量基价调整为每千瓦时0.3707元。

有关电厂调整后的上网电价水平见附件一。

二、理顺发电企业上网电价与销售电价关系。2008年8月全国火力发电企业上网电价提高影响电网企业增加的购电成本，通过调整销售电价予以疏导。

三、根据可再生能源发展需要，按照《可再生能源法》和《可再生能源发电价格和费用分摊管理试行办法》（发改价格［2006］7号）有关规定，将可再生能源电价附加标准提高到每千瓦时0.40分钱。

四、将各省（市）销售电价每千瓦时提高0.20分钱，暂用于解决电网企业“一户一表”改造投资还本付息等问题。

五、为逐步完善跨省跨区电网输电价格机制，此次上海市、浙江省、江苏省、安徽省、福建省提高的销售电价中每千瓦时含华东电网公司输电价格0.05分钱。

六、同意江苏省在销售电价中每千瓦时提取0.05分钱，用于解决地方水库、水电站移民后期扶持问题。

七、适当提高电网销售电价。各省（市）销售电价平均提价标准每千瓦时分别为：上海市3.60分钱、浙江省2.90分钱、江苏省3.10分钱、安徽省2.72分钱、福建省3.32分钱。各类用户调价后具体电价标准见附件二～附件六。

八、进一步优化销售电价结构。上海市一般照明、非普动力用电价格合并为“工商业及其他用电”电价类别；福建省商业、非居民照明与非普工业用电价格合并为“一般工商业及其他用电”电价类别，分三年过渡到位。合并后同步执行峰谷分时电价等需求侧电价管理制度。

九、同意福建省实行居民生活用电、农业生产用电全省同价；两年内实现其他类别用电全省同价，具体方案另行报我委批复。

十、以上电价调整自2009年11月20日起执行。其中，电力用户11月20日后的用电量，可按对应抄表周期内日平均用电量乘以应执行调整后电价的天数确定。

十一、各地价格主管部门要精心组织，周密安排，做好宣传解释工作，确保本通知规定的各项措施及时得到贯彻落实。执行中如有问题，请及时报告我委。

附件：一、华东电网部分电厂上网电价表（略）
　　　二、上海市电网销售电价表（略）
　　　三、浙江省电网销售电价表（略）
　　　四、江苏省电网销售电价表（略）
　　　五、安徽省电网销售电价表（略）
　　　六、福建省电网销售电价表（略）

国家发展改革委关于调整华中电网电价的通知

为疏导电价矛盾，完善电价结构，促进可再生能源发展，国家发展改革委经商国家电监会、国家能源局，决定适当调整电价水平。2009年11月18日以发改价格［2009］2925号文就调整华中电网电价有关事项通知如下：

一、调整发电企业上网电价

（一）为合理反映燃煤电厂投资、煤价、煤耗等情况变化，适当调整统调燃煤机组标杆上网电价水平。江西省统调燃煤机组标杆上网电价每千瓦时上调0.2分钱，现行上网电价低于标杆电价的机组，同步上调；四川省统调燃煤机组标杆上网电价每千瓦时上调1分钱；重庆市统调燃煤机组标杆上网电价每千瓦时上调0.4分钱，其他燃煤机组同步调整；河南省统调燃煤机组标杆上网电价每千瓦时下调0.3分钱，现行上网电价高于标杆电价的机组，同步下调。

（二）为合理补偿燃煤机组脱硫成本，将重庆市统调燃煤发电机组脱硫加价标准由每千瓦时1.5分钱调整为2.0分钱。

（三）为促进水电站库区和移民安置区经济社会发展，缓解水电企业亏损严重、更新改造资金不足等问题，适当提高部分水电企业的上网电价。湖北省水布垭电站3号机组上网电价暂按照1、2号机组上网电价执行；江西省上犹江、洪门、江口、廖坊、柘林电厂上网电价每千瓦时分别提高3分钱，万安水电厂上网电价每千瓦时提高1分钱；四川省水牛家、洛古、硗碛、瓦屋山、大桥、仁宗海、狮子坪、紫兰坝水电站上网电价每千瓦时提高3分钱；葛洲坝电厂送湖北基数电量上网电价调整为每千瓦时0.18元，其余上网电量执行电价调整为每千瓦时0.24元。重庆市装机容量5万kW以上的水电企业，2008年7月份以前投产的上网电价为每千瓦时0.30元，2008年7月份以后投产的上网电价为每千瓦时0.31元；5万kW以下的水电企业上网电价由重庆市物价局另行制定。

（四）由于水电项目开发的政策环境变化较大，新建水电暂停执行我委核定的水电标杆电价。四川省瀑布沟电站暂执行临时上网电价每千瓦时0.30元。

（五）江西省分宜发电公司和分宜第二发电公司国产循环流化床机组上网电价调整为每千瓦时0.447元。同意江西省矶山湖风电场、长岭风电场、大岭风电场执行中标价格。

有关电厂调整后的上网电价水平见附件一。

二、理顺发电企业上网电价与销售电价关系。2008年8月全国火力发电企业上网电价提高影响电网企业增加的购电成本，通过调整销售电价予以疏导。

三、根据可再生能源发展需要，按照《可再生能源法》和《可再生能源发电价格和费用分摊管理试行办法》（发改价格［2006］7号）有关规定，将可再生能源电价附加标准提高到每千瓦时0.4分钱。其中，四川省列入国家地震灾后重建规划的39个县、市、区可再生能源电价附加标准每千瓦时提高0.2分钱。

四、各省（市）销售电价每千瓦时提高0.2分钱，暂用于解决电网企业“一户一表”改造投资还本付息等问题。

五、为逐步完善跨省跨区电网输电价格机制，此次湖北、河南、湖南、江西、重庆省（市）提高的销售电价中含华中电网公司输电价格每千瓦时0.05分钱。

六、适当提高电网销售电价。有关省（市）销售电价平均提价标准每千瓦时分别为：湖北省3.20分钱、湖南省2.70分钱、河南省3.45分钱、江西省2.84分钱、四川省2.24分钱、重庆市3.20分钱。各类用户调价后具体电价标准见附件二～附件七。

七、进一步优化销售电价结构。同意江西省推进城乡工业用电同价，实现全省各类用电同价；湖北省将非居民照明及商业电价与非普工业电价合并为“一般工商业及其他电价”；河南省将一般工商业电价与非居民照明电价合并为“一般工商业及其他电价”；四川省实行商业与非居民照明用电同价；重庆市实行商业与非居民照明用电同价。

八、以上电价调整自2009年11月20日起执行。其中，电力用户11月20日后的用电量，可按对应抄表周期内日平均用电量乘以应执行调整后电价的天数确定。

九、各地价格主管部门要精心组织，周密安排，做好宣传解释工作，确保本通知规定的各项措施及时得到贯彻落实。执行中如有问题，请及时报告我委。

附件：一、华中电网部分电厂上网电价表（略）
二、湖北省电网销售电价表（略）
三、湖南省电网销售电价表（略）
四、河南省电网销售电价表（略）
五、江西省电网销售电价表（略）
六、四川省电网销售电价表（略）
七、重庆市电网销售电价表（略）

国家发展改革委关于调整南方电网电价的通知

为疏导电价矛盾，完善电价结构，促进可再生能源发展，国家发展改革委经商国家电监会、国家能源局，决定适当调整电价水平。2009年11月18日以发改价格［2009］2926号文就调整南方电网电价有关事项通知如下：

一、调整发电企业上网电价

（一）为合理反映燃煤电厂投资、煤价、煤耗等情况变化，适当调整统调燃煤机组标杆上网电价水平。广东省统调燃煤机组标杆上网电价每千瓦时下调

0.8 分钱，其他燃煤机组同步下调；海南省统调燃煤机组标杆上网电价每千瓦时上调 0.32 分钱；云南省统调燃煤机组标杆上网电价每千瓦时上调 0.7 分钱，现行上网电价低于标杆电价的机组，同步上调。

（二）为合理补偿燃煤电厂脱硫成本，将贵州燃煤发电机组脱硫加价标准由每千瓦时 1.5 分钱调整为 1.7 分钱。

（三）为促进水电站库区和移民安置区经济社会发展，缓解水电企业亏损严重、更新改造资金不足等问题，适当提高部分水电企业的上网电价。云南省鲁布革、以礼河、大寨、西洱河、绿水河、六郎洞等原厂网分离电厂平水期和枯水期上网电价的上浮幅度由 10%提高至 20%，丰水期电价保持不变。云南省单机容量 25 万 kW 以下中小水电站上网电价每千瓦时提高 0.7 分钱。海南省大广坝水电站、牛路岭水电站上网电价每千瓦时分别提高 1 分钱、2 分钱。广西长洲水电站上网电价每千瓦时提高 1 分钱。广东省南告、潭岭、新丰江、枫树坝、流溪河、南水、长湖、长潭水电站上网电价每千瓦时提高 2 分钱。贵州省洪家渡、鱼塘、普定、引子渡、光照、清溪水电站上网电价每千瓦时提高 0.5 分钱，红枫、索风营、大花水电站上网电价每千瓦时提高 0.2 分钱。

（四）由于水电项目开发的政策环境变化较大，新建水电暂停执行我委核定的水电标杆电价。贵州构皮滩水电站和思林水电站暂执行临时上网电价每千瓦时 0.277 元；云南小湾水电站暂按每千瓦时 0.300 元结算；广西龙滩水电站上网电价按每千瓦时 0.307 元执行。

（五）同意广东南海发电一厂、汕头万丰电厂、坪石发电厂 3 号机上网电价每千瓦时分别提高 1.5 分钱、1.5 分钱、2 分钱。

二、理顺发电企业上网电价与销售电价关系。2008 年 8 月全国火力发电企业上网电价提高影响电网企业增加的购电成本，通过调整销售电价予以疏导。

三、根据可再生能源发展需要，按照《可再生能源法》和《可再生能源发电价格和费用分摊管理试行办法》（发改价格［2006］7 号）有关规定，将可再生能源电价附加标准提高到每千瓦时 0.4 分钱。

四、各省（区）销售电价每千瓦时提高 0.2 分钱，暂用于解决电网企业“一户一表”改造投资还本付息等问题。

五、适当提高电网销售电价。有关省（区）销售电价平均提价标准每千瓦时分别为：广东省 1.90 分钱、广西自治区 2.40 分钱、云南省 2.28 分钱、贵州省 2.61 分钱、海南省 3.45 分钱。各类用户调价后具体电价标准见附件一～附件五。

六、进一步优化销售电价结构。同意广东省缩小商业与非普工业用电价差，扩大峰谷电价比价，拉大电压等级差价；广西自治区商业与非普工业用电价格合并为“一般工商业及其他电价”类别；贵州省缩小商业与非普工业和非居民照明用电价差。

七、以上电价调整自 2009 年 11 月 20 日起执行。其中，电力用户 11 月 20 日后的用电量，可按对应抄表周期内日平均用电量乘以应执行调整后电价的天数确定。

八、各地价格主管部门要精心组织，周密安排，做好宣传解释工作，确保本通知规定的各项措施及时得到贯彻落实。执行中如有问题，请及时报告我委。

附件：一、广东省电网销售电价表（略）
二、广西自治区电网销售电价表（略）
三、云南省电网销售电价表（略）
四、贵州省电网销售售电价表（略）
五、海南省电网销售电价表（略）

国家发展改革委、国家电监会关于 2009 年 1～6 月可再生能源电价补贴和配额交易方案的通知

国家发展改革委、国家电监会根据《可再生能源发电价格和费用分摊管理试行办法》（发改价格［2006］7 号）和《可再生能源电价附加收入调配暂行办法》（发改价格［2007］44 号），于 2009 年 12 月 17 日以发改价格［2009］3217 号发文，就 2009 年 1～6 月可再生能源电价附加调配、补贴等有关事项通知如下：

一、电价附加补贴的项目和金额

可再生能源电价附加资金补贴范围为 2009 年1～6 月可再生能源发电项目上网电价高于当地脱硫燃煤机组标杆上网电价的部分、公共可再生能源独立电力系统运行维护费用、可再生能源发电项目接网费用。对纳入补贴范围内的秸秆直燃发电项目继续按上网电量给予临时电价补贴，补贴标准为每千瓦时 0.1 元。

具体补贴项目和金额见附件一、二、三、四。

二、电价附加配额交易

对收取的可再生能源电价附加不足以支付本省可再生能源电价补贴的省级电网企业，按照短缺资金金额颁发同等额度的可再生能源电价附加配额证，以配额交易方式实现可再生能源电价附加资金调配。2009 年 1～6 月电价附加配额交易方案见附件五。

配额卖方向买方出售配额证，配额买方应在收到配额证后 10 个工作日内，按额度将款项汇入卖方账

户，完成交易。

三、电费结算

（一）可再生能源发电项目上网电价在当地脱硫燃煤机组标杆上网电价以内的部分，由当地省级电网负担；高出部分，通过本次电价附加补贴解决。

（二）2009年1～6月电价附加有结余的省级电网企业，应在本通知下发之日起10个工作日内，对可再生能源发电项目结清2009年上半年电费（含接网费用补贴）。2009年1～6月电价附加存在资金缺口的山东、新疆等15个地区的电网企业，应在配额交易完成10个工作日内，对可再生能源发电项目结清2009年上半年电费（含接网费用补贴）。

（三）对2009年1～6月公共可再生能源独立电力系统的电价附加补贴，按本通知附件三所列的项目和金额，由所在省（区）的价格主管部门会同省级电网企业负责组织实施。

（四）本次配额交易完成后，电价附加有结余的省级电网企业，对已纳入补贴范围内的可再生能源发电项目按月结算电费，高于当地脱硫燃煤机组标杆上网电价的部分从电价附加中支付。

（五）各省级电网企业对可再生能源电价附加继续单独记账，余缺逐期滚存。

四、加强监管

各省（区、市）政府价格主管部门和各区域、城市电力监管机构要加强对可再生能源电价附加征收、配额交易、电费和补贴结算行为的监管，坚决纠正和查处违反本通知规定的电费结算行为，确保可再生能源电价附加补贴按时足额到位。

附件：一、2009年1～6月可再生能源发电项目补贴表（略）

二、2009年1～6月秸秆直燃项目临时电价补贴表（略）

三、2009年1～6月公共可再生能源独立电力系统补贴表（略）

四、2009年1～6月可再生能源发电接网工程补贴表（略）

五、2009年1～6月可再生能源电价附加配额交易方案（略）

财政部关于加强大中型水库库区基金征收管理有关问题的通知

财政部为落实《国务院关于完善大中型水库移民后期扶持政策的意见》（国发［2006］17号）和《财政部关于印发〈大中型水库库区基金征收使用管理暂行办法〉的通知》（财综［2007］26号）的规定，经商水利部，于2009年8月12日以财综［2009］51号文，就加强大中型水库库区基金（以下简称库区基金）征收管理有关问题通知如下：

一、凡财政部已批复库区基金征收使用管理实施细则的省份，要严格按照批复的征收范围、对象、标准和期限征收库区基金，确保应收尽收，不得擅自减免、缓征或停征。

二、凡行政区域内有装机容量在2.5万kW及以上有发电收入的水库和水电站，且尚未制定库区基金征收使用管理实施细则的省份，要抓紧制定本地区库区基金征收使用管理实施细则，并于2009年9月30日前按规定程序上报财政部，由财政部会同国家发展改革委、水利部批准后实施。

三、确因特殊情况需减免、缓征或停征库区基金的省份，应由省级财政部门报省级人民政府同意后，由省级人民政府向国务院提出申请。

四、各相关省、自治区、直辖市要高度重视库区基金征收使用管理工作，切实采取有效措施，加大征管力度，确保基金足额征收。财政部驻相关地方财政监察专员办事处和相关省级财政部门要各司其职，加强对库区基金的征收管理和监督检查，对未经国务院批准擅自减免、缓征或停征库区基金的，要按照《财政违法行为处罚处分条例》（国务院令第427号）的有关规定进行处罚，追究有关责任人的行政责任。

财政部关于征收跨省际大中型水库库区基金有关问题的通知

财政部根据《国务院关于完善大中型水库移民后期扶持政策的意见》（国发［2006］17号）和《财政部关于印发〈大中型水库库区基金征收使用管理暂行办法〉的通知》（财综［2007］26号）的相关规定，于2009年9月5日以财综［2009］59号文，就征收装机容量在2.5万kW及以上有发电收入的跨省、自治区、直辖市（以下简称跨省际）大中型水库库区基金有关问题通知如下：

一、跨省际大中型水库库区基金，由财政部驻水库发电企业所在省份财政监察专员办事处（以下简称专员办）负责征收，征收标准按照水库发电企业所在省份的大中型水库库区基金征收标准执行。

缴纳大中型水库库区基金的跨省际大中型水库名单，具体负责征收跨省际大中型水库库区基金的专员办名单，以及各水库适用的大中型水库库区基金征收标准见附件。

二、跨省际大中型水库为独立法人的，由水库（水电站）缴纳大中型水库库区基金；跨省际大中型水库为非独立法人的，由其归属企业缴纳大中型水库库区基金。

三、专员办征收跨省际大中型水库库区基金，实行直接缴库。水库（水电站）或其归属企业应于每月10日前向专员办申报上月实际销售电量和应缴纳的大中型水库库区基金，专员办应于每月12日前完成对申报的审核，并向申报企业开具《非税收入一般缴款书》。水库（水电站）或其归属企业应在每月15日前，按照专员办开具《非税收入一般缴款书》所规定的缴款额，足额上缴资金。专员办应根据水库（水电站）全年实际销售电量，在次年3月底前完成全年应缴大中型水库库区基金的清算和征缴。

四、跨省际大中型水库库区基金收入在政府收支分类科目中填列第1030150项“大中型水库库区基金收入”。

五、跨省际大中型水库库区基金收入全额缴入中央国库，由中央财政按相关省份应分配的比例，并根据资金入库情况按季拨付给相关省级财政。跨省际大中型水库库区基金在相关省份的分配比例，按照有关部门和相关省份共同确认的跨省际大中型水库移民人数比例核定，具体分配比例详见附件。

六、中央财政向省级财政拨付大中型水库库区基金时，填列政府收支分类科目第2300401项“政府性基金补助支出”。相关省份收到时，填列政府收支分类科目第1100401项“政府性基金补助收入”，在安排最终支出时，2009年填列政府收支分类科目第2130336项“大中型水库库区基金支出”。2010年填列政府收支分类科目第2130380项“大中型水库库区基金支出（基础设施建设和经济发展）”、第2130381项“大中型水库库区基金支出（解决移民遗留问题）”、第2130382项“大中型水库库区基金支出（库区防护工程维护）”、第2130384项“其他大中型水库库区基金支出”。

七、已经审定但未列入本通知附件的跨省际大中型水库，其库区基金征收政策，待水库发电企业所在省、自治区、直辖市按规定程序向财政部报送该地区大中型水库库区基金征收使用管理实施细则时一并考虑，并按财政部会同国家发展改革委、水利部批准后的相关征收政策执行。

八、符合征收条件的新建跨省际大中型水库，其库区基金征收政策，由水库发电企业所在省、自治区、直辖市按规定程序上报，经财政部会同国家发展改革委、水利部批准后执行。

九、本通知自2009年10月1日起实施。

附件：跨省际大中型水库名单、库区基金征收标准、征收机关和分配比例表

附件：

跨省际大中型水库名单、库区基金征收标准、征收机关和分配比例表

序号	工程名称	征收标准 [厘/(kW·h)]	征 收 机 关	涉及省份	分配比例
1	桓仁水库	8	财政部驻辽宁财政监察专员办事处	辽宁	75.00%
				吉林	25.00%
2	水丰水库	8	财政部驻辽宁财政监察专员办事处	辽宁	66.00%
				吉林	34.00%
3	万家寨水利枢纽	8	财政部驻山西财政监察专员办事处	山西	2.80%
				内蒙古	97.20%
4	丹江口水库	8	财政部驻湖北财政监察专员办事处	湖北	61.00%
				河南	39.00%
5	江垭水库	8	财政部驻湖南财政监察专员办事处	湖南	85.00%
				湖北	15.00%
6	纳吉滩水电站	8	财政部驻湖北财政监察专员办事处	湖北	38.40%
				湖南	61.60%
7	塘口	8	财政部驻湖北财政监察专员办事处	湖北	40.00%
				湖南	60.00%

续表

序号	工程名称	征收标准[厘/(kW·h)]	征收机关	涉及省份	分配比例
8	碗米坡电站	8	财政部驻湖南财政监察专员办事处	湖南	93.80%
				重庆	6.20%
9	宝珠寺电站	8	财政部驻四川财政监察专员办事处	四川	81.40%
				陕西	9.40%
				甘肃	9.20%
10	炳灵水电站	8	财政部驻甘肃财政监察专员办事处	甘肃	31.30%
				青海	68.70%
11	张窝电站	8	财政部驻四川财政监察专员办事处	四川	5.40%
				云南	94.60%
12	大洪河水库	8	财政部驻重庆财政监察专员办事处	重庆	37.00%
				四川	63.00%
13	向家坝电站	8	财政部驻四川财政监察专员办事处	四川	45.40%
				云南	54.60%
14	溪洛渡电站	8	财政部驻四川财政监察专员办事处	四川	33.00%
				云南	67.00%
15	彭水电站	8	财政部驻重庆财政监察专员办事处	重庆	34.60%
				贵州	65.40%
16	龙滩电站	8	财政部驻广西财政监察专员办事处	广西	42.20%
				贵州	57.80%
17	鲁布革电站	8	财政部驻云南财政监察专员办事处	云南	48.50%
				贵州	51.50%
18	天生桥一级水电站	8	财政部驻贵州财政监察专员办事处	广西	43.60%
				云南	5.70%
				贵州	50.70%
19	天生桥二级水电站	8	财政部驻广西财政监察专员办事处	广西	74.50%
				贵州	25.50%
20	洞巴水电站	8	财政部驻广西财政监察专员办事处	广西	54.80%
				云南	45.20%
21	百色水利枢纽	8	财政部驻广西财政监察专员办事处	广西	67.50%
				云南	32.50%
22	平班水电站	8	财政部驻广西财政监察专员办事处	广西	58.60%
				贵州	41.40%

财政部、国家税务总局关于再生资源增值税退税政策若干问题的通知

财政部、国家税务总局根据各地的反映，于2009年9月29日以财税［2009］119号文，对《财政部、国家税务总局关于再生资源增值税政策的通知》（财税［2008］157号）的有关政策问题明确如下：

一、财税［2008］157号第四条第（一）款“通过金融机构结算”，是指纳税人销售再生资源时按照中国人民银行《关于印发〈支付结算办法〉的通知》（银发［1997］393号）规定的票据、信用卡和汇兑、托收承付、委托收款等结算方式进行货币给付及其资金清算。纳税人销售再生资源发生的应收账款，应在纳税人按照银发［1997］393号文件规定进行资金清算后方可计入通过金融机构结算的再生资源销售额。

纳税人销售再生资源按照银发［1997］393号文件规定取得的预收货款，应在销售实现后方可计入通过金融机构结算的再生资源销售额。

纳税人之间发生的互抵货款，不应计入通过金融机构计算的再生资源销售额。

纳税人通过金融机构结算的再生资源销售额占全部再生资源销售额的比重是否不低于80％的要求，应按纳税人退税申请办理时限（按月、按季等）进行核定。

二、财税［2008］157号文件所称再生资源的具体范围，操作时按照2008年底以前税务机关批准适用免征增值税政策的再生资源的具体范围执行，但必须符合财税［2008］157号文件第六条的规定，其中加工处理仅限于清洗、挑选、破碎、切割、拆解、打包等改变再生资源密度、湿度、长度、粗细、软硬等物理性状的简单加工。

三、财税［2008］157号文件第四条第（一）款规定按照《再生资源回收管理办法》（商务部令2007年第8号）第七条、第八条规定应当向有关部门备案的，应当自备案当月1日起享受退税政策。

四、纳税人申请退税时提供的2009年10月1日以后开具的再生资源收购凭证、扣税凭证或销售发票，除符合现行发票管理有关规定外，还应注明购进或销售的再生资源的具体种类（从废旧金属、报废电子产品、报废机电设备及其零部件、废造纸原料、废轻化工原料、废塑料、废玻璃和其他再生资源等8类之中选择填写），否则不得享受退税。

五、负责初审的财政机关和税务主管机关应当加强联系，及时就纳税人的征税和退税等情况进行沟通。负责初审的财政机关应当定期向税务主管机关通报受理和审批的申请退税纳税人名单及批准的退税额，税务主管机关对在日常税收征管、纳税检查、纳税评估、稽查等过程中发现的纳税人的异常情况及时通报给负责初审的财政机关。

对于税务主管机关通报有异常情况的纳税人，负责初审的财政机关应将有关情况及时上报负责复审和终审的财政机关，各级财政机关应暂停办理该纳税人的退税，并会同税务主管机关进一步查明情况。对于查实存在将非再生资源混作再生资源购进或销售等骗取退税行为的，除追缴其此前骗取的退税款并根据《财政违法行为处罚处分条例》（国务院令第427号）的规定进行处罚外，取消其以后享受再生资源退税政策的资格。

六、本通知自2009年10月1日起执行。

水利建设市场主体信用信息管理暂行办法

为解决水利建设领域存在的市场主体信用意识薄弱和信用缺失等突出问题，推进水利建设市场信用体系建设，规范水利建设市场主体行为，加强水利建设市场秩序监管，水利部制定了《水利建设市场主体信用信息管理暂行办法》，2009年10月15日以水建管［2009］496号发布执行。全文如下：

水利建设市场主体信用信息管理暂行办法

第一条 为贯彻落实《中共中央办公厅国务院办公厅关于开展工程建设领域突出问题专项治理工作的意见》（中办发［2009］27号）、《国务院办公厅关于社会信用体系建设的若干意见》（国办发［2007］17号）和中央治理商业贿赂领导小组《关于在治理商业贿赂专项工作中推进市场诚信体系建设的意见》（中治贿发［2008］2号）的精神，促进水利建设市场信用体系建设，规范水利建设市场主体行为，加强水利建设市场秩序监管，促进水利事业又好又快发展，根据有关法律法规，结合水利建设行业实际和特点，制定本办法。

第二条 本办法适用于水利建设市场主体信用信息采集、审核、发布、更正和使用的管理。

第三条 本办法所称水利建设市场主体，是指参与水利工程建设活动的建设、勘察、设计、施工、监理、咨询、供货、招标代理、质量检测、安全评价等企（事）业单位及相关执（从）业人员。

第四条 水利建设市场主体信用信息管理遵循依法、公开、公正、准确、及时的原则，维护水利建设市场主体的合法权益，保守国家秘密，保护商业秘密和个人隐私。

第五条 水利部、水利部在国家确定的重要江河湖泊设立的流域管理机构（以下简称流域管理机构）和省级人民政府水行政主管部门是水利建设市场主体信用信息管理部门，按照各自的职责分工负责水利建设市场主体信用信息管理工作。

水利部负责组织制定全国水利建设市场主体信用信息制度和标准，建立全国水利建设市场主体信用信息平台，采集和发布全国水利建设市场主体信用信息，指导全国水利建设市场主体信用信息管理工作。

各流域管理机构和各省级人民政府水行政主管部门依照管理权限，分别负责其管辖范围内的水利建设市场主体信用信息管理工作，建立水利建设市场主体信用信息管理平台，采集和发布水利建设市场主体信用信息，同时将信用信息及时报送水利部。

第六条 水利建设市场主体信用信息包括基本信息、良好行为记录信息和不良行为记录信息。

基本信息是指水利建设市场主体的名称、注册地址、注册资金、资质、业绩、人员、主营业务范围等信息。

良好行为记录信息是指水利建设市场主体在工程建设过程中遵守有关法律、法规和规章，受到县级以上人民政府、水行政主管部门、流域管理机构或相关专业部门、有关社会团体的奖励和表彰，所形成的信用信息。

不良行为记录信息是指水利建设市场主体在工程建设过程中违反有关法律、法规和规章，受到县级以上人民政府、水行政主管部门、流域管理机构或相关专业部门的行政处理，或者未受到行政处理但造成不良影响的行为，所形成的信用信息。

第七条 各水利建设市场主体自主填写信用信息，按以下程序报送：

（一）中央企业、水利部所属企（事）业单位向水利部报送。

（二）流域管理机构所属企（事）业单位向流域管理机构报送，经流域管理机构审核后报水利部。

（三）其他企（事）业单位向其注册所在地省级人民政府水行政主管部门报送，经省级人民政府水行政主管部门审核后报水利部。

水利建设市场主体报送的信用信息应真实、合法。信用信息的采集、审核、更正，必须以具有法律效力的文书为依据。

第八条 建立水利建设市场主体不良行为记录公告制度。对水利建设市场主体在工程建设过程中违反有关法律、法规和规章，受到县级以上人民政府、水行政主管部门、流域管理机构或相关专业部门的行政处理，所形成的不良行为记录进行公告。未受到行政处理的不良信用信息可在公告平台后台保存备查。

水利建设市场主体不良行为记录公告办法及认定标准由水利部另行制定。

第九条 水利建设市场主体信用信息实行实时更新。水利建设市场主体基本信息发布时间为长期，良好行为记录信息发布期限为3年，不良行为记录信息发布期限不少于6个月，法律、法规另有规定的从其规定。

第十条 水利建设市场主体对公告信息有异议的，可向信用信息管理部门提出书面更正申请，并提供相关证据。信用信息管理部门应当立即进行核对，对确认发布有误的信息，及时给予更正并告知申请人；对确认无误的信息，应当告知申请人。

行政处理决定经行政复议、行政诉讼以及行政执法监督被依法变更或撤销的，不良行为记录将及时予以变更或撤销，并在信息平台上予以公告。

第十一条 水利部、流域管理机构和省级人民政府水行政主管部门应推进信用信息平台的互联互通，实现网络互联、信息共享和实时发布，维护水利建设市场的统一开放、竞争有序。

第十二条 水利部、流域管理机构和省级人民政府水行政主管部门应依据有关法律、法规和规章，按照诚信激励和失信惩戒的原则，逐步建立信用奖惩机制，在市场准入、招标投标、资质（资格）管理、信用评价、工程担保与保险、表彰评优等工作中，利用已公布的水利建设市场主体的信用信息，依法对守信行为给予激励，对失信行为进行惩处。

第十三条 水利部、流域管理机构和省级人民政府水行政主管部门要明确分管领导和承办机构、人员及职责，加强对水利建设市场主体信用信息管理工作的监督检查，保证信息公告、传送及时准确。鼓励社会各界监督水利建设市场主体信用信息管理工作。

第十四条 有关水行政主管部门、流域管理机构及其工作人员，违反本办法规定的，责令改正；在工作中玩忽职守、弄虚作假、滥用职权、徇私舞弊的，依法给予行政处分；涉嫌犯罪的，移送司法机关依法追究刑事责任。

第十五条 中国水利工程协会在水利部指导下，研究制订统一的信用信息分类及编码、信用信息格式和信用数据库建设标准等；建立统一的水利建设市场主体信用信息平台，并采集、记录和管理信用信息；组织开展水利建设市场主体信用知识培训教育。同时，要完善行业内部监督和协调机制，建立以会员单位为基础的信用信息平台，加强行业自律，提高企

（事）业单位及相关执（从）业人员的信用意识。

第十六条　各流域管理机构和各省级人民政府水行政主管部门可根据本办法，制定具体实施细则。

第十七条　本办法自2009年12月1日起施行。

水利建设市场主体不良行为记录公告暂行办法

为促进水利建设市场信用体系建设，健全水利建设市场失信惩戒机制，规范水利建设市场主体行为，水利部制定了《水利建设市场主体不良行为记录公告暂行办法》，于2009年10月27日以水建管［2009］518号文发布。全文如下：

水利建设市场主体不良行为记录公告暂行办法

第一章　总　　则

第一条　为贯彻《中共中央办公厅国务院办公厅关于开展工程建设领域突出问题专项治理工作的意见》（中办发［2009］27号）、《国务院办公厅关于社会信用体系建设的若干意见》（国办发［2007］17号）、《关于印发〈招标投标违法行为记录公告暂行办法〉的通知》（发改法规［2008］1531号）和《水利建设市场主体信用信息管理暂行办法》（水建管［2009］496号），促进水利建设市场信用体系建设，健全水利建设市场失信惩戒机制，规范水利建设市场主体行为，根据相关法律规定，制定本办法。

第二条　对水利建设市场主体的不良行为记录进行公告，适用本办法。

第三条　本办法所称水利建设市场主体，是指参与水利工程建设活动的建设、勘察、设计、施工、监理、咨询、供货、招标代理、质量检测、安全评价等企（事）业单位以及相关执（从）业人员。

第四条　本办法所公告的不良行为记录，是指水利建设市场主体在工程建设过程中违反有关法律、法规和规章，受到县级以上人民政府、水行政主管部门或相关专业部门的行政处理所做的记录。

水利建设市场主体不良行为记录认定标准见附件。

第五条　水利部、水利部在国家确定的重要江河湖泊设立的流域管理机构（以下简称流域管理机构）和省级人民政府水行政主管部门（以下统称公告部门）负责水利建设市场主体不良行为记录公告管理。

水利部负责制定全国水利建设市场主体不良行为记录公告管理的相关规定，建立全国水利建设市场主体不良行为记录公告平台，并负责公告平台的日常维护。

各流域管理机构和各省级人民政府水行政主管部门按照规定的职责分工，建立水利建设市场主体不良行为记录公告平台，并负责公告平台的日常维护。

第六条　水利建设市场主体不良行为记录的公告应坚持准确、及时、客观的原则。

第七条　水利建设市场主体不良行为记录公告不得公开涉及国家秘密、商业秘密、个人隐私的记录。但是，经权利人同意公开或者行政机关认为不公开可能对公共利益造成重大影响的涉及商业秘密、个人隐私的不良行为记录，可以公开。

第二章　不良行为记录的公告

第八条　公告部门应自不良行为行政处理决定作出之日起20个工作日内对外进行记录公告。

流域管理机构和省级人民政府水行政主管部门公告的不良行为行政处理决定应同时抄报水利部。

第九条　对不良行为所作出的以下行政处理决定应给予公告：

（一）警告；

（二）通报批评；

（三）罚款；

（四）没收违法所得；

（五）暂停或者取消招标代理资格；

（六）降低资质等级；

（七）吊销资质证书；

（八）责令停业整顿；

（九）吊销营业执照；

（十）取消在一定时期内参加依法必须进行招标的项目的投标资格；

（十一）暂停项目执行或追回已拨付资金；

（十二）暂停安排国家建设资金；

（十三）暂停建设项目的审查批准；

（十四）取消担任评标委员会成员的资格；

（十五）责令停止执业；

（十六）注销注册证书；

（十七）吊销执业资格证书；

（十八）公告部门或相关部门依法作出的其他行政处理决定。

第十条　不良行为记录公告的基本内容为：被处理水利建设市场主体的名称（或姓名）、违法行为、处理依据、处理决定、处理时间和处理机关等。

公告部门可将不良行为行政处理决定书直接进行公告。

第十一条　不良行为记录公告期限为6个月。公告期满后，转入后台保存。

依法限制水利建设市场主体资质（资格）等方面的行政处理决定，所认定的限制期限长于6个月的，公告期限从其决定。

第十二条 公告部门负责建立公告平台信息系统，对记录信息数据进行追加、修改、更新，并保证公告的不良行为记录与行政处理决定的相关内容一致。

公告平台信息系统应具备历史公告记录查询功能。

第十三条 公告部门应对公告记录所依据的不良行为行政处理决定书等材料妥善保管、留档备查。

第十四条 被公告的水利建设市场主体认为公告记录与行政处理决定的相关内容不符的，可向公告部门提出书面更正申请，并提供相关证据。

公告部门接到书面申请后，应在5个工作日内进行核对。公告的记录与行政处理决定的相关内容不一致的，应当给予更正并告知申请人；公告的记录与行政处理决定的相关内容一致的，应当告知申请人。

第十五条 行政处理决定在被行政复议或行政诉讼期间，公告部门依法不停止对不良行为记录的公告，但行政处理决定被依法停止执行的除外。

第十六条 原行政处理决定被依法变更或撤销的，公告部门应当及时对公告记录予以变更或撤销，并在公告平台上予以公告。

第三章 监督管理

第十七条 公告部门应依法加强对不良行为记录被公告的水利建设市场主体的监督管理。

第十八条 公告的不良行为记录应当作为市场准入、招标投标、资质（资格）管理、信用评价、工程担保与保险、表彰评优等工作的重要参考。

第十九条 有关公告部门及其工作人员在不良行为记录的提供、收集和公告等工作中有玩忽职守、弄虚作假或者徇私舞弊等行为的，由其所在单位或者上级主管机关予以通报批评，并依纪依法追究直接责任人和有关领导的责任；涉嫌犯罪的，移送司法机关依法追究刑事责任。

第四章 附 则

第二十条 各流域管理机构和各省级人民政府水行政主管部门可根据本办法，制定具体实施办法。

第二十一条 本办法自2009年12月1日起施行。

附件：水利建设市场主体不良行为记录认定标准（略）

供电监管办法

国家电力监管委员会于2009年11月26日以电监会27号令颁布《供电监管办法》，自2010年1月1日起施行。《供电监管办法》全文如下：

供电监管办法

第一章 总 则

第一条 为了加强供电监管，规范供电行为，维护供电市场秩序，保护电力使用者的合法权益和社会公共利益，根据《电力监管条例》和国家有关规定，制定本办法。

第二条 国家电力监管委员会（以下简称电监会）依照本办法和国家有关规定，履行全国供电监管和行政执法职能。

电监会派出机构（以下简称派出机构）负责辖区内供电监管和行政执法工作。

第三条 供电监管应当依法进行，并遵循公开、公正和效率的原则。

第四条 供电企业应当依法从事供电业务，并接受电监会及其派出机构（以下简称电力监管机构）的监管。供电企业依法经营，其合法权益受法律保护。

本办法所称供电企业是指依法取得电力业务许可证、从事供电业务的企业。

第五条 任何单位和个人对供电企业违反本办法和国家有关供电监管规定的行为，有权向电力监管机构投诉和举报，电力监管机构应当依法处理。

第二章 监管内容

第六条 电力监管机构对供电企业的供电能力实施监管。

供电企业应当加强供电设施建设，具有能够满足其供电区域内用电需求的供电能力，保障供电设施的正常运行。

第七条 电力监管机构对供电企业的供电质量实施监管。

在电力系统正常的情况下，供电企业的供电质量应当符合下列规定：

（一）向用户提供的电能质量符合国家标准或者电力行业标准；

（二）城市地区年供电可靠率不低于99%，城市居民用户受电端电压合格率不低于95%，10kV以上供电用户受电端电压合格率不低于98%；

（三）农村地区年供电可靠率和农村居民用户受电端电压合格率符合派出机构的规定。派出机构有关农村地区年供电可靠率和农村居民用户受电端电压合格率的规定，应当报电监会备案。

供电企业应当审核用电设施产生谐波、冲击负荷的情况，按照国家有关规定拒绝不符合规定的用电设施接入电网。用电设施产生谐波、冲击负荷影响供电质量或者干扰电力系统安全运行的，供电企业应当及时告知用户采取有效措施予以消除；用户不采取措施或者采取措施不力，产生的谐波、冲击负荷仍超过国家标准的，供电企业可以按照国家有关规定拒绝其接入电网或者中止供电。

第八条　电力监管机构对供电企业设置电压监测点的情况实施监管。

供电企业应当按照下列规定选择电压监测点：

（一）35kV专线供电用户和110kV以上供电用户应当设置电压监测点；

（二）35kV非专线供电用户或者66kV供电用户、10（6、20）kV供电用户，每10 000kW负荷选择具有代表性的用户设置1个以上电压监测点，所选用户应当包括对供电质量有较高要求的重要电力用户和变电站10（6、20）kV母线所带具有代表性线路的末端用户；

（三）低压供电用户，每百台配电变压器选择具有代表性的用户设置1个以上电压监测点，所选用户应当是重要电力用户和低压配电网的首末两端用户。

供电企业应当于每年3月31日前将上一年度设置电压监测点的情况报送所在地派出机构。

供电企业应当按照国家有关规定选择、安装、校验电压监测装置，监测和统计用户电压情况。监测数据和统计数据应当及时、真实、完整。

第九条　电力监管机构对供电企业保障供电安全的情况实施监管。

供电企业应当坚持安全第一、预防为主、综合治理的方针，遵守有关供电安全的法律、法规和规章，加强供电安全管理，建立、健全供电安全责任制度，完善安全供电条件，维护电力系统安全稳定运行，依法处置供电突发事件，保障电力稳定、可靠供应。

供电企业应当按照国家有关规定加强重要电力用户安全供电管理，指导重要电力用户配置和使用自备应急电源，建立自备应急电源基础档案数据库。

供电企业发现用电设施存在安全隐患，应当及时告知用户采取有效措施进行治理。用户应当按照国家有关规定消除用电设施安全隐患。用电设施存在严重威胁电力系统安全运行和人身安全的隐患，用户拒不治理的，供电企业可以按照国家有关规定对该用户中止供电。

第十条　电力监管机构对供电企业履行电力社会普遍服务义务的情况实施监管。

供电企业应当按照国家规定履行电力社会普遍服务义务，依法保障任何人能够按照国家规定的价格获得最基本的供电服务。

第十一条　电力监管机构对供电企业办理用电业务的情况实施监管。

供电企业办理用电业务的期限应当符合下列规定：

（一）向用户提供供电方案的期限，自受理用户用电申请之日起，居民用户不超过3个工作日，其他低压供电用户不超过8个工作日，高压单电源供电用户不超过20个工作日，高压双电源供电用户不超过45个工作日；

（二）对用户受电工程设计文件和有关资料审核的期限，自受理之日起，低压供电用户不超过8个工作日，高压供电用户不超过20个工作日；

（三）对用户受电工程启动中间检查的期限，自接到用户申请之日起，低压供电用户不超过3个工作日，高压供电用户不超过5个工作日；

（四）对用户受电工程启动竣工检验的期限，自接到用户受电装置竣工报告和检验申请之日起，低压供电用户不超过5个工作日，高压供电用户不超过7个工作日；

（五）给用户装表接电的期限，自受电装置检验合格并办结相关手续之日起，居民用户不超过3个工作日，其他低压供电用户不超过5个工作日，高压供电用户不超过7个工作日。

前款第（二）项规定的受电工程设计，用户应当按照供电企业确定的供电方案进行。

第十二条　电力监管机构对供电企业向用户受电工程提供服务的情况实施监管。

供电企业应当对用户受电工程建设提供必要的业务咨询和技术标准咨询；对用户受电工程进行中间检查和竣工检验，应当执行国家有关标准；发现用户受电设施存在故障隐患时，应当及时一次性书面告知用户并指导其予以消除；发现用户受电设施存在严重威胁电力系统安全运行和人身安全的隐患时，应当指导其立即消除，在隐患消除前不得送电。

第十三条　电力监管机构对供电企业实施停电、限电或者中止供电的情况进行监管。

在电力系统正常的情况下，供电企业应当连续向用户供电。需要停电或者限电的，应当符合下列规定：

（一）因供电设施计划检修需要停电的，供电企业应当提前7日公告停电区域、停电线路、停电时间；

（二）因供电设施临时检修需要停电的，供电企业应当提前24小时公告停电区域、停电线路、停电时间；

（三）因电网发生故障或者电力供需紧张等原因需要停电、限电的，供电企业应当按照所在地人民政府批准的有序用电方案或者事故应急处置方案执行。

引起停电或者限电的原因消除后，供电企业应当尽快恢复正常供电。

供电企业对用户中止供电应当按照国家有关规定执行。

供电企业对重要电力用户实施停电、限电、中止供电或者恢复供电，应当按照国家有关规定执行。

第十四条 电力监管机构对供电企业处理供电故障的情况实施监管。

供电企业应当建立完善的报修服务制度，公开报修电话，保持电话畅通，24 小时受理供电故障报修。

供电企业应当迅速组织人员处理供电故障，尽快恢复正常供电。供电企业工作人员到达现场抢修的时限，自接到报修之时起，城区范围不超过 60 分钟，农村地区不超过 120 分钟，边远、交通不便地区不超过 240 分钟。因天气、交通等特殊原因无法在规定时限内到达现场的，应当向用户作出解释。

第十五条 电力监管机构对供电企业履行紧急供电义务的情况实施监管。

因抢险救灾、突发事件需要紧急供电时，供电企业应当及时提供电力供应。

第十六条 电力监管机构对供电企业处理用电投诉的情况实施监管。

供电企业应当建立用电投诉处理制度，公开投诉电话。对用户的投诉，供电企业应当自接到投诉之日起 10 个工作日内提出处理意见并答复用户。

供电企业应当在供电营业场所设置公布电力服务热线电话和电力监管投诉举报电话的标识，该标识应当固定在供电营业场所的显著位置。

第十七条 电力监管机构对供电企业执行国家有关电力行政许可规定的情况实施监管。

供电企业应当遵守国家有关供电营业区、供电业务许可、承装（修、试）电力设施许可和电工进网作业许可等规定。

第十八条 电力监管机构对供电企业公平、无歧视开放供电市场的情况实施监管。

供电企业不得从事下列行为：

（一）无正当理由拒绝用户用电申请；

（二）对趸购转售电企业符合国家规定条件的输配电设施，拒绝或者拖延接入系统；

（三）违反市场竞争规则，以不正当手段损害竞争对手的商业信誉或者排挤竞争对手；

（四）对用户受电工程指定设计单位、施工单位和设备材料供应单位；

（五）其他违反国家有关公平竞争规定的行为。

第十九条 电力监管机构对供电企业执行国家规定的电价政策和收费标准的情况实施监管。

供电企业应当严格执行国家电价政策，按照国家核准电价或者市场交易价，依据计量检定机构依法认可的用电计量装置的记录，向用户计收电费。

供电企业不得自定电价，不得擅自变更电价，不得擅自在电费中加收或者代收国家政策规定以外的其他费用。

供电企业不得自立项目或者自定标准收费；对国家已经明令取缔的收费项目，不得向用户收取费用。

供电企业应用户要求对产权属于用户的电气设备提供有偿服务时，应当执行政府定价或者政府指导价。没有政府定价和政府指导价的，参照市场价格协商确定。

第二十条 电力监管机构对供电企业签订供用电合同的情况实施监管。

供电企业应当按照国家有关规定，遵循平等自愿、协商一致、诚实信用的原则，与用户、趸购转售电单位签订供用电合同，并按照合同约定供电。

第二十一条 电力监管机构对供电企业执行国家规定的成本规则的情况实施监管。

供电企业应当按照国家有关成本的规定核算成本。

第二十二条 电力监管机构对供电企业信息公开的情况实施监管。

供电企业应当依照《中华人民共和国政府信息公开条例》、《电力企业信息披露规定》，采取便于用户获取的方式，公开供电服务信息。供电企业公开信息应当真实、及时、完整。

供电企业应当方便用户查询下列信息：

（一）用电报装信息和办理进度；

（二）用电投诉处理情况；

（三）其他用电信息。

第二十三条 电力监管机构对供电企业报送信息的情况实施监管。

供电企业应当按照《电力企业信息报送规定》向电力监管机构报送信息。供电企业报送信息应当真实、及时、完整。

第二十四条 电力监管机构对供电企业执行国家有关节能减排和环境保护政策的情况实施监管。

供电企业应当减少电能输送和供应环节的损失和浪费。

供电企业应当严格执行政府有关部门依法作出的对淘汰企业、关停企业或者环境违法企业采取停限电措施的决定。未收到政府有关部门决定恢复送电的通知，供电企业不得擅自对政府有关部门责令限期整改的用户恢复送电。

第二十五条　电力监管机构对供电企业实施电力需求侧管理的情况实施监管。

供电企业应当按照国家有关电力需求侧管理规定，采取有效措施，指导用户科学、合理和节约用电，提高电能使用效率。

第三章　监 管 措 施

第二十六条　电力监管机构根据履行监管职责的需要，可以要求供电企业报送与监管事项相关的文件、资料，并责令供电企业按照国家规定如实公开有关信息。

电力监管机构应当对供电企业报送信息和公开信息的情况进行监督检查，发现违法行为及时处理。

第二十七条　供电企业应当按照电力监管机构的规定将与监管相关的信息系统接入电力监管信息系统。

第二十八条　电力监管机构依法履行职责，可以采取下列措施，进行现场检查：

（一）进入供电企业进行检查；

（二）询问供电企业的工作人员，要求其对有关检查事项作出说明；

（三）查阅、复制与检查事项有关的文件、资料，对可能被转移、隐匿、损毁的文件、资料予以封存；

（四）对检查中发现的违法行为，可以当场予以纠正或者要求限期改正。

第二十九条　电力监管机构可以在用户中依法开展供电满意度调查等供电情况调查，并向社会公布调查结果。

第三十条　供电企业违反国家有关供电监管规定的，电力监管机构应当依法查处并予以记录；造成重大损失或者重大影响的，电力监管机构可以对供电企业的主管人员和其他直接责任人员依法提出处理意见和建议。

第三十一条　电力监管机构对供电企业违反国家有关供电监管规定，损害用户合法权益和社会公共利益的行为及其处理情况，可以向社会公布。

第四章　罚　　则

第三十二条　电力监管机构从事监管工作的人员违反电力监管有关规定，损害供电企业、用户的合法权益以及社会公共利益的，依照国家有关规定追究其责任；应当承担纪律责任的，依法给予处分；构成犯罪的，依法追究刑事责任。

第三十三条　供电企业违反本办法第六条规定，没有能力对其供电区域内的用户提供供电服务并造成严重后果的，电力监管机构可以变更或者吊销电力业务许可证，指定其他供电企业供电。

第三十四条　供电企业违反本办法第七条、第八条、第九条、第十条、第十一条、第十二条、第十三条、第十四条、第十五条、第十六条、第二十一条、第二十四条规定的，由电力监管机构责令改正，给予警告；情节严重的，对直接负责的主管人员和其他直接责任人员，依法给予处分。

第三十五条　供电企业违反本办法第十八条规定，由电力监管机构责令改正，拒不改正的，处10万元以上100万元以下罚款；对直接负责的主管人员和其他直接责任人员，依法给予处分；情节严重的，可以吊销电力业务许可证。

第三十六条　供电企业违反本办法第十九条规定的，电力监管机构可以责令改正并向有关部门提出行政处罚建议。

第三十七条　供电企业有下列情形之一的，由电力监管机构责令改正；拒不改正的，处5万元以上50万元以下罚款，对直接负责的主管人员和其他直接责任人员，依法给予处分；构成犯罪的，依法追究刑事责任：

（一）拒绝或者阻碍电力监管机构及其从事监管工作的人员依法履行监管职责的；

（二）提供虚假或者隐瞒重要事实的文件、资料的；

（三）未按照国家有关电力监管规章、规则的规定公开有关信息的。

第三十八条　对于违反本办法并造成严重后果的供电企业主管人员或者直接责任人员，电力监管机构可以建议将其调离现任岗位，3年内不得担任供电企业同类职务。

第五章　附　　则

第三十九条　本办法所称以上、以下、不低于、不超过，包括本数。

第四十条　本办法自2010年1月1日起施行。2005年6月21日电监会发布的《供电服务监管办法（试行）》同时废止。

水利部、国家工商行政管理总局、国家安全生产监督管理总局、国家电力监管委员会关于加强小水电站安全监管工作的通知

水电［2009］585号

我国5万kW以下的小水电资源十分丰富，广泛分布在1700多个县，技术可开发量1.28亿kW。在

党中央、国务院的高度重视下，小水电建设取得了举世瞩目的成就。目前，全国已建成小水电站45 000多座，总装机容量5100多万kW，在建规模达2000万kW。小水电在农村社会经济发展、农民脱贫致富、节能减排和应急救灾等方面发挥了重要作用。但近年来，在小水电快速发展和体制转轨过程中，由于职责不清、监管缺位，一些小水电站安全隐患严重，事故时有发生，危及人民群众的生命和财产安全。为加强小水电站安全监管，消除安全隐患，保障公共安全，现就小水电站安全监管工作通知如下：

一、明确安全生产责任主体和监管主体

小水电站业主是安全生产的责任主体。业主负责人实行“一岗双责”，既要承担生产管理职责，也必须承担安全管理职责。业主单位要建立完善安全生产责任制度，保障安全投入，落实安全措施，不安全不允许生产。

审批、核准小水电项目的地方人民政府是小水电站的安全生产监管责任主体。各级水行政主管部门、安全监管部门和电力监管机构要按照综合监管与专业监管相结合的原则，明确各部门职责分工。有关部门和单位要各司其职，各负其责，协同配合，确保监管到位。

二、切实加强建设项目安全监管

小水电站是以开发水能资源为主要目标的水利工程，根据水利工程的特点，小水电建设要抓好关键环节的安全监管工作。

（一）严格项目审批、核准前的安全把关

从事小水电开发的项目业主，应取得工商行政管理部门核发的营业执照，其经营范围应包括水电开发业务。

小水电项目必须符合河流水能资源开发规划，取得有管辖权的水行政主管部门签署的水工程建设规划同意书；必须获得水能资源开发权，提交取水许可预申请，通过建设项目洪水影响评价、水资源论证、水土保持方案审批、初步设计审批和其他法定行政许可程序。

凡不满足上述要求的小水电项目，一律不得申请、审批或核准。

（二）严格项目的审批、核准

小水电项目按投资来源不同实行审批制或核准制。对于政府投资的小水电项目实行审批制，按国家相关规定履行审批手续；对不使用政府投资的小水电项目实行核准制，其项目申请报告必须达到初步设计深度。为确保“小电站大水库”的安全，库容达到或超过1000万m^3的水库电站项目必须根据水库库容的大小，按同等规模的水库项目进行初步设计审批。

各省（自治区、直辖市）水行政主管部门应明确辖区内小水电项目初步设计分级审批权限和具体要求，项目业主按工程规模向县级以上人民政府水行政主管部门申报审批。

已经通过初步设计审批的小水电项目，任何单位或个人不得擅自变更建设规模和内容。凡涉及水库大坝及溢洪设施、总体布置、建设规模、工程特性、主要设备等重大设计变更，项目业主应及时以书面形式报原审批部门批准后方可变更。

（三）严格项目建设过程的监管

小水电项目开工前，业主应提出开工申请，经有审批权的水行政主管部门审批后，方可开工建设。小水电工程建设应执行项目法人责任制、招标投标制、建设监理制和合同管理制。

小水电项目业主在主体工程招标工作完成并与施工、监理承包单位签订合同后，应向有监督管理权的水行政主管部门申请办理工程质量与安全监督手续，并接受工程质量安全监督机构的监督；要认真执行建设项目安全设施“三同时”工作的规定和要求，切实保证安全设施与主体工程同时设计、同时施工、同时投入生产和使用。

各级水行政主管部门、安全监管部门要加强对小水电工程建设过程的专业监管与综合监管，进一步加强小水电在建工程施工安全的监督检查，督促落实各项审批意见和安全生产措施。各级水利工程建设质量安全监督机构要切实履行职责，做好工程建设各环节的质量安全监督工作。

（四）严格项目验收制度

小水电建设项目验收应参照执行《水利水电建设工程验收规程》（SL 223—2008）的有关标准，实行分类验收制度。

截流前验收、重要隐蔽工程及基础处理工程验收、单位工程验收由项目业主负责，水行政主管部门参加；工程蓄水验收由项目业主提出申请，水行政主管部门主持；其他专项验收按相应规定和规程规范，由项目业主商相关部门负责组织。

竣工技术预验收，由项目业主提出申请，水行政主管部门主持，有关部门和单位参加。政府投资的小水电工程的竣工验收，按国家有关规定办理；不使用政府投资的小水电工程的竣工验收，由水行政主管部门负责组织。小水电工程竣工验收合格，取得工程竣工证书和电力业务许可证、取水许可证后，方可正式投入运行。

凡未经蓄水验收的小水电工程一律不得蓄水，凡未经竣工验收的小水电工程一律不准投入正式运营。

三、不断强化已建工程安全监管

已建成运行小水电站的大坝管理单位应按规定向大坝主管部门或指定的注册登记机构申请登记。

按照“属地管理”的原则和职责分工，各地各有关部门要摸清本地区小水电工程的基本情况，逐站落实安全监管责任主体。小水电站的安全监管责任已经落实的地方，可继续执行现行职责分工；职责尚未明确的地方，各省级水行政主管部门与当地电力监管机构，要按照职责分工和全面覆盖、利于监管、协商一致的要求，在2010年汛前全面落实本行政区域内小水电站的安全监管责任主体。

各地各有关部门应定期对已经投运的小水电站进行安全执法检查。重点检查工程设备设施是否存在安全隐患，安全生产责任制是否落实，安全生产管理机构是否健全，安全生产管理制度是否完善，安全保障措施是否到位，安全隐患是否得到及时整改。

各级水行政主管部门要与有关部门密切配合，进一步落实农村水电安全管理分类和年检制度以及安全监察员持证上岗制度，做好安全运行监管、标准化管理和教育培训工作。

电力监管机构要与有关部门密切配合，进一步加强对并入电网运行的小水电站的涉网安全监督管理，确保电网安全和并网机组安全。

四、严格落实防汛安全责任制度

小水电工程防汛安全实行地方行政首长负责制，统一指挥、分级分部门负责，明确防汛行政责任人和防汛指挥调度权限。小水电站业主要编制汛期调度运用计划和防洪抢险应急预案，并报防汛指挥部门审批。要与所在河流水文测报机构保持联系，建立健全包括各参建、运行单位在内的安全应急机制，落实汛情预警、信息传输、物资储备、抢险队伍等应急措施。

汛期所有施工、维修作业都要严格遵守相关技术规程，并落实安全防护措施。特别是在涉及重大公共安全、施工人员生命安全的危险区域进行施工、维修作业的，施工前应制定应急预案，并向当地防汛指挥机构报告，得到批准后方可施工。一旦出现险情，有关防汛责任人要第一时间到达现场，组织抢险。

各级水利、安全监管、电监等有关部门和单位要在当地防汛指挥机构统一指挥下，认真履行相关职责，切实加强监管，及时消除隐患，确保工程安全。

五、继续加大违规水电站清查整改力度

违规水电站普遍存在审批手续不全、设计不够合理、管理制度缺失、质量安全隐患严重等问题，一旦发生事故，后果十分严重。地方各级水利、工商、安全监管、电监等部门和单位要在地方人民政府统一领导下，在各自的职责范围内，认真履行监管职责，并加强协作配合，采取有效措施，实施联合执法。要区分不同情况，在登记造册基础上，明确重点和范围，有针对性地实行分类整改，挂牌督办，限期销号。要建立长效防控机制，确保清查、整改和监管等各项工作落实到位，防止产生新的违规水电站。

六、严厉查处各种违法违规行为

我国小水电站分布广泛、数量众多，安全监管难度很大。各有关部门和单位要通力协作，加强监管。要依法规范小水电建设市场准入，禁止无资质、无许可证的单位和无执业资格的人员进入小水电建设市场。

对违反规划、未经审批擅自开工的小水电项目，水行政主管部门应责令其立即停工并予以处罚。对违规建设的小水电工程，水行政主管部门、安全监管部门应依法进行查处并责令其限期整改。对于安全隐患严重、整改不力或拒绝整改的，根据地方政府下达的关闭决定，工商行政管理部门依法吊销企业营业执照；电力监管机构不予办理电力业务许可；水行政主管部门不予办理取水许可。

对未经验收擅自蓄水或投运的小水电工程，水行政主管部门应责令其放空库容，不予办理取水许可，并报请地方人民政府立即采取措施。根据地方政府下达的关闭决定，工商行政管理部门依法吊销企业营业执照；电力监管机构不予办理电力业务许可。

对已投运的小水电站，凡存在工程安全隐患严重、安全责任制不落实、安全管理制度不健全、持证上岗不规范、安全投入无保障等违规问题的，由水利、安全监管、电监等部门和单位责令其限期整改；对于整改不力或拒绝整改的，依照有关法律法规予以查处。根据地方政府下达的关闭决定，工商行政管理部门依法吊销企业营业执照；电力监管机构取消其电力业务许可；水行政主管部门取消其取水许可。

对发生生产安全事故的小水电站，要依照《生产安全事故报告和调查处理条例》，认真做好事故调查和处理工作，坚持“四不放过”原则，查明事故原因，依法追究责任，强化警示教育，落实整改措施。

小水电站的安全监管工作事关人民群众生命财产安全和社会稳定，各地各有关部门要站在落实科学发展观、构建社会主义和谐社会的高度，进一步提高认识，加强领导，统一协调，周密部署，认真研究制定适合本地实际的小水电站安全监管办法，进一步落实责任，完善制度，提高监管水平，促进小水电又好又快发展。

二〇〇九年十一月三十日

领 导 讲 话

胡锦涛在第64届联大讲话强调加紧研发新能源和可再生能源

国家主席胡锦涛2009年9月23日在纽约出席第64届联大一般性辩论时发表重要讲话。胡锦涛强调，中国的前途命运日益紧密地同世界的前途命运联系在一起。中国将始终不渝走和平发展道路，始终不渝奉行互利共赢的开放战略，坚持在和平共处五项原则的基础上同所有国家发展友好合作。中国越是发展，对世界的贡献就越大，给世界带来的机遇也越大。中国过去、现在、将来都是维护世界和平、促进共同发展的积极力量。

联大一般性辩论在联合国总部大会厅举行，与会领导人主要就国际形势、联合国作用及重大国际和地区问题阐述看法。当地时间16时30分许，在热烈的掌声中，胡锦涛登上联合国庄严的讲台，发表题为《同舟共济　共创未来》的重要讲话。

胡锦涛指出，当今世界正处在大发展大变革大调整时期，和平、发展、合作的时代潮流更加强劲。世界多极化、经济全球化深入发展，多边主义和国际关系民主化深入人心，开放合作、互利共赢成为国际社会广泛共识，国与国相互依存更加紧密。同时，国际形势中的不稳定不确定因素给世界和平与发展带来严峻挑战。

胡锦涛强调，面对前所未有的机遇和挑战，国际社会应该继续携手并进，秉持和平、发展、合作、共赢、包容理念，推动建设持久和平、共同繁荣的和谐世界，为人类和平与发展的崇高事业不懈努力。

第一，用更广阔的视野审视安全，维护世界和平稳定。在人类历史上，各国安全从未像今天这样紧密相连。安全不是孤立的、零和的、绝对的，没有世界和地区和平稳定，就没有一国安全稳定。我们应该坚持互信、互利、平等、协作的新安全观，既维护本国安全，又尊重别国安全关切，促进人类共同安全。坚持联合国宪章宗旨和原则，坚持用和平方式解决地区热点问题和国际争端，反对任意使用武力或以武力相威胁。坚持反对一切形式的恐怖主义、分裂主义、极端主义，不断深化国际安全合作。

第二，用更全面的观点看待发展，促进共同繁荣。没有发展中国家普遍发展和平等参与，就没有世界共同繁荣，就无法建立更加公正合理的国际经济秩序。我们应该把促进共同发展作为解决全球发展不平衡和实现可持续发展的重要途径。联合国应该加大对发展问题的投入，促进经济全球化朝着均衡、普惠、共赢方向发展，努力营造有利于发展中国家发展的国际环境。国际金融机构应该把新增资源首先用于帮助发展中国家脱困。国际金融体系改革应该着力提高发展中国家代表性和发言权。我们应该采取负责任的应对国际金融危机举措，坚定反对保护主义，积极推动多哈回合谈判早日取得全面、均衡的成果。发达国家应该向发展中国家开放市场、减免关税，兑现官方发展援助和减债承诺。发展中国家应该立足自主发展，探索有利于实现发展、消除贫困的发展模式。

第三，用更开放的态度开展合作，推动互利共赢。在气候变化、粮食安全、能源资源安全、公共卫生安全等全球性挑战面前，任何国家都不可能独善其身。加强国际合作，是应对挑战、确保和睦安宁的必由之路。我们应该坚持《联合国气候变化框架公约》及其《京都议定书》主渠道地位，坚持共同但有区别的责任原则，坚持“巴厘路线图”的授权，推动哥本哈根大会取得成功，努力实现互利共赢。我们应该加大农业投入，发展先进技术，抑制市场投机，增加粮食援助，加强农业和粮食合作。加强能源开发利用方面的互利合作，加紧研发新能源和可再生能源，构建先进能源技术研发和推广体系，实现能源供应多元化。

第四，用更宽广的胸襟相互包容，实现和谐共处。不同文明交流借鉴、兼容并蓄，是社会进步的不竭动力。国家不分大小、强弱、贫富一律平等。我们应该承认各国文化传统、社会制度、价值观念的差异，尊重各国自主选择发展道路的权利，使不同文明和发展模式在竞争比较中取长补短、在求同存异中共同发展。

胡锦涛指出，中国人民即将迎来中华人民共和国成立60周年。60年前，中国人民经过长期艰苦奋斗实现了民族独立、人民解放，建立起人民当家做主的新中国。而今的中国，综合国力显著增强，人民生活总体上达到小康水平。中国发展对世界和平与发展作出了重大贡献。

胡锦涛强调，中国作为一个负责任的发展中大国，历来把促进共同发展作为外交政策的重要内容，尽力向其他发展中国家提供支持和帮助。为进一步帮助发展中国家，中国还将采取以下举措。一是继续加强对受国际金融危机影响严重的发展中国家的支持，认真落实有关增资融资计划，加强贸易和投资合作，增强有关国家抵御金融风险和可持续发展能力。二是继续落实中国在联合国千年发展目标高级别会议上提出的帮助发展中国家加快发展的举措，促进联合国千年发展目标的实现。三是继续落实中非合作论坛北京峰会确定的各项援非举措，增加对非援助，减免非洲国家债务，扩大对非贸易和投资，提供人力和技术支持，加大人力资源培训。四是继续参与和推动地区货币金融合作，维护地区金融和经济形势稳定，促进地区金融合作和贸易发展。

胡锦涛最后表示，让我们携起手来，共同分享发展机遇，共同应对各种挑战，为建设持久和平、共同繁荣的和谐世界而不懈努力。

（摘自中国水电工程顾问集团公司《水电风电信息汇编》）

国务院副总理李克强在全国能源工作座谈会上强调保能源供给推进结构调整和产业升级

中共中央政治局常委、国务院副总理李克强2009年2月在全国能源工作会议的座谈会上强调，要认真贯彻党中央、国务院关于保增长、扩内需、调结构的决策部署，按照科学发展观的要求，切实保障能源有效供给，不断提高能源效率，加快发展现代能源产业，推进能源结构调整升级，促进经济社会又好又快发展。

李克强说，能源关系国计民生，是经济社会发展的重要基础，是我国现代化建设的基本保障。进入新世纪以来，我国能源发展取得显著成绩。当前世界金融危机仍在蔓延，对我国经济造成较大冲击。能源发展中既存在结构不合理、环境压力大等老问题，也出现了需求减缓、效益下降等新情况。要立足当前、着眼长远，化挑战为机遇，积极应对金融危机带来的影响，在保持能源生产稳定增长的同时，大力推进能源结构调整，构筑稳定、经济、清洁、安全的能源供应体系，以能源的健康发展支持经济增长，以能源的稳定发展支持经济社会可持续发展，以能源的安全供应支持国家现代化建设。

李克强指出，加强能源基础设施建设，有利于扩内需保增长，也有利于增强发展后劲。要针对当前能源领域存在的突出矛盾和问题，加大投入力度，重点推进农村和城镇电网改造、节能减排改造、西电东送、西气东输、大型煤炭基地、石油化工基地、大型核电等工程建设，更好地保障人民生活和经济社会发展。

李克强强调，国内国际能源供需矛盾的缓解，为解决能源领域深层次矛盾提供了有利时机。必须把促进增长与调整结构有机结合起来，大力推进能源结构战略性调整，加快转变能源发展方式。要着力推动科技创新，积极开发水电、风电、太阳能等清洁能源、可再生能源，加快发展循环经济和节能环保产业，培育现代能源产业，形成新的经济增长点。

李克强说，改革是发展的动力。加快能源结构调整步伐，促进能源产业可持续发展，必须深化能源领域各项改革。要积极稳妥地推进能源产品价格改革，理顺能源资源价格关系，加快能源市场体系建设进程，不断探索和改进新形势下政府能源管理体制，促进能源产业转入科学发展的轨道。加强战略规划，完善政策法规，创新工作方式，充分利用国际国内两个市场两种资源，提高能源领域对外开放水平，实现互利共赢。

（摘自中国水电工程顾问集团公司《水电风电信息汇编》）

国家发展改革委副主任、国家能源局局长张国宝在水电可持续发展中心成立大会上的讲话

国家水电可持续发展研究中心成立大会暨高层论坛于2009年9月19日在北京隆重召开，国家发展改革委副主任、国家能源局局长张国宝在成立大会上作重要讲话。

昨天十七届四中全会刚刚闭幕，全国人民现在正在喜迎国庆60周年，大家都沉浸在欢乐的气氛当中，在四中全会刚刚闭幕，我们就召开了成立水电可持续发展研究中心，我对此中心的成立表示热烈的祝贺。

刚才陈雷部长作了一个非常重要的讲话，不仅是对可持续发展研究中心今后工作指明了方向，同时也是对我国水利事业、水电事业的发展阐明了重要的指导意见，大家要很好的去学习和领会。

昨天的四中全会，加上后来的活动，我估计陈雷部长两点多以后才睡觉，我也是，但是我们今天早晨还是很兴奋，很早就起来了，就是要来参加发展研究中心的成立大会，因为我觉得这个中心的成立，意义

非凡。中国水利水电科学研究院一直是国家发展改革委在水能领域的重要机构，我在国家发展改革委分管这项工作以后，很多难事、大事都是委托中国水利水电科学研究院来帮助我们国家发展改革委来处理。

下一步比如包括太阳能，有多少太阳能是可以利用的，都要进行科学的研究，光凭探讨是不行的，我们现在科学研究当中，有很多拍脑瓜的事，也有很多人云亦云的事，都要用科学的事实来说话。比如说，我们的水电发展现在确实面临着很多争论，也面临着很多的问题。我在主管这项工作，我也感到很苦恼，各种各样的理论都会出来，哪个是科学，哪个是不科学，我想凭我的精力和我的知识，我无法准确地回答。比如讲关于发展水电，就有一种观点：你们说水电是清洁能源，我看不是，它产生沼气，比火力发电站排出的二氧化碳温室气体还要多呢。这只是一句话，科学不科学，我不知道持这种观点的人，他有没有算过？我们不同意这种观点的人，有没有算过？恐怕都没算过。如果你要说他这个观点不对，你要批驳他，你要拿出数据，要拿出科学论证来；他要说这一条我是很站得住脚，那他应该拿出数据来，支撑自己的观点。现在一个人发表一个意见，讲一句话，就成了一个经典了。大家你也有理，我也有理，不是真理的也变成真理了。那不行，那不是一种科学的态度。所以这方面的问题，作为政府机关来讲，没有这个能力来解决这件事。我们需要成立的这个研究中心，让科技工作者去深入研究一下，去做一些科学的研究，用科学的态度来回答这些问题。如果确实是，将来我们在发展水电中，我们都要注意；如果不是这样，那你也要拿出科学的论据来，去批驳错误的观点，所以这都需要有人去论证。

现在水电建设取得了重大的成就，待会儿我可以讲一讲，刚才陈雷部长也讲了，但是我们水电发展现在确实面临着很多重大的问题，有些问题我也不太清楚，我非常希望你们能帮我回答这个问题。比如最近我去了一趟江西，江西的领导就告诉我，鄱阳湖是我们国家两个最大的淡水湖之一。在我脑子当中，鄱阳湖起码也都有好几百亿立方米的水。他告诉我不到两亿，我说怎么可能，密云水库还有好几亿呢，你这鄱阳湖怎么就那么少？我说你这是不是开玩笑，他说不是。我问那是为什么呢？他说因为三峡工程建了。过去鄱阳湖水面大，主要因为长江水位经常高于鄱阳湖水位，有长江顶托输水的作用。现在三峡水库建了以后，有时候经常需要对三峡的下游的长江水位进行调剂，有些时候长江水位就低于鄱阳湖的水位，这样鄱阳湖的水都流到长江里面去了。现在只剩下几亿立方米。我真的不太清楚，因为我没有主管这件事情，但是我听了以后，我说我现在不敢轻易相信，究竟怎么回事，我得回去问问。问谁啊，我就得问你们，是不是这样。

当然建三峡这样大的工程，以后会产生什么样的变化，确实在筹建的时候，应多加研究。但是建了以后呢，我们要进行重要的后评估。我觉得像类似于这样的课题或者问题，总是需要有一个职能机构来进行研究，来进行归纳总结。要举这样的例子，我可以讲一上午，你们把时间都给我，我也讲不完；而且都不是给你们讲故事，都是我眼下碰到了马上要解决的问题。比如说对湄公河的开发，国际上又要开会了。对于湄公河资源的开发，各种声音越来越大，很多都是国际上的一些机构，包括非政府机构，也包括政府组织，他们认为在湄公河，特别是湄公河上游，我们中国境内建水电站就会影响湄公河水位，就会影响它的鱼类的繁殖等。各种各样的危害都渲染得比较严重。但是客观情况到底怎么样，我觉得我们需要拿科学的事实来说话，要拿出科学的办法。如果真有问题，那你如何来解决这些，如果没有问题你要具体去驳斥这种观点。在很多国际会议上，我想我们要拿出有说服力的讲话或者文章来，都需要你的科学研究作为支撑。

因此我们在工作当中，深切地感到，需要有这样一个职能机构，所以，我们国家发展改革委、国家能源局是非常支持成立一个水电的可持续发展的研究中心，来认真研究水电发展当中我们碰到的一些问题，帮助政府进一步搞好我们的水电建设。刚才很多同志都讲到了，像陆佑楣部长现在是院士，他既有实践经验，又有领导经验，是我非常尊重的我们水电战线上的一位领导，一位科学家，他为水电的发展，到处奔走、呼号。但是我们现在水电真是有点举步维艰。还有潘家铮院士，这两名院士都是我们水电界最受尊敬的老领导。

汶川大地震发生以后，当人们都担心岷江流域，四川境内的一些水电站会不会发生灾难性的影响的时候，潘家铮院士在医院里面亲自写了很长的一篇文章，送给温总理。阐述了他在四川汶川大地震以后，奔赴于四川各条河流上的水电站的科学的看法。我也认真读了他这篇文章，甚至都叫好，不仅为他的这种精神所感动，而且对他科学严谨的工作态度，我也很折服。我觉得我们在研究水电问题的时候，需要有更多像潘家铮院士这样科学的态度，并且是要为我们这个事业负责任，甚至于献身的一种精神。

水电事业确实取得了很大的成绩，刚才同志们都讲，2008年年底我们全国的装机容量到了1.72亿kW，现在已经超过1.8亿kW，从装机容量本身来讲，稳居世界第一已经毫无疑问。但是和我们国家蕴藏的水能资源相比，这还是一个小数字。刚才陈部长讲的里面列举了两个数字，我想各位都认真听了，一个我国拥有的理论的水能蕴藏量大约7亿kW，其中技术可开发的5亿多千瓦。陈部长说的是经济可开发的4.02亿kW，和我们现在的1.8亿kW来比，还有很多可开发的水电资源。为什么没有得到开发？关于水电的好与坏，该不该开发，或者应该怎样开发，确实长期以来都存在着激烈的争论。我们过去建设的一些水电站，现在也确实有很多需要总结的经验和教训，以及要处理的后续问题。这些问题处理不好，就会极大的影响我们水电的发展。

我不是学水电的，因为我在国家发展改革委工作，才有机会接触到水电，也有机会接触到国际上水电开发的一些情况。但是慢慢地，我对水电也有了我自己的一些看法，我所接触到的发展比较早的发达国家，水力资源的开发比例都相当高。包括美国，没有说百分之十几、二十几的，都是70%、80%的水力资源都得到开发。而且都是在它经济起飞那一段时间开发的。比如讲美国，大部分都在罗斯福新政前后，比较著名的胡佛水坝；像田纳西州流域，都是在这段时间开发的。所以它现在剩余的可开发的水能资源可以说已经很少了。所以他们讲的一些话，用中国的话说得不好听，就是站着说话不腰疼，他已经都开发完了，没有我们现在面临的这些问题。其他国家也是一样，我过去也分管工业，接待过很多国际上来的大老板。其中美国铝业多次找过我，他曾经也想在中国发展铝业。我就向他请教一个问题，我说搞铝最大问题就是电能，电能便宜就有竞争力，电价高就没有竞争力。我问他最愿意把电解铝，放在哪个国家搞？他说冰岛，我问你怎么会放在冰岛？因为我就是在这方面知识比较欠缺，他说冰岛是水能资源最丰富的，也是最便宜的。他说那里一度电才两（美）分钱。从他嘴里边我才知道冰岛的情况，过去我对冰岛确实不是很了解。另外水力资源比较丰富，像挪威这些国家占的比重都相当高，95%以上都是靠水电。

有的时候我也不同意一些说法，虽然我不敢直接说不同意，但至少对我们有些专家的一些论点，我还不敢轻易相信。比如我们过去有人讲一定要水火搭配，水电比例不能超过多少。也经常有这样的论文，因为峰谷差，所以水电不能搞太多。相应的一定要配合火电，经常有这样的论文。我就奇怪，我真的是知识很欠缺，那挪威99%的水电，它的水火比比我们要高得多，人家怎么过的日子呢？冰岛的水电比例也很大，人家怎么过这个日子呢？

现在这样的理论非常多。比如说我们现在搞风能，现在又有理论出来了，说风能在整个电网当中占的比重不能超过10%，超过了就如何如何？我也感到很困惑，如果这样的话，我们发展风能，就根本解决不了减排问题。因为如果你要搞10个风力发电，你就得搞90个火力发电。因此，风电开发越来越多，越解决不了减排问题。但是呢，又有资料说丹麦风力发电占20%以上，那人家怎么过的日子呢？这个比例是怎么出来的，是拍脑瓜想出来的，还是科学计算出来的？我看好像是拍脑瓜，我没有看到有什么科学计算的数据。

像这样的例子非常多。比如说最近又有一个问题，也非常困扰我。我们前一段时间太阳能炒得很热，现在大不一样了，风水轮流转。反对太阳能的文章突然比赞成的要多了。其中有一篇，昨天领导刚刚批到我这儿，就说获得太阳能的光伏设备在制造过程当中，所消耗的能量要比它20年应用期所能发出的电能要多得多。要是这样的话，那你发展它干啥？你花了那么多能量，你20年当中才能让它恢复，而且还没赚回来。所以越搞太阳能，能量消耗越多。我觉得这个问题太重要了，但是我确实回答不了，我不能说人家这个说法是假的，是吧，我不能说。但是我也确实没有看到准确的计算，所以我讲，我们科学研究部门，你们应该拿数据来说话。你们应该去算算，是不是这样。如果是那样，肯定会影响政府的一些决策；如果不是，我们就要拿科学的数据来驳斥。我觉得现在我们一些互相传抄，拍脑瓜出来的数据，或者人云亦云的东西都特别多。

我也是一个学工科出身，所以养成一个毛病，我不喜欢轻易的相信人云亦云的话，包括我下面同事给我打的签报，他们可能对我有一点不满，他们写的东西，我经常在上面说，你这东西哪儿来的，是你自己算出来的，还是你从哪儿听来的？你听来的是不是考证过它的可靠性？因此我们需要有一个制度，如果我们碰到这样的困扰和问题的时候，我们要请科技工作者来帮助我们做深入的、科学的研究，来回答这些问题。

现在水电开发在中国确实潜力很大。我个人认为它是一个很好的清洁的可再生能源，只要地球上还有太阳照着，还有日月星辰，还有春夏秋冬，还刮风下雨，那水电站总还有水。它就是可再生能源，而且它不会排出二氧化碳。除了个别人说的，水库里面有沼气，我想一般来讲，大家都会认可水电的减排作用。在全球都关注碳减排，我们也面临极大的减排压力的情况下，中国低碳能源的出路到底在哪里？我跟美国能源部长朱棣文都辩论过，他是大哲学家，诺贝尔奖获得者。他到中国来也很友好，我半开玩笑半认真地问了他一下。我跟他讲，我说我在你面前，最多是小学生，你是诺贝尔奖获得者。我说我有好多问题要跟你两个人探讨探讨，请教请教。我说美国宣传氢能源，有的曾经一度把氢能源作为未来清洁能源的主力这样来描述，我说对这个观点您同意吗？我说我自己有点困惑，我说氢从哪儿来，一个从有机物当中来，或者天然气，或者是煤，或者是石油，或者是秸秆、有机物，从这里来，那么这些东西本身也是能源。

另外呢，制造氢的过程又增加了消耗20%到30%的能源，又都排出二氧化碳，你还得把这部分扣掉，我说氢只是改变了能源使用的形态，可能把风能变成了液体，确实也需要这种液体。我说真不错，它一定会有它专门的用途。在有些特定的工作环境下，不适合用别的能源，就适合用氢能。举个例子，仓库里开的叉车，都是用柴油在开，如果改成用氢能源，那是非常好的，但是我说你没有增加能源。

除此之外，你去电解水，你需要耗费电能产生氢能，然后再燃烧，又恢复到水，你又放出能量。这个过程，理论上都是平衡的，实际上肯定要少，因为你中间还消耗很多能量。你没有产生出什么新能源。他私下讲，我跟你观点一样，所以我把氢能源汽车的拨款给停了。但是停了以后，国会就反对我，有关利益集团也反对我，所以我不得不再给它恢复点。我说那你为什么要给它停了，他说“要我看，10年、20年不会实用化，所以我给它停了”，但是他说我也面临很大的压力，他们肯定不同意我的观点，因此我还得给它拨点钱。

接着我就问，我说你非常主张碳捕捉，我说到底能捕捉多少，全世界一年排出二氧化碳250多亿吨，我说你算过没有，全世界能捕捉到1亿t吗？他也一样，他说太多了，他说没有数据，我问他，他也说不上来。

然后我再问，我说烧煤的二氧化碳体积有多大，大家老说排放多少，到底排的体积有多大，他说我也不知道，我说那咱们再简单一点，我说我手上有一捧煤烧掉了，产生多大气体的二氧化碳，他说我也不知道，我说我告诉你22.4L，他说怎么会呢，我说假设我的手上有12g炭，燃烧了，需要消耗32g的氧，加在一块是44g的二氧化碳给产生了，44g的二氧化碳就是22.4L。他说不会吧，会不会比这个少一点或者多一点？我说朱部长，你不要问这个问题，那是初中课本上的东西。

实际上，我接触到好多美国人，他对碳捕捉也是持某种异议，要花很大的代价。对好多事要用科学去判别，不要拍脑瓜。我们现在喜欢拍脑瓜的人很多，还有一种喜欢顺竿爬的人也很多，领导一问，到底多少，他就顺嘴给你说个数字出来。是这个数字吗？再问就完了，就回答不出来了。我陪很多领导考察，尤其朱镕基任职的时候，他经常这样。到了湖北，他就问粮价是多少，粮食局局长站起来了，2块钱。他说你说错了，我特地派警卫到外头去看过了，现在粮价是1块5，你怎么说2块。顺嘴说的人非常多，人云亦云的人也很多，所以，我们需要一个科学的态度才能很好的去发展。

水电这问题，现在困扰很大，一个是移民，我们口号写得很好，叫做建设一个水电，造福一方人民。所以，希望能落实，溪洛渡开工的时候打了很大的一条标语，我当时致辞的时候，就有一句话，我说希望一定能做到这个，建设一个水电，能造福一方人民。可是我们现在接触到的呢，尤其过去老水电站，不停在告状，几十年过去了还在告。陆部长过去也当过能源部的领导，你们都是老部长了，你们都清清楚楚的，岩滩的问题也在告状，包括新安江它也没消停。是吧，还在告状。岩滩的问题你再进一步了解，岩滩水电是1毛4分钱一度电，原来还要低，后来调到1毛4。我说你多加点电价，解决移民的问题行不行。他说这不行，水电有怎么样的缺点，有季节性的问题，调节性能不好，所以它价钱就应该很便宜。

我说它的优点呢，它不排二氧化碳，你怎么说。另外说水电挣钱多，我说过去我们水电的投资少，其中也有一个因素，就是我们对移民，对建水电站地区的一些基础设施，可能我们帮助得还不多。确实我们把造价都压得很低，如果按照现在的那些思维，以人为本的态度，就是要提高一些。在移民搬迁，实施地方建基础设施方面，今后在水电当中，要增加一项。

我现在还有个身份，是政协常委。叫我提提案，我说提啥提案，我就自己给自己提了个提案，我说要求水火同价。结果这个提案一转回来，让国家发展改革委自己来回答。他们也回答不了，反正他一回答，就是这个理由，那个理由，我就给他驳回去。他一看我这个老主任有意见，所以他们处理这个提案以前，就先征求我的意见。最后我说算了。现在就让你们确实做到水火同价有一点困难，但是你朝着这个方向慢慢做。他们也同意了，准备拿一个省出来先做做试点，把矛盾比较突出的一个省拿出来做试点。

这个问题确实不是那么简单。搞水火同价，会带来一系列的问题，比如说电的售后价格，你怎么去平摊这些价格；另外多增加的这一块收益，是交给业主，还是给别的人；会不会引起别的移民攀比？这一系列的问题都出来了。所以水火同价也要请你们做课题。这个好处要给的话，你还得研究研究会引起什么反应？这都不简单，做好事也不容易。你说你把水电从1毛4给它调到2毛4，一度电就增加1毛，收益大大增加。但这1毛钱呢，大家都说，不能光给你们发电公司，不能光给业主，要补移民欠账。你补移民欠账怎么补，对不对，形成一个什么样的机制等。

另外我也在想，你说移民问题老这么突出，成为我们水电继续推行的一个重大的障碍。现在连农民都在试行社会养老保险，那么移民能不能在这方面去试行，研究研究，也要搞养老保险。像这些大课题，不是拍脑瓜能出得来的，需要有人坐得下来，下去调查研究，认真分析，拿出科学数据来，才能解决。这要靠谁啊，靠你们。你们人比我们多，你们知识也比我们强。你有这个时间去做这些课题，但是政府要给予支持，但是需要有人提出来。

今天我为什么要赶来参加这个会议，就是想每逢这种场合，我就要阐述一下我的观点。我认为你们给我们提供了一个讲台。当然，我自己的观点有的也对，有的也不对。有人可能喜欢，有人也不喜欢，但是这毕竟是我的想法，我讲出来了，供大家参考。也希望新成立的水电可持续发展研究中心能够充分发挥你们的作用，完成好政府委托的职能，为我们水电建设和可再生能源的建设，发挥你们重要的作用。

（摘自中国水电工程顾问集团公司《水电风电信息汇编》）

水利部部长陈雷在全国农村水电工作会议上的讲话

这次会议的主要任务是：认真贯彻党的十七大、十七届三中全会和中央一系列重要会议精神，深入贯彻落实科学发展观，总结工作，交流经验，分析形势，理清思路，部署当前和今后一个时期的农村水电工作，努力开创农村水电工作新局面。

一、认真总结近年来的农村水电工作

新中国成立以来，在党中央、国务院亲切关怀下，地方各级党委、政府和广大山区群众治水办电，以小水电为主体的农村水电得到了快速发展。特别是进入新世纪，在国家政策引导和水电农村电气化县建设的带动下，农村水电发展迅猛。截至 2008 年底，已建成农村水电站45 000座，总装机容量 5100 多万千瓦，年发电量 1600 多亿千瓦时，约占全国水电装机和年发电量的 30%，在建规模达 2000 万 kW。这几年农村水电工作有以下几个突出特点。

第一，坚持服务“三农”，治水办电结合，水电农村电气化建设迈上新台阶。积极开发农村水电，建设中国特色农村电气化，是邓小平同志亲自倡导的一条解困富民道路。进入新世纪，党中央、国务院把加快农村电气化建设作为实现农业和农村现代化的重要条件，加大政策扶持力度。“十五”期间建成了 409 个水电农村电气化县，其中 80%以上的县位于老少边穷地区，治水办电结合治理了上万条中小河流。通过五年的电气化建设，累计完成投资 1151 亿元，增加农村水电装机 1060 万 kW；人均年用电量 644kW·h，比 2000 年增长 76.6%，比全国平均增长率高 10 个百分点；409 个县 GDP 年均增长率达到 15%，是全国平均水平的 1.7 倍。根据农村经济社会发展需要，2006 年又启动了更高标准的 400 个水电农村电气化县建设。三年来，农村水电电气化建设各项工作进展顺利，已累计完成投资 125 亿元，建成 397 个项目，增加装机容量 126 万 kW。

第二，坚持面向山区，统筹农民利益与生态建设，小水电代燃料试点成效显著。为巩固退耕还林等生态建设成果，解决农民燃料和长远致富问题，党中央、国务院作出实施小水电代燃料工程的英明决策，并于 2003 年在 5 个省、自治区的 26 个县、市开展试点。2006 年，国家又在 21 个省、自治区、直辖市及新疆生产建设兵团的 80 个县开展了扩大试点建设。水利部党组高度重视，将小水电代燃料工程作为水利三大亮点工程之一，通过政府扶持、企业运作、农民参与、低价供电，探索了一条农村水能资源开发与生态建设有效结合的新路子，试点山区 20 多万户、80 多万农民告别了祖祖辈辈上山砍柴、烟熏火燎的日子，过上了现代、文明、健康的新生活。同时保护森林面积 350 多万亩，被群众誉为点燃大山希望的德政工程。党中央、国务院对小水电代燃料试点给予充分肯定，温家宝总理批示，小水电代燃料经验宝贵。回良玉副总理指出，小水电代燃料工程一举多得，能够实现经济、社会、生态效益三赢，是山区解决“三农”问题的有效途径，应扩大小水电代燃料建设规模和实施范围。

第三，坚持开拓创新，理顺体制机制，水能资源管理初见成效。各级水行政主管部门把水能资源管理作为农村水电工作的重点，采取行政、法律、经济等手段遏制无序开发势头，取得明显效果。浙江省在水能资源开发中率先提出资源、生态、经济等三大补偿机制，并采取招标、拍卖、挂牌等方式有偿出让水能资源开发使用权。目前，水能资源开发使用权有偿出让和市场化配置工作已在全国 10 多个省、自治区、直辖市推开。湖南、吉林省人大常委会出台了水能资源开发利用管理条例，贵州省政府出台了水能资源使用权有偿出让办法，浙江、重庆、新疆、安徽、湖北、陕西等省、自治区、直辖市在地方性法规中明确了水能资源管理的有关原则，福建、广西等 7 个省、自治区、直辖市出台了水能资源开发利用的规范性文件。国务院批准的水利部新“三定”规定中，明确水利部负责开展水能资源调查和指导农村水能资源开发，这是首次明确水利部水能资源管理职能。同时，全国有 12 个省明确由水行政主管部门负责水能资源统一管理。

第四，坚持多管齐下，强化整改落实，农村水电安全监管逐步到位。针对农村水电建设管理中出现的违规建设突出、安全事故频发、水事纠纷增多等问题，从2003年起，在全国范围内开展了违规水电站清查整改工作，清理出违规水电站3400多座。广东省政府整改违规水电站380多座，拆除了一批不符合河流规划、严重威胁公共安全的违规水电站；湖南省组成由水行政主管部门牵头，发改、经委、工商、安监、电监等五个部门参加的联合执法组，对有重大安全隐患的水电站进行了集中整治。截至2008年底，全国75%的违规水电站完成了整改任务，福建、湖北、重庆、贵州等9个省、直辖市的整改率达到100%，其他省、自治区、直辖市也都落实了整改措施。加强与国家安监总局、电监会等部门的配合，组织开展重大安全事故联合督查。全国农村水电安全事故逐年减少，安全形势逐步好转。

第五，坚持深入实际，科学编制规划，农村水电基础工作得到加强。2006年组织开展了建国以来首次全国农村水能资源专项复查，全面系统地梳理了165 00多条河流的流域、水系脉络关系，并首次对单河水能资源理论蕴藏量1万kW以下的11 400多条河流进行了详查，填补了我国水资源调查和水能资源普查工作的空白。通过调查评价，查明农村水能资源遍布30个省、自治区、直辖市的1715个县、市；技术可开发量为1.28亿kW，比1980年普查的0.89亿kW增加了44%，为加强农村水能资源管理奠定了基础。编制完成了全国农村水电中长期发展规划、全国小水电代燃料生态保护工程规划、2009～2015年全国小水电代燃料工程规划、“十一五”全国水电农村电气化规划等一批重要规划。农村水电技术标准体系逐步完善，编制、修订了农村水电站工程环境影响评价规程等17项技术标准。农村水电统计制度纳入了国家统计序列。

第六，坚持对外开放，增进国际合作，小水电国际影响不断扩大。我国开发小水电、建设农村电气化的经验，得到了国际社会的普遍赞誉。近年来，国际小水电中心和亚太小水电中心先后为30多个国家提供了小水电技术咨询和服务，为发展中国家培训了大批小水电技术骨干，带动了国内小水电设备出口和劳务输出。由联合国工发组织和国际小水电中心共同倡导的“点亮非洲”项目得到了联合国有关机构和非洲国家的充分肯定和欢迎。组织召开了“今日水电论坛”等一系列国际会议，成为世界各国同行加深相互了解、分享成功经验、促进交流合作的重要平台。建成了郴州、张掖等国际小水电示范基地，为加强国内外技术合作，加快小水电发展提供了示范。小水电国际合作在促进我国对外交往，维护国家利益，提升国际威望方面发挥了重要作用。

经过多年发展，农村水电已成为我国农村经济社会发展的重要基础设施、山区生态建设和环境保护的重要手段。目前，农村水电遍布全国1/2的地域、1/3的县市，累计解决了3亿多无电人口的用电问题，农村水电地区的户通电率从1980年的不足40%提高到2008年的99.6%，供电质量和可靠性大大提高。按照2008年全国6000kW及以上电厂供电标准煤耗349g/(kW·h)时计算，我国农村水电一年的发电量相当于节约标准煤5600多万吨，相当于减少二氧化碳排放1.4亿t、二氧化硫排放70多万吨。农村水电不仅在增加能源供应、改善能源结构、保护生态环境、减少温室气体排放方面作出了重要贡献，还在电力应急保障中显示了独特作用。去年南方低温雨雪冰冻灾害和“5·12”汶川特大地震灾害期间，在电力主网因灾解列、大面积停电的情况下，小水电发挥了分散分布式供电的优势，迅速恢复供电，保障了受灾地区在电力主网恢复重建期间的供电，减轻了灾害损失，有力地支援了救灾工作。

这些成绩的取得，是党中央、国务院高度重视的结果，是中央有关部门大力支持、地方各级政府精心组织的结果，也是水利系统广大干部职工开拓进取、扎实工作的结果。借此机会，我代表水利部向长期关心、重视、支持农村水电工作的各有关部门，地方各级党委、政府和社会各界表示衷心的感谢！向奋战在农村水电一线的广大水利干部职工致以诚挚的问候！

二、充分认识农村水电发展面临的形势

当前，我国经济社会发展正处在新的历史起点上，农村水电工作面临着新的形势。

从实施可持续发展战略看，农村水电肩负着重要使命。党的十七大强调坚持节约资源、保护环境的基本国策，大力发展清洁能源和可再生能源。国民经济和社会发展“十一五”规划纲要要求，加快资源节约型、环境友好型社会建设，坚持节约发展、清洁发展、安全发展，实现可持续发展。水电是清洁可再生能源，技术较成熟，运行成本低，是全球清洁发展机制项目（也称碳排放交易机制，简称CDM）的重点，也是我国可再生能源发展的优先领域。目前，在国家发展改革委批准的CDM项目中，水电项目有702个，占已批准总数的35.4%，是所有批准项目中比例最高的，其中农村水电占水电项目的90%以上。根据可再生能源中长期发展规划，2020年我国农村水电装机容量将超过7500万kW，按照目前的发电煤耗标准相当于节约标准煤8200多万吨，减少二氧化碳排放2亿多吨，减少二氧化硫排放100多万吨。另外，我国农村水能资源分布在全国1700多个山区

县，与退耕还林区、自然保护区、天然林保护区和水土流失重点治理区的分布基本一致。通过开发农村水能资源，实施小水电代燃料工程，逐步改变我国山区农民靠烧柴做饭、取暖的传统生活方式，既可大量减少烧柴产生的温室气体，还可长期稳定地解决山区农民生活燃料问题，巩固退耕还林、天然林保护等生态建设成果，保护和改善生态环境。

从加强"三农"工作看，农村水电发挥着突出作用。解决好农业、农村、农民问题，事关全面建设小康社会大局，始终是全党工作的重中之重。贫困地区农村经济社会发展滞后，是"三农"发展的难点地区、"硬骨头"地带。目前，全国相对贫困人口大都分布在中西部地区，这些地区农村水能资源十分丰富，可开发量1亿多千瓦，占全国总量的82%，目前开发利用率仅为32%。592个国家扶贫开发工作重点县中，398个县农村水能资源丰富，可开发量达5600万kW，开发率仅为24.3%，是贫困山区脱贫致富的一大资源优势。农村水电建设具有规模小、周期短、见效快、技术成熟、农民增收效果显著等特点，有助于把当地资源优势变成经济优势。因此，近几年中央一号文件都把农村水电列入农村中小型基础设施建设重点领域。农村水电广泛分布在偏远山区，适宜就地开发，就近供电，与大电网长距离输送供电相比，具有明显的价格优势，可减少经济发展成本和农民用电支出。山区农民可以在农村水电建设中通过提供劳务、入股等方式增加收入，加快脱贫致富步伐。

从扩大国内需求看，农村水电承担着新的任务。农村水电产业链长，开发农村水能资源既可增加建材、机电设备等方面需求，又可为广大山区农民提供廉价的电力保障，促进家电下乡，繁荣农村市场，对于增加就业，扩大内需具有重要作用。当前，中央把加强水利等基础设施建设作为应对国际金融危机、扩大国内需求、保持经济平稳较快发展的重要措施，把增加水利投入作为安排新增建设资金的重点领域。今年全国水利工作会议把农村水电及电气化建设列为"十大水利工程"之一，要求大力发展农村水电，加大中央投资力度，引导社会资金参与，加快建设步伐。同时，2009年中央加大中西部农网完善工程投资力度，目前已下达中央投资50亿元，重点是中西部地区仍未进行农网改造的农村，目标是实现同网同价。这一系列拉动经济增长的政策措施为农村水电加快发展提供了宝贵机遇。

从促进行业健康发展看，农村水电面临着新的挑战。我国农村水电发展迅速，潜力巨大，前景广阔，但也存在一些不容忽视的问题。一是发展很不平衡。东中部地区开发程度相对较高，西部边远地区开发程度很低。主要原因是西部贫困地区地方自筹能力有限，融资困难。二是水电开发亟待规范。我国数量众多的中小河流尚未制定河流规划，特别是在一些水能资源丰富的河流上，水电资源无序开发问题仍很突出。加之一些地方把关不严、管理职责不清、行政监管不力，出现了一些无立项、无设计、无监管、无验收的"四无"电站。三是对生态环境保护重视不够。一些地方片面追求经济效益，忽视河流生态环境保护和水能资源可持续利用，导致局部河段生态恶化。四是安全生产形势严峻。近年来一些地方违规建设屡禁不止，安全隐患突出，有的甚至酿成安全事故。20世纪90年代以前建设的2万多座农村水电站，受当时的技术和经济条件制约，建设标准低，设施老化失修，资源利用效率不高，安全隐患较多。这些问题对农村水电行业的持续健康发展带来了严峻挑战。

总之，我们必须从战略和全局高度，充分认识加强农村水电工作的重要性和紧迫性，准确把握农村水电工作面临的新形势，顺应全面建设小康社会新要求，努力开创农村水电工作新局面。

三、准确把握农村水电发展的目标和任务

当前和今后一个时期农村水电工作总体要求是：全面贯彻党的十七大、十七届三中全会精神，深入贯彻落实科学发展观，积极践行可持续发展治水思路，按照全面建设小康社会和推进城乡经济社会发展一体化的要求，统筹流域水资源综合利用，严格资源管理，强化安全监管，创新体制机制，完善政策法规，推动技术进步，加快小水电代燃料和水电农村电气化建设，提高贫困山区农民用电水平，增加农民收入，改善农村生产生活条件，保护生态环境，促进经济社会可持续发展。

到2020年，要努力实现以下目标：

——农村水能资源开发科学有序。法规制度体系基本完善，发展规划体系基本健全，权责统一的农村水能资源管理体制基本建立。农民权益得到充分保障，生态环境得到有效保护，农村水能资源基本实现有序开发、可持续利用。

——小水电代燃料得到广泛实施。到2015年，基本解决生态环境特别脆弱、以烧柴为主的200万户农民的生活燃料问题，户均年生活用电量不低于1200kW·h。到2020年，基本解决退耕还林区、天然林保护区、自然保护区和水土保持重点治理地区1000万户农民的生活燃料问题，户均年生活用电量不低于1500kW·h，农村能源结构进一步优化。

——水电农村电气化水平大幅提高。建成与社会主义新农村建设要求相适应的600个水电新农村电气化县和一大批水电新农村电气化乡村，全国农村水电

装机容量超过 7500 万 kW，农村水电供电区无电和缺电人口用电问题全面解决，用电水平大幅度提高。

——农村水电技术进步全面推进。农村水电新材料、新技术、新设备和现代化管理手段广泛应用，农村水电技术标准体系进一步完善，农村水电站更新改造规划任务基本完成，无人值班、少人值守的农村水电站及其配套电网到 2015 年达到 50%，到 2020 年达到 90%以上。

做好农村水电工作，必须坚持以下原则：

第一，坚持把保障和改善民生放在农村水电发展的首要位置。要把发展小水电代燃料和水电农村电气化，作为贫困山区新农村建设的重要内容，作为改善农民生产生活条件的重要手段，作为增加山区农民收入的重要途径，切实解决好人民群众最关心、最直接、最现实的利益问题。农村水电建设必须严格执行国家规定的征地补偿、移民安置和有关扶持政策，有效保障农民合法权益，妥善解决受影响地区农民生产生活问题。

第二，坚持把促进人与自然和谐作为农村水电发展的核心理念。要正确处理农村水能资源开发与生态建设和环境保护的关系，坚持在保护生态基础上科学有序开发利用农村水能资源，既满足农村经济社会发展的合理需求，又维护河流健康的基本需要。要严格执行农村水电建设环境影响评价和水土保持方案审批制度，做到水土保持设施、环境保护设施与主体工程同时设计、同时施工、同时投产使用。已建农村水电站要实行有利于生态保护的调度方式，建立生态补偿机制和环境恢复治理责任制，实现经济效益、生态效益、社会效益的三赢。

第三，坚持把政府调控和市场配置相结合作为农村水能资源开发的重要手段。水能资源是水资源的重要组成部分，是有限的自然资源，必须采取政府调控和市场配置相结合的方式进行开发管理。要建立健全农村水能资源开发的法规和制度，制定有利于市场主体公平竞争的市场规则，加强对市场的监管和调控。对于综合利用和直接改善民生的农村水能资源开发项目，政府要给予积极扶持。对社会投资为主的农村水能资源开发项目，应采取市场配置的方式有偿出让水能资源开发使用权。

第四，坚持把加强工程质量和安全监管作为农村水电工作的重要任务。农村水电站点多、面广、量大，其工程质量和安全不仅关系到自身功能效益的发挥，还关系到人民群众的生命财产安全。要高度重视农村水电工程质量和安全监管工作，建立权责统一的监管体制，完善监管制度，明确监管职责，强化监管措施，不断提高工程质量和安全水平，确保工程质量经得起检验，防止发生重特大安全事故。

四、扎实做好农村水电发展的重点工作

当前和今后一段时期，要着力抓好以下六个方面重点工作：

第一，突出抓好水能资源管理。水能资源管理是水资源管理的重要内容。一要严格水能资源开发许可管理。各级水利部门要建立健全规范高效、协调有序的水能资源开发管理内部工作机制，严格执行水工程建设规划同意书、水资源论证和取水许可等制度，形成水能资源管理合力，从源头上遏制过度开发、无序开发。认真总结推广各地有偿出让水能资源开发使用权的经验，逐步完善水能资源有偿使用和市场配置制度。加强水能资源开发分区管理，按照国家和区域主体功能区管理要求，合理控制重点开发区、优化开发区、限制开发区的开发强度，严禁在禁止开发区内开发利用水能资源。二要编制和修订农村水能资源开发规划。中小河流水能资源开发规划是农村水能资源开发利用的基本依据。各地要根据流域和区域综合规划，统筹协调好发电与防洪、供水、灌溉、生态和环境保护等的关系，用三年左右时间完成辖区内中小河流水能资源开发规划编制或修订工作，科学合理确定开发程度和开发方案。三要加强水能资源调查评价工作。要建立水能资源调查评价制度，完善水能资源管理标准体系，组织开展水能资源调查评价，掌握水能资源开发利用情况及其变化规律，动态分析评价水能资源开发利用产生的影响，提出相应对策措施。四要建立健全流域与区域相结合的水能资源管理体制。各级水行政主管部门要切实履行本行政区域内水能资源统一管理的行政职能，各流域机构要高度重视水能资源管理工作，建立管理机构，加强与流域内各省、自治区、直辖市的协调与配合，共同做好水能资源管理工作。

第二，突出抓好小水电代燃料工程建设。小水电代燃料对于巩固退耕还林、天然林保护等生态建设成果，保护生态环境，改善农民生产生活条件，促进农村发展，具有十分重要的作用。一要全面实施2009～2015 年全国小水电代燃料工程规划。进一步细化规划内容，实化政策措施，强化责任机制，确保解决170 万户、677 万农村居民生活燃料问题，新增代燃料电站装机容量 170 万 kW。根据规划实施情况，积极争取进一步扩大建设规模。二要高标准搞好项目建设。加强项目前期工作，强化工程建设管理，大力推进技术进步，统一标准标识，统一管理制度，把小水电代燃料项目建成农村水能资源开发利用的示范工程。三要切实降低代燃料电价。在采取有力措施，降低工程建设费用，节约运行管理成本的同时，各地要积极向当地政府汇报，主动与有关部门协调，加强与

电网企业沟通，在具备条件的地区采取就近直接供电，其他地区也要努力降低供电环节费用。在保证代燃料电站保本微利的前提下，最大限度地降低代燃料电价，让农民用得起、用得好、长受益。四要完善管理体制和运行机制。建立健全国家投资出资人制度，完善代燃料电站法人治理结构，加强电站内部管理和发供用电管理，保证电站良性运行。完善代燃料项目监督制度，充分发挥农民用电户协会的作用，全过程监督代燃料项目实施。

第三，突出抓好水电农村电气化建设。加快农村电气化建设，是实现农业和农村现代化的重要条件。一要完成好“十一五”水电农村电气化建设任务。“十一五”只剩不到两年时间，电气化建设任务繁重，各地要加强指导和督促检查，加快项目建设进度，确保水电农村电气化建设取得实实在在成效。二要明确新时期水电新农村电气化建设重点。按照城乡统筹和社会主义新农村建设要求，结合我国农村水电工作新情况、新特点，以中西部地区为布局重点，完善配电网络结构，提高供电可靠性和供电质量。三要抓紧编制2010～2020年水电新农村电气化规划。农村水能资源开发程度较低的地区，重点是规范水能资源开发秩序，加快水能资源开发步伐。农村水能资源开发程度较高的地区，重点是优化配置农村水能资源，进行挖潜改造，提高水能资源利用效率和效益。

第四，突出抓好农村水电供电区建设。农村水电供电区大多处于大电网末端或大电网没有延伸覆盖的老少边穷地区，农村水电对于确保这些地区电力供应，促进经济社会可持续发展具有十分重要的作用。一要加强农村水电供电区电网建设与改造。抓住中央加大中西部农网完善工程投资的机遇，加强与有关部门沟通协调，加大农网完善工程投资力度，扩大实施范围，优先安排无电地区和未改造地区，提高农村水电供电区的供电能力。二要加强农村水电供电区管理和服务。农村水电供电企业要建立和完善现代企业制度，加强经营管理，提高供电质量和服务水平，增强市场竞争能力。三要推动农村水电就近直接供电。分散分布式供电是国际上公认的安全、便捷、节能的供电方式，也是解决负荷分散的广大山区农村用电问题的重要途径。各地要创造条件，积极推动农村水电就近直接供电。

第五，突出抓好农村水电行业管理。一要严格执行国家基本建设程序。严格项目前期工作，严格项目法人责任制、招标投标制和建设监理制，严格工程开工报告和工程验收制度，切实加强工程质量和安全管理。二要继续开展违规水电站清查整改。各级水行政主管部门要在当地政府统一领导下，加强部门之间配合，尽快完成整改任务，建立长效机制。三要加强农村水电安全生产工作。贯彻“安全第一”的方针，落实安全生产和防汛行政首长责任制，完善农村水电安全监管体系，建立农村水电安全监管联合执法机制，加强安全检查和隐患排查。督促农村水电企业建立健全安全生产管理制度，加强水库大坝安全管理，完善应急预案，落实管理措施，确保工程安全和社会公共安全。四要实施农村水电增效减排工程。改造老化、低效的农村水电设施，对消除安全隐患，确保安全运行，提高资源效率，增加生产能力，降低农村电价，具有十分重要的作用。要搞好规划，明确目标，规范标准，创新模式，在试点基础上逐步推开。五要加强农村水电基础工作。完善农村水电技术标准体系，建立农村水能资源基础数据库和农村水电管理信息系统，提高农村水电信息化管理水平。

第六，突出抓好农村水电国际交流与合作。水电国际交流与合作是水利国际交流与合作的重要内容。一要按照温家宝总理在联合国千年发展目标高级别会议提出的，未来五年内为发展中国家援建100个小水电等小型清洁能源项目的要求，加快组织实施“点亮非洲”等小水电合作项目。二要引进、消化、吸收当今国际先进水电技术以及管理经验，进一步提高我国水电技术水平、装备水平和管理水平。三要充分发挥我国在小水电建设领域的技术、设备、经验及性能价格优势，推动我国小水电技术、设备出口和劳务输出。四要把按照国际惯例管理与创造中国特色模式有机结合起来，加强国际小水电中心和亚太小水电中心建设。

五、切实加强对农村水电工作的领导

当前和今后一个时期，农村水电工作任务重、要求高、难度大。要与时俱进，开拓创新，真抓实干，切实加强和改善对农村水电工作的组织领导，促进农村水电事业取得新发展，再上新台阶。

一是进一步强化责任。各级水行政主管部门要把农村水电工作作为水利工作的一件大事和要事来抓，认真研究加强本地区农村水电工作的对策措施，及时解决工作中遇到的困难和问题，扎实推进农村水电工作。要建立健全责任机制，一把手要亲自过问，分管领导要直接抓，班子要形成合力。要把农村水电发展的目标任务、建设管理、安全监管、环境保护等责任落实到具体单位和具体岗位，在工作部署、资金安排、干部配备上给予大力支持。要加强与发展改革、财政、环保、税务、物价等部门的沟通、协调与配合。

二是进一步增加投入。要不断增加小水电代燃料、水电农村电气化建设的投资，扩大建设规模，让更多的山区农民受益。要积极拓宽资金渠道，争取财政资金用于农村水电增效减排等工程建设。各地也要争取地方财政对农村水电建设的支持，落实配套资金。要充分发挥政府投资的引导作用，扩大政策性信贷规模，吸引社会资金参与农村水电开发。

三是进一步完善法规。要建立农村水电管理法规体系，研究制定农村水电条例和水能资源调查评价管理办法，尽快出台农村水能资源管理办法。各地要根据实际情况，建立健全相关政策法规，依法加强农村水电管理。

四是进一步深化改革。要按照国家电力体制改革的总体要求，以培育独立市场竞争主体为核心，以就近直接供电为重点，深化农村水电体制改革，提高农村水电服务“三农”的能力和水平。继续深化中央投资形成的农村水电资产的产权制度改革，建立农村水电促进农民增收的长效机制。建立和完善水能资源开发生态补偿机制，促进水能资源开发与生态环境保护相协调。

五是进一步加强宣传。要充分发挥新闻媒体的作用，大力宣传农村水电在改善农村生产生活条件、增加农民收入、促进农村经济社会发展以及节能减排、保护生态环境等方面的重要作用，大力宣传农村水电法律法规和政策措施，争取社会各界对农村水电的重视和支持，进一步调动农民群众参与农村水电建设的积极性，为农村水电发展营造良好氛围。

六是进一步抓好队伍。要高度重视农村水电队伍建设，通过选派优秀人才，加大教育培训力度，建设一支政治坚定、业务精通、作风优良、廉洁勤政的高素质水电干部队伍。广大农村水电工作者要大力弘扬“献身、负责、求实”的水利行业精神，积极投身农村水电事业，不断提高农村水电管理水平。

农村水电工作使命光荣，责任重大，任务艰巨。让我们在以胡锦涛同志为总书记的党中央领导下，坚持以邓小平理论和“三个代表”重要思想为指导，深入贯彻落实科学发展观，积极践行可持续发展治水思路，开拓进取，扎实工作，开创农村水电工作新局面，为全面建设小康社会作出新贡献，以优异成绩迎接新中国成立60周年！

（水利部农村水电及电气化发展局）

水利部副部长胡四一在全国小水电代燃料工程建设现场会上的讲话（摘要）

（2009年8月27日）

今天我们在这里召开小水电代燃料工程建设现场会，贯彻落实2009年全国农村水电工作会议精神，总结小水电代燃料扩大试点经验，研究部署下一阶段小水电代燃料工程建设工作。下面我讲三点意见。

一、小水电代燃料扩大试点成效明显

根据党中央国务院的决策部署，2003年在5个省开展了小水电代燃料试点建设，取得了显著成效。在试点基础上，2006年在全国开展了更大规模的扩大试点建设，涉及21个省（区、市）和新疆生产建设兵团的81个项目。目前工程进展顺利，有43个项目的代燃料电站已投产运行，年底前将有76个项目实施代燃料供电，基本完成了扩大试点建设任务。

（1）小水电代燃料从根本上解决了农民的燃料问题，有效保护了生态环境。据统计，小水电代燃料扩大试点建设保护森林200多万亩，每年减少薪柴消耗75万t，项目区走上了以林蓄水、以水发电、以电护林的良性发展道路。

（2）小水电代燃料解除了农民砍树烧柴的艰辛，提高了生活质量。过去农民为了砍柴翻山越岭，斧砍肩扛，受苦受累。农村妇女烧柴做饭，三餐围着灶台转，要四、五个小时，烟熏火燎，负担沉重，有的还得了红眼病和肺气肿病等。现在用电做饭，方便、快捷、省时、省力，减轻了农民负担。

（3）小水电代燃料显著改善了农民生活条件，美化了人居环境。小水电代燃料建设带动项目区改厨、改厕、改圈，通电、通水、通路，项目区人居环境发生了显著变化，缩小了城乡差距，农民过上了现代文明的新生活。

（4）小水电代燃料解放了受砍树烧柴束缚的农村劳动力，增加了农民收入。据初步统计，实施小水电代燃料后，项目区群众平均每户每年增加收入上千元。

（5）小水电代燃料增加了可再生能源比重，促进了节能减排。砍树烧柴不但破坏植被，削弱生态建设成果，还会增加大量温室气体。小水电代燃料工程建设增加了小水电装机，改善了农村能源结构，减少了温室气体排放。

各地在小水电代燃料扩大试点建设中进行了大量的实践探索，积累了许多好的经验和做法：一是领导高度重视。各级水行政主管部门把小水电代燃料作为水利工作的重点，主要领导亲自过问，分管领导直接抓，保证了项目的顺利实施。二是群众积极拥护。小水电代燃料最大限度地降低了代燃料电价，让农民用得起、长受益，显著改善了生活条件，真正得到了实惠。三是建立体制机制。各地在扩大试点实践中探索建立了“国家所有、企业经营、农民使用”的管理体制和“国家补助、企业运作、农民受益、协会监督”的运行机制，保证了代燃料工程长期发挥效益。四是

出台扶持政策。河北省政府出台了允许小水电代燃料就近直接供电的政策，湖北省政府出台了小水电代燃料电价的一系列优惠政策等。

当前，小水电代燃料试点工作虽然取得了显著成效，但也还存在前期工作不扎实、代燃料电站余电上网电价低、代燃料供电过网费偏高等问题，在一定程度上影响了工程建设进度和代燃料的效果。

二、着力抓好小水电代燃料工程建设

小水电代燃料是民生水利的重要内容，利在当代、功在千秋。到2015年基本解决200万户农民的生活燃料问题，到2020年基本解决1000万户农民的生活燃料问题。为此，在当前和今后一段时期，小水电代燃料建设要着力抓好以下四个方面的重点工作：

（1）做好项目前期工作，夯实代燃料工程建设基础。小水电代燃料工程是中央补助投资的地方项目，前期工作是基础，其程序要严格按照《中央预算内投资补助和贴息项目管理暂行办法》（国家发展改革委第31号令）、《国家发展改革委关于改进和完善中央补助地方投资项目管理的通知》（发改投资［2009］1242号）有关规定执行。各地要依据《2009～2015年全国小水电代燃料工程规划》选择建设项目。要按照水利部《关于做好小水电代燃料项目实施方案编制工作的通知》要求，由县级水行政主管部门负责组织编制项目实施方案并会同发展改革部门上报，省级水行政主管部门会同发展改革部门组织对实施方案进行审查和批复，报水利部备案，批复后的实施方案作为项目建设和验收的依据。

（2）强化工程建设管理，打造农村水电示范工程。一是严格按公司法组建代燃料项目法人。负责电站、项目区的建设和管理。从试点情况看，国有独资、国有控股和集体企业作为项目法人，有利于项目的顺利实施和效益的发挥。二是高质量搞好代燃料电站建设。要严格实行项目法人责任制、招标投标制、建设监理制和合同管理制。要建立健全工程质量管理和监督机制。按照《小水电代燃料项目技术进步和标准化管理指导意见》的要求，大力推进技术进步。三是高标准搞好项目区建设。要结合新农村建设、国土整治和村镇建设规划，以行政村为单元，按照就近供电的原则，科学合理选择项目区。要统一标识，统一管理制度，把小水电代燃料工程建设成环境友好、社会和谐的农村水能资源开发利用典范。

（3）加强供用电管理，切实降低代燃料电价。一是保障长期稳定供电。代燃料电站由代燃料项目法人自主经营、自负盈亏。项目法人要与供电公司签订并网和供电协议，明确上网电量和电价，确保代燃料供电长期稳定。二是加强用电管理。代燃料用电要按照“核定基数、定额限量、分类计费、按月结算”的办法管理。供电公司要与代燃料用户签订用电协议，明确代燃料电量、电价和安全用电等。代燃料电量和电价要公开，切实将农民的利益保护好。三是努力降低代燃料电价。国家投入大量资金用于小水电代燃料建设，项目法人要千方百计降低建设费用和运行成本，最大限度地降低代燃料到户电价，使农民得到实惠，生态得到保护。

（4）建立管理体制机制，确保工程长期发挥效益。要按照“国家所有、企业经营、农民使用”和“国家补助、企业运作、农民受益、协会监督”的要求，进一步完善管理体制和运行机制，保证代燃料工程长期稳定运行。建立健全国家投资出资人制度，明确代燃料电站的所有权、经营权和使用权，实现所有者、经营者和使用者权利和义务的统一。小水电代燃料项目是社会公益类项目，任何单位和个人不得从中牟取私利。小水电代燃料涉及广大山区农民的根本利益，需要农民的参与、支持和配合，要成立以代燃料户为主体的小水电代燃料用户协会，对小水电代燃料工程进行民主管理和监督。

三、切实加强小水电代燃料工作的领导

（1）落实责任。各级水行政主管部门要切实负起责任，有关各方要层层签订目标责任书，落实责任，明确权利和义务。通过层层签订协议，确保代燃料工程的顺利实施和长期稳定发挥效益。

（2）搞好协调。各级水行政主管部门要主动向政府汇报，主动与发展改革、财政、税务、国土、林业、环保、扶贫等部门沟通，争取投资、税收等政策支持；主动与供电企业协调，落实就近供电政策和借网供电按成本价收取过网费政策，落实小水电代燃料电站余电全额上网、电价不低于全网平均电价等政策；主动与中国农业发展银行和国家开发银行等金融机构联系，落实小水电代燃料工程贷款。

（3）强化监督。各级水行政主管部门要加强对小水电代燃料项目的监督和检查，重点是建设程序和内容，工程质量、安全和进度，资金筹措和使用，管理体制和机制，建设目标和任务等，确保工程安全、资金安全和代燃料目标任务的实现。要充分发挥代燃料用户协会和社会舆论的监督作用，保证代燃料工作公平、公开、公正。

（4）广泛宣传。要深入细致地做好宣传工作，让项目区群众充分了解小水电代燃料的重要意义，理解和支持项目建设。采取多种形式，积极向有关部门和社会宣传小水电代燃料的作用和效果，关心和支持小水电代燃料工程。要做好项目区周边群众的思想工作，为小水电代燃料工程建设创造良好的环境和氛围。

小水电代燃料是一项创新性工作，正处于从试点转向全面实施的重要阶段。要真抓实干，扎实做好小水电代燃料工作，全面开创农村水电工作新局面！

（水利部农村水电及电气化发展局）

新中国水电60年

新中国60年水电发展的历程

新中国60年水电发展的历程，大致可以改革开放为界划分为前后两个30年。

（一）前30年发展历程

1. 三年经济恢复和第一个五年计划时期

1949年中华人民共和国成立，中央政府就开始了组织水电规划建设的工作。1950年召开的全国水力发电工程会议这样评价新中国成立以前的状况："中国的水力发电工业建设比较迟、规模小、数量少、技术水平低，但经过长期的努力，也获得了一定的成绩。"这次由朱德出席并讲话，会议代表受到毛泽东周恩来接见的重要会议，决定了恢复与建设水电工程的方针和任务，决定了成立燃料工业部水力发电工程局（之后改为水力发电建设总局）统一领导全国水电建设。在新中国水电历史上具有重要意义。

在很短时间内，全国组建起了8个勘测设计院，12个工程局（处）和1个科学研究院。拥有了一支近4万名建设者的队伍。开始了对14座水电站施工和51项水电站的勘测设计工作。其中，很重要的是对丰满水电站进行的加固补强和改扩建，使这座日本帝国主义侵占时为掠夺我国资源而修建的水电站旧貌换新颜。丰满的加固扩建保证了大坝安全，满足了向东北地区供应电的需要，也为我国大型水电站的施工安装和机组制造，培养了一批管理干部、技术干部和技术工人。解放初的三年国民经济恢复时期和第一个五年计划期间，在对龙溪河、古田溪、永定河、以礼河等中小河流进行开发规划的基础上，我国自行设计施工建设了狮子滩、古田一级、黄坛口、上犹江、流溪河、官厅、大伙房、佛子岭、梅山、响洪甸等一批中型水电站以及新疆乌拉泊、西藏拉萨和海南东方等小水电站。这些中小型水电站，以工期短、投资少的优越性满足了所在地初期发展的需要。

1953～1955年，根据地形、水文和实地查勘的资料，水力发电建设总局组织统计估算了全国1598条干支流，第一次普查汇总了全国的水力资源，得出我国水能资源蕴藏量为5.45亿kW。后经1956～1958年由电力工业部和水利部联合组织各流域机构和各地勘测设计院进行的全面复查，得到第二次普查的全国水能资源蕴藏量为5.83亿kW。

1957年7月，第一届全国人民代表大会第二次会议批准了由黄河规划委员会为主编制的《黄河流域除害兴利综合利用规划报告》，拟定了黄河防洪、灌溉、航运和水土保持等综合利用任务。接着进行了淮河、海河、辽河、珠江等流域规划，以及资水、沅水、汉江上游、岷江上游等梯级开发规划和浙江、福建、广东、广西等地区的水电开发规划。

1955年，中央决定开展长江流域规划工作，由水利部会同燃料工业部、交通部、地质部组建长江流域规划办公室（简称长办），并聘请苏联专家帮助进行规划。长办和苏联专家认为，应该把流域规划工作分为两个阶段，第一阶段的任务是编制出流域规划要点，内容包括规划长江干流和最重要的支流对防洪和国民经济各部门综合利用要求拟定梯级开发方案；第二阶段的任务是对已经选出的干流和某些大支流编制综合利用规划。长办1959年提出《长江流域规划要点报告》[1]上报，之后又按照中央制定的"统一规划，全面发展，适当分工，分期进行"的原则分批分期进行规划。在编制规划要点的过程中，1956年曾经对长江先干流开发还是先支流开发等问题展开过认真深入的讨论。

上述水力资源普查和大小河流的规划，为此后的水电建设提供了依据。

新中国成立以前，没有专门培养水电专业人才的高等院校。1952年，南京大学、上海交通大学、同济大学、浙江大学的水利系或土木系水利组及华东水利专科学校共同组建了华东水利学院，1952年起，水力发电建设总局先后与长春、成都、武汉等地质学院合办水文地质和工程地质专业，1956年又成立了

[1] 1983年国务院批复任务书要求在1959年报告的基础上修订补充《长江流域综合利用规划要点报告》，1988年，经水利部会同能源部审议，长办提出了报告的修订本。

武汉水利水电学院，培养了大批水电专业人才。1955～1959年水力发电建设总局先后派遣4批60余人赴苏联学习进修，这些人多数回国以后成为本专业的领导和技术骨干。

1957年10月在北京北海公园举办了全国水电建设展览会，展示了我国水力资源分布情况，水电建设成就河流规划及发展前景。周恩来、朱德等党和国家领导人亲临展览会并题词，中央委员和各部部长100多人前来参观，对我国水电事业取得的成就给予肯定，极大地鼓舞了水电建设者。

至1957年底，全国水电装机容量达到101.9万kW，为1949年的2.8倍，年发电量48.2亿kW·h，为1949年的4倍。1949～1957年的八年内，装机容量和年发电量年增长率分别达到14%和19%，世界排名分别上升至第16位和第17位。这一时期是中国水电建设史上的第一次高潮。更为重要的是它为我国水电的更大发展奠定了基础，储备了人才，积蓄了经验。

2. 大跃进和国民经济调整时期

为了满足国民经济进一步发展的需要，1957年开始建设新安江和三门峡两座大型水电站。新安江水电站装机容量66.25万kW，大坝高105m，总库容216亿m^3。1952年规划，是我国自行设计施工和制造机电设备的第一座大型水电站。得益于前期勘测设计完善和施工队伍扎实工作，从1957年4月开工到1960年4月第一台机组发电仅仅用了3年时间，及时满足了向上海和华东地区供电。同期建设的并请苏联帮助设计的三门峡水电站，蓄水后短短时间就出现了泥沙严重淤积并向上游渭河发展的“翘尾巴”，直接威胁西安等城市安全，刚刚建成的三门峡水利枢纽被迫进行两次大的改建，水库降低水位运行，从原来“蓄水拦沙”的高坝大库改成“蓄清排浑”的低水头径流式水电站，这是设计思想和建设决策的失误，是我国在多泥沙河流筑坝修水库应吸取的一个重大教训。

从1958～1965年，水电建设虽经历了一个坎坷曲折的历程，但是，这一时期的水电建设从整体上仍然得到了进一步的发展。这期间投产的大型水电站都是在20世纪50年代后期按照原计划开工建设的，前期工作做得较好，选择对象合理，勘测设计比较完善，施工队伍工作比较扎实，因此工期较短，造价较低。从工程开工到第一台机组发电，新丰江用了25个月，新安江为36个月，盐锅峡为38个月，柘溪为42个月。不少中型水电站也有类似的情况，从工程开工到第一台机组发电只有2年左右，例如大洪河只有14个月，百丈漈一级和六郎洞都是22个月，流溪河和水府庙都是24个月，水槽子25个月等。在装机容量方面，刘家峡水电站是中国自行设计、制造、施工的第一座装机容量超过100万kW的大型水电站，其规模不但是当时国内最大的，其147m高的整体式混凝土重力坝、开挖跨度31m高59m的地下厂房、流速达35～45m/s的高速水流泄水建筑物、单机容量22.5万kW的水轮发电机组、330kV的超高压输变电工程等，均居当时国内首位。在施工上，混凝土坝施工的机械化水平得到提高，如新安江机械化程度为48%，三门峡为64%，丹江口后期达到75%。在“大跃进”时期，广大水电建设者出于对改变中国落后面貌的迫切愿望和迅速建设社会主义的强烈责任心，怀着要“让高山低头，令河水让路”的豪迈精神，尽管施工条件十分简陋，生活条件非常艰苦，工程任务相当艰巨，建设者们还是意气风发，斗志昂扬，干劲冲天。

“大跃进”期间的下放机构和精简人员，分散削弱了水电队伍，至1962年重建机构时回调近17 000人。1959年的“反右倾”运动中，批判“大水电主义”，错误地打击了水电系统的一批领导干部和技术骨干，造成了不应有的损失，影响了水电事业的健康发展。

1962年，水利电力部发出《关于当前电力工业工作的几点指示》，水利水电建设总局贯彻中央“调整、巩固、充实、提高”八字方针，强调严格按照基本建设程序，重视规划，设计先行，保证质量，建立概预算制度。经过几年调整，国家经济状况有所好转。1964年开始刘家峡、丹江口等水电站陆续复工，映秀湾、猫跳河四级和五级、碧口等新工程相继开工。

3. “文化革命”十年

水电建设经过3年调整，逐步走上正轨。1966年开始，又经历了十年“文化大革命”，“文革”运动和极“左”思潮再次严重干扰和破坏水电建设，肆意制造冤假错案，打击陷害广大干部、知识分子和工人。1967年，水利电力部实行军管，军代表进驻水利水电建设总局领导运动，全国各地水电建设的管理工作基本陷于停顿，绝大多数干部“斗、批、改”以后，下发到宁夏“五七”干校参加劳动。1969年，军管会宣布撤销水利水电建设总局，北京、上海、昆明、中南、西北直属勘测设计院，水利水电科学研究院也同时撤销机构，人员下放分散到各个工程局。造成水电前期工作和科研工作长期落后被动的局面，严重影响了水电建设正常推进，其深刻的历史教训显现在之后的发展过程中。

1966年开始的第三个五年计划，立足于备战，要求改变工业布局，加快三线建设。这期间安排的基本建设投资，重点是国防工业和重工业，包括解决能源问题的电力项目。项目大部分分布在西南、西北三线。1970～1975年的“四五”计划，继续执行战备方针，要求电力先行。由于1970年前后电力增长跟不上经济回升的需求，出现了拉闸限电和电网长时间低频率运行的缺电状况。因此，电力建设是“三五”计划和“四五”计划的重点。虽然这个时期国家陷入文化大革命运动中，水电建设遇到人才、物资、技术等各种困难，但三线建设的战略决策还是为水电发展提供了机遇，推动了水电的建设，并且取得了较好的成绩。这主要得益于“文化大革命”前打下的工作基础和水电战线广大职工的努力，这个时期先后有刘家峡、丹江口、龚嘴、碧口、富春江、青铜峡等大型水电站和桓仁、黄龙滩、陈村、石泉等43座中型水电站建成投产。这个时期开工或复工建设的有万里长江第一坝——葛洲坝水电站及龙羊峡、乌江渡、凤滩、大化和白山等大型水电站。

1969年，小水电建设加快了步伐。水利电力部在福建永春召开了全国小水电现场会，提出了“谁建、谁管、谁有、谁受益”的政策，保护建设者利益。1975年，水利电力部还对大电网扶持小水电、小水电联网后的互供电量的电价和小水电入网的电力要保证质量等作了规定，极大地促进了小水电的发展。这一年，小水电达到6.8万座，308万kW，发电量66.9亿kW·h，占全国发电量的3.4%。小水电成为我国电力的重要补充力量。

至1976年底，全国水电装机容量达到1465.5万kW，为“一五”期末的14倍，年发电量456.4亿kW·h，接近“一五”末发电量的10倍。从数字上看，可以说中国水电出现了第二次建设高潮，但是许多投产项目在“文化大革命”前早已动工或做了大量的前期工作。由于文革中前期工作停顿，长期吃老本，设计储备不足，这个时期的建设比例是失调的。至于在“左”的思想影响下出现的设计与施工质量下降，劳动生产率低下，制度与管理混乱等现象，影响更为深远。

1966～1976年的“文化大革命”期间，水电建设再次遭到“左”的严重干扰和空前破坏。尽管如此，由于“文化大革命”期间的社会经济秩序混乱，火电建设受到煤炭供应和铁路交通运输等影响发展缓慢，而水电建设受此方面影响较少，在国家关于加快三线建设方针政策的推动下，西部水电资源得以加快开发。同时，在深山峡谷中，广大水电建设者尽量减少干扰，克服困难，坚持生产，因而这一期间的水电建设仍然继续发展。新安江、柘溪、云峰、盐锅峡、新丰江、青铜峡等电站相继建成竣工，乌江渡等一批水电工程开（复）工建设，一些大型电站从工程规模、建设难度、施工强度等方面，均达到新的高度。

（二）后30年发展历程

1. 调整改革整顿提高

1976年10月，以粉碎“四人帮”为标志，我国结束了持续十年之久的“文化大革命”。1978年12月，党的十一届三中全会提出了改革开放的战略决策，全党工作的着重点向社会主义现代化建设转移。水电系统在清理“左”的错误，拨乱反正，落实政策，平反冤假错案方面做了大量工作；恢复和重建了被撤销的总局、勘测设计院和科研机构，建立健全必要的规章制度，推行经济责任制，加强精神文明建设；重新规划与部署了水电前期工作，围绕提高水电建设这个中心，开始进行全面的整顿和改革。

1977年4月～1980年10月，在全国开展了新中国成立以后的第三次全国水力资源普查，水利和电力部系统约2700人参加了此项工作。按1万kW以上的河流和装机容量1万kW以上的水电站统计，全国水力资源理论蕴藏量为6.76亿kW，年发电量5.92万亿kW·h；可开发装机容量为3.79亿kW，年发电量1.92万亿kW·h。第一次查明了技术可开发的水力资源，并按照前期工作的深度将技术可开发的资源分为四类，这对于安排项目开发的时序和进一步投入前期工作很有意义。

1979年，在全国水力资源普查的基础上，提出了《十大水电基地的设想》。这十大水电基地是：黄河中上游水电基地、大渡河水电基地、雅砻江水电基地、澜沧江水电基地、乌江水电基地、红水河水电基地、长江上游水电基地、闽浙赣水电基地、湘西水电基地、金沙江水电基地。1989年水利水电规划设计总院根据各勘测设计单位的大量基础工作，又增加了东北水电基地和黄河北干流水电基地，编印了《十二大水电基地》的规划性文件。最新的水力资源普查结果显示，怒江水电装机容量排在第六位，水能资源极为丰富。在综合考虑怒江建设条件的前提下，十二大水电基地又加入了怒江，形成十三大水电基地。我国水力资源主要分布在十三大水电基地，十三大水电基地装机容量为27 796万kW，年发电量12 030亿kW·h。按技术可开发量计算分别占51.3%和48.6%。

规划是河流和河段水电开发的战略性工作。为了开发利用好红水河基地这一水能“富矿”，1978年水利电力部下达任务，第四次对红水河进行开发规划。1959年、1960年的两次规划过多强调防洪，1973年的规划提出“红水河钢铁运输线”的口号，过多强调航运。第四次红水河规划对历次查勘的20个梯级坝进行研究分析，提出了“红水河开发以发电为主，兼顾防洪、航运、灌溉、水产等综合利用效益”的方针。1981年，红水河规划经国家能源委员会和国家计划委员会批准，国务院还作了加快开发红水河的批示。

1978年3月，水利、电力两部再次合并为水利电力部以后，为了加强水电，水利电力部决定成立水利水电建设总公司（水利水电建设总局）和水利水电规划设计总院（水利水电规划设计管理局），赋予行政职能，挂两块牌子，代部归口管理大中型水利水电工程的建设和前期工作，同时代部管理部直属的工程局和勘测设计院。这一时期，水电前期工作加快，至1983年底，已储备初步设计23项，共计1243万kW；可行性研究报告7项，共计2012万kW。以施工企业为主的企业整顿是围绕推行经济责任制展开，企业由生产型向生产经营型转变，1983年，全系统摘掉了亏损帽子，实际成本比预算成本降低了8.7%。

1983年完成水电建设投资1639亿元，其中水利水电建设总公司所属企业完成1488亿元，全面完成施工和投产的年度计划。1981年1月，葛洲坝工程在长江干流上胜利完成大江截流，至1983年已完成一期工程，7台机组96.5万kW投产发电，开始兴建二期工程。建设过程中的龙羊峡在1981年遇到特大洪水，水电建设者用临时围堰挡住了洪水，保证了工程和下游的安全。这个时期开工的东江、安康、万安、鲁布革、岩滩、红石和渔子溪二级等水电站，多数被列为国家经济建设重点项目。其中一些电站坝高、洞长，工程艰巨，它们的兴建，标志我国水电建设达到了一个新的水平。

1980年6月，在电力工业部和中国科技协会支持下，由七十多位水电专家和教授发起，中国水力发电工程学会在新安江水电站召开成立大会。学会理事113人，中国水电教学创始人，清华大学著名教授施嘉炀先生任第一届理事会理事长。中国水力发电工程学会成立之后，又相继成立了省、区分会和专业委员会。29年来，中国水力发电工程学会在中国科协领导下的全国一级学会，经历了六届理事会，现有会员43 000多人。1982年，《水力发电学报》创刊。

2. 改革创新的发展阶段

调整整顿带来了水电建设规模扩张的新势头。同时，由于水电建设投入大，工期长，以中央财政拨款及以后拨改贷的方式，财政很难支持大规模的水电建设。寻找建设资金的出路，探索引导发展的体制改革，成了中国水电人继续前进的重要思考。

党的十一届三中全会以后，水利电力部决心拿出一两项目水电工程作为对外开放，引进外资的试点。经过与世界银行接触和商谈，报国家计委和国家外资管理委员会批准，决定鲁布革和水口两个项目作为引进外资试点。1984年1月，世界银行执董会批准了鲁布革项目额度为1.454亿美元的贷款，成为中国第一个使用世界银行贷款的大型水电工程。鲁布革建设管理局作为水利电力部的派出机构，也是最早按市场模式进行项目管理的建设单位，负责对9.4km的引水隧洞工程实行国际招标。日本大成公司以低于标底43%的投标价中标，合同工期提前4个月，高质量地完成了该项目。开创了管理体制和建设模式的先河。招标前以自营方式承担该项目施工的十四局变成了“打工者”，形成了轰动全国的“鲁布革冲击波”。水电建设体制受到了冲击，全国基本建设行业上上下下的思想观念也受到了冲击。

随后，广州抽水蓄能、岩滩、漫湾、水口、隔河岩等五个百万级水电站纷纷实行了业主负责制、招标承包制、建设监理制的管理模式。其中，除漫湾外的四个项目都是利用外资的。新的管理体制和运行机制使这些项目在工期、质量、造价等方面取得了公认的成绩和进步，被业内誉为“五朵金花”。根据统计资料，1986～1990年的“八五”计划期间，实行新的建设体制的水电项目与自营体制的相比，用工减少1/2～2/3，工期缩短1～2年，劳动生产率提高1～3倍，质量合格率100%，优良率85%。投资得到了有效控制。因此，在水电行业，市场化的建设管理模式很快替代了自营制模式。之前，部分自营制项目开展以工程概算总承包为特征的责任制，打破“大锅饭”，强化内部管理，也为水电体制改革打下了一定的基础。

1993年党的十四届三中全会召开前夕，理论界对公司制进行了讨论。水电建设推行了业主负责制，但是新旧制度的关系没有从根本上理顺。根据《公司法》，电力工业部指导帮助水电建设系统按照现代企业制度的要求，进一步把业主负责制推进到公司制，先后把清江、二滩、乌江、桂冠、五凌组建或改制成为水电开发公司。改制以后的水电开发公司作为“独立电厂”，为电力体制的改革和建立电力市场创造了有利条件。

1993年12月，为了适应水电体制变革的需要，与国家基本建设项目审批程序相协调，电力工业部颁发了调整设计阶段的通知。调整以后的水电设计阶段为：预可行性研究阶段；可行性研究（等同初步设计）阶段；招标设计阶段和施工图设计阶段。1997年，电力部和水利部组织专家，参照国际工程师联合协会FIDIC合同条件的一般原则，结合国内水利水电工程的情况，编写和颁发的《水利水电施工招标和合同条件范本》（简称红皮本，2000年修订），为建立公平公正的水电市场提出了规则和规范。

改革开放给举世瞩目的三峡工程建设带来了历史性的机遇。1984年国务院原则批准《长江三峡工程可行性研究报告》后，三峡工程建设摆上了中央和国务院的议事日程，成立了三峡工程筹备领导小组和中国长江三峡工程开发总公司筹备组。为了积极而又慎重决策兴建三峡工程这样关系千秋万代的大事，以求更加细致、精确和稳妥。1986年6月开始，根据1985年全国人大和政协两会的意见和建议，三峡工程论证领导小组组织全国412位专家，进行了14个专题、历时两年八个月的重新论证。通过了坝顶高程185m，正常蓄水位175m，初期蓄水156m的“一级开发，一次建成，分期蓄水，连续移民”的建设方案。之后，国务院三峡工程审查委员会于1991年8月3日通过了水利电力部根据上述方案正式报送的《长江三峡工程可行性研究报告》。1992年4月3日，全国人大七届五次会议以1767票赞成，177票反对，664票弃权的结果批准了《关于兴建长江三峡工程的决议》。1993年9月，中国长江三峡工程开发总公司挂牌成立，同时开始了紧锣密鼓的施工准备和一期工程。1997年大江截流后进入二期工程，三期工程2004年开始。2006年大坝全线浇筑到顶，2005年9月和2008年10月，左右岸26台70万kW机组全部投产发电，比原设计工期提前一年。截至2009年8月，三峡累计发电3450亿kW·h，获得了巨大的效益。三峡工程在建设过程中创造的“四制”，将合同管理提升到业主负责制、招标承包制、建设监理制的同一层面，使以市场机制为核心的项目管理模式更加充实和完善。

1997年，国家电力公司成立，国务院授权其经营中央电力资产，也从生产关系上形成了一个中央水电投资主体。得益于亚洲金融危机后国家拉动经济的宏观环境，国家电力公司在成立后先后在中西部布局和开展了“五大一小”水电项目的前期工作，卓有成效地推动了龙滩、小湾、公伯峡、洪家渡、三板溪和岷江杂谷脑流域的前期工作，这些工程均在“十五”初期开工建设。也积极有序地推动和布置了泰安、桐柏等一批抽水蓄能电站的开工准备和前期工作。

进入20世纪90年代以后，我国水电继续高速发展。1992～1999年，水电投产连续七年超过300万kW，1998年和1999年分别达到了534万kW和633万kW，是中国水电建设史上的第三次高潮。至1999年底，全国水电装机容量7279万kW，年发电量2129亿kW·h，分别居世界第2位和第4位。

3. 跨越发展的新世纪初期

进入21世纪，在国家继续推进西部大开发，振兴西部经济，建设水电大基地，加速了金沙江、红水河、黄河上游、澜沧江、雅砻江等水电基地的开发建设。“十五”和“十一五”计划安排了龙滩、公伯峡、拉西瓦、小湾、构皮滩、洪家渡、瀑布构、彭水、三板溪、水布垭、溪洛渡、锦屏一级、向家坝、锦屏二级、长洲等大型和巨型水电站相继开工建设。大型抽水蓄能电站西龙池、张河湾、惠州、黑糜峰等也在“十五”相继开工，中小河流梯级滚动开发蓬勃展开，迎来了我国水电建设的第四次高潮。

进入21世纪，三峡工程建设一步一个脚印，先后实现了右岸明渠截流、双线五级船闸试水、大坝全线浇筑到顶，蓄水至156m高程等里程碑，完成了水库移民的搬迁安置工程，2008年10月30日，随着右岸最后一台15号机组完成调试和投产，三峡水电站左右岸26台机组全部建成，提前一年投产发电。2003年至2009年8月，已累计发电3450亿kW·h，创造了巨大的效益。

进入21世纪，中国水电进一步打开国门，走向世界。2005年国际可再生能源大会在北京召开，中国以水电发展的斐然成就获得了全球同行的赞许，《北京宣言》也呼吁各国通过开发本地能源资源如水力、风能等，以增强对世界能源市场不稳定性的抵抗力。中国水电顾问集团公司、中国水利水电建设集团公司、葛洲坝集团公司、中国长江三峡开发总公司以及两个电网公司和五个发电公司积极推进国际化战略，在50多个国家和地区进行规划设计和工程建设，有近60部国内现行使用的水电标准已经或正在翻译成英文推广海外。中国水利水电建设集团公司（Sinohydro Corporation）拥有全球约50%的水电建筑市场份额，该集团公司入选美国《工程新闻纪录》2008年度全球最大225家国际承包商排行榜第50位，在中国对外承包工程企业中排名第4位。中国已建和在建高于30m的大坝近5200座，其中高于100m的140余座，高于200m的14座。在2009年5月举行的第77届国际大坝委员会年会上，中国水利水电科学研究院副院长贾金生当选为第22任主席，这是中国代表首次担任国际大坝委员会主席。

2002年12月，根据国务院颁布的《电力体制改革方案》（国发［2002］5号），国家电力公司进行了分拆重组，成立了国家电网和南方电网两个电网公司，华能、大唐、华电、国电、中电投等五个发电集团公司，水电和电力两个设计集团公司，水利水电建设集团和葛洲坝集团两个水电施工集团公司。基本上实现了厂网分开的第一步改革目标。长期以来，电力工业垂直一体化垄断经营的局面被打破，发电侧竞争态势基本形成。并且形成了中央办电和众多地方、外资、民营等企业多家办电、多种所有制办电的竞争格局，企业办电的积极性高涨。2002～2006年的三年多时间就扭转了全国大范围缺电的局面。

2000～2003年期间，国家发展和改革委员会组织全国1000余名工程技术人员，历时3年，对我国水力资源总量进行了复查。复查结果，大陆水力资源理论蕴藏量 6.944 亿 kW，年发电量60 829亿 kW·h；技术可开发为 5.416 亿 kW，年发电量24 740亿 kW·h；经济可开发为 4.017 9 亿 kW，年发电量17 534亿 kW·h。2006 年，为了查勘西藏丰富的水力资源，受国家发展和改革委员会委托，水电水利规划设计总院组织了本部、中国水电顾问集团成都勘测设计研究院和西藏自治区电力公司的 33 位专家，对雅鲁藏布江下游河段和其第一支流帕隆藏布进行了历时 26 天的野外实地查勘，取得了极其珍贵的第一手资料。

2000～2009 年[1]，全国水电装机容量从 7279 万 kW 增长至18 210万 kW，增长量为建国前 50 年的 1.5 倍。2000～2009 年累计发电量35 519亿 kW·h，占 60 年水电累计发电量67 273亿 kW·h 的 52.8%，装机容量和年发电量双双位居世界第 1 位，实现了新世纪的跨越式发展。

（摘自中国水力发电工程学会主编的《中国水电 60 年》）

新中国 60 年水电建设体制的变革

新中国成立至今，我国水电建设体制经历了由计划经济模式向市场经济模式的变革。计划经济模式主要就是自营制，市场经济模式则是从改革开放以后的投资包干责任制、概算总承包等过渡模式，经历了鲁布革招标承包制的冲击，形成了以业主负责制、招标承包制和建设监理制为内容的三项制度，进而发展到按现代企业制度组建的项目法人负责制。

（一）计划经济与自营制模式

1978 年改革开发以前，我国水电建设体制一直采用自营制模式。所谓自营制，即由国家指派建设单位施工，建成后移交生产单位。而在建设过程中，施工单位既当项目施工生产的主体，又是建设项目管理的主体。是施工和管理由一家单位承担的建设体制。从新中国成立初期的古田溪工程处等十二个施工局（处、公司），到 1978 年以前的十五个水利电力部直属的工程局，都是使用这种模式展开施工和管理工程的。自营制项目建成后，生产运行是移交给与项目建设没有干系的另外一家单位。这一制度根本性的弊端是人为地割裂了投资收益链，没有人对项目的投入产出的全过程负责。因为建设项目和建设资金都是由国家计划统一安排和财政统一分配的，干部和工人也都是吃“皇粮”的。因此，国家负责对水电开发负有无限责任。而施工单位按照国家计划调遣，代表国家建设水电站，各级领导更多关心的是完成任务和维持队伍，承担行政责任而缺乏经济责任；队伍实行大兵团作战，技术装备落后，拖家带口随工程走，包袱沉重，劳动生产率低下；分配上普遍吃“大锅饭”，没有积累，发展缓慢。因此，在财政的建设资金总体上安排不足的情况下，实行自营制的工程，经常发生工程费用短缺，工期拖长。这种情况，在那些在建项目少，受“左”倾思想影响大的地区和时段，尤其表现得严重和突出。

（二）改革探索过渡管理模式

1982 年，党的十二大提出了“到 20 世纪末全国工农业年产值翻两番”的奋斗目标。为了实现“翻两番”的战略目标，水电建设以管理体制改革为突破口，解放思想，“百花齐放”，转变观念，积极实践。出现了以水电概算总承包为内容的投资包干责任制、以设计院为主体的建设总承包制和以招标投标为主要特征的建设责任制。

1. 投资包干责任制

1982 年，遵照中央领导关于“一定要降低建设造价，选择最优方案，缩短建设周期”的指示，水利水电建设总公司积极“做好第二篇文章”，选择部分所属工程局进行了投资包干责任制试点。确定吉林红石水电站为“降低造价，加快建设”的样板，内容是实行“三自一包”，即自己做施工设计，自己带设备，自己施工和经济承包责任制。采取了总承包方统一指挥，其余施工方大流水协作的施工方法，加快了进度。电站用不到 3 年时间建成，概算节约 2000 万元，全员劳动生产率由 4344 元提高至 9825 元。

进而，水利电力部在葛洲坝二期工程等 19 个项目开展“五定”，是当时控制水电站投资超概算的重要工作。“五定”是定建设规模、定总投资、定建设工期、定投资效益、定外部协作条件。五定概算核定的 19 个项目装机总规模 1202.5 万 kW，概算 193.66 亿元，单位千瓦投资 1610 元。在此基础上，葛洲坝水电工程局和第十二水电工程局分别对葛洲坝二期工程和紧水滩水电站实施了概算总承包。

1983 年，水利电力部成立了作为建设单位的葛洲坝代表处，代表水利电力部与葛洲坝工程局签订合同，实行概算包干。合同规定结余按 6∶1∶3 分成，即葛洲坝工程局 60%，葛洲坝代表处 10%，水利水电建设总公司 30%。1983～1986 年，按包干结余分成，葛洲坝工程局实现利润 7539 万元，实际留成和各项利润指标与一期工程相比有很大提高。由于有了明确的奖励办法和经济责任制，调动了各方面的积极性，整个工程提前一年建成。工程质量比一期工程明

[1] 数据统计至 2009 年 7 月。

显提高，混凝土浇筑优良率一直保持在90%以上。概算包干改变了过去实报实销的吃“大锅饭”状况，也有代表处代表甲方，但是甲方只局限于代表国家将概算包给乙方，由施工单位自建自营的那种方式没有根本改变。

2. 建设总承包制

以设计院为主体的建设总承包制也是水电建设体制改革探索的模式之一。石塘水电站为瓯江流域一座7.8万kW的中型电站，初步设计审定概算1.775亿元，原来安排由水电十二局自营方式施工，最终水利电力部决定以浙江省电力局为业主，由华东勘测设计院组建工程咨询公司进行主体工程建设总承包。总承包实施中引入了竞争机制，通过招标择优选定施工、制造和安装单位，发挥了设计工作和设计优化贯穿于建设全过程，设计人员既考虑技术，又重视经济效益，在进度控制、质量和投资管理方面取得了经验。在物价上涨和政策性调整的情况下，仍然将投资控制在批准概算的范围内。同时，这次试点也发现和暴露了一些问题，诸如业主与总承包单位的关系的问题，设计单位自身经济实力有限，缺少流动资金和自有资金的问题；投资包干风险大，责任不明确，总承包容易偏向于包盈不包亏损等问题。由于这种总承包责任制虽然有业主，但是仍然只是作为总承包方的行政上级存在，总承包最终变成了在建设过程中下级对上级负责，成了节约投资，提高效率的一种管理手段。

3. 建设责任制

鲁布革水电站引水洞工程实行国际公开招标之初，鲁布革建设管理局作为水利电力部的派出机构，只是受业主云南省电力局的委托，行使按市场模式进行的项目管理职能，行政上不属于业主领导。鲁布革模式的意义是在于它通过公开的招标投标，真正用市场方式和经济原则来组织建设，摒弃了依靠行政方式组织水电建设的旧体制。

“鲁布革冲击”使招标承包制得以在水电系统乃至全国的基本建设行业全面推行，最终冲开了实行了几十年的自营体制。水电建设体制改革迈出重要的一步，同时也引进了国际建设市场规则。

（三）创建业主负责制、招标承包制和建设监理制

1986年起，随着在水电建设系统和全国推广鲁布革经验，广州抽水蓄能、岩滩、水口、漫湾、隔河岩等“五朵金花”水电站也竞相开展了业主管理、招标投标和建设监理为主要内容的建设管理体制改革的尝试。1991年12月在广东从化抽水蓄能电站召开的建设经验交流会（广蓄会议），对实践几年的体制改革和管理改革进行了总结，形成了一个以业主负责制、招标承包制和建设监理制为内容的建设管理体制的框架，业主、监理、施工和设计各方关系的大格局已经形成。

1. 业主负责制

在全面推行招标承包制的过程中，业主在水电建设的项目策划、资金筹资、建设实施、生产经营、还贷和资产保值增值的全过程中的核心地位逐渐凸显，业主负责制的形成是一种必然趋势。作为一种制度，针对的是自营制业主缺位的主要弊端，它根本上是要把水电站的建设与运营作为一个完整的项目经济周期，用业主负责制整合起来。而在20世纪80年代初期，由于国家金融财税体制改革，水电建设资金由原来中央拨款全部改为贷款性质。此时，必须让负责运行和经营水电站的、具有还贷能力的单位或机构当业主。因此，电力局理所当然地被指定作为业主单位，而水电工程局也就作为承包商，全面进入了水电建筑市场的竞争激流之中。同时，由于计划经济时期的电力局没有水电建设管理的职能，因此必然要派生一种机构代行业主职能。包括鲁布革和这一时期的“五朵金花”水电站，在项目组建之初，都有这样一个由业主派出的、负责建设管理的机构，而这个被称为建设单位的管理机构并非真正意义上的业主。也给之后水电建设体制的进一步改革留下了需要研究的问题。

2. 招标承包制

竞争是市场经济的重要原则和前进推动力，招标投标是基本交易方式，其实质和主要特征就是体现竞争。鲁布革冲击波正是因为选择了招投标为突破口，才在中国的市场经济来临之际，显现出如此强大的威力。鲁布革虽然只是部分土建工程国际招标，但其引进的国际招标的市场规则。却为日后水口、二滩、小浪底等水电站利用外资的全面国际招标提供了样板。另外，石塘水电站以及之后由中央与地方集资建设的漫湾水电站是国内公开招标，又为国内招标积累了经验。到1991年，当时在建的26项大中型水电站有14项实行招标投标，装机容量占全部在建规模的75%，投资占93%。

招标投标带来了竞争意识的增强和对企业信誉的重视，带来了效率和质量的提高，带来了造价和人员的减少。与当时仍然维持自营方式的工程比较，施工水平提高，进度明显加快。岩滩1989年11月10日浇筑碾压混凝土10 619m^3，刷新了美国1987年埃尔克克里坎工程日浇筑碾压混凝土9474m^3的世界纪录；为了在投标中有良好的信誉，水电施工企业十分重视严把施工质量关。1991年6月，能源部检查组对水口水电站100万m^3混凝土进行检查的结果表明，大坝轮廓尺寸符合设计要求，外形工整光滑，各

种标号混凝土的强度保证率和离差系数达到部颁优良标准。检查的隔河岩、岩滩、漫湾和五强溪等其他实行招投标的大型水电站的质量，也是好的和比较好的。控制造价方面，石塘、岩滩、漫湾、广蓄等水电站的中标价，分别依次比标底降低 18.8%、18.8%、16.3%和 12.1%，效果显著。由于招标竞争，促使施工企业更新装备，精选队伍，轻装上阵。以往一个百万级别电站工地上需要施工人员上万人和几万人的家属子女，招投标以后减少到 3000～5000 人，效率提高了，也减少了大量临建费用。

3. 建设监理制

建设监理制引进了工程师单位对项目实施监督控制。业主管理人员通过监理，保证了质量、进度、付款的责任到位，管理也更加专业化。施工企业不再承担项目管理和施工生产的双重责任，专心致志地组织项目的施工生产，施工技术水平和内部管理水平都得到了显著的提高。

广州抽水蓄能电站最早成建制聘请建设监理，一期工程四年中，监理对设计、施工提出了许多有益的建议，对工程部位实行旁站监理，对关键部位组织质量跟踪，对设计图纸、施工方案等进行全过程监督检验，从而保证了工程质量。广蓄实行建设监理招标，择优选择建设监理队伍，对推动和完善建设监理制有较大的意义。

（四）项目法人责任制

从以业主负责制为核心的“三制”到项目法人责任制是一次根本性的转变。根据 1993 年党的十四届三中全会提出的建立社会主义市场经济体制和《公司法》，水电建设体制在前一阶段改革的基础上，通过规范化运作，对老项目（已经实行了三项制度的公司）进行了改制，对新项目按照《公司法》组建成立了有限责任公司。在电力工业部指导帮助下，先后对清江、二滩、乌江、桂冠、五凌等公司进行改制或新组建。

1987 年成立的清江水电开发公司，由原国家能源投资公司和湖北省合资组建的。1994 年，国家能源投资公司撤销，湖北省政府和清江公司在与电力工业部和国家开发银行磋商清江流域开发的衔接工作时，遇到了企业改革的深层次问题。因为清江水电开发公司只是一个“负责隔河岩电站建设和管理”的经营者，不是投资人代表，无权与华中电力公司签订合资协议，也不能沿用清江水电开发公司的名称。直到湖北省成立了清江水电投资公司作为湖北省的出资代表，才得以与华中电力公司签订合资协议。按照《公司法》清江水电开发公司改组为“湖北省水电开发有限责任公司”。投资公司的总经理担任有限责任公司的董事长，投资权和所有权在主体形式上分离，又由企业家通过企业机制结合起来，是中国水电行业第一家由业主责任制公司向现代企业制度转变的企业。这样，公司通过建成运行的隔河岩水电站得到的收入，再用于梯级电站开发，基本上形成了“业主负责，建管结合，流域开发，滚动发展”的清江模式。

二滩水电开发公司组建之初没有董事会。代表出资人利益项目投资主体一直没有在企业到位。企业不能按照“谁投资、谁决策、谁收益、谁承担风险”的原则承担投资全过程的风险责任，这种情况不符合《公司法》，也不符合世界银行贷款的要求。1995 年原国家能源投资公司和四川省投资公司、四川省电力公司签订了《合资建设经营二滩水电站协议书》，将二滩水电开发公司改组为二滩水电开发有限责任公司，同意共同投资建设经营二滩水电站。公司制订了章程，成立了董事会，聘任了总经理和经营班子，建立起决策、经营、监督、激励和约束机制。合资三方出资的股份比例分别为 48%，48%，4%。融资责任按三方的股份比例承担。公司具有独立法人地位，享有各方投资形成的全部法人财产产权，依法享有民事权利，承担民事责任。在构建和运行市场经济模式的公司中，二滩水电开发有限责任公司不断改革，积极创新，对中国水电企业建立现代企业制度提供了重要的示范作用。这一套先进的体制和机制，为推动二滩水电站优质高效的建设与运营奠定了基础。

广西桂冠电力股份有限公司是全国水电行业 2000 年以前唯一一家上市公司。它是现代企业的一种组织形式，也是按照现代企业制度建立起来的。桂冠公司由广西电力有限公司广西开发投资公司、工商银行广西分行信托投资公司和交通银行南宁分行共同发起成立，而百龙滩水电站则是全国第一家依靠股份制集资兴建的中型水电站。电站从开工到投产发电，工期不到 3 年，为国内同规模水电站少见的建设速度，之后又有大化水电站入股。充分证明是水电行业最先从实践中总结出业主责任制、招标承包制和建设监理制的公司。公司股票上市以后，资本金比例达到 75%以上，确实为水电建设企业资本金比例偏低的问题提供了一种解决方式。

水电体制改革最实质、最有突破性的改革是进行市场化的改革。我国水电建设体制的改革走过了 3 个里程碑，形成了以项目法人负责制为核心，招标承包制、合同管理制和建设监理制的“四制”配套管理的体系以后，已经实现了向市场经济接轨和与国际接轨。

（摘自中国水力发电工程学会主编的《中国水电 60 年》）

新中国60年水电科技国家级攻关项目

我国水电科学研究工作有着悠久的历史，“1956～1967年科学技术远景规划”就已经把长江三峡工程重大科技列入其中。从20世纪70年代长江上兴建第一座坝——葛洲坝水电枢纽工程起，国家级水电科研开始提速。

1. “五五”期间

大型水电工程建设技术研究开始列入国家科技重点项目中，国家还组织制定了《1978～1985年水利工程学科规划》、《1978～1985年水利水电科学技术发展观》和《1986～2000年水力发电科学发展规划》，这三个规划有力地指导水电科学的发展。

2. “六五”期间

依托天生桥一级和鲁布革电站的设计和施工所提出的技术问题，国家第一次把“水电建设关键技术”纳入国家科技攻关计划中。

3. “七五”期间

1986～1990年再次把“水电工程筑坝技术”、“高土石坝技术研究”、“高混凝土坝技术研究”、“高坝坝基技术研究和定向爆破筑坝技术研究”等四个大课题二十多个专题，列入国家科技攻关项目。

4. “八五”期间

1991～1995年，在“七五”攻关成果的基础上，我国再次把“高坝建设关键技术研究”作为国家重点科技攻关项目列入第八个五年发展计划中。针对高坝建设中尚存在的高难技术，分高拱坝关键技术、高土石坝关键技术、高边坡稳定及处理技术和碾压混凝土拱坝筑坝技术等四个课题进行研究。

经过五年的联合攻关，取得了4项成套技术，13项新理论、新方法、新技术、新工艺、新材料，6项新仪器、新设备和12项重要的计算机软件等一系列成果。

5. “九五”期间

1996～2000年第九个五年计划内，再次把高坝建设中的关键课题，如小湾水电站，拱坝最大坝高295m；龙滩水电站碾压混凝土筑坝，最大坝高216.5m；水布垭水电站混凝土面板堆石坝，最大坝高233m等，列入国家攻关计划中。

6. “十五”和“十一五”期间

“十五”国家科技攻关，由于电力体制改革，没有归口申报政府部门，故没有水电项目列入其中。国家水电科技攻关任务出现缺位和断档。

为了不中断三峡工程的科研任务，中国长江三峡工程开发总公司成立了三峡工程科学技术委员会承担起三峡科研工作，并会同国家科委、自然科学基金重新组织科技攻关，取得了一系列技术上的重大突破，保障了三峡工程建设的顺利进行。

（摘自中国水力发电工程学会主编的《中国水电60年》）

新中国60年水电科技取得的主要成就

新中国水力发电科学技术的发展，主要是依托于国家重大工程建设，本着有所为有所不为，重点突出，急工程所急，全面服务于工程建设和运行。在坝工建设及机电设备研制上，全面突破200m级特高碾压混凝土筑坝技术（RCC），200m级特高混凝土石板堆石坝（CERD），300m级特高拱坝（AD）及100m级特高碾压混凝土拱坝筑坝技术难关，在复杂特殊地质条件下，深度达150m的基础处理和浇筑成功超深的混凝土防渗墙工程，以及700m级的高边坡开挖、加固技术；高速水流的消能工技术创新；70万kW大型水轮发电机组的国产化，突破了国际同类机组所没有过的技术难关；在大型机组的冷却方式上，具有自主知识产权的蒸发冷却技术属世界首创。

（一）完成了水力资源的普查与复查

新中国成立以来，燃料工业部、水利电力部分别于1955年、1958年和1977～1980年组织了三次全国水力资源的普查与核查。2000～2003年期间，国家发展和改革委员会组织全国1000多名工程技术人员，历时3年，对我国水力资源总量进行了复查。复查的范围是我国大陆境内河流装机容量1万kW及以上的3886条河流。复查结果为，大陆水力资源理论蕴藏量6.944亿kW，年发电量60 829亿kW·h；技术可开发为5.416亿kW，年发电量24 740亿kW·h；经济可开发为4.017 9亿kW，年发电量17 534亿kW·h。本次复查较第三次普查增加了867条河流的资料，其理论蕴藏量增加了6.7%，技术可开发量增加了46.4%，成果可信度高，可供我国能源发展长期规划之用。

此外，根据台湾1995年水力资源普查成果，其水力资源理论蕴藏量为1165.2万kW，年发电量1020.7亿kW·h；技术可开发量为504.8万kW，年发电量201.5亿kW·h；经济可开发量为383.5万kW，年发电量138.3亿kW·h。

我国沿海海岸曲折漫长，北起鸭绿江口南至北仑河口，全长18 000多公里，蕴藏着丰富的潮汐能，1978年开始进行普查工作，着重对可开发装机容量

500kW 以上的站点进行研究和评估。截至 1983 年前后，在我国沿海 156 个海湾和 33 个河口，选出了可装机容量 500kW 级以上的潮汐站站址共 191 处，年发电 619 亿 kW，相应可开发装机容量 2158 万 kW（未计西沙和南沙诸岛）。

我国地域辽阔，山川众多，地形起伏，不仅常规水能资源丰富，而且抽水蓄能发电资源也相当多，据全国 23 个省市区初步研究和普查结果，已查明的优良抽水蓄能电站站址 250 余处，总装机容量可达 3.1 亿 kW，工程技术经济指标优越，开发价值高，能满足我国能源优化结构和电网安全运行的需要。

（二）土石坝工程技术

我国 20 世纪 50 年代建有 10 余座土坝，坝高大都在 40～50m；20 世纪 60 年代建成的坝高大都在 60～80m，共有如毛家林、松涛等 10 余座；20 世纪 70 年代建成超 100m 高土石坝，如甘肃碧口、台湾曾文等 5～6 座。进入 21 世纪，已建成的小浪底为壤土斜心墙堆石坝，最大坝高 160m；建设中的糯扎渡是心墙堆石坝，坝高 261.5m，均具有代表性。

（三）高混凝土面板堆石坝筑坝技术

混凝土面板堆石坝是一种年轻而富有竞争力的坝型。该坝型对筑坝坝址地形、地质、恶劣自然条件和筑坝材料等的适应性大，同时还具有投资省、工期短、运行安全等优点。1980 年我国开始学习国外先进技术和经验，同时重视自主开发，并将此项新技术列入国家科技攻关项目和国家自然科学基金项目进行研究。30 多年来，我国混凝土面板堆石坝的发展经历了湖北西北口 95m 级，天生桥一级 178m 级，洪家渡 200m 级，水布垭 230m 级的历程，已具备在强地震区、深覆盖层、深风化层、岩溶地区、窄谷峡谷高边坡、河道拐弯不对称地形及严寒地区等建混凝土面板堆石坝的技术。在坝体材料的采用上，突破了不少规范，在软岩坝料的采用上也有了新的突破。

（四）超高碾压混凝土筑坝技术

碾压混凝土筑坝技术是采用类似土石坝填筑施工技术和工艺，将干硬性混凝土振动压实的一种新型施工技术。此技术具有机械化程度高、工期短、投资省等优点，备受世界坝工界青睐。1979 年我国开始对碾压混凝土筑坝技术进行探索研究，1986 年在福建坑口建成当时世界第一座高碾压混凝土（高 75m）重力坝，取得了令人瞩目的技术成就。20 世纪 90 年代，结合岩滩百米级碾压混凝土技术的开发和技术推广工作，提供一些工程作为碾压混凝土科学实验实践工程，先后把坑口、普定、沙牌及龙滩工程建设中的关键技术列入国家重点攻关项目，创新硕果累累，其中福建坑口碾压混凝土重力坝和普定碾压混凝土重力拱坝的科技成果荣获了国家科技进步一等奖。近年来，我国碾压混凝土筑坝技术全面提升，目前已经建成的碾压混凝土高坝 66 座，在建的 35 座，最近要兴建的 24 座，已建碾压混凝土围堰工程 21 座。已建超过 100m 的 16 座，其中龙滩超过 200m。从统计上看，我国的碾压混凝土在坝型上、数量上及成套施工技术水平均居国际领先。我国现已成为碾压混凝土技术创新的大国，坝工理论和筑坝的新技术、新工艺、新材料不断创新、不断提高，并突破在高温多雨的夏季和高海拔严寒低温冬季筑坝的禁区，形成了具有自主知识产权的不同类型、不同坝型的特色技术和国际先进的筑坝工法。筑坝的低水泥用量、中胶凝材料、掺粉煤灰技术、薄层排铺、大仓成全断面连续上升浇筑等特色工艺，均是我国自主知识产权，属原创新型技术，有效地支撑着我国碾压混凝土筑坝技术向更高、更新、更快的方向发展。

（五）特高拱坝设计理论的突破

经过“七五”、“八五”和“九五”国家科技攻关计划中的水电项目的研究，基本解决了 300m 级的设计和施工的有关技术问题，诸如：特高拱坝的设计理论、试验和模拟分析计算方法，坝体结构和体型优化，抗震结构和设计标准，温度控制及温度应力计算方法，坝体线型优化组合，应力设计标准，温度控制标准等，从理论到设计均有较大的进展和系统的自主创新。具有中国特色的拱坝设计理论和施工工艺，既为我国的高拱坝建设又为坝工科学作出了重大贡献。这些创新的理论和设计方法指导着我国乃至世界数一数二的二滩（高 240m）、小湾（高 292m）和锦屏一级（高 305m）特高拱坝建设，并把高拱坝建设技术推向到世界坝工的巅峰。

（六）坝工基础工程技术

20 世纪 90 年代以来，我国水电工程的地基处理技术得到了快速发展，这是由于大规模水电建设而出现的新的工程问题。水电工程规模不断扩大，高坝、大库和大电站的相继出现，对地基处理的技术要求更高，特别是西南水电基地的建设遇到世界少有的复杂和不良的地质条件，对地基处理提出了一些挑战性技术问题，要一一解决。例如四川南桠河冶勒水电站右岸台地处，坝基覆盖层最大厚度超过 420m 的胶结卵石层，是世界上罕见的，该覆盖层的处理采用两层防渗墙加墙下帷幕灌浆处理，总深度超过 200m；贵州乌江渡水电站的坝基溶洞甚多，采用了孔口封闭灌浆法防止坝基渗漏；三峡永久船闸开挖岩质高壁陡坡，采用了预应力锚索技术解决稳定问题。

水电工程的地基处理不同于其他工程，它的处理工作必须与工程建设同步，而且要求质量高、施工速度要快。地基处理与基础工程技术，大体可分为：防渗墙、灌浆、振冲和锚固等五大类。

防渗墙是工程体（坝、堤、堰）基础和工程体的主要防渗结构。目前我国已建成的防渗墙最深100m，最大厚度1.5m，单项工程最大截水面积为27.15万m^2。灌浆技术广泛应用于大坝基础、隧洞围岩等加固处理以及地下洞室和水工混凝土结构的裂缝、接缝的修补上。目前我国灌浆孔的最大深度已达206m。振冲技术主要应用于软土地基液化工程处理中，目前国内已超过深度30m左右的振冲加密地基水平，近年来研制了150kW振冲器，广泛应用到三峡工程和飞来峡工程中的振冲作业上，效果良好。振冲技术应用到坝体和坝基的加固和防地震液化上，也是一种有效的工程措施之一。预应力锚固主要应用于边坡稳定、混凝土结构加固及混凝土裂缝处理上，目前我国单索锚固吨位已达10MN。以往我国采用黏结式锚索，后来在二滩、小浪底等工程中采用了无黏法锚索。在锚索结构上，研制成功了拉力分散型等型式的全长防腐锚索，并在漫湾、潘家口及十三陵抽水蓄能电站工程上成功应用。拉力复合型锚索，在大桥水库成功实现。目前的预锚抗拉强度可达1860MPa。预锚边坡加固最多的是漫湾水电站，其一次采用2600余根1～6MN锚索来稳定山体滑坡；三峡永久船闸加固边坡中使用近4000根水平锚索。此外，预应力锚索锚固技术与抗滑桩结合加固山体，在李家峡水电站使用了3000多根6MN、8MN和10MN吨位的锚索加固抗坝坝肩高陡边坡，在隔河岩水电站4条引水隧洞、小浪底3条排沙洞、天生桥一级引水洞均成功应用。实践证明，我国水电工程地基处理与基础工程技术，在工艺、材料、设备等方面，已取得很大的进展。今后水电工程中一定还会面临一些新的难题，地基处理工程技术前景和空间潜力很大，尚需依靠科技进步来解决。

（七）高速水流与消能工

消能防冲是泄水建筑物中最重要的水力学问题之一。在我国水电建设中，常会遇到大流量、高水头、大功率的泄洪、消能防冲、防空化空蚀、防振动等工程问题。结合工程建设，在水工建筑物枢纽布置开展消能工型式和结构的系统研究，取得了有特色的创新技术。

新中国成立以来围绕着消除水工建筑物的防冲蚀、防空化、防自激振动、防雾化等问题，研究创新出许多新型的消能工型式，减少了对建筑物的破坏，保障了工程的运行安全。具有我国特色的消能工类型主要有：窄缝式挑坎消能工［如贵州东风电站大坝，单宽流量可达600m^3/（s·m）］；高低坎碰撞消能工［如吉林白山大坝）；挑射水流平面碰撞消能工（如广东泉水大坝）；表孔、中孔对撞加水垫塘联合消能工（如四川二滩水电站大坝）；宽尾墩联合消能工［如“宽尾墩＋台式坝面＋消力池”，云南大朝山大坝，单宽流量193.6m^3/（s·m）］；洞内消能工（如孔塞式泄洪洞，运行水头达140m）；孔板式泄洪洞（如河南小浪底工程）；旋流式消能泄流洞（如青海公伯峡工程，消能率达85%左右）。以上是我国创新的几种适用有效的消能工结构和类型，在不同工程条件下，满足了工程安全运行要求。

（八）大型水电机组国产化

我国水电机组国产化道路，选择了一条引进先进设备和引进核心技术并举的方针，依托国家重大工程，引进、消化、吸收、再创新。新中国成立60多年来，我国水电装备有了显著的进步，前后经历了刘家峡、龙羊峡、岩滩、广州抽水蓄能、天荒坪抽水蓄能等一批单机容量30万kW级机组投入运行后，单机容量40万kW的李家峡，单机容量55万kW的二滩，特别是30多台单机容量70万kW的三峡、小湾、龙滩机组顺利投产；正在建设中的溪洛渡、向家坝、拉西瓦、白鹤滩、乌东德等电站，单机容量从70万kW向着80万kW直至100万kW机组发展。在遵循自主创新的战略方针下，我国大型水电机组的制造能力和水平正逐步达到世界先进水平。

经过多年的努力，大型混流、轴流和冲击式水轮机关键技术开发和国产化进程上，已经有了单机容量840MVA、推力轴承负荷达55000kN、转轮直径10.6m的三峡混流式机组；有了最大水头109.2m、单机最大出力61万kW、空冷每极容量达14.57MVA、转轮直径6.247m的二滩混流机组；有了最大水头57.8m、单机容量20万kW、转轮直径为8m、推力负荷4100tf、世界最大、水头最高的水口轴流机组；有了最大水头637.2m、额定容量12万kW、转轮直径2.6m的冶勒冲击式机组；有了具有我国自主知识产权的蒸发冷却方式、单机容量40万kW的刘家峡机组；采用双排机组布置电站厂房结构也在李家峡实现。

在灯泡贯流水电机组的国产化开发方面，通过近十多年的国内外合作开发研制，实现了已达水头3～16m，单机容量4万～6万kW的制造水平。正在建设的广西长洲水电站装有16台4万kW、运行水头3～6m、转轮直径7.5m的国产化机组，电站的规模居世界第一。广西桥巩电站安装8台5.7万kW、额定水头13.8m、转轮直径27.5m的机组，单机容量位居世界第二。

抽水蓄能机组的国产化历程：双向可逆水泵水轮机组，在20世纪70年代，我国开始起步，研制成功单机容量1.1万kW的机组，并安装在北京密云水电站，在运行情况不佳之后，研制工作停止。在20世纪80年代末又启动大规模的抽水蓄能电站建设，

1992年河北潘家口首台单机容量9万kW抽水蓄能机组并网发电，1993年6月29日广州抽水蓄能电站首台单机30万kW机组并网发电，从此我国抽水蓄能电站又掀起了新的建设高潮。机组的供货问题，不能继续依靠国外，故国产化问题引起了有关部门的高度关注。机组的国产化道路同样是走“三峡大机组国产化模式”。国家决定，依托宝泉、惠州、白莲河3座电站16台30万kW可逆水泵水轮机组捆绑一起引进、合作设计和制造、专利转让来实现我国抽水蓄能机组的国产化。为了巩固技术和发挥创新潜力，国家还以蒲石河、桓仁、深圳、呼和浩特、仙游和黑糜峰等六个抽水蓄能电站作为装备国产化机组的后续依托工程，以保障大型抽水蓄能机组和辅机设备国产化任务的顺利完成。

（九）三峡工程取得了一系列重大技术突破

举世瞩目的三峡工程既是一座巨型电站，又是一项技术工程和智慧工程，也是新中国成立60多年来最具有影响力的30件大事之一。三峡工程规模巨大，涉及学科众多，技术复杂，许多内容都是世界独一无二的，技术难题也是世界顶级的。在工程建设中所采用的新理论、新技术、新工艺不胜枚举，先后创造了150余项水电工程技术世界之最。三峡是一个科技工程，在建设中所突破世界级的技术比比皆是，它既是中国水电工程技术创新的成就展示，也是水电工程技术的缩影。三峡工程开工以来，建设者们坚持科技第一生产力，以科技引领建设全过程，刷新了水电工程多项世界纪录，取得了一系列重大技术的突破，解决了五大工程领域关键技术，攻破了十大工程难题，创造了百余项工程技术世界之最，谱写了水电史上的新篇章。

（十）流域梯级水电站群调度技术

梯级水电站群联合运行，首先要统筹兼顾上下游水量、水头和科学利用水能资源的原则，以发挥电站群的整体综合效益最大化功能。流域梯级水电站群联合运行与电站群的监测监控系统、水情自动测报系统、水调自动化系统、通信系统及流域梯级水电站群联合优化运行决策支持系统有关联，也是联合优化运行的基础。

随着我国大型水电基地的开发和大型水电站群梯级的形成，电站运行管理系统（对各电站进行统一运行管理）、生产体系（以调度为龙头，以效益为核心）、集中监控方式（梯级运行业务系统）的科学规划和协调成为当务之急的管理问题。在探索新型管理模式的过程中，我国首个流域滚动开发发电项目——清江公司，率先成立了“清江梯级调度管理中心”。梯调可以从全面整体最优、效益最大原则运行梯级中的各个电站。在这种模式指导下，三峡梯级调度中心、乌江流域梯级水电站群集中控制管理中心、黄河上游梯级水电站群集中控制管理中心及雅砻江流域水电梯级调度管理中心相继建立。另外，国家电网公司设立了“国家水电调度管理中心”，采用现代的通信技术、数据库技术、专家咨询决策技术，有效地控制着全国电网骨干水电电源最优化运行。

新中国成立60年来，中国水电科技伴随着电力建设的发展和所取得的累累硕果，吸引着全球同行的目光。我国水电建设所走过的历程，科学研究工作始终能走在设计工作的前面，主要原因是我国科技界、水电界中有科学决策的主帅，有一批献身水电事业的精英，有一批特别能战斗的和技艺高超的水电队伍。目前，我国水电总装机容量为1.82亿kW左右，它全面、系统地记录了中国水电人辛勤劳动和无私奉献的丰功伟绩，记录了中国水电人从追求创造物质财富，转向实现可持续发展的新观念和建设山川秀美的绿色工程和生态环保电站的全过程。

（摘自中国水力发电工程学会主编的《中国水电60年》）

六十“而立”的中国水电

关心水电的人不难察觉，国家对于开发水电的态度已有微妙的变化。2009年4月，国家能源局局长张国宝发表在《求是》上的署名文章提出，要“积极推进水电开发”。这与我国“十一五”规划关于水电的表述“在保护生态基础上有序开发水电”显然有所不同。虽然，“十一五”还没有结束，虽然，新的能源规划还没正式出台，虽然，前不久又有两个水电项目被叫停，但这无法改变国家“积极推进水电开发”态度的基本走向。我们有理由相信，人们对水电的认识已更加理性，也更加成熟。

其实，水电作为清洁能源，早已为国际社会所认同。我国政府也早有大力发展水电的努力。1958年，国家曾提出“水主火辅”办电方针，但因多方原因，未能实现。20世纪60年代国家提出“水电火电并举”，70年代提出“在有水力资源的地区多发展水电”，但直到改革开放前的1978年底，全国水电装机容量只有1728万kW，尚不足我国水电能源技术可开发量的10%，在整个电力总装机容量中只占33%，既没“主”起来，也没“并”起来。

进入21世纪后，国家在“十五”规划中明确提出“积极发展水电”，我国水电事业进入了一个大发展时期。从2000年开始，中国水电人用8年时间，实现了水电总装机容量比新中国成立50年的总和翻一番的超越，水电能源开发利用率也从不足10%提高到了27%。而早在2004年，我国水电装机容量即已突破1亿kW，超过美国跃居世界第一。

然而，正当我国水电快速发展之时，随着国际反坝思潮的高涨以及我国水电建设自身所存在的问题，人们对水电的清洁能源属性产生了怀疑，甚至是反感，有人提出要“让河流自由流淌”，有人警告“中国已进入水电伤害时代”。因之“十一五”规划对水电作了“在保护生态基础上有序开发”的修订。而在2009年的人民代表大会上，一向属于清洁能源的水电，还险些从清洁能源的队伍中滑出。

青山遮不住，毕竟东流去。人们对水电的认识也就在这种忽左忽右、大起大落的反复中走向成熟。

认识到位并不意味着技术到位。我国的水电技术现在又是怎样一个水平呢?

随着大量的水电工程的实践，我国各种坝型和各种复杂地形地质条件下的水工建筑物的设计和施工皆已趋于成熟。20世纪50～60年代，一个水电项目的设计需要15～20年，从90年代起，缩短至7～10年，大坝、电站的设计质量和速度空前提高。双曲拱混凝土坝、面板堆石坝以及碾压混凝土重力坝和大洞室地下厂房等施工都有在世界上获誉的成功实例，我国的水电坝工技术已领跑世界。2008年“5·12”汶川地震即用极端的形式验证了中国坝工技术的水平，国际水电界公认，水库的长期使用在中国已是成熟技术。

大型机电设备设计制造曾是制约我国水电发展的一个瓶颈，经三峡工程特大机组的引进、消化、吸收和再创新，目前我国已具备了设计制造当今世界最大机组实力，部分技术已处世界领先。

而总里程3580km的三峡500kV交、直流输电工程的建设则使我国500kV输电等级的技术水平跃上台阶；其1087km500kV直流输电工程的建设，使得我国一跃成为世界第一的直流输电国家。据报道，2009年4月投运的国家电网晋东南—南阳—荆门1000kV特高压交流工程，是目前世界上正在运行的电压等级最高、技术水平最高、输送能力最强的输变电工程。而尤可喜者，该工程主要设备上没有一个外国商标。

制度体制方面，国家加大了对水电开发的宏观调控及实施各个环节（如环保、水土保持、土地使用及银行贷款）的把关，加强了河流的综合规划、专业规划以及项目实施过程监管和项目完结的后评估工作，人水和谐、可持续发展观念已深入人心，工程项目完全市场化运作，投资主体已由国家财政拨款发展为多方持股灵活多元，而流域开发公司的大量出现，又使得“流域、梯级、滚动”的水电开发模式得以实现，移民工作一改过去单一的安置补偿的做法，也探索出了一条将移民的开发性安置与社会主义新农村建设结合起来的新路子。

中国水电，六十“而立”。

（摘自《中国三峡》杂志，田宗伟）

中国坝工技术走在世界前列

新中国成立以后，特别是改革开放30年来，中国的大坝建设和坝工技术有了突飞猛进的发展。据国际大坝委员会统计，到1986年底，全世界大坝共有36 226座，中国有18 820座，占52%；截至2007年底，世界共有15m以上大坝47 500多座，中国有26 278座，约占55%。

我国现代坝工技术的发展大体可以20世纪80年中期为界划分为两个时期。从新中国成立到80年代中期为第一时期。丰富的水力资源和众多条件优越的坝址，使得我国的坝工建设一起步就得到了迅猛的发展。据国际大坝委员会统计，1951～1977年间，世界其他国家平均每年建坝335座，中国为420座；1982年全世界15m以上大坝为34 798座，中国为18 595座，占总数的53.4%。这一时期坝工技术的特点是：在我国传统工艺的基础上土洋并举，修建了数量众多、型式多样的各类大坝。除了传统的土坝外，建成了连拱坝、大头坝、宽缝重力坝、重力拱坝、空腹重力坝、空腹拱坝等多种型式的中高坝，坝的高度已达到100m以上。在中小型工程中，利用当地材料及我国传统的坝工工艺，修建了型式多样的土石混合坝、水坠坝、淤地坝、草土坝、竹木坝以及橡胶坝等极具中国传统风格的坝型。

20世纪80年代中期到现在是我国坝工技术发展的第二时期。改革开放促进了国民经济高速发展，水电建设管理新体制极大地推动了水电建设的发展，高坝建设的数量和速度明显上升。通过学习和引进国外坝工新技术，开展国家重点科技攻关，研究解决了一些复杂条件下的高坝建设技术难题。新坝型和新的坝工技术得到了广泛应用和进一步的深化研究，如混凝土面板堆石坝、碾压混凝土坝、高拱坝等。截至2007年底，中国已建在建的坝高30m以上的大坝共有5191座，其中坝高300m以上有1座，坝高200～300m有9座，坝高100～200m有132座。

我国水坝规模之大，数量之多，独步全球。目前已经拥有了多项世界之最：世界上混凝土量最大的、泄洪能力最大的大坝——三峡大坝，坝高181m，坝顶长2309m，混凝土量约2000万m^3，泄洪能力为102 000m^3/s；世界上最高的混凝土面板堆石坝——清江水布垭大坝，坝高233m；世界上最高的碾压混凝土重力坝——广西龙滩大坝，坝高216.5m；世界上最高的碾压混凝土拱坝——四川沙牌大坝，坝高132m；世界上最高的拱坝——雅砻江锦屏一级大坝，坝高305m。这些大坝的建成，标志着我国的坝工建设水平在数量、规模、难度和技术创新等方面走在了世界前列。

（一）混凝土面板堆石坝

我国在20世纪80年代中期引入混凝土面板堆石坝技术，在借鉴了国外经验的基础上，通过实践积累了自己的经验，并在全国范围内推广应用。截止到2007年底，我国已建成高30m及以上的面板堆石坝160座，高100m及以上的40余座。已建成的清江水布垭大坝坝高233m，目前为世界最高的混凝土面板堆石坝。

我国地域辽阔，自然条件千差万别，混凝土面板堆石坝以其良好的适应性遍布全国各地，在恶劣的自然条件下也能得到成功修建。如高海拔山区，西藏的查龙坝，坝顶高程4388m，为世界上海拔最高的混凝土面板堆石坝，坝区年最低气温−41.2℃；高纬度地区，黑龙江莲花水电站大坝，坝区年最低气温−42.5℃，每年冰期达5个月；强地震高发地区，黑泉、茄子山、吉林台、大桥、海潮坝、查龙等水电站位于Ⅷ度区，天生桥一级、乌鲁瓦提、柴石滩、紫坪铺、公伯峡等水电站位于Ⅶ度区；深厚覆盖层上，新疆察汗乌苏坝，趾板置于覆盖层上，坝高107.6m，覆盖层最深约50m；窄深峡谷和不规则地形条件下，常以高混凝土挡墙来改造地形，以使混凝土面板与挡墙相连接组成完整的防渗体系，小干沟坝的挡墙高25.2m，龙首二级坝的上游挡墙高39.8m，公伯峡坝的挡墙高达50m。

我国的混凝土面板堆石坝在数量、规模、难度和技术创新等方面都已进入世界最前列。在大坝性态研究和科学试验方面，提出了坝体粗料大尺度效应、应力应变、土工离心机模拟技术，开展了坝体与坝基动力研究，提出了抗震防震技术，研究了坝体变形规律和破坏机理；在设计准则方面，提出了面板接缝止水结构的设计参数及控制指标准则、坝体填筑分区、程序标准，制定设计和施工规范；在筑坝材料方面，拓宽了材料的使用范围，在坝体一定部位使用软岩和风化岩石，充分利用开挖料；在防止面板裂缝技术方面，提出了大坝主堆石体与下游次堆石体的科学分区，采用了面板混凝土的改性工艺，面板混凝土掺加粉煤灰、掺加复合外加剂，采用补偿收缩混凝土、纤维混凝土及高性能混凝土等技术；在施工工艺方面，实现了无轨滑模、围坡防护和挤压边墙等施工新技术、新工艺。

（二）碾压混凝土坝

我国于1986年建成第一座碾压混凝土坝——福建坑口碾压混凝土重力坝，2007年已建在建碾压混凝土坝有126座。1993年建成坝高75m的普定大坝，为当时世界最高的碾压混凝土重力拱坝。1996年建成的福建溪柄溪拱坝，为世界上第一座碾压混凝土薄拱坝。2001年建成的沙牌拱坝是目前世界上最高的碾压混凝土拱坝。近期建成的龙滩大坝是世界最高碾压混凝土重力坝（坝高216.5m）。三峡三期上游碾压混凝土围堰，其月、日最高浇筑强度分别创造了47.5万m^3和2.1万m^3的世界纪录。

我国在引进碾压混凝土筑坝技术的同时强调走自己的路，结合我国的实际情况不断自主创新。坝工理论和筑坝技术、工艺、材料不断创新、不断提高，并突破了在高温多雨夏季和高海拔严寒低温冬季筑坝的禁区，形成了具有自主知识产权的特色技术和国际先进的筑坝工法。我国碾压混凝土多采用低水泥用量、高掺粉煤灰、中胶凝材料干硬性混凝土，薄层连续碾压，二级配碾压混凝土防渗，变态混凝土过渡，广泛采用诱导缝，不设纵缝，全仓面或全坝面碾压施工。

我国在碾压混凝土筑坝技术的创新主要有以下几个方面：①采用高掺粉煤灰和低稠度碾压混凝土配合比；②防渗层采用二级配富浆碾压混凝土；③周边采用变态混凝土（1999年中国成都RCC国际讨论会后，变态混凝土工法传至约旦、哥伦比亚、伊朗、巴西和印度等国家）；④斜层平推法碾压施工，在拌和能力受限的情况下，有效地减小了仓面摊铺面积、缩短层间覆盖时间，保证碾压混凝土层间结合质量和大仓面连续浇筑；⑤负压溜槽运送碾压混凝土，在狭窄河谷以负压溜槽作为碾压混凝土垂直运输的重要手段（伊朗的加根坝在碾压混凝土围堰施工中，仿中国的负压溜槽采用了钢板溜槽）；⑥采用简便快速的造缝技术，在棉花滩碾压混凝土坝施工中，创造了用手提式振动夯改装的振动切缝机，在碾压后切缝的同时将PVC编织布条压入碾压混凝土中；⑦在普定碾压混凝土拱坝设计中，首先采用了在坝体设置横缝和诱导缝相结合的分缝模式的拱坝坝体结构，并设置了可用于重复灌浆的预埋灌浆系统；⑧三峡工程围堰碾压混凝土，首次采用了埋冷却水管通水降温，突破了国外“碾压混凝土不宜在坝内埋冷却水管”的规定。

（三）高拱坝

我国在1958年建成第一座混凝土拱坝——响洪甸拱坝。1980年以后，我国拱坝建设有很大的发展，特别是100m以上的混凝土拱坝，由1980年以前的3座发展到2005年的25座。目前在建的锦屏坝（高305m）、小湾坝（高292m）和溪洛渡坝（高278m），高度都超过了世界最高的英古里坝（高272m）。

我国混凝土高拱坝建设体现了如下主要特点和趋势：放宽对坝址地形和坝基岩体条件的要求，拱坝体形多样化，厚度越来越薄，重视枢纽布置和泄洪消能。

我国对拱坝技术的研究和实践不断深化和发展，特别是经过“七五”、“八五”和“九五”国家科技攻关计划中的水电项目的研究，基本解决了300m级高拱坝的设计和施工的有关技术问题。如：特高拱坝的设计理论、试验和模拟分析计算方法，坝体结构和体形优化，抗震结构和设计标准，温度控制及温度应力计算方法，坝体线型优化组合，应力设计标准，温度控制标准等，从理论到设计都有较大的进展和系统的自主创新。

（四）高水头大流量泄洪建筑物及消能工技术

我国高坝泄洪单宽流量、总泄量和泄洪功率均居世界前列，目前泄洪量超过20 000m^3/s的有20多座大坝，其中三峡大坝泄量102 500m^3/s，溪洛渡、五强溪、水口等大坝泄量均大于50 000m^3/s。我国的高坝一般能量集中，消能要求高，如二滩、构皮滩、小湾和溪洛渡等工程，都在河床宽80～110m的范围内，其泄洪功率：构皮滩31 600MW，二滩39 000MW，小湾46 000MW，溪洛渡98 000MW，不仅泄洪功率大，泄洪建筑物的单宽流量和流速均很大。据统计，泄洪、导流设施流量超过20 000m^3/s的工程就有30多座，如三峡工程，校核洪水流量达124 300m^3/s。另外，我国还有多座水头超过200m以上的高坝泄洪建筑物，流速大于50m/s，泄洪建筑的单宽流量都大于200$m^3/(s\cdot m)$，这使我国处理泄洪消能问题难度增大。

根据不同的坝型和泄洪规模，采用了不同的泄洪布置及其组合：重力坝主要通过坝身泄洪，以表孔为主，辅以深孔并兼作排沙等用途；拱坝通常以坝身孔口为主，辅以岸边泄洪设施；土石坝则一般采用岸边式溢洪道和泄洪隧洞为主。随着高坝建设的实践，经过科技攻关，我国的消能技术不断创新，在多种联合消能、加大坝身泄洪、强化水舌空中扩散与碰撞、分散落水点和减小冲击力、建立二道坝形成水垫塘消能和隧洞内消能等方面均有新的发展，并研究创新出许多新型的消能工形式，有效减少了对建筑物的破坏，保障了工程的运行安全。具有我国特色消能类型主要有：窄缝式消能工、宽尾墩式联合消能工、掺气分流墩消能工、挑射水流平面碰撞消能、高低挑坎碰撞消能、挑流＋水垫塘联合消能、淹没跌坎式底流消能、洞内孔板消能工、洞内漩流消能。

（五）大流量深水截流技术

通过长江、黄河等大江大河截流的科学研究和工程实践，特别是长江上三次截流的圆满实施，中国的截流技术已从总体上达到了国际领先水平。长江三次截流涵盖了大江大河截流的所有高难点且各有特点：葛洲坝截流的特点是大流量、高流速、大落差、高填筑强度，其关键在于突破水力学难关；三峡大江截流的特点是大流量、大水深、高填筑强度，其关键在于大水深导致堤头坍塌进而引发进占安全问题；三峡三期截流的特点是大流量、高流速、大落差、大水深、高填筑强度，其关键包含上述二者，故综合难度最高。

衡量截流施工水平的指标有截流流量、截流落差、流速、水深以及物料抛投强度等。按截流流量大于3000m^3/s，落差大于3.5m，水面流速大于7m/s或平均流速大于5m/s的截流水力学指标综合统计，在三峡明渠截流前达到上述指标的，世界上曾出现过4次。它们分别为巴西巴拉圭的伊泰普截流（流量8100m^3/s，最大落差3.76m，最大平均流速5.0m/s）、原苏联的Bratzk截流（流量3660m^3/s，最大落差3.51m，最大水面流速7.4～5.0m/s）、美国的Menny截流（流量3935m^3/s，最大落差5.4m，最大水面流速9.1m/s）和罗马尼亚与南斯拉夫的铁门截流（流量3390m^3/s，最大落差3.72m，最大水面流速7.5m/s）。中国的三峡工程导流明渠截流综合指标排名第一，设计截流流量1.03万m^3/s，截流落差4.11m，截流流速7.5m/s。三峡工程的两次截流还突破了三项截流的世界最高指标，即截流流量10 300m^3/s，截流水深达到60m，截流抛石强度达到194 000m^3/d。

三峡工程大江截流采用了预平抛垫底，有效防止了大规模的堤头坍塌。三峡工程明渠截流，成功地采用并实施了从设计到施工的双戗配合立堵截流实践，完善了双戗截流理论。三峡工程明渠截流上戗采用先铺设混凝土四面体然后再镶嵌覆盖一定量大块石型式拦石坎，下戗采用合金钢网石兜拦石坎成功地降低了截流难度，为工程实践积累了经验。

（六）坝基覆盖层防渗处理技术

我国1958年引进防渗墙技术，首先在大坝地基防渗处理中应用。1958年山东月子口水库在砂砾石地基中建成了深20m连锁桩柱式混凝土防渗墙。1959年北京密云水库白河主坝砂砾石地基中创造出一套用钻劈法建造深44m的槽孔型混凝土防渗墙的新方法，取得了巨大成功。混凝土防渗墙作为覆盖层地基和土石坝（围堰）工程的主要防渗措施，其形式、规模和适用范围发展很快，并且扩展到其他领域，在有特殊要求的工程中作为防冲、挡土、承重墙等。40年来，尤其改革开放以来通过大量的工程实践和科学实验，防渗墙施工设备和方法不断改进，施工效率不断提高，我国的防渗墙施工水平已经跨入了世界先进水平的行列。

防渗墙深度方面，继四川狮子坪水电站和新疆下坂地水利枢纽突破 100m 后，2008 年西藏旁多水利枢纽坝基防渗试验创造了 146.3m 的成槽深度记录，超过了加拿大马尼克Ⅲ大坝的 131m，随即在 2009 年在四川泸定水电站主坝防渗墙施工中以 154.8m 的最大孔深刷新了这一记录，成为新的“世界最深墙”。

防渗墙规模方面，河北黄壁庄水库加固工程副坝混凝土防渗墙长度 4860m，防渗面积 27.1 万 m^2，该工程是我国工程量最大的混凝土防渗墙。

施工强度方面，金沙江向家坝一期围堰混凝土防渗墙，面积近 5.2 万 m^2，厚 0.8m，最大深度81.8m，最大施工强度达到 2.4 万 m^2/月。汉江兴隆水利枢纽工程围堰防渗墙总面积 25 万 m^2、墙壁厚 80cm、平均深度超过 60m，2009 年 5～6 月，实际施工强度达到了 5.36 万 m^2/月。

施工条件方面，四川冶勒水电站坝基覆盖层深度超过 420m，坝基及岸坡混凝土防渗墙分上下两段建造，下墙在专门开挖的隧洞中施工，最大深度达到 84.85m，为国内在隧洞中建成的最深防渗墙。

综合难度方面，长江三峡二期上游围堰是综合难度最大的代表性工程。堰基为水下抛填卵石、原始砂卵石层、粉细砂层、风化花岗岩体等，架空卵石、不稳定粉细砂、风化花岗岩中的块球体，以及河槽侧面基岩陡坡等不利地质条件给施工带来了极大的困难。围堰防渗曾咨询国外著名承包商，提出采用 2 道混凝土防渗墙和 5 排高喷防渗墙，工期需要 2 个枯水期。我国设计和施工单位联合攻关，实际采用 1 道塑性混凝土防渗墙，河床深处局部 2 道防渗墙，最大墙深 73.5m，成墙面积 4.1 万 m^2，自 1997 年 11 月至次年 5 月一个枯水期内完成。

墙体材料方面，呈现多样化。为与地基变形相适应，推广了塑性混凝土；出于结构受力的需要，采用了高强混凝土，小浪底水利枢纽防渗墙强度达到 35MPa，冶勒水电站混凝土强度等级为 $C_{90}40$；为加快施工进度和降低造价，在多个工程中采用了自凝灰浆和固化灰浆防渗墙。

施工设备方面，在传统的钢绳冲击钻机基础上研制成功了冲击反循环钻机并不断改进，引进并研制了抓斗式挖槽机，引进了液压铣槽机。

施工方法方面，探索形成了多种不同机具组合成槽工艺，如“两钻一抓（铣）”、“上抓（铣）下钻”、“铣、砸、爆”等，以适应不同地层；采用先进的泵吸反循环、气举反循环清孔技术；研制了拔管专利技术，使墙段接头技术达到了国际领先水平，拔管深度不断加大，四川狮子坪水电站达到 93.5m，泸定水电站达到 113.6m，在我国承建的越南拜尚水闸的防渗墙施工中，成功地采用了在墙段接缝中安设 PVC 止水片的技术。在润扬长江公路大桥北锚旋地连墙墙段接缝中采用了 V 形钢板连接技术。

（摘自《中国三峡》杂志，长江勘测规划设计研究院　颜家军）

中国大型水电机组制造瓶颈已彻底打破

新中国对电器工业非常重视，共和国成立三个月后的 1950 年 1 月，中央就召开全国电器工业工作会议，要加强国内电器工业建设，决定在东北建立发电设备制造工厂。当时，抗美援朝已经开始，沈阳地区的工业北迁。做变压器的沈阳电工五厂和做开关的十五厂部分人员与设备于 1950 年 11 月迁到哈尔滨成立东北电工四厂，后来演变成哈尔滨电机厂（以后简称哈电）。这是我国自己设计建设的第一个发电设备制造工厂。“一五”期间，我们引进苏联技术，在东北还成立了哈尔滨汽轮机厂、哈尔滨锅炉厂。东北三大动力厂就是这么建立起来的。做出 2.5 万 kW 的汽轮发电机组于 1958 年开始运行。

同时，上海地区把原来有的老工厂组织起来，加上改建新建的厂，也成立了三大动力厂：上海电机厂、上海汽轮机厂、上海锅炉厂。引进捷克技术，制成 1 万 kW、1.2 万 kW 火电机组。

1958 年，国家加强三线建设，哈尔滨三大动力厂支援内地，在四川也建立了一套三大动力厂：东方电机厂（以后简称东电）、东方汽轮机厂、东方锅炉厂。1966 年，这三大动力厂正式投产。

这样全国就有了三大动力制造基地。

其中，真正最早做水电的，就是哈电。1948 年，国民党撤退时炸坏了四川下硐水电厂 800kW 机组，周总理批示东北电工局组织制造设备恢复发电。当时新厂房还没盖，就在一个老的农机厂里做的，在沈阳高压开关厂水轮机车间组装试验，1951 年底做成，安装后运行很好。接着，又给四川上硐水电站做 3000kW 水电机组，给福建古田水电站做 6000kW 水电机组。这些机组都是从国外回来的一些工程师带领下搞出来的。

到了 1954 年，全学苏联一边倒。设计制造的第一台机组是官厅水库 1 万 kW 水轮发电机组，1955 年就发电了。这后来就多了，1.2 万 kW 的，1.5 万 kW 的，1.6 万 kW 的，1959 年就做出了7.25 万kW 的水轮发电机组。这可视为一个阶段。第一阶段是自己的，最大做到 1 万 kW，第二阶段学苏联，最大做到新安江 7.25 万 kW 水轮发电机组，共 9 台。

1960 年苏联专家撤走，全国贯彻“自力更生、奋发图强”的方针，自主设计制造了中朝合建云峰电厂单机10万kW机组，首台苏联供货、后3台自己设计制造。1964年自己做出了首台10万kW机组。但这时水轮机模型试验还是苏联的，那时苏联是全民的，数据都是公开公布的，采用转轮型式，直径达到4.1m。此型号的共做了10台，云峰外，湖南风滩4台、甘肃白龙江3台，运行都很好。国家还给了个质量银奖。这是中国水电制造的头个奖项。

1958年，我国第一个百万千瓦水电站甘肃刘家峡电站（122.5万kW）开始建设，3台22.5万kW、1台25万kW、1台30万kW机组，1974年12月5台全部发电，也是哈尔滨电机厂设计制造的（转轮技术还是苏联的）。这个时候我们的机组设计制造技术与国际上是相当的。我们设计制造22.5万kW机组时，苏联当时还只有21万kW的机组。

至1978年末，全国电站装机总容量达5712万kW，其中水电站1728万kW，占30.3%，水电机组国内制造比例达80%。

改革开放以后，全国加强水电规划、勘测、设计前期工作，提出开发十二个水电基地（后加上怒江为十三个），充分开发利用清洁可再生水能源，西电东送，加快了水电建设。机组设计制造一方面立足自主研发，一方面为进口机组分包制造非核心部件，机组设计制造技术有较大提高。但与国外机组设计制造水平差距也很大。

20世纪80年代，哈电为吉林白山水电站设计制造了5台30万kW机组，东方电机厂为青海龙羊峡水电站设计制造了4台32万kW机组，为青海李家峡电站设计制造了5台40万kW机组，其4号发电机成功采用蒸发冷却技术，国内首创。这期间，哈电和东电还为葛洲坝电站制造了2台17万kW和19台12.5万kW世界尺寸最大的转桨式机组。这些机组投运后运行良好，获国家质量金奖，葛洲坝工程获国家科技进步特等奖。

与此同时，由于看到国内外水电机组技术的巨大差距，一些新建大型水电站纷纷采用进口机组，国内企业只能分包制造一些非核心部件，分包中没有技术转让项目，但还是起到了解世界的作用，技术上也有收获。这期间国内分包制造的机组有：云南鲁布革372m水头15万kW机组、湖南五强溪混流式轮轮直径8.3m的24万kW机组、河南小浪底30万kW水轮机、四川二滩55万kW机组。

另外，这期间还在哈尔滨大电机研究所、东电和天津电气传动研究所建成了符合IEC标准的水力试验台，从而可以开展水轮机水力设计与模型试验，在哈尔滨大电机研究所建立3000t推力轴承试验台、在东电建立1000t推力轴承试验台，有效保证了推力轴承以及机组的可靠性。

1992年4月3日，全国人大七届五次会议通过《关于兴建三峡工程决议》，1994三峡工程开工建设。鉴于当时国外已有20多台70万kW级机组在运行，而我们自主研发的能力还只能做出40万kW机组，与国外合作（制造非核心部件）只做到55万kW机组，党中央、国务院明确提出依托三峡工程，实行国际采购招标，以“技贸结合、技术转让、联合设计、合作生产”方式，引进、消化吸收国外先进技术，全面提升我国水电装备制造整体水平。国家决定，三峡工程左岸电站14台机组通过国际招标采购，但外商投标时必须以向中方转让技术为前提条件。标书要求，投标者对设备的经济和技术负全部责任，投标者必须带上中国有资格的企业参与设计、合作制造，中国制造企业分包的份额不低于合同总额的25%，且最后两台机组必须以中国企业为主制造。这就不同于改革开放初期各个电站的国际采购只着眼设备，而是引进核心技术。

技术转让的内容由国内制造企业提出清单，实际上就是转让我们所需要的全部设计制造技术。技术转让的深度，须将外商计算机软件连同源程序带回国内，在计算机运算能够得到相同的结果，并稳定运行一年以上。国内制造厂家对转让的技术满意签字后，中国长江三峡工程开发集团公司方向外商支付技术转让费用。条件可以说是十分苛刻。

1996年6月，左岸电站一次采购14台70万kW水轮发电机组消息公布，这个全球最大的水电设备采购项目，立刻吸引了全球著名水电设备制造厂商组成5个联合体竞争投标，形成激烈的竞争局面。经过议标，Alstom采用挪威Kvaerner水力设计和ABB中标8台，与哈电合作；VGS（Voith，GE，Siemens）中标6台，与东电合作。

国家的这个决策很英明。由于从1983年国务院成立重大技术装备领导小组，把三峡机组列入专项，哈电和东电就开始自主研发，并做出方案设计，有了一定技术基础，因此，合同的执行也很顺利并取得成功。2005年9月，三峡工程左岸电站14台机组全部投产发电。以哈电为主制造的14号、以东电为主制造的9号机组的国产化率分别达到了71%和85%。包括哈电、东电为主制造的两台机组，所有机组目前运行良好。我们用不到10年时间实现了30年的跨越，包括国家支持的两厂技术改造，现在我们已完全具备了设计制造70万kW特大型水轮发电机组的能力。

2003年，三峡右岸电站12台机组国际招标，哈电、东电与Alstom“三分天下”，各拿到了4台机组的合同。通过左岸机组的引进、消化、吸收加上自主创新，我们也具备了独立设计制造目前全球单机容量最大的机组的能力了。2008 年 10 月，三峡右岸电站 12 台机组全部投产发电。从运行的情况看，哈电与东电设计制造机组的稳定性达到了国外机组的同等水平。因此可以说，我国大型水电机组制造瓶颈已彻底打破，甚至有些技术已达到国际领先水平。比如：国产机组就已消除了长期困扰水轮机特殊压力脉动带现象，大型机组空冷技术和右岸地下电站将采用的蒸发冷却技术都达到了世界一流的水准、绝缘技术也达到了世界级先进水平。

除了三峡外，20 世纪末，我国还建设了一批大型水电站，如广西龙滩、云南小湾、贵州构皮滩、青海拉西瓦等。在三峡机组引进技术中，我们在大型机组的设计制造上消化吸收并不断创新，已能够自主设计制造全球巨型水电机组，技术瓶颈已彻底打破，已跻身世界机组设计制造大国，在有些方面，已是世界领先。比如哈电自主开发 70 万 kW 全空冷水轮发电机就打破了此前业界普遍认为的全空冷水轮发电机不能超过 60 万 kW 的限制。近年来我国设计制造已开始从“引进”转向“输出”。每年都有数量不小的机组出口。我们的机组设计制造已开始走向世界。而同时，我国还有数量巨大的水能资源尚未开发，我们有巨大的水电发展空间，国家规划的常规水电总装机容量在 2010 年、2015 年、2020 年要分别为 19 400 万 kW、27 100 万 kW、32 800 万 kW，抽水蓄能电站装机容量分别为 1800 万 kW、3400 万 kW、5000 万 kW。发电设备设计制造有着巨大的市场。

目前，哈电和东电已具有研究开发能力，能独立开展水轮机水力设计与模型试验和发电机试验研究，现在正在设计制造单机容量 80 万 kW 级的大型水电机组。2007 年分别生产总容量 603 万 kW 和 519 万 kW 水电机组，是国内自主开发设计制造大型发电设备的国有骨干企业。另外，中外合资的上海福依特西门子水电设备有限公司、天津阿尔斯通水电设备有限公司、杭州通用电气亚洲水电设备有限公司和东芝水电设备（杭州）有限公司，皆具有较强的焊接加工能力，依托其母公司的技术开发与管理的支持，也能够制造大型水电机组。我们既有技术，又有市场，可以预见，不久我国将成为水电机组设计制造强国。

（摘自《中国三峡》杂志，中国工程院院士　梁维燕）

特高电压输电构筑中国电力高速公路（摘要）

我国电网输电线路，从高压、超高压到特高压线路 60 年的发展历程看，大型水电站的建设推动电网输电电压的等级在一个台阶又一个台阶地大幅度跨进。刘家峡、葛洲坝及向家坝水电站的先后建设，无不推动着这一历程大步向前！

选登的“特高电压输电构筑中国电力高速公路”一文，从另一方面见证中国水电建设的巨大成就。

1000kV 晋东南—南阳—荆门特高压试验示范工程成功投入商业运营和±800kV 云南—广州和向家坝—上海两条特高压直流示范工程的开工建设标志我国大容量远距离输电和电网建设进入新时期。特高压交、直流大容量远距离输电工程的继续发展，形成特高压输电网，将构筑我国大容量远距离输电骨干通道——中国电力高速公路。它的建设将更好地推动全国电力资源优化配置，更好地促进未来大型水电、大型风电等可再生新能源的开发利用和传统煤电基地的建设。

（一）特高压提升大容量远距离输电能力

交流输电线路输送的功率与电网电压平方成正比，与线路电抗成反比。线路电抗随输电线路长度成比例增加，因此线路输送的功率与电网电压平方成正比，与输送距离成反比。电网输电线路的输电能力与电网电压平方成正比的关系是推进输电电网的电压等级由高电压、超高电压向特高电压发展的基本动力。

在保持同样稳定运行水平条件下输电线路的输电能力通常用线路的自然功率评价。

高压、超高压和特高压三相交流线路输送自然功率的能力，如表 1 所示。

表 1　高压、超高压和特高压三相交流线路输送自然功率的能力

电压等级（kV）	220	330	345	500	750	1000
输送功率（10MW）	13.2	29.5	32.0	92.6	216.3	454.5

1000kV 相对于 500kV 来说电压提升了 1 倍，线路的输电能力却提升了将近 5 倍。

1000kV 特高压输电线路，与 500kV 相比，不仅输电能力可提升将近 5 倍，而且输电距离可增加 1 倍。1000kV 输电线路构成的电网可在更广的地域范围优化配置电力资源，可更好地解决发电资源与负荷中心在地域上极不均衡的问题。

直流输电是大容量远距离输电的重要方式。直流输电系统由整流站、逆变站和直流输电线路组成。直流输电线路输送的功率是直流电压与直流电流的乘积，即 $P=V_{dc}\cdot I_{dc}$，V_{dc}为极线对地电压，I_{dc}为直流电流。直流输电的距离主要由直流线路电压降和线路功率损耗决定。

目前，世界上正在运行的高压直流输电工程共 78 项（含 23 项背靠背直流工程），共计额定输电容

量 73 347MW，主要用于水电站电力送出工程或电网之间联络线工程。中国 500kV 远距离高压直流输电总容量已达 18 000MW，占世界上运行的高压直流输电总容量的 24.5%，占主要大容量远距离直流输电容量的 39.7%，居领先地位。

±800kV 直流输电绝缘与 1000kV 交流输电绝缘水平相当，被称为特高压直流输电。基于 4000A 晶闸管构成的±800kV 特高压直流输电，额定输送容量 6400MW，输电距离可达 2000km 及以上。

（二）特高压构筑大容量远距离输电通道

我国未来水电开发主要集中在长江上游、金沙江、大渡河、雅砻江、怒江、澜沧江、乌江和雅鲁藏布江以及黄河中、上游。未来大型风电场的开发主要在甘肃、内蒙古、新疆、东北和江苏东部海上风电场。未来的煤电开发主要集中在西北的蒙西、宁夏、陕西、山西、新疆东部及云贵等省区，而负荷中心将仍然主要在东部地区，特别是沿京广线以东的地区。未来主要发电资源与负荷中心在地区上的不均衡性将更加突出。跨大区输电距离将主要在 1000～2000km 及以上，发展特高压大容量远距离输电是未来输电电网建设的必然趋势。

特高压交流和特高压直流输电都可实现大容量远距离输电，构筑强大的大容量远距离输电通道。如果长输电线路中间能建开关站，中间接入电源或动态无功补偿获得电压支持，采用交流特高压输电不仅安全、稳定性和经济性好，而且容易形成特高压电输电网络，对能源和负荷变化的适应性和灵活性好。对于远离负荷中心，地处边远山区的水电站及水电站群送出工程，在沿线路建设中间开关站困难时，为了节省线路走廊用地，大容量远距离输电采用特高压直流将会有较好竞争性。特高压大容量远距离输电总体上主要应建设特高压交流输电工程并形成特高压输电网，辅之特高压直流输电。

（三）自主创新跨越式发展

特高压大容量远距离输电技术是在超高压输电技术基础上的发展和创新。先进的超高压输电技术及其设备研发和成功的应用经验促进了特高压输电技术的研究和在大容量远距离输电的应用。

1981 年，主要依靠进口输变设备建成我国第一条 500kV 交流输电线路姚孟—双河—荆门—武昌线路，全长 595km，输送功率 1000MW。在引进、消化、吸收国外先进技术和经验基础上，坚持自主创新，采用国产化输变电设备，1985 年建成 500kV 元宝山—锦州—辽阳—海城输电线路，线路全长 602km。500kV 输变电设备国产化后，推进了 500kV 输变电工程的快速发展，形成六大跨省的，比较坚强的区域电网。500kV 输变电设备国产化为自主研制 1000kV 特高压输电工程开辟了广阔前景。

我国第一个高压直流输电工程，±500kV 葛洲坝—南桥高压直流输电工程，线路长 1046km，额定输送容量 1200MW，于 1999 年双极投入运行。该项工程的设备全部从国外引进。随着自主创新能力和设备国产化率逐步提高，在三峡±500kV 直流输电工程中，设备国产化率由三常直流工程的 30%提高到三广直流工程的 50%，进而到三沪直流工程的 70%，2005 年投运的西北—华中联网工程，灵宝背靠背工程实现了 100%国产化。这为±800kV 直流输电工程设备国产化，从而降低工程建设成本奠定了基础。

电网技术发展走自主创新、集成创新和引进再创新相结合的道路，开展的电网发展关键技术研究取得了一系列具有国际先进技术水平成果，用于电网，包括输变电工程建设实际已产生显著效益。跟踪国外提出先进的灵活交流输电（FACTS）概念，已自主研制成功串联电容补偿加可控串联补偿（TCSC）用于 500kV 东北电网的伊—冯输电工程，在确保电力系统稳定条件下提升了线路的大容量远距离输电功率。静止无功补偿装置（SVC）已有多套装于 500kV 输电线路，20 套串联电容补偿已安装 500kV 远距离输电线路。它们的应用对提高线路输电能力，提高电力系统稳定性发挥了重要作用。超高压大容量远距离输电先进技术的应用经验为研究 1000kV 特高压大容量远距离输电提供了成功的借鉴。

交流特高压输电技术虽然是在超高压输电技术基础上的发展，但面临四大主要的关键技术挑战。空气绝缘间隙放电特性进入特高压将呈现明显的饱和特性。绝缘子串的闪络电压特性进入特高压呈现的非线性饱和特性更为明显。特高压空气绝缘间隙和绝缘子串长度的增加比电压的提高更快。如果按超高压的试验数据设计特高压输电工程，其绝缘成本的增加将使特高压输电在经济上不可行。输电导线的表面电场强度随输电电压的提升而增加，从而使电晕放电的概率增加。电晕放电将产生可听噪声、无线电和电视信号干扰以及电晕电能损失。特高压输电的电晕将更为突出。特高压输电的更高电压和更大的输电电流将产生更强的工频电场和磁场。如果按超高压试验数据处理特高压输电的环境影响将难于接受。发展特高压输电必须解决以上所述的关键技术问题，即：①特高压输电的绝缘特性和绝缘要求；②特高压输电的电晕特性及输电导线结构；③特高压输电的工频电磁场及其对环境的影响；④特高压输电的系统特性。

发展特高压直流输电面临更多的关键技术挑战，同样不能简单地用高压直流试验数据处理特高压直流输电工程设计和安全经济运行问题，必须研究解决如下关键技术问题，即：①外绝缘，包括特长的大尺寸穿墙套管绝缘；②内绝缘，包括变压器绝缘和阀厅绝缘；③过电压，特别是限压器（避雷器）的容量、耗能限制；④电晕与导线结构；⑤电磁场与环境影响；⑥与交流输电系统的相互影响等。

我国开展特高压研究始于20世纪90年代后期。进入21世纪，特别是电力体制改革、厂网分开管理以后，结合工程需要才全面开展特高压关键技术试验研究和系统分析研究。在特高压关键技术研究方面与国外相比晚了25年左右。在借鉴国外研究成果和研究经验基础上，走自主创新、集成创新和引进吸收再创新相结合的发展道路，电网和电力设备制造企业、厂学研协同攻关，短短几年时间解决特高压输电建设和运行的一系列关键技术难题。基于国产化特高压输变设备的1000kV晋东南—南阳—荆门特高压试验示范工程，已于2009年1月投入商业运行。这是世界上第一个投入商业运行的特高压输电工程。我国特高压从技术开发和输变电设备研制到工程投入运行在不到5年时间走完国外20年才能完成的过程。±800kV云南—广州和向家坝—上海两条特高压直流示范工程在主要依靠自主创新，解决了一系列关键技术和主要设备制造技术后，已分别于2006年和2007年开工建设。这标志我国特高压输电已走在世界前列，技术研究成果和应用处于国际领先水平。我国已形成交流特高压输变设备批量生产能力，已具备大规模应用交流特高压技术，继续建设特高压输电工程的条件，实现特高压大容量远距离输电的跨越式发展。

（四）优化成本管理提升社会经济效益

发展特高压大容量远距离输电的出发点和落脚点是：在全国范围优化配置电力资源，降低输电建设成本、运行成本、输电功率损失，从而降低输电成本，节省变电站和架空线占地面积，保护环境。特高压大容量远距离输电在解决我国未来电力资源与电力负荷地区间不均衡的同时，可显著降低输电成本，保护环境。

特高压交流和直流输电有不同特点。特高压交流输电由升变电站、三相输电线路和降压变电站组成。变电站相对直流换流站来说占地面积小，建设成本低。线路长度超过输送自然功率的经济距离需要加中间开关站、串联电容补偿和并联动态无功补偿，这样，超过输电经济距离的更长线路才能达到输送自然功率及以上的能力，因而，随输电距离的增长线路建设成本较高。特高压直流输电由整流站、两极线直流输电线路和逆变站组成。相对交流变电站来说占地面积大，建设成本高，但架空输电线路建设成本相对较低。在确保线路电压降在5%左右情况下，线路越长单位输电容量成本越低。

±800kV直流输电的绝缘水平与1000kV绝缘相当。直流输电架空线路与交流架空线路建设成本的差别主要决定于分裂导线的根数、总截面和总重量。直流输电与交流输电比，架空导线总截面少，总重量轻。±800kV单回直流输电线路的建设成本约为1000kV线路的50%，但两端换流站的建设成本比特高压变电站高得多。直流输电的线路功率损失率比交流输电高不少。±800kV、2000km输电线路电阻功率损失率约为额定输送功率的7%～8%，而1000kV交流输电在同样情况下仅为2.8%～3.4%，两者几乎相差2倍及以上。直流输电线路走廊与交流线路猫头塔线路相当。由于直流输电输送功率大，±800kV单位输送容量所占线路走廊约为1000kV交流输电的70%。特高压交流输电一般采用双回路输电，当一回线路因故障跳开时，另一回线可短时承担原两回线输送的总功率，并保持稳定运行。特高压直流输电，当一极线路跳开时，剩下的另一极线路仅能短时增加20%左右功率输送，此时需要在送端采取切机，并同时在受端采取切负荷措施才能保持稳定运行。大容量远距离输电工程是采用交流输电还是采用直流输电一般采用全寿命周期成本管理，选用全寿命周期最小的输电方案。全寿命周期成本指的是工程一次建设成本和工程经济寿命周期内各年的运行、功率损失、维修成本和故障及检维停电造成的可靠性损失成本之和。采用全寿命周期成本最小选取的特高压大容量远距离方案，因综合考虑了整个寿命周期各种成本因素，将显著提升特高压输电企业和发电企业的经济效益和社会经济效益。

（摘自《中国三峡》杂志，中国电力科学研究院　曾庆禹）

新中国60年小水电波澜壮阔的发展历程

新中国小水电发展经历了三个阶段。新中国成立到20世纪70年代末的30年是第一阶段，从实行改革开放到20世纪末的20年为第二阶段，21世纪以来至今为第三阶段。

（一）从起步到巩固发展

新中国成立到20世纪70年代末的30年，是中国小水电发展的第一阶段。国家实行“两条腿走路”的方针，结合江河治理，兴修水利，开发小水电。到20世纪70年代末，小水电从无到有，从小到大，从单站发电到联网运行，从建设地方小电网到与国家大电网联结，初步形成了大小电网并举、各有侧重、余缺调剂、共同发展的格局。

1. 20世纪50年代

新中国成立初期，为适应农业合作化用电的需要，党和政府十分重视小水电的发展，1952年水利部设置了小水电的专管机构。1955年，全国水利工作会议提出积极试办小型水电站。1956年1月，中央在《1956年到1967年全国农业发展纲要》中明确提出："凡是能够发电的水利建设，应当尽可能同时进行中小型水电建设"。

1958年2月，第一届全国人大第五次会议调整国务院所属组织机构，水利部和电力部合并成立水利电力部，水利部农田水利局主要职能划出并入农业部，小水电业务随同划归农业部。

1958年5月，党的八届二中全会提出建设农村电气化设想。8月，农业部在天津召开了全国小水电工作会议，决定在第二个五年计划期内以较快的速度发展小水电，以满足不断增长的农村用电需要。

到1960年，全国有1100多个县建成小水电站8975处，装机容量25.15万kW。

2. 20世纪60年代

1960年，党的八届八中全会提出了"以农业为基础，以工业为主导"发展国民经济的总方针。兴建电力排灌站，解决农业用电成为发展农业生产，提高粮棉产量的一项重要措施。

1963年，中央批准在水利电力部设立农村电气化局，管理农村电力和小水电，小水电管理职能回归水利电力部。

1969年，国务院业务组在福建省永春召开了"南方山区小型水利水电座谈会"。会议制定了"小型为主、地方群众自办为主、设备地方自制为主"的方针。小水电发展被正式列入国家计划。

1960～1969年，全国小水电新增装机容量58万kW，平均年新增装机容量5万～6万kW。至1969年底，建成小水电站近1.9万处，装机容量72.95万kW。

3. 20世纪70年代

20世纪70年代，水利电力部连续在广西、广东、湖北、北京召开小水电工作会议，贯彻"谁建、谁有、谁管、谁受益"政策，小水电范畴上，明确当时小水电系指单机6000kW及以下，总容量12 000kW及以下的水电站和配套的送变电工程。

1975年，水电部［75］水电生字第27号文件指出："在电网供电区和电网邻近地方的小水电，在自发自用的基础上联入电网，实行余缺调剂。"

到1979年底，全国累计建成小水电站近9万处，装机容量632.94万kW，年发电量119.20亿kW·h。全国一半以上的县开发了小水电，近千个县主要依靠小水电供电，小水电建设使1.5亿无电人口用上了电。

（二）点亮农村

从实行改革开放到20世纪末的20年，是中国小水电发展的第二阶段。在邓小平同志的倡导下，开发小水电、建设中国特色农村电气化，为农村水电及电气化事业的改革发展开创了新时期，开辟了新道路。到2000年底，全国1500多个县开发了小水电，1/2的地域、1/3的县、1/4的人口主要靠小水电供电，建成了653个农村水电初级电气化县。

1. 农村水电初级电气化县建设

1983年12月，国务院以《批转水利电力部〈关于积极发展小水电建设中国式农村电气化试点县的报告〉的通知》（国发［1983］190号）文件，批准了在100个县实施中国式农村电气化试点建设。

1986年3月，水利电力部在北京召开全国100个农村初级电气化试点县工作会议。向提前达到农村初级电气化的县颁发了证章和证书。

1991年，国务院以国发［1991］17号文部署第二批农村水电初级电气县建设，要求更好地完成第二批200个试点县的工作。1995年10月，第二批农村水电初级电气化县胜利建成。

1996年国务院以国办通［1996］2号文部署第三批农村水电初级电气县建设。

第一、二、三批分别达标验收109个、209个和335个县，共建成653个农村水电初级电气化县，超额完成了国务院下达的600个县的建设任务，实现了97%以上的农户通电，比20世纪70年代末全国农户通电率增加了一倍多；解决了1.2亿无电人口的用电问题，年人均用电量增加到236kW·h，是20世纪70年代末的6倍多；这些县基本上实现了国内生产总值、财政收入、农民人均纯收入、人均用电量5年翻一番、10年翻两番。

2. 两改一同价

1999年2月，水利部在成都召开了全国水利系统农电体制改革会议，全面贯彻落实国务院2号文件，研究部署全国水利系统农电"两改一同价"、农村水电初级电气化县建设和小水电行业管理工作。

至2000年底，小水电供电区农网改造完成投资80亿元，超过到位资金20%。累计新建和改建高低压变电容量475万kVA，高低压线路16.6万km，改造配电台区45352个，累计完成1828个乡镇电管站改革，实现了乡村用电"三公开、四到户、五统一"，大幅度降低了农村电价，提高了供电质量和安全性，农村用电量显著增加。

至2000年底，全国共建成小水电站4.8万座，装机容量2485万kW，占全国水电总装机容量的32.4%；年发电量800亿kW·h，占全国水电总发电量的36.2%。建成800个县电网和40多个跨县地区性电网，高低压线路100多万千米。

（三）十年飞跃

进入21世纪，中国小水电的发展也进入了第三阶段。以贯彻落实党的十五大、十六大、十七大精神和党中央、国务院关于加强“三农”工作的一系列文件为标志，小水电及农村电气化事业的改革发展进入新阶段、肩负新使命、实现新任务。水电农村电气化建设实现新跨越，小水电代燃料生态工程开创新领域，股份制开发小水电开辟农民增收新途径，水能资源统一管理依法确立和加强。

1. 水电农村电气化建设实现新跨越

2001年10月国务院批准“十五”期间全国建设400个水电农村电气化县。11月全国农村水电暨“十五”水电农村电气化县建设工作会议在北京人民大会堂举行。提出了“十五”水电及农村电气化建设总的目标、任务、要求以及主要对策和措施。

水利部商有关部委，并经专家论证，2003年7月发布了《水电农村电气化标准》（SL 30—2003），2004年7月发布了《水电农村电气化验收规程》（SL 296—2004）。水利部还下发了《水电农村电气化建设管理办法》和相应的规章制度，认真组织实施，实行分类指导。

截至2005年底，全国建成409个水电农村电气化县，超额完成了国务院部署的建设任务。“十五”水电农村电气化县建设新增小水电装机容量1060万kW，平均每县新增装机容量2.6万kW；村、户通电率分别达到99.37%和98.79%；人均年用电量达到644kW·h，5年增长86%；国内生产总值年均递增13.1%，是全国年均增速的1.5倍；县财政收入年均增长12.1%；人均年纯收入增加592元，年均增加118.4元，小水电建设负献率达23.1%。

2006年又启动了“十一五”更高标准的400个水电农村电气化县建设。3年来，农村水电电气化建设各项工作进展顺利，已累计完成投资125亿元，建成397个项目，增加装机容量126万kW。

2. 小水电代燃料工程开创新领域

2001年4～8月，朱镕基总理赴湖南、四川、贵州考察时指出：“保护和改善生态环境，已到了刻不容缓的地步。”“要推广蜂窝煤、沼气，特别要大力发展小水电，这方面要给予扶持。”“大力发展小水电、沼气等，解决农民的燃料和农村能源。”“要通过发展小水电、沼气等解决农民的燃料和农村能源问题，防止滥伐山林，保护退耕还林成果。”

为贯彻落实国务院领导指示精神，水利部组织开展了《小水电代燃料生态工程规划》编制工作。

2003年12月30日，全国小水电代燃料试点启动仪式在四川、广西、云南、贵州和山西同时举行，主会场设在四川广安。这次试点选择了26个项目，涉及5个省（自治区）、26个县。

2004～2005年，26个小水电代燃料试点建设取得圆满成功。小水电代燃料解除了农民砍柴烧柴的辛劳，减轻了农民负担，解放了农村劳动力，增加了农民收入，带动了改厨、改厕、改厩、改水、改路等农村基础设施建设，大大改善了农民的生产生活条件。

2006～2008年，开展了小水电代燃料扩大试点建设，涉及21个省（自治区、直辖市）和新疆生产建设兵团的81个项目。同时编制完成了《2009～2015年全国小水电代燃料工程规划》并已获批复，继续扩大小水电代燃料建设规模。

3. 股份制开发小水电开辟农民增收新途径

党中央、国务院中发［2002］2号、中发［2003］3号等文件把小水电列为“周期短，见效快，覆盖千家万户，促进农民增收效果更显著”的农村基础设施和“六小工程”，以开发小水电为载体，实行国家扶持指导农村集体与农民股份制办电，开辟了农民增收、农业增效、农村发展的新途径。

4. 水能资源管理实现新突破

2005年2月颁布的《可再生能源法》，确立水能作为可再生能源重要组成部分的独立能源的法律地位，明确了可再生能源在能源主管部门统一管理下的分部门分级管理的体制，规定：“国务院有关部门在各自的职责范围内负责可再生能源开发利用管理工作。”“县级以上地方人民政府有关部门在各自职责范围内负责可再生能源开发利用管理工作。”

水利部依据《可再生能源法》，重新制定了农村水电及电气化发展局的“三定”职责，新增了水能资源管理职能，充实了农村水电建设管理职能。2008年7月，国务院办公厅印发的水利部“三定”方案明确水利部开展水能资源调查，指导农村水能资源开发。

5. 资产重组、配电端改革、农网改造深入进行

截至2008年，实行小水电资产战略性重组，全国水利系统先后组建了四川、重庆、吉林、广西、湖南、新疆、浙江、云南、湖北、青海、广东、河南、贵州、福建、山西、辽宁、陕西、安徽、河北等19家省（市）级水电集团公司与水电公司。全国水利系统还组建了70多家跨县的地区性水电集团公司与水电公司，并巩固壮大。

截至2009年初，全国水利系统共有“乐山电力”、“明星电力”、“岷江水电”、“西昌电力”、“广安爱众”、“三峡水利”、“乌江电力”、“涪陵水电”、“闽东电力”、“钱江水利”、“桂东水电”、“郴电国际”、“文山电力”、“汇通水利”、“安徽水利”以及河南九

龙水电集团有限公司等16家公司实现了上市或控股上市公司，在中国股市上形成了业绩稳健的中小水电与水利板块。

水利系统农网改造，严格执行国家有关规定和技术标准，在注重改善农网结构、提高农网供电能力的同时，重视应用新技术、新设备、新工艺，提高农村电网的现代化水平。农网改造和乡镇电管站改革完成的地方，农民的到户电价大幅度下降，每年可直接减轻农民负担20亿元。

6. 全面清查整改“四无”水电站

2003年，水利部紧急部署全国水利系统全面开展清查“无设计、无审查、无管理、无验收”的“四无”水电站，接连下发了《关于清查“四无”水电站确保安全度汛的紧急通知》和《关于加强领导，清除“四无”水电站事故隐患的紧急通知》，要求各地认真清查整顿。各地非常重视，立即紧急部署清查整顿工作，全国共查出“四无”水电站3000多座。

7. 逐步落实小水电管理机构和职责

进入新世纪，根据小水电是农村基础设施、公共设施和“六小工程”的定位，水利部在明晰小水电管理机构、职能的基础上，突出加强了小水电行业监管，强调要切实履行政府职责和有效实施行业管理。归纳起来：一是依法行政，实施水能资源统一管理和开发利用许可制度；二是加强小水电建设和运行的安全监管，清理“四无”电站；三是继续加大水电农村电气化和小水电代燃料等惠农民生工程建设；四是加强法律法规建设，促进依法行政。

8. 抗击雨雪冰冻和地震灾害取得重大胜利

在2008年初南方发生低温雨雪冰冻灾害、“5·12”汶川大地震造成大面积停电的情况下，小水电发挥分散分布式供电的优势，在迅速恢复供电、保障电网安全等方面发挥了重要作用。据不完全统计，在低温雨雪冰冻灾害中，小水电保障了200多个县城、2000多个乡镇春节和电力主网恢复重建期间的供电，保障了京九、鹰厦、渝怀、湘黔等电气化铁路的应急供电。汶川大地震造成发供电设施严重损毁，当地迅速组织抢修震损小水电站及其配套电网，短时间内恢复了汶川、茂县、理县、彭州县城和部分乡镇的供电，及时有力地支援了抗震救灾。

9. 小水电快速发展，国际影响显著提高

中国开发小水电、建设中国特色农村电气化，得到了国际社会的高度评价和赞扬，包括欧美发达国家都积极推广中国发展小水电的经验。中国已为100多个国家和地区培养了数千名小水电专家，向50多个国家出口了小水电设备。有60多个国家和地区、300多个政府机构、国际组织和单位组成的国际小水电组织总部设在中国杭州。2000年，联合国工发组织在中国杭州成立了国际小水电中心，成为联合国在中国境内设立的第一个法律框架内的组织。

新中国成立60年来，小水电既是“建设中国特色农村电气化”诞生的生命源泉，又是“中国农村水电及电气化事业”发展的动力源泉。小水电装机容量从新中国成立时的3634kW，发展到2008年底的5100万kW，增长了1.4万倍。中国小水电60年为中国农村经济社会发展作出了不可磨灭的贡献。

（摘自水利部农村水电及电气化发展局编《中国小水电60年》）

专 家 论 坛

水电要为减排作更多的贡献

——中国科学院、中国工程院院士潘家铮

我国水电装机总规模将突破2亿kW大关，成为当之无愧的全球水电大国，这是在中央各项正确方针的指引下，全体水电同志们用心血和汗水取得的成绩，来之不易，为国家的经济发展、社会进步、节能减排作出了巨大贡献。

当前，全球都在关注气候变化及减排问题。科学家们对此还存在不同见解，而且减排问题（或说排放权问题）已变成了一个政治工具，在哥本哈根会议上，西方国家用尽心机搞些动作，企图隐瞒和推卸自己的历史责任，力求尽量由发展中国家来替他们还债。尽管如此，主流观点是温室气体的无限制增排将对地球环境产生灾难性后果，而且一旦出现这种后果，人类就无法使之逆转。再说节能减排对每个国家毕竟都是件好事，所以尽管争论激烈，各国政府原则上都愿为减排做努力。中国是最大的发展中国家，中国减排面临的困难比任何国家都大，但我国政府为了大局，还是作出庄严承诺，为会议的成功作出重大贡献，赢得全世界人民的赞扬。中国是言出必行的，今后，如何实施减排承诺将成为影响我国发展的头号问题。

电力行业是排放CO_2的大头，任务更为艰巨。尤其我国一次能源中煤占极大比例，电力结构中煤电比例一直居高不下，如何减排是我们面临的严峻挑战。现在"减排"是最热门的议题，从科学专家到网民，提出了种种见解。对此我们要保持清醒头脑，能分辨轻重缓急，能辨别哪些是真减排，哪些是假减排；哪些持续可行，哪些在材料上、经济上是不可持续的；哪些是当务之急，现在就能大发展；哪些需长远安排，或最近十几年、几十年中做不到或形不成气候，甚至还在设想阶段。要知道最近这段时期（从现在起到2020年或再稍后一些）是我国经济高速发展和大翻身的关键时期，也是电力供需还将剧增的时期，同时又是考验我国是否实施减排承诺的时期，如果处理不当，丧失了这段发展时机或未能实施减排，后果都是灾难性的。水电在当前乃至相当长的时期内是数量最大、技术最成熟、电网吸纳最现实的可再生清洁能源，中国又拥有极其丰富的水电资源，作为水电人，我们要急国家之所急，任劳任怨"任骂"，尽我们一切努力多建水电，多发水电，为中国和全球的减排作出自己的贡献，这是历史赋予我们的神圣责任。

在此还必须指出，水电（包括抽水蓄能）对减排是起双重作用的。首先，水电本身是清洁能源，替代化石能源后，可直接减排温室气体。对于我国在2020年GDP将达到什么规模，实施单位GDP排放量削减40%～50%（与2005年相比）要减排多少吨CO_2/年，人说不一，我也算不清楚，总之是数十亿吨/年的规模。但水电对减排的大账是很清楚的［发1kW·h的煤电需燃烧原煤0.5kg，排放CO_2 1kg，用1kW·h的水电代替它就减排1kg CO_2，这是不会错的。我们如能把每年经济可开发的2.4亿kW·h的水电都利用起来，可代替12亿t原煤，可减排24亿t CO_2！如果2020年只利用50%，即1.2亿kW·h（这大致相当于水电装机容量达3.2亿kW），可减排12亿t CO_2。我想象不出还有什么其他措施能够达到如此的减排效果］。

其次，为了减排，我们今后要大力发展风电和太阳能，要建设规模惊人的核电站，使它们在改变电源结构中起重大影响，但风电、太阳能都有间断性、随机性和不可控性，而且还在一定程度上是"反调峰"的，不采取有效措施，只强调要全额吸纳，电网不仅难以解决负荷平衡、需求侧管理和远距离输电问题，连控制电网的频率和电压都做不到，甚至导致全网失稳和解体。而核电又是另一极端，为了保证安全经济运行，核电站宜在不变的出力下运行，同样给电网运行带来困难。总之，要改变和优化我国的电力结构，离开水电和抽水蓄能是很困难的。我们一定要把这种情况向社会反复讲，讲清楚。

（一）管好用好已建水电，挖掘最大潜力

历尽千辛万苦建成的水电站十分可贵，水电站一旦建成，就可以持续利用，就是一只下金蛋的鹅。能够多发1kW·h水电，就减少排放1kg CO_2。但目前许多已建水电站还未能发挥最大作用。根据我的分析，其原因有三：

第一是许多水电站承担着防洪任务。在汛期内必须将水库降到防洪限制水位，腾出库容，调蓄可能出现的洪水，到汛后才能蓄水，但那时也无多少水可蓄了。这个矛盾不但影响水电的利用，还影响下游的需水供水。最理想的办法是能蓄一点汛期的水，皆大欢喜，但又有风险。防洪规范和批准的设计文件当然应该尊重，但随着科技水平的突飞猛进，现实条件的变化，通过严密的研究和法定审批程序，可以做适当调整。许多专家建议利用现代预报预测手段，进行灵活防洪调度，确实值得重视。今后流域中水电站多了，各水库可以联合优化调度，与一些工程初设时的情况已有很大差别，这些都值得深入研究改进。当然，各座工程的具体条件是不同的，例如，流域的雨情、水情、监测的精度、信息传递处理水平、枢纽的规模、库容的大小、对防洪能起到的作用、枢纽泄洪能力及下游河道容纳能力等等都不相同，因此不可能有统一之规，而需因地制宜地研究调整。

第二是由于受电网调度上的制约，有些水电站汛期即使有大量电量可发，电力系统无法全部吸纳，被迫大量弃水。"弃水调峰"是常见的。这就要增建以抽水蓄能为主体的调峰电厂加强智能电网建设和需求侧管理，通过电网优化调度来解决。

第三是受枢纽建筑物、设备和输电线路的限制，无法多发多供水电。例如建设时装机容量偏小，机电设备的陈旧老化，输电线路能力不足和系统稳定上的要求，下游淤积减小的发电水头，库容缩减降低了调节能力，枢纽建筑物有缺陷被迫降低水位运行等等，这需要对每座电站进行诊断，或增容、或更新、或扩建、或疏浚、或补强……使老厂焕发青春，有些工程还有条件加高大坝，扩大库容，分期建设的工程更应及时按最终规模完建，所有这些方面有很多潜力可挖。我曾建议过由一些学术组织（例如中国水力发电工程学会及各地分会）来组织推动，联合有关部门（包括水电厂和其上级公司、设计和科研院校、电网或电力公司以及水利部门），对全国现有水电站进行全面调查研究，明确还能挖多少潜力，应采取什么措施，作出规划，提出方案，经过审批，予以实施。

总之，提高现有水电站的运行管理水平是件非常重要的事，首先要确保枢纽、设备和防洪的安全。去年俄罗斯发生的萨扬舒申斯克水电站惨痛事故，值得我们每位水电运行管理同志反复研究，引以为训，对比查找，改进工作。在此前提下，又要尽我们最大努力，挖掘可以利用的潜力，最大限度地增发、增供、增纳，为国家作贡献，这是我们的共同责任和义务。

（二）抓紧建设好在建水电，及早发挥效益

我国在建的水电规模是空前的，面临的挑战和困难也是空前的。希望大家发挥优良传统，迎难而上，艰苦奋斗，努力创新，全面攻关，不骄不躁，抓紧建设，争取及早发挥效益。这里我想强调两个问题。

第一，重视面临的挑战。

水电建设要在复杂的自然条件下进行，从来就不能掉以轻心。尤其随着水电开发的深入，工程规模越来越大，过去百万千瓦的电站就是了不起的大型工程，望穿秋水才能开工一座，现在动辄建设数百万乃至一千数百万千瓦巨型工程；过去百米大坝就是高坝，现在最高的坝高超过 300m 了。而建设地点的自然条件则越来越不利，这是必然的。因为在开发初期，我们当然要选择最靠近经济发达地区和条件最优越的地方先搞，然后不断向西部、向边疆、向地质最复杂、交通最困难的地方进军。我看过有关大渡河、雅砻江、金沙江、澜沧江等流域一些水电开发的规划和预可、可行性报告文件，我的印象是：穷山、恶水、高坝、大库、地震、滑坡、大断裂、深覆盖……没有一块好啃的骨头！

现在我们的勘测、设计、施工和管理水平已有极大提高，正如一些外国专家说的，中国工程师能够在中国任何江河上修建需要的任何工程，这是值得自傲的事，但千万别因此而自满和急躁。还须特别指出，由于任务重，现在学生们一出校门就肩挑重担，几乎没有培训和反复实践充实提高的阶段。现在的一些分析计算工作，多用计算机而不是计算尺完成，实际上无法一一追踪其运算过程，进行复核，加上一些业务领导同志的忙碌，在科技工作以外还要做许多“关系工作”，这和过去又完全不同。而我们工作中最微小的缺陷疏忽，都逃不出大自然的严峻考验，并实施无情惩罚。萨扬水电站的悲剧虽产生严重后果，还限于水电站本身，我们在建工程如果出现重大事故，不仅毁了工程本身，还会对下游产生灾难性后果，而且会影响整个水电声誉，会影响国家形象。所以我们不仅要对工程负责，而是要对水电行业负责，对国家负责，这一点我们要永铭于心。

因此，在任何情况下要保持谦虚谨慎态度，要坚持安全和质量第一。对一些重要决策，如无确切把握，要留余地，要有预案，要慎之又慎。有人说这是不是保守，是不是影响新技术的采用，我的理解是，安全和创新并非绝对不相容。一位成功的工程师，就是能够通过创新来增加安全度。我还呼吁各层领导要悉心研究业务，掌握大规律，对重大课题要平行复核，对重要文件要字字审读或自行起草，切莫做签字工程师。我们要向国家庄严保证：中国水电特别是大坝的安全是绝对有保证的。

第二，建设中要把移民和生态环境问题放到重要的位置上。

现在开发水电的阻力主要来自移民和生态环境问题上，其实，水电开发总是利大于弊的，水电和移民及生态环境之间并非零和游戏，只要努力，可以做到双赢。我们要听得进反面意见，改进工作，向上进言，争取政策，经常站在弱势群众一边，设身处地为他们着想。尽我们之力去做到：建好一座电站，带动一方经济，改善一片环境，造福一批移民，使水电开发成为建设和谐社会的巨大动力，用我们的至诚和实际成绩来回答和消除社会上对水电的误解与质疑。

（三）掀起更大的水电建设高潮

我国还有巨大的水电资源，许多工程在等待审批，或在规划设计中，更多的则尚待开展工作。为了今后吸纳核能、风能、太阳能还要修建无数抽水蓄能电站，我们要排除万难，抓紧战斗，积极呼吁，争取水电理应享受的政策，掀起更宏伟的建设高潮，把我国能够合理利用的水电，无论大、中、小型，都开发出来，我相信以前调查的资源数据还会被突破。抽水蓄能资源要再次普查，包括在电网末端地区和风能、太阳能大基地地区。现在水电陷入“停批期”，我非常担忧，这是很不正常、很不合理的。

我们要开发尚未开发的江河，要从江河的下游进军中游、上游，直达西部等边境地区。尤其是西藏，目前还较落后，没有石油、天然气、煤，却有得天独厚的水电宝藏和太阳能，我们要通过开发水电，让西藏电力工业以几十倍、上百倍的规模腾飞，使西藏来一个跨越式的发展，率先进入富裕和谐社会，给叛国分裂分子以致命的打击。

西藏水电开发公司的领导邀请我去西藏参观，说哪怕是站在江边向大河湾望上一眼也好。去西藏当然是我的梦想，但我现在去西单也困难，去西藏会给人家带来什么麻烦真不敢说。不过我即使身体去不了，我的灵魂会去的。我去不去没有影响，一定会有大批的年轻同志高举红旗进军西藏，西藏的水电一定会得到充分而科学的开发利用。

在建设中国水电的同时，我们还要毫不犹豫地继续大踏步走向世界，进军东南亚、进军非洲、进军拉美。把中国的技术和产品带到全世界，开拓国外市场，使全世界有更多的水电资源得到开发，为全球减排作出贡献。这方面中国水利水电建设集团公司和许多设计院已有很好的基础，今后一定会有更大的发展。在水电领域，21 世纪就应该是中国世纪。在进军海外时，对生态环保问题要特别重视，少数水电站如确有较大负面影响，其开发就要慎重，我们并不是唯利是图的开发商。

当前的能源危机对水电来说是最大的机遇，我再次呼吁，紧紧抓住当前有利形势，尽一切努力加快开发水电；呼吁国家尊重水电是再生清洁能源这一客观事实，给予政策；呼吁国家加快安排和审批水电建设项目；呼吁国家把开发水电和改变山区落后面貌及农业经济转轨、农民改变身份的国策结合起来，彻底解决移民问题；呼吁大家联合起来改革创新，依靠科技进步，使中国的水电开发和管理技术再登高峰！

（摘自《中国三峡》）

叫停电站折射中国水电开发困局

——访中国工程院院士陆佑楣

“生态环境”既是不合理的能源结构和电价形成机制的受害者，某种意义上，又成为它们的替罪羊。它直接导致了人们对于水电开发的重重误解，一方面，迫在眉睫的西南水电开发屡屡受阻，另一方面，依旧紧张的能源结构下“电荒”随时可能再度而来。

2009 年 6 月，在金沙江中游水电项目“鲁地拉”和“龙开口”两个水电项目被叫停后，国务院三峡工程建设委员会原副主任、原中国长江三峡工程开发总公司（以后简称三峡总公司）总经理、中国工程院院士陆佑楣在接受记者采访时如是说。

问题的本质在于决策程序

记者：最近金沙江中游有两个水电项目被叫停，是怎么回事？我记得 2007 年，三峡总公司在金沙江下游的溪洛渡、向家坝工程也被叫停过。

陆佑楣：这些项目本身没什么问题。像水电这样大规模的工程项目，需要一个严格的科学决策程序。这些工程不是哪个业主自己拍板就可以干的，都是高层领导来决策的。它们的前期工作 20 世纪 80 年代就已开始，经过了几十年的研究和论证。现在出现了问题，本质是决策程序混乱，要追查一下这些电站是怎么起源的。

但环保部门说要一票否决，这点我是反对的。你能一票否决，能一票赞成吗？像三峡工程，从孙中山先生提出起已有 72 年历史，经过多少论证，其他水电站也都如此。金沙江中游两个项目被叫停事件被报道后，误导了很多人，造成舆论又一次认为“水电站破坏生态环境”的一边倒，其实并非如此。实际上，这些项目自始至终没有被否认。

不少工程对自然界客观的状态还没有认识透，就开始建设，我说这是一种浮躁情绪，应该坚决制止。同时，我也坚决反对风暴式地搞“环保运动”，叫停 30 个项目。叫停多少个项目不是环保问题，而是政府决策程序的问题。对待水电与环境保护的问题要更理性一点更科学一点。

记者：水电项目的决策程序是怎样的？

陆佑楣：任何一个水电工程项目的建设必有三个阶段。项目前期工作是第一阶段，是项目决策过程。对于水电工程来说，百万千瓦级以上的大电站一般需要 10 年左右的论证时间，应该完成以下工作内容：流域规划的复核，全面的地质调查、社会调查、生态环境调查，市场分析预测，规划设计，地质勘探，设计方案，科学试验，提出可行性和必要性的论证，最终完成决策审批程序。第二阶段是工程的实施阶段，第三阶段是工程的运行经营阶段。

根本问题是利益分配

记者：前不久，我们采访了水电水利规划设计总院（以后简称水规总院）前任副院长何根寿，这几个工程的前期工作他基本上都参与了，他告诉我，20 世纪 80 年代以后，电力部恢复了水电建设总局，加快了上海、成都等八大设计院的重建工作，开始安排全国性的河流资源普查与规划，部署了近期可开工项目的可行性研究，所需经费由财政部以事业费名义每年划拨 3000 多万元。他说，这 3000 多万元是有任务的，水规总院每年必须要保证手上有一定数量的勘测规划储备。一个水电项目开工，马上要启动另一个规划储备项目补上。后来，前期工作的经费越来越紧张，电力体制改革后，这项原来在严密计划领域的工作，也市场化了。

陆佑楣：是这样。进入 21 世纪以来，每年投产 1000 万 kW 以上，实际上已经把 20 世纪积存的前期工作储备逐渐消耗完了，开始出现了一些前期工作周期过短、投入力量不足、设计质量下降、科研论证不到位、决策程序模糊的现象。造成一些工程建设走了弯路，不能健康有序地建设。

记者：为什么会这样？过去水电发展的瓶颈不就是资金问题吗？现在电力公司抢地盘也是引入竞争主体后的必然结果。我采访的所有水电专家都认为，现在对于水电开发来说，钱不再是问题了，资金问题解决了，为什么又会出现新的问题？您能帮我们梳理一下我们国家水电发展的背景吗？

陆佑楣：我在水利电力部任副部长的时候，虽然修建了一些大型水电站，但当时是极其困难的，全部靠国家财政给钱，水电站造价比火电站要高很多，水电建设成本大概每千瓦 4000～5000 元，火电当时才 3000 元。所以很多工程当时是干干停停，等钱。水电部工程局干一个工程，没钱了，就来部里要钱，干一年没钱了，等着，工期拉得特别长。当初水利电力部所谓“水火之争”无非也就是争钱、争项目。相比之下，火电建设成本低，周期还短，我们国家能源结构里“火主水辅”的格局也是必然的。

所以发展水电必须要在投资方法上想办法。不能让施工单位去要钱，要走“鲁布革”的道路，它是用世界银行贷款，它的一套管理模式是全新的。后来我在水利电力部、能源部时期，基本上是在沿着这个方向走，业主对工程负责，钱由业主自己去找，包括三峡。

记者：三峡工程应该说为中国水电开发探索出了一种资金模式和开发模式。但问题是，三峡工程太特殊了，它决策时的高度一致性，在未来的水电开发上是不可复制的。我想，当这种模式要向金沙江、怒江继续复制时，就会面临困难。

陆佑楣：一个流域一个业主本来是一个很好的模式，但投资渠道一放开，利益就更多元化。电力体制改革伴随着“圈地”，也没有正式批文，这块地谁占住就是谁的了。

任何一个工程刚开始一定要把关系弄顺，而金沙江上的关系一开始就已经成为这个格局。金沙江一面是云南省，一面是四川省，政策不一样，谈也谈不拢。像移民补偿的问题，一个高了，一个低了，结果当然就高不就低，低的这一方提高标准，那你一提高标准，就肯定不能只是一个水库的移民，而要引起全省标准的变动。省里跟县里又是一个博弈关系，现在好几个电站工程建完了，因为移民问题没解决，不能蓄水，不能发电。现在流域上又出现了公司与公司的关系，就更为复杂。这些问题不是解决不了，而是要确定由谁去解决。

其实根本问题是一个利益分配问题。水电开发的资金来源解决了，水电开发的收益分配也要解决，所有关系都要理顺。

缺少一个制度化的补偿机制

记者：水规总院的何根寿先生也提到类似问题。他说，大藤峡水电站在正常高水位确定问题上，广东和广西争了几十年，最终这个项目没有结果。广东希望增加蓄水水位，但这就要牺牲更多的土地，广西就要为土地损失和移民承担更大成本。过去计划经济体制下“淹上游保下游”现在行不通了，更关键的是，广西穷广东富，结果是广西受损广东受益，这当然无法平衡。

陆佑楣：现在库区移民是水电所有矛盾的焦点所在，我前面说的层层博弈关系最后都集中到这上面。为什么说这是一个利益分配问题呢？拿三峡来说，因为它的水能资源在西部，发的电，能源大量给了发达地区，广东以及其他南部和沿海省市，一直到华中。他们得到了 0.25 元/（kW·h）的廉价电力，得到了可再生的清洁能源，这是发达地区享受了。

但水能资源应该是全民共享的，自然界的资源经过开发利用后变成社会财富也应该共享。党中央提出改革发展的成果应该全民共享。水电开发后变成的社会财富需要进行一次重新分配。现在，库区居民、资源所在地的居民没有得到好处，没有享受到社会财富的合理分配。

这个分配包括两部分，一是移民补偿，一是电站建成后收益的合理分配，也就是说，除了当时给的一笔补偿，还要有一个源源不断的利益分配。现在移民总是不满意，这制约了水电的开发和发展。说到底，是缺少一个制度化的补偿机制。

现在的问题是，水电开发成本和收益之间的合理机制没有形成。投资问题解决了，我的电价上不去，本身还亏着呢，还在还债呢，怎么去补贴流域里利益分配不均的不同地区呢？假如我三峡的电价从 0.25 元提高到 0.3 元，提高 5 分，从东部收上来，这其实完全可以接受。提高的这一部分不是给开发商的，而是返还给西部，这样，一年 800 亿 kW·h 电，40 个亿，每年这么多拿给西部，给库区发展经济，可以平衡很多矛盾。这需要变革，现在这个速度进展得太慢了。

记者：水电价格最初怎么定的？它的原则依据是什么？

陆佑楣：三峡工程建成以后的电价到底是多少，讨论了很长时间。国务院最后定了一个原则，就是不要引起当地原来电价的上涨，要起到平抑电网销售价格的作用。

现在三峡总公司发电成本，把所有折旧、还贷、税收加在一起，我说个大概数，每千瓦时电 0.2 元，电价 0.25 元，也就是说每千瓦时电净利润 5 分钱。这 5 分钱，我们用来扩大再生产，滚动开发下面的水电站。

还有一些水电站，像二滩、小湾电价更低，都只有 1 毛多钱。三峡电价是国家发展改革委定的，而那些电价定价权各省也有一定权力，地方上为了促进经济发展，压低资源价格，所以水电根本无利可图。这很不合理，开发商滚动开发时只有去银行贷款，维持高负债，这是危险的。

生态环境的矛盾被人为夸大了

记者：那么水电开发商也就难以保证开发水电的同时兼顾环境保护了。我想知道，水电价格机制无法体现成本的关键原因在哪？电力体制改革的壳卡在哪儿了？

陆佑楣：这就又得回过头说我们国家的能源结构了。当初为了迅速发展能源，过度依赖火电，形成了火电主导的能源格局。而电力体制改革把投资一放开，市场的主角仍是原来的火电部门，他们想自己得到大发展，要竞争，就要占有资源。五大发电集团拼命圈地搞发电，当然他们也看到煤炭处于一个涨价周期，也开始在金沙江等流域圈一些地搞水电，但更多的，还是想发展火电。因此我们国家在又一轮能源发展中盲目发展了很多火电，有的企业甚至是在煤炭资源还没有落实的情况下，就盲目发展，这进一步加剧了能源结构的紧张。

记者："水火"失衡变得更严重?

陆佑楣：现在全国的装机容量当中，74%～76%是以煤为主的火电，火电利用小时数很高，按照发电量来说，煤电量占85%，这个比例很高。

这样，以煤为主的能源消费由此产生环境污染、生态破坏、地表塌陷、酸雨等问题日益严重，减排温室气体、应对气候变化压力也越来越大。在这种能源结构下什么都是紧张的：一年25.3亿t煤有13亿t用在发电上。铁道部说整个铁路一半的运力是在运煤，这其中又有60%是发电运煤，对铁路压力也很大。另外，矿难频发，生产成本、安全治理成本高昂。用在煤矿安全治理方面费用光是中央拿出的钱就是好几十亿元。现在要关掉这么多小煤矿，本来中国煤炭产量里，小煤矿占了一半左右，小煤矿一停，供给减少，而煤炭成本又继续增加，资源税，治理费，谁污染谁治理，谁塌陷谁治理。这一来，煤炭价格肯定高居不下，加上火电厂又大量建设，供需矛盾更紧张，在煤电矛盾下电价上涨的冲动极为强烈。

在保证销售电价稳定的前提下，正由于火电发展过快，火电涨价的需求太强，那作为低价能源的水电不仅不能涨，还要用这钱来分摊平衡整个电价，水火同质不同价的问题就越来越突出。

电力本身可以成为一个商品，煤炭也是一个商品，水电也是商品，但现在国家控制着。国家控制是需要的，但过度的价格扭曲，实际上把很多成本掩盖住了。现在水电站上网电价普遍偏低，水库造成后续影响的成本被掩盖了，矛盾也就掩盖了。

记者：这些成本压力实际上转移并表现在一些水电站的环境生态维护、移民安置这些问题上了。说到底，其实是电力成本问题掩盖住了这些问题，而这些问题又遮蔽了能源结构问题的本质。人们如今总是把板子打在环境问题上，反过来还影响了水电开发的正常进程。

陆佑楣：对。生态环境实际上并不是水电站的主要矛盾，只是被人为夸大了。水质污染，不是水库引起的。长江自古以来，就是一个排污的通道，经济不发达，人口不多的情况下，这些污水就自然净化。现在时代不一样了，庞大的工业和城市，集中的人口，决定了把长江当成一个排污口的古老习惯要彻底颠覆了。源头是在陆地上，治理也是在陆地上，这跟水电发展没有任何关系，这是一个简单的道理。

为什么现在老把水电和环境生态破坏概念化联系在一起，对水电的认可度那么低？这跟国外的NGO组织，反坝组织不无关系。那些在中国反水坝的人，没有概念，缺乏科学知识。水资源是时空分布不均匀的，当然应该通过工程措施来合理配置。以前，人类是自然地向有水源的地方移动，现在人口不用大迁移了，想办法用工程的措施让它尽可能均衡一点这是一个很自然的过程。

事实上，全球有多少座坝？全球有40万座，美国7万多座。20世纪30年代到70年代是发达国家水电建设的高峰期，目前发达国家的水能资源已基本得到开发。法国被视为新能源利用出色的国家，我去那儿什么感觉呢，它们的水能几乎都开发了，几乎每一滴水都利用了。大坝的使用寿命都长达百年以上，西方国家并不是说不建坝了，而是已经完成了这个大规模建坝的过程。中国现在水电站建设规模应该说不小，但还差得远，和他们当时情况比，大体上类似于罗斯福新政的时候。

那些认为国外现在到了"拆坝时代"的观点也完全是一种误导。这涉及不同国家对坝的定义问题。美国5m到8m都称为坝，如果按这种标准，中国有多少坝？8.6万多座。美国垦务局局长告诉我，美国每年会拆一部分坝，其中有些水坝仅仅是为了灌溉或者是为了小农庄的电力自给，比如自己的领地里面修建一个小电站等等。目前，美国的大电网领土覆盖率非常之高，有了大电网，小电站就完成了历史的使命，就可以拆了。美国大型水坝没有被拆。中国也拆掉了一些小电站，最古老的石龙坝电站已经停止发电了，因为这是一座很小的电站，已经过时了，但并不是说已经进入了拆坝时期，到了停止建设水电站的时期。

记者：现在比较麻烦，西南水电占到我们国家未开发水电的绝大部分，大力开发势在必行。但围绕金沙江、怒江水电开发的争论从前几年开始就没停止过。

陆佑楣：有些人太情感化了。他说河流必须要自然地流淌，没有这个道理！河流是自然存在的东西，如果没有水坝，你人类怎么利用这个水资源呢？如果没有密云水库，能有今天的北京吗？

西南地区的河流，是世界自然遗产。修了十几个梯级电站，难道能把三江并流变成两江并流吗？没有，还是三江并流。他们太夸大了，就是不去了解真实情况。淹没区我都去看过，有人说建电站有一片原始森林要淹没？不存在。其实低海拔的树都已经被砍光了，这些树都是从岩石缝里长出来的，没有几百年恐怕也长不出来。它是经过几百年甚至上千年，不断地筛选才能长出来的。实际上这十几个梯级电站，每个电站，水位都远低于裸露的山体。但是如果你不去开发，当地的居民非常贫困，他要靠山吃山，过去一直以来的生态破坏是贫困跟人口的同步增长造成的。三峡工程不建，那些老县城的人怎么发展？没有土地资源，没有太丰富的矿产资源，如果在矿产上打主意，环境破坏只会更大。

对鱼类的保护确实是一个难题。长江里面有一些很珍贵的鱼类，像中华鲟，过不了坝了。国外做了很多试验，修了很多鱼道，鱼梯，升鱼机等。像美国哥伦比亚河上这么多梯级电站，建成后现在才逐步研究鱼类怎么过坝的问题。我们长江里的鱼已经很少，少的原因是捕捞过度和污染。像中华鲟的产卵本来不是在金沙江，而是在长江的中下游。由于中下游人类的活动太多，把它们赶到了金沙江去。那么现在建葛洲坝，修三峡水库，已经切断了。现在用人工繁殖的办法来繁殖，是不是成功还有待于长期观测。

这些问题要在水电合理有序的开发过程中解决，研究具体的办法，研究水电的收益怎么合理地使用，而不是不去开发。开发和保护是两个问题，不是简单对立的。有些是生物多样性的需要，应该把这些鱼类保护住，不要让它灭亡，但保持“生物多样性”也还是要从人类可持续发展的角度来考虑。

4亿kW水电可以代替6亿t煤炭的燃烧

记者：水电未来在我们能源结构究竟将占据什么样的位置？

陆佑楣：水电能源完全取决于落差，中国正好在帕米尔高原和喜马拉雅山脉隆起，落差很大，长江就是5400m的落差，这些落差都集中在西部，这是天赋的资源。前一阶段国家发展改革委组织水规总院进行普查，又进行了一次论证，提出理论上水能资源是6.9亿kW左右，这是理论上的，实际上是不可能全部开发的。技术上可行、经济上合理的，只有4亿kW左右，但就是这4亿kW也可以代替6亿t煤炭的燃烧。

现在已经开发了多少？到2008年底，1.7亿kW，4亿kW里有这么多已经发电了，这是几十年积累下来的。到2008年底，在建的有7000万kW，等于有2.4亿kW已经到手了。还有1.6亿kW没有开发，这是从经济的角度计算的。国外通常计算开发利用程度，都是按技术可行，随着你经济水平再发展，能源利用效率的提高，也就是说，它的可开发量还会增加，如果算上这部分，4亿kW外，还有1.4亿kW。举个例子说，雅鲁藏布江到我们的大拐弯墨脱，这地方有2000m的落差，有非常丰富的水力资源，这里一个电站就能有3500万kW到5000万kW，这都没算在4亿kW里面，因为从现在看，它还不具备开发条件，经济上很困难，电怎么送出来都是问题。

这是未来的事，但我想眼前这4亿kW是必须得到充分利用的，不用就浪费了。现在的能源结构中，火电比例那么大，煤炭每年的产量已经不宜再增加，我的观点是，能保持在每年27亿t就可以了。水电一定要继续发展，这部分水电如果还得不到有效开发，结构不合理的状况就会加剧。

最近全国人大常委会通过了《可再生能源法》，肯定了水能是可再生能源，我们国家可再生的商品化的电力从目前来看只有依靠水电。现在媒体上一讲新能源，似乎风能就可以解决整个中国的电能需求，实际上不可能，完全脱离实际。我不是说反对发展风能，而是要大力发展风能；太阳能也要发展，但是离商品化还有很长的时间，需要国家政策积极扶持和推动。这部分能源的成本很高，要发展它们，就需要大力发展水电，通过水电来平抑电价，要不然谁有动力去发展那些新能源呢？

记者：水电一方面发展要加速，这样才能扭转水火失衡的能源格局，但另一方面，水电发展又要避免火电发展中已经出现的种种问题，比如跑马圈地，过度扩张。而水电发展还需要能逐渐扭转一个不合理的能源结构和价格体系，种种问题交错在一起，这的确很困难。

陆佑楣：电价一定要合理调整，不是说一定要调得很高。我曾经说过，三峡的电，你每年调个半分也可以啊。你要是一直不动，总是担心影响下游物价，这事就做不了。老百姓移民工作要顺利推进，一定要给他利益分配。我同意这句话，为穷人做事，为富人讲话。有了体制化的支付转移办法，也可以多少避免在无序开发中破坏环境和上下游扯皮的事情。

至于控制无序开发的问题，为什么我们国家彩电发展的时候，一下子全国会上几百条生产线？汽车工业一上，每个省甚至每个市都要上自己的工业，我们还是从计划经济转过来的，为什么这个管不住？在种种博弈关系下，应该由政府找到一个平衡点。流域应该完善流域机构，还拿三峡工程为例，建成之后怎么调度？这也是极其复杂的，你要满足防洪、用水、航运、发电，综合起来，电站怎么运行？现在汛期是水利部调度，发电是电网调度，谁都管，接下来，要综合管理的事情更多。鱼类的生存也要调度，这些都应该照顾到，但最终怎么来统一调度？应该适当上收权限，这样才能保证水电开发有序推进，水资源得到最有效和最充分的运用。而不是像现在这样环保部不认水利部，水利部也不认环保部。

现在政府把投资开发权下放了，这是大势所趋，但有的权力应该回收，权责明确，而不能让开发商跟政府混淆。我一直主张，所有水电项目的立项过程，前期工作，移民的代价，生态环境代价，这些工作都由政府来推动。政府推动了，各种成本都算清了，然后公开，开发商投标，国家根据开发商的能力财力再选择开发商。

把水规总院划归能源局管，成立一个水电开发基金，你前期工作需要投入的费用，由国家发展改革委出，最后谁中标了，这笔钱由谁来掏，这就理顺了。

我想，水电资源 4 亿 kW 里剩下的 1.6 亿 kW，应该在 2050 年以前开发完，我也不像有的人认为，要在 2030 年以前干完，我觉得不用这么急。前期工作一定要做充分。

（摘自《中国三峡》）

破解发展难题　有序开发水电

——访中国水力发电工程学会副理事长、中国华电集团公司原总经理贺恭

我国已探明的水能资源世界第一，但水电开发的程度远低于国外发达国家水平。虽然水电装机容量持续增长，但由于受到环保、移民等因素制约，水电发展速度还不够快，水电比重还不够合理。如何看待我国水电发展现状？如何认识和破解这些难题？2009 年 6 月 4 日，《中国能源报》记者专访了有丰富水电工作经验，先后担任过中国长江三峡工程开发总公司副总经理、国家电力公司副总经理、中国华电集团公司总经理的中国水力发电工程学会副理事长贺恭。

（一）近期重点推动西南水电的开发

中国能源报：我国水电的开发现在处于一种什么水平？近期的开发重点是什么？

贺恭：截至 2008 年底，水电装机容量已突破 1.7 亿 kW，占全国发电装机容量的 21.6%，居世界第一位。预计 2010 年将突破 2 亿 kW，2020 年将达到 3 亿 kW 或以上。但是，开发利用程度还比较低，远低于美国、挪威等发达国家，发展潜力巨大。按照水能资源的总量和技术、经济可开发量及电力结构的合理需求，当我国人均用电达到 1kW（中等发达国家水平）时，水电比重以 30%为宜，即如果电力总装机容量达到 14 亿 kW，水电开发应达到 4 亿 kW 左右（相当于我国水能资源经济可开发总量）。近期我国经济进入了一个调整周期，为我国调整能源结构，加快开发水电提供了有利契机。如果说世界水电在中国，中国水电则在西南，仅川、藏、滇三省区的技术可开发量就约占全国的 61%，并且未开发的资源也主要在西南。因此，不论从调整国家能源结构、推动能源基地、包括后续能源基地建设看，还是从促进区域发展、改善当地民生计，重点应大力推动西南水电特别是云南、四川、贵州以及西藏等地区若干主要江河的有序开发。

中国能源报：您在刚才的谈话中，强调“有序开发”，请进一步谈谈您的看法。

贺恭：实现水电有序开发，前提是要有一个科学的水能资源开发规划。多年来，中国水电在规划上做了大量工作，特别是本世纪初组织普查，较彻底地搞清了家底。存在的问题一是综合规划和专业规划如何结合；二是二、三级支流规划做的深度不够；三是规划的权威性和严肃性不够。一些地区水电无序开发，特别是审批权在地方的小水电，其根本原因在于规划的全面、权威及执行力的弱化。目前二、三级支流的规划或是空白，或是形同虚设。因此，针对河流的重要等级，应加强分级（并适当上收权限）管理。有规划和严肃执行规划，才能谈得上有序开发。至于综合规划和专业规划的结合，则应在国家发展改革委统一协调下，综合各方面的因素，科学合理处理流域和项目的功能定位问题，以免因扯皮而影响开发时机的选择。

中国能源报：中国经济的发展阶段和能源集中分布的特点，决定了西南水电必然以“外送”为主。最近国家电网提出到 2020 年将全面建成统一的坚强智能电网，西南水电开发与智能电网如何协调？

贺恭：纵观中国水电和电网的发展史，水电开发特别是大水电基地的开发，都是与电网建设相辅相成、休戚相关的。国家电网顺应世界电力发展新趋势提出建设坚强智能电网，核心是建设具有长距离、大容量输电特征的特高压电网，这将使水电的输送和调配更加方便快捷，促进能源布局结构调整和能源资源优化配置。同时，大水电也有力地推动着智能电网的建设和支撑着电网的稳定运行。西南地区的水电送出，国家电网公司与南方电网公司应加强协调，两个电网公司合作方能奏效。当前应当从电力总体规划和水资源开发规划的结合入手，加强水电开发企业和电网企业的合作，使西南水能资源开发和电网在新的台阶取得双赢的效果。

（二）建议设置高层次的移民管理机构

中国能源报：目前影响我国水电发展的主要问题是什么？

贺恭：以前阻碍我国水电发展主要是技术和资金问题，随着我国水电技术的不断发展和经济实力的不断壮大，以中国长江三峡集团公司为代表，我国水电已经进入百万千瓦级水电机组的研发阶段，技术和资金现在已经不是主要问题。现阶段看主要有两大问题：环保与移民。

中国能源报：水电开发的环保问题，近年来一直

是舆论关注的焦点，对此您如何看待？

贺恭：毫无疑问，水能资源开发必须以保护环境为基础。从总体上看，水电作为清洁能源的科学利用本身就是对环保的巨大贡献，但毕竟水电开发是对自然形态山川的改造，会对植被、河流形态、水生物、水质等环境因素产生不同程度的影响。因此，在水电开发中，环保是必须下工夫进行论证和设计的重要内容。

同时，在重视环保的基础上，要看到国家能源需求总量在不断增加，而化石能源资源越来越稀缺，新型能源还在逐步启动和成熟。分析这几方面因素，水能资源开发力度应加大。应合理地处理开发和环保的关系，把环保作为推动水电科学发展的动力因素，动态、系统地分析水能开发对环保的利弊，全面权衡、科学决策。当年决策上三峡工程时，专家们对工程的评价是“利大于弊”、“晚上不如早上”，对如今仍有重要的指导和借鉴意义。事实上，近几年有不少流域和项目在开发的同时，认真履行环保职责，采取具体措施减少负面影响，效果是显著的。而且，许多水电开发项目还开展了环境保护后评估工作。这些都说明，水电开发对生态文明建设是能够起到应有的积极作用的。

中国能源报：移民搬迁安置近年来不断引发社会问题，解决这一难题的思路是什么？

贺恭：移民搬迁历来是水电站建设必须要解决好的问题，移民工作做得好坏是水电站建设成败的关键。解决好移民问题，需要真正做到“移得出、稳得住、能致富”。

移民问题的关键在于合理的补偿，包括工程补偿和后期扶持两个部分的物质补偿，以及长期的政策扶持。已有一些流域和区域做得比较成熟，应予以总结交流。但各地情况不尽相同，在总体政策平衡的情况下，各地要从本地实际出发解决好相关问题。鉴于移民工作涉及工程建设、民生和社会稳定，政治性、政策性很强，建议国家权威部门设置高层次的移民管理机构，各地亦应根据具体情况设置相应机构。工程业主要按照国家政策及当地实际情况，把移民安置规划和补偿概算做好，并在工程投资及运行电价中落实好。地方政府则必须承担做好此项工作的主体责任。只要地方政府和工程业主合作良好，协调一致，就能够把移民工作做好。

（三）坚持“流域、梯级、滚动、综合”方针

中国能源报：您一直是水电流域梯级开发模式的倡导者，并曾组织领导了澜沧江、金沙江和乌江等流域的梯级开发。对于这种模式，您是如何看待的？

贺恭：“流域、梯级、滚动、综合”是20世纪80年代以来，国家确定的流域水电开发的方针，中国的水力资源集中于大江大河，十三大水电基地的装机容量约占全国技术可开发量的51%，占经济可开发量的60%，有利于集中开发和大规模外送。可依据各电站的自身特点、地理位置、调节性能、装机规模、上下游关系及电力需求等因素进行综合分析，结合所在电网的发展规划和电力需求，统一规划，有序建设。一些已在某个流域上初步形成梯级规模开发的企业，如乌江流域，其水能资源利用效率和调节能力大为提高，对区域电网稳定的支持和跨区域调剂能力大为加强，充分说明在流域规划指导下，流域梯级有序开发和连续开发是非常必要的。因此，应继续坚持这个方针。同时，必须加强对梯级电站的有效管理，流域公司应当承担起梯级电站集中控制或梯调的职责。目前，不少流域公司都有着相应的机构和办法，有的取得了电网的支持，有的还在协调之中。流域机构须与电网调度很好合作，方能使流域水能资源的利用取得节能增效的最优成果。

关于流域开发的“综合”问题，主要是要解决好流域水电开发如何带动地方经济社会发展的问题。胡锦涛总书记2005年2月视察乌江索风营电厂作出的“围绕贵州能源优势做好乌江开发下篇文章”的指示，就是对“综合”两字内涵的高度概括。一些发达国家已有较成熟的例证，国内一些流域公司亦在进行着拓展产业链的尝试和实践。我认为，水电工作者值得为此付出巨大努力，以实现所在地区水电开发和经济社会的同步、和谐发展和共赢。

（摘自中国水电工程顾问集团公司《水电风电信息汇编》）

从全国能源工作会议透视我国能源发展新情况

全国能源工作会议2009年2月5日在京闭幕，这是我国17年来首次举行的全国性能源工作会议。在全球能源形势剧烈波动，我国能源发展面临一系列新情况、新考验的形势下，这次会议备受关注。

问题与希望同在，机遇和挑战并存。当前，国际金融危机影响日益加深，如何更好、更有效地解决能源安全问题，推动能源发展上水平、上台阶，成为摆在我国面前的一项紧迫而重大的任务。

（一）锻造可持续保障的能源链条

能源是经济社会发展的基础，是现代化建设的基本保障。

2008年的能源形势，经历了过山车般的“梦幻起伏”。上半年，从“油荒”、“电荒”的不时出现，到煤价、油价的持续飞涨，令人印象深刻。煤、电、

油、气、运的一度紧张，使能源供应这个“瓶颈”在经济运行中再次突显。

然而，能源形势的迅速变化让人始料不及。从2008年三季度起，“油荒”、“电荒”似乎在一夜之间变成了相对“过剩”，煤炭、石油价格也一路下滑，能源消费需求下降，能源企业效益减少，能源投资增速放缓。

“经济形势的变化对我国能源发展造成了一些不利影响。”国家发展改革委副主任、国家能源局局长张国宝说。

2008年，全国煤炭消费量、全社会用电量、原油表观消费量年度增幅，分别同比回落1.6个、9.57个和2个百分点。同时，全年煤炭、石油天然气投资增幅分别比前三季度下降8个、17.4个百分点，电源项目基建投资完成额也同比下降10.78%。

近年来，能源供应始终是制约我国经济建设的突出问题。目前，我国石油对外依存度已经超过50%，国内优质能源少、人均占有量低，能源偏紧、资源约束是一个长期的矛盾。

“当前能源需求增长减缓，但不能因此停止能源项目建设。”张国宝指出，从全面建设小康社会的进程看，我国能源需求仍有很大的增长空间，能源发展仍处于增长较快的历史阶段。

在全社会投资中，能源投资比重较大，占10%左右。尽管能源企业投资有所减少，但从2008年第四季度起，作为扩大内需举措的一个重要方面，我国政府加大了能源投资力度，加强重大能源基础设施和重大能源项目建设。

2008年底，福建福清、浙江方家山、广东阳江3个核电站，宁东煤电化基地等已经开工建设。2009年，我国将提速13个亿吨级大型煤电基地建设，开工建设浙江三门、山东海阳和广东台山等核电站和西气东输二线东段工程。

专家指出，利用当前扩张性的政策环境，推进关系全局和战略安全的能源投资，既可以有效拉动内需，又有利于锻造能源长远保障的链条，增强能源整体抗风险的能力。

（二）让能源结构更优更加洁净

近几年，我国的发电装机容量几乎以每年增加1亿kW的速度增长。2008年底电力总装机容量达到7.92亿kW，在世界上仅次于美国。

然而，电力高速发展的同时，问题也在不断累积。其中，电力结构中火电所占比重不降反升，火电装机容量和发电量占80%左右，水电、石油、天然气、核电等优质能源仅占20%左右。

当前，在我国一次能源消费中，煤炭消费所占比重为70%左右，比世界平均水平高40个百分点。我国煤炭消费量世界第一，煤炭的大量开采利用，带来的环境、运输等问题日益严重。

过于依赖煤炭的能源结构，给能源安全供应带来很多问题。“能源供需形势的相对缓和，为结构调整提供了难得的战略机遇。”张国宝指出，2009年要把结构调整作为能源工作主线。

电力工业结构调整，被列在2009年我国能源工作的首位。根据部署，新一年国家在推进大型煤电基地建设、推进电力工业“上大压小”的同时，将把“大力发展核电”作为重要任务。

目前，核电装机容量仅占我国电力总装机容量的1.1%，仅占一次能源消费的0.77%，不仅同世界一些发达国家相比差距很大，而且远远低于世界平均水平。

“我国发展核电潜力很大。当前，无论是人才队伍，还是技术水平和装备制造能力，都具备了加快发展核电的条件。”张国宝说。据了解，2009年我国将开工建设多个核电项目，新核准开工规模840万kW。

积极发展水电、风能、太阳能、生物质能等可再生能源与新能源，不断提高清洁能源在中国一次能源消费中的比重，成为我国优化能源结构的另一个突破口。

本次全国能源工作会议已经特别提出，要促进风电规模化发展。按照规划，国家将力争用10多年时间在甘肃、内蒙古、河北、江苏等地形成几个上千万千瓦级的风电基地。

据了解，为了适应核电、风电等清洁能源快速发展的需要，国家今年将加快研究调整核电中长期发展规划、风电发展目标和建设规划，此前公布的预期目标都将作大幅调整。

（三）用改革促进能源行业健康发展

2008年底，由于主要供煤企业与五大发电集团在电煤价格上互不相让，历时7天的“2009年全国煤炭产销衔接合同汇兑会”未能打破近年来煤、电博弈的僵局，双方一单未签。

中国煤炭运销协会负责人对此直言，煤电双方僵持不下的原因根本不在于价格，而是煤炭和电力企业身处市场和计划两种不同体制的博弈。

“市场煤”和“计划电”之间矛盾突出，煤炭行业内部也存在着“合同煤”与“市场煤”的“双轨制”。而且，由于大煤矿集中度不高，小煤矿多、散、乱，国家对煤炭生产供应的调控能力受到限制。

在石油方面，出于经济发展和民生考虑，我国成品油价格与国际价格并不完全接轨。2008年上半年国际油价一路高涨时，国内国际价格曾一度严重倒挂，影响了企业的生产积极性，进而影响到市场供应。

“电煤供应紧张，国内局部时段的油荒，都与现行体制机制和财税价格体系有很大关系。”张国宝指出，受各方利益影响，继续推进改革难度很大，但如果不推进改革，这些问题不可能彻底解决。

从 2009 年 1 月 1 日起，我国决定实施成品油价格和税费改革，取消了原在成品油价外征收的六项收费，提高了燃油消费税水平，完善了成品油价格形成机制。

专家指出，虽然从现在看，因为需求不足，油价下降后石化企业利润压力较大。但从长期看，改革确立了市场机制，有利于能源企业的长远发展。

成品油价格和税费改革的顺利推进，关键在于抓住了国际原油价格下跌的空间。受国际金融危机的影响，世界经济增长减缓，对石油的需求也随之大幅减少，国际油价一路下跌。

“金融危机发生后，我国通货膨胀压力减轻，有利于理清能源产品价格关系。”张国宝指出，当前要抓住有利时机，更加注重推进体制机制创新，用改革的办法解决发展中的问题。

当前，我国面临能源需求不足的严峻局面，但业内人士指出，加快能源发展方式转变，构筑“稳定经济清洁安全”的能源供应体系，深化能源领域的改革是必由之路。

（摘自中国水电工程顾问集团公司《水电风电信息汇编》）

中国如何避免水电惨案
——俄罗斯萨扬惨案启示

2009 年 8 月 17 日，俄罗斯一座拥 10 台 64 万 kW 机组的巨型水电站——萨扬—舒申斯克水电站，发生了世界水电史上最大的惨案。正在担负电网 440 万 kW 负荷的大电站，出力在 8 时 13 分 25 秒瞬间变为零。3 台 64 万 kW 的机组严重毁坏，其余 7 台受到重创。当时正在电站工作的 300 多名员工，有 75 名不幸遇难，13 名受伤。事故的教训永远铭刻在世界水电史上，留给人们许多反思与启示。

中国水电站应如何从萨扬惨案中吸取教训以避免惨剧发生？就此，《中国能源报》记者采访了曾访问考察过俄罗斯萨扬—舒申斯克水电站的中国长江三峡集团公司科技委委员、原副总工程师黄源芳教授。现将该报采访整理的相关报道摘要如下。

（一）萨扬惨案是一面镜子

中国是世界水电大国，水电站的总装机容量世界第一，也有与萨扬—舒申斯克相同年代建设、安装、运行的水电站。当年我国机电设备的技术水平并不如那时的苏联。特别是早期制造投产的机组设备，遗留的问题较多，仍有许多老机组设备未被提到“现代化改造”的日程上。

我国对水电机组修复与现代化改造，更多地着眼于“增容”，相对缺乏科技内涵，忽略了“安全”和“环保”等因素，致使有的隐患未经消除就被放行。在电站、机电设备运行的规章制度、责任范围、问责体制等方面还未系统化，容易造成事故责任不清。萨扬惨案是一面镜子，水电工作者都应以此为戒，杜绝一切隐患，使之不会在中国重演。

1. 设计应一切从安全出发

对于新建、升级改造以及现代化改造的水电站机电设备，不应选用技术落后、技术性能不稳定、安全性差甚至已淘汰的机电设备，而应采用成熟先进且经运行被证明是安全、高效的设备。同时，水轮机的总体技术要求不应轻易触动“底线”。包括运行水头范围、应力水平、试验标准、运行范围等，不经详细论证和试验，不应随意提出“超标准”、“超世界水平”的技术要求。对于已证明成熟的传统结构形式不应轻易改变。

作为在系统中担任负荷调节的机组，水轮机必须具有良好的调节性能，有较宽的运行稳定范围。水轮机调节需保证计算，特别是高水头、长引水管、长尾水管过渡过程，不但在做可行性研究时要计算，在机组招标文件中也要明确提出要求。在水轮机性能经过模型验收试验后，还应根据水工布置、水轮机性能的最新成果，复核计算各种危险组合工况下的各种数据是否在原先设定的安全范围内。此项成果应经业主单位主管领导专门批准，以示负责。

在电站厂房机电设备布置方面，厂房内的行政办公室、生活用房以及检修车间应尽可能不布置在正常下游水位以下。在任何情况下应保证电厂内通信、通道（包括电梯）畅通的措施。根据各水电站运行的特点，设计时应考虑水工建筑物在发生事故或非常情况下，例如设备爆炸、水淹厂房时的避难场所和保护人身安全的设施，并在电站运行维护规程中以正式条文予以明示。

高水头电站必须设进水口快速闸门，不应以任何理由，例如以设置圆筒阀为由取消进水口快速下落闸门。进水口快速闸门应有“双电源”并可手动关闭，重要大型电站的备用电源应接至电厂保安自备电厂。自备柴油发电机作为紧急备用电源，必须如同检查消防系统一样，要有定期检查、试运行检验的机制，确保紧急时能发挥作用。

2. 设备体检、健身、修复，一个都不能少

国际电工委员会水轮机技术委员会一份文件说，

水力发电设备是稳固的、可靠的、使用寿命长的设备。其稳固性可在很长时间内不需进行重要修复而能维持连续运行。水轮机可以不需要进行重要的修复改造，工作30～50年，这主要取决于机组的型式、设计、制造质量、运行条件和其他因素。当然，发电设备不可避免地会随着时间的推移，性能、可靠性、可利用率下降。

萨扬惨案是水轮机寿终正寝导致的吗？相比之下，已年过半百的中国第一座自主设计的水电站——新安江电站7.5万kW级机组，不但未见“老态龙钟”之相，而且“神采奕奕”，“光彩照人”。新安江水电站员工仔细为长期运行的机组做了完善的检修和修复，这一语道破维持水电设备“长生不老”的秘诀，就是要经常“体检”，要有“健身方案”，要有足够的经费支付体检、换心术（换转轮）和日常护理费用。

因此，对巨型水电设备机组要有完善的检修制度和修复计划，对有缺陷的大机组的更新、修复计划要落实，对自动化元件、保护元件和系统进行及时的升级换代。对设备运行状况应有专人负责记录，要进一步研究更准确检测机组外特性（振动、摆动、频率、温升、间隙）的方法，并应对检测结果进行快速研判和果断决策。发现水电设备问题、缺陷应及时修复，更换部件、进行现代化改造，而不是让其长期“带病”运行。特别是新机组、大修后重新投运的机组，发现了问题还未安排大修的机组更应成为重点定期巡视的对象。

应对水电设备的技术实行淘汰机制。根据水轮机的技术发展和原型机的运行研究，在一定时期内提出技术落后的、欠安全的“淘汰机型、应用材料”清单，经国家有关部门，例如国家生产安全局或国家标准委批准公布。应通过“技术换市场”方式将替代的机型、技术转让给中、小设备制造厂家，使新投产的水电站机电设备的安全性能更有保障。

应在把握现状基础上，提出水电机电设备升级改造的方案，落实资金，分步实施。在此基础上，根据现有水电站的特点、运行参数及其现状、修复改造后重新投入运行的机组状况，提出运行限制区域的建议，以及参与电网功率和频率调节的方法和管理的建议。

3. 机组应分区运行保证安全

萨扬惨案引发水电机组如何安全运行的大讨论最终达成一致：分区运行才能确保安全。大型水电站，必须严格按照运行区域分区运行。运行分区应通过原型水轮机试验，参照水轮机模型验收试验成果，由电厂（或发电集团公司）与国家（地方）电网研究提出，并经国家安全生产总局聘请的有经验的专家组评审后，以合同或法律形式作出规定。

应明确大型水电机组（例如30万kW以上）不参与电网“频率调节”。对巨型水电机组（例如60万kW以上）宜安排长期在稳定高效运行区内运行。即使出于电网安全的考虑，巨型机组也宜快速通过不稳定运行区。应坚持只有设备状态为“优良”的水电机组才能参与负荷调整和无功调节运行。

4. 业主是决策和负总责的关键

“水电站事故是由一系列原因造成的，其中包括水电站本身设计缺陷，使用、维护不当及管理不善等因素。”在俄罗斯萨扬事故的报告中，责任人不包括30年前的工程设计单位和水轮机设备制造厂的负责人，设计和制造并不承担责任。很明显，俄罗斯当局认定，从萨扬水电站工程设计、产品制造、部件安装、设备运行、电厂检修、突发事故处理方面存在的所有这些缺陷或不足，都是业主技术管理的漏洞。业主应负总责。

业主要科学决策，不赶进度，坚持质量，才能保证不出事故。坚持保证质量、顾及安全的原则，尽量不把缺陷带到现场。在市场经济中处于“强势”的业主应该有清醒的认识：业主技术管理的严格与否，业主的决策正确与否，科学的措施落实与否，对及时发现和避免设计、制造、安装、运行、维修过程中的某些安全漏洞至关重要。当然，业主并不是什么都懂的“通才”，但业主可以依靠有理论有实践经验的各专业人士组成的专家组，在安全和高效生产方面严格把关。

5. 事故处理公开迅速才能警示业界

萨扬事故的处理，从事发当天的2009年8月17日，到媒体报道的2009年10月5日公布事故原因分析报告，仅用了52天的时间。在表述“事故原因”时，媒体报道强调了事故直接原因是超负荷运转导致水轮机组螺栓脱落。初步指定责任者25人，首要责任人为原“俄罗斯统一电力公司”总裁丘拜斯，其余所有原水电站站长和总工程师等无一免责。

事故报告充分体现了以“事实为依据”的原则，全面公布了萨扬水电站事故基本经过、人员伤亡、设备毁坏、事故原因、有关责任人名单及违规违法事实、经济损失等情况。媒体迅速报道分析了这份报告披露的内容，使这件震惊世界的惨案不再继续“漫燃”。

这“快刀斩乱麻”的处理突发重大事故的方式，体现了俄罗斯处理此事的效率和决心，也体现了一个发达的工业大国迅速处理事故尽快恢复电力生产的信心。

在当今的中国，发生重大惨案，都有媒体跟踪报道。造成重大事故者故意隐瞒不报者，将受到政府纪律或法律的惩处。然而，对于未造成人员伤亡的“技术性”事故，情况就不同了。据悉，近年来国内有的新建抽水蓄能电站机组在试运行时，电机曾发生重大事故。但由于没有死人，使“关门”处理成为可能。然而，这样的关门处理不但造成了外界的各种猜测怀疑，业内人士也无法在公开的技术刊物上看到“事故报告”这类文章，更无法从“已交的学费”中，举一反三，吸取有益的教训。

突发重大事故的处理，即使在今天，仍然存在“公开”与“掩盖”两种不同处置方法。当然，前者可能会“丢面子”，但最终彻底丢掉面子的是“掩盖”这种并不高明的做法。

（二）萨扬事故原因

根据俄罗斯政府公布的萨扬事故原因技术调查报告披露情况看，事故发生的原因和暴露的问题是多方面的：机组运行中水轮机轴承振动幅值严重超标而未按规定“卸荷并停机”；在制造厂商文件和电站运行文件中，均无保证检查紧固件状况的标准和紧固件的使用期限；在机房受淹，保护和控制回路电压消失时，导水机构不能自动关闭；中控室没有关闭进水口快速事故闸门的控制开关……所有的一切应急预案、应急措施、应急通信似乎都没有发挥作用。

1. 49个螺栓未能起到“联结紧固”的作用

事故调查人员发现，躺在萨扬—舒申斯克2号机坑内的油混水中的机件，除了水轮机大轴、转轮、发电机转子等转动部件外，竟还有机组的承重部件顶盖和支撑在顶盖上的发电机推力支架等固定部件。这“一串”部件中的顶盖从原来的位置与浇灌在混凝土内的联结部件——座环脱开了，窜升10m左右倒在发电机层楼板上。而用于将顶盖紧固在水轮机座环上的80个螺栓中的49个螺栓，在事故发生时未能起到“联结紧固”的作用，成为酿成这一悲剧的直接原因。

在对这关键的49个螺栓检验后发现，有6个螺栓无螺帽，有41个螺栓螺纹断裂的疲劳断口面积平均达64.9％。断口面积占螺栓面积70％以上的螺栓有14个，甚至有8个螺栓断口断裂面积超过90％！也就是说，螺栓已完全失去承载能力。用探伤方法检验后还发现螺母上有较长不连续的裂缝，螺圈上也有本不容许存在的缺陷。

萨扬水电站的10台64万kW水轮发电机组，首台在1978年12月投入运行，最后一台于1985年12月投产发电。制造厂家规定的紧固件使用寿命与设备本身的使用寿命都是30年。而至事故发生时，水轮机已运行29年10个月。早在1997年，俄罗斯就制订计划，提出对功率在30万kW以上的64座水电站进行设备更新，其中包括更换154台转桨式和29台混流式水轮机。可是，直到2002年，俄罗斯只更换了8台机组。

2. 运行安全限制的缺失

水电站水轮机的运行区域是经过设计、模型试验和电站运行试验确定的。萨扬水轮机分成4个区域：容许运行区、不推荐运行区、推荐运行区、临时禁止运行区。但是，限于当时的技术水平，推荐运行区的负荷调整范围太窄，在事故发生前的负荷调整范围只有7万kW。

惨案发生前一天，电站内的2号机组，负荷变化幅度超过7万kW达12次。事故当日零时至2时30分，发电负荷从44.15万kW降低至28万kW，而从4时12分至7时5分发电负荷又增加至41万kW，变化达16万kW。计划出力的这种变化迫使2号机组从其投入工作时刻起，相继6次通过不推荐运行区域。从前次维修结束重新投入运行后，2号机组总共210次处于不推荐运行区域，总共运行时间超过2500s，水轮机轴承振动幅值严重超标。这种运行方式，是造成“惨案”的主要原因之一。

萨扬机组设计上明确了不同运行分区，但是没有设定在各区域运行的安全限制，电网调度部门以首选的负荷调整机组——2号机作为“自动发电控制”运行机组，这个外部原因加之联接顶盖和座环的49个“不作为”的螺栓，导致了惨案的最终发生。

3. 机电设备“配角”也惹祸

水工专业和机电专业是支撑整个水电工程建设和运行管理的两大支柱。我们通常将调控水库水位、监测大坝安全、“将水变成电”和“把电送出去”的设备统称为机电设备，这是水电工程总体建设中不可或缺的重要组成部分。一般认为，机电设备不是在施工现场“造就”出来的，而是在工厂“加工”出来的。机电设备是“钢”的，材料好，加工精确，一般不应该会引发事故。因此，在水电工程建设中“机电设备”往往处于“配角”地位，引发事故的风险也似乎要小些。

萨扬水电站在水工技术方面创造了多项世界纪录，但也出现过不少问题和事故。例如，施工初期一些柱状混凝土浇筑块出现裂缝，坝基渗水，消力池受破坏。在未加控制的条件下泄洪，曾使水电站厂房受淹，使消力池底护面严重破坏，导致消力池底护面受到严重损毁。这些发生在水工建筑物上的事故，后来通过修复也就可以正常运用了。人们怎么也不曾想到，正在电站厂房内运行的2号机组，是惨案发生的源头。紧接着电站厂用电系统、通信系统、保护系统、自动化系统均遭到破坏，殃及其他9台机组，拉垮了3台机组的厂房。

这次直接由机电设备引发的萨扬惨案，使人们认识到了机电设备对水电工程也同样重要。这将会使人们对水电站机电设备的规划设计、工程建设和运营管理方面的重要性重新定位，将改变过去“水工是老大，机电无所谓”的片面认识。

（摘自《中国能源报》）

央 企 工 作

国家电网公司 2009 年工作情况

2009 年是我国经济社会发展面临严峻考验的一年。国家电网公司在（以下简称公司）继上一年电网遭受历史罕见的特大冰灾和震灾之后，又受到金融危机的严重冲击，形势非常严峻，挑战前所未有。面对复杂的国际国内环境，面对艰巨繁重的经营发展任务，公司党组团结带领广大员工坚决贯彻中央关于保增长、保民生、保稳定的决策和部署，认真落实国资委的工作要求，将公司工作与党和国家工作大局紧密结合，将开展深入学习实践科学发展观活动与应对国际金融危机紧密结合，继续推进公司发展方式和电网发展方式转变，在应对挑战中把握机遇，在战胜困难中开拓前进，各方面工作不断取得新进展、实现新突破，公司保持了平稳健康发展的良好态势。

2009 年，公司完成固定资产投资 3111 亿元，其中电网投资首次突破 3000 亿元，达到 3058.6 亿元，增长 22.5%；完成拉动内需投资 312.4 亿元。110（66）kV 及以上输电线路开工 6.1 万 km，投产 5.8 万 km；变电开工 2.8 亿 kVA，投产 2.9 亿 kVA。完成售电量 22 748 亿 kW·h，增长 7.1%；国家电力市场交易电量 2944 亿 kW·h，增长 11.6%；营业收入 12 660 亿元，增长 11%。在受到国际金融危机严重影响、售电量增速大幅下滑、上网电价单边上调的情况下，实现利润 45.2 亿元，完成利税 681.7 亿元。资产总额 18 600 亿元，增长 13.2%；资产负债率 65.41%，同比上升 2.35 个百分点。全员劳动生产率 29.8 万元/（人·年）。

（一）深入学习实践科学发展观活动取得显著成效

在参加中央第二批学习实践科学发展观活动中，公司高度重视、精心组织，紧紧围绕“科学发展上水平”的核心目标，结合企业特点和工作实际，以“深化‘两个转变’、推动科学发展”为载体，超前调研、创新形式，高标准、高质量地开展学习实践活动，做到了“两手抓、两不误、两促进”。通过学习实践活动，广大员工深化了对电网功能定位、电力发展规律以及清洁能源发展带来的新挑战等重大问题的认识；公司作出了加强“三个建设”、推进人财物集约化管理等重大工作部署，确定了建设坚强智能电网的发展目标，解决了一批影响和制约公司科学发展的突出问题，“两个转变”和“四化”工作的内涵进一步丰富，电网建设、经营管理、优质服务等各方面工作得到新的加强，公司在服务国家宏观调控和维护安全稳定大局方面发挥了重要作用。党中央、国务院领导同志和中央企业学习实践活动指导检查组对公司学习实践活动的整体效果，特别是创新活动载体、注重活动实效等做法给予了充分肯定。

（二）为经济社会发展提供了安全可靠的电力保障

针对电力供需形势明显变化、发电装机继续大量投产、清洁能源迅猛发展、影响电网安全的不确定因素增多的新情况，公司始终坚持安全第一的方针，认真组织安全生产“三项行动”、“全国安全月”活动和秋季“三查一整改”活动，加强隐患排查治理，不断夯实安全基础，健全完善应急机制。在基建、辅业、农电等所属企业开展专项治理行动，对煤矿、化工等重要用户开展供用电安全隐患治理，按照“四不放过”原则，加大事故责任追究力度，公司安全工作水平有了新的提升，电网事故和设备事故同比分别下降 56.5%和 15.6%。针对去年入冬以来华中等地区出现的缺电局面，公司充分发挥特高压和跨区跨省输电优势，精心调度，大范围优化资源配置，落实政府批准的有序用电方案，有效缓解了供电紧张矛盾。从现场作业、管理流程、状态检修、装备配置等方面，全面加强设备标准化管理和运行维护，提高了设备健康水平。组建了直升机公司。总部和各网省公司应急指挥中心全部建成。自觉规范市场行为，加大交易价格等重要信息公开力度，“三公”调度水平进一步提高。积极应对新疆“7·5”事件对电网和公司造成的影响，确保了电网安全和队伍稳定。圆满完成了新中国成立 60 周年庆典、全国两会、全运会、迎峰度夏（冬）等重要保电任务。

（三）电网发展实现重大突破

公司在应对危机中把握发展机遇，坚持以科学规划引领电网发展，认真落实国家拉动内需建设项目，加大电网投入，统筹推进特高压、跨区跨省输电、省级电网主网架和城乡配电网建设，电网结构得到改善，资源配置能力有了明显提升，为促进经济增长发挥了积极作用。

电网规划继续加强。结合大型能源基地特别是清洁能源基地的开发建设，完成了国家电网总体规划的滚动优化，以及蒙东、新疆等电网规划；初步完成了国家电网智能化规划；各地以电力为中心的能源规划研究进一步深化；启动了国家电网“十二五”发展规划编制工作。

各级电网建设取得重大进展。特高压交流试验示范工程自2009年1月初建成投运，已安全运行一周年，输送电量超过90亿kW·h，发挥了显著的综合效益，验证了特高压输电的可行性、安全性、优越性，被评为新中国成立60周年百项经典工程，列入“国家重大工程标准化示范”项目。向家坝—上海特高压直流示范工程成功实现800kV全线带电，锦屏—苏南特高压直流工程开工建设。灵宝背靠背扩建工程竣工投产。西北750kV主网架基本形成。青藏联网以及新疆—西北联网等工程前期工作取得重要进展。宝鸡—德阳直流工程单极投运，呼辽直流、宁东—山东等重要跨区跨省电网项目加快建设。一批500kV输变电工程建成投产，网架结构得到加强。完成提高电网输送能力工程190项，提高输送能力1719万kW。组织实施拉动内需农网完善工程，大力推进西藏“户户通电”。全年建成新农村电气化县132个、电气化乡镇1687个、电气化村3万个。全面推广“三通一标”成果，公司首条750kV同塔双回线路、首条220kV同塔六回线路建成投运。电网智能化工作全面推进。发布了建设坚强智能电网的战略报告，制定了智能电网技术路线和技术标准框架，用电信息采集系统、智能调度技术支持系统、智能变电站等关键技术研究取得阶段性成果。首批智能电网试点工程全面实施。上海世博园智能电网综合示范工程扎实推进。

（四）经营管理取得显著成效

在电力需求大幅下挫、电价矛盾不断积累、经营环境中不确定因素明显增多的情况下，公司上下坚持“过紧日子”，采取从严从紧的经营策略，以开展“三节约”活动为主线，严格综合计划和预算管理，充分发挥集团优势，深入挖掘内部潜力，在规划建设、生产运行、营销服务的全过程严格控制成本，大力增收节支、降本增效。输变电工程本体造价同比下降3.2%；可控费用同比下降3.3%，比营业收入增幅低14.3个百分点；出国、车辆、办公经费同比分别下降29.7%、15.9%和6.2%。全年低成本融资1700亿元，在电网投资持续加大的情况下，银行长期借款下降269亿元，资金运作效益累计达66亿元。各单位加强经济形势和电力供需分析，千方百计开拓市场。严控欠费风险，严打窃电行为，当年电费回收率达99.99%，陈欠电费下降56.5%。积极配合国家出台电价调整政策，电价矛盾得到部分疏导，为公司可持续发展提供了重要保障。

金融产业在完成清理、整合基础上，基本形成金融控股集团架构。英大人寿成功引进战略投资者，金融产业体制机制不断创新。通过深入推进产融结合，金融产业盈利能力稳步提高。深入推进直属产业重组整合和优化布局，积极拓展勘测设计、设备制造等领域并取得了重要突破。运营管理菲律宾国家电网平稳有序、取得实效。认真落实国资委法制工作三年目标要求，扎实推进依法治企，取得明显成效。社团组织规范清理工作全面完成，初步健全了公司社团组织和工作体系。网省公司层面多经资产的清理处置工作基本完成。稳妥推进电力用户与发电企业直接交易。积极配合审计署、财政部等部委完成了对三峡输变电工程的审计和评审、中央扩内需促增长政策落实情况检查等工作。理顺蒙东电力管理体制，成立了内蒙古东部电力有限公司。

（五）人财物集约化管理全面推进

公司着眼于提高管理效率和经济效益，以加强人财物资源整合和优化配置为重点，着力构建集约高效的管理体系，基本形成了总部、网省公司两级人财物管理体系和工作机制，初步实现了人财物管理由粗放到集约的转变，管理的集中度和调控力有了明显提升，有效减少了经营风险。

公司制订了人力资源战略规划和特高压、科技、金融等专项人才规划，加强了人力资源年度计划管理；规范网省、地市公司本部机构编制和职级序列，实施供电企业劳动定员标准，改进了公司绩效考核评价体系；员工入口得到有效管控。着力构建以“六统一、五集中”（“六统一”即统一会计政策、统一会计科目、统一信息标准、统一成本标准、统一业务流程、统一组织体系，“五集中”即会计集中核算、资金集中管理、资本集中运作、预算集约调控、风险在线监控）为基础的新型财务管理模式，试点工作取得重要进展。全面推行财务管理标准化，规范会计政策，统一的标准成本体系开始运用。实施资金集中运作，撤销了网省公司资金结算中心。网省公司资金归集率超过98%。加快建设统一的物资管理体系，建立了公司两级物资管理部门和三级物流服务机构。制定了统一的物资采购标准，扩大了集中招标采购规模。大力推行“总部统一组织，网省具体实施”的招标采购新模式，总部集中招标采购范围和比重进一步扩大。全年集中招标累计中标金额1863.2亿元，节约资金 167.9 亿元。物资仓储配送管理、设备集中监造等工作取得了新进展。

全面加强农电人财物管理。落实管理责任，完善管理标准，着力解决用工不规范、混岗等问题，实现供电所人员全部持证上岗。直供直管县供电企业全部实现财务集中统一管理，物资采购全部纳入公司两级招标体系，农电企业规范管理取得明显成效。

（六）科技创新和信息化建设取得丰硕成果

公司以支撑“两个转变”为目标，坚持走自主创新的内涵式发展道路，继续实施“一流四大”科技发展战略，整合科研资源，加大科技投入，加快构建适应可持续发展需要的自主创新体系。“电力系统全数字实时仿真”项目获得国家科技进步一等奖，同时，获得国家科技进步二等奖 5 项，获得中国专利金奖和优秀奖各 1 项，获国家级奖励的数量创历史最好水平。发布特高压企业技术标准 130 项；申请专利 2528 项，获得授权专利 1517 项。

“四基地两中心”全面建成投运，形成了目前世界上功能最完整、试验能力最强、技术水平最高的特高压、大电网试验研究体系。新能源开发利用示范工程——“国家风光储输示范工程”全面启动。获准建设国家风能、太阳能发电研发（实验）中心。智能电网研究院筹建工作进展顺利。公司科技研发能力迈上新台阶，取得了一批具有国际领先水平的创新成果。研制成功全球容量最大的直流换流阀，标志着±800kV直流输电技术实现关键性突破。特高压交流灵活输电、450 万 kVA 大容量变压器等技术研发取得阶段性成果。具有自主知识产权的国际首套 500kV 故障电流限制器成功研发并投入运行。碳纤维复合芯扩容导线研制成功并推广应用。

经过近四年的努力，完成了公司信息化 SG186 工程，提前一年实现了公司“十一五”信息化发展规划目标，建成了覆盖总部、网省、地市县公司，纵向贯通、横向集成的一体化信息平台，实现了公司经营业务应用的全面推广，健全完善了保障体系，公司信息化水平整体进入国内先进行列。公司在中央企业年度信息化评价中连续被评为 A 级企业。

（七）教育培训和人才建设进一步加强

公司坚持以人为本，立足于提高队伍综合素质，整合培训资源，完善培训体系，强化全员教育培训，同时加大高层次人才引进力度、岗位交流力度，着力解决人才结构性矛盾、西部地区人才短缺等突出问题，员工的业务素质、工作能力有了新的提升。国家电网技术学院完成了 1500 名新进员工的培训。管理学院正在加快建设。全年公司系统培训员工超过 200 万人次，新增高级技师 1100 名、技师 7800 名。9 名员工获得中央企业技术能手称号。落实国家“千人计划”，围绕智能电网、新能源、新技术等领域积极引进海外高层次人才。面向国内外公开招聘高级管理人才和科技人才 193 名。与知名高校合作培养了 120 名特高压技术人才。为西部五省区和西藏公司培养了 240 名优秀青年人才，从东部地区选拔 44 名管理和技术骨干支援西藏公司。组织三期共 54 名高级管理人员完成境外培训。

（八）党的建设和精神文明建设全面加强

公司认真组织学习贯彻党的十七届四中全会精神，落实全国国有企业党的建设工作会议部署，大力推进“三个建设”（党的建设、企业文化建设、队伍建设）。创建“四好”领导班子取得新成效，各级领导班子的领导力和执行力进一步提高。高度重视加强党风廉政建设，按照中纪委《建立健全惩治和预防腐败体系 2008～2012 年工作规划》，着力构建国家电网特色惩防体系，取得了显著成效。在“三重一大”决策制度执行、工程建设、成本控制等重点领域，深入开展效能监察。积极开展“电网先锋党支部”创建活动，基层党支部和广大党员在深入推进“两个转变”中发挥了关键作用。广泛开展群众性精神文明创建活动，公司总部等 112 个单位荣获“全国文明单位”称号。充分发挥职代会作用，开展职工代表巡视检查和调查研究，132 条代表提案全部落实。制定了班组建设三十条重点要求，全面推进班组建设。充分发挥各级工会和团组织作用，大力开展劳动竞赛和建功立业活动。近 25 万名青年志愿者积极投身各类志愿服务行动。公司 44 个单位荣获“全国五一劳动奖状”，37 名员工荣获“全国五一劳动奖章”，39 个集体荣获中央企业先进集体称号，62 名员工荣获中央企业劳动模范称号。逐级落实信访维稳责任，维护了公司和谐稳定局面。全面落实离退休老同志的政治待遇和生活待遇。实施品牌引领战略，全面履行社会责任，“国家电网”品牌名列 2009 中国 500 最具价值品牌第二名，公司名列 2009 中国服务企业 500 强第一名。

回顾过去的一年，是公司成立以来经营压力最大、发展非常困难的一年，是公司发展战略实现重大提升、“四化”工作深入推进、创新发展取得突出成绩的一年，是公司开放合作、国际影响力明显提升的一年。回顾过去的一年，广大员工弘扬“努力超越、追求卓越”的企业精神，以高度的事业心和责任感，以顽强的毅力和过硬的作风，爱岗敬业，勤奋工作，自我加压，勇挑重担，历经许多艰辛和考验，熬过许多不眠之夜，全面完成了一届四次职代会暨 2009 年工作会议确定的各项任务，为公司发展作出了积极贡献。回顾过去的一年，我们深切地体会到：坚决贯彻党中央、国务院的决策和部署，落实科学发展观，主动把公司工作融入党和国家工作大局，是我们战胜挑战、科学发展的基本前提；坚定不移地深化以集团化运作为核心、以提升执行力为关键的“四化”工作，是我们推进“两个转变”的主要着力点；始终保持战略上的前瞻性、工作上的创新性，是我们把握机遇、争取主动、加快发展的重要经验；始终坚持以人为本，大力加强“三个建设”，打造高素质员工队伍和优秀企业文化，是建设“一强三优”现代公司的根本保证。

（摘自刘振亚在国家电网公司一届五次职代会暨2010年工作会议上的报告）

中国长江三峡集团公司2009年工作情况

（一）概况

2009年，中国长江三峡集团公司以邓小平理论和“三个代表”重要思想为指导，深入贯彻落实科学发展观，按照党中央、国务院的部署和国资委的要求，积极应对金融危机挑战，精心组织工程建设和电力生产，稳步实施主营业务整体上市，加快推进公司战略转型，保持持续稳定增长态势，全面超额完成国资委下达的年度业绩考核指标。

2009年，中国长江三峡集团公司年发电量971.95亿kW·h，其中：三峡电站发电798.53亿kW·h，葛洲坝电站发电162.43亿kW·h，小水电发电8.3亿kW·h，风电及余热发电2.68亿kW·h。营业收入263.68亿元，同比增长3.52%。利润总额126.84亿元，同比增长8.60%。其中，经营利润94.05亿元，同比增长7.05%。净资产收益率（按考核口径）9.59%。成本费用总额占营业收入比重64.83%。安全生产形势总体平稳，没有发生重大安全事故。

（二）电力生产经营安全平稳

中国长江三峡集团公司坚持统筹兼顾，以确保满足防汛抗旱、航运、供水等要求为前提，实施优化调度，充分利用可调库容，不断提高电站经济运行水平。2009年三峡—葛洲坝梯级电站完成发电量960.96亿kW·h，节水增发电量50.6亿kW·h，水能利用提高率5.6%。三峡电站26台机组首次全部并网发电，首次达到全厂额定出力1820万kW，实现三峡电站全面投产后首个完整年度安全稳定运行。

加强电力市场营销，全面完成三峡—葛洲坝梯级电站上网电量销售任务。按照国家批复的上网电价，实现电量按期结算、电费足额回收。抓住国家调整火电价格机遇，加强与各个方面的沟通和协调，提高葛洲坝上网电价2分/（kW·h），为葛洲坝电站实施重大技术改造创造条件。

（三）风电、国际水电等新业务不断拓展

中国长江三峡集团公司顺利完成与中国水利投资集团公司的重组和融合，在共同研究的基础上调整中国水利投资集团公司和中国水利电力对外公司的战略定位和发展规划，加大资金等方面的支持力度，加快风能开发和国际水电业务的发展步伐，在新业务培育和市场开拓方面取得突破，重组效益开始显现。2009年，中国水利投资集团公司完成营业收入8.89亿元，同比增长64.8%；实现利润总额3.53亿元，同比增长20.2%。中国水利电力对外公司完成主营业务收入37.6亿元，实现利润约8000万元。

风电开发的区域布局初步形成。中国长江三峡集团公司与内蒙古自治区政府签订战略合作框架协议，以抽水蓄能和风电组合方式开发内蒙古的清洁能源，获取449万kW风电场资源，为近期大规模开发风电增加储备。中国水利投资集团公司积极开拓内蒙古、新疆、辽宁、甘肃等地风电市场，内蒙古化德风电场一期工程、吉林白城风电场二期工程等相继投产发电。浙江慈溪风电场全部并网发电。完成国家“十一五”科技支撑计划海上风电课题的主体工作任务，江苏响水近海2MW试验风机吊装成功，浙江和江苏两个近海风场的预可行性研究通过咨询和审查，为中国长江三峡集团公司未来开发海上风电做必要的技术准备。

国际水电业务发展顺利。中国长江三峡集团公司以EPC方式承建的马来西亚沐若项目施工情况良好，被当地媒体称为水电开发的示范性工程，初步树立中国长江三峡集团公司在国际水电市场的品牌和形象。中国水利电力对外公司积极开拓国际市场，市场占有率不断提高，首个BOT项目老挝南立水电站成功下闸蓄水，承建的苏丹麦洛维电站正式发电。中国长江三峡集团公司与中国水利水电建设集团公司、中国南方电网有限公司签订战略合作框架协议，明确由中国长江三峡集团公司作为中方的牵头方，联合开发缅甸萨尔温江流域水电项目，塔山项目的前期工作已经展开。

（四）主营业务整体上市圆满完成

为进一步深化改革，促进企业持续发展，经国务院同意，在国资委、证监会等部委大力支持下，中国长江三峡集团公司于2008年5月正式启动主营业务整体上市工作。将中国长江三峡集团公司拥有的价值约1073亿元的三峡工程发电资产及相关专业化公司股权注入长江电力；三峡工程公益性资产继续保留在中国长江三峡集团公司，由中国长江三峡集团公司负责运行、管理及维护。2009年9月28日，中国长江三峡集团公司与长江电力顺利实现资产交割。

主营业务整体上市，对三峡工程公益性资产运行维护做出阶段性安排，有利于三峡工程综合效益的发挥；以划拨方式获得与发电资产相关的坝区土地的使用权，并由中国长江三峡集团公司授权经营；减少中国长江三峡集团公司与上市公司的经常性关联交易，两者的功能定位更加清晰；提升上市公司质量，促进长江电力与中国长江三峡集团公司的协同发展，实现更高层次的国有资产保值增值。主营业务整体上市得到国家有关部门和资本市场的充分认可。

（五）企业管理水平和经济效益逐步提升

面对全球金融危机的冲击，中国长江三峡集团公司以风险防范为重点，以经济效益为目标，以信息化为手段，不断强化内部管理，夯实企业发展的基础，中国长江三峡集团公司经济效益稳步提升。

加强资金集中管理，统筹安排筹融资活动，以内部资金拆借替代部分外部融资，全年共减少集团合并利息支出7.7亿元。成功发行100亿元三峡债（其中5年期70亿元、利率3.45%，7年期30亿元、利率4.05%），在较低水平上锁定融资成本。强化预算管理和成本管理，严格控制非生产性支出，加强管理费用控制，降低管理成本。加强对外投资管理，制定对外投资管理办法，规范投资决策程序，加强投资项目的前期分析研究和评估审查，有效防范投资风险。

各专业化公司注重强化内部管理，不断提升服务质量。各公司经营稳定，营业收入、利润总额较上年有所增长，完成主营业务收入13.74亿元，同比增长6.73%；实现利润总额1.47亿元，同比增长35.37%。

立足于服务中国长江三峡集团公司整体战略，编制中国长江三峡集团公司信息化总体规划，实施“信息化发展登高计划”。信息化建设全面覆盖中国长江三峡集团公司工程建设、电力生产、专业化经营和内部管理等各项业务，实现信息管理的不断延伸和管理能力的移植复制，促进中国长江三峡集团公司管理的规范化、科学化、集约化。中国长江三峡集团公司在中央企业信息化水平评价中晋升A级，中国长江三峡集团公司报评的电力生产管理信息系统（ePMS）被列为中央企业首批信息化示范工程。

（六）学习实践科学发展观活动取得实效

中国长江三峡集团公司扎实开展深入学习实践科学发展观活动。通过学习实践活动，进一步深化科学发展理念，理清发展思路，提出创建大型清洁能源集团的战略目标，并滚动修编2009～2011年发展规划。认真抓好整改方案落实工作，初步解决制约企业科学发展的一些突出问题，为中国长江三峡集团公司成功应对全球金融危机、实现又好又快发展提供保障。职工群众对学习实践活动的总体满意度测评达到99.12%。

（七）履行社会责任、树立良好企业形象

中国长江三峡集团公司认真落实“建好一座电站，带动一方经济，改善一片环境，造福一批移民”的“四个一”水电开发理念，主动履行社会责任，树立良好的企业形象。

加大扶贫工作力度。不断探索扶贫工作新思路和新方法，按照“输血与造血相结合，近期与远期相结合，支援与合作相结合”的原则，采取干部支援、智力帮扶、项目帮扶、送温暖等多种形式，加大对中央和国家确定的定点扶贫、对口支援县以及三峡、溪洛渡、向家坝库坝区的扶持和支援力度。全年共投入扶贫帮困资金7560多万元，重点支持改善民生和促进就业项目，为促进边疆稳定、促进贫困地区经济发展作出贡献，为三峡工程的长期安全运行和金沙江下游水电开发营造和谐、稳定的外部环境。2009年中国长江三峡集团公司被国务院三峡工程建设委员会授予三峡工程移民培训工作先进集体。

加强环境保护和资源节约。坚持在保护生态的基础上有序开发水电，全面落实环境保护措施。中华鲟全人工繁殖研究取得成功，世界上第一尾全人工繁殖的中华鲟在中华鲟研究所三峡坝区基地降生，标志着中华鲟物种保护实现重大突破。中国长江三峡集团公司节能减排系列活动获得圆满成功，增强全员节能减排意识，有力推进节能减排工作。中国长江电力股份有限公司发布环保节能规划，把绿色理念贯穿到电力生产经营的每个环节，着力打造绿色电站。

（八）固定资产投资完成情况

2009年，中国长江三峡集团公司固定资产投资完成情况见表1。

表1 中国长江三峡集团公司固定资产投资完成情况汇总表 万元

项　目	2009年计划	2009年完成	占年计划（%）	自开工累计完成
总投资	3 435 026	2 232 849.45	65.00	20 198 641.71
（一）水电项目投资	3 300 637	2 164 865.79	65.59	20 030 447.72
1. 在建项目	3 095 718	2 124 447.27	68.63	19 870 472.47
三峡工程	1 871 726	1 094 186.04	58.46	15 921 618.07
三峡地下电站工程	113 946	89 873.94	78.87	345 665.26

续表

项　目	2009年计划	2009年完成	占年计划（%）	自开工累计完成
溪洛渡水电站项目	514 180	422 804.32	82.23	2 131 159.92
向家坝水电站项目	595 865	517 582.97	86.86	1 472 029.21
2. 筹建项目	204 919	40 418.52	19.72	159 975.25
乌东德水电站项目	23 952	5 943.47	24.81	45 803.94
白鹤滩水电站项目	131 600	26 599.66	20.21	91 988.73
天荒坪二抽水蓄能电站	19 767	7 258.24	36.72	11 265.24
小南海工程	29 600	617.15	2.08	10 917.34
（二）风力发电工程	134 389	67 983.66	50.59	168 193.99
1. 在建项目	119 089	67 983.66	57.09	168 193.99
慈溪风力风电	3554	1 012.89	28.50	60 491.75
响水风力风电	115 535	66 970.77	57.97	107 702.24
2. 筹建项目	15 300			
海上风电	15 300			

（中国长江三峡集团公司　张立先　乔仁贵）

中国水利水电建设集团公司2009年工作情况

2009年是进入新世纪以来我国经济发展最为艰难的一年。在这一年里，中国水利水电建设集团公司（以下简称公司）以深入学习实践科学发展观活动为强大动力，积极应对国际金融危机的严峻挑战和建筑行业发展的新形势，齐心协力，顽强拼搏，各项工作取得了积极进展，保持了持续快速发展势头，取得了显著成绩。

（一）经营成效显著，公司实力进一步增强

（1）营业收入持续增长。2009年，公司实现营业总收入778.61亿元，为年计划的109.93%，比2008年增长28.04%。其中，国内水电建筑业营业收入335.57亿元，比2008年增长2.35%，占总营业收入的43.10 %；国内非水电建筑业营业收入208.65亿元，比2008年增长56%，占总营业收入的26.8%；国际业务营业收入193.17亿元，比2008年增长31.8%，占总营业收入的24.81 %。营业收入按行业板块划分：建筑业94.41%，其中：水电建筑51.60%，非水电建筑42.81%；设计制造0.73%；发电2.10%；房地产0.96%；租赁0.38%；其他业务1.41%。

（2）市场开发成效显著。实现新签合同额929.88亿元，是年计划的131.9 %。合同存量为1787.26亿元（其中国内水电688.95亿元，国内非水电358亿元，国际740.05亿元，国内水电仍然保持核心主业位置，国际业务合同存量首次超过国内水电），比2008年末增长15.5%。新签国内水电工程合同额346.70亿元，同比增长7.13%，占总签约额的38%；新签国际项目合同额375.61亿元，同比增长25.5%，占总签约额的40.49%；新签国内非水电建筑合同额207.57亿元，占总签约额的22%。新签合同额总量比2008年减少4%，主要由于中标国内非水电建筑大项目减少。

（3）经营效益大幅提升。实现利润总额30.74亿元，比2008年增长90.23 %。其中，国内业务实现利润11.53亿元，占利润总额的37.5%；国际业务实现利润19.21亿元，占利润总额的62.5%。子公司盈利面为82%，较2008年增加6个百分点。利润总额按业务板块细分为：建筑77.38%，其中：水电建筑51.47%，非水电建筑25.91%；电力投资16.03%；房地产2.56%；租赁1.48%；设计制造1.22%；其他业务1.32%。

（4）经营质量继续提高。公司总资产突破1000亿元大关，达到1022.63亿元，比2008年增长33.88%。净资产增加到156.05亿元。营业收入利润率3.95%，成本费用利润率4.11%，净资产收益率12.95%，国有资产保值增值率152.96%。资产负债率同比下降1.91%。全员劳动生产率60.55万元/(人·年)，同比增长19.56%。在岗员工人均工资40 081元，同比增长14.98%。公司全年上缴各种税金35.59亿元。

（二）主营业务持续健康发展，转型升级取得明显成效

水利水电建筑业务板块得到巩固发展。一是公司

在国内水利水电建筑市场继续巩固保持行业主导地位，彰显了“中国水电建设第一品牌”的核心竞争力优势。在水电站招标项目减少，水电市场竞争更为激烈的情况下，实现了水电项目新签合同214.7亿元，水利项目新签合同132亿元，中标机组安装98台，占招标机组的75.4%，中标装机容量3664万kW，占招标总装机容量的67.6%，确保了公司在国内水利水电建筑市场的主导地位。二是水电建筑业务经营质量有了很大提高，经营利润水平继续好转。三是水电在建项目进展顺利，全年完成国内水电机组安装119台，总装机容量1934万kW。截至2009年底，公司累计完成水电装机容量1.3亿kW，为我国绿色能源开发和低碳经济发展作出了历史性重大贡献。

国际经营业务板块持续快速健康发展。面对国际金融危机的严重冲击和国际市场大环境萧条的挑战，公司坚定实施国际业务优先发展战略。公司新签约国际项目59个，成功开辟了贝宁、多哥、马里、科特迪瓦、科威特、厄瓜多尔等十国市场，并积极开发南部非洲市场及拉美市场，初步形成了9个以项目群为特点的大型国际市场。成立了卡塔尔、安哥拉、利比亚三个区域业务总部，推动了公司国际业务向区域化管理方式的转型。截至2009年底，公司在48个国家有在建项目211个，合同总额1029.49亿元。在46个国家设立了59个驻外机构。国际业务涵盖了水利水电、非水利水电和投资项目，形成了业务多元化格局。海外投资业务稳步推进，经营业务升级取得新突破。目前，在海外投资建设的电站装机31万kW，已签订电源占有协议的项目计划装机约500万kW。公司投资兴建的老挝甘蒙塔克水泥厂运行顺利，2009年销售水泥46万t，营业收入超2650万美元。老挝万象平原钾盐矿首期年产12万t钾盐生产项目开始建设。公司参股的刚果（金）铜钴矿项目完成可行性研究编制等待批复。公司的国际声誉和影响力进一步彰显。

非水电建筑业务板块持续增长。按照“大集团、大土木、大市场、大品牌”的战略思路，公司加快推进经营结构的战略性调整和优化转型，确立了基础设施业务在公司持续发展中的重要战略定位，使基础设施建筑业务成为公司重要的经济增长源。在铁路市场方面，以29.5亿元中标新建南宁至广州铁路5标段，以49.4亿元中标南京至杭州铁路客运专线2标段，实现了公司在铁路建设业务领域的进一步拓展。在公路市场方面，中标了广东惠深高速公路路面工程，实现新的突破。在城市轨道交通市场方面，中标西安地铁一号线10标段工程，为公司纵深开拓轨道交通市场奠定了基础。京沪高铁项目在各参建子公司的大力支持下，得到了业主、监理等相关方的肯定和认同。港口航道疏浚吹填业务在市场开拓、设备配置、资源整合方面取得新进步。租赁业务以融资租赁为核心，向经营租赁、贸易租赁业务发展，经营质量效益有新的提升。

国内投资业务板块稳步发展。按照经营结构调整战略总体部署，重点推进新能源、房地产、基础设施领域投资发展。投资业务板块已经成为公司经营性资本集中区域和营业收入增长源。截至2009年底，公司控股开发项目共59个，其中电站项目43个、房地产项目10个、路桥项目4个、股权投资水务项目1个、国外水泥项目1个。控股开发电力项目总装机容量约918万kW，权益装机约659万kW，投产运营电力项目总容量约245万kW，项目涉及总投资规模约678亿元。重点投资项目建设取得新突破：沙湾水电站及洪一、色尔古电站共8台机组提前投产发电。长岭风电二期10万kW项目全部投产，酒泉瓜州风电20万kW项目完成了项目核准和前期工作。华亭火电项目二期扩建前期工作取得新进展，崇信2×60万kW火电项目继续推进。路桥项目开发投资总额约166亿元，开发总里程达175km，武邵高速、邛名高速、成简快速公路项目建设有序推进。房地产开发项目初步形成了全国性的战略布局，2009年实现营业收入9.97亿元，较2008年有较大幅度增长，“中国水电地产”品牌在行业内也有了一定的知名度。

（三）企业改制、公司战略引领和经营管控措施得当，企业经营管理能力不断增强

（1）整体改制上市工作取得重大进展。2009年，公司把加快公司制股份制改革步伐，推进企业科学发展上水平作为一项重要工作来抓。2009年11月27日，中国水利水电建设股份有限公司胜利召开创立大会，提前实现了“跨越工程”“12·31”节点目标，为公司科学发展上水平奠定了体制基础，在公司改革发展历史上具有里程碑意义。

（2）公司发展战略的引领作用明显，控制力、凝聚力不断增强。围绕建设具有较强国际竞争力的质量效益型跨国企业集团的战略目标，继续加强集团化建设，战略管控坚持一手抓内部经济关系、利益关系的管控调整，另一手抓公司发展战略及管理制度的落实、企业发展方向的把握、出资人意志的实现，使公司资源的利用效率及经营效益大幅提升。

（3）与相关企业的重组工作继续推进。于2009年12月10日签署了辽宁省水利水电工程局整体无偿划转集团公司的协议，已经得到国务院国资委批准。与广西水电工程局的重组工作也已经取得积极进展。与同类业务企业的重组有利于强化公司的行业地位，有利于区域市场的战略布局。

（4）财务资金管理不断加强，公司风险管控体系

继续完善。全面执行《企业会计准则》，财务及资产管理制度进一步完善。《建造合同准则》的推行也取得积极进展。加强对国际经营风险的系统性防范，制订应急预案，对银行和业主支付能力、资金、汇率、保函和担保、安全、履约等方面的风险实行重点防控，对在建国际项目进行系统风险源排查，加强国际业务资金管控力度特别是国外应收款回收。成功发行了五年期企业债券和一年期融资券。深化高端银企关系，拓宽了融资渠道，在各银行的授信额度达到2285亿元，进一步改善了公司外部融资环境。

（5）管理重心向项目前移，精益化管理取得新进展。坚定不移地走质量效益型发展之路，不断健全完善经营管理制度并加强落实，推动实施目标成本管理和项目精细化管理。把工作重点前移，工作重心下移，着力解决经营管理中的突出问题，提高了项目经营质量和效益，促进了企业经营管理水平的有效提升。在京沪、贵广、南广等铁路项目着力推动架子队管理模式，优化了资源配置，促进了项目的精益化管理。公司成立了科学管理委员会，进一步推动了公司管理转型升级上水平。

（6）业绩考核制度不断深化，激励约束机制进一步优化。发挥业绩考核制度的战略导向与杠杆作用，以正确的业绩观落实科学发展观，推行分类考核、分类指导，试行EVA考核制度。完善激励约束机制，强化业绩考核的客观性、严肃性。加强了效能监察工作，强化了对各子公司主要负责人的离任和任期经济责任审计、评价，加大了对投资项目、非水电项目的监督力度，强化了对国际项目的审计监督。

（7）选人用人新机制不断健全，人事用工向市场化改革方向进一步转变。继续推进“面向社会，内部优先，公开竞争，优中择优”的人才选聘工作。进一步健全干部考核机制并加强对企业领导班子和领导人员的考核工作，进一步规范薪酬管理并推动市场化薪酬制度改革。对企业领导人员进行轮训，促进了企业高管人员综合素质的提高。

（8）依法治企工作不断推进。法律风险防范工作契合经营管理需要进一步加强，历史遗留法律纠纷处理取得明显成效，为公司在高风险期持续稳步发展发挥了积极作用。

（9）设备物资集团化采购与管理进一步规范。按照“围绕集团战略，防范采购风险，建设两个平台，夯实两项基础，实现两个创新”的工作思路，设备物资的规范化管理进一步加强。

（10）信息化整体水平显著提高。公司已经实现了和各子公司的VPN广域网连接，为经营管理系统的部署和实施提供了基础保证，公司核心业务管理系统在特级资质子公司全面推广。2009年，在国资委组织的中央企业信息化水平评测中达到了B级，位列中央企业第34名。在中央企业网站绩效评估中，公司网站被评为A级，位列中央企业第3名。

（11）积极履行企业社会责任。公司坚持互利共赢的开放战略，积极构建社会责任体系，关注和谐企业建设。公司“5·12”特大地震灾后恢复重建工作进展顺利，生产经营恢复工作基本完成，灾区办公与生活设施恢复重建工作全部完成。加大节能减排工作力度，完成了国资委的考核目标。2009年，公司荣获中国对外承包工程企业社会责任奖。

（四）安全管理不断强化，安全生产形势持续稳定

以“安全生产年”活动为主线，深入开展安全生产“三项行动”，全面加强“三项建设”，推进安全生产管理工作标准化。与2008年相比，安全生产责任事故伤亡人数下降，未发生较大以上安全生产责任事故。工程技术管理和现场控制得到强化。

（五）保持行业科技领先地位，自主创新能力不断提升

公司科技创新体系作用有效发挥，科技资源配置得到优化，实现了较好的经济效益和社会效益。科技创新投入加大，自主创新能力不断增强，取得了一批先进科技成果。公司承建的山东泰安抽水蓄能电站、西安市黑河金盆水利枢纽工程、海南省大隆水利枢纽工程、伊朗塔里干水利枢纽工程获得“鲁班奖”；公伯峡水电站工程等3项工程荣获国家优质工程金奖和银奖；小浪底斜心墙堆石坝、紫坪铺面板堆石坝获得国际堆石坝工程里程碑工程奖；获得中国电力优质工程奖7项、中国水利工程优质（大禹）奖3项、“新中国成立60周年百项经典暨精品工程”12项；获得国家发明专利9项、实用新型专利55项。

（六）企业党建、精神文明建设和反腐倡廉工作扎实开展

党建工作坚持“融入中心、服务大局”，党组织的政治优势、组织优势和群众工作优势得以有效发挥，促进了企业科学可持续发展。以“战略转型升级上水平”、着力实现“五个转变”作为学习实践科学发展观活动的载体，解决了一批制约企业科学发展和职工群众反映强烈的突出问题。完善了创建“四好”领导班子工作体系，建立了创建“四好”班子长效机制。进一步落实《关于加强国内项目党建工作的指导意见》和《关于加强海外工作机构党建工作的指导意见》。以党风廉政建设责任制和惩防体系建设为抓手，全面推进反腐倡廉建设，有效发挥了监督保障作用。开展“三创建”活动收到了实效。2009年，公司所属各单位有17个项目申报公司文明工程项目。公司总部连续5届荣获首都文明单位称号、连续10年荣

获中央国家机关文明单位。企业品牌形象建设和宣传工作进一步加强，提高了公司的社会声誉和市场影响力。

（中国水利水电建设集团公司）

中国水电工程顾问集团公司2009年工作情况

2009年，国际金融危机全球蔓延，对世界和我国经济产生严重影响，是我国新世纪以来经济发展最困难的一年。面对严峻复杂的经济形势，党中央、国务院全面分析、正确判断、果断决策、坚定信心、从容应对，制定和实施了应对国际金融危机的一系列措施和政策，团结带领全国各族人民奋力拼搏，攻坚克难，有效遏止了经济增长明显下滑态势，率先实现经济形势总体回升向好，经济社会发展取得显著成效。中国水电工程顾问集团公司（以下简称集团公司）在国资委的正确领导和监事会的有效监督指导下，深入学习实践科学发展观，认真落实国资委各项部署，冷静分析形势，沉着应对各种挑战和风险，较好地把握住发展机遇，积极经营，努力工作，进一步提高管理水平和核心竞争力，通过广大干部职工不懈努力，各方面都取得了较好的成绩，继续实现了平稳较快的发展。

（一）以学习实践活动为契机，理清发展思路，明确发展目标

2009年，按照中央和国资委党委的统一部署和要求，开展了深入学习实践科学发展观活动。在此基础上，通过系统调研和分析检查，基本查清了在发展战略、集团化经营、国际化发展、企业管理等8个方面制约集团公司科学发展上水平存在的问题；并针对存在的问题，以推进集团公司科学发展为目标，制定和实施了修订新一轮发展战略、进一步加强企业发展战略管理，进一步做好经营工作、保持集团公司平稳较快发展，促进我国水电风电科学发展等9个方面整改落实项目，取得了较好的成效。

同时，全面开展了集团公司发展战略的修编工作。初步形成了“巩固和扩大国内市场、强力拓展国际市场，进一步做强做大传统主业、努力开拓新业务，实施多元化、国际化发展”的整体发展思路和“高端切入、规划先行、技术领先、融资推动、服务优良、风险可控、效益明显”的国际发展思路，提出了把集团公司建设成为“以技术和管理为核心竞争力的国际型工程公司”的发展战略目标。

（二）扎实工作，努力经营，继续保持了企业平稳较快发展

2009年，在党组的正确领导下，继续保持了集团公司平稳较快发展。

（1）经营效益稳步提高，资产质量进一步改善。全年，实现经营收入88.2亿元，比上年增长15%；实现利润总额11.7亿元，比上年增长60%，其中净利润10.1亿元，比上年增长63%；净资产收益率40.75%，同比上升近5个百分点；总资产报酬率9.16%，同比提高了近2个百分点。到2009年底，集团公司资产总额达到158亿元，资产负债率79%，比上年降低了3个多百分点；归属于母公司所有者权益28.9亿元。但是，2009年新签合同136.5亿元、比上年减少16.8%，其中国内合同121.2亿元、比上年增加22%，国际合同15.3亿元、比上年减少77%。

（2）国际经营取得新进展。在我国有关部门和埃塞俄比亚政府的支持下，集团公司与埃塞俄比亚电力公司签订了埃塞俄比亚乃至东非的第一个51MW风电场，这是我国在境外的第一个风电EPC并采用中国设备和技术标准的项目，有望近期获得我国有关部门批准生效实施。通过努力，2009年初，在中共中央政治局常委、中央书记处书记、国家副主席习近平和哥伦比亚桑托斯副总统的见证下，集团公司与哥伦比亚柯玛格达莱纳公司签署了玛格达莱纳河综合规划项目谅解备忘录，目前工作任务和大部分工作经费已经获得哥伦比亚政府有关部门的认可，待我国商务部批准后即可正式签订合同开展工作。2009年底，在习近平和缅甸联邦和平与发展委员会貌埃副主席见证下，集团公司与缅甸电力一部签署了缅甸瑙帕与曼栋两水电站的开发谅解备忘录，现已开展项目的前期工作。此外，集团公司还与埃塞俄比亚矿产能源部签订埃塞俄比亚风电和太阳能规划的备忘录。集团公司还组织了一系列国际项目投标。利比亚房建EPC项目克服了海水埋藏深度浅导致基础处理难度大和与外国监理沟通难等困难，各项工作正平稳推进，没有发生劳资纠纷和不安全的事故；土耳其和越南的机电设备成套业务也克服了劳务签证等困难，努力按合同实施；国际勘测设计咨询项目克服金融危机造成的影响等困难，继续取得了新的进展。

（3）新业务开拓取得新突破。中国水电顾问集团中南勘测设计研究院与有关单位联合中标承担了我国首批四座地下石油洞库中的三座的勘察设计任务，中国水电顾问集团昆明勘测设计研究院承担了中缅输油管道的部分勘察工作，实现了集团公司首次进入石油行业。

（4）投资业务继续稳步发展，投资效益开始显现。全年，共完成固定资产投资21.05亿元，其中新开工项目1.46亿元、续建项目19.6亿元。截至2009年底，集团公司投资水电风电权益容量411.68万

kW（其中风电 48.26 万 kW），其中开展前期工作项目 169.82 万 kW（其中风电 16.15 万 kW），在建项目 170.07 万 kW（其中风电 32.11 万 kW），投产运行 71.79 万 kW（2009 年新投产权益容量 18.37 万 kW）。投资建设水务项目规模达 51.1 万 t/d，其中已投入商业运营 6 万 t/d。集团公司第一个独立投资并由子公司以 EPC 方式建设张北风电场一期工程（10 万 kW）的机组已全部安装完毕，送出工程完成后即可投产发电，其他在建的水电风电工程建设总体顺利。全年，控股投资电站的销售电量 17.15 亿 kW·h，实现权益发电销售收入 2.3 亿余元、占集团营业收入的 2.6%。投资的水务工程开始产生收入，实现营业收入 940 万元，并在当年基本实现收支平衡。

2009 年，通过广大干部职工不懈努力，集团公司全面完成了国资委下达的经营业绩考核目标，其中实现利润总额完成目标值 146%，净资产收益率完成目标值 132%，成本费用总额占主营业务收入比重比目标值下降近 5 个百分点，技术投入比率超过目标值近 2 个百分点。

根据 2009 年发布的排名结果，集团公司 2008 年业绩在全球 150 名设计公司中排名第 38，在国际 200 名设计公司中排名 156；在全球 225 名承包商中排名第 161，在国际 225 名承包商中排名第 214，在中国工程设计企业 60 强排名第 1。

（三）直面困难、努力工作，保证国家水电风电发展需要

2009 年，全国新投产水电发电装机容量 2527 万 kW、风电发电装机容量 1180 万 kW，均是我国水电、风电发展历史上新投产容量最多的年份，令人振奋。同时，又是近十年来国家核准新开工建设水电项目最少的一年，全年共核准水电装机容量 516 万 kW，其中常规水电 372 万 kW，抽水蓄能 144 万 kW，我国水电发展新近面临的困难局面仍然严峻。为了促进我国能源和电力可持续发展，全集团广大干部职工直面困难、坚定信心、攻坚克难、努力工作，有效地保证了在建项目的顺利建设、前期项目论证的积极推进，从而保证国家水电风电等可再生能源发展需要。

（1）风电规划又有新成果。按照国家能源局的要求，又完成 4 个千万千瓦级、3 个百万千瓦级风电能源基地规划，通过了国家主管部门的批准，并已开始组织实施。同时，正在开展 2 个海上千万千瓦级和 4 个百万千瓦级风电能源基地规划的编制工作，为国家风电发展战略的顺利实施提供必备的规划依据。

（2）水电规划取得新进展。基本协调好了金沙江、怒江等河流的水电规划与综合规划的有关问题，为这些河流的水电规划顺利审查并获得批准打下了重要的基础，进而为国家大力开发水电提供必需的规划支撑。

（3）项目勘测设计等工作顺利进行。所承担的预可行性阶段的 67 项水电、4 项抽水蓄能电站、12 项风电总装机容量共 6542 万 kW，可行性阶段的 80 项水电、8 项抽水蓄能电站、67 项风电总装机容量共 7620 万 kW，建设阶段的 124 项水电、12 项抽水蓄能电站、105 项风电总装机容量共 10 587 万 kW 的勘测设计，保证了酒泉千万千瓦级风电能源基地的顺利开工建设，保证了拉西瓦、小湾和瀑布沟等特大型水电站按计划投产发电，保证了其他在建水电风电项目的建设顺利，保证了前期论证项目的有效推进，从而保证了国家水电风电发展需要。

（4）法规政策研究取得新成果。受国家有关部门的委托，完成了《水电开发管理条例（建议稿）》、《汶川地震灾区大中型水电站震损调查和初步分析》、《在保护生态基础上有序开发水电政策措施研究》和《中国水电中长期（2030、2050）战略规划研究》等近 10 项重大法规政策课题研究，按计划开展水电价格形成机制改革研究、长江宜宾至重庆河段开发问题综合研究论证、金沙江虎跳峡河段开发方案深入研究论证等重大课题研究工作，为促进我国大力开发水电提供政策依据。根据对西藏自治区发展及需要的前瞻分析，超前安排并垫资开展了数个水电项目的前期工作，为贯彻落实 2010 年 1 月召开的中央第五次西藏工作座谈会有关精神创造了必需的条件。

（四）加强内部管理，企业经营进一步规范

（1）启动并推进战略管理。成立了由集团公司领导、总部有关部门和各子公司主要负责人组成的战略管理委员会，组织了集团公司战略修编工作组，全面开展了集团公司的战略修编工作，现已取得了许多重要的阶段性成果，为集团公司进一步推进有效的战略管理打下了基础。

（2）进一步建立健全规章制度。根据新的形势和新的要求，结合企业发展的实际，集团公司和各子公司对运行数千项制度进行了全面清理，新出台各类规章制度 295 项，修改完善 486 项，废止制度 192 项。

（3）加强水电项目的经营管理。2009 年陆续按新收费标准签订了藏木、果多、阿海、景洪、硬梁包及缅甸乌托、腊撒等常规水电项目以及抽水蓄能项目的勘察设计合同，为下一步全面推行创造了条件。初步建立了内部协调机制，维护了集团公司的整体利益。

（4）初步形成了集团化国际经营的管理制度体系。通过大量的总结和调查研究，编制完成了集团公司《国际经营管理办法》等四项管理制度，并经集团公司国际经营工作会议讨论完善，将于近期颁发，初步形成集团化国际经营的管理制度体系，将对加强管

理、防范风险，推进集团化国际发展发挥重要作用。

(5) 加强财务、资金管理。为了适应新的要求，重新颁布了集团公司《资金管理办法》等财务管理制度，预算编制和管理效果总体上好于2008年。除个别子公司外，各子公司基本能够按集团公司60%资金集中度的要求上划资金，资金管理进一步加强，但个别子公司还存在一些问题。初步建成了覆盖七个子公司的资金在线监控系统，实现了资金存量和流动的在线监控。

(6) 严格投资管理。在按照有关规定对投资项目进行进一步的严格管理同时，开始推行集中招标采购。第一次对投资和EPC总承包的风电场塔筒和箱变实施集中招标采购，就分别节省资金1.2亿元和0.3亿元，为项目概算的27%和43%，进一步提高投资和EPC项目的效益。

(7) 质量管理扎实稳步推进。对七个设计院的42个项目进行评审，产品质量“好”占52%，“合格”占48%，未出现“差”等级产品。组织开展了“质量和安全年”活动，通过顾客意见调查，对各子公司的满意率、基本满意率达到96.5%。开展工程质量问题剖析活动，通过对存在问题的深刻剖析，制定了严防类似问题发生的措施。

(8) 以抓制度执行力为重点，进一步加强安全生产。深入开展“安全生产年”各项工作。认真组织开展安全生产“三项行动”大检查，着力强化制度的执行力，抓好生产一线及重点岗位、重点部位的从严管理。以专题会议的方式，对已发生的典型安全生产责任事故进行深刻剖析，促进全集团充分吸取教训，更有针对性地加强安全生产管理，有效缓和了安全生产形势。

(9) 进一步加强内部监督管理，保障企业和职工健康发展。继续实施党风廉政建设责任制考核，落实述职述廉、任前廉政谈话等制度，坚持开展多种形式的党风党纪教育。进一步扩大内部审计范围和内容，继续加大过程控制力度，不断促进审计意见落实，全年开展各类审计91项，内部审计覆盖面达到了79%，累计提出审计意见和建议264条，按已下达审计意见和建议统计整改落实率为95%。开展了清理账外资金（“小金库”）专项检查，首次在各子公司自查的基础上，组织中介机构进行核查，对进一步加强资金管理、防范违规违纪行为起到了重要作用。对昆明勘测设计研究院所属勘察分院设立账外资金（“小金库”）进行了认真查处，按照有关规定对相关责任人进行了纪律处分或通报批评，对昆明勘测设计研究院领导班子的年度考核进行了扣分和扣减绩效工资处理，经过努力，在有关单位的帮助下，所有资金已全额追回。利用昆明勘测设计研究院勘察分院出现的问题，深刻剖析产生问题的原因及应吸取的教训，进行警示教育，取得了很好的效果。

（五）推进科技创新，加强队伍建设

(1) 积极推动科技创新。坚持研究开发和开发应用相结合，积极推进水电工程三维设计专项研究，对水电规划设计理念、方法、标准进行研究和改进已初有成效，完成了“拱坝辅助设计系统开发研究”等30项集团公司科研成果和3项集团技术标准，特别是《水电站气垫式调压室设计规范》填补了国内空白，也是国际上技术先进、系统完整的技术标准，且具有知识产权。“中国数字水电”研制取得了阶段性初步成果。完成了“风电技术标准体系专题研究”，获得国家能源局批准成为光伏发电技术负责归口管理单位，启动了光伏发电设计技术标准的工作。

(2) 进一步加强科技成果、工程“四优”和专利申报工作。2009年，集团公司荣获省部级科技进步奖26项，《中华人民共和国水力资源复查》等2项成果荣获中国电力科技进步一等奖。获得优秀工程设计奖6项（金奖、银奖、铜奖各2项），优秀工程勘察奖4项（金奖1项、银奖1项、铜奖2项），优秀工程勘察设计软件银奖1项。获得授权专利35项（其中发明专利9项），到2009年底，集团公司拥有专利124项，其中：发明专利19项。此外，还有一大批规划设计、咨询成果荣获年度全国优秀咨询成果奖。

(3) 进一步加强信息化建设。制订并实施了“登高计划”，通过国资委的评审，集团公司网站实现了从D级向A级的提升。为促进企业管理水平提升，启动建立集团公司决策支持系统研制工作。

(4) 加强教育培训，提高队伍素质。为更好地应对金融危机，进一步促进可再生能源发展，全年邀请国家有关部门领导和专家学者共举办了10场专题辅导报告。举办了集团公司首次国际项目经理培训班，集中了46名骨干职工接受培训，为国际发展加快人才准备。举办集团公司首次青年技术论坛，进一步激励青年职工科技创新的热情。

（六）认真开展学习实践活动，加强和改进党的建设

(1) 认真开展深入学习实践科学发展观活动，取得较好实效。2009年3～8月，按照中央和国资委党委的统一部署和要求，圆满完成三个阶段六个环节各项工作，取得了较好的实效，为集团公司继续保持平稳较快发展发挥了十分重要作用。8月底，在群众中进行满意度测评，对集团公司党组和各子公司领导班子的满意率、比较满意率之和分别达到98.99%、99.49%。12月底，在群众中对整改落实后续工作进行满意度测评，对集团公司党组和各子公司领导班子的满意率、比较满意率之和分别达到100%、99.7%。

（2）继续开展“四好”领导班子创建活动。持续加强子公司领导班子和领导班子成员队伍的建设，着力提高素质和能力、树立优良作风。进一步加强了对子公司领导班子和领导班子成员监督管理，实行了对子公司领导班子从政治素质、经营业绩、团结协作和作风形象四个方面进行民主测评。紧紧围绕提高党员素质、全面推进党的基层组织建设，充分发挥党组织战斗堡垒作用和党员先锋模范作用。支持工会工作，健全职代会制度，进一步推进企业的民主管理。

（3）继续加强精神文明建设、企业文化建设。2009年，集团公司总部被首都文明委授予“首都文明单位”称号，华东勘测设计研究院、昆明勘测设计研究院荣获“全国精神文明建设工作先进单位”称号。集团公司成功举办了“祖国颂——庆祝新中国成立60周年职工文艺汇演”，各子公司也举办文艺汇演活动，增强了企业的凝聚力。

在肯定成绩的同时，必须清醒地看到，集团公司的发展还面临一些困难和问题：对标先进企业，集团公司的经营能力和管理水平还存在较大差距；收入仍主要依赖于国内水电，我国水电发展要摆脱当前面临的困境还需时日，对集团公司经营工作的不利影响仍将继续加深；国际经营竞争激烈、风险增加，集团公司的应对措施不足；个别在建工程出现了一些问题，集团公司的技术和产品质量面临考验；个别子公司成本费用偏高、利润水平偏低等等。这些困难和问题必须引起高度重视，在今后的工作中认真加以改进。

（摘自晏志勇在中国水电工程顾问集团2010年工作会议上的工作报告）

中国葛洲坝集团公司 2009年工作情况

一、主要业绩

2009年是中国葛洲坝集团公司（以下简称集团公司）统一认识，上下齐心，积极、智慧、有效地应对国际经济危机，经受住严峻复杂考验，战胜困难，实现企业又好又快发展的又一丰收之年。一年来，面对异常严峻的经济形势和空前繁重的生产经营任务，集团公司始终保持清醒头脑，以科学发展观为指引，准确判断抢机遇，从容应对抗风险，果断决策保增长，取得了前所未有的骄人业绩，创造了十二项历史之最：

一是资产总额创造历史之最。预计全年公司资产总额将达到430亿元，同比增长30%以上。这不仅是总量的历史之最，而且是增量的历史之最。并且在资产总量增长100亿元的同时，资产负债率下降了近3个百分点。

二是投标签约创造历史之最。全年新签合同508亿元，占年计划的127%，同比增长67.33%。

三是产值规模创造历史之最。预计全年完成企业总产值260亿元，占年计划的108.33%，同比增长40.33%。

四是实现利润创造历史之最。预计全年实现利润总额14.25亿元，同比增长55.37%。公司产值利润率在9家建筑中央企业中位列第一。

五是筹融资创造历史之最。首先，成功配股募集到20.54亿元资本金；其次，公司权证成功行权，达到99.68%，创造了中国证券市场权证交易品种设立以来行权比例最高纪录，共募集资金13.59亿元。这两项融资，使股份公司资产负债率大幅降低。同时，还成功发行短期融资券8亿元、中期票据5亿元，和基准利率相比，节约财务费用达2600万元。

六是银行授信额度创造历史之最。全年获得银行授信首次突破1000亿元，与2003年底40亿元相比，翻了25倍。

七是获得科技成果数量创造历史之最。全年申报专利54项，获得专利授权43项。完成3项电力行业标准、1项电力行业英文标准报批，编写工法22项，6项工法被评为湖北省工程建设工法，6项工法被评为国家级工法。全年共获得国家科技进步二等奖1项、湖北省科技进步特等奖1项、其他省级和行业科技奖12项。

八是国际经营创造历史之最。全年完成产值50亿元、实现利润3亿元，同比分别增长52.16%、50%。目前，已经有14家子分公司走向国际，国际化程度呈现良好局面。

九是投资兴业创造历史之最。预计全年完成投资85.17亿元，占年计划的121.67%。二次创业、转轨变型取得阶段性重大成果。

十是争取政策项目创造历史之最。可称之为“全面争取”，全年共争取到3.52亿元政策资金支持。

十一是银行存款创造历史之最。在增加100多亿元资产总量，大幅降低企业负债的同时，银行存款仍然有所增加，年末银行存款41.72亿元（实际为63亿元），同比增长46.28%。各单位的财务状况根本好转。

十二是职工收入创造历史之最。预计全年职工人均收入3.82万元，同比增长10.3%。其中，一线职工和关键技术岗位职工收入同比增长12%。

二、工作特点

回顾2009年的各项工作，具有以下五个方面的显著特点：

（一）是抢机遇、抗风险、保增长，企业综合实力显著提升的一年。一年来，认真落实年初职代会确立的“抢机遇、抗风险、保增长”的工作方针，经营业绩逆势而上，资产总额、营业收入、投标签约、盈利水平保持了快速大幅增长的强劲态势，各项经济指标再创历史新高，财务状况进一步好转，综合实力显著增强，公司进入全球225家最大承包企业百强，在中国企业500强排名第279位，提升38位。

（二）是加快实施企业转轨变型，企业获得全面发展的一年。一是投资兴业突飞猛进。按照“三主”目标，抓好质量、进度、投资“三控制”，加快在建投资项目建设。水泥年产能达到2000万t，名列全国特大型水泥集团前茅。炸药产能达到17.5万t，也位居全国前列。大广北高速公路通车，进入收益期；内遂高速公路全线开工。新疆战略稳步推进，斯木塔斯水电站开工建设。上海葛洲坝大厦竣工投入使用，武汉、宜昌300多万平方米高档楼盘项目建设进展顺利，销售良好。工业产值完成41亿元，同比增长73.96%，投资业利润同比增长220.58%，投资业从业人员7698人，占职工总人数的20.83%，同比增长20%。二是国际化程度不断提高。集团公司沉着应对国际金融危机，坚定不移地实施国际化战略，加快子分公司“走出去”步伐。各单位高度重视，对走出去闯荡国际市场认识空前统一。对国际经营管理体制机制、方式方法也高度认可，运作模式逐渐向高端项目运作。三是子分公司独立闯市场能力显著增强。全年以子分公司自有资质中标个数达350项，中标总额113.05亿元，占集团股份公司中标总额的42.09%，同比增长87.05%。四是非水电市场开拓取得新进展。全年共中标244项，合同金额226.18亿元，占总签约合同金额的53.68%。

（三）是坚持“依法、从严、精细”六字治企方针，企业管理水平快速提升的一年。一是初步建立了全面风险管理体系，风险管控得到强化，风险管理认识得到全面提高。二是信息化建设提速，企业业务流程、管理模式发生深刻变革。全年签订信息化项目合同22个，计算机中心机房、服务器存储设备及平台软件、网络及安全设备、财务报表系统、视频会议系统等7个项目顺利通过验收，集团数据中心初具规模，覆盖各子分公司的网络平台基本形成，部分系统开始运用于企业的日常管理。三是大力实施人才强企战略，企业发展后劲进一步增强。我们牢固树立人才资源是第一资源的理念，紧密结合生产经营，加大了对国际经营、投资、房地产等行业，以及铁路等非水电建筑市场专业人才的培养，全年引进大学毕业生1193名，培训职工100期7635人次。薪酬待遇逐步向一线职工和关键技术岗位倾斜。四是加大科技创新力度，企业核心竞争力进一步增强。2009年，公司取得了一系列重大科技创新成果，承建的水布垭大坝获得第一届堆石坝国际研讨会“面板堆石坝国际里程碑奖”、黄河公伯峡水电站工程获得青海省科技进步一等奖；参与的“大滑坡体中深长防淘墙施工关键技术研究与应用”获得中国电力建设科学技术成果一等奖、“碾压混凝土拱坝的新设计理论与实践”获得大禹水利科学技术一等奖、“三峡巨型水轮发电机组创新研究与国产化实践”获得湖北省科技进步特等奖。2009年，公司治理和资本运作的突出业绩受到社会各界的高度评价，获得上市公司“典型并购重组案例奖”。公司良好的经营业绩和发展潜力得到广大投资者充分认可，一直保持着沪深300指数、沪深300成长指数和上证公司治理指数样本股地位，去年又入选“上证180公司治理指数”、“上证180成长指数”、“上证中央企业50指数成份股”、“中证中央企业综合指数”、“中证中央企业100指数”样本股、被评为“2008年度中国上市公司价值百强”和“2009中国最具竞争力上市公司20强”。公司还创造了8项中国企业新纪录。

（四）是全力深化改革，企业享受政策优惠项最多的一年。一年来，加大资产资源重组整合力度，加快子分公司重组整合步伐，做大做强各子分公司，增强了子公司的抗风险能力。公司成为首家完成厂办大集体改革试点工作的中央企业。各单位、各业务板块、各部门千方百计争取优惠政策，并将政策学精、吃透、用活，为企业发展注入了强劲的“助推剂”。不仅争取到了2008年度离休人员医药费补贴470万元、基建贷款贴息资金1381.9万元、厂办大集体改革试点企业资金6690万元、灾后重建补贴2.5亿元、节能减排资金补助1700万元、中国进出口银行优惠贷款10.13亿元，还争取了对外承包工程专项资金补助、进口设备贴息、申报高新技术企业、原集体工参加养老保险等一系列优惠政策。

（五）是秉持强企富民宗旨，和谐企业建设稳步推进的一年。一年来，抓住召开第二次党代会和深入学习实践科学发展观活动的契机，秉持强企富民宗旨，全体职工分享到了企业又好又快发展的成果，切身感受到了安居乐业、丰衣足食的实惠。

三、存在的问题与不足

在肯定成绩的同时，还必须清醒地看到，企业经营管理的各个环节中还存在许多问题和不足：一是发展不平衡的矛盾突出，表现在建筑业中水电与非水电市场之间、三大主业之间、各单位之间依然没有实现全面协调发展。二是任务储备严重不足，缺乏可持续快速发展后劲。三是在建工程项目优秀管理人才、核心设备、合格劳务组织等优质资源不足，在建项目和投资项目管理粗放、基础工作薄弱。四是应收款项增速过快，资产负债率、主营业务成本费用率偏高。五是安全生产形势不容乐观。六是企业保稳定的任务依然艰巨。这些问题严重制约企业的快速发展，务必引起高度重视。

四、主要经验

第一，必须坚定不移地走管理型之路。集团公司制定了“一型三化大强富”目标，这里的一型就是管理型。多年来，集团公司强力推行“依法、从严、精细”的治企方针，实现由承包商向既是承包商又是投资开发商转变，由单纯劳务型承包施工向管理型转变，由经营粗放型向经营集约型转变的“三个转变”，实现了在从事建安职工逐年减少，管理队伍日益精干的情况下，企业的规模、签约、产值、利润的大幅增长。

第二，必须坚定不移地走现代化之路。企业的现代化，首先在于是否建立了一个产权清晰、权责明确、政企分开、管理科学的现代企业制度。集团公司主业资产上市，建立起了现代企业制度的基本框架，企业发生了脱胎换骨式的变化，从一个积弊深重、严重亏损的老企业蜕变成为具有了完善健全的现代企业制度的跨国企业集团。其次，管理手段上的现代化。集团公司信息化平台已经建立，要进一步推广应用，不断完善，要走到同行业管理手段现代化的前列。

第三，必须坚定不移地走国际化之路。集团公司成立了国际公司并将其总部迁往北京，吸收高素质人才，学习先进的管理经验，国际化进程逐年加快。先从支持条件具备的建筑子企业大胆走出去，到目前基本上所有建筑子企业已走出去，大力开拓国际市场，国际市场的签约、产值和利润贡献率逐年大幅提高。

第四，必须坚定不移地走科技兴企之路。集团公司提出技术经济的理念，逐年加大科技资金投入，建立博士后流动站，提高参与国家重点工程的建筑施工技术科学含量。申报和获得的国家专利和专有技术、编制国家级工法、参与制定的行业标准、获得以鲁班奖为代表的各种奖项逐年增多。我们要牢牢掌握行业发展的制高点，大大提高企业核心竞争能力和开拓国际市场的能力。

第五，必须坚定不移地走人才强企之路。集团公司每年引进近两千名大学生，一批思想活跃、视野开阔、有知识、懂技术的新一代葛洲坝人涌现在生产前沿。集团公司的人才强企战略不仅应该，而且必须要实现三个转变，这就是：管理人员必须由单纯生产型向生产经营型转变；技术干部必须由单纯技术型向技术经济型转变；工人必须由单纯劳务型向知识技能型转变，变成工头、工长。只有不断转变，才能提升企业的经济附加值。

第六，必须坚定不移地走投资兴业之路。集团公司确定投资兴业的产业定位和价值取向，就是要使投资业与建筑主业一样，真正成为营业收入的主渠道、利润的主来源、职工从业的主平台，这是投资兴业的产业定位，也是成功实现转轨变型、二次创业的重大标志。必须坚定不移地走下去，这是集团公司实施跨越式发展，建设大强富集团的重要战略选择，是公司二次创业、转轨变型的主要途径，是葛洲坝未来发展的重要依托，是强企富民的必由之路。

这些是集团公司过去成功的经验总结，也是集团公司现在必须坚持的制胜法宝，更是集团公司将来应当继承和发扬的宝贵财富。

（摘自杨继学在中国葛洲坝集团公司2010年工作研讨会上的讲话）

2

水能及风能开发

流域规划与开发

金沙江中游河段水电开发建设总体规划

金沙江是长江的上游，发源于唐古拉山中段的各拉丹东雪山和尕恰迪如岗山之间，径流丰沛且稳定、河道落差大、水能资源丰富、开发条件较好，是规划的全国最大水电能源基地。习惯上将金沙江干流分为上、中、下三段。直门达至石鼓为上段；中段从石鼓至攀枝花市雅砻江口；雅砻江口至宜宾为下段。金沙江中游河段长约564km，落差838m，按国家批准的《金沙江中游河段水电规划报告》推荐的金沙江中游河段“一库八级”开发方案，河段规划总装机容量20 580MW，保证出力8946MW，年均发电量883亿kW·h。

2005年12月，为充分发挥金沙江中游水电开发整体效益，加快金沙江中游梯级电站开发，国家发展和改革委员会以发改能源［2005］2609号文正式批准成立云南金沙江中游水电开发有限公司（以下简称公司），要求公司按已批复的规划方案全资开发龙盘、两家人、梨园、阿海四个梯级电站，参股建设金安桥、龙开口、鲁地拉和观音岩电站，全面负责金沙江中游梯级水电站开发建设的协调和管理工作。公司自成立以来认真贯彻落实国家发展改革委批复要求，按照统一规划、统一调度和统一运行的原则，为充分发挥金沙江中游梯级电站发电、防洪、供水等综合利用效益，组织开展了梯级水电站开发建设的环境保护规划、移民安置、输电网架规划、水资源利用综合效益分析规划等流域总体规划工作，从流域层面统筹水电开发与环境保护、移民安置及地方经济社会发展的关系，努力实现流域水资源综合开发的经济、社会、环境效益最大化。

（一）流域水电开发环境保护规划

1. 流域环境影响评价规划

为总体把握金沙江中游水电开发的环境影响问题，充分协调水电梯级开发、经济增长、社会进步与环境保护要求的关系，系统性地提出环境、生态保护措施，促进流域水电开发与环境保护相协调，公司委托开展了流域水电开发规划环境影响评价及对策措施研究，开展流域水环境、水生生物、陆生生态、局地气候、社会经济、景观旅游资源及环境监测方案研究，提出合理开发利用和保护水资源、减少流域梯级电站建设对下游水资源利用不利影响的评价体系和对策。

该环境影响评价规划于2007年5月完成了研究大纲，2008年9月完成了《金沙江干流中游河段水电开发规划环境影响及对策研究报告》的编制工作，2009年5月通过环保部组织的评估并取得了《关于金沙江中游河段水电开发规划环境影响评价及对策研究报告审查意见的函》（环办函［2009］436号）。

环保部印发的审查意见指出“从生态与环境保护角度考虑总体布局及开发规模，除金沙江中游河段龙盘和两家人电站需进行深入研究确定环境可行性外，其他水电梯级开发总体可行”。公司按照项目研究成果组织开展各梯级水电站环境影响评价研究及项目筹建工程施工环保方案实施、景观景点、库区优势产业及移民安置、生物多样性保护、交通规划、三江并流保护区局地气候影响研究及流域环保管理等工作，取得了阿海水电站环境影响批复、金沙江中游流域移民安置创新政策等应用成果，流域各梯级电站施工筹建项目建设与流域环境保护工作同步较好的开展，逐步形成水电开发与环境保护共赢的流域开发局面。

2. 开展流域水生生物影响总体评价研究

为全面了解和掌握金沙江中游河段水生生物资源状况，公司委托开展了流域梯级电站区水生生物的调查与评价专题研究和金沙江虎跳峡—旭龙河河段龙头水库建设与生物多样性保护专题研究工作。设计单位针对金沙江中游梯级水电站，提出了《金沙江中游阿海等五个梯级水电站水生生物影响总体评价》、《虎跳峡—旭龙河河段龙头水库建设与生物多样性保护关系研究》专题。两专题报告分别通过了水电水利规划设计总院，云南省环境保护局等单位组织的评审验收。

此项研究为全面了解和掌握金沙江中游河段水生生物资源提供了科学的依据，为电站建设能更好地进行水生生物保护制定了详细的规划，提出了科学可行的解决方案，是研究大中型水电建设项目与生物多样性保护的关系的一项基础性、开创性工作，为我国生物多样性影响评价制度建设提供了研究案例。

3. 玉龙、哈巴雪山自然保护区保护规划研究

为明确金沙江中游“一库八级”梯级电站与玉龙雪山和哈巴雪山省级自然保护区关系，公司配合相关

单位开展保护区的边界范围界定和功能区划研究工作，为掌握第一手珍稀动植物资源分布、数量、种类等基础资料提供基础，也为如何在保护的基础上合理地开发利用提供科学依据。根据科考研究成果，云南省世界遗产管理委员会办公室批复并确认梨园水电站工程建设区域不在保护区和风景名胜区范围内。

此外，为把握龙盘水库建成后对区域气候的总体影响、是否会导致玉龙雪山雪线下降的问题，公司开展了《金沙江龙头水库水体局地气候效应研究》、《龙盘水库局地气候效应对本区冰川与雪线的影响研究》等专题研究。设计单位利用多年来对玉龙雪山冰川与环境变化观测所获得的大量基础数据，通过水库局地气候效应的数值模拟，结合冰川变化预测模型，分析了龙盘水库局地气候效应对冰川与雪线的影响。研究结果表明，龙盘水库建设对区域气候影响很小，不会诱发新的气象灾害如暴雨、高低温天气、雾等，总体上有利于冰川的发育和保护，对目前由于全球变暖引起的本区冰川强烈退缩和雪线上升具有显著的减缓作用。此项研究为解决玉龙雪山地区水资源短缺、保护冰川等问题提供了科学依据，论证了水电开发与环境保护共赢等问题。

4. 完成了虎跳峡河段景观保护和旅游发展规划工作

为落实好“在发展中落实保护，在保护中促进发展”方针，既做好电站开发，又促进库区旅游发展，保护好环境，深入研究电站建设期、电站建设后给库区旅游、景观带来的影响，云南省设计院、城乡规划设计研究院及有关知名专家、学者完成了《龙盘水电站坝址至其宗坝址河段景观景点总体规划》和《其宗水电站规划区景观景点总体规划》。研究表明金沙江虎跳峡河段开发对景观景点的影响，可以通过保护利用措施及开发方案加以解决。通过规划实施，龙头水库开发建设与地方区域资源保护利用、移民生活安置与旅游产业支撑及地方经济社会发展之间的关系能够较好地相互协调。通过电站的建设，可以对上、中、下虎跳峡峡谷交通道路进行综合规划改造，进一步开发中、下虎跳峡旅游资源，按照生态环保的理念，合理布局整个虎跳峡景区两岸旅游资源，开发峡谷景观，使其得到更好的利用。

5. 建立流域环境保护监测管理协调机构

金沙江中游水电开发环境保护涉及责任主体多，环境保护措施落实难度大，为统一流域梯级电站开发环境保护协调管理，公司成立国内首家大型流域水电开发环境保护监测管理中心，充分协调流域水电开发、经济增长、社会进步与环境保护之间的关系，以促进金沙江中游梯级水电开发和环境保护要求相互协调推进。

流域环保中心的职能是充分协调流域各梯级电站的环保责任部门，加强与国家和地方环保管理与监督部门对口衔接。开展流域环境保护综合技术研究及流域环境影响后评价等工作；统一各项目环境监测技术标准和工作要求，开展流域环境监测实施规划设计、协调监测管理等，对各项目监测成果进行统计、分析和研究；收集、整理和上报流域各项目分年度的环保工作计划、主要工作内容和资金安排计划；指导、协调流域各项目生态环保方案和措施的实施、完善。

成立流域性的环境保护机构，在水电开发领域尚属首次，这是公司按照环保部要求，合理解决流域水电开发环境累积问题，统筹环保措施，提高项目环境保护工作的质量和效果，在“统一规划”的基础上履行好国家发展改革委赋予的“统一调度”职能进行的一次开拓性的创举，将为我国流域水电开发的环境保护工作做出有益探索，提供宝贵的经验。

（二）创新移民安置方式研究

水电开发过程中，解决好移民的脱贫致富和长远发展是当前面临的普遍困难，也是引发环境次生问题的重要原因。金沙江中游水电开发移民搬迁安置任务较为繁重，流域“一库八级”电站共需要搬迁安置移民15.2万人，土地资源较为紧张，以土安置容量难以承载。此外，少数民族区域性强，需要保证民族文化的传承。为此，公司按照云南省委、省政府的总体安排，配合云南省发改委、移民局、国土局、环保厅等21个厅局和4个地州，开展了“创新移民补偿安置方式”重大课题研究。经过近两年的艰苦努力，根据国家《大中型水利水电工程建设征地补偿和移民安置条例》[2006]（国务院令第471号），最终完成了《云南金沙江中游水电开发移民安置补偿补助意见》及八个实施办法的编制工作，并取得云南省政府批复意见。这项重大课题研究成果被称为“16 118移民安置政策”。

本着“和谐水电”的理念，为实现移民的可持续发展，公司委托开展了《金沙江梨园—观音岩河段水电开发移民后续产业发展规划》研究，龙头水库比选方案库区经济调查、优势产业规划、移民的可持续发展以及相关的具体措施和组织保障方案、民族文化保护方案的研究。从库区及周边社会经济与资源环境条件分析，对优势产业规划，分库区优势产业规划布局及就业容量测算、发展资金筹措与管理等对移民后续产业发展进行了规划，并通过了相关主管部门组织的审查。金沙江中游流域水电开发移民安置政策及产业发展规划自实施以来得到广大移民群众的支持拥护，也得到国家有关部委、各级地方政府和水电行业专家的认可和支持，为解决金沙江中游水电开发移民问题提供了强有力的政策支撑。

（三）流域电站重大件运输及对外公路规划

金沙江中游流域地处滇西北高山峡谷地区，交通条件极为有限。为了统筹协调金沙江中游梯级电站开发与地方交通发展规划的关系，使电站对外交通与地方交通发展规划协调一致，改善沿江地州交通状况，促进地方经济发展，2006 年 8 月国家林业局昆明勘察设计院开展了金沙江中游梯级水电站重大件运输及对外公路规划工作，2008 年 1 月通过云南省发展改革委批复。

该规划符合云南省综合交通的实际情况和发展要求，对于促进金沙江中游沿线区域的全面、协调和可持续发展具有重要意义。公司依托该项研究成果开工建设的丽江市鸣音—阿里恒—梨园公路工程和丽江苹果园—鸣音—阿海公路是梨园水电站和阿海水电站常规及大件运输的重要对外通道，项目同时是玉龙县公路网络的重要组成部分，是规划的丽江小南环线的组成部分，较好地结合了地方交通发展规划，有效促进了地方经济社会发展。

（四）流域地震监测台网设计规划

汶川地震后，为加强对金沙江中游流域梯级水电站工程建设区域地震活动的监测管理，提高地震监测能力，确保金沙江中游流域梯级水电站的建设、运行安全以及库区居民的生活稳定，按照《国家发展改革委关于加强水电工程防震抗震工作有关要求的通知》（发改能源［2008］1242 号）的要求，公司开展了梨园、阿海、龙开口、鲁地拉和观音岩水电站防震抗震专题研究工作。在各梯级电站防震抗震设计专题研究的基础上，2009 年，中国水利水电科学研究院开展了全流域的地震监测台网规划和建设工作，目前流域地震台网规划报告已完成，并通过了中国水利水电规化设计总院组织的审查。

金沙江中游流域梯级水电站水库地震监测台网设计规划顺利开展并实施，为保证梯级电站运行安全和稳定库区正常生产、生活秩序，减轻地震灾害和地震次生灾害所造成的损失，最大限度维护流域移民及公司经济利益具有重要作用。

（五）流域梯级水电站综合调度规划及水情测报系统规划

为充分发挥各梯级电站的发电、防洪、供水等综合利用效益，确保流域水资源开发利用整体效益的充分发挥，公司开展了集控中心调度自动化及通信系统规划工作，为实现全流域电站集中控制调度运行目标打下了基础，现流域集中控制调度中心建设基本完成，具备投入使用的条件。同时，为满足各梯级电站截流及施工期水情信息预报的要求，公司提前开展了流域水情自动测报系统的规划及可研工作，并于 2008 年汛前投入使用，为流域各项目安全度汛提供了保障。

（六）流域梯级水电受电市场及输电网架规划

根据国家发展改革委《国家发展改革委办公厅关于开展西南地区水电受电市场及输电网架规划研究工作的通知》（发改办能源［2005］2518 号文）要求，在电能消纳研究成果基础上，电力规划设计总院编制完成了《金沙江中游梯级电站输电系统规划报告》，并通过了中国南方电网有限责任公司组织专家评审。

在此研究成果的支撑下，金沙江阿海、梨园水电站接入系统设计及其外送输电工程可行性研究通过了南方电网批复，各项目公司据此开展了电站接入系统设计工作。输电系统规划工作有效地推动了流域各梯级电站接入系统设计及审批，为梯级电站顺利并网外送提供规划基础和条件。

（云南金沙江中游水电开发有限公司）

湖南省湘资沅澧“四水”干流水电开发方案

在 2007 年开始的全国新一轮的流域规划修编中，湖南省水利水电勘测设计研究总院在湖南省水利厅的领导下，按照长江流域规划修编工作大纲的要求，对湘江、资水、沅水、澧水“四水”原流域规划中的水电开发方案，根据流域防洪保安和水资源综合利用以及水生态环境保护的要求，进行了复核和调整。调整后的“四水”水电开发方案为：

（一）湘江

1985 年湘江干流规划以来，梯级处数未发生变化，但梯级位置发生了较大变化。规划修编湖南境内湘江干流布置 11 个梯级进行开发，分别为：

白滩河(123m)＋湘江(118m)＋太洲(105m)＋潇湘(97m)＋浯溪(88m)＋湘祁(75.5m)＋近尾洲(66m)＋土谷塘(58m)＋大源渡(50m)＋株洲航电(40.5m)＋长沙综合枢纽(29.7m)。

目前湖南境内干流上已相继建成了湘江、潇湘、近尾洲、大源渡、株洲航电等梯级，太洲、浯溪、长沙综合枢纽正在建设中，白滩河、湘祁、土谷塘梯级都已开展前期工作。

（二）资水

1995 年规划资水干流罗家庙以下规划为 13 级，2004 年将敷溪口梯级调整为珠溪口。规划修编湖南境内资水干流双江口以下按 13 级布置为：

孔雀滩（222m）＋神滩渡（215m）＋晒谷滩（207.2m）＋筱溪（198m）＋浪石滩（175m）＋柘溪（167.2m）＋东坪（96.5m）＋珠溪口（87.5m）＋金塘冲（78.0m）＋马迹塘（55.7m）＋白竹洲（49.0m）＋修山（43.0m）＋史家洲（34.5m）。

目前晒谷滩、筱溪、浪石滩、柘溪、东坪、珠溪口、马迹塘、修山已建成，白竹洲、孔雀滩、史家洲正在建设，神滩渡、金塘冲正在进行前期工作。

（三）沅水

2003年编制的《沅水干流规划复核报告》沅水干流湖南境内有9个梯级，2009年增加了桃源梯级。规划修编湖南境内沅水干流河段10级开发方案为：

托口(247m)＋洪江(190m)＋安江(166m)＋铜湾(154m)＋清水塘(140m)＋大洑潭(130m)＋鱼潭(115m)＋五强溪(108m)＋凌津滩(51m)＋桃源(39.5m)。

目前，洪江、铜湾、清水塘、大洑潭、五强溪、凌津滩已建成投产，托口正在建设，安江、鱼潭、桃源正在进行前期工作。

（四）澧水

1991年《澧水流域规划报告》澧水干流有16个梯级，2009年对贺龙梯级进行了调整。规划修编澧水干流河段17级开发方案为：

凉水口(420m)＋山羊溪(304m)＋贺龙(288m)＋八斗溪(257.8m)＋渔潭(250m)＋花岩(204m)＋木龙滩(166m)＋红壁岩(156m)＋黄家铺(148m)＋宜冲桥(140m)＋岩泊渡(105m)＋茶庵(95.5m)＋城关(87m)＋茶林河(81m)＋三江口(69.2m)＋青山(48.2m)＋艳洲(40.2m)；在中源规划了新街梯级。

澧水干流经几十年的建设，现已建成11个梯级，分别是贺龙、八斗溪、渔潭、木龙滩、红壁岩、茶庵、城关、茶林河、三江口、青山、艳洲。

（湖南省水利水电勘测设计研究总院　李建坤）

西藏玉曲河流域水电开发规划

（一）流域概况

玉曲河位于西藏自治区昌都地区境内怒江和澜沧江分水岭的西侧，发源于西藏自治区昌都地区类乌齐县的瓦合山南麓，河流总体由北向南流，在林芝地区察隅县察瓦龙乡目巴村附近汇入怒江。玉曲河流域面积9379km^2，干流总长444.3km，天然落差3122m，河口处多年平均流量为114m^3/s，全流域水力资源理论蕴藏量2510MW，经济技术可开发量2000MW。流域流经昌都地区察雅县、洛隆县、八宿县、左贡县和林芝地区察隅县。流域内农牧业相对发达，工业规模小，经济社会发展相对缓慢，目前，流域内只有主要城镇通电，且孤网运行，其余居民照明均以酥油、蜡烛为主。

（二）开发任务

科学利用玉曲河流域的水资源，合理开发水能资源，可促使该地区资源优势转变为经济优势。开发玉曲河水力资源，不仅可缓解流域内用电紧张的局面，而且还可形成昌都南部地区的支撑电源，解决昌都地区南部的电力供需矛盾，有力地支持地方经济发展，提高当地人民群众生产生活水平和生活质量。

（三）流域规划情况

玉曲河流域水电规划于2008年3月开始，2009年11月，《玉曲河干流水电规划报告》（送审稿）完成，并于2009年12月通过审查。在充分考虑有效治理域内水土流失、生态环境保护和改善、减少水库淹没、合理开发水能资源的原则下，规划推荐玉曲河流域采用“一库七级”开发方案：成德（3760m）—扎玉（3550m）—吉登（3400m）—中波（3200m）—碧土（3080m）—扎拉（2810m）—轰东（2100m），规划总装机容量1984MW，联合运行时保证出力717.40MW，多年发平均电量98.25亿kW·h，推荐碧土等梯级为近期开发梯级水电站。随着上述规划梯级电站的开发，有望实现“藏电外送”实质性的突破。

（中国大唐集团公司）

新疆阿克苏库玛拉克河流域和台兰河流域水电开发情况

（一）库玛拉克河流域开发情况

新疆阿克苏河支流库玛拉克河全长293km，其中中国境内河长118km，多年平均年径流量约48.7亿m^3，多年平均流量约154m^3/s。国内河段规划《新疆阿克苏河支流库玛拉克河河段水电规划报告》（2006年版）“一库四级”开发，依次是大石峡、小石峡、塔尕克和吐木秀克水电站。大石峡枢纽工程是库玛拉克河控制性工程，设计坝高250m，库容约12亿m^3，电站总装机容量600MW。工程任务是：在保证向塔里木河流域生态供水的前提下，承担灌溉、防洪和发电等任务。

大石峡水利枢纽项目建议书已于2009年3月初通过自治区水利厅上报水利部。小石峡水电站承接大石峡尾水，坝高约65m，水库总库容6900万m^3，装机容量110MW；工程主要任务是发电并对大石峡水库出水过程进行反调节；2009年9月已完成项目核准，11月正式开工建设。塔尕克水电站（49MW）和吐木秀克水电站（48MW）均是协合拉水利枢纽东岸总干渠上的引水式电站，其中塔尕克水电站已由新华水利开发建成，吐木秀克水电站已由国电阿克苏河流域水电开发有限公司于2009年12月建成发电。大石峡、小石峡和吐木秀克三个电站年发电总量约28亿kW·h。

（二）台兰河流域规划情况

台兰河流域位于阿克苏地区温宿县境内，发源于西南天山托木尔峰南麓，上游由大台兰河、小台兰河在距出山口前 8km 处汇合后称台兰河，出山口后由西向东汇入支流塔克拉克河，为典型的内陆河。台兰河流向为自北向南，全长约 90km，流域总面积 $5824km^2$，其中山区面积 $1324km^2$，平原区 $4500km^2$。台兰河多年平均径流量为 7.501 亿 m^3，多年平均流量为 $23.79m^3/s$（1957～2006 年观测资料），全流域水能资源理论蕴藏量为 230.3MW。

台兰河流域水电规划主要以中游河段为主。受温宿县人民政府委托，2008 年初，新疆生产建设兵团勘测规划设计研究院编制完成了台兰河河段（大桥三级尾水—台兰河总干渠东风闸）规划报告。为充分利用该河段水能资源，2009 年新疆水利水电勘测设计研究院在此规划报告基础上，通过优化，对山区段和出山口段的水能资源进行了初步规划，提出了“一库五级”（依次为大桥一级电站 30MW＋大桥二级电站 25MW＋台兰河一级电站 45MW＋台兰河二级电站 47MW＋台兰河三级电站 30MW＋台兰河四级电站 10MW）。目前台兰河一级电站（45MW）和台兰河二级电站（47 MW）正在积极进行项目核准前期工作。

（三）库玛拉克河上游境外河段—萨雷扎兹河的水电规划前期工作

萨雷扎兹河水资源和水能资源比较丰富，吉尔吉斯斯坦境内萨雷扎兹河全河水能理论蕴藏量约 1770 MW，开发规模 1500 MW 以上。中吉《萨雷扎兹河—库玛拉克河联合考察报告》中方报告已于 2009 年 3 月完成编制，2009 年 9 月完成《中吉萨雷扎兹河流域联合考察及水能资源联合开发规划报告》中、俄文本，分别提交两国政府。

（中国国电集团公司）

四川绰斯甲河流域水电开发情况

国电四川阿水电力开发有限公司由国电四川发电有限公司和阿坝藏族羌族自治州政府国有资产监督管理委员会分别以 90％、10％的比例出资组建。公司现阶段主要负责开发 4 个水电项目，分别是大渡河一级支流绰斯甲河干流（曾克寺—麦斯卡段）的绰斯甲、观音桥、上寨水电站与足木足河（属大渡河干流）的卜寺沟水电站，总装机容量 1239 MW，总投资约 183 亿元。

（一）绰斯甲河流域规划

2009 年 4 月，四川省发展和改革委员会以《关于印发〈绰斯甲河干流（曾克寺—麦斯卡段）水电规划报告审查意见〉的通知》（川发改能源［2009］341 号），正式批复绰斯甲流域规划。

2009 年 5 月，四川省发展和改革委员会以《关于同意阿坝州绰斯甲河上寨、绰斯甲、观音桥水电站开展前期工作的函》（川发改能源函［2009］579 号），正式确立国电四川发电有限公司对绰斯甲河上寨、绰斯甲和观音桥水电站开发权的主体地位。

（二）项目基本情况

1. 绰斯甲电站　为大渡河一级支流绰斯甲河干流（曾克寺—麦斯卡段）水电规划的第三级电站，具有日调节性能，长引水式开发，Ⅱ等大（2）型工程，调节库容 47.9 万 m^3，初拟装机容量 390MW，年发电量 174 300 万 kW・h，年利用小时数 4717h。

2. 观音桥电站　为绰斯甲河干流水电规划的最后一级，混合式开发，800 万 m^3 调节库容，初拟装机容量 135MW，年发电量 60 300/67 400 万 kW・h，年利用小时数 5000h。

3. 上寨电站　为绰斯甲河干流水电规划的“龙头”水库，坝式开发，最大坝高 229m，总库容 103 800 万 m^3，调节库容 70 400 万 m^3，具有年调节性能，初拟装机容量 354MW，年平均发电量 161 400 万 kW・h，年利用小时数 4560h。

4. 卜寺沟电站　位于阿坝州马尔康县，系大渡河干流水电规划“三库 22 级”的第 4 级水电站，坝式开发，最大坝高约 133m，库容 24 600 万 m^3，初拟装机容量 360MW，年发电量 164 000 万 kW・h，年利用小时数 4555h。

（三）开发时序优化

按照中国国电集团公司要求，结合阿坝水电四个项目的技术经济特点和开发难易程度，公司将以前的“211”开发时序调整为“2＋2”，即先期开发绰斯甲、观音桥水电站，再开发卜寺沟、上寨水电站，实现滚动开发。

（四）项目进展情况

2009 年，公司加快推进前期勘测设计工作，加强设计优化和重大问题的研究咨询，加大施工准备工程工作力度，各项前期工作取得新的实质性进展。

1. 绰斯甲电站　于 2009 年 9 月完成预可行性研究报告审查，2009 年 12 月启动接入系统设计工作。

2. 卜寺沟电站　于 2009 年 1 月启动了接入系统的设计工作，2009 年 11 月完成可研阶段正常蓄水位选择专题报告审查工作，2009 年 12 月完成可研阶段坝址、坝型、坝线及枢纽布置格局专题研究报告咨询工作。

3. 上寨和观音桥电站　按照中国国电集团公司招投标管理办法规定，于 2009 年 8 月完成勘察设计招标开标工作。2009 年 9 月中国国电集团公司工程招标管理办公室批复确定了上寨、观音桥水电站勘察设计的中标单位。2009 年 11 月 3～4 日，公司分别与北京国电水利电力工程有限公司、中国水电顾问集团贵阳勘测设计研究院签订了上寨水电站、观音桥水电站勘察设计合同，预可行性研究工作全面启动。

4. 施工供电工程　2009 年 7 月，公司完成绰斯甲水电站、卜寺沟水电站施工电源工程勘测设计招标工作。2009 年 8 月，公司分别与阿坝州马尔康电力有限责任公司和太阳河流域水电开发有限公司签订了《绰斯甲水电站施工用电框架协议》，达成了施工用电相关事宜。2009 年 10 月，绰斯甲水电站、卜寺沟水电站施工电源工程可行性研究报告通过审查。

5. 马尔康管理集控中心工程　2009 年 4 月，公司与马尔康县国土资源局完成了马尔康管理集控中心工程建设用地的购买工作，先后完成该宗土地的测量、地质灾害评估、矿产压覆、文物调查等专项报告；2009 年 4 月，完成工程设计招标评标工作；2009 年 12 月，与中标单位四川大学签订了设计合同。

（中国国电集团公司）

四川东义河流域水电开发及规划

2009 年 9 月，国电四川发电有限公司与深圳市玉湖投资集团有限公司对四川民和水电投资有限公司进行了战略重组。重组后，国电四川发电有限公司持有四川民和水电投资有限公司 65％的股权，深圳市玉湖投资集团有限公司持股比例为 35％。四川民和水电投资有限公司注册地点为成都市高新技术产业开发区，负责四川省东义河流域水电资源开发建设和运营，下辖两个子公司，其中：稻城县民和水电有限公司负责东义河流域稻城县境内水电开发任务；木里民和水电有限公司负责东义河流域木里县境内水电开发任务。

（一）东义河流域基本情况

1. 流域概况　东义河是水洛河一级支流，金沙江二级支流，发源于稻城县杂内垭卡山，流经稻城、木里两县汇入水洛河。东义河干流长 127km，流域面积 2940km²，总落差 2778m（4340～1562m 高程），河道的平均坡降 21.8‰。

2. 地质地貌　东义河流域地处青藏高原东南边缘、横断山脉中段的高山高原峡谷地带，两岸山顶高程一般在 3500～5000m，相对高差为 1000～2000m，区域内群山起伏，峰峦重叠，地貌崎岖。地质构造上以断裂构造为主；区内岩层受强烈挤压、变形，节理、片理非常发育，岩体破碎，易风化剥蚀；暴雨季节易发生滑坡、泥石流，区域内冲洪积、崩坡积广布。

3. 气象气温　由于青藏高原复杂地形的影响，本地区呈现青藏高原型气候和大陆性气候特征，属大陆性季风高原型气候。总的气候特征为春秋相连，长冬无夏，日照充足；干、雨季节分明，地方性大风明显。冬半年，空气干燥，多晴冷冰冻天气；夏半年气温较高，雨水、冰雹和雷雨天气频繁。根据稻城县气象站气象资料统计：多年平均降水量 622.8mm，多年平均气温 4.2℃，极端最高气温 27.9℃，极端最低气温－27.6℃；多年平均相对湿度 56％；多年平均风速 2.4m/s；多年平均蒸发量 1783.3mm；多年平均日照时数 2641.7h。

4. 行政区划　东义河流域水电开发共 14 级电站（含干流、支流龙达河和 6 个支沟电站），初拟装机容量 519.4MW，其中：位于甘孜州境内电站 11 级，装机容量合计 300.4MW；位于凉山州境内电站 3 级，装机容量合计 219MW。工程所在地区均为藏族或藏文化影响地区。

5. 交通条件　东义河流域规划河段交通极为不便。东义梯级以下色苦、益地电站及龙达河的俄桠、洋那梯级尚无通车道路，前期勘测设计工作均需步行进出。东义河流域附近地区工业水平落后，工程所需的材料、设备多需从云南昆明或四川西昌、成都运入。据统计，自东义河口经由西昌至成都约 947km，至西昌 435km；自东义河口经由康定、泸定至成都 902km；经由丽江、大理至昆明 825km。而且，沿途要翻越崇山峻岭及复杂的强对流气象地区，交通运输难度大，安全保障差。

（二）项目基本情况

1. 东义河干流梯级

东义河干流规划采用“二库六级”开发方案，初拟装机容量 419MW。

（1）卡斯电站，为东义河干流规划中的上游第一级电站，具有季调节能力，于 2007 年 6 月 7 日完成流域规划工作，规划装机容量 31MW，年发电量 14 104万 kW·h。

（2）尼隆电站，为东义河干流梯级开发的第二级电站，引水式开发，无调节能力，装机容量 30MW；电站单独运行时，年发电量 13 082 万 kW·h，与卡斯电站联合运行时，年发电量 13277 万 kW·h。

（3）浪都电站，为东义河干流梯级开发的第三级电站，径流引水式开发，规划装机容量 33MW，电站单独运行时，年发电量 15 140 万 kW·h，与上游卡斯电站联合运行时，年发电量 15 695 万 kW·h。

（4）东义电站，为干流梯级开发的第四级电站，采用混合式开发。东义水库规划正常蓄水位 2288.5m，死水位2210m，正常蓄水位以下库容18 520万 m^3，调节库容15 845万 m^3，具有年调节能力。电站规划装机容量106MW，年发电量43 825万kW·h。

(5) 色苦电站，为东义河干流梯级开发的第五级电站，采用引水式开发，具有日调节能力。电站装机容量51MW，单独运行时，年发电量20 897万kW·h；与上游卡斯、东义电站联合运行时，年发电量23 170万kW·h。

(6) 益地电站，为东义河干流梯级开发规划中的第六级，采用引水式开发，具有日调节能力。电站装机容量168MW，单独运行时，多年平均年发电量69 950万kW·h；与东义水电站联合运行时，多年平均发电量73 740万kW·h。

2. 东义河支流龙达河梯级

龙达河为东义河的最大支流，规划采取两级开发，即俄椏和洋那水电站，总装机容量51MW。

(1) 洋那电站，为东义河支流龙达河规划两级开发的第一级电站，采用引水式开发，规划装机容量25MW，年发电量11 935万kW·h。

(2) 俄椏电站，为东义河支流龙达河规划的第二级电站，采用闸坝引水式开发，无调节性能。电站装机容量26MW，年发电量10 742万kW·h。

3. 东义河6个支沟电站基本情况

东义河稻城境内6个支沟电站总装机容量49.4MW，均为单级开发，开发任务单一，建设工期较短。

(1) 往子沟电站，位于东义河支流往子沟上，采用引水式开发，无调节性能。电站装机容量7.4MW，年发电量3334万kW·h。

(2) 夹依龙巴电站，位于东义河支流夹依龙巴沟上，采用引水式开发，无调节性能。电站装机容量6.4MW，年发电量2897万kW·h。

(3) 小水牙电站，位于东义河支流小水牙沟上，采用引水式开发，无调节性能。电站装机容量4.2MW，年发电量1955万kW·h。

(4) 高羊古电站，位于东义河支流高羊古沟上，采用引水式开发，无调节性能。电站装机容量4.4MW，年发电量1984万kW·h。

(5) 尼隆沟电站，位于东义河支流尼隆沟上，采用引水式开发，无调节性能。电站装机容量17MW，年发电量7726万kW·h。

(6) 开江宫电站，位于东义河支流开江宫沟上，采用引水式开发，无调节性能。电站装机容量10MW，年发电量4609万kW·h。

(三) 项目进展情况

1. 项目前期工作情况

尼隆、浪都水电站开展了预可行性研究，完成外业勘测工作；东义电站开展了预可行性研究阶段的勘测，启动了东义电站坝址和色苦电站厂址的联合设计优化工作；完成了色苦电站外业勘测工作；益地电站预可研报告已由四川省发展改革委完成审查，正在开展正常蓄水位和施工总布置专题报告的编制。完成往子沟、夹依龙巴沟电站可研报告审查，并取得甘孜州发展改革委关于两座电站的可研报告审查意见。

支流小水牙、高羊古、尼隆沟、开江宫电站已取得甘孜州发展改革委关于开展前期工作的批复，同时取得甘孜州发展改革委同意上述支流电站开展预可行性研究工作的通知；其中小水牙水电站已完成水土保持方案、水资源论证、行洪与河势稳定论证、环保报告的专题审查等，并将电站可行性研究报告（送审稿）上报至甘孜州发展改革委待审。

高羊古、尼隆沟、开江宫电站的环境影响与评价审查申报表已上报甘孜州环保局待审；水土保持方案、水资源论证、行洪与河势稳定论证已由设计院完成编制，近期将提交相关部门审查。

2. 配套工程建设情况

(1) 东义河沿河通村公路工程。制约益地、色苦等电站开发的主要因素——东义河沿河通村公路工程正加紧向前推进，该段道路工程分为稻城县、木里(1)、木里(2)三个标段。稻城县标段全长10.88km，已完成道路开挖及平整工作，初步具备通车条件；木里(1)标段全长7.6km，已完成了6km的道路开挖工作；木里(2)标段公路全长11.71km，已完成道路开挖及平整工作，整个沿河道路工程有望2010年5月初全线贯通，并基本具备通车条件。

(2) 东义河往子沟通村公路工程。东义河往子沟通村公路工程为往子沟水电站进场施工道路。公路全长9.1km，已完成约3.5km的道路开挖工作。其中，往子沟电站引水隧洞3号支洞已经具备进场施工条件。

3. 电力输出工程

东义河流域地处偏远的四川西南部，属川藏高原地区，所在地尚无国家电网，电力输出是一个亟待解决的问题。为此，公司十分重视，积极协调，于2009年3月顺利取得东义河流域电力输出规划方案的批复。目前，正在开展往子沟、夹依龙巴和益地电站的接入系统方案设计工作。

（中国国电集团公司）

柳江梯级规划

(一) 柳江概况

柳江是珠江流域西江水系的第二大支流，是珠江流域的重要跨省界河流，流域面积为58 520km²，涉及黔、桂、湘三省（自治区）8个州（市）的34个县。柳江干流全长750.5km，上游都柳江绝大部分为中高山峡谷，中游融江多为低山丘陵地区，龙江汇合口以下的柳江为低山丘陵与台地平原相间地区。由于柳江流域面积的98.9%在黔、桂两省，地理位置较偏、少数民族聚居、基础设施和区域经济发展较为滞后，贫困人口众多，尤其是都柳江干流经过的独山、三都、榕江、从江、三江等县，均为国家级贫困县。

（二）已有规划情况

为开发利用柳江干流水资源，从20世纪50年代末期就开始了柳江干流水资源的设计研究工作，主要有以下几次规划（普查）：1959年原珠江流域规划办公室编制的《珠江流域开发治理方案》（草案）提出柳江采用5级开发方案、1979年全国水力资源普查成果题提出8级开发方案、1989年珠委西江局编制《珠江流域西江水系柳江综合利用规划报告》提出9级开发方案（以下简称“89规划方案”）。历次规划成果中“89规划方案”被纳入《珠江流域综合规划报告》，对指导干流梯级开发发挥了重要作用。“89规划方案”提出柳江干流以航运、水力发电、防洪统筹兼顾的综合开发任务，自上而下推荐了榕江、板寨、从江、洋溪、麻石、浮石、古顶、大埔和红花9级开发方案。目前，柳江中下游的麻石、浮石、大埔、红花、古顶梯级已相继建成，而洋溪以上的都柳江干流4个梯级，由于库区淹没大，且淹没区几乎都在贵州省境内，贵州省土地资源匮乏，淹没造成的移民安置困难，由此制约了规划梯级的实施。

（三）梯级开发情况

“89规划方案”提出柳江干流以航运、水力发电、防洪统筹兼顾的水资源综合开发任务，从上到下推荐了榕江、板寨、从江、洋溪、麻石、浮石、古顶、大埔和红花9级开发方案，总装机容量为954.6MW，多年平均发电量46.94亿kW·h（联合运行）。

目前，柳江干流水资源开发以水电开发为主，其中，都柳江干流水资源开发利用程度较低，已建电站规模较小，总计13.15MW，主要有三都—从江河段已建的红岩电站（榕江县城上游，1982年建成），装机容量2.5MW，永福电站装机容量7.5MW（1994年建成）；而干流中下游的融江和柳江“89规划方案”各梯级均已相继建成，即麻石（1972年建成）、浮石（2002年建成）、古顶（2006年建成）、大埔（2004年建成）、红花（2005年建成），装机容量分别为100MW、54MW、80MW、90.4MW、220MW，比“89规划方案”装机容量大41.9MW，多年平均发电量相应增加2.17亿kW·h。现状情况下，柳江干流已建电站装机容量为557.55MW，占干流理论蕴藏量1091.1MW的51.1%。

柳江干流已建规划梯级基本情况见表1。

表1 柳江干流已建规划梯级基本情况表

项目		单位	红岩	永福	麻石	浮石	古顶	大埔	红花
所在河流			都柳江	都柳江	融江	融江	融江	融江	柳江
综合利用			发电	发电	发电、航运	发电、航运	发电、航运	发电、航运	发电、航运
开发方式			引水式	坝后式	河床式	河床式	河床式	坝后式	河床式
坝址以上集水面积		km²	4157	6675	19 940	21 870	24 273	26 765	46 770
多年平均流量		m³/s	91.4	146	575	618	724	790	1260
校核洪水	频率	P（%）	1		0.2	0.33	0.1	0.33	0.05
	水位	m	254.98		139.9	121.35	113.37	101.78	93.05
设计洪水	频率	P（%）	5		2	2	2	2	1
	水位	m	253.36		136.3	117.82	109.74	98.1	86.43
正常蓄水位		m	248	238	134	113	102	93	77.5
死水位		m			130	110.2	101.5	92	77
调节性能			无调节	无调节	日调节	无调节	日调节	日调节	日调节
电站尾水位		m	239.7	229.2			94.15		

续表

项　目	单位	红岩	永福	麻石	浮石	古顶	大埔	红　花
装机容量	MW	2.5	7.5	100	54	80	90.4	220
保证出力	MW		1.14	17.9	12.7	12.464	18.7	27.4
多年平均发电量	亿 kW·h	0.15	0.38	4.55	2.878	3.3181	4.52	8.8
年利用小时数	h	6010	5110	4550	5329	4147	5000	4001
最大坝高	m			30.6	28.9	23.6	35.3	67.65
通航建筑物（长×宽×门槛水深）	m		（预留）	47.5×8×1.2	80×8×1.5	80×8×1.5	80×8×1.5	180×18×3
建成时间		1982 年	1994 年	1973 年	2002 年	2006 年	2004 年	2005 年

（四）梯级开发存在的主要问题

（1）水力资源丰富，但开发程度不高。根据柳江流域水力资源复查结果，都柳江干流水力资源丰富，可开发潜力较大，但由于历次规划提出的开发方式均采取高坝大库的形式，造成耕地淹没和动迁人口较多，投资大且移民安置困难，如榕江梯级将淹没三都县的拉揽、打鱼、坝街，榕江县的新华、定威、八开、腊西、下都江等乡镇，规划淹没耕地 26 346 亩，迁移人口 51 180 人（2004 年指标），实施难度大，致使都柳江干流水力资源迟迟不能开发，丰富的水能资源未能造福于当地社会。

（2）干流已建工程实施时与“89 规划方案”目标有差距。“89 规划方案”确定柳江的开发任务为防洪、航运、发电统筹兼顾，综合开发，部分河段是以航运为主。柳江流域水系具有发展航运的优越条件，但由于种种原因，流域内水运发展缓慢，与同时期的铁路、公路、民航事业相比明显处于落后地位，水运在交通运输中所占比重逐年下降，不能适应国民经济发展的需求，是当前交通运输网络中最薄弱的环节。而在都柳江河段，已建的红岩梯级未能考虑航运要求，永福梯级也仅留有 50t 级的航道位置，造成了都柳江事实上已断行。而融江河段的浮石、古顶和大埔的航道均按 100t 级规模建设，1972 年建成的麻石电站航道尺寸仅能通航 50t 船舶，与“89 规划方案”和航运部门要求的 300t 级航道要求不相应，使得柳江优越的水运条件未能得到充分发挥。仅有 2005 年初建成的红花水电站，其航道建设规模符合航运部门要求的 1000t 级标准。

（五）调整规划情况

随着经济社会的发展，都柳江干流原规划方案引起的淹没耕地和移民问题更加突出，省际间矛盾加大，以建设高坝大库追求电站效益的河流开发方式与国家新时期的治水思路及社会环境的承受能力不相协调，规划方案的实施难度进一步加大。为此，为了加快开发利用上游都柳江水力资源，造福贫困地区，“89 规划方案”实施以来又先后提出了以下梯级规划调整方案：1995 年贵州省院编制《贵州省都柳江干流（贵州河段）梯级开发方案研究报告》、2003 年 12 月《中华人民共和国水力资源普查成果·珠江流域》、2005 年 12 月贵州省院提出《贵州省都柳江干流水电开发规划报告》及 2006 年 3 月的补充材料。

以上调整规划成果尚未得到正式审批，而随着流域内经济社会不断发展及水资源开发程度的不断提高，对柳江的开发利用提出了新的要求，迫切需要与时俱进地编制新一轮流域规划，指导和规范建设项目，不仅是地区经济发展的迫切需要，也是水行政管理部门实施管理的需要。2003 年，水利部珠江水利委员会（以下简称珠江委）以珠水规计［2003］55 号文上报了“柳江流域综合利用规划任务书”，水利部以水规计［2005］356 号文对任务书进行了批复。2005 年 7 月，珠江委在柳州市主持召开了柳江综合规划修编工作会议，成立了珠江水利委员会、贵州省水利厅、广西自治区的规划修编领导小组，正式启动柳江规划修编工作。中水珠江规划勘测设计有限公司于 2009 年 7 月提出《柳江干流梯级补充规划报告》，并计划在 2010 年初提出《珠江流域西江水系柳江综合规划修编报告》。这些成果将纳入《珠江流域综合规划修编》报告中。

本次调整后的柳江干流规划方案为白梓桥、柳叠、坝街、寨比、榕江、红岩（扩机、改建）、永福（扩机）、温寨、朗洞、大融、从江、梅林、洋溪、麻石、浮石、古顶、大埔、红花 18 个梯级，总装机容量 961.2MW，详见表 2。

表 2 柳江干流推荐方案技术指标成果表

序号	项目		单位	白梓桥	柳叠	坝街	寨比	榕江	红岩	
									总规模（改建）	原有
1	梯级序号			(1)	(2)	(3)	(4)	(5)	(6)	
2	所在河流			都柳江	都柳江	都柳江	都柳江	都柳江	都柳江	
3	建设地点		县、市	三都	三都	三都	榕江	榕江	榕江	
4	建设性质			新建	新建	新建	新建	新建	改建	
5	综合利用			航运/发电	航运/发电	航运/发电	防洪/航运/发电	航运/发电	航运/发电	
6	坝址以上集水面积		km^2	1580	2444	2846	3811	4127	4157	
7	多年平均流量		m^3/s	35.5	54.2	62.9	83.8	90.7	91.4	
8	校核洪水	频率	P（%）	0.5	0.1	0.1	0.05	0.1	1	
9		流量	m^3/s	5760	9710	10 600	13 800	13 100	8860	
10		水位	m	381.25	360.69	335.21	312.78	270.28	254.98	
11	设计洪水	频率	P(%)	3.33	1	1	0.2	1	5	
12		流量	m^3/s	3600	6470	7080	11 300	8820	5980	
13		水位	m	381.2	357.48	331.75	310.64	267.23	253.36	
14	正常蓄水位		m	381.2	357.2	331.5	310	267	248	
15	死水位		m	380.5	355		300			
16	正常蓄水位相应库容		万 m^3	984	2170	2080	12 100	2130	43.3	
17	调节库容		万 m^3	90	460		5930			
18	调节性能			日调节	日调节	无调节	季调节	无调节	无调节	
19	最大毛水头		m	24	25.7	21.5	43	19	8.3	
20	最小净水头		m	23.28	24.93	20.85	32.01	18.43	8.05	
21	算术平均水头		m	23.28	24.93	20.85	40.3	18.43	8.05	
22	出力加权平均水头		m	23.28	24.93	20.85	41.14	18.43	8.05	
23	装机容量	单独运行	万 kW	0.63	1.5	1.7	4.4	1.8	0.7	0.25
24		联合运行		0.63	1.5	1.7	4.4	2.3	0.85	0.25
25	多年平均发电量	单独运行	亿 kW·h	0.266 3	0.566 2	0.596 8	1.617 1	0.727 1	0.303 6	0.150 3
26		联合运行		0.266 3	0.566 2	0.596 8	1.617 1	0.813 8	0.336 4	0.169
27	装机利用小时数	单独运行	h	4226	3775	3511	3675	4039	4337	6010
28		联合运行		4226	3775	3511	3675	3538	3957	6760
29	保证出力（$P=90\%$）	单独运行	万 kW	0.06	0.14	0.14	0.52	0.2	0.09	
30		联合运行		0.06	0.14	0.14	0.52	0.26	0.11	
31	水量利用率	单独运行	%	43.39	56.34	61.14	63.18	58.48	55.42	
32		联合运行		43.39	56.34	61.14	63.18	65.02	60.99	
33	水库淹没耕地		亩	30	400	920	945	352	60	
34	迁移人口		人		234	771	1716	293	45	
35	工程静态总投资（不含通航设施）		万元	10 440	15 571	20 281	39 548	23 637	13 706	
36	单位千瓦投资（不含通航设施）		元/kW	16 571	10 381	11 930	8988	10 277	22 843	
37	单位电度投资（不含通航设施）		元/(kW·h)	3.92	2.75	3.4	2.45	2.9	7.36	
38	工程静态总投资（含通航设施）		万元	18 117	23 322	26 991	49 855	29 879	25 295	

续表

序号	项目		单位	永福			温寨	郎洞	大融	从江	梅林
				总规模	新增	原有					
1	梯级序号			(7)			(8)	(9)	(10)	(11)	(12)
2	所在河流			都柳江			都柳江	都柳江	都柳江	都柳江	都柳江
3	建设地点		县、市	榕江			从江	从江	从江	从江	从江
4	建设性质			扩机			新建	新建	新建	新建	新建
5	综合利用			航运/发电			航运/发电	航运/发电	航运/发电	航运/发电	航运/发电
6	坝址以上集水面积		km^2	6675			6851	8564	8632	10 111	11 160
7	多年平均流量		m^3/s	146			150	191	192	227	253
8	校核洪水	频率	$P(\%)$				0.1	0.1	0.1	0.5	0.1
9		流量	m^3/s				17 400	19 300	19 400	16 400	21 700
10		水位	m				235.38	224.13	209.94	194.45	187.7
11	设计洪水	频率	$P(\%)$				1	1	1	3.33	1
12		流量	m^3/s				11 900	13 300	13 400	11 200	15 200
13		水位	m				231.74	220.78	207.24	191.46	187.5
14	正常蓄水位		m	238			229.2	217	207	191	176
15	死水位		m								167.3
16	正常蓄水位相应库容		万 m^3	980			2150	1290	2300	846	3900
17	调节库容		万 m^3								
18	调节性能			无调节			无调节	无调节	无调节	无调节	日调节
19	最大毛水头		m	8.8			12.2	10	16	14.5	13
20	最小净水头		m	8.54			11.83	9.7	15.52	14.06	0
21	算术平均水头		m	8.54			11.83	9.7	15.52	14.06	6.5
22	出力加权平均水头		m	8.54			11.83	9.7	15.52	14.06	11.5
23	装机容量	单独运行	万 kW	1.3	0.55	0.75	1.9	1.9	3.2	3.3	3.9
24		联合运行		1.6	0.85	0.75	2.4	2.4	4	4	3.9
25	多年平均发电量	单独运行	亿 kW·h	0.549 3	0.166 1	0.383 2	0.794 7	0.831 4	1.365 6	1.453 8	1.37
26		联合运行		0.604	0.220 8	0.383 2	0.879 6	0.919 1	1.499 5	1.579 1	1.378
27	装机利用小时数	单独运行	h	4226	3020	5110	4182	4376	4268	4406	3523
28		联合运行		3775	2598	5110	3665	3829	3749	3948	3533
29	保证出力($P=90\%$)	单独运行	万 kW	0.17	0.06	0.11	0.24	0.27	0.44	0.47	0.386
30		联合运行		0.19	0.06	0.13	0.27	0.28	0.46	0.49	0.416
31	水量利用率	单独运行	%	59.29		51.2	60.04	60.23	61.46	61.15	
32		联合运行		64.91		51.2	66.19	66.37	67.27	66.24	
33	水库淹没耕地		亩				250	90	190	30	675
34	迁移人口		人				209	75	160	25	0
35	工程静态总投资(不含通航设施)		万元		6261		23 572	25 402	31 472	28 590	99 112
36	单位千瓦投资(不含通航设施)		元/kW		7366		9822	10 584	7868	7148	25 413
37	单位电度投资(不含通航设施)		元/(kW·h)		2.84		2.68	2.76	2.1	1.81	7.23
38	工程静态总投资(含通航设施)		万元		10 584		29 810	31 229	38 430	35 267	110 700

续表

序号	项目		单位	梅林	洋溪	麻石	浮石	古顶	大埔	红花
1	梯级序号			(12)	(13)	(14)	(15)	(16)	(17)	(18)
2	所在河流			都柳江	都柳江	融江	融江	融江	融江	柳江
3	建设地点		县、市	从江	从江	融安	融安	融水	柳城	柳州市
4	建设性质			新建	新建	已建	已建	在建	已建	已建
5	综合利用			航运/发电	防洪/航运/发电	航运/发电	航运/发电	航运/发电	航运/发电	航运/发电
6	坝址以上集水面积		km^2	11 160	13 165	19 940	21 870	24 273	26 765	46 770
7	多年平均流量		m^3/s	253	296	575	618	724	790	1260
8	校核洪水	频率	$P(\%)$	0.1	0.05	0.2	0.33	0.1	0.33	0.05
9		流量	m^3/s	21 700	25 300	25 000	27 300	36 000	30 600	44 800
10		水位	m	187.7	187.2	139.9	121.35	113.37	101.78	93.05
11	设计洪水	频率	$P(\%)$	1	1	2	2	2	2	1
12		流量	m^3/s	15 200	16 500	18 000	20 700	23 800	23 400	32 700
13		水位	m	187.5	187.2	136.3	117.82	109.74	98.1	86.43
14	正常蓄水位		m	176	163	134	113	102	93	77.5
15	死水位		m	167.3	162.5	130	110.2	101.5	92	77
16	正常蓄水位相应库容		万 m^3	3900	1716	16 050	11 500	6915	23 700	57 000
17	调节库容		万 m^3		720	6250		440	2340	2900
18	调节性能			日调节	日调节	日调节	无调节	日调节	日调节	日调节
19	最大毛水头		m	13	28.17	21.2	13.46	10	15.6	17
20	最小净水头		m	0	10	10	3	3.9	4	10.42
21	算术平均水头		m	6.5	19.09					
22	出力加权平均水头		m	11.5	26.54					
23	装机容量	单独运行	万 kW	3.9	12	10	5.4	8	9.04	22
24		联合运行		3.9	12	10	5.4	8	9.04	22
25	多年平均发电量	单独运行	亿 kW·h	1.37	4.28	4.55	2.878	3.318 1	4.52	8.8
26		联合运行		1.378	4.304	4.573	2.890 6	3.324 3	4.537 7	8.811 1
27	装机利用小时数	单独运行	h	3523	3567	4550	5329	4147	5000	4001
28		联合运行		3533	3587	4573	5353	4155	5020	4005
29	保证出力($P=90\%$)	单独运行	万 kW	0.386	1.34	1.79	1.27	1.25	1.87	2.74
30		联合运行		0.416	1.39	1.85	1.31	1.28	1.89	2.76
31	水量利用率	单独运行	%				72.9	71.2	62.4	64.2
32		联合运行								
33	水库淹没耕地		亩	675	3215					
34	迁移人口		人	0	5223					
35	工程静态总投资(不含通航设施)		万元	99 112	309 167					
36	单位千瓦投资(不含通航设施)		元/kW	25 413	25 764					
37	单位电度投资(不含通航设施)		元/(kW·h)	7.23	7.22					
38	工程静态总投资(含通航设施)		万元	110 700	339 232					

(中水珠江规划勘测设计有限公司 陈俊贤)

功果桥水电站水能利用综述

功果桥水电站坝是澜沧江中下游河段梯级规划开发的第一个梯级电站，下游为在建的小湾水电站，上游为规划的苗尾水电站。坝址控制流域面积 9.72 万 km^2，多年平均流量 1010m^3/s，多年平均径流量 318.51 亿 m^3。功果桥水电站以发电为主，水库正常蓄水位 1307m，相应库容 3.16 亿 m^3，调节库容 0.49 亿 m^3，为日调节水库。电站装机容量 900MW，年发电量 40.41 亿 kW·h。功果桥水电站的供电范围为云南省电网，将作为保证云电外送及省内用电的重要电源。

（一）正常蓄水位选择

功果桥水电站在可行性研究阶段，正常蓄水位拟定 1306m、1307m、1308m、1309m 共 4 个方案进行比选。

该电站正常蓄水位抬高，其装机容量、年平均发电量和工程总投资等都随之增加。水位从 1306m 起，每增加 1m，差额电量单位电度投资分别 2.45、3.17、4.82 元/(kW·h)；差额经济内部收益率分别为 9.30%、6.19%、1.73%。正常蓄水 1306m 增至 1307m，增加电量单位电度投资为 2.45 元/(kW·h)，差额经济内部收益率大于 8%。正常蓄水 1307m 增至 1308m 以及自 1308m 增至 1309m，差额经济内部收益率分别降至 6.19%、1.73%，小于 8%的基准收益。说明在上游古水电站投入前功果桥电站正常蓄水位（考虑与上游苗尾电站尾水位衔接因素）不宜高于 1307m。

在古水水库调节后，该工程年平均发电量有所增加。正常蓄水位从 1306m 起，每增加 1m，发电量依次净增加 0.28 亿、0.22 亿、0.18 亿 kW·h，差额经济内部收益率分别为 10.82%、7.30%、3.60%。差额电量单位电度投资分别 2.19、2.88、4.01 元/(kW·h)。当正常蓄水 1306m 增至 1307m，差额经济内部收益率大于 8%，而从 1307m 增至 1308m 及 1308m 增至 1309m 时，差额经济内部收益率降至 7.3%、3.6%，小于 8%的基准收益，经济性较差。说明考虑古水电站投入后，功果桥电站正常蓄水位亦不宜高于 1307m。

根据回水计算成果，功果桥水电站蓄水位 1306m、1307m、1308m、1309m，枯水期（流量 400m^3/s 左右）苗尾电站尾水位分别抬高 3.48m、4.36m、5.31m、6.28m；流量 1000m^3/s 时（约为平均流量），苗尾电站尾水位分别抬高 2.73m、3.36m、4.18m、5.05m。当水位从 1307m 增加到 1308m 时，仅多利用水头 0.15m，相当于功果桥水电站正常蓄水位提高 1m，净得水头 0.15m，增幅已较小。

功果桥水库淹没损失不对正常蓄水位方案比选产生制约性作用。从环境保护角度分析，功果桥水电站工程正常蓄水位变化的环境影响效应不明显。

综上所述，结合工程地质地形条件、水库淹没情况，功果桥水电站正常蓄水位推荐为 1307m。

（二）装机容量选择

可行性研究阶段装机容量比选方案拟定为 860MW、900MW、940MW、980MW 共四个方案进行比较。方案比较中采用云南省新投产机组标杆上网电价 0.305 3 元/(kW·h)计算发电效益；费用计算中，水电运行费率取固定资产投资的 2.0%；经济基准收益率采用 8%。

综合分析比较认为功果桥水电站单独运行情况下电站装机容量以 900MW 为宜，相应的年利用小时 4490h。位于功果桥水电站上游的古水水库具有年调节能力，能够对功果桥水电站的发电出力过程进行补偿。经过电力电量平衡计算，各方案吸收电量差与单独运行吸收电量差相同，说明古水水库调节后，功果桥水电站装机容量亦为 900MW，相应的年利用小时为 4657h，基本可满足外送电源年利用小时数要求。

综上所述，从动能经济比较分析，功果桥水电站装机容量在 900MW 左右比较合适；从云南、广东电力市场需求情况分析，功果桥水电站装机容量 900MW 左右均可被系统吸收。因此，功果桥水电站可行性研究阶段选择装机容量 900MW。

（三）经济评价

功果桥水电站工程装机容量 900MW，多年平均年发电量 40.41 亿 kW·h，固定资产投资 792 906 万元，单位千瓦投资 8810 元/kW，单位电度投资 1.96 元/(kW·h)；总投资 919 774 万元，单位千瓦投资 10 220 元/kW，单位电度投资 2.28 元/(kW·h)。

以资本金财务内部收益率 10%，经营期出厂电价为 0.271 5 元/(kW·h)[含增值税为 0.317 7 元/(kW·h)]，投资回收期 14.2 年，全部投资财务内部收益率为 8.57%(税后)，投资利润率为 5.26%，投资利税率为 7.48%，资本金利润率 25.56%。

以全部投资内部收益率(税后)8%，经营期出厂电价为 0.253 0 元/(kW·h)[含增值税为0.296 0元/(kW·h)]，投资回收期 14.7 年，资本金财务内部收益率 8.61%，投资利润率为 4.38%，投资利税率为 6.45%，资本金利润率 21.27%。

功果桥水电站建成后，每年向电网提供 40.41 亿 kW·h 电量（古水投入后将增加为 41.91 亿 kW·h），可缓解能源紧缺问题，减轻火电机组对环境的污染，优化电网电源结构，有利于社会经济的可持续发展。该项目在经济上是合理的，财务上是可行的，而且社会经济效益显著。

（华能澜沧江水电有限公司　李云汉　肖海斌）

贵州省芙蓉江沙阡水电站规划调整

根据贵州省发展和改革委员会通知，经贵州省水利厅组织对开发方案进行技术审查，同意芙蓉江良坎至鱼塘河段由原一级开发（沙阡 516m）方案调整为两级开发（土溪 516m+沙阡 503m）方案。

芙蓉江是乌江最大的一级支流，地跨贵州、重庆两省市，发源于贵州省绥阳县的石翁子，流经黔渝两省市八县，于重庆市武隆县江口镇汇入乌江。干流全长 233km，主河道平均比降 2.84‰，全流域面积 7793km²，其中贵州省境内河段长 194.1km，流域面积 6859km²，占全流域面积的 88.0%，贵州省内河段水力资源理论蕴藏量 597.7MW。

1992 年，贵州省计委批复同意的芙蓉江规划梯级开发方案为小河口（655m）＋朱老村（621.5m）＋牛都（605m）＋田坝（570m）＋良坎（548.3m）＋沙阡（516m）＋鱼塘（465m）＋石门坎（409m）＋浩口（360～369m）＋江口（300m）共 10 级，装机容量 403.5MW。沙阡水电站（516m）是芙蓉江干流规划梯级中的第 6 级，位于贵州省北部正安县格林乡的芙蓉江干流河段上，电站距正安县城 9km，对外交通方便。规划沙阡水电站正常蓄水位 516m，与上游已建成的良坎电站尾水位衔接，沙阡水电站尾水接下游已建成的鱼塘电站正常蓄水位 465m，电站利用落差 51m。

随着社会经济的发展，沙阡水电站正常蓄水位 516m 的方案水库淹没较大，经济指标较差，为了尽量减少水库淹没，合理利用水力资源，提高资源开发利用效益，中国水电顾问集团贵阳勘测设计研究院于 2009 年 10 月开始开展沙阡水电站开发方案论证工作，2009 年 12 月完成了论证报告。经本次研究，原规划沙阡水电站河段现分为两级开发。一级土溪水电站坝址位于芙蓉江干流良坎坝址下游约 3.5km 处，水库正常蓄水位 516m，装机容量 8MW，多年平均年发电量 2661 万 kW·h，装机年利用小时 3326h。二级沙阡水电站坝址位于芙蓉江干流正安县鱼塘河段，鱼塘大桥上游 300m，原规划沙阡水电站上坝址处，水库正常蓄水位 503m，装机容量 50MW，多年平均年发电量 15 717 万 kW·h，装机年利用小时 3143h。两级电站坝址间河道距离 14.2km。

（中国水电顾问集团贵阳勘测设计研究院　龚兰强）

风　能　开　发

我国的风能资源与风力发电

风能是取之不尽、用之不竭、洁净无污染的可再生能源。发展风力发电对于调整能源结构、减轻环境污染、解决能源危机等方面有着非常重要的意义。我国风能资源丰富，风力发电建设速度迅猛。

（一）风能资源

我国风能资源丰富，据最新风能资源普查初步统计成果，我国陆上离地 10m 高度风能资源总储量约 43.5 亿 kW，居世界第一位。其中，技术可开发量为 2.5 亿 kW，技术可开发面积约 20 万 km²，此外，还有潜在技术可开发量约 7900 万 kW。另外，海上 10m 高度可开发和利用的风能储量约为 7.5 亿 kW。全国 10m 高度可开发和利用的风能储量超过 10 亿 kW，仅次于美国、俄罗斯居世界第三位。陆上风能资源丰富的地区主要分布在三北地区（东北、华北、西北）、东南沿海及附近岛屿。

1. “三北”（东北、华北、西北）地区风能丰富带　包括东北三省、河北、内蒙古、甘肃、青海、西藏和新疆等省（自治区）近 200km 宽的地带，风功率密度在 200～300W/m² 以上，有的可达 500W/m² 以上，可开发利用的风能储量约 2 亿 kW，占全国可利用储量的 80%。另外，该地区风电场地形平坦，是我国连成一片的最大风能资源区，有利于大规模开发风电场。

2. 东南沿海地区风能丰富带　沿海及其岛屿风能丰富带，年有效风功率密度在 200W/m² 以上，风功率密度线平行于海岸线，沿海岛屿风功率密度在 500W/m² 以上，如台山、平潭、东山、南鹿、大陈、嵊泗、南澳、马祖、马公、东沙等，年有效风速（4～25m/s）时数约在 7000～8000h。这一地区特别是东南沿海，由海岸向内陆是丘陵连绵，风能丰富地区仅在距海岸50km之内。

3. 内陆局部风能丰富区　在两个风能丰富带之外，风功率密度一般在$100W/m^2$以下，年有效风速（4～25m/s）时数在3000h以下。但是在一些地区由于湖泊和特殊地形的影响，如鄱阳湖附近较周围地区风能就大，湖南衡山、湖北的九宫山、河南的嵩山、山西的五台山、安徽的黄山、云南太华山等也较平地风能为大。

4. 海上风能丰富区　我国海上风能资源丰富，10m高度可利用的风能资源约7.5亿kW。海上风速高，很少有静风期，可以有效利用风电机组发电容量。一般估计海上风速比平原沿岸高20%，发电量增加70%，在陆上设计寿命20年的风电机组在海上可达25～30年，而且海上风电场距离电力负荷中心很近。

图1和图2分别为中国全年风速大于3m/s小时数分布图和中国有效风功率密度分布图。

（二）风力发电

1. 风力发电的发展阶段　我国风力发电始于20世纪80年代，发展相对滞后，但起点较高，主要经历了三个重要的发展阶段。

（1）第一阶段（1985～1995年），为试验阶段，主要是利用丹麦、德国、西班牙政府贷款，进行一些小项目的示范，积累了大量的经验。同时国家“七五”“八五”设立的国产风机攻关项目，也取得了初步成果。

（2）第二阶段（1995～2003年），中国各级政府相继出台了各种优惠的鼓励政策。科技部通过科技攻关和国家863高科技项目促进了风电技术的发展，原经贸委、计委分别通过双加工程、国债项目、乘风计划等项目促进风电的持续发展。

（3）第三阶段（2003～至今），国家发展和改革委员会通过风电特许权经营，下放50MW以下风电项目审批权，要求国内风电项目风电机组设备国产化比例不小于70%等政策，扶持和鼓励国内风电制造业的发展。我国2006年新增装机容量1347MW，比以前翻了一番还多，比2005年增加106.4%，2006年风电累计装机容量为2604MW，是世界第6大市场；我国2007年新增装机容量3304MW，比2006年增加126.9%，2007年风电累计装机容量为5908MW，是世界第5大市场；我国2008年新增装机容量6300MW，比2007年增加106.6%，2008年风电累计装机容量为12 210MW，是世界第4大市场。

自从2006年1月1日开始实施《可再生能源法》后，中国风电市场稳步发展，2007年提前三年实现了2010年中国风电5000MW的发展目标，并且2008年新增装机容量超过了2007年以前装机容量的总和。

2. 风力发电现状　目前，我国的风电开发势头迅猛。主要表现在以下几个方面：

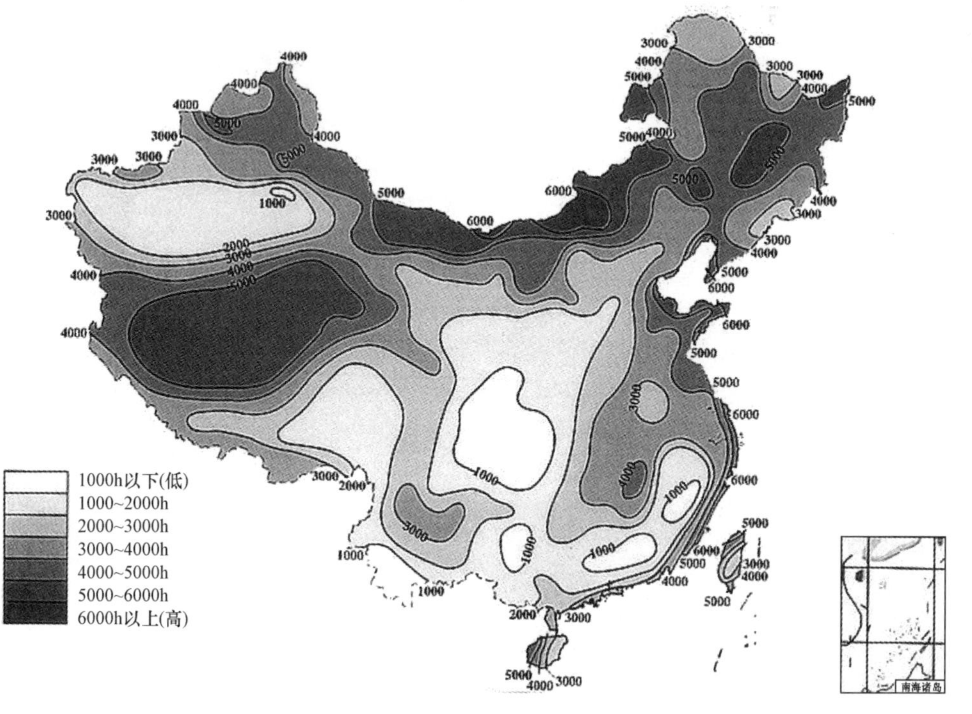

图1　中国全年风速大于3m/s小时数分布图

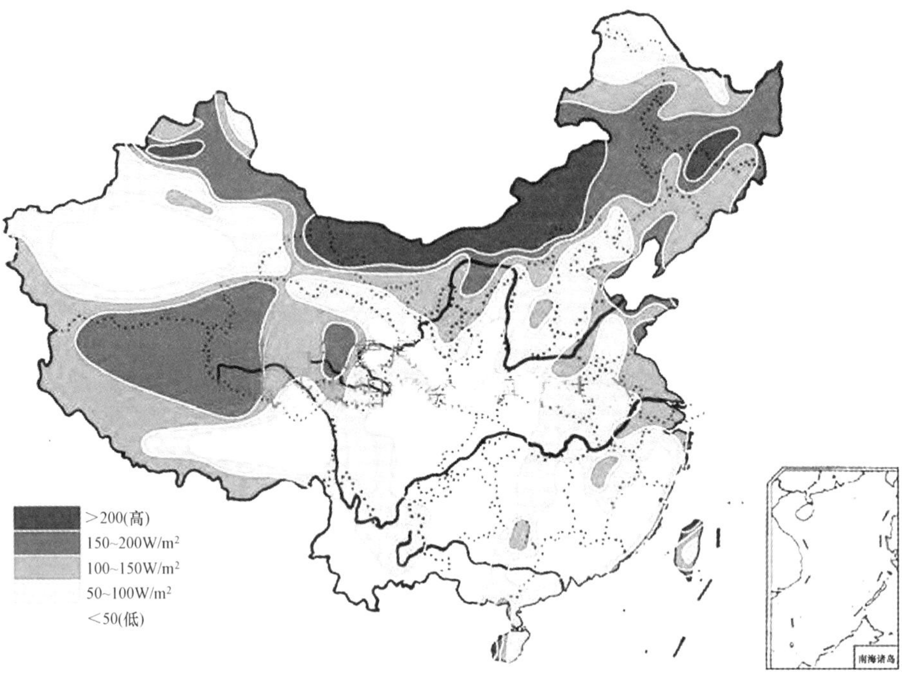

图 2 中国有效风功率密度分布图

（1）风电建设规模不断扩大，管理逐步规范。到2006年底，全国已建和在建的风电场约91个，装机总容量达到2604MW；到2007年底，全国已建和在建的风电场约158个，装机总容量达到5908MW；到2008年底，全国风电装机总容量达到12 210MW。单个风电场工程规模从过去的1万kW左右发展到目前最大的30万kW；风电场工程规划从过去的几万千瓦发展到目前的百万千瓦级、千万千瓦级风电基地。同时，有关部门正组织编制有关风电前期、建设和运行规程，风电场管理在逐步走向规范化。

（2）风电设备制造能力不断增强。我国风电设备制造起步较晚，2002年前后仅能小批量生产600kW级风电机组，而同期国际风电设备兆瓦级风电机组已经成为主流机型。目前，我国已基本掌握了大型风电机组的制造技术，全国已经生产或准备进入大型风电机组制造的整机生产企业有50多家，已能够批量生产单机容量为1.5兆瓦级的风电机组。与此同时，国内已有一批企业进入了风电机组零部件的配套生产，初步形成了风电设备制造和配套零部件专业化产业链。

（3）风电法规政策环境不断完善。为了促进可再生能源的发展，确立了可再生能源总量目标、强制上网、分类电价、费用分摊和专项资金等基本制度，国家发展改革委、财政部等有关政府部门研究制定了有关配套政策，为可再生能源的加快发展奠定了重要基础。

（4）风电发展前景良好。国家将把实施可持续发展战略放在更加突出的位置，按照国家能源局"打造陆上'三峡'、建设大基地、融入大电网"的风电开发和发展思路，我国将重点陆续建设甘肃酒泉、新疆哈密、河北坝上、蒙东和蒙西以及江苏沿海等千万千瓦级风电基地。目前，甘肃酒泉千万千瓦级风电基地首批开发项目已经开始建设，其他几个千万千瓦级风电基地规划已经通过审查。到2010年，全国风电累计装机容量预计超过2000万kW。到2020年，全国风电开发建设规模有望达到1亿kW，远远超过原先规划的3000万kW目标。风电技术水平和装备能力基本达到国际水平。

表1为我国1995～2008年风电装机容量统计表。

3. 风力发电趋势

（1）风力发电成本将大幅度降低。在过去20多年里，风力发电技术不断取得突破，规模经济性日益明显。增大风力发电机组的单机容量就减少了基础设施的投入费用，而且同样的装机容量需要更少数目的机组，节约了成本。随着融资成本的降低和开发商的经验丰富，项目开发的成本也相应得到降低。风力发电机组可靠性的改进也减少了运行维护的平均成本。

（2）风电设备国产化比例提高。2005年7月，国家发展改革委《关于风电建设管理有关要求的通知》中明确规定：风电设备国产化率要达到70%以上。实现风力发电技术装备国产化的目的是提高我国风力发电装备的制造能力和技术水平，降低风力发电

表 1　我国 1995～2008 年风电装机容量统计表　MW

年份	1995	1996	1997	1998	1999	2000	2001	2002	2003	2004	2005	2006	2007	2008
新增装机容量	23	41	91	54	44	76	56	68	98	197	503	1347	3304	6300
累计装机容量	38	79	170	224	268	344	400	468	567	764	1266	2604	5908	12 210
增长率（%）		107.9	115.2	31.8	19.6	28.4	16.3	17	20.9	34.7	65.8	106.4	126.9	106.6
	61.35													

成本，提高市场竞争能力，为推动我国风力发电技术大规模商业化发展奠定基础。

（3）海上风力发电悄然兴起并将成为重要能源形式。随着风力发电的发展，陆地上的风机总数将趋于饱和，海上风力发电场将成为未来发展的重点。海上发电也是近年来国际风力发电产业发展的新领域，是“方向中的方向”。我国海上风能资源储量远大于陆地风能资源储量，10m 高度可开发利用的风能资源超过 7.5 亿 kW，而且海上风电场距离电力负荷中心很近。到 2010 年，海上的风力发电总装机容量将达到 200～300MW。目前，我国正在进行江苏近海风电规划研究，上海已经开始海上风力发电项目的建设准备工作。上海东海大桥海上风电场示范工程位于杭州弯北岸，风电场布置在东海大桥两侧，设计装机容量为 102MW（34×3MW），年利用小时数 2624h，年上网电量 2.68 亿 kW·h。风电机组选用大连华锐 SL3000/90 型，目前该工程正在建设之中。

（4）风力发电机组不断向大型化发展。风力发电机组正不断向大型化发展。2002 年前后，国际风力发电市场上主流机型已经达到 1500kW 以上。目前，欧洲已批量生产安装 3600kW 风力发电机组，美国已研制成功 7000 kW 风力发电机组，而英国正在研制巨型风力发电机组，我国研制成功的最大功率风力发电机是 2000～3000kW，国产风电机组目前的主流机型为 1500kW。

4. 21 世纪中国风力发电展望（略）

（中国水电顾问集团西北勘测设计研究院　申宽育）

上海市海上风电场工程规划简介

（一）项目背景

开发新能源是我国能源发展战略的重要组成部分。为鼓励风力发电的发展，国家发展和改革委员会提出了到 2020 年全国建设 1 亿 kW 风电装机的目标，并配合国家颁布实施的《可再生能源法》，相继出台了《可再生能源发电有关管理规定》、《可再生能源发电价格和费用分摊管理试行办法》等政策，积极支持风能资源的开发。

2009 年国家能源局发布了《国家能源局关于印发海上风电场工程规划工作大纲的通知》（国能新能［2009］130 号）通知，要求沿海各省市做好海上风电场工程规划工作。

上海市位于东亚季风盛行区，受冬夏季风影响，风力资源较为丰富，尤其是近海区域，地域开阔、障碍物少，具有良好的风能资源开发利用价值。上海市发展和改革委员会对上海市的风能资源开发利用十分重视，为实现国家发展改革委和上海市制订的风电发展目标，促进中国海上风电场的发展，填补国内海上风电规划空白，上海市发展改革委委托上海勘测设计研究院开展上海市海上风电场工程规划工作。

编制上海市海上风电场工程规划是国家可再生能源和新能源发展规划的要求，要摸清资源和潜力，规划工作必须先行，为风电场建设和实施提供科学的、可靠的决策依据。

海上风电产业是新能源产业发展的重要领域，海上风电装备制造又是主要发展方向，积极开发上海市海上风能资源，是推进上海市风电产业发展的重要支撑；加大建设海上风电场的力度和步伐，彰显上海市的综合经济实力，提升城市形象，进一步带动上海市风力发电设备制造、海上工程施工、设计咨询、运行维护管理等相关产业的发展。

（二）工作过程

为了摸清上海海上风能资源和海上风电开发潜力，按照《国家能源局关于印发海上风电场工程规划工作大纲的通知》（国能新能［2009］130 号）的部署和要求，上海市发展改革委于 2009 年 5 月委托上海勘测设计研究院开展上海市海上风电场工程规划工作。上海勘测设计研究院于 2009 年 6 月编制完成了《上海市海上风电场工程规划选址报告》（送审稿），上海市发展改革委就海上风电场工程规划场址，发函征询了市建设交通委、经委、农委、规划局、环保局、海洋水务局、海事局、气象局、交通港口、崇明县、浦东新区、奉贤、金山、市规划设计院、市电力公司、东海风力发电有限公司、军事等单位的意见，并于 2009 年 7 月组织召开了征求意见会。根据以上相关职能部门和单位的具体书面意见和要求，对《上海市海上风电场工程规划选址报告》（送审稿）进行了相应的修改、对海上风电场规划选址方案进行调整和优化，形成了《上海市海上风电场工程规划选址报告》（审定稿）。

综合考虑《上海市海上风电场工程规划选址报告》（审定稿）、上海电网“十一五”发展规划及2020年远景目标等规划的基础上，按照《近海风电场工程规划报告编制办法（试行）》（FD005－2008），2009年11月编制完成了《上海市海上风电场工程规划报告》（送审稿）。2009年12月，国家能源局、水电水利规划设计总院在北京主持召开了《上海市海上风电场工程规划报告》审查会议，并形成初步审查意见，上海勘测设计研究院根据审查意见要求进行了修改、完善，最终形成《上海市海上风电场工程规划报告》（审定稿）。

（三）规划概况

《上海市海上风电场工程规划报告》按照“有效利用、保护环境、合理布局、有序开发”的规划思路，坚持以资源定规划、以规划定项目，先规划、后开发的原则；坚持开发利用与经济、社会和环境相协调的原则；坚持规范化开发与产业发展互相促进的原则。根据确定的规划范围和水平年，通过对上海海域的详尽调查论证，确定了规划风电场场址。同时对风电场的建设条件、接入系统、环境影响、开发规模及投资匡算进行了科学、详尽的分析，主要结论如下：

上海市近海海域具备建设大型海上风电场的条件。根据上海市海域风资源条件，从满足海洋功能区划、相关专业规划的要求；协调与城市规划、航运、渔业及环境生态保护的关系，具备较好的建设海上风电场条件出发，选择出东海大桥、奉贤、南汇、崇明、长江北支、横沙岛、金山、深远海域共8个区域海上风电场场址，推荐场址规划总面积约1449km²，总装机容量约595万kW。其中，潮间带及潮下带滩涂风电场规划总面积约89.9km²，总装机容量约30万kW；近海风电场规划总面积约1359km²，总装机容量约565万kW。

在东海大桥主通航孔以南至洋山深水港的洋山港海域，该报告规划了东海大桥洋山港海域场址，该场址规划面积约135.4km²，总装机容量约65万kW。考虑采用目前洋山深水港和东海大桥建设的运作模式，建议场址内海上风资源采取上海市和浙江省合作开发的模式。该报告将该区域作为一个独立的单元单独进行规划。

考虑海上风电场建设投资的均衡性，及电网对风电场接入的承受能力，结合规划风电场开发顺序，上海市海上风电场分期建设、滚动开发。2010年世博会前完成正在实施的东海大桥风电场（10万kW）建设；2010～2015年的前5年期间，近期优先开发东海大桥、奉贤、南汇大部分海上风电场，其装机规模达到40万～80万kW；2015～2020年期间的中期，后续开发东海大桥、奉贤、南汇余下的小部分风电场，以及崇明风电场，其装机规模达到65万～105万kW。2020～2030年的远期，后续开发奉贤、崇明、长江北支、横沙岛、金山、深远海域余下的风电场，其装机规模达到440万kW，到2030年底，争取实现上海市海上风电装机达到595万kW。

上海市海上风电场规划装机容量合计为595万kW，其中近海风电场单位千瓦投资约为23 000元/kW，滩涂风电场单位千瓦投资约为18 000元/kW，深远海域风电场单位千瓦投资约为26 000元/kW，匡算海上风电场工程投资约1587亿元（含东海大桥洋山港海域）。根据上海市海上风电场工程投资，按照资本金内部收益率8%的要求，参考已建海上风电场工程经验，初步测算含增值税的上网电价为1.0413元/(kW·h)（滩涂）～1.1866元/（kW·h)（海上）。

（四）规划意义及影响

《上海市海上风电场工程规划报告》是上海市“十二五”期间新能源产业发展的纲领性报告。

（1）该工程规划的必要性阐述透彻、论证充分翔实。风能资源是清洁的可再生能源，上海市近海风能资源丰富，沿海地区经济较发达，电力需求量大。开发利用海上风能资源，对于满足电力需求、改善能源结构、减少环境污染、应对全球气候变化、促进经济可持续健康发展具有重要作用，符合国家能源可持续发展战略的要求。

上海市位于东亚季风盛行区，受冬夏季风影响，风力资源较为丰富，尤其是近海区域，地域开阔、障碍物少，具有良好的风能资源开发利用价值。开发建设上海市海上风电场，符合国家能源结构调整和国民经济可持续发展战略的要求，是科学发展观在新能源领域的具体实践，同时对发展和推动我国风电设备产业建设具有重要现实意义。

本次编制上海市海上风电场工程规划，是国家可再生能源和新能源发展规划的要求，要摸清资源和潜力，规划工作必须先行。上海市海上风电场工程规划，为风电场建设和实施提供科学的、可靠的决策依据。

海上风电产业是新能源产业发展的重要领域，海上风电装备制造又是主要发展方向，积极开发上海市海上风能资源，是推进上海市风电产业发展的重要支撑；加大建设海上风电场的力度和步伐，彰显上海市的综合经济实力，提升城市形象，进一步带动上海市风力发电设备制造、海上工程施工、设计咨询、运行维护管理等相关产业的发展。

（2）规划工作方法及原则可靠，工程建设布局合理。本次规划提出了按照“有效利用、保护环境、合理布局、有序开发”的规划思路，坚持以资源定规划、以规划定项目，先规划、后开发的原则；坚持开发利用与经济、社会和环境相协调的原则；坚持规范化开发与产业发展互相促进的原则。上述规划原则符合可持续的科学发展观要求。本次规划在上海市5～15m水深内的海域规划近海风电场的基础上，对上海市沿海多年平均大潮高潮线以下至理论最低潮位以下5m水深内的潮间带和潮下带滩涂区域、理论最低潮位以下5～50 m水深内的海域风能资源丰富的场址进行分析研究，从风能资源、海洋水文、工程地质、接入电力系统、交通运输、施工安装及自然环保、投资匡算等方面进行比较，并综合考虑港口、航道、管线等其他用海需要，规划上海市海上风电场的装机规模共计595万kW，其中潮间带和潮下带滩涂风电场装机规模总计30万kW；近海风电场装机规模总计565万kW。并提出上海市海上风电场按照近、中、远期开发建设的工程布局是技术可行、经济合理，符合国家新能源发展战略及上海市新能源行业发展要求。

（3）海上风资源评估难度大，本次规划分析手段国内领先，成果合理。本次规划收集南汇、奉贤、东海大桥海上测风塔的实测资料，结合数值模拟技术分析，上海地区风资源以海上最大，西北部中部沿岸次之，由沿岸向内陆逐渐减小。根据TAMP模式计算结果，上海市海域10m高度层近海海域多年平均风速在5～6m/s之间，年平均风功率密度在150～250W/m^{2}之间；在90m高度层近海海域多年平均风速在7～8m/s之间，年平均风功率密度在350～500W/m^{2}之间；风能资源较为丰富，主风向为N和S～SE方向。本次规划采用国内外在风资源分析方法上最先进分析方法进行计算分析外，尤为重要地是利用我院多年在风资源分析中的经验，研究风沿海岸线及垂直海岸方向的变化情况，并对海上测风塔的测风数据建立数学模型，进行详细、深入的计算分析，对风电场风资源进行推算和验证，为风电场工程选址提供了依据。该分析方法在国内处于领先地位，并得到评审专家的好评。

（4）海上风电场建设条件分析全面，风电场选址合理。本次规划对上海市风电场区域的海洋水文及工程地质、风电机组基础结构型式、交通运输和施工安装条件等进行了全面分析，海上风电场的规划选址应尽量满足相关区划、规划的要求；协调与城市规划、海事、海洋、军事、航运、渔业及环境生态保护的关系；具备较好的水文地质、并网、交通运输和施工安装等场址建设条件和多方面综合考虑确定，海上风电场工程规划选址主要考虑：①场址区域具有丰富的风能资源；②规划风电场场址应符合上海市海洋功能区划及岸线规划；③避开港区、锚地、航道、通航密集区以及主管机关公布的航路；④避开军事用海限制区域；⑤避开通信、电力、油气等海底管线及其保护范围；⑥符合有关海洋自然环境保护规定；⑦不影响其他已明确的特殊用海，如科研活动、灾害观测、导航设施等；⑧考虑基础施工条件和施工设备要求，提高风电场建设的经济性，场址区域水深条件一般控制在5m以下和5m～50m范围内。选择出东海大桥、奉贤、南汇、崇明、长江北支、横沙岛、金山、深远海域共8个区域海上风电场场址合理可行。

（5）结合海上风机建设条件及布置，提出合理的规划装机容量。上海地区海上风能资源丰富，但可用于建设海上风电场的场地有限，尤其是场址地区地下管线众多，航道避让区域、上海和浙江海域分界线等，为最大限度地利用丰富的海上风能资源，发挥风电场规模和经济效益，本次规划从风机型式、单机容量、风机布置、风机间距、轮毂安装高度等各方面进行分析，提出初步方案，为后续海上风电场的开发建设提供技术可行，经济合理的决策依据。

（6）国内先进理念的海上风电场输电规划的初步方案。由于海上风电场集电线路主要依靠海缆将风机所发电能送至升压变电站，经升压站升压后再接入系统变电站。因此风电场位置设置的主要受制因素是海缆的损耗和充电功率，规划中提出建设海上升压平台、陆上升压站的原则。对于规模较大、离海较远的大规模海上的风电场，可分片区建造220kV海上升压平台，再经220kV海缆送至陆上电网。建在陆地上的升压变电站位置选择应综合考虑海缆登陆路径、高压出线走廊/通道、周边电网的接入情况、交通运输、地质水文等因素，经综合比较择优选择。合理选择接入系统的电压等级。本次规划提出电压稳定、谐波防治、系统稳定措施，从电网的电力电量平衡出发，按照系统的负荷需求和系统消纳能力，合理安排风电开发进度；并根据当地电网的变电容量和高电压等级网络的建设情况，合理确定风电的接入规模、接入点和接入等级；提出了大规模、大容量的海上风电场输电规划的初步方案和地理位置接线图。

（7）国内先进的海上风机基础及其安装设计理念和设计初步方案。海上风力发电机组基础结构具有重心高、承受的水平风力和倾覆弯矩较大等受力特点，设计过程中还须充分考虑离岸距离、海床地质条件、海上风、浪以及海流、冰等外部环境的影响。因此，海上风电机组基础的造价是海上风电工程总造价的主要组成部分之一，研究合理的基础结构是国内外海上风电场研究开发的重要课题。本次规划提出的海上、滩涂风电场风力发电机组基础结构方案在国内处于领先水平。海上风电场施工受海上风、浪、潮、雾、台风的影响较大，施工作业区在一年中的有效天数为188天左右，而且为避开大风大浪天气，海上施工船只需要经常往返避风，也降低了施工作业效率，经分析台风多发季节前夕的风浪最小，有利于风电场施工。在充分研究海上风机的施工特点后，本次规划推荐采取陆上整体拼装或在陆上完成部分风机拼装后再运输到风机安装点、分体安装方案，对今后海上风电场的建设具有指导作用，为海上风机的施工安装提供有力技术支持和借鉴。

（8）投资匡算及财务分析，为确定海上风电场上网电价提供依据和借鉴。本次规划编制的投资匡算，以及测算的海上风电场的上网电价，为分析确定各规划风电场具备一定的开发价值提供依据。

（9）国内首次审查通过的大规模、大区域的海上风电场工程规划，评审专家评价认为上海市海上风电场工程规划内容翔实，规划方法和原则合理，属国内领先，是可持续科学发展战略的具体体现，在我国风电建设行业，值得推荐和借鉴。

（上海勘测设计研究院　胡志坚）

江苏省海上风电场工程规划工作简介

（一）规划背景

国家相继出台了《可再生能源法》、《可再生能源发展“十一五”规划》、《可再生能源中长期发展规划》指导可再生能源的发展。其中提出了风电发展的具体目标，国家发展改革委也提出了规划目标的实现方式——“建设大基地，接入大电网。”在特许权政策的支持下，江苏省发展改革委积极推进陆地风电场建设，至2009年12月底，已建风电场总容量94.53万kW，在建容量27.15万kW，预计2010年左右全部建成投产，另有177.2万kW风电场正在开展前期工作。在开发陆地风电的同时，江苏省发展改革委积极推进如东、大丰和响水等海上风电示范项目前期工作。

我国风能资源丰富区主要集中在“三北”地区和东南沿海，在特许权政策的推动下，条件较好的江苏沿海陆地风电场陆续开工建设，风电建设的重心向资源丰富、成本较低的“三北”地区转移。但“三北”地区远离受电市场，送出是这一地区风电大规模建设的限制因素，目前正在研究远距离输送风电问题。江苏沿海海域风能资源丰富，虽处沿海地区，但受台风影响较小，开发条件相对较好；地处“长三角”负荷中心，风电并网条件较好；江苏海域广阔，海底地形平坦，规划风电场容量较大，适合建设千万千瓦级风电基地，并为规模化建设先行示范。江苏省海上风电场工程规划也是江苏千万千瓦级风电基地规划，是唯一一个海上千万千瓦级基地。

国家能源局2009年1月15日在北京召开“海上风电开发及沿海大型风电基地规划工作会议”，会上对“江苏沿海千万千瓦级风电基地的规划工作”进行部署。2009年4月底，国家能源局颁发了“海上风电场工程规划工作大纲”（国能新能［2009］130号），大纲对海上风电场工程规划的工作内容和深度提出了明确要求。

2009年2月，中国水电顾问集团华东勘测设计研究院（以下简称“华东院”）根据“海上风电开发及沿海大型风电基地规划工作会议”的精神，开始江苏省海上风电场工程规划工作。经过资料收集，规划工作，省级职能部门意见征求，地方政府意见征求等环节，2009年8月完成《江苏省海上风电场工程规划报告》（初稿），并于2009年9月10日由江苏省发展改革委、省能源局组织审查。

2010年1月27～28日，江苏省人民政府组织召开了《江苏省海上风电场工程规划》论证会，会议邀请了王景全院士等专家以及省沿海办、经信委、交通厅、环保厅、海洋与渔业局、气象局、海事局、电力公司、滩涂公司、省军区等部门，与会人员对规划提出了宝贵的意见，华东院修改后于2010年2月完成《江苏省海上风电场工程规划报告》（送审稿）。

（二）规划结论

江苏省位于我国东部沿海，地处长江中下游平原和淮河冲积平原，地势平坦，沿海地区和近海海域风能资源丰富，开发建设海上风电场的资源条件较好。江苏省是“长三角”经济发达地区核心成员，国内生产总值和增长水平均位于各省前茅，2008年全省地区生产总值突破3万亿元，经济总量大，发展速度快，对电力需求量也大。江苏省煤炭、油气资源储量非常有限，基本无可开发水力资源，火电占电网装机比例超过90%，能源依靠省外供应为主。江苏电网属于华东电网，是“长三角”负荷中心的一部分，规划的风电场靠近负荷中心，可就近接入电网，所发电量在网内消纳条件较好。江苏省海岸线总长954km，除北部滨海海域外，基本为淤积性海岸线，近海海域水深在25m以内，绝大部分在15m左右，建设近海风电场的条件较好，航运、军事等制约因素相对较少，适于作为海上风电示范基地，先行开发建设。

本次规划坚持以资源定规划、以规划定项目的原则。通过对江苏沿海风能资源、岸线资源、海域资源的综合分析，在离岸100km以内，水深25m以下，包括沿海滩涂，规划建成装机规模为2100万kW的风电场。其中陆上300万kW，海上1800万kW。随着经济社会发展和江苏沿海规划的落实，风电场前期工作逐步推进，可能出现部分项目不具备开发条件或容量减少的情况。为确保规划发展目标，共规划2303万kW风电场，其中陆上风电场项目36个，规模为378万kW；海上风电场项目包括潮间带和近海共68个，规模为1925万kW。规划主要结论如下：

（1）江苏省近海风能资源丰富，根据江苏省气象局《江苏省风能资源评价报告》，风能资源总储量为3469万kW，主要分布在沿海滩涂和近海海域。沿海滩涂70m高度年平均风速在6.8m/s左右，潮间带和近海海域80m高度平均风速在7.5m/s左右，据估算，近海部分海域80m高度平均风速超过7.5m/s，接近8.0m/s。风能资源开发价值较好。

（2）江苏陆上规划36个风电场，总装机容量378万kW。根据风能资源分布、近海海域使用现状及规划、海洋功能区划，按照《海上风电场工程规划工作大纲》的要求，考虑项目之间相互影响，规划风电场场址，并划分成若干个30万kW左右的单元，江苏省潮间带及近海风电场规划海域总面积为9280km^2，规划装机容量为1925万kW，其中，潮间带风电场290万kW，近海风电场1635万kW。

（3）按照江苏沿海潮间带和近海风电场规划布局，从北至南规划4个百万千瓦基地，分别为废黄河口以北的连云港及盐城北部百万千瓦基地，总容量300万kW；废黄河口与射阳河口之间的盐城东部百万千瓦基地，总容量为295万kW；射阳河口以南至盐城、南通边界的盐城南部百万千瓦基地，总容量为910万kW；盐城南通边界以南的南通百万千瓦基地，总容量420万kW，潮间带风电场全部在盐城南部和南通百万基地。

（4）根据《江苏沿海地区发展规划》和《江苏省风力发电发展规划（2006～2020年）》，结合风电场规划布局和建设条件，本次规划确定的发展目标为：2010年建成170万kW；2015年建成580万kW；2020年建成1000万kW；远期建成2100kW。根据建设时序安排：2010年规划建设171万kW，陆地151万kW，潮间带20万kW；2015年规划建设716万kW，陆地256万kW，潮间带260万kW，近海200万kW；2020年规划建设1278万kW，陆地333万kW，潮间带290万kW，近海655万kW；远期规划建设2303万kW，其中陆地风电场378万kW，潮间带风电场290万kW，近海风电场1635万kW。

（5）根据国内外近年来海上风电发展的情况，潮间带推荐选用单机容量2000kW及以上的风电机组；近海风电场推荐选用3000kW及以上风电机组，中远期开发的风电场建议选用5000kW级风电机组，可以选择IECⅡ～Ⅲ类风电机组。本规划坚持规模化开发与产业发展相互促进的原则，选择风机时，要以本地化程度作为一个衡量指标，在满足技术、质量要求的条件下，优先选择本地化率高的风电机组。

（6）沿海风电场距离江苏电网接入点距离远，接入系统投资高，因此，根据规划布局，小型风电场宜与附近的风电场合成一个风电场，风电场容量约在20万～50万kW，宜采用一个升压站，由1～2回220kV线路接入系统；个别较单独的容量在10万kW以下风电场以110kV线路接入系统。

（7）江苏省陆地风电场投资约为9500元/kW；潮间带风电场投资约为15 000～17 500元/kW，其中盐城南部基地高于南通基地；近海风电场投资在21 000～23 000元/kW之间，其中盐城东部和盐城北部基地高于盐城南部基地和南通基地。

（中国水电顾问集团华东勘测设计研究院　李睿元）

江苏响水近海2MW试验风机项目实施情况

（一）概况

为提高我国海上机组设备制造产业的技术能力，解决近海风电有关关键技术难题，2006年国家科技部提出了“大功率风电机组研制与示范”的计划，响水近海2MW试验风机是该计划的支撑性课题。课题目的是通过试验风机的建设及后期的运行维护，为今后大规模开发海上风电提供宝贵经验，并探索海上风电机组设计制造、风电场设计、海上机组施工等关键性环节的技术问题。

江苏响水近海2MW试验风机位于响水县灌东盐场外侧的海域，试验风机距海岸线约3km，水深约3.5m。试验风机采用上海电气风电设备有限公司生产的W2000-93机型，单机容量2MW，转轮直径93m，轮毂高度70m。试验风机以一回35kV海底电缆接入已建的响水陆上风电场，并通过已建的响水陆上风电场35kV集电线路接入220kV升压站，最终接入系统。

（二）设计施工情况

1. 风机基础设计　试验风机所在海域主要为深厚覆盖层地基，海床面以下10m深度范围内均为高压缩性的新近沉积土和淤泥质粉质黏土，承载力低、变形大，没有天然地基条件，故风机基础需采用桩基础。试验风机基础设计时，综合比较了单桩、导管架、高桩承台等多种基础型式。因为试验风机仅一台，基础型式选择时考虑尽量采用目前已有的施工设备，采用目前成熟的施工手段，所以试验风机基础最终选用高桩承台方案。高桩承台的基础结构型式为：8根直径为1.4m、长66.5m的钢管桩作为基桩，以密实粉砂层作为持力层，8根钢管桩在承台底部沿10m直径的圆周均匀分布。承台为现浇钢筋混凝土结构，承台直径14m，厚度3.0～4.5m，承台混凝土强度等级C40，采用高性能混凝土。风机基础钢结构部分防腐蚀设计采用物理防护与电化学保护相结合的联合保护方式，即钢管桩整体采用牺牲阳级保护，在浪溅区和水位变动区涂刷双层熔结环氧粉末。混凝土结构防腐蚀设计采用基本防腐蚀措施和特殊防腐蚀措施相结合的方式，基本防腐蚀措施主要是提高混凝土本身的密实性和抗氯离子渗透性，包括采用高性能混凝土、严格控制混凝土质量、适当增加混凝土保护层厚度等措施；特殊防腐蚀措施包括设置混凝土表面防腐涂层，混凝土中掺加钢筋阻锈剂等措施。

2. 风机基础施工　风机基础的钢管桩在陆上预制厂加工制作，钢管桩采用整桩统长不分段制作，在预制厂加工制作并做好防腐后，用驳船运输至试验风机现场，用大型打桩船施打。钢管桩施工完成后，进行桩基承载力检测。桩基施工完成并达到规定的停止时间后，开始浇筑上部承台混凝土。首先在桩顶安装承台的底模，在底模上安装钢套箱，钢套箱作为混凝土浇筑的侧模，也作为临时的挡水结构。承台混凝土分两次浇筑，先期浇筑封底混凝土，封底混凝土内配置少量的钢筋。封底混凝土达到一定强度后，就被用作二期混凝土浇筑的施工平台，在封底混凝土上绑扎二期混凝土的钢筋和安装塔筒连接段。二期钢筋绑扎完成、塔筒连接段安装并调平后，浇筑二期混凝土。全部承台混凝土采用混凝土搅拌运输船在现场搅拌、泵送入仓。

3. 风电机组安装　欧洲国家同类风电机组的安装一般采用专业的安装船。这种专业的安装船带有四个或六个支腿，安装作业时支腿支撑在海底，形成海上平台，但国内尚无这种专业的安装船。也有风电机组采用整体安装方式，即风电机组整体在陆上组装场装配后，整体运输至现场，用大型起重船一次性起吊安装，但试验风机处水深较浅，目前国内的大型起重船无法进入，因此也不能用整体安装的方式。另外试验风机数量少，所以风机安装方案设计时考虑尽量利用国内目前现有的船机设备，尽量采用在现有船机设备少量改装的方案。经对国内现有船机设备的大量调研，并综合考虑现场条件和经济性等因素后，最终选定用半潜驳作为主要安装设备，在半潜驳上加装大型履带吊用于风机安装。风电机组采用分体运输、分体安装，机舱、轮毂和2个叶片在陆上组装场预装后，整个风电机组分为下段塔筒、上段塔筒、机舱＋轮毂＋2个叶片、第3个叶片共四部分运输，并在现场依次起吊安装。因为半潜驳能座底作业，半潜驳座底后海上风浪对半潜驳的影响很小，安装作业非常稳定，各部件顺利起吊、安装。

4. 电气设计　试验风机出口电压为690V，在塔筒底部配套设置一套机组升压设备，将电压升至35kV后以一回35kV海底电缆接入已建的响水陆上风电场场内集电线路。机组配套升压设备选用干式变压器，高压侧选用SF_6绝缘负荷开关熔断器组合电器柜体，低压侧配置低压断路器柜，全部设置在塔筒底部。海底电缆选用铜导体3芯交联聚乙烯分相铅护套钢丝铠装光复合海底电缆。

（三）工程建设情况

江苏响水近海2MW试验风机由上海电气风电设备有限公司设计制造，由中交第三航务工程局安装，工程于2009年9月开工建设，10月完成风机基础浇筑，11月23日试验风机全部安装完成。

（中国水电顾问集团华东勘测设计研究院　俞华锋　赵生校）

江苏东台20万kW风电场介绍

（一）工程概况

江苏东台风电场属国家发展改革委第三期特许权项目，风电场位于江苏省东台市东南约70km弶港镇滩涂地区，场区南北长约14.4km，东西宽约2～5km，全区地势低洼，地面高程为1.7～4.5m。

风电场65m高度年平均风速6.7～6.9m/s，风功率密度等级为302～369 W/m²。风电场共安装134台1.5MW的风力发电机组，总装机容量201MW，年上网电量43 631.60万 kW·h，年等效满负荷小时数为2170h。

风电场建设一座220kV升压站，以一回220kV输电线路接入220kV金东变电所，送出线路长度为31km。

该项目于2006年6月28日正式开工建设，2007年5月31日220kV升压站调试完成，6月20日完成倒送电，具备并网发电条件。

2007年4月30日完成首台风机的吊装，5月20日完成首批4台机组吊装完成，5月底首批4台机组并网发电。

2008年6月底完成了92台风电机组并网发电，剩余42台机组于2009年完成并网发电。

（二）风能资源

根据风电场范围内测风塔实测数据分析得出，8

月风功率密度最大，65m高度风功率密度达到585W/m^2；10月风功率密度最小，65m高度风功率密度约为200W/m^2。从全年看，年平均风功率密度等级达到3级，65m高度平均风速为6.9m/s。

该风电场主要受来自海上的季风影响，以SE和NE两个风向风能较为集中，风速、风功率密度春夏季节较大，秋季较小；白天风速、风功率密度较大，夜晚风速、风功率密度较小；从风能密度分析风能资源较好，是一个较为理想的风电场场址，具有良好的开发前景。

（三）风力发电机选型和布置

该项目所选用的风力发电机组机型有通用电气和华锐大重，单机容量均为1500kW机组，轮毂高度均为65m，转轮直径分别为70m和77m，分别安装了41台和93台。

风电机组沿着与海岸线大体平行的方向布置，行间距约为700m（超过9D），行走向基本呈南北向，行内相邻风机间距约为550m（超过7D），同时结合现场用地规划和征地限制等条件，分成北区、南区和东区三个区块分别布置且依次开发建设。

该项目年上网电量为43 631.6万kW·h，折合有效年利用小时数为2170h。

（四）工程地质

风电场场区属黄海潮间带滩涂地貌单元。场区呈T字形分布，南北长约14.4km，东西宽约2～5km，场区地形为沿海滩涂，场区内沟渠呈树根状分布，局部野生植物丛生。全区地势低洼，地面高程为1.7～4.5m。

场区地层主要为海相及冲积～海积相地层，地形平坦，建筑物施工期对场区地质影响不大，不会形成破坏性的地质灾害。风电场建成后，场区地形地貌基本恢复到原状，也不会对场区原来地质构造产生不利影响。

场地抗震设防烈度为Ⅶ度，设计地震分组为第二组，场区20m深范围内分布的液化土层为场地上部的②-1层砂质粉土、②-2层砂质粉土、③-1层粉砂夹砂质粉土，属轻微～中等液化土层。

（五）电气设计

根据接入系统推荐方案，该项目由一回220kV出线接入220kV（金东）变电所（原三仓变），线路长度为31km。该项目在风电场中心位置建造220kV升压站，风电场电能经2台220kV主变压器升压后，通过一回220kV架空线路送至220kV金东变电所。

由于风电机出口电压为690V，每台风电机配置一台箱式变电站，变压器将风电机出口电压升高至35kV，升压后通过集电线路接入220kV升压站中压开关柜。

风电场设2台220/35kV升压变压器。变电站35kV侧共有11回进线和2回出线，另外还有2回场用变出线，35kV采用单母线分段接线，220kV配电装置采用GIS设备。

该风电场由江苏省调调度管理，采用少人值守方式运行。在风电场控制室设通信工作站。风电场采用计算机监控，风力发电机组计算机监控系统由风力发电机组厂家配套提供，专供风力发电机组的自动监视和控制。220kV线路、主变压器、35kV线路的集中监控和调度部门远方监控“四遥”功能由升压站计算机监控系统完成。风电场分三级监控：现场单机监控、中央控制室集中监控、江苏省调实行远方监控。

（六）土建设计

1. 风电机组基础　该项目全部风电机组位于沿海滩涂的软基上面，覆盖层较厚。因风机为高耸结构建筑物，受水平风荷载时，其水平力和底部弯矩很大，并且风机对塔架倾斜较敏感，对基础不均匀沉降要求较高。该项目场地土②-1层和②-2层工程性能较差，若采用天然地基或碎石振冲桩复合地基，其承载力和变形不能满足风机要求。而桩基础具有承载力高，沉降速率低、沉降小且均匀等特点，能够较好的承受垂直荷载、水平荷载、上拔力及由风机产生的振动或动力作用。故该项目风机基础采用桩基础。③-2粉砂，中密，全区分布稳定，层厚7.8～19.8m，工程性能较好，可用为风机基础桩基持力层。④粉质黏土，埋深中等，土的工程性能较好，但仅局部分布，厚度不大，不适合作为持力层。⑥粉砂，中密，标贯击数N=11～47击，全区分布较广，其工程性能较好，也是较好的桩基持力层，但埋藏较深。风机基础设计选用③-2作为持力层，较为合适。根据项目场地土的特征，初设及招标技施阶段对风机基础采用灌注桩和预制管桩（PHC桩）进行了比较，综合工程造价、施工时间、施工工艺及安全可靠等多方面考虑，风机基础最终选用PHC桩基础。

（1）通用电气（GE）风电机组基础（预埋地脚螺栓）：采用现浇钢筋混凝土基础，为圆盘形，直径17m，埋深2.5m，厚1.0～2.0m，立柱直径6.0m，高0.8m。圆盘形基础底下布置两圈桩基，桩基采用直径600mm的预应力混凝土管桩，桩长11～18m，每台风机下布置26根管桩。

（2）华锐大重（FL）风电机组基础（预埋基础环）：采用钢筋混凝土基础，为圆盘形，直径18m，埋深2.5m，厚1.0～2.0m，圆墩直径8.0m，高0.5m。圆盘形基础底下布置两圈桩基，桩基采用直径600mm的预应力混凝土管桩，桩长11～13m，每台风机下布置30根管桩。

基础设计结合已施工的江苏同类地区的风电场经

验，并有效利用了我院研究取得的实用新型专利——用于滩涂地区的风力发电机基础结构（ZL 2007 20112818.8）。由于风电场风机采用两种类型，所以风机基础也有两种类型，该基础设计得到了建设单位委托的基础设计科研单位浙江大学的认可和好评。由于地勘工作到位，桩基设计合理，基础钢筋合理布置，所以基础施工简便，得到了施工单位、监理单位的一致认可。

2. 220kV 升压站　升压站内设有生产综合楼、生产辅助楼各一幢，另外还布置有 650m 深水井及泵房、事故油池、消防水池及水泵房等建（构）筑物。GIS、220kV 主变压器均为户内布置，风场 11 回 35kV 架空集电线路进线通过电缆沟从变电站东、北两侧进入站内，一回 220kV 出线从南侧经铁塔架空出线。

（七）大型机组吊装

风电机组由设备制造厂家负责运抵施工现场。新建的场内施工道路能满足每台风电机组设备运输及吊装的要求。设备吊装采用一台主起重机、两台辅助起重机，主起重机为德马克的 600t 履带式起重机 CC2800-1，负责塔筒、机舱、叶片的组装和吊装；辅起重机为 1 台 100t 汽车起重机和 1 台 50t 汽车起重机，负责小件的组装，并协助主起重机完成组装。

1. 塔筒安装　塔筒安装分三节进行。安装时，先利用履带式起重机提升下塔筒，慢慢将塔筒竖立，使塔筒的下端准确坐落在基础法兰钢管上，按设计要求连接法兰盘，做到牢固可靠。中塔筒、上塔筒的安装方法与下塔架相同。

2. 风电机组安装　风速是影响风电机组安装的主要因素之一，当风速超过 12m/s 时，不允许安装风电机组。机舱安装时，施工人员站在塔架平台上，利用履带式起重机提升机舱，机舱提起超过安装高度后，再慢慢下落，机舱应完全坐在塔架法兰盘上，按设计要求使之与法兰盘连接。转子叶片和轮毂在地面组装好后，利用履带式起重机整体提升，轮毂法兰和机舱法兰按设计要求连接。上述作业完成并经验收合格后，移去施工设施，进行风电机组调试，完毕后投入运行。

（中国水电顾问集团华东勘测设计研究院　陈德春）

中水珠江规划勘测设计有限公司风电技术发展情况

（一）加强国际交流与合作

为了更加开阔视野，走在新能源设计的前沿，掌握国际的专业设计理念，长期以来，中水珠江规划勘测设计有限公司新能源设计研究中心和德国新能源研究机构及知名企业等进行了广泛的技术交流培训及合作研究工作。

2005 年 7 月 26 日～8 月 6 日游赞培董事长、总经理一行六人对德国进行了商务考察，先后参观考察了德国 REPOWER 风力发电公司以及德国科隆尼尔热电厂等多家新能源和环保产业公司，学习外方在清洁能源开发、环保指标市场交易补偿机制、废水深度处理工艺，电力负荷调峰机制等方面的先进经验。作为回访，德国 REPOWER 风力发电公司的 Carsten Covino 先生于 2006 年、2007 年两次抵穗与新能源中心进行技术交流。

2006～2008 年度新能源设计研究中心三期四人赴德国参加德国 InWent 基金会风能利用培训（短期一月、长期一年），主要培训内容有：风能技术培训、海上风电技术及风力发电领域新技术与新政策培训。

同时，新能源中心也承担起对外新能源业务培训，2007 年 9 月 30 日德国柏林技术经济专业大学可再生能源专业学生 Jürgen Edinger 来新能源中心进行为期半年的实习，并于 2008 年 3 月 15 日圆满完成实习内容回国，新能源中心被培训机构给予 A+评价。

长期的中德新能源技术交流开阔了新能源设计人员的视野，学习先进的科研技术，对更好地引进国际先进技术起到积极作用，同时也为建立国际合作研究关系打下了基础。

（二）研究解决风电关键技术

1. 复杂条件下的风电场微观选址技术　目前的微观选址技术，主要是应用相关工具软件，如应用较为广泛的有 WaSP、WinPro、WindFarmer 等进行分析和优化，它是通过一个对数或指数风廓线分析层高对风流影响而得出风能资源为基础的。而在复杂地形和气候条件下，驱动风流的因素并不唯一，一个典型的拟合结果是：风速并不随高程的上升而升高，而在某一高度后，风速随高程的上升而不再升高或降低。我国地域辽阔，自然环境、风能资源状况不尽相同，依据或依赖国外标准制造风电设备或选址相对而言更加复杂，微观选址技术的标准不明确，引起的选址技术结果差异显著，直接导致在复杂的地形和恶劣的气候条件下现有风电设备的安全可靠性大打折扣，运行控制变得更加困难，实际出力也比预测评估的要低。其中一个主要原因是：风电场建设时采用的微观选址技术较为简单有关。

对复杂条件下的风电场进行微观选址技术研究，是基于场址地形的研究，合理的微观选址方法的选择、风场风能资源分析、风场条件对风机设备的影响等进行综合分析。

“复杂条件下的风电场微观选址技术”是中水珠江规划勘测设计有限公司胡立伟等基于 CFD 软件提

出的建立风电场动态模型的研究成果。该技术于2008年在全国风电技术协作网第三届年会公开发布，在业界引起较大的影响，目前对复杂条件下的风电场设计正逐步接受和采用CFD软件建立风电场动态模型。动态模型能够进行场点验证设计，微观选址成果可详细列出设计机位点环境湍流、尾流影响、入流角、切变指数、极值阵风系数等，给工程设计提供有效支持，其功能先进、全面、规范、使用方便，能提高风电场设计技术指标。

在华能文昌风电厂一期和二期项目评估及项目审查工作中，应用"复杂条件下的风电场微观选址技术"对风电场建立风电场动态模型，以及风资源各项参数、风电场设计技术指标进行复核计算，结果表明其功能先进、全面、规范，使用方便。

2. 风能资源小尺度拟合技术 "风能资源小尺度拟合技术"是基于"复杂条件下的风电场微观选址技术"衍生出的新技术。广东省气候中心在陆丰甲湖风电场特许权项目前期风能资源评估及预可行性研究工作中，采用"风能资源小尺度拟合技术"对风场进行中尺度分析，并局部加密进行小尺度拟合和场点验证设计。研究表明，计算结果更为真实、准确，各种参数计算不但满足国家规范要求，还能显著提高风电场设计技术指标，为工程设计提供了有效的技术支持，取得了良好的社会经济效益。

（中水珠江规划勘测设计有限公司 胡立伟）

中水珠江规划勘测设计有限公司参与的几个风电项目简介

（一）粤水电新疆吉木乃风电场

粤水电新疆吉木乃风电场位于新疆维吾尔族自治区吉木乃县拜格托别区域及合孜勒哈巴克区域，总面积约120km²。

广东省水利水电第二工程局经与吉木乃县人民政府达成投资协议书，获权开发吉木乃县境内50万kW的风电场建设项目。

中水珠江规划勘测设计有限公司受广东省水利水电第二工程局的项目公司——布尔津县粤水电能源有限公司（以下简称"粤水电"）委托，编制风电场规划报告。

新疆吉木乃县是有名的风口，根据风速拟合分析，规划风场各场区的年平均风速在7～9m/s之间，有很高的开发价值。

根据风能资源分布及当地情况，拜格托别区域可开发容量为20万kW，合孜勒哈巴克区域可开发容量为30万kW。按照以上的风电场初步规划选址，粤水电新疆吉木乃风电场规划开发容量为50万kW，规划场址面积为100km²。

根据吉木乃风电场以及吉木乃的实际情况，结合电网发展和用电负荷的预测，规划分10期开发，每两期容量5万kW（亦可根据新疆的实际情况及施工条件两期一起开发），最迟至2020年建成。

粤水电新疆吉木乃风电场规划容量为50万kW，年理论发电量为181 386万kW·h，年上网电量为126 971万kW·h，年满发小时数为2544h。

（二）华能文昌风电厂

华能文昌风电厂规划规模为120MW，位于海南省东部文昌市境内木兰头的东南方海岸，属于海边风电场。场址距海口市城区约70km，距文昌市约75km，地处东经110°43′，北纬20°05′。

受项目建设方华能海南发电股份有限公司的委托，中水珠江规划勘测设计有限公司于2007年9月开始进行华能文昌风电厂（一期）的可行性研究及勘测设计工作。

风电场场址位于海岸线附近海滩上，场内地势开阔平坦，一年四季风向较稳定，以东北风和东风为主导风向和主导风能风向。场区内10m高度平均风速为4.5～5.2m/s，平均风功率密度为114～149W/m²；50m和70m高度平均风速可分别达7.1、7.4m/s，平均风功率密度分别为331、434W/m²，场区靠近沿海一带的大部分地区风资源可达3级（较好），具有较好的开发利用价值。

华能文昌风电厂（一期）装机容量49.5MW，安装33台单机容量为1500kW的风力发电机组，轮毂高度65m，设计年上网电量10 330万kW·h，容量系数为23.8%，全年满负荷运行时间为2086.9h。华能文昌风电厂（一期）已于2008年12月建成并网发电，运行情况良好。

华能文昌风电厂（二期）装机容量70MW，目前正在施工图设计中，其中一台单机2MW的样机已经于2009年12月建成并网发电，也是目前海南省最大的风电单机设备。

（三）徐闻勇士风电场

徐闻勇士风电场位于广东省湛江市徐闻县曲界镇勇士农场的丘岗地带，属于台地风场，地理位置在北纬20°29′～20°33′和东经110°14′～110°17′，场内海拔高度在147.9～221.0m之间。

受项目建设方广东粤电湛江风力发电有限公司的委托，中水珠江规划勘测设计有限公司于2009年4月开始进行徐闻勇士风电场的勘测设计工作。

场区70m高度处代表年平均风速为6.74m/s，风功率密度为243.0W/m²，50m高度处年平均风速为 6.41m/s，风功率密度为 206.7W/m²，根据《风电场风能资源评估方法》（GB/T 18710—2002）判定该风电场风功率等级为 2 级。主风向和能量主要集中在 ENE 和 NE 两个方向。

风电场建设规模为 49.5MW，安装 33 台单机容量为 1500kW 的风力发电机组。预计年上网电量为 10 372万 kW·h，装机利用小时数为 2095h。

（四）珠海高栏岛风电场

珠海高栏岛风力发电场场址位于珠海市西南部的高栏岛，属复杂山地风电场。受项目建设单位珠海富华风能开发有限公司委托，中水珠江规划勘测设计有限公司于 2009 年 6 月开始进行珠海高栏岛风电场工程的勘测设计工作。

高栏岛陆地面积约为 34.2km²，通过连岛大堤公路与珠海市区相连，岛内多数为复杂山地地形，最高海拔达 418.0m。高栏岛属亚热带海洋性季风气候。冬季多偏北风，空气干燥；夏季多东南风，且常受台风影响。春季冷暖气流交替，是全年天气多变的季节，季内以偏东风为主，风向多变。

珠海高栏岛风电场地形复杂，受地形的加速或阻碍的影响，不同区域风速变化较大。高栏岛长年平均风速处于 6.75～7.91m/s 之间，平均风功率密度处于336.7～561.5m/s 之间，风电场等级为 3～5 级。

珠海高栏岛风电场装机容量为 49.5MW，工程安装浙江运达风力发电工程有限公司单机容量 750kW 的 WD49-750 风力发电机组，安装 66 台。

珠海高栏岛风电场年理论发电量为12 798万kW·h，年上网电量为 9582.6 万 kW·h，年满发小时数为 1936h，容量系数为 22.10%。

（五）粤水电新疆布尔津城南风电场

粤水电新疆布尔津城南风电场位于新疆布尔津县西南侧，属于内陆风电场。2007 年 11 月广东水电集团有限公司与新疆布尔津人民政府签署《布尔津县塑克拉克哲腊风电项目投资协议书》，拟在布尔津县规划投资建设 60 万 kW 风电场项目。按照协议书的要求，首先在规划风电场场址范围内开展一期 49.5MW 的风电场项目的工作。

2008 年 12 月受广东水电集团有限公司的委托，中水珠江规划勘测设计有限公司承担了布尔津一期 49.5MW 风力发电场工程可行性研究及勘测设计工作。

布尔津县位于新疆维吾尔自治区北部，阿尔泰山脉西南麓，准噶尔盆地北沿。西北部与俄罗斯、哈萨克斯坦接壤，是中国西部唯一与俄罗斯交界的县，国界线长 218km，东北部毗邻蒙古国，东邻阿勒泰市，西邻哈巴河县，南与吉木乃县和福海县相连。全县总面积10 369.45km²。布尔津县地势由东北向西南倾斜，分三部分：北部为高、中山区，中部为低山丘陵、河谷地，南部为半荒漠低山区。

该风电场场区 50m 和 70m 高度平均风速分别为 7.41m/s 和 7.56m/s，平均风功率密度分别为 470.8W/m² 和 502.9W/m²，该区风资源等级属 4 级（好），具备较好的开发利用风资源条件。测风塔 70m 高度的主导风向均来自于西、偏西以及东南偏东。

风电场建设规模为 49.5MW，风电场厂区位于布尔津县城西南测位置，位于布尔津县至吉木乃县的国道 319 两侧，场址开阔，交通便利。该风电场工程建筑物主要由风电机组及箱变、变电所、生产及生活用房等组成。风电场拟安装 33 台单机为 1.5MW 的风力发电机，设计年上网电量12 909.6万 kW·h，年发电小时数为 2608h。

（六）潮州饶平海山风电场

潮州饶平海山风电场场址位于广东省潮州市饶平县海山镇南岛，属山地风电场。中水珠江规划勘测设计有限公司负责海山风电场项目总承包。

饶平县依山傍海，属亚热带海洋性季风气候，北回归线自县境南部穿过，气候温和，季风明显，雨量充沛，年平均气温 21.4℃，降雨量 1475.9mm。海山镇处在台湾海峡喇叭口西南端，受台湾海峡的影响，每当冷空气南下到达时，由于狭管效应的结果使风速增大，这里是我国风能资源最佳的地区之一。

风电场场址选定在海山岛内的丘陵山岭，主要坐落在中部的猫地山—烟楼山—埠尾山及东北部烛台山—羊头山及其延展形成的丘陵的山坡上，区内地形高程变化较大，主要为丘陵。经订正计算，多年平均状况下，埠尾山、烟楼山和羊头山测风站距地面 70m 高度年平均风速分别为 7.9、7.5、6.7m/s，年平均风功率密度分别为 548.9 、441.8、332.5W/m²，参考国家标准 GB/T 18710—2002 给出的风能资源评估的等级标准，埠尾山风资源等级为 5 级，烟楼山为 4 级，羊头山为 3 级。观测年度各测风站主导风向为东风，年风能密度主要集中在 ENE-ESE 扇区。

潮州饶平海山风电场拟安装 33 台 1500kW 的风力发电机组，总装机容量 49.5MW。设计年发电量为 10 920.4万 kW·h，容量系数为 25.19%，全年标准运行时间为 2206h。

（中水珠江规划勘测设计有限公司　胡立伟）

中国水电顾问集团华东勘测设计研究院获批成立“华东海上风电省级高新技术企业研究开发中心”

2009 年 9 月 27 日，浙江省科学技术厅正式发布

“关于下达 2009 年第一批省级高新技术企业研究开发中心建设计划的通知”［浙科发条（2009）197 号］，中国水电顾问集团华东勘测设计研究院获批成立“华东海上风电省级高新技术企业研究开发中心”。这为中国水电顾问集团华东勘测设计研究院科技创新，特别是海上风电研发创立了新的平台与品牌。近年来，在国家政策扶持下，风电建设快速发展，截至 2008 年底，全国累计建成装机容量 1200 余万千瓦，但这其中仅以陆上风电为主，海上风电尚处于起步阶段。而我国海上风能资源可开发量约 1 亿～2 亿 kW，国家《可再生能源“十一五”规划》提出：要在苏沪海域和浙江、广东沿海探索近海风电开发经验，打造百万千瓦级海上风电基地的目标。中国水电顾问集团华东勘测设计研究院在风电领域已积累较丰富的工程项目经验，近几年，正发挥自身综合优势不断加强海上风电承接与研发力度，正在开展 10 多项海上风电项目勘测设计，先期开展的几个示范和科研项目已进入实施阶段。

（中国水电顾问集团华东勘测设计研究院　程　平）

3

大中型水电工程

常规水电工程

三峡工程2009年建设情况

2009年是三峡工程初步设计工期的最后一年，三峡工程初步设计建设目标如期实现。经过数万名三峡建设者17年的艰苦奋斗，三峡工程初步设计建设任务除国家批准缓建的升船机外，均提前或如期完成。顺利通过175m蓄水前验收，三峡工程由以建设为主转入以运行为主的阶段。三峡工程防洪抗旱、发电、航运、供水等综合效益全面发挥。

（一）固定资产投资完成情况

2009年，三峡工程投资计划187.17亿元，实际完成投资109.42亿元，占年度计划的58.46%。其中：建筑安装工程完成投资22 990万元，比计划投资55 642万元减少32 652万元；设备费完成投资7907万元，比计划投资18 236万元减少10 329万元；其他费用完成投资12 388万元，比计划投资23 659万元减少11 271万元；水库移民费完成投资100亿元，比计划投资169亿元减少69亿元。

截至2009年底，三峡工程累计完成投资1592亿元，其中：枢纽工程静态投资完成477.4亿元，占枢纽工程概算500.9亿元的95.31%；库区移民完成静态投资505亿元，占库区移民静态投资530亿元的95.28%；价差458.4亿元；贷款利息151.3亿元。静态、动态投资均控制在国家批准的概算投资范围内。

2009年三峡工程固定资产投资完成情况详见表1。

（二）完成工程量及主要工程形象进度

2009年，三峡主体工程完成工程量详见表2。

表1　三峡工程固定资产投资完成情况汇总表

项　　目	单位	2009年计划	2009年完成	占年计划（%）	自开工累计完成
三峡工程投资	万元	1 871 726	1 094 186.04	58.46	15 921 618.07
1. 建筑安装工程	万元	55 642	22 990.31	41.32	3 135 797.30
其中：建筑	万元	54 340	22 089.58	40.65	2 982 495.97
安装	万元	1302	900.73	69.17	153 301.33
2. 机电设备费	万元	5981	4781.94	79.95	938 715.43
3. 金结设备费	万元	12 255	3124.76	25.50	193 092.12
4. 其他费用	万元	21 892	8681.51	39.66	426 566.33
5. 基本预备费	万元	1761	3706.94	210.49	79 846.86
6. 水库淹没处理补偿费	万元	636 579	376 674.00	59.17	5 050 041.61
7. 价差预备费	万元	1 137 615	674 226.58	59.27	4 584 283.83
其中：枢纽工程	万元	84 194	50 900.58	60.46	1 778 662.48
水库淹没处理补偿费	万元	1 053 421	623 326.00	59.17	2 805 621.35
8. 贷款利息	万元				1 513 274.61

表2　三峡工程主要工程量完成情况汇总表

项　　目	单位	2009年计划	2009年完成	占年计划（%）	自开工累计完成
主要工程量					
土石方开挖	万m^3	0.00	2.16		14 017.72
土石方填筑	万m^3				5349.37
混凝土浇筑	万m^3	7.60	4.42	58.16	2832.00

续表

项目	单位	2009年计划	2009年完成	占年计划（%）	自开工累计完成
固结灌浆	万m	0.00	0.33		49.58
帷幕灌浆	万m	1.13	0.83	73.63	34.14
接缝灌浆	万m^2				50.11
钢筋制作安装	万t	1.57	0.27	17.39	59.67
锚杆	万根	0.00	1.12		57.00
混凝土防渗墙	万m^2				28.35
机电安装	万t				19.06
金属结构安装	万t	0.15	0.10	69.33	22.04

2009年，三峡右岸地下电站形象进度超过年度计划目标，完成6台机组基础环、座环的安装和验收，完成4台机组的蜗壳安装并向土建施工交面，基本满足2011年和2012年各投产3台机组的目标要求。升船机建设完成船厢室段塔机安装，塔柱混凝土浇筑有序上升。工程建设实现“双零”管理目标。

2009年1～11月，三峡主体工程土建与金属结构安装工程单元质量评定完成795个，合格率100%，优良率92.6%。实现全年无质量事故管理目标。

（三）枢纽运行和管理情况

2009年，三峡水利枢纽运行安全平稳。三峡大坝、船闸高边坡变形、渗流量等各项参数均处于正常范围内，枢纽建筑物运行正常。三峡水库水质同比无类别变化。库首区地震和库岸基本稳定。枢纽运行安全平稳，坝区内外平安和谐。

水库优化调度研究和实践取得初步成果。取得“防洪限制水位有条件上浮1.5m、汛末试验性蓄水提前至9月15日开始”两项研究成果，并应用于批复的度汛方案、试验性蓄水方案及水库优化调度方案中。2009年，三峡电站通过优化调度节水增发电量39.5亿kW·h；春秋两季为下游实施航运补水调度125天，补水总量96亿m^3，有效保障了枯水季节下游航运和生产生活用水需求。

试验性蓄水工作全面完成。试验性蓄水于2009年9月15日启动，2009年11月24日达到最高水位171.43m。蓄水过程严格执行长江防汛抗旱总指挥部下达的6次调度令，加大下泄流量，缓解了洞庭湖及鄱阳湖流域旱情。

枢纽管理进一步强化。对26台机组启闭机房进行改造，对电站环境进行整治，为机组安全发电提供保障；2009年船闸通航率达到95.9%，远高于84.1%的设计指标；启动《三峡船闸运行管理手册》编制工作；积极开展三峡通航管理体制研究及协调工作；制定10余项茅坪溪大坝管理制度。

水库管理工作有力推进。开展水文泥沙原型观测和多个科研项目，完成价值1061万元的设备招标采购和安装，水文泥沙监测实时性和准确性大大增强；联合中国科学院建立香溪河生态系统实验站，为库区水质监测提供技术支撑；继续开展漂浮物清理，全年清理漂浮物10万m^3；进行库首区地震流动观测，完成地震监测系统技术升级改造准备；开展近坝库岸查勘和野猫面滑坡体监测；6次巡查上游水库和下游河段，掌握三峡库区消落区、地质灾害治理、水环境和下游河势等方面第一手资料。

（中国长江三峡集团公司　张立先　乔仁贵）

溪洛渡水电站工程2009年建设情况

（一）概况

2009年是溪洛渡工程开工的第四年，主体工程于本年全面展开。2009年3月27日开始大坝主体混凝土浇筑，10月29日开始二道坝混凝土浇筑，6月29日开始水垫塘底板混凝土浇筑。

2009年，溪洛渡水电站工程计划投资51.4亿元，实际完成投资42.3亿元，占计划的82.3%。其中：建筑安装工程完成投资177 229万元，比计划投资198 894万元减少21 665万元；设备费完成投资98 003万元，比计划投资174 884万元减少76 881万元。

截至2009年底，溪洛渡水电站工程累计完成投资213.12亿元，其中：建筑安装工程完成投资125.17亿元，永久设备完成投资13.93亿元，建设征地及移民安置费完成投资29.44亿元，其他费用完成投资37.28亿元，贷款利息7.3亿元。

2009年溪洛渡固定资产投资及主要工程量完成情况详见表1。

表 1 溪洛渡固定资产投资及主要工程量完成情况汇总表

项 目	单位	2009 年计划	2009 年完成	占年计划（%）	自开工累计完成
一、溪洛渡水电站投资	万元	514 180	422 804.32	82.23	2 131 159.92
（一）枢纽工程	万元	374 777	275 232.13	73.44	1 390 953.20
1. 建筑安装工程	万元	199 894	177 228.80	88.66	1 251 661.74
建筑工程	万元	198 894	169 685.67	85.31	1 242 246.09
施工辅助工程	万元	32 840	27 678.04	84.28	459 079.79
建筑工程	万元	155 573	137 270.12	88.24	752 656.62
环保工程	万元	10 481	4737.51	45.20	30 509.68
安装工程	万元	1000	7543.13	754.31	9415.65
2. 永久设备	万元	174 884	98 003.33	56.04	139 291.46
机电设备费	万元	153 784	89 151.54	57.97	130 358.18
金属结构设备费	万元	21 100	8851.79	41.95	8933.28
（二）建设征地和移民安置费	万元	37 362	58 548.23	156.71	294 385.00
（三）独立费用		46 376	34 889.57	75.23	219 025.01
（四）基本预备费	万元				
（五）价差预备费	万元	37 665	35 039.72	93.03	153 811.24
（六）贷款利息	万元	18 000	19 094.67	106.08	72 985.47
二、主要工程量					
土石方明挖	万 m^3	136.45	355.68	260.67	5459.75
石方洞挖	万 m^3	179.47	175.10	97.57	1970.77
混凝土浇筑	万 m^3	161.82	116.84	72.20	495.86
锚杆（锚筋）	万根	24.95	34.81	139.52	203.92

2009 年，溪洛渡主体工程共评定单元工程 4690 个，合格 4690 个，优良 4478 个，优良率为 95.50%。

（二）主要工程形象进度

1. 大坝工程

大坝主体 11～20 号坝段混凝土最低浇筑至高程 341m，最高浇筑至高程 359m。

2. 水垫塘及二道坝工程

二道坝混凝土最低浇筑至高程 341m，最高浇筑至高程 348m。水垫塘底板混凝土浇筑完成 84 仓。

3. 地下厂房工程

左岸 1 号机组和 7～9 号机组混凝土分别浇筑至高程 353.6m 并向机电安装交面；2～6 号机组混凝土浇筑分别至高程 348.5、346.53、335、335、344.53m。右岸 10、11、18 号机组混凝土均浇筑至高程 355.8m 并向机电安装交面；12～14 号机组混凝土浇筑分别至高程 352.5、349.1、336.72m。左岸主变压器室技术供水泵房和主变压器室上游运输通道混凝土浇筑完成；4、5、9 号机组母线洞大洞段边墙混凝土浇筑至高程 383m；1、2 号机组出线竖井下段开挖支护全部完成，竖井混凝土浇筑至高程 387m；3、4 号机组出线竖井开挖支护全部完成，竖井混凝土浇筑至高程 400m。右岸主变压器室技术供水泵房、上游运输通道和尾水调压室渗漏集水井混凝土浇筑完成；10、11、13～15 号机组母线洞大洞段边顶拱混凝土浇筑完成。左岸 1～3 号尾水洞底板混凝土浇筑分别完成 1055.71、361.41、197.76m；1、9 号机组尾水管底板混凝土浇筑完成 67.88m。右岸 4～6 号机组尾水洞底板混凝土浇筑分别完成 223.81、615.2、1030.87m；10、18 号机组尾水管底板混凝土浇筑完成 60.16m。

4. 泄洪洞

左岸 1、2 号泄洪洞有压段、中闸室、无压段开挖完成，龙落尾段开挖完成 50%，进口护坦混凝土浇筑完成设计工程量的40%，出口最低开挖至高程370m；1号泄洪洞有压段底板混凝土浇筑完成49m，2号泄洪洞无压段底板混凝土浇筑完成198m。右岸3、4号泄洪洞有压段、中闸室、无压段和龙落尾斜井段开挖完成，龙落尾下平段上层、中层开挖分别完成383m、86m，进水塔底板及边墙混凝土浇筑完成，胸墙混凝土浇筑至高程571m，出口开挖至高程370m；4号泄洪洞无压段底板混凝土浇筑完成99m，3号泄洪洞有压段底板混凝土浇筑完成49m。

（中国长江三峡集团公司　张立先　乔仁贵）

向家坝水电站工程 2009年建设情况

（一）固定资产投资完成情况

2009年，向家坝水电站计划投资59.59亿元，实际完成投资51.76亿元，占全年计划投资86.86%。其中：建筑安装工程完成投资158 089万元，比计划投资195 151万元减少37 062万元；设备费完成投资51 167万元，比计划投资83 094万元减少31 927万元；独立费用完成投资34 218万元，比计划投资56 385万元减少22 167万元。

截至2009年底，向家坝水电站累计完成投资147.2亿元，其中：建筑安装工程完成投资59.92亿元，设备费完成投资7.79亿元，建设征地和移民安置费完成投资53.73亿元，基本预备费用完成投资1.82亿元，其他费用完成投资20.51亿元，贷款利息3.43亿元。

2009年向家坝工程固定资产投资完成情况详见表1。

（二）主要工程量完成情况

2009年向家坝工程建设按照年度计划稳步推进，主要工程项目进度受控。其中，左岸主体及导流工程汛前满足度汛条件，年底左非岸坡坝段基本浇筑到高程382.5m；二期土石围堰汛前填筑完成，二期基坑10月完成大面开挖，年底基本完成齿槽开挖，具备开始浇筑混凝土的条件；右岸地下电站主厂房1号机完成锥管安装，2号机完成肘管安装和肘管二期混凝土浇筑，3号机完成肘管安装，主厂房关键线路进度满足年度计划要求。

2009年向家坝工程主要工程量完成情况详见表2。全年主体工程共评定单元工程2318个，合格率100%，优良率92.36%。

表1　向家坝固定资产投资完成情况汇总表

项　目	单位	2009年计划	2009年完成	占年计划（%）	自开工累计完成
	万元	595 865	517 582.97	86.86	1 472 029.21
（一）枢纽工程	万元	278 246	209 225.66	75.19	677 125.47
1. 建筑安装工程	万元	195 151	158 058.69	80.99	599 189.57
建筑工程	万元	194 251	154 124.94	79.34	594 889.37
施工辅助工程	万元	63 014	60 432.60	95.90	268 484.94
建筑工程	万元	128 125	91 160.54	71.15	311 523.89
环保工程	万元	3113	2531.81	81.34	14 880.53
安装工程	万元	900	3933.75	437.08	4300.21
2. 永久设备	万元	83 094	51 166.97	61.58	77 935.91
机电	万元	72 763	47 038.93	64.65	73 807.87
金属结构	万元	10 332	4128.04	39.96	4128.04
（二）建设征地和移民安置费	万元	237 499	241 572.00	101.71	537 322.00
（三）独立费用	万元	56 385	34 217.54	60.69	149 173.44
（四）基本预备费	万元	2100	1177.84	56.09	18 150.79
（五）价差预备费	万元	11 636	19 072.75	163.91	55 970.40
（六）贷款利息	万元	10 000	12 317.18	123.17	34 287.12

表 2 向家坝工程主要工程量完成情况汇总表

项目	单位	2009 年计划	2009 年完成	占年计划（%）	自开工累计完成
土石方明挖	万 m^3	940.01	1050.41	111.74	4580.46
石方洞挖	万 m^3	29.16	21.28	72.98	290.89
土石方填筑	万 m^3	128.49	111.15	86.50	1139.56
混凝土浇筑	万 m^3	80.72	89.98	111.47	481.91
固结灌浆	万 m	9.70	4.75	49.01	17.48
帷幕灌浆	万 m	12.00	12.53	104.42	23.04
钢筋	万 t	0.77	3.78	490.91	13.14
锚杆（锚筋）	万根	6.09	4.34	71.26	84.42

（三）主要工程形象进度

1. 左岸主体及导流工程

（1）基础处理工程，除左岸非溢流坝段 14 号坝段外，其余左岸非溢流坝段固灌全部完成；左岸非溢流坝段 1～4 号坝段主帷幕全部完成，冲沙孔、左岸非溢流坝段主帷幕基本完成；冲沙孔～左岸非溢流坝段 5 号坝段、左岸非溢流坝段 8 号坝段封闭帷幕全部完成，左岸非溢流坝段 6 号坝段封闭帷幕基本完成。

（2）混凝土工程，冲沙孔坝段年底全部浇到一期设计高程 340m；左岸非溢流坝段 1～6 号坝段，2009 年 2 月前浇到高程 280m；左岸非溢流坝段 7～18 号坝段，年底除左岸非溢流坝段 13、14 号坝段外，均浇筑到高程 382.5m。接缝灌浆，汛前完成左岸非溢流坝段 7 号以右坝段高程 280m 以下大部分，2009 年 12 月完成冲沙孔坝段高程 311m 以下部分。

（3）金属结构机电工程，1～5 号导流底孔封堵门于 2009 年 4 月门槽二期埋件埋设至高程 279.5m，槽塞安装完成；6 号导流底孔事故门二期埋件埋设至高程 330.5m，主反轨安装于 2009 年 12 月底完成，槽塞安装到高程 280m；6 号导流底孔工作门二期埋件埋设至高程 296m，槽塞安装到高程 275m；冲沙孔于 2009 年 4 月完成复合钢衬安装；2009 年 5 月完成左岸非溢流坝段 7 号坝段进厂交通洞、冲沙孔、上围堰施工支洞等部位防洪门的封堵；大坝集水泵站完成深井泵安装。

2. 二期厂坝工程

（1）土石方工程，2009 年 5 月 31 日下游围堰填筑至设计高程 291.5m，6 月 12 日上游围堰填筑至设计高程 305m，二期土石围堰汛前填筑完成。2009 年 8 月中旬泄洪坝段坝基开挖至设计高程 240m，12 月基本完成齿槽开挖，具备碾压混凝土浇筑施工条件。

（2）混凝土浇筑，右岸非溢流坝段 6 号坝段浇筑至高程 298m；泄洪坝段及消力池于 2009 年 11 月 15 日开始泄 1 号坝段高程 240m 平台找平混凝土浇筑，12 月 18 日开始泄 5 号坝段深齿槽找平混凝土浇筑，年底完成泄 2～4 号坝段和消力池高程 235m 平台填塘混凝土浇筑；厂 1～3 号坝段乙块于 2009 年 12 月 8 日浇筑找平混凝土，年底厂 1、厂 2 号坝段丙块浇到高程 243m；7 号机年底Ⅰ区、Ⅱ区浇筑 2 层，8 号机Ⅰ区、Ⅱ区浇筑 1 层（1m），6 号机Ⅱ区浇筑 1 层。

3. 右岸地下电站

（1）进水口 1～4 号进水塔混凝土浇筑分别至高程 337.1～342.3m。

（2）引水系统，完成引水洞全部开挖支护，启动渐变段和下弯段混凝土浇筑；压力钢管（共 88 节）制造完成，基本完成吊装，其中 1 号洞完成钢管焊接。

（3）主厂房于 2009 年上半年完成开挖支护，2009 年 5 月开始机组段混凝土浇筑。截至 2009 年底：1 号机组完成锥管一期混凝土浇筑（高程 251m）和锥管安装；2 号机组完成肘管安装，肘管二期混凝土浇筑至高程 241m；3 号机组完成肘管安装，肘管二期混凝土浇筑至高程 231m；4 号机组完成垫层混凝土浇筑。集水井边墙混凝土浇筑至高程 263.24m。

（4）主变压器室完成垫层混凝土浇筑，母线洞完成全部衬砌。

（5）1～4 号尾水扩散段开挖支护完成，1、2 号尾水支洞第Ⅰ层开挖支护完成；1 号尾水主洞（洞长 263.8m），完成洞顶拱混凝土衬砌和第Ⅱ层开挖；2 号尾水主洞（洞长 199.8m），完成顶拱混凝土衬砌 120.6m。

（6）尾水渠，Ⅰ区大面开挖至高程 250m，Ⅱ、Ⅲ区大面开挖至高程 269m。

（7）开关站完成高程 509.5m 以下边坡锚索施工；电缆竖井（共 217m）全断面开挖支护至高程 306.7m，累计开挖 202m，剩余 15m。

（8）1、2 号排沙支洞（分别长 100m、40m），各完成开挖进尺 10m；排沙主洞（共 338m），完成开挖进尺 87m；排沙洞闸门室交通洞（共 163m），全部开挖完成。

(9) 帷幕灌浆，第三层帷幕（即高程 274m 以下度汛关键帷幕）全部完成，第二层帷幕完成 70%。

4. 灌溉取水口

(1) 左岸灌溉取水口连接隧洞，计划 2010 年 1 月开始开挖。

(2) 右岸灌溉取水口连接隧洞，完成开挖支护 140m，剩余部分待进水塔浇到高程 360m 后再开挖。

5. 金属结构与机电

(1) 第一阶段金属结构设备已开始制造的项目有：左岸冲沙孔检修门及门槽、地下电站的各类闸门及埋件（快速门除外）。

(2) 第二阶段金属结构及启闭机采购完成招标工作。

(3) 机电设备已完成水轮发电机组、500kV 主变压器和 GIS 设备等主要机电设备以及部分辅助机电设备的采购；完成调速系统、励磁系统、厂用电系统等专题设计和审查；完成地下厂房 2 台桥机安装。

(四) 翻坝转运

截至 2009 年 12 月 31 日，全年共转运货物 58.36 万 t，其中煤矿 19.97 万 t，磷矿 38.39 万 t，最高日运量 0.61 万 t。

（中国长江三峡集团公司　张立先　乔仁贵
中国水电顾问集团中南勘测设计研究院　潘江洋）

拉西瓦水电站工程 2009 年建设情况

2009 年，拉西瓦水电站工程实现了按期下闸蓄水、首批机组发电和“一年四投”的目标。2009 年 3 月 1 日成功下闸蓄水，4 月 15 日 6 号机组和 5 号机组并网发电，9 月 27 日 3 号机组投产发电，12 月 25 日 2 号机组投产发电，全年实现了 4 台 70 万 kW 机组投产发电的目标，在我国水电工程建设中创造了诸多第一和亮点。其中，6 号机组的投产发电，被国家发展改革委、中国电力企业联合会授予我国“电力装机容量突破 8 亿 kW 标志性机组”称号；2 号机组的投产发电，被青海省政府授予“青海省电力装机容量超千万千瓦标志性机组”称号。

2009 年，完成混凝土浇筑 74.91 万 m^3，钢筋制作安装 6918.24t。截至 2009 年底，大坝最低坝段浇筑至 2444m 高程，最高坝段浇筑至 2458.5m 高程；大坝底孔、深孔、坝后水垫塘全部完成；电站进水口、压力引水管道及尾水系统全部完成并投入使用，厂房除 4 号机组以外土建工程全部完成。左右岸 2405m 高程以下固结灌浆、帷幕灌浆全部完成。

为实现拉西瓦水电站按期下闸蓄水、首批机组发电和“一年四投”的目标：

(1) 加强工程进度管理。一是加强现场施工进度管理，严格执行 2009 年初制定的进度计划，并逐一分解到季、月、周，实时进行进度目标控制。对没有按期完成的节点计划，认真分析原因，采取赶工措施。二是加强机电设备的催交、检查验收工作，确保机电安装工程有序进行。三是实行现场碰头会制度，及时解决现场需要协调的问题。四是重视合同结算管理，及时进行工程结算，确保各参建单位的资金到位和施工资源的投入。

(2) 加强安全施工管理。落实安全生产责任，形成横向到边、纵向到底、不留死角的安全监管体系。针对拉西瓦水电站边坡高陡、安全风险大的实际情况，制定切实可行的应急预案，对不安全岩体进行监控和加固，确保施工高峰期的安全。

(3) 加强工程质量管理。工程质量始终处于受控状态，满足设计和规范要求，单元工程优良率达到或超过质量考核目标。混凝土工程已验收单元全部合格，单元工程优良率为 96.2%；机电设备安装工程已验收单元工程优良率为 97.9%；金属结构已验收单元工程优良率为 95.2%。

在拉西瓦水电站工程建设中，始终坚持“以科技创新打造精品工程”的理念，注重新技术的开发和应用，成功使用了多项新工艺、新技术。在国内首次采用反拱水垫塘，经受了泄水的考验，运行工况正常；70 万 kW 机组蜗壳采用弹性垫层的埋入方式，750kV 超高压 GIS、GIL 设备的安装、投运等，处于国际领先水平。反拱水垫塘水力试验及结构计算研究、坝基无盖重固结灌浆试验研究分别荣获黄河上游水电开发有限责任公司科技进步一、二等奖；钢蜗壳垫层材料研究荣获中国电力投资集团公司科技进步三等奖和黄河上游水电开发有限责任公司科技进步三等奖。

（黄河上游水电开发有限责任公司
胡耀斌　许为宁　张文俊）

积石峡水电站工程 2009 年建设情况

积石峡水电站是国家 2009 年唯一核准的百万级水电项目，总装机容量 102 万 kW。黄河上游水电开发有限责任公司建设分公司紧紧把握这一有利契机，根据 3 个主体标段实际开工时间均晚于合同要求时间的实际情况，组织参建各方详细编制年度进度计划，在实施过程中严格控制施工进度，组织召开进度专题会议，研究赶工方案，强化赶工措施的落实，并加大施工资源投入，确保了 1 号机组定子吊装、坝体填筑等各关键节点目标按期实现。2009 年完成大坝填筑 279.07 万 m^3，混凝土浇筑 34.79 万 m^3，钢筋制作安装10 148.98t。

截至 2009 年底，大坝填筑至 1857m 高程；中孔泄洪洞及排沙底孔混凝土浇筑全部完成；进水口混凝土浇筑基本完成，引水压力钢管安装全部完成；溢洪道堰闸段混凝土浇筑完成；安装间、1 号机组混凝土浇筑全部完成；1 号机组定子吊入机坑（2009 年 10 月 22 日），转子焊接完成；3 号机组蜗壳安装完成向土建交面；GIS 设备本体安装完成。

在安全施工方面，2009 年继续把重大危险源（点）的预测、预警、预报、预控、预防作为重中之重，进一步落实安全生产责任，逐步形成了横向到边、纵向到底、不留死角的安全监管体系。针对积石峡水电站工程施工面窄、起重设备多、布置集中、交叉干扰大、设备运行安全矛盾突出等问题，黄河上游水电开发有限责任公司建设分公司制定了专门的设备安全运行措施，组织专家对工地起重设备进行了专项检查，对检查发现的问题及时整改，同时加强对施工单位的安全指导和安全考核，杜绝了事故的发生。

工程质量始终处于受控状态，满足设计和规范要求，2009 年积石峡水电站单元工程优良率达到或超过质量考核目标。混凝土工程已验收单元全部合格，单元工程优良率为 95.2%；机电设备安装工程已验收单元工程优良率为 100%；金属结构已验收单元工程优良率为 100%。

在投资控制方面，一是进一步加强了招标管理，重点加强招标文件的审查，主要对招标文件的设计方案、招标图纸、工程进度、技术参数、工程量清单等进行详细审查，着力提高招标文件的编制质量，为工程投资控制奠定了良好的基础。二是充分调动参建各方的技术力量，加强设计优化工作，缩短工程工期，降低工程投资。

积石峡水电站建设始终坚持“以科技创新打造精品工程”的理念，注重新技术的开发和应用，成功使用了多项新工艺、新技术。水电站面板堆石坝多岩性混合开挖料筑坝分析理论与施工优化技术研究、大直径压力钢管整体卷制研究荣获黄河上游水电开发有限责任公司科技进步一等奖。

（黄河上游水电开发有限责任公司
胡耀斌　许为宁　张文俊）

瀑布沟水电站工程 2009 年建设情况

2009 年，瀑布沟水电站工程按照“安全发展、科学发展、和谐发展、加快发展”的工作取向和“不留尾工、不留隐患、不留遗憾，一举成功”的总体要求，圆满实现了年度各项建设任务。大坝工程全面填筑完成，共计 2213 万 m^3；机组安装按计划推进，圆满实现了首批 2 台机组投产发电的目标；溢洪道工程土建工程施工全部完成；放空洞工程完工并通过竣工验收，实现了成功过水；尼日河引水工程全线开挖贯通，进入衬砌阶段；泄洪洞工程全部完工。2009 年实现安全无事故，工程累计实现安全生产 1961 天。共计验收评定建筑单元工程 5918 项，质量合格率达 100%，优良率达到 94.1%。安装单元工程 34 项，合格率 100%，优良率达到 100%。完成枢纽建筑物投资 19.73 亿元，占全年计划投资的 131.17%。

经过 8 年建设，2009 年 11 月 1 日 10 时 16 分，瀑布沟水电站工程正式下闸蓄水；11 月 10 日，蓄水至 790m 高程，完成了第一阶段蓄水任务。2009 年 11 月 10 日，电站 GIS 开关站布坡三线、四线及母线反送电一次成功，500kV 送出工程东线正式进入系统分部试运行阶段。2009 年 12 月 13 日 15 时 55 分，瀑布沟水电站首台机组（6 号机组）顺利通过 72h 试运行，并投入商业运行。2009 年 12 月 23 日 11 时，瀑布沟水电站第二台机组（5 号机组）顺利结束 72h 试运行，并投入商业运行。瀑布沟水电站在同一个月内实现了 2 台单机容量 60 万 kW 大型水轮发电机组的投产目标。

瀑布沟水电站位于四川省雅安市、凉山州境内，是大渡河上最大的水电站，其水库是大渡河流域的控制性水库之一。电站总装机容量 6×60 万 kW，设计多年平均发电量 147.9 亿 kW·h。水库总库容 53.9 亿 m^3，其中调洪库容 10.56 亿 m^3，调节库容 38.82 亿 m^3，具有季调节能力。瀑布沟水电站于 2003 年 1 月获得国家批准立项，2004 年 3 月 30 日工程正式开工，2005 年 11 月成功截流。计划 2010 年 10 月前，后续 4 台机组全部投运，2010 年完工。

（中国国电集团公司）

深溪沟水电站工程 2009 年建设情况

深溪沟水电站是大渡河干流规划的第十八级电站，位于四川省雅安市汉源县和凉山州甘洛县境内，是瀑布沟水库的反调节电站。电站设计最大坝高 49.5m，电站装机容量 4×16.5 万 kW，设计年发电量 32 亿 kW·h。工程于 2006 年 4 月核准开工，计划 2010 年 7 月首台机组发电，年内两台机组投产，2011 年完工。

2009年，深溪沟水电站工程坚持"突出一个'快'字，狠抓一个'精'字，落实一个'细'字"的总体要求和"一个突出、两个突破、三个确保"的工作思路，瞄准2010年7月1日首台机组发电目标，扎实推进"攻坚年"各项工作。

投资超额完成，工程造价全面受控。2009年累计完成建筑安装工程投资10.70亿元，为年计划的116%，其中枢纽建筑物完成投资8.42亿元。

实现"双零"目标，安全生产全面稳固。未发生任何重大及以上责任安全事故，2009年12月31日实现连续安全生产1360天。

确保工程质量，施工质量全面优良。2009年完成土建单元工程评定1394个，合格率100%，优良率96.1%；完成金属结构安装单元工程评定4个，合格率100%，优良率100%。未发生任何质量事故和设备损坏事故。

工程顺利推进，节点目标全面实现。2009年2月19日，提交1号机组锥管安装工作面；2月25日，4号机组混凝土整体浇筑到580.55m设计高程；6月23日，提交1号机组座环安装工作面；9月15日，完成安装间封顶、止漏；9月30日，1号机组进口段混凝土浇筑至坝顶设计高程；12月28日，完成了1号机组定子组装及磁化试验；12月29日，1号机组发电机层楼板混凝土浇筑提前17天完成。

（中国国电集团公司）

大岗山水电站工程2009年建设情况

大岗山水电站位于四川省雅安市石棉县境内，为大渡河干流规划的第十四级电站，总装机容量4×65万kW。电站枢纽建筑物由混凝土双曲拱坝、水垫塘及二道坝、泄洪隧洞、引水及尾水建筑物、发电厂房、开关站等组成，发电厂房为地下式。最大坝高约210m，总库容7.42亿m^3，调节库容1.17亿m^3，多年平均年发电量109.8亿kW·h。工程施工总工期95个月。

2009年，大岗山水电站工程沉着应对复杂情况，不断开拓创新，稳步推进工程建设，顺利实现了各项年度目标。

枢纽工程稳步推进。顺利完成了左、右岸坝顶以上开挖支护工程；坝顶以下工程开挖最低已开挖至1050m高程；提前完成右岸深部卸荷裂隙补充勘探和加固处理措施。引水发电系统各项进度考核目标均提前完成：主厂房岩锚梁开挖完成，岩锚梁混凝土施工启动，Ⅳ层拉槽开挖完成；主变压器室、母线洞开挖基本完成；尾调室Ⅴ层开挖启动。大坝高线混凝土拌和系统一期土建已完成。大坝低线混凝土系统已投产。大坝砂石系统棱子坝料场开采运输通道已基本联通，海流沟生产系统完成并投入运行，料场开始顶部覆盖层剥离，粗碎车间正在施工。大坝深部基础处理工程按计划顺利推进。上下游围堰已填筑至设计高程并经受住了汛期考验。1、2、3号缆机安装顺利完成，并投入试运行。

安全形势保持平稳。国电大渡河流域水电开发有限公司坚持"落实责任、过程控制、严格考核"的安全强势管理思路，进一步落实了"管工程必须管安全"的责任制，加强现场安全管理力度。积极推进安全隐患责任追究制，不放过任何一个隐患背后的安全责任。不断完善重奖重罚安全管理手段，切实提高了安全管理水平。加强各种安全知识培训，增强了参建人员的安全意识和安全防护技能，切实抓好施工现场的安全管理工作。2009年，未发生任何安全责任事故。截至2009年12月31日，大岗山水电站工程连续安全生产1605天。

质量管理得到强化。围绕2009年质量控制重点，狠抓质量管理责任的落实，充分发挥监理和三大中心的监管作用，进一步明确了从设计到施工的各级质量管理职责。强化了质量管理培训工作，邀请专家开展质量控制现场专项培训，组织人员到溪洛渡、向家坝等工程学习取经，提升了质量管理人员水平。加大了质量考核力度，充分利用质量奖罚基金和质量管理考核办法，采取强抓严管措施，对质量控制不符合要求的部位采取重罚。针对大坝拱肩槽开挖、地下厂房岩锚梁开挖浇筑等重点部位制定了严格的质量达标要求和控制方案措施。2009年，工程建设质量合格率100%，土建单元优良率达93.1%，安装单元优良率96%，未发生工程质量事故。

（中国国电集团公司）

亭子口水利枢纽工程

（一）工程概况

亭子口水利枢纽位于四川省广元市苍溪县境内，是嘉陵江干流的控制性骨干水利枢纽工程，开发任务以防洪、灌溉及城乡供水、发电为主，兼顾航运，并具有拦沙减淤等综合利用效益。该水利枢纽是《长江流域综合利用规划简要报告（1990年修订）》和《嘉陵江干流广元至苍溪河段规划报告》中推荐的近期建设项目，也是国务院批转水利部《关于加强长江近期防洪建设若干意见》（国发［1999］12号）确定的完善长江防洪工程体系近期建设的防洪工程之一。

亭子口水利枢纽为一等大（1）型工程。枢纽布置为：河床中间布置8个表孔、5个底孔及消能建筑物，底孔（兼作排砂孔）布置在表孔左侧；河床左侧布置坝后式电站厂房，河床右侧布置垂直升船机，两岸布置非溢流坝段。大坝为混凝土重力坝，坝轴线总长995.4m，坝顶高程465m，最大坝高115m。水库正常蓄水位458m，总库容40.67亿m^3，可灌溉农田292.14万亩。电站装机容量4×275MW，保证出力163～187MW，设计年平均发电量29.67亿～31.94亿kW·h。通航能力为2×500t级。

工程建成后，将是川东北地区规模最大的具有年调节能力的大型水电电源，可有效地缓解川东北地区电网调峰容量不足的紧张局面；同时，还可提高下游15座梯级电站的保证出力188MW，增加多年平均发电量约4.5亿kW·h。亭子口水利枢纽在防洪、灌溉及城乡供水方面具有不可替代性，工程社会效益显著，并具有较好的经济和环境效益。

（二）前期工作情况

亭子口水利枢纽项目建议书于2007年8月3日获得国家发展改革委批准（发改农经［2007］1924号文）。2008年11月12日，水利部将亭子口水利枢纽项目可行性研究报告以水规计［2008］479号文报国家发展改革委；2009年6月30日，国家发展改革委以发改农经［2009］1746号文正式批复了项目可行性研究报告。

2009年10月30日，水利部以水总［2009］526号文批复了嘉陵江亭子口水利枢纽初步设计报告，同日，水利部以办建管［2009］448号文批复了项目开工报告。2009年11月25日，由中共四川省委、中国大唐集团公司共同举办了开工仪式。

自2006年12月左岸进场公路开工至2009年底，相继完成了左岸进场公路、亭子口嘉陵江大桥、左右岸场内公路，建成了两岸施工供水系统、两岸混凝土生产系统和亚洲最大的天然砂石骨料加工系统，完成了导流工程、左岸前期工程土石开挖等施工任务。

前期建设共计完成土石方开挖约900万m^3，浇筑混凝土约100万m^3，钢筋、金属结构约11 000t。

（三）工程建设管理

亭子口水利枢纽由嘉陵江亭子口水利水电开发有限公司负责开发建设及建成后的运行管理。

嘉陵江亭子口水利水电开发有限公司（以下简称亭子口公司）成立于2006年6月，是由中国大唐集团公司、四川省投资集团有限责任公司、四川省港航开发有限责任公司、四川省水电投资经营集团有限公司、四川省苍溪嘉陵江水利水电开发有限责任公司按55%、20%、16%、5%、4%的股份比例共同组建的有限责任公司，由中国大唐集团公司四川分公司管理。

亭子口公司成立了创建优质精品工程领导小组，编制了《嘉陵江亭子口水利枢纽创建优质精品工程策划书》。质量总目标是：工程合格率100%，土建优良率90%，机电优良率95%，关键部位优良率100%；管理制度表格健全、档案资料完整有效；不发生人身死亡和责任性重大生产事故；不发生重大社会影响事件；工程安全稳定，按时达标投产，运行一年后不出现影响使用的质量问题；建成创新、环保、经济、和谐、友好的水利枢纽；获国家电力优质工程奖，创鲁班奖，争国家优质工程金质奖。2009年，将质量总目标分解到各施工项目、各工序，渗透到工程建设全过程，使亭子口工程质量管理水平得到全面提升；年内完成单元工程评定3217个，合格率100%，优良率92.62%，未发生重大质量事故，实现了质量管理目标。

亭子口公司严格工程招标和合同管理各项制度，规范开展各项招标活动，未发生重大设计变更和索赔事项；重点完成了大坝Ⅰ标、大坝Ⅱ标、厂房标三大主标招标工作，保证了主体工程开工工期。2009年，工程造价控制在设计概算之内，执行的主要合同199个，合同总额约51亿元。亭子口公司通过改变合同关系以及结算方式、减少流转环节，减轻了砂石骨料增值税税负。通过反复与中国工商银行沟通，将2008年贷款在2009年要到期的、利率高的贷款提前归还，节约融资费用约40万元。

截至2009年底，亭子口水利枢纽工程完成投资13.63亿元；完成单元工程评定4335个，合格率达到100%，机电工程优良率95%，土建项目优良率93.1%；未发生重大及以上质量事故。

（嘉陵江亭子口水利水电开发有限公司）

藏木水电站工程

（一）工程概况

藏木水电站是雅鲁布江中游规划建设的第一座大型电站，是雅鲁藏布江中游河段水电站规划的第四级电站，位于西藏中部电网负荷中心。工程场址位于西藏自治区山南地区加查县境内，地处雅鲁藏布江中游桑日至加查峡谷段出口处，坝址区距下游加查县县城17km，距拉萨直线距离140km，距下游右岸藏木村5.0km。

藏木水电站为堤坝式开发，开发任务主要为发电，兼顾生态环境用水要求，无航运、漂木、防洪、灌溉等综合利用要求。坝址控制流域面积15 766km^2，占中国境内流域积的65.61%，多年平均流量

1010m^3/s。电站采用左侧河床布置6孔溢流坝，右侧河床布置6台水轮发电机组的坝后式地面厂房方案。水库总库容为0.93亿m^3，正常蓄水位3310m以下库容为0.866亿m^3；死水位3305m以下库容为0.735 8亿m^3，调节库容0.130 2亿m^3，具有日调节能力。电站引用流量1070.3m^3/s，额定水头53.5m，总装机容量510MW，年发电量25.008亿kW·h，工程静态总投资79.141 3亿元，按国家拨款50%计算，总投资95.613 4亿元，首台机组发电工期为75个月，总工期为90个月。

藏木水电站可行性研究报告于2008年10月通过水电水利规划设计总院组织的审查，2009年4月完成《西藏自治区雅鲁藏布江藏木水电站可行性研究报告（审定本）》；2009年5月完成资金筹措专题报告和工程建设的可行性报告，10月通过中国国际工程咨询公司的项目评估。预计2010年主体工程开工建设。

（二）枢纽布置及建筑物

藏木水电站工程水库总库容0.93亿m^3，电站装机容量510MW，依据《水电枢纽工程等级划分及设计安全标准》（DL 5180—2003），工程等别为二等工程，工程规模为大（2）型，其永久性主要水工建筑物按2级设计，永久性次要水工建筑物按3级设计，临时建筑物为3级建筑物。

考虑到藏木水电站是雅鲁藏布江上兴建的第一座大型水电站的重要性，电站下游17km处为加查县县城，雅鲁藏布江干流历史洪水资料少的情况，确定混凝土重力坝、泄水建筑物按500年一遇洪水设计，2000年一遇洪水校核；电站厂房按200年一遇洪水设计，500年一遇洪水校核；2级建筑物消能防冲设施按50年一遇洪水设计。

坝轴线位于横Ⅱ勘线，方向为NE54°58′0″。水库正常蓄水位3310.00m，设计洪水位3310.00m，校核洪水位3310.61m，死水位为3305m，坝顶高程为3314.00m。枢纽建筑物主要由拦河大坝、泄洪消能防冲、排沙、发电厂房等建筑物组成。导流明渠布置在左岸和两孔表孔溢流坝结合，前期为导流明渠，后期改建为两表孔溢流坝。

拦河大坝自左向右分别为左岸挡水坝、溢流坝、左冲沙底孔坝段、厂房坝段、右冲沙底孔坝段和右岸挡水坝段，坝顶总长度389.50m，其中左岸挡水坝段长48.0m，溢流坝长度为127.0m，左冲沙底孔坝段坝顶长度为15.0m，厂房坝段长135.5m，右冲沙底孔坝段长度15m，右岸挡水坝长为49m。坝后式厂房布置在左、右冲沙底孔坝段之间，位于河床右侧，安装间设置为地面安装间，邻主机间靠山内侧布置。溢流坝及左冲沙底孔坝段下游接综合消力池及海漫。右冲沙底孔采用冲沙管的形式，从地面安装间底部穿过至下游，采用底流消能的方式，出口布置在厂房尾水反坡段下游水平段。

（三）主要建筑物

1. 左岸挡水坝段

为1、2号两个坝段，坝顶长度均为24.0m，共计48.0m，坝顶高程3314.00m，最低建基面高程为3238.0m，最大坝高76.0m，坝顶宽度19.0m，上游坝坡为直立面，下游坝坡坡度为1∶0.75，下游面折坡点高程3304.0m。

2. 溢流坝

为3～8号共6个坝段，共中3、4号溢流坝段由左岸导流明渠改建而成；各坝段长度分别为24.5m、23.0m、20.0m、20.0m、20.0m、19.5m，总长度为127.0m；最大坝高109.0m，最低建基面高程3205.00m，坝基最大宽度88.0m。溢流坝段共布置6个溢流表孔，孔口尺寸15m×19m（宽×高）。溢流坝闸墩顺水流方向51.0m，边墩厚4.5m，中墩厚5.0m。溢流坝消能防冲按50年一遇洪水设计，采用底流消能方式，消力池采用综合式消力池。因枢纽布置方案采用和导流明渠结合的方式，导流明渠外导墙将消力池分左右两个。

3. 左冲沙底孔坝段

为9号坝段。为便于运行期冲沙、兼顾水库放空和向下游泄放生态流量，设左冲沙底孔。该坝段坝顶长度15.0m，坝顶宽度25.0m，最大坝高116.0m，最低建基面高程3198.00m，坝基最大宽度95.1m。冲沙底孔宽5.0m、高6.0m，采用两段弧过渡与消力池底板相接，底槛高程3246.0m，洞身采用钢板衬护。

4. 厂房挡水坝段

为10～15号共6个坝段，按一机一缝布置，各坝段长度分别为27.90m、22.40m、19.5m、22.40m、19.5m、23.8m，全长135.5m；顺水流方向最大宽度89.10m。坝基置于弱风化花岗岩上，最低开挖高程3198.00m，坝顶高程3314.00m，最大坝高116m。坝内分别布置一条灌浆廊道、一条交通廊道和2条排水廊道，并同冲沙底孔坝段廊道连通。

5. 厂房

主机间和安装间呈“一”字形布置，纵轴线与坝轴线平行，距坝轴线间距104m，主机间段顺水流方向宽度为60.5m，厂房跨度为26.0m，高度48.15m。厂内安装6台单机容量85MW的混流式水轮发电机组，采用“两机一缝”布置方式，机组间距19.50m，机组安装高程3237.20m。主机间建基面高程3217.65m，置于弱风化的花岗岩上。厂房内设有

250t/50t桥式起重机一台。主机间分为两层，发电机层高程3249.80m，水轮机层高程3241.80m，两层之间分别布置楼梯作为上下层的交通。安装间布置于主机间右侧，顺水流方向宽度同主机间为26.0m，沿机组纵轴方向长38.5m。主变压器及GIS楼布置于厂房挡水坝段与主机间之间，长131.68m，宽15.0m，主要布置有主变压器、GIS及屋面出线场。下游副厂房布置于厂房主机间下游与尾水平台之间，长度与主机间相同，宽10.50m。

6. 进厂交通洞

由下游公路经右岸山体内，在安装间右端墙进入厂房，总长487.95m，其中靠安装间的平段长度44.0m，后接坡段长度443.91m，坡度为2.97%。考虑便于大件运输，尺寸初拟8m×8m。交通洞顶拱及边墙均采用ϕ22@1.5m×1.5m、长4m的系统锚杆，并采用50cm厚钢筋混凝土全断面衬砌，顶拱及边墙设置排水孔，并在顶拱部位进行回填灌浆，出口段100m范围内进行固结灌浆；洞脸采用100cm厚钢筋混凝土衬砌，边坡进行喷混凝土、挂钢筋网及锚杆支护处理。

7. 右冲沙底孔坝段

为16号坝段，坝顶长15.0m，宽27.0m，最大坝高80.00m。冲沙底孔孔口尺寸4.0m×5.0m，洞身采用钢板衬护，出口段表面采用C40抗冲耐磨混凝土。进出口设平板检修闸门和工作闸门，进口检修闸门下游，采用直径4.0m圆形断面，即采用20mm钢板内衬，外包混凝土的方式。冲沙底孔穿过地面安装间，出口采用底流消能的方式，消力池出口布置在厂房尾水反坡段下游水平段。

8. 右岸挡水坝段

为17、18、19号共3个坝段，坝顶长度分别为17.00m、20.00m、20.00m，共计57.00m，坝顶高程3314.00m，最低建基面高程为3238.0m，最大坝高76.0m。

（中国水电顾问集团成都勘测设计研究院　刘吉祥　唐　兰）

银盘水电站工程建设情况

银盘水电站位于乌江下游河段，地处重庆市武隆县，是乌江干流水电开发规划第十一梯级，是其上游彭水水电站的反调节电站。枢纽工程等别为二等，工程规模为大（2）型。电站以发电为主，兼顾航运，装机容量600MW，保证出力161.7MW，多年平均年发电量27.08亿kW·h，以2回220kV输电线路接入重庆市电网；设500t级船闸，库区改善通航里程55km。水库淹没耕地2102.0亩，淹没园地50.3亩，淹没林地955.9亩，迁移人口4235人。

（一）水文和水库特性

坝址以上流域面积74 910km^2，为乌江流域面积的85.20%，多年平均流量1390m^3/s，多年平均径流量436亿m^3。百年一遇设计洪水流量27 100m^3/s，相应库水位219.00m；千年一遇校核洪水流量35 600m^3/s，相应库水位225.57m。水库总库容3.20亿m^3；正常蓄水位215m，相应库容1.83亿m^3；死水位211.50m，死库容1.46亿m^3；调节库容0.37亿m^3，为日调节水库。电站额定水头26.5m，最大工作水头35.12m，最小工作水头13m，单机额定流量635.8m^3/s。

（二）枢纽布置

坝址系页岩、砂岩、灰岩，岩体致密。坝址区地震基本烈度为Ⅵ度。枢纽由右岸船闸、河床溢流表孔、左岸河床厂房、220kV开关站等组成。大坝为混凝土重力坝，最大坝高78.5m，坝顶高程227.50m，坝顶长600.10m。泄洪建筑物有10孔溢流表孔，单孔15.5m×20.0m，堰顶高程195m，采用面流和底流消能。河床式厂房长142.1m、宽93.4m、高82.8m（不含安装场），水轮机安装高程175.80m。厂内安装4台单机容量为150MW的轴流转浆式水轮发电机组；2台主变压器容量均为340MVA，电压等级220kV。

根据航运规划，该河道为Ⅳ级航道，通航建筑物为500t级单级船闸。船闸有效尺寸120m×12m×4m（长×宽×槛上最小水深）。船闸设计最大水头为36.46m，代表船型500t级货船的尺寸为67.5m×10.8m×1.6m（总长×型宽×设计吃水），年通航天数为336天，设计水平年（2030年）货运量309万t/年。

（三）工程量与施工导流方案

银盘水电站总工程量：土石方开挖1268.58万m^3，混凝土259.65万m^3，喷混凝土23.48万m^3，帷幕灌浆6.27万m，固结灌浆6.33万m，钢筋钢材6.7万t，金属结构安装18 520t。设计总工期77个月（不包括工程筹建期），其中施工准备期22个月，主体工程施工33个月，工程完建期22个月，首台机组发电55个月。

施工导流采用三期导流方式：一期原河床导流；二期上、下游全年挡水土石围堰挡水，明渠导流；三期上下游全年挡水土石围堰挡水，汛期由已建成的河床溢流坝段8孔表孔泄流。

（四）项目投资与申报情况

建设单位为重庆大唐国际武隆水电开发有限公司，股东方投资比例为：大唐国际发电股份有限公司

51%、重庆鼎泰能源有限公司24.5%、重庆航运建设发展有限公司24.5%。设计单位为长江勘测规划设计研究院。2005年5月，预可行性研究报告通过了水电水利规划设计总院审查。2007年底，可行性研究报告通过了水电水利规划设计总院审查。中国国际咨询公司以咨能源［2008］1130号文下发了银盘水电站核准评估报告的审查意见。根据核准评估意见，按2008年二季度末价格水平，银盘水电站工程（不含送出工程）总投资为804 478万元，其中静态投资723 465万元，建设期贷款利息81 013万元。2008年12月29日，国家发展改革委以发改能源［2008］3635号文下发了银盘水电站项目核准意见。计划2011年4月中旬第一台机组发电，2013年6月工程全部完工。

（五）2009年工程建设形象面貌

1. 厂房及围堰工程

2009年3月16日，1～4号机组尾水管顶板全部封顶；9月23日，第一台机组Ⅱ区15层移交机电安装，进行座环安装；10月18日，4台机组进水口底板全部浇筑完成；11月13日，厂房左非坝段全线到顶。厂房标段全年完成混凝土浇筑53.91万m^3，累计完成混凝土浇筑66.83万m^3，占总设计量的83.0%；完成基础固结灌浆10 444.4m，累计完成14 569.4m，占设计量的100%。

2. 大坝工程

2009年4月18日，泄5～8号表孔溢流面全部施工完毕；5月5日，纵向围堰坝身段上游块混凝土浇筑到设计高程227.3m；6月10日，左中区护坦全部施工完毕。全年完成大坝混凝土33.52万m^3，累计完成混凝土49.46万m^3，占总设计量的91.4%；完成大坝基础固结灌浆1150.45m，占设计总量100%。2009年3月开始基础帷幕灌浆施工，全年完成11 184.3m，占设计总量的98.8%。

3. 机电及金属结构安装工程

4台机组尾水锥管安装调整加固验收完成，尾水管以下部分测量、电缆及水、气管路埋设完成，安Ⅰ坝段193m高程以下水管、油管路埋设完成，安Ⅱ坝段193m高程以下水管、气、油管及电缆管等埋设完成，1、4号机组座环、转轮室安装调试完成并移交土建进行蜗壳顶板钢钎维混凝土浇筑，2、3号机组座环安装调整完成并移交土建进行蜗壳顶板备仓。泄洪坝段完成弧门底槛、侧轨安装，完成检修门门槽、底槛安装，完成临时叠梁门底槛、门槽以及5～9号闸墩锚栓架安装，完成6～9号闸墩油缸支铰座等安装，共完成埋件约750t，并完成该坝段门机安装。1～4号机组厂房尾水闸门底槛、门槽（门楣以下部分）安装也完成。

（六）移民、环保水保工作情况

银盘水电站按照“三同时”原则，委托了环保、水保监理实施专业归口管理，健全了环保、水保管理制度，构成完整的环境保护、水土保持监督和保证体系。建立了与地方政府可靠的环保、水保联动应急机制，开展尘、毒、噪声治理，合理排放废渣、生活污水和施工废水，最大限度地减少施工活动给周围环境造成的不利影响。为了打造“绿色银盘”工程，提前启动了施工区域内的水土保持和绿化工作，目前正按规划分阶段实施。

银盘水电站积极配合地方政府共同打造“重庆市样板移民工程”。在实施过程中，关注移民遇到的实际困难，化解各类矛盾，最大限度满足移民提出的合理要求，确保移民稳定。2009年10月24日，《乌江银盘水电站移民安置实施规划报告》正式获得重庆市的批准，成为银盘水电站移民安置工程实施的重要依据。重庆市召开了“重庆乌江银盘水电站移民工作会”，副市长谭栖伟分别与彭水、武隆两县分管移民工作的县领导签订了“责任书”，确定了2010年10月底具备下闸蓄水的目标。目前，彭水、武隆两县移民工程全面启动，各项工程节点工期基本满足蓄水目标进度。

（大唐国际发电股份有限公司　余圣刚
重庆大唐国际武隆水电开发有限公司）

彭水水电站工程尾工建设情况

彭水水电站5台单机容量350MW的水轮发电机组已于2008年全部投产发电，2009年工程建设进入收尾。截至2009年底，工程形象面貌如下：

大坝工程的所有项目全部完成。大坝、引水洞、主厂房、尾水洞、开关站单项工程竣工验收完成。

通航建筑物土建部分：上游引航道、船闸、中间渠道、下游引航道、升船机混凝土及屋面网架等均已全部施工完成；升船机高程290m以上装修砌体全部完成，剩余墙面装饰、门窗安装及地面装修施工。

通航建筑物金属结构安装：船闸金属结构全部安装完成，并完成无水调试。升船机下闸首工作门安装完成3节（共4节），升船机主提升设备基座安装调整完成，主提升设备全部吊装就位。承船厢已全部吊装至高程203m船厢室内，开始就位调整和焊接组装。

鱼类增殖放流站一期场坪全部施工完成，二期养鱼池土建完成80%，配套设施同步进行。

（大唐国际发电股份有限公司　余圣刚）

潘口水电站工程简介及建设情况

潘口水电站位于湖北省十堰市竹山县境内，地处堵河干流上游河段，坝址距竹山县城 13km，经鲍峡镇至十堰公路里程 162km。工程开发任务以发电、防洪为主，电站建成后还具有增加南水北调中线可调水量、提高南水北调的供水保证率、改善库区通航条件等综合利用效益。水库正常蓄水位 355.00m，相应库容 19.70 亿 m^3，总库容 23.38 亿 m^3，调节库容 11.20 亿 m^3，为完全年调节水库。电站装机 2 台，总装机容量 500MW，年平均发电量为 10.5 亿kW·h。工程静态投资405 791万元，总投资439 735万元。

潘口水电站可行性研究报告于 2005 年 11 月 13 日通过了审查，国家发展改革委于 2007 年 9 月 27 日核准了该项目，主体工程于 2007 年 10 月 28 日正式开工建设，2009 年 9 月 26 日成功实现了截流，同年 11 月 22 日开始大坝填筑。

（一）水文和地质概况

潘口坝址控制流域面积 8950km^2，占堵河流域面积的 71.6%，多年平均流量为 164m^3/s，年径流量 51.7 亿 m^3，多年平均含沙量为 0.962kg/m^3，多年平均输沙量 497 万 t。

坝址位于潘口河口至上游 1.2km 长的峡谷段内，河道弯曲呈“S”形，总体上右岸为凸岸，河流流向自北北西转向北东东，两岸坡度 40°～50°。坝址由上游至下游出露有元古界武当山群化口组（P_{twdh3}）（俗称副片岩）的白云母石英片岩、下寒武统水沟口组（$\in_{1sg}$）绢云绿泥石英片岩、炭质千枚岩地层。加里东期辉长—辉绿岩沿上述两地层接触线，似层状侵入到下寒武统水沟口组中，后期变质为绿泥钠长片岩（γ_3^{1n}）（俗称正片岩）。

库区出露的地层岩性变化较大，主要有元古界武当山群、震旦系、寒武系、奥陶系、志留系、泥盆系、二叠系、第四系地层以及加里东期基性侵入岩。岩性主要有结晶片岩、千枚岩、板岩、砂页岩等。两岸分水岭高程大于 490m，山体雄厚。库盆基岩多裸露，岩层走向北西，与河谷呈直交或斜交，大多为斜交谷或横谷，水库蓄水后不会造成大规模顺层坍滑。库盆主要由隔水的结晶片岩、千枚岩、板岩及砂页岩组成，仅南支官渡河库尾段为灰岩，两岸地下水露头高于库水位，水库不存在向邻谷渗漏问题。

工程区地震基本烈度为Ⅶ度，对壅水建筑物取基准期 100 年内超越概率 P_{100} 为 0.02 的基岩水平加速度峰值为 0.228g，工程设防烈度为Ⅷ度。对非壅水建筑物取基准期 50 年内超越概率 P_{50} 为 0.05 的基岩水平加速度峰值为 0.134g。

（二）枢纽布置及主要建筑物

枢纽建筑物主要由混凝土面板堆石坝、右岸岸边开敞式溢洪道、右岸泄洪洞、左岸引水隧洞、地面厂房和开关站等组成，属一等大（1）型工程。

混凝土面板堆石坝坝顶高程 362.0m，趾板最低建基面高程 248.0m，最大坝高 114.0m。坝轴线长 292.0m，顶宽 9.2m，上下游坝坡均为 1∶1.4，下游坝坡在高程 333.0m、308.0m 处各设置一条 2.0m 宽的马道，在高程 283.0m 处设置一条 5.0m 宽的马道。采用 1000 年一遇（洪峰流量17 800m^3/s）设计，采用10 000年一遇（洪峰流量22 700m^3/s）校核。溢洪道布置在右岸，位于大坝和泄洪洞之间，采用岸边开敞式，由进水渠、闸室段、泄槽段、挑流鼻坎等部分组成，进水渠底板高程 330.0m，最小渠底宽度 69.0m；闸室段长 35.0m，前缘宽 69m，堰顶高程 337.0m，闸室共分为 3 孔，孔口尺寸 20.0m×18.0m（宽×高）；泄槽净宽 69.0m，底坡 0.15，水平长度为 300m；挑流鼻坎采用连续扩散式斜鼻坎。泄洪洞布置在溢洪道右侧山体内，为明流隧洞，采用岸塔式进水口，进口底板高程 300.0m，孔口尺寸 8.0m×10.0m（宽×高），无压隧洞长 635.0m，纵坡 $i=0.038$，洞身过水断面尺寸 8.0m×13.0m（宽×高），城门洞形，出口采用连续式挑流鼻坎。

引水发电系统布置在左岸，进水口采用岸塔式，底板高程 309.0m；采用单机单洞引水，两条引水隧洞长度分别为 492.3m 和 428.3m，混凝土衬砌段内径 9.5m，衬砌厚度为 0.7m，钢衬段内径为 8.5m，回填混凝土厚度 0.6m。厂房采用岸边地面厂房，内设两台单机容量为 250MW 的混流式水轮发电机组，主厂房尺寸为 94.3m×31.1m×59.0m（长×宽×高），开关站布置在左岸上坝公路内侧，地面高程 381.00m，尺寸为 160m×106m（长×宽）。

（三）施工安排

1. 施工导流

潘口水电站坝址河谷属狭窄形河谷，施工导流采用河床一次拦断，隧洞导流的导流方式，围堰采用土石围堰结构，导流时段选择为枯水时段 10 月 1 日～次年 4 月 30 日，导流流量采用时段 20 年一遇洪峰流量 4350m^3/s。导流隧洞布置在右岸，采用城门洞型，尺寸为 15.0m×18.0m（宽×高）。

2. 料场选择

为充分利用当地材料，堆石坝采用了多种料源：溢洪道开挖利用料（片岩），河床天然砂砾料以及潘口河石料（硅质岩、灰岩）。混凝土骨料采用天然砂砾料。

3. 主体工程施工

主体及导流工程量：土石方明挖 546 万 m^3，石方洞挖 35 万 m^3，混凝土浇筑 46 万 m^3，坝体填筑 276 万 m^3。大坝填筑安排 15.3 个月，分 5 期填筑，其中Ⅰ期为坝体抢筑临时拦洪度汛断面，填筑高程 248.00～322.00m，填筑方量 143.86 万 m^3，要求 2010 年 4 月 30 日前完成。

4. 施工总进度

工程首台机组发电工期为 3 年 6 个月。工程于第一年 10 月开工，第二年 9 月底截流，第二年 12 月开始大坝堆石填筑，第三年 4 月 30 日临时拦洪度汛断面达到高程 322.00m，第三年年底坝体全断面填筑至高程 358.00m，第四年 10 月初水库下闸蓄水。

（四）水库淹没处理及环境保护

水库淹没涉及竹山、竹溪县的 10 个乡（镇）、69 个村、244 个村民小组。淹没土地总面积 61.45km^2（其中陆地面积 53.16km^2），淹没耕地面积 2.46 万亩、林地面积 2.89 万亩，塌岸影响耕地 69.8 亩，水库淹没和滑坡影响的人口为31 043人，淹没影响房屋建筑面积 120.4 万 m^2。水库淹没二级公路 8.05km、三级公路 48.57km 以及四级公路 20.04km。

施工区征地面积 3803.2 亩（含水库淹没区 1033.3 亩），其中耕地面积 744.4 亩、林地 1582.7 亩。在施工区征地面积中，永久征地面积为 3353.7 亩，临时占地面积为 449.5 亩。施工区占地搬迁人口 610 人。

工程建设虽然存在一定不利环境影响，但没有制约工程建设的重大不利影响因素，其大多数不利影响可以采取一定的环境保护措施加以减少和避免，工程区域自然环境质量不会明显下降，在切实落实各项环境保护措施的情况下，社会环境质量将有所提高。

（五）工程建设计划及进展情况

潘口水电站 2009 年完成土石方明挖 249 万 m^3，石方洞挖 8.2 万 m^3，混凝土浇筑 5.2 万 m^3，钢筋制作安装 0.55 万 t，压力钢管制作 17 节（572t），固结灌浆 0.8 万 m。工程全年完成投资108 523.77万元，累计完成投资222 577.42万元。

截至 2009 年底工程形象面貌如下：

1. 导流洞工程

全年主要集中在导流洞进口及洞身段施工，完成混凝土浇筑 3 万 m^3，钢筋制作安装 0.2 万 t，固结灌浆 0.8 万 m。2009 年 3 月 10 日通过过水验收，3 月 16 日导流洞过水。

2. 泄洪洞工程

泄洪洞洞挖于 2009 年 7 月 19 日全部结束，全年完成土石方明挖 3.8 万 m^3，石方洞挖 4.9 万 m^3，2009 年洞挖最大月强度达到 0.9 万 m^3。洞身混凝土浇筑于 2009 年 7 月 30 日开始，截至 2009 年底完成 1.70 万 m^3；进水塔混凝土浇筑于 2009 年 8 月 1 日开始，截至 2009 年底完成 0.52 万 m^3，浇筑最大月强度达到 0.5 万 m^3，钢筋制作安装 0.35 万 t。

3. 大坝工程

大坝坝肩及趾板开挖于 2009 年 12 月 23 日完成，全年完成坝基土石方明挖 26 万 m^3，完成边坡支护 0.6 万 m^2。完成大坝填筑料砂砾石备料 33.3 万 m^3，完成潘口河石料场剥离料开挖 12.5 万 m^3，完成有用料开挖 70.4 万 m^3，其中备料 41.7 万 m^3。截至 2009 年底大坝拦洪度汛断面累计填筑 24.00 万 m^3，坝体最高部位填筑至 283.00m 高程。

4. 溢洪道工程

溢洪道主要进行了开挖和支护工作，基本完成了进水渠的开挖，完成了闸室段和泄槽段的大部分开挖。全年完成土石方明挖 73.8 万 m^3，完成边坡支护 1.84 万 m^2，2009 年开挖最大月强度达到 8 万 m^3。

5. 引水系统工程

进水口开挖支护工作于 2009 年 9 月底全部完成，全年完成土石方明挖 31.95 万 m^3，完成边坡支护 2.2 万 m^2，其中预应力锚索 60 根，2009 年开挖最大月强度达到 7 万 m^3。两条引水隧洞通过施工支洞同时开挖，地质条件好的洞段取消了系统支护，对地质条件差的部位采取了挂网锚喷支护，全年石方洞挖 3.97 万 m^3。压力钢管于 2009 年 11 月开始制作，制作了 17 节。

6. 发电厂房

截流前，基本完成了水上部分的开挖，截至 2009 年底，完成了厂房基坑及尾水渠的大部分开挖，全年完成土石方明挖 22.7 万 m^3，完成边坡支护 1.2 万 m^2，2009 年开挖最大月强度达到 6 万 m^3。

7. 机电设备

水轮发电机组图纸设计、机组模型验收已于 2009 年 4 月初完成，一期埋件于 2009 年 12 月底运抵现场；导流洞进口门槽埋件安装于 2009 年 6 月底完成。

（中国水电顾问集团中南勘测设计研究院　胡　伟）

龙口水利枢纽工程 2009 年建设情况

2009 年是龙口水利枢纽工程建设攻坚的一年。黄河万家寨水利枢纽有限公司坚持以科学发展观为指导，紧紧围绕龙口工程建设总体部署和年度工程建设目标安排，狠抓工程质量、安全、进度和投资控制，积极协调参建各方关系，较好地完成了年度工程建设管理目标，首台机组提前并网发电。

（一）投资计划完成情况

2009年，上级批复龙口水利枢纽投资92 020万元，实际完成总投资87 981万元。其中：建筑工程15 120万元，机电27 415万元，金属结构2659万元，独立费用4665万元，移民9383万元，环保228万元，水保523万元，融资利息27 988万元。

截至2009年底，龙口水利枢纽完成总投资251 610万元。其中：建筑工程72 504万元，机电62 182万元，金属结构10 249万元，临时工程29 190万元，独立费用26 222万元，移民21 031万元，环保537万元，水保1707万元，融资利息27 988万元。

（二）土建工程进展情况

2009年完成混凝土浇筑5.8万m^3。自开工建设以来，累计完成主体混凝土浇筑92.7万m^3，钢筋制作安装20 900t，帷幕灌浆20 950m，固结灌浆22 702m。

2009年4月30日，龙口大坝全部达到900.0m设计顶高程；7月18日上游二期围堰拆除到设计高程；8月21日下游围堰拆除完成；10月25日主厂房全部封顶，11月18日机组坝段机窝混凝土全部完成，尾水渠及左右岸护岸全部完成，主厂房、副厂房和GIS开关站装修全部完成。

（三）机电工程进展情况

2009年9月8日，龙口水利枢纽1号机组及相关电气设备分部及阶段通过验收，具备启动运行条件；9月18日，首台机组（1号机组）成功实现并网发电，提前一年实现首台机组投产发电；12月5日，2号机组完成72h试运行，顺利投入商业运行。

截至2009年底，龙口水利枢纽工程金属结构设备已全部安装完成；全厂公用系统机电设备基本安装完成；3号机组涉网试验前的所有安装调试、试验工作已全部完成；4号机组安装工作完成，充水实验结束；5号机组安装基本完成。

（四）工程质量管理情况

2009年，在黄河龙口水利枢纽工程质量管理委员会组织领导下，进一步完善了《黄河龙口水利枢纽工程质量管理办法》、《龙口水利枢纽工程混凝土质量管理考核细则》、《龙口水利枢纽工程监理工程师工作考核细则》、《黄河龙口水利枢纽工程施工进度管理考核办法》等制度，完善了工程建设质量管理体系。

结合工程建设实际，重点组织开展工程质量检查、考核工作。2009年5月，组织进行了龙口工程机电安装工程单元评定资料及相关资料的检查活动，并在检查结束后对发现的问题提出了整改意见；严格按照监理合同要求，每月对现场监理人员到位情况进行考核，确保现场监理人数；配合水利部建管总站质量与安全监督巡查工作，按照巡查组检查整改报告要求，组织施工单位限期整改，并将整改材料上报建管总站核备；对蓄水安全鉴定中提出的问题，及时组织缺陷处理，确保施工质量满足规范要求。

2009年4月16日，黄河龙口水利枢纽工程通过了由水利部水利水电规划设计总院组织的龙口水利枢纽工程蓄水安全鉴定。

2009年9月1日，黄河龙口水利枢纽工程通过水利部黄河水利委员会组织的下闸蓄水验收。

2009年12月18～20日，黄河龙口水利枢纽工程首台机组通过了水利部黄河水利委员会的启动验收。

（五）工程安全管理情况

2009年，认真落实《中华人民共和国安全生产法》，贯彻“安全第一、预防为主、综合治理”的方针，深入开展“三项行动”，全面加强“三项建设”，全力推进“安全生产年”，依法规范安全生产行为，完善安全生产监督体系和工作机制，大力整治事故隐患，安全生产保持稳定局面，保证了龙口水利枢纽工程建设的顺利进行。

一年以来，共排查整改了事故隐患211项，有效遏制了安全生产事故的发生。根据国家关于特种设备管理的规定，全年完成15台套特种设备的告知、检验取证、登记等手续。对失效的23具灭火器进行维修，为员工宿舍配置950型微型水系家用灭火器，确保灭火器材的良好。

（六）征地移民情况

移民安置方面，组织完善了库区准格尔旗侧魏家峁移民安置点基础设施建设和房屋建设工作，具备了搬迁条件，已有25户移民搬进了新家。淹没线下的43人已经妥善安置，其余淹地影响人口待把新房装修后入住。组织完成了偏关县关河口移民安置点的基础设施和房屋的建设，共计完成移民房建设18 000m^2。组织对关河口村庄进行临时防护，确保了水库水位如期上升。

库底清理方面，组织完成了库底硫磺矿渣清理工作，并通过环境保护部下闸蓄水阶段库底清理验收；组织完成了库区淹没线下移民的征地补偿、移民搬迁和库底清理工作，并分别通过了山西省移民办、内蒙古自治区移民办和黄河水利委员会移民局的下闸蓄水验收。协调两省区文物部门及时完成了库区已查明文物的发掘和保护工作，保证了下闸蓄水正常进行。组织完成了库区偏关县林地报批工作，准格尔旗的林地报批工作正在抓紧进行。

（七）水土保持和环境保护

组织完成了副厂房污水处理系统的建设和设备安装工作。按照环境保护、水土保持报告书要求对施工阶段的污染源、水土流失情况开展了日常监测工作。

组织完成了龙口水利枢纽工程申请CDM项目的

资料准备和相关协议谈判工作，完成了龙口项目DOE现场审定工作。

2009年，龙口工程建设管理局荣获晋陕蒙水土保持监督局“大型生产建设项目水土保持工作先进单位”称号。

（黄河万家寨水利枢纽有限公司 董四全 赵 欣）

马鹿塘水电站二期工程建设情况

（一）工程概况

马鹿塘水电站二期工程，位于云南省文山州麻栗坡县境内的盘龙河上，距麻栗坡县城公路里程34km，距昆明公路里程448km，是盘龙河11个梯级规划中的第八个梯级，以发电为主，混合式开发，工程分两期建设。坝址以上流域面积5878km^2，为盘龙河流域面积的95.72%，多年平均流量80.3m^3/s，多年平均径流量25.3亿m^3。大坝为混凝土面板堆石坝，最大坝高154m；水库正常蓄水位627m，总库容5.5亿m^3，调节库容4.22亿m^3，具有年调节能力；电站额定水头容量340m，安装3台混流式水轮发电机组，总装机容量240MW（增容后为300MW）。加上一期装机容量100MW，马鹿塘水电站总装机容量340MW，保证出力150.28MW，多年平均发电量18.14亿kW·h，其中二期多年平均发电量为11.42亿kW·h。接入系统采用四回线路“Π”接至220kV马河线（马关—越南河江），其中，两回送至马关变电站，两回送至河江变电站。

电站枢纽工程等别为二等，工程规模为大（2）型。坝址区地震基本烈度为Ⅵ度。大坝按500年一遇洪水设计，10 000年一遇洪水校核，相应洪水流量分别为2680m^3/s、3970m^3/s。水库淹没耕地5551亩，迁移人口4363人。

马鹿塘二期工程总工程量：土石方明挖331.30万m^3，石方洞挖71.61万m^3，土石方填筑699.97万m^3，混凝土31.58万m^3，帷幕灌浆1.41万m，固结灌浆3.22万m，回填灌浆5.09万m^2，钢筋钢材1.88万t，金属结构安装3566t（未含机组设备）。施工导流采用隧洞导流方式。工程静态投资186 159.72万元（2004年6月底价格水平），总投资205 827.41万元，其中：枢纽工程投资158 915.82万元，水库淹没处理费43 318.59万元。根据国务院471号令，2008年3月经政府主管部门审查，水库淹没静态补偿总投资调整为69 641.87万元。工程建设总工期为56个月，第一台机组发电工期为47个月。

（二）枢纽布置

总体布置为：首部位于盘龙河与畴阳河汇口下游峡谷入口处，拦河大坝为混凝土面板堆石坝，左岸设开敞式溢洪道、放空隧洞；一期首部上游右岸修建引水发电系统，引水至盘龙河与猛洞河汇口上游侧地下厂房。

二期工程枢纽建筑物主要由混凝土面板堆石坝，左岸岸边溢洪道、放空隧洞，右岸引水隧洞、调压井、压力管道、地下发电厂房及附属洞室等组成。大坝最大坝高为154.00m，坝顶宽度10m，坝顶长度493.40m，坝顶高程634.00m。溢洪道布置3孔，堰顶高程617.0m，孔口尺寸10m×10m（宽×高），采用挑流消能。引水隧洞（一、二期共用）全长约3.2km，内径7.00m；阻抗式调压井内径22m，高115.63m。放空洞全长540.08m，进口高程538.00m，洞径6.60m，由有压洞段、闸门井段、无压洞段和出口明槽及挑流鼻坎段组成。地下建筑物主要由主厂房、副厂房、主变压器GIS室、尾闸室、尾水洞和进厂交通洞等组成。主副厂房总尺寸为97.4m×18.2m×42.3m（长×宽×高），主变压器室尺寸为77.0m×15.0m×27.0m（长×宽×高）。主变压器GIS室分两层设置，下层为主变压器，上层为GIS开关站；3条尾水洞经厂房机组尾水检修闸室后合并为一条尾水洞。机组间距16.5m，水轮机安装高程238.00m，发电机层高程249.00m，蜗壳层高程233.80m，尾水肘管底板高程228.20m。

（三）工程进展情况

1. 工程主要建设进度

2005年6月27日，云南省发展改革委以云发改能源[2005]536号文下发了项目核准意见；8月21日，导流洞开工；11月28日，主体工程开工。2006年11月23日，实现大江截流。2009年11月10日，成功下闸蓄水；12月30日，1、3号机组投产发电。

2. 截至2009年底累计完成工程量

明挖333.7万m^3，洞挖72.2万m^3，填筑615.3万m^3；喷混凝土3.1万m^3，浇筑混凝土27.274万m^3，钢筋1.764 5万t；锚杆4.164 8万根；排水孔1.373 9万m；回填灌浆5.98m^2，固结灌浆2.89万m，帷幕灌浆1.41万m^2；金属结构安装3783t。

3. 2009年工程形象面貌

（1）首部枢纽工程：大坝、放空洞土建工程已完工；溢洪道土建工程基本完成，泄槽段剩左边墙一块混凝土因闸门安装需留作运输通道暂时未完成。

（2）引水发电系统工程：引水洞、调压井、压力钢管道工程已完工；连接洞设计长度236.474m（水平投影长），开挖完成；钢筋混凝土衬砌段长168.345m，基本完成；钢衬段长104.677m，从一期调压井穿过后与一期压力钢管连接，回填混凝土累计完成12.2%；临时钢堵头已安装完成。临时钢堵头上游的5节钢管安装完成，并回填完混凝土。

(3) 一期改造工程：一期引水洞桩号0+780处堵头施工已完成并成功挡水；一期机电设备改造工程进行中。

(4) 地下厂房工程：主副厂房、主变压器GIS室、出线井、出线场、尾水洞、尾闸室混凝土浇筑完成，装修工程进行中；除2号机组之外，其他机电设备安装工程全部完成。

(5) 金属结构安装工程；除溢洪道工程外，引水系统、放空洞、厂区系统金属结构工程全部的完成。

(四) 建设管理情况

马鹿塘水电站的业主为云南大唐国际文山水电开发有限公司。该公司由大唐国际发电股份有限公司、文山电力股份有限公司和中国水电顾问集团昆明勘测设计研究院3家单位分别按总投资的60%、25%和15%共同出资组建。

马鹿塘二期水电站采用EPC总承包方式建设。2005年8月26日，云南大唐国际文山水电开发有限公司（以下简称公司）与中国水电顾问集团昆明勘测设计研究院（以下简称昆明院）正式签订了《文山马鹿塘水电站二期工程工程总承包合同》。工程设计、施工和设备、材料采购由昆明院完成。公司与总承包单位在承包合同中商定承包总价。总承包单位按可行性研究报告及设计概算的项目投资包干，节省归己，超支不补。工程月进度款依据总承包单位完成的工程形象进度支付。

工程建设执行项目法人制、合同管理制、招投标制和建设监理制，充分发挥业主的核心主导作用，充分发挥总承包单位的设计优势。对施工单位，要求总承包单位选择国家有水电施工总承包特级、壹级资质的水电施工企业。对设备，公司在招标前对潜在投标人进行资质预审，确定入选投标人；总承包单位在公司认可的设备制造单位中招标选定制造商；在总承包单位招标全过程，公司均参与监督。

施工质量管理，主要从原材料、设计、施工过程对总承包进行管理监督。对用于本工程的原材料质量，要求各参建单位进行严格控制。对于钢材、水泥等主材，由总包单位统购，总承包单位每月对各施工单位所用原材料、混凝土试验资料进行统计，报公司备查。

建设过程中的施工安全管理，主要是督促各参建单位建立健全安全管理组织机构、安全责任制、安全管理规章制度，并做好日常安全管理工作。

施工进度管理，主要按工程施工组织设计总进度计划进行控制。要求总承包单位把总进度计划按重要节点、按年度进行分解，制定年度进度计划；根据年度进度计划，制定月度进度计划。根据总承包单位制定的各种进度计划，对比检查实际进度计划完成情况，发现工期滞后即要求赶工，必要时召开参建各方领导参加的工程协调会解决进度问题。

根据总承包合同约定，马鹿塘二期水电站的枢纽工程中分部工程验收由总承包单位组织完成，单位工程验收、阶段验收，以及工程各专项验收、竣工验收由公司组织进行。2009年，工程先后完成了蓄水安全鉴定、蓄水阶段验收、机组启动验收。

（大唐国际发电股份有限公司　余圣刚
云南大唐国际文山水电开发
有限公司　彭春平　刘万里）

蜀河水电站工程2009年建设情况

(一) 工程概况

蜀河水电站位于陕西省旬阳县境内汉江干流上，坝址在旬阳县蜀河镇上游约1km处，距旬阳县城51km，距上游已建成的安康水电站约120km，距下游已建成的丹江口水电站约200km，是汉江上游梯级开发规划中的第六个水电站。

蜀河水电站装有6台46MW贯流式水轮发电机组，总装机容量276MW，年利用小时3530h，保证出力57.4MW，年平均发电量9.53亿kW·h。水库库容1.76亿m^3，正常蓄水位217.30m，为日调节水库。

蜀河水电站工程规模为大（2）型，地震基本烈度和设防烈度均为Ⅵ度。大坝、厂房等主要建筑物按百年一遇洪水设计，千年一遇校核。百年一遇洪水流量为30 740m^3/s，千年一遇洪水流量为38 100m^3/s。

工程总投资为220 387万元。施工总工期52个月，第一台机组发电工期42个月。

枢纽布置采用厂顶溢流式方案，除右副坝和右岸泄洪闸坝段布置有泄洪表孔外，厂房机组坝段和安装间坝段在机组流道顶板以上亦布置有泄洪表孔。泄洪闸消能方式为底流消能，厂房和安装间表孔消能方式为面流消能。坝顶总长度290m，最大坝高72m。

蜀河水电站电气主接线采用两机一变扩大单元单母线接线方式，采用户内型GIS组合电器开关。共3回110kV出线，一回与蜀河变电站连接，另两回与旬阳白柳变电站连接。

蜀河水电站工程由大唐陕西汉江投资开发有限公司投资兴建。该公司现有股东为：大唐陕西发电有限公司（出资比例为53%），陕西省水电开发有限责任公司（出资比例为30%），陕西省交通厅航运管理局（出资比例为10%），中国水利水电第三工程局有限公司（出资比例为5%），安康市国有资本经营公司（出资比例为2%）。

（二）2009年项目建设情况

蜀河水电站工程2009年的主要目标是：6月底厂房具备过流条件，确保安全度汛；年内首台机组投产发电。围绕这两大目标，业主单位组织设计、监理和施工单位反复研究，不断优化和调整施工方案，加大施工资源投入，昼夜拼抢，按期完成了工程建设目标。

为实现2009年6月底厂房具备过流条件的目标，确保安全度汛，采取了以下主要工程措施：①多台机组管型座同时安装，并及时浇筑二期混凝土；②及时将坝顶门机切块在右岸泄洪闸坝顶提前安装，在安装间下游增加门机轨道，使尾水门机在安装间下游平台提前安装，为厂房上下游闸门安装创造条件；③先进行5、6号机组管型座上部倒T型梁施工，为防水钢盖板创造安装条件；④为解决钢盖板因缺起重手段而无法整体安装的问题，及时研究采取用钢板条临时焊接替代水封的方案。

蜀河水电站厂房主体工程于2009年6月29日完成了所有与厂顶过流有关的土建和金属结构安装的施工；2009年12月13日，电站下闸蓄水；2009年12月29日，首台机组（1号机组）完成72h试运行，正式投产发电。

2009年，蜀河水电站工程共完成混凝土浇筑16.15万m^3，其中右岸泄洪闸工程完成0.35万m^3，左岸厂房工程完成15.8万m^3；完成砖砌体近3万m^2；共完成钢筋制作安装7744t，其中右岸泄洪闸工程完成148t，左岸厂房工程完成7596t；共完成金属结构安装约12 000余吨，完成机电设备安装2000余吨100多台套。

2009年共完成基建工程投资78 818万元，其中建筑工程投资24 546万元，安装工程投资1374万元，设备费投资18 352万元，其他费用34 546万元，年度投资计划完成率为103.5%。截至2009年12月底，蜀河水电站工程累计完成工程投资204 336万元，其中建筑工程投资88 584万元，安装工程投资1997万元，设备费投资41 400万元，其他费用72 355万元。

（三）项目管理情况

1. 安全管理

蜀河水电项目通过全面开展安全隐患排查、治理、样板工地建设等活动，使得施工安全管理规范有序，安全管理做到了可控、在控，促进蜀河水电站安全文明样板工地建设水平持续攀升，打造更加安全有序的安全建设环境，并受到了中国大唐集团公司领导的肯定，年度未发生不安全事故和质量缺陷，完成了年度安全目标。

2. 质量管理

截至2009年12月底，蜀河水电站主体土建工程共验评了2523个单元，全部合格，合格率100%；2315个单元评定为优良单元，优良率91.76%。金属结构安装工程虽未评定，但从已完成的单元工程质量验评情况看，工程施工质量可控、在控，施工质量总体优良。

3. 投资管理

蜀河水电站工程建设中，认真执行业主负责制、建设监理制和招投标制，强化监督约束机制。以合同为主线，加强管理，控制承包合同价，防止合同价升值。建立内部协调、制约机制和专业部门联审制，在制定确保全面履行合同的体系和措施的基础上，抓好3个工作重点：

（1）在确保工程质量、安全的前提下，抓进度、保工期。采取各种有效措施，千方百计保证资金及时到位，实行重奖重罚等；尽力为施工创造良好的外部条件，寻求缩短工期的途径，以减少时间的消耗，减少贷款利息和管理费、风险费等各种费用，达到降低造价和提前发挥投资效益之目的。

（2）严把设计变更关。对设计变更实行“双签制”，即变更设计须有技术部门和计经部门共同签字才生效。

（3）狠抓投资的静态控制、动态管理。对设计变更、地质情况变化、国家政策性调整、物价和设备价格的调整以及不可预见因素引起的费用变化等，都要进行认真分析，尽最大可能进行控制。

蜀河水电站工程建设过程中，为解决施工期的争议与索赔，建立了一套完整的组织机构和程序，并与有资质单位签订了造价咨询协议，为处理索赔提供技术支持，有效地解决工程索赔问题，有效地进行投资控制。

（大唐陕西汉江投资开发有限公司 崔增华 孟玲）

苗家坝水电站工程建设情况

（一）工程概况

苗家坝水电站位于甘肃省文县境内白龙江中下游，距下游已建成的碧口水电站31.5km。工程主要任务是发电。枢纽建筑物主要由混凝土面板堆石坝、溢洪洞、泄洪排沙洞、引水发电洞及岸边厂房等组成。电站正常蓄水位800m，相应库容2.68亿m^3；总装机容量240MW（3×80MW），保证出力43MW，设计年发电量9.24亿kW·h，装机年利用小时3850h。

工程规模属二等大（2）型，主要建筑物挡水坝级别为1级，其他主要建筑物级别为2级，次要建筑物级别为3级。挡水建筑物混凝土面板堆石坝按500

年一遇洪水设计，5000年一遇洪水校核，相应入库洪峰流量分别为2930m^3/s和3880m^3/s。厂房按100年一遇洪水设计，500年一遇洪水校核。下游消能防冲建筑物按50年一遇洪水设计，相应洪峰流量1990m^3/s。

电站导流工程主要建筑物由导流洞进水口、导流洞（后期改为溢洪洞）洞身、出口挑流鼻坎、消能段及下游护坡组成。过流部位全长935m。

苗家坝水电站由甘肃大唐白龙江发电有限责任公司建设。该公司位于甘肃省文县碧口镇，注册资本10 093万元。苗家坝水电站工程是该公司开发兴建的水电项目之一。

（二）工程建设情况

2007年1月4日，导流洞工程开工。在2008年“5·12”汶川地震中，工程受到严重破坏，对外交通中断，部分施工单位人员受伤，被迫停工。在甘肃省地方政府、中国大唐集团公司、大唐甘肃公司的关怀支持下，经过甘肃大唐白龙江发电有限责任公司及各参建单位的共同努力，在最短的时间内就恢复了施工。地震发生后的第三天，开始对外道路的清理，2008年6月25日，开始震后第一仓混凝土浇筑。2008年12月18日，导流洞洞身全线浇筑完成，12月24日，导流洞（溢洪洞）出口段水面以下全部浇筑完成。截至2009年底，大坝填筑达727m高程（设计805m高程），填筑量83万m^3（总量360万m^3）；厂房工程开始基础混凝土浇筑，发电引水洞3台机组岔管贯通。

（甘肃大唐白龙江发电有限责任公司）

万家口子水电站工程建设情况

（一）工程概况

万家口子水电站位于云南省宣威市及贵州省盘县的交汇地界的珠江流域北盘江干流革香河上，是北盘江干流的第四级电站，距云南省宣威市75km，距贵州省盘县120km。电站开发任务以发电为主，兼顾下游工农业用水；安装2台9.0万kW立轴混流式发电机组，总装机容量为18.0万kW，保证出力3.329万kW，多年平均发电量为71 039万kW·h，装机年利用小时3947h。电站坝型为碾压混凝土双曲拱坝，坝顶高程为1452.5m，最大坝高167.50m，坝顶长413.157m，为目前世界最高的碾压混凝土双曲拱坝。水库总库容27 926.0万m^3，正常蓄水位为1450.0m，相应库容26 929.0万m^3，死水位1415.0m，死库容9950.0万m^3，调节库容16 979.0万m^3，具有不完全年调节性能。该电站建成后，可提高下游梯级水电站的保证出力56.86MW，增加下游梯级电站的年发电量2.07亿kW·h，是实现流域梯级滚动开发的关键工程。

工程静态总投资144 028.2万元，动态总投资163 537.65万元。项目资本金为32 707.53万元，占动态总投资的比例为20%。资本金以外的融资由业主向金融机构贷款解决。

2009年3月12日，云南省和贵州省发展改革委联合下文，正式批复核准万家口子水电站项目，随后主体工程正式开工。工程施工总工期36个月，计划2012年机组全部投产发电。

（二）参建设单位

万家口子水电站的建设单位为大唐宣威水电开发有限公司。该公司于2007年10月22日正式成立，注册资本1亿元人民币，中国大唐集团公司控股80%，广西壮族自治区水电工程局占有股比20%。

广西电力工业勘察设计研究院负责大坝工程设计，吉林省水利水电勘测设计研究院负责除大坝工程以外的设计工作；施工单位为广西壮族自治区水电工程局；监理单位为广西桂能集团工程咨询有限公司。

（三）2009年工程形象面貌

万家口子水电站于2009年10月大江截流。

截至2009年12月底，大坝基坑全面开挖至1288m高程；大坝左岸上下游侧边坡全部支护至1315m高程，右岸下游侧边坡支护至1340m高程，上游侧边坡支护至1315m高程；水垫塘左岸边坡全部挖至1315m高程，坝基前段开挖至1290m高程，左岸边坡支护至1340m高程。

右岸施工生产、生活用水系统已建设完成，并投入使用；右岸砂石加工系统、混凝土拌和系统已建设完成，并投入使用。

2009年累计完成土石方开挖204万m^3，混凝土0.8万m^3，钢筋安装385t。

（大唐宣威水电开发有限公司）

汉江崔家营航电枢纽工程

（一）工程概况

崔家营航电枢纽工程是汉江中下游梯级开发中湖北省境内9级枢纽中的第五级，坝址位于襄樊市下游17km处。该枢纽是以航运为主，航电结合、综合利用的工程，正常蓄水位62.73m，相应库容2.45亿m^3，装机容量90MW，多年平均发电量3.898亿kW·h，年利用小时4331h，工程等别为二等。枢纽主要建筑物由船闸、电站、泄水闸和土石坝组成。枢纽船闸的闸首和闸室、泄水闸、电站、土石坝为2级，船闸上下游导航墙、泄水闸的导墙为3级，施工导流围堰为4级。主要建筑物洪水设计标准采用50年一遇，相应流量为19 600m^3/s；校核洪水标准为300年一遇，洪峰流量25 380m^3/s。枢纽总布置自右至左分别为：右岸连接坝段（长103.5m)、船闸（44.0m)、泄水闸（长474.5m)、厂房（长167.55m)、门机检修平台（长40m)、鱼道、土坝（长1350.45m)，坝轴线总长2180.0m。

（二）工程建设情况

1. 船闸

船闸布置在汉江主河道右侧，轴线与坝轴线正交，等级为Ⅲ级，按通航双排双列一顶四驳船队设计。闸室有效尺寸180m×23m×3.5m（长×宽×门槛水深)，设计水头8.82m，采用闸墙长廊道短支管分散输水系统，引航道底宽75m。船闸设计年通过能力为768万t。上游最高通航水位为62.73m，最低通航水位为62.23m。下游最高通航水位为61.21m，最低通航水位为53.91m。

2. 泄水闸

泄水闸布置于船闸和电站厂房之间，闸址位于主河床上，前缘总宽474.5m。泄水闸采用平底闸型式，由闸室段、上游防冲板、闸下护坦、下游海漫和下游防冲槽等组成，闸底板顶高程48.23m。泄水闸共布置20孔20m×14.5m（宽×高）的泄水孔口，消能形式采用9孔底流消能护坦消能；闸顶高程70.5m，门机采用大门机方案。

3. 电站厂房

电站厂房为河床式，布置于主河道左侧，右连泄水闸，左接土石坝；安装6台单机容量15MW的灯泡贯流式水轮发电机组；分缝采用一机一缝。安装场位于主厂房左侧，门机检修平台紧临安装场布置。开关站布置于厂房左侧门机检修平台下游。鱼道紧靠电站厂房左侧布置，进出口各设两平板闸门。

4. 左岸土石坝

左岸土石坝为塑性混凝土防渗墙砂砾石坝，建在河心洲、左河汊和左岸Ⅰ级阶地、漫滩上，地面高程53.0～63.0m，左接汉江防洪大堤，右接电站厂房；坝顶高程为67.2m，坝顶宽度为7.0m。

在溢流闸坝下游与副厂房顶设一宽度为7.0m的交通桥与两岸非溢流土坝连接，通过两岸公路与外沟通，厂房进厂采用平面进厂方式。

崔家营航电枢纽工程的业主单位为湖北省港航局，湖南省水利水电勘测设计研究院负责电站部分设计。2005年10月正式开工建设，2009年2月首台机组投产发电。

该工程采用左岸设置导流明渠、主河床一次截断的导流方案；基岩为白垩系钙泥质砾岩，上部呈强溶蚀风化状态，属不同于灰岩岩溶（喀斯特）问题的另类强溶蚀地基。其施工期基坑排水及基础防渗、不均匀变形处理方案，对在汉江上建设其他航电工程和其他大江大河上类似工程提供了很好的成功经验和借鉴。

（湖南省水利水电勘测设计研究院　胡正福）

安江水电站

安江水电站位于湖南省洪江市境内沅江干流中游，下距安江镇约7.9km，距怀化市约70km，是沅江干流规划中的第九级电站。

安江水电站为低水头径流式电站，以发电为主，兼顾航运等综合利用。坝址控制流域面积40 101km^2，多年平均流量830m^3/s。水库总库容2.32亿m^3，正常蓄水位165.0m。电站设计水头8.8m，安装4台单机容量为35MW的灯泡贯流式机组，总装机容量为140MW，年发电量5.62亿kW·h，年利用小时4014h。

枢纽工程由船闸、土石坝、溢流坝、厂房和开关站等主要建筑物组成，坝顶全长1109m，呈“一”字形拦河布置。溢流坝居中布置在左右汊河床，河床式电站厂房紧靠河心洲布置于左汊主河道的右侧，船闸布置于河道左岸阶地上。

该电站业主单位为广水安江水电开发有限公司，设计单位为湖南省水利水电勘测设计研究院。计划2010年9月主体工程正式开工，2013年4月首台机组投产发电。

（湖南省水利水电勘测设计研究院　谢育健）

浯溪水电站

浯溪水电站位于湘江干流中上游湖南省永州市祁阳县境内，上距永州市53km，下距祁阳县城2.5km。该工程是湘江干流流域规划11个梯级中的第五级，下接湘祁电站库尾，上与潇湘电站尾水衔接，是一个以发电为主，兼有旅游、航运、灌溉、交通及城市开发建设等综合利用的水电工程。工程坝址控制流域面积23 380km^2，占湘江流域总面积的24.7%，坝址多年平均流量697m^3/s。水库总库容2.757亿m^3，正常蓄水位88.5m，相应库容1.778亿m^3，回水长度54.04km，可改善湘江航道53km。电站为径流式低水头电站，设计水头9.7m，安装4台单机容量为2.5万kW的灯泡贯流式水轮机发电机组，总装机容量为10万kW，年发电量3.955亿kW·h，年利用小时 3955h。

枢纽工程由左岸土坝、厂房、溢流坝、船闸、右岸土坝等建筑物组成。大坝呈“一”字形拦河布置，最大坝高 28m，坝顶全长 910.2m。溢流坝居中，坝段长 310.6m，共布置 13 孔泄流闸孔，孔口尺寸为 20m×12.5m，堰型为“WES”实用堰，堰顶高程为 76.0m。河床式厂房布置在河床左侧阶地上，安装 4 台机组，主厂房长 71.1m，机组间距 16m（17.1m）。永久船闸级别为Ⅳ级，布置于河床右侧阶地上，为单级船闸，由上游引航道、上闸首、闸室、下闸首及下游引航道等组成，全长 569m；闸室长 120m，最大过坝船舶为 500t 级，年通航能力 200 万 t。

浯溪水电站的业主为湖南浯溪水电开发有限公司（由湖南新华水利电力有限公司控股），设计单位为湖南省水利水电勘测设计研究院。

工程总投资 12.3 亿元，2005 年 12 月正式开工建设；2009 年 12 月 19 日，电站首台机组正式并网发电；计划 2010 年 8 月全部机组投产发电。

（湖南省水利水电勘测设计研究院　姚敦呈）

湘祁水电站

湘祁水电站位于湖南省永州市祁阳县和衡阳市祁东县交界处，为湘江干流 11 个梯级开发的第六级，是一个以发电、航运为主，兼顾灌溉、旅游等综合效益的工程。坝址右岸属祁阳县黄泥塘镇范围，距祁阳县城约 48km；坝址左岸属祁东县归阳镇范围，距祁东县城约 32km。坝址上距祁阳县境内浯溪水电站 60.8km，下距衡南县境内近尾洲水电站 46km。坝址控制流域面积 27 118 km^2，占湘江总流域面积的 28.7%；多年平均流量为 777m^3/s。电站水库总库容 3.131 亿 m^3，正常蓄水位 75.5m，相应库容 1.609 亿 m^3；总装机容量为 80MW，设计水头 7.2m，为径流式低水头电站，年发电量 3.18 亿 kW·h，年利用小时 3975h。

枢纽工程由左岸接头土坝、重力坝、左岸船闸、溢流闸坝、右岸电站厂房、右岸重力坝及右岸接头土坝等建筑物组成，坝顶全长 626.27m，呈“一”字形拦河布置。河床式电站厂房布置在河床右侧的一级阶地上，永久船闸布置于河床左侧山坡上，溢流坝居中。溢流闸坝堰型为“WES”实用堰，共布置 19 孔泄流闸孔，孔口尺寸为 14m×12m，堰顶高程为 73.5m，溢流坝段长 318.5m。电站厂房安装 4 台灯泡贯流式水轮机发电机组，主厂房长 79m，机组间距 18.5m（19m）。船闸级别为Ⅲ级，最大过坝船舶为 1000t 级，由上游引航道、上闸首、闸室、下闸首及下游引航道等组成，全长 557m。

湘祁水电站的业主为华能湖南湘祁水电有限责任公司，设计单位为湖南省水利水电勘测设计研究院。

2009 年 10 月 27 日，该电站正式开工建设。

（湖南省水利水电勘测设计研究院　王旭斌）

白竹洲水电站

白竹洲水电站位于湖南省桃江县境内资水干流下游，下距桃江县城 24km，距益阳市 51km，系资水干流柘溪下游规划中的第五级。坝址以上控制流域面积 26 600km^2，占资水流域面积的 94.9%，多年平均流量 723m^3/s。工程以发电为主，兼有航运等综合效益。水库正常蓄水位 49.0m，总库容 0.978 亿 m^3；电站设计水头 3.9m，安装 5 台单机容量为 9MW 的灯泡贯流式机组，总装机容量为 45MW，保证出力 10.42MW，多年平均发电量为 2.01 亿 kW·h，年利用小时 4464h。按水库库容，该电站为三等中型工程。

该工程枢纽总平面布置主要建筑物从左至右依次为左汊左岸土坝段、电站厂房、左汊溢流闸坝段、船闸、中洲土坝、右汊溢流闸坝段及右岸连接段，坝顶总长 758.605m。

白竹洲水电站的业主单位为湖南锦源白竹洲水电有限公司，设计单位为湖南省水利水电勘测设计研究院。

工程于 2006 年 12 月正式开工建设；2007 年 5 月因资金问题停工；2008 年湖南新华水利电力有限公司投资控股湖南锦源白竹洲水电有限公司，2008 年 8 月工程复工；到 2009 年底，土建工程基本完成，机组正在紧张安装；计划 2010 年 3 月首台机组投产发电。

（湖南省水利水电勘测设计研究院　王小玲）

铁川桥水电站

（一）工程概况

铁川桥水电站为云南大理州宾川县与楚雄州大姚县交界的金沙江一级支流渔泡江上第四级电站。坝址以上流域面积 3994km^2，多年平均流量 23.6m^3/s。水库正常蓄水位 1272m，相应库容 2529 万 m^3。电站装机容量为 42MW，年利用小时数 2975h，多年平均发电量12 490万 kW·h。大坝为碾压混凝土双曲拱坝，坝顶高程 1274.50m，最大坝高 94.50m，泄水建筑物采用3孔溢流表孔和1孔冲沙泄洪中孔。引水发电系统由岸塔式进水口、引水隧洞、调压井、压力管道、地面厂房组成。

项目核准前业主为大理辉煌水电有限公司，勘察设计工作由中国水利水电第十四工程局科研设计院完成，2007年1月通过预可行性研究报告审查，8月通过可行性研究报告审查，11月取得项目核准批复。2008年4月，中国大唐集团公司云南分公司取得电站开发权，6月进行总承包邀请招标，11月大唐宾川水电有限责任公司与中国水电顾问集团中南勘测设计研究院签订了《云南渔泡江铁川桥水电站工程设计、采购和施工（EPC）总承包合同》。

（二）2009年工程建设情况

截至2009年底，主要工程形象进度为：完成渔泡江大桥、施工供电工程、业主综合楼、大坝缆机安装、工地实验室、引水隧洞1～4号施工支洞、导流洞、17km长的左岸永久进场公路、右岸坝肩边坡开挖等项目。左岸坝肩边坡开挖至高程1240m，大坝坝基河床覆盖层开始开挖，厂房导流明渠和基坑开挖基本结束，全长6380m的引水隧洞完成洞挖约1000m，调压井溜渣井开挖16m，776m长的过坝交通洞和长约8km的扶贫公路完成2/3。砂石系统开始试运行，拌和楼安装基本完成。

（大唐宾川水电有限责任公司　李孟德）

巴山水电站建成发电

巴山水电站工程位于重庆市城口县境内的任河干流上，是任河规划7个梯级开发方案中的第三个梯级，为任何梯级开发中的控制性工程。工程以发电为主，兼有旅游和改善生态环境等综合利用。枢纽由拦河大坝、溢洪道、引水系统及发电厂房等组成。坝址位于巴山镇上游约1km的冉家坝处，厂址位于巴山下游雷打石任河左岸山坡处。拦河大坝为混凝土面板堆石坝，坝高155m；水库正常蓄水位680.00m，总库容3.165亿m^3，具有年调节性能；电站安装2台单机容量为70MW的混流式水轮发电机组，总装机容量140MW。

该工程大坝采用断流围堰、隧洞导流。前期导流选用枯水时段10月至次年5月，10年一遇标准，由围堰挡水，隧洞导流；当大坝填筑升高超过围堰，则坝体临时挡水，导流洞泄流，度汛标准为全年50年一遇，相应设计流量为3670m^3/s。大坝上下游围堰采用堆石填筑，上游采用复合土工膜防渗，最大堰高31.20m，下游采用黏土斜墙防渗，最大堰高7.80m。导流隧洞采用城门洞形断面，衬砌后洞径为10m×13m，洞身段长839.10m，明渠进口段长25.0m，出口段长35.00m。

厂房围堰设计标准采用10年一遇，相应设计流量2820m^3/s；考虑厂房布置的地形条件及筑堰所需建筑材料等因素，围堰采用下部预留岩埂，岩埂上部设置浆砌石，最大堰高约17.00m。

电站主体工程及临时建筑混凝土总量约26.07万m^3，大坝小区料2.45万m^3，垫层料13.67万m^3。按2005年四季度价格水平编制的工程总投资125 295.75万元，静态总投资111 929.44万元，静态单位千瓦投资7995元/kW，单位电量投资2.79元/(kW·h)。设计施工总工期为49个月，第一台机组发电工期为3年8个月。

工程于2005年12月1日开工，开始导流隧洞施工；2006年10月18日截流；2006年12月18日开始坝体填筑，2007年汛前填了82m高，至612m度汛高程；2008年1月30日，大坝填筑到640m临时断面，3月底开始浇筑一期面板，10月12日，除右岸溢洪道缺口外，大坝填筑至681.6m高程；2009年4月12日，三期面板浇筑完成，4月28日下闸蓄水；2009年7月4日，2号机组投产发电，8月10日1号机组投产发电；2009年底完工。

（中国水电顾问集团华东勘测设计研究院　陈振文　齐立景）

大化水电站扩建工程

（一）工程概况

大化水电站位于广西壮族自治区大化县城，是1980年《红水河综合利用规划报告》推荐的十级开发方案中的第六级，坝址上游约83km接岩滩水电站，下游27.6km有百龙滩水电站，坝址以上集雨面积112 200km^2，占红水河全流域面积的85.9%，多年平均流量2000m^3/s，年径流量632.6亿m^3。电站以发电为主，兼顾航运等综合利用效益，水库正常蓄水位155m，死水位153m，调节库容0.39亿m^3，水库具有日调节性能。水库校核洪水位169.63m，总库容8.74亿m^3。电站安装4×100MW轴流转桨式水轮发电机组，于1975年10月动工兴建，1985年6月全部竣工投产。2002年5月，经增容改造，电站装机容量为4×114MW。电站船闸于2006年12月29日通过竣工验收，近期通航规模为250t级。

大化水电站扩建工程主要任务是发电，位于大坝左岸预留位置，安装1台110MW轴流转浆式水轮发电机组；主要建筑物为圆筒厂房、挡水土坝、刺墙坝、引水渠、尾水渠等；采用220kV电压等级接入系统，以1回220kV线路送出，接至电站右岸开关站220kVⅡ段母线，通过右岸开关站220kV出线送出。扩建工程利用现有水库，不改变水库的特征水位，不新增水库移民；按2007年三季度价格水平，总投资为63 313万元。

扩建工程可提高电站承担系统调峰调频的能力及电厂备用。扩建后，大化水电站总装机容量为566MW，年发电量28.85亿kW·h（龙滩水电站正常蓄水位400m时为29.98亿kW·h）。

（二）工程建设情况

大化水电站扩建工程于2006年底被列为中国大唐集团公司、广西桂冠电力股份有限公司重点开发项目，2007年11月25日，国家发展改革委以发改办能源[2007] 2910号文予以批复同意开展大化扩建工程项目前期工作。2008年2月20日，水电水利规划设计总院以水电规水工[2008] 0003号文批复《大化水电站扩建工程可行性研究报告审查意见》。2008年11月6日，国家发展改革委以发改能源[2008] 2938号《国家发展改革委关于红水河大化水电站扩建工程项目核准的批复》文件，同意建设红水河大化水电站扩建工程。

广西桂冠电力股份有限公司在大化水电站扩建工程中，努力协调各参建方的关系，按发电工期倒排计划和优化流程，逐级落实责任。参建各方克服地质条件差、施工场地狭窄、主机设备供货严重滞后等不利因素，创造了国内同类型水电站建设机组投产工期的奇迹。2009年6月26日，扩建机组开始72h试运行，7月5日正式投入商业运行。

（广西桂冠电力股份有限公司
广西桂冠大化水力发电总厂　韦贵岗）

中国水利水电建设集团公司投资的7个水电站2009年建设情况

（一）沙湾水电站

沙湾水电站位于四川省乐山市境内，是大渡河干流下游河段（铜街子以下）的一个梯级电站，安装4台单机容量为12万kW的轴流转桨式水轮发电机组，总装机容量48万kW，保证出力15.1万kW，年发电量24.07亿kW·h。

2009年，沙湾水电站完成开发投资92 785万元，自初始投入起累计完成投资429 595万元，3台机组投产发电。2009年4月15日，该电站首台机组（1号机组）完成72h试运行，4月23日投入商业运行。随后，4号、3号机组分别于2009年7月10日、12月14日投入商业运行。投产机组当年发电76 977.5万kW·h。

（二）毛尔盖水电站

毛尔盖水电站位于四川省阿坝藏族羌族自治州黑水县境内，是黑水河流域水电规划“二库五级”中的第三级，装机容量42万kW，年发电量17.17亿kW·h。2009年，完成投资137 498万元；截至2009年底，累计完成投资269 530万元。

主要工程形象面貌：上下游围堰满足度汛并达到设计要求；大坝防渗墙完成心墙料填筑至2029.5m高程；大坝基础灌浆廊道施工完成；厂房基础开挖至2035m高程；溢洪道开挖基本完成；调压井、压力管道斜井、放空洞、引水隧洞等地下工程，满足合同工期进度或有所提前。

（三）柳坪水电站

柳坪水电站位于四川省阿坝藏族羌族自治州茂县境内，是黑水河水电梯级开发的最末一级低闸引水式电站，装机容量12万kW，年发电量为5.28亿kW·h。2009年5月27日，3号机组发电。至此，该电站3台机组全部投入商业运行。2009年发电量为48 730万kW·h。

（四）色尔古水电站

色尔古水电站位于四川省阿坝藏族羌族自治州黑水县境内，是黑水河水电梯级开发的第四级电站，位于毛尔盖电站与柳坪电站之间。电站装机3台，总装机容量15万kW，年发电量为5.94亿kW·h，总投资18.29亿元。

2009年，色尔古水电站2号、3号、1号3台机组分别于6月22日、6月29日、7月22日投入商业运行，基建工程进入尾声，全年发电量38 789.98万kW·h。

（五）洪一水电站

洪一水电站是松林河支流洪坝河最下游的一级水电站，位于四川省雅安地区石棉县与甘孜州九龙县交界的松林河次源洪坝河上，安装2台4万kW机组，总装机容量8万kW，年发电量为4.09亿kW·h，动态总投资3.97亿元。

2009年，洪一水电站克服地震灾害影响，主要土建工程项目全部完工，两台机组分别于5月28日、6月2日投入商业运行。

（六）五一桥水电站

五一桥水电站位于甘孜州九龙县九龙河上，是九龙河“一库五级”中的第二个梯级，装机容量13.2万kW，多年平均发电量6.247亿/6.576亿kW·h（单独/联合）。

该电站2005年底开工，2008年3台机组全部投入商业运行。2009年仅余尾工完建工程，全年发电量44 461.55万kW·h，受枯水期水量不足的影响，尚未达到设计保证出力水平。

（七）甲米河一级水电站

甲米河一级水电站位于四川省凉山州盐源县境内的甲米河上，为径流引水式电站，设计装机3台，共3.6万kW，年发电量为15 509万kW·h，投资概算4.6亿元。

该电站于2008年5月31日开工建设。2009年11月28日截流，同年底完成厂房部位开挖，并开始基础混凝土浇筑。2009年完成投资5310万元，自开工累计完成投资7707万元。

（中国水电建设集团四川电力开发有限公司）

中国国电集团公司在新疆、江西和云南的几个水电站2009年建设情况

（一）小石峡水电站

小石峡水电站位于新疆阿克苏地区库玛拉克河中下游温宿县与乌什县交界处，是库玛拉克河第二级梯级电站，距上游大石峡水利枢纽工程11km。工程的主要任务是发电，上游大石峡水电站投入运行后，同时承担大石峡水库发电用水的反调节任务。小石峡水电站坝高约65m，水库总库容6900万m^3，总装机容量为11万kW，供电范围为整个阿克苏地区。该电站由国电阿克苏河流域水电开发有限公司建设管理，于2009年9月10日获得新疆维吾尔自治区发展改革委的核准批复，10月启动施工准备工作。2009年12月26日，举行开工仪式，标志着小石峡水电站正式开工建设。

（二）吐木秀克水电站

吐木秀克水电站是库玛拉克河第四级梯级电站，安装2台单机容量为2.4万kW的水轮发电机组。该工程投资约5亿元人民币，由国电阿克苏河流域水电开发有限公司建设管理。2009年12月14日19时35分、19时55分，两台机组分别完成72h试运，正式开始商业运营。

吐木秀克水电站是协合拉水利枢纽东岸总干渠上的引水式电站，渠基土最小渗透系数为1.6×10^{-2}cm/s，最大渗透系数为3.5×10^{-2}cm/s，具中等～强透水性，且渠水渗漏时渠基土可能发生管涌，因此，采取措施对渠道进行全断面防渗处理。局部渠道存在粉土层，该层具有冻胀性，采取砂砾石换填措施。压力前池位于库玛拉克河左岸Ⅳ级阶地上，地面高程1325～1322m，建基面高程1323.51m，前池底板基本置于地表。前池进口前发育一条E向的冲洪沟，沟顶宽15m，沟底宽8m，切割深度3～5m，相应采取了防洪措施。压力前池的布置，原为正向进水、侧向排冰，后改为正向排冰、侧向进水；压力钢管由明管改为外包钢筋混凝土管。厂房位于库玛拉克河左岸Ⅲ级阶地前缘阶坎边坡处，设计基础高程1242.10m，基坑开挖深度50m，地下水位高程1260.20m，施工难度较大。

（三）吉林台二级电站

吉林台二级水电站位于新疆维吾尔自治区伊犁自治州尼勒克县境内，为伊犁喀什河流域梯级开发的第十一级，共安装2台立轴混流式水轮发电机组，装机总容量为5万kW。该电站为引水发电工程，由国电新疆艾比湖流域开发有限公司建设管理。

2009年，国电新疆艾比湖流域开发有限公司严格控制施工队伍素质、施工作业方法、施工机械设备和材料质量，确保每个单项工程质量，实现了大坝混凝土浇筑合格率100%、优良率85.4%，厂房混凝土单元质量评定合格率100%、优良率86.26%，金属结构及机电安装工程单元质量评定合格率100%、优良率98.2%。2009年8月1日，大坝具备初期蓄水条件；9月20日，第一台机组正式并网发电；9月27日，第二台机组正式并网发电，如期实现中国国电集团公司确定的机组双投目标。

（四）国电井冈山水电站

国电井冈山（原名泰和）水电站是赣江流域治理开发的重要工程之一，是赣江流域规划中的第四个梯级水电站。原规划泰和坝址淹没损失过大，难于开发，经多方论证，将原泰和坝址上移8km至万安县窑头镇。该项目由中国国电集团公司建设和管理，已分别由中国国电集团公司和江西省发展改革委上报国家发展改革委、国家能源局申请开展项目前期工作的请示。

国电井冈山水电站（窑头坝址）位于江西省吉安市万安县境内，在万安水电站下游35km处，总装机容量14.8万kW，年利用小时3455h，年平均发电量5.11亿kW·h。该电站投运后可以渠化库区赣江35km航道，满足赣江航运规划要求；作为上游万安水电站的反调节梯级，增强万安水电站的调峰能力，改善江西电网的供电质量。项目的建设，对促进井冈山革命老区的社会经济发展具有重要意义。

（五）三江口水电站

三江口水电站位于云南省墨江县，是阿墨江流域水电梯级开发中的第三级电站，总装机容量9.9万kW，由国电云南阿墨江发电有限公司（中国国电集团公司控股）开发，工程总投资84 150万元，于2007年5月23日开工。中国葛洲坝集团一公司三江口项目部承担了电站面板堆石坝、左岸溢洪道、冲沙道、引水发电系统及导流建筑物等项目建设。2009年是三江口水电站截流、度汛、保发电的关键年。经过近21个月的紧张施工，2009年2月28日成功实现截

流。截流后，电站大坝、厂房等主体工程立即开工。中国葛洲坝集团一公司三江口项目部倒排工期，科学组织生产，使大坝形象面貌一天一个样，并创下了月最高填筑强度 40 万 m^3、日最高填筑逾 2 万 m^3 的单产纪录。经过几个月的艰苦奋战，已完成大坝填筑 82 万 m^3，2009 年 6 月 20 日，大坝顺利填筑至防御百年一遇洪水的 598m 度汛高程。电站安全度汛，施工进展顺利，预计 2010 年 6 月实现首台机组发电。

（中国国电集团公司）

国电大渡河流域水电开发有限公司前期项目 2009 年筹建情况

2009 年，国电大渡河流域水电开发有限公司认真贯彻“科学、有序、合规”和“组织最优、开发最快、效益最好”的原则要求，强化“一抓三保”各项措施，前期项目筹建取得重要进展。

（一）双江口水电站

该电站规划装机容量 200 万 kW，是大渡河干流的龙头电站，位于阿坝州马尔康县境内。2009 年，可行性研究工作进入收口阶段，300m 级心墙堆石坝关键技术研究专题完成初步验收，枢纽工程可行性研究设计工作基本完成，结合科研工作进一步优化完善。防震抗震研究报告、环境影响报告书、水土保持方案报告书、工程安全预评价报告、水资源论证报告书、工程建设规划符合性论证报告及防洪评价报告等专题，相继通过审查。移民安置规划大纲通过核定，移民安置规划报告基本编制完成。

（二）金川水电站

该电站规划装机容量 76 万 kW，位于大渡河上游阿坝州金川县境内。2009 年开展可行性研究阶段移民安置规划工作，面板堆石坝科研报告完成，工程安全预评价、水资源论证报告书、防震抗震研究等专题报告通过审查，移民安置规划大纲（征求意见稿）编制完成。

（三）猴子岩水电站

该电站规划装机容量 170 万 kW，位于大渡河上游甘孜州境内。2009 年可行性研究工作完成，可行性研究阶段移民安置规划大纲、移民安置规划报告、水保报告、环保报告通过审查。可行性研究报告于 2009 年 11 月通过了审查，同年 12 月取得水电水利规划设计总院印发的审查意见。

（四）枕头坝水电站

该电站分两级开发，规划总装机容量 95 万 kW，位于瀑布沟水电站下游。枕头坝一级水电站可行性研究报告枢纽部分完成，防震抗震研究、工程安全预评价等专题报告通过审查。水土保持方案报告书完成咨询。水资源论证、防洪评价、建设规划符合性论证等专题报告编制完成正在报审。枕头坝二级水电站已开展预可行性研究阶段勘测设计工作。

（五）沙坪水电站

该电站分两级开发，规划总装机容量 78 万 kW，位于枕头坝水电站下游。沙坪二级水电站可行性研究报告枢纽部分完成，防震抗震研究报告、工程安全预评价报告、对成昆铁路影响专题报告通过审查，水资源论证报告、防洪评价报告、建设规划符合性论证报告编制完成正在报审。沙坪一级水电站已开展预可行性研究阶段勘测设计工作。

（六）安宁、巴底水电站

原规划的巴底水电站分为安宁、巴底两个梯级开发，规划装机容量 110 万 kW，位于大渡河上游阿坝州境内。已开展预可行性研究工作，金川至丹巴河段开发方式研究报告及相应环评报告通过审查。

（七）丹巴水电站

该电站规划装机容量 110 万 kW，位于大渡河上游甘孜州境内。已开展预可行性研究工作，预可研报告（咨询本）编制完成。

（八）老鹰岩水电站

该电站规划装机 64 万 kW，位于大渡河中游雅安市境内。已开展开发方式研究工作。

（中国国电集团公司）

四川一些水电站建设情况

（一）金窝水电站机组都已投入商业运行

四川田湾河流域金窝水电站首台（2 号机组）和第二台机组（1 号机组）分别于 2008 年 12 月 21 日、2009 年 1 月 14 日顺利通过 72h 试运行，2 台水轮发电机组都已投入商业运行。金窝水电站位于四川省雅安市石棉县境内，大渡河中游右岸的一级支流——田湾河中段界碑石——喇嘛沟河段上，是田湾河流域梯级开发 3 级规划中的第二级（第一级为仁宗海水电站，第三级为大发水电站），为引水式电站。该电站装设 2 台单机容量 140MW 的水斗式水轮发电机组，最大运行水头 619m，总装机容量 280MW，多年平均发电量 12.87 亿 kW·h。该电站采用的水斗式水轮发电机组，为目前亚洲该水头段已投入运行的单机容量最大的水轮发电机组。

（二）阴坪水电站机组全部投产发电

2009 年 7 月 1 日，经过中国水利水电第五工程局有限公司、中国水利水电第十工程局有限公司、中国水电基础局有限公司建设者的不懈努力，四川阴坪水电站实现了2台机组全部投产发电的目标。该电站是火溪河一库四级梯级开发的最后一级电站，这是四川省绵阳市在“5·12”特大地震后投产的投资规模最大、装机容量最大的水电项目。阴坪水电站位于四川省绵阳市平武县，装机容量2×5万kW，电站闸址为深厚覆盖层软基，地层结构复杂，最大闸高达到35.5m，为目前我国在软基上建成的第二高闸坝。在基础处理中，使用了大范围振冲加固地基，振冲处理量和处理深度均在国内水电工程中名列前茅。阴坪水电站于2006年12月20日开工。

（三）龙头石水电站机组全部投产发电

龙头石水电站位于四川省石棉县安顺场上游10km处，是大渡河干流规划22级方案的第十五级电站，上接在建的大岗山水电站，下连待建的老鹰岩水电站；装设4台单机容量17.5万kW的混流式水轮发电机组，总装机容量70万kW，多年平均发电量31.21亿kW·h。该电站自2005年开工以来，经历了2006年冬季的雪灾和2008年“5·12”汶川地震的考验，建设者们克服重重困难坚持施工，在保证工程质量的同时加快工程进度。2008年10月3日，首台机组（1号机组）投产发电；2009年3月13日，龙头石水电站2号机组顺利结束72h试运行正式并网发电；2009年5月28日，3号机组顺利完成72h试运转，并转入商业发电；2009年7月20日，龙头石水电站最后一台机组（4号机组）投入商业运行，比原计划提前36天实现了发电目标。

（四）宝兴水电站机组全部投产发电

宝兴水电站位于四川省宝兴县境内，属宝兴河流域水电站梯级开发的第三级，为长隧洞（约18.05km）引水式、高水头（额定水头305m）电站，主要由首部枢纽、引水系统和地下厂房枢纽三部分组成；共安装3台6.5万kW混流式发电机组，总装机容量19.5万kW，年平均发电量8.74亿kW·h。2009年9月，电站3台机组同时进行调试，11月初均完成所有试验项目，具备72h试运行条件，并分别于2009年11月10日、15日、18日顺利完成1号、3号、2号机组72 h试运行，正式投入商业运行。至此，该电站3台机组全部发电建成投产。

（五）一道桥水电站正式并网发电

一道桥水电站位于四川省甘孜藏族自治州九龙县境内，为九龙河右岸一级支流铁厂河梯级开发自下而上的第一梯级水电站；安装2台单机容量4万kW冲击式机组，总装机容量8万kW。该水电站系无调压井高压引水式电站，设计突破常规，取消调压井设置，采用台阶式深埋高压引隧洞，降低对当地环境的影响。一道桥水电站由中国水利水电第七工程局有限公司控股的四川久隆水电开发有限公司投资开发建设，主体工程于2006年12月正式开工建设。2009年6月13日，一道桥水电站正式并网发电。

（六）仙女堡水电站正式投产发电

仙女堡水电站位于四川省平武县境内涪江流域，于2006年初开工建设，设计装机容量7.6万kW，多年设计平均发电量为3.801亿kW·h。该电站是广西桂冠电力股份公司继收购四川茂县天龙湖、金龙潭水电站之后，于2009年8月又一次成功收购的四川水电项目。四川仙女堡水电站1、2号机组顺利通过72h试运行，分别于2009年12月23日和12月24日正式投产发电。

（七）洛古水电站投产发电

洛古水电站坝址位于四川省昭觉县洛古乡，距西昌市约118km，为西溪河流域两库5级电站中的第二级，由四川华电西溪河水电开发有限公司负责建设和运行管理。其水库为西溪河流域水电梯级近期开发的龙头水库，水库正常蓄水位2043.00m，相应库容3730万m^3。电站共安装2台5.5万kW水轮发电机组，总装机容量11万kW。洛古为长引水式电站，拦河坝为碾压混凝土重力坝，最大坝高82m，坝顶长221m，引水隧洞全长15.83km，引用流量35m^3/s。洛古水电站项目2006年8月获四川省发展改革委核准，同年11月实现大坝截流。2009年6月10日，洛古水电站1号机组完成72 h试运行，正式投产发电；6月27日，2号机组结束72h试运行，顺利投产发电。

（八）联补水电站投产发电

联补水电站位于凉山州布拖县境内的西溪河上，西溪河二库五级电站梯级开发规划中的第三级，由四川华电西溪河水电开发有限公司负责建设和运行管理。该电站是一座以发电为主的混合式电站，正常蓄水位1674m，共安装2台6.5万kW水轮发电机组，年平均发电量可达5.67亿kW·h。2005年5月，四川省发展改革委批复核准西溪河联补水电站项目，同年12月电站实现大坝截流。2007年12月19日，电站总长13 970m的引水隧洞全线贯通。2009年6月24日12时09分和16时，联补水电站1、2号机组分别完成72h试运行，两台机组在同一天投产发电。

（九）地洛水电站1号机组投产发电

地洛水电站位于凉山州境内金沙江左岸的一级支流西溪河上，是西溪河两库5级电站梯级开发规划中的第四级。该电站是以发电为主的低闸高水头引水式电站，共安装2台5万kW水轮发电机组，总装机容量10万kW，年发电量可达3.7亿kW·h。地洛水电站由四川华电西溪河水电开发有限公司建设与管理，2006年6月开工。2009年12月20日，地洛水电站1号机组通过72h试运行，顺利投产发电。

（十）江边水电站截流成功

江边水电站位于四川省甘孜藏族自治州东南部九龙县，为九龙河干流一库五级开发的最后一级，电站总投资20.5亿元，装机容量330MW，是四川省甘孜藏族自治州境内规模最大的引进外资合作开发的水电项目，也是九龙河各梯级电站装机规模最大、效益最好的一座低闸引水式水电站。江边水电站于2006年4月完成了可行性研究报告并通过审查，2007年10月底完成项目核准。2008年1月10日主体工程正式开工建设，2009年1月18日，江边电站九龙河主河床截流成功。计划2011年2月首台机组投产发电，2011年7月最后一台机组投产发电。

（十一）毛滩水电站开工建设

毛滩水电站位于夹江县境内的青衣江上，是青衣江干流千佛岩至河口段水电规划3级开发方案中的第一级，也是夹江县境内青衣江河段梯级开发的第二个梯级电站。该电站为混合式开发，以发电、防洪、灌溉为主，兼顾城市景观用水；安装3台3.4万kW轴流转浆式水轮发电机组，总装机容量10.2万kW，多年平均年发电量4.8亿kW·h。2009年12月16日，毛滩水电站开工仪式在四川夹江县甘江镇河西村举行，项目预计总投资12亿元。

（十二）上通坝水电站项目核准

2009年12月16日，四川省发展改革委以《关于木里河上通坝水电站项目核准的批复》（川发改能源［2009］1343号），同意木里河上通坝水电站工程开工建设。上通坝水电站是木里河干流水电梯级开发一库六级方案中的第一级，闸址位于四川省甘孜州理塘县，厂址位于凉山州木里县，电站设计安装3台8万kW混流式水轮发电机组，总装机容量24万kW，多年平均发电量10.99亿kW·h。

（十三）官帽舟水电站开工建设

官帽舟水电站位于四川省乐山市马边县境内，距马边县城9km左右，是马边河（系岷江下游右岸一级支流）干流水电规划报告推荐的7级开发方案中的第一个梯级龙头水库。电站采用混合式开发方案，为三等中型工程。水库正常蓄水位为674m，校核洪水位677.44m，总库容为0.973 3亿m^3，设计洪水流量3180m^3/s（$P=1\%$），校核洪水流量4860m^3/s（$P=0.05\%$）。发电厂房安装2台机组，装机容量共11万kW。考虑马边河生态基流需要，坝后设置生态基流电站，安装2台机组，其总容量为1万kW。2009年11月10日，官帽舟水电站正式开工建设。

（本年鉴编辑部摘编）

四川几个水电项目前期工作情况

（一）桐子林水电项目申请报告通过评估

桐子林水电站位于四川省攀枝花市盐边县境内，距上游二滩水电站18km，是雅砻江下游最末一个梯级电站，以发电任务为主，兼有下游综合用水要求。2009年4月19～20日，水电水利规划设计总院会同四川省发展改革委在成都京川宾馆主持召开了《四川省雅砻江桐子林水电站可行性研究报告（重编）》审查会议。会议听取了中国水电顾问集团成都勘测设计研究院关于《四川省雅砻江桐子林水电站可行性研究报告（重编）》主要研究成果及设计变化情况的汇报，并分规划、地质、水工、机电、施工、水库、造价等7个专业组进行了认真的讨论和审议。综合历次审查及收口会议意见，审查认为2008年12月成都院提出的《四川省雅砻江桐子林水电站可行性研究报告（重编）》达到了可行性研究阶段的深度要求，基本同意该报告。

2009年11月30日，桐子林水电站项目申请报告顺利通过评估，标志着该项目向通过国家核准迈出了重要一步。

（二）安谷水电站可行性研究报告通过审查

2009年4月27～29日，水电水利规划设计总院会同四川省发展改革委在四川省峨眉山市主持召开了四川省大渡河安谷水电站可行性研究报告审查会议。安谷水电站位于四川省乐山市市中区安谷镇与沙湾区嘉农镇接壤的大渡河干流上，为大渡河干流梯级开发中的最后一级，上游为在建的沙湾水电站。坝址控制流域面积7.67万km^2，多年平均流量1490m^3/s，工程的开发任务为发电、防洪、航运、灌溉和供水等。电站总装机容量760MW，多年平均发电量32.57亿kW·h，枢纽工程主要由左岸面板堆石坝、泄洪冲沙闸、厂房坝段、通航建筑物、右岸混凝土接头坝等拦河枢纽建筑物及主坝上游左岸长副坝、右岸太平镇防护副坝、下游长泄洪渠、长发电尾水渠等组成。会前，部分专家和代表查勘了工程现场。会议听取了四川省水利水电勘测设计研究院关于报告设计成果的汇报，并分组进行了认真的讨论和审议。审查认为，报告基本达到可行性研究阶段工作内容和深度要求，需按审查意见（初稿）对有关问题进行补充研究和完善。

（三）卡基娃水电站可行性研究报告通过审查

2009年5月25～27日，水电水利规划设计总院在成都主持召开了木里河卡基娃水电站可行性研究报告审查会议。会议听取了中国水电顾问集团成都勘测设计研究院关于报告主要勘测设计成果的汇报，并分组进行了认真的讨论和审议。会议认为，报告的内容和工作深度基本达到了可行性研究阶段的要求，基本同意该报告。木里河卡基娃水电站位于凉山州木里县境内，坝址距西昌市约424km，系木里河干流（上通坝—阿布地河段）水电规划一库六级的第二个梯级，是该河段梯级开发的“控制性水库”工程，总库容3.745亿m^3，具有年调节能力。电站采用混合开发方式，拦河大坝为混凝土面板堆石坝，引水隧洞长约6.36km，总装机容量452.4MW（含12.4MW生态流量小机组），年发电量16.51/17.14亿kW·h（单独/联合）。卡基娃水电站面板堆石坝坝高171m，坝址区河床覆盖层厚4.7～22.3m，坝址处为不对称“V”形河谷，大坝宽高比为1.89∶1，堆石料采用砂板岩筑坝。工程区地质条件复杂，受坝址区上、下游多个巨（大）型滑坡制约，首部枢纽布置困难，特别是因不能采用挑流消能而导致泄洪消能难度极大。在预可行性研究基础上，中国水电顾问集团成都勘测设计研究院不畏艰苦，开展了大量的勘察设计和研究工作，联合河海大学、四川大学等科研单位，攻克重重技术难题，在全面完成可行性研究阶段所有专题专项工作的基础上，于2008年12月编制完成了《四川省木里河卡基娃水电站可行性研究报告》。

（四）立洲水电站可行性研究报告通过审查

2009年5月22～24日，水电水利规划设计总院会同四川省发展改革委在成都主持召开木里河立洲水电站可行性研究报告审查会议。立洲水电站位于四川凉山彝族自治州木里藏族自治县境内，是木里河干流水电规划的第六个梯级，开发任务为发电，总装机容量355MW。立洲水电站预可行性研究报告于2006年9月通过审查后，中国水电顾问集团贵阳勘测设计研究院开始可行性研究阶段工作，于2009年4月编制完成《四川木里河立洲水电站可行性研究报告》。立洲水电站可行性研究报告通过审查，对木里河立洲水电站顺利通过核准具有推进作用。

（五）黄金坪水电站可行性研究报告通过审查

2009年11月11～13日，水电水利规划设计总院会同四川省发展改革委在成都市主持召开了四川大渡河黄金坪水电站可行性研究报告审查会议。黄金坪水电站系大渡河干流水电规划调整推荐“三库22级”开发方案的第十一个梯级电站，位于四川省康定县，上游与长河坝水电站衔接，下游为泸定梯极。工程主要任务是发电。坝址控制流域面积5.69万km^2，多年平均流量847m^3/s。水库正常蓄水位1476m，总库容1.4亿m^3，具有日调节性能。电站总装机容量85万kW，多年平均发电量38.61亿kW·h。枢纽工程由沥青混凝土心墙堆石坝、左岸溢洪道、泄洪放空洞坝身泄洪、左岸地下引水发电系统及右岸生态机组电站等建筑物组成，最大坝高95.5m。审查认为，报告达到水电工程可行性研究阶段设计深度要求，基本同意该报告。

（本年鉴编辑部摘编）

贵州几个水电站建设情况

（一）构皮滩水电站

构皮滩水电站位于贵州省余庆县境内乌江干流河段，是乌江梯级水电开发的第七级电站，水库总库容64.51亿m^3，装机容量300万kW（5×60万kW），设计多年平均发电量96.67亿kW·h。构皮滩水电站是国家“十五”期间开工建设的大型水电工程项目及贵州西电东送的标志性工程，也是乌江流域水电开发规划中最大的水电站，由贵州乌江水电开发有限责任公司负责开发管理。工程于2003年11月正式开工建设，2004年11月16日顺利实现大江截流，2008年11月底导流洞下闸蓄水。2009年7月14日21时17分，构皮滩水电站首台机组（5号机组）第一次启动成功，7月31日顺利完成72h试运行，正式并网发电投入商业运行；8月21日，4号机组正式投入商业运营；11月22日，3号机组顺利通过72h试运行后，正式投入商业运行；12月22日，电站第四台机组（1号机组）顺利通过72h试运行；12月28日，电站最后一台机组（2号机组）顺利完成72h试运行，正式投产发电。在2009年一年的时间里，成功实现了5台大型机组全部投产发电目标，并在11月30日，拱坝混凝土浇筑全线达到了设计要求的640.5m高程。

（二）思林水电站

乌江思林水电站位于贵州省思南县境内的乌江中游河段，为乌江干流梯级规划开发的第八级电站，由贵州乌江水电开发有限责任公司负责开发管理。电站安装4台26.25万kW水轮发电机组，总装机容量为105万kW，设计年发电量为40.64亿kW·h，水库总库容为12.05亿m^3。工程项目于2006年10月经国家发展改革委核准，同年11月8日正式开工建设。在地方各级政府的大力支持下，贵州乌江水电开发有限责任公司及所属思林水电站建设公司充分发挥业主的主导和核心作用，克服了工程地质条件复杂、库区移民任务艰巨、2008年初特大冰冻灾害及汛末超标洪水对工程建设带来的严重影响，在强化安全和投资管理中，优质、高效地按计划推进工程进度。2009年5月28日，首台机组（4号机组）投产发电；7月21日，第二台机组（3号机组）顺利完成72h试运行，并直接转入商业运行；9月19日，第三台机组（2号机组）一次性通过72h试运行，不需停机消缺直接转入商业运行；12 月 11 日，第 4 台机组（1 号机组）顺利通过 72h 试运行，具备投产发电条件。2009 年实现了“一年四投”的工程建设目标。

（三）董箐水电站

董箐水电站为北盘江干流梯级的第三个电站，下游尾水与龙滩电站水库衔接，装机容量 4×22 万 kW，由贵州黔源电力股份有限公司控股开发。2009 年 12 月 1 日，首台机组（1 号机组）投产发电；12 月 18 日，2 号机组在成功完成 72h 试运行后，正式投入商业运行。2009 年实现了“一年两投”目标。

（四）沙沱水电站

沙沱水电站为乌江干流规划梯级电站的第九级，也是乌江干流贵州境内在建的最后一级水电站。电站位于贵州省铜仁地区的沿河县，其上游为乌江思林水电站，下游为彭水水电站，总装机容量 112 万 kW。其枢纽工程由拦河大坝、坝后发电厂房及通航建筑物等 3 部分组成，工程总投资 107 亿元。该工程由贵州乌江水电开发有限公司负责开发管理，是贵州“西电东送”项目规划的第二批“四水六火”的标志性骨干电源项目。2009 年 4 月 17 日，通过参建各方的不懈努力和艰苦奋斗，沙沱水电站成功实现二期截流。此举标志着沙沱水电站主体工程施工全面展开，为工程早日投产发电奠定了坚实的基础。计划首台机组于 2011 年发电。

（五）善泥坡水电站

善泥坡水电站是北盘江综合规划的第八个梯级电站，地处六盘水市腹地，总装机容量 18.55 万 kW，设计多年平均发电量 6.788 亿 kW·h，水库正常蓄水位 885m，相应库容 7760 万 m^3。工程总投资 16.9 亿元，由黔源公司控股的贵州西源发电有限责任公司负责项目开发建设。2009 年 12 月 15 日，贵州黔源善泥坡水电站项目获贵州省发展改革委核准；12 月 26 日，在六盘水市水城县顺场乡举行开工仪式。电站首台机组预计于 2013 年投产发电，2014 年两台机组全部投产。

（六）格里桥水电站

格里桥水电站为乌江支流清水河梯级开发的第二级，其上游是大花水电站（装机容量 200MW，2007 年 11 月建成投产），由贵州乌江水电开发有限责任公司控股开发。其枢纽工程由碾压混凝土重力坝、左岸引水发电系统组成，坝高 124m，装机容量为 150MW。工程于 2007 年 1 月截流。2009 年 12 月 29 日，乌江清水河格里桥水电站成功下闸蓄水，两台水轮发电机组的安装工作已结束，正在进行机组投产发电前的调试。

（七）大田河大地、落生两级水电站

2009 年 9 月 23～25 日，贵州大田河大地、落生两级水电站枢纽工程通过专项验收。贵州大田河水电站引水河流为北盘江右岸的一级支流大田河，包含落生、大地两级电站，概算总投资约6.194 8亿元，总装机容量 10 万 kW，设计年发电量约 4.13 亿 kW·h，是黔西南州实施“电力兴州”战略的重要电源点之一，也是“西电东送”的电源点之一。落生水电站是大田河引水式开发的第一级电站，安装有 2 台 4 万 kW 的水轮发电机组，设计水头 256.3m，水库淹没耕地约 276 亩；大地水电站是大田河引水式开发的第二级电站，安装有 2 台 1 万 kW 的水轮发电机组，直接引用落生电站的尾水发电，设计水头 69.7m。两级水电站主体工程于 2003 年 11 月开始动工，2006 年 6～10 月，4 台机组相继并网发电。经过 3 年的生产运行考验，两级水电站各工程建筑物运行状态良好。2009 年 9 月 23 日，受贵州省经贸厅委托，黔西南州经贸局主持的贵州大田河水电站枢纽工程专项验收会议在黔西南召开。验收委员会分别听取了关于水电站工程建设、设计、施工、运行、监理、质量监督等方面的汇报，并就工程建设质量、竣工验收应满足的条件等问题进行了认真的讨论。验收委员会认为，贵州省大田河落生、大地两级水电站的设计合理，符合相关规程、规范，工程各建筑物及机电安装、金属结构安装的质量总体满足规范和设计要求，且工程验收资料齐全，工程造价控制在总概算以内，根据 DL/T 5123—2000《水电站基本建设工程验收规程》，大田河落生、大地两级水电站枢纽工程通过专项验收。

（本年鉴编辑部摘编）

云南几个水电站建设情况

（一）金沙江龙开口水电站

2009 年 1 月 6～9 日，水电水利规划设计总院会同云南省发展改革委，在昆明主持召开了龙开口水电站可行性研究报告审查会议。会前，部分专家和代表查勘了工程现场。会议听取了中国水电顾问集团华东勘测设计研究院关于《金沙江中游河段龙开口水电站可行性研究报告》的汇报，并分组进行了认真的讨论和审议，审查认为：报告满足本阶段设计工作内容和深度的要求，基本同意该报告。龙开口水电站位于云南省大理州鹤庆县境内，是金沙江中游河段规划“一库八级”开发方案的第六个梯级，电站总装机容量 1800MW，为一等大（1）型工程，工程以发电为主，兼顾灌溉和供水。枢纽工程主要由碾压混凝土重力坝及坝后式厂房等建筑物组成，最大坝高 119.00m，坝顶长 768.00m。2007 年 5 月，由中国水电顾问集团华东勘测设计研究院编制的《金沙江龙开口水电站预可行性研究报告》通过水电水利规划设计总院组织的审查。在预可行性研究报告和审查意见的基础上，中国水电顾问集团华东勘测设计研究院通过大量地质勘察、方案比较、计算分析和科研试验工作，提出了45个专题报告、近20余个单项科研报告，于2008年12月提交了《金沙江中游河段龙开口水电站可行性研究报告》。《金沙江中游河段龙开口水电站可行性研究报告》通过审查，标志着龙开口水电站的建设进入了一个新的里程。

（二）澜沧江功果桥水电站

2009年5月26日，国家发展改革委以发改能源[2009] 1352号文对云南澜沧江功果桥水电站项目的核准请示予以批复：为了合理开发利用澜沧江丰富的水能资源，增加云南电网电力供应，满足电网用电增长及“西电东送”需要，变资源优势为经济优势，促进民族地区经济和社会发展，同意建设云南澜沧江功果桥水电站工程。功果桥水电站是澜沧江中下游河段梯级开发的最上游一级电站，下游为在建的小湾电站，上游为规划的苗尾水电站。本工程以发电为主，挡水建筑物为碾压混凝土重力坝，坝顶高程1310m，坝顶长356m，最大坝高105m。水库正常蓄水位1307m，相应库容3.16亿m^3，调节库容0.49亿m^3，为日调节水库。电站地下厂房安装4台22.5万kW机组，总装机容量90万kW，年均发电量40.4亿kW·h。建成后，将增加云南电网电力供应，满足电网用电增长及“西电东送”需要，变资源优势为经济优势，促进民族地区经济和社会发展。

（三）景洪水电站

2009年6月7日，云南景洪水电站最后一台机组完成72h试运行，正式投入商业发电，至此，电站5台机组全部投产。景洪水电站是我国西部大开发和“西电东送”的重点工程，也是云南“十一五”期间投产的第一个百万千瓦级水电站，位于云南省西双版纳州景洪市，澜沧江下游，坝高108m，装机5台，总装机容量175万kW，年均发电量79.3亿kW·h。

（四）那邦水电站

那邦水电站是云南省勐乃河流域规划的第四级电站，由首部枢纽、引水系统和厂区枢纽3部分组成，安装3台6万kW立轴冲击式水轮发电机组，装机年利用小时4518h。工程由中国水利水电第十四工程局有限公司承建，于2008年11月3日开工，计划于2011年10月首台机组发电。该电站的建设，对实现当地农村电气化、保护生态环境、促进民族地区的经济发展具有重要意义。水电十四局那邦项目部按照工程提出的“又好又快建设”的要求，认真落实施工组织措施，确保工程建设稳步推进，2009年11月16日，电站顺利截流。

（五）等壳水电站

等壳水电站位于云南省保山龙陵县龙江流域，安装3台单机4万kW水轮发电机组，总装机容量12万kW，由中国水利水电第三工程局有限公司云南分局承建。2009年1月8日，该水电站截流成功。在前期施工中，项目部克服了没有施工道路、工期紧、先后遭遇因地质条件差导致的多达11次的塌方以及“10·28”特大洪峰导流洞翻堰进水等困难，积极采取应对措施，加大资源投入，根据工程进展制定赶工计划和施工措施，适时动员全体员工掀起大干高潮，保证了施工进度，实现了当年进点、当年截流的目标。

（六）大盈江四级水电站

大盈江四级水电站位于云南省盈江县，是大盈江干流中国境内规划的最后一个梯级电站，电站装机容量4×17.5万kW。2009年4月14日，大盈江四级水电站4号机组顺利并网发电。

（七）凤凰谷水电站

凤凰谷水电站是南盘江干流一库十级综合开发方案的最后一级电站，位于南盘江中游河段师宗县境内，为单一发电功能的河床式电站，装设2台5万kW水轮发电机组，总装机容量10万kW。2009年3月14日，该电站首台机组（2号机组）投入商业运行；7月3日，1号机组顺利通过72h试运行并网发电。至此，凤凰谷水电站全部机组投产。

（本年鉴编辑部摘编）

青海、新疆等地7个水电站开工建设

（一）黄丰水电站

2009年7月27日，青海黄丰水电站主体工程正式拉开施工序幕。黄丰水电站是黄河上游龙羊峡至刘家峡段的第十个梯级电站，位于青海省循化县境内的黄河干流上，总装机容量22.5万kW，工程以发电为主，兼顾少量农业灌溉等综合利用。

（二）纳子峡水电站

大通河纳子峡水电站位于青海省门源回族自治县境内，项目属于大（2）型水电工程，设计为混凝土面板坝，坝高121.5m，装机容量8.7万kW，年均发电量3.1亿kW·h，总投资7.6亿元。2009年9月15日，青海省大通河纳子峡水电站破土动工，计划2013年建成投产。

（三）尕曲水电站

2009年10月13日，青海省黄河支流上的又一水电站——总投资6亿元的兴海县尕曲水电站正式开工。尕曲水电站距兴海县城70km，是曲什安河中下游流域梯级开发的第三级电站。该电站坝高124.7m，库容9675m³，设计装机容量8万kW，多年平均发电量3.3亿kW·h，计划于2013年建成并投入试运行。

（四）吉勒布拉克水电站

2009年6月26日，新疆吉勒布拉克水电站工程正式开工。吉勒布拉克水电站是额尔齐斯河一级支流——哈巴河规划的第三个梯级水电站，总装机容量14万kW。中国水利水电第十一工程局有限公司五分局承建吉勒布拉克水电站深孔泄洪洞暨导流洞工程，洞身段总长755m。

（五）别迭里一级水电站

别迭里一级水电站为新疆阿克苏河流域两库十一级中的第八级，属引水式电站，共设8台机组，总装机容量24.8万kW。电站主要由拦河引水枢纽、引水渠、引水洞、压力前池、压力管道、电站厂房、泄水槽、尾水渠、退水渠、渠系交叉建筑物等组成，2009年5月工程正式开工。

（六）白河（夹河）水电站

2009年6月2日，由中国广东核电集团公司、陕西省安康市人民政府、湖北省十堰市人民政府联合主办的汉江白河（夹河）水电站开工庆典暨中国广东核电集团汉江开发有限公司挂牌仪式，在陕西省白河县麻虎乡隆重举行。汉江白河（夹河）水电站位于陕西省白河县和湖北省郧西县的界河上，属两省共同拥有的资源开发项目，是汉江流域中上游梯级规划的第七级电站，也是陕西、湖北两省"十一五"重点建设项目。电站设计装机容量18万kW，多年平均发电量5.54亿kW·h，建设期50个月。

（七）林海水库项目

2009年9月28日，黑龙江林海水库开工。该项目位于海浪河上游，距黑龙江省牡丹江市115km，总库容3.77亿m³，电站装机容量6万kW，估算工程总投资约21亿元，计划工期4年半。该工程建成投产后，每年可向牡丹江市及周边城镇提供优质源水2亿～3亿m³，年发电量1.03亿kW·h，增加灌溉面积1.2万hm²，并能有效提高海浪河沿岸村镇和农田的防洪标准。

（本年鉴编辑部摘编）

乐滩水电站工程简介

乐滩水电站工程，于2006年11月建成，2009年6月获"中国电力优质工程奖"，12月获2009年度"国家优质工程银质奖"。

（一）工程概况

乐滩水电站是红水河规划开发的第八个梯级，位于广西省忻城县红渡镇址上游3.0km处，上下游分别是百龙滩水电站和桥巩水电站，是一座以发电为主，兼有航运、灌溉等综合利用效益的大型水利水电枢纽。坝址控制流域面积118 000km²，多年平均流量2180m³/s。水库总库容9.5亿m³，正常蓄水位112.0m，为减少水库淹没损失，汛期限制水位110.0m，死水位110.0m。电站总装机容量60万kW，保证出力30.18万kW，多年平均发电量34.95亿kW·h。船闸设计船只吨位近期2×250t，远期可达2×500t，年货运量180万t。电站建成后，可渠化至百龙滩水电站的河段76.2km，淹没险滩22处，改善航运条件，并可为库区提水灌溉农田9.38万亩。

乐滩水电站工程是恶滩水电站的扩建工程。2003年5月15日，"恶滩水电站"更名为"乐滩水电站"。

恶滩水电站系利用已建航运枢纽的拦河坝所壅高的水位发电，航运部分包括左岸船闸一座、开敞式溢洪道一座，堰顶高程94.3m，于1976年4月蓄水。电站建筑物有短引水渠、进水闸、圆筒式厂房、尾水渠、开关站等，安装一台6万kW机组，于1977年兴建，1981年5月机组投产发电。乐滩水电站的坝轴线位于原恶滩坝轴线下游22.7m处，工程的扩建使原6万kW机组机不能再运行。

（二）枢纽布置

工程主要建筑物有溢流坝、河床式厂房、左岸船闸、左右岸重力坝和开关站等。本电站为二等大（2）型工程，按地震基本烈度Ⅵ度设防。其永久性挡水建筑物的拦河坝、厂房、船闸上闸首和冲沙闸闸首为2级建筑物，按百年一遇洪水设计，千年一遇洪水校核，其他永久性建筑物按3级建筑物设计。

坝轴线上自右至左布置：①右岸重力坝段，长93.8m；②溢流坝段，长157.0m；③厂房段，长208.5m；④船闸段，长32.5m；⑤冲沙闸段，长23.0m；⑥左岸重力坝段，长32.0m；⑦左岸土石坝段，长39.5m。混凝土溢流坝布置在主河槽，分8孔。发电厂房为河床式，布置在左岸滩地，最大高度82.0m，基础总宽85.5m，安装有4台单机容量15万kW的水轮发电机组。

（三）机电及金属结构

1. 水轮机

型号ZZA813a-LH-1040，额定出力153 100kW，额定水头19.5m，最大水头31.5m，最小水头8.65m，额定流量863.9m³/s，额定转速65.2r/min。

2. 发电机

型号SF150-96/15640，额定容量150 000kW/171 400kVA，额定电压15.75kV，额定电流6284A，额定转速65.2r/min，功率因数0.875，频率50Hz，励磁方式为晶闸管励磁。

3. 电气主接线

发电机电压采用单元接线，4台发电机、变压器均组成单元接线，220kV侧采用双母线带旁路接线。升压后接入220kV系统，出线5回。

4. 主要金属结构

溢流坝共8孔，每孔设1扇15m×15.3m工作闸门、1扇15m×15.3m检修闸门。4台机组的进水口共设置12扇7.5m×17.9m事故闸门，动水关闭静水启门，设3扇7.5m×20.6m检修闸门。厂房尾水管共设12扇7.86m×12.86m检修闸门。

（四）工程建设情况

红水河乐滩水电站工程可行性研究报告于1992年8月完成，1992年11月水利水电规划设计总院会同广西壮族自治区发展计划委员会在南宁市主持召开“可行性研究审查会议”，并提出审查意见。1993年3月5日，能源部以能源水规［1993］203号发了“关于广西红水河恶滩水电站扩建工程可行性研究审查意见的批复”同意审查意见。1995年4月，广西电力工业勘察设计研究院完成了该工程的全部初步设计工作，并上报有关单位。1995年8月24～26日，电力部水电水利规划设计管理局会同广西壮族自治区建设委员会在南宁市共同主持召开红水河乐滩水电站工程初步设计报告审查会，并通过审查。

本工程分两期施工，一期工程（主体建筑物Ⅰ标）主要施工发电厂房、溢流坝10～12号坝段、船闸、船闸冲沙闸及左岸接头坝；二期工程（主体建筑物Ⅱ标）主要施工溢流坝和右岸接头坝。

工程于2001年11月8日开工兴建，2005年底4台机组全部投产发电。截至2006年底，完成土方开挖213.4万m^3、石方开挖373.6万m^3、混凝土浇筑119.5万m^3、钢筋制作安装4.69万t、金属结构1.22万t、固结灌浆1.84万m、帷幕灌浆2.72万m。2007年8月1日，环境保护专项通过了国家环保总局组织的验收。2008年6月19日，枢纽工程通过了国家发展改革委组织的专项验收。2009年8月23日，劳动安全与工业卫生通过了国家安全监督总局组织的专项竣工验收。库区移民工作仍在进行，尚未具备验收条件。

（广西桂冠开投电力有限责任公司
乐滩水电厂　阮启业　韦爱华）

乐滩水电站老厂房利用改造情况

乐滩水电站工程是恶滩水电站的扩建工程。恶滩水电站是利用原有航运枢纽建成的红水河干流最早的一座中型水电站，装机1台，容量60MW，于1977年1月开工建设，1981年5月建成发电。2004年，在原坝址处建设的乐滩水电站开始发电，水库正常蓄水位112m，总库容9.5亿m^3，电站装机4台，总容量600MW。由于水库水位抬高后超出了老电站的设计水头范围，引水渠也被新的大坝阻断，老电站停运。

随着上游龙滩水电站建成发电，其良好的水库调节作用使乐滩水电站发电量明显增加，装机利用小时数较高。为更好地利用水能资源，提高电站的调峰能力，适应电网发展与运行需要，2008年4月起，受广西桂冠开投电力有限责任公司委托，广西电力工业勘察设计研究院开展了乐滩老厂房利用改造的研究工作。

研究的大方案分为拆除老厂房进行扩建和利用老厂房进行改造。在拆除老厂房进行扩建的方案中，分别比较了安装一台100MW、120MW、150MW的方案，但由于建设新厂房投资太大、经济指标太差而被否定。在利用老厂房的方案中，根据原有机组转轮直径、机组埋件、转轮室尺寸及流道尺寸的特性，同样比较了多个方案，包括安装60MW、70MW、80MW以及不同的额定水头、不同的机组运行水头范围等的各种方案。经初步比较，安装70MW（额定水头18.0m）、安装80MW（额定水头19.0m）、安装80MW（额定水头19.5m）三方案较优越，故选定该三方案进行详细比较。经详细比较后，安装70MW（额定水头18.0m）机组方案技术可行，获得的电量较多，容量效益较好，投资最少，经济指标优越，故推荐该方案为采用方案，并于2009年10月提出了《乐滩老厂房利用改造工程预可行性研究报告》。

2009年11月21～22日，水电水利规划设计总院会同广西壮族自治区发展改革委，在南宁市主持召开了乐滩老厂房利用改造工程预可行性研究报告审查会议，审查并通过了《乐滩老厂房利用改造工程预可行性研究报告》。

现正在进行乐滩老厂房利用改造工程的可行性研究工作。

（广西桂冠开投电力有限责任公司　方显能）

下只恩水电站建设情况简介

下只恩水电站位于云南省迪庆州香格里拉县三坝乡境内，距昆明公路里程744km，是金沙江一级支流格基河流域规划的4个梯级电站中的最后一级。

该电站采用引水开发方式，枢纽工程由首部枢纽、有压引水隧洞、调压室、压力管道、地面厂房、升压站和开关站等建筑物组成。电站装机两台，总装机容量 40MW，多年平均发电量 2.0 亿 kW·h，年利用小时数为 5017h。可研概算总投资 18 598.10 万元。

该工程为四等小（1）型工程，主要建筑物级别为 4 级，次要及临时水工建筑物级别为 5 级。首部枢纽按 50 年一遇洪水设计，200 年一遇洪水校核；厂房按 50 年一遇洪水设计，100 年一遇洪水校核。

首部枢纽主要建筑物由拦河闸坝和进水口组成。水库总库容 2 万 m^3，正常蓄水位 2022.0m，死水位 2017.0m。坝顶高程 2023.0m，最大坝高 13.5m，坝顶全长 45.7m。左岸挡水坝段长 10m，为混凝土重力坝。河床中部设 2 孔泄洪闸和 1 孔冲沙闸，每孔净宽 3.0m，堰顶高程均为 2013.0m。下游设长 20m 的消力池。坝基采用水平铺盖防渗，闸坝上游侧设 60m 长的钢筋混凝土＋土工膜铺盖，水库左岸边坡采用贴坡混凝土支护，右岸采用衡重式挡墙支护。进水口布置在右岸，为拦河坝的一部分，紧靠冲沙闸，正向冲沙、正向取水。进水口后部通过引水涵洞与隧洞相连。首部枢纽主要建筑物基础均位于崩积层和冲洪积层上。

引水隧洞全长约 9267m，为方便施工，隧洞采用相同的开挖断面，过水断面根据不同的围岩类别分别采用不支护、喷锚、混凝土衬砌等永久支护型式。

调压室为阻抗式，高约 132.5m。阻抗孔直径 2.0m，高 77.5m。大井内径 7.0m，总高约 55m。上部通气洞总长约 60m，部分洞段兼上室。

高压管道分为埋管和明管两部分，均采用钢衬，钢管内径 1.9m，壁厚 12～30mm，采用 Q345R 钢材。埋管段为长约 204.65m 的平洞，钢衬外回填素混凝土。明管段总长（埋管出洞口至钢岔管中心）约 826.0m，高差约 271m。厂房上游钢岔管采用对称“Y”形月牙肋型式，分岔角 70°，岔管后支管长度 17.557m，在厂房前渐变为 0.9m 与球阀连接。钢岔管采用 600MPa 级高强钢，管壳厚度 28mm。

厂房位于格基河河口（入金沙江）处金沙江左岸台地上，主厂房由主机间和安装间组成，主机间平面尺寸 24.2m×17.1m（长×宽），最大高度 30.7m，布置两台 20MW 的立轴混流式水轮发电机组，安装高程 1617.0m。主机间内布置发电机层、水轮机层和球阀层。安装间布置在主机间右侧，与发电机层同高。副厂房位于主厂房和安装场的上游侧，由中控室、高压开关室、厂用变压器室等组成。

升压站布置在主厂房上游侧引水钢岔管顶部回填形成的平地上，地面高程 1625.4m，布置两台主变压器。开关站位于厂区上游侧平缓的台地上，地面高程 1661.0m，开关站平面尺寸 47m×35m（长×宽）。

该电站由中国水电顾问集团华东勘测设计研究院进行工程总承包，2007 年 9 月 31 日临时工程开工，2009 年 8 月 28 日隧洞全线贯通，预计 2010 年 7 月底发电。

（中国水电顾问集团华东勘测设计研究院　孙　健）

河口水电站工程建设有关情况

（一）工程概况

河口水电站位于甘肃兰州市西郊黄河干流，距上游八盘峡水电站 8km，距下游柴家峡水电站约 10km，距兰州市区约 45km，是黄河龙—青段梯级第十七座水电站，坝址以上流域面积 22 万 km^2，多年平均年径流量 328 亿 m^3，多年平均流量 1040m^3/s。该电站以发电为主，兼有一定的灌溉、旅游及改善环境等综合利用效益，属三等中型工程。

河口水电站为河床式，枢纽建筑物从左至右为：安装间坝段、厂房坝段、1～2 号冲沙闸、3～7 号泄洪闸、右岸挡水坝段及 GIS 开关站。枢纽前沿总长度 317.65m，混凝土闸坝，坝顶高程 1562.0m，最大坝高 37.0m。水库总库容 1638.4 万 m^3，正常蓄水位 1558.0m，相应库容 1364 万 m^3。电站安装 4 台单机容量 18.5MW、转轮直径 7.3m 的灯泡贯流式水轮发电机组，总容量 74MW，年发电量 3.85 亿 kW·h。

工程分两期施工，一期由束窄河床导流，进行安装间、厂房及冲沙闸坝段施工；二期采用机组发电及 2 孔冲沙闸导流泄洪，进行泄洪闸及右副坝的施工。总工期 34 个月，第一台机组发电工期 26 个月。

河口水电站整个工程按施工时段及专业分为主体一标（HKF-CⅠ）、主体二标（HKF-CⅡ）和机电安装标（HKF-JD-AZ）3 个标段。中国水利水电第三工程局有限公司中标承担 CⅠ标段施工。

（二）CⅠ标段施工情况

中国水利水电第三工程局有限公司于 2008 年 12 月初收到甘肃电投炳灵水电开发有限责任公司下发的中标通知书，工程于 2008 年 12 月 20 日正式开工。CⅠ标段主要建筑物有安装间坝段、厂房坝段、1～2 号冲沙闸、GIS 开关站；主要工程量为：土石方开挖 58.63 万 m^3（其中砂砾石开挖 10.14 万 m^3，石方开挖 46.17 万 m^3），喷混凝土 776.6m^3，各种锚杆 1516 根，帷幕灌浆 2037m，固结灌浆 8764m，接触灌浆 440m^2，各种砌体11 119m^3，各种混凝土浇筑 24.76 万 m^3，钢筋制作安装10 695.25t，钢结构制造和安装 54.4t，闸门及启闭机安装 2942t，建筑装修及施工导流及水流控制工程等；合同额为 1.975 亿元。该标段施工主要情况如下：

1. 2009年完成情况

截至2009年底，累计完成产值131 559 835.09元，完成合同额的66.61%。完成建基面清理1.58万m^2，土石方开挖约57.24万m^3，混凝土浇筑约19.64万m^3，钢筋制作安装约6624.15t，锚喷混凝土4690m^2，锚杆施工6778m，锚筋桩施工5883m，金属结构制作安装339.837t，帷幕灌浆792m，固结灌浆6091.5m。

2. 主要工程进展情况

（1）1、2号导墙及冲沙闸工程：2009年3月底进入正常施工，同年5月1日冲沙闸首块混凝土具备浇筑条件。2号导墙及冲沙闸右边墩位于原河床中央部位，岩层透水性强，导墙基础开挖过程中有大量水从导流河床渗入，层间走向又略平行于开挖方向，施工中曾多次出现层间滑裂、坍塌现象。为实现2009年6月30日前2号导墙全部达到设计高程，具备挡水度汛要求，项目部加大人员、设备及物资的投入，在业主、监理及设计等单位的大力支持及项目部全体成员的共同努力下，按期实现了一期度汛目标。

（2）厂房机组段工程：河口水电站属于河床式电站，基坑开挖主要为原河床泥沙土、砂砾石覆盖层、深层基础黏土岩及周边体型边坡的开挖。黏土岩开挖面遇水再经过阳光照晒后，其表面20～50cm岩体会完全风化，组织结构破坏，但岩体未发生移动，仍残留有原始结构痕迹，增加了岩体塌方率，对工程施工带来极大隐患。尤其是左岸安装间边坡在开挖过程中因其岩体走向偏向于基坑边坡开挖方向的缘故，造成已开挖成型的左岸边坡大体积塌方，且根据其岩体层间结构存在有再次坍塌的迹象，因此，在基坑边坡及齿槽边坡增设9～15m锚筋桩，用以稳固开挖边坡。经努力，2009年6月12日，机组段首块混凝土浇筑，工程由土石方开挖转入混凝土施工阶段。考虑到前期工期的滞后，为满足后续混凝土工程按期完成，组织了6家施工队伍对1～4号机组同时展开作业。施工中坚持以首台机组为主线，其他机组为辅线的施工原则进行宏观调控，即以4号机组为重点，3～1号机组逐步次之的原则进行施工调配及资源组织。2009年9月28日，提前4个月实现首台机组管型座土建向安装交面，同年11月23日，实现首台机组管型座安装向土建反交面。预计2010年4月底实现厂房机组段4台机组一期混凝土全线封顶，同时完成中控楼、GIS开关站主体结构的施工任务，2010年6月底具备挡水条件。

3. 施工管理情况

（1）河口水电工程建设过程中，项目部坚持安全第一的理念，从安全基础工作入手，完善安全生产考核办法，进一步落实安全生产责任制，定期培训与动态培训相结合，不断提高全员安全生产意识，强化现场标准化管理，使安全工作按照安全目标责任制的要求一直保持较好水平。施工过程中未发生任何安全事故。

（2）河口水电站的建设过程体现了管理创新的理念，项目部以狠抓质量管理和质量保证体系为重点，进一步完善了工程质量体系的运行工作，工程质量的控制能力不断得到增强。在施工过程中加强质量监督制度的执行，层层落实质量责任书，完善质量奖惩机制，完善作业层指导书，坚持执行国家工艺规范要求，实现了工程质量目标。共验收单元工程756个，其中优良工程728个，合格率为100%，优良率为96.3%。

（3）项目部坚持工程建设与保护生态环境并举的施工原则，对各项施工措施计划认真把关，确保其在便于施工操作的同时满足节能耗、减排放的环保要求。在实际施工中加强过程控制，把各项环保措施落实到位并结合现场实际情况不断创新管理使全体员工树立了环保意识，积极主动地做好环保工作。

（中国水利水电第三工程局有限公司　崔佰奎　马丽琼）

橙子沟水电站发电引水隧洞C标段工程建设简况

（一）电站概况

橙子沟水电站位于甘肃省陇南市境内，为白龙江干流水电开发规划的第十五个梯级，引水式开发，装机容量115MW，坝高18.5m，库容280万m^3。枢纽主要建筑物由泄洪冲沙闸、左岸堆石坝、右岸岸边式电站进水口、引水发电隧洞、调压井、压力管道、发电厂房及开关站等建筑物组成。

引水隧洞沿白龙江右岸布置，全长约17.2km，为有压引水隧洞，纵向坡比为0.194 3%。引水隧洞为圆形断面，Ⅲ、Ⅳ类围岩采用钢筋混凝土全断面砌衬，开挖洞径为11.7m、12.1m，衬砌后洞径均为10.5m，洞内流速3.01m/s；Ⅱ类围岩采用底部素衬及顶部喷混凝土衬砌，开挖洞径为12.50m，衬砌后洞径为12.20m，洞内流速2.21m/s。

电站主体工程分5个标段施工，其中首部枢纽、厂房工程各为一个标段，引水系统3个标段。

（二）C标段工程

中国水利水电第三工程局有限公司中标承担白龙江橙子沟水电站引水发电隧洞工程C标段施工，中标合同额总价为2.068亿元，合同范围及主要工程量如下：

1. 合同范围

该标段合同范围为引11＋566.27m～引17＋

000.00m之间发电引水隧洞工程及5号、6号施工支洞工程，其中发电引水隧洞工程包含引水隧洞开挖、支护、钢筋混凝土衬砌、水泥回填灌浆及固结灌浆、集石坑等；施工支洞的开挖、支护及封堵；隧洞检修进人门及埋件安装；环境保护及水土保持工程；永久工程移交前的管理维护及保修期内的维修等工作。为沟通引水隧洞、施工支洞、弃渣场等各施工区的左右岸交通，该标段需修建部分施工道路及2座跨江大桥。在5号施工支洞附近的4号施工大桥跨度为51.82m（主跨43.98m），在6号施工支洞附近的5号施工大桥跨度为48.77m（主跨41.39m），均为桥面宽4.5m、荷载按公路Ⅱ级设计的加强型装配式公路钢桥（常称贝雷桥）。

2. 主要工程量

该工程合同工程量如下：土方明挖432m³；石方明挖1008m³；石方洞挖65.64万m³；喷混凝土85 047m²；挂网钢筋813.01t、钢支撑制作安装1647.56t；锚杆16 972根，混凝土浇筑10.816万m³；钢筋制作安装13 178t；固结灌浆93 923m；回填灌浆58 849m²；钢制防水门安装2t。

（三）C标段工程进展情况

中国水利水电第三工程局有限公司于2008年10月中标，并于当年10月21日进点。施工进展情况如下：

1. 合同额及主要工程量完成情况

截至2009年底，累计完成产值4284.16万元，占合同额20.7%；完成土方明挖3933.83m³、石方明挖14 874.28m³、石方洞挖25.42万m³、喷混凝土72 431m²、挂网钢筋220t、钢支撑制作安装740t、锚杆33 899根、混凝土浇筑167.86m³、固结灌浆758.26t。

2. 施工支洞进展情况

2008年12月25日、2009年1月15日，5号和6号施工支洞分别完成洞脸土石方明挖，开始洞身段开挖。由于两条施工支洞长度均在400m以上，并需长期使用，结合运输车辆行驶情况，经与各方代表沟通，调整了开挖洞径，即支洞内Ⅱ类围岩开挖洞径为7.0m×6.5m（宽×高），Ⅲ类围岩开挖洞径为7.2m×6.6m（宽×高），Ⅳ类围岩开挖洞径为7.4m×6.7m（宽×高）。2009年3月，5号施工支洞0＋176.50m～0＋227.00m段发生塌方，主要原因为该段围岩为灰黑色千枚岩，遇水软化，造成卸荷，导致钢支撑变形。项目部积极组织人员设备，制定了相应的处理措施，在一个月的时间内，分阶段进行钢支撑修复、加固，增设补强钢支撑，挂网喷混凝土，随机锚杆，固结灌浆等处理，使围岩处于稳定状态。在Ⅳ类围岩段，遵循“短进尺、弱爆破、强支护”的施工方法，保证了施工进度和质量。5、6号施工支洞分别于2009年5月31日和2009年4月28日按期修建完成。

3. 引水隧洞进展情况

该标段引水洞施工段全长为5.4km，共分为4个工作面，单工作面最短为1.2km。施工线路较长，洞内通风、照明、排水是施工过程中的主要辅助措施，对此进行了统一规划布设，即在支洞口安装两台2×75kW隧洞轴流风机向洞内供风，保障洞内施工作业面的空气质量；照明线路沿洞壁拱肩处布设，每隔10m安装25W节能灯一盏；沿洞室单侧设排水沟，局部设集水坑，不间断进行抽排水。通过各项措施，保障洞室内施工作业环境，并做到节能减排。根据开挖洞径及岩石类别，项目部制定了相应的开挖及支护措施，紧抓工序衔接，确保各类支护随开挖掌子面进行。应施工需要，各个工作面依据开挖高度，自行设计并制作了钻爆台车和支护台车，合理配置施工作业人员和机械设备，以保证施工强度。引水洞内围岩类别常发生变化，为保障钻爆质量，项目部技术人员不断调整并优化爆破设计。对洞内施工道路进行经常性维护，确保道路畅通，保障车辆通行方便，从而提高施工进度。截至2009年底，共已完成2489m隧洞开挖。

（中国水利水电第三工程局有限公司　冯　彦）

抽 水 蓄 能 工 程

蒲石河抽水蓄能电站 2009年工程建设进展情况

（一）工程进展情况

2009年是蒲石河抽水蓄能电站工程建设主体开工建设的第三年，经过各参建各方的共同努力，年度安全、质量、投资、进度目标均已完成。全年主体工程共完成土方开挖10.63万m³、石方明挖0.87万m³、石方洞挖2.7万m³、土石方回填10.53万m³；喷混凝土3202m³、混凝土浇筑20.5万m³；钢筋制作安装7199t；锚筋、锚筋桩19 710根，预应力锚索212根；固结灌浆11 630m、帷幕灌浆3543m、回填灌浆 4716m²；金属结构制作安装约 6000t；预埋各种水机、电气、给排水等管路 3 万延米。全年完成工程投资 8.37 亿元，截至 2009 年末累计固定资产投资 26.92 亿元。完成工程主要形象面貌如下：

1. 上水库工程

面板堆石坝的面板混凝土浇筑完成，防浪墙混凝土挡墙混凝土浇筑完成。趾板基岩固结、帷幕灌浆全部完成。库岸开挖完成 80%，库岸防护完成 68%。

2. 下水库土建及金属结构安装工程

下水库泄洪闸及挡水重力坝段浇筑到坝顶，坝后消力池底板和边墙全部浇筑完成。大坝基础和坝肩岩体灌浆完成，坝基排水孔施工完成。大坝泄洪弧形闸门安装完成，坝顶弧门启闭机房主体结构完工。

3. 地下厂房土建工程

地下厂房系统洞室开挖全部完成，4 台机组混凝土全部浇筑至发电机层。安装间、副厂房混凝土工程、副厂房砌体施工全部完成，安装间和主厂房吊顶施工完成。4 条母线洞全部浇筑到电机层，主变室混凝土浇筑完成，高压电缆洞混凝土完成 375m（完成总长度的 80%）。地面开关站 GIS 室已浇筑 55%。设备支架基础混凝土浇筑完成。

4. 输水系统

引水隧洞上平圆洞段、扩散段混凝土浇筑完成，闸门井混凝土浇筑完成，闸门井交通桥吊装完成。两条引水斜井开挖全部完成，两套斜井混凝土衬砌滑模施工台车已安装到位。4 条压力钢管安装、混凝土浇筑、回填灌浆、固结灌浆、接触灌浆全部完成。2 个引水岔管混凝土浇筑完成 1 个。尾水系统全部开挖完成，尾水主洞混凝土完成 1012m，完成总长度的 88%。4 条尾水支洞钢衬安装完成、混凝土浇筑完成。尾闸室混凝土全部浇筑完成、吊顶安装完成。尾水调压井混凝土施工全部完成，开始进行固结灌浆施工。下库进出水口扩散段、闸门启闭机排架混凝土浇筑完成，启闭机房主体结构完成。

5. 机电设备及金属结构安装工程

（1）4 号机（为第一台发电机组）座环研磨完成，定子机座、定位筋安装完成，开始定子铁芯叠片。3 号机埋件安装完成。2 号机和 1 号机的座环、蜗壳、机坑里衬安装完成。

（2）主厂房 300t＋300t/50t/2×10t 桥式起重机安装已完成，尾闸室 800kN 尾闸桥机安装完成。

（3）下水库进出水口两台 1250kN 固定卷扬式启闭机安装完成，一台 2×400kN 移动式启闭机安装完成。

（4）引水系统上、下水库进出水口闸门安装就位，具备进行无水试验条件。

（5）下水库坝 7 孔泄洪弧形闸门安装、坝顶门机安装、平面检修闸门安装已完成。

（二）生态建设情况

蒲石河抽水蓄能电站位宽甸县境内，地处于山岭重丘区，以林地为主，人均耕地占有量少。因此节约电站建设用地，有效保护自然环境显得尤为重要。在电站建设过程中，从设计和施工组织布局上入手，优化进场公路路径、优化弃渣方式、调整石料取用途径；调整施工区营地使用方式，尽量减少使用临时用地，将永久生活占地与临时用地结合使用，在满足施工需要的情况下将部分施工临建生活区优化后取消，在工程永久占地区布置临建区，共计减少占地 1500 多亩。

为加强环境保护和生态恢复，引入环境恢复的理念，为确保高边坡的稳定与安全，对高边坡采取了喷护植草等措施，并取得了良好的效果。

（三）建设管理情况

1. 工程质量管理

（1）建管单位：建立健全了工程质量管理体系，制定了系列质量管理规章制度，明确参建各方在质量管理中的义务和责任，设立质量管理机构和专职人员。坚持工程建设质量例会制度，充分发挥建管单位在工程建设中的主导与核心作用。在工地成立中心试验室对工程原材料、混凝土、砂浆等中间产品以及施工质量进行监督性的抽样检查工作。建管单位委托有水电站建设试验资质和经验的单位进行第三方质量抽样检测。

（2）勘测设计单位：严格执行设计公司质量体系文件，按照国家和行业有关法规、规范内容和深度要求进行各设计阶段的设计。安排一名院副总工程师分管工程技术，在工地组建了工程设代处并保持至少一名副总工常驻工地。在工程建设过程中发挥了技术保障作用。

（3）监理单位：建立健全质量保证体系，完善监理工作制度。制定了监理实施细则，内部机构和监理人员的分工明确。施工质量控制的内容、程序、流程清晰。检查施工单位的资源投入情况，审批施工单位报送的施工组织设计或施工方案、组织技术交底，签发开仓令等方式控制施工质量，严格履行监理合同赋予的“四控制、两管理、一协调”监理职责。

（4）施工单位：各施工项目单位均通过了标准质量体系认证，具有水电施工壹级资质，均在工地现场组建了施工项目部，建立了质量管理体系，设立了专门的质量管理机构，配备了一定数量的专职质量管理人员，编制了项目质量计划和系列质量管理办法。施工单位内部实行“三检制”，对控制工程的施工质量发挥了重要作用。

2. 工程质量情况

2009 年主体土建工程共评定单元工程 1298 个，合格率 100%，其中优良单元 1221 个，单元工程优良率到94%。机电及金属结构安装工程单元评定307个，合格307个，合格率100%，优良304个，优良率99%。

3. 合同及造价管理

制定合同及变更管理办法，从变更程序到变更单价审核等方面加强内控管理，做到规范化操作。对土石方工程量以及土石方分界线的确定，进行全程控制。严格索赔项目审核，对属于工程保险范围的索赔项目与保险公司积极沟通进行理赔，冲减工程费用。对于结算工程量超出合同量的项目采取预警机制，分析超出原因。对于施工单位违约进行反索赔。这些措施有效地控制了工程造价。

4. 工程安全管理

坚持“安全第一、预防为主、综合治理”的方针，2009年制定了基建安全策划指导各参建单位落实危险点及危险源的预控，制定落实重大危险源应急预案管理；组织开展“反违章”、安全生产“三项行动”、“三查一整改”和“安全生产月”等安全活动；定期组织召开季、月、周安全例会，指导和督促参建单位落实工程各项安全措施。进一步加强工程安全设施标准化建设，被国网新源控股有限公司命名为安全设施标准化达标合格单位。

与当地公安部门联合成立工地派出所，对电站施工区域进行封闭管理，对于火工材料管理、综合治安、交通安全、流动人口的管理统一由工地派出所负责。确保施工区域的治安环境，为创建平安工地、和谐工地提供了有力的保障。

（辽宁蒲石河抽水蓄能有限公司　赵忠文）

仙居抽水蓄能电站

（一）概况

仙居抽水蓄能电站位于浙江省仙居县湫山乡境内，距仙居县城50km，是一座日调节纯抽水蓄能电站。电站额定水头437m，安装4台单机容量375MW的混流可逆式机组，总装机容量1500MW，设计年发电量25.125亿kW·h，年平均抽水耗电量32.63亿kW·h，综合效率77%。电站建成后，以两回500kV输电线路接入义乌变电站，主要服务于浙江电网，承担系统调峰、填谷、调频、调相及事故备用等任务。

工程总投资为58.51亿元人民币，静态投资为48.91亿元人民币。由国网新源控股有限公司、浙江省电力公司、华东电网有限公司、上海市电力公司、浙江省仙居县国有资产经营有限公司分别按照50%、25%、10%、5%、10%出资比例共同投资兴建。

仙居抽水蓄能电站可行性研究报告于2006年12月完成，并通过了水电水利规划设计总院审查。2009年4月，中国国际工程咨询公司受国家发展改革委委托，在浙江省仙居县主持召开了《浙江仙居抽水蓄能电站项目申请报告》核准评估会议，项目通过了评估。

（二）水文气象及水源

1. 水文气象

该流域地处亚热带湿润季风区，全年季节变化明显，气候温和，雨量丰沛。降水量年内分配不均匀，多集中于梅雨和台风季节。多年平均降水量1548.0mm，主要集中在3～9月，实测最大年降水量2215.3mm、最小年降水量1065.0mm；多年平均气温17.3℃，极端最高气温41.3℃，极端最低气温−9.9℃；多年平均相对湿度79%；多年平均水面蒸发量1094.3mm；多年平均风速1.5m/s，实测最大风速19.0m/s。

2. 水源

电站上水库集水面积为1.21km^2，多年平均流量为0.035 1m^3/s，天然来水量少；下水库利用已建的下岸水库，坝址以上流域面积257km^2，多年平均流量为8.26m^3/s，水库有多年调节性能。下岸水库作为电站初期蓄水和正常运行补水水源。

（三）工程地质

工程区大地构造单元属华南褶皱系（$Ⅰ_2$）浙东南褶皱带（$Ⅱ_3$）温州—临海拗陷（$Ⅲ_8$）内黄岩—象山断拗（$Ⅳ_{11}$），褶皱不发育，构造形迹以北东～北北东、南北向的断裂为主，与北西向的断裂构成了工程区的构造格局，其他走向的断裂亦有发育，但规模较小。

上水库库（坝）区出露一套侏罗系上统高坞组、西山头组火山碎屑岩地层，岩性主要为含砾晶屑熔结凝灰岩、玄武岩、角砾熔岩等。断层不发育，节理发育。库区全～强风化层厚度不大，无大的顺坡缓倾角结构面分布，岩体弱～微透水性，除北库岸及西北库岸有渗漏之虞外，其余库岸山体雄厚，不存在库水外渗问题，库岸稳定性好。主坝址区冲沟狭窄，基岩裸露，风化浅，岩体完整性好，坝基渗漏问题不大，建坝条件优良。副坝址区地形较平缓开阔，岩性复杂、性状差异较大，局部覆盖层、全风化层较厚，岩体完整性差～较破碎。

输水系统深埋于下水库右岸山体内，沿线地层岩性为高坞组含砾熔结凝灰岩、角砾凝灰岩及凝灰质砂岩等，其间有北西向岩脉侵入；断层、节理发育，以北西～北北西向为主，北东向次之。引水隧洞以块状～次块状结构的Ⅱ类围岩为主，尾水隧洞以层状结构岩体为主，少部分为镶嵌碎裂结构，围岩以Ⅲ类为主，局部为Ⅳ～Ⅲ类。

地下厂房上覆岩体厚405～465m，围岩以块状～次块结构的角砾凝灰岩为主，少部分为中厚层状结构的凝灰质砂岩，岩体新鲜、较完整～完整，属中等地应力区，围岩以Ⅱ类为主，Ⅲ次之，整体稳定性好。

下岸水库库岸主要由相对不透水的火山岩组成，进出水口岩性主要为高坞组（J_{3g}^{1}）晶屑熔结凝灰岩，其间发育花岗闪长斑岩、英安玢岩及玄武岩等，地表呈强～弱风化，块状～次块状结构，断层发育，围岩以Ⅲ类为主，断层为Ⅴ类。

（四）主要建筑物

电站枢纽由上水库、输水系统、地下厂房、地面开关站及下水库等建筑物组成。

1. 上水库

上水库利用湫山乡梧桐村所在的天然盆地在主、次冲沟口筑坝形成，总库容1294万m^3，有效库容1066万m^3，正常蓄水位675m，死水位633m。上水库建筑物主要包括一座主坝和一座副坝。主坝为混凝土面板堆石坝，坝顶长255m，坝顶宽7m，最大坝高86.7m，坝顶高程679.2m，坝体上游面坡比1∶1.4，下游面坡比1∶2.0～1∶2.2；副坝也采用混凝土面板堆石坝，坝顶高程、上下游坝坡均与主坝相同，最大坝高59.7m，坝顶长度222m，坝顶宽度7m。

2. 下水库

下水库利用永安溪上已建的下岸水库，是一座以防洪、灌溉（供水）为主，结合发电的综合性水利枢纽。其主要建筑物为一座64m高的拱坝和一座装机容量16MW的电站。总库容13 504万m^3，有效库容9261万m^3，正常蓄水位208m，死水位178m。为解决本电站投入运行后发电流量和台汛期洪水叠加问题，在下岸水库增建直径为7.4m的泄放洞。泄放洞布置在下水库右岸，全长791m，在下水库校核洪水位213.87m时，工作闸门全开，最大下泄流量736.7m^3/s。

3. 输水系统

输水系统采用两洞四机布置，分两个水力单元，总长度为2176.1～2219.9m，其中引水系统全长1181.2～1219.2m，尾水系统全长994.9～1000.7m。主要建筑物包括：上水库进/出水口、上水库事故检修闸门井，引水隧洞上平段、上斜井段、中平段、下斜井段、下平段、引水岔管、引水高压钢支管、尾水支管、尾水岔管、尾水调压室、尾水隧洞、下水库事故检修闸门井、下水库进/出水口等。

（1）上水库进/出水口采用侧向岸边竖井式，下水库进/出水口采用侧向塔式。

（2）引水隧洞直径7.0m，引水岔管采用“卜”形，分岔角55°，采用钢筋混凝土结构。引水高压钢支管直径4.2m，长166.0～181.0m，以81°斜向进入厂房与球阀相接。引水隧洞发电工况额定流速为5.16m/s，抽水工况最大流速为4.43m/s；钢支管发电工况额定流速为7.16m/s，抽水工况最大流速为6.16m/s。

（3）尾水主隧洞直径为7.4m，尾水支管直径5.2m，除机组尾水管出口后100.0m长钢衬外，其他均采用钢筋混凝土结构。尾水岔管布置在距厂房约210.0m处，采用Y形，分岔角50°。尾水调压室布置在尾水岔管后35.0m处，采用阻抗+上室式，调压室大井直径10.0m，阻抗孔直径4.8m，总高约110.0m；上室采用城门洞形，断面10m×12.0m。尾水隧洞发电工况额定流速为4.61m/s，抽水工况最大流速为3.97m/s；支管发电工况额定流速为4.67m/s，抽水工况最大流速为4.02m/s。

4. 地下厂房及开关站

地下厂房位于输水线路的中部，由主副厂房洞、主变洞、尾闸洞、母线洞、交通洞等附属洞室组成。

（1）主副厂房洞尺寸为181m×25.5m×54.5m（长×宽×高），拱顶高程153.5m。机组安装高程113.0m；主变洞开挖尺寸为168m×19.5m×21.5m（长×宽×高），底板高程129.0m，拱顶高程149.5m；尾闸洞开挖尺寸为110m×8.2m×18.7m（长×宽×高），4条母线洞垂直布置在主厂房与主变压器洞之间的岩体中。

（2）主副厂房总长181.0m，其中机组段长113.0m，机组间距为26.5m，安装场段长48.0m，副厂房长20.0m。机组段分5层布置，副厂房分9层布置，主变压器洞分3层布置。

（3）地面GIS开关站布置在下水库进/出水口东北侧约270m的山坡上，地面高程230.0m，平面尺寸为134m×42m。场内设一条环向道路，供消防用，建筑物有GIS室、500kV出线场及地面副厂房。从主变压器洞二层接出的二回500kV高压电缆经出线斜井进入开关站GIS室。

（中国水电顾问集团华东勘测设计研究院　徐文仙）

黑麋峰抽水蓄能电站工程2009年建设情况

黑麋峰抽水蓄能电站装机4台，单机容量300MW，总装机容量1200MW，是我国抽水蓄能电站机组设备打捆招标第二批次项目和抽水蓄能电站机组设备国产化后续工作的依托项目之一。2009年，工程主要施工项目有：地下输水隧洞灌浆、充水试验、厂房系统机电设备安装、调试和试运行以及土建装修、道路完善和场地绿化等。经努力，电站首台机组于2009年8月23日完成30天试运行，进入商业运行。

（一）主体工程量及投资完成情况

2009年主体土建完成工程量为：钢筋混凝土及混凝土浇筑完成1.93万m^3，水泥固结灌浆完成1.53万m，化学固结灌浆完成0.23万m。

2009年，工程完成投资7950万元，其中土建工程实际完成投资4250万元，机电设备安装完成投资3700万元。截至2009年底，工程开工以来累计完成投资25.34亿元。

（二）主要项目工程形象进度

1. 上、下水库工程

(1) 2009年，完成上水库环库公路安全防护，完成上、下水库进/出水口启闭机房装修剩余工作，完成上、下水库场地绿化剩余工作。截至2009年底，上、下水库尾工项目全部完成。

(2) 上、下水库于2007年8月1日正式下闸蓄水，至2009年8月23日首台机进入商业运行时，上、下水库总蓄水量803.4万m^3，总有效蓄水640.3万m^3，占水库设计调节库容的75.4%。

2. 输水系统工程

(1) 2009年，完成剩余引水洞及堵头混凝土浇筑（引水施工支洞外侧堵头混凝土于2009年8月18日浇筑完成）；完成3、4号尾水洞剩余混凝土及堵头浇筑（尾水施工支洞外侧堵头混凝土于2009年12月23日浇筑完成）；完成2号引水洞剩余的灌浆（含回填灌浆、高压超细水泥分段循环固结灌浆、高压化学固结灌浆和普通水泥固结灌浆）。

(2) 2009年4月，1号流道（含1、2号机引水流道和1号机尾水流道）一次充水成功；2009年11月，2号流道（含3、4号机引水流道和3号机尾水流道）一次充水成功，测得地下洞群渗水总量均小于5L/s。截至2009年底，4台机全部引水系统和尾水系统充水试验完成。

3. 厂房系统

主厂房二期混凝土于2009年3月28日浇筑完成。截至2009年底，厂房土建工程除进厂交通洞洞口建筑施工以及主厂房部分精装修外均已全部完成。

4. 机电设备安装工程

(1) 500kV送出工程及配电装置、10kV及400V厂用电系统、公用油气水系统、照明系统、消防及通风系统全部施工完成，并投入运行。

(2) 电站1号机组于2009年2月16日全部安装完成，同年6月16日成功并网发电，同年8月23日完成30天试运行，进入商业运行。截至2009年底，2号机已完成调试，并于2009年12月6日进入30天试运行；3、4号机组安装全部完成，待并网调试。

5. 安全监测系统

安全监测仪器安装埋设全部完成，仪器读数自动化采集，可在中控室计算机读取。

（三）工程建设质量情况

2009年度，土建共评定374个单元工程，优良率92.5%；自开工至2009年底，金属结构制造及安装质量共评定529个单元工程，优良率94.3%；机电设备安装质量共评定205个单元工程，优良率96.6%。

（中国水电顾问集团中南勘测设计研究院　张孝松）

白莲河抽水蓄能电站工程2009年建设情况

白莲河抽水蓄能电站装机4台，单机容量300MW，总装机容量1200MW，是我国第一批抽水蓄能电站机组设备打捆招标项目之一。2009年，工程主要施工项目有：地下输水隧洞施工支洞混凝土堵头接缝灌浆，2号流道充排水试验，上水库抽蓄水，厂房系统机电设备安装、调试和运行以及土建装修、道路完善和场地绿化等。经努力，电站4号机组和3号机组分别于2009年11月22日和2009年12月24日先后投入商业运行。

（一）主体工程量及投资完成情况

2009年，主体土建完成工程量为：钢筋混凝土及混凝土浇筑完成0.27万m^3，水泥固结灌浆完成0.215万m。

2009年，土建工程实际完成投资1019.9万元，机电设备安装完成投资867.45万元。截至2009年底，工程开工以来土建工程累计完成投资5.605亿元。

（二）主要项目工程形象进度

1. 上、下水库工程

(1) 2009年，完成上水库环库公路安全防护，完成上、下水库进/出水口启闭机房及地面中控楼开关站装修，完成电站上、下水库场地绿化剩余工作。截至2009年底，上、下水库尾工项目全部完成。

(2) 上水库于2007年7月正式下闸蓄水。2009年8月，首台机组并网发电时，上水库已抽蓄至正常蓄水位308.00m。

2. 输水系统工程

(1) 完成输水系统施工支洞堵头混凝土浇筑与灌浆（含回填灌浆、高压超细水泥分段循环固结灌浆）。

(2) 2009年2月，2号流道（含3、4号机组尾水流道）充水成功。

3. 厂房系统

(1) 主厂房三期混凝土于2009年11月25日全部浇筑完成。

(2) 厂房土建工程除进厂交通洞洞口建筑施工以

及主厂房部分精装修外，均已全部完成。

4. 机电设备安装工程

（1）500kV送出工程及配电装置、10kV及400V厂用电系统、公用油气水系统、照明系统、消防及通风系统全部施工完成投入运行。

（2）电站首台机组（4号机组），2008年11月22日全部安装完成；2009年2月14日，充水成功；2009年5月22日，机组在低扬程的情况下，实现水泵工况抽水成功；2009年11月22日投产，进入商业运行。2009年12月24日，电站3号机组投产，进入商业运行。截至2009年底，1、2号机组安装已全部完成，正在并网调试。

5. 安全监测系统

安全监测仪器安装埋设全部完成，仪器读数自动化采集尚在调试中。

（三）工程建设质量情况

上水库于2009年8月6日利用机组水泵工况开始分阶段抽蓄水，库水位从281.50m上升至正常蓄水位308.00m。电站运行期最高水位达308.01m，最低水位296.06m，水位最大变幅11.95m。

实测主坝最大沉降量为325.72mm，占最大坝高的0.54%，主坝坝体内横向水平位移最大实测值为0.45mm，纵向水平位移基本无变化，主坝沉降已趋稳定；面板最大横向水平位移为2.03mm，面板混凝土与钢筋应力增幅很小；主坝渗漏量变化主要受降雨的影响，量水堰实测最大值为1.21L/s，降雨后3～5天，测值随之减小至小于1L/s；导流洞与施工支洞堵头混凝土与围岩接缝基本无变化，无明显渗漏。

上、下水库进/出水口边坡及库岸边坡与塔体稳定；地下厂房围岩最大累计变形13.01mm，锚杆最大应力值280MPa；主变洞围岩最大累计变形8mm，锚杆最大应力值195.83MPa；球阀室围岩最大累计变形9.88mm，锚杆最大应力值198.25MPa；尾闸室围岩最大累计变形3mm，锚杆最大应力值91.75MPa，洞室群围岩稳定。岩锚吊车梁未发现裂缝，工作状况良好。流道系统衬砌混凝土应力、钢筋应力与钢衬应力等因水压作用而有所增加，但远低于材料的屈服强度。

已投运的机电设备运行稳定，各建筑物工作状况良好。

2009年度，土建共评定45个单元工程，优良率100%；自开工至2009年底，金属结构制造及安装质量共评定56个单元工程，优良率98.2%；机电设备安装质量共评定163个单元工程，优良率99.8%。

（中国水电顾问集团中南勘测设计研究院　熊卫亚）

南水北调工程

南水北调有关工程建设情况

（一）丹江口大坝加高工程

1. 右岸混凝土坝段全线贯通

2009年1月7日，伴随着丹江口大坝加高工程最后一罐混凝土顺利入仓，由中国水利水电第三工程局有限公司承建的南水北调中线水源丹江口大坝加高工程右岸混凝土坝段全线贯通。大坝加高工程2007年3月开始加高施工，由于丹江口大坝要以防汛为主，所以主要施工集中在枯水期。中国水利水电第三工程局有限公司在整个混凝土坝段加高过程中，经历了特大冰雪灾害的洗礼，克服了施工场地狭小、老坝体裂缝处理等一系列难题。深孔坝段于2008年5月全部达到176.6m新坝顶设计高程，随后，右岸各个坝段加高混凝土浇筑也陆续完成，共完成混凝土浇筑345 900m^3，钢筋安装1270t。至此，右岸加高混凝土坝段已全线贯通。按照丹江口大坝加高工程“四枯”施工进度计划提前完工，满足了2009年度汛要求。

2. 右岸土石坝全部填筑到设计高程

2009年12月2日，丹江口大坝加高工程右岸土石坝已经全部填筑达到设计高程176.6m，上游护坡已建设完成。由中国水利水电第十一工程局丹江口大坝加高工程项目部承建的丹江口大坝右岸土石坝施工项目，自2005年9月26日开工以来，施工单位精心组织，科学施工，在确保安全、质量的前提下，不断加快施工进度。监理部门严把工程质量关，确保每项施工合格率达到100%。汉江集团南水北调项目部加大与业主和施工单位的沟通协调力度，确保大坝右岸土石坝加高施工按计划稳步推进。目前，大坝右岸土石坝上游护坡已经建设完成。坝顶防浪墙除右岸坝头和水源公路结合部位20余米外，其余全部浇筑完成。施工单位正按照业主要求，做好下一步施工准备工作。

（二）兴隆水利枢纽工程开工

2009年2月26日，南水北调中线兴隆水利枢纽工程在湖北省天门市多宝镇举行隆重的开工典礼，总投资84亿元的汉江中下游治理工程由此拉开序幕。国务院南水北调办公室主任张基尧在开工仪式上讲话并宣布工程开工，湖北省省长李鸿忠代表湖北省委、省政府致辞，中国水利水电建设集团公司副总经理李跃平、中国水电基础局有限公司董事长张源智等应邀出席开工典礼。南水北调中线一期工程从丹江口水库调水95亿 m^3，将使汉江中下游水环境容量减少26%。为缓解调水对汉江中下游的不利影响，国务院将“汉江中下游治理”纳入中线一期工程，包括兴隆水利枢纽、引江济汉、部分闸站改造、局部航道整治等4项工程。率先开工的兴隆水利枢纽位于汉江下游潜江、天门市境内，距武汉河口273.7km。大坝正常蓄水位36.2m，相应库容4.85亿 m^3，可灌溉农田327.6万亩；库区回水长度76.4km，规划航道等级为Ⅲ级；电站装机容量4万kW。该工程静态总投资30.5亿元，总工期4年半。作为汉江干流规划的最下一个梯级，该水利枢纽的主要任务是枯水期壅高库区水位，改善库区沿岸灌溉和河道航运条件，兼顾发电，不仅将有效缓解南水北调中线工程对汉江下游的影响，保障和促进南水北调中线工程顺利推进，而且对加快汉江中下游综合治理开发，促进汉江中下游经济社会可持续发展具有十分重要的意义。承担兴隆水利枢纽围堰防渗墙基础工程的中国水电基础局有限公司承诺，将用先进的技术和卓越的诚信把南水北调汉江兴隆水利枢纽围堰防渗墙基础工程做成世纪精品工程。

（三）江都站更新改造成功

2009年3月11日下午3时，随着最后一台机组的顺利投运，南水北调江都站更新改造项目——江都三站机组发电试运行取得圆满成功。经现场测试，在5m的扬程下，机组发电功率为3400kW，各发电设备相关技术性能、技术参数均达到了预期效果。江都三站位于江都二站东侧，是江都水利枢纽的主力泵站之一，建于1966年12月。该站装有10台套立式全调节可逆式轴流泵，配用立式可逆电动发电机，总装机容量16 000kW，设计流量135 m^3/s，正转可抽水，反转可发电。经过30多年的运行，机电设备严重老化，存在很多安全隐患。江都三站更新改造工程于2006年11月正式开工，改造主要项目有：更换水泵电机、电气设备、检修闸门及拦污栅，对进水流道进行改造，增设自动控制系统等。工程总投资5993万元。在前一阶段淮北地区旱情较重时，为使机组具备投入抗旱排涝运行的工程条件，江都三站全体职工加班加点，于2009年2月24日提前完成了10台机组的安装工作。此次发电试运行圆满成功，标志着江都三站在发挥抽水抗旱排涝社会效益的同时，还可在淮河来水较多的情况下，反转发电，充分发挥江都水利枢纽工程的综合效益。

（四）南水北调中线河南郑州段工程开工

2009年，7月28日，南水北调中线河南郑州段工程开工建设，标志着中线黄河以南工程建设进入新阶段。南水北调中线河南郑州段工程起点位于新郑市观音寺镇英李村，终点位于穿黄工程隧洞入口，途经新郑、中牟、管城、二七、中原、高新、荥阳等7个县（市、区），全长128.94km，占中线一期工程总长的1/10。工程起点设计流量305 m^3/s，加大流量365 m^3/s，终点设计流量265 m^3/s，加大流量320 m^3/s。工程总投资约135亿元。

（五）南水北调中线天津干线河北境内工程开工

2009年，7月29日，南水北调中线天津干线河北境内工程开工建设，标志着中线一期工程天津干线在途径的天津、河北两省市全面开工建设。天津干线工程是南水北调中线一期工程的重要组成部分，全长约155km。其中的天津1段和天津2段主体工程已于2008年11月17日开工建设。天津干线河北境内工程，西起河北省保定市徐水县西黑山村，东至廊坊市安次区，全长131km，为地下箱涵输水结构。起点设计流量为50 m^3/s，加大流量60 m^3/s；终点设计流量45 m^3/s，加大流量55 m^3/s。工程总投资约为74.6亿元。

（本年鉴编辑部摘编）

4

工 程 勘 测

工程地质勘察与评价

潘口水电站工程地质勘察与评价

（一）工程概况

潘口水电站位于湖北省十堰市竹山县境内，地处堵河干流上游河段，坝址下距竹山县城约13km。枢纽建筑物由大坝、右岸岸边开敞式溢洪道、右岸泄洪洞、左岸引水隧洞、地面厂房和开关站等组成。水库正常蓄水位355.00m。拦河坝为混凝土面板堆石坝，坝顶高程362.00m，最大坝高114.0m。电站装机2台，总装机容量500MW。工程于2007年10月开始动工兴建。

潘口水电工程规划工作始于1966年，由原水利电力部长沙勘测设计院（即现中国水电顾问集团中南勘测设计研究院）提交了规划报告。

1982～1985年进行初步设计工作，并通过原水利电力部与湖北省计委联合组织的审查。2003年受湖北省潘口水电发展有限公司委托，在新编项目建议书的基础上补充了大量的地质钻探、洞探、地质测绘与试验工作，重编了可行性研究报告。各阶段共完成岩芯钻孔11 816.15m，洞探2911.25m，槽坑探11 578.27m^3，地震勘探14 600m，现场抗剪试验15组，还进行了岩基、建材、水力学模型等多项室内外试验，查明了工程区及建筑物地段的主要工程地质问题。工程于2007年10月开工建设。

（二）主要工程地质条件与评价

1. 区域构造稳定性

区域展布有3条大的断裂带，将区域分为3个大地构造单元：扬子准地台、南秦岭加里东褶皱带、武当隆起区。新构造运动以间歇抬升为主，工程区位于武当隆起区。根据工程场地地震安全性评价，50年超越概率10%的动峰值加速度为0.098g，地震基本烈度为Ⅶ度；100年超越概率2%的动峰值加速度为0.228g，地震烈度为Ⅷ度。

2. 水库工程地质

水库为峡谷型，两岸分水岭高程大于490.00m，不存在向邻谷渗漏问题；库岸存在滑坡、崩塌、坍岸等现象，但规模较小或分布远离坝区，对水库及工程运行影响不大；库区亦无较大的淹没问题。

3. 河床坝基及趾板地基地质条件及开挖处理

河床砂砾石层厚度10～16m，需在趾板线至下游60m范围将河床砂砾石层全部清除。基岩为灰白色白云母石英片岩，弱风化，片理较发育，地质构造简单，无不良地质缺陷，可满足建坝地基要求。趾板地基，河床先清除覆盖层，基岩开挖深度2～6m；两岸开挖到弱风化岩带中上部。垂直开挖深度，左岸4～25m，右岸6～20m。右岸高程330.00m以下至河床基岩为下武当群化口组白云母石英片岩夹云母片岩，高程330.00m以上为加里东期灰绿色绿泥钠长片岩，岩体呈弱风化。左岸高程340.00m以下至河床基岩为下武当群化口组白云母石英片岩夹云母片岩，高程340.00m以上为加里东期灰绿色绿泥钠长片岩，岩体呈弱风化。趾板基础开挖表明右岸及河床基岩较完整，且无明显的超挖现象；左岸基岩风化相对强烈，节理裂隙相对发育，在高程260.00～295.00mm（Z22～Z30）岩体较破碎，出现超挖现象，施工中已采用混凝土回填处理。趾板基础布设系统锚杆并进行固结灌浆处理，系统锚杆间、排距1.5m×1.5m，深入基岩5m，外露0.35～0.55m。

4. 厂房基础地质条件及开挖处理

发电厂房布置在左岸岸边，自然岸坡坡角40°～45°，河床水位261.00m，厂房纵轴线方向为北东20°。开挖基岩面高程236.10～237.60m。建基岩石主要为绿泥钠长片岩夹透镜状大理岩与绢云绿泥石英片岩及含炭石英质千枚岩，为微风化至新鲜岩体，均能满足建基要求。厂房基础工程地质良好。

5. 边坡开挖及处理

潘口水电站主要建筑物边坡有左岸引水隧洞进水口边坡、左岸地面厂房后边坡、右岸泄洪洞进出口边坡、右岸溢洪道边坡等。

（1）左岸引水隧洞进水口边坡，分正面坡（下游）及上游侧坡。正面坡为斜交坡，最大坡高142m，自上而下开挖坡比为1∶0.75～1∶0.25，岩石主要为白云母石英片岩、绿泥钠长片岩，节理裂隙较发育并伴有层间软弱夹层，开挖过程中局部出现垮塌及掉块。边坡支护措施采用系统锚杆挂网喷护，挂网喷护厚度10～15cm，系统锚杆为ϕ28～32，长7.5～9.0m，排间距3m×1.5m，考虑在水位变动带高程362.00～347.00m增设2排预应力锚索，锚索长25m，间距6m，设计锚固力1000kN。根据变形观测资料，目前边坡处收敛稳定状态。上游侧坡多为顺向坡，最大坡高130m，自上而下开挖坡比为1∶0.75～1∶0.5，岩石为白云母石英片岩，节理裂隙较发育，岩体扭曲变形较严重，由于各结构面相互切割，开挖过程中局部出现垮塌。边坡支护措施主要采用系统锚杆挂网喷护，挂网喷护厚度10cm，同时在地质条件较差坡段增设预应力锚索及锚桩进行加强支护。系统锚杆为ϕ28，长7.5～9.0m，排间距3m×1.5m、2.5m×2.5m、2m×2m。在高程312.00～342.00m，桩号0－034.66～0－080.54地段，开挖过程中出现顺层垮塌，为确保其边坡稳定，增设了4排锚桩加强支护，锚桩长度15～20m。考虑在水位变动带高程362.00～347.00m增设2排预应力锚索，锚索长25m，间距6m，设计锚固力1000kN。根据变形观测资料，目前边坡处于收敛稳定状态。

（2）左岸地面厂房后边坡，为斜交坡，最大坡高约90m，自上而下开挖坡比为1∶0.75～1∶0.15，岩石为绿泥钠长片岩，夹透镜状大理岩与绢云绿泥石英片岩及含炭石英质千枚岩，节理裂隙较发育，在开挖过程中局部出现垮塌及掉块。边坡支护措施采用系统锚杆挂网喷护，挂网喷护厚度10cm，系统锚杆为ϕ28，长6.5～9.0m，排间距3m×3m，2.5m×2.5m，在地质条件较差坡段增设锚桩进行加强支护，锚桩长度20m，间距4m。根据变形观测资料，目前边坡处于收敛稳定状态。

（3）右岸泄洪洞进口边坡，为反向坡，最大坡高180m。高程482.00～315.00m开挖坡比为1∶0.75～1∶0.25，高程315.00～297.50m为垂直开挖。高程362.00m以上岩石为绿泥钠长片岩，其下为白云母石英片岩，片理产状335°～340°/NE∠40°～50°。节理裂隙较发育，开挖过程中局部出现垮塌。边坡支护措施采用系统锚杆挂网喷护，挂网喷护厚度15cm，同时在不同高程共增设预应力锚索98根、锚桩91根进行加强支护。系统锚杆为ϕ32，长8.7mm，排间距3m×1.5m；预应力锚索长度30～40m，间距6～12m，设计锚固力1000～1500kN；锚桩长度20m，间距6m。根据变形观测资料，目前边坡处于收敛稳定状态。

（4）右岸溢洪道边坡，最大坡高80m，为白云母石英片岩及绿泥钠长片岩。片理走向340°～350°，倾向北东，倾角45°～50°。片理走向与溢洪道轴线近垂直，侧坡开挖自上而下开挖坡比为1∶1～1∶0.25。边坡支护措施主要采用系统锚杆挂网喷护，挂网喷护厚度10cm，系统锚杆为ϕ25、ϕ28、ϕ32，长5～9m，排间距3m×1.5m，在地质条件较差坡段增设锚桩进行加强支护，锚桩长度20m，间距4m。

6. 洞室开挖及处理

（1）导流隧洞，布置在右岸，进口底板高程262.00m，洞向41°，设计净断面为15.0m×18.0m（宽×高）。断面采用城门洞形，洞长约530m。岩性为进口段白云母石英片岩夹云母片岩、绿泥钠长片岩，岩层（片理）走向：310°～320°/NE∠45°～55°。经开挖表明洞室围岩大多为Ⅲ类围岩，局部为Ⅳ围岩。总体评价洞室工程地质条件较好。支护措施主要采用系统锚杆挂网喷护，挂网喷护厚度15cm，洞顶拱及侧墙上部系统锚杆参数为ϕ28，长8.5m，排间距3m×1.5m；侧墙中上部系统锚杆参数为ϕ28，长5.5m，排间距3m×1.5m。在地质条件较差洞段增设随机锚杆，进出口采用锁口锚杆和钢支撑。

（2）泄洪洞，布置在右岸，长约690m，为无压隧洞。进口底板高程300.00m，设计净断面为8.0m×13.5m（宽×高）。断面采用城门洞形。洞轴方向北东58°。岩性为进口段白云母石英片岩夹云母片岩、绿泥钠长片岩、炭质千枚岩。岩层（片理）走向：300°～350°/NE∠45°～60°。经开挖表明洞室围岩大多为Ⅲ类围岩，局部为Ⅳ围岩。总体评价洞室工程地质条件较好。支护措施主要采用系统锚杆，系统锚杆参数为ϕ28，长5.7m，排间距3m×3m，在地质条件较差洞段增设随机锚杆，进出口采用锁口锚杆和钢支撑。

（3）引水发电隧洞，位于左岸，平行布置2条。进口底板高程307.00m，设计净断面直径为9.5m。1号引水隧洞长461.90m，2号引水隧洞长461.90m。岩性为白云母石英片岩夹云母片岩、绿泥钠长片岩。岩层（片理）走向：320°～330°/NE∠40°～55°。经开挖表明洞室围岩大多为Ⅲ类围岩，局部为Ⅳ围岩。总体评价洞室工程地质条件较好。支护措施为$Ⅲ_1$类围岩采用随机锚杆（ϕ25，$L=4.5$m，外露0.5m，梅花型布置），视现场开挖情况喷0.10m厚C20混凝土。$Ⅲ_2$类和Ⅳ类围岩采用系统锚杆（ϕ28，$L=6$m，外露0.5m，排距2.5m，梅花型布置），喷0.10m厚C20混凝土。进出口采用锁口锚杆和钢支撑。

7. 天然建筑材料

潘口水电站经过多次勘测设计和方案比选，为充分利用当地材料，挡水建筑物采用混凝土面板堆石坝，大坝堆石填筑总方量259.30万m^3，由11种不同要求的料物构成。

潘口水电工程在可行性研究阶段共勘察了4个石料场，最后在招标阶段确定黄茅观料场为主堆石料场。

2008年10月，作为主堆石料场的黄茅观石料场经开挖后现场碾压试验表明，渗透及沉降变形参数难以满足设计要求。

为解决堆石坝料源问题，设计考虑将利用一部分天然砂砾料作为大坝填筑料源并要求在坝址附近寻找新的石料场。因此，2008年12月又对坝址上游犁湾滩至下游四湾总长约13km河段沿河分布的10个砂砾石料场进行了补充勘探和复核，同时在潘口河口上游约2km处选定了潘口河石料场并进行了详细勘察，于2009年4月提交了《潘口水电站大坝料源补充规划专题报告》。经勘探表明：砂砾石总储量186.17万m^3；潘口河石料场地层岩性为寒武系下统水沟口组的硅质岩、灰岩、硅质板岩等，岩石具有抗风化能力强，压缩性小等特点，是堆石坝适用的填筑石料，有用层勘探储量为420万～450万m^3。

潘口水电站所选各砂砾料场产地分布零散，但通过精心安排，在考虑满足混凝土骨料的前提下，充分利用天然砂砾石料作为大坝填筑料。根据勘探和现场试验成果资料，设计重新调整了大坝填筑分区，较好地解决了潘口工程大坝填筑料源问题，确保潘口工程可在2010年4月底前大坝拦洪度汛断面达到高程322.00m。

（中国水电顾问集团中南勘测设计研究院　唐朝旺）

西龙池抽水蓄能电站利用深厚覆盖层建坝工程地质研究

西龙池抽水蓄能电站下水库为岸边式水库，修建于滹沱河左岸一大型冲沟内，库底高悬于河床之上，库区深厚洪积覆盖层分布广泛，如何充分利用其修坝建库，需对其进行全面系统研究。

（一）深厚洪积覆盖层成因分析

受地壳差异性升降及掀倾运动的影响，河流溯源侵蚀增强，西河村段的滹沱河于第四纪早更新世晚期开始发育，至中更新世基本形成现今河流发育的方向、形态。在此期间沟谷的出口处洪积扇极为发育，为本区的第一期洪积扇（Q_2^{pl}），它形成时代较早，相应时代为第四纪中更新世。随着河流的发育，在形成河流Ⅲ级阶地（Q_3^{al+pl}）的同时，沟谷的出口处的第二期洪积扇（Q_3^{pl}）也生成了，相应时代为第四纪晚更新世，由于洪积物的规模较大，它不但将第一期洪积扇切穿，并在其前缘堆积，沿滹沱河与第一期洪积扇呈内迭式接触，而且还将滹沱河推向右岸，与Ⅲ级阶地堆积物呈交互相的成生形态，致使滹沱河切割右岸的Ⅲ级阶地，产生小范围的河流改道，而形成现今的滹沱河河床。到了第四纪全新世，地壳处于间歇性的升降运动状态，使得第三期洪积物（Q_4^{pl}）及对应的滹沱河的Ⅱ、Ⅰ级阶地（Q_4^{al+pl}）成生。Ⅱ、Ⅰ级阶地在滹沱河左岸有少量堆积，而洪积物仅限于较大的冲沟内有堆积，其洪积舌未延伸到滹沱河河床，大龙池沟沟口也未形成洪积扇，少量的洪积物多堆积在沟脑部位，堆积的厚度也较薄，与前两期洪积物呈上迭式的堆积形式，河流阶地为内迭式的堆积形式。

（二）深厚洪积覆盖层工程地质特性评价

按成因和形成时代对覆盖层的物理力学性质进行了研究，并结合建筑物对覆盖层物理力学性质进行了评价。

Q_4^{pl}、Q_3^{pl}、Q_2^{pl}的洪积物组成物质以碎、块石土为主，夹有土层、土夹碎石和碎、块石层的透镜体以及大孤石，其在三度空间上的分布极不均匀，但在上部土层压密作用和地表、地下水的长期淋滤作用下，使得第一期（Q_2^{pl}）和第二期（Q_3^{pl}）洪积物的结构较为密实，碎、块石颗粒间呈连续的紧密状接触，同时在不同的部位形成不同程度的胶结，胶结形式主要有泥钙质基底式、孔隙式、接触式和松散团块状胶结，不同程度的胶结体在三度空间上分布亦极不均匀，连续性较差。

通过地质、勘探、物探和试验工作，并对各期洪积物的工程地质特性作了较系统的分析，包括覆盖层的颗粒级配、物理特性、弹性波特性、地震动反应特性、抗剪强度、承载能力、变形特性、压缩特性、渗透特性和应力应变特性等。而早期洪积物的上述物理力学性质均优于一般河床冲积的砂卵砾石，与堆石坝堆石基本相同，与其他工程类比，其具有较为优良的工程地质特性，可以满足百米级堆石坝地基的设计要求。

主堆石区的坝基可利用较早形成的Q_2^{pl}和Q_3^{pl}洪积物，大龙池沟沟底主堆石区范围内的Q_4^{pl}全部挖除；对沟两侧的Q_2^{pl}洪积物，除考虑沟梁间的开挖坡比必须满足变形要求需要加大对洪积物的开挖外，原则上Q_2^{pl}、Q_3^{pl}洪积物在清除表层1～2m的坡积土夹碎石或人为的耕植土后，即可作为堆石坝主坝坝基；位于左右两坝肩缓坡上的$Q_{2\sim4}^{col+dl}$和瓦窑沟沟底的Q_4^{pl}应全部挖除。

次堆石区坝基可以考虑利用Q_4^{pl}洪积物的中下部，位于大龙池沟沟底次堆石区范围内的Q_4^{pl}上部予以挖除；对沟两侧的Q_2^{pl}及Q_3^{pl}洪积物除考虑沟梁间的开挖坡比必须满足变形要求需要加大对洪积物的开挖外，原则上Q_2^{pl}及Q_3^{pl}洪积物在清除表层1～2m的坡积土夹碎石或人为的耕植土后，即可作为堆石坝次堆石区坝基；对位于右坝肩附近缓坡上的Q_4^{col+dl}和瓦窑沟沟底的Q_4^{pl}，应全部挖除。

库盆范围内第四系堆积物厚度19～28m，据勘探揭示Q_4^{pl}的厚度均大于10m，需将Q_4^{pl}覆盖层全部清除；利用其下伏的较老洪积物和基岩作为库盆地基；对分布在库岸面板范围的$Q_{2\sim4}^{col+dl}$全部予以清除，使库岸面板均坐落在基岩上。

从勘探、试验成果看，下水库库坝区上部清除的$Q_{2\sim4}^{pl}$覆盖层，其物理力学性质指标，能够满足堆石坝次堆石区对筑坝料的设计要求，可将其做为次堆石区的筑坝材料。

通过施工开挖揭示及施工期、工程运行期坝基覆盖层变形监测成果，进一步验证了前期勘察研究结论是符合实际的。

（中国水电顾问集团北京勘测设计研究院 李院忠）

张河湾抽水蓄能电站上水库软弱夹层特性

张河湾抽水蓄能电站位于河北省石家庄市井陉县，装机容量为1000MW。电站利用甘陶河上未完建的张河湾水库为下水库，选定其左岸老爷庙山顶建设上水库。上水库为半挖半填形成库盆，围库大坝为堆石坝，采用复式沥青混凝土面板进行全面防渗。

（一）一般地质条件

张河湾上水库为一北东向展布的高悬平台，南北长约2km，东西宽250～700m，周边有高约50m的陡崖，东、北、西三面受沟谷深切，西侧发育有西沟、西南沟两大冲沟。

与上水库工程有关的岩体为寒武系馒头组灰岩、泥岩、砂泥岩、粉砂岩和长城系大红峪组石英砂岩、铁质砂岩、长英砂岩，寒武系地层假整合盖在长城系地层之上。

上水库位于走向近SN的区域性断裂F_7、F_8之间，单斜岩层，产状：NW350°～NE10°SW（NW）∠6°～10°，局部产状有变化。受F_7、F_8影响上水库发育次一级断层100条左右，按走向分为近SN、近EW、NE、NW 4组；岩体内裂隙较为发育，走向与断层基本一致，岩体为中厚层状结构，局部为镶嵌碎裂结构或薄层状结构。

上水库地下水主要为基岩裂隙水，由于周边为深切沟谷，排泄条件好，地下水埋藏很深，为284m。岩体透水性不均一，埋深50m以内垂直分带的规律不明显，岩体以弱透水和中等透水为主。

上水库山体普遍受卸荷作用影响，主要表现为平行于陡壁的裂隙张开并充填次生泥，大致可以分为强、弱两个风化卸荷带，强卸荷带在台坪东侧宽20～40m，西侧宽50～60m。

（二）软弱夹层

上水库地层中普遍发育有软弱夹层，间距一般在0.5～5.0m，按物质组成及结构特征分为泥夹碎屑型和碎屑岩片型两类：

（1）泥夹碎屑型（Ⅰ类）：物质组成以白色、灰白色泥质物（岩粉）为主，间夹透镜体状角砾岩、岩片、碎屑等，夹层厚度0.1～12.0cm，其中含泥厚0.1～3.0cm；层面呈稍舒缓波状起伏，起伏差为4.0～12.5cm，充填度为0.2～0.9，层面较光滑并可见到NW向的擦痕。

（2）碎屑岩片型（Ⅱ类）：物质组成以原岩岩片、碎屑为主，局部夹少量泥质物；层面不规则，无明显界面，夹在软硬相间岩层内，呈舒缓波状，其起伏差也很小。

软弱夹层矿物成分主要为伊利石，有部分蒙脱石、绿泥石、高岭石。为取得软弱夹层的抗剪指标，针对上水库具有代表性的夹层分别进行了室内直剪、三轴剪切、中型剪切和室外大型剪切试验，以其为基础，类比已建工程同类型夹层抗剪强度指标，提出上水库软弱夹层抗剪指标建议值（见表1）。

表1 上水库软弱夹层抗剪指标建议值

层位	夹层类型	抗剪强度指标建议值				主要夹层编号
		饱和状态		天然状态		
		f	C (MPa)	f	C (MPa)	
寒武系馒头组	Ⅰ	0.30～0.32	0			R_{m1-2}、R_{m1-3}，R_{m1-4}，R_{m1-8}，R_{m1-8-1}
	Ⅱ	0.35	0			R_{m1-3-1}，R_{m1-3-2}
长城系大红峪组	Ⅰ	0.22～0.25	0	0.30～0.32	0	R_{d3-1}～R_{d3-10}，R_{d3-13}，R_{d3-15}，R_{d3-16}
	Ⅱ	0.35	0			R_{d3-1}～R_{d3-6}，R_{d3-8}，R_{d3-8-1}，R_{d3-14}

对本工程影响较大的主要是长城系大红峪组中延伸长远、连续性好、含泥量高、分布稳定的R_{d3-1}、R_{d3-2}、R_{d3-3}。

（三）上水库坝基抗滑稳定分析

上水库地层中发育的众多的软弱夹层，特别是长城系大红峪组中的R_{d3-1}、R_{d3-2}、Rd_{3-3}，埋藏在坝基下，且规模大、连续性好、泥化程度高，对坝基抗滑稳定不利。

根据上水库三维渗流值模拟研究的等水位线图，结合软弱夹层建议值，取半饱和状态下抗剪参数，$f=0.275$，$C=0$，计算方法分别采用了拟静力法和动力法。拟静力法结果正常运行工况安全系数均大于1.3，地震工况下都大于1.1，符合安全要求；动力法表明，正常蓄水位下上水库基础安全系数均大于1.0，是安全的，死水位下沿软弱夹层R_{d3-1}虽有小于1.0的时刻，但持续时间很短，不会产生较大的滑移而整体失稳破坏。

（四）结语

张河湾抽水蓄能电站上水库地处高悬台坪，存在软弱夹层等诸多不利的地质因素，以及高山动力反应的影响。经过大量的室内外试验和认真深入的研究分析，掌握了软弱夹层的特性和力学性质，在此基础上对上水库基础沿软弱夹层的深层抗滑稳定问题进行了充分的分析计算和研究论证。通过地震危险性分析及坝料动、静力三轴试验，提出了地震参数和坝料的力学参数，据此进行了上水库动力分析。通过选取合理的库盆防渗方案和相关的辅助工程措施，确保了工程的安全性、可靠性。

（中国水电顾问集团北京勘测设计研究院　赵国刚）

琅琊山抽水蓄能电站上水库岩溶渗漏特征

琅琊山抽水蓄能电站上水库建在岩溶较发育的地区，渗漏问题是上水库的主要工程地质问题。工程区出露的地层岩性主要为上寒武统琅琊山组（$\in_{3Ln}$）薄层灰岩和车水桶组（$\in_{3C}$）薄层与中厚层灰岩互层、厚层灰岩。其中，车水桶组中段厚～巨厚层致密块状灰岩是岩溶最为发育的地层，其在地下形成的岩溶管道是库水外渗的主要通道。

受地质构造控制，岩溶多沿陡倾角层理裂隙面和NW～NWW的断裂构造发育，故岩溶发育的型式以垂直形态为主，在平面上常循层理裂隙（NE）、断裂（NW）呈“之”字形分布，但总的趋势为NE～SW向成线型断续分布。地下溶洞延伸及地下水在灰岩中储存、径流以NE向为主，NE向溶蚀宽缝与断层交汇后一般形成较大的洞穴空腔。

地面岩溶形态以溶隙、溶蚀宽缝、落水洞等形式与地下岩溶直接或间接连通。根据上水库108个钻孔的溶蚀率统计结果，岩溶的发育程度随深度的增加而减弱，190m高程以上岩溶最为发育，为强发育带，80～190m高程为弱岩溶发育带，80m高程以下只局部出现零星溶蚀现象。

上水库各分水岭的岩性和岩溶发育规律差异较大，根据各分水岭的地下水位和岩溶发育规律，小狼洼分水岭、副坝区、进/出水口、主坝坝基及主坝左坝肩单薄分水岭和龙华寺地下水位凹槽部位需要做防渗处理，大狼洼和库盆不存在库水外渗问题，不需要做防渗。

（1）主坝坝基和主坝左坝肩至龙华寺车水桶地层之间以及进/出水口为琅琊山组薄层极薄层灰岩，岩溶相对不发育，为裂隙型渗漏。对主坝坝基进行40m深度的帷幕灌浆处理，主坝左坝肩防渗帷幕底线为140m高程，进/出水口防渗帷幕底线以穿过F_{15}断层为底界，底高程为85m高程。

（2）小狼洼分水岭地层由$\in_{3Ln}$条带灰岩组成，岩溶相对不发育，地表灰岩沿层面和风化裂隙有微弱溶蚀现象。上水库同位素示踪试验以溶蚀裂隙性渗漏为主。防渗处理措施为防渗帷幕北侧与副坝帷幕相接，南侧延伸至F_1上盘岩脉出露部位，帷幕底高程为120m高程。

（3）副坝分水岭岩溶发育最强烈，渗漏量大。从岩溶发育规律、充填物性质、水文地质条件等综合考虑，防渗处理的原则以垂直防渗为主，水平黏土铺盖防渗为辅，对副坝坝基清基后和3条灌浆洞开挖后所发现的溶洞全部进行了掏挖，并进行了素混凝土回填，确保帷幕线的形成。对于岩溶最为发育的水桶组地层中段和上段（$\in_{3C}^{2\sim3}$）的防渗底线为30m高程。

（4）龙华寺分水岭断层F_{39}以北，存在一个110m宽的低于水库正常蓄水位的地下水凹槽，不存在地下水分水岭，地下水直接通过分水岭排向外侧。渗漏型式为溶蚀管道渗漏，防渗帷幕底线定为80m高程。

经过各阶段的勘察工作，查清了上水库存在库水外渗范围和渗漏型式。处理措施以半库环绕的垂直防渗体系为主，并辅之岩溶强烈发育区（副坝区）的溶洞回填、黏土铺盖等防渗处理措施，满足了上水库防渗要求。

（中国水电顾问集团北京勘测设计研究院　宫海灵）

琊琊山抽水蓄能电站地下厂房蚀变岩工程地质特性

地下厂房布置于蒋家洼和丰乐溪之间的条形山体内，与上水库水平距离约250m，洞室平均埋深150m左右。厂房区围岩主要为上寒武统琅琊山组（$\in_{3Ln}$）薄层灰岩及薄层夹中厚层灰岩、车水桶组（$\in_{3C}$）薄层和中厚层灰岩互层及燕山期侵入的花岗闪长斑岩岩脉。地下厂房位于②号背斜NW翼，厂房区主要发育一花岗闪长斑岩蚀变带及F_{209}、f_1、f_2等7条断层。

受紧闭褶皱虚脱架空的影响，蚀变花岗闪长斑岩空间展布的规律性差，由于蚀变岩存在水稳定性差易膨胀崩解、结构构造被后期构造变动破坏，存在软弱结构面等特殊的工程地质问题，且与围岩的物理力学性质差别较大，因此对蚀变岩的发育规模、膨胀特性（膨胀力、膨胀率）需要进行必要的研究，判断其对厂房稳定性及基础承载力的影响，提出支护处理措施。蚀变岩整体上呈NE向展布，与厂房轴线大角度相交，并向下游倾伏，倾伏角约35°，宽度和产状变化较大，空间形态规律性较差，出露宽度 3～15m。

蚀变岩矿物成份检测成果表明，其成分主要为斜长石、蒙脱石、石英，其次为黑云母、方解石、绢云母、高岭石等。按受风化及地下水等的影响程度将蚀变岩分为轻微蚀变、中等蚀变和严重蚀变。另外，在强烈应力的作用下，蚀变岩体内形成了次生裂隙及断层型结构面，岩体呈碎裂结构，局部呈次块状结构，岩体整体稳定性差，属Ⅳ～Ⅴ类围岩。

根据室内及现场原位试验资料，蚀变岩的比重一般为 2.65～2.67kN/m^3；天然容重为 24.6～25.7kN/m^3，天然含水率随着蚀变的加重而增大，一般为 2.54%～3.14%，平均值为 2.84%；自由膨胀率（轴向）为 0.4%～4.2%，径向为 1.2%～2.4%，膨胀力（体积不变）为 11～38kPa，均随着蚀变岩蚀变的加重而增大；耐崩解性指数（二次循环）为 89%～98%，5 次循环的耐崩解性指数为 80%～97%，随着蚀变的加重和循环的增加而减小；软化系数轻微蚀变岩的平均值为 0.75，中等蚀变为 0.55，严重蚀变为 0.3。轻微蚀变、中等蚀变、严重蚀变的饱和抗压强度建议值分别为 50～60MPa、20～40MPa、0.5～10MPa；轻微蚀变、中等蚀变、严重蚀变的变形模量建议值分别为 6～8GPa、0.5～1GPa、0.05～0.5GPa；蚀变岩本身、蚀变岩/灰岩及蚀变岩/混凝土之间的凝聚力及摩擦系数见表 1，但该指标只适合作为岩体锚固的参数，蚀变岩滑动稳定分析受严重蚀变带泥化结构面的控制，其抗剪指标类比给出：C'小于等于 0.05MPa，f'小于等于 0.2。

表 1　　蚀变岩抗剪试验参数建议值

试验项目		轻微蚀变	中等蚀变	严重蚀变
蚀变岩/蚀变岩	凝聚力(MPa)	0.8～0.9	0.5～0.7	0.1～0.3
	摩擦系数	0.8～0.9	0.4～0.45	0.3～0.35
蚀变岩/基岩	凝聚力(MPa)	0.6～0.8	0.3～0.4	0.1～0.2
	摩擦系数	0.75～0.8	0.45～0.5	0.3～0.35
蚀变岩/混凝土	凝聚力(MPa)	0.7～0.8	0.4～0.6	0.05～0.1
	摩擦系数	0.8～0.9	0.35～0.4	0.3～0.35

影响蚀变岩变形破坏的因素很多，而起主要控制作用的因素为蚀变岩所含的蒙脱石、高岭石等矿物的物化变形力学机制，即吸水膨胀引起的变形破坏，因此施工期支护的关键是减少地下水及潮湿等的影响。首先蚀变岩开挖后尽快喷护一层混凝土，一方面可以防止地下水及潮气的侵蚀，另一方面可以暂时起到柔性支护的作用，限制其塑性变形，避免松动破坏的发生。其次是最佳支护时间的选择问题，蚀变岩部位开挖以后，原有的天然应力状态被破坏，切向应力在洞壁附近发生高度集中，致使这一区域岩层屈服而进入塑性状态。蚀变岩塑性区的出现使应力集中从岩壁向纵深偏移，当应力集中强度超过其屈服强度时，又将出现新的塑性区，如此逐层推进，使塑性区不断向纵深发展，若不采取适当的支护措施，临空塑性区将随变形加大而出现松动破坏。松动破坏区没有任何承载能力，而塑性区具有一定的承载能力，最佳支护时间的选择就是最大限度地发挥塑性区承载能力而又不出现松动破坏。

通过室内及现场试验，查明了蚀变岩的物理力学性质，在此基础上，分析其破坏机理及可能产生的破坏形式，最终采取了有针对性的支护措施。

（中国水电顾问集团北京勘测设计研究院　宫海灵）

金沙江鲁地拉水电站麦叉拉沟内滑坡稳定性分析

（一）滑坡基本特征

麦叉拉沟内滑坡位于金沙江左岸麦叉拉沟内左岸，距沟口约 500m，距鲁地拉中坝址约 800m。现场调查资料显示，该滑坡前缘高程 1280m，后壁高程 1480m。两侧各以冲沟为界，形态上为圈椅状地形，前缘邻近麦叉沟。后缘地形较陡，坡度在 45°左右，中上段地形渐缓，坡度从 41°变化至 20°，中下段坡度保持在 34°左右。滑坡体前缘厚度为 20～30m，中部厚度为 40～50m，后缘厚度则相对较薄，为 15m 左右。滑坡主滑方向倾向麦叉拉沟，主滑方向 275°，体积约 80 万 m^3。

麦叉拉沟内滑坡周边及滑床的岩性为侏罗系中统（J_{2s}）蛇店组砂岩、板岩，风化严重，岩体被多组结构面切割，滑坡附近发育多处崩塌。麦叉拉沟左右岸地形坡度均较陡，滑坡所处左岸斜坡为顺向坡，总体上是前缘和后缘较陡，中部较缓。滑坡前缘下部有水渠通过，水渠高程 1260m 左右，水库正常蓄水位 1223m，因此麦叉拉沟内滑坡位于库水位以上。

（二）滑坡变形破坏机制分析

麦叉拉沟内滑坡坡面坡度在 45°左右，属于中陡倾斜坡，据野外现场调查，确定其为顺层岩质边坡。岩体受平行于斜坡走向倾向坡内的中陡倾裂隙以及走向垂直于边坡走向的陡倾裂隙切割，变形破坏多沿同向缓倾角的层间弱面蠕滑，后缘沿稍陡的裂面拉开，在长期的蠕变后，超过弱面强度后形成滑坡，滑坡的变形破坏方式为滑移—拉裂型。滑坡形成前期，在重力的作用下，斜坡岩体沿层面或追踪结构面向麦叉拉沟临空方向发生蠕变，逐步使后部、中部岩体产生拉裂。随着沿层面滑动的进一步加剧，上述蠕滑逐渐向滑移过渡，岩体中后部迅速产生大量拉裂缝，进而发生破坏。由于麦叉拉沟内滑坡所处层面倾角与坡角接近，所以滑坡的前期主要为顺层面的蠕变，变形比较缓慢，逐步使上部岩体开裂，直到最后坡体发生破坏。

（三）滑坡物理力学参数的确定

计算参数的合理选取，是评价滑坡稳定性的关键所在。其中，滑带土的参数选取尤为重要。首先对滑带土原状样进行物理力学指标的试验确定，然后将野外获取的滑带土样在重塑的状况下进行力学试验，进而确定滑带土力学参数。在不同含水率条件下，滑带土样表现出了不同的物理力学性质。在充分考虑滑带土所处应力环境的条件下，经过试验与计算分析，来综合选取计算所需的力学参数。

1. 物理性质

由于滑带土取样后已经离开了其赋存环境，再加上水分的蒸发和外界的扰动，在室内试验得到的强度参数已经不能完全代表真实环境下的抗剪强度。但考虑到软弱夹层、滑带土的各种物理力学指标有着内在的联系，在现场取出滑带土样后马上进行含水量和密度的测试，然后把试样在实验室作重塑样试验，调整试样使其含水量接近现场滑带土的含水量，然后进行抗剪强度试验得到在这种含水量条件下的 C、ϕ 值。因此滑带土初始的物理性质指标显得尤为重要。在室内完成了天然状态下土的含水率、密度、颗粒比重、塑限及液限的测定，得出的滑带土物理指标见表 1、表 2。

表 1　　滑带土基本物理指标

天然状态土的物性指标				塑限	液限	塑性指数
含水率	密度		颗粒比重			
	湿	干				
%	g/cm^3	g/cm^3		%	%	
3.0	2.29	2.22	2.79	12.8	23.3	10.5

表 2　　滑带土颗分成果表

颗粒组成								有效粒径		不均匀系数	曲率系数
粗粒土						细粒土					
砾石			砂粒			粉粒或粘粒					
粗	中	细	粗	中	细						
粒径大小（mm）											
＞10	10～5	5～2	2～1	1～0.5	0.5～0.25	0.25～0.074	0.074～0.005	＜0.005	d_{10}	C_u	C_c
%	%	%	%	%	%	%	%	%			
1.7	4.7	18.1	19.3	8.3	10	11.5	17	9.4	0.0553	21.54	0.0907

2. 力学参数

（1）进行滑带土室内压缩试验。在室内将现场取回的滑带土配制成接近液限的试样，放入高压固结仪中，分别以 25kPa、50kPa 一直到 1600kPa 进行加压，获得各级压应力下的孔隙比 e。从试验的结果可知，孔隙比 e 和正应力 p 之间具有很好的相关性，可建立 e 与 p 之间的关系式，根据有限元计算获取滑带上不同位置的正应力，就可以得到不同部位的孔隙比。再根据土力学公式，可以得到滑带上不同部位的含水率 w，平均为 12.1%。

（2）进行滑带土重塑样室内直剪试验。配置不同含水率的 4 个试样，分别在不同正应力 p 的作用下，施加水平剪应力进行剪切，试验采用应变控制式直剪仪，测得剪切破坏时的剪应力 τ。

（3）通过试验结果，根据库仑定律可得出在不同含水率条件下抗剪指标 C 和 f。滑带土在饱和度为 85%情况下的强度参数为 $C=48\text{kPa}$、$f=0.520$；折减 0.9，综合分析得到滑带土的饱和条件下抗剪强度参数为 $C=43\text{kPa}$、$f=0.47$。

（四）滑坡稳定性计算

关于滑坡稳定性计算的方法很多，如摩根斯坦法、萨尔码法、递系数法、毕肖普法等极限平衡法等，这些方法在解决实际问题时各有长短，其中摩根斯坦法简化条件最少，计算方法最复杂，计算精度最高。结合麦叉拉滑坡实际地层岩性、剖面形态等多方面因素，本文选用大型商用程序 Rocscience-SLIDE 5.0 中的摩根斯坦算法来分析稳定性。

从麦叉拉滑坡沟内的形态可以看出，滑面总体上较有规律，前缓后陡，将滑坡剖面均匀条分为 25 个条块。计算主要分 4 种工况进行：天然条件；暴雨条件；地震条件；地震＋暴雨条件。不同工况下的计算结果见表 3。

表3　不同工况下的滑坡稳定性计算结果

工　况	稳定性系数
天然条件	1.42
暴雨条件	1.27
地震条件	1.10
地震+暴雨条件	1.06

从计算结果可以看出，滑坡在天然条件下的稳定性系数 $K=1.42$，量值较高，与现场调查滑坡体上无任何变形相符合；滑坡在暴雨条件下稳定性，考虑滑面1/2的部分饱水，计入孔隙水压力计算模型，计算得到的稳定性系数 $K=1.27$；滑坡在地震条件下，水平地震系数取0.131g，稳定性系数 $K=1.10$；同时考虑地震与暴雨时，稳定性系数为 $K=1.06$，此时滑坡仍处于稳定状态，不会危及鲁地拉电站大坝的安全。

（五）结论

麦叉拉沟内滑坡方量约为80万 m^3，发育在侏罗系中统青灰～灰绿色变质砂岩夹泥质板岩地层中；滑坡为顺层岩质滑坡，其成因机制为滑移—拉裂模式；借助试验，较为合理地选取了滑面的强度参数；在现场获得滑坡的形态与边界条件的基础上，用大型商用程序计算了滑坡的稳定性。计算结果表明，在同时考虑暴雨及地震工况下，滑坡稳定性系数为1.06，因此滑坡不会危及大坝的安全。

（中国水电顾问集团西北勘测设计研究院
陈　龙　李治民）

溧阳抽水蓄能电站输水发电系统主要工程地质特征与评价

溧阳抽水蓄能电站输水系统采用2洞6机布置方案，最大发电水头290m。输水线路总长约2100m，地下厂房采用首部式布置，装机容量6×250MW。主厂房开挖尺寸为219.9m×23.5m×55.05m（长×宽×高）。工程已于2008年12月正式开工建设。本工程地质条件复杂，地下洞室围岩质量总体较差。

1. 输水发电系统主要工程地质特征

（1）工程区位于伍员山背斜的南东翼，基岩主要为志留系上统茅山组上段（S_{3m}^3）岩屑石英砂岩夹泥质粉砂岩及粉砂质泥岩，仅尾水出口段为侏罗系上统龙王山组（J_{3L}）角砾凝灰岩，另有多条岩脉分布。志留系地层整体上走向NE，但由于次级小褶皱发育及断层错动影响，岩层产状变化较大，部分地段产状较凌乱。

（2）断层、层间软弱带及节理裂隙密集发育。厂区PD5勘探平洞共揭露大小断层110多条，断层平均发育间距10～15m。断层发育方向分散，最发育的主要有NWW、NEE两组。层间软弱带包括层间挤压破碎带、泥化夹层、层间错动面等，发育间距为5～30m，尤其是尾水系统层间破碎带发育密度高，厚度大，性状差。工程区节理裂隙十分发育，且发育方向分散，规律性较差，难以找出优势节理组。间距一般为0.2～0.5m，同时节理密集带较多。由于构造发育，故岩体完整性差，勘探平洞内平均 *RQD* 值为25%～30%，钻孔岩心平均 *RQD* 值为7%～42%。

（3）岩体普遍风化强烈，强风化带深度为16～58m，弱风化带下限埋深则一般大于150m；岩体风化除遵循随深度增大而风化程度减弱的一般规律外，风化深度与岩性，尤其与构造关系密切，囊状及带状风化特征明显，钻孔中在高程－10.0m以下（埋深超过300m）多处遇有强风化囊。弱风化带虽岩块本身强度较高，但沿断层及节理裂隙面风化强烈，各类破裂面上普遍有铁锰质浸染，部分裂隙附有黄色泥膜。而尾水洞部位的薄～中厚层砂岩内则岩体风化深度相对较浅，强风化下限埋深为9～20m，弱风化下限埋深为15～50m。

（4）地下水丰富、岩体透水性较强是地下厂房区的一大主要地质特征。岩体总体上透水性较强，沿部分断层，尤其是NNE、NEE两组断层及裂隙则形成集中透水带，平洞开挖时沿单条断层最大透水量可达300～350L/min。PD5平洞开挖时总渗水量最大达到约150m^3/h，勘探平洞的开挖改变了引水系统及厂区地下水排泄条件，厂区部位已形成最低水位为70m左右（平洞高程）的地下水低槽。据估算，施工开挖期厂区排水廊道排水总量与地下洞室开挖时涌水量之和约为5000m^3/d；运行期厂区排水廊道排水总量与地下洞室涌水量之和约为3000m^3/d。尾水隧洞区岩层较平缓，因层间泥化夹层等较发育，透水性相对较小，安山岩脉则相对不透水。

2. 地下洞室主要工程地质评价及工程处理建议

（1）地下厂房区山体雄厚，洞室埋深200～300m，洞室围岩主要岩性为岩屑石英砂岩夹少量泥质粉砂岩，岩性坚硬，多数呈中厚～巨厚层状。地应力量级较低（最大主应力为6.3MPa）。断层及节理裂隙发育，F_{54}、F_{57} 等多条断层斜穿厂区主要洞室，除断层带本身稳定性较差外，也是围岩块体稳定的主要控制面。其他小型断层、层间弱面及节理裂隙相互组合形成不稳定块体，岩体完整性较差。断层普遍填充有次生黄泥，沿裂隙透水性强，围岩大部分位于弱风化带内。岩体呈镶嵌结构或块裂结构，少量为碎裂结构，洞室围岩质量以Ⅲ～Ⅳ类为主，局部Ⅴ类。围岩稳定性主要是受断层、层间软弱面及节理所组成的块体的稳定性控制。厂区洞室围岩不稳定块体是围岩支护处理的重点，支护措施须尽量满足及时、快速的要求，拟采用系统锚杆＋系统预应力锚索＋喷钢纤维混凝土（或喷素混凝土＋挂钢筋网）＋格栅钢拱架等系统支护措施，厂房、主变压器洞顶拱均须进行高压预固结灌浆处理。同时，大型地下洞室群施工开挖前做好排水处理是提高围岩稳定性的重要措施。

（2）引水隧洞岩性为志留系岩屑石英砂岩、泥质粉砂岩及粉砂质泥岩，断层及节理裂隙发育，岩体完整性差，风化较强烈，围岩以Ⅲ～Ⅳ类为主，局部Ⅴ类。高压岔管及高压支洞围岩主要为Ⅳ类，因引水隧洞围岩质量差，地下水活动较强，需采用钢管衬砌。

（3）尾水隧洞穿越志留系岩屑石英砂岩、泥质粉砂岩及侏罗系凝灰岩，围岩大部分地段以倾角较平缓的薄～中厚层砂岩为主，断层、层间挤压破碎带、泥化夹层及节理裂隙十分发育，围岩主要为Ⅳ类，少量Ⅴ类，局部Ⅲ类，同时尾水洞需跨越宽度较大的 F_{10} 断层、蚀变岩脉等不良工程地质段。因围岩质量差，尤其是顶拱稳定性差，施工难度较大，施工开挖时大部分地段必须采取有效的超前支护措施。

（中国水电顾问集团中南勘测设计研究院 胡梦蛟）

红花水电站工程地质条件及评价

红花水电站位于广西柳州市境内，是柳江下游一座发电、航运、灌溉相结合的综合利用的大型水利水电工程。挡水建筑为重力式混凝土拦河闸坝，最大坝高 47m。水库正常蓄水位 77.5m，总库容 30 亿 m^3，电站总装机容量 230MW。2005 年 10 月第一台机组发电，现已建成。

（一）库区工程地质条件及评价

（1）工程区位于构造相对稳定地区，未发现现代活动性断裂，根据《中国地震动参数区划图》（GB 18306—2001），工程区地震动峰值加速度为 0.05g，地震动反应谱特征周期 0.35s，相应地震基本烈度为Ⅵ度。

（2）水库为河槽式，库岸基本由黏性土组成，上、中库段两岸分水岭宽厚，不存在向邻谷渗漏问题。下库段与洛清江分水岭处，两江相距约 7km，观测地下水位也高于正常蓄水位。考虑喀斯特地下水特殊性及灰岩沟通两江，概算其渗漏量仍是很小的，不存在严重渗漏问题。

（3）水库两岸为宽阔、平坦阶地耕植地带，地下水埋深一般大于 10m，对其进行壅水计算的结果，水库蓄水后地下水位壅高后大部分地区仍低于地面 3.3～11.2m，不会产生大面积的浸没问题。阳和高速公路桥下游地段低佳处沿淹没线两侧会产生狭窄条带状浸没。鸡喇地区部分低洼地带预测蓄水后会产生浸没问题，可能存在因水库蓄水导致加剧柳州市城区内涝问题。

（4）土质库岸的黏土、壤土，天然岸坡坡角大多大于 40°，属不稳定或临界稳定状态类型，每年洪水期均发生不同程度的坍塌。计算水库蓄水后 2～3 年内的短期坍岸宽度为 3～5m，最终坍岸带（柳洲市附近）宽度为 20～30m。

（5）水库蓄水后，沿江两岸喀斯特发育地带，可能产生喀斯特塌陷和喀斯特气爆型的水库诱发地震，其震级 $MI<3$ 级，低于本区地震基本烈度值。

（二）枢纽建筑物区工程地质条件

1. 地形地貌及地层岩性

坝址区地貌为侵蚀溶蚀低山丘陵区，该处河宽 490m，河床为横切岩层的宽阔箱状河谷，河床高程 57.5～62.6m，河床覆盖层为厚 1.2～6.3m 的含泥砂卵砾石层。坝址出露的岩层主要有石炭系下统大塘阶中的黄金组上、下段，寺门组上、下段及第四系。黄金组下段 C_{1h}^{1} 分布于坝址下游，上部为灰黑色中厚层灰岩、炭质灰岩夹薄层硅质岩、含锰泥岩、页岩、含棘屑灰岩，下部为深灰色～灰黑色中厚层灰岩夹薄层炭质灰岩、硅质岩条带和炭质页岩、含锰泥岩，厚约 115m。黄金组上段 C_{1h}^{2} 为坝基主要地层，按岩性组合划分为 3 个岩组：第一岩组 C_{1h}^{2-1}，深灰～灰黑色中厚层～薄层灰岩夹硅质岩及极薄层炭质页岩，厚30～50m；第二岩组 C_{1h}^{2-2}，深灰～灰黑色薄～中厚层灰岩、炭质灰岩及极薄层硅质岩互层夹极薄层硅质泥岩及炭质页岩，局部夹透镜状劣质煤，厚 25～40m；第三岩组 C_{1h}^{2-3}，灰黑色中厚层～薄层灰岩、炭质灰岩夹极薄层炭质页岩、硅质泥岩等，厚 20～40m。寺门组下段 C_{1s}^{1} 分布于坝址两岸及Ⅰ线上游河床，上部为深灰色～黄绿色粉砂质泥岩夹泥质粉砂岩、硅质岩、含锰硅质岩；下部为灰～灰绿色薄层状泥岩、泥质粉砂岩；底部为深灰色硅质岩、泥岩，局部为团块状劣质煤，厚 40～70m。寺门组上段 C_{1s}^{2} 分布于坝址上游，上部为褐灰色厚层状砂岩、石英砂岩夹页岩；中部为褐灰色中厚层石英砂岩夹粉砂质泥岩；下部为灰色薄层状石英砂岩夹粉砂岩、页岩，厚 100～140m。第四系主要为含碎石黏土、壤土、砂壤土、黏土、砂卵砾石。

2. 地质构造

坝址区位于新华夏系构造带的穿山向斜、穿山断裂和长沙背斜、呈村断裂之间，主构造线方向北东10°～30°，是本区占主导地位的构造形迹。坝址区发育了一组相互平行的挤压断层带，呈北北东或北北西方向雁行排列，伴生一组北西向发育的扭裂带，形成了多字行扭动构造的格局。坝址区位于倒转向斜的倒转翼，应力比较集中，形变较为剧烈，各种小型褶皱均有发育，且轴向亦多变化，其宽度一般10多米，没有发现宽度几十米向下游延伸的宽缓褶皱。

3. 水文地质条件

坝址区主要分布有第四系松散层，碎屑岩类，碳酸盐岩，形成第四系孔隙含水层和基岩喀斯特裂隙含水层，两岸地下水基本上是直线型补给河流，左岸地下水位67.77～84.69m，右岸地下水位62.84～80.02m，河床处地下水位与河水位相近。第四系孔隙含水层主要受大气降水补给，向柳江排泄。基岩喀斯特型含水层透水性取决于裂隙喀斯特的发育程度及相互连通情况。坝轴线基岩平均透水率在高程10～40m之间随高程增长而缓慢增长，而在高程40m以上则随高程增长而呈直线型增长。相对隔水顶板($q<3lu$)高程在12～70.29m之间，河床及右岸比较平缓，左岸略高，隔水顶板平均高程39.08m。

4. 岩溶发育特征

坝址区基岩主要为碳酸盐岩夹硅质岩，岩溶发育微弱，地表只发现个别小型溶洞和落水洞，主要为钻孔揭露的覆盖型岩溶，多数属于溶孔溶隙类型，极少数为小型溶槽。坝址基岩主要为黄金组上段岩组，主要为含泥灰岩、泥炭质灰岩，方解石含量一般少于70%，而泥炭含量达10%～43%，且常夹薄层硅质岩、炭质页岩，难以形成岩溶发育的环境，因此该段岩溶发育较弱。坝址区左右岸及河床均发现岩溶溶隙，左岸船闸处相对发育，厂房次之，河床泄水闸及土坝段最弱。坝址岩溶发育主要是层间溶蚀或沿裂隙、断层溶蚀，相与之间连通性差。

5. 岩体风化特征

坝址区出露的寺门组粉砂岩、泥岩为全、强风化层相间出现，单层较薄，实际难以分层，称全强风化层。黄金组岩石以化学风化的溶蚀为主，抗风化能力强，除局部有少量强风化层外，一般均为弱～微风化层。坝址两岸风化较深，且右岸比左岸深，河床处部分缺失全强风化层，一般在砂卵石层下即为弱风化层。在坝轴线附近，有多个风化槽。

6. 软弱夹层分布特征

坝址岩层有炭质页岩等软弱岩层，受后期构造运动及地下水影响，形成构造型软化～泥化软弱夹层和风化次生软弱夹层，单层厚1～15cm，原生沉积，黑色，夹于薄层～中厚层灰岩之间，顶底面平整，顺层连续，层数多，层位稳定，倾角大部分大于30°，坝轴线局部在6.75m深处发现有倾角为25°的软弱夹层，其余均在较深处发现。通过计算，软化、泥化夹层在最不利的组合情况下，仍基本能满足稳定要求，但下游抗滑岩体在运行中不能被水流破坏。

（三）枢纽建筑物工程地质评价

（1）枢纽建筑物区的基岩，除两岸上部有寺门组全强风化层外，其余均为黄金组弱风化灰岩、炭质灰岩，其岩体力学强度较高，属AⅢ～BⅢ类岩体。断裂、褶皱较发育。灰岩中所夹的软弱泥化夹层经验算符合稳定要求，具备修建低水头河床式电站的工程地质条件。

（2）初步设计阶段所选的Ⅰ线和Ⅴ线两比较坝轴线，经综合比较后选用Ⅴ线为坝轴线。

（3）布置于河床上的混凝土闸坝基础置于黄金组弱风化灰岩、炭质灰岩上，坝基下断层如F_3、F_{16}等需作专门处理，局部坝基抗滑稳定问题需设计进一步验算。由于浅部基岩因裂隙发育及局部岩溶导致透水性不均一，需做好防渗帷幕和固结灌浆。

（4）两岸土坝需做好地基土层与基岩面接触带及强风化层的防渗帷幕灌浆处理，以防产生渗漏及渗漏稳定问题。

（5）厂房的主要工程地质问题是开挖形成的高边坡的稳定问题，需做好防护及安全监测工作。

（6）通航建筑物船闸上、下闸首及闸室基础均置于弱风化灰岩上，岩体完整性较好，力学强度较高，具有较好的工程地质条件，但需注意上、下引航道左侧边坡的稳定。

（四）施工期开挖验证

通过施工开挖和地质编录可以看出，电站建筑物区工程地质条件与初设阶段工程地质结论基本一致。除土坝段和右岸门库段外，电站其他主要建筑物地基均置于石炭系下统黄金组上段弱～微风化灰岩、炭质灰岩上，岩体主要为中厚层状结构，岩体完整，局部完整性较差，岩体质量为AⅢ～BⅢ类岩体，力学强度高；坝轴线附近（约20m范围）处于岩层陡倾部位（大于50°），顺层软弱夹层倾角陡（大于50°），坝基抗滑稳定性较好。通过建筑物区的一些断层经过地基开挖后，大部分尖灭或没有在弱～微风化岩中通过，开挖所揭露的断层破碎带宽度较小，分布较零散，经处理后对上部结构不产生影响。地基局部出现的溶槽经挖除和置换钢筋混凝土塞处理，工程地质条件满足设计要求。

（中水珠江规划勘测设计有限公司 吴 飞）

工程地质问题处理

龙开口水电站右岸变形体工程地质勘察评价及处理

(一) 工程概况

龙开口水电站坝址位于云南省鹤庆县中江乡境内，系金沙江中游河段8个梯级电站的第六级。电站大坝为碾压混凝土重力坝，最大坝高119.0m，坝顶高程1301.0m，水库正常蓄水位1298.0m，总库容5.58亿m^3，电站装机容量1800MW。

坝址右岸有大面积变形体，分A、B、C区及风化破碎区，总体积达760.0万m^3，分布在大坝右坝头及其上、下游范围内，其稳定性对大坝的影响较大。为此，进行了边坡稳定性专题研究，并提出了相应的处理方案。处理工作于2008年4月开始，2009年底完工。

(二) 变形体特征及其稳定性

1. 基本地质条件

(1) 右岸山体总体为台地和斜坡相间的地貌，山坡走向约N10°W。自上游向下游发育有水板沟、涧槽沟及水阱沟等3条冲沟，高程1265m以下发育三级阶地。

(2) 基岩为二叠系上统上段的玄武岩组（$P_2\beta$）角砾熔岩及致密块状玄武岩、杏仁状玄武岩，按岩流层可进一步划分为10个旋回，其间为凝灰岩相隔，自下而上凝灰岩为t_0～t_9，其中t_1和t_2两层凝灰岩在涧槽沟上游（往北）缺失。凝灰岩岩层产状不稳定，总体倾向坡外，t_4～t_9凝灰岩层走向NE缓倾向SE，即倾下游偏坡外；t_0、t_3凝灰岩层表层走向NW缓倾向SW，山体内NE缓倾向SE。上接触面常见灰绿色的玄武岩蚀变矿物，形成层间错动带。

(3) 右岸边坡岩体中构造形态，表现为规模较小的断层（宽度均小于1m）、平行发育的成组裂隙、少量的柱状节理。倾向坡内和坡外的两组结构面最发育，这两组裂隙对坡体变形的侧裂和后缘有明显的控制作用。

(4) 通过地下水位观测分析，右岸山体的地下水位变化大，干旱季节地下水位埋深大，雨季时地水位埋深浅，水位相差达21.7m，说明山体的透水性大，但凝灰岩层有相对隔水层作用，持续性大雨、暴雨时，地下水可在凝灰层面形成面流。

2. 变形体分区特征及其稳定性

(1) A区分布于水板沟～涧漕沟之间，下部以凝灰岩层t_3为界，上部约至坡顶，即为勘Ⅰ～勘Ⅵ的右坝肩边坡，为右坝头所在区域。可分为强变形体、AⅠ区变形体、AⅡ区卸荷倾倒岩体和风化破碎岩体4个带，总体积约546.6万m^3。强变形体分布于坝轴线上游AⅠ区变形体内，垂直厚约41.0m，呈碎块、碎屑状的散体结构，已产生蠕滑，方量约39.0万m^3。AⅡ区卸荷倾倒岩体主要分布于AⅠ区以内及边坡后缘，水平厚7.8～33.0m，垂直厚3.8～37.1m，岩体以碎裂结构、块裂结构为主。体积约160.8万m^3。风化破碎区岩体分布于水板沟至涧漕沟的凝灰岩t_0～t_3之间山体，岩体裂隙发育，岩体破碎。A区变形体外侧以沿凝灰岩层蠕滑—拉裂变形为主的变形岩体，呈碎块状散体结构，后缘剪切带岩体呈碎屑状散体结构；中部以卸荷倾倒拉裂变形为主的岩体，呈碎裂结构；内侧为弱卸荷岩体，陡倾裂隙发育，岩体较完整。稳定性分析表明，A区变形体边坡在天然状况下整体稳定，但在设计暴雨工况下局部组合抗滑安全储备尚不满足规范的要求，可能失稳方向为下游偏左岸（涧槽沟方向）。持久、短暂、偶然等各种工况条件下的凝灰岩夹层与AⅠ区后缘剪切带组合为最不利组合，应采用适当的工程措施提高其稳定性。

(2) B区变形体涧漕沟南侧边坡，为右坝下游侧边坡，边坡较顺直，坡度较陡，达40°～45°，体积约66.7万m^3。岩体为碎块状散体结构～碎裂结构岩体，裂隙面大量的次生黄泥充填，顺坡延伸倾向山体的裂隙倾倒特征较明显，未发现有明显的剪切带。B区变形体主要由于涧漕沟快速下切使得边坡较陡、前缘临空，引起岩体卸荷、顺坡向裂隙的产生倾倒及山体发育的断层错动形成，属于松动、卸荷倾倒拉裂成因的变形岩体。分析表明，B区整体稳定，安全系数满足规范要求。暴雨季节受沟内洪水淘刷，浅表层局部会发生塌滑。

(3) C区分布于水阱沟北侧边坡，为厂房尾水后边坡。可较明显的分为3个带，即H4滑坡体、CⅠ区变形体及CⅡ区卸荷倾倒体，总体积约144.3万m^3，其中：CⅠ区垂直厚度14.2～41.5m，表层2～10m岩体呈碎块状散体结构，后缘岩体倾倒变形强烈，中下部岩体呈碎裂结构、部分块裂结构，岩体变形稍弱，体积约37.4万m^3；CⅡ区垂直厚度17.3～24.9m，表层岩体呈碎裂结构，中下部岩体呈块裂～块状结构，体积约85.4万m^3；H4滑坡体内为松散的碎石、块石堆积体，岩屑、角砾充填为主，体积约21.5万m^3。C区变形体是由于水阱沟快速下切，凝灰岩软弱夹层顺坡分布且倾坡外，坡面临空，以及节理发育，岩体卸荷变形发展的结果，属下挫—拉裂型变形体。稳定性分析表明，C区中CⅠ、CⅡ区的安全系数满足规范要求；H4滑坡体在暴雨和Ⅵ度地震状态下，安全系数不能满足规范要求，其失稳下滑对主体建筑物无直接的影响，但影响进厂公路的正常通行，并淤积尾水渠，需采取适当的工程措施减免其对工程的影响。

（三）右岸变形体工程处理措施

变形体主要对右岸坝头稳定有影响，因此对变形体的处理重点是对坝头区t_3以上的A区变形体，主要工程措施是提高AⅠ后缘与t_3、t_4、t_7组合滑动的安全系数。鉴于A区变形体厚度大，AⅠ区水平厚度最大达96.5m，AⅡ区最大厚度达37.1m，锚索施工难度较大，所以综合分析及方案筛选后，重点研究了抗滑桩加锚索阻滑和削坡减载两个方案。经综合比较，最后采用以锚索抗滑桩为主，同时清除脊部松动岩体的综合处理方案。A、B、C 3个区处理措施如下：

1. A区变形体处理

（1）该区边坡稳定安全系数总体满足规范的要求，天然和暴雨工况下沿t_3、t_4、t_5和t_7凝灰岩夹层沿真倾向滑动的安全系数不足，总的处理原则是不对坡面进行大范围开挖，采取以锚索抗滑桩为主的综合处理方案。

（2）沿t_3、t_4涧漕沟侧布置11根4m×5m的抗滑桩，每根桩的上部设4根200t预应力锚索。

（3）清除拟布置的抗滑桩上部突出山脊的松动岩体，使坡面平顺，喷混凝土保护。

（4）为了提高暴雨条件边坡的安全储备，在变形体边坡表面布置表面截排水沟网。设4层排水洞，通过变形体内部的排水洞及排水孔排水，以提高其整体稳定性。

（5）坝肩采用桩板墙的连接方式，以减少开挖对变形体稳定带来的牵引影响。

（6）同时加强变形体在工程施工期及运行期的安全监测。

（7）缆机布置形式调整：右岸由平移式改为辐射式，固定端置于原状岩体的涧槽沟内。

鉴于右岸坝肩边坡开挖可能对其上部的变形体产生不利的牵引影响，锚索抗滑桩应在右岸坝肩开挖之前施工完成。

2. B区变形体边坡工程处理

该区边坡整体稳定，但该区边坡坡脚布置有辐射式缆机的固定端，边坡的局部塌滑也可能危及人员和设备的安全，因此实际施工时，对施工临时建筑物范围内边坡坡面进行清坡，下部采用混凝土护坡和锚索的处理方式。

3. C区H4滑坡体的处理措施

CⅠ和CⅡ区整体稳定，未进行处理。H4滑坡体各工况条件下安全储备不满足规范要求。考虑H4滑坡体失稳后主要堆积在水阱沟内，对主体工程无直接的不利影响，在H4滑坡体外、水阱沟上游设置挡水坝将水阱沟水引至下游，消除沟水的不利影响；结合过境公路改造，在水阱沟口设置挡渣坎利用弃渣压坡；在坡面设置截排水网，改善坡体在暴雨工况下的稳定条件。

（中国水电顾问集团华东勘测设计研究院
周会信　黄春华）

锦屏二级水电站引水隧洞高地应力围岩破坏及其控制

（一）工程概况

锦屏二级水电站位于四川省凉山彝族自治州木里、盐源、冕宁三县交界处的雅砻江干流锦屏大河弯上，利用150km长的大河弯，截弯取直，开挖隧洞引水发电。电站最大水头321.0m，额定水头288.0m，总装机容量4800MW。电站枢纽主要由首部拦河闸、引水系统、地下厂房三大部分组成，为一低闸、长隧洞、高水头、大容量引水式电站。4条引水隧洞平行布置，横穿跨越锦屏山，进水口至上游调压室的平均洞线长度约16.7km，隧洞中心距60m，洞主轴线方位角为N58°W。4条引水隧洞组成的水工洞群采用钻爆法（2、4号引水隧洞和1、3号引水隧洞东西端洞段）和TBM法（1、3号引水隧洞中部洞段）相结合的施工方案。钻爆法施工洞段为马蹄形断面，开挖直径13m，混凝土衬砌段洞径11.8m；采用TBM施工的引水隧洞段，开挖隧洞直径为12.4m，衬后洞径为11.2m。

锦屏深埋隧洞洞室群由4条引水隧洞、两条辅助洞和一条排水洞共7条隧洞组成，辅助洞和排水洞平行布置于引水隧洞南侧，全长各约17.50km，施工排水洞与辅助洞的洞轴线间距为35m，与4号引水隧洞的洞轴线间距为45m。洞室群一般埋深1500～2000m，最大埋深约为2525m，具有规模大、埋深大、洞线长、洞径大的特点。隧洞将横穿地质条件复杂的锦屏山，高地应力岩爆、高压涌（突）水是隧洞的主要工程地质问题。

两条辅助洞已于2008年8月全线贯通，单条引水隧洞也已开挖7km左右，在施工过程中遭遇了多次单点流量大于$1m^3/s$的涌水点，最大达$7.3m^3/s$；遭遇了因高地应力引起的岩爆、应力型破坏、大变形等围岩破坏，影响了正常施工，后期采用应力解除爆破、强支护等手段，较有效地控制了围岩破坏，保证了隧洞的正常施工。

（二）隧洞开挖高地应力破坏现象

1. 岩体基本条件

（1）锦屏辅助洞目前实测最大主应力46MPa，回归分析最大主应力70MPa左右，其特征是：①最大主应力、中间主应力和最小主应力均随埋深增加而增大，递增关系呈非线性；②σ_1/σ_3地应力比值随洞深的增加而减小；③最大主应力方位角为20°～50°转向120°～140°，显示工程区的主应力随埋深增加由NE～SW转为NWW～SEE；④最大主应力倾角自6.45°转为75.4°，表明随着埋深增加，地应力从岸坡近水平应力状态转变为以竖直为主的自重应力状态；⑤地应力沿隧洞线存在进/出水口区域的河谷地应力带、隧洞中段的重力应力带和断层穿越区域的断层应力带。

（2）锦屏隧洞岩体主要为大理岩，岩石平均饱和单轴抗压强度65～90MPa，抗拉强度3～6MPa，围岩强度应力比大多小于2；实测岩体岩爆倾向性指数为1.32～5.8，反映了隧洞沿线的不少岩石具有高储能性质，具备发生高地应力破坏的强度条件。

（3）岩体开挖卸荷作用不仅引起岩体应力分异，造成围岩应力重分布和集中，而且还会因差异回弹而在围岩中形成一个被约束的残余应力体系，岩体的变形和破坏的发生正是由于应力状态的上述两个方面的变化引起的。

2. 围岩破坏方式及特征

（1）岩爆：其破坏方式有片/层状剥落、弯曲鼓折破裂、穹状/楔状爆裂；其破裂面特征有平整破裂面、阶梯状破裂面、贝壳状破裂面、穹状破裂面和弧形破裂面。岩爆多发生在围岩为整体结构、块状结构等岩体结构类型中，岩体坚硬、干燥、裂隙不发育，一般为Ⅱ类以上围岩。Ⅰ、Ⅱ级岩爆的破坏方式主要为层状/片状剥落和穹状爆裂为主。层/片状剥落岩石呈薄片或板状，单层厚度0.5～10cm，破裂面大多平直，局部有花纹；穹状爆裂岩爆坑上部发生张性破裂，形成粗糙的破坏面，下部发生剪切滑移，形成平行条纹状破裂面。Ⅲ级岩爆的破坏方式主要为张裂—剪断和楔状（穹状）爆裂。张裂—剪断形式的岩爆破坏面往往呈条带状，岩爆规模较大；楔状（穹状）爆裂式的岩爆破裂面往往呈团状或近似圆形，现场可以见到明显的岩爆坑。隧洞岩爆发生的烈度级别主要以轻微（Ⅰ级）为主，占隧洞总长的11.3%～14%；其次为中等岩爆（Ⅱ级），占2.9%～4.0%；深埋地段存在少量强烈岩爆（Ⅲ级）和极强烈岩爆（Ⅳ级），分别占隧洞总长的1.5%～1.7%和0.2%。不同埋深条件下，埋深2000～2500m洞段岩爆发生最多，占相应埋深分段长度的34.9%～36.1%；其次为埋深1500～2000m和1000～1500m洞段，占相应埋深分段长度的10.8%～17.0%、8.2%～20.1%；最小为埋深0～1000m洞段，占相应埋深分段长度的9.3%～11.3%。其中埋深2000～2500m洞段最高发生Ⅲ、Ⅳ级岩爆，埋深1500～2000m洞段最高发生Ⅲ级岩爆，埋深1000～1500m洞段发生Ⅰ、Ⅱ级岩爆，埋深0～1000m洞段仅发生Ⅰ级岩爆。可见，随着埋深的增加，发生岩爆等级和长度越来越高。岩爆发生的部位大多在东端掌子面右侧（西端掌子面左侧为同一侧），占岩爆总长度的38.1%～52.6%；其次为东端掌子面左侧（西端掌子面右侧）和洞顶，占岩爆总长度的23.3%～36.8%、24.1%～25.1%。岩爆发生的次数与掌子面距离以及开挖时间的关系分析表明，岩爆多发生在距掌子面5～20m的范围内（以6～12m居多），多发生在掌子面开挖后的5～50h。少量岩爆也发生在掌子面，数月后某些发生过强烈岩爆部位仍有可能再次剥落和发生岩爆。

（2）应力型破坏：有非断层应力型破坏和断层应力型破坏两种，其特征是岩体在高地应力作用下，发生松弛或坍塌，但未产生岩爆。非断层应力型破坏方式在锦屏隧洞施工中较多见，主要表现为岩体松弛和垮塌，松弛深度一般为0.8～2.0m，最深达到6m，时效变形明显。断层应力型破坏是在高地应力作用下沿结构面发生破坏，界面受结构面控制，其破坏主要有3种情况：①洞室顶拱、边墙、端墙存在结构面的不利组合，在高地应力作用下出现垮塌；②当深埋岩体中结构面相对发育，但胶结良好时，高应力常常导致结构面胶结物发生破坏，造成围岩强度破坏，出现结构面应力型坍塌；③单一结构面对围岩稳定性的影响与结构面性质及其与洞周围岩中应力分布密切相关。当结构面出现在应力松弛区、且受力状态不良时，往往表现为松弛张开；当结构面出现在应力集中区时，相对软弱的结构面与最大主应力交角较小具有剪切趋势且临空相对较好时，可产生较大范围的围岩破坏；软弱结构面端部为完整脆性岩体时，开挖面逼近这一区域时可能导致强烈的破坏；坚硬刚性结构面、特别是刚性剪切带出现在应力集中区附近时，可能影响岩体应力集中区的受力状态，并反过来影响到结构面的受力状态，可导致强烈破坏。断层应力型破坏往往规模大、破坏力强，对施工安全影响很大。

(3) 大变形：在隧洞西端 T1 绿泥石片岩段，由于岩体抗压强度较低（20～40MPa），洞室开挖后引起的应力重分布超过围岩强度，围岩因塑性化而产生大变形；洞室变形达 30cm 以上，使洞室发生挤压变形，喷混凝土产生较大裂缝和垮塌。

（三）高地应力围岩破坏的控制

1. 大理岩（硬岩）的高地应力围岩破坏控制

(1) 改变爆破和作业方式：①应力解除爆破，具体方法是在掌子面正常爆破前，增加应力解除爆破，解除围岩部分能量，改变局部岩体的受力状态，降低风险和支护工作量，强烈与极强岩爆洞段应将应力解除爆破作为日常性爆破作业的一部分；②采取短进尺、弱爆破，并控制炮眼利用率，可以降低岩爆的发生频率。

(2) 对冲洗的开挖面进行立即的初喷处理，其中顶拱和边墙的喷层厚度 10cm，掌子面厚度 5cm，岩爆强烈洞段开挖前应考虑超前锚杆预支护。

(3) 围岩支护同时满足支护强度和抗冲击能量两个方面的要求，利用其支护能力给围岩提供足够的锚固力限制冲击变形和防止冲击破坏。当冲击变形量较大、围岩积累的能量很高时，锚杆设计需要考虑其抗冲击变形和能量吸收能力，利用随同变形和吸收能量的方式达到围岩破坏控制的目的。一般采用锥杆、螺纹钢锚杆、水胀式锚杆、机械胀壳式锚杆、摩擦锚杆、锚索，按岩爆强度不同采用不同锚杆组合进行支护。在掌子面和周边洞壁喷护完成后，进行洞周防岩爆锚杆的钻设施工，防岩爆锚杆要求设置钢垫板，并通过锚杆垫板固定挂网钢筋网片。防岩爆锚杆可采用机械胀壳式中空注浆锚杆或水胀式锚杆等。

(4) 以上工作应在掌子面出渣以后 4～5h 以内完成，最迟也必须在下一个爆破循环开始之前完成。

(5) 在初喷混凝土、钢筋网片、防岩爆锚杆等措施的保护下，及时进行全断面系统锚杆的施工和二次混凝土的喷射，隧洞的系统支护跟进工作面距离开挖掌子面不宜大于 1 倍洞径，在岩爆强烈洞段根据具体情况布置钢拱架。

2. 绿泥石片岩（软岩）围岩大变形的控制

(1) 设计断面尺寸必须在开挖净空轮廓的基础上，预留围岩周边相对位移变形量。

(2) 分期支护、先柔后刚。初期支护采用既具有一定柔性又能快速实施的喷锚支护，包括可缩式钢拱架，使围岩塑性区得到一定的发展，以完成适度的岩体应力释放和卸压作用，二次支护采用网喷、钢拱架喷混凝土或现浇、预制块钢筋混凝土复合结构。初期喷锚支护（包括可缩式钢拱架）应尽快实施，一般在开挖后的 2h 内施作喷混凝土，8～16h 内完成锚喷支护。

(3) 采用仰拱封底，形成全封闭结构，避免隧洞底部没有约束，围岩裸露，形成膨胀和应力释放的集中部位，产生底鼓，造成隧洞墙脚内移和支护结构的严重破坏。

(4) 在大变形特征明显、稳定性差的洞段，应考虑实施超前支护措施，包括超前锚杆与超前管棚。

（中国水电顾问集团华东勘测设计研究院 单治钢）

喜河水电站右导墙高陡边坡基础抗滑处理

喜河水电站位于陕西省石泉县境内汉江干流上，电站总装机容量为 180MW（3×60MW）。右导墙（含导墙坝段）紧邻厂房基坑布置，厂房基坑边坡高 20m，设计开挖坡比 1∶0.21。根据施工导流程序和施工进度安排，右导墙需在Ⅰ汛、Ⅱ汛、Ⅱ枯及Ⅲ枯时段挡水。

（一）右导墙布置特点

右导墙坝段建基面高程 323.0m，Ⅰ汛前先浇筑形成临时断面，顶高程 355.0m。下游右导墙顶高程 349.0m，建基面高程 323.0～327.0m，施工期设计挡水水位 348.5m，紧邻的厂房基坑开挖坡比 1∶0.21，基坑最低开挖高程 305.0m，设计挡水位距基坑底部高差 43.5m。右导墙平面布置如图 1 所示。

（二）右导墙基础地质特性

右导墙基础位于弱风化岩体中部，为弱风化凝灰岩，岩体主要为 BⅢ类，局部为 BⅡ、BⅣ类。施工过程中在右导墙左侧边坡坝下 0+050.00m～坝下 0+106.00m、高程 323.0m 附近出露倾向基坑的 fk11 缓倾角贯穿性断层，其产状为 NE10°～45°NW20°～40°，断层面起伏、粗糙，断层带宽 5～15cm，带内为棱岩、角砾岩、碎裂岩。fk11 断层的抗剪断参数 $f'=0.30\sim0.35$，$C'=0.05$MPa；岩体的抗剪断参数 $f'=1.1$，$C'=1.0$MPa；岩体与混凝土接触面抗剪断参数 $f'=1.1$，$C'=0.5$MPa。

（三）右导墙基础抗滑分析

右导墙（含导墙坝段）基础 fk11 缓倾角断层及裂隙发育范围深层抗滑稳定问题突出，为确保安全，采用概率极限状态设计原则，以分项系数极限状态表达式对右导墙（含导墙坝段）各部位进行抗滑稳定分析。根据 fk11 的分布特点及对右导墙稳定的影响程度，分段采用以下两种方法进行抗滑稳定分析：

(1) 坝下 0+047.00m～坝下 0+089.00m 段倾向基坑的 fk11 缓倾角断层在开挖边坡上出露，采取挖除 fk11 断层的上盘，并用混凝土回填。为减小开

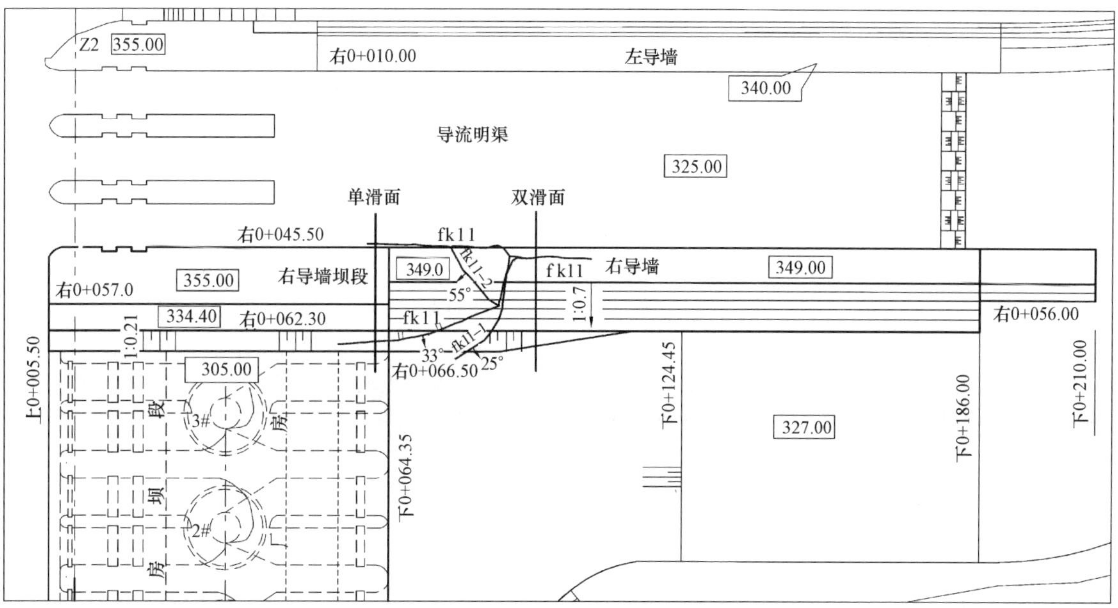

图 1　右导墙平面布置图

挖量，将该段基础开挖为两个台阶，台阶高程分别为 316.8m、312.7m，稳定分析采用单滑面模型进行计算，以厂房基坑边坡坡脚为滑动面底部出露高程作为最不利控制条件进行深层抗滑稳定计算。

（2）坝下 0＋089.00m～坝下 0＋115.00m 段采用双滑面进行计算，双滑面计算模型中抗力体部分最不利滑动面的位置经试算确定。

两种模型计算简图如图 2 所示。

（四）右导墙基础抗滑处理

根据右导墙（含导墙坝段）边坡抗滑分析结果，右导墙各段采用的抗滑处理措施如下：

（1）坝下 0＋047.00m～坝下 0＋64.35m 段：挖除 fk11 断层上盘，导墙坝段基础在 316.8m、312.7m 高程开挖为两个台阶，台阶宽度分别为 11.58m 和 6.72m；导墙基础增设 8 个排水孔，孔距 2m，岩石下孔深 15～18m；设置 12 根 2000kN 锚索（1 排，间距 1.5m），对基础边坡进行加固。

（2）坝下 0＋064.35m～坝下 0＋089.00m 段：挖除 fk11 断层上盘，导墙坝段基础在 316.8m、312.7m 高程开挖为两个台阶，台阶宽度分别为 11.58m 和 6.72m；导墙基础设置有防渗帷幕和排水孔，挖除 fk11 断层上盘后的右导墙能满足基础深层抗滑稳定要求，不用采取其余工程措施。

（3）坝下 0＋090.00m～坝下 0＋115.00m 段：设置 11 根 2000kN 锚索（2 排，间距 2.5m），对基础边坡进行加固。

（中国水电顾问集团北京勘测设计研究院
薛宝臣　陈　浩　伊　军）

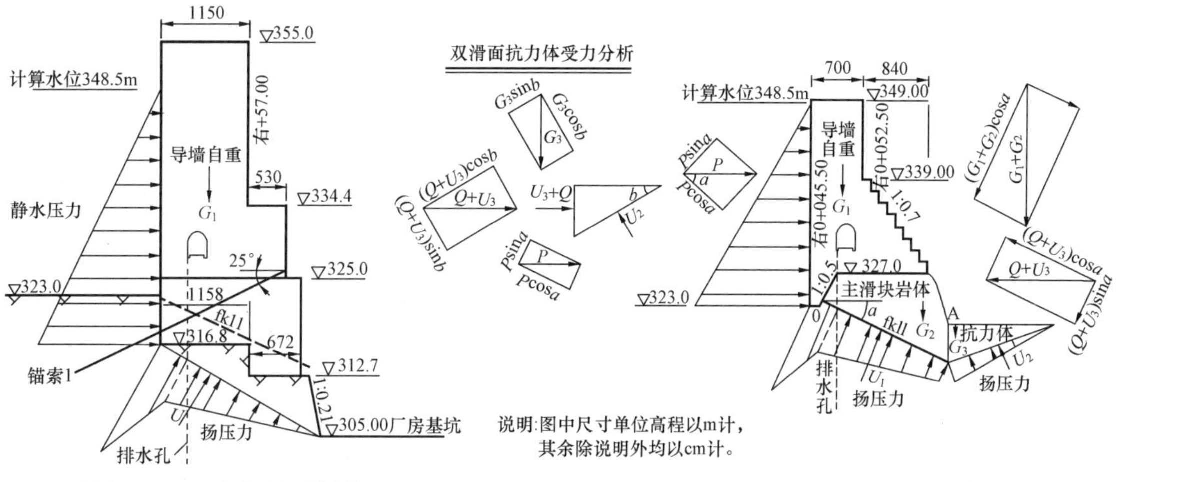

坝下0+047~0+089段典型断面计算简图　　坝下0+089~0+115段典型断面计算简图

图 2　计算模型简图

岩溶通道涌水堵漏新技术

（一）概况

乌江沙沱水电站建设采用分期截流施工，10号坝段位于一、二期截流分界线上。该坝段在基坑开挖时，已揭示多个岩溶通道，涌水很大，当时虽经处理，但未能将漏水通道成功封堵，为了确保安全度汛，采用了埋设集水钢盒加排水钢管的方式将水引出，再浇筑大坝混凝土。因涌水量大，涌水除大部分从排水钢管引出外，另有一部分从集水钢盒经混凝土与基岩接触面流出，并汇集至11号坝段（一期基坑内）涌出，参见图1。

在10号坝段混凝土顺利浇筑至设计度汛高程后，随着汛期河床水位的不断升高，通过10号坝段排水钢管和基础面的涌水越来越大，并在11、12号坝段基岩面形成多处流量很大的渗漏通道，总涌水流量超过2m³/s，涌水压力最大为0.2MPa。根据钻孔勘探结果，10号坝段混凝土与基岩面结合差，接触面多为砂、砾石等。如此大的涌水不仅严重影响到大坝右岸基坑开挖与混凝土浇筑，还给10号坝段运行带来了极大的安全风险。为确保大坝安全度汛和二期截流目标实现，需及时对10～12号坝段坝基渗水进行有效封堵。

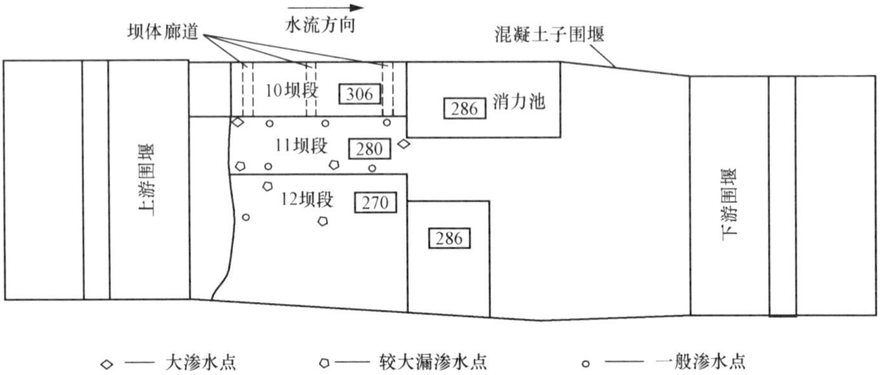

图1 一期基坑主要涌水点位置示意图

（二）模袋灌浆封堵

1. 模袋加工及安装

模袋采用双层土工布和一层机织帆布制作，根据探明的涌水点形状，制作不同直径的模袋，安装前在袋内插入灌浆管，并用铁丝将袋口扎死。模袋下入至指定位置后，将灌浆钢管焊接固定在预先安装在涌水出口的钢管格栅上。

2. 模袋灌浆

(1) 灌浆材料，采用0.5∶1纯水泥浆液灌注，特殊情况下如水流流速增大、压力增大时在浆液中加入水玻璃灌注，以促进浆液凝固。

(2) 灌浆顺序，先进行埋在出水口中间的模袋的灌浆，后进行四周模袋的灌浆，最后视情况进行补强。

(3) 灌浆浆液，采用水泥水玻璃双液。水灰比采用0.5∶1，水玻璃在配浆桶中直接加入，加入量为2%左右，在条件允许的情况下再适当加浓，以促使浆液尽快凝固。

(4) 灌浆方法，采用纯压式。灌浆结束标准采用两种标准：当灌入量达到规定量，或灌浆压力达到规定的压力时，即可结束该模袋的灌浆。灌浆压力应超过涌水压力且控制在模袋能承受的压力范围之内，根据该涌水点的情况，初步拟定为0.5MPa，在实际施工时，将视灌浆效果以模袋的承受能力进行调整。

3. 涌水封堵

模袋灌浆结束后，由于模袋之间存有一些间隙仍然漏水，故需要进一步对涌水进行封堵。通过在廊道内预先钻孔与涌水通道连通，待模袋灌浆完成并凝固具备一定强度后，通过灌注速凝膏浆、纤维膏浆等材料进行封堵。同时，为了防止灌浆过程中所加纤维材料被涌水冲出，在涌水出口部位安装钢筋格栅和钢筋笼进行阻挡，灌浆过程中，通过灌注水玻璃材料加速浆液凝固，效果良好。

（三）泵送混凝土封堵

模袋灌浆结束后，有效地封堵了原集中涌水，涌水全部由集水钢管引出至基坑外，为11、12号坝段基坑开挖创造了条件。

然而，在11号坝段基坑开挖过程中，又揭示出多条涌水通道，而且，根据水流情况分析，这些涌水点大多与集水钢管内的涌水是相通的。由于涌水点在基坑内，形状不规则，上面有大量浮渣，用模袋灌浆的方式无法进行封堵。经分析，决定采用泵送混凝土砂浆灌注的方式，首先在10号坝段上游廊道内打孔与涌水通道连通（由于距离近、深度浅，钻孔容易连通），再通过该孔灌注混凝土砂浆。

采用泵送混凝土封堵的原则是：利用混凝土泵输送的连续性和大排量的特点，在混凝土被水冲散、离析前将水堵住。混凝土采用一级配泵送混凝土，混凝土泵安在混凝土运输车辆可以到达的地方，通过输送管送到孔内进行封堵，由于钻孔孔口涌水大，混凝土输送管与孔口连接处采用了特殊的封闭方式，确保混凝土不返出孔外。

（四）充填及固结灌浆

10号坝段集中涌水点封堵成功后，为确保安全度汛及大坝安全，又在10号坝段坝体廊道内进行了充填及固结灌浆，以进一步封堵坝体混凝土与基岩面之间的缝隙和基岩的岩体力学性能，提高大坝的整体性和稳定性。

充填及固结灌浆在同一孔内进行施工，由于10号坝段涌水大，部分涌水经集水钢盒漏出后，经基岩与大坝混凝土接触面涌出。同时，该坝段在浇筑时，由于涌水大，底部砂浆存在一定的砂、浆分离现象，在长时间的水流作用下，砂被带出，该坝段接触面存在一定程度地脱空。因此，各孔第一段钻至基岩面并进入基岩10cm后，需进行充填灌浆。随后分段进行固结灌浆。

（五）灌浆效果分析及结论

（1）10号坝段渗漏涌水流量大，压力高，在岩溶地区也少见。坝基堵漏灌浆施工前，10～12号坝段多处出现大量涌水，导致11、12号坝段无法施工。经堵漏灌浆后，10～12号坝段仅出现少量渗水，模袋灌浆和泵送混凝土灌注混凝土砂浆工法在本工程中得到了成功应用，确保了基坑开挖和混凝土浇筑顺利进行。

（2）10号坝段坝基涌水出露点形成空腔，采用在空腔内安放自制模袋灌注水泥浆液，起到了很好的封堵效果。模袋形成后，为防止集中渗漏通道封堵后被涌水再次击穿，采用了锚杆进行加固，证明是有效的。

（3）对固结和充填灌浆钻孔过程中涌水大的孔通过混凝土泵注入混凝土砂浆后，效果明显。

（4）通过本次施工，使模袋灌浆和泵送混凝土应用于大涌水封堵和岩溶通道封堵的工艺更加成熟，灌浆效果也证明了以上工艺的可行性，为类似工程的处理提供了有益的经验。

（中国水利水电第八工程局有限公司　姜命强　向红利）

台江水电站挡水建筑物基础处理

（一）工程简况

台江水电站位于福建省三明市沙溪干流上，为沙溪流域规划第三个梯级电站。电站装机容量30MW，为低水头径流式水电站，河床式布置，枢纽主要建筑物包括溢流坝、河床式厂房、船闸上闸首、右岸重力式挡水坝段及左岸土坝接头。拦河坝为混凝土闸坝，拦河坝最大坝高38m，坝顶全长372.50m。

（二）坝址工程地质条件

坝址地层自上而下为：第四系覆盖层（Q_4）、古生界二叠系文笔山组泥质粉砂岩（P_{1w}）、栖霞组灰岩（P_{1q-2}）、栖霞组粉砂质泥岩和泥岩（P_{1q-1}）。

坝基主要地层基岩岩性为中～薄层状粉砂质泥岩、泥质粉砂岩，成互层状，属软质岩石，易泥化、力学强度较低。岩石结构面发育，风化破碎强烈，呈强风化、全风化状且不均匀，弱风化岩层埋藏较深，厚度大，一般都大于25.0m。受构造变动影响，坝址区褶皱、断裂较发育，其中F_3、F_4断层对工程影响较大，F_3断层N70°～85°W/SW∠65°～80°，宽2～3m，近平行于坝线，位于坝线下游约60m，对坝线选择影响较大。F_4断层N60°～80°E/SE∠60°～75°，宽2～5m，斜穿坝基上、下游，由糜棱岩组成，炭质泥岩富集，带内物质全风化，工程性质软弱，易形成渗漏通道。

（三）基础处理设计

1. 基础加固处理

（1）发电厂房主机段受结构控制，建基高程较低，置于弱风化岩层上。溢流坝段、厂房装配场段、重力式挡水坝段及船闸上闸首基础应力较小，抗滑稳定安全余地较大，经技术论证，基础置于强风化岩层上。为保证强风化岩层满足坝基强度和变形要求，从两个方面给以解决：一是上部结构设计时，通过调整断面，尽量减少基础面应力，要求建筑物平均基底应力不大于地基容许承载力，基底应力最大值和最小值之比不大于2～2.5；二是沿结构基础面进行全断面固结灌浆，提高基础岩石的完整性、均匀性、变形模量和容许承载力指标，改善坝基岩石强度。固结灌浆孔孔距、排距均为3.0m，孔深5.0m，梅花型布置。

（2）施工过程中，厂房2号主机段下游尾水段和厂坝中导墙下游段灰岩面高程突降，原建基高程为全风化粉砂岩；厂房机组段流道中段右侧与护坦交界处开挖时，揭露了一条溶蚀深槽，充填砂卵砾石和全风化土、灰岩块石等混合物。这3处可利用基岩埋藏深，周边为尾水边坡或基坑边坡，为确保尾水边坡、基坑边坡稳定，避免大开挖引起边坡失稳，采用了钢筋混凝土冲孔灌注桩处理方式。灌注桩直径为110cm，桩距为3m×3m，桩尖嵌入弱风化灰岩1m以下。对于基岩埋藏较浅的部位，采用先开挖至弱风化灰岩，然后回填C15混凝土。

2. 基础防渗和断层破碎带处理

(1) 坝基岩石虽较破碎，但由于上、下游最大水位差仅 8m，故帷幕灌浆采用一排灌浆孔，孔距 2m。帷幕灌浆孔深至相对不渗水层以下 3m，河床部位普遍为 15～20m。土坝接头部位水文地质条件复杂，相对隔水层埋藏深度普遍较深，达 35～52m，为此进行了渗流分析。渗流分析平均渗流坡降小于 0.057，满足渗透稳定的要求，土坝接头部位采用黏土截水槽+悬挂式帷幕的防渗处理方式。右岸 205 国道下覆 5～7m 厚堆渣及残坡积土，堆渣下部即为强风化泥质粉砂岩。堆渣及残坡积土渗透性强，是该地段防渗处理的重点。设计布置了 3 排帷幕灌浆，排距、孔距为 2m，梅花型布置，帷幕孔深 5～12m。

(2) 坝址处共 15 条断层，其中规模较大或对结构、基础渗漏有不利影响，需进行专门处理的断层或断层影响带一条 (F_4)。其他断层或距坝线较远对结构及坝基渗漏无明显不利影响或断层规模较小可结合基础开挖、固结灌浆、帷幕灌浆、边坡处理一并考虑，不需作专门处理。

(3) F_4 断层斜穿溢流坝 1～2 号坝段坝基，为逆断层，贯通上、下游。其主要问题是易产生集中渗漏，在此部位加深了帷幕灌浆以截断渗漏通道。由于其对坝基应力影响不大，采用刻槽回填混凝土置换部分断层破碎带物质，刻槽宽约 4m，深约 2m。根据该断层破碎带岩石破碎程度，局部增补了固结灌浆孔。

3. 1～2 号机流道中段溶蚀深槽处理

厂房机组段 1～2 号机流道中段深槽灰岩埋藏深，深槽内充填砂卵砾石和全风化土、灰岩块石等混合物，最大宽度约 9m，由于基岩埋藏深，受现场施工条件等因素的限制，无法进行开挖置换处理，考虑到灌注桩施工周期较长，为确保流道中段混凝土的浇筑进度，该部位采用钢筋混凝土厚板结构进行处理。即通过加大底板厚度，提高基础的整体刚度，对深槽分布范围内倒悬的岩体、凸出的蚀石进行挖除、清理、冲洗干净，并在深槽周围侧面设置系统锚杆。底板以下部分的充填物用混凝土进行局部置换，在深槽范围内布置孔排距为 2×2m 的固结灌浆孔，以提高基础的整体性。

(四) 结语

台江水电站工程虽规模不大，但地质条件复杂，坝基地质结构面较发育，风化破碎强烈，还有边坡稳定及基坑涌水等工程地质问题，加之两岸紧邻工厂和国道，环境约束多，使工程处理难度加大。设计因地制宜地采取了有针对性的处理措施，使工程得以顺利进行。工程已于 2008 年 2 月蓄水发电，蓄水后的观测资料表明，大坝变形、两岸渗流、边坡稳定等均处于正常状态，说明大坝的建基面选择、基础及边坡处理措施是合适的。

(中国水电顾问集团华东勘测设计研究院　熊立刚)

红花水电站工程地质问题的处理

红花水电站位于广西柳州市境内，是柳江下游一座发电、航运、灌溉相结合的综合利用的大型水利水电工程，水库总库容 30 亿 m^3，电站总装机容量 230MW。对坝址区存在的软弱夹层和岩溶地质问题的处理情况如下：

(一) 坝基软弱夹层抗滑稳定问题的处理

在初步设计勘察查明软弱夹层成因、分布及其产状变化规律的基础上，推荐软弱夹层产状较陡的Ⅴ线作为坝轴线，并被设计采纳及付诸实施。施工开挖表明，坝轴线恰好落在岩层陡倾（大于 50°）的部位。如果坝轴线上下移动超过 20m，都将进入缓倾软弱夹层发育区，对坝基抗滑稳定非常不利。极限平衡法及有限元法计算成果均表明：存在倾角缓于 25°的软弱夹层的坝基抗滑稳定安全系数不能满足规范要求，倾角陡于 30°的软弱夹层的坝基抗滑稳定安全系数满足规范要求。坝轴线如果进入缓倾（倾角缓于 25°，下同）软弱夹层发育区，为提高坝基抗滑稳定性的工程处理措施（工程量）将大幅增加。

施工开挖后发现，坝基岩体中存在由极薄层炭质页岩、硅质泥岩受构造运动和地下水作用软化、泥化而形成的软弱夹层，夹于薄～中厚层灰岩之间，坝轴线附近（约 20m 范围）倾角陡（大于 50°），倾角平缓（小于 30°）的夹层集中分布于下游护坦段。根据其在坝基分布所占比例，采用面积加权法提出了地质参数，建议设计进行坝基抗滑稳定计算；同时，8～10 号坝段建基面高程普遍降低 1.0～4.0m，0+579.0～0+611.0 段整个建基面进行固结灌浆，闸坝下游护坦地基布置锚筋，增强坝基抗滑稳定能力，上游局部边坡放缓坡度，从而保证了泄水闸的施工和运行安全。

开挖后所揭露的软弱夹层分布、产状与前期勘察评价一致，所采取的处理措施被证明是有效的。

(二) 岩溶地质问题的处理

1. 勘察期间的处理

该工程地质勘察期间，勘察单位极为重视地质测绘和地质（构造和岩溶）分析，运用“先有地质认识后作勘探验证”的勘察思路，把勘探作为验证手段，将有限的勘探工作量针对主要工程地质问题布置，主要体现在：

(1) 抓住岩溶河谷选择坝址的关键，在正确划分岩溶分区的基础上，果断提前放弃岩溶较发育的长沙坝址，可行性研究阶段集中力量开展处于弱岩溶区的红花上坝址、下坝址的比选勘察，推荐软弱夹层较少且产状较陡的上坝址，并被设计采纳并付诸实施。

(2) 充分利用柳州地区已有岩溶水文地质资料，加强分析研究，预测水库蓄水的岩溶浸没问题不是库水倒灌问题，而是淹没岩溶管道出口可能导致的局部短时的内涝问题。分析结论为近一年的水库运行情况初步验证。

2. 施工期间的处理

泄水闸坝段只在14号坝段中部靠近13号坝段处有一小型溶凹，充填褐黄色淤泥，施工时，溶凹充填物全部挖除，局部小溶穴上覆岩层用风镐打掉，其中充填物全部掏挖，用清水冲洗干净后，再浇筑混凝土。从施工开挖结果可以看出，泄水段闸地基的工程地质条件和勘察期工程地质结论基本一致，第四系砂卵石层下即为石炭系下统黄金组上段弱风化灰岩、炭质灰岩夹硅质泥岩及炭质页岩，基本无全强风化层，该段岩溶也不发育，建基面岩体为中厚层状结构，岩体较完整，局部完整性较差，岩体质量为AⅢ～BⅢ类。

（中水珠江规划勘测设计有限公司　吴　飞）

勘测技术与设备

物探数据计算解译系统及规范化成图

在水电工程领域，物探是进行地质勘察的重要手段之一。中国水电顾问集团北京勘测设计研究院（以下简称北京院）紧跟国内外技术发展的步伐，逐步将计算机的分析、统计、解释优势应用到物探领域，20世纪90年代中期，在国内同行还处于半手工作图状态下，已实现百分之百物探计算机成图率。近年来，一方面随着项目增多，物探内业工作量大增；另一方面，随着社会进步和市场化进一步深入，对勘测成果的要求也越来越高。为了提高勘测成果质量，提高绘图效率，实现内业成图标准化、自动化，并利于工程信息、资料的存储保管，北京院开发了物探数据计算解译系统及规范化成图（以下简称WTCAD2.0）系统。

（一）系统构成

WTCAD2.0系统包括4个子系统内容：浅层地震折射分析解释绘图子系统（含面波剖面、地震映像剖面和地震横河剖面）；声波及综合测井分析解释绘图子系统（含剪切波速度测井、电阻率测井）；平洞（竖井）弹性波测试分析解释绘图子系统；高密度电法数据处理和成图子系统。

1. 浅层地震折射分析解释绘图子系统

该子系统下涵盖了目前常用的4种分析解释方法——t_0法、哈莱斯法、共轭点法和时间场法，对这4种方法系统开发的难点和关键是如何实现非水平地形下进行计算和精确绘制基岩界面。该子系统应用循环内插法彻底解决了非水平地形的计算和绘图工作。

t_0法计算和构图相对简单，其技术原理是采用相遇观测系统获取相遇时距曲线。哈莱斯法对于地表比较平坦、基岩面起伏较大、基岩内有速度变化的情况，能获得较好的效果和较高的解释精度。此法过去应用不多，主要是因为其解释成图比较复杂。共轭点法所依据的折射波路径与哈莱斯法完全相同，两者不同之点在于共轭点法是从数学推导出发，利用计算机作逻辑演绎并自动成图的一种方法。时间场法是一种比较精确的方法，它适用于规则和不规则的各种界面情况。根据实测时距曲线上波到达各接收点的时间值，按照波传播过程中的波前原理绘制波在不同时刻的等时面，再根据波传播的几何规律来确定出折射界面的形态和位置。这种方法作图复杂、步骤烦琐，计算机编程有一定困难，是一直以来没有得到广泛应用的主要原因。

2. 声波及综合测井分析解释绘图子系统

该子系统涵盖了目前国内市场上常用的声波测井仪器（包括SY-1、RSM、RS等声波测井仪器）和综合测井仪器（JGS-1和MS3等综合测井仪器）所采集的数据处理和成图，具有自动判别数据文件的功能，可直接调用所列仪器采集的数据，无需进行任何变换，减少了不必要的环节，降低了差错率。该系统又具有必要的智能功能，在数据处理和成图过程中，可作智能判别并解释。

3. 平洞（竖井）弹性波测试分析解释绘图子系统

该子系统也是集分析、计算、解译、绘图于一身，是目前物探界功能最全、最强大的子系统。首先，该子系统提供的参数最全，包括纵波、横波、泊松比、动弹模量、完整性系数、风化系数、岩体分级；其次，该子系统具有智能判别的功能，有自动筛选、自动归类的功能，有自动判别、自动标识的功能。

4. 高密度电法数据处理和成图子系统（略）

（二）系统特点

WTCAD2.0 系统具有以下特点和优势：

（1）基于国际上先进成熟的计算机辅助设计系统 AutoCAD 平台进行开发。WTCAD2.0 系统以闻名世界的 Autodesk 公司开发的 AutoCAD 软件为支撑平台。AutoCAD 是当今最流行的二维绘图软件，同时有部分三维功能，具有功能强大、体系开放、易于开发、高精确度等特点，与同类软件相比，无论在实用性还是在可操作性方面都具有明显的优势。作为植根于 AutoCAD 环境下的 WTCAD2.0 系统，能充分发挥 AutoCAD 软件的优势。由于 AutoCAD 软件应用广泛，因此 WTCAD2.0 系统更易于被接受和使用。

（2）具有数据和图形的自动识别功能。当前，物探仪器设备已都具有自动采集和存储功能。每种方法和同一种方法不同的仪器设备采集来的原始数据文件格式都不相同。这些原始数据文件总体上可分为波形文件（二进制文件）和数据文件（文本文件）两类。对于波形文件，需要应用专用软件作进一步的处理；对于各种数据文件，可直接用于数据的分析和处理。WTCAD2.0 系统具有自动识别各种数据文件（文本文件）的功能，可直接对采集来的各种文本文件进行数据分析、处理、成图。在计算机处理成图时，有的需要根据计算出的参数进行解译和判断，解译和判断的依据是给定的阀门值和规定的标准范围。WTCAD2.0 系统具有自动解译和判别图形的功能，这不但提高了解释的准确性、科学性，而且丰富了解释手段。

（3）运行高效。电脑只是工具，WTCAD2.0 系统也仅是辅助系统，都不能脱离人脑而自主运行，特别是在数据的分析、处理及方案的选择上离不开人脑的参与，这就是说，必要的人机交互是不可或缺的。WTCAD2.0 系统的 4 部分，每一部分都有独立的参数输入对话框，在主程序运行过程中，仅保留了必要的人机交互，这样既可以保持程序的高效运行，又能保证成果的完整性。

（4）成图规范。规范化成图是 WTCAD2.0 系统最基本的功能。WTCAD2.0 系统的成图部分是严格按照有关规程规范编制而成的，无论是图例、图框、线性，还是实体属性、图案，都是标准和规范的，绘制的图件不会因人而异。

（5）具有广泛的兼容性。WTCAD2.0 系统适用于 AutoCAD2000 至目前 AutoCAD2007 的任一版本平台，具有广泛的兼容性。

（6）具有良好的可操控性和简洁、实用的用户界面。WTCAD2.0 系统操作简单，界面简洁、实用。除了必要的人机交互外，输入参数都在相应的对话框中进行，数据的格式、参数的属性都在对话框中有相应的说明，极大地方便了用户的准确选择。

（7）采用模块化设计，提高了运行稳定性。模块化设计是现代程序设计中一种很重要的技巧，有着众多优点：便于分工合作，提高效率，提高质量；便于维护、维修，增强通用性、易读性；增强模块的独立性，降低相互之间的依赖程度。

（三）应用情况

从对国内同行多年的了解和近期的调研情况来看，目前很多大单位的物探软件自成体系，有从国外引进的 mapgis、grapher、surfer 等软件，也有自主编制的各种数据采集、处理、成图解释软件，可谓百花齐放、各具特色。但不少单位编制的软件，都是从各单位实际需要出发的，有不少处理成图方法脱离了规程规范的要求，在目前国内市场经济还很不完善的情况下，这种状况很难短期内解决。另外，从数据处理和成图过程及成图效果来看，在自动化、标准化、规范化等方面都不同程度地存在这样那样的问题。迄今，仍有不少兄弟单位，包括个别的大单位仍在手工计算机作图，效率可想而知。

自 WTCAD2.0 系统开发完成以来，先后应用于马吉、松塔、乡城、许曲河、呼和浩特抽水蓄能、丰宁、旬阳、文登等多个水电工程，不但提高了工作效率，而且成果质量也得到了明显提高。

在工作效率方面：由于 WTCAD2.0 系统集成化和自动化程度高，数据处理和成图效率明显得到了提升。如绘制一个地震剖面，从数据建立、选参、处理成图到插入图例、图名等完成整个流程，现在只需 10min（单纯选参、处理成图 1min 足够），而在手工绘图阶段，一个熟练的技术人员首先要绘制各种参数的剖面，进而比选最佳剖面，则需要 1 天时间。

在成果质量方面：WTCAD2.0 系统进一步优化了算法，修正了 WTCAD1.0 存在的各种不足，弥补了 WTCAD1.0 的遗漏；进一步提高了解释精度，使成图流程化、标准化，保证了一流的成果质量，达到了最佳的测试成果，为多快好省地进行工程建设，发挥物探技术的先进作用，使其达到“技术可靠、经济合理”。

（中国水电顾问集团北京勘测设计研究院
常 伟 刘善军）

地质雷达在西龙池抽水蓄能电站岩溶地层探测中的应用

西龙池抽水蓄能电站位于山西省五台县境内的滹沱河水系，距太原市及忻州市的公路里程分别为154km和74km，主要建筑物包括上水库、输水系统、地下厂房系统、下水库、补水系统等，总装机容量1200MW，额定水头640m。

根据西龙池抽水蓄能电站前期勘察成果预测，上、下水库库盆基础在开挖到设计高程时，其建基面以下的岩土体内还分别存在溶洞、溶蚀宽缝和土质透镜体、碎石架空带等不良地质现象，面板地基不均一。因此，在施工期需要利用以物探方法查明地基及以下一定深度范围内的溶洞、溶蚀宽缝和土质透镜体等的发育情况，并依据不同规模评价其对面板地基变形的影响，建议相应处理措施。

根据西龙池抽水蓄能电站前期勘察成果，区内奥陶系上下马家沟组、冶里组、寒武系凤山组、崮山组岩层岩性为质纯层厚的灰岩和白云质灰岩，属可溶岩，岩溶较发育。输水系统穿越以上地层部分，可能揭露或在隧洞周围岩体内隐伏有溶洞或溶蚀宽缝，对隧洞尤其是高压管道段运行期围岩的稳定不利。因此，在施工期需要利用以物探手段查明高压管道段周围岩体一定深度范围内的溶洞、溶蚀宽缝等的发育位置。

(一) 可能造成不均匀沉陷的地质单元

上水库库盆基岩为灰岩、白云岩、泥质白云岩互层，存在有不同程度的溶蚀，主要表现为溶蚀宽缝及溶洞，全充填或半充填，如果其处于坝基及面板下一定深度范围内，将会对大坝及面板地基造成不均匀沉陷。

下水库大坝及库盆大部分坐落于深厚覆盖层上，覆盖层组成物质极不均匀，主要为碎石土，夹有粉质土及块石、碎石架空带透镜体，若此两类透镜体处于坝基及面板地基一定深度范围内，将会对大坝及面板地基造成不均匀沉陷。

输水系统存在岩溶问题的岩层层组为上、下马家沟组、冶里组、凤山组、崮山组岩层的质纯层厚的灰岩和白云质灰岩，主要表现为溶蚀宽缝和溶洞，全充填或半充填。在上、下马家沟组岩层底部，分别发育一层泥质角砾状白云岩，为相对隔水层，长山组下段、张夏组上段也为相对隔水层，隔水层附近岩溶相对更发育。岩溶的发育不仅与岩性有关，还受构造的控制，且追踪现象十分明显，发育方向主要沿NE向构造发育。因此，高压管道段岩溶发育部位即为隧洞穿越上述岩层部位，如果其隐伏于输水隧洞周围的岩体内，将对高压管道运行期压力管道结构稳定不利。在薄层灰岩出露部位，虽然从岩性上看，岩溶发育程度较厚层灰岩出露部位低，但沿构造面仍有可能发育溶洞，另外在地表地质测绘的过程中，在亮甲山组岩层出露部位，零星可见溶蚀空洞，因此，薄层灰岩出露部位及亮甲山组岩层出露部位也应在本次地质雷达探测范围内。

(二) 任务要求和测线布置

上水库库盆岩溶探测要求探明建基面以下10m深度范围内发育的岩溶洞穴和溶蚀宽缝，确定溶洞、溶蚀宽缝的数量、分布和范围，为地基处理提供资料。

下水库库区地质雷达探测要求：探测面积大于1m×1m的土质透镜体、松散碎石土架空层等不良地质体，为地基处理提供资料。

根据设计要求，输水系统的岩溶探测要求探明洞壁以内10m深度范围内发育的岩溶洞穴和溶蚀宽缝，确定溶洞、溶蚀宽缝的数量、分布和规模，为洞壁处理提供资料。

上、下水库库盆测线间距为2.5m，与工区主要地质构造线垂直或大角度斜交。现场测试时先进行人工放线、放点，沿测线方向每2m标注一个点位，每10m标注一个控制点。

输水系统测线布置沿洞轴线方向，共布置5条测线，分别为洞顶中心线一条、两拱角各一条、两侧壁各一条。在输水系统高压管道段的上平段、中平段等近水平段处采用车载移动、伸缩臂固定雷达天线方式进行资料采集工作。在上斜井段、下斜井段等倾斜段处视具体情况考虑采用在爬罐车内、运输平台上加固伸缩臂并固定雷达天线，仪器操作人员在爬罐车内、运输平台上操作的方式进行资料采集工作。

(三) 探测结果

上水库雷达探测工作共探测出溶洞异常51个、溶蚀宽缝异常94条，合计145处之多，其分布规律为：

(1) 岩溶发育方向基本沿NE向，发育方向多为NE∠40°～60°，受构造控制的方向性明显，溶洞直径一般在1～3m，少数大于3m，溶蚀裂隙宽度一般小于0.5m；从开挖揭露的情况看，溶洞及溶蚀宽缝大多数为充填型，少数为无充填或半充填型；溶洞多充填黏土，少量夹有碎石；宽缝以黏土碎块石充填为主。

(2) 所探测到的较明显的岩溶分布规律，基本分布于原始地形条件下的沟底部位。

(3) 第五层灰岩及第四层灰岩与白云岩互层部分岩溶较发育，而第四、六层泥质白云岩部分岩溶相对不发育。

地质雷达探测到的溶洞和溶蚀宽缝经开挖验证，与实际均是吻合的，仅在范围上有所差别，说明本次测试所采用的技术方法和参数是合适的，解释是合理的，测试成果满足要求。

下水库雷达探测工作共探测出土质透镜体异常19个、松散碎石土架空层异常14条，合计33处，其分布规律为：

(1) 下库库底探测区不良地质体较发育，主要沿冲沟方向发育，多呈长条状。

(2) 下库库盆西边坡探测区覆盖层较薄，不良地质体不发育。

雷达探测还较好地揭示了探测区内部分区域基岩与覆盖层的分界面，与原始地貌吻合，即测线在冲沟处覆盖层较厚，基岩界面在冲沟边界较陡。

通过对一号输水隧洞上平段、上斜段及下斜段的探测，大于等于1m的溶洞或溶蚀宽缝异常体主要有：

(1) 上平段：在S1 0+90桩号左壁发育溶洞，其规模沿洞壁深12～13m、宽5m、高3m，在S1 0+105桩号左壁发育一出露的溶洞，宽2m、高3m。

(2) 上斜井上段：左壁0+103～0+106剖面，深0～5m发育溶洞，溶洞规模沿剖面长约3m、高5m，已经进行回填处理。

(3) 其余洞段在探测范围内未发现较大异常，仅在局部发育裂隙、小溶蚀及破碎岩体，裂隙宽度一般小于10cm。

二号输水隧洞上平段、上斜段及下斜段，大于等于1m的溶洞或溶蚀宽缝异常体主要有：

(1) 上平段：右壁0+35～0+38剖面，发育一充填型溶缝，溶缝宽2～3m，局部已出露；底部0+50剖面，埋深7～8m，发育一宽3m、高1.5m的充填型溶洞或溶蚀破碎。

(2) 上斜井上斜段：顶部0+110～0+114剖面，深0～2m发育溶蚀，其规模沿剖面长4m、高2m，已经进行回填处理；右壁0+117～0+121剖面，深0～3m发育溶洞，溶洞规模沿剖面长4m、高3m，已经进行回填处理。

(3) 其余洞段在探测范围内未发现较大异常，仅在局部发育裂隙、小溶蚀及破碎岩体，裂隙宽度一般小于10cm。

综合一、二号输水隧洞探测成果分析：该输水系统岩溶、溶蚀宽缝等不良地质体主要发育于上平段及上斜井上段，该洞段岩体裂隙相对较发育，岩体较破碎。上斜井下段及下斜井仅在局部发育裂隙，岩体相对较完整。

地质雷达有无损、快速、准确的优点，能够很好地解决工程上的疑难问题。其高精度、高效率、高分辨率、快速经济、灵活方便、剖面直观等优点，日益受到工程技术人员的青睐。

(中国水电顾问集团北京勘测设计研究院 常 伟)

AutoMeas自动测量技术在控制测量中的应用

水利水电工程控制测量工作多在深山峡谷中进行，其主要特点是：测区范围小，精度要求高，外业作业劳动强度大，同时要求操作人员要具备丰富的实践经验和熟练的操作技能。因此，如何快速、准确地获得控制测量野外测量数据，缩短外业时间，减轻外业人员的劳动强度，提高控制测量作业效益，成为测绘领域普遍探究的课题。中国水利水电第八工程局有限公司科研设计院测绘中心在湖南省碗米坡、五强溪、黑麋峰及云南向家坝、龙开口，贵州构皮滩等水电工程建设和京沪高速铁路施工控制测量工作中，引进了AutoMeas自动测量系统，通过对瑞士徕卡测量系统股份有限公司（以下简称瑞士徕卡公司）生产的TCA系列全站仪的开发应用，成功解决了控制测量工作中这一困扰多年的难题，同时，避免了人工观测时容易出现的读错和记错测量数据现象，免除了大量测量数据需要现场计算和校核的工作量，取得了良好的经济效益。

(一) 特点

水利水电工程控制测量采用AutoMeas自动测量技术，外业作业不需要人工瞄准目标，避免了观测人员长时间重复瞄准目标，体力下降，眼睛疲劳，导致观测成果质量降低问题；仪器自动瞄准锁定目标后进行测量，数据自动记录到随机的PC卡中，不需要人工干预，从而避免了测量数据读错或记错的现象。

采用AutoMeas自动测量技术进行控制测量外业作业时，可按照国家、行业规范要求预先设定好各种限差。测量过程中，如果出现测量数据超限，仪器将自动报警，并提示超限的内容以及是否进行重测，操作人员只需根据提示选择“yes”或“no”即可，仪器将自动重新进行测量，超限的测量数据将不进行记录。每个测站的全部观测作业结束后，仪器自动计算全部观测数据，比较各种限差，全部合格以后，仪器自动将所有观测数据记录在随机的PC卡中，因此，不存在测站观测数据超限需要重新补测的情况，也不需要人工进行记录。

AutoMeas自动测量技术以瑞士徕卡公司生产的TCA系列全站仪为平台，具有马达驱动自动瞄准锁定目标功能，采用内置的ATR发射出激光束，经过反射后由内置的CCD相机接收，相对于CCD相机中心的接收光点位置被计算，其偏移量用来控制仪器马达，转动仪器以便使十字丝照准棱镜中心。由于观测过程不依赖可见光，在夜晚同样可以进行正常观测作业，故适用于大多数水利水电工程控制测量作业、大坝及高边坡变形观测作业，以及采用常规全站仪测设控制网的其他工程建设控制测量作业。

（二）工艺原理

瑞士徕卡公司的TCA系列全站仪具有自动跟踪锁定目标功能，仪器自带的Monitoring测量程序可以自动重复测量，但不能按照规范要求预先设定各种限差，观测过程中限差超限时不报警，目标失锁后自动跳转到下一步进行测量，所有数据（无论是否超限）一律进行记录。而AutoMeas自动测量软件则是利用瑞士徕卡公司的GeoBASIC编译语言作为二次开发平台，按照我国现行的规范要求设计开发的一套自动观测软件，充分利用TCA系列全站仪具有自动马达驱动和目标自动跟踪锁定功能，实现了仪器自动观测、自动记录和计算。

（三）质量控制

（1）AutoMeas自动测量系统遵照国家、行业颁布的如下规范：GB/T 17942—2000《国家三角测量规范》、DL/T 5173—2003《水电水利工程施工测量规范》、GB/T 16818—2008《中、短程光电测距规范》。

（2）作业开始前，收集测区范围内有关的测绘资料、图纸，了解测区范围内已有的控制点埋设情况，实地查看有无损坏、位移，相临控制点间是否通视等。

（3）根据规范、工程设计技术要求等，编写控制测量作业指导书，提前向所有参加作业的人员进行技术交底，使每一位队员明确了解各自的分工以及作业过程中的注意事项。

（4）作业开始前，认真做好准备工作，按照分工提前清理好所需携带的工器具，查看工器具的工况是否完好，配件是否齐全，电池是否充好电等。

（5）作业开始前，应对仪器设备和工器具进行检校，作业过程中应随时检查和校正，严格按照操作规程进行，确保仪器设备和工器具状态良好。

（6）作业过程中，同一方向上禁止同时出现两个反射棱镜或其他反光物体，尽量避免使用对讲机，以免出现干扰。

（7）野外作业结束后，仪器设备应按照要求装箱搬运，装箱时应检查各部件是否复位，同时认真清点设备和配套工具。

（8）控制测量作业受外界自然天气条件影响较大，应尽量选在阴天有微风、成像稳定清晰的天气条件下进行作业。采用AutoMeas自动测量技术，有条件也可以选在温度、湿度和气压变化较小的夜间进行。

（四）安全措施

（1）在软件上载过程中，仪器必须有充足的电量，如果在传输过程中停电，全站仪将损坏不能再使用，只有送维修中心维修。

（2）所有仪器、仪表和配套的工器具，在搬运和使用过程中，应有防震措施，防止摔碰。

（3）晴天或雨天作业时，仪器和棱镜务必打伞，雷雨大风或大雾天气应停止，严禁野蛮作业。

（五）环保措施

（1）控制网选埋标点时，在保证控制网的精度要求和有利于今后施工放样需要的前提下，尽量不占、少占耕地、田土。确需占用时，应会同业主、监理和当地政府有关部门及时进行协商。

（2）控制测量野外作业，除保证必要的通视条件外，不要随便砍伐当地植被，随时注意保护当地生态环境。

（六）效益分析

（1）采用AutoMeas自动测量技术，一般每个测站需要30～40min即可完成以往半天的作业，且无返工问题。

（2）观测过程中，跟踪锁定目标、测量和记录等完全由仪器自动完成，不需要人工瞄准读数和记录观测数据，避免了读错、听错和记错等现象。

（3）采用AutoMeas自动测量技术，只需要将仪器设置好后，整个观测过程全部由仪器自动完成，降低了观测人员的劳动强度。

（4）常规的控制测量作业要求观测人员有比较熟练的操作技能和观测经验，采用AutoMeas自动测量技术，只要求观测人员具备一般的操作常识即可完成。

（5）由仪器自动完成测站现场观测数据的计算和比较，完全符合要求以后，仪器才记录全部观测数据，省去了现场计算和内业校核的大量工作，提高了工作效率。

（中国水利水电第八工程局有限公司　刘坤华）

红花水电站勘测中新技术新方法的应用

红花水电站位于广西柳州市境内，是柳江下游一座发电、航运、灌溉相结合的综合利用的大型水利水电工程，水库总库容30亿m^3，电站总装机容量230MW。在工程勘测中，新技术、新方法的应用情况如下：

（一）勘察思路

（1）选坝阶段，规范要求比选坝址之间需要同精度比较。因此，国内水利水电勘察设计单位一般均对主要参选坝址安排基本相同的较大勘察工作量。该工程在充分分析 1∶10 000 地质测绘成果和少量物探资料的基础上，结合广西地区岩溶勘察经验，得出“长沙坝址明显地存在岩溶渗漏问题”的地质认识，据此建议不再安排钻探工作，提前放弃岩溶较发育的长沙坝址，可行性研究阶段集中力量开展处于弱岩溶区的红花上坝址、下坝址的比选勘察，减少了不少勘探工作量。

（2）选线阶段，规范要求比选坝线之间需要同精度比较。因此，国内水利水电勘察设计单位一般均对主要参选坝线安排基本相同的较大勘察工作量。该工程根据坝址区小构造（褶皱）发育特点，利用两岸实测地质剖面进行详细的地质构造（褶曲）分析，沿一倒转背斜的陡倾（倒转）翼布置主（V）勘探线，并把主要勘察手段和工作量针对V线布置，最终推荐V线作为坝轴线，并被设计采纳及付诸实施，使拦河闸坝等主要建筑物成功避开缓倾软弱夹层，为工程快速（提前一年）优质建成奠定了良好的基础。

（二）勘察技术

该工程基岩中软弱夹层发育，软弱夹层控制的坝基抗滑稳定问题是坝址区主要工程地质问题。查明软弱夹层的分布，特别是其产状（主要是倾角陡缓）及延伸情况，是计算、判断其抗滑稳定的关键。国内探查软弱夹层的先进技术主要有跨孔 CT 技术、钻孔电视录像技术和综合测井技术，其中跨孔 CT 技术既有昂贵的地震法、电磁波法，也有经济适用的声波法。国内对软弱夹层的先进勘探手段除了强调改进金刚石双管单动钻具外，多采用植物胶。

该工程首先加强钻孔取芯技术控制，采用金刚石双管单动钻具，但严格控制钻探回次进尺，确保岩芯采取率高达 95%以上，成功取到不少软弱夹层并量测到准确的夹层倾角，再选用经济适用的声波法，结合钻孔电视录像技术，查明缓倾角软弱夹层确实分布于局部地段，据此提出只需进行局部（存在倾角缓于25°软弱夹层）坝段的深层抗滑稳定验算。

（三）强岩溶区的水库浸没分析预测

强岩溶区的水库浸没问题因岩溶的复杂性而成为复杂的环境地质问题。该工程需要重点研究的水库浸没问题是鸡喇谷地可能存在因水库蓄水导致的柳州市城区内涝问题。自然条件下，鸡喇谷地洪水期遇雨即涝，水库蓄水后，是否会因库水倒灌而“无雨也涝”?

在查明鸡喇谷地洪水期遇雨即涝的主要原因的基础上，为了阐明鸡喇暗河天然排洪能力，还需要进行水文地质定量分析，但其中的管道断面等关键参数如何获取？有充足勘探经费的工程项目可能采用地质雷达探测管道部位，再利用重型勘探（钻探和平洞或竖井等）揭露管道，但仍存在只能取得部分点信息而难于取得全线综合参数的问题。本工程为民营企业投资项目，勘探经费不足，勘测单位选择利用大量长期观测成果进行的岩溶水文地质反演分析，取得岩溶暗河全线综合参数。

分析认为：鸡喇谷地洪水期遇雨即涝的最主要原因是暗河系统的天然排洪能力不足（通道断面太小），其次是柳江洪水顶托对岩溶内涝的影响（减小岩溶地下水水力梯度）非常显著。据此预测：鸡喇谷地在暴雨时可能存在因水库蓄水导致的局部短时内涝问题——延长低洼地带的内涝时间，增加泵站抽排时间；正常蓄水非降雨期，防护区不会出现“倒灌式”浸没（内涝），无需进行专门处理。工程运行情况表明，强岩溶区的水库浸没分析预测与实际相符，利用反演分析是较好的选择。

（中水珠江规划勘测设计有限公司 吴 飞）

5

水 工 设 计

大 坝 设 计

锦屏二级水电站拦河闸坝设计

锦屏二级水电站位于四川省凉山彝族自治州木里、盐源、冕宁三县交界处的雅砻江干流锦屏大河湾上，是雅砻江干流上的重要梯级电站。电站总装机容量4800MW，属一等大（1）型工程，主要由首部拦河闸坝、引水系统、尾部地下厂房三大部分组成，首部拦河闸坝按1级建筑物设计。

拦河闸坝位于雅砻江锦屏大河湾西端的猫猫滩，距上游锦屏一级水电站约7.5km。水库正常蓄水位1646m，相应库容为1401万m^3，死水位1640m，日调节库容为496万m^3。拦河闸坝采用500年一遇洪水设计，相应洪水流量为12 109m^3/s，上游设计洪水位1649.58m；2000年一遇洪水校核，相应洪水流量为13 980m^3/s，上游校核洪水位1651.80；下游消能防冲建筑物的洪水标准为100年一遇，相应洪水流量为9100m^3/s。

工程区域地震基本烈度为Ⅶ度。拦河闸坝按甲类工程抗震设防，在基本烈度基础上提高1度作为设计烈度，即地震设计烈度为Ⅷ度。闸址区河谷呈V形，枯水期河水面宽70～100m。河床覆盖层厚5～42m，自下而上分别为：Ⅰ（Q_3^{al}）含漂石卵砾石层、Ⅱ（Q_3^{pl+al}）含砂壤土碎砾石层、Ⅲ-1（Q_4^{al}）含孤块石卵砾石层、Ⅲ-2（Q_4^{Col+al}）块碎石夹砾卵石层、Ⅳ（Q_4^{Col+al}）层在两岸侧所分布的现代崩坍堆积物。闸址区两岸出露主要地层为三叠系上统（T_3）之变质砂岩、板岩。

根据闸址区地形地质条件以及水文和枢纽布置的特点，拦河闸坝施工采用枯水期断流围堰、隧洞导流方式。上、下游围堰采用土石过水围堰结构，围堰在汛期需过水度汛。

（一）拦河闸坝总体布置

拦河闸坝主要由河中泄洪闸、两岸挡水坝段、上游铺盖和下游消能防冲设施等组成。泄洪闸布置在主河床，基础为卵砾石覆盖层，共设置5个闸室段，每个闸室宽20m、泄洪净宽13m，泄洪闸段总长100m，闸顶高程1654m，最大闸高34m。闸室上游设长30m、厚4m的混凝土铺盖。闸室下游接长60m、厚3m的混凝土护坦。护坦上部设有导流墙用于调整急流流态。护坦末端接100m长的大块石海漫。闸室左、右岸接分别27m和38m混凝土重力坝段，重力坝段均建在基岩上。泄洪闸工作门采用开敞式弧形闸门、启闭设备为液压启闭机，并在上游侧设有平板检修钢闸门，门机启闭。

（二）泄洪闸闸室结构设计

综合考虑泄洪、消能、排沙、水流流态、对锦屏一级的影响、枢纽布置及工程投资等因素，经首部拦河闸坝水工水力学模型试验验证，泄洪闸采用5孔、单孔过流净宽13m的闸孔型式，闸室溢流堰采用平底宽顶堰型式，闸室底板顶高程为1626m，底板厚6m。泄洪闸采用弧形闸门挡水，弧形闸门尺寸为13m×22m（宽×高）。考虑到闸墩需承受较大的作用力，闸墩中混凝土出现较大的拉应力，经比较分析采用预应力闸墩结构型式，闸墩厚度3.5m。

闸顶高程由校核洪水位情况控制，同时考虑到闸顶交通桥、门机轨道梁等布置的需要，闸顶高程确定为1654m。卵砾石覆盖层基础上的闸室顺水流长度一般为上下游水位差的1.5～2.5倍，本工程上下游水头差最大为25m左右，经闸室应力稳定验算，确定闸室沿水流向长47m。

为提高建筑物抗震性能和适应基础变形等要求，泄洪闸闸室均采用单孔独立缝墩式结构，闸底板与闸墩整体浇筑，每个闸室段长度为20m。垂直水流方向相邻闸室间设变形沉降缝，缝间设止水铜片、橡胶止水片各一道，止水布置在工作弧门附近。

（三）防渗设计

拦河闸坝河床覆盖层采用全封闭混凝土防渗墙、两岸采用水泥帷幕灌浆的基础防渗措施。

混凝土防渗墙布置在闸室上游的铺盖底部，墙底嵌入弱风化基岩以下1.0m，两岸接基岩，墙顶嵌入铺盖0.5m。防渗墙厚度为0.8m，混凝土强度为C25，抗渗标号为W8，全断面配筋。防渗墙的质量采用钻孔取芯、压水试验、单孔声波、声波CT、钻孔变模检测等多种检测方法，检测防渗墙各项物理力学参数，从而评价防渗墙质量。

防渗墙与铺盖之间设置10cm的周边缝以适应变形，缝内嵌填SR柔性止水材料，并设置一道铜片止水和一道橡胶止水。

防渗墙通过灌浆帷幕与两岸重力式坝段基础的灌浆帷幕衔接。考虑到两岸坝肩岩体有一定的卸荷影响，岩体渗透性较好，同时，水库蓄水后可能给岩体及边坡带来不利影响，帷幕灌浆深度按深入5Lu线以下5m控制。

（四）覆盖层基础灌浆加固设计

拦河闸坝工程基础覆盖层深厚，成分较复杂，地基存在不均匀沉降问题，分布在埋深15m范围内的砂层透镜体在Ⅷ度地震条件下可能发生液化。结合抗液化设计，考虑对闸室基础、上游铺盖基础、护坦上游侧5m范围基础采用固结灌浆加固处理，以减小闸坝基础沉降和相对沉降差，加强地震时地基与闸底板的连接，并改善闸底板和防渗墙应力状况。固结灌浆孔、排距2.5m，梅花形布置，灌浆深度15m。覆盖层固结灌浆采用自上而下分段、孔口封闭、孔内循环灌浆法。灌后质量采用声波测试、压水试验、钻孔取芯、孔内变模、孔内电视等多种措施检测，进行综合评定。

（五）左岸强卸荷处理设计

拦河闸坝左岸卸荷强烈，距坡面12～13m范围内岩体裂隙较发育，孔内电视显示孔内掉块现象较明显，局部有10cm左右的裂隙存在。设计对其进行灌浆处理，灌浆要求优先灌注水泥砂浆，由低高程到高高程分序施工。由于坡表裂隙发育，灌浆时坡面易出现冒浆等现象，要求采用混凝土嵌缝、表面封闭等方法处理，并视情况待凝后再复灌。

（六）消能防冲设计

拦河闸坝闸址区河谷狭窄，泄洪时洪水流量和流速均较大，上下游水位差较小。下游河床为砂卵石覆盖层，抗冲流速较小，抗冲刷能力弱。工程具有洪水流量大、流速大、消能率低、河床抗冲能力弱、岸坡为岩体抗冲能力强的特点。

根据水工水力学模型试验成果，工程采用护坦后铺设大块石海漫作为消能防冲方案。护坦长60m，厚3m，上、下游底部设齿槽，以提高护坦抗冲稳定性。护坦下游接100m长的大块石海漫，护坦下游40m范围内铺厚5.0m、粒径大于1.5m的大块石；其余60m铺厚3.0m、粒径大于1.0m的大块石。

过堰水流平顺通过混凝土护坦段及大块石海漫段，在海漫末端形成冲坑后以底流形式与下游衔接，保证闸坝建筑物及下游护坦的防冲安全要求。

（七）抗冲磨设计

水工水力学模型试验结果表明，本工程泄洪闸闸室内最大流速为17.7m/s，洪水期水流携带卵石或块石等大粒径的推移质过闸，携带有推移质的水体在闸底翻滚，对混凝土表面将产生严重的冲刷和磨损。为避免混凝土表面因冲刷磨损而影响工程的耐久性和安全性，在闸室底板及闸墩距离底板5m高度范围内的过水表面、上游铺盖和下游护坦表面均采用了50cm厚C40硅粉混凝土。为提高混凝土的抗裂性能，在每方硅粉混凝土中掺加1.2kg的聚乙烯醇纤维。抗冲耐磨混凝土要求与底板常态混凝土连续浇筑，不能留施工缝。同时还需特别注意早期养护，本工程采用蓄水养护的方式进行抗冲耐磨混凝土早期的养护。

（中国水电顾问集团华东勘测设计研究院
史 彬 陆 欣）

宜兴抽水蓄能电站下水库大坝设计

（一）坝型与结构

宜兴抽水蓄能电站下水库挡水坝经坝型比较，黏土心墙堆石坝对地基的要求较低，对地基变形的适应性也更强，坝基开挖对右岸顺坡岩层稳定的影响较小，选定黏土心墙堆石坝为下水库大坝坝型。

该黏土心墙堆石坝，由于地形限制，坝轴线平面上呈折线型，左坝头折向上游；坝顶高程83.40m，防浪墙顶高程84.60m，坝顶宽度设计为8m，最大坝高为50.40m，坝顶长度485.79m，最大底宽182.94m。上游坝坡1∶2.0，不设马道。为了利用下进/出水口及库盆扩容开挖风化料筑坝，减少弃渣，下游坝坡放缓为1∶2.5，在下游坝坡中部设宽为2.0m的马道一条。上游坝面为混凝土预制块；下游坝面为草皮护坡。结构断面按部位和受力特点的不同分为黏土心墙防渗区、上下游坝壳堆石区以及两者之间的反滤、过渡料区，即自上游向下游依次为上游堆石区，上游过渡层区、反滤层区，黏土心墙防渗区，下游反滤层区、过渡层区，下游混合料堆石区。黏土心墙顶部宽3.0m，心墙上、下游边坡均为1∶0.2。坝基防渗帷幕深入相对隔水层（$q \leqslant 3Lu$）以下5m，并向左、右岸分别延伸344m和475m。

本电站是最早采用黏土心墙堆石坝坝型的抽水蓄能电站。

（二）关键措施

针对抽水蓄能电站库水位骤降骤落的特点，设计主要采取了加强排水，加强反滤和加强坝体与岸坡、基础连接等措施。

1. 加强排水

（1）为保证库水位骤降后上游堆石区的孔隙水迅速排出，在分区设计中将上游堆石区分设为堆石Ⅰ区和堆石Ⅱ区：正常发电消落水位58.00m高程以上为堆石Ⅰ区，58.00m高程以下为堆石Ⅱ区。上游堆石Ⅰ区是库水位骤降骤升区域，要求采用地下洞室开挖的新鲜或微风化料，渗透系数$\geqslant 2\times10^{-1}$cm/s，堆石Ⅱ区则可采用下进/出水口开挖的弱风化料，渗透系数≥1×10^{-1}cm/s。

（2）在黏土心墙下游过渡区与下游堆石区之间原会坞水库的槽挖部分，设置长181m、高5.0m、上下底平均10.0m宽的纵向排水通道。在河槽部位设置有两条横向排水通道，穿越原会坞水库挡水坝，断面与纵向排水通道相同。排水区要求采用地下洞室开挖的茅山组岩屑砂岩料，即堆石Ⅰ区料。

（3）在坝后布置长度约500m的双层D200软式透水管，接场区D200软式透水总管，汇水至集水井。在坡脚布置净断面为500mm×400mm的浆砌块石排水沟，并通过排水暗涵将其与集水井相接。

2. 加强反滤

（1）由于库水位骤降骤升，向上游排泄的渗透比降相对较大，心墙土料孔隙含水也相对较多，上游反滤是关键部位。因此，本工程心墙反滤层厚度设计上游为1.5m，下游为1m。后经设计修改，上游反滤层厚度从高程70m开始由1500mm逐步收缩，至高程73m厚度为1200mm。同样，将下游反滤层逐步收缩，至高程73m厚度为700mm。由于水头较低，经计算一层反滤即能满足要求。反滤层设计指标见表1。

表1　　反滤层设计指标

项目	设计及质量控制指标					
	干密度（g/cm³）	相对密度	渗透系数（cm/s）	最大粒径（mm）	不均匀系数	小于0.075mm颗粒含量（%）
	≥1.78	≥0.7	（1～30）$\times10^{-3}$	4	平均≤8 最大<15	≤5

（2）为了检测反滤料技术指标，验证设计计算的正确性，委托南京水利科学研究院进行了渗透变形试验。试验的主要内容包括渗透系数、临界坡降、破坏坡降、破坏形式；试验共做一个试样，反滤层厚度25cm；主要试验结果见表2。

表2　　反滤料渗透变形试验成果表

名称	渗透系数（cm/s）	临界坡降 J_{cr}	破坏坡降 J_c	破坏形式
反滤料	2.27×10^{-3}	1.04	1.12	流土破坏

渗透变形试验的结果表明：①试验反滤层厚度25cm，临界坡降$J_{cr}=1.04$，而心墙上游反滤层实际厚度达1.5m，不会造成流土破坏；②渗透系数2.27×10^{-3}cm/s，符合设计指标值（1～30）$\times10^{-3}$要求，能满足大坝水位升降的要求；③无黏性土允许渗透比降，当不均匀系数大于5时一般为0.5～0.8，而本工程反滤料试验临界坡降$J_{cr}=1.04$，大于0.5～0.8，因此本工程反滤料抗渗透变形能力比较强。

3. 加强心墙与基础、边坡及建筑物的连接

（1）为了使大坝心墙与基岩保持良好接触，防止接触面渗流，在黏土心墙与基础岩体接触面设置混凝土垫层。砂岩基础上的混凝土垫层厚度为1m，花岗斑岩岩脉基础上的混凝土垫层厚度为3m。混凝土垫层上填筑黏土时，先洒水湿润，并边涂刷3～5mm厚的浓黏土浆，边铺黏土、边压实，严禁泥浆干涸后铺料压实。混凝土垫层上部50cm范围内，用纯黏土薄层填筑，干密度调整为≥1.56g/cm³，含水率控制在大于最优含水率的1%～3%，并严禁振动碾压，以防止防渗土料与混凝土垫层脱开。对于心墙防渗体的砂岩基础，要求岸坡应大致平顺，不应成台阶状、反坡或突然变坡。岸坡上缓下陡时，变坡角应小于20°。

（2）坝基廊道为钢筋混凝土结构，在穿越黏土心墙防渗体时，为防止渗透水流沿接触面的渗透破坏，一般需要设计截水墙延长渗径。根据工程资料，黏土沿混凝土接触面的安全渗透坡降为2.5～5.0，取允许渗透坡降$J_0=3.0$，按最大水头$H=40$m计算，本工程已经满足沿接触面的渗径要求，可以不设截水墙。但考虑混凝土接触面施工质量难以保证及考虑一定的安全裕度，在廊道顶部设置一道梯形断面混凝土截水墙。在廊道混凝土截水墙的周边填筑了高塑性黏土，并在齿墙顶部1m范围内铺设高塑性黏土（液限大于42%）。在心墙下游6m范围内，用50cm厚的反滤料和50cm厚的过渡料，把泄水建筑物混凝土廊道包围起来，以加强反滤，防止心墙细料被渗水带走，从而在泄水建筑物周边形成渗流通道。

（三）多功能的泄水建筑物

根据江苏宜兴抽水蓄能电站下水库的地形和地质情况，设计在黏土心墙堆石坝右坝肩布置了泄水建筑物。该泄水建筑物由进水口、电动蝶阀、坝基廊道、泄水钢管、管理房、电动锥形阀及阀门室、消力池和尾水渠组成，全长390m；布置在靠右坝肩的坝基下廊道内，进口采用竖井式，廊道底部置于坝基弱风化岩体开挖的沟槽中，廊道上部置于坝体内。

下水库泄水建筑物具有泄洪、放空、补水、施工导流四大功能，即：①电站遭遇洪水时宣泄多余水量；②下水库检修时放空水库；③电站初期蓄水及运行期补水时由补水工程二级泵站通过泄水钢管向下水库输水；④大坝施工期间利用围堰和坝体挡水，泄水建筑物泄流。

（四）结语

宜兴抽水蓄能电站下库大坝2005年6月竣工后4年多的监测数据表明，大坝心墙和堆石体的累计最大沉降均小于坝高的0.5%，而且沉降已经趋于稳定。坝体实测最大水平位移30.1mm，远小于计算值。运行期库水位每天的骤降骤升变化对心墙水平位

移影响很小。渗压监测成果表明大坝的浸润线正常，下水库渗漏量仅 2～3L/s，小于总库容的 1/5000。

（上海勘测设计研究院 傅方明）

江边水电站闸坝工程设计

（一）工程概况

江边水电站位于四川省甘孜藏族自治州东南部九龙县，为九龙河干流梯级电站最末一级，发电为主。电站为低闸高水头引水式，水库正常蓄水位 1797m，相应库容 133.0 万 m^3，死水位 1789m，日调节库容 90.6 万 m^3；额定水头 272m，安装 3 台单机容量 110MW 的水轮发电机组，总装机容量 330MW，多年平均发电量 16.20 亿 kW·h，保证出力 62.44MW，装机年利用小时 4909h，是九龙河上装机规模最大、效益最好的一座水电站。

该水电站为二等工程，引水系统和发电厂房为 2 级建筑物；挡水、泄水等主要建筑物按 3 级建筑物设计。拦河闸坝设计洪水重现期为 100 年，校核洪水重现期为 1000 年；消能防冲建筑物按 30 年一遇洪水设计；厂房设计洪水重现期为 100 年，校核洪水重现期为 500 年。主要建筑物按Ⅶ度设防。

（二）地质条件

闸址区河谷为不对称的 U 形，两岸山体雄厚，谷坡陡峭，谷底地形宽缓；出露地层主要为二叠系下统甲黄沟群（P_{1jh}）和第四系冲洪积、冲湖积、崩坡积地层，二叠系下统甲黄沟群（P_{1jh}）以黑云母石英片岩为主，弱～微风化黑云母石英片岩单轴饱和抗压强度大于 60MPa，属坚硬岩；岩层产状为 N40°～60° WNE∠50°～60°；断裂构造稀疏，以小断层和大裂隙为主，无区域性断层或较大规模的断层分布。

勘探揭示河流右侧至堆积台地前缘一带分布有埋藏古河槽，槽底高程 1684m 左右，第四系覆盖层最厚达 109.2m。闸基第四系覆盖层深厚，是影响建闸坝的主要地质条件。按岩性和埋藏条件分为 5 大层：第①层为崩坡积（Q_4^{col+dl}）碎石土，厚度 2.9～18.6m，结构松散，局部架空，承载力低，不能作为闸坝基础；第②层为冲洪（Q_4^{al+pl}）漂（块）卵（碎）石层，总厚度 7.5～40.7m，漂（块）卵（碎）石，主要由卵（碎）石组成，漂（块）石散布其中，上部局部架空，下部较密实，地层较均一，承载力为 600～700kPa，变形模量为 50～55MPa，可作为闸坝基础持力层。在闸址处分布有中细砂、含砾粉土及泥质粉砂透镜体夹层，其中中细砂夹层分布规模最大，埋深 1.2～32m，厚 0.4～10m，存在液化的可能，不宜作为闸基持力层；第③层为冲湖积（Q_4^{al+l}）砂质粉土，夹有粉质黏土及粉砂透镜体，厚度一般为 10.5～66.3m，最大厚度达 71.65m，分布于第②层以下，呈密实状，平均渗透系数为 1.78×10^{-5} cm/s，属微透水性，与坝基两岸弱风化微透水岩体直接相连，是较好的天然铺盖，可利用其作为坝基防渗依托；第④层为冲洪积（Q_4^{al+pl}）卵（碎）砂砾，杂色，泥质弱胶结，密实，仅分布于古河槽底部；第⑤层为冲洪积（Q_4^{al+pl}）卵（碎）石，为古河道两岸阶地堆积物，颗粒岩性以黑云母石英片岩为主，泥质弱胶结，密实。

（三）工程枢纽总体布置

江边水电站为一低闸、长隧洞、高水头引水式电站。枢纽主要由首部枢纽、引水系统、发电系统三大部分组成。

首部枢纽拦河闸坝位于九龙河干流和支流踏卡河汇合处下游约 800m 位置，采用正向泄洪排砂、侧向引水的方式布置。拦河闸坝由二孔泄洪闸和一孔冲沙闸及左右岸混凝土挡水重力坝段、右岸黏土心墙坝段组成，其中泄洪闸和冲沙闸位于主河床处，冲沙闸位于左侧进水口附近。

引水系统进水口布置在左岸坝上游侧，靠近冲沙闸，侧向取水，采用岸塔式结构，由拦污栅段和闸室段组成，进水口轴线与坝轴线交角为 15°。在进水口与坝顶设有交通桥。闸坝左右两侧均设有上坝道路，左岸上坝道路与原 S215 省道连接，右岸上坝道路与改建后的 S215 省道连接。

引水系统沿九龙河左岸直至雅砻江锦屏大河湾拐弯处，采用一洞三机布置方式，洞线长度 8.57km。受地形的限制，引水隧洞经三个平面转弯后接至阻抗式调压室。引水隧洞位于新鲜的黑云母石英片岩和黑云母花岗岩中，隧洞底坡 0.3%，埋深为 70～1677m，采用相同的马蹄形开挖断面，开挖洞径 8.4m，底宽 7.0m，采用喷锚衬砌和钢筋混凝土衬砌两种衬砌型式。在调压室后设有高压管道，采用钢筋混凝土衬砌，内径为 5.5m，总长 413m。高压管道由上平段、斜管段和下平段组成，斜管段与水平面夹角为 55°。高压管道后设有“卜”字形岔管，岔管后接压力钢管，内径 3.0m，采用斜进厂方式，钢管轴线与机组纵轴线夹角为 55°。

地下厂房位于九龙河汇入处下游约 5km 的雅砻江左岸 S215 省道里侧。主要洞室有主副厂房洞、主变压器洞、母线洞、进厂交通洞、通风及安全出口兼顶拱施工支洞、220kV 出线洞、排水廊道等。

尾水隧洞接于地下厂房尾水管出口，由尾水支洞与尾水主洞组成，断面形式均采用城门洞形，尾水闸门洞介于尾水支洞与尾水主洞之间，三条尾水支洞汇流于尾水闸门洞。

（四）拦河闸坝结构布置

拦河闸坝自左至右依次为左岸混凝土挡水坝段、冲沙闸段、泄洪闸段、右岸混凝土挡水坝段和右岸岸坡黏土心墙坝段。坝顶高程为1799.50m，最大坝高27.50m，坝顶总长179.10m，分为8个混凝土坝段和一个岸边黏土心墙坝段，混凝土坝段长为15.50～22.0m。

1. 左岸混凝土挡水坝段　左岸混凝土挡水坝段长42.20m，坝顶宽13m，最大坝高27.50m，分为2个坝段（原设计3个坝段，现场根据实际揭露地质条件，已将1号坝段取消）。2、3号坝段坐落在覆盖层上，上游坝坡在1789.0m高程以下坡比为1∶0.5，下游坝坡在1790.00m高程以下坡比1∶1。为满足坝底应力分布的均匀性要求，在坝体上、下游均设置了贴角：坝踵贴角宽度为3m，坝趾贴角宽度5.0m，贴角厚度均为5.0m。

2. 冲沙闸、泄洪闸段　拦河闸坝设有2孔泄洪闸和1孔冲沙闸。闸孔均为胸墙式孔口结构，泄洪闸孔口尺寸为8.0m×6.0m（宽×高），冲沙闸孔口尺寸为4.0m×4.5m（宽×高），闸室底板顶高程为1776.0m，底板厚为4.0m，闸高为27.50m。冲沙闸与相邻1号泄洪闸为一个闸室段，闸段宽为22.0m，底板长为36.0m。闸室左边墩厚为3.0m，中墩厚度为4.0m。2号泄洪闸为独立闸室段，宽为14.0m，底板长为36.0m，边墩厚3.0m。泄洪闸及冲沙闸在胸墙孔口下游设有弧形工作闸门，采用液压启闭机操作。在胸墙前设一道平板检修闸门，采用门机启闭。

3. 右岸挡水坝段　坝顶长100.90m，由混凝土坝和黏土心墙坝组成。其中混凝土坝段长50.55m，分3个混凝土坝段（6～8号），坝顶宽12m，最大坝高28.50m。断面型式与左岸相同。在6号坝段，设有生态流量泄放孔和溢流管，以保证下游生态用水和控制上游最高运行水位。黏土心墙坝段坝顶长50.47m，最大坝高24.50m，坝顶高程为1799.50m，坝顶宽35m，兼作回车场。心墙顶高程为1798.0m，宽为3.0m。坝壳回填料采用石渣回填，上游坝坡为1∶1.5，下游坝坡为1∶1.8。上、下游均采用干砌石护坡，厚度为30cm，在干砌石下面铺设计20cm厚的卵砾石垫层和一道无纺布。

（五）消能防冲设计

冲沙闸及泄洪闸消能建筑物采用30年一遇洪水设计，并经过模型试验确定。闸室后设混凝土护坦，长55m，宽32.8m，底板顶高程为1774.0m。首端设1∶5坡度与闸室底板顺接。在护坦上设有混凝土隔水墙，两侧采用直立混凝土挡墙，右侧混凝土挡墙上设有生态流量泄放孔出口和溢流管出口。在护坦末端齿墙底部设有混凝土防冲墙，深10.0m，厚0.80m。护坦下游设有大块石海漫，长60m，与护坦同宽，海漫上游30m段厚2.5m，下游30m段厚1.0m。护坦直立边墙与下游护坡采用30m长的混凝土扭曲墙连接。下游护坡采用混凝土结构，厚度为0.50m，坡度为1∶1.5。根据地形条件和工程需要，左岸护坡长30m，右岸护坡长130m。

（六）基础防渗与加固处理

江边水电站基础覆盖层防渗设计采用垂直混凝土防渗墙与水平混凝土铺盖联合防渗。防渗墙厚度为0.8m，考虑施工要求，轴线为折线布置，在泄洪闸与冲沙闸前设在铺盖下面，然后折向两侧挡水坝进入坝基后平行于坝轴线布置。

防渗墙横贯河床及岸坡覆盖层，两端与坝肩基岩相连并嵌入基岩1.0m，并在左岸基岩设灌浆帷幕，形成左右封闭结构；在防渗墙顶部与坝体和混凝土铺盖间，设置一道铜片止水和一道橡胶止水，在缝间充填沥青玛蹄脂，底部深入相对隔水层砂质粉土层5m，形成垂直封闭。

拦河闸坝基础除2号坝段左侧5m宽位于基岩上，其余建于覆盖层上。为了满足地基承载力的要求，对基础采用固结灌浆进行处理。灌浆孔距、排距均为2.5m，孔深为建基面以下10m。

（七）结语

江边水电站最大的特点就是建在100m以上深度的覆盖层上，坝基沉降成为设计控制的重点，基础处理措施选择是否合适，直接关系到工程安全和工程造价。由于江边水电站还未投入蓄水运行，但通过对坝体施工期坝体变形的观测，沉降变形量远小于设计计算变形量。

（中国水电顾问集团华东勘测设计研究院
丁玉财　史　彬　黄　维　陆　欣）

向家坝水电站高水头大单宽流量底流消能技术研究

（一）概况

向家坝水电站装机容量6400MW，最大坝高162m。校核洪水（$P=0.02\%$）入库流量49 800m^3/s，上下游水位差约85m，最大下泄总功率约40 000MW，消力池内最大单宽流量225$m^3/(s\cdot m)$，表孔、中孔理论入池流速达40m/s左右。坝址多年平均悬移质输沙量为2.47亿t，多年平均含沙量为1.72kg/m^3。

向家坝泄洪消能具有高水头、大单宽流量、多泥沙的特点。电站下游紧临水富县城和大型企业云南天然气化工厂，消能方式只能采用底流消能，以尽可能减轻泄洪雾化对环境带来的影响。可行性研究报告推荐采用高低坎底流消能作为向家坝泄洪消能的选定方案。

（二）招标阶段成果

招标阶段延续以水力学条件为主要考虑因素，对高低坎方案的跌坎型式进行了进一步的优化研究，在保持泄洪消能总体布局不变的前提下，对中、表孔出口跌坎高程等参数进行调整，将可行性研究阶段要求的必须先开中孔优化为中孔、表孔均可单独开启。

优化后推荐体形为：中孔出口坎顶高程253.00m，水平出口；表孔出口坎顶高程261.00m，水平出口，出口设20m长的线性收缩段，两侧对称收缩各1m。

（三）深化研究阶段成果

深化研究是在消力池池内及上下游的水力学指标满足泄洪消能总体要求的前提下，对池内中导墙墙顶高程、跌坎下局部水流流态、跌坎上坝面中隔墙顶高程、中表孔泄槽的掺气减蚀、水弹性模型试验、减压试验及坝面中隔墙和消力池导墙上的脉动压力等进行进一步的深化研究。现将主要成果介绍如下。

1. 中表孔泄槽的掺气减蚀　中表孔泄槽流速均较高，需要设掺气设施保护泄槽过流面。中孔为短有压段接明流泄槽型式，最大运行水头约83m，在中孔弧门下游0＋030.00m桩号设突跌掺气，跌坎高度1.5m，两侧通气孔直径1.60m，掺气跌坎下游坝面采用直线斜坡，并与下游反弧段相切。表孔采用孔口尺寸为8m×26m，沿程流速及水深均较大，在泄槽底板溢流面直线段高程329.81m设掺气槽，坎高1.00m，两侧边墙加设贴角，贴角水平方向坡度1∶25，桩号0＋044.05m处贴角出口厚度0.2m，两侧边墙通气孔直径1.90m。中表孔掺气试验成果表明：跌坎后均能形成稳定空腔，空腔内无回水，掺气效果良好；表孔贴角出口断面后形成较为稳定的侧空腔，并与底部空腔完全连通；水舌底部空腔负压均不超过－5kPa；中孔通气孔最大风速41m/s，表孔通气孔最大风速30m/s，均小于规范允许值60m/s。中表孔掺气浓度沿程逐渐减小，在泄槽出口，底部最小掺气浓度约在1%左右。考虑到模型试验通气孔直径类比其他类似工程偏大，而通气孔最大风速较规范允许值还有较多富裕，掺气减蚀下阶段试验考虑适当减小通气孔直径来进行对比优化。

2. 大比尺模型试验　主要对招标设计采用的高低坎方案跌坎下游局部漩涡进行研究，大比尺模型试验比尺1∶36，模拟3个表孔和2个中孔。该试验的主要目的是研究高低坎消力池跌坎下游立轴漩涡和横轴漩涡的特性，判断该漩涡对消力池底板和边墙的影响。试验成果表明：大比尺模型的水流流态与前阶段单池模型大体一致，消力池底板压强和临底流速也与单池模型基本相当；跌坎立面和消力池底板压强均为正压，未测到负压。消力池底板压强平顺，没有体现立轴漩涡对底板压强的影响；表孔处跌坎立面有立轴漩涡间歇临底，但强度较低，尺度较小，漩涡呈游离和间歇性；在底板与表孔跌坎形成的三角形区域，间歇性生成横轴漩涡，位置游移；立轴漩涡与横轴漩涡相互干扰，对消力池底板尚不致造成威胁。

3. 高低坎数值模拟计算　数值模拟计算主要配合大比尺模型试验，重点研究消力池内立轴漩涡和横轴漩涡的产生机理、漩涡强度及其分布，判断漩涡对消力池底板和边墙的影响。研究结果表明：泄洪时泄槽及消力池各部位的壁面压力均为正压。消力池底板压力变化平缓，没有明显的冲击点。消力池前部形成形状各异、大小不同的游离性立轴漩涡和横轴漩涡，漩涡强度均很小，漩涡中心具有200kPa以上的正压，漩涡结构对消力池底板和边墙的影响均较小，底板不会发生空化空蚀破坏。

4. 泄洪中孔及跌坎出口段减压模型试验　高低坎底流消能各股水流淹没射流会在消力池跌坎附近形成游离性的立轴漩涡和横轴漩涡，可能会对附近固壁产生空化空蚀破坏。故选取1个边表孔、1个中孔和半个中表孔进行减压箱试验，试验模型比尺1∶45，重点研究中孔及跌坎出口段的空化空蚀问题。试验成果表明：中孔进口四周及检修门槽区均无空化发生，中孔泄槽掺气坎下游发生空蚀的可能性不大；跌坎上坝面隔墙处中、表孔侧壁，跌坎垂直面及其附近消力池底板发生空蚀破坏的可能性不大；边表孔出口消力池边导墙水流剪切区存在发展阶段空化，且空化泡崩溃触及边壁，水下噪声谱级差最大值约为15dB，发生空蚀破坏的风险较大，需采取一定的表面抗蚀措施；表孔检修门门槽区存在明显空化，水下噪声谱级差最大值约为12dB，应采取表面抗蚀措施。鉴于消力池边导墙发生空蚀破坏的风险较大，按现有体形又无调整的余地，除在混凝土配合比方面进一步加强导墙的抗冲磨性能并在表面喷涂抗冲磨涂料外，下阶段进行闸门调度试验时，需考虑尽量限制边表孔的使用，以降低边导墙发生空蚀破坏的概率。

5. 水弹性模型试验　坝面隔墙、消力池底板与导墙的水弹性模型试验主要研究高速水流对坝面隔墙、消力池导墙和底板的流固相互作用，进而评价其稳定和应力特性。水弹性试验模型比尺1∶80，选取左消力池整池作为研究对象，为保证流态的相似性，左消力池左导墙以左坝后电站尾水渠模拟宽度20m，中导墙以右模拟一个表孔和一个中孔。现该试验正在进行之中。

6. 抗冲磨材料研究　根据各部位流速的不同，消力池导墙上游段迎水面采用$C_{90}55$抗冲磨混凝土，消力池底板上游段表面采用 $C_{90}50$ 抗冲磨混凝土，其余部位迎水面采用 $C_{90}40$ 抗冲磨混凝土，消力池及导墙内部混凝土采用 $C_{90}30$ 混凝土。抗冲磨混凝土 $C_{90}55$、$C_{90}50$ 两种混凝土采用“硅粉＋粉煤灰”的技术路线，其余部位采用粉煤灰混凝土，粉煤灰最大掺量按 30%～35%控制，硅粉掺量采用 5%左右。在一些冲磨强度大的部位，还可考虑使用聚脲等在抗冲磨混凝土表面增加一层防护涂层，以进一步提高其抗冲磨性能。

（中国水电顾问集团中南勘测设计研究院 张永涛）

混凝土面板堆石坝潜没式混凝土高趾墙设计

在混凝土面板堆石坝设计时，为弥补地形、地质条件的缺陷，协调坝肩相邻水工建筑物的布置衔接，通常采用混凝土高趾墙结构方式。混凝土高趾墙是坝体趾板结构体的一部分，其中大部分墙体位于库水位以下的高趾墙称为潜没式高趾墙。

黄河公伯峡水电站混凝土面板堆石坝右坝肩采用潜没式高趾墙，墙体总长 84.99m，最大高度 50m，是目前国内已建工程中高度最大的高趾墙。新疆开都河察汗乌苏水电站右岸趾板线跨六坎沟，采用潜没式高趾墙，墙体总长 72.7m，最大高度 25.0m。由于大部分墙体位于水库正常蓄水位以下，受力情况复杂，同时又作为趾板，因此对稳定、应力、位移要求严格。

（一）潜没式高趾墙体形设计

潜没式高趾墙体形设计，是在坝体及趾板线布置基本确定的条件下进行的。高趾墙通常是大体积重力式结构体，根据其承担的功能，体形设计时需考虑以下因素：

（1）墙内侧（坝体侧）设计有周边缝和止水，墙顶部的坡度应与大坝混凝土面板布置相协调，墙顶宽度应与上、下游相邻趾板的宽度相协调。同时墙体坡度不宜过陡，应满足坝体堆石填筑的要求。

（2）墙的外侧坡体形通常是与其他相邻水工建筑物或山体开挖边坡相衔接，根据高趾墙承担的功能，外侧坡的体形通常应由相邻水工建筑物的体形要求确定。

（3）高趾墙底面宽度和建基面高程，应结合工程地质条件和相应的工程处理措施来确定。

（4）高趾墙基础底面一般为斜坡式，墙体施工分缝位置宜保留一定宽度的开挖平台。

（5）高趾墙的断面尺寸设计要重点考虑墙内帷幕灌浆排水廊道和排水措施。

（6）高趾墙在施工期受大坝填筑施工荷载，在正常运行期主要受库水压力，需综合考虑工作状态受双向控制。

（二）潜没式高趾墙作用荷载

在公伯峡水电站、察汗乌苏水电站混凝土面板堆石坝右岸潜没式高趾墙设计中，参考国内工程经验，高趾墙设计荷载做如下考虑：

（1）高趾墙墙体自重。

（2）水压力。墙体承受两侧、顶部和上、下游方向的水压力作用，这是与其他型式高趾墙的主要区别。

（3）土压力。墙体于坝体侧有堆石体的侧向土压力，墙体外侧有填土时的侧向土压力，按规范规定，坝体堆石体按主动土压力计算。

（4）基础扬压力。潜没式高趾墙布置帷幕排水廊道，是坝体防渗帷幕的组成部分，墙体基础扬压力是一项重要荷载，计算时对扬压力图形需一些必要的假定。

（5）地震作用力。高趾墙是大坝的一个组成部分，应按规定进行抗震设计，可参照相关规范的规定进行。

（6）风浪压力、冰压力、泥沙压力忽略不计，主要考虑到这些荷载作用影响很小，是从简化计算出发考虑的。

（三）潜没式高趾墙结构设计

潜没式高趾墙结构设计的计算工况为：① 正常蓄水位情况；② 校核洪水位情况；③ 竣工情况（大坝施工完成，水库未蓄水）；④ 正常蓄水位＋地震情况。

1. 计算方法　潜没式高趾墙是一个三向受力的结构体，通常采用材料力学法和有限元法对高趾墙的稳定和应力应变进行计算分析。在公伯峡水电站、察汗乌苏水电站混凝土面板堆石坝潜没式高趾墙设计计算时，情况如下：

（1）平面单宽材料力学法计算。分别选择 4 个代表设计断面，进行了 4 种工况的计算。根据计算结果，对初拟的趾墙体形进行了修正调整，基本确定了高趾墙体形。通过计算成果发现，潜没式高趾墙的最大断面并不是最危险断面，而是最大断面控制基础应力，最小断面确定趾墙体的稳定。因此，在墙体断面体形设计时，不能只取最大断面计算，应根据墙体的长度和分块情况，选取几个断面计算，综合计算成果，基本确定墙体断面尺寸体形。

（2）三维整体材料力学法计算。平面单宽材料力学法计算时不能计入沿上下游方向作用的水压力，采用三维整体材料力学法计算可以解决这个问题。潜没式高趾墙墙体长度较大，需设置横向施工缝将墙体分成若干个块体，公伯峡水电站右岸潜没式高趾墙长84.99 m，分为4个块体，察汗乌苏水电站右岸潜没式高趾墙墙体长72.68 m，分为4个块体。对潜没式高趾墙的三维计算是采用单个块体三维计算还是采用整个墙体的三维计算，是一个值得研究的问题。经研究分析，提出了将潜没式高趾墙的横缝作为临时施工缝，在缝面布置键槽并进行接缝灌浆，将高趾墙体作为一个整体的设计方案。这种方案充分利用墙体自重和底面积，设计的体形较经济合理。公伯峡、察汗乌苏水电站潜没式高趾墙的设计采用三维整体计算方案。两电站水库蓄水运行后，潜没式高趾墙工作性态正常，证明设计方案是可行的。三维整体设计方案较平面单宽法设计确定的体形工程量可减少10%左右，相对比较经济。

(3) 有限元法计算。分为平面有限元和三维整体有限元法进行。平面有限元法取几个代表性墙体断面进行。三维整体有限元法计算是结合坝体三维仿真模拟计算同时进行的，可以较好地解决潜没式高趾墙的边界条件模拟问题，只是在计算网络划分时应考虑高趾墙的体形和成果整理的需要。计算研究主要针对施工期、蓄水运行期、地震工况情况下高趾墙体的应力、变形特征，评价高趾墙的工作性态和安全性。

2. 成果分析　从计算的成果分析，可得出以下结论：

(1) 平面有限元法计算各块体的抗滑稳定安全度差异较大，其规律性和采用平面单宽材料力学法的计算成果总体是一致的，沿建基面的抗滑稳定是由某个块体控制的。高趾墙基础、块体的基础压应力值均不大，且基本无拉应力区，块体位移变形以沉降变形为主，且数值不大，各项指标满足要求。

(2) 在三维整体情况下，由于潜没式高趾墙的体形特征和受力条件复杂性，高趾墙体发生有受扭力作用特征，反映了潜没式高趾墙的应力、变形与一般重力坝不同的特性。高趾墙的抗滑稳定、应力、变形工作性态，均能满足要求，墙体内出现拉应力区域，但范围和拉应力值均不大，应力条件不成为控制因素。墙体的位移量值均不大，以垂直变位为主，不会对混凝土面板周边缝止水产生不良影响。地震工况情况，墙体应力、变形量值有变化，但没有成为高趾墙设计的控制工况。

(3) 通过对有限元法和材料力学法计算成果的对比分析，认为高趾墙结构设计采用材料力学法计算结果是可行的。故对潜没式高趾墙结构设计可先采用材料力学法进行，对于大于100m坝高的1、2级混凝土面板堆石坝的高趾墙设计应进行有限元计算复核，必要时调整修改设计方案的方法是合适的。

（四）几个问题的讨论

1. 潜没式高趾墙地基条件问题　对高趾墙的地基一定要求坐落在微、弱风化岩体，可能因开挖深度较大、增加较多的工程量而不经济。遇到这种情况，采用工程处理的办法来满足墙体对基础的要求，国内工程经验证明是可行和经济的方法。

2. 潜没式高趾墙抗滑稳定计算　对沿建基面的抗滑稳定计算，通常是参考混凝土重力坝规范的相关公式来进行的。现行《混凝土重力坝设计规范》(SL 319—2005) 规定采用抗剪、抗剪断公式计算，《混凝土重力坝设计规范》(DL 5108—1999) 规定采用极限状态法。这应该都是可行的，但两个规范计算方法中对混凝土与基岩的抗剪参数 f'、C' 取值规定是有差别的。有关文献曾提出了这两个规范规定不统一的问题。有些工程在设计时，两种方法都进行计算，且要求都能满足要求。但对 f'、C' 取相同的值，这也是不恰当的。笔者认为，采用抗剪断公式计算高趾墙沿建基面的抗滑稳定的方法是可以满足设计要求的，但应注意对建基面抗剪断参数取值的正确性。

3. 潜没式高趾墙沿建基面抗滑稳定安全度问题　混凝土重力坝设计规范中规定计算坝体抗滑稳定时，基本组合工况的抗剪断安全系数 $k'\geqslant 3.0$。对潜没式高趾墙在采用抗剪断公式计算时，安全系数采用多少，国内工程一般参考采用混凝土重力坝设计规范的规定，但对这个问题讨论不多。国外文献曾有报道，提出潜没式高趾墙的抗滑稳定安全系数 k' 值应达到8～10，甚至更高。为什么有这么高的安全系数，可能主要因高趾墙的稳定性直接关系到混凝土面板周边缝的变形量，保证止水不被破坏，任何情况下不因高趾墙体的稳定而影响大坝的安全运行，也可能是因对高趾墙这种结构体受力情况下的工作状态认识不深等原因，故采取保守的设计应是可以理解的。近几年来，由于计算分析手段的快速发展、工程实践经验的积累，对潜没式高趾墙这种结构体认识的深入，通过多种计算手段可较全面正确地了解高趾墙体的工作性态，抗滑稳定安全系数不需采用较高的值。但沿建基面抗滑稳定安全系数是设计的一个重要指标，采用多少合适，有待在工程实践进行总结和研究。

4. 潜没式高趾墙是否允许产生拉应力问题　对高趾墙体是否允许产生拉应力在规范中没有明确规定，有文献曾提出，高趾墙在任何情况下不允许出现拉应力。高趾墙趾板是面板堆石坝的重要组成部分，若产生拉应力值超过混凝土允许抗拉强度，致使混凝土产生裂缝、发生渗漏等破坏，处理和补救将是十分困难的。因此，高趾墙块体不允许产生拉应力的要求应该是合理的。

（中国水电顾问集团西北勘测设计研究院　安盛勋）

张河湾抽水蓄能电站上水库沥青混凝土防渗设计

（一）工程概况

张河湾抽水蓄能电站位于河北省石家庄市井陉县测鱼镇附近的甘陶河上，电站装机容量1000MW。电站建成后，并入河北省南部电网，担任调峰、填谷、调频、调相及事故备用等任务。

电站枢纽主要由上水库、水道系统、地下厂房系统和地面出线场、下水库拦河坝及拦排沙工程等组成。工程等别为一等，主要建筑物级别为1级。地震设防烈度Ⅶ度。

上水库位于甘淘河左岸的老爷庙山顶，通过开挖和填筑堆石坝围库而成。主要包括堆石坝、库盆沥青混凝土防渗面板、排水系统、库岸基础处理和电站进/出水口等。上水库正常蓄水位810.00m，死水位779.00m，总库容为770万m^3，其中，调节库容为715万m^3，死库容为55万m^3。上水库采用沥青混凝土复式面板全库盆防渗，总防渗面积33.7万m^2，其中，库坡为20万m^2，库底为13.7万m^2。

（二）上水库地质条件

上水库所在的老爷庙山顶为古夷平面，呈北东—南西向不规则的条形展布，台坪南北长约2km，东西宽250～700m。台坪的总体地势东北高，西南低，地面高程740～846m。

上水库地层由寒武系馒头组与长城系大红峪组组成，二者呈平行不整合接触。寒武系地层大多为薄层状砂质泥岩、砂泥岩夹泥灰岩，其性质软弱，强度较低，遇水可软化，失水易崩解。长城系大红峪组为石英砂岩和铁质砂岩，质地坚硬、性脆，强度高，陡倾角裂隙发育，透水性强。因层间错动寒武系馒头组与长城系大红峪组岩层中顺层发育有多层缓倾角软弱夹层，其矿物成分含有蒙脱石及绿泥石，亲水性较强，力学性质较差，对坝基抗滑稳定不利。其中延伸长远、连续性好、含泥量高、分布稳定的3条，编号分别为Rd3-1、Rd3-2、Rd3-3，在上水库西侧的西沟和西南沟陡壁上出露。

台坪上部岩体陡倾角裂隙发育，岩体完整性差，风化层厚度大，岩体渗透性强，渗透系数可达0.2～3m/d，地下水埋深约284m，上水库地基存在严重的水库渗漏问题。如果蓄水后一旦产生渗漏，水库将成为稳定的补给水源，使馒头组泥岩及基础软弱夹层受到水的浸泡，强度会明显降低，对坝基及边坡的抗滑稳定极为不利。综上所述，上水库必须做好全面防渗，尽可能控制和减少渗漏。

（三）库盆防渗方案

设计充分考虑了上水库地层存在软弱夹层的特殊地质情况，采用了防渗性能优异的沥青混凝土面板全库盆防渗方案，沥青混凝土面板则采用了更为安全可靠的复式断面形式。

通过大量的原材料和沥青混凝土配合比试验研究，收集国内外已建工程的成功经验，以安全可靠、经济合理为原则对沥青混凝土面板复式断面进行了创新优化，将防渗面板的防渗底层和整平层合并为一层，优化方案有效减少了投资、缩短了工期。

（四）沥青混凝土面板设计

上水库为开挖和填筑堆石坝围库而成，库内坡为1∶1.75，下游坝坡1∶1.5。坝料根据作用不同和料源情况分为三个区，分别为碎石垫层区、过渡区和主堆石区。

为给沥青混凝土面板提供一个平整、坚实、稳定的基础，起到坝体粒径过渡、减小基础不均匀变形、排水（包括渗漏水和天然地下水）、防冻胀等作用，并为沥青混凝土面板施工的摊铺机械行走提供工作面，沥青混凝土面板与坝体填筑体、库岸岩坡和库底基础之间设置了碎石垫层。其中库岸填筑坝体部分的垫层水平宽度2.0m，库岸基岩开挖部分的垫层厚度60cm，库底垫层厚度50cm，要求压实后的垫层变形模量不小于45MPa。

防渗面板结构型式优化后采用三层的复式结构，从上至下依次为防渗层、排水层和兼有收集渗水起到相对隔水作用的整平胶结层，为提高面板的抗老化能力，面板表面涂刷一层2mm厚的沥青玛蹄脂封闭层。

(1) 防渗层：为厚度10cm的密级配沥青混凝土，沥青含量不低于7.5%，压实后的密度不低于2.3g/cm^3，孔隙率不大于3%，渗透系数不大于10^{-8} cm/s，斜坡流淌值不大于2mm，冻断温度不高于－35℃，20℃的拉伸应变不低于0.8%，2℃的弯曲应变不低于2%，柔性（圆盘挠度试验）25℃时不低于10%，2℃时不低于2.5%。

(2) 排水层：库底为10cm、库坡为8cm的开级配沥青混凝土，沥青含量为3.5%，压实后的密度不低于1.9g/cm^3，孔隙率不小于16%，渗透系数不小于10^{-1}cm/s。

(3) 整平胶结层：为厚度8cm的密级配沥青混凝土，沥青含量不应低于5%，压实后的密度不低于2.2g/cm^3，孔隙率不大于5%，渗透系数不大于5×10^{-5}cm/s，斜坡流淌值不大于1.5mm。

(4) 封闭层：为2mm厚的沥青玛蹄脂封闭层，应在工程区当地温度条件下在1∶1.75的斜坡上保持稳定，应与防渗层紧密结合，不产生相对移动。

（五）排水系统

为将防渗面板后的渗漏水顺畅排走，避免面板因反向水压引起破坏，保证面板和上水库的安全运行，并便于监测渗水情况及检修维护，设置了完备的排水系统。由以下几部分组成：

1. 沥青混凝土防渗结构内设排水层　在沥青混凝土面板防渗层和整平胶结层之间设置了库底10cm、库坡8cm的沥青混凝土排水层。为便于监测和维修，在排水层中设置了隔水带，库坡间距为100m左右，库底60～75m，库底周边和中间排水廊道上部沿廊道中心线布置了宽度1m的隔水带。

2. 沥青混凝土面板下面设置碎石排水垫层　堆石坝段水平宽2m，库岸开挖岩坡段垂直厚度60cm，库底厚50cm。

3. 排水检查廊道　库盆内部沿库底周边、库底中间、进出水口周边设置了排水检查廊道（断面$b \times h = 1.5m \times 2m$），汇水经进/出水口底层排水检查廊道进入外排廊道，渗水由外排廊道排到库外。为了使渗水及时由排水垫层排入排水检查廊道，在排水廊道设置了ϕ100mm的排水管，排水管间距3m。

为了减少上水库西侧和西南侧坝基软弱夹层的饱和范围，提高该部位的深层抗滑稳定性，在库周排水廊道的下部沿软弱夹层Rd3-3布设了160m长的深层排水廊道，两层排水廊道之间设置了间距3m的排水孔。

（中国水电顾问集团北京勘测设计研究院　张向前）

响水涧抽水蓄能电站上水库设计

（一）概况

响水涧抽水蓄能电站位于安徽省芜湖市峨桥镇，装机容量1000MW，是一座日调节纯抽水蓄能电站。电站上水库由主坝、南副坝、北副坝和库周山岭围成，正常蓄水位222.00m，死水位190.00m，总库容1748万m^3，有效库容1282万m^3。主坝和南、北副坝均为钢筋混凝土面板堆石坝。上水库库盆及主、副坝坝址区基岩为燕山晚期侵入的中粗粒花岗岩。

（二）主、副坝坝体设计

受坝基地形条件所限，主坝建在向下游倾斜的基础面上，最大坝高87m（从趾板基础面计算），从下游坝趾算起坝高达163m。主坝坝顶高程225.00m，上游防浪墙顶高程226.20m，坝顶长度为520m，坝顶宽8.0m，上游面坝坡1∶1.4，下游面每隔25.0m高差设有4.0m宽马道，马道之间坝坡1∶1.25。

坝体堆石料全部采用库区开挖料，在垫层区和过渡层区下游为主堆石Ⅰ区和主堆石Ⅱ区。主堆石Ⅰ区、Ⅱ区分区线倾向下游，坡度1∶0.4。考虑到主坝下游基础面偏陡，为减少下游贴坡式坝体的沉降，主堆石Ⅱ区在高程135m以下设置了增模区。增模区与高程135m以上的主堆石区相比，铺层厚度由800mm减薄为600mm，碾压遍数由8遍增加为10遍，孔隙率控制标准为19%，相应干容重20.7kN/m^3。高程135m以上主堆石Ⅱ区在设计指标上与上游主堆石Ⅰ区没有差别，孔隙率控制标准为20%，相应干容重20.5kN/m^3。之所以分为两个区，是考虑到上水库主、副坝均取自于库内同一料场，施工过程中现场开挖出来的筑坝石料在质量上会有差异，设计要求将新鲜、微弱风化的石料填筑在增模区和上游主堆石Ⅰ区，而允许主堆石Ⅱ区上部含少量强风化石料上坝。

南副坝最大坝高65m，坝顶长339m，坝顶高程225.00m，上、下游坝坡设计同主坝。南副坝基础在上、下游坝脚位置虽然地形高差不大，但坝轴线附近的垭口较高，形成不对称马鞍形状，马鞍顶部与上游趾板开挖面高差约20m。考虑减少垭口处坝基排水槽的开挖量和坝体填筑量，坝基排水槽没有挖至趾板深槽高程。为防止上游坝体渗水在施工期对坝体结构产生反向渗压破坏，在趾板上部布置了六根管径150mm的排水钢管，排水钢管在上游铺盖填筑前予以封堵。封堵后反向渗压由上游铺盖区和盖重区的重量平衡。

北副坝最大坝高53.5m，坝顶长174m，坝顶高程225.00m，上、下游坝坡设计同主坝。北副坝基础在上下游方向亦呈马鞍形状，与南副坝一样存在反向渗压的问题。由于北副坝垭口底部有F_1断层穿过，结合基础处理，采用混凝土座垫置换断层破碎带的方式，趾板置于座垫之上。为保证帷幕灌浆效果，创造后期补充灌浆的条件，谷底座垫内设灌浆兼排水廊道，左岸趾板下设交通廊道。上游反向渗水通过排水管进入廊道，再通过集水井与排水泵集中抽排。

在主坝坝基设置了泄水廊道，用于施工期导流排水和运行期降低水位（或放空水库）。廊道平面上沿主坝沟底布置，城门洞形，断面为2.6m×3.5m（宽×高），廊道内架设一根内径80cm的泄水钢管，钢管头部设闸阀室，钢管尾部设锥阀室。考虑到钢管出口紧邻下游坝脚，下泄水流对坝脚会有冲刷，因此在廊道末端设置消力池及尾水渠，将水流送离坝脚以外。

（三）库区防渗

上水库除南、北侧各有一垭口需建副坝挡水外，库周山岭浑厚。库盆除F_1断层外，无其他较大断层通过。F_1断层产状N0°～15°W，SW∠80°～85°，断层破碎带由北向南逐渐变窄。除主坝～北副坝之间的山脊相对隔水层顶板线及地下水位低于正常蓄水位222.00m之外，库周其余地段地下水位均在正常蓄水位以上。因此，库周的防渗设计，只需要做好主、副坝坝址区以及主坝～北副坝之间的马鞍形山脊的防渗处理，水库不存在向邻谷渗漏问题，库盆不需要采取专门防渗措施。

上水库防渗主要采取水泥帷幕灌浆的型式。对F_1断层破碎带穿过的南、北副坝坝址局部区域，北副坝趾板基础下挖除断层破碎及影响带后浇筑混凝土座垫，南副坝趾板基础下对出露的F_1断层破碎带表层置换混凝土塞，经处理后再配合进行帷幕灌浆。F_1断层贯穿的库盆区域，由于表层覆盖类似天然铺盖的密实壤土层，故不再做防渗处理。

（上海勘测设计研究院　成卫忠）

景洪水电站左岸坝肩锚拉板设计及防渗设计

（一）左岸坝肩地质条件

景洪水电站左岸坝肩边坡主要为闪长岩。岩体风化较深，高程595m以上总体为全风化，散体结构；高程595～579.7m为强风化，碎裂结构；高程579.7m以下为弱风化，镶嵌结构。同时Ⅱ级结构面G_{23}与坝轴线近乎平行且通过坝肩，G_{23}破碎带物质主要为片状岩、碎裂岩、构造透镜体、糜棱岩，挤压紧密、胶结差。

（二）左岸坝肩锚拉板设计

景洪水电站河谷较宽阔，施工缆机跨度较大。由于左岸坝肩边坡基岩风化较深，受Ⅱ级结构面G_{23}的影响严重，为保证缆机的跨度不超过1000m，且为确保上坝公路形成，故在上坝公路以上采用较缓的边坡开挖，上坝公路以下采用1∶0.1的边坡开挖并配合锚拉板等“弱开挖、强支护”的手段，以尽量减少坝肩开挖，达到减短非溢流坝段的长度、节省工程量的目的。

1. 左岸坝肩边坡稳定分析

(1) 岩土物理力学参数见表1。

表1　景洪水电站边坡稳定计算岩土物理力学参数表

岩体	天然容重 (kN/m³)	饱和容重 (kN/m³)	抗剪断强度		承载力 (MPa)	中缓倾节理连通率 (%)
			ϕ' (°)	C' (kPa)		
全风化	18	18.5	23～25	25～40	0.2～0.3	
强风化	23	24	29	100～150	0.5～0.7	60
弱风化	25.7	26.2	39	400～500	3～4	40
G_{23}挤压带			17	30		

(2) 计算假定：①计算中仅考虑边坡沿剖面方向的顺层滑移或圆弧破坏；②岩体孔隙水压力按孔压系数0.13确定，不考虑动水压力和内部渗压；③仅考虑水平向地震作用，取50年超越概率10%的地震基本烈度（为Ⅶ度）相应的基岩地震水平峰值加速度为0.109g。

(3) 边坡平面稳定计算考虑了正常运行、地震、水位骤降三种工况，作用在滑体上的荷载有：①滑体自重；②地下静水压力；③地震惯性力；④锚固力。预应力锚索或抗滑支挡结构（抗滑桩）提供的阻滑力，需要时施加。

(4) 边坡按Ⅱ级设计。其平面抗滑稳定最小安全系数控制标准：正常运行工况为1.2；地震工况为1.05；水位骤降工况为1.1。

(5) 计算剖面见图1，计算成果见表2。根据计算结果，左岸坝肩边坡在高程609.00m、604.00m、599.00m、592.00m和586.00m布置5排1800kN级预应力锚索，长度分别为45m、40m、35m、25m和20m。锚索水平间距6m，水平下倾20°。

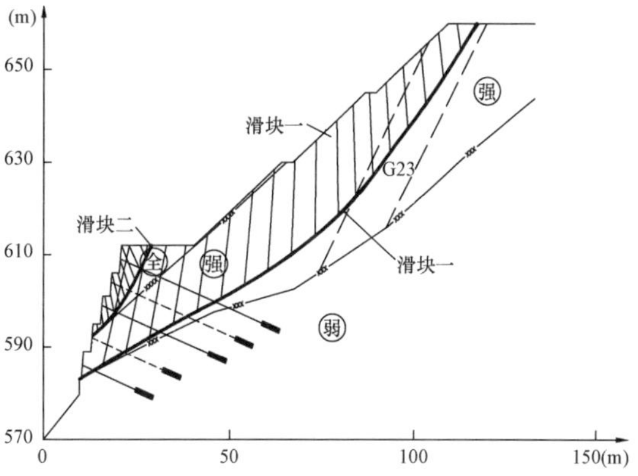

图1　计算剖面

表2　计算成果表

名称	滑面位置高程 (m)	设计工况 岩体孔隙水压系数取为0.13			需锚固力 (t/m)
		运行工况	水位骤降	地震工况	
滑面一	583～660	1.16	1.16	1.04	90
滑面二	590～612	0.76	0.76	0.66	70
安全系数控制标准		1.2	1.1	1.05	

2. 锚索结构设计　左岸坝肩所布置锚索的承载地基均为全风化岩体，承载力很低，仅为0.2～0.3MPa，需对锚索结构进行专门的设计。锚索结构设计主要包括钢绞线计算、内锚段长度计算、锚墩尺

寸拟定及承载力强度、刚度、承压、开裂和配筋计算。经计算，1800kN级全风化无黏结预应力锚索主要参数见表3。

表3　　　　锚索主要参数表

项目	钢绞线			锚墩顶宽(mm)	锚墩底宽(mm)	孔径(mm)	锚墩混凝土强度等级	内锚固段长度(m)
	规格	束	强度(MPa)					
技术参数	$7\phi5$ (d=15.24mm)	12	1860	400	2700	165	C40	10

3. 锚拉板结构设计　左岸坝肩边坡采用阶梯形开挖，开挖坡度近于垂直，且上部有全风化岩体出露。为满足左岸坝肩边坡稳定的要求，在开挖边坡上浇筑一块钢筋混凝土板，板上布置锚索，这样可对该部位全风化岩体达到很好的封闭效果。施工时，板与锚墩同时浇筑，共同承担锚索张拉荷载。锚拉板采用C25混凝土，厚度为50cm，每隔12～16m左右设一道伸缩缝，缝宽2cm，不设填缝材料。锚拉板根据锚索张拉荷载计算配筋，计算后配筋采用ϕ25@200和ϕ16@200纵横向布置，混凝土保护层5cm，钢筋不过缝。锚拉板上共设置91根1800kN级预应力锚索，水平间距6m，梅花形布置，锚索方向水平下倾20°。锚拉板典型剖面及纵向剖面见图2、图3。

（三）左岸坝肩防渗设计

1. 锚拉板与左岸非溢流坝段间防渗设计　主要措施为：在上游迎水面锚拉板混凝土与左岸非溢流坝施工缝间设永久止水，对锚拉板与非溢流坝接触面进行接触灌浆，对左岸非溢流坝基进行固结灌浆。此外，为顺利进行帷幕灌浆，设计中锚拉板布置的锚索避开了帷幕灌浆范围，确保帷幕灌浆施工顺利进行。

2. 左岸岸幕防渗布置　左岸612.000m高程以下岩体在坝肩部分有近20m长、最深达20m的全风化三角体。该三角形全风化岩体，由于岩体松散，无论采用帷幕灌浆的方式，还是采用深固结灌浆的方式，

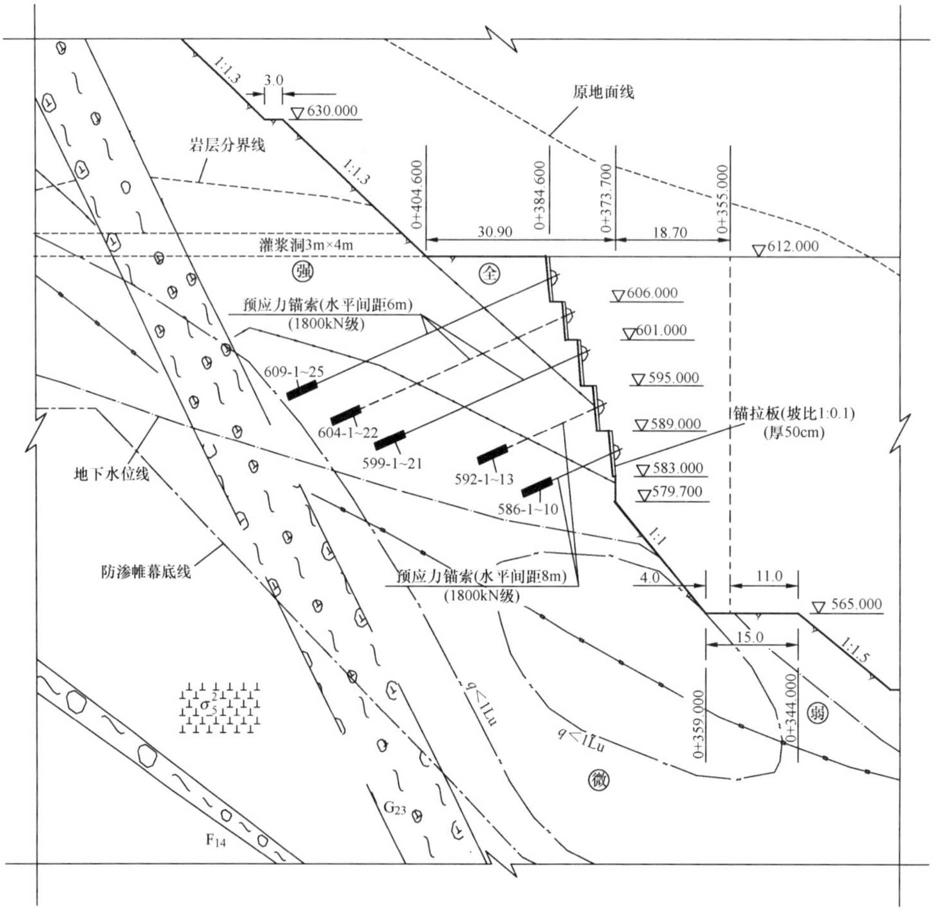

图2　锚拉板典型剖面

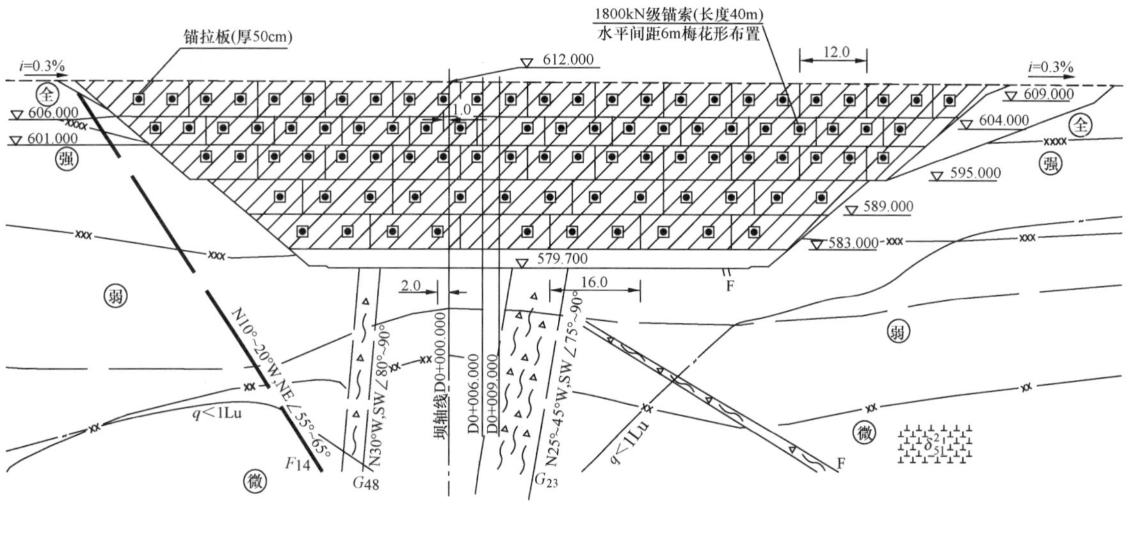

图 3 锚拉板纵向剖面

或者采用高压旋喷的方式进行防渗处理，均很难达到良好的灌浆效果，难以满足坝肩防渗要求。考虑工程蓄水后部分岩体长期处于水位变幅区，为保证工程的永久运行，最终确定在此全风化三角体部分采用防渗墙与帷幕灌浆相结合的方式进行防渗，而其余岸幕采用常规的帷幕灌浆的防渗方式。

3. 左岸岸幕防渗帷幕设计

(1) 景洪水电站防渗帷幕的防渗控制标准为3Lu。左岸岸幕的防渗底界为：伸入相对不透水层3Lu线以下3～5m或者正常蓄水位与地下水位线相交处，两者取大者来控制灌浆底界。左岸坝头部位的岸幕应伸入到地下水位线与正常蓄水位相交处，岸幕的长度为241.743m，最大灌浆深度为107m。

(2) 考虑到左岸岸幕帷幕灌浆深度较深，在左岸布置了两层帷幕灌浆洞。由于布置的两条灌浆洞位于同一坝横桩号，若只考虑一条竖向帷幕灌浆不能形成防渗封闭区域，所以又在下层灌浆洞侧墙内设置一条水平帷幕与竖向帷幕相衔接。这样，两条帷幕形成连续的封闭的区域，能达到良好的防渗效果。左岸坝肩防渗采用单排帷幕防渗，孔距为1.5m，分三序施工。

(3) 为了使帷幕灌浆线穿过更多的结构面，竖向防渗帷幕线倾向上游，原则上所有的帷幕灌浆孔倾角为6°。由于防渗墙的设置，为保证防渗帷幕的顺利施工，采取在防渗墙内预埋灌浆管而在防渗墙下部钻孔的方法成孔，并对该区域帷幕孔进行加密处理，孔距为0.75m，长短相间布置，长灌浆孔方向倾向上游3.5°～5°，短灌浆孔为铅直孔，且严格控制短灌浆孔底部离下层灌浆洞顶部衬砌1m。

4. 防渗墙设计

(1) 防渗墙布置在左岸上坝公路以及左岸1号灌浆洞进口段、左岸锚拉板后全风化和强风化上部，顶长26.5m，底界伸入强风化基岩2.5m，最大墙深20m，与锚拉板间设两道U形铜止水。

(2) 防渗墙最大承受的水压为17.4m，选取C_{28} 25W8F100混凝土，墙厚度取2m。

(3) 防渗墙槽孔采用人工跳槽开挖，分两序进行施工，每序开挖段长4.5m，槽孔底部开挖成阶梯状。各序槽孔施工缝间布置一道铜止水。槽孔采用钢筋混凝土固壁，厚度0.2m左右，在岩石条件较差的部位适当增加横向支撑或锚杆，确保开挖过程中侧向围岩的稳定。

(4) 在防渗墙底界竖向进行帷幕灌浆钻孔，钻孔直径150mm。在防渗墙后横纵向预埋MHY-200K塑料盲沟管，外包300g/m^{2}的土工布，间排距9m×6m，排水孔相互连通，并与防渗墙以下排水孔相连；在坝后边坡锚拉板上钻孔预埋排水管，孔径不小于60mm，预埋塑料盲沟管，外包300g/m^{2}的土工布，间排距6m×6m，长度8m，梅花形布置，水平上仰5°。

(四) 结语

景洪水电站左岸坝肩锚拉板于2005年6月施工完成至今，左岸坝肩边坡稳定性良好，自2008年4月下闸蓄水至今，左岸坝肩坝后排水孔未发现明显渗水，所布置的监测设备未观测到异常情况，这表明景洪水电站左岸坝肩锚拉板设计及防渗设计是成功的。

采用锚拉板作为非溢流坝段与边坡的连接方式，是在混凝土重力坝坝肩接头方案选择上一个新的尝试，为今后类似工程提供了宝贵经验，具有一定的借鉴和指导意义。

(中国水电顾问集团昆明勘测设计研究院 闫会宗)

戛洒江一级水电站坝基冲积层利用研究

（一）工程概况

戛洒江一级水电站位于云南省玉溪市新平县水塘镇的戛洒江河段上，是红河（元江）干流梯级综合规划十二级开发方案的“龙头”电站。工程开发以发电为主，兼顾下游农田灌溉和城镇供水，建成后可发展库区航运，促进地区旅游业的发展。电站装机容量270MW；水库总库容17.41亿m^3，具有年调节能力。枢纽主要由混凝土面板堆石坝、左岸溢洪道、左岸放空冲沙（兼导流）洞、左岸引水发电系统等组成。

（二）坝基冲积层特性

据钻孔资料，河床冲积层厚15～35m，主要为卵、砾石，夹中、细砂及少量块石，小于5mm的粉细砂粒含量平均为15%～20%，未见连续的粉细砂层或淤泥层分布。卵、砾石直径为2～6cm，磨圆度中等～较好，分选性较差；主要为砂岩、花岗片麻岩及泥岩、石英。

据钻孔抽水试验资料，河床冲积层渗透系数为（1.5～1.695）$\times 10^{-2}$cm/s，属强透水层。为了解河床冲积层的密实程度及物理力学性质，选择坝址左岸河漫滩进行了河床冲积层钻孔重型动力触探、物探剪切波及荷载试验。综合测试成果，结合工程经验，与同类工程类比分析，该电站河床冲积层呈中等密实状态，物理力学综合参数建议值见表1。

表1 戛洒江一级水电站枢纽区河床冲积层物理力学综合指标建议值表

密度(g/cm^3)	比重	干密度(g/cm^3)	相对密度	孔隙比	剪切波(km/s)	变形模量(MPa)	泊松比	标准承载力(kPa)
2.16	2.68	2.11	0.62	0.27	0.78	23～30	0.30	350～450

（三）趾板置于河床冲积层上的研究

国内外利用河床冲积层作为面板坝堆石基础或趾板基础的面板堆石坝已有多座。对其中的Bou Hanifia（阿尔及利亚）、凯姆波·莫洛（意大利）、Santa Juana（智利）、Puclaro（智利）、Los Caracoles（阿根廷）、柯柯亚（新疆鄯善）、铜街子左副坝（四川乐山）、横山（浙江奉化）、槽鱼滩（四川洪雅）、梅溪（浙江鄞县）、梁辉（浙江余姚）、塔斯特（新疆）、岑港（浙江）、楚松（西藏）、汤浦（浙江上虞）、那兰（云南金平）、汉平嘴（甘肃文县）、九甸峡（甘肃）、察汗乌苏（新疆和静）、多诺（四川九寨沟）、斜卡（四川九龙）、双溪口（浙江余姚）和乌鲁瓦提（新疆）等混凝土面板堆石坝的相关建设情况及河床冲积层的特性进行了资料收集与分析研究。这些面板堆石坝，坝高超过100m的有：智利Santa Juana坝（113.4m）、阿根廷Los Caracoles（138m）、云南那兰（109 m）、甘肃九甸峡（136.5m）、新疆察汗乌苏（110m）、四川多诺（108.5m）、四川斜卡（108.2m）；冲积层厚度达100m的有：智利Santa Juana（113m）、四川斜卡（100m）。

戛洒江一级如将面板坝的趾板置于河床冲积层上，冲积层以上坝高146.5m，冲积层最大深度20～35m。该规模的坝目前国内外尚无成功的实践经验。经对开挖冲积层方案（只开挖趾板区及其下游0.3H范围）和趾板置于冲积层上（坝基采用防渗墙防渗）两方案进行比较，结果：①开挖冲积层方案要多开挖河床冲积层50万m^3左右，坝体填筑多30万m^3，导流洞、泄洪冲沙洞及引水隧洞的长度略有增加，工程投资略大；②开挖冲积层方案要多花4个月时间，但后期蓄水，主要受上游流量影响，实际上本工程在1月下闸与5月下闸所能达到的蓄水效果相差不大，两方案首台机组发电时间相同，采用保留河床冲积层的方案，发电工期无明显优势。

考虑本工程面板坝较高，而河床冲积层类比其他工程变形指标略微偏低，从安全角度考虑，最终确定按开挖冲积层将趾板置于基岩上的布置方案设计。

（四）河床冲积层作为面板堆石坝堆石基础研究

1. 物理力学特性分析

（1）从已建工程实例可知，柯柯亚坝基冲积层的卵砾石含量为67%，乌鲁瓦提坝的含砂量为15%～16%，梅溪坝冲积层内含泥量大于9%，圣塔扬那坝河床沉积物有厚8m的黏性土层，那兰坝卵砾石含量80%，说明对冲积层的级配没有限制，都允许冲积层内有薄的不连续的细颗粒透镜体。本工程坝基冲积层的卵砾石含量80%～85%，小于5mm颗粒含量15%～20%，无连续的粉细砂层或淤泥层分布，从坝基冲积层的颗粒组成来看，与已建工程利用的冲积层性状相当，甚至略好。

（2）本工程纵波速平均为2.19km/s，剪切波波速平均为0.78km/s，动弹性模量平均值为3.88GPa，动剪切模量平均值为1.37GPa，动泊松比平均值为0.43。察汗乌苏上部漂石砂卵砾石层的剪切波速度为583m/s，动剪切模量为751MPa，下部漂石砂卵砾石层的剪切波速度为615m/s，动剪切模量为835MPa。从物探剪切波成果看，戛洒江一级的坝基河床冲积层密实度也较好。

（3）对比钻孔动力触探（N63.5）试验成果，戛洒江一级平均击数8～12击（修正后），那兰为8～9击（未修正）、察汗乌苏为13～14击，戛洒江一级略微偏低。

（4）对比载荷试验成果，戛洒江一级承载力最小值为199kPa，最大值为597kPa，平均值为360kPa，那兰坝为780～1450kPa，察汗乌苏为494～724kPa，平均为590kPa，水布垭为280～770kPa，戛洒江一级略微偏低。

（5）冲积层变形模量指标，戛洒江一级为20～30MPa，那兰坝为50～100MPa，察汗乌苏为45～55MPa，水布垭为25～70MPa，柯柯亚为60MPa，乌鲁瓦提为118MPa。相比较而言，戛洒江一级偏低。

（6）坝基渗透系数，戛洒江一级为（1.5～1.695）$\times10^{-2}$cm/s，那兰坝为$1.7\times10^{-2}\sim4.7\times10^{-1}$cm/s，察汗乌苏为$6.7\times10^{-2}$cm/s，乌鲁瓦提为（1～1.2）$\times10^{-2}$cm/s，九甸峡为$3.5\times10^{-2}\sim1.7\times10^{-1}$cm/s，戛洒江一级坝基冲积层渗透系数在类似工程范围内，略微偏小。

综上所述，戛洒江一级河床冲积层基本具备作为面板堆石坝堆石基础的条件。

2.不同挖除宽度对应力变形的影响　为了研究冲积层对应力变形的影响，特委托河海大学分别计算了挖除50m、100m、150m三种情况。河海大学采用Duncan *E-B* 模型参数进行应力变形计算，共有计算参数5种，分别为室内试验参数、敏感性分析1、敏感性分析2、敏感性分析3和设计参数；5种计算参数和3种冲积层挖除宽度组合后，共有15种计算结果。根据计算成果分析得出以下结论：

（1）15组计算结果均显示坝体部分的变形量总体上较小，沉降量集中在底部冲积层上方，最大为1.53m，占坝高的1%左右。坝体应力水平最大值为0.77 MPa，5组计算参数均可计算通过，说明坝体的应力变形能满足设计要求。

（2）混凝土面板的应力数值在一般面板坝正常范围，完建期面板应力较小，压应力和拉应力均远小于混凝土强度（未考虑温度应力）。

（3）采用室内试验参数计算时，蓄水期面板轴向应力以压应力为主，最大压应力为3.54MPa，位于河谷中部，岸边拉应力未超过0.58MPa。顺坡压应力为4.07MPa，顺坡拉应力数值为2.19MPa，受拉区集中在面板下部接近趾板的部位。

（4）敏感性分析考虑最不利材料参数时，轴向应力和顺坡应力都有较大增加，轴向拉应力和顺坡拉应力分别达到1.97MPa和4.29MPa。

（5）设计方案冲积层挖除50m，面板挠度的计算结果为0.284～0.383m，占面板长度的0.1%～0.14%；如果冲积层挖除150m，面板挠度的计算结果为0.204～0.300m，占面板长度的0.075%～0.11%。面板挠度与坝高和河谷宽度有关，本工程河谷宽高比为2.6左右，对照国内外几个工程，计算的面板挠度处于正常范围的上限，其原因是冲积层存在增加了一定的面板挠度。

（6）根据3种挖除宽度（50m、100m、150m）的冲积层计算，虽然增加开挖宽度有利于减少面板应力，但对比计算结果发现，冲积层存在对坝体沉降、面板挠度、接缝相对变形的影响较大，对坝体应力水平和面板应力的影响相对较小。开挖宽度为50m时，面板变形受冲积层影响较大，挠度集中在底部，开挖宽度达到100m时，面板挠度分布趋于正常形状，说明冲积层对面板的变形较小。开挖宽度达到150m时，挠度形状基本没有改变。因此，建议冲积层挖除的宽度取50～100m。

（7）本工程周边缝张开量最大达到41.2mm（室内试验参数，开挖50m），随开挖宽度增加，周边缝张开量有所减小。建议加强周边缝的止水构造，防止止水拉开增加渗漏。

根据以上试验结论分析，不同的冲积层挖除宽度存在对坝体沉降、面板挠度、周边缝张开量、接缝相对变形有较大影响，对坝体应力水平和面板应力的影响相对较小。综合考虑技术难度、工程安全性及经济性，戛洒江一级电站拟将趾板冲积层向下游挖除60m宽度。

戛洒江一级电站面板堆石坝最后布置剖面见图1。

（中国水电顾问集团昆明勘测设计研究院
赵云秀　冯业林）

土石坝抗滑稳定分析的分项系数设计法使用简介

DL/T 5395—2007《碾压式土石坝设计规范》将土石坝抗滑稳定分项系数设计法列为资料性附录，以便在需要用可靠度法计算坝坡稳定时使用。

（一）分项系数的确定

经研究，认为坝坡抗滑稳定计算的分项系数设置体系以五系数为好。

对于土石坝在施工期、稳定渗流期、水库水位降落期以及正常使用遇地震等四种工况下的稳定计算，这五项系数为：γ_0为结构重要性系数，反映不同工程等级的土石坝抗滑稳定安全度水平的差异；ψ为设计状况系数，反映不同运行条件、不同荷载组合对土

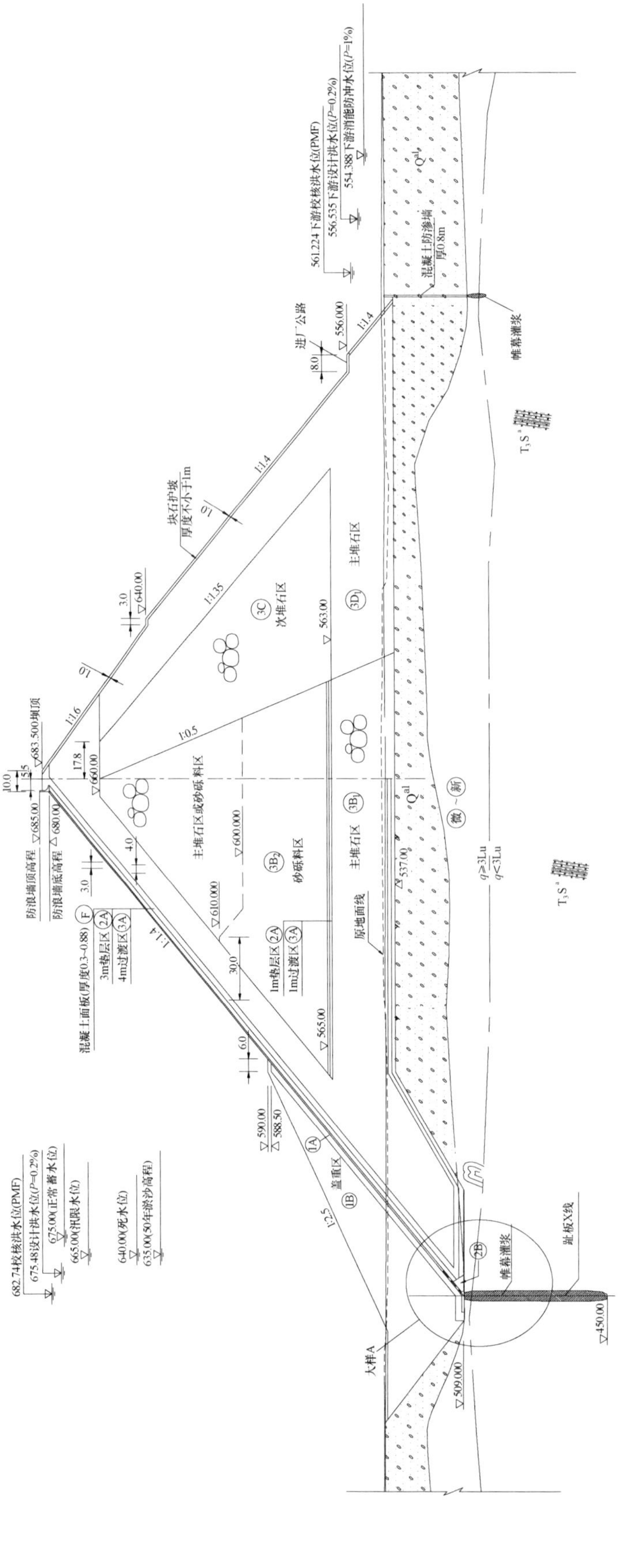

图1 戛洒江一级水电站坝体剖面图

石坝抗滑稳定安全度水平的不同要求；γ_G、γ_Q 为作用分项系数；γ_c、γ_f 为土体抗剪强度设计指标的材料性能分项系数；γ_d 为结构系数。

1. 结构安全级别及结构重要性系数　参考 DL/T 5395—2007 各级坝安全系数间的比例关系，各级土石坝的结构重要性系数 γ_0 与结构安全级别规定见表 1。

表 1　土石坝的结构安全级别及结构重要性系数

土石坝级别	土石坝的结构安全级别	结构重要性系数 γ_0
1	Ⅰ	1.1
2、3	Ⅱ	1.0
4、5	Ⅲ	0.9

2. 设计状况及设计状况系数　土石坝稳定分析宜考虑三种设计状况：

(1) 持久状况（正常运用条件）：正常蓄水位及经常运行的上游水位，或设计洪水位下，稳定渗流期的上、下游坝坡，以及水库水位经常性降落期的上游坝坡。

(2) 短暂情况（非常运用条件Ⅰ）：施工期的上、下游坝坡；非常运用洪水位下，稳定渗流期的上、下游坝坡；水库水位的非常降落的上游坝坡。

(3) 偶然状况（非常运用条件Ⅱ）：正常运用条件遇地震的上、下游坝坡。

参考现行规范不同设计状况安全系数的比值，设计状况系数 ψ 取值如下：①持久状况为 1.00；②短暂状况为 0.90；③偶然状况为 0.85。

3. 作用分项系数

(1) 地震作用分项系数 γ_E 应取为 1.0；

(2) 土体自重作用分项系数 γ_G 采用 1.0。

(3) 孔隙水压力的作用分项系数 γ_Q 的确定，需要大量实测统计资料。但目前这方面的资料还很少，难于定出较为合理的孔隙压力作用分项系数，因此，暂不考虑孔隙压力作用的变异性，直接取 $\gamma_Q=1.0$，待以后逐步积累这方面的资料，条件成熟后再确定比较合适的孔隙压力作用分项系数。由于孔隙压力作用的变异性较大，其作用分项系数一般大于 1.0。

4. 材料性能分项系数　《碾压式土石坝设计规范》（DL/T 5395—2007）规定，土体抗剪强度的标准值宜按小值平均值确定。若按正态分布考虑，小值平均值相当于取其概率分布的 0.25 分位值，保证率为 75％ 。

根据统计分析结果：当土体抗剪强度标准值与设计值分别按其概率分布的 0.25 分位值及 0.15 分位值确定时，利用国内外土体抗剪强度的统计参数求得的土体抗剪强度材料性能分项系数 γ_c、γ_f 都比较接近，γ_c 大约在 1.2 左右；当内摩擦角分别采用对数正态分布及正态分布时，γ_f 均为 1.05 左右。因此，土体抗剪强度的材料性能分项系数 γ_c 取为 1.2，γ_f 取为 1.05。对于采用对数函数抗剪指标时，由于只用 Φ 表示，实际上，线性指标中的凝聚力（或称咬合力）c 已包含在 Φ 内。因此，抗剪强度材料性能分项系数仅用 $\gamma_f=1.10$ 即可。

5. 结构系数　按可靠度分析法与按工程经验校准法所确定的结构系数是非常接近的。基于不计条块间作用力的瑞典圆弧法进行坝坡抗滑稳定计算时，可取结构系数 $\gamma_d\geqslant 1.10$；基于计及条块间作用力的简化毕肖普法等方法进行坝坡抗滑稳定计算时，可取结构系数 $\gamma_d\geqslant 1.20$。

对坝坡抗滑稳定的结构系数 γ_d，采用 $\gamma_d\geqslant 1.10$（或 1.20）的形式，算出结构系数 γ_d，而不是像其他结构设计规范采用的规定 $\gamma_d=1.10$（或 1.20，或各规范规定的其他定值）使结构功能函数式成立的形式，可能更符合土石坝坝坡稳定分析的习惯。也可使大家直观地看到，土石坝坝体结构有多大的安全裕度。

（二）抗滑稳定计算方法

坝坡抗滑稳定计算方法，DL/T 5395—2007《碾压式土石坝设计规范》规定了：瑞典圆弧法、简化毕肖普法、摩根斯顿—普赖斯法、滑楔法等 4 种，且以简化毕肖普法为基本方法。当然，也不排除使用其他方法。

除不计条块间作用力的条分法（源自瑞典圆弧法）可直接计算结构系数 γ_d 外，其余各种方法均通过相当安全系数 γ_R 来推求结构系数 γ_d。

条块间侧向作用力为水平向的条分法（源自简化毕肖普法），其相当安全系数 γ_R 为

$$\gamma_R=\frac{\gamma_0\psi\gamma_d(1+\rho_c)}{\dfrac{1}{\gamma_d}+\dfrac{1}{\gamma_c}\rho_c} \tag{1}$$

其中土条的凝聚力与摩擦力的比值

$$\rho_c=\frac{c'b\sec\alpha}{(W\sec\alpha-ub\sec\alpha)\tan\varphi'} \tag{2}$$

式 (1)、式 (2) 由单一安全系数计算公式直接导出（推导略）。此处假定各作用分项系数为 1.0。

如材料抗剪指标采用非线性的对数函数式，材料性能分项系数仅有 γ_f，则 $\gamma_R=\gamma_0\psi\gamma_f\gamma_d$；如令材料性能分项系数 $\gamma_f=1.0$，则 $\gamma_R=\gamma_0\psi\gamma_d$。

对于条块间作用力为任意方向的条分法（源自摩根斯顿—普赖斯法），相当安全系数仍为式 (1)，其土条的凝聚力与摩擦力的比值

$$\rho_c=\frac{c' \mathrm{d}x\sec\alpha}{(\mathrm{d}W\sec\alpha-u\mathrm{d}x\sec\alpha)\tan\varphi'} \tag{3}$$

对基于滑楔法的抗滑稳定计算公式，相当安全系数还用式(1)表示，其土条的凝聚力与摩擦力的比值

$$\rho_c=\frac{c' \Delta x\sec\alpha_i}{(W_i\sec\alpha_i-u\Delta x\sec\alpha_i)\tan\varphi'} \tag{4}$$

上述式（2）、式（3）、式（4）中，条分宽度分别用 b 或 $\mathrm{d}x$ 或 Δx 表示，条块重分别以 W 或 $\mathrm{d}W$ 表示。其中式（3）、式（4）是近似公式。

（三）结语

土石坝坝坡抗滑稳定分析的分项系数设计法，以概率设计准则为基础，以可靠指标度量结构可靠性，采用以基本变量的标准值和分项系数表达的极限状态实用设计表达式进行设计。现行《碾压式土石坝设计规范》（DL/T 5395—2007）将分项系数设计法作为对传统的单一安全系数法补充的另一种方法列入附录。中国水电顾问集团西北勘测设计研究院与武汉大学合作编制了计算程序，使该法可用于土石坝工程设计。

（中国水电顾问集团西北勘测设计研究院　陈洪天）

地 下 工 程 设 计

小湾水电站超大型圆筒尾水调压井设计

（一）调压室工程地质条件

小湾水电站尾水调压室地段分布的岩层为黑云花岗片麻岩夹薄层透镜状片岩。Ⅲ级断层 F_{27} 在 2 号尾水调压室通过，产状 N65°～80°W，NE∠65°～80°，破碎带宽约 1m，顺片岩发育，由多个宽 5～15cm 的挤压面组成，挤压面物质主要为碎裂岩、糜棱岩，挤压面间岩体破碎，主要为片状岩、碎块岩，沿面渗水，局部地段见有 30cm 宽的石英脉；Ⅳ级结构面较发育，均为顺片麻理面挤压面，宽度一般不超过 10cm，物质主要为片状岩和碎块岩；Ⅴ级结构面主要分为三组：顺片麻理节理、近 SN 向陡倾角节理和少量的中缓倾角节理。地段未发现较大规模的不稳定分离块体，围岩总体稳定条件较好。裂隙水压力较高，对围岩稳定不利，较高的地应力也有可能产生中等～轻微的岩爆现象。

（二）尾水布置概况

经过多方案比选，结合引水发电系统枢纽布置、工程地质条件和水力过渡过程计算成果，小湾尾水调压室最终采用带连通上室的双圆筒阻抗式调压井方案。该方案不但改善了围岩稳定条件，减少了支护工程量，并且降低了地下厂房洞室群的支护难度。小湾水电站尾水系统采用单机单尾水管，三机共用一座尾水调压室和一条尾水隧洞的布置形式，自厂房尾水肘管后（厂横 0＋032.200 桩号）向下游依次布置有：1～6号尾水支洞，机组尾水检修闸门室，1、2 号尾水调压室，1、2 号尾水隧洞及尾水出口检修闸门等相关建筑物。2 个调压室中心间距 99.504m。尾水调压室采用“三机一井”布置，结构型式采用带连通上室的双圆筒阻抗式尾调室。1、2 号尾水调压室上部之间有连通上室连接，在底部上游侧与尾水支洞相接，下游侧与尾水隧洞相接。调压井选定方案平面布置见图 1。

尾调室顶拱为球冠形，球冠中心角 120°，半径 R＝18.65m，穹顶高程 1039.50m；下部为圆筒形，圆筒内径 D＝32.0m，自 1005m 高程以下井壁部位衬砌厚度 1.0～2.85m 不等；圆形阻抗孔孔口直径 D＝11.0m，孔井面积比 11.8%，孔板厚度自孔口至井壁部位为 2～4m 渐变；调压室底部为平面四岔口（上游与 3 条尾水支洞连通，下游与 1 条尾水隧洞连通）、立体五岔口（顶部与调压井井筒连通）结构型式。

（三）水力设计

尾水道设计引用流量为机组额定流量 365m³/s；尾水支洞断面为 10m×15m（宽×高）的城门洞形断面，流速为 2.28m/s；尾水隧洞断面尺寸为 D＝18m 的圆形断面，同一单元 1 台机运行时流速为 1.43m/s，2 台机运行时流速为 2.87m/s，三台机运行时流速为 4.30m/s，当过流量为设计引用流量时，可计算得同一单元 3 台机尾水道（尾水肘管末至尾水出口）水头损失为 4.38m。根据《水电站调压室设计规范》（DL/T 5058—1996）的规定，对尾水调压井的稳定断面积进行了计算。经计算，所需托马稳定断面积为 630m²，相应的井筒直径约为 28m。为使最高、最低涌波水位控制在一个适当的范围内，经计算

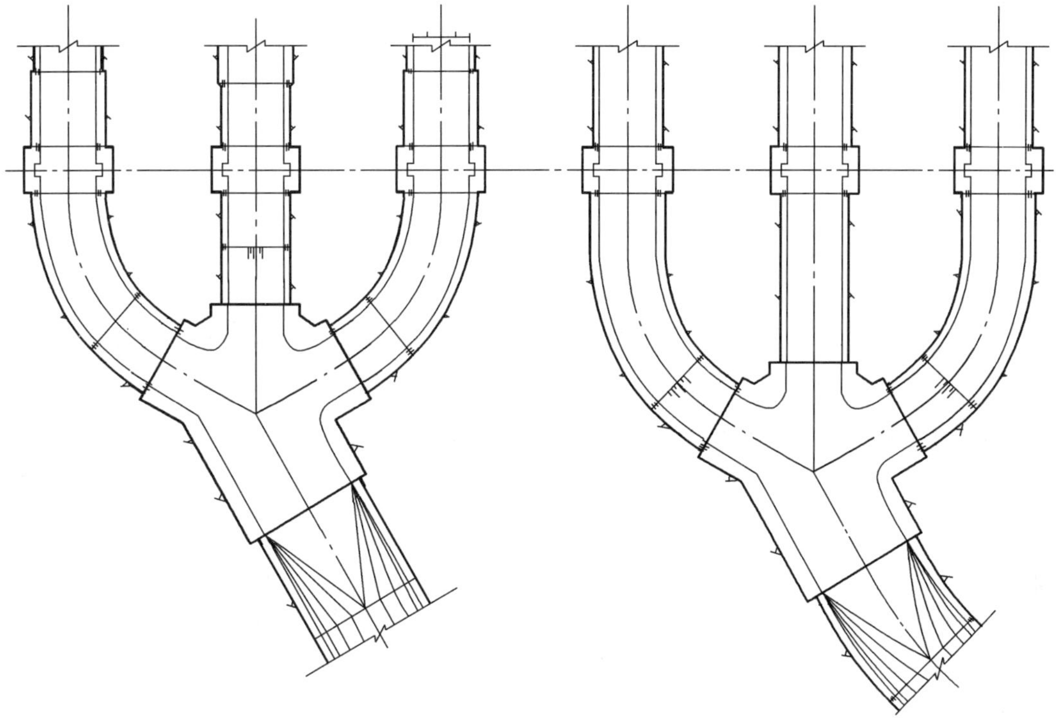

图 1　调压井选定方案平面布置图

比较和带模型机组的水力过渡过程试验分析，取尾水调压井的井筒直径为 32m。1 号尾水隧洞长度为 958.8m，最小及最大流量水头损失系数分别为 1.197×10^{-6}、2.329×10^{-6}，尾水调压井阻抗孔流量水头损失系数为 8.132×10^{-6}（阻抗孔孔径 11.0m，流量系数取 0.7）。经计算，叠加工况即 3 台机相应尾水位，同一单元 2 台机运行、一台机增荷，在最不利时刻丢弃全部负荷工况是最低涌波水位较危险的工况，相应的最低涌波水位为 973.4m；设计尾水位时同一单元 2 台机运行、1 台机增荷，在最不利时刻丢弃全部负荷工况是最高涌波水位较危险的工况，相应的最高涌波水位为 1020.4m。阻抗板上下最大压差为 7.10m 水头。

（四）开挖支护设计

尾水调压室及连通上室一次锚喷支护参数设计见表 1。

表 1　尾水调压室及连通上室一次锚喷支护参数表

部　位	支　护　参　数
球冠/顶拱	砂浆锚杆 ϕ36/ϕ28@2.0m×2.0m，L=9.0m/4.5m，喷 C30 钢纤维混凝土，厚 0.2m
连通上室边墙	砂浆锚杆 ϕ32/ϕ25@2.5m×2.5m，L=9.0m/4.5m，喷 C20 聚丙烯微纤维混凝土，厚 0.15m
井　筒	1000m 高程以上：砂浆锚杆 ϕ32/ϕ25@2.0m×2.0m，L=9.0m/4.5m，喷 C20 聚丙烯微纤维混凝土，厚 0.15m； 1000m 高程以下：砂浆锚杆 ϕ32/ϕ25@2.5m×2.5m，L=9.0m/4.5m，喷 C20 聚丙烯微纤维混凝土，厚 0.15m
不良地质段	对顶拱部位断层破碎带以钢筋肋拱结合 125kN 级预应力锚杆进行缝补式加强支护；井筒、边墙部位断层破碎带采用随机（预应力）锚杆进行加强支护，并喷 C30 钢纤维混凝土，厚 0.2m
洞室交叉部位	调压井顶拱与连通上室顶拱相交部位：采用 2 排 450kN 级锁口预应力锚杆 ϕ32@1.5m×1.5m，L=9.0m 进行加强支护； 调压井井筒与连通上室边墙和底板、尾水支洞、尾水隧洞、通风洞交叉部位，连通上室与通风洞交叉部位：采用 2 排 125kN 级锁口预应力锚杆 ϕ32@1.5m×1.5m，L=9.0m 进行加强支护

在尾水调压室开挖过程中，根据现场揭示的实际情况，并结合监测资料综合分析，主要进行的动态跟踪设计及优化如下：根据开挖揭示的实际地质情况，节理密集带和断层出露部位以挂双层 ϕ6.5@0.15m×

0.15m钢筋网结合喷C30钢纤维混凝土进行了加强支护；对特定部位采用一定数量的预应力锚索进行加强支护。

（五）结构设计

调压井下部为五岔管，调压井洞室的围岩稳定及混凝土结构十分复杂。为了全面分析调压井洞室稳定和衬砌结构受力特性，采用三维非线性有限元方法和结构力学法对尾水调压室筒壁、阻抗板、下部五岔管结构及其邻近的围岩施工期的稳定、安全，运行期机组各种运行工况下的结构安全稳定进行分析计算，为工程提供设计依据。

根据内力计算结果，考虑到结构计算中未考虑一次支护及固结灌浆的作用，所采用的水位和压差为极端情况下的计算值等情况，实际配筋应适当减少，结合调压井具体结构体形，并参考同类工程经验，最终确定的结构配筋如下：

1005.00～993.70m高程范围井筒衬砌内、外侧均配ϕ36@150mm的环向主筋和ϕ25@228mm的竖向分布筋；

993.70～971.00m高程范围井筒衬砌内、外侧均配ϕ36@125mm的环向主筋，内侧配ϕ32@111mm的竖向分布筋，外侧配ϕ32@130mm的竖向分布筋；

971.00～950.00m高程范围底部四岔口边墙和底板内、外侧均配ϕ32@125×125mm钢筋网；

971.00～975.00m高程范围阻抗板底面和顶面均配ϕ36@125mm的环向和径向钢筋，并在阻抗板与井筒交界处内侧配置倾角为45°的ϕ32@250mm加强筋。

为适应结构变形和不均匀沉降，调压井底部岔口部位与尾水支洞和尾水隧洞间均设置有结构缝，结构缝宽均为2cm，缝内充填高压聚乙烯泡沫塑料板。为防止内水外渗，尾水调压井与尾水支洞间结构缝内均设置2道止水。

（六）监测成果分析

根据尾水调压室的工程地质条件和结构设计，对调压室围岩和结构进行了相应的监测设计，对监测成果分析，可以得出如下主要结论：

（1）尾水调压室变形主要受施工期开挖及不良地质条件的影响，在开挖结束后大部分围岩变形随时间趋于收敛，目前尾水调压室多点位移计孔口位移介于0～66.72mm之间，测值趋势变化平稳。

（2）锚索测力计受施工干扰影响较大，锚杆应力计测值普遍不大。目前各围岩支护监测效应量测值变化较小，绝大部分测点已收敛，小部分测点呈小幅波动状态。

（3）阻抗板各钢筋应力基本趋于平稳，钢筋应力介于－2.45～34.02MPa之间。阻抗板处于正常工作状态。

小湾水电站工程尾水调压室较好地适应了工程地质和水力学条件，布置合理，结构设计可靠。监测成果表明，调压室围岩变形收敛，围岩整体稳定，阻抗板结构处于正常工作性态。该调压室结构型式可供类似工程借鉴。

（中国水电顾问集团昆明勘测设计研究院
杨宜文 许 晖）

锦屏二级水电站地下厂房开挖支护动态设计

（一）概况

锦屏二级水电站地下厂房洞室群规模巨大，主要由上游调压室、高压管道、主副厂房洞、主变压器洞、尾水隧洞和尾水闸门室组成。厂内安装8台600MW机组，主厂房纵轴线为NE35°，全长352.44m，吊车梁以上开挖跨度为28.30m，以下为25.80m，开挖总高度为72.20m；主变压器洞长374.60m，宽为19.80m，最大高度为34.10m。

锦屏二级水电站主副厂房洞于2007年5月1日开始开挖，2008年8月完成岩梁浇筑，2009年12月完成开挖支护；主变压器洞于2007年8月开始开挖，2009年2月完成开挖支护。由于洞室群规模巨大，工程地质条件复杂，整个厂区均为高倾角地层且有不利断层F_{16}和F_{65}穿越洞室，加上不利的地应力方向和岩层走向，对地下厂房的稳定都是个考验。设计根据地质条件，精心对地下厂房开挖做了支护设计，又以现场实际情况、监测数据和反馈分析为理论依据，应用“动态支护”的设计理念，及时调整支护参数，保证了地下厂房洞室的围岩稳定。目前变形收敛，各项监测数据稳定。

（二）地质条件

地下厂房区域地层岩性为中三叠统盐塘组（T_{2y}）及第四系（Q）地层，围岩类别以Ⅲ、Ⅱ类为主，无区域性断裂或次一级的断层（Ⅰ类结构面）通过，小型断层及破碎带等Ⅲ级结构面发育。厂内裂隙主要发育有五组：① N10°W～N30°E，NE～NW∠73°～85°；② N60°～80°W，SW∠20°～40°、∠70°～90°；③ N40°～60°E，SE∠20°～40°；④ EW S∠20°～40°；⑤ N70°～85°E，SE∠60°～80°；其中以①、②组为主，③、④组次之，⑤组少量。实测厂区最大主应力量级一般在10.1～22.9MPa之间，以近垂直岸坡方向为主，其平均方向为S43.1°～47.4°E，与区域最大主应力NWW方向基本一致，属中高地应力区。

本工程地下厂房洞室群规模巨大，工程地质条件复杂，整个厂区均为高倾角地层且有不利断层F_{16}和

F_{65}穿越洞室；厂房位于深切河谷山体内部，初始地应力水平较高且复杂。此外，受厂区枢纽总体布置的限制，主副厂房洞、主变压器洞等大型洞室与地应力大角度相交，与主要裂隙小角度相交，对大型洞室高边墙的围岩稳定极为不利。

（三）技术施工阶段地下厂房支护参数

技术施工阶段，锦屏二级水电站地下厂房洞室群围岩系统支护参数见表1。对特定块体、断层或节理密集带部位加强支护。

表1　锦屏二级水电站地下厂房洞室群围岩系统支护参数一览表

岩体类别 洞室部位		Ⅲ类围岩	Ⅳ类围岩
主厂房	顶拱	预应力中空注浆锚杆：T=120kN，ϕ28，L=6m，ϕ32，L=8m，@1.5m×1.5m矩形间隔布置。 挂网喷混凝土：δ=15cm	预应力中空注浆锚杆：T=120kN，ϕ28，L=6m，ϕ32，L=8m，@1.0m×1.0m矩形间隔布置。 挂网喷混凝土：δ=15cm
	上游边墙	预应力锚索：高程1321.50～1350.00m，T=1750kN，L=20m，@4.5m×4.5m矩形间隔布置。 普通砂浆锚杆：ϕ28，L=6m；中空注浆锚杆：ϕ32，L=9m，@1.5m×1.5m矩形间隔布置。 挂网喷混凝土：δ=15cm	预应力锚索：高程1321.50～1350.00m，T=2000kN，L=20m，@4.5m×4.5m矩形间隔布置。 普通砂浆锚杆：ϕ28，L=6m；中空注浆锚杆：ϕ32，L=9m，@1.0m×1.0m矩形间隔布置。 挂网喷混凝土：δ=15cm
	下游边墙	与主变压器洞上游边墙对穿预应力锚索：高程1321.5～1350.00m，T=2000kN，@4.5m×4.5m矩形间隔布置。 普通砂浆锚杆：ϕ28，L=6m；中空注浆锚杆：ϕ32，L=9m，@1.5m×1.5m矩形间隔布置。 挂网喷混凝土：δ=15cm	与主变压器洞上游边墙对穿预应力锚索：高程1321.5～1350.00m，T=2000kN，@4.5m×4.5m矩形间隔布置。 普通砂浆锚杆：ϕ28，L=6m；中空注浆锚杆：ϕ32，L=9m，@1.0m×1.0m矩形间隔布置。 挂网喷混凝土：δ=15cm
主变压器洞	顶拱	预应力中空注浆锚杆：T=120kN，ϕ28，L=5m，ϕ32，L=7m，@1.5m×1.5m矩形间隔布置。 挂网喷混凝土：δ=12cm	预应力中空注浆锚杆：T=120kN，ϕ28，L=5m，ϕ32，L=7m，@1.0m×1.0m矩形间隔布置。 挂网喷混凝土：δ=12cm
	上游边墙	与主厂房下游墙对穿锚索：高程1337.00～1358m，T=2000kN，@4.5m×4.5m矩形间隔布置。 普通砂浆锚杆：ϕ28，L=5m；中空注浆锚杆：ϕ32，L=7m，@1.5m×1.5m矩形间隔布置。 挂网喷混凝土：δ=12cm	与主厂房下游墙对穿锚索：高程1337.00～1358m，T=2000kN，@4.5m×4.5m矩形间隔布置。 普通砂浆锚杆：ϕ28，L=5m；中空注浆锚杆：ϕ32，L=7m，@1.0m×1.0m矩形间隔布置。 挂网喷混凝土：δ=12cm
	下游边墙	普通砂浆锚杆：ϕ28，L=5m；中空注浆锚杆：ϕ32，L=7m，@1.5m×1.5m矩形间隔布置。 挂网喷混凝土：δ=12cm	普通砂浆锚杆：ϕ28，L=5m；中空注浆锚杆：ϕ32，L=7m，@1.0m×1.0m矩形间隔布置。 挂网喷混凝土：δ=12cm

（四）地下厂房开挖支护动态设计

地下厂房洞室群规模巨大，工程地质条件复杂，施工开挖过程中产生的卸荷作用，实际上是岩体应力场不断调整的过程，由此将引起岩体结构、能量集散及宏观力学性质发生相应的变化。结合现场的地质条件、监测数据、施工过程，锦屏二级地下厂房开挖支护秉承“动态支护”的设计理念，进行了实时动态的反馈分析，对现场实际出现的问题进行理论解释、分析，客观地对围岩稳定性进行综合评价，并预测开挖完成后的围岩稳定和支护状态，及时提出局部补强措施。

实际开挖支护过程中，地下厂房的支护参数主要的动态调整如下：

(1) 2008 年 4 月，在厂房第二层岩锚梁成形和厂房第三层开挖过程中，与厂房轴线小夹角的陡倾层面和较发育的缓倾结构面（F_{65}及同组结构面）切割，导致表层 4m 范围内围岩松弛严重，上游边墙多个监测断面显示围岩变形增长较大，多根监测锚索荷载接近或超过设计吨位。设计及时调整上下游边墙 1339m 高程以下的锚索排距，加密锚索间距并降低锁定值，所有系统锚杆加设垫板；对高边墙施加一定的表面法向应力控制表层围岩的变形，抑制围岩表层松动范围和向内部扩展，提高围岩的承载能力。

(2) 2008 年 11 月，地下厂房洞室群开挖较快，支护滞后，导致主厂房围岩应力调整过快、过大，主厂房上下游侧岩锚梁以上至拱肩出现一系列喷层裂缝，多为 45°斜向，局部拱肩部位喷层整片脱开，最宽开裂宽度约 6mm。设计及时增加在主厂房上下游边墙 1353.25m 高程处预应力锚索，对裂缝发育的部位进行裂缝锁边锚杆支护，对局部渗水区域施打随机排水孔。

(3) 2009 年 8 月，母线洞内出现了不同程度的环向贯穿性裂缝，裂缝宽度最大约 2cm，有向主变压器洞侧发展的趋势，主变压器洞上游边墙中下部锚索荷载增长较快，主厂房和主变压器洞之间隔墙塑性区加深。设计及时调整支护参数，在主变压器洞上游侧增加两排锚索，并相应增加监测。

(4) 主变压器洞开挖完成后，下游拱肩应力集中，最大主应力 30MPa 左右，结构面发育，出露 F_{16} 等断层和破碎带，性状较差，围岩渗滴水严重；下游拱肩喷层破坏较严重，多处出现喷层开裂、外鼓、剥落，钢筋格栅拱架受围岩的挤压出现了不同程度的破坏，变形严重，拱架与洞壁完全脱开并产生了明显的倾向洞内的弯曲。2009 年 11 月 27 日，主变压器洞厂右 0+010m～厂右 0+025m 段下游拱肩发生掉块。原有系统支护略显不足。根据以上实际情况，设计及时调整支护参数：在下游拱肩系统锚杆之间内插预应力锚杆，增设两排系统锚索，增设两排排水孔，相应增加监测。

（中国水电顾问集团华东勘测设计研究院　万祥兵）

响水涧工程地下厂房的优化调整设计

（一）概况

响水涧抽水蓄能电站地下洞室由主副厂房洞、主变压器洞、母线洞、进厂交通洞及通风兼安全洞等组成。该电站前期由上海勘测设计研究院负责可行性研究，招标和施工详图阶段由中国水电顾问集团华东勘测设计研究院和上海勘测设计研究院合作设计，其中，中国水电顾问集团华东勘测设计研究院负责地下工程和机电设备部分的勘测设计工作。在设计过程中，中国水电顾问集团华东勘测设计研究院根据可行性研究复核审查意见以及项目核准意见，并充分利用天荒坪、桐柏、宝泉、泰安的设计经验或教训，复核了原有设计，并进行细化、优化设计，使本阶段设计更加安全可靠，更能满足施工、安装、检修、运行、管理需要，同时，使工程运行后环境舒适，投资合理。

（二）地下厂房轮廓尺寸的调整优化

1. 主厂房宽度的设计调整　可行性研究阶段主厂房引水钢管中心线与机组中心线夹角为 60°，净宽为 21.5m，上下游边墙厚各为 1m，厂房总宽度 23.5m。其中，厂房上游边线距机组中心线为 13.3m，下游边线距机组中心线为 10.2m，机组段长度为 28m。招标阶段对厂房平面尺寸进行复核，对主厂房宽度作了如下调整：

(1) 厂房上游侧宽度 13.3m，按初定的蜗壳控制外形尺寸及蜗壳＋Y 方向的外包混凝土厚 2.4m 计算，蜗壳层上游侧布置技术供水设备所占据的通道宽度为 3.15m，人行通道最小宽度只有 0.65m。由于蜗壳层下游侧无贯穿全厂的巡检通道，此通道为蜗壳层的主通道，根据辅助系统设备布置的要求，水泵等设备的巡检、维护通道应不小于 1.2m，则主厂房上游需增加宽度 0.55m，实际加宽 0.60m。因此，厂房上游侧宽度调整为 13.9m。

(2) 厂房下游侧宽度，参考相似工程下游侧宽度、发电机机坑尺寸、中间层下游通道等，厂房下游侧宽度比上阶段增加 0.9m，最终定为 11.10m。

(3) 厂房总宽度由 23.5m 调整至 25.0m。

2. 安装场长度设计优化调整　可行性研究阶段安装场总长为 40.0m，与主厂房同一洞室布置。考虑安装场左端部要布置通风系统的宽度为 5m 的机房（房内设的楼梯也作为上桥机及上厂顶网架的检修通道），同时，为兼顾安装场定子、转子等安装布置需要，安装场总长调整为 42.5m。

（三）厂房渗漏检修排水系统的优化

厂房内部排水系统由集水井、深井泵、排水管等组成。可行性研究阶段在主厂房右端底部设置一个渗漏集水井（1 号机组右侧位置），渗漏水直接排至 1 号、2 号尾水隧洞。机组检修排水由布置在 3 号机组段管道廊道内的检修排水泵沿尾水隧洞直接抽排至下水库。可行性研究复核审查意见认为“同意机组技术供水采用水泵供水、下游取水的供水方案。下阶段需研究适当提高厂房渗漏排水的可靠性，优化厂房渗漏排水系统的设计。”

为了寻求一种相对可靠的排水方式，设计考虑了两个方案作为厂内渗漏排水。方案一：为保证排水在最高尾水以上，将排水口布置在下库校核洪水位以上，可沿尾水隧洞借尾水事故闸门井上行至下游最高尾水以上。该方案排水管路总长将比排至尾水隧洞方案更长，并增加尾水闸门后地面布管的固定和保护措施，且影响美观。方案二：渗漏、检修排水通过渗漏、检修排水泵先抽至上部排烟兼排水洞（利用 PD7 排风洞改建），再自流排至厂外。通过排烟兼排水洞排水的方式可消除渗漏排水和检修排水系统故障导致的尾水倒灌的可能性，增加了排水系统的可靠性。由于两种方案工程量基本相当，考虑到在尾水隧洞埋设两根 ϕ600mm 钢管对尾水隧洞施工以及隧洞灌浆影响较大，方案二更能满足实际情况。

现阶段集水井位置改至安装场右端的底部，渗漏水泵室的地面高程由上阶段的蜗壳层高程抬高至水轮机层高程，增加了地下厂房的安全可靠度。集水井位置修改后与 1 号机组段及副厂房之间的施工干扰减小，并可与安装场底板以下透平油处理室统一考虑，节省 1 号机机组段由于渗漏水泵房的布置而增加的长度。同时，集水井下游紧靠厂房下部施工支洞，其开挖及施工运输也更方便。

（四）厂区排水形式的优化

本工程由于输水线路短，因此地下厂房洞群距上、下水库都比较近，约 200～300m。据勘探资料，厂区地下水位较高，在 176.85m 高程左右。地下水主要为岩基裂隙水，在探洞内存在沿裂隙滴落或渗流，并受季节降雨影响。电站投入运行后，上、下游输水道的内水外渗也将成为地下水的补给源。为了保护厂内电气设备的安全运行以及围岩的稳定，需要引排上下游来的渗漏水，为此，在厂房洞室群四周设置上中下三层排水廊道，下层排水廊道与厂房渗漏集水井相接。各层排水廊道之间设排水幕，形成了厂区完整的排水网络。

厂房围岩的渗水，通过厂房周边的排水廊道汇集至集水井，再通过渗漏排水泵，经上层排水廊道将水抽至厂房顶部的排烟兼排水洞最终水自流至厂外。为了防止地下水透过厂区顶部岩体进入厂房，根据工程经验，在上层排水廊道中部（主厂房与主变压器洞之间）增设一道排水廊道，使得厂房和主变压器洞顶部分别能形成封闭的“人”字形排水幕，将顶部渗水引至上层排水廊道，最终引至集水井。

（中国水电顾问集团华东勘测设计研究院　谭建梅）

糯租水电站厂区防渗设计

（一）概况

糯租水电站位于南盘江干流中游河段上。工程为低坝引水式开发。枢纽由首部拦河坝、左岸冲沙洞、左岸引水系统、地下厂房、地下尾水系统和地面升压站等组成。

地下厂房采用浅埋式布置，距南盘江悬崖边仅 40～120m。厂房全长 87m，内装 3 台单机容量为 25MW 的混流式水轮发电机组。自右至左依次为电气副厂房、主机间、安装间和送风机房，按“一”字形布置，纵轴方位为 NE60°。厂房发电机层、水轮机层、蝶阀层的地坪高程分别为 1164.50m、1157.00m、1152.00m，机组安装高程 1155.00m，尾水管底板高程 1148.66m，尾水管建基面高程 1147.60m。

尾水闸门室位于主厂房下游 22.1m 处，与主厂房纵向平行布置，地坪高程 1177.00m。尾水闸门井深 26.67m，底板高程 1150.33m。在闸门井前尾水支洞长 20.1m；闸门井后三条支洞逐渐汇合为一主洞，主洞长 62.0m。

厂房为 3 级建筑物。按 100 年一遇洪水设计、200 年一遇洪水校核，下游河床设计洪水位为 1171.56m、校核洪水位为 1172.42m。三台机发电尾水位 1161.00m。

（二）厂区工程地质条件

地下厂房和尾水建筑物部位分布岩层为 S_{2m}^{b-3} 中厚～厚层灰岩，岩体单层厚度一般为 60～120cm，局部夹少量薄层。微风化～新鲜岩体，岩层产状较平缓，一般为 N10°～50°E，SE∠10°～30°。厂房顶拱上覆岩体厚度在 63～80m，岩体地质构造发育，Ⅱ级破裂结构面 F_{103} 断层展布于地下厂房东侧，距离主厂房东侧边墙大于 70m，是一条阻水断层，地下厂房及尾水建筑物在断层的下盘。厂区Ⅲ级结构面较少，Ⅳ级破裂结构面较发育。

根据地质测绘、平洞资料和地质雷达探测显示，厂区喀斯特现象较发育，主要表现为溶洞和溶蚀裂隙。大小溶洞共发现 17 个，其中 R_1、R_4、R_5 三个溶洞规模较大，连通性较好，洞径一般为 1.4～3.5m，人可进入深度达 30～40m；其他均表现为局部溶蚀（或称为溶穴），洞径一般 0.5～1m，连通性不好。溶洞发育方向多受层面控制，总体走向 N30°～50°E，并沿 N30°～ 50°W 和 SN 向及 EW 向陡倾节理呈树枝状分布。溶洞发育高程一般为 1149～1205m。溶洞（如 R_1、R_4、R_5 等）多为半充填，底部一般有 30～70cm 厚的钙质砂质黏土夹灰岩碎石；

溶穴一般为全充填，充填物多为红泥和灰岩角砾。溶蚀裂隙主要沿顺层挤压面和 N30°～50°W、近 EW 向、近 SN 向陡倾节理发育，宽一般 10～40cm，多为红泥夹灰岩碎、块石充填。

厂区下层岩溶地下水水位低，接近河水位，枯期地下水位高程约 1160.5～1166m，比厂房底板高出 10.5～16m，洪水期地下水位要高出厂房底板 20m 左右。厂区有一泉水出露于尾水洞出口下游约 40m，流量约 6～10L/s，流量较稳定。

（三）防渗设计

2006 年 5 月 5 日晚约 11 点，岔管施工支洞（桩号约 0＋143.000）右侧边墙脚部的溶洞出现涌水。洞内涌水水位约 1160m，涌水口处淹没水深约 1.5m。经地质分析判断，此涌水来源于岩溶地下水和江水倒灌。涌水发生后，组织专家进行现场查勘和会议研究讨论，决定采用帷幕灌浆封闭地下建筑主要回灌通道，永久与施工期处理措施结合考虑。为了减少施工期建筑物开挖排水难度，下游侧尾水施工支洞和上游侧的岔管施工支洞都封闭在帷幕灌浆内。

根据上述情况，设计采用帷幕灌浆与阻水断层 F_{103} 结合形成一个封闭的阻水幕，封闭地下建筑主要回灌通道。帷幕灌浆底线高程 1142.00m，在机组尾水管底板以下 5.6m；顶部高程 1172.50～1177.20m，在下游河床校核水位 1172.42m 以上；底部两端伸出 F_{103} 断层，采用单排孔，孔距 1.5m 并局部加密。根据施工进度安排，靠河床侧采用地面钻孔进行帷幕灌浆，其余打绕厂区环形灌浆隧洞进行地下灌浆。地面灌浆段长度 91.5m，帷幕灌浆洞长 283.2m，断面尺寸 3.4m×4.0m。洞内设排水沟，断面为 0.35m×0.25m。灌浆隧洞顶部内打向上排水孔 ϕ110mm，孔深 12m，孔距 3.0m。因开挖灌浆洞的施工支洞布置需要，灌浆洞底坡排水由主厂房电梯井的交通支洞处向两头排水，一侧通过扩挖 20 号勘探平洞排出洞外，一侧排到尾水施工支洞的集水坑中。

在岔管施工支洞堵头和尾水施工支洞堵头附近布置集水坑，设抽水站进行抽排。

由于主厂房顶拱 F_{11}、F_{12} 断层有阻水作用，厂房顶拱没有设置排水孔，通过三个汛期观察洞顶渗水不严重。采用洞顶拱形镀锌钢板吊顶，把渗水汇集到岩壁吊车梁的排水沟（断面尺寸：0.15m×0.15m）和防潮夹层底部的排水沟（断面尺寸：0.2m×0.2m），再汇入集水井后抽走。

（四）防潮设计

地下厂房发电机层以下边墙采用 65cm 厚的钢筋混凝土衬砌，发电机层以上的边墙、顶拱采用喷锚支护。在发电机层以上的厂房四周均设有防潮夹层，利用防潮墙保持厂内干燥，改善设备和运行人员的工作条件。

（五）结语

厂区灌浆帷幕形成后，对电站施工期和运行期主要体现在以下几方面：

（1）地下建筑物施工期间，由于其出水量减少，降低了施工期的抽排水难度。

（2）通过 2007 年、2008 年及 2009 年三个汛期的考验，帷幕防渗效果较好。地下厂房渗漏集水井渗水量较小，上游岔管施工支洞及尾水施工支洞内渗水量都不大，保证了机电设备的运行安全。

（3）电站首台机组于 2008 年 8 月发电后，第二台、第三台机组正也相继发电。经过近两年的运行验证，证明各建筑物运行情况良好。

（中国水电顾问集团昆明勘测设计研究院 孟桂萍）

岩壁吊车梁在地下洞室大范围Ⅳ～Ⅴ类围岩中的应用

琅琊山抽水蓄能电站位于安徽省滁州市西南郊，装机容量为 4×150MW，电站建成后承担电网的调峰填谷、调相、调频和事故备用任务。

电站地下厂房区地质条件复杂，围岩稳定性差，在 1、2 号机组段发育蚀变花岗闪长斑岩带，宽约 20m，横贯厂房上、下游边墙以及顶拱、底板，属Ⅳ～Ⅴ类围岩。蚀变岩蚀变程度具有随机性和不均一性，严重蚀变岩体力学指标非常低，抗压强度只有 10～20MPa，变模 0.5GPa，摩擦系数 0.28。地下厂房蚀变岩范围大，强度低，易软化，对可否建造岩壁吊车梁进行了专题研究。通过现场试验、计算分析等研究，认为该Ⅳ～Ⅴ类围岩可以作为岩壁吊车梁的基础，并在琅琊山工程成功建造了岩壁吊车梁。具体的处理措施如下。

（1）利用蚀变岩承载能力，采用悬吊锚杆承受部分吊车荷载。蚀变岩遇水或潮气加速蚀变，但未经扰动的原岩仍有一定的承载能力，锚杆在轻度、中度蚀变的蚀变岩体锚固效果较好。因此，施工时，尽量减少对蚀变岩的扰动，开挖后对蚀变岩及时喷混凝土保护封闭，保持原岩的力学特性。在梁体上部设置两排悬吊锚杆 ϕ36@75，$L=9.75$m，锚入岩石 8m，孔口 1m 范围内涂抹沥青，使锚杆应力向深部围岩传递；下部锚杆 ϕ28@75，$L=7.15$m，锚杆锚入岩石 6m，共同承受部分吊车荷载。

（2）设置 L 形悬吊刚性基础垫座。蚀变岩抗压强度低，变形模量低，当承受巨大的吊车荷载时，提供的地基反力将不能维持梁体平衡，易发生塑性变形，使梁体失稳。为了形成与岩壁吊车梁计算假定相仿的稳定基础，将吊车梁蚀变岩基础侧壁和底部扩挖 1m，先锚喷支护，再浇筑 L 形基座混凝土，形成刚性基础垫座。该基础沿厂房纵轴方向长 19.9m，跨过蚀变岩出露范围，延伸支撑至灰岩基础。考虑到厂房下部开挖可能使垫座混凝土底部的蚀变岩塌方脱落，导致该刚性基础悬空，仅靠简支在两端灰岩基础，无法承受巨大的吊车运行荷载，并且蚀变岩具有易软化、易膨胀的特性，因此设置悬吊锚索锚固刚性基础垫座。预应力锚索均为无黏结式，设计吨位 1000kN，间距 2.5～3m，长度 20m。上游设置 8 根与排水廊道对穿锚固，其中 4 根锚固于蚀变岩内，另外 4 根穿过蚀变岩锚入灰岩中。下游设置 4 根内锚式锚索，全部穿过蚀变岩锚入灰岩中。L 形的断面形式，使吊车梁由斜壁支撑改为平台支撑，减轻了悬吊锚杆的拉拔力，使受力更为合理。经过处理，将软弱的蚀变岩基础置换成稳定的刚性基础垫座，该垫座既能约束蚀变岩膨胀、变形，又能抵抗蚀变岩软化、脱空的影响，为吊车梁提供了良好的承载基础，如图 1 所示。此结构“新型地下厂房岩壁吊车梁 L 形悬吊刚性基础垫座结构”已获得实用新型专利授权（专利号：200920176291.4）。

(3) 悬空混凝土墙辅助支撑吊车梁。蚀变岩段岩壁吊车梁除了依靠悬吊锚杆承受拉力，L 形悬吊刚性基础垫座提供支撑力，还利用下部悬空混凝土边墙作为辅助支撑。为维持蚀变岩段高边墙稳定设置的直立倒悬混凝土边墙，支撑在 L 形基础垫座外侧，避免 L 形垫座横断面呈悬臂结构，使吊车轮压作用线刚好位于墙体内，充分利用墙体的承压能力。厂房开挖至基础后，先期限制桥机起吊吨位（15t）提早将吊车投入运行，后期倒悬边墙与底板基础连接后，吊车全负荷投入运行。

琅琊山抽水蓄能电站地下厂房先后安装了 2 台桥机，1 台 32/5t 桥机用于厂房下部开挖和混凝土浇筑辅助施工，1 台 QE180＋180/25-20.5 双小车桥机用于大型机电设备安装。岩壁吊车梁的成功建成，使桥机能较早投入运用，加快了施工进度，节约施工工期 2 个月，节省投资约 100 万元。岩壁吊车梁建成至今已有丰富的监测资料和安全运行经验，这些资料表明，对大范围Ⅳ～Ⅴ类围岩基础的岩壁吊车梁处理措施是合理的，吊车梁运行安全可靠。

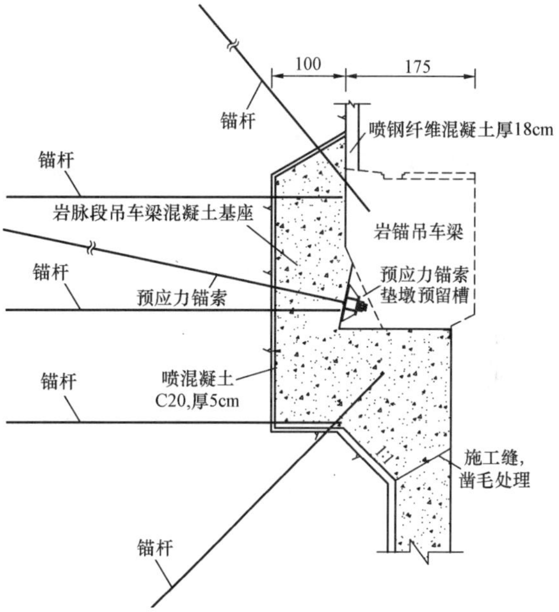

图 1 蚀变岩段岩壁吊车梁 L 形悬吊刚性基础垫座横剖面图

琅琊山抽水蓄能电站地下厂房在大范围Ⅳ～Ⅴ类围岩基础上修建岩壁吊车梁，为其他工程提供了宝贵经验，填补了国内大型地下厂房在Ⅳ～Ⅴ类围岩基础上修建岩壁吊车梁的空白，具有广泛的推广应用价值。

（中国水电顾问集团北京勘测设计研究院
王阳雪　吴　奎）

枢 纽 布 置 设 计

江苏宜兴抽水蓄能电站设计特点

（一）工程概况

宜兴抽水蓄能电站位于江苏省宜兴市西南郊约 10km 的铜官山区，装机容量 4×250MW，以 2 回 500kV 出线接入岷珠变电站，在电网中承担调峰、填谷、调频、调相和事故备用等任务。电站主要由上水库、下水库、输水系统、地下厂房洞室群和地面开关站等组成。

宜兴抽水蓄能电站由中国水电顾问集团华东勘测设计研究院和上海勘测设计研究院负责勘测设计，勘测工作由中国水电顾问集团华东勘测设计研究院承担。电站主体工程于2003年7月31日正式开工，2008年5月1日1号机组投入商业运行，同年12月全部机组投入运行，实现“一年四投”，比原计划提前13个月。

（二）工程技术特点

该工程已顺利通过消防、建设征地移民安置、水土保持、环境保护、职业病、枢纽工程、劳动安全与工业卫生、档案等专项验收。各验收委员会和水电专家对工程设计和建设成果给予了充分肯定和高度评价。宜兴抽水蓄能电站设计具有枢纽建筑物布置紧凑、边坡工程难度不大、施工及运行管理方便、投资相对较省等特点。

1. 上水库　主坝选用钢筋混凝土面板混合堆石坝坝型，即钢筋混凝土面板坝加下游重力挡墙。挡墙顶长347.75m，最大高度45.9m，悬臂段最大高度25.0m，基础布置钢筋混凝土抗剪桩和预应力锚索。该坝型为国际首创，节省大量投资；建成后最大沉降值为220mm（变形值比例仅0.29%，小于设计1%标准），最大水平位移73.05mm（小于设计标准100mm）。库盆和坝基总渗漏量最大值16.84L/s（占总库容的0.274‰，小于不大于总库容0.5‰的设计标准），变形和渗漏指标达到国际先进水平，获得了世界银行特别咨询团和国内外水电专家的高度评价。

2. 下水库　下水库设计集功能性和生态景观于一体，库周边坡采用客土吹附复绿技术，充分利用水库和山形地势，打造园林式山水景观。大坝在国内抽水蓄能电站中第一个采用黏土心墙堆石坝，经精心设计与施工，实测心墙最大沉降量235mm，为坝高的0.47%，小于设计标准1%；渗流量在3～5L/s，小于下水库日平均渗流量20L/s的计算值和0.5‰有效库容（30L/s）的设计标准，大坝变形和渗漏指标达到国际先进水平。

3. 地下厂房　地下厂房洞室群位于Ⅳ～Ⅲ类为主、局部Ⅴ类的中～厚层岩屑砂岩夹薄层泥质粉砂岩围岩中，节理较为发育，地下水丰富，断层构造带发育，在我国已建的类似工程地下厂房中，其地质条件最差。设计首次采用以锚杆＋喷钢纤维混凝土＋拱肋＋预应力锚索的复合型柔性支护方案，提出了排水先行的设计理念，保证了施工安全；创造性地采用复合式分期承载岩壁吊车梁结构，主机段岩梁下部结合防潮墙构造柱布置设置支撑柱，使地下厂房桥机如期投入运行；开展机组和厂房抗振技术、蜗壳结构联合受力和配筋优化研究，成功避免了国内高水头蜗壳外包混凝土开裂问题。主厂房围岩变形值为0.41～17.39mm，开挖结束后已经稳定收敛；锚杆受力已收敛并趋于稳定，应力在50～100MPa之间。该地下厂房的成功建造，开创了国内复杂工程地质条件和水文地质条件下兴建大型地下工程的成功典范。

4. 输水系统

（1）招标设计阶段进行了高边坡方案与下库进/出水口外移200m方案的比较，最终采用下库进/出水口外移200m方案。外移后下进/出水口边坡高度降低了75m，地质条件也有所改善，避开了较大断层F_{110}。

（2）将引水钢岔管位置向下游调整约40m，缩短高压支管的长度，减少工程投资，经水力学过渡过程计算分析，两台机组间水力干扰也较小。

（3）将两条尾水隧洞轴线距离从51.8m缩小为35m，使下水库2个进/出水口间距减小16.8m，明挖范围减小；检修闸门井平台与拦污栅平台之间的工作桥均减短了16.8m，工作桥的安全性和经济性也得到提高；另外，还避开了F_{14}断层对尾水调压室的高边墙稳定的影响。

（4）将尾水钢衬向下游延伸至尾水事故闸门洞中心线下游28.5m处，与尾水事故闸门洞下游侧排水廊道及帷幕灌浆形成了一道阻水防线，避免了尾水隧洞内水向尾水事故闸门洞渗漏，改善了液压启闭设备的工作环境。

5. 地面开关站　将原布置在厂房顶部地面（310m高程）的地面开关站移到位于厂房北侧约500m处的山坡（195m高程）上，改原竖井出线为斜洞出线，使开关站边坡高度大为减少，降低了工程潜在风险，节约投资约1000万元。

6. 金属结构　上、下水库拦污栅设备全部采用接近流线型断面设计，着重研究拦污栅安装工艺要求，解决了抽水蓄能电站特有的双向水流作用下的拦污栅振动问题。

7. 机电工程

（1）将额定水头从353m提高到363m，机组运行稳定性得到改善，电动机的最大入力降低8%左右，降低发电电动机造价约1000万元。

（2）取消主变压器有载调压方案，采用发电电动机机端调压的方式，提高了设备可靠性。

（3）技术供水系统由原2台机组分两组集中供水方案改为单元供水，每台机一主一备，增加了供水可靠性，简化了控制程序。

（4）检修排水系统根据不同排水量要求，设置了大、小两种容量的水泵，减小厂用电，便于控制和操作。

（5）渗漏排水系统从两个集水井改为一个，布置位置从主厂房移到尾水闸门洞，提高了厂房安全性。

（6）从中压压气系统减压作为吹扫和主轴密封用气源，提高供气可靠性，同时节省一台检修空气压缩机。

(7) 主厂房桥机由 250＋250/50t 双小车桥机改为单小车桥机，减小了桥机轮压对岩壁吊车梁的影响，可减少发电机层支柱，也节约了工期。

(8) 安装场下中间透平油罐室移入施工支洞，减少了土建开挖量。

(9) 本工程的地下厂房排水不具备自流排水条件，增设柴油发电机组，确保地下厂房运行安全，同时可满足本电站作为系统黑启动电源点，承担系统的安全保障任务功能。

8. 环境保护与水土保持　工程建设各项环保水保方案及设施实施后，扰动土地整治率 99%，水土流失总治理度 99%，土壤流失控制比 1.4，拦渣率 99%，林草植被恢复率 98%，各项指标均优于防治目标要求。世界银行督察团对电站工程环保水保工作的评价为："项目的整个环境质量令人高度满意。"在水土保持专项竣工验收中，验收组推荐申报水利部水土保持示范项目工程。

（三）结语

本电站工程总投资为 47.63 亿元人民币，由于优化设计，采用多项"四新"技术和先进的建设管理，实际投资 41.6 亿元，节约投资约 6 亿元，取得显著的工程效益。截至 2009 年底，本电站已安全运行 609 天，产生了可观的经济效益。

该工程已以平均分 95.70 的高分通过国家电网公司达标投产验收。

（中国水电顾问集团华东勘测设计研究院
陈顺义　姜长飞　时雷鸣）

巴山水电站枢纽布置设计

巴山水电站工程位于重庆市城口县境内的任河干流上，是任河规划 7 个梯级开发方案中的第三个梯级，为任河梯级开发中的控制性工程，水库具有年调节性能。工程以发电为主，兼有旅游和改善生态环境等综合利用。坝址位于巴山镇上游约 1km 的冉家坝处，厂址位于巴山下游雷打石任河左岸山坡处。水库正常蓄水位 680.00m，总库容 3.165 亿 m^3；电站安装 2 台单机容量 7 万 kW 的水轮发电机组。

任河是汉江上游右岸一条较大的支流，干流总长 212km。坝址以上控制集水面积 1712km^2，多年平均流量为 44.0m^3/s，年径流总量 13.9 亿 m^3。

坝址区地层岩性为含砾凝灰质岩屑砂岩，无区域性大断层通过，小规模断层、挤压破碎带和节理裂隙较发育。工程区地震基本烈度为Ⅵ度。

本工程枢纽由钢筋混凝土面板堆石坝、溢洪道、引水系统及发电厂房等组成。工程等别为二等。拦河大坝为混凝土面板堆石坝，坝高 155m，超过 100m 提高一级，为 1 级建筑物；泄水进水口、引水系统进水口等主要建筑物为 2 级建筑物，引水隧洞、发电厂房等次要建筑物为 3 级建筑物，临时建筑物为 4 级。拦河大坝及其泄洪建筑物按 500 年一遇洪水 (4920m^3/s) 设计，5000 年一遇洪水 (6100m^3/s) 校核；发电厂房按 100 年一遇洪水 (4060m^3/s) 设计，200 年一遇洪水 (4430m^3/s) 校核，下游消能防冲按 50 年一遇设计。

（一）大坝

大坝为面板堆石坝，坝顶路面高程 685.00m，坝顶宽 10.00m，建基面最低高程 530.00m，最大坝高 155.00m，坝顶长 477m，防浪墙顶高程 686.20m。坝顶下游侧设挡墙。下游坝坡不设"之"字形上坝公路，而是沿高度方向每隔 30m 设 2m 宽的马道，上面两级坡度为 1∶1.3，下面两级坡为 1∶1.4，下游平均坝坡为 1∶1.4。上游面坝坡为 1∶1.4。坝线转弯处混凝土面板设连接板。沿冲沟布置的趾板局部由于面板坡度缓于原地形，面板与原地形间有高差，趾板须用高趾墙连接。

坝体堆石分成六区，即辅助防渗区（粉土铺盖及石渣回填）、垫层区、过渡层区、上游堆石区（中部为砂砾石）、下游堆石区、下游大块石区。其中垫层区水平宽度 3.0m，过渡层区水平宽度 5.0m。面板上游 595m 高程以下设粉土铺盖和盖重区，下游面干砌石护坡和坝脚下游回填超径石压坡。

混凝土面板厚度：顶部为 0.3m，底部随高度变化，计算式为：$d=0.3+0.0035H$（H 为计算断面至面板顶部的垂直距离）。面板纵向分缝，缝间距 12m，横向不分缝。

两岸岸坡段趾板采用"$4+x$"型式，水平段长 4.5m，其余顺着岸坡为斜坡趾板，两趾板间设缝止水。斜坡段长按不同作用水头，高程 635.00m 以上、585.00～635.00m、585.00m 以下三个部位，趾板宽度分别为 4.0m、7.0m、10.0m，斜坡段厚均为 0.3m，水平段与上述三个高程段匹配相应厚度分别为 0.6m、0.7m、0.8m。趾板按单层双向配筋，纵横向配筋率均为 0.35%，布置在趾板顶部，保护层厚 10cm。

在工程施工过程中，为实现一枯拦水，加快施工进度，确保度汛断面的按期完成，将内置防渗板修改为挂网喷混凝土，厚 20cm，同时取消了防渗板上的固结灌浆，适当加长喷混凝土长度，并在趾板上游面增加贴坡混凝土并设加强固结灌浆和帷幕灌浆。

（二）溢洪道

溢洪道位于右坝头，利用右岸山坡开挖而成，溢洪道轴线与坝轴线夹角132.2°。由进水渠、控制段、泄槽、挑流鼻坎及尾水渠等建筑物组成。溢洪道宽45m，总长约519.5m，共设3孔，每孔净宽13.0m，闸墩厚度为3.0m，每孔设弧形闸门采用液压启闭机操作。进水渠底高程661.50m，堰顶高程667.50m，堰面曲线为WES型。

泄槽段纵坡分别为1∶20和1∶2，中间设掺气槽连接，共设三道掺气槽，以减小空蚀影响。挑流鼻坎为分条复式扭曲挑流鼻坎，共分3条，每条宽15m。坎顶高程568.85～574.39m，挑角为10.28°～33.99°，反弧半径30～40m。鼻坎后设30m混凝土护坦。尾水渠渠底高程565.30m。

（三）引水发电系统

采用一洞二机布置。建筑物包括进水口、引水隧洞、调压室、高压管道竖井、钢筋混凝土岔管、高压钢支管等部分。

进水口采用岸塔式布置，进水口底板高程637.00m。进水口由分流隔墩分成2孔，每孔净宽为5.0m，高12.0m，设一道拦污栅。进水口与闸室段之间采用方洞连接。闸室段长7.2m，闸门孔口尺寸为5.3m×6.6m（宽×高）。

引水隧洞为马蹄形断面，洞径7.6m，底宽4.5m，全长2181.28m，纵向按“一坡到底”布置，坡度1.593‰。在桩号0+102.634m处的第一个平面转弯点，隧洞走向由N52°E转为N82°W。

调压室为升管阻抗式地下调压室。引水高压管道采用竖井布置。竖井中心线距调压室中心线30.3m，总长118.23m（含上下弯段），洞径6.6m。竖井中心处为平面转弯点，竖井后高压管道下平段走向为N40°W，下平段长30m，中心线高程511.1m。岔管距电站厂房机组中心线约164m，将高压管道分成2条高压钢支管。

（四）发电厂房

巴山电站厂房位于巴山下游雷打石左岸山坡，距坝址区5.0～6.0km。厂区主要建筑物有主厂房、下游副厂房、端副厂房、升压站、开关站等。主厂房总长度52.70m，其中机组段长31.70m，安装场长21.00m。下部宽度为37.00m，上部宽为21.00m，总高度为40.10m，地面以上高度16.00m。安装场及尾水平台与厂区地面同高，高程为523.10m，进厂公路由左侧与安装场联系。

巴山电站升压、开关站布置在厂房右侧，升压、开关站尺寸宽为21.00m，长为40.80m；开关站地面高程523.10m，与厂区地坪高程同高；升压站、开关站通过电缆廊道与厂房联系。

（中国水电顾问集团华东勘测设计研究院
陈振文　齐立景）

石虎塘航电枢纽工程设计简介

（一）工程概况

石虎塘航电枢纽工程位于江西省赣江中游泰和县城公路桥下游26km的石虎塘村附近，下游距吉安市井冈山大桥33km，是赣江赣州至湖口河段自上而下6个规划梯级中的第3个梯级，是渠化赣江航道的重要梯级。兴建石虎塘枢纽工程后，可渠化坝址上游38km的航道，使该河段能通过千吨级船舶，对促进江西省对外物资调节和经济发展有十分重要的影响。

石虎塘航电枢纽工程以改善航运条件为主，兼顾发电，结合兴建防护工程对库区两岸有防洪作用。工程正常蓄水位56.5m，相应库容约1.668亿m^3，航道及船闸等级为Ⅲ级，电站装机容量为12万kW。工程于2009年7月开工建设，总投资24.41亿元。

（二）设计标准

石虎塘航电枢纽校核洪水位61.03m，相应水库总库容约7.43亿m^3，航道及船闸等级为Ⅲ级，电站装机容量120MW。根据《防洪标准》（GB 50201—1994）、《渠化工程枢纽总体布置设计规范》（JTJ 220—1998）和《水电枢纽工程等级划分及设计安全标准》（DL 5180—2003），石虎塘航电枢纽工程为二等大（2）型工程。由于本工程挡水高度10.3m，在各级洪水情况下，坝前水位壅高值小于0.3m，接近天然水流流态，失事后造成损失不大，经过主管部门批准，本工程主要建筑物泄洪冲沙闸、船闸挡水部分、发电厂房、左右岸接头土石坝段按3级建筑物设计，次要建筑物按4级设计。

（三）工程布置

枢纽建筑物从左到右依次为左岸土坝、船闸、泄水闸、厂房、右岸连接坝段和右岸土坝，鱼道和导排渠从右岸土坝穿过。枢纽建筑物坝顶总长度1639.7m，其中左岸土坝长度438.4m，船闸宽度43.4m，泄水闸长度532m，主厂房长度136m，连接段长度86.5m，右岸土坝长度403.4m。

（四）主要建筑物

1．泄水闸　本枢纽泄水建筑物由23孔泄水闸组成，前缘总长532.0m，每孔净宽20.0m。采用孔中分缝，分为22个坝段，除两个边孔坝段宽为36m外，其余每个坝段宽度均为23.00m。堰顶高程46.7m，闸室顺水流方向长度32.8m。从上游往下游，设一道平板检修门，利用坝顶移动式门机启闭；

一道弧形工作门，液压启闭机启闭。泄水闸闸顶高程66.0m，闸顶宽37.0m。坝顶下游侧设9.5m宽公路桥，是贯穿整个枢纽的交通通道，紧临公路桥上游侧是油管电缆箱梁和20.8m间距的两根坝顶门机轨道梁。闸墩中部设油压泵房。

泄水闸堰型采用宽顶堰，上游堰顶高程均为46.7m，桩号坝0+017.0m后，以1∶4.0的坡度和消力池相接，消力池顶面高程43.0m。

泄水闸下游分三区，Ⅰ区（7孔）、Ⅲ区（7孔）设消力池，消力池长37.5m，Ⅱ区（9孔）设护坦，长30.0m。区与区中间设中隔墙，中隔墙结合施工纵向围堰，墙顶高程均定为54.9m。泄水闸和厂房之间设导墙，长160m，墙顶高程54.9m。

2. 船闸　船闸布置在泄水闸左侧；设计年通过能力近期为605万t，远期为880万t；按千吨级驳船队标准设计，设计船队尺寸：160m×10.8m×2.2m（长×宽×吃水），闸室有效尺度：180m×23m×3.5m（长×宽×门槛水深）。上闸首长29.50m，宽43.4m，顶高程为62.5m，右侧与泄水闸闸墩连接，左侧与左岸接头坝连接。闸室结构长度为180m，宽23m，顶高程为58.70m。下闸首长32.2m，宽43.4m，顶高程为59.50m。

3. 电站厂房　发电厂房布置在泄水闸右侧；厂房前缘总长176m，其中主机间长136m，安装6台单机容量2万kW的贯流式灯泡机组，一机一缝，自右至左依次为1～6号机组，其中1、2号机组为4叶片机组，3～6号机组为3叶片机组。根据设备布置、流道尺寸和水工结构要求，标准机组段前缘长21.71m，左、右边机组段前缘长均为26.01m。安装间位于主机间右侧，长40m，净宽与主机间相同。副厂房由尾水副厂房和安装间上、下游副厂房组成。变电站布置于主机间下游侧。

4. 连接坝段及左右岸土坝　船闸左侧采用438.4m长土坝与左侧岸坡相连。厂房主机间右侧设86.5m长混凝土连接坝段，连接坝段右侧采用403.35m长土坝与右侧岸坡相连。

（中水珠江规划勘测设计有限公司　刘元勋）

官帽舟水电站枢纽布置设计

官帽舟水电站位于四川省乐山市马边县境内，距马边县城9km左右，是马边河干流水电规划报告推荐的7级开发方案中的第1个梯级龙头水库，马边河为岷江下游右岸一级支流。2009年11月10日，官帽舟水电站正式开工建设。

官帽舟水电站采用混合式开发方案。水库正常蓄水位为674m，校核洪水位677.44m，总库容为0.9733亿m^3，设计洪水流量3180m^3/s（$P=1\%$），校核洪水流量4860m^3/s（$P=0.05\%$）。工程等别为三等中型工程。发电厂房安装2台机组，装机容量共110MW。考虑马边河生态基流需要，坝后设置生态基流电站，安装2台机组，其总容量为10MW。

官帽舟水电站的地震设防烈度为Ⅷ度。坝址区岩性主要为泥质粉砂岩、长石石英砂岩夹粉砂质泥岩，主要为软质岩。

（一）拦河坝

沥青心墙混合坝最大坝高为109m，坝顶长为242.8m，宽高比为2.23，是目前国内高沥青心墙坝之一。坝顶高程为679m，坝顶宽度为10m；坝基河床高程为580.5～582m，河床宽度为40m左右。上下坝坡分为4级，3级马道，马道之间高差主要为30m，除了坝顶下迎水侧的第一级坝坡为1∶2，背水侧的最下面一级坝坡为1∶1.75外，其余坝坡均为1∶2.25。拦河坝与施工上游全年围堰结合，坝体材料分为7个分区，填筑料主要为粉砂岩和砂岩的石渣混合料；泄洪道开挖泥岩料主要布设在坝体下游干燥区，填筑方量为260万m^3。沥青心墙顶部厚度为0.6m，底部厚度为1.5m。在坝高超过72m以上河床坝基内沥青心墙底部设置带有灌浆廊道的C25混凝土基座，河床基座建基高程为570m，两岸沥青心墙底部设置C25混凝土垫座。由于坝基覆盖层厚度仅为2～8m，坝基均采用帷幕防渗系统。

（二）泄洪建筑物

1. 敞开式溢洪道　挡水坝右侧680m高程有一平台。为了减少高边坡，敞开式溢洪道紧邻右坝肩，其控制段闸墩布置在弱风化泥质粉砂岩上。闸孔尺寸为2孔14m×12m（宽×高），堰顶高程为662m。由于枯期有很长时间库水位低于堰顶高程，因此不设检修闸门，只设弧形工作闸门。进水渠底板高程为658m。泄槽为由堰后宽度的31m收缩到28m宽度的矩形槽，泄槽纵坡为1∶4.2，水平长度238.67m。溢洪道设计洪水泄量为2355m^3/s（$P=1\%$），校核洪水泄量为3483.3m^3/s（$P=0.05\%$），最大单宽流量为124.4m^3/s，最大流速为36.64m/s，出口采用曲面贴角鼻坎挑流消能工。

2. 泄洪放空洞　泄洪放空洞采用龙抬头结合利用导流洞，位于溢洪道轴线右侧平行32m处，其优先开启闸门宣泄。检修闸门井与工作闸门井合并布置在泄洪洞上半部分，检修闸门尺寸为6m×7.5m，弧形工作闸门尺寸为6m×6m，闸门底坎高程为620m。进水口轴线与闸门井轴线角度为52°，两轴线以30m半径的圆弧段连接。闸门井前采用有压圆形段，洞径为7.5m，总长197.234m。闸门井后采用无压城门洞形，龙抬头尺寸为 7.5m×10.0m。龙抬头渥奇曲线方程为 $y=0.003\ 561x^2$，长约 116.024m。结合导流洞改建的泄洪洞尺寸为 7.5m × 11.5m，长为 259.025m 左右，纵向坡度为 0.2%。洞出口高程为 584m，采用挑流消能。泄洪放空洞设计洪水泄量为 $814.69m^3/s$（$P=1\%$），校核洪水泄量为 $845.69m^3/s$（$P=0.05\%$），泄洪放空洞最大单宽流量为 $117.87m^3/s$，最大流速为 33.731m/s。

（三）引水发电系统

1. 引水发电隧洞　发电引水系统采用一洞二机引水方式，额定引水流量为 $2\times59.94m^3/s$。引水隧洞长度为 6.38km，包括岸塔式进口、钢筋混凝土衬砌段、水室式调压井和钢衬段。进口底板高程为 629m，位于坝轴线上游左岸约 151.6m 处。进口采用 3 孔拦污栅，孔口尺寸为 4.5m×9m；设事故检修门一道，共 1 孔，孔口尺寸 6.2m×6.2m（高×宽）。钢筋混凝土衬砌段洞径为 6.2m，全长为 6.094km，最大洞内流速为 3.971m/s。水室式调压井包括竖井和上室。竖井为直径 20m 的圆形，井顶部高程为 699.5m，井底部引水隧洞底板高程为 608.0m，井深为 91.5m，其最高涌波水位为 698.44m，最低涌波水位为 616.57m。上室为长方形 10.3m×20.6m（长×宽）（顺水流向×垂直水流向），顺水流向下游与竖井直径 20.6m 半圆相连，上游半圆与下游竖井半圆相对称。水室式调压井内设一快速事故闸门，闸门孔口尺寸为 5.4m×5.4m。闸门井后主管钢衬段直径为 5.4m，纵向长 205.699m；2 条支管的直径为 3.5m，每条支管纵向长 70.633m。支管中心线高程即机组进水管安装高程为 545.65m。

2. 发电厂房　电站厂房为岸边引水式厂房，厂址位于坝址下游约 10km、马边河左岸、洞子口冲沟上游，厂区地面高程 568.3m。电站额定水头 102.6m，安装 2 台单机容量为 55MW 的混流式水轮发电机组。单机额定引用流量为 $55.94m^3/s$。厂房前缘总长 62.661m，其中主机间长 39.161m，安装间长 23.5m。厂房顺水流向宽 28.338m。主机间净宽 16.53m。安装间位于主机间左侧，净宽与主机间相同，地面高程 568.5m。副厂房主要位于主机间和安装间上游。

（四）生态流量引水系统

1. 生态流量隧洞　生态流量隧洞采用一洞二机引水方式，额定引水流量仅为 $2\times7.74m^3/s$。生态流量隧洞包括进水口、钢筋混凝土衬砌隧洞段和钢衬段，顺水流向长度为 471.724m。生态流量隧洞进水口采用与发电引水洞进口并列布置的独立进水口。进口底板高程 629m，拦污栅孔为 1 孔 4.5m×4.5m，检修闸门为 1 孔 2m×2m。钢筋混凝土衬砌隧洞段内径为 2m，全长 429.771m。钢衬主管段内径为 2m，顺水流向长 21m。主管直径为 2m，顺水流向长 21m。2 条支管内径为 1.5m。支管中心线高程即机组进水管安装高程为 580.35m。

2. 生态流量电站　生态流量电站为岸边引水式厂房，厂址位于坝后左岸。电站安装间、主机间、副厂房沿山坡脚“一”字形布置，厂区地面高程 594.1m。发电厂房装有 2 台单机容量 5MW 的混流式水轮发电机组，总装机容量 10MW。电站厂房由主机间、安装间和副厂房组成，前沿长度 51.2m（其中主机间 21.2m，安装间 14.6m，副厂房 15.4m），厂房顺水流向长度 17.4m。机组间距 8.25m，安装高程 580.35m，厂房顺水流向宽度 17.4m。安装间位于主机间左侧，安装场地面高程 594.3m。

（中水珠江规划勘测设计有限公司　韩小妹）

红花水电站枢纽布置及建筑物优化设计

（一）工程概况

广西柳江红花水电站位于广西壮族自治区柳江县境内，是《珠江流域西江水系柳江综合利用规划报告》确定的柳江干流最下游一个梯级。坝址控制流域面积 $34\ 097km^2$，占柳江流域面积的 80%。电站是一个以发电、航运为主，兼顾灌溉、旅游、养殖的综合利用工程。

红花水电站正常蓄水位为 77.5m，相应库容为 5.7 亿 m^3，总库容为 30 亿 m^3，总装机容量 238MW，保证出力 27.4MW，多年平均发电量 8.8 亿 kW·h，为日调节水库，承担系统部分调峰任务。枢纽建成后，可渠化库区干支流河道 108km，与上游的大埔电站尾水位衔接，使柳州市以下的 60km 航道不需整治可通航 1000t 级的船舶；可灌溉农田 15 万亩；可促进养殖业、旅游业发展，改善生态环境，将对柳州腹地社会经济的发展起重要作用。

（二）主要建筑物布置

红花水电站为一等工程，挡水建筑物为 2 级，混凝土挡水建筑物按 100 年一遇洪水标准设计，1000 年一遇洪水校核，土坝按 2000 年一遇洪水校核。红花水电站主要建筑物包括泄水闸、船闸、厂房、门库连接坝、土坝。电站布置自右向左依次为右岸土坝、右岸门库、厂房、泄水闸、船闸、左岸门库、左岸土坝。

坝顶长度 885m，其中左岸土坝长 62m，最大坝高 29.65m，为均质土坝。左岸门库连接坝段长 94m，最大坝高 36.65m。船闸为单线一级，闸室有效尺寸为 180m×18m×3m（长×宽×槛上水深）。泄水闸坝段长 366m，最大坝高 52.3m，堰型为改进机翼堰型，堰顶高程 60.0m，闸孔净宽 16m，共 18 孔，消能方式为底流消能。电站厂房为河床式，安装 6 台单机容量为 38 MW 灯泡式水轮发电机组。右岸门库连接坝段长 60m，最大坝高 39.65m；右岸土坝长 103.8m，最大坝高 29.65m，为均质土坝。

左岸为河道深泓线，河床高程在 56～61m 之间，可利用基岩面高程在 56～59m 之间，覆盖层很少，又是天然状态下的主航道线。船闸布置在左岸，有利于上、下游引航道与原航道相接，通航水流条件较好，且船闸能够与厂房同步于一期施工，这对于尽早恢复柳江的通航、电厂尽快发电以提高枢纽的社会经济效益极之有利。

厂房布置于右岸基岩风化深槽上，石方开挖量较小；对外交通公路在右岸，利于厂房发电设备的进场安装及施工区布置；电站进水渠须避开 220kV 跨河高压线塔基础。

左岸门库连接坝段共 4 段，挡水前缘长 94m，除了停放船闸上游挡洪门和泄水闸上游检修门外，还起连接坝段的作用。右岸门库连接坝段共 3 段，挡水前缘长 60m，除了停放厂房上游备用拦污栅外，还起连接坝段的作用。

（三）枢纽布置及建筑物优化

（1）泄水建筑物取消原来的排漂孔坝段，右岸的厂房向河床中间移动 44m，减少了原厂房上下游进出口的开挖，避免了高压输电线塔的搬移，改善了厂房的进出口水流条件。同时，右岸门库坝段建基面抬高，设计成空箱型结构，减少开挖工程量及混凝土、钢筋用量。

（2）厂房进口拦污栅墩经过优化，在墩上采取圆孔通排式，改善了拦污栅墩的通水条件，减少水头损失。

（3）利用船闸上、下闸首和右边墙兼作泄水闸二期纵向围堰，减少围堰工程量，缩短施工工期。

（4）主机间布置成一层即发电运行层，在主机间流道顶板内设计电缆廊道和管道廊道，省了一层楼板，使布置更加简洁，同时电缆线、油气水管道各入各廊道，使厂房管理显得有序，运行、维护也很方便。

（5）电站由于汛期尾水位高，厂房的挡水墙也相应高，厂房的自然采光通风条件不好。为了尽可能利用有限的自然条件，主副厂房屋面均设采光罩，同时利用错层和天井增加自然采光和通风面积，尽可能减少能耗，降低运行成本。

（6）由于采用 2 个制造厂家的机组设备，机组流道长度、进出口闸门尺寸都不同，机组附属设备选型和布置形式不同。经与制造厂家多次的联系研究，把机组流道尺寸整合为相同的尺寸，把附属设备的型号和布置形式也整合得基本相同。这有利于土建施工、设备安装和电站运行管理。

（7）优化变压器的结构设计，减少变压器室的面积，优化主变压器和 GIS 设备的连接方式，设备布置更加紧凑。

（8）将原设计尾水门机改成尾水台车，尾水闸墩体形优化设计，减少了混凝土、钢筋用量。

经过优化设计后，工程投资节省超过 3000 多万元。

（中水珠江规划勘测设计有限公司　凌春海）

导流建筑物设计

向家坝水电站截流设计与施工

（一）工程概况

向家坝水电站位于金沙江下游河段，河流大体自西向东流，河谷形态呈不对称的 U 形，底宽 500m 左右。枯水位 266.50m 时，主河槽在右侧，水面宽度 160～220m，水深 3～10m。河床覆盖层上游深、下游浅，两侧深、中间浅，一般厚度 10～50m。

工程枢纽由混凝土重力坝、左岸坝后厂房、右岸地下厂房、左岸垂直升船机和两岸灌溉取水口等组成。施工采用分期导流方式，一期施工左岸，由右侧束窄后的主河床泄流；二期施工右岸；主河床截流时，由左岸坝体中预留的 6 个进口高程 260.0m、10m×14m（宽×高）的导流底孔分流。

（二）截流设计

1. 截流时段和设计流量　根据施工总进度安排，主河床截流计划于 2008 年 12 月中旬进行，截流设计流量选择为 12 月中旬 10 年一遇，旬平均流量 2600 m^3/s。

2. 截流方式与戗堤布置　根据本工程主河床截流时的分流条件和截流水力参数，采用单戗立堵双向进占的截流方式。截流戗堤与上游土石围堰填筑体相结合，布置于堰基混凝土防渗墙的下游侧，戗堤轴线与围堰轴线平行，平距约为 30m。截流戗堤轴线全长为 297m，其中一期纵向围堰与二期纵向围堰之间段长 41m，一期纵向围堰占压段长 70m，右岸河床段 186m，堤顶高程 272.0m。戗堤顶宽 25m，上、下游边坡和堤头边坡均为 1∶1.5。

3. 截流预进占及龙口宽度　根据施工总进度及河流水文特性，截流预进占需在 11 月下旬至 12 月上旬进行。戗堤预进占料采用右岸工程开挖料和一期土石围堰拆除料，预进占料粒径为 5～40cm。综合分析计算与截流模型验证，在 11 月下旬开始戗堤非龙口段的预进占抛投（导流底孔分流前），设计流量为 11 月下旬 10 年一遇，$Q=3500m^3/s$，龙口宽度束窄至 110m；12 月上旬导流底孔具备过流条件，进一步束窄河床，设计流量为 12 月上旬 10 年一遇，$Q=3000m^3/s$，预留龙口宽度 60m，龙口位置设于河床中部偏左岸（靠近一期纵向围堰）。龙口河床覆盖层经过一期束窄河床 3 年汛期行洪，表面覆盖层粗化，抗冲流速增加。对预进占戗堤进行适当裹头保护后基本不流失。

4. 截流龙口水力学计算　合龙设计流量为 $Q=2600m^3/s$，合龙过程中龙口水力学参数计算结果见表 1、图 1。

表 1　合龙过程中龙口水力学参数计算结果

龙口宽度 (m)	上游水位 (m)	落差 (m)	底孔流量 (m^3/s)	龙口流量 (m^3/s)	龙口流速 (m/s)	单宽流量 [$m^3/(s\cdot m)$]	单宽功率 [$t\cdot m/(s\cdot m)$]
60	268.72	0.78	1389	1211	3.18	42.00	32.80
50	268.93	0.99	1565	1034	4.12	53.30	52.59
40	269.38	1.44	1917	683	4.78	46.70	67.23
30	269.94	2.00	2283	317	4.75	31.70	63.52
20	270.29	2.35	2511	89	4.12	15.60	36.79
10	270.42	2.48	2593	7	2.45	3.30	8.13
0	270.43	2.49	2600	0	0.00	0.00	0.00

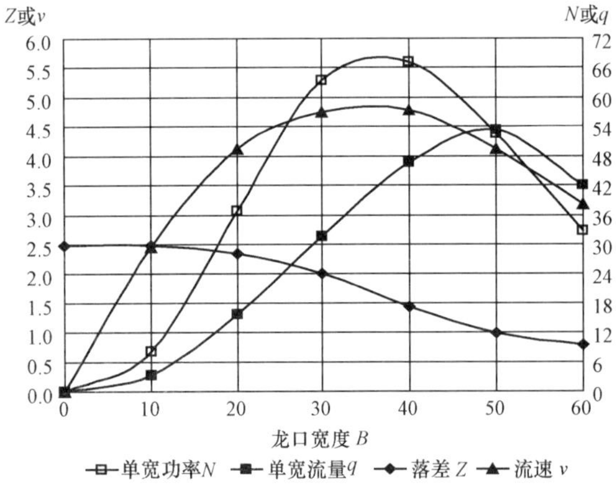

图 1　龙口水力学参数图

5. 截流材料选择及抛投物数量确定

(1) 上戗堤预进占区段，抛投材料以 0.4m 以下的粒径混合石渣料或河床卵砾石为主，对堤头采用粒径 0.7m 左右块石适当保护。

(2) 根据合龙过程中不同龙口宽度的水力学指标，将上游截流龙口划分为 3 个区段。各区抛投材料：①第 1 区段，龙口宽从 60m 束窄至 50m，最大流速 4.12m/s，最大落差 0.99m，以抛投粒径 0.4～0.7m 混合石渣料为主，在上挑角处抛投少量大石；②第 2 区段，龙口宽从 50m 束窄至 20m，当龙口宽度束窄至 40m 左右时，出现最大流速 4.78m/s，最大落差 2.35m，以抛投粒径 0.7～1.0 m 的大石为主，占 70%，另外采用 10%的一般石渣料和 10%的中石；③第 3 区段，龙口宽从 20m 束窄至合龙，最终落差为 2.49m，以抛投粒径 0.1～0.4m 的一般石渣为主，占 70%，另外采用 20%的中石和 10%的大石。

(3) 经工程类比分析，只需采用挑选过的大块石作为合龙抛投特殊材料，但作为安全储备，可制作部分钢筋石笼，规格以 1.0m×1.0m×1.5m 为宜，以备使用，备料数量按合龙困难段的 10%计算。

(4) 抛投材料数量计算，非龙口段抛投考虑 1.15 的流失系数，龙口段抛投考虑 1.3 的流失系数。截流各阶段抛投料粒径及数量见表 2。

表 2　上游截流戗堤抛投料特性表

部 位	进占长度（m）	龙口宽度（m）	抛 投 料				
			一般石渣料（40cm 以下）（m^3）	中 石（40～70cm）（m^3）	大块石（70～100cm）（m^3）	钢筋石笼或（100～130cm 块石）	设计抛投量（m^3）
非龙口段	126		98 559	24 640			123 199
龙口段	10	60～50	2199	6598	2199		10 997
	30	50～20	1993	1993	13 953	1993	19 933
	20	20～0	1972	563	282		2817
合计	186		104 724	33 795	16 434	1993	156 946

注　非龙口段工程量不包括一期纵向围堰与二期纵向围堰之间的先期填筑量。

（三）截流施工

抛投材料备料数量计算，非龙口段抛投考虑 1.3 的备料系数，龙口段抛投考虑 1.5 的备料系数。上游戗堤抛投总量为 17.82 万 m^3。上游截流堤备料特性详见表 3。

表 3　上游截流戗堤备料特性表

项 目	上游戗堤	备料场地
石 渣（万 m^3）	11.85	上游新滩坝弃渣场
中 石（万 m^3）	3.84	下游尾水出口
大 石（万 m^3）	1.90	下游尾水出口
钢筋石笼或特大石（万 m^3）	0.23	下游尾水出口
合 计（万 m^3）	17.82	

截流戗堤所需的各类抛投料均来源于右岸工程的开挖利用料，其中大石和特大石主要从右岸进水口和坝肩明挖料中选取。截流备料选择堆存于上游新滩坝弃渣场和下游厂房尾水渠出口。下游戗堤备料结合围堰填筑料一并考虑，堆存于下游尾水出口部位。

为增加截流的可靠性，增大抛投强度，除在右岸备足截流材料外，在左岸利用一、二期纵向围堰之间的场地形成了“岛式”截流平台，创造了双向进占的有利条件。一般石渣料主要利用一期围堰拆除料；钢筋笼在“岛式”平台上利用一期围堰拆除料进行填充；大块石料采用地下厂房开挖利用料；特大块石料从开挖料拣选后集中备料。为确保截流合龙成功，另备部分单个体积为 4.8m^3 的混凝土四面体用于龙口抛投。

向家坝大江截流实际施工分为三个阶段进行：

第一阶段为截流预进占，2008 年 12 月 1 日正式开始，至 12 月 20 日，左岸戗堤共完成岸坡段进占 108.80m，完成工程量 5.10 万 m^3，形成口门宽度 79.10m、水面宽度为 67m 的龙口。

第二阶段为截流阶段性进占，即封航令下达后，在主河槽进占施工，这一阶段是截流施工的最关键阶段。截流阶段性进占于 12 月 21 日上午 9 时正式开始，至 22 日上午 9 时，共持续 24h，形成宽度约 10m 的合龙龙口。进占期间最大截流流量 2350m^3/s，最大水深 20m，龙口最大流速 6.10m/s，最终落差 2.34m，最大单宽功率 74.48t·m/（m·s），最大小时抛投强度 3225m^3/h，共抛投材料 5.60 万 m^3，使用特大石特种截流材料 2.90 万 m^3。

第三阶段为截流龙口合龙。2008 年 12 月 28 日上午 10：58 合龙进占正式开始，经过 28 分钟的奋战，胜利完成截流。

（中国水电顾问集团中南勘测设计研究院
李勇刚　盛乐民）

巴山水电站大坝施工导流设计

（一）工程概况

巴山水电站系汉江支流任河干流梯级开发规划中确定的控制性骨干梯级电站，工程位于重庆市城口县巴山镇，以发电为主，兼有旅游和改善生态环境等综合利用功能。电站装机容量 2×70MW，总库容 3.154 亿 m^3。拦河坝为钢筋混凝土面板堆石坝，最大坝高 155.0m。

电站导流隧洞工程于 2005 年 12 月 1 日开工建设，2006 年 10 月 18 日截流；2009 年 4 月 28 日下闸蓄水，7 月第 1 台机组投产发电，年底工程完工。

（二）导流方案设计

巴山水电站施工导流共分为五个阶段：

（1）第一阶段为截流后的第一个枯水期（2006

年10月底至2007年5月底），主要进行围堰填筑、基坑开挖、趾板混凝土浇筑等，要求坝体临时断面在2007年5月底填筑至607.00m高程。该阶段由土石围堰挡水，导流隧洞泄流；导流标准选择枯水时段（10月～次年5月）10年一遇洪水，相应流量1570m³/s。

(2) 第二阶段为截流后的第一个汛期（2007年6～9月），继续填筑坝体，根据度汛要求，6月底大坝上游侧顶高程不低于611.50m，顶宽不小于30.0m，以满足主汛期坝体临时断面的挡水要求。该阶段由大坝临时断面挡水，导流隧洞泄流，大坝度汛标准：6月采用10月～次年6月时段50年一遇洪水，相应流量2940m³/s；7～9月的主汛期采用全年50年一遇洪水，相应流量3670m³/s。

(3) 第三阶段为截流后的第二个枯水期（2007年10月底至2008年5月底），主要进行大坝一期混凝土面板浇筑、坝体继续填筑等。该阶段由土石围堰挡水，导流隧洞泄流；导流标准选择枯水时段（10月～次年5月）10年一遇洪水，相应流量1570m³/s。

(4) 第四阶段从2008年6月至2009年4月导流隧洞下闸封堵前，2008年汛期由坝体临时断面挡水度汛、导流隧洞泄流，继续进行坝体填筑、大坝面板混凝土浇筑等。该阶段大坝度汛标准选择全年100年一遇洪水，相应流量4060m³/s。

(5) 第五阶段自2009年4月导流隧洞下闸封堵、水库开始蓄水至12月工程完工前，主要进行导流隧洞堵头、坝顶结构的施工。该阶段由坝体挡水，溢洪道泄流，大坝度汛标准选择全年200年一遇洪水，相应流量4430m³/s。

（三）导流建筑物设计

1. 导流隧洞　导流隧洞断面为城门洞形，衬砌后尺寸为10.0m×13.0m（宽×高）。进口底板高程545.0m，出口底板高程541.0m，设计底坡0.4734%，导流隧洞总长845.0m，其中直线段长约799.4m，转弯段长45.6m，平面转弯半径为60.0m，转角43.5°。隧洞进口段、出口段及洞身局部地质条件较差的Ⅲ～Ⅳ类及以上围岩地段，采用钢筋混凝土全断面衬砌，衬砌厚为2.5～0.5m，其余洞段不做受力衬砌，但为了减小糙率，提高泄流能力，采用锚杆混凝土薄衬，衬砌厚度为0.35m。

导流隧洞施工过程中，由于前期开挖占用工期较多，导致后期衬砌工期紧张。根据导流隧洞上层贯通后揭露的实际地质条件，为满足工程顺利实施的要求，及时对洞身中间段的Ⅱ、Ⅲ类围岩洞段的衬砌进行优化，优化洞段总长约586m。

2. 上游围堰　根据上游围堰处的地形地质条件，结合本地区建筑材料情况，可行性研究阶段上游围堰采用堆石填筑、复合土工膜防渗的结构型式。堰顶高程572.20m，最大堰高31.20m，堰顶宽度10.0m，上、下游堆石堰体边坡1∶1.5，在迎水侧高程561.00m及背水侧高程557.00m处各设一宽5.0m的马道，围堰迎水侧坡面设置60cm厚的块石护坡。堰基防渗采用黏土截水墙，截水墙底宽10.0m。堰体防渗采用双面复合土工膜，主膜厚0.8mm，土工膜两侧设置砂砾料，砂砾料宽度为4.0m。

导流隧洞衬砌优化设计后，需相应调整大坝上游围堰和大坝2007年度汛临时断面的顶高程。根据水力学计算，在围堰挡水时段内（枯水期$P=10\%$频率情况下），上游围堰挡水位将抬高4.41m，需加高上游围堰4.4m；在大坝2007年度汛时段内（全年$P=2\%$频率情况下），大坝度汛临时断面的上游水位将抬高5.08m，大坝临时挡水度汛断面汛前需填筑至611.50m高程以上。通过上述调整，保证了大坝施工导流的安全性，保证了工程的顺利实施。

3. 下游围堰　下游围堰采用堆石填筑、黏土斜墙防渗的结构型式。堰顶高程547.20m，最大堰高7.80m，堰顶宽度10.0m，堆石戗体边坡1∶1.5。黏土斜墙迎水面边坡1∶2.5，设置60cm厚的块石护坡和100cm厚的铅丝笼，铅丝笼沿坡脚水平铺设长度为10m。

（四）截流设计

截流时间安排在2006年10月中旬，根据规范规定，截流设计流量采用10月5年一遇月平均洪水，相应流量为76.3m³/s。

截流戗堤与上游围堰结合，采用黏土斜墙堆石结构，顶高程551.00m，宽度15.0m。截流采用单戗立堵、右岸单向进占的方式。截流前先进行备料，截流抛投材料分别取自棕坝中转堆料场和大坝岸坡及河床基础开挖料。

（五）导流隧洞永久封堵

导流隧洞堵头按一级永久建筑物设计，设计洪水采用500年一遇，相应水位为681.79m；校核洪水采用5000年一遇，相应水位为683.66m。堵头的设计水头及校核水头分别为139.49m和141.36m。

因导流隧洞堵头需与大坝防渗帷幕连成整体，故堵头位置应设置在大坝上游趾板下，堵头上游端位于坝轴线上游约35m左右，桩号为导0+545m～导0+575m。堵头段围岩为含砾凝灰质岩屑砂岩，微风化或新鲜，岩体呈较完整状，局部较破碎；断层及破碎带不很发育且规模较小（一般宽度3～20cm），属$Ⅲ_1$类围岩洞段。

堵头体形按照楔形体断面设计，最大断面为10.46m×13.15m（宽×高）。堵头内设置灌浆廊道，廊道长20.0m，断面尺寸为2.5m×3.0m（宽×高）

的城门洞形廊道，廊道上游端面距堵头上游面10m。

堵头施工时按楔形体断面进行开挖。为有效排除堵头前的渗水，在堵头前缘设置混凝土挡水围堰，并在底部埋设排水钢管，设置封堵阀门和后期灌浆管及连通管。

（中国水电顾问集团华东勘测设计研究院
陈义军　陈永红）

天花板水电站导流隧洞设计

天花板水电站位于云南省昭通市境内的牛栏江上，是牛栏江中下游梯级规划的第七级水电站。天花板水电站为混合式开发水电站，主要由碾压混凝土拱坝、引水系统、地面厂房等组成。最大坝高107m，总库容0.787亿m^3，装机容量180MW，为三等中型工程。天花板水电站采用围堰一次拦断河流、导流隧洞导流、基坑全年施工的导流方式。

（一）导流隧洞布置

导流隧洞布置于坝址区左岸，进口位于坝轴线上游280m处，出口位于坝轴线下游约380m处，洞线在平面上呈曲线布置，其中进、出口直线段长98.4m、170.6m，中间为335.4m转角60°、转弯半径320m的圆弧段。导流隧洞长604.4m，进口底板高程989.0m，出口底板高程987.2m。断面型式采用12m×14m（宽×高）城门洞形，顶拱中心角120°，隧洞过水面积155.91m^2。导流隧洞进口设置长约80m的进口引渠和进水塔，出口设置长约77m的导流明渠。

（二）导流隧洞地质条件

导流隧洞进口段坡度相对较缓，约30°；出口段坡度较陡，约60°。洞身经过岩层依次为东龙潭组上段（Z_{2dl}^3）灰色、灰白色粉晶白云岩，东龙潭组中段（Z_{2dl}^2）灰、灰黑色富藻粉晶白云岩。隧洞埋深19.7～240m，地下水主要为岩溶裂隙水和基岩裂隙水，沿线大部分洞段地下水位高于洞顶。导流隧洞进口段38m以及出口段31.9m为Ⅳ类围岩，洞身段Ⅱ、Ⅲ类围岩为主，总长484.8m，占整个隧洞的80.2%，其余为Ⅳ类。

（三）导流隧洞水力条件

天花板导流隧洞按有压隧洞设计，设计导流标准为全年10年一遇洪水，设计洪峰流量2130m^3/s，设计平均流速13.66m/s，通过设计洪水时相应上下游水位为1027.04m、999.26m。坝体临时挡水度汛标准为全年20年一遇洪水，洪峰流量2730m^3/s，相应上下游水位为1043.7m、1000.84m，导流隧洞封堵期间上游水位1053m，封堵闸门挡水水头63m。

（四）导流隧洞支护衬砌设计

1. 洞身支护设计　导流隧洞支护设计利用新奥法施工的原理，充分利用围岩的自承作用，在进出口及Ⅳ类围岩条件较差洞段，采用初期锚喷支护、后期全断面钢筋混凝土复合支护型式；在Ⅲ类围岩洞段，采用初期锚喷支护、后期底板和边墙浇筑30cm厚钢筋混凝土复合支护型式；在Ⅱ类围岩洞段底板浇筑30cm找平素混凝土，边顶拱采用锚杆加喷聚丙烯纤维混凝土的支护方式。为降低锚喷支护段糙率系数，要求喷混凝土洞壁起伏差小于15cm。导流隧洞衬砌结构采用概率极限状态设计原则，以分项系数极限状态设计表达式进行计算，结构配筋按《水工混凝土结构设计规范》（DL/T 5057—1996）有关规定进行计算。

2. 导流洞进出口稳定加固措施

（1）导流隧洞进口段埋深19.7～28.5m，开挖跨度16.4m，开挖高度21.3～18.2m。洞脸1028.0m高程以上为崩坡积碎石土，989.0～1028.0m范围为全、强风化粉晶白云岩，属Ⅳ类围岩，围岩自稳时间很短。为确保进口段及洞脸稳定，洞脸采用两排ϕ25@2m×2m、$L=4.5$m的锁口锚杆，并布置两排水平1000kN的预应力锚索进行加固。上部采用全断面开挖，开挖后架设钢支撑。受雨季降雨影响，进口后边坡洞顶及直立洞脸出现多条卸荷变形裂缝。为确保安全，后边坡表面裂缝填塞水泥浆并对洞顶喷混凝土封闭，同时新增7根1000kN的斜向锚索进行加固，保证了进洞安全。

（2）导流隧洞出口处地形陡峻，坡度约60°。为减小开挖，导流隧洞出口采用斜交出洞，边坡按断层走向挖成直坡，坡面采用ϕ25@2m×2m、$L=5$m，挂网ϕ10@25cm×25cm喷混凝土20cm进行支护，并施打27根1000kN、$L=25$m的锚索进行加固。

（五）导流隧洞施工

天花板导流隧洞设置两条施工支洞，施工时从两条施工支洞进入主洞进行洞身土石方开挖和混凝土衬砌施工。导流隧洞石方洞挖分两层施工，上层高度7.0m，下层高度7.65～9.15m，先开挖上部导洞，手风钻造孔，光面爆破，侧卸装载机装自卸汽车出渣。主洞下部开挖两侧及底部预留2m保护层，采用液压钻造垂直孔，梯段爆破，反铲装自卸汽车出渣。两侧及底部保护层手风钻造水平孔，光面爆破。混凝土衬砌段先浇筑底板，边顶拱采用一台简易钢模台车一次浇筑成型。

从施工支洞进入导流隧洞主洞开挖至导流隧洞具备过流条件，共用时约10个月。

（中国水电顾问集团北京勘测设计研究院
薛宝臣　赵万青　陈　浩）

锦屏二级水电站进水口纵向围堰的设计与实施

锦屏二级水电站进水口，2008～2009年汛期施工水上部分，2009年汛期停工，2009～2010年枯期在围堰围护下进行1640m高程以下的开挖支护、基础处理、底板混凝土浇筑及底板固结灌浆施工，2010年汛期围堰基坑过水，2010～2011年枯期完成1653m高程以下混凝土浇筑，2011～2012年枯期完成进水口剩余部分施工。其施工围堰为一枯水期挡水的纵向围堰，为4级建筑物。

（一）施工围堰设计

1. 洪水设计标准及堰顶高程　电站进水口围堰挡水时段为12月至次年4月枯期挡水，设计标准$P=10\%$，$Q=1010m^3/s$，相应原始状态天然河道水位高程为1639.34m。围堰设计时考虑河床积渣影响，并充分考虑下游拦河闸坝围堰及本工程围堰束窄河床造成水位壅高，遂将堰顶高程定为1641.00m，如遇枯水期超标洪水，考虑在围堰顶部人工码砌1.5m高黏土草袋子堰加高。围堰过水度汛标准按全年洪水频率$P=5\%$设计，$Q=8850m^3/s$。施工期场地及施工区防洪标准$P=10\%$，施工场地及施工设施布置时按该标准要求设计。

2. 围堰平面布置　围堰布置紧密结合实际地形，在满足挡水的前提下，尽量不占压进水口施工部位及少占河床，并保证原河道水流平顺。围堰平面布置见图1。

3. 围堰结构型式　该围堰充分利用原始地形，按设计断面填筑施工形成。围堰轴线长248.60m，堰顶高程1641.00m、宽5.00m，最大堰高约22.6m，内外侧坡比均为1∶1.4。围堰堰体防渗采用80cm厚

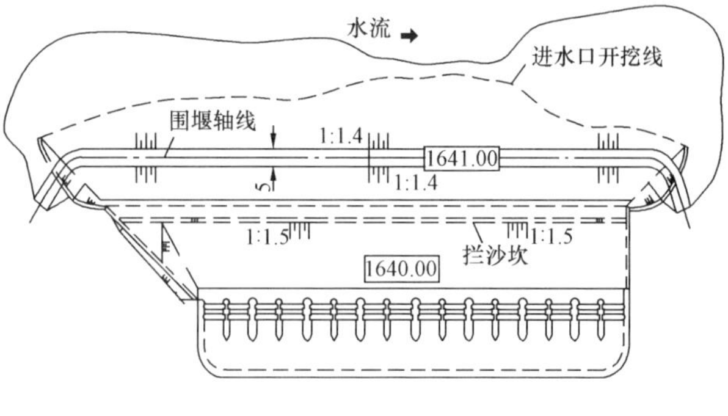

图1　进水口纵向围堰平面布置图

的塑性混凝土防渗墙，防渗墙深入T13岩层0.5m以下。为防止水流对围堰外侧的冲刷及围堰过水后影响围堰稳定，围堰外侧整个迎水坡面设置钢筋石笼，内侧采用干砌石护坡进行防护。其断面结构如图2所示。

临时加高子堰在堰顶靠外侧码砌，迎水面坡比为1∶1、内侧坡比为1∶0.5，在堰顶留出约1.25m宽的人行通道，用于黏土草袋码砌。

（二）围堰设计的安全验证

为了确保围堰的安全，特委托四川大学水力学与山区河流开发保护国家重点实验室对该纵向围堰进行了安全验证。采用$1010m^3/s$，$4000m^3/s$、$8850m^3/s$三级流量状态下对围堰段水流流态、堰前水位与流量的关系、堰前流场、对纵向围堰的冲刷等四个方面进行验证。验证主要情况如下：

（1）$1010m^3/s$、$4000m^3/s$、$8850m^3/s$三级流量下，堰前水流都较平顺；围堰上游端头部有明显壅水，在$4000m^3/s$左右最明显，下游尾部靠右岸侧有一定的回流。

（2）围堰下游支流溪口清淤后，围堰段水流流速明显增大，流量在$4000m^3/s$时平均增加较大，局部增幅超过1.5m/s。

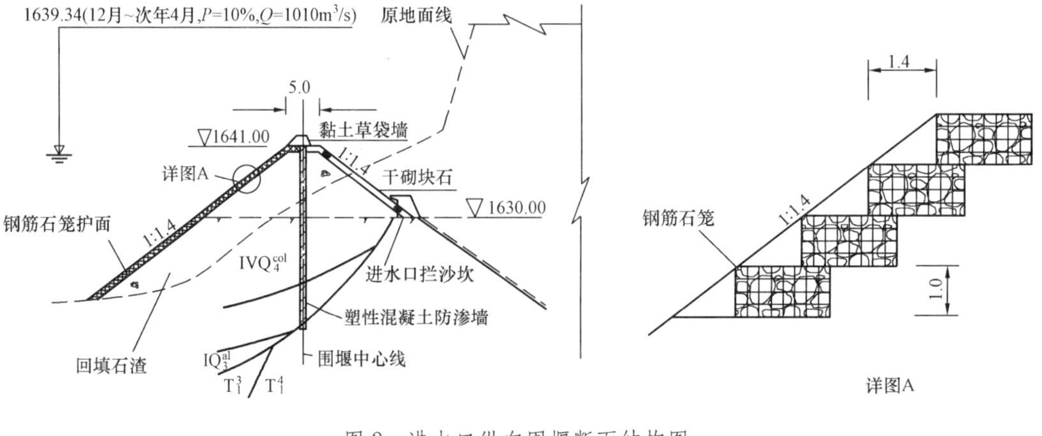

图2　进水口纵向围堰断面结构图

(3) 各级流量下围堰前断面平均流速最大值为4～5m/s，局部达5.5m/s左右，表面流速最大值局部达6.7m/s，故围堰采用抛填大于0.5m^3的钢筋石笼或抛填粒径0.50～0.75m大小的块石对围堰进行护坡与护脚，能够满足不被冲刷的要求。

(三) 围堰施工

围堰填筑安排在2008年2～4月枯期施工，内侧边坡在2009～2010年进水口1640m高程以下开挖过程中形成，开挖过程中在堰后预留了约7.0 m宽的道路作为下基坑施工道路，堰后护坡块石在围堰内侧边坡形成后施工。

围堰填筑料源主要采用进水口开挖石渣料和土石混合料。水下部分直接抛填，水上部分分层填筑压实。

水下部分抛填采用15～20t自卸汽车进占法卸料，推土机及运输车辆压实。围堰外侧抛填大块石或钢筋石笼，石块要求抗风化、抗水蚀变性能良好，块度不小于0.5m^3。

水上部分填筑前首先采用反铲或推土机对覆盖层进行清理，并将围堰轴线范围内的块石清理至轴线外侧，填筑料采用TY320推土机整平，18t振动碾碾压，铺料厚度为80～100cm，碾压6～8遍，实际施工参数根据碾压试验确定。堰前护坡钢筋石笼在同层堰体填筑前进行，钢筋石笼主筋采用ϕ18，分布筋采用ϕ12。上下游裹头受力较复杂，其钢筋石笼经过一年汛期后若出现不稳定现象，则将采取在钢筋石笼表面喷射10cm厚的C20混凝土加以保护。钢筋石笼采用8t汽车吊或人工搬运就位，回填块石后封顶，堆砌时上下层错开50cm并收坡约1.4m，钢筋石笼之间采用焊接或其他可靠的连接方式以提高其整体稳定性。堰后护坡块石在堰后坡形成后从下至上分层码砌。为防止汛期基坑过水对干砌石护坡产生较大破坏，必要时采用ϕ6.5@ 30cm×30cm钢筋网护面，钢筋网与伸入堰体的锚筋焊接牢固。

(四) 运行效果评价

进水口围堰于2008年1月开始填筑施工，2008年3月填筑、防护完成，在2008年5～10月的汛期中经历了约5000m^3/s流量的洪水冲刷，汛后经检查发现围堰上游端头局部有少量冲刷现象，整体运行与试验验证基本吻合，达到了经济、安全、合理、适用的标准。

(中国葛洲坝集团第二工程有限公司　陈　刚)

6

土 建 施 工

大坝与围堰施工

河口水电站基坑大体积黏土岩开挖施工

河口水电站位于兰州市西郊黄河干流上，是黄河龙—青段梯级第十七座水电站。其基坑基岩主要由黏土岩（29%）、粉砂质黏土岩（56%）、黏土质砂岩、砂岩组成。岩体层间节理发育完全，多呈片层状分布，层间有1～2.5mm厚次生泥质填充。

（一）施工难点分析

（1）坝址区域内岩石大多为黏土岩，在施工过程中开挖面遇水后再经过阳光照晒后其表面20～50cm范围内岩体会完全风化，组织结构破坏，但因岩体未发生移动，仍残留有原始结构痕迹，增加了岩体塌方率，对工程施工带来极大隐患。

（2）黏土岩坚硬系数在2.0～4.0之间，其层状厚度在1～5m，边坡开挖施工中对预裂孔的孔深、间距、装药量、线装药密度及最大单响药量的精确度要求较高，施工难度较大。

（3）岩层走向呈北东偏西，在基坑左岸边坡开挖施工中，容易将岩层底端嵌入层切断，造成岩体整层塌滑，需在每个开挖阶层开挖完毕后进行岩层走向的观察及推断，确定支护方案及下层开挖方案。

（4）由于厂房坝段基坑基岩面地下水位较高，在进行开挖施工作业时需多个井点抽水，但线路、管路布置错综复杂，不利于开挖作业面的全面展开。

（5）在施工现场没有固定渣场，临时渣场就设在厂房尾水下游侧，占用部分施工场所，造成施工作业面狭小，在开挖过程中需根据开挖面的进展不断地调整布置施工道路，存在多次重复循环施工。

（二）施工方案

1. 爆破方案

（1）考虑到施工部位地质结构的特殊性，在厂房开挖施工时采用深孔预裂、浅孔爆破的施工方案，即在预裂爆破施工时采用一次性造孔12～20m（1～2个开挖循环），而主爆孔造孔施工时按10～12m为一个作业循环进行爆破施工。

（2）主爆区控制爆破参数为：①炮眼直径100mm；②底盘抵抗线3.0m；③炮孔间距3.0m；④炮孔排距，厂房边坡开挖时取3.0m，厂房基坑开挖时根据岩石情况可取3.0～4.0m；⑤钻孔深度10.5m；⑥单位体积耗药量，一般边坡石质较软取0.18～0.20kg/m³，基坑岩石取0.25～0.32kg/m³，每个炮孔装药量最大孔装药量为28.8kg；⑦选用直径32mm的2号岩石乳化炸药，装药时把3支药卷捆成一组连续装药，炮孔底部1m左右为加强段，起爆药包用2个同段的毫秒雷管，反向捆在炸药药卷上，放在距孔底30cm处；⑧堵塞长度2.5m，最小堵塞长度不得小于2.0m，采用黏土和细砂的混合物堵塞；⑨起爆方式采用排间微差顺序起爆。

（3）边坡预裂爆破参数为：①线装药密度 $q_{max}=450g/m$，$q_{min}=300g/m$；②炮眼直径100mm，间距取90cm、100cm、120cm（岩石结构完整，无节理裂隙发育取大值120cm，岩石结构较完整节理裂隙发育取100cm，岩石结构破碎，节理裂隙完全发育取90cm）；③孔深 $L=2.15H$，H 为单个爆破循环作业主爆层高度；④装药结构采用不耦合间隔装药法，选用直径32mm的2号岩石乳化炸药，不耦合系数为3.13，将炸药间隔捆装在竹片上，再装入炮孔，炮孔堵塞长度1.5m；⑤预裂炮孔采用同段毫秒雷管传爆，并先于主爆网大于50ms提前起爆；⑥在扭面、两坡交线及基坑齿槽部位布置导向孔，孔深、孔斜及布置位置根据现场岩体结构及开挖控制线进行控制。

2. 厂房边坡开挖时的支护措施　前期厂房边坡开挖施工时由于不知道岩层走向，开挖台阶过大，将安装间边坡岩层底端嵌入层切断，造成该处岩体整层塌滑。通过已开挖面的岩层走向，判断岩体大体走向及嵌入层大致位置，调整开挖台阶高度，并制定了相应的支护措施。在厂房边坡开挖施工时采用分段、小台阶、多作业面的开挖方式，台阶高度为3～5m。每次爆破作业面出渣完毕后，根据岩体走向及片层厚度分别采用9、12、15m不等的锚筋桩（3ϕ28）进行锚固、喷混凝土支护，待支护完毕后方可进行下阶层开挖施工。锚筋桩的布置根据岩体走向、片层分布情况随现场实际情况而布置，其间距为2～3m，造孔向垂直于岩体走向方向，其两者夹角小于90°布置。

3. 基坑开挖时的降水措施　基坑开挖过程中，随着基坑基岩面的下降，河床水通过地下岩层反渗到基坑内，造成炮孔内积水填充，大大减弱了爆破效果，并增大了炸药的单耗量约12%。鉴于此，在开挖过程中采用“井点排水法”降低地下水位，方便基坑开挖。即在施工时根据开挖面的布置，分别在其周边布置若干个集水深井，利用潜水泵抽水用以降低开挖作业面的地下水位，保证基坑开挖的顺利进行。根据开挖面的不断变化，集水深井的布置位置及井深也随之变化。通过实际施工工程中的灵活布置，大大提高了基坑内岩体的破碎率，为基坑开挖过程中出渣道路的布置提供了极大的便利。在整个基坑开挖过程中其效果是显著的。

（三）施工布置

通过施工前期对爆破参数、基础降水及地质岩层的研究分析后，根据优化的施工方案、排水措施和修改后爆破参数，对整个开挖面进行重新布置：

厂房边坡开挖施工布置中，由于将原来10m的开挖台阶修改为3～5m的开挖台阶，为保证该处的施工进度，将原来的1个作业面调整为4个作业面，开挖、支护两两交替施工，以满足其施工进度要求。

厂房基坑段施工时在基坑布置树状施工道路，倒退式开挖，以满足基坑多面开挖的施工要求。同时按照已展开的开挖面在基坑内布置网状井点以降低基坑内地下水位高度，从而达到减小施工难度、增强爆破效果，同时降低炸药单耗的施工效果。

（四）效果分析

通过对河口水电站片层状黏土岩、砂岩的开挖施工中开挖台阶、爆破参数、支护方案及基础降水措施的研究、分析，最终优化后的各项施工参数及措施方案均满足现场施工进度和施工质量要求，取得了良好成果。

厂房边坡片层状岩层开挖中，其半孔率高达85%，且半孔周边岩体基本未遭到结构破坏。爆破作业共用炸药量为83 664kg，开挖土石方约54万m^3，炸药平均单耗0.155kg/m^3，比原设计0.2～0.3kg/m^3的单耗量降低约38%，节约炸药约51.3t，降低了土石方开挖的施工单价。

通过采取优化后的开挖、支护方案，在厂房边坡及基坑沟槽开挖中未出现塌滑事故。在基坑施工道路布置方面采用树状道路，倒退式开挖，极大地改善了基坑内道路的循环挪移施工，减少了施工过程中的重复施工项目。

（中国水利水电第三工程局有限公司 崔伯奎 陈小祎）

河口水电站贯流式机组坝段施工技术

（一）概况

河口水电站位于兰州市西郊黄河干流上的一座中型水电站，额定水头5.3m，安装4台单机容量18.5MW、转轮直径7.3m的灯泡贯流式水轮发电机组，总装机容量74MW，多年平均发电量3.85亿kW·h。

厂房坝段布置在安装间左侧，采用两机一缝布置，机组坝段长41.2m，总长82.4m，顺水流方向底宽70.1m。坝顶高程1562.0m，厂顶高程1582.0m，尾水平台高程1557.5m，机组安装高程1542.4m。

灯泡贯流式机组水电站在施工时具有混凝土浇筑高峰集中、各机组坝段几乎同步上升的施工特点。在整个机组坝段施工中，管型座安装及二期混凝土回填的进度直接影响机组蓄水发电工期。

（二）机组坝段结构布置

河口水电站厂房机组段结构布置为两机一缝，1、2号机组为一个坝段，3、4号机组为一个坝段。每个坝段施工时从上游至下游又分为进水口段（Ⅰ）、机组安装段（Ⅱ）、尾水管段（Ⅲ）。混凝土浇筑，Ⅰ、Ⅱ、Ⅲ段几乎同步上升，高峰强度达到3.3万m^3/月。

电站4台机组分别设有独立的流道。每条机组流道分为进口段、管型座安装段及尾水扩散段三部分。流道进口段呈喇叭口形状，管型座安装段呈直上直下竖井状，尾水管段呈直锥形扩散状。在流道管型座安装段空腔内布置水轮发电机系统，同时在其上部设有竖井，作为发电机、水轮机安装的施工通道及运行维修通道。竖井与流道顶板贯穿处设有异型流道钢盖板，以保证流道内壁整体的流线型。

（三）主要施工技术

1. 土石方开挖　灯泡贯流式机组基坑开挖深度相对较浅，且机组进水口段、机组安装段及机组尾水段基坑开挖深度没有大的阶梯，在施工时可通过相邻作业面连续层间开挖。开挖施工以首台机组（4号）为重点、其他机组面同步展开的开挖顺序进行，以保证首台机组Ⅰ、Ⅱ、Ⅲ段建基面尽早形成，为后续混凝土施工提供进度保障。

2. 混凝土施工　主要分为基础、流道进口方变圆、尾水管段圆变方、板梁柱混凝土施工及其他部位大体积混凝土施工。

（1）其水平运输主要为自卸汽车运输，垂直运输主要为门机吊运。

（2）厂房混凝土施工以3、4号机为主线，1、2号机为调节辅线的总体原则进行安排，避免了混凝土浇筑集中在同一施工时段。这样安排实现了3、4号机板、梁、柱等结构混凝土模板、支撑材料向1、2机及副厂房部位的调节使用，极大地降低了一次性投入量，同时提高了周转性材料的周转次数，使施工设备、模板、支撑材料效益最大化。

（3）考虑到机组流道异型曲面体形，如采用钢模和木模结合拼装的施工方法不能保证工期要求，且模板、木材用量大，耗时长，施工费用高，外观棱角、接缝多，决定采用定型钢木模板，对流道曲面段进行分段整体吊装、浇筑，以保证机组流道快速、优质的施工。

3. 管型座施工

(1) 按照以往电站施工程序，管型座安装需等到厂房全部封顶、坝顶桥机投运后再进行管型座安装。河口水电站在厂房主机层一期混凝土浇筑完成后，便利用坝前2台MQ600/30型高架门机开始管型座分瓣吊装施工，工期提前4个月，为首台机组按期发电提供了保障。

(2) 为保证管型座周边混凝土的密实性，避免管型座底部二期混凝土发生脱空现象，在管型座安装完成后沿其底部120°范围内预埋钢衬灌浆管，进行钢衬灌浆，使二期混凝土与管型座的结合充分密实。

4. 流道顶板施工　电站流道顶板原设计为现浇混凝土结构，必须等到流道两侧闸墩施工完成后方可进行，存在以下缺点：①模板及支撑材料耗用量大；②备仓时间长，顶部侧立面模板不易加固；③作业危险系数高。经与监理、业主、设计沟通，将原设计现浇流道顶板结构更改为预制梁结构，提前组织预制施工，待流道两侧闸墩施工完成后直接利用坝前门机进行预制梁架设、梁间缝及梁端浇筑施工。采用该方案后不仅使流道顶板施工计划比原定计划提前整整一个月，而且极大地减少了模板、支撑材料的投用量，降低了该部位的混凝土的施工成本。

（四）结语

河口水电站灯泡贯流式机组坝段的施工，通过对施工工艺、技术措施、总体施工程序及过程控制管理进行优化调整，使施工进度安排、资源配置更趋于合理化。这为今后该类电站的施工提供了较为成熟的施工工艺及更为科学的管理经验。

（中国水利水电第三工程局有限公司
崔佰奎　骆星　陈小祎）

莲麓一级水电站主体工程混凝土防渗墙施工

（一）工程概况

莲麓一级水电站工程区位于甘肃省西南部渭源、康乐交界处的洮河干流九（甸峡）—海（甸峡）河段上，装机容量66MW（3×22MW），属三等中型工程。该电站为河床式，混凝土闸坝，最大坝高51.5m，坝顶总长230.31m，其中左副坝段长29.7m，电站厂房挡水段长71.46m，泄冲闸段长45.03m，右副坝段长30.03m，右岸防渗墙54m。

右岸混凝土防渗墙施工分9个槽段，1～5号槽段沿坝轴线方向布置，全长为27m，坐落于右副坝靠山侧回填砂砾石区上；6～9号槽段沿坝轴线向上游偏转51°，墙体末端接右岸灌浆平洞，全长为26.4m。混凝土28天抗压强度为4～5MPa；初始切线弹性模量700～1000MPa；渗透系数$K=1\times10^{-5}$ mm/s；抗渗等级W10。墙体厚度为80cm，墙内布置有钢筋笼，考虑到后期防渗墙底部帷幕灌浆，在钢筋笼间顶部6m埋设钢管，减少后期帷幕灌浆钻混凝土量。防渗墙造孔深入基岩2m，最深孔为右副坝回填区上1号槽段槽孔达到39m，最浅孔为靠山侧9号槽段槽孔达到11.2m，而且所有槽段墙体以下有28m基岩帷幕灌浆。

（二）施工前准备

导墙断面采用倒L形C20钢筋混凝土。施工平台、导墙断面结构见图1。

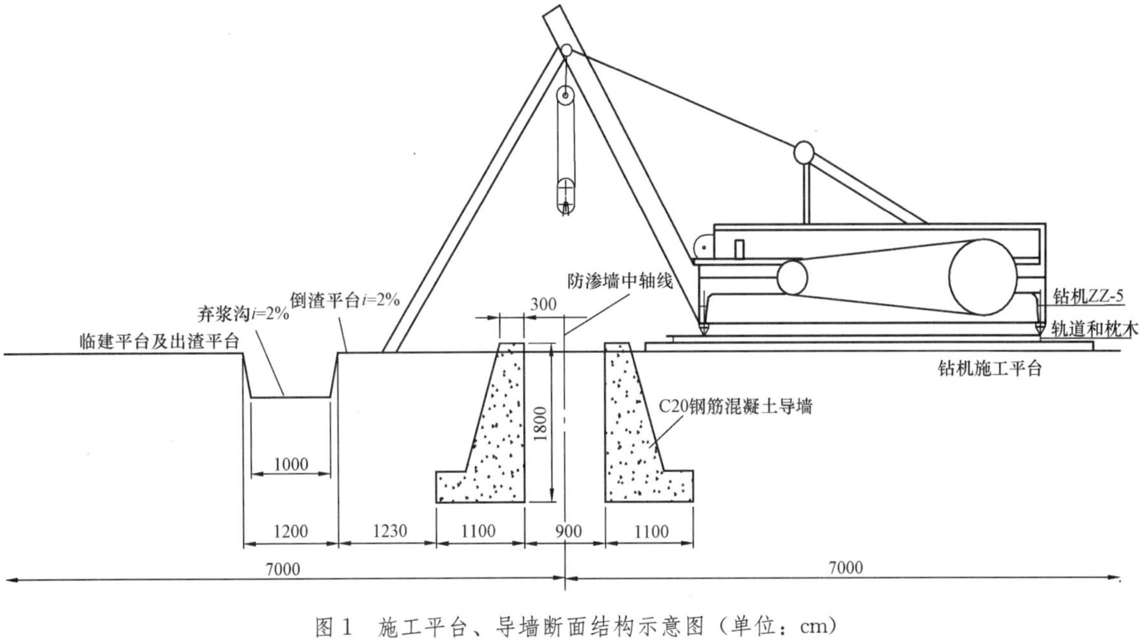

图1　施工平台、导墙断面结构示意图（单位：cm）

考虑覆盖层深厚、组成物粒径变化大、防渗墙墙体深度大、工作面场地狭小等特点，采用 ZZ-5、ZZ-6两种型号冲击钻机（乌卡斯）造孔成槽，以适应各种复杂地层条件。

沿防渗墙轴线划分 9 个槽段，其中Ⅰ期槽段 4 个（2、4、6、8 号），Ⅱ期槽段 5 个（1、3、5、7、9 号）。Ⅰ期槽段划分为 11 个孔，其中主孔 6 个、副孔 5 个；Ⅱ期槽段划分为 13 个孔，其中主孔 7 个、副孔 6 个。

（三）防渗墙体施工

1. 墙下回填施工　墙下砂砾石回填料源一部分取自二期基坑开挖时原始河床砂砾石，另一部分取自一期基坑开挖弃料场，随一期副坝混凝土浇筑上升进行回填施工。回填料不含杂草等腐殖质，含水量小于5%，20t 振动碾 6 遍碾压，层高 80cm，碾压后指标为内摩擦角为 31°～33°，相对密度不小于 0.75，现场控制干容重指标为 21.5～22kN/m³。

2. 固壁泥浆　泥浆采用黏土与膨润土结合的方式进行拌制，固壁面保持在导墙顶面以下 300～500mm，其性能指标见表 1。实际施工中，如会出现塌孔，则要通过增加膨润土剂量，调整泥浆比率来解决。

表 1　　固壁泥浆性能指标

密度（g/cm³）	漏斗黏度（s）	含砂量（%）	胶体率（%）	稳定性
1.05～1.2	20～25	≤10	≥96	≤0.03

失水量（mL/30min）	1min 静切力（N/m²）	泥饼厚（mm）	pH 值
10	2～5	≤3	7～9

3. 造孔施工

（1）先施工双号槽段，再施工单号槽段。每个槽段内两侧主孔先施工，待主孔钻至设计深度后，再钻凿中部的其他主孔和副孔，直到整个槽段达到设计深度。

（2）采用 ZZ-5 型钻机主孔钻凿副孔劈打法成槽，造槽过程中，用泥浆泵不断向槽孔内补充漏失的泥浆，并保持泥浆具有良好的固壁性能。

（3）槽段连接采用“钻凿法”进行槽段连接，即施工二期墙段时在一期墙两端套打一钻的连接方法，其接缝呈半圆弧形。

（4）施工中应注意控制孔形、孔斜；为了避免对已浇筑墙体造成不利影响，接头孔在槽孔浇筑结束后48h 开钻，并宜提前形成一个 2～3m 深的导向坑。

4. 清孔换浆与验收　槽孔终孔后，进行孔位、孔深、槽孔长度及孔斜等全面检查验收，验收合格后进行清孔换浆。清孔换浆结束 1h 后，孔内泥浆密度小于1.3g/cm³，黏度小于 30s，含砂量不大于 10%；二期槽清孔换浆前，用钢丝钻头刷洗两端一期槽混凝土孔壁上的泥皮，使刷子钻头上基本不带泥屑为合格。

5. 混凝土浇筑

（1）按设计要求设置钢筋。

（2）预埋 ϕ114×4mm 钢管。预埋管弯曲率应小于 1%，采用 ϕ16 钢筋与钢筋笼的水平筋焊接牢固。

（3）采用直升导管法浇筑混凝土。每个槽段布置 2 套内径为 300mm 的导管，导管距孔端接头管间距为 1.0m；下入导管后，将导管提离孔底距离为 15～25cm；开浇前，导管内置入可浮起的隔离塞球。首罐料浇筑时，先在浇筑漏斗内注入适量的水泥砂浆，随即浇入足够的混凝土，以使导管内混凝土面上升速度不小于 2m/h；导管埋深控制在 1～6m，每 30min 测量一次混凝土面，每 2h 测定一次导管内混凝土面，使混凝土面均匀上升，高差控制在 0.5m 内；混凝土终浇高程，高出设计顶面高程 0.5m；在墙体混凝土浇筑升至距墙顶高程 5m 时，视为终浇阶段，一般情况下，此时泥浆稠度大，导管内混凝土冲力减小，为保证混凝土面上升速度不小于 2m/h，采用人工辅助方式，降低孔内泥浆面，以减小导管外压力，利于混凝土浇筑面上升；混凝土浇筑连续进行。

（4）现场施工用的混凝土配合比经试验确定，主要性能指标为：出机口坍落度 18～22cm，扩散度 34～40cm；拌和析水率少于 3%；初凝时间不小于 8h，终凝时间不大于 24h。配合比见表 2。

表 2　　混凝土配合比材料用量表　　kg/m³

水灰比	水	水泥	粉煤灰	砂子
0.75	210	130	80	787
中石	小石	膨润土	LSP	DH9
415	508	70	1.44	0.007 2

6. 特殊处理

（1）底层严重漏浆，应迅速填入锯末等堵漏材料，必要时采用黏土回填槽孔，进行二次钻孔。

（2）钻进过程中，如果发现块（漂）石埋藏较浅、不适宜爆破时，选用重锤冲凿、砸碎大块（漂）石进行钻进；对于特大孤石可以采用岩芯钻的方法，先在巨石上钻出很多密集的孔洞（梅花孔），破坏岩石的完整性，然后再使用重锤击碎。

（3）遇到直径较大的单个块球体时，可采用水下钻孔爆破。其主要方法是：当冲击钻钻至巨型块（漂）石时，将钻头提出槽孔外，先下套管到达大块石表面，然后在套管下口周围用黏土进行封堵，之后选用岩芯钻配金刚石钻头在块石内钻爆破孔，孔径75mm；爆破筒径取 60mm，炸药装入爆破筒内，每筒长 200mm。爆破筒根据钻孔长度由一个或几个小筒组成，其总长度小于钻孔深度 200～300mm。每个小筒内安放两个雷管，小筒支线与导线采取并联形式，爆破筒底部配加沉重装置。采用2号岩石炸药、8号电雷管，利用220V/380V的电源起爆，炸药量按每米钻孔2kg控制。对探头石、槽底硬岩部分，可使用爆破筒进行聚能爆破。爆破筒为内外双层筒结构，两筒之间用黏土填实。爆破筒外层选用1.5～2.0mm厚铁皮焊制而成。水下聚能爆破筒结构见图2。

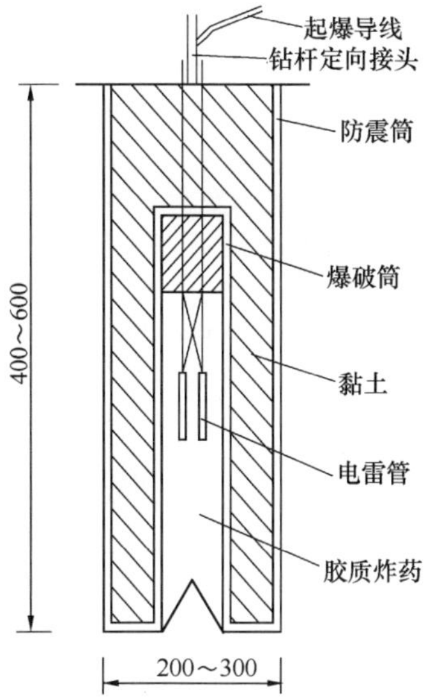

图2　水下聚能爆破装置示意图
（单位：mm）

（四）墙下帷幕灌浆施工

莲麓一级水电站右岸混凝土防渗墙用于主体工程砂砾石层段挡水，墙下布置有帷幕灌浆孔，需在墙体上部沿埋管位置进行穿墙打孔施工。此种设计方式比较特别，施工中相应采取特殊的施工方法。

1. 钻孔

（1）钻孔使用XY-2地质钻机、XY-1B地质钻机，钻孔孔径59～91mm。

（2）在墙内低速挡操作，控制孔斜，确保孔在混凝土墙体内。在进入基岩段钻孔中，若出现不返水、漏水现象时，先进行固结密实灌浆，压力控制在0.2～0.5MPa，再进行帷幕钻孔灌浆。

2. 测斜　鉴于防渗墙墙宽只有0.8m，要求在混凝土防渗墙段钻孔垂直度要求较高。每孔按5m/次测斜，进入基岩按第一次（段长2m）、第二次（段长8.5m）检查。相应的钻孔允许偏差高于帷幕灌浆规范要求，详见表3。

表3　帷幕灌浆孔孔底允许偏差　m

孔　深	20	30	40	50	60
允许偏差(单排孔)	0.25	0.45	0.7	1.0	1.3

3. 钻孔冲洗和压水试验

（1）灌浆孔各孔段灌浆前采用压力水进行裂隙冲洗。冲洗至回水清净无岩粉沉淀时再延续10min后结束，压力为灌浆压力的80%，并不大于1MPa。

（2）裂隙冲洗、压水试验和灌浆过程中安装千分表监测灌浆坝块抬动变形。以变位小于0.2mm为控制，变位大于此值时要降低灌浆压力。

（3）灌浆孔灌浆前的压水试验应在裂隙冲洗后进行，试验采用简易压水，压水试验压力值取该段灌浆压力的80%，并不大于1MPa，压水20min，每5min测读一次压水流量，取最后的流量值作为计算流量，其成果以透水率表示。

（4）主帷幕终孔段灌前压水试验透水率大于5Lu时，增加一个灌浆长度（6.5m）段长。

4. 灌浆

（1）采用孔内循环自上而下分段灌浆法。鉴于此段地层破碎、岩溶泥质充填物较多以及塌孔较多，选用孔口封闭装置进行灌浆。根据一期帷幕灌浆试验数据，段长划分和灌浆压力定为表4的值。终孔段段长不得大于10m。

表4　帷幕灌浆段长和压力

段　次		1	2	3	4	5
单排帷幕	段长（m）	2	6.5	6.5	6.5	6.5
	压力（MPa）	0.5	0.9	1.0	1.2	1.3

以上压力指回浆管的压力表中值，指针摆动范围应小于灌浆压力的20%，并对摆动范围做记录。灌浆过程中使用自动记录仪监测灌浆压力和流量，并随时观测底板的抬动变位值，以变位小于0.2mm为控制，变位大于此值时要降低灌浆压力。

（2）浆液水灰比采用称量和测浆液比重来控制。帷幕灌浆的浆液水灰比采用5∶1、3∶1、2∶1、1∶1、0.8∶1、0.6（或0.5）∶1六个比级。灌浆中浆液水灰比顺序渐变，当发生任何漏浆、冒浆时，不得越级变换浓度。当某一级水灰比浆液的灌入量已达300L以上，而灌浆压力及吸浆量均无改变或改变不显著时，改浓一级灌注，如此一直变至灌浆结束。当注入量大于30L/min时，可根据具体情况越级变浓，但不允许采用间歇灌浆。

（3）水泥灌浆要在较短时间内达到设计压力。如开始时因吸浆量大等原因不能立即达到设计压力时，则应保证在正常操作的条件下，加大浆液浓度，尽快达到设计压力。当注入率大于30L/min时，为了防止串浆过远，造成浪费和防止底板抬动，则应分级升压。

（4）帷幕灌浆各灌浆段的结束条件为：在该灌浆段最大设计压力下，当注入率不大于1L/min后，继续灌注 60min，可结束灌浆。帷幕灌浆孔封孔采用“全孔灌浆封孔法”，封孔压力为终孔段灌浆压力。

5. 灌浆过程中特殊问题的处理

（1）灌浆过程中如发生串浆时，被串孔正在钻进的应立即停钻，如为已完成的钻孔且具备灌浆条件，则可采用一泵一孔进行并联灌注，但须注意，并灌孔不得多于 3 个；控制灌浆压力不得抬动混凝土底板。被串孔无条件同时灌注时，应塞住串浆孔，待灌浆孔灌浆结束后再对串浆孔进行扫孔、冲洗、钻进。

（2）若因故中断，应按以下原则进行处理：①当中断时间超过 30min，应立即冲洗钻孔，再恢复灌浆，若无法冲洗或冲洗无效，则应在重新灌浆前进行扫孔；②恢复灌浆时，应使用开灌比级的水泥浆进行灌注，如注入率与中断前比较相差在 10%以内，则采用中断前的浆液比级继续灌注；如注入率与中断前比较相差在 10%～30%之间，则应逐级加浓浆液继续灌注；如注入率与中断前比较相差大于 30%，且在短时间内停止吸浆，则认为该灌浆段不合格，需采取补救措施。

（3）在有涌水的孔段灌浆时，特别在涌水压力大于 0.2MPa 时，可采用掺用速凝剂、灌后屏浆等措施，屏浆时间不少于 60min。

6. 质量检查方法　混凝土防渗墙帷幕灌浆划分为一个单元工程验收项目进行检查孔的布置，检查孔 F_5 断层处布置一个，其他段再布置一个。整个单元完成 14d 后，经明确帷幕灌浆质量检查孔的具体位置，采用钻孔压水试验的方法，试验采用五点法。质量的评定标准为：经检查孔压水试验检查，坝体混凝土与基岩接触段及其下一段的透水率的合格率为 100%；其余各段的合格率不小于 90%。当设计防渗标准大于或等于 2Lu 时，不合格段的透水率不超过设计规定的 150%，且不合格试段的分布不集中，灌浆质量可评为合格。灌浆后的设计透水率标准为 q 小于 5Lu。

（中国水利水电第三工程局有限公司
雷子祥　柳洪丹）

锦屏二级水电站复杂地层围堰基础塑性混凝土防渗墙快速施工技术

一、工程概况

锦屏二级水电站首部拦河闸坝施工，枯期采用上、下游围堰挡水，右岸导流洞过水；汛期采用导流洞和围堰联合泄洪。上、下游围堰全长分别为 129.23m、98.18m，基础防渗采用塑性混凝土防渗墙。防渗墙最深分别为 60m、55.5m。主要采用 CZ-30 型冲击钻机造槽，成槽采用“钻劈法”施工，槽孔分二期进行，Ⅰ、Ⅱ期槽孔采用套接；塑性混凝土采用直升导管浇筑的施工工艺。

区域地质情况复杂，河床为 V 形，地基主要为崩塌体组成，无级配良好砂砾石。右岸河床上部为崩坡积堆积，两岸坡均为基岩裸露。河床覆盖层较厚，为 20～43m，按物质组成及颗粒大小由下至上可分为含漂石卵砾石层、含粉土质砂碎砾石层、含孤块石群卵砾石层及块碎石夹卵砾石层四层。围堰基础置于河床覆盖层上。

二、防渗墙设计要求

1. 塑性混凝土的力学性能指标　防渗墙墙厚 0.8m，墙底入岩 0.5m，抗压强度 $R_{28}=4\sim6$MPa；弹性模量 800～1500MPa；渗透系数 $K\leqslant1\times10^{-7}$ cm/s；28d 破坏比降≥200。

2. 混凝土性能设计指标　初凝时间大于 8h；终凝时间不大于 48h；入槽坍落度 20～24cm；坍落度保持在 15cm 以上的时间不少于 1h；扩散度34～40cm。

三、防渗墙快速施工技术

（一）施工特点难点

（1）按要求，上下游围堰近 10 000m² 塑性混凝土防渗墙须在 2008 年 12 月 15 日～2009 年 3 月 15 日 90d 内完成，施工工期紧、强度高，且场地狭窄、相互干扰大、组织困难。

（2）河床主要由含漂块石群等粗颗粒组成，级配不良，结构变化大，局部架空现象严重，属强透水地层。在该地层建造地下连续混凝土防渗墙难度大，不确定因素多，制约防渗墙施工进度和质量。

（3）截流戗堤位于防渗墙轴线上游仅 36.75m，截流水力学指标高，龙口底槽水力坡降大，截流合龙施工中抛填了大量的块石串等特殊材料，部分冲积到防渗墙轴线，不但影响施工进度，而且造孔固壁困难。

（4）由于围堰填筑水下只能采用石渣抛填，密实度差，渗流量大，特别在龙口段合龙后其初期渗流量达 80～100m³/s，防渗墙平台填筑过程中，部分细颗粒流失，河床以上 5～8m 架空严重，其上下游水头差达 4.6m，形成动水压力，导致了防渗墙施工中泥浆固壁效果大大减弱，塌孔、漏浆情况十分严重。

（5）下游围堰在合龙后，由于上游围堰渗流量大，水位变幅大，在防渗墙施工同时必须安排围堰下游脚防护施工，造孔废弃浆液也只能排到基坑，因此槽孔内外水位差难以控制在 1.5m 以上，成槽困难，塌孔严重。

（二）工程处理措施

1. 戗堤上游增设斜墙铺盖　在戗堤上游先铺 1m 左右反滤料，然后铺设 3m 厚洞渣垫层料，再填 2m 厚黏土斜墙铺盖进行堰体初期防渗，以减少动水压力对防渗墙施工影响。

2. 加高下游围堰施工平台　由于上游围堰渗流大，基坑水位与下堰原设计施工平台高程 1631m 相近，不能满足防渗墙槽内外水位差大于 1.5m 的要求。为避免塌孔影响成槽质量，采用加高防渗墙施工平台到高程 1632m，同时在两岸Ⅱ期浅槽段内预埋涵管导流，最后施工涵管段槽孔，确保了下游围堰防渗墙施工的正常进行。

3. 优化槽段划分及设备布置　在常规槽段划分的基础上，采用“短、多、快”重点突破深孔槽段的原则，以减少塌孔，有利于快速成槽，保证施工质量和进度。“短”就是Ⅰ期槽段缩短，“多”就是同一槽段安排多台设备同时钻进，“快”就是采用快速成槽钻进的施工措施。具体为：①上下游围堰造孔全部采用 CZ-30 型冲击钻，上游投入 20 台，下游先期投入 16 台；②上游围堰防渗墙槽段优化后，Ⅰ、Ⅱ期槽各 12 个，其中槽孔深度超过 55m 的有 5 组，槽孔划分均是 3 主 2 副，长为 4.8m，其他Ⅱ期槽段及槽孔较浅的部位分别采用 4 主 3 副、5 主 4 副进行划分槽孔；③下游围堰防渗墙共划分 17 个槽孔，其中 8 个Ⅰ期槽、9 个Ⅱ期槽，槽孔深度在 50m 以上的槽段有 4 个Ⅰ期槽、3 个Ⅱ期槽，槽孔划分原则同上游围堰。

4. 优化勘探实施方案　由于河床覆盖层结构复杂并含有孤块石较多，施工过程中无法准确鉴定基岩面，采用上下游围堰每 20m 做补勘一次，上游围堰补勘 7 个孔，下游围堰补勘 5 个孔。为不影响施工进度，根据现场情况采用冲击钻先行钻凿主孔，当距离设计基岩面高程 3～5m 时，挪开冲击钻机，改用岩芯钻钻孔取芯，快速确定基岩面，减少工序衔接时间，从而确保施工进度。

5. 因地制宜优化泥浆性能指标加快成槽速度　由于块巨石架空，渗流量大，为了有效形成泥皮，抵制外界渗流水压力影响，保证有效成槽，对于Ⅰ期槽孔泥浆重点控制，不但要考虑固壁而且还须堵漏。通过实验，Ⅰ期槽优化试验泥浆配比见表 1。对于Ⅱ期槽孔主要采用黏土泥浆固壁。

表 1　Ⅰ期槽优化试验泥浆配比

组分 / 加量 / 类型	水 (kg)	膨润土 (kg)	纯碱 (kg)	CMC (kg)	正电胶 (kg)	烧碱 (kg)
泥　浆	1000	100.0	2	0.375	0	0

在施工中，严格按规范要求控制泥浆性能指标，并不断调整。同时加大制浆站储浆、制浆能力，采用上述的固壁措施不但保证成槽进度，而且较为经济。

6. 塑性混凝土配合比优化设计　根据设计指标，塑性混凝土配制强度按 5MPa 控制。通过多组试验对比分析，各种材料掺量对设计强度和弹模的影响分析，确定最终实施塑性混凝土施工配合比（见表 2）。

表 2　塑性混凝土施工配合比

编号	水胶比	砂率 (%)	材料用量 (kg/m^3)						
			水	水泥	膨润土	砂	小石	减水剂	引气剂
1	0.947	80	275	150	140	1266	319	1.16	0.064

（三）特殊情况处理

1. 塌孔、漏浆严重地层处理　当钻进到 40m 左右时，SFS-11 和 SFS-17 槽段多次发生塌槽，SFS-11 槽经过 5 次向槽孔内分层（厚度约 0.5～1.0m）投入黏土、碎石土、锯末、水泥后再用重凿冲击挤密，最终钻进达到要求深度；SFS-17 槽塌孔严重，在钻机平台下形成了大的空腔，存在极大的安全隐患，采用在槽孔内回填 C15 塑性混凝土，待凝 24h 后继续钻进，成功处理了本次塌槽事故。

2. 漂石、孤石、坚硬基岩以及地下障碍物施工处理　XFS-14 槽段在施工过程中，施工进度缓慢，钻具被破坏，经勘探查明为孤石。由于地层结构松散，原方案准备采用聚能爆破，可能影响槽孔安全。后通过加重钻具、勤焊钻头，对孤漂石进行重锤冲凿穿透基岩，虽然工效较聚能爆破低，但确保了槽段安全，而确保了施工进度。

3. 架空层施工的处理　施工时储备一定数量的黏土球与碎石土石掺合料，当钻进至架空层时，迅速投入这种掺合料至孔口，然后用钻机进行不排渣钻进，反复多次冲击，用回填挤压密实的方法逐步改善架空地层的结构，增强了槽壁的稳定性。

4. 孔斜的处理　由于孤块石等的影响，各个槽段施工中均在 8～20m 范围内发生孔斜，使墙体的有效厚度减少，以及影响墙体的连续性。为了保障质量，采用在钻头上加焊耐磨块，在孔口垫方木进行强制性修正，以达到最终效果。

5. 掉钻、埋钻处理　下游围堰在施工过程中突发基坑水位升高，距离防渗墙施工平台不足 1m，XFS-2、XFS-4、XFS-6、XFS-8、XFS-10、XFS-15、XFS-16 槽段均同时发生了掉钻、埋钻事故。出现掉钻或埋钻后，采用加大基坑排水，及时把水位差控制在 1.5m 以上，并采用主副孔换位和槽段合并法等方式进行打捞处理。

四、施工过程质量控制与检查

（一）孔深、孔斜检查及基岩鉴定控制

本工程塑性混凝土设计墙厚0.8m，Ⅰ期槽两端的主孔孔斜率按不大于0.3%控制，其他槽孔孔斜率按不大于0.4%控制，遇有含孤石、漂石的地层及基岩面倾斜度较大等特殊情况时，孔斜率按0.6%控制，要求相邻孔不得异向；要求整个槽孔孔壁平整无梅花孔、探头石和波浪形小墙等。施工过程采用重锤法进行检测，经检测槽孔孔斜率均满足要求。

（二）浇筑混凝土前清孔质量检查

（1）槽孔清孔换浆结束后1h，使用特制的取浆器从孔底以上0.5m处取试验泥浆，膨润土泥浆应达到下列标准：密度≤1.15g/cm^3；黏度（马氏漏斗）32～50s；含砂量≤6%。

（2）孔内淤积厚度采用测针和测饼进行测量，其厚度严格按规范控制。

（3）Ⅱ期槽在清孔换浆结束之前，用刷子钻头清除Ⅱ期槽孔端头混凝土孔壁上的泥皮。结束标准为刷子钻头上不再带有泥屑，刷洗过程中，孔底淤积不再增加为准。

在清孔验收合格后4h内浇筑混凝土，如因下设预埋件不能按时浇筑，则重新按上述规定进行检测，如不合格应重新进行清孔。

（三）防渗墙墙体质量检查

（1）混凝土浇筑过程中，在机口或槽口由试验室试验员随机取样，测试混凝土熟料主要性能指标。

（2）防渗墙工程完工后，根据监理工程师要求上游防渗墙取2个检查孔，下游取1个检查孔，采用钻孔取芯注水试验进行了质量检查。经检查渗透系数$K=7.918\ 49\times10^{-9}\sim8.132\ 8\times10^{-8}$cm/s，满足设计要求。

（四）混凝土强度等物理力学性能检查

（1）混凝土强度，上游围堰共计取样23组，最小值4.8MPa，最大值6.3MPa；下游围堰共计取样16组，最小值4.3MPa，最大值5.6MPa，满足设计4～6MPa。

（2）弹模检查共41组，一般为1400～1600MPa，几组略有超标，根据已建工程的经验和评定规范要求，弹模不作为主要检测项目，验收小组评审认为满足使用功能要求。

（五）渗压计渗压检查

经防渗墙上下游渗压计检测数据对比，防渗墙上游渗压值为112～131.2kPa、防渗墙下游为－1～18.2kPa，经计算分析，上下游塑性混凝土防渗墙的防渗性能满足设计要求。

（六）Ⅰ、Ⅱ期槽接头孔检查

开挖检查显示，接头孔呈圆弧形、平顺、致密，满足规范要求。

（二滩水电开发有限责任公司 杨培洲
中国水利水电第五工程局有限公司 常明云 舒向东）

地 下 工 程 施 工

锦屏辅助洞工程施工

（一）工程概况

锦屏辅助洞工程位于四川省凉山彝族自治州冕宁、盐源、木里县境内，为锦屏一级、二级水电站工程的关键前期施工项目，是锦屏一级、二级工程的交通洞，锦屏二级引水隧洞的施工辅助、超前勘探试验洞。

锦屏二级水电站利用雅砻江150km长的大河湾，截弯取直，开挖隧洞引水发电。引水洞线自景峰桥至大水沟，引水隧洞共4条，平均长度16.67km。电站装机容量4800MW，单机容量600MW。闸址上游约7.5km是具有年调节能力的锦屏一级水电站，装机容量3600MW。目前，锦屏一级、二级水电站工程正在建设中。

工程位于锦屏二级四条引水隧洞南侧，平面上与引水隧洞呈平行布置，北侧的B线辅助洞距4号引水隧洞的中心间距为80m。辅助洞全长约17.50km，由相互平行、中心距为35m的两条单车道隧洞组成。两洞设计断面均为城门洞形，位于南侧的A线辅助洞设计净宽5.5m，净高4.5m；位于北侧的B线辅助洞设计净宽6.0m，净高5.0m。断面按满足运输锦屏一级水电站最大件的净空要求设计。

工程隧道最大埋深2525m，是国内第一深埋隧道。本工程地质条件极为复杂，主要由三叠系下统（T_1），三叠系中统杂谷脑组（T_{2z}）、白山组（T_{2b}）和盐塘组（T_{2y}），三叠系上统（T_3）等地层及第四系角砾岩地层组成。受地形条件限制，无法从辅助洞中间设置施工平洞或斜井，仅能从东、西两端向中间掘进，独头开挖长度超过9km，工程具有深埋长隧洞的特点。在施工过程中遇到了高压大流量地下水、高地应力引起的不同等级的岩爆等工程技术难题。本工程的洞长、埋深、地应力、外水压力等指标位于已建隧道前列。

工程于2003年底开工，2008年年中贯通，2009年底建成通车。

（二）高压大流量地下水处理

辅助洞地下水具有“高水头、大流量、强交替、突发性”的特点。经对洞内地下水出水情况的统计，洞内共揭露了12条出水带、突发性涌水点5个、涌泥点2个；单点突发性最大涌水量为5～7.3m^3/s；集中涌水段外水压力约5～6MPa，其他一般为3～4MPa及以下。

根据揭露地下水的不同类型，通过大量的研究和实践探索，对辅助洞地下水处理有针对性地制定了四种处理方式，分别是：引流处理、局部封堵处理、系统的高压固结灌浆处理和大涌水点的处理。

1. 引流处理　引流处理是为保证辅助洞的通车环境，将隧洞无序地下渗水归流的工程措施。该处理方式主要用于量少、渗水面小、随季节性变化的密集滴水段。

2. 局部封堵处理　局部封堵处理是封堵隧洞周边围岩地下出水裂隙，减少出渗水量的灌浆工程措施。该处理方式主要用于量少、水压力低、出水结构连通性差的密集滴水、线状流水和股状涌水段。局部封堵处理根据裂隙结构面的走向、产状布置封堵灌浆孔，使钻孔与裂隙在不同深度斜向相交，通过灌浆施工，将该涌水点出露的主裂隙充填满水泥浆液，在较大的范围内，堵塞涌水通道。辅助洞施工过程中，采用引流处理和局部封堵处理的方式占大多数。

3. 系统的高压固结灌浆处理　系统的高压固结灌浆处理通过系统的、全断面布置的固结灌浆，封闭辅助洞周边岩体渗水裂隙和通道，增强围岩抗渗性和长期渗透稳定性，从而减小外水内渗，防止辅助洞围岩发生水力渗透破坏，影响辅助洞内正常的交通运营。该处理方式主要用于出水流量大、压力高、连通性好的线状、股状涌水段。

4. 大涌水点的处理　大涌水点的处理通过“分流减压”方案，降低施工难度和施工风险，最终达到封堵地下涌水目的。在无法采用灌浆封堵的特大涌水点，采用分流导洞、预埋低压钢管和高压钢管导水分级提升压力、施工混凝土堵头，最后关闭高压闸阀等方法，将动水转化为静水，封堵涌水点。该种处理方式用于压力高、流量大的岩溶管道出水，如A线辅助洞的14+762m段的出水处理。

在辅助洞的施工实践中，成功地实施了上述四种地下水的处理，为混凝土路面浇筑、机电设备安装及早日贯通运行创造了重要条件，积累了丰富的地下水处理经验。

（三）强岩爆、极强岩爆处理

辅助洞一般埋深为1500～2000m，最大埋深达2525m，实测（埋深1305m）地应力最大主应力值达到44.18MPa，地应力场反演的辅助洞沿线最大主应力值达70MPa。自A线辅助洞在AK1+155.5m发生第一次岩爆以来，发生不同烈度等级的岩爆近500次。经统计，A洞发生岩爆的洞段长3222.5m，占全洞线长度的18.48%；B洞发生岩爆的洞段长2838.7m，占全洞线长度的16.29%。局部洞段发生强烈岩爆（Ⅲ级），A洞发生301.5m，占总洞长的1.73%，B洞发生196.0m，占总洞长的1.12%；极强岩爆（Ⅳ级），A洞发生15m，占总洞长的0.09%，B洞发生30m，占总洞长的0.17%。

通过参建单位的共同努力和经验积累，研究和总结了一套比较完善的岩爆防治体系，采用应力解除爆破、喷超细粉纳米混凝土、机械涨壳式锚杆或水胀式锚杆等系列岩爆处理技术，较好地解决了辅助洞强岩爆的预防和处理问题，为辅助洞的早日贯通和安全施工打下了基础。应力解除爆破原理如图1所示。

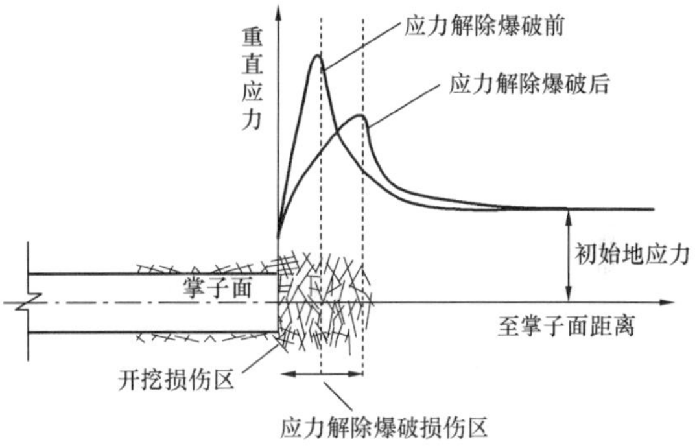

图1　应力解除爆破原理图

（四）辅助洞开挖

为实现辅助洞的早日贯通，通过对辅助洞布置方案的不断比选优化，最后通过设置“人”字形底坡，化解了地下水等施工风险，为异常恶劣地质条件下的辅助洞快速掘进创造了条件。

辅助洞东端洞口800m洞段采用导洞法施工，其余洞段采用全断面钻爆法施工。施工中借助A、B线辅助洞间横通道作为施工横通道，利用三臂钻机钻孔，大直径空眼柱形掏槽，周边光面爆破，非电引爆毫秒、半秒雷管顺序起爆。洞内采用四轨双线轨道，梭式矿车运输出渣，配置312挖掘装载机装渣。

辅助洞西端采用全断面钻爆法施工。施工中也借助A、B线辅助洞间横通道作为施工横通道，局部通过横通道反向施工。利用三臂钻钻孔，采用无轨运输，配置装载机和挖掘机配合装渣，自卸汽车运输。

本工程于2003年底开工，虽然施工过程中遇到岩爆、突涌水等地质问题，但在参建各单位的共同努力下，2008年5月16日实现A、B线辅助洞横向贯通，2008年8月8日实现双线辅助洞全线贯通。连续一年以上时间平均月掘进进尺接近200m，创造了无轨运输独头掘进9750m的纪录。2009年底，双线隧道投入运行。

（中国水电顾问集团华东勘测设计研究院 李 军）

思林水电站导流洞工程施工

（一）工程概况

思林水电站采用枯期围堰挡水、隧洞过流的导流方式。导流隧洞共布置有2条，左右岸各1条，过流断面尺寸13m×15m（宽×高）。左岸导流隧洞全长932m，进出口明渠混凝土段分别长41.16m、25.0m，进出口高程分别为370.0m、364.0m。右岸导流隧洞全长820.89m，进水塔高47.5m，内设平面闸门，进出口明洞分别长15.0m、70.0m，进出口明渠混凝土段分别长20m、35m，进出口高程分别为364.0m、362.0m。主要工程量：土石方明挖25.6万m^3，石方洞挖42.1万m^3，喷混凝土1.4万m^3，锚杆5.0万根，衬砌混凝土14.0万m^3，钢筋9417t，回填灌浆2.0万m^2，固结灌浆3.0万m，闸门及启闭机安装577t。

工程建于石灰岩地区，工程地质条件复杂。左岸导流隧洞于2004年11月5日开工，2006年4月施工结束；右岸导流隧洞于2004年10月26日开工，2005年11月20日完工。由于前期道路不通、停电及溶洞涌水等原因造成了工期延误，因此右岸导流洞工程有效工期仅有10个月左右，工期紧，任务重。

（二）施工情况

1. 进出口

（1）采用潜孔钻及手风钻造孔、边坡预裂、自上而下梯段爆破、建基面预留保护层的开挖方式，台阶高度不大于10m，反铲或装载机配合自卸汽车出渣，开挖渣料运往指定渣场。

（2）搭设脚手架进行边坡支护施工。锚杆采用岩石电钻或手风钻造孔，注浆机注浆后，人工安插，干喷混凝土。左岸导流洞进口在366.5m高程以上左侧边坡岩层走向顺坡、结构松散、裂隙及溶蚀带发育，稳定性差，先后坍塌3次，未形成马道；采用了挂网喷射C20混凝土，打9m长ϕ32锚杆、15m长3ϕ25钢筋束、18m长3ϕ25钢筋束及浇筑贴坡混凝土等加强支护措施，保证了边坡稳定。右岸导流洞进口发生一次塌方，采用了挂网喷射C20混凝土，打9m长ϕ32锚杆等加强支护措施。

（3）为确保左岸边坡的稳定，先开挖喇叭口段，并浇筑完成喇叭口段混凝土，而后开挖明渠段岩埂及进行明渠段混凝土浇筑。喇叭口及进水塔段采用满堂脚手架支撑组合钢模板，按3～5m一层分层浇筑。

2. 洞身施工

（1）导流洞分2层开挖，上层高约7.5m，下层高约9.0m（含2m厚的底板保护层），上部洞室开挖采用自制移动台车配合手风钻钻孔及人工装药，中导洞或全断面爆破，周边光面爆破；下部洞室开挖采用梯段开挖、两侧预裂，主爆孔采用潜孔钻机造孔，预裂采用支架式电动钻机造孔，挖掘机或装载机配合自卸汽车出渣。

（2）洞身段的锚喷支护分上半洞和下半洞施工。锚杆采用岩石电钻或手风钻造孔，注浆机注浆后，人工安插，干喷混凝土。在取消边墙或顶拱混凝土衬砌段，做了喷钢纤维混凝土或聚丙烯纤维混凝土的支护。左岸导流洞开挖、支护手段与右岸导流洞基本一致，但上部为11号交通洞影响段及出口施工道路影响段，顶部岩层较薄（约0.8倍洞径），因此顶拱进一步采用钢格栅、喷混凝土加强支护，并在洞口采用9m锚杆束锁口，确保了安全。

（3）边顶拱混凝土衬砌以钢管台车为主，分为边墙钢管台车和全断面钢管台车，左岸导流洞采用液压全断面钢模台车1台、自制全断面钢管台车1台、自制边墙钢管台车1台、钢拱架2套。右岸导流洞工程混凝土衬砌共投入自制边墙钢管台车5台，自制顶拱钢管台车3台。每台钢管台车长度12m，安装时间为15～20d（其中材料需提前准备，模板需提前制作），浇筑速度边墙4d/仓，顶拱5d/仓。主要采用混凝土搅拌运输车配混凝土泵输送混凝土入仓，采用软轴式插入振捣器振捣。

（三）施工方案调整优化

1. 左岸导流洞出口改明挖为洞挖　为减少出口明挖工程量及便于施工道路布置，根据监理部组织的设计交底会上参建各方达成的共识，左岸导流洞出口按轴线不变进行了调整，延长洞身约25m，相应明渠缩短25m，改明挖为洞挖。调整后保留了顶部高程392m的施工道路，隧洞上覆及外侧岩体厚度不足1倍洞径，明挖工程量从2.8万m^3减少到1.1万m^3，锚杆减少408根，喷混凝土减少340m^3，缩短明渠段的施工工期，确保了2005年度出口的度汛面貌。

2. 优选2005年度汛方案

（1）右岸导流洞进口，承包人投标时采用浆砌石围堰挡水，堰高11～13m，工程量约8000m^3，可靠性差。施工中根据现场实际情况，监理组织四方研究决定采用在明渠 0～20m 桩号设置混凝土拱围堰的方案，防洪标准为全年 10 年一遇洪水，堰顶高程为 375m，堰高 11m，顶宽 1m，底宽 3m。2005 年汛期进水口最高洪水位 374m，低于堰顶高程 1m，围堰达到了保障汛期连续施工的目的，又经济稳妥。

(2) 汛期水流控制，按原投标方案右岸导流洞进口是利用闸门下闸挡水。由于工期滞后，该方案不能实现，采用了在洞内 0＋43～0＋48 留岩塞的方案；出口采用在明洞段 0＋843 浇筑混凝土拱围堰挡水。

(3) 为确保 2005 年 11 月截流目标的实现，进水塔施工、闸门安装与洞身开挖、支护必须同步进行，因此导流洞进口 0＋43～0＋48 岩塞的拆除必须在没有进口闸门保护的情况下进行。经过对历年来水情况、当年中长期水情预报及进口堰顶高程等综合分析，利用乌江流域完善的水情测报系统作指导，决定 10 月初对岩塞进行拆除，同时不封堵进口喇叭口的方案，确保了右岸导流洞进口闸门安装、岩塞拆除及混凝土衬砌的按期完成。

3. 优化四条尾水洞与右岸导流洞相交段的施工　招标阶段四条尾水洞与右岸导流洞相交段的施工要求是挖除尾水洞顶部与导流洞之间的岩体，尾水洞顶戴帽、回填混凝土后浇导流洞底板混凝土，各工序均位于直线工期上。此法影响导流洞的工期，施工难度大，工艺复杂，经优化设计后降低尾水洞的高程，该主要矛盾得以解决，节约工期 3 个月。

4. 优化导流洞混凝土衬砌　右岸导流隧洞全长 820.89m，城门洞形，衬砌后断面 13m×15m，招标阶段要求隧洞全断面衬砌。施工中根据围岩地质条件进行了优化，全断面衬砌段只有 393.89m，顶拱取消混凝土衬砌段长 403m，0＋718～0＋742m 段顶拱采用钢格栅、喷混凝土、回填及固结灌浆支护。左岸导流隧洞全长 932m，全断面衬砌段只有 525.94m，顶拱取消混凝土衬砌段长 257.06m，边墙顶拱取消混凝土衬砌段长 149m。取消混凝土衬砌段Ⅱ类围岩采用喷钢纤维（掺量 50kg/m^3）混凝土，Ⅲ类围岩采用喷聚丙烯（掺量 0.9kg/m^3）混凝土支护。

5. 实际采用单洞截流双洞度汛　导流隧洞共布置有 2 条，左右岸各 1 条。由于前期道路不通、停电及溶洞涌水等原因造成了工期延误，左岸导流洞不能按时完成。根据现场实际条件，截流时只采用右岸导流洞单洞分流。同时要求左岸导流洞增加资源投入，加强组织管理，确保 2006 年 3 月底具备过流条件，参与度汛。

（中国水电顾问集团昆明勘测设计研究院
宗宪金　刘富万　王国强）

橙子沟水电站施工支洞塌方处理

（一）概况

橙子沟水电站位于甘肃省陇南市境内，为白龙江干流水电梯级开发规划的第 15 级电站。中国水利水电第三工程局有限公司中标承担了该工程 C 标段施工任务。标段引水隧洞全长 5433.73m，沿途布置有 5、6 号两条施工支洞，开挖断面呈城门洞形。

5 号施工支洞全长 462.8m，开挖断面尺寸（宽×高）有 7.4m×6.7m、7.2m×6.6m、8.0m×7.0m 三种，进口高程 868.5m，与引水洞相交处高程 851.59m，段坡比为 3.5%～ 3.84%。洞身开挖施工过程中，按照围岩类别的相应支护措施，随掌子面跟进支护。但该支洞在 0＋175.00m～0＋227.00m 段洞身发生变形，导致局部发生塌方。经分析，该洞段围岩为灰黑～黑色千枚岩，层理极发育，部分岩层揉皱（扭曲），属Ⅳ类围岩，或者略次Ⅳ类，遇水后易于软化，凝聚力差，易卸荷变形；岩层产状 NW290°～300° NE∠60°～70°，与洞轴线夹角较小，对洞室稳定不利。

本次塌方处理共分为三个阶段，即为变形段初期控制、变形段中期控制、变形段后期控制，每个处理阶段都紧密结合，环环相扣。

（二）变形段初期控制

根据变形段各部位的变形程度，先进行不同方式的初期变形控制。

0＋175.00m～0＋200.00m 段，在原已安装的钢支撑之间加密安装钢支撑，保证其平均间距不大于 50cm，且在拱脚处垂直向下安装锁脚锚杆，锚杆为 ϕ25 钢筋，单长 250cm，入岩 220cm。根据该洞段围岩特性，为防止钢支撑拱脚处岩石遇水软化，造成拱脚下沉，以及稳固钢支撑拱脚，防止其向内侧滑动，在钢支撑两侧拱脚处进行纵向混凝土浇筑，混凝土强度为 C20，以增强抗滑稳定能力。

在 0＋200.00m～0＋227.00m 段，为防止变形的钢支撑变形位移量继续增大，在原已安装的钢支撑拱脚内侧采用 18 号工字钢横向安装水平钢支撑，支撑两端分别与原钢支撑焊接牢固，并垂直向下安装锁脚锚杆，锚杆为 ϕ25 钢筋，单长 250cm，入岩 220cm，随后浇筑底板混凝土，防止新增水平支撑变形和该部位岩石遇水软化导致钢支撑下沉或变形。混凝土强度为 C20，厚度不小于 50cm，保证混凝土面覆盖工字钢的保护层 15cm，底部清理淤泥至基岩面。

（三）变形段中期控制

经初期变形控制后，立即进行其他各项支护措施，加强该变形段的抗变形能力。加强支护施工过程由外向内进行，从 0+200.00m 向洞内方向先进行钢支撑加密安装，随后进行各部位锁脚锚杆施工。上述工序完成后，及时进行了混凝土喷护施工，封闭已完成的工作面。之后转入下一循环作业面，按照上述顺序继续施工，每个循环作业段为 3m。

具体施工方法及步骤如下：

(1) 在原间距为 1.5m 的钢支撑之间增加两榀钢支撑，保证其平均间距不大于 50cm，按照断面要求，对钢支撑制作加工尺寸进行相应的适当调整，使新增钢支撑紧贴原喷混凝土面。钢支撑之间纵向采用 ϕ25mm 钢筋焊接连接，间距为 50cm。

(2) 钢支撑安装完成后，在钢支撑两侧墙及拱肩处安装锁脚锚杆，单榀钢支撑为 16 根，锚杆采用 ϕ25mm 钢筋，单长 450cm，入岩 400cm，外露部分与钢支撑环抱焊接牢固，靠底部一排锚杆向下倾角 45°，以上三排向上倾角 10°～15°。拱脚处锁脚锚杆为 4 根，单长 250cm，入岩 220cm，外露部分与钢支撑腹板焊接牢固。锁脚锚杆全部采用锚固剂安装。

(3) 在钢支撑之间顶拱及侧墙喷混凝土，要求封闭所有已施工完成的裸露工作面，混凝土强度为 C20，厚度为 20～50cm。

(四) 变形段后期控制

通过初期的变形控制，以及随后的钢支撑安装加强支护，围岩基本稳定，在此基础上，根据需要进行了固结灌浆施工。

本次固结灌浆施工钻孔为 251 个孔。根据施工进度及工序要求，0+175.00m～0+200.00m 范围固结灌浆施工在喷混凝土达到 50％设计强度后进行，环内全断面布孔；0+201.00m～0+209.00m 段环内全断面布孔，0+210.00m～0+227.00m 段只在左侧墙进行布孔，待喷混凝土完成且混凝土达到 50％设计强度后，先进行侧墙灌浆施工，再进行顶拱灌浆施工。

由于该施工段岩石遇水后易于软化，凝聚力差，易卸荷变形，故取消灌浆施工前的裂隙冲洗和简易压水试验。主要施工要求如下：

(1) 按照图纸要求进行布孔，0+175.00m～0+209.00m 段孔间距为 2.0m×1.4m；0+210.00m～0+227.00m段孔间距为 2.0m×2.0m。所有灌浆孔全部采用 YT-28 手风钻造孔，孔深 5.0m，孔径为 50mm。

(2) 固结灌浆采用硅酸盐水泥，水泥强度等级为 42.5 级。制浆材料采用重量称量法，称量误差小于 5％。由集中制浆站的高速搅拌机制备水灰比为 0.5∶1的原浆，由灌浆泵经输浆管路输送至洞内灌浆站，灌浆站按照浆液比重配制成 3∶1、2∶1、1∶1、0.5∶1 的水泥浆供灌浆使用。

(3) 采用单孔内循环，全孔一次灌注方式灌浆。灌浆压力视不同地段和孔深采用 0.2～0.3MPa，采用水灰比 3∶1 的浆液开灌，按照 3∶1、2∶1、1∶1、0.5∶1 浆液由稀到浓逐级变换。在规定压力下，当注入率不大于 0.4L/min，继续灌注 20min，灌浆结束。

(4) 灌浆孔封孔采用“压力灌浆封孔法”。封填前，排除孔内稀浆和污物，以保证钻孔孔口段封填密实。

(五) 处理结果

(1) 在 0+175.00m～0+227.00m 段左侧墙中部每隔 5.0m 设一个检查孔，共计 9 孔。各检查孔孔深均为 5.0m，孔径为 50mm。灌浆结束后 3～7d 后，进行钻孔，检查灌浆密实度及原边顶拱空腔灌浆填实厚度，检查灌浆密实度及原边顶拱空腔灌浆填实厚度。通过钻孔过程及孔壁观察，各检测孔钻孔进钻速度均衡、持续无卡钻现象。

(2) 在整个处理过程中以及处理完成后的一段时间，对不稳定段设变形观测点，分时段进行观测，及时整理观测数据，并及时将观测成果上报相关部门。根据塌方段处理完成 1 个月后的观测成果分析，该洞段趋于稳定，测量数值显示无明显变化。

（中国水利水电第三工程局有限公司
冯　彦　李鸣豪）

斜井施工的测量控制

水电工程输水系统采用斜井，可减少输水管线长度，充分利用水能，但斜井的施工测量一直是技术难题。

斜井施工，包括导井开挖和扩挖，按施工导向分为正导井法和反导井法；按照采用的施工手段分为人工辅助设备施工法（掘进升降机爬罐）和机械施工法（反井钻）。目前国内在长斜井常用爬罐法进行施工，它具有快速、安全、高效、经济等优点。但是斜井施工，尤其是导井施工到一定长度，通视条件差，测量问题是一个值得关注的技术问题。为此，中国水利水电第三工程局有限公司编写了斜井施工测量方法，在山西西龙池抽水蓄能电站斜井施工中应用并得到完善；之后又运用于仁宗海电站、拉西瓦电站的施工测量。

斜井施工测量，首先需布设近井控制点，而且近井控制点必须纳入控制网中。

(一) 正导井施工测量

1. 近井控制点的布设　正导井近井控制点布置

在导井中心轴线反向延长线上斜井上部平段（或弯段），并尽可能位于导井中心线上。施测后求得近井控制点成果，根据其桩号、高程等数据计算出在实际斜井中的位置关系。

2. 具体方法

（1）采用全站仪对正导井进行测量放样。放样时在近井控制点架设仪器，后视上一个基本导线点，水平角转至引水洞设计中心线方向，用正倒镜法于掌子面上放出两点，坡度符合设计坡度，并标出一条方向线，然后根据该点与方向线在设计导井中的位置，用钢尺采用支距法放样形成导井轮廓线。

（2）在导井施工长度超过 15m 后，安装激光指向仪，在距激光器 5m 处安装激光觇牌，用激光控制导井方向。觇牌为一块棱形铁板，下面焊接一个伸缩管，可以使觇牌上下调整位置。觇牌固定在激光定向仪前方的岩壁上，让激光束从觇牌的目标孔穿过，起到定位的作用，目标孔孔径小于 8mm。

（3）采用全站仪测量导井位置、桩号及高程并进行精确的检测，以提前预计贯通误差及制定贯通计划，调整作业导井的位置，提高贯通精度。

（二）反导井施工测量

在反导井施工中，采用在近井控制点架设仪器进行测量放样，存在以下问题：①每次由于仪器架高不同，测量数据必须重新进行计算，测量比较繁琐；②由于爬罐的结构导致只有轨道两侧可以有空隙通视，仪器架设的高度也很难控制；③每次架设仪器均需对近井控制点所在之处的堆渣进行处理，增加了测量放样的时间和测量人员及设备的危险性；④随着开挖深度的增加，通视条件逐步恶劣，所需要的通风时间成倍增加。而采用激光定向仪，不但可以连续提供中心方向线，而且可以定期检测，与施工可以融洽配套，减少了工序，降低了测量危险程度，具有既保证精度又安全快捷的优点。反导井施工采用激光定向仪控制的测量方案，包括激光指向仪的安装、使用，激光束的定位、检核，放样。

1. 近井控制点布设　布置原则仍然是保证精度、便于放样，根据导井中心在各个桩号的设计坐标来设置。如采用爬罐作业，要考虑爬罐本身的结构。为了便于控制激光，近井控制点设在下平段与斜井相交处底板上，埋设两点，分别埋在中心线偏左约 80cm 及中心线偏右 60cm 处；各埋设一块铁板，上面定点，同样纳入基本导线进行施测。

2. 激光定向仪安装

（1）在反井开挖一定距离（大于 20m）后，安装激光定向仪。为了减少爆破石渣对激光定向仪的撞击，以及便于利用爬罐平台控制和实测激光，激光定向仪安装在距斜井反导井口 3～5m 的顶拱上，位置在中心线偏左约 80cm，要求顶拱岩壁开挖平整，并超挖约 20cm。

（2）安装前，首先在近井控制点上架设全站仪，在预先确定的安装位置上，将激光仪安装中心线在岩壁上放出；再用膨胀螺栓将激光定向仪安装在岩壁上。用同样方法，将激光定向仪的两目标孔位点位放出，并安装激光指向仪光觇牌。

3. 激光定向仪的控制检查　激光定向仪安装固定以后，首先通过测设激光管底部末端管中心线的三维坐标及激光管口中心的三维坐标，对激光管进行粗调，顾及激光管的直径（约 6cm），计算后求出激光束的基本位置，然后进行精确调整及校正。在激光定向仪调整好以后，将激光定向仪的厚钢板保护罩安装就位。

4. 斜井轴线测量数据计算　利用大地坐标转换施工坐标的方法（见图 1），具体公式为

$$E=(X_1-X_0)\sin\alpha+(H_1-H_0)\cos\alpha$$

$$S=(H_1-H_0)\cos\alpha-(X_1-X_0)\sin\alpha$$

式中　E——斜长；

S——与中心距离；

X_0——旋转点桩号；

H_0——旋转点高程；

α——旋转角度；

X_1、H_1——测量点坐标。

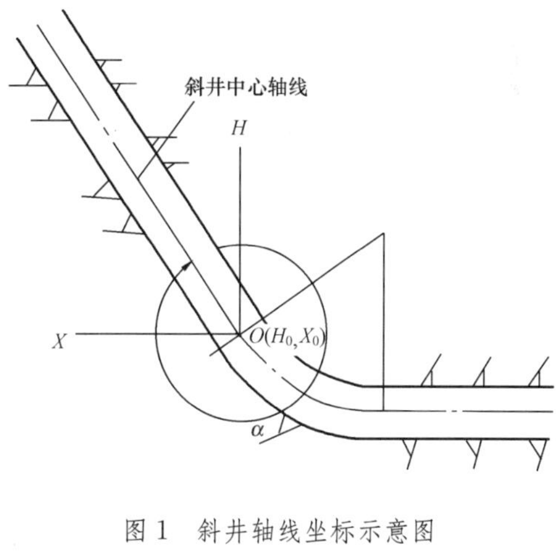

图 1　斜井轴线坐标示意图

5. 误差分析　经计算，20m 内 3′角度可以使激光束点最大偏移 1.7cm。根据实际作业，目标觇牌随开挖进尺向前延伸，当导井开挖到 80m 以后，为保证导井的方向准确性，将觇牌安装在距激光指向仪 60m 处。为了减小系统误差，激光定向仪要经常性检查校正，5、6 个施工循环校正调整一次，而且要让调整偏差正负值以均等概率出现。要求开挖作业人员在每次作业前，必须调正激光穿过觇牌，作业面用激

光点控制放样作业边线。理论和实践证明，随着进尺延伸，前排目标孔上移后，在一定的距离（200m）内，由于调整校正激光束的基线延长，非常有利于将激光束调整至相对精度相当高的程度。按照比例概念，设100m的基线误差为20mm，即使延伸控制500m，误差也仅为100mm，满足导井开挖精度要求。

（三）反井钻安装及导孔的测量

（1）反井钻的钻孔孔位布置在导井中心轴线反向延长线上斜井上部平段（或弯段）。

（2）在反井定位前，首先放出反井钻的位置和孔口位置。反井钻定位时，用全站仪测量，安装误差不大于3mm。由于测量反井钻钻杆很困难，通常测量主机架面四角（取A、B、C、D）点，再计算出反井钻的定位数据。经反复调整，使反井钻定位满足要求。

（3）在反井钻导孔施工到25m后，拆出钻杆，将钻杆滑架升到最高处，用全站仪按间距2m测量出已钻孔的偏斜数据，并画出孔位的曲线。这既可以检查钻孔偏斜是否满足要求，又可以推算出最后的偏斜数据是否满足钻孔标准，从而决定该孔位是继续钻，还是重新造孔。

（四）斜井扩挖的测量放样

1. 扩挖时测量控制点加密　在斜井进行扩挖时，控制点的加密点距按斜距50～80m布设，点位测量方法按支导线进行，加密点的精度要求为平面控制网Ⅲ等。同时要进行贯通测量平差。

2. 扩挖测量放样

（1）斜井扩挖采用全站仪进行测量放样，计算工具用CASIO FX4500P（或FX4800P），根据设计图的数据进行编程计算。编程必须同设计图数据校对，无误后方可运用。

（2）在放样时，开挖边线要加支护厚度，不能出现欠挖，控制超挖。

（3）当开挖满足设计体形尺寸后，按规范要求进行开挖断面测量，作为竣工资料上报、存档。

（4）不要用激光指向仪控制开挖边线（这种设备控制边线是在全站仪不具备无棱镜测距时用）。激光指向仪控制边线，易出现超欠挖，影响进度和经济效益。

（五）结语

在西龙池抽水蓄能电站大坡度超长斜井的施工中，上斜井上段采用了反井钻施工，钻孔方向由测量控制，140m长56°钻孔，偏斜率为0.44%；上斜井下段采用爬罐施工，382m，激光指向偏差小于100mm，贯通误差为40mm，满足测量规范要求。

（中国水利水电第三工程局有限公司　皮高华）

安全监测科技手段在南水北调东线穿黄隧洞工程安全管理中的应用

（一）工程概况

南水北调东线穿黄河隧洞工程，位于山东省东阿县位山村和东平县解山村之间，隧洞上方筑有黄河大堤，从勘探洞揭示的地质资料看，该洞穿越岩层构造发育，共有断层13条，产状多为北东走向，陡倾角，宽度在0.5～3.0m之间，均通向黄河底部。该隧洞按100m³/s进行设计，为圆形有压隧洞，开挖洞径8.9～9.5m，洞长585.38m。穿黄隧洞包括南岸竖井、过河平洞、北岸斜井及进、出口埋管，其中竖井段实长82.25m，平洞段实长307.17m，斜井段实长195.96m。

为加强施工管理，确保施工生产的正常、顺利进行，项目部积极倡导科学管理理念，推行科技管理手段，确保项目安全生产。

（二）安全监测手段配置情况

1. 多点位移计　多点位移计由位移传感器、位移传递杆、保护管、锚头等组成。目前共埋设多点位移计3套设备，埋深16.0m，分别布置在隧洞上半拱180°范围。初期每天观测一次，后期每周观测一次，将收集的观测数据及时分析总结，与设计理论值进行对比分析，以指导安全管理。

2. 锚杆应力计　锚杆应力计由振弦、磁芯和不锈钢外壳等部件组成。目前共埋设锚杆应力计3支，埋深3m，分别布置在隧洞上半拱180°范围。为确保施工期对系统锚杆应力状况的监测，埋设完成初期每天观测一次，后期每周观测一次，并对观测数据及时分析总结，与设计理论值进行对比分析，以指导安全管理。

3. 渗压计　渗压计由振弦、磁芯和不锈钢外壳等部件组成。为长期观测隧洞基岩内部孔隙水压力和渗透水压力状况，并监测埋设点温度的变化情况，穿黄隧洞工程目前共埋设渗压计2支，埋深0.8m，分别布置在隧洞上半拱180°范围。为确保施工期对孔隙水压力和渗透水压力状况的监测，埋设完成初期每天观测一次，后期每周观测一次，并对观测数据及时分析总结。

4. 收敛计　收敛计由百分表、钢尺、恒力弹簧、调节装置等部件组成。隧洞变形收敛观测是直接检验围岩是否稳定、支护是否合理的手段，对施工安全具有重要意义。目前穿黄隧洞工程收敛观测点埋设3个断面，每个断面埋设6个收敛测点。收敛测点埋设完成后，通过收敛仪每天监测一次，后期每周观测一次，以防止围岩变形造成隐患。

5. 视频监控系统　结合穿黄隧洞工程实际施工特点，洞内采用矿用提升绞车牵引平台车进行有轨运输，运送开挖弃渣、机械设备、物资材料等。在矿用提升绞车使用过程中，如果没有视频监控系统，操作员只能依据绞车的运行标尺和洞内人员发出的铃声信号进行操作，不能看到平台车在20°近200m的斜坡道上运行状况，只能凭经验进行控制。为了做到对平台车和运行轨道情况的掌握，配置了视频监控系统，在隧洞的斜井段和掌子面安装了可视探头，可连续采集15d斜井段工作运行资料。这不仅使绞车操作员对轨道和平台车安全情况有了直观了解，同时，也可为安全情况的调查、取证提供了可靠依据。

6. 钢丝绳电脑探伤仪　矿用绞车的运用，大大降低了隧洞施工过程中的运输成本。但是安全控制系统欠缺是矿用绞车在使用过程中的难题。钢丝绳是卷扬机和平台车之间的薄弱环节，一旦发生断裂事故，后果不堪设想。项目部在做好日常人工检查的同时，为了加强对钢丝绳的安全状态监控，对矿用绞车钢丝绳安装了MTC电脑钢丝绳探伤仪。其工作原理是通过MTC磁传感器与采集模块相结合，通过RS232（或USB）总线驱动，直接将数据存储到计算机中。操作过程中，通过采样、断丝分析、磨损分析完成探伤仪的检测工作，并对被检测的钢丝绳的原始信号进行采集控制与处理分析。

（三）科技管理与安全生产现状分析

（1）管理费用高，投入落实难。在采用科技手段管理安全施工过程中，安全生产投入成本相对较高，使项目在投入上承担很大压力。矿用绞车运行过程中的监测、检测系统，费用高达十几万元。科技产品费用高，科研观测费用、操作人员培训费用、检测设备费用投入等一系列投入费用问题，均制约着科技产品的应用与推广。

（2）管理方法先进，培训频次高。在采用科技手段管理安全施工过程中，对新产品认知的人员少，由于施工人员的流动性大、人员变动频繁等情况，使得每次操作人员岗位更换，都必须进行培训，不但增加管理成本，同时也发生短时间管理中断。

（四）结语

穿黄隧洞工程项目部充分利用科技手段进行施工安全生产管理，通过一年多的时间应用，取得了良好效果，值得在更广范围内推广投入使用。

（中国水利水电第五工程局有限公司
赵慧仙　廖成林　朱海亚　孙宝山）

截　　流

锦屏二级水电站高水力学指标窄戗堤截流方案关键技术研究与实施

（一）概况

锦屏二级水电站拦河闸坝工程，受地形限制和建筑物布置需要，采用右岸单洞导流（14m×16m城门洞形）、基坑枯期施工、汛期围堰过水的施工导流方案。工程截流采用窄戗、单戗单向进占合龙。由于特殊的地形和地质条件，雅砻江经过该段时，水流急，流态变化大，给截流带来了较大的困难。为保证截流顺利实施，与三峡大学联合对截流进行水工模型实验，同时根据实际边界条件对截流关键要素展开研究，制定详细实施方案和预案，多次通过专家审查，并对截流期的水文要素进行了实测，用于指导施工。在导流洞分流条件达不到设计要求，龙口流态较实验模型发生变化的情况下，因地制宜，改进特殊材料结构、抛填工艺、抛投方法，使龙口关键段进占成功。

（二）截流模型实验研究

1. 模型设计　试验在三峡大学土木水电学院水工试验大厅进行。模型试验采用恒定流的试验方法，以尾门水位控制模型下游水位。

2. 实验研究工况

（1）试验采用流量标准：11月中旬20%旬平均流量$Q=890m^3/s$；11月下旬20%旬平均流量$Q=746m^3/s$；12月上旬20%旬平均流量$Q=637m^3/s$；12月中旬20%旬平均流量$Q=549m^3/s$。

（2）导流洞进口在设计分流工况及在1m、2m残埂分流工况下截流，对戗堤顶宽10m、18m，分别在11月中旬、11月下旬、12月上旬流量进行定床和局部动床预进占试验，研究水力要素及相关参数；采用单戗立堵左岸单向进占及左岸为主、右岸为辅双向进占水力要素及相关参数研究。

3. 主要成果及结论

（1）导流洞在设计分流条件、截流流量为746～549m^3/s时，截流戗堤未闭气情况下，最大落差为

4.28～3.14m，戗堤头部最大垂线平均流速为6.97～5.96m/s。综合定床和局部动床的试验成果，上述流量截流合龙时，截流龙口以预留大于50m、50～45m、45～40m为宜；非龙口段预进占以左岸单向进占为主，但为改善最终龙口合龙时的水流流态，右岸也宜适当预进占一定的长度，以20m为宜。

（2）导流洞进口存在围堰残埂2m、截流流量746～549m^3/s时，截流戗堤末闭气终落差为4.61～3.48m，比设计分流条件增加0.33～0.34m；戗堤头部最大垂线平均流速为7.37～6.44m/s，比设计分流条件增加0.40～0.48m/s。导流洞进口岩埂1m时，上述指标增加相应减少。岩埂的存在使截流难度有所增大。

（3）截流戗堤宽度由设计10m增加到18m有利于截流合龙施工强度的提高。

（4）局部动床试验成果表明，截流流量746～549m^3/s进占合龙过程中，河床覆盖层最大冲刷深度为2m左右，考虑本工程的实际施工条件，建议不进行专门的龙口护底。

（三）截流实施方案

1. 截流实施方案

（1）综合各种因素，按$Q=746m^3/s$在导流洞2.0m残坎的工况下进行截流设计，龙口段合龙过程中各阶段主要水力学参数（模型实验）见表1。

（2）采用右岸非龙口段预进占35m，单戗立堵、从左向右单向进占为主，右岸为辅（部分特殊材料抛填）的截流方式，龙口初始宽度确定为50m，水面宽度37m。

（3）戗堤设计顶宽18.0m，顶高程1636.00m，顶长162m，上游边坡1∶1.5，下游坡为1∶1～1∶1.5，进占端头边坡大于1∶1。

（4）上下游围堰相距370m左右，为确保下游围堰防渗墙施工进度，在上游围堰截流合龙前预留50m左右龙口，上游围堰合龙后跟进合龙。

2. 截流关键技术措施制定

（1）对50.00m宽龙口段分4个区进行抛填设计，确定备料系数和备料粒径。如图1所示，每区宽度分别为10m、10m、10m和20m，编号分别为龙1、龙2、龙3和龙4。以模型试验参数为指导，经验计算复核，数学几何仿真模型模拟河床坡降对抛填物各质点进行受力分析，抛填设计为：①龙1区（$B=50\sim40m$），最大流速4.28m/s，抛投含大石20%以上石渣和一般石渣；②龙2区前半段（$B=40\sim35m$），最大平均流速6.49m/s，在上挑角抛投大石、特大石，跟进抛投含大石20%以上石渣；③龙2区后半段和龙3区（$B=35\sim20m$），最大流速7.37m/s，准备总重20t特大块石串、钢筋石笼串和混凝土四面体串等特殊抛投料在戗堤上下游角凸抛进占，中间跟进抛投大块石和含大石20%以上的石渣；④龙4

表1 $Q=746m^3/s$岩埂2m左岸单戗单向龙口段合龙截流水力学主要参数表

流量 (m^3/s)	龙口口门宽 (m)	水面宽度 (m)	戗堤上游水位 (m)	戗堤落差 (m)	导流洞分流量 (m^3/s)	龙口流量 (m^3/s)	戗堤渗流量 (m^3/s)	左堤头最大流速 (m/s)	右堤头最大流速 (m/s)
746	65	53	1631.07	0.26	302	432	12	1.90	1.92
	50	37	1631.37	0.60	319	404	23	3.05	3.03
	40	26	1631.83	1.07	354	356	36	4.28	4.17
	30	18	1633.03	2.37	448	233	65	6.49	6.49
	20	13	1634.3	3.66	540	111	95	7.37	7.37
	0	0	1635.14	4.59	620	0	126	0	0

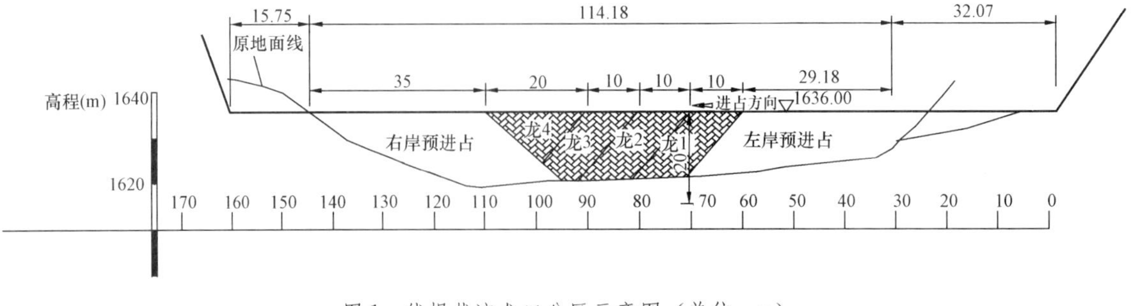

图1 戗堤截流龙口分区示意图（单位：m）

区，流量及流速有较大回落，落差却有较大的增长，合龙终落差 4.59m，抛投特大块石料、钢筋石笼和含大石 20%以上石渣，以加大抛投强度使龙口尽快合龙。各区备料系数：龙 1 区为 1.5，龙 2 区前半部和龙 4 区为 1.6，龙 2 区后半部和龙 3 区为 1.8。

(2) 因地制宜进行备料粒径设计（特殊抛填材料）。模型实验认为使用最大粒径为 5t 的掺合料能顺利合龙，但通过经验计算和数学仿真模型试验分析，考虑到龙口河床底部水力坡降大，冲刷严重，单宽功率增大，高速水流冲击作用下，抛填料稳定性差，模型实验难以真实反映其实际受力特点。经计算与分析，15t 以上特殊材料才能稳定，确定准备单重 20t 以上特殊材料。

(3) 制定单洞分流恶劣条件下满足不了设计要求的截流合龙备用预案。考虑导流洞可能分流差，必须采取措施分散落差改善龙口流态。经过研究，采取：①在现窄戗堤基础上向上游加宽 10.0m 左右，既分散落差（相当潜堰作用），又可作为上游凸抛特殊材料专用道路，以加大抛填强度；②加大特殊材料的粒径，即把块石串成“糖葫芦状”，单串在 60t 以上，在该加宽部分进行上挑角进占，钢筋石笼下压角，块石中部跟进进占补齐。

(4) 根据水力学指标，制定抛填技术，主要有：①上挑角凸抛按 30°～60°方向进占，实际采用 45°方向进占；②在堤头采用 8%坡度下压进行抛投，抛投料出水面后即采用石渣加高，并用级配较好的石渣料进行铺筑，形成良好进占路面以提高进占速度；③右岸预进占 35m，钢筋石笼裹头，大孤石抛入河谷深槽局部护底。

(5) 鉴于唯一备料场距戗堤 5km，为满足高抛填强度，通过优化设计，形成截流进料运输环形路；并在左岸 1 号道路设中转料场，导流洞开挖洞渣直接卸在该部位，作为预进占和龙 1 区填筑料，截流施工时作为环形施工道路基础。

3. 截流备料确定　参照模型实验提供的参数，结合经验计算和截流关键技术研究成果，戗堤顶宽 18m 时，龙口 50m 设计抛填量为 25 265m^3，启动预案上游加宽设计量备料为 12 000m^3，根据龙口分区采用 1.5～1.8 备料系数，备料总量为 55 000m^3。

（四）截流实施

2008 年 10 月下旬流量 Q=1280m^3/s 开始右岸预进占，11 月 8 日开始左岸预进占，11 月 14 日上午 11 时预留龙口 65m 时开始对导流洞进出口同时爆破破堰。此实测流量 Q = 859m^3/s，导流洞分流量为 129m^3/s，导流洞分流量仅 15%，模型实验分流量应为 40%～50%，主要原因为进口围堰前河床在破堰前未做深挖处理。采用垫渣退挖进行部分深挖处理后，分流量得到改善。

2008 年 11 月 22 日上午 8 时流量为 765m^3/h 开始截流演习，在龙 1 区和龙 2 区前 5m 使用掺合料 3 个点卸料全段面进占比较顺利，流失量很小，推进速度平均为 1.5m/h，在进入龙 2 区后 5m，采用中石、大块石凸出上游挑角、中下游掺合料跟进进占 2m 后，继续进占，速度减慢，出现大块石向下游滚失现象，后改用 10～20t 块石串凸出上游挑角、中下游掺合料跟进进占，进入龙 3 区，20t 块石串无法稳定。经分析对比，各种水力学指标高于模型实验，主要原因是流量略高于模型实验，导流洞分流条件比设计条件差，河床底床淘深，水力坡降增大，单宽能量增大，经研究启动截流备用预案。

2008 年 11 月 26 日上午 9 时实测流量为 746～750m^3/s，与模型实验流量接近，开始截流，采用在戗堤上游加宽部位专门采用 40t 块石串凸抛 2～3m 左右，下游采用 20t 块石串平抛压脚，中部块石补齐的方案进占，避免大块石冲集到防渗墙轴线。当进占到龙口宽 27m 左右，进尺缓慢，上游角 40t 块石串无法稳定，致使龙口推进速度非常缓慢，速度在 0.1～0.15m/h 持续 3h。后上游角改用 60t 块石串向上游 20°方向凸抛进占，当进占龙口宽 25.5m 左右，进尺缓慢，此时最大表面流速达 7.4m/s。调整上游角块石串按 45°方向凸抛进占，为使串体易于稳定，先把串体的一大块石串置于戗堤上游侧低流速区入水，相当锚桩作用，然后把其余块石串连成糖葫芦状用推土机推入水中。戗堤下游侧采用钢筋石笼 3～4 个一组串连用推土机推入水中，在未全部入水时，立即与后面一组串联，再用推土机推赶，如此多组串接入水，类似“赶羊”进行下游压角，中部及时用块石补齐。在该段虽水力学指标较高，流失量很少，当进占水面宽度 7.5m 时难度大大降低，改用上游角 20t 大块石凸抛进占、下游特大块石压角、中部掺合料及时补齐，该部分平均进尺 1.2m/h。龙口表面流速变化在 5.1～7.4m/s。

锦屏二级水电站在截流实施中根据水文、水力学监测数据，及时调整措施，增加抛投物料，加大抛投粒径，不断改进抛填工艺，累计经过 30 多个小时紧张施工，到 2008 年 11 月 27 日 15 时截流施工基本完成，龙口宽约 5m，龙口流速 3.1m/s，龙口流量为 50m^3/h。此后主要进行戗堤围堰加高、加固及下游围堰跟进合龙施工，上游围堰龙口暂停推进，各种水力要素基本稳定。11 月 30 日 10 时 16 分历时 16min 完全闭合，锦屏二级水电站截流取得了圆满成功。

（五）实测相关参数与模型实验对比分析

1. 水位及落差　随着龙口推进和束窄，水位逐渐提高，在流速达到 7.4m/s 以前，落差比模型实验高出 0.6m 左右，与导流洞分流条件比设计条件差有关，龙口宽度小于 20m 后开始与模型实验相近。经对比分析，下游围堰预进占对改善龙口落差有利。当上游围堰基本合龙后，落差最大达 4.6m。经过分析总结，虽分流条件差于设计状态，但其变化趋势规律与理论和水工模型的结论基本一致。

2. 龙口流速　在龙门宽度 50m 左右时，龙口表面平均流速为 2.6m/s，前期随龙口的束窄，流速逐渐增大，但各流速大于模型实验同等条件的流速，在达到最大流速 7.4m/s 时，门口宽度 25.5m 左右，随着龙口进一步束窄，龙口流速进一步减少，合龙后龙口流速、流量减少为零，经总结分析其变化趋势规律与理论和水工模型的结论基本一致。

3. 龙口口门　前期推进平均速度为 1.5m /h，随着龙口的束窄，龙口流速加大，进入龙 3 区按实验模型抛填料粒径进占无法稳定，进尺仅 0.15m /h，经分析由于分流条件差于设计状态，采用加长块石串、改进抛填工艺等措施渡过难关，龙口流速开始发生转折，推进速度又逐渐加快。

4. 截流期间流量　在截流期间没有大的洪水过程，总流量按 $10m^3/d$ 左右逐渐减少，期间虽有回升现象，但最大回升流量仅 $40m^3$ 左右，变化幅度比较平缓。导流洞分流虽比设计条件差，但分流比变化过程与总流量变化过程相应；从 11 月 26 日 8 时开始到 27 日 15 时，其分流比直线上升，以后随着上游围堰龙口推进暂停，分流比维持在一个稳定的水平，到 11 月 30 日龙口完全合龙后，分流达到 80%。由于龙 3 区抛填大量特殊材料，龙口渗流量近 20%，合龙后在戗堤上游增加 5m 左右细粒料斜墙铺盖，以减小渗流对防渗墙施工的影响。

5. 抛填实测资料　在围堰戗堤进占中实测各类抛填物 3.8 万 m^3（包括龙口上游加宽 $12000m^3$）；其中特殊材料抛填 $4993m^3$，占龙口设计总量 20%，占高水力学指标抛填区域 38%左右。模型实验显示在 $746m^3/s$ 流量时流失量为 5.56%，且在进占过程中在戗堤下游形成 50m 长、17m 宽、最大堆积厚度 5m 的石舌。由于实际进占加大了抛投直径，改进了抛投工艺，减小了流失量，且基本未超过防渗墙轴线。总体分析抛投物料的量与模型实验的结论趋势基本一致。

（中国水利水电第五工程局有限公司
赵　玉　常明云　舒向东）

毛尔盖水电站大坝枢纽工程截流与度汛施工

毛尔盖水电站位于四川省阿坝州黑水县境内黑水河中游红岩乡至俄石坝河段，坝址距成都 290km，总库容 5.35 亿 m^3，总装机容量 420MW，拦河大坝采用碎石土心墙堆石坝，最大坝高 147m。大坝枢纽工程由中国水利水电第五工程局有限公司施工，并已于 2008 年 4 月开工，其截流与度汛施工情况如下。

（一）截流设计

1. 截流时段与截流流量　根据工程总工期安排，河床截流安排在 2008 年 11 月。截流设计流量为 10 年一遇流量，取 11 月平均流量为 $80.4m^3/s$。

2. 截流方式　采用单戗单向立堵进占方式，自右岸向左岸进占，龙口位置布置在河道左岸。

3. 截流戗堤断面型式　截流戗堤布置在导流洞进口下游，呈直线布置，轴线位于上游土石围堰轴线上游侧并与之平行，两轴线相距 62.00m。戗堤顶高程为 2000.5m，上、下游边坡均为 1 ∶ 1.5，顶宽为 25m。

4. 截流水力计算　计算水位时，假设龙口上游水位与导流洞进口水位相等，其总泄流量为截流设计流量 $80.4m^3/s$，以此上游水位求出截流龙口流量和导流洞分流流量，水力计算成果见表 1。

（二）截流准备和实施

1. 截流材料备料　戗堤预进占材料主要为洞渣料及西尔料场堆石开挖料，预进占抛投量为 $4499m^3$，龙口段特殊抛投料为 $3696m^3$，截流材料备料见表 2。

表 1　龙口水力特性指标参考表

龙口宽度 (m)	龙口流量 (m^3/s)	上游水位 (m)	下游水位 (m)	龙口落差 (m)	平均流速 (m/s)	单宽功率 [t·m/(s·m)]	最大块石粒径 (m)
20	29.76	1996.5	1996.28	0.27	1.91	1.06	0.21
15	26.23	1996.68	1996.28	0.39	2.12	1.79	0.26
12	23.44	1996.77	1996.28	0.48	2.29	2.46	0.30
10	21.18	1996.84	1996.28	0.55	2.41	3.05	0.33
8	18.59	1996.92	1996.28	0.64	2.57	3.86	0.37
6	15.59	1997.03	1996.28	0.75	2.77	5.07	0.43
0	0	1997.48	1996.28	1.20	0.00	0.00	0.00

表 2　截流施工计划备料表

项 目 名 称	预进占段	龙 口		
		Ⅰ区	Ⅱ区	Ⅲ区
		$L=8$m	$L=6$m	$L=6$m
设计抛投量（m^3）	3749	1304	744	168
流失及备料系数	1.2	1.5	2	1.5
总备料量（m^3）	4499	1956	1488	252
特殊抛投料	一般石渣	含较多中石的石渣	中石和大石	中石和大石
龙口截流材料备料总量	中石 1848m^3，大石 870m^3，一般石渣 5477m^3			

2. 截流施工道路布置　截流材料进料线来自上下游两个方向，施工道路利用已有 S302 省道运至卸料点，只需在预进占右端填至一个宽阔的施工回转平台即可。龙口截流戗堤按四车道布置：第一道和第四道为特殊料卸料线，第二道为空车道，第三道为洞渣料及开挖料卸料线。不同材料的运输车辆进入指定道路，空车从空车道返回，并设专人指挥。

3. 截流强度与辆车配备　龙口抛投强度与戗堤前沿能同时布置的抛投点成正比。龙口合龙总抛投量为 3696m^3，按 6h 合龙计算，抛投强度为 616m^3/h，按 20t 汽车一次运 10m^3 估算，每 0.5h 运输 1 趟，配备 31 辆车即可满足要求。

4. 截流方案审查与截流验收　2008 年 11 月 1～4 日，毛尔盖水电站截流验收委员会工程专家组在毛尔盖工程现场召开了专家组截流验收会议，对截流设计及施工方案进行了技术评审，提出了 2008 年 11 月底可以择机截流的建议。2008 年 11 月 28 日，中国水利水电建设集团公司会同四川省发展改革委共同组织工程截流验收，主任委员由中国水利水电建设集团领导担任，验收委员会在成都召开会议，通过截流验收。

5. 截流现场组织　为保证截流施工顺利进行，由承担大坝主体施工的单位成立现场截流指挥中心，由项目经理担任指挥长，统一指挥戗堤进占与截流合龙的施工。

6. 截流过程　尽管“5・12”地震给工程建设造成了一定的影响和损失，截流时段仍然不变。2008 年 11 月 17 日导流洞开始分流，11 月 18 日开始预进占，由于分流条件比预期要好，加之投入设备多达 50 余台套，预进占 8h 后，仅剩龙口宽度 12m；2008 年 11 月 28 日通过截流验收后，随着“开始截流”的一声令下，2h 即顺利完成合龙。

（三）围堰施工与安全度汛

1. 度汛标准与工程形象要求　设计防洪标准为 20 年一遇洪水，相应设计流量为 1030m^3/s，上游围堰上游水位 2034.00m，上游围堰堰顶设计高程为 2036.00m。为满足工程度汛要求，2009 年 3 月底应完成上游围堰防渗墙施工，2009 年 4 月 15 日应将上游围堰填筑至 2036m 度汛高程。

2. 围堰填筑施工

（1）上游围堰为坝体堆石的一部分，围堰填筑施工是保证安全度汛的关键项目，设计填筑工程量为 66 万 m^3，最大堰高 43m。

（2）为了减轻后期上游围堰的填筑强度和为截流施工场地创造条件，提前进行了上游围堰右侧临时断面填筑，围堰填筑主要施工道路布置三条，分别布置在 2000m、2020m、2036m 高程。

（3）围堰填筑堆石料源主要有 1 号洞开挖利用料、磨子沟料场、西尔料场三个料源。截流前仅用洞渣料，截流后磨子沟料场和西尔料场已具备出料条件，其中洞渣料可运输填筑量为 5 万 m^3/月，磨子沟出料强度为 6 万 m^3/月，西尔料场出料强度为 12 万 m^3/月。过渡料主要来源于河滩砂砾料。

（4）堰体堆石料填筑按照料场开采、运输、卸料、摊铺、洒水、碾压、质检几道工序控制，采用 20t 自卸汽车运料，推土机散料，25t 轮式振动碾碾压。摊铺厚度 10～1.2m，碾压遍数为 10 遍。满足堆石料孔隙率小于 23%的要求。

（5）为了确保围堰填筑达到度汛要求，制定了 2009 年 2 月底填筑至 2020m 高程，3 月底填筑至 2030 高程，4 月 15 日填筑至 2036 高程的工期节点目标，实际填筑过程中由于措施得力，工期均有所提前，并于 2009 年 3 月 18 日将围堰全断面填筑至 2036m 度汛高程，提前 28d 实现了安全度汛目标，创造了月高峰填筑强度达 25 万 m^3 的好成绩。

（中国水利水电第五工程局有限公司
高印章　李法海）

钢筋石笼土石围堰在中小型水电站导截流工程中的应用

（一）在云南几个水电站的应用情况

在云南槟榔江二级猴桥水电站的横向、纵向围堰和三级苏家河口水电站的厂房纵向围堰，采用了钢筋石笼土石围堰。在保山市龙江等壳水电站优化防洪度汛的方案中，新增度汛临时围堰也采用了钢筋石笼土石围堰。这些围堰均为中小型围堰，其结构设计型式如下：

1. 猴桥纵向围堰　一枯水期围护右岸基坑，完成导流明渠开挖及混凝土浇筑、泄洪冲沙底孔等工程。洪水由束窄河床通过，导流设计标准 $P=20\%$，$Q=400m^3/s$，河道比降大，水流急。围堰采用梯形断面钢筋笼块石结构，夹钢管桩固定。基础防渗采用黏土截水墙，堰体防渗采用黏土心墙，钢筋石笼与黏土心墙之间采用黏土麻袋加强防渗并加强堰体稳定。围堰最大高度 6.5m，堰顶宽 3m，迎水、背水面坡比均 1∶0.5。

2. 猴桥横向围堰　为二期全年围堰，采用 $P=5\%$洪水标准，为Ⅴ级临时建筑物。上游围堰采用块石钢筋笼、土石混合料与土石麻袋结合的形式，堰体防渗采用黏土心墙，基础防渗采用黏土铺盖；下游围堰采用块石钢筋笼与土石麻袋结合的形式，堰体防渗采用黏土心墙，基础防渗采用黏土铺盖。为防止渗水对黏土心墙的冲刷，在黏土心墙两侧包裹一层土工膜。上游围堰最大堰高 13.7m，迎水面坡比 1∶1，背水面坡比 1∶0.8，顶宽 7m；下游围堰最大堰高 10.9m，迎水面坡比 1∶0.8，背水面坡比 1∶1，顶宽 7.0m，顶部采用 0.5m 厚石渣回填作为交通道路。

3. 苏家河口厂房纵向围堰　分一期围堰及二期围堰，最大堰高 10.5m，迎、背水面坡比均为 1∶0.8。一期围堰防洪设计标准 $P=5\%$，$Q=1320m^3/s$（全年）；二期围堰防洪设计标准 $P=10\%$，$Q=388m^3/s$（11 月～次年 4 月），使用时段 2008 年 11 月～2009 年 4 月。由于围堰所处河段河床狭窄，围堰布置又受到尾水渠限制，对右岸岸坡进行 40m 范围扩挖，确保过流量。

4. 龙江等壳水电站临时度汛围堰　为确保汛期右岸基坑大坝及坝后厂房的施工，汛前浇筑中部 7～8 号坝段至度汛高程 979m，同时沿右岸增设临时围堰围护右岸基坑。该临时围堰是在枯期横向围堰围护下实施，堰基处理及防渗施工条件较好，堰后坡有坝体防护，确保围堰稳定，最大堰高 14m，迎水面采用钢筋石笼防护，坡比 1∶0.5，堰体采用土石渣回填，黏土心墙防渗。

（二）钢筋石笼土石围堰的特点

（1）堰高较小，多数在 10m 左右，导流等级不高，根据《水利水电工程施工组织设计规范》（SDJ 338—1989），导流建筑物为Ⅴ级临时建筑物。

（2）以纵向围堰为主，水流冲刷应力相对较小，堰体结构断面较小，堰顶宽度小，一般没有交通要求，两侧堰坡坡比较小，小于 1∶1，可以通过基础增设钢管桩加强堰体抗滑稳定性。

（3）河道狭窄，不宜布置体形庞大的土石围堰，导流技术要求尽量少束窄河床，以增加汛期过流量，增强度汛能力。

（4）多采用黏土心墙防渗，并根据当地黏土质量，可增加土工膜加强防渗，黏土心墙与堰面钢筋石笼之间采用土石麻袋或过渡料回填，增强防渗效果，同时利于堰体稳定。

（5）堰基多为冲积层或洪积层，覆盖层厚度相对较大，不适合大面积基础开挖出露基岩，而钢筋石笼对基础承载和整体性要求较低，不会因为基础不均匀沉降发生整体性破坏。

（6）施工强度相对较低，投资成本低，多采用小规模施工机械和器具，便于施工布置，对周边主体建筑物施工影响较小。堰基处理难度小，不必增设大体积临时围堰后组织施工，钢筋石笼甚至可以直接组织水下作业。

（三）结构设计

以苏家河口厂房围堰设计为代表作简要叙述如下。

采用钢筋石笼土石（黏土）麻袋围堰，主要结构为钢筋石笼堰面、土石麻袋和黏土麻袋堰体构、黏土心墙；钢筋石笼堰面坡比 1∶0.8，以尽量少束窄河床，同时减少右岸河床扩挖量；堰体防渗采用 1m 厚黏土心墙，心墙按照 1∶0.1 坡比设置，并分别在心墙迎、背水面设置土工膜（$350g/m^2$，0.3mm，两布一膜）加强防渗层及土工布反滤层；堰基防渗采用深挖换填黏土心墙方式，迎水面的钢筋石笼基础开挖齿槽，增强抗冲刷能力；堰体布置 $\phi42@2m\times3m$ 钢管桩，同时钢筋石笼之间采用 $\phi16$ 的钢筋连接，并与钢管桩焊接使之成为整体，增加整体抗滑稳定性。

一期围堰最大堰高 10.5m，顶宽 5.8m，心墙至背水面堰面部分堰体直接占压尾水渠底板，汛后需挖除占压部分；在此基础上实施二期枯期围堰，提交尾水渠底板工作面。故二期围堰在一期围堰不完全拆除的基础上实施，一期围堰堰后坡按照 1∶1.5 坡比拆除至心墙中心线时直坡下挖与一期堰体黏土心墙相接，同时将心墙土工膜延伸连接至二期围堰堰顶，与堰体黏土麻袋共同形成防渗体，之后采用 60cm 厚土石麻袋回填护坡，最大堰高 7.0m，顶宽 1.0m。

纵向围堰设计结构见图 1。

围堰边坡稳定计算采用中国水利水电科学研究院陈祖煜编制的 STAB 土质边坡稳定分析程序进行计算，采用圆弧滑裂面。堰体填筑料计算参数参照类似工程的经验数值，计算采用计及条块间作用力的毕肖普法计算。

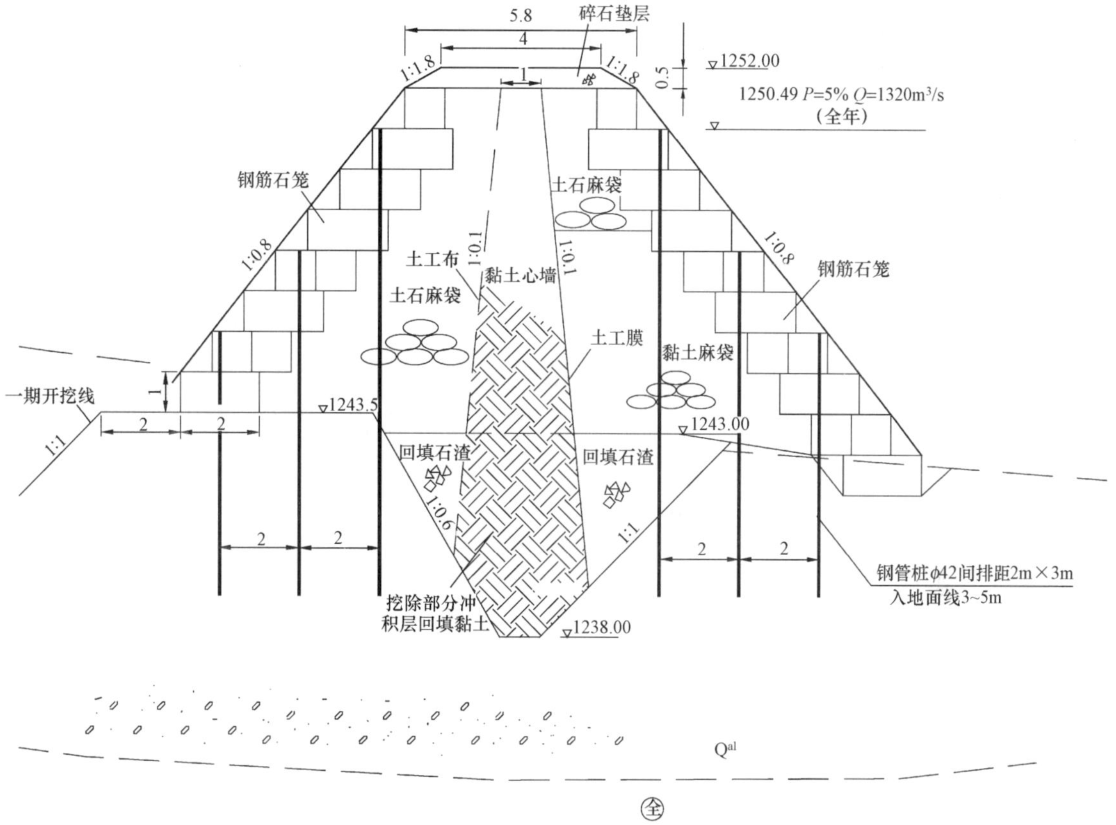

图 1　苏家河口厂房围堰结构示意图

根据《水利水电工程施工组织设计规范》(SDJ 338—1989)中的要求，在正常运用条件下，Ⅴ级建筑物的坝坡抗滑稳定最小安全系数不小于1.05。按照施工完成时核算边坡稳定，上游为设计水位时核算上下游边坡的稳定性，上游为最高水位骤然降落时核算迎水面边坡的稳定性等工况进行验算，经验算围堰满足稳定要求。

（四）施工方法

1. 堰基开挖　按照测量放样的结果确定开挖施工的范围，利用CAT320液压反铲在开挖区内结合厂房基坑开挖道路直接挖除，按照从下游至上游依次进行覆盖层、部分冲积层、基础齿槽的顺序组织开挖。对于堰基出露的孤石进行解爆处理，开挖弃渣直接用反铲装20t自卸汽车运至指定渣场，对可用料进行集中堆存。黏土心墙基础开挖要求严格控制开挖界限，原则上挖除冲洪积层，至密实层为止，并控制大面平整，开挖完成后及时分层回填黏土。同时特别注意控制堰头开挖，要求开挖成槽状，使心墙嵌于两侧山体或岩层，避免洪水绕堰渗漏。

2. 钢筋石笼　按照设计配筋图在工厂焊接加工成钢筋笼。主骨架钢筋ϕ16@1m×1m×2m（宽×高×长），钢筋网ϕ6.5@15cm×15cm。钢筋下料按照骨架、钢筋网尺寸考虑搭接后切割，确保接头搭接焊接牢靠，在焊接时要确保钢筋的正确就位、根数和间距，并按规范焊接牢固。检验合格后，采用载重汽车运往施工现场。根据设计要求逐层人工码放，错缝搭接，设备配合人工进行块石回填，要求块石直径不小于20cm，通过错层码放钢筋石笼控制位置及堰体坡比。回填完成后相互之间采用钢筋焊接连接牢靠，确保钢筋笼组成整体，加强整体稳定性。

3. 黏土心墙

(1) 在铺料时应考虑铺料层厚均匀并对已压实合格土料不产生剪力破坏，采用自卸汽车在已摊铺好的松土层上卸料，推土机向前进占平料，蛙式夯机跟进压实。

(2) 填筑过程中严格控制含水量、分层厚度，并根据料源及土工试验结果及时调整碾压参数，保证设计要求心墙料压实标准：最大干密度1.8g/cm³，最优含水率13%，压实度不低于96%。

4. 土石（黏土）麻袋回填　土石料直接采用厂房边坡及基坑开挖出的可用料，黏土选用心墙料源，根据现场考察在厂房上游500m处所取。把所取的土石混合料及黏土料装入标准麻袋，按照设计坡比分层错缝堆放，夯机碾压密实即可。施工中黏土料可以使用花岗岩全风化料代替，但需通过土工试验确定施工技术参数。

5. 钢管桩　钢管选用普通脚手架管，采用SM-3000型风动锚杆钻机造孔并跟入钢管，上部采用焊接或管箍连接加长，每层钢筋石笼施工完成后及时与钢管桩点焊连接。

6. 监测分析　为了观测围堰的运行状况，主要进行了堰体稳定沉降观测、基础渗流监测等监测项目。堰体表面埋设变形监测点，采用TCR402全站仪测量，结果反映围堰完成后沉降速率较大，之后趋于稳定，符合土石围岩沉降规律及技术要求；在内侧堰脚最低点设置简易渗流量监测装置，测量数据表明渗透量较小，布置1台水泵进行常规排水即可。在汛期加强观测，围堰运行正常，监测结果符合技术要求，表明围堰和防渗心墙均能在水位变化导致的荷载应力变化下满足使用要求。

（五）结语

在中小型水电工程，钢筋石笼土石围堰在适用性、自身稳定性、堰体防渗能力、经济投资等方面较传统围堰均存在优势，在施工组织、施工进度方面可行，可推广应用。

（中国水利水电第三工程局有限公司
江　燕　孟宪坤）

其　　他

柔性防护网系统在拉西瓦右岸高边坡防护的应用

拉西瓦水电站右岸高边坡顶部高程约为2950.0m，底部高程为2460.0m，上、下高差高达450m，坡度大约为40°，边坡陡峻，坡面岩石风化严重危石发育。右岸高边坡下方的主要建筑物有：水电站的进水塔、出线楼及右岸上坝公路等。风化崩落的岩石顺高边坡坡面而下，落石在坡面上经碰撞变成分散的石块，覆盖面又变大，这对下方的建筑物和行人都造成相当大的安全隐患。在综合考虑各方面因素后，拉西瓦右岸高边坡采用了柔性防护网系统（SNS）作安全防护。

（一）柔性防护网系统简介

边坡柔性防护网系统是以高强度柔性网作为主要构成部件，并以覆盖和拦截两大基本类型来防治各类斜坡坡面地质灾害、岸坡冲刷、爆破飞石、坠物等危害的安全防护系统。目前，可分为主动防护网系统和被动防护网系统。

1. 被动防护网系统　主要是拦截高边坡滚石、飞石及崩塌的岩石。该系统通过锚杆、钢柱、支撑绳和拉锚绳将钢丝网在坡面上形成栅栏形式的拦石网，实现对落石和崩落岩块的拦截，从而保证主要建筑物及施工人员的安全。其主要特点就是允许整个系统有一定的变形和位移，安全性能高，不受地形影响，运输方便，施工简便且经济，在狭窄的场地和冲沟区域更能显示出其优势。拉西瓦右岸高边坡及青石梁高边坡被动防护网采用的是X-50型，防护能量为500kJ。该防护网高7m，钢柱间距为5m；钢柱基座与地脚螺栓相锚固，基座的4根地脚螺栓锚杆是由ϕ28螺纹钢加工制作而成，锚杆长1.5m，拉锚绳采用双股ϕ16钢丝绳，钻孔注浆采用M10水泥砂浆。

2. 主动防护网系统　用以钢丝绳为主的各类柔性网覆盖或包覆在需防护的斜坡或危石上，以限制岩体的风化剥落以及危岩的坍塌。其明显的特征是采用系统锚杆固定，并根据其柔性的特点，通过支撑绳和缝合绳拉伸来对柔性防护网部分实现预张拉，从而对整个边坡实现连续支撑。其作用原理类似于锚喷和土钉墙等面层护坡体系，并且由于柔性的开放性，雨水可以沿山坡排泄，避免了挂网喷混凝土存在的雨水涌入对喷混凝土造成破坏，甚至引起边坡失稳。该系统还能不破坏原有地面形态和植被，实现最佳的防护和环境保护的目的。拉西瓦水电站右岸出线楼高边坡和青石梁高边坡采用了大量的GPS2型主动防护网对坡面进行防护。根据现有情况的观察，防护效果明显。

（二）SNS防护网系统的实施

1. 施工布置　由于该种防护系统是在施工区域现场组装而成，且组装成防护网的各部分构件重量都较轻，施工时在材料运输的布置上相对较为简单。现有布置于右岸出线楼的高边坡卷扬机系统可满足大部分部位防护网材料的运输，防护网运输至施工区域后，由人工分散运输至各个施工面。人工无法到达的区域通过搭设钢爬梯或简易通道来满足材料的运输。施工用风主要为现场的锚杆造孔方面，现有的布置于施工现场的系统供风装置即可满足施工现场的需要。

2. 被动防护网施工　主要流程为：边坡浮石清理→测量确定锚杆及基座位置→锚杆造孔及清空→锚杆安装→基座及钢柱安装→钢丝绳安装→格栅网安装。

（1）施工前需将基座安装部位基础的浮石及覆盖层清理彻底。清理完毕后，进行钢柱基座位置测量放点。

（2）锚杆孔采用 YT-28 型手风钻造孔，用高压水进行清孔，合格后进行锚杆安装、注浆等工序的施工。

（3）锚杆安装完成浆液达到一定的强度后进行钢柱基座的安装，人工辅助小型的工器具将基座套入地脚螺栓并用螺帽拧紧贴死。

（4）安装及调试钢柱和拉锚绳，使钢柱尽可能地垂直，拉锚绳必须绷紧且加固牢靠。接着在钢柱间安装及调试支撑绳，用手动 1t 葫芦拉紧后其两端用绳卡固定连接。

（5）铺挂钢丝绳网，与支撑绳间用 $\phi 8$ 钢绳进行缝合；再铺挂格栅网，重叠宽度不小于 5cm，格栅网间及格栅网与钢绳网间用 $\phi 1.5$ 的铁丝进行绑扎。

3. 主动防护网施工

（1）在施工区域内搭设一定数量的施工脚手架，清理施工区域周围的危石及浮石。脚手架管的间距要充分考虑防护网的网片大小，在安全的前提下，保证施工简便。

（2）根据图纸设计测量确定固定防护网的锚杆孔。采用 YT-28 手风钻造孔，孔深应大于设计锚杆长度的 5～10cm。高压风进行清孔后，用挤压式注浆泵向锚杆孔内注浆。当孔内注满浆后，由人工立即插入锚杆，注浆锚杆水泥砂浆强度等级不应低于 20MPa。锚杆安装后，其养护时间不得小于 3d，且养护其间不得敲击、碰撞和拉拔锚杆。

（3）安装纵横向支撑绳，张拉紧后两端用绳卡与锚杆外露环套固定连接。如果因为边坡岩石凹凸不平导致支撑绳张拉不紧的时候，可采用小型的手拉葫芦施加一定的拉力，使其满足需求。支撑绳安装完成后，人工自上而下铺挂格栅网，重叠宽度不小于 5cm，两张格栅网间的缝合及格栅网与支撑绳间用 $\phi 1.5$ 铁丝进行绑扎。坡面坡度小于 45°，扎结点间距不得大于 2m；坡面坡度大于 45°，扎结点间距不得大于 1m。

（4）在铺挂格栅网的同时在格栅网的上部自上而下地铺挂钢丝绳网，用 $\phi 8$ 钢绳将钢丝绳网与支撑绳进行缝合，并用 1t 手动葫芦将钢绳网进行张拉。缝合绳两端各用两个绳卡与钢绳网进行固定连接。

（三）结语

该边坡防护网系统的先进性和创新点如下：

（1）充分利用了柔性材料易铺展性和高防冲击能力，通过系统的开发和大量的现场试验和现场应用形成了适用各种坡面的地质灾害防护系统化技术。通过定性化的均衡设计和部件的工厂式生产，实现了该种系统的标准化和最优化。

（2）充分利用了系统的开放性来减小系统对原有植被系统的破坏，并且还给实施人工绿化提供了可能，将工程治理与环境保护融为一体。

（3）该种系统在其表面采用了镀锌材料的防腐以保证系统在将来长时间内的寿命，一般使用时间可达 30～50 年，必要时只需更换少量的部件即可延长其使用寿命。

该防护网系统施工方便、简单、经济，在拉西瓦右岸高边坡的高位边坡应用，作用明显。

（中国水利水电第三工程局有限公司　赵　琦）

土锚杆在土质边坡处理中的应用

（一）概况

在水电站高边坡开挖、支护施工中，为了加快工程进度，减小边坡开挖范围，缩短施工工期，较好地保护植被，适应环保要求，对地质不良的边坡采用尽量减小开挖工程量、加强边坡支护的处理方式，已成为水电站边坡施工的主导思路。但采用何种支护方式，必须结合工程的地质情况综合确定，达到既经济合理又满足工程需要的效果。

苏家河口水电站位于云南省边陲腾冲县西北部中缅交界附近中方一侧的槟榔江河段上，总库容 2.26 亿 m^3，大坝为混凝土面板堆石坝。坝基开挖形成的边坡，中、上部主要由全风化岩体构成，局部有少量坡积物；中部含部分强风化岩体，以散体结构为主，含少量碎裂结构，除构造节理外，风化节理及卸荷裂隙都很发育，总体上边坡介质以散体为主。下部边坡主要为弱风化岩体构成的岩质边坡，岩块坚硬。坝基边坡开挖高度 250m 左右，月均开挖工程量 80 万 m^3，施工强度高，且集中在雨季施工，对边坡支护质量及进度提出了非常高的要求。设计采用了网格梁支护型式，节点采用专用中空自进式锚杆或土锚杆，长度 6.0m。根据两种锚杆实施试验情况，实际采用了节点土锚杆的支护体系。

（二）土锚杆简介

土锚杆为自制锚杆，主要材料为 $\phi 48\times 3.5$mm 普通钢管、8mm 厚普通钢板、$\angle 30\times 30$ 角钢，锚杆体主体结构为钢管。苏家河口电站采用的 6m 长土锚杆，需要 6m 长普通钢管加工制作。土锚杆结构型式见图 1。

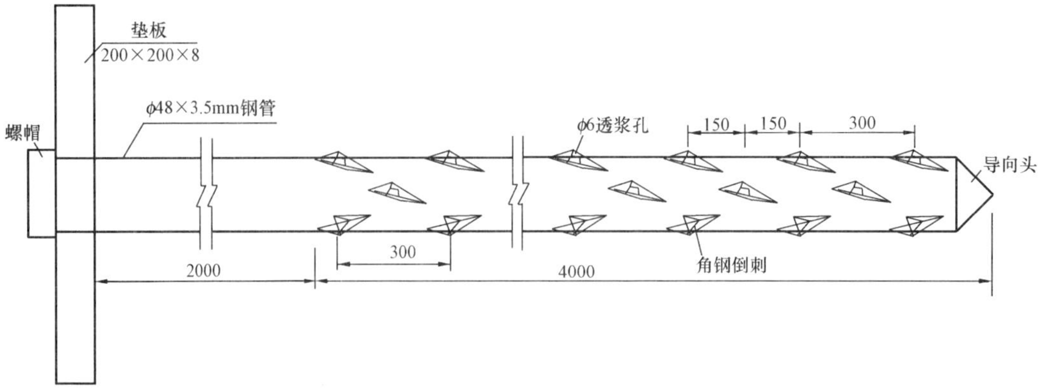

图 1 土锚杆结构型式图（单位：mm）

6m长土锚杆由4m注浆段、2m非注浆段、垫板、螺帽及前端加工成锥形的导向头组成，其中4m长注浆段在杆体设置φ6透浆孔，环向布置3孔，排距0.3m，梅花形布孔，透浆孔利用与杆体焊接在一起的角钢倒刺覆盖，防止杆体插入过程中土体进入杆体内部，影响注浆效果。注浆过程中通过插至孔底的注浆管沿透浆孔自内向外固结周边围岩，形成以土锚杆为中心的锚固岩圈；2m长非注浆段、垫板及螺帽起到孔口封闭，防止表层围岩冒浆、跑浆，加强锚固效果的目的；当进浆管和回浆管浆液流量、浓度、压力相当时闭浆，之后结束，最后对杆体内部进行浆液充填和补充灌浆，这样既确保了土锚杆周边土层围岩固结效果，又可以使杆体与围岩形成整体，大大加强锚杆孔壁摩阻力、砂浆握裹力，进而提高锚杆抗拔力，起到锚固、固结、抗拉、抗剪等作用，从而达到稳固边坡的作用。

（三）钻具与注浆试验

1. 钻具试验及选择　在苏家河口水电站边坡的施工中，通过几种钻具的现场试验确定施工机具，试验情况如下：

（1）YT28手风钻在全风化土层、堆积体、岩石破碎或土夹石等不良地质条件的施工中能够钻进深度小于6m的孔，但成孔效率约60%，且注浆效果不太理想；大于6m后钻进效率大大降低，成孔难度极大，不适合土锚杆钻进。

（2）液压钻（ROC-D7）在试验中钻进速度较快，并能保证钻进深度，但须在开挖过程中同步完成。开挖与锚杆钻进需逐层穿插施工，每层开挖高度需控制在2～3m，与开挖干扰较大。由于液压钻推进压力较大，施工中需密切注意孔口的石粉吹出情况，以免杆体中孔堵塞，影响注浆效果。

（3）将QZJ-100D潜孔钻简易改装后用于土锚杆造孔，由于是电动机直接驱动，不用压缩空气，较YQ100B潜孔钻机成本明显较低。试用结果表明，在较破碎的岩体、堆积体中，钻孔深度在12m左右较为适用。对较为完整、坚硬岩石，钻进深度可达30m。

根据以上的现场钻孔试验，苏家河水电站边坡土锚杆的造孔采用以QZJ-100D潜孔钻机为主导设备、液压钻作为补充的手段，确保了锚杆造孔速度，有效地保证了支护及时跟进。

2. 注浆试验

（1）通过室内配合比试验，确定用于土锚杆注浆的配合比为水∶水泥∶砂＝0.45∶1∶1，注浆压力为0.15～0.3MPa。

（2）注浆密实度试验：选取与现场相同的锚杆、锚孔孔径与倾斜度、砂浆，并按现场施工相同的注浆工艺进行注浆，养护7d后剖管检查其密实度。经试验验证，土锚杆通过透浆孔注浆密实、效果良好。

（四）施工工艺控制

1. 钻孔工艺　造孔主要采用QZJ-100D轻型潜孔钻机，孔径φ76；干钻法施工，以防止卡钻、破坏边坡；成孔后要验孔，保证平面位置、孔深、孔径、倾角等符合设计要求。安装土锚杆前，及时进行清孔，用高压力风将孔内残留物或岩粉清除干净。

2. 锚杆安装　采用人工辅助钻机安装，钻机经改装后直接推送杆体入孔。成孔后立即安插，以防塌孔，之后用水泥砂浆（或细石混凝土）封闭孔口。

3. 注浆工艺　这是保证土锚杆与周围土体紧密贴合的关键步骤。

（1）在孔口处设置止浆塞并旋紧，使其与孔壁紧密贴合。在止浆塞上将注浆管（最好采用镀锌钢管）插入注浆口内，插至孔底，通过快速注浆接头将注浆管端部与注浆泵相连，边注浆边向孔口方向拔管，直到注满为止。采用纯压式注浆，灌浆压力为0.15～0.3MPa，管口周围回浆或虽未见回浆但灌浆压力达到0.5MPa时结束灌浆。

（2）为保证注浆效果，钻进完成与注浆时间间隔不宜过长，锚杆钻进后应在2h内进行注浆，且注浆顺序应遵循从低到高的注浆顺序，以免在破碎岩体中串浆堵塞上部锚杆。

(3) 灌浆结束后，在砂浆凝固前，不得敲击、碰撞、拉拔土锚杆。当水泥砂浆强度达到设计值的75%后，即可施工面层结构，安装垫板及螺帽，用扳手旋紧螺母，如开挖坡面不平整采用M20砂浆找平。

（五）支护效果

苏家河口水电站土锚杆设计要求抗拔力为8～12t。为检验土锚杆在边坡支护后的锚固效果，经工程师抽检，对完成28d之后的锚杆进行了3根有代表性的破坏性检测。检测选择造孔过程中塌孔严重、注浆吃浆量大、断层节理发育部位，采用穿心式千斤顶进行拉拔，当施载18t时出现松动现象，25t荷载能够拉出。对拉出的土锚杆进行了锚固圈测量、浆液渗径观察，3根锚杆锚固周边土体呈环状，平均直径20～30cm,同时沿裂隙渗透现象明显，呈穿透状态，表明注浆效果良好，锚固力接近于岩石砂浆锚杆。

（六）结语

通过苏家河口水电站坝基高边坡土锚杆施工的各种工序试验，结合实施后支护效果，说明土锚杆用于土质高边坡锚固可行，对边坡处理进度、边坡稳定效果明显。但土锚杆的施工工艺及控制标准仍需进一步研究、完善，特别是与土锚杆配套的施工机具尚待进一步研发。

该支护方式与传统的岩石锚杆支护方式相比：①通过压力注浆可提高软弱围岩、破碎岩体的整体稳定性，对土质、堆积体边坡具有较好的固结效果；②在钻孔过程中不受塌孔影响，用料简单，制作方便，成本较低，且施工速度快；③成孔孔径、杆体内径大，固结围岩范围远大于中空自进式锚杆；④杆体长度选择性强，可根据需要选择。

（中国水利水电第三工程局有限公司
孟宪坤　江　燕　孙家俊）

砂浆加钢丝网截水沟在工程中的应用

（一）概况

仙游抽水蓄能电站位于福建省仙游县境内。其进场公路路线全长11913m，为三级公路，水泥混凝土路面，路面宽度为6m，是该电站工程建设的组成部分。沿线开挖边坡高度在1.5～70m之间，边坡坡度为1∶0.75、1∶0.5、1∶0.25三种形式，部分地段自然坡度较陡，距边坡开挖开口线5m以外设计有截水沟。截水沟原设计采用M7.5浆砌片石结构，分为Ⅰ型（500mm×500mm梯形）、Ⅱ型（800mm×800mm梯形）和600mm×600mm梯形三种形式，其中Ⅰ型截水沟总长1287m，Ⅱ型截水沟总长390m，600mm×600mm梯形总长1273m。

浆砌片石截水沟需要石料，但有的部位有石方开挖可利用，有的部位需要从其他工作面运来。对于边坡很高的部位，汽车无法运输石块到位，需要大量的人工搬运，而人工费的不断提高，会造成施工成本大大增加，且存在很大的安全隐患，对施工进度也有很大影响。

根据现场实际，施工单位与业主、设计、监理进行了大量的沟通，提出了改变截水沟原设计方案。经研究，采用了砂浆加钢丝网结构。

（二）砂浆加钢丝网截水沟的结构与经济性

1. 结构型式　采用5cm厚M7.5水泥砂浆中间加钢丝网的结构型式，具体见图1。钢丝网采用直径1mm的钢丝加工成定型的网片产品，钢丝间距10mm×10mm，钢丝网无其他特殊要求，主要起到加筋的作用，市场上有大量的成品可以购买。

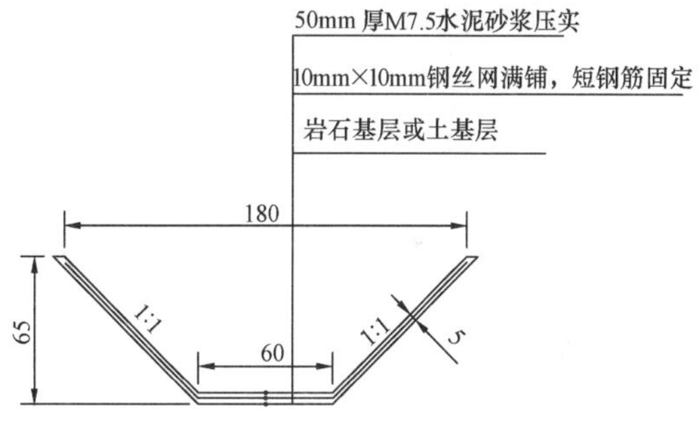

图1　砂浆加钢丝网截水沟结构型式（单位：cm）

2. 经济比较　以Ⅰ型浆砌片石截水沟为例，每延米需要砂浆用量0.737 9×30%（定额数据）=0.221 4m³，预算得出M7.5浆砌石截水沟140元/m³，则每延米截水沟衬砌造价为：0.737 9×140=103.31（元/m）。而砂浆加钢丝网截水沟，每延米需要砂浆0.119 4m³，预算得出5cm厚砂浆抹面600元/m³，每延米截水沟衬砌造价：0.119 4×600+0.6×2.25=72.99（元/m）。砂浆加钢丝网截水沟每延米砂浆用量减少0.102m³，增加钢丝网的价格0.6元/m²，但砌筑用石块全部取消，减少了搬运石块的人工费和开挖量，因此从施工成本上具有很大的优势，同时减少了材料运输，从施工进度上也能大大加快施工进度。

（三）砂浆加钢丝网截水沟施工方法

1. 开挖和修整　在进行边坡开挖时，如果机械能到达的部位，按照测量放线首先进行截水沟的开挖，人工配合机械将截水沟开挖成型，机械不能到达的部位采用人工进行开挖。开挖的渣料随着边坡开挖料一起运至业主监理指定的部位。一段边坡开挖施工结束后，人工从上至下再按照设计尺寸进行体形修整。边坡开挖完成后再进行截水沟下步施工，以避免人工与机械的互相干扰，减少安全隐患。

2. 基础面验收　截水沟开挖成型后，人工将沟内的松动岩块或土颗粒清理干净，保证结构尺寸和基底的密实，坡度要平顺，不要存在突变部位。自检合格后报请监理工程师进行验收，基础面验收合格后开始进行下一道工序施工。

3. 钢丝网固定　钢丝网一般为成卷购买，根据设计将钢丝网裁剪成合适的大小尺寸，裁剪好的钢丝网片运到施工现场备用。钢丝网采用 ϕ6mm 的钢筋固定，ϕ6mm 的钢筋单根长度 15cm，顶部加工成 3cm 的弯钩用于固定钢丝网，钢筋提前加工好运到现场备用。基础面经过验收合格后开始铺网，网片之间搭接 10cm，用铅丝绑扎牢固，钢丝网保护层厚度为 2.5cm，放在 5cm 厚砂浆的中间，钢丝网下部用合适的砂浆块垫好，保证保护层的厚度。固定用钢筋根据现场地形情况随机布置，保证在砂浆施工过程中钢丝网不移动即可，钢筋在土基部位直接打入基础内，在岩石基础部位用手持冲击钻钻孔将钢筋插入岩石内。

4. 铺砂浆

(1) 砂浆采用 M7.5 的水泥砂浆，水泥采用建福牌普通硅酸盐 32.5 水泥，砂料采用河砂，配合比见表 1。砂浆在边坡底路基旁用砂浆搅拌机拌好后人工运至坡顶施工部位，随拌随用；稠度控制在40～60mm。

表 1　　M7.5 砂浆每立方米各种材料用量表

材料名称	P.O32.5 水泥（kg）	河砂（kg）	水（kg）
用 量	330	1270	365

(2) 铺砂浆前先将基底进行湿润，保证砂浆和基础面的良好黏结。砂浆施工从一端向另一端顺序铺筑，用铁抹子拍打密实，最后人工抹面，保证砂浆表面平整、光滑、密实。砂浆铺筑施工过程中特别注意与两侧边坡接触要顺坡过渡衔接，结合边线部位不要高出基础面，要嵌在两侧基础面内。砂浆抹面施工完成后要进行保护，禁止人员踩踏。

5. 养护　砂浆施工完成后及时进行养护，养护采用覆盖编织物洒水的方式，洒水养护期保证在 14d 以上。

（四）结语

浆砌石截水沟和混凝土截水沟在工程上是普遍应用的结构型式，施工过程中需要投入大量的人工，随着市场上人工费的不断提高，浆砌石截水沟的施工成本会大大提高。

福建仙游蓄能电站进场公路沿线的截水沟全部采用砂浆加钢丝网的结构。当地雨水多，已经经过了 2 年多的考验，截水沟未发生破坏现象。砂浆加钢丝网截水沟能满足截水沟功能要求，而且在经济上、外观上、施工进度上都具有很大的优势。

（中国水利水电第五工程局有限公司　潘福营）

混凝土摩擦桩在复杂地质桥梁基础处理中的应用

（一）概况

白龙江橙子沟水电站引水隧洞位于白龙江右岸，左岸有 212 国道，施工跨江交通采用加强型装配式公路钢桥（常称贝雷桥），其中 5 号桥跨度为 51.82m，6 号桥跨度为 48.77m。

坝址至厂房区河床覆盖层厚度一般为 47～71m。上部、下部为漂石砂卵砾石层（Ⅲ岩组），其间夹含砾粉细砂层（Ⅱ岩组）透镜体。漂石砂卵砾石层及含砾粉砂层具有结构较紧密、压缩性较低、压缩模量较大及透水性强的特点。但含砾粉细砂层（Ⅱ岩组）在Ⅷ度地震烈度条件下，有发生振动液化的可能性；同时砂层多以透镜体分布，厚度不均，且承载力低，抗变形性能差。

根据上述地质资料及合同工期，确定施工跨江桥基础采用混凝土摩擦桩。

（二）桥基设计

桥梁设计荷载为汽－20 挂 80，承台以上基本荷载为 6200kN，安全系数取值为 2。每个桥基采用 3 根钻孔灌注混凝土摩擦桩承担上部荷载，单根直径为 1.2m，深度为 10m。每个桥墩下混凝土灌注桩采用三角形布置，临河侧布置两根，后面布置一根。

根据《公路桥涵地基与基础设计规范》（JTGD—2007），经计算，单桩轴向受压承载力容许值为 4372.32kN，三根灌注桩轴向受压承载力容许值为 13 116.96kN,大于 2×6200kN ＝12 400kN，满足承载要求。

（三）灌注桩施工

1. 施工准备

(1) 由于桥台紧靠河床边缘，需采用石渣填筑施工作业平台。施工平台 18m×20m，高于水面 1.5～2.0m，迎水侧采用片石和块石自然堆砌。

(2) 采用全站仪进行孔位放样，测量偏差不大于 10mm，并用木桩进行定位，同时标明灌注桩孔深。

(3) 护筒直径 1.5m，高 2m，采用 5mm 厚钢板制作，在上、下段及中部外侧各焊一道加劲肋，以此增加护筒强度。埋设护筒，上口与钻孔台车架平齐，下部埋入地下，周围 60cm 范围内以黏土分层夯填到与护筒顶部齐平。

2. 造孔

(1) 钻机采用冲击钻机。安装好起吊系统，调整使钻塔垂直，根据四角控制拉好的“十字线”对准桩位。钻进过程中经常检查，如有问题及时纠正。

(2) 泥浆比重为 1.1～1.2，黏度 18～22s，含砂率小于 8%。在正常循环中，大量泥沙在开挖的沉淀池沉淀下来，需要人工及时清理。施工中备有蓄浆池，将废浆暂时储存，调节外运，以保持场内清洁。

(3) 成孔检查主要检测内容有：孔口、孔底标高，孔的倾斜度，实际孔深，直径，护壁高度，清空情况，孔底沉淀层厚度，孔内渗水情况。要求：①尺寸误差不得大于 5cm；②垂直控制误差不得大于 1%；③孔底沉渣厚度不得大于 15cm。

(4) 单根桩基施工完成后，拔出护筒，以做重复利用，并对场地进行清理，将钻机移至下一孔位，24h 后开始下一根桩的钻进。

3. 灌注

(1) 钢筋笼在加工厂分段制作，运到现场组焊成形。为使钢筋笼下到孔内时不靠孔壁而有足够的保护层，在钢筋笼主筋上每隔 2m 左右对称设置四个“钢筋耳朵”。利用 25t 汽车式起重机吊入孔内，达到标高后，将对称焊接在钢筋笼顶部主筋上的四根吊耳与孔口护筒相焊接，以防掉笼或浮笼。

(2) 导管在安装前进行组拼和压水试验，试验压力不小于灌注时导管可能承受的最大压力的 1.5 倍。吊放导管时位置居中，轴线顺直，稳步沉放。导管下口距孔底为 30cm，以便剪球时球塞能顺利排出管外。导管上口设漏斗和储料斗。

(3) 灌注的混凝土为 C25（一级配），配合比见表 1。

表 1　　混凝土配合比表

强度	级配	每立方米材料用量				
		水 (kg)	水泥 (kg)	砂 (kg)	小石 (kg)	中石 (kg)
C25	一	190	422	796	972	

(4) 在漏斗的底部内事先放置一个直径略小于套筒的皮球；按照事先计算的首灌混凝土量，将足够量的混凝土盛放到漏斗中；迅速全开漏斗阀门，让混凝土把导管内的水完全压出并使混凝土顺利封底，达到埋管 1m 以上。以后灌注可根据设备条件进行适当的调节。灌注应连续进行，导管埋入混凝土的深度不得小于 2m，并不宜大于 6m；在最后灌注时，要核对混凝土的灌注量。为了保证桩头混凝土质量，最后灌注时导管在 1～2m 范围内上下移动，桩顶超灌 1m 左右的混凝土。

(四) 结语

白龙江橙子沟水电站跨江施工大桥采用摩擦桩进行地基处理。大桥经过一年多的运行，基础未发生沉降及位移。这一地基处理方法，可为类似工程施工借鉴。

（中国水利水电第三工程局有限公司　孙　波）

钢纤维混凝土的耐久性

混凝土的耐久性是指混凝土在实际使用条件下抵抗各种破坏因素的作用，长期保持强度和外观完整性的能力。正常使用条件下混凝土的耐久性主要取决于混凝土的密实性。碳化作用、氯离子渗透、硫酸盐侵蚀都与水泥基体的渗透力成正比。

依照推荐方法掺入 Dramix 钢纤维，不会降低混凝土的密实性，因此不会增加侵蚀物质的渗透。

(一) 钢纤维碱性保护

水泥颗粒在水化作用过程中，形成了许多游离石灰（氢氧化钙），使混凝土的 pH 值≥12。在该 pH 值环境下，钢材表面形成细微的氧化膜。该氧化膜具有钝化作用，可以防止钢材锈蚀。当 pH 值降低到 8～9时，这种保护环境消失。如果有水和氧出现，钢材就会腐蚀。

水泥颗粒周围的材料，如骨料、钢纤维及传统的钢筋，加到水泥浆中形成了一个局部密实性较差的区域。水泥的水化作用使这些材料的周围形成了一个过渡区。该区域主要由氢氧化钙组成，厚度约为 50μm，强度低于水泥基材料（见图 1）。

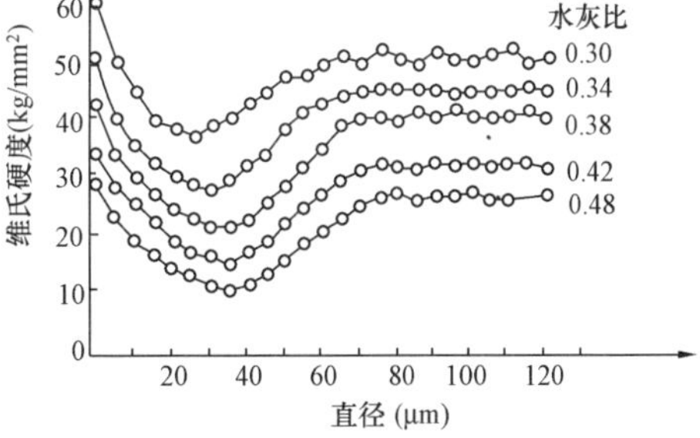

图 1　直径对纤维表面影响及水灰比对抗压强度影响（维氏显微硬度值）

如上所述，钢纤维周围存在大量氢氧化钙，使钢纤维混凝土具有良好的防腐蚀性能。钢纤维直径小，比表面积大，与传统钢筋混凝土中直径较大的钢筋相比，氢氧化钙保护层的作用更有效。

（二）碳化作用

混凝土的碳化作用是空气中的二氧化碳使混凝土逐渐变成弱碱性的一个自然过程。游离石灰转变成碳酸钙，混凝土的 pH 值降低。

碳化作用从混凝土表面开始，只要有充足的二氧化碳，碳化作用将持续向混凝土内部发展。碳化作用的渗透率由混凝土的渗透性决定，并随时间减小，是一个自我减速过程。

当 pH 值为 8～9 时，钢纤维表面的钝化保护层被破坏，水分的进入将引起钢纤维腐蚀。

事实上，由于钢纤维周围有大量的氢氧化钙，碳化作用达到钢纤维时，停止向前发展。在长期作用下，钢纤维可能会失去钝化保护层，但埋置较深的纤维仍是安全的。实验证明，高品质混凝土中钢纤维埋置深度大于 5mm 时，在长期作用下不会腐蚀。

钢纤维腐蚀产生的腐蚀产物导致了体积增加，不足以使混凝土保护层开裂。使用镀锌保护层 Dramix-CN 纤维（镀锌纤维）可避免这种腐蚀。

（三）氯离子渗透

当混凝土暴露在海水、海边空气或除冰盐环境下时，氯离子会渗透进入混凝土。如果有氧气存在，这些游离的氯离子就会削弱钢筋表面的钝化保护层，从而导致表面腐蚀和孔蚀。实验证明，具有明显粗糙表面的钢纤维与冷拉钢丝制造的钢纤维相比更容易产生孔蚀。钢纤维周围有丰富的氢氧化钙物质包裹时，会减小氯离子渗透引起的腐蚀作用。

在海浪飞溅区进行了 5 年试验，结果显示，埋置在钢纤维混凝土梁中的钢筋由于钢纤维的存在而受到保护。图 2 表明，冷拉钢丝纤维可获得最好的效果。

处于开裂状态的钢纤维混凝土，分别在饱和氯离子环境下和氯化物游离环境下进行了完整试验。图 3 结果表明，当裂缝宽度小于 0.25mm 时，在海水中进行 650 次循环交替暴露后，试件的弯曲强度没有损失。

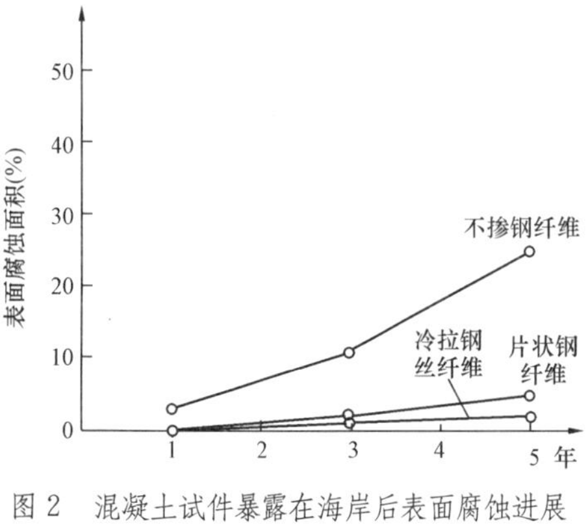

图 2 混凝土试件暴露在海岸后表面腐蚀进展百分比(钢筋直径为 10mm，保护层厚度为 30mm)

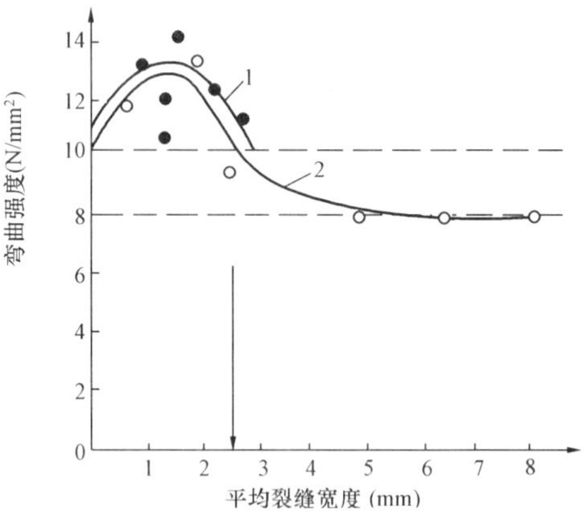

图 3 在海水中进行 650 次循环后平均裂缝宽度对应的弯曲强度

1—Dramix 钢纤维；2—熔化萃取钢纤维

（四）结语

混凝土中的钢纤维比表面积大于钢筋，所以钢纤维的氢氧化钙保护膜的钝化作用大于钢筋，同时抵抗碳化作用的能力也大大提高。

在海洋性环境下，氯离子侵入到混凝土中钢筋的周围并产生化学反应，从而导致钢筋的腐蚀，而钢纤维混凝土中氯离子渗透远低于钢筋混凝土，基本不会产生腐蚀，极大地提高了混凝土的耐久性。

如果腐蚀对混凝土表面的美观产生不利影响，应优先使用镀锌 Dramix 钢纤维，其耐久性更加优良。

与钢筋相比，钢丝纤维能减少混凝土的裂缝，限制侵蚀物质的渗透，而且当裂缝宽度小于 0.25mm 时钢纤维混凝土试件不会产生破坏。

（上海贝卡尔特—二钢有限公司
董 帅 王 荣 孙 斌）

船坞沉箱围堰基床升浆技术研究及在青岛船坞围堰工程的应用

在港口码头、船坞建设中，为增加地基承载力和沉箱围堰的止水防渗，需要对码头地基和沉箱围堰以下部位进行基础处理。船坞沉箱围堰采用双层土工布包裹抛石形成长方形基床室，沉箱坐落在土工布包裹抛石的基床顶面上，基岩、土工布包裹与沉箱地板形成透水不透砂浆的空间；利用沉箱底部的预埋管将升浆管锤击入基岩强风化面，提升升浆管，将配比砂浆泵入基床内，形成整体混凝土体，增加基础承载和密闭止水。中国水利水电第一工程局有限公司对船坞沉箱围堰基床升浆技术进行了研究，并在青岛船坞围堰工程应用。该沉箱围堰段长570m。

（一）施工准备

1. 沉箱施工平台搭设　施工平台采用预制钢结构块体拼装结构，用船吊吊放至沉箱上已经安装好的施工平台轨道上，在预制钢结构块体拼装结构上密集铺设跳板，形成沉箱施工平台。沉箱施工平台顶标高为+5m，沉箱顶标高+2.3m，北码头M1～M3沉箱底标高-9.5m。

2. 机械设备　沉箱施工平台上升浆机械设备主要采用UB4.0砂浆泵、1.5m³储浆桶、龙门式起重机、三脚架及100～150kg吊锤。施工前对机械设备进行检查及维护，确保设备完好以满足升浆施工要求。

3. 清孔　沉箱基床升浆造孔前应对吹填砂后的沉箱预埋升浆管进行测孔，详细记录每个预埋升浆孔的孔深，发现满孔或堵孔现象及时进行冲洗。如堵孔采用冲洗无法清除，则调用地质钻机进行扫孔处理，一般这种情况都是孔内预存混凝土块。

（二）造孔

基床升浆造孔采用锤击方式，孔位为沉箱上直径110mm的预埋管；利用钻机卷扬提拉100～150kg吊锤施打底部带脱落式冲尖的直径50mm压浆管，将其施打至设计所规定深度或岩面。本次造孔施工先采用地质钻机在抛石基床内进行钻孔，将抛石缝隙扩大，最后在扩大的抛石缝隙内进行锤击造孔施工。造孔施工以贯入度（下沉量除以锤击数）来判别沉管是否达到岩面标高。当造孔接近给定基槽底标高，平均贯入度小于5mm/次时，即认为达到岩面标高。

（三）砂浆制作与运输

1. 拌和站制浆

（1）制浆材料的要求为：①水泥为P.O32.5R普通硅酸盐水泥，受潮结块不得使用，从出厂到用完不得超过3个月；②砂为中细砂，粒径不大于2.5mm，细度模数在1.8～2.2之间；③水应满足拌制水工混凝土用水要求；④外加剂有减水剂和膨胀剂，应满足其技术指标。

（2）基床升浆材料为水泥砂浆，其应具备如下的性能：①良好的流动性和注入性，能完全充填粗骨料的空隙；②施工中不能有太大的离析；③具有适当的膨胀率；④硬化后具有必要的抗压强度和黏结力；⑤具有足够的耐久性和水密性。

（3）砂浆技术指标如下：①流动度为（18±2）s；②泌水率≤3%；③初凝时间为12～14h；④与基床的结合混凝土抗压强度≥20MPa。

（4）施工中砂浆的控制要求：①对砂、水泥、水等原材料及浆液的温度进行检测；②流动度每40～50m³检测一次，泌水率、初凝时间每个施工段检测一次，结合混凝土抗压强度试块每个施工段检测一组；③对每批次水泥、砂、外加剂等主要原材料进行抽检复验。

（5）浆液配合比，比初拟为水：灰：砂=0.5：1：1，掺入1.0%的高效减水剂。施工中实际浆液配合比根据砂浆性能指标进行具体调整。

2. 砂浆输送　将拌和好的水泥砂浆经卧式混凝土泵送至升浆施工平台上储浆罐内。南侧施工采用混凝土罐车进行短距离运输。

（四）基床升浆施工

1. 施工方法　基床升浆就是制备合格的砂浆通过砂浆泵、输浆管、连接器和压浆管，在自流压力作用下把砂浆压入基床块石空隙内，形成封闭止水系统。砂浆泵采用UB4.0型砂浆泵，输浆管采用爆破压力为1.5MPa的普通胶管。施工现场两侧各布置2个1m³储浆槽及6～8台UB4.0型砂浆泵，以满足两侧同时施工要求。升浆前，首先进行现场浆液性能调试，使浆液性能满足可灌入要求。其次对注浆设备进行施工前调试，保证设备完好。最后对注浆管进行起拔、试水试验，使注浆管离开基坑底面。确定注浆管贯通后即开始对坞外侧一排进行升浆施工，根据升浆管的埋深和升浆方量控制升浆管的提升，如果孔口溢出浆液可提出升浆管进行第二排预埋管的施工。以此类推直至孔内全部溢出浆液，第二、三排孔对整个基床升浆进行补充施工，施工结束。

2. 施工要求

（1）应保证施工的连续性，每个施工段施工不允许中断时间过长，如中断时间超过12h，应对上、下两层的结合部位进行处理。

（2）应进行分段施工，分段应与制浆站的生产能力相适应，每个施工段升浆量在200～400m³之间，一般一个沉箱为一个施工段，对个别基床体积小的沉箱采用两个沉箱为一个施工段。

（3）对基床升浆混凝土深度大于2.0m的孔段，升浆过程中起拔注浆管时，保证注浆管埋深在0.6～2.0m之内，严禁注浆管管口提出浆面。

3. 施工控制

（1）避免堵塞压浆管路，影响升浆质量；

（2）保证一泵一孔，不允许一泵多孔同时灌浆；

（3）浆液的配合比严格按试验最终确定的配合比执行；

（4）随时检测砂的含水量，避免因砂含水量变化引起所制备浆液不合格；

（5）施工中随时检查浆液性能，做到不合格浆液不得灌入孔内，避免影响升浆质量。

4. 质量检查 基床升浆主要起止水作用，其质量检查以检查孔压水试验为主，并结合基床升浆资料综合评定。升浆质量检查标准应满足渗透系数 $K\leqslant 3\times10^{-5}$cm/s（相当于 $q\leqslant$3Lu）的要求，压水试验检查应结合帷幕灌浆压水试验进行。

（五）经济效益和社会效益

（1）船坞沉箱围堰的沉箱预制完成后，在船坞堵口和码头部位，直接安装，施工简便，易于操作。

（2）施工安全性提高。由于沉箱属于预制安装，船只在海面配合安装，安装简单，易于操作。同时该工艺在船坞基床内形成水下混凝土，只能有少量渗漏，不会形成管涌式的大型漏水，对船坞内的主体施工提供了安全保障，没有安全隐患存在。

（3）码头部分不需要进行二次开挖围堰填筑材料，对码头上部结构施工，一次成型。码头本身作为船坞围堰直接应用。

（4）缩短船坞直线工期 3～4 个月，对比传统工艺的挖除填筑料和码头建造安装等，该工艺不需要对围堰形成后的围堰进行海底清除。码头和船坞堵口围堰的沉箱预制可在填筑其他部位时同时进行。在最后进行沉箱安装及沉箱基床升浆止水，全部完工一般只需 10d，与传统工艺的施工工期比较是不同层次的施工。

（5）经济效益显著。施工节省大量填筑料和废弃料，减少了人工费及海上大型船只设备的使用。取消了船坞堵口土石围堰的开挖，至少降低工程造价 20%～30%。

（六）结语

船坞沉箱基床升浆技术属国内外首创，该项技术施工台车已申请国家发明专利并被受理。该项技术成果已于 2009 年 12 月通过鉴定，鉴定意见认为：该项技术属自主创新，在船坞海域围堰施工领域内达到了国际领先水平，具有良好的应用前景，可在各种码头加固、船坞围堰止水工程中推广。

（中国水利水电第一工程局有限公司
宫模松 张发林 部绪锋）

玻璃钢管道施工技术

（一）工程概况

苏夫项目Ⅰ期工程位于阿尔及利亚人民民主共和国 EL OUED 省内，工程兴建的目的在于解决当地地下水位呈现周期性的上涨，对当地农业区和市区造成很大影响的问题。死水和露出地面的水含盐量很高，威胁到了棕榈林和所有植物。苏夫项目Ⅰ期工程业主为阿尔及利亚人民民主共和国水资源部水净化管理司，简称 ONA。

中国水利水电第三工程局有限公司中标承担该项目，合同价格折合美元 1.21 亿，2005 年 10 月 8 日正式开工，工期 34 个月。该工程管线部分难度较大且占合同额最大的就是玻璃钢管（PRV）的施工，主要工程量详见表 1。

表 1 PRV 管工程量表

管 径（mm）	各部位长度（m）						合 计（m）
	EU01～EPI	EPI～ET01	ET01～ET03	ET03～ET04	ET04～ET05	ET05～REJET	
DN1000	6798			4467	8248	10125	47608
DN800		2600	15370				

（二）PRV 管道的施工技术

1. 管道及其附件的装卸与运输

（1）在管道装卸的过程中，宜用纤维质吊带等柔性材料，若用铁链或钢索起吊，需在吊索与管道棱角处填橡胶或其他柔性物。起吊时应轻起轻放，必须采用双点起吊，严禁单点起吊，切不可用绳子贯穿其两端来装卸管道。

（2）运输时应固定牢靠，底部嵌入木楔，并确保管道不相接触；最大挠曲量不要超过 1.5%。

2. PRV 管的连接

（1）连接时应逆水流方向连接，连接前在沙垫层上对应承口的位置挖一个凹槽，承插安装后，用沙回填密实。

（2）连接时检查承口和插口，在承口上安装打压嘴，在承口表面上均匀涂润滑剂，将 O 形胶圈套在插口上，均匀涂刷润滑剂。分别在玻璃钢管两侧安装手扳葫芦，两侧同时均匀地、对称地加力，使插口端匀速向承口端移动。

（3）当承口和插口接触时，人工辅助对齐管口，均匀地、对称地加力直至承口和插口结合。预先对插入深度在管外壁上进行刻度标示，当达到刻度线时，即可终止该过程。如图 1 所示。

（4）对于垂直和水平方向有借转角度的情况，在管子连接完成后由人工进行微调。承插口连接完成后，通过打压嘴用动打压泵加水压至 1.5 倍管路工作压力，保持 3min，以检验承插安装之后的质量。

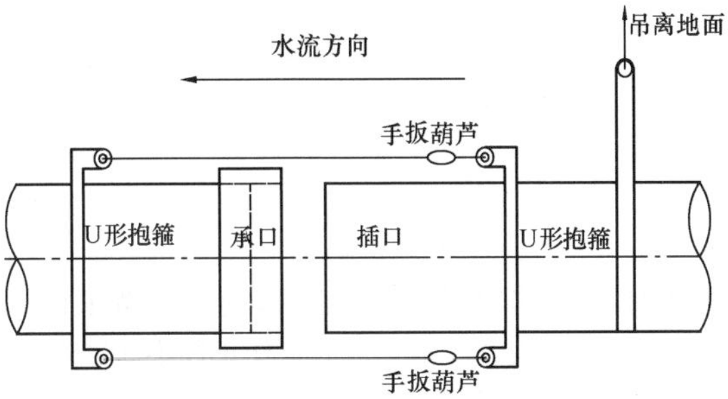

图 1　承插口连接示意图

3. 无板箱挡护段的安装

(1) 依托新修道路，将设备、管材及附件运至施工现场。使用全站仪在已开挖的沟槽内对管轴线进行放样，设置控制轴线桩，控制水准点设置在控制轴线桩上。

(2) 用四驱轮胎起重机直接吊装入槽，送管道至沟槽内，起吊用四点平吊，吊点在管两端四分之一处。

(3) 在管沟内利用简易三脚架将管子吊离沟底，人工用倒链调整管子高度和距离。

4. 有板箱挡护段的安装

(1) 受板箱横撑的制约，管道无法直接吊装入槽，安装时，需要从管槽开挖端沿斜坡通道入槽，斜坡坡度按 1∶3 进行控制。

(2) 用吊车将管子入槽后，将管子小心放置于预先安装的滚筒托架上（见图 2），管道入槽及运输过程如图 3 所示。

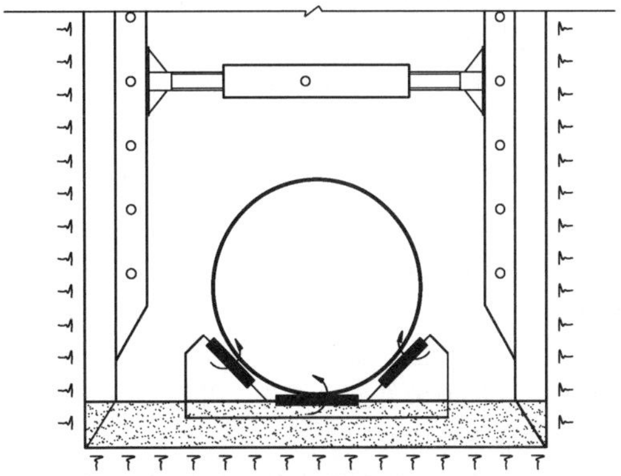

图 2　滚筒托架水平运管

5. 上、下坡段的安装　对于上、下坡段，在安装管子时，要将承口的安装方向随上坡和下坡进行转向。上坡段承口顺水流方向，下坡段承口逆水流方向。

6. 与构筑物结合部的安装　PRV 管路沿线经过的构筑物有阀门井、排气井、放空井、泵站和镇墩等。安装管道时，应以镇墩部位定位，向两侧进行。安装至泵站部位时，应保持一定距离，待泵站施工完成后再连接该段管道。

(三) 施工质量控制

1. 管沟开挖技术质量要求

(1) 管沟开挖应确保沟底土层不被扰动，下管之前需平整沟底。超挖15cm以内时，采取开挖料回填

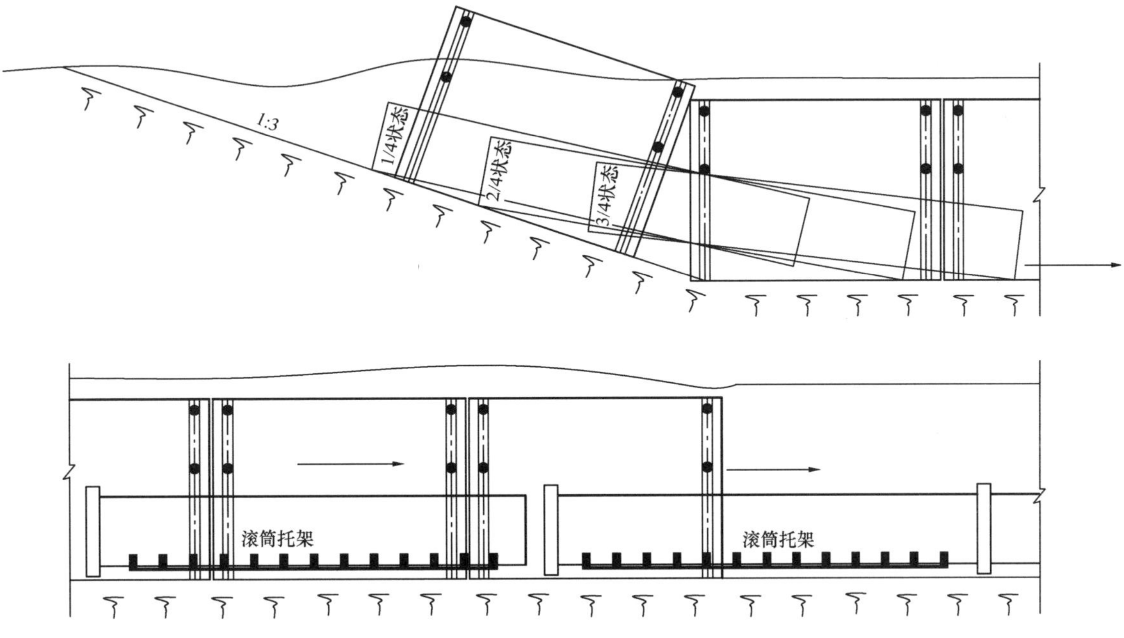

图 3　入槽过程示意图

夯实，压实度不小于 93%。机械开挖时，沟槽平直，中心线及纵坡符合施工图要求。

(2) 有地下水的管沟开挖前要采取降水措施，要求水位降至基底以下 50～100cm 以下后方可开挖。

(3) 将路面切除的沥青覆盖层运往垃圾场，而将基层和底层材料分别进行储存，以便日后再使用。要小心拆除道路边石和其他构筑体，以便工程完工后再使用。

(4) 如果开挖作业与现有水网或者地下障碍物发生冲突，需提前做好勘察工作，并采取必要的措施，且需要与业主达成共识。

(5) 在施工地点附近有住家、植被、建筑体、管道或者电缆的情况下，必须要求采用手工作业方式。

(6) 开挖中，必须确保槽壁的稳定性防止坍塌。根据沟槽开挖深度、土质、地下水情况等，采取相应的挡护措施，挡护方案要合理并得到业主的许可。

(7) 不扰动天然地基或地基处理符合设计要求。槽底高程的允许偏差，开挖土方时应控制在±20mm 以内。管槽开挖深度、纵坡、宽度及平面位置要符合施工图设计要求。

2. 管沟回填技术质量要求

(1) 在管道安装完成进行管道压力试验并经业主验收后，按照图纸要求回填 PRV 管两侧、周围和上面。

(2) 填筑时必须在拆除钢板箱后才可以进行。严禁先填筑后拆除钢板箱的做法，填筑作业时不得损坏 PRV 管道。

(3) 严格控制填筑料的最优含水量，并合理安排填筑分区及分段长度。当土料含水量偏离最优含水量较多时，应采取措施来调整土料含水量。做好土石料的室内外试验研究工作，并在施工期间不断进行检测以便及时调整施工参数。

(4) 首先将管道两侧拱腋下 40°范围内均匀回填，两侧管道同时进行分层夯实，以对管道形成骨架支撑。

(5) 回填材料分 RE 填料和 RR 料。RE 填料是指经分拣的用作垫层和水管保护层的填料，主要来自坑道挖方，去除了其中可能会损害水管外层的成分和植物残骸和根茎；填筑应分层进行，每层厚度 10～15cm，注意不要移动已铺设管，夯实度要达到 93%。RR 料是指填方混合料，用于填筑水管埋设坑道的上部。最大粒径不得大于 150mm，要尽量利用开挖的土石料，不得含有植物根茎和残骸或其他不洁净物。填筑应分层，每层厚度 20～30cm，夯实度一般要达到 92%，主干道下面的夯实度要达到 100%。

(中国水利水电第三工程局有限公司　任　强)

中國水力發電年鉴

7

机电及金属结构

水电机组及辅机

拉西瓦水电站水轮机主要参数选择设计

（一）装机容量和机组台数

拉西瓦水电站是黄河流域规模最大、电量最多、具有优越开发条件的水电站，是“西电东送”北通道的骨干电源。也是实现西北水火电“打捆”送往华北电网的战略性工程。装机容量考虑西北和华北联网及南水北调西线工程并为远景发展适当留有余地，装机容量确定为4200MW。

针对拉西瓦水电站总装机容量4200MW，通过7×600MW、6×700MW、5×840MW的3个方案装机台数的技术经济分析比较，6台单机容量700MW机组方案制造难度适中，与同期开发的龙滩和小湾电站机组容量相当。各水轮机制造厂家通过三峡工程700MW机组的设计制造以及引进各种先进设计软件之后，其技术开发和制造能力日趋先进与增强，具备承担拉西瓦700MW机组的设计制造能力。经审查同意拉西瓦水电站推荐的6台单机容量700MW水轮发电机组方案。

（二）水轮机主要参数选择与优化

拉西瓦水电站地处高海拔地区，水轮机功率P_r=711MW，额定水头H_r=205m，属中高水头巨型水轮机。采用统计设计法进行水轮机参数选择，然后请制造厂分析计算，进行CFD计算，并经初步模型试验，召开机组技术研讨会并邀请国内有关专家共同对水轮机主要技术参数进行了讨论与优化。

1. 基本原则

（1）保证水轮机具有良好的水力稳定性，把长期安全稳定运行放在首位。鉴于20世纪90年代新投运的大型混流式机组运行稳定性方面出现的不少问题，影响到机组与电站的安全运行，为此，把保证拉西瓦水轮机具有良好的水力稳定性，保证能长期安全稳定运行贯穿到设计阶段的全过程。

（2）水轮机参数宜适中，具有较宽的高效率区，以获得较高的加权平均效率。拉西瓦水电站水头范围192～220m，水头变幅小（不考虑提前发电水头），且电站上游有龙羊峡水库蓄水，水中含沙量较小，有这两个有利条件，应当说，可以适当提高水轮机参数。但是，考虑到电站要求水轮机能在较大的运行范围内稳定运行，因此，水轮机参数宜适中，不宜片面追求高效率。针对拉西瓦运行实际情况，要求水轮机应具有较宽广的高效率区，适应较宽的负荷变化，以获得较高的加权平均效率，使电站能获得较大的经济效益。

（3）参数选择时不考虑初期发电时的低水头。拉西瓦水电站水头变幅小，长期运行条件良好。在参数选择设计时，应只考虑192～220m的运行，不考虑初期低水头发电对机组参数选择的影响，但应在模型试验中对低水头运行的稳定性进行分析研究。

2. 水轮机比转速选择　拉西瓦电站水头高，若选择高比转速，则水轮机过机流速较高，水轮机空蚀能力要求较高，另外要提高水轮机的过机流量，水轮机出口环量相对增大，这样会直接带来两个问题：①使水轮机出口损失增大，降低水轮机的效率；②出口环量增大会使水轮机的振动增大。因此，拉西瓦电站水轮机比转速的选择，应建立在稳定可靠同时又不失先进水平的基础上。在前期设计和发包设计阶段中统计了前苏联萨扬舒申斯克、努列克、齐吉凯、泽林丘格斯克，加拿大麦卡，瑞典塞得瓦尔、奇奥卡津，墨西哥奇森科，日本喜撰山、有峰第二，中国天生桥Ⅱ、二滩、水布垭、小湾等额定水头在200m左右的水轮机比转速。结合国内外上百座电站大中型混流式水轮机比转速n_s随水头H_r变化的关系曲线及经验统计公式综合分析，考虑到该电站建成后，机组的运行条件比较好（如水头变幅小；水质好；又是地下厂房，容易满足水轮机安装高程的要求，减轻空化），拉西瓦水电站水轮机比转速取155（m—kW制），相应的比速系数为2219，与萨扬舒申斯克和同期小湾等水轮机水平相当，是比较先进的，也是切实可行的。

3. 单位转速n_{11}和单位流量Q_{11}　单纯地通过提高n_{11}或Q_{11}来达到某一比转速n_s都是不切实际的。国内外水电站的实际运行经验表明，水轮机的综合性能的优劣，在很大程度上与n_{11}、Q_{11}的匹配好坏关系极大，只有当n_{11}与Q_{11}处于最优匹配时，才可能获得最优的水轮机综合性能。拉西瓦水轮机，设计推荐水轮机模型转轮最优工况点单位转速n_{10}=65～68r/min，单位流量Q_{10}=420～460L/s；额定工况点单位流量Q_{11}=540～570L/s。模型转轮经验收确认最优工况点单位转速为67r/min，单位流量为442L/s；额定工况点单位流量554.5L/s，与设计推荐值相吻合。

4. 额定转速的选择　拉西瓦水轮机额定转速选择中进行了同步转速136.4r/min、142.8r/min与不同的转轮直径搭配下，全水头区域运行范围的单位转速比较。由于拉西瓦水电站的水头变幅较小，两转速均能满足水轮机要求，但综合对发电机选择中并联支路数和合适的槽电流来考虑，通过比较确定额定转速选择 n_r＝142.8r/min。该方案对水轮机低水头性能的影响不大，同时，也有利于发电机设计，水轮机亦可在较优工况运行。

5. 效率　可研阶段额定点的效率要求在91%左右，在编制水轮机招标书中，要求水轮机在规定的水头范围和导叶开度较宽广的范围内有较高的效率，且效率曲线变化平缓。对额定点的效率不提出具体要求，而是要求模型水轮机最高效率不低于93.5%，原型水轮机的加权平均效率不低于93.5%。经水轮机模型验收，该模型转轮最优区有较宽的水头范围，最优点模型效率为94.62%，原型效率为96.14%；额定点的模型效率为92.76%，原型效率为94.32%；原型加权平均效率为95.03%，比设计要求值均有所提高。

6. 装置空化系数及吸出高度的确定

（1）拉西瓦水电站水轮机过机水质较清，可按清水考虑，预计机组投运后，泥沙磨损和空蚀的问题不会突出。但从有利于机组运行稳定性的角度出发，装置空化系数的选取也不宜太小。考虑到电站对“无空化运行”趋势的要求，电站采用地下厂房，增加挖深对土建工程量影响不大，拉西瓦水电站 σ_p 确定为0.095～0.1之间，要求：最优工况，模型临界空化系数 $\sigma_m \leqslant 0.045$；额定工况，$0.06 \leqslant \sigma_m \leqslant 0.065$。经水轮机模型验收试验见证其额定点临界空化系数为0.063，所需电站空化系数0.103，能满足水轮机招标文件要求转轮的空化性规定的 $\sigma_p/\sigma_i \geqslant 1.2$ 和 $\sigma_p/\sigma_{0.2} \geqslant 1.6$ 要求。

（2）通过计算水轮机吸出高度为－13.4m，考虑最不利因素（即尼那电站在死水位时）工况，1台机运行时下游水位，确定水轮机的安装高程为2220.0m。经各典型工况的水头与 H_s 进行计算并复核其他工况，拉西瓦水电站水轮机在各种工况下，空蚀安全系数 K_p 都比较大，具有足够的安全裕度，最不利工况下 $K_p \geqslant 1.49$，一般均在2.0以上。针对高海拔并设置尾水调压井的电站，在确定水轮机安装高程中，还应特别满足电站水力过渡过程调节保证计算结果的要求。

7. 水轮机稳定性的要求　在设计参数选择中以水轮机稳定运行为前提，强调选用较高的水轮机设计水头，使水轮机的最优点偏向高水头，优化水力参数，改善拉西瓦水轮机高水头部分负荷运行区转轮内的流道旋涡特性，对于机组应避免在小负荷区运行，应在45%额定负荷区域以上运行，以避免发生有害的压力脉动及其引起的机组振动。同时配合水工专业进行厂房尤其是机墩的动态特性计算，防止厂房发生共振现象，以及应避免产生钢管水力共振，并提出加强水轮机结构刚度计算要求。机组设置主轴中心孔补气装置，并在顶盖上预留强迫补气孔以备必要时使用。拉西瓦水电站尾水管压力脉动主要以负荷变化控制指标，原型水轮机尾水管压力脉动混频双振幅峰—峰值（97%置信度）：稳定运行区（$45\%P_r \sim 100\%P_r$），$\Delta H/H \leqslant 4\%$，其他区域 $\Delta H/H < 5.5\%$。初期发电工况 $\Delta H/H < 6.5\%$。通过模型试验尾水管压力脉动在不同的负荷范围均满足相应的要求。

8. 提前发电的可行性分析　针对拉西瓦电站提出提前发电的要求，进行了专题论证，并在模型试验中进行了见证。在初期发电工况下，根据 H＝130m的压力脉动试验结果，水轮机尾水管压力脉动、蜗壳进口的压力脉动混频双振幅峰峰值均满足相应的合同保证值。通过试验验证拉西瓦水电站在初期水头130～192m提出提前发电是可行的。

（三）原型水轮机参数

通过各设计阶段的水轮机主要参数的优化设计以及招标、技术协议的讨论和签订及模型验收后，最终确定的水轮机主要技术参数为：

型号：	HLV155-LJ-690
转轮直径 D_1：	6.9m
额定转速 n_r：	142.9r/min
额定流量 Q_r：	378m³/s
额定功率 P_r：	711MW
飞逸转速 n_f：	255r/min
临界空化系数 $\sigma_{0.2}$：	0.54
装置空化系数 σ_p：	0.102
吸出高度 H_s：	－13.4m
额定效率 η：	94.32%
最高效率 η_{max}：	96.14%
水轮机总重：	1800t

水轮机制造厂为上海福伊特西门子水电设备有限责任公司。

（四）结语

从1977年开始，中国水电顾问集团西北勘测设计研究院对拉西瓦水轮机参数进行了30年设计分析，并曾与国内有关厂家、高校进行了相应试验研究工作，为设计优化打下了良好的基础。在机组招标前召开了多次技术研讨会，听取了国内有关专家的丰富经验与宝贵建议，从而进一步保证了拉西瓦水轮机运行性能良好，可达到安全稳定运行的要求。

（中国水电顾问集团西北勘测设计研究院
苑连军　刘慧凤　田树棠）

金川水电站水轮机主要参数选择

（一）概况

金川水电站工程为大渡河干流规划22级方案的第6个梯级电站，属二等大（2）型工程，水库正常蓄水位2253m，相应库容4.878亿m^3，调节库容0.498亿m^3，具有日调节性能。电站总装机容量4×215MW，电站保证出力215.7MW，年平均发电量35.287亿kW·h，年利用小时4103h。该电站的开发任务主要为发电，电站采用500kV一级电压接入四川电网，出线两回（一回备用）。

电站枢纽主要由挡水坝、右岸岸边溢洪道、右岸泄洪洞和左岸引水发电系统及地下厂房等建筑物组成。引水系统采用"单机单管"布置，尾水系统采用两台机共用一条尾水洞形式，地下厂房、主变洞、尾闸室三大洞室依次平行布置。

电站最大水头为99.5m，最小水头为86.6m，额定水头为93m，加权平均水头95.1m，多年平均含沙量0.27kg/m^3，中值粒径（悬移质）0.034mm。

（二）机型及额定水头

金川水电站水头范围为86.6～99.5m，经预可行性和可行性研设计阶段分析、对比，最终确定金川水电站采用立轴混流式机组。

对92m、93m、94m三个额定水头方案，从投资经济性比较，推荐93m；从水头保证率分析，保证率分别约为100%、99%、94%。经综合考虑，推荐额定水头93m较为合适。

针对H_r=93m进行复核计算，H_{max}/H_r=99.4/93=1.07<1.15，H_{min}/H_r=86.6/93=0.93>0.65，H_r/H_a=93/95.1=0.978，所选额定水头在加权平均水头的0.95～1倍的范围内，满足DL/T 5186—2004《水力发电厂机电设计规范》相关规定。

（三）比转速和比速系数

该电站水头范围在86.6～99.4m之间，额定水头为93m，水轮机属大型混流式。首先采用各种经验或统计公式进行统计计算，n_s的平均值约为230.5（m—kW制，下同)。其次，参考国内外部分与金川水电站机组水头相近的混流式水轮机，其n_s在210～232之间，K值为2136～2349。再按$n_s=2357/H_r^{0.538}$公式所绘回归曲线及按$n_s=47\,406/(H+108.5)$所绘曲线，可看出百米水头段按照统计曲线计算得n_s=205左右，这明显低于目前的发展水平。考虑到目前水轮机设计水平，新建电站n_s均可取至240左右。

综合上述三种方法的比较，结合目前国内大中型制造厂家的咨询资料，认为在百米水头段内，目前水轮机比转速应在220～240间取，相应K值2200～2400。因此，金川水电站水轮机比转速n_s取为232，相应K值取为2237，水平为中等偏上。

（四）最优单位转速n_{110}和单位流量Q_{110}

根据水轮机比转速与单位转速之间的统计曲线，百米水头段比转速选择范围为220～240，则相应的额定点单位转速在74.2～77.8r/min之间选择。

表1为目前国内外同水头段电站相关机组参数对照表，从表中额定点单位转速可反算出，按照目前的发展水平，本水头段最优单位转速n_{110}应控制在72.5～76r/min。鉴于金川水电站水头变化范围较小，泥沙含量不大，故最优单位转速n_{110}选择中等偏上，取为74r/min，并确定该电站额定转速为142.9r/min，水轮机转轮直径为5.15m。由此计算出转轮出口圆周速度v_r=38.1m/s，针对该电站的泥沙含量及中值粒径，比较适中。

表1　国内外部分大容量、相近水头混流式水轮机主要参数

项目 / 电站	国家	水轮机出力 N_t (MW)	额定水头 H_t (m)	转轮直径 D (m)	额定转速 n_r (r/min)	单位转速 n_{11} (r/min)	单位流量 Q_{11} (m^3/s)	投产年份
大古力Ⅲ	美国	612.0	87.0	9.78	72.0	89.86	1.014	1975
卢阿丰索Ⅳ	巴西	425.0	115.0	6.5	120.0	82.22	1.295	1976
卡伯拉巴沙	莫桑比克	415.0	103.5	7.2	107.1	75.8	0.84	1975
哈斯普兰格特	瑞典	469.0	103	6.6	107.1	69.65	1.136	1980
李家峡	中国	408.2	122	6.03	125.0	68.24	0.918	1995
公伯峡	中国	306.0	99.3	5.8	125.0	72.755	1.013	2003
宝珠寺	中国	178.6	84.4	5.0	136.4	74.236	1.015	1995

续表

电站＼项目	国家	水轮机出力 N_t (MW)	额定水头 H_t (m)	转轮直径 D (m)	额定转速 n_r (r/min)	单位转速 n_{11} (r/min)	单位流量 Q_{11} (m^3/s)	投产年份
漫湾	中国	255.1	89	5.5	125	72.875	1.107	1991
隔河岩	中国	310	103	5.73	136.4	77.01	0.983	1993
天生桥一级	中国	310	111	5.775	136.4	74.766	0.865	1997
大朝山	中国	250	72.5	5.8	115.4	78.608	1.327	2001
安康	中国	200.0	76.2	5.5	107.1	67.5	1.118	1990
百色	中国	137.8	88	4.3	166.7	76.41	1.015	
鲁地拉	中国	367	80	7.1	100		1.12	在建
金安桥	中国	612	111	7.8	93.8	69.44	0.94	
漫湾扩机	中国	306	89	6.3	115.4	77.06	1.039	

机组单位流量，从表1看，已建的百米水头段电站大约为1.0～1.1m^3/s；从已掌握的混流式水轮机最大水头与单位流量的关系曲线看，最大水头在100m时，推荐使用的单位流量在1.18m^3/s左右，前苏联型谱曲线的取值1.0～1.23m^3/s，综合考虑，认为就目前的设计、制造水平，百米水头段单位流量宜在1.0～1.1m^3/s之间选取，金川水电站取1.03m^3/s。

（五）水轮机效率

近年来，随着水电建设事业的开发逐步成熟，国内外水轮机水力设计中广泛利用计算机等精确设计手段，使得水轮机原、模型机的效率均有不小的提高。国内目前水平先进的转轮真机最高效率达到94%以上，如岩滩94.44%，天生桥94.48%，漫湾94.4%，公伯峡94.8%，新近招标的云南鲁地拉水电站真机最高效率达96.26%；国内目前水平先进转轮模型最高效率可达92%以上：如岩滩92.04%，天生桥92.75%，漫湾92.23%，新近招标的云南鲁地拉水电站模型最高效率达94.65%等。统计资料表明，国外大中型水轮机模型转轮的最高效率值最高已达95.2%。

金川水电站机组在安全稳定运行的前提下，可以对水轮机的最优效率水平提出较高的预期值，最大可能提高水轮机的加权平均效率，额定效率不宜预期过高，如果额定效率过高，将使水轮机的最优点偏向大流量区，从而使小流量时的运行恶化。因此，本阶段其目标值为：真机最高效率不低于95%，加权平均效率不低于93.5%。

（六）水轮机装置空化系数及吸出高度

电站装置空化系数σ_p的大小，直接影响电站开挖深度和水轮机运行寿命。

按国内外常用的经验公式统计计算本水头段内的空化系数，百米水头段的平均值为0.157～0.170。

按不同的比转速下装置空化系数统计曲线，百米水头段的空化系数范围为0.153～0.181。

金川水电站多年入库平均含沙量0.27kg/m^3，预计机组投运后，过机水流含泥沙状况还可进一步改善。从有利于机组长期运行稳定的角度出发，装置空化系数的选取不宜太小。考虑到电站对“无空化运行”趋势的要求，一方面，采用CFD转轮叶片水力设计优化，使压力分布和速度分布更合理，减小空化；另一方面，由于金川水电站采用的是地下厂房，降低机组安装高程对土建工程量影响不大，如果岩石地质条件允许，应考虑保证水轮机的吸出高度要求的条件下预留一定的余量，故根据金川水电站水轮机比转速值，按照上述各经验公式，计算其空化系数平均值为0.161。结合国内一些厂家百米水头段模型转轮临界空化系数大多在0.10左右，初步确定该电站装置空化系数σ_p=0.165，反算可知安全系数为1.65左右，最终取得该电站吸出高度H_s为－7.8m。

（七）结语

通过上述水轮机比转速、单位转速、单位流量及空化系数的计算选择，大致估算得出在百米水头段各参数的取值范围，并从中初步拟定金川水电站各参数值，具体数据见表2。

表2 百米水头段水轮机主要参数选择范围

主要参数	比转速（m—kW制）	K值	最优单位转速（n_{110}）	单位流量（Q_{11}）	装置空化系数σ_p
取值范围	220～240	1977～2545	72.5～76	1.0～1.1	0.153～0.181
金川水电站	232	2237	74.5	1.03	0.165

在百米水头段，国内各大中型制造厂所研制的转轮参数差别不大，在实际的选型设计中可根据电站的泥沙含量、中值粒径等因素酌情选取。金川水电站水质条件较好，在可研设计阶段水轮机各参数值选取中等偏上水平，这样既可以保证参数的先进性，又在安全稳定运行要求之内，待下阶段机组定标时，可根据国内各厂的先进技术进一步优化该电站机组参数。

（中国水电顾问集团西北勘测设计研究院　赵有东）

景洪电站水轮发电机组转子组装

（一）概况

景洪发电机转子主要由转子中心体、支臂、磁轭、磁极及其他附件组成；转子上部与上端轴相连，下部与发电机主轴连接，连接方式均为法兰连接。转子圆盘支架由1个中心体和10瓣支臂在工地组焊成整体。转子支架的下部设有80块制动块；磁轭由6mm厚单重66.8kg的高强度铁片在现场叠装而成并热套于转子支架外侧，磁轭铁芯高度为2020mm，并用磁轭键、调节键、切向键和加强键连成整体。磁轭的外侧挂装80个磁极，转子最大外径为ϕ18 071mm。

（二）景洪发电机转子结构特点

（1）磁轭为整体结构，无专用通风槽片，利用磁轭铁片间接头间隙形成通风通道。

（2）磁轭压紧连接螺杆只有一种规格，提高磁轭压紧螺杆的互换性。

（3）磁轭热打键加热使用薄片状加热片，加热片置于磁轭冲片接头处，该加热方式保证了磁轭加热的均匀、高效。

（4）磁轭与转子支架采用多种形式的键联结：①转子磁轭键，共计20对，自立筋底端到顶端全长连接，主要承受径向力，并可以调整磁轭的圆度、同心度和垂直度。②转子磁轭调节键，共计100对，磁轭调节键与磁轭键共同组成磁轭热胀键，分段布置于立筋上，在每对磁轭键背部匹配5对切向键，斜度1∶50,辅助调整磁轭的圆度、同心度和垂直度，并改善磁轭键在长度方向受力的均匀性。③磁轭切向键，共计20套，磁轭旋转形成的扭矩主要通过切向键传递给转子支架。④磁轭加强键，共计40套，用于与切向键共同传递所有磁轭旋转形成的扭矩，同时在分离转速下，保证磁轭与转子支架的同心度。

（三）转子支架组装与焊接

1. 转子支架组装

（1）将转子中心体吊放在支墩上，检查上法兰面水平度不大于0.03mm/m，检查上下法兰止口的同心度，用螺栓将中心体把紧固定。

（2）调整测圆架与转子中心体的同心度在0.05mm内，检查测圆架支臂水平应不大于0.02mm/m，旋转测量支臂一周，用百分表检查测头上下跳动量不大于0.50mm，任意一点半径误差不得大于0.02mm。

（3）按照制造厂厂内预装标记，吊装第1瓣转子支架扇形支臂，利用千斤顶调整支架水平，制动环基础面与中心体下法兰的高差，初步把紧扇形支臂与中心体的组合块的螺栓。根据立筋的半径、垂直度的实测数据确定在扇形支臂与中心体的组合块间的加垫厚度，使立筋的半径、垂直度均满足要求。转子支架组装尺寸见表1。

表1　转子支架组装尺寸　mm

序号	检查项目	测点位置	允许公差	实测值
1	中心体下法兰面与制动环基础板高差	制动环、下法兰面	410 （−2～0）	408
2	制动环基础板水平度	径向 周向	≤0.5 ≤1.5	0.4 1.5
3	立筋半径	立筋加工面	*R*8042 （+5.0～+7.0）	8046.8～8050.3
4	测圆架与中心体同心度	下法兰止口	≤0.05	0.03

从上表可看出，转子支架组装后的半径小数点不满足要求，主要由于转子组合块在厂内预装时已焊接定位，因其限制使转子支架拼装尺寸不能调整，造成两个支臂半径偏大。

2. 转子支架焊接

（1）按照制造厂焊接工艺要求，转子支架焊接顺序为：①转子中心体与支架腹板间连接板焊接；②圆盘支架上、下扇形板与中心体周向环形对接缝；③圆盘支架上、下扇形板径向对接缝；④磁轭挂钩（制动板基础板）径向对接缝、制动闸板加强板焊缝。

（2）焊接变形控制：对转子整体进行焊前、焊前加固后、焊接过程各阶段、焊接后的变形随时进行测量，以此作为调整焊接顺序的依据。焊接变形监测项目包括：制动板至中心体下法兰面的高差、中心体水平、闸板制动板基础水平、支架下挠度、立筋垂直度、立筋半径、立筋弦长等。监测时间为：①制动板基础径向对接焊缝随时监控；②挂钩加强环板的对接立焊缝，焊完主缝，背缝清根，并完全冷却后测量；③上、下翼缘板的对接焊缝，完成15%的焊接工作量，背缝清根、并冷却后测量一次，以后每完成25%的焊接工作量即测量一次；④转子支架上下翼缘与中心体的环向对接焊缝，完成15%的焊接工作量测量一次，以后每完成5%的焊接工作量即测量一次；⑤中心体与支架腹板连接的角焊缝，一侧的焊缝全部焊完后测量一次，另一侧焊完后再测量一次。当焊接过程中出现焊接变形过大时，立即进行产生的原因分析，采取相应的改变焊接参数、焊接方向、跳焊顺序、焊工人数，并控制焊接热输入，控制层间温度，采取消应等措施以确保尺寸控制。对组装后间隙较大的焊缝，采用镶边堆焊的方式以减小焊接应力对支架几何尺寸的影响。转子支架焊接后尺寸见表2。

表2 转子支架焊接后尺寸 mm

序号	检查项目	测点位置	允许公差	实测值
1	中心体下法兰面与制动环基础板高差	制动环、下法兰面	410±1	409.8
2	制动环基础板水平度	径向 周向	≤0.5 ≤2.0	0.5 1.8
3	立筋半径	立筋加工面	R8042.5（−3～1.5）	8043.08～8046.22
4	测圆架与中心体同心度	下法兰止口	≤0.05	0.03
5	焊接后转子支架半径收缩			3.65

（四）转子磁轭叠装

1. 下压板调整及磁轭预叠

（1）利用楔子板、花篮螺栓调整转子下磁轭压板高程、水平及周向波浪度，检查、处理下磁轭压板与转子立筋挂钩间隙，最大不超过0.5mm。

（2）按照图纸要求的层间错位方式，在转子下磁轭压板上预叠5层磁轭铁片，用定位销临时进行定位并调整磁轭铁片使其圆度满足±0.30mm（±1%空气间隙），调整下磁轭压板上的拉紧螺杆孔与磁轭铁片拉紧螺杆孔同心。

2. 磁轭调节键、磁轭键及磁轭叠片导向键安装

（1）利用预叠后的磁轭铁片进行周向定位，安装磁轭键和调节键，调整磁轭键的绝对半径、径向垂直度，磁轭键的绝对分布半径为8110.5±0.15mm，各磁轭键径向、周向垂直度均不大于0.05mm/m，合格后将各键点焊固定。

（2）调整各叠片导键的外径、弦距和切向、径向垂直度。要求各叠片导键的外径为8110.5±0.15mm；各导键间的弦距为2537.5mm，各导键的切向、径向垂直度均不大于0.05mm/m，合格后将其点焊固定。

3. 磁轭叠装

（1）转子磁轭分3次进行预压，其预压高度分别为666mm，1341mm及2016mm，利用磁轭叠片临时定位销，在下磁轭压板上先叠装1个节距的磁轭铁片，用临时定位销将磁轭螺杆孔调整对齐。调整合格后，按要求插入转子磁轭叠片圆柱销，其中每张磁轭铁片上插入圆柱销数不得少于2个，相邻两根定位销插入的方式，定位销应长短交错布置，插入圆柱销后，检查调整该段磁轭的外径、圆度、同心度和垂直度。当转子磁轭分别叠装到666mm、1341mm、2016mm时，利用风动扳手、力矩扳手和磁轭预压工具对磁轭预压，分别按850、1275、1700N·m逐渐加大压紧力矩，采用中圈→内圈→外圈→中圈的顺序进行多次压紧。每段磁轭预压时，在磁轭内、外侧的点焊拉筋用于紧固磁轭铁片。

（2）最后一段磁轭铁片叠装完成并预压后，对称用专用圆拉刀逐一拉削磁轭铁片的拉紧螺孔，并穿入所有的M42的永久压紧螺杆，按要求的力矩值（1700N·m）拧紧螺杆。将永久拉紧螺杆更换完成后，松开磁轭支撑钢支墩，分上、中、下三个断面测量转子磁轭半径，每个断面半径与该断面设计半径之差不大于±0.74mm（±2.5%空气间隙），转子磁轭整体偏心不大于0.3mm；沿周向高度差不大于8mm，径向高度差不大于5mm；叠压系数不小于0.99。检查下磁轭压板与立筋挂钩间隙，允许个别立筋挂钩与下磁轭压板存在最大间隙不超过0.5mm。用1.0m平尺检查磁轭与磁极间的接触面，应平整且接触良好，对局部高点进行打磨处理。

4. 磁轭热套

（1）根据冷打键和热打键对磁轭键长度的要求，核查磁轭键长度；在监测磁轭圆度情况下，用18磅大锤将磁轭键冷态打紧（间隔12h打三遍）；打紧过程中，利用冷打磁轭键进一步调整磁轭圆度、垂直度以及偏心（先打半径较小的磁轭键）。检查磁轭键上端长度满足磁轭热打键要求，根据转子磁轭热打键及磁轭圆度调整的要求，在相应位置的磁轭长键上划出磁轭热打键长度标记。

（2）磁轭热打键：支架与磁轭间采取隔热措施，用石棉被隔离开。在加热过程中，每30min检查磁轭顶、底部内外温度及转子支架顶、底部温度和磁轭涨量，当磁轭不同温控点温差大于10℃，适当降低高点的升温速度，使温升基本一致。根据磁轭键的单边紧量计算出磁轭与转臂温差$\Delta t=33.6$℃，当温差达到33.65℃，进一步检查磁轭被加热的膨胀量，达到2.7mm的间隙要求后停止加热。对称均匀打紧磁轭

键。热打键完成后，在磁轭冷却过程中采取保温措施，使磁轭按从下向上的顺序冷却，以防止磁轭上窜，同时应控制磁轭冷却的速度，以免温度骤然降低使转子中心体变形。磁轭冷却后，检查磁轭的同心度、圆度及垂直度和绝对半径值。

（五）转子磁极及附件安装

1. 转子磁极挂装　计算出磁极挡块的安装高程，将磁极挡块焊接在鸽尾槽底部相对应位置，因为磁极挂装后产生一定的挠度，安装定位块时应比图纸所示尺寸高出0.6mm；根据厂家编号对称挂装磁极，第1号磁极和第80号磁极挂装位置与转子励磁引线的位置相对应。检查各磁极挂装高程的平均高差不大于±1.5mm，分上、中、下三个断面测量各磁极铁芯对称位置处的半径，检查磁极的偏心、圆度、垂直度。

2. 附件安装

（1）安装阻尼环联结片，用0.05mm塞尺检查阻尼环接头的接触面，塞入深度不大于5mm。

（2）将极间连接线安装就位，用0.05mm塞尺检查极间连接线和磁极引线头间间隙，塞入深度不得超过5mm。

（3）按要求将所有极间连接线和磁极引线头间的把合螺栓以及其绝缘支撑垫块把合螺栓的制动垫圈锁定牢靠。

（六）结语

景洪发电机转子，采用自由状态下焊接、叠片、磁极挂装方式，消除转子挠度对转子外形尺寸的影响；利用磁轭片本身形成通风通道；采用薄片状电阻加热器加热磁轭，热量从磁轭内部往内外两侧传递，从而取得较好加热效果；采用多种组合键对磁轭叠片进行调整控制，使转子圆度、垂直度、整体偏心值均得到了良好的控制。

（中国水利水电第八工程局有限公司　何　毅　冯黎明）

彭水水电站ALSTOM机组水轮机接力器安装调整

彭水水电站位于重庆市彭水县的乌江上，是乌江干流水电开发的第10个梯级，安装5台单机容量350MW水轮发电机组。该机组由ALSTOM制造，其接力器活塞直径750mm，活塞杆直径280mm，活塞截面积4417cm^2，接力器总容积346L，设计行程783mm，预留压紧行程8.0mm；安装采用后端盖加一调整板，以调整接力器的水平、中心及与X轴的距离，要求调整板和接力器基础板接触良好。

（一）安装准备

1. 前期准备　根据机组安装轴线进行放样，将样点转至机坑里衬上进行标记；彻底清扫接力器坑衬及接力器基础板，直至接力器基础板表面呈现金属光泽；用丝锥对基础板与接力器联接螺栓孔进行二次攻丝，并清扫干净；检查接力器的基础板基础螺栓是否与设计扭力值相符；检查基础板的中心线是否与设计值相一致；检查基础板的垂直平面度是否合格，以及基础板与接力器联接螺栓孔是否对位，对不合格的项目进行处理，使之达到验收标准。

2. 接力器检查及压力试验　选择合适的场地，拆卸接力器端盖固定螺栓并用透平油对其进行保养，用起吊设备将活塞杆垂直提起，随后对接力器缸体、活塞及其附件进行全面检查，检查缸体、活塞是否存在毛刺、凹点等缺陷，检查密封圈是否存在裂纹、断裂等影响接力器密封、运行的问题；上述检查项目完成后将接力器缸体、活塞等零部件进行全面清洗，满足回装要求后在主管监理工程师、设备制造厂家现场代表检查下完成接力器回装工作。接力器端盖固定螺栓需涂抹专用螺纹紧固胶，紧固必须达到设计扭力值要求。随后用接力器试压专用工装向接力器缸体注满经质量检验部门校验合格的透平油，做好接力器试压准备。将接力器活塞杆和端盖外露部分进行清洗，清洗完成后用试压泵将接力器的活塞推进、推出约500mm，检查接力器活塞杆动作情况无卡阻现象，动作应灵活可靠；然后逐渐升压至6.3MPa，保压1h，检查接力器无渗漏及其他异常现象后，再逐渐升压至9.6MPa，保压2h，检查无渗漏及其他异常现象后，缓慢降压至6.3MPa，保压4h，检查无渗漏和其他异常现象后，最后缓慢降压至0。

（二）安装工艺

1. 预装及调整　用16个临时螺杆、螺母将接力器及到货的调整板固定在基础板上，按75%额定扭力拧紧；采用在调整板与基础板之间加铜垫的方法，调整接力器的中心、水平、高程，使其水平偏差不超出±0.10mm/m，中心偏差不超出±3.0mm，高程（相对于控制环）偏差不超出±1.5mm。

2. 调整板加工量确定

（1）两接力器调整完成后，在两接力器活塞都推进到底和控制环两轴套孔心连线与机组X轴线重合的情况下，测量接力器耳孔与控制环耳孔的间距L_1（见图1）。

（2）按确保推拉杆两轴套孔心尺寸（设计值2085mm，以到货设备现场实测孔心距为准），并考虑压紧行程及精调需要，计算出调整板加工量。如1、2号接力器测量的接力器耳孔与控制环耳孔的间距分别为$L_{a1}=2452$mm、$L_{b1}=2458$mm，则1号接力器调整板的加工量：$\delta_1=2085-(2452-392)+8+8=$

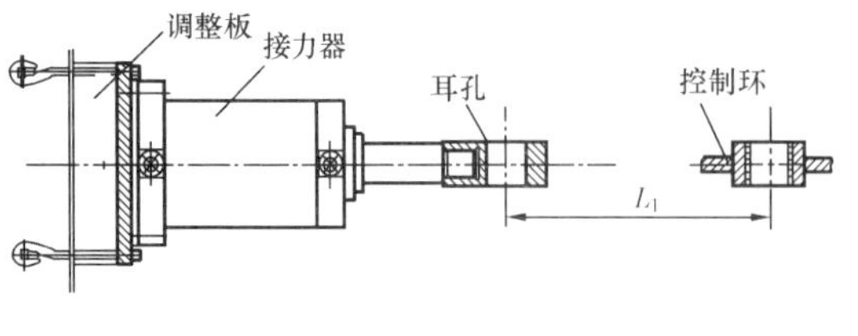

图1　接力器安装示意图

41mm(2085mm为推拉杆两轴套孔心尺寸；392mm为接力器行程的一半；第一个8 mm为预留压紧行程；第二个8 mm为考虑测量存在偏差需运用活塞杆与耳孔连接螺纹调节的预留量)；2号接力器调整板的加工量：$\delta_2 = 2085-(2458-392)-8+4=15$mm(各数值含义同上)。

(3) 实际加工还要根据加垫的方位和厚度确定倾斜加工量。最终加工量确定后，在调整板上作出详细的方位、方向等标记，为接力器正式安装提供方便。

3. 接力器的正式安装及调整　接力器调整板加工完成后，清理接力器基础板和调整板，将接力器及加工后调整板安装至标记位置处，并将每个连接螺杆涂上洛克泰243，按75%额定扭力对称均匀拧紧螺母，检查、调整接力器的中心、水平、高程，合格后再按100%额定扭力对称均匀拧紧螺母。用0.05mm塞尺检查接力器调整板与基础板之间应无间隙。

(三) 注意事项

清扫检查时发现，有些基础板中心与四周边缘成一伞形的凸状，如不处理就预装，加垫数据则不真实，加工出的调整板不能满足安装要求。因此，对这种基础板要进行打磨处理，以便安装达到要求。

(中国水利水电第八工程局有限公司　刘博学)

彭水水电站水轮机埋件吊装技术

乌江彭水水电站地下厂房安装5台混流式水轮发电机组，总装机容量1750MW。地下厂房长度252m，宽度为28.5m，内设2台350t/50t+15t−27m型双小车桥式起重机。由于现场条件的限制或施工安排需要，水轮机尾水管、座环、基础环吊装采取了一些特殊措施。

(一) 尾水肘管吊装

每台机尾水肘管总重141.997t，分为7节(制造时分为8节)，进口第1节安装高程为190.765m，尾水管底板安装高程为174.90m。单节最大外形尺寸ϕ10260mm×7700 mm，最大重量约40.824t。

肘管第7节(最大件)吊装是整套肘管吊装的难点。首先是桥机不能直接就位，原因有两点：一是厂房桥机吊装扬程不够，只有34m，而就位时需要45m；二是安装位置有2/3位于厂房下游墙尾水洞内，在桥机小车行程之外。其次，需要在空中进行翻身。

初步设想的吊装方案是：该管节立在安装间整体组圆后，吊到189m高程岩台(桥机起升高度可以满足)，接长吊装千斤绳，利用桥机另一大钩将肘管空中翻身，用一个大钩吊往安装位置；在安装位置肘管支墩上架设临时滑移轨道和拖移小车，在尾水洞侧墙和下游面布置地锚。肘管通过临时滑移轨道和拖移小车，侧向的缆风拉绳，地锚，利用链条葫芦向下游牵引移动，牵引到安装位置后通过千斤顶顶升、拆除滑移轨道后调整就位。但该方案施工工期预计需要5d，且拖移作业不是很安全。

后来，经过仔细斟酌，并结合现场试验，决定将临时滑移轨道和拖移小车取消，在桥机吊装到位后，采用25t汽车吊做动力，辅以滑轮、地锚、钢丝绳将肘管拖移到位，拖移过程中，桥机配合降钩，见图1。结果施工工期缩短为2d，安全性大大增加。

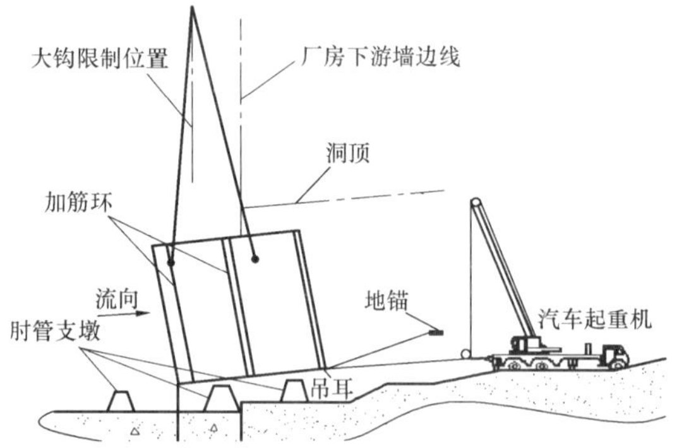

图1　肘管拖移就位示意图

(二) 基础环与座环整体吊装

基础环垂直高度为1648.5mm，分为四瓣到货，总重为44.991t。座环分为四瓣供货，总重约261.768t。基础环上部与座环下围板采用焊接连接。由于基础环、座环的整个安装工期只有20d。为节省安装时间，减少机坑工作量，降低作业人员的劳动强度和规避安全风险，拟将基础环、座环在地下厂房安装间组拼成整体吊装，组装后总重约为320t(含吊具等)，外形尺寸为15 564mm×11 800mm×4037mm(长×宽×高)。

经研究，采用8点吊装，采用吊耳板，布置在座环下环板上。吊耳板材料为16Mn，厚60mm，焊接按照Ⅰ类焊缝操作。吊装示意图见图2。

在实际吊装过程中，由于座环等分的四瓣重量不均，带舌板的一瓣比其余三瓣平均重量重约20t，故在第Ⅰ象限的两个吊点采用两套50t滑轮组代替千斤绳对座环、基础环调平后起吊，整个吊装过程安全平稳，吊耳板一切正常。

（三）座环翻越定子吊装

彭水电站最后一套座环（1号机）的安装，考虑到定子进场组拼，挡住吊往机坑的通道，原吊装方法不能满足需要，计划在机坑现场组装。机坑现场组装存在几个不利因素：一是支撑加固极为困难；二是施工质量不易保证；三是作业时需搭设大量的施工脚手架平台；四是作业安全风险大。经过充分讨论，认为在安装间组拼整体吊装是有可能实现的，关键在于控制吊装高度。桥机在安装间的有效起吊高度是11.5m，定子最高位置是测圆架中心柱，高度接近5m。为保证座环起吊后翻过定子，吊钩中心距座环最下部不得超过6m（考虑0.5m的余量，消除吊装不平及钢丝绳伸长偏差）。

吊装设想：单套座环装配总重约261.768t，考虑吊具等重量，吊装时按照280t考虑。采用双小车并车抬吊，以座环X轴线等分双钩并车的距离（7m），还是采用8点吊装，吊耳板布置分$+Y$方向4个一组，$-Y$方向4个一组，吊耳板材料为16Mn，吊耳板焊接按照Ⅰ类焊缝操作。以吊钩中心到吊耳板的直线确定吊耳板焊接偏角，吊钩中心到吊耳板的水平距离满足吊装钢丝绳夹角需要。吊装示意图见图3。

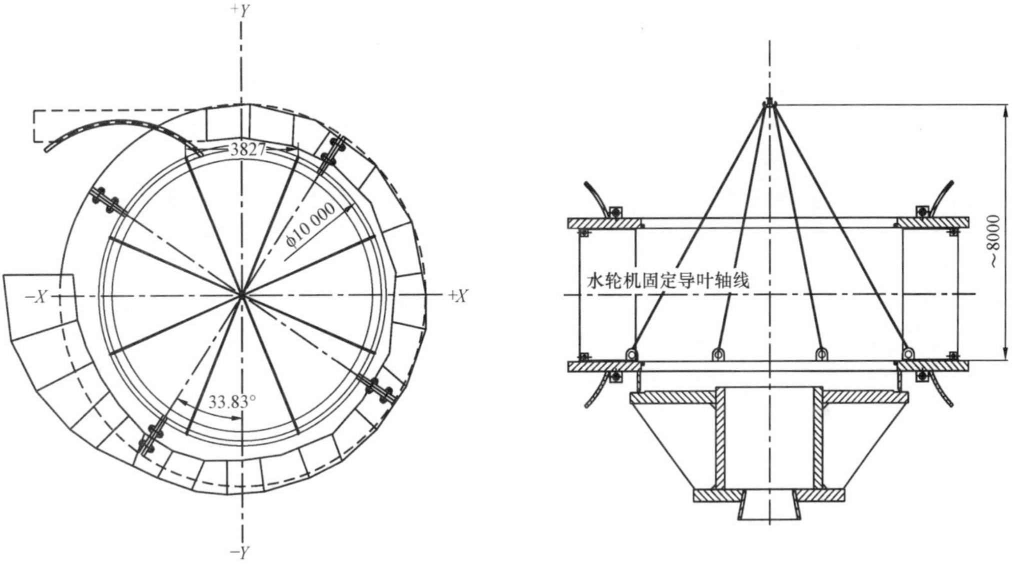

图2 基础环、座环整体吊装示意图（单位：mm）

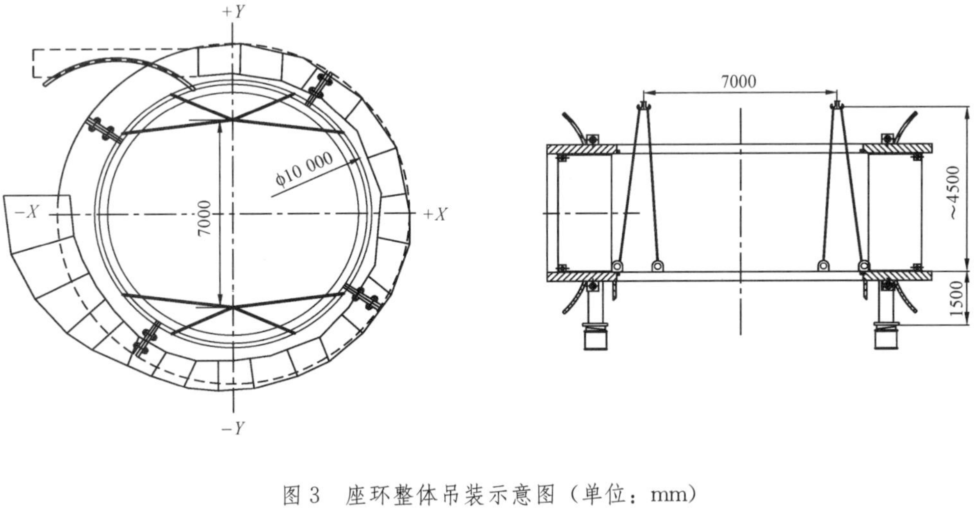

图3 座环整体吊装示意图（单位：mm）

在实际吊装过程中，由于座环带舌板的一瓣比其余三瓣平均重量重约20t，故在第Ⅰ象限的两个吊耳板增加加劲板，以提高其强度。同时对+X侧千斤绳缩短1.2 m，使整个座环基本调平后起吊，在越过定子时，其空间与计算值差别不大，整个吊装过程安全平稳，吊耳板一切正常。

（中国水利水电第八工程局有限公司 周德和）

水轮机金属蜗壳安装施工技术

大型水轮发电机组由于其流量大、水头高等特点，水轮机蜗壳一般为金属蜗壳。它们结构尺寸大、重量重、钢板厚度大；现场安装、焊接工作量大，安装质量要求高，安装难度大。

为确保安全、优质、高效的完成特大型金属蜗壳安装，中国水利水电第八工程局有限公司在施工中充分使用新材料、新工艺、新技术，经精心组织研究，经过多次优化形成了特大型蜗壳安装技术，在承建的许多电站多次使用，可靠性高，其工艺及技术达到了国内外先进水平。

（一）施工工艺流程及操作要点

蜗壳安装工艺流程为：施工准备→蜗壳管节瓦块拼装、焊接→管节运输吊装→舌板吊装、调整、焊接→定位节吊装、调整→蜗壳其他管节吊装、调整、焊接、探伤→蜗壳凑合节安装、焊接→蜗壳与座环过渡板焊接、探伤检查→座环导流板安装、焊接→蜗壳支墩混凝土浇筑→蜗壳内、外支撑拆除及附件安装→蜗壳焊缝防腐→蜗壳检查验收。

蜗壳施工操作要点如下：

1. 管节瓦块拼装 在蜗壳安装现场起重设备起吊能力许可情况下，将所有的管节组装成整节，并完成所有焊接、探伤工作。将进口直管段尽可能组装成摞节。

2. 测量放样及施工平台安装 利用座环测量中心控制点和操作平台，校核机组中心线，使设置的中心线处于基础环最佳位置。在座环及混凝土仓面上测放蜗壳定位节安装控制点和位置线；在座环蝶形边上放出每管节分缝的位置；并在与每节蜗壳相连的蝶形边固定挂装挡板。在座环上下环板上制作并安装铁板平台，布置施工设备、工器具。在距蜗壳外缘线500mm左右处搭设施工脚手架；架设至蜗壳管节梯子；在蜗壳顶部搭设防雨设施。

3. 座环舌板与蜗壳定位节挂装

（1）舌板吊装到位后，底部采用型钢支承，然后利用舌板上的对位锁定装置、拉紧器等对舌板进行调整，使舌板进口定位尺寸满足设计要求，并按工艺要求点焊和焊接。

（2）在舌板焊接后或焊接完成50%后进行定位节吊装，初步调整到位后，在管节底部和腰部用千斤顶支承，然后用千斤顶、拉紧器调整管节的准确位置，合格后将管节与过渡板点焊。

4. 其他管节挂装

（1）定位节挂装、调整好后，在每个定位节两侧、蜗壳尾端依次挂装其他蜗壳管节。管节主要采用分批次集中挂装，每个方向挂装的管节数量根据整体平衡进行控制，以减少座环的位置变动。

（2）管节间隙调整在压缝时进行，控制在2～5mm。环缝压缝从腰部远点开始，到上、下蝶形边处结束，保证错牙不超标。调整合格后，点焊管节环缝及管节与座环过渡板之间的焊缝，点焊适宜在背缝侧，点焊时用烤枪预热。

（3）当一个定位节两侧方向挂装三节，焊缝间隙与错牙调整合格并验收通过后，即可开始焊缝的焊接。

5. 凑合节制作与安装 凑合节瓦块采取在现场进行画线配割安装的方法，采用从下至上的安装顺序。将瓦块调整到位，使瓦块尽量贴近蜗壳，从蜗壳内按实际位置划切割线；然后将瓦块垫高，采用火焰切割；切割完毕后，将瓦块调整到位，按要求点焊瓦块。焊缝坡口采用气刨加工，并用角磨机打磨出金属光泽。

6. 蜗壳焊接 焊接前，需按要求做焊接工艺评定，焊接过程中严格按照焊接工艺评定的参数进行焊接。参加蜗壳焊接的所有焊工必须持相应焊接位置的有效合格证上岗。以三峡右岸电站的AH蜗壳（为舞阳钢厂生产的610D级高强调质钢）焊接为例。工艺如下：

（1）采用手工电弧焊，选用GB9018ϕ3.2mm、ϕ4.0mm、ϕ5.0mm焊条。焊条首先经350～400℃烘烤1～2h，然后缓冷至100℃左右进行保温，随用随取。

（2）焊接顺序为：舌板焊接→蜗壳管节环缝焊接→凑合节焊接→蜗壳与座环上、下蝶形边环缝焊接→蜗壳与钢管环缝焊接。

（3）蜗壳焊接前对母材预热，在焊缝两侧各100mm处布置电加热片进行均匀预热，预热升温速度不超过1.5～2℃/min。用红外测温仪进行温度监测。预热温度80～120℃，最高层间温度不大于220℃。焊后消氢，升温170～200℃，保温2h缓慢降温。

（4）施焊前检查焊缝坡口的组对质量，对于间隙偏大的焊缝，先进行镶边焊，当间隙和成型坡口满足要求后再行施焊。所有焊缝均采取多层多道分段退步焊，用 ϕ3.2mm 焊条打底和盖面，其余各层用 ϕ4.0mm、ϕ5.0mm 焊条焊接。焊接工艺参数见表 1。

表 1 蜗壳焊缝主要焊接工艺参数

焊条规格	电压（V）	电流（A）			焊接速度（mm/min）
		平、横焊	立焊	仰焊	
ϕ3.2mm	21～24	90～140	80～120	90～130	60～200
ϕ4.0mm	22～25	140～200	120～170	130～185	60～200
ϕ5.0mm	22～28	190～240	150～200		60～200

（5）焊接前需将焊缝及其两侧至少各 20mm 内的铁锈、油脂等打磨干净，使其露出金属光泽；清根后须将渗碳层完全去除；焊接完成后，蜗壳内表面焊缝打磨至与内表面平齐。

（6）蜗壳环缝焊接：正缝焊接 70%～80%→进行背缝清根、打磨、PT 探伤→焊接背缝 70%～80%→再焊接正缝→再焊接背缝。每段焊接长度 200～400mm，焊接层间接头错开 50mm 以上。

（7）凑合节焊接，采用先纵后环焊接顺序，将纵缝焊接完成后，再依次焊接两侧环缝。

（8）上、下蝶形边焊缝同时沿圆周方向对称施焊，焊接工艺与蜗壳环缝相同。

（9）舌板先在背缝点焊，正缝焊至坡口的 1/3 后，进行清根打磨，交替进行背缝与正缝的焊接。

（10）蜗壳与钢管环缝焊接时应力较大，焊接采用锤击消应。采用风铲锤击，第一层和盖面层不锤击，其余各层锤击至焊缝发亮即可，焊接工艺与蜗壳管节环缝焊接工艺一样。

7. 焊接变形监测与控制　在焊接过程中安排专人定时监视蜗壳、座环变形，并做好变形记录，根据变形情况及时调整焊接顺序。在舌板末端设置上、中、下三个监测点，在舌板焊接过程中，用经纬仪与线锤对舌板末端进行监视，随时根据舌板的位置变化调整焊接顺序。

8. 焊接质量控制与检查　现场焊缝焊接完成，由焊工或质检员进行外观检查，及时消除表面缺陷，外观检查合格后，进行无损探伤检查，一般执行 ASME 锅炉压力容器规范第Ⅴ卷规定的无损检验标准或 GB 8564—1988 中 3.1.9 款之规定。

9. 导流板安装与蜗壳支撑拆除

（1）采用保压方案浇筑蜗壳二期混凝土的蜗壳，内支撑在焊缝的探伤合格之后、蜗壳充水前拆除，蜗壳外支撑在支墩混凝土浇之后拆除。

（2）铺设弹性垫层的蜗壳，内支撑在蜗壳二期混凝土浇筑完成且土达到龄期后拆除，外部支撑及拉杆浇筑在混凝土内，当蜗壳外包混凝土浇到一定高程时，割除蜗壳外部支撑板。

（3）导流板安装在蜗壳内支撑上部割除后进行。先检查、测量每块导流板长度并记录。在座环上、下导流板安装处放置机组轴线控制点，以控制点为标准，根据导流板安装图纸及导流板实测尺寸，划出各筋板安装位置，安装、焊接筋板。筋板焊接、探伤检查合格，再进行导流板安装。

10. 蜗壳防腐

（1）蜗壳内表面焊缝部位、支承位置，主要采用喷沙除去表面焊渣、铁锈、焊缝底漆等，局部不能喷沙处理的采用手工处理，处理合格后方可进行油漆涂装。

（2）油漆涂装采用高压无气喷涂机喷涂、局部采用手工涂装，喷涂时蜗壳的环境温度与湿度必须符合相关要求，喷涂现场应通风良好，空气相对湿度超过 85%或钢材表面温度低于周围露点 3℃时不得进行涂装。喷涂采用分层进行，油漆分层标准要求为：一道环氧底漆，50μm，二道环氧面漆，各 150μm，最小干膜总厚度，350μm。各层涂装时间间隔应满足表 2 的要求。

表 2 油漆涂装时间间隔

相对湿度（%）	50	60	70	85
最大时间间隔（h）	8	6	4	3

（3）每层漆膜涂装前应对上一层涂层外观进行检查，要求外表光滑、颜色一致、无皱皮、起泡、流挂、漏涂等缺陷，并用测厚仪对上一层涂层厚度进行检查。

（4）涂装完成后进行漆膜附着力检查，使用专用硬质刀具在涂层上画一个 60°夹角的切口进行检查。用胶带粘贴划口部位，撕开胶带涂层无剥落为合格。

（二）技术特点

（1）通过合理的施工设备布置，合理的人员安排及采用合适的吊装手段，保证蜗壳安装施工安全以及工作的连续性、高效性。

（2）蜗壳管节瓦块在后方拼装场地组装成整节，减少工地焊接工程量的同时，最大限度地减少安装工期。

（3）设置合理的凑合节数量，减少凑合节数量及凑合节瓦片，缩短蜗壳安装工期。

（4）蜗壳管节采用大批量集中挂装，可减少起重设备的占有时间，充分提高吊装效率，减少对其他工种作业的影响。

（5）安排足够数量的焊接工作面，集中大批量的、高水平的合格焊工同时焊接，在保证焊接质量的同时可以大大缩短施工工期。

（三）结语

该技术已成功应用于三峡左岸、右岸电站、景洪水电站、彭水水电站等蜗壳的安装。目前，已投运的三峡左岸、右岸电站、景洪电站、彭水电站机组蜗壳运行安全、稳定，各项技术质量指标均满足设计及有关标准、规程规范要求。

（中国水利水电第八工程局有限公司
冯黎明　刘运华　曾　辉）

三峡水轮发电机组的国产化及创新

三峡电站装机26台，单机容量700MW，总装机容量达18 200MW，是目前世界上最大的水电站。三峡水轮发电机组是当今世界上最大的混流式水轮发电机组之一，技术要求高、制造难度空前，是一项跨世纪的挑战性工程。世界上几乎所有的知名水电设备制造公司都在承制三峡机组的部件。造好三峡机组，是东方电气集团东方电机有限公司（以下简称“东电”）作为中国发电设备重点骨干企业义不容辞的历史使命。东电在国家有关部委和中国长江三峡工程开发总公司的大力支持下，在三峡这个发电设备奥林匹克竞技场上，与世界知名厂商展开了一场面对面的较量。通过引进技术，消化吸收到自主创新取得了巨大成功，实现了三峡右岸水轮发电机组的自主研制。

（一）三峡左岸机组引进技术消化吸收

三峡水轮发电机组是全球容量最大、直径最大、重量最重的机组，其设计和制造难度对世界著名的制造商也具有很大挑战。国家实施的“以市场换技术”战略，为东电的三峡水电机组技术引进与分包制造创造了历史性的发展机遇。1997年，在国家有关部门和中国长江三峡工程开发总公司的支持下，东电获得了引进国外先进技术并分包制造单机容量700 MW三峡左岸水轮发电机组的合同。

东电经过三峡左岸机组5年的技术引进和消化吸收以及潜心攻关，实现了三峡水轮发电机组定子、转子绕组绝缘材料的国产化以及制造的本地化，并通过VGS联合体承制的6台左岸水轮发电机组中2.5台份的分包制造，全面掌握了700MW级大型水轮发电机组的开发、设计和制造技术，大大提高了东电的技术水平。发电机绝缘技术的突破和自主化，电压20kV，主绝缘工作场强2.51kV/mm，实现了多胶模压线棒全面达到国外VPI少胶绝缘体系先进性能指标；叶片数控加工、转轮等大部件焊接、主轴窄间隙焊接、转轮等大部件加工工艺技术都是在这一时期发展起来的，具备了立足国内自主研制700MW级巨型水轮发电机组的能力和条件。

通过参与制造三峡左岸水轮发电机组，东电掌握了700MW级大型水轮发电机组的核心技术，推动了技术创新，实现了水电单机容量从300MW到700MW的历史性跨越，分包制造的三峡左岸水轮发电机组质量精良，为三峡左岸水轮发电机组提前一年发电作出了积极贡献。

（二）三峡右岸机组的创新开发

转轮是水轮发电机组的“心脏”，其性能的优劣直接影响到水轮机的效率、空化性能和压力脉动。国外多家知名发电设备商经过多年研究推出的三峡左岸转轮虽然效率达到了要求，但由于电站运行水头变化大，压力脉动不甚理想，且之前中国从国外引进的小浪底、大朝山等水电站水轮机转轮都出现了“卡门涡”问题，国务院三峡质量检查组建议三峡右岸水轮发电机组待左岸水轮发电机组转轮问题解决之后再招标。国务院三峡办紧急召集国内水力专家进行了多次研讨，提出了在三峡右岸开发出性能优于左岸的转轮，东电接受了这项最具有挑战性的研究任务。

东电在消化吸收国外公司流体计算软件的基础上，又进行了二次开发和创新，创建了集水轮机转轮水力设计、流态分析和性能预测于一体的水力开发软件系统。在试验台上对国外公司的三峡转轮进行了复核试验，在对压力脉动高的区域进行模拟分析的基础上，利用自行开发的软件系统和多年来积累的水力设计经验，对三峡右岸转轮进行水力优化设计，优化了水轮机各过流部件尤其是转轮的内部流动，降低水轮机的水压脉动，消除高部分负荷压力脉动带。经过几轮试验，新开发的转轮压力脉动已明显优于国外的三峡左岸转轮，水轮机水力稳定性有了实质性突破，自主开发出了比左岸国外机组性能更优越的转轮核心技术，完全消除了困扰国内外水轮机行业的特殊压力脉动问题，为国内企业赢得了与跨国公司同台试验对比水轮机模型的资格，引领和激发了国内外同行对三峡右岸机组新一轮转轮优化的竞争开发。

在中国水利水电科学研究院试验台与国际著名公司进行的三峡右岸模型水轮机同台对比试验中，东电最终以自主开发的达到了世界先进水平的转轮赢得了三峡右岸4台机组的自主研制合同，并拥有从水力设计到真机制造的自主知识产权，保证了三峡电站建设工程的顺利实施。

在三峡右岸转轮取得突破的同时，东电通过对右岸发电机电磁方案进行优化改进，解决了三峡左、右岸VGS发电机振动噪声问题，又取得三峡右岸发电机关键技术的突破。

三峡左、右岸VGS发电机方案存在较大的振动问题，东电的技术人员通过分析和论证，制定了详细的改进方案。结构及安装工艺改进方案的实施，达到降低低频振动近50%的效果，振动改进方案的实施，将引起电磁振动的激振分数次谐波幅值削弱达90%，基本消除了定子铁心的100Hz工频振动，同时使发电机噪声大幅下降，达到优良指标。尤其是15号机各部位振动噪声数据创下了三峡右岸机组最好纪录，机组摆度也达到了国产机组最好水平。

东电在研制三峡右岸机组中取得的两项国际尖端关键技术的突破，即自主开发出了比左岸机组性能更优越、完全消除了困扰国内外水轮机行业的特殊压力脉动问题的右岸转轮和解决了三峡左、右岸发电机中存在的振动噪声问题，提升了国际发电设备行业的技术水平，为三峡项目之后的近百台巨型水电机组的开发奠定了坚实的技术基础，对我国能源工业的发展和安全具有重大的意义。

中国长江三峡工程开发总公司组织召开的三峡电站水轮发电机组性能评审会认为，经过国内多年的研究和科技攻关，三峡电站机组设计制造由左岸电站以国外厂商为主、国内厂商分包制造，到右岸电站国内厂商独立设计制造其中的8台机组（其中东电4台、哈电4台），走出了一条“技术引进—消化吸收—再创新”的成功之路，实现了700MW级水轮发电机组的国产化。国产三峡机组在水力设计、电磁设计、冷却方式、绝缘技术等方面达到了国际同等水平，三峡右岸电站机组总体性能优于左岸电站机组。

（三）三峡地下厂房蒸发冷却技术的应用

大容量发电机采用何种冷却方式是发电机设计、制造中的重大问题，也是制约大型发电机发展的主要因素。随着发电机容量的增大，电机各部分的损耗也明显增加。因此，改进电机的冷却，有效地带走各种损耗所产生的热量，降低电机各部分温升，是设计、制造大容量发电机的一个重要课题。

为了适应自主研制大型水轮发电机的需要，建立起我国拥有自主知识产权的大型水轮发电机冷却技术体系势在必行。多年来，东电在大型水轮发电机的冷却技术上与中国科学院电工所等单位合作研发了具有自主知识产权的蒸发冷却水轮发电机技术，研制的云南大寨10MW蒸发冷却水轮发电机、陕西安康50MW蒸发冷却水轮发电机和青海李家峡400MW蒸发冷却发电机皆获得国家科技进步二等奖。蒸发冷却技术与国外一些公司的水冷却发电机技术相比无论在技术上，还是安全可靠性以及操作维护等方面都有它独特的优点，而且还能够突破空冷发电机设计制造的极限容量。充分体现出该技术的先进性。

线圈是水轮发电机组的“血管”。在成功建设三峡左岸电站700MW水轮发电机蒸发冷却改造试验台，完成系统的试验研究基础上，东方电机又针对三峡地下厂房电站700MW水轮发电机建设了1∶1蒸发冷却模拟试验台进行了真机结构的工业试验。经过中国长江三峡工程开发总公司、长江水利委员会设计院、中国科学院电工所的专家和代表组成的业主见证和评审组的仔细评审，东电为三峡地下电站设计的蒸发冷却水轮发电机模拟试验通过了业主见证及评审，认为模拟试验台仿真性能较好，设计制造达到了预期的效果。试验结果满足合同的相关要求，地下厂房电站蒸发冷却发电机可根据试验结果进行设计。

目前，东电以独特的技术优势承接的三峡地下厂房电站2台700MW蒸发冷却机组的技术准备工作已经完成，正在进行制造。2010年，东电制造的世界最大的700MW蒸发冷却机组将在三峡电站投产发电。

（四）结语

东电以三峡左岸电站水轮机技术引进为契机，完整构建和全面提升了水轮机水力设计、流体动力分析、水轮机和发电机模型测试技术的硬软件平台，培养了新一代设计人员，采用新的设计理念和设计方法，在消化吸收引进技术再创新上下工夫，实现了跨越式的飞跃。在短短的几年内，陆续在巨型混流式、大型轴流转桨式和大型贯流式水轮发电机组开发中取得重大突破，技术开发已达到了世界先进水平。

东电紧紧抓住左岸水轮机特殊压力脉动和左、右岸VGS发电机方案存在较大的振动等问题实施再创新，开发出没有特殊压力脉动的右岸转轮，解决了三峡左、右岸VGS发电机振动噪声问题，各项指标达到国际先进水平，实现了以三峡水轮发电机组为代表的大型水轮发电机组全面自主化，推进了瀑布沟、构皮滩、金安桥、锦屏一级、官地、糯扎渡、溪洛渡等系列大型水轮发电机组的自主化。东电开发的模型转轮最高效率在93.5%～95.3%之间，处于国际先进水平。在空化性能和水力稳定性方面，可确保在电站运行范围内转轮进口无空化，尾水管及导叶后转轮前无叶区压力脉动水平略优于国外，尤其有独到技术消除高部分负荷压力脉动带，体现了自己的技术优势和特色。特别值得一提的是，锦屏一级、溪洛渡200～250m水头段水力开发性能达到世界领先水平，稳定性已独有特色，在同台对比中勇夺技术第一标，结束了国外公司在这一水头段的长期垄断。目前，东电正在进行单机1000MW巨型水轮发电机组的研发。

当今的中国正在成为世界工厂，有人认为制造业全球化进程中“中国制造”将面临严峻的挑战。如何克服“技术殖民化”——只有引进没有创新、只有加工没有制造、只有模仿没有原创；如何克服“中国制造”始终处于价值链的低端等问题，这些都是中国企业绕不开的现实问题。东电三峡机组的“引进、吸收、消化、再创新”的自主创新研发模式，从三峡左岸的“中国制造”走向三峡右岸的“中国创造”的现实，从正面完全回答了这个问题。

（东方电气集团东方电机有限公司 贺建华 石清华 余小波）

中国水利水电第四工程局有限公司2009年机电安装取得好成绩

2009年，中国水利水电第四工程局有限公司（以下简称水电四局有限公司）全年共投产水电机组3226MW，创本公司年投产发电机组容量最高纪录；同时，创本公司一年在一个电站投产700MW机组台数最多纪录，平同行业一年在一个电站投产700MW机组台数纪录，并创2台700MW机组仅间隔4d时间完成72h试运行工作的好成绩。

水电四局有限公司2009年安装投产的机组分布在青海拉西瓦、广西长洲水电站和埃塞俄比亚的泰可泽水电站。

（一）拉西瓦水电站机组安装投产情况

拉西瓦水电站安装6台水轮发电机组，单机容量700MW，总装机为4200MW。电站以750kV一级电压接入西北电网，750kV出线两回，分别送至西宁变电站（78.5km）和官亭变电站（184km）。电站建成后，除满足西北电网用电需求外，还将在西北电网及“西电东送”中承担调峰和事故备用。

2006年7月1日，水电四局有限公司中标黄河拉西瓦水电站A标工程安装和调试工作。A标工作内容为：6台套水轮发电机组及其辅助系统埋件安装；5台套水轮发电机组及其辅助设备的安装调试；5台套调速系统安装调试。后又从B标分得5台套励磁盘柜及其直流电缆安装调试、5台套机组监控系统安装调试。

经过近三年的精心施工，其中6号、5号、3号和2号4台机组在2009年先后投产发电，共计2800MW。这4台机组的主要安装、调试情况如下：

(1) 6号机组埋件安装于2006年10月13日开工，2009年3月21日开始充水试验，4月23日结束72h试运行，不停机移交运行单位投产发电。

(2) 5号机组埋件安装于2007年1月6日开工，2009年3月26日开始充水试验，4月27日结束72h试运行，不停机移交运行单位投产发电。

(3) 3号机组埋件安装于2007年1月12日开工，2009年9月13日开始充水试验，9月26日结束72h运行，停机小修4h后，开机移交运行单位投产发电。

(4) 2号机组埋件安装于2007年5月10日开工，2009年12月10日开始充水试验，12月22日结束72h试运行，不停机移交运行单位投产发电。

（二）长洲水利枢纽机组安装投产情况

广西长洲水利枢纽包含有内江、外江水电站，在全国灯泡贯流式电站中，装机台数最多，总容量最大。内江安装6台42MW灯泡贯流式机组，由水电四局有限公司承担安装任务。2008年内江水电站已投产3台机组。

2009年，内江水电站13号、14号和15号机组分别于6月2日、7月30日和10月28日完成72h试运行，并投产发电。水电四局有限公司2009年在长洲内江水电站完成3台42MW灯泡贯流式机组的安装调试工作，共126MW发电容量投产。至此，长洲内江6台42MW灯泡贯流式机组全部投产发电。

（三）泰可泽水电站机组安装投产情况

泰可泽水电站为埃塞俄比亚最大的电站，安装4台单机容量为75MW的水轮发电机组。水电四局有限公司机电安装分局承担的埃塞俄比亚泰可泽水电站的机电安装与调试工作。

2009年8月15日4号机组首先投产发电；随后，1号、3号和2号机组分别于9月5日、9月28日、10月11日投产发电。水电四局有限公司在该水电站完成4台机组的安装调试，共有300MW投入商业运行。

（中国水利水电第四工程局有限公司 郑少平）

运用知识经济观念指导水机设计优化

一、石泉扩机工程设计优化及其实践

（一）概况

在石泉水电站扩机工程设计中，采用了如下设计优化措施：取消调压井；以水轮机筒形阀代替蝶阀；采用新型机组取代老机组等，累计节省电站建设投资5495万元。实践与试验证实设计优化是成功的，可保障电站与机组安全运行。

（二）取消调压室

石泉扩机工程进口调压室处在设置与否边缘状态。压力引水隧洞经优化后其长度 $L_1=227.5$m，洞径 $D_1=9.0$m，分叉后较长一根支管 $L_1=46.844$m，直径原为5.5m；再计及水轮机过流部件的 LV 值，计算得 $T_W=4.0$s；后将支管直径增大为6.0m，使 $T_W=3.65$s，可以满足规定要求。决定取消调压室。

通过过渡过程调保计算，结果参见表1。

石泉扩机工程在2001年3月，由业主会同有关

单位进行了两台机同时甩负荷试验，试验时正好是额定水头工况，实测最大转速上升值仅 48.5%，远小于计算值。

这里值得指出的是，中国水电顾问集团西北勘测设计研究院（以下简称西北院）计算的最大转速上升值 58.07%，大于厂家保证值与过去的有关规范值 55%，曾有人提出不同意见。但是，发电机结构设计是按机组飞逸转速设计，对该机组为 280r/min，是额定转速 136r/min 的 205.8%；并且按机组临界转速校核，东电公司给出的飞逸转速下转动部分的安全系数≥1.33。可见，即使转速上升达到 60%左右，对于发电机的结构不会造成任何危害，也不会影响机组安全可靠运行。这是符合价值工程的观点——利用设备的剩余功能。

表 1 石泉扩机工程调保计算与实测值比较

机组过渡工况	东电保证值	西北院计算值	两台机甩负荷实测值
机组在额定水头，额定出力运行时突甩满负荷的最大转速上升	≯55%	58.07%	48.5%
机组在最大水头，额定出力运行时突甩满负荷的蜗壳最大压力上升	0.75MPa	0.75MPa	

石泉扩机工程所取消的调压室设计直径 25m，高 43m，其预算投资约占总投资的 11.3%，按该扩机工程总投资 3 亿元计，约可节省投资 3390 万元人民币。而且降低了施工难度，缩短了施工周期。

（三）采用筒形阀代替蝴蝶阀

1. 采用筒形阀的原因　由于石泉扩机工程采用一洞两机岔管引水方案，无法利用进水口快速门作为每台机组的防飞逸措施。筒形阀装设于固定导叶与活动导叶之间，在导水机构事故无法关闭时，可以实现全流量动水关闭；机组运行全开时阀筒缩入顶盖与座环形成的腔内，下端与顶盖平齐，完全在流道之外，水轮机的效率不受影响。如果设置蝶阀等进水阀，则因过流面积减少而使机组效率受影响在 0.1%～0.2%之间。该扩机工程如采用蝴蝶阀，其直径为 ϕ5.3m，不仅制造困难，国内当时也没有制造经验，而且无法整体运输（没有水运及公路运输条件），须在工地拼装更增加了制造难度。为此，采用筒形阀代替蝴蝶阀。

2. 采用筒形阀的优势

（1）节省投资。采用筒形阀整体投资仅为相应进水蝶阀的 1/3～1/5，而且不需要专门的阀室或专用廊道，可以缩减厂房宽度、减少石方开挖、缩短建设周期，累计节省工程投资约 1000 万元以上。

（2）密封性能好，减少能量损失。在工作水头为 47.5m 时，导叶的漏水量为 0.52m^3/s，筒形阀的漏水量仅为 0.016 m^3/s，仅相当于导叶的漏水量 1/32。

（四）用新型机组取代老式机组

1990 年进行扩机工程初步设计时，限于当时的国内水轮机技术水平，仍采用了原水轮机型号。当然这也是为了与老厂机型一致，有利于备品备件一致性。

到 1997 年底，扩机工程获准开工时，国内水轮机行业因国际合作或合资公司成立，45m 水头段已有了良好的混流式转轮。为了优化工程设计与获得更好的经济效益，1998 年 5 月通过机组招投标，采用东方电机股份有限公司新研制的 HLD260B-LJ-386 混流式水轮机，不仅提高水轮机能量参数水平，而且提高了水轮机效率：额定点效率提高 5.53%，最高效率也提高了 3.65%。水轮机比转速 $n_s=301$（m—kW 制），达到国内先进水平。

由于能量参数的提高，使机组重量减轻了 2×120t，关键是发电机转速由 107.1r/min 提高到 136.4r/min，重量减轻较多。水轮机由于增加了筒形阀（重约 31t）、金属蜗壳（过去是有钢板里衬的混凝土蜗壳），则增加了 10t。机组招投标后，合同价为 4895 万元，比概算价 6000 万元节省 1105 万元（含机组调速器等辅助设计价）。

石泉扩机工程于 1998 年 8 月开工，2000 年 8 月、11 月两台机分别并网发电，已安全运行 9 年有余。而且，进行了筒形阀动水关闭试验与两台机同时甩负荷试验。

上述试验与机组运行实践表明，西北院的优化设计是成功的。不仅累计节省建设投资 5495 万元，而且减轻了施工难度，保证了建设周期，具有明显的技术经济意义。再者，由于水轮机效率的提高，尚可增加 4%左右的年发电量。

二、促进大型灯泡机组发展

从 1990 年前后，西北院即开展大型灯泡机组设计工作。在西部地区推广技术先进的灯泡机组，不仅仅是技术问题，更重要的是要打破陈旧观念。虽然开始比较困难，但经过努力终于从尼那电站打开缺口——2003 年尼那机组发电之后，灯泡机组在西部地区的应用才普遍开展，详见表 2。

表2 西北院设计的灯泡机组参数

河流	电站	装机容量（台×MW）	H_{max}（m）	H_r（m）	n_r（r/min）	D_1（m）	备注
黄河	尼那	4×40.0	18.1	14.0	107.1	6.0	2003年发电
黄河	直岗拉卡	5×38.0	17.5	12.5	100.0	6.1	2005年发电
黄河	康扬	7×40.7	22.5	18.7	125.0	5.46	2007年发电
黄河	炳灵	5×48.0	25.7	16.1	107.1	6.2	2008年发电
黄河	柴家峡	4×24.0	10.0	6.8	68.2	7.2	2007年发电
黄河	乌金峡	4×35.0	13.5	9.2	78.95	7.0	2008年发电
黄河	黄丰	5×45.0	19.1	16.0	115.4	5.98	在建
黄河	河口	4×18.5	6.8	5.3	68.2	7.2	在建
汉江	蜀河	6×46.0	26.0	19.6	125.0	5.45 5.46	在建
白龙江	紫兰坝	3×35.0	19.9	15.4	136.4	5.35	2006年发电
嘉陵江	凤仪	3×28.5	10.2	8.3	75.0	6.7	在建
白水江	横丹	2×12.5	19.0	17.2	200.0	3.3	在建
恒河	真纳	8×12.0	6.2	4.8	75.0/750	6.5	在建
甘再河	PH2	3×3.1	10.0	6.8	166.7	2.75	在建

灯泡机组有着明显的技术经济优势，采用灯泡机组比轴流机组可节省投资10%～20%，而且每年多发3%的电量。而利用灯泡机组卧式布置的优势，采取厂顶溢流方案的炳灵、蜀河两电站，不仅解决河谷狭窄，枢纽布置困难问题，而且节省了巨大建设投资（蜀河节省4.75亿元投资）。

在灯泡机组发展的同时，也促进了设计部门技术水平的提高，拓展了低水头径流电站的一些设计理念。例如，要用全厂发电的上、下游水位差，并扣除0.5m水头损失来确定灯泡机组的额定水头 H_r，不能用调蓄电站加权平均概念，而要用径流电站的概率概念来对待 H_r 等问题。另外，从尼那机组运行初期故障较多，认识到灯泡机组的特殊问题，即疲劳破坏问题。在其后的灯泡机组招投标，以及合同谈判中，都加强了机组刚强度计算、疲劳分析的要求，强调灯泡机组主要部件（叶片、转子支架等）必须保证40年寿命周期等。

三、公伯峡采用整体运输的全不锈钢转轮

近年来，随着欧美高参数转轮的引进与应用及异种钢转轮直径的增大，在运行中叶片裂纹事故屡有发生，且产生裂纹的时间也有缩短的趋势，从而引起设计运行与水电设备制造部门重视。

经研究，为了减少可能高达500MPa的残余应力发生，对于大型混流式启停频繁的调峰机组转轮，宜采用全不锈钢——上冠、下环采用与叶片同一钢种的不锈钢材料，甚至连焊丝、焊料也要与之相匹配，以减少残余应力、防止裂纹发生。

在工厂将大型转轮组装加工与热处理结束后，再整体运往工地方案有利于提高转轮制造质量与可靠性，并加快工地安装进度。南方电站大多具备水运条件，采用整体转轮运输方案较多。而北方过去较少采用，但随着高速公路建设日趋发展，已有莲花、万家寨等转轮采用公路整体运输方案获得成功。黄河公伯峡水电站，装机5台，单机容量300MW，转轮直径 $D_1=5.8$m，西北勘测设计研究院设计与水轮机中标厂家哈电公司研究决定采用公路整体运输方案。公伯峡采用整体运输的全不锈钢转轮，已运行数年，转轮叶片未发生裂纹。

四、混流式水轮机提前发电技术研究

黄河龙羊峡水电站，水库有247亿 m^3，但来水

量较小，要想蓄满非常困难。西北院在设计之初，考虑了低水头提前发电问题。为此，开展了一系列模型试验与原型测试，结论是，低水头发电不会影响机组的运行稳定性。龙羊峡机组设计 $H_{min}=99.5m$、$H_r=122.0m$、$H_{max}=148.5m$，实际上，在水头 80m 左右的低水头运行区运行了十多年，最低发电水头 76m，没有因水头低发生的故障。

近年设计的黄河拉西瓦水电站（6×700MW），装机容量大，水头高（$H_{max}=220m$、$H_r=205m$、$H_{min}=192m$）。但是，枢纽河谷狭窄、两岸坝肩陡峭，坝高 256m 的拱坝施工困难。为保障施工人员生命安全，不能过于强化施工进度。为了缩短电站发电工期，地下厂房的 6 个进水口，分三个高程设置，最低的 2 台机组可在水头 130m 时开始发电。

为此，西北院做了大量分析研究工作。曾请哈尔滨大电机研究所专门作模型试验；在福伊特水力试验室进行模型验收试验时，亦对低水头发电工况进行了模型试验工作。2009 年 4 月 15 日拉西瓦 2 台机组投入运行，发电水头 130m，机组运行正常，与我们预测的结果基本一致。

（中国水电顾问集团西北勘测设计研究院
田树棠　段宏江　刘国峰）

电液同步控制筒形阀水电机组在多泥沙水电站的应用

许多中高水头和多泥沙河流的水电站，要求停机后必须立即关闭水轮机进口阀。如果不设进口阀或不关进口阀，导叶立面间隙和端面间隙处不可避免地存在高速水流（漏水量大约为额定流量的 0.3%～0.5%），使导叶上下抗磨板甚至转轮叶片的进口边发生空蚀损害。

我国西北西南地区分布着丰富的水力资源，但该地区的水力资源泥沙含量较高，对水电站设备及阀门耐泥沙磨损提出了更高要求。云南红河干流的南沙水电站，装机容量为 3×50MW，电站最大水头 51.06m，最小水头 31.46m，额定水头 44.5m，加权平均水头 46.34m；其多年平均含沙量 5.08 kg/m^3，实测最大含沙量 11.8 kg/m^3。业主要求水轮机采用筒形阀。经投标，天津市天发重型水电设备制造有限公司中标承担了该电站机组制造工作。

筒形阀是水轮机的一种新型进水阀门，装设于固定导叶与活动导叶之间，具有结构紧凑、重量轻的优点；全开时缩入顶盖与座环形成的空腔内，下端面与顶盖平齐，不产生水头损失；全关时密封性能良好，对多泥沙电站，可有效保护导水机构停机时免遭间隙空蚀与泥沙磨损；当机组产生飞逸时，可动水关闭，以保护机组免遭损坏。

该机组筒形阀采用 6 只直缸接力器操作，由电液系统实现同步。

（一）电液同步控制筒形阀

筒形阀采用直缸接力器操作，较之油马达操作，具有油压设备较小的优点。

操作筒形阀的接力器由一个伺服比例阀集中控制，以控制整个筒形阀的启闭及开关速度。整个筒形阀同步由专用液压调节分配系统实现；而专用液压调节分配系统同步，又分开环调节系统和闭环调节系统。

开环调节系统，用同排量分配马达，使通往直缸接力器的流量相等，以保障直缸接力器的运动速度基本相同。此为纯机械形式，靠操作压力油流自动驱动，以实现均流功能。这种机械同步控制，用于粗调。

闭环调节系统，由装在电气控制单元内的位置测量单元与安装在直缸接力器内的位移变送器完成，在上升时，以最慢的一只缸为准，对运行较快的缸放油，以达到同步；下降时，以最快的缸为准，对慢的缸实现放油，以实现同步。这种电液同步控制，用于精调。

筒形阀开启、关闭时接力器活塞在两端部和中部的速度是不一样的，通常刚开始时比较慢，在中部时达到设定的最大速度，然后速度下降直至到达端部时速度为 0。正常全部开启时间约为 90s，全部关闭时间约为 60s。

如果接力器中任何一处的位置偏差超过允许值，控制系统将停止筒形阀操作并向相反方向移动以纠正偏差，如果偏差得以纠正，则筒形阀继续沿原方向操作；如果不能消除偏差，将再次向相反方向移动以纠正偏差，如果偏差被纠正则恢复操作；经过 2 次调整均不能有效消除偏差，便发出筒形阀发卡的信号，同时筒形阀操作被停止。当有筒形阀发卡信号出现时，意味着筒形阀无论向上、向下均不能移动，就需要人工干预。

当机组事故时，筒形阀动水关闭，由机组过速保护装置提供油压力信号，此时筒形阀在 60 s 内关闭，如果此时位移监控系统发出发卡信号，则控制系统切除位移监控系统，按既定程序关闭筒形阀。

筒形阀开启及关闭时间可由控制系统按设计时间调整关闭规律，进行调整。

筒形阀开启达 95%开度时，由位移传感器发出的信号，控制油管路系统流量，慢开启筒形阀，避免筒体撞击顶盖，损坏筒形阀部件。

筒形阀只处于全开或全关位置，不作流量调

节用。

（二）电液同步控制筒形阀同步控制系统

1. 液压系统的组成　由于系统的同步控制性能要求高，液压系统采用模块化布置方案，主要包括一套控制阀组模块、配油模块等。

2. 电气控制系统的组成

（1）电气控制系统采用“触摸屏＋可编程控制器”的方式，触摸屏监控压力、位移和液位等，PLC进行实际控制，操作方式采用现地自动/手动控制。

（2）PLC控制系统中配有位置检测模块，该模块由PLC控制系统中的位置测量程序和与其配套安装在筒阀接力器内部的位移传感器组成，主要用于实时监测接力器的位移值。

（3）传感器内部数据的采集与外部时钟频率同步，保证控制器最优化的计算速率。位移传感器可以直接将液压缸的位移值转换为高精度、高可靠性和高线性度的模拟量值，送入PLC进行后续处理。

3. 电气控制系统的工作原理

（1）结合筒形阀接力器行程允许位置偏差曲线，通过调整配油模块中的电磁球阀实现接力器的精确位置同步。电气同步通过PLC和同步电磁球阀来实现。为每个接力器配置两个电磁球阀，它们的调节精度不同，通过实时通断电磁球阀，实现同步调整功能。

（2）在筒形阀上升或下降过程中，每个接力器顶端的位置传感器实时地将接力器的位置信号反馈至PLC，由PLC比较各个接力器的位置，将位置最低的接力器的位置作为基准位置。然后分别将其他接力器的位置与之相比较，得出每个接力器的位置偏差。同时根据接力器允许位置偏差曲线得出基准位置的允许偏差。如果某个接力器的位置偏差超过允许偏差的30％小于70％时，对应的微调电磁阀励磁，将接力器下腔的油适量的排回油箱；当位置偏差超过允许偏差的70％时，粗调电磁阀励磁，将该接力器下腔更多的油排回油箱。通过排油，减缓该接力器上升速度或加快其下降速度，与其他接力器运动速度渐趋一致，从而保证各个接力器运动过程中的同步。

（3）筒形阀在全关位置时，由于水力因素，需要较大的提升力才能使其开始运动。因此初始启动时，运动速度较小。同时，为了防止筒形阀在其行程的起始段和终止段产生发卡或撞击相邻部件，在接力器的起始段和终止段，筒形阀的运动速度远小于中间段的运动速度。在筒形阀的运动过程中，PLC按照相应速度曲线向电磁比例方向阀发送调节信号，比例阀根据接收到的调节信号，控制开启侧或关闭侧的油口开度，进而控制接力器的开启和关闭速度。

（三）筒形阀运行效果

云南红河南沙电站筒形阀在2007年12月投入商业运行以来，完全能够满足合同规定要求，效果非常好，特别是其同步误差精度小于5mm，完全能够实现动水关闭，在机组切除一切电源后，仍然能够关闭筒形阀从而关闭机组。它的成功运行，一是通过采用筒形阀可以减少由于采用大的蝶阀的成本增加，同时也增加了动水关闭的可靠性；二是此次控制完全采用电液同步系统对筒形阀进行控制，是在原纯机械保持同步的升级换代产品，从而使控制更加先进可靠。

由于南沙电站筒形阀的成功运行，天津市天发重型水电设备制造有限公司又进一步开拓了市场，成功承揽了3×100MW的马堵山电站水电机组的制造项目。

（天津市天发重型水电设备制造有限公司
单庆臣　孙　江　马恩君　周学钧　王惠明）

电　　气

小湾电站700MW水轮发电机组励磁系统研制与应用

（一）概况

小湾水电站系澜沧江中下游河段梯级开发的第二级电站和“龙头水库”，电站装机6×700MW。小湾水电站以500kV电压接入电力系统，是电力系统中的主力电站，在系统中担负基荷及调频、调峰和事故备用任务。国电南瑞科技股份有限公司（以下简称南瑞）负责小湾电站励磁系统及附属设备的研制、制造及投运工作。为积极调动各方面的有利条件，成立了小湾项目组，攻克重重难关，并借助三峡励磁系统的技术再创新，全面提升了该励磁系统整体设计制造水平，相关部分技术已经超越国外产品，达到了国际领先水平。

700MW 水轮发电机组是目前国内最大的巨型水电机组，对励磁系统的可靠性稳定性要求非常高。该项目是在充分考虑到国内电力行业特点，通过充分消化吸收国外先进的控制技术，并将其与南瑞先进稳定可靠的灭磁技术完美结合起来，取长补短优化互补并进行自主创新；同时，在充分考虑国情的基础上，修改完善国外励磁系统控制系统中诸多不合理的逻辑关系，开发出适合国情的运行软件。另外，在满足各种工况需要并实现可靠稳定控制的前提下，励磁系统的不断简单化也是该项目的特色之一。它的完成是对国内 700MW 机组励磁系统控制技术的进一步完善和提高。

（二）系统硬件配置

硬件系统设计方面，结合自身技术经验，针对巨型水轮发电机组励磁系统的具体技术特点，开发出了包含励磁变压器、整流系统、灭磁及过电压保护系统在内的全套励磁系统的设计算法，同时针对系统中关键器件的设计、选型进行了详细的理论和实践论证，为整套系统的可靠稳定运行提供了最大程度的保证。最终整套励磁硬件系统基本配置如下：①3 台单相环氧浇注干式励磁变压器；②1 台双通道数字式励磁调节器；③4 台大功率晶闸管整流柜；④2 台灭磁及过电压保护柜（含起励装置）；⑤1 台辅助控制柜；⑥相关配套的连接电缆和附属备品。

小湾励磁系统由西门子调节器、功率柜和南瑞灭磁及过压保护装置共同组成。在保证其安全可靠运行的前提下，合理利用盘柜空间，将灭磁开关与非线性电阻（SIC）集成在两个盘柜中，缩减了励磁盘柜的总数量，大大简化了一次回路的接线，降低了主回路设计的复杂性，同时合理充分地利用了现有资源，大大减少了设计成本。

（三）系统软件设计方案

小湾励磁系统采用了最新的 SIMOREG 励磁调节器。通过对该调节器进行充分的消化、吸收，完全掌握了其核心设计思想及理念，并且根据国情及现场情况改进了软件中种种复杂的甚至不合理的逻辑关系，以满足小湾项目的实际需要。

1. 调节器总体控制流程　调节器直接采样电子三相电压、三相电流、转子电压、转子电流，并由此计算出发电机的有功功率、无功功率、功率因数、有功电流、无功电流、电压频率等。其控制模式包括电压闭环（AVR）、电流闭环（ECR）、无功调节（Q-Regulator）以及功率因数调节（$\cos\phi$）。辅助控制功能包括欠励限制器、过励限制器、定子电流限制器、伏/赫限制器、无功补偿器（调差）、电力系统稳定器（PSS）。其中，电力系统稳定器（PSS）采用现阶段比较先进的 PSS2B 模型，不仅保证了对有功低频振荡的抑制效果，同时也有效地避免了反调现象的发生。总体控制流程见图 1。

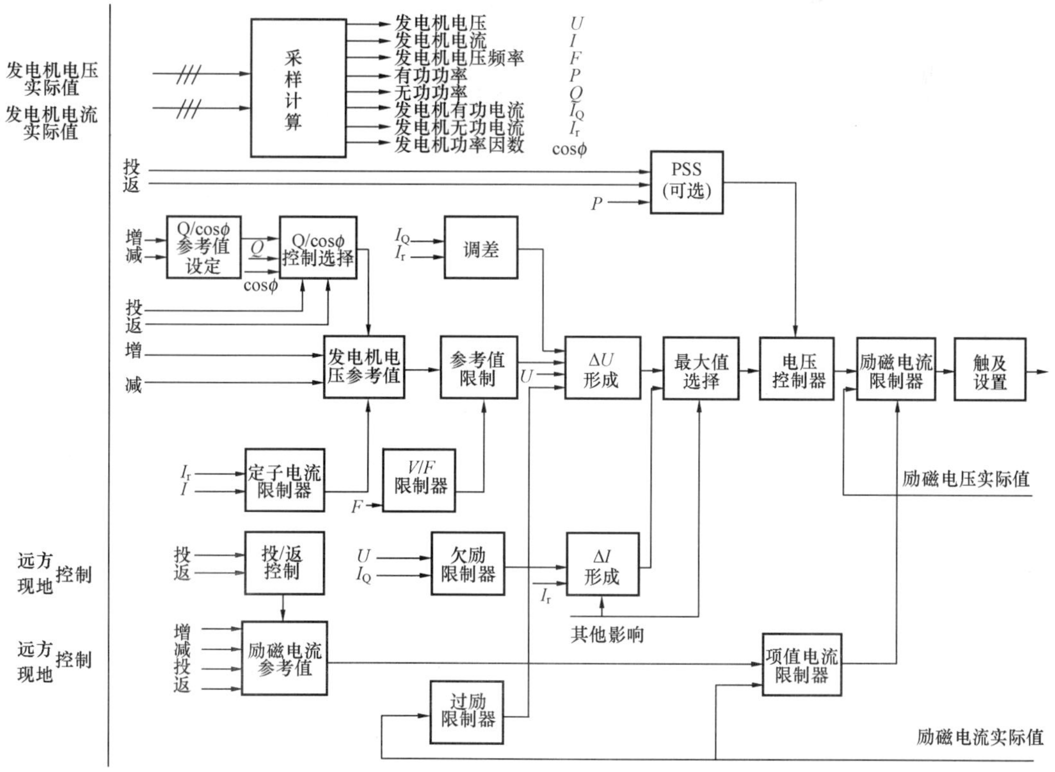

图 1　电压调节器逻辑结构图

2. 励磁系统投入流程 现地控制模式分为正常模式和试验模式（即unlocked模式），试验模式与正常模式相比较，其开机条件以及AVR/ECR的给定范围限制都放宽了，这就为静态或动态情况下模拟励磁系统各种工况的试验提供了很大的便利。

3. 励磁系统退出流程 励磁系统退出运行分为正常情况退励磁和事故情况退励磁两种：

（1）正常情况退励磁主要指逆变灭磁。逆变灭磁时，功率柜晶闸管的触发角度为150°，逆变5s之后晶闸管的触发脉冲将被闭锁，调节器发出跳闸指令，灭磁开关跳开。

（2）事故情况退励磁一般指发变组保护动作停机、内部转子回路过电压保护动作、低频保护动作、给定值越限保护动作等。

（四）主要创新点

（1）励磁系统总体方案实现了中外设备接口的完美对接，实现接口信号的准确设计，减少了励磁盘柜的数量，简化了励磁系统一次回路的接线，提高了设备运行的可靠性；

（2）改进了西门子设计理念中的诸多不合理方面，设计思路更加符合中国国情，如：风机切换逻辑、起励过程控制、故障录波功能、主从跟踪控制等程序的改进；

（3）励磁系统一次回路取消交流开关，采用交直流冗余灭磁的方法，优化了灭磁时序，并首次成功应用于700MW容量水电机组；

（4）采用跨接器和过流继电器配合完成过电压保护回路的设计，同时兼具发电机组非全相运行保护功能；

（5）在国外设备通信主站无需进行编程配置的前提下，成功实现了现场通信总线Profibus-Modbus通信协议的转换，完成了下位机通信协议转换程序的编制，运行效果良好。

（五）应用情况及意义

小湾电站首台机组于2009年9月25日正式投产发电，第二台和第三台机组也相继于2009年11月12日、12月11日投产发电。励磁系统零故障稳定运行，为机组的安全稳定运行提供了可靠的保障。这标志着国内引进吸收消化国外先进技术再创新进入了一个崭新的阶段，推动了现代励磁系统国产化的进程，积累了巨型水电机组重大设备的研发和生产调试的宝贵经验，进一步为以后国家大规模大容量水力发电建设奠定了良好的基础。

（国电南瑞科技股份有限公司 许其品）

长江三峡水利枢纽船闸安全监测自动化系统开工建设

由南京南瑞集团公司承担的长江三峡水利枢纽船闸安全监测自动化系统于2009年3月顺利开工建设，计划于2010年2月完成。

三峡永久船闸是三峡工程的三大主要建筑物之一，也是确保长江黄金水道通畅的关键工程。船闸位于大坝左岸坛子岭以北约200m处，线路上起祠堂包，下迄坝河口，总长6442m，其中上游引航道长2113m，主体段长1621m，下游引航道长2708m，总水头113m，设计年单向通航能力5000万t。

该船闸系在天然山体中深切开挖兴建，船闸轴线方向110.96°，单级闸室有效尺寸280m×34m×5m（长×宽×槛上最小水深），闸室墙采用锚固于边坡上的薄衬砌式结构。船闸开挖后形成南、北两侧岩质高边坡，边坡坡高一般100～160m，南坡最大坡高170. 28m，北坡最大坡高为137.8m，闸室边墙部位为50～70m的直立坡，两线船闸间保留高50～70m、宽55～57m的岩体中隔墩。南、北两侧高边坡岩体内，各设置有7层排水洞，中隔墩和两侧边坡岩体内各开挖一条输水隧洞，每级闸首两侧上游岩体内开挖阀门井和检修门井，共36个。

三峡船闸安全监测自动化系统纳入的测点共约468点，其中已安装传感器并接入数据采集单元（data acquisition unit，缩写DAU）的测点共134点，仅安装了传感器未接入数据采集单元的测点183个，尚未安装传感器的测点151个。现场已安装的数据采集单元共26台（已接入测点134点）。系统需对以上传感器及现场数据采集单元进行检查，并根据现场情况配置和安装必要的传感器、数据采集单元及设备将以上468个测点接入一个完整的安全监测自动化系统。

南京南瑞集团公司经过对系统的兼容性和技术成熟性进行了详细的调研，充分考虑分析了系统对每一类传感器的接入可能和接入经验。经过充分的考虑，选用技术成熟可靠、兼容性强的DAMS-IV型智能分布式大坝安全监测系统及其DAU2000型数据采集单元。

南京南瑞集团公司研制的DAU2000型数据采集单元已经拥有10大类共22种NDA系列智能模块用于不同类型仪器的采集和通信，是行业内公认的目前兼容性最强的大坝安全监测数据采集单元。

系统完成后，可对现场准备接入自动化系统的测点传感器及原有数据采集单元（DAU）进行监测；为离线信息分析软件开放原始数据库（包括所有测点的位置、类型、参数、观测原始数据等）、成果数据库（经转换计算的物理量）等资料，并协助离线信息分析软件编制方进行现场软件调试；完成原有人工观测数据（已入三峡监测中心数据库管理系统）转入本自动化系统数据库的工作。

由于系统复杂，三峡船闸安全监测自动化系统克服了众多技术难点。

安全监测传感器类型多，工作原理与输出信号形式各不相同，一套系统同时接入这些仪器难度大。若前期安装的数据采集单元性能不能满足要求，新安装的系统要能接入该数据采集单元原接入的仪器。前期安装了国内、外 4 个厂家的外观仪器和至少 6 个厂家的内观仪器，各厂家的仪器类型、输出信号形式、输出信号范围、测量方式均不相同，一套系统需同时接入这些仪器。

前期已有多种数据采集单元，系统结构与总线类型各不相同，系统集成难度大。自动化系统建设时将多家的数据采集系统集成到一个平台，实现数据统一管理，监测统一控制。

三峡水利枢纽船闸安全监测自动化系统经过多方努力，到 2009 年底，该项目完成电缆铺设、仪器安装和仪器接入等基础工作，为下一步设备联网、系统调试打下良好基础。

（国网电力科学研究院　汤祥林）

拉西瓦水电站安全稳定控制工程

（一）系统概况

拉西瓦水电站位于青海省贵德县与贵南县交界的黄河干流上，安装 6 台单机容量 700MW 混流式水轮发电机组，装机容量 4200MW，是黄河流域装机容量最大、大坝最高、发电量最多、单位千瓦造价最低的水电站；主要承担西北电网的调峰和事故备用，是“西电东送”北通道的骨干电源点，也是实现西北水火电“打捆”送往华北电网的战略性工程，对西北电网 750kV 网架起重要支撑作用。2009 年是西北电网建设高速发展的一年，750kV 网架主体结构逐步形成，大大增强了省间电网的联络，提高了系统的动态稳定水平，但此时，热稳定问题成为制约省间电网输送能力的主导因素，同时在 2009 年 12 月连接四川德阳和陕西宝鸡的 500kV 德宝直流工程单极投运，又引起西北电网的稳定性问题。拉西瓦水电站机组的运行工况对西北电网的稳定性起着重大的影响，并且当电网发生故障时通过切除拉西瓦水电站机组，能更好地保持稳定性。为保障电网安全稳定运行，南京南瑞集团公司电网安全稳定控制技术分公司 2009 年 10 月承担建设了西北主网架建设核心工程——“750kV 兰州东—平凉—乾县输变电工程”的安全稳定控制系统，其中在拉西瓦水电站设置了切机执行站。

（二）系统配置

750kV 兰州东—平凉—乾县输变电工程安全稳定控制系统在乾县变电站建区域稳控主站，在平凉、兰州东建子站，同时在青海李家峡、刘家峡、拉西瓦水电站、甘肃平凉、崇信、景泰和陕西彬长电厂等七个大型水、火电站建切机执行站；系统共 10 个厂站组成，每站双重化配置两套南瑞稳定公司生产的 SCS-500E型分布式稳定控制装置，站间以 2Mbps 光纤数据通道互联，构成双主运行方式的安全稳定控制系统。该系统监测德—宝直流运行信息以及陕甘输电断面潮流和故障信息，根据主网架各元件的运行工况，过载和故障情况，实施综合切机、切负荷控制和直流极控控制，以确保系统的安全稳定运行。

各厂站通道联系图如图 1 所示。

（三）功能配置

拉西瓦电站稳控装置主要监测 750kV 拉宁线边开关、750kV 拉宁线中开关、750kV 拉官线中开关、750kV 拉官线边开关和 1～6 号主变高压侧的运行工况，判别系统高周切除本厂机组，并接收兰州东变稳控装置发来的指定切机命令切除本厂机组。具体如下：

(1) 高频率功能：当装置监测到系统发生高频率时，按照事前整定的高频率定值和延时定值分 4 轮动作，每轮高频率切除 1 台机组，按机组出力从大到小顺序切除，优先切出力最大的机组。为了更好地防止误动作，装置判断高频率所用频率为出线中频率最高的出线的频率，系统高频率动作时需要机组高压侧频率确认。

(2) 接收远方命令功能：拉西瓦电厂与兰州东变稳控装置之间采用 2M 口通信装置，将本厂机组出力、投停及允切信息经兰州东上送至平凉变、宝鸡变，同时接收经兰州东转发的平凉、宝鸡变的切除本厂指定机组的命令，按照命令切除指定机组。

（四）社会及经济效益

750kV 兰州东—平凉—乾县安全稳定控制系统的投运，可以确保拉西瓦水电站更有效地送出，保障了西北—华中（四川）电网联网跨区跨流域水火电的互供调节和西北网西部水电与东部、北部火电、风电的互补调节战略的有效实施，获得最佳的经济效益、环境保护效益和社会效益。

（南京南瑞集团公司　尹旭阳）

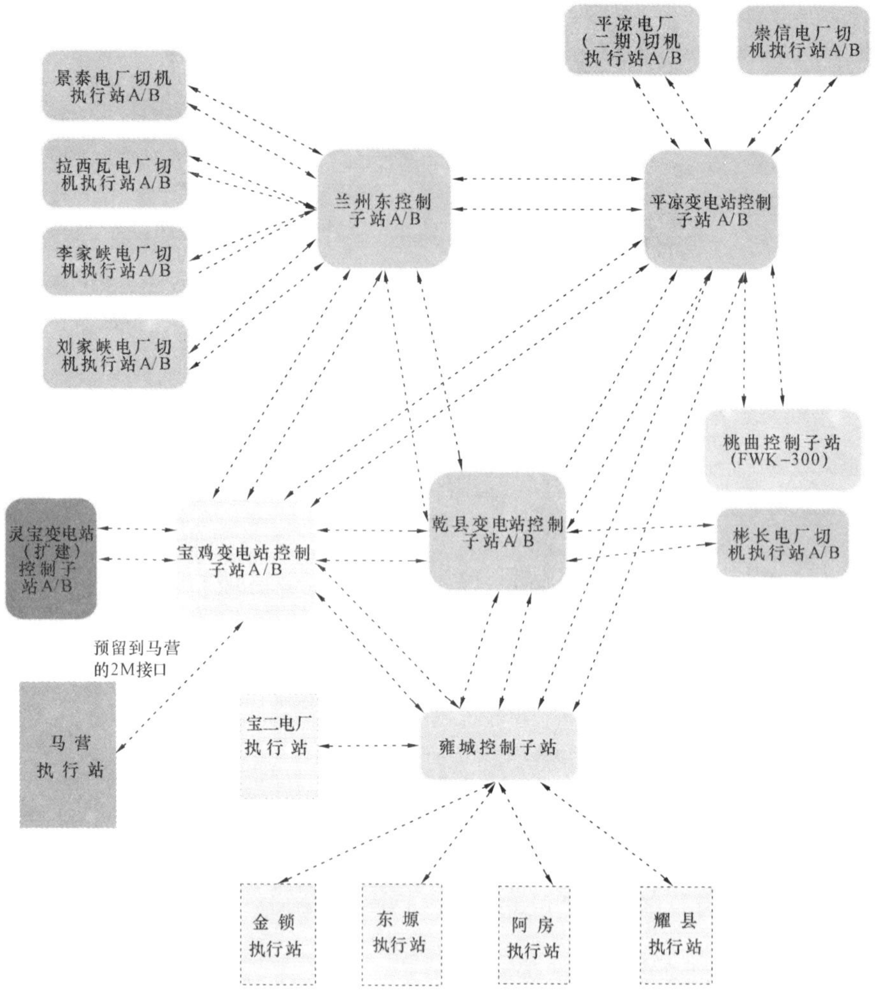

图1　系统厂站通道联系示意图

瀑布沟水电站送出安全稳定控制系统

（一）系统概况

瀑布沟水电站位于大渡河中游四川省汉源县和甘洛县境内，是一座以发电为主，兼顾漂木、防洪的综合利用水利水电工程，总装机容量3600MW，是目前四川最大的也是距四川省腹地最近的一座具有大水库的水电站。瀑布沟水电站汇合下游深溪沟水电站的电力通过4回500kV线路送出至眉山东坡变电站，再经华阳500kV尖山变电站、500kV资阳变电站、500kV南天变电站接入四川主网。瀑布沟送出安全稳定系统的主要作用是：监测外送输电线路和机组运行方式，在线路故障情况下，按照控制策略实施切瀑布沟电厂机组或向深溪沟水电站发送远方切机命令措施；在高频率高压事故情况下，实施高频率切机措施，或解列电厂送出线路；在系统振荡情况下，对送出线路实施解列。

（二）系统配置

瀑布沟电站送出工程安全稳定系统主要由瀑布沟水电站和东坡变电站组成。瀑布沟水电站配置有南京南瑞集团公司电网安全稳定控制技术分公司生产的FWK-300型分布式稳定控制装置（双套配置）、UFV-200F型失步解列装置及UFV-200M多功能综合解列装置各一套，主要监测机组及出线的运行状况，在线路故障时按照事先制定的策略表进行切机控制；同时还监测判断系统的高频率及失步故障，在满足设定的条件时采取切机或者解列线路的措施。东坡变电站配置由南瑞稳定公司生产的SCS-500型稳定控制装置，主要监测东坡变电站出线及主变电站的运行状况，在出线故障时按照策略表采取切机措施。

系统电气接线图及各厂站通道联系图见图1及图2。

（三）功能配置

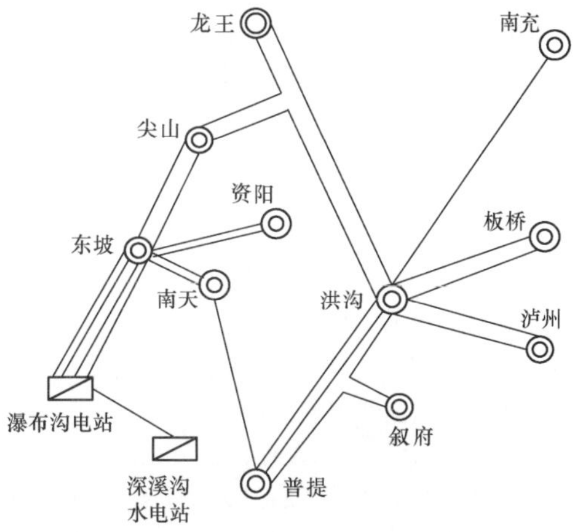

图 1　瀑布沟电站送出系统电气接线图

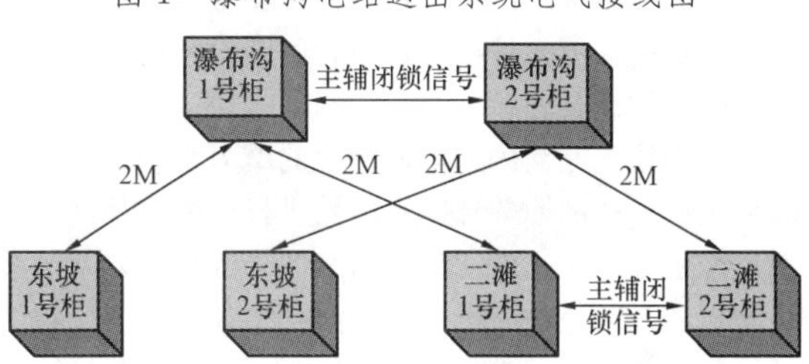

图 2　瀑布沟电站送出工程通道联系图

1. 瀑布沟电站　瀑布沟电站稳控装置采用双套配置主/辅方式运行，防止由于采样误差引起机组排序不一致而导致过切机组。主要监测 500kV 瀑布沟坡东坡 4 回线及布深线的运行状况，具有线路跳闸联切、高频切机和收远方命令切机等功能。

(1) 跳闸联切功能：装置监测布坡 4 回线的电气量，根据元件投停及特殊方式压板投退情况判断相应的运行方式，当元件出现故障时，根据事故前的电网运行方式、事故时判出的故障元件及故障类型，查找控制策略表的内容，确定本站切机的总容量。

(2) 高频切机功能：装置监测两段 500kV 母线的电压，如果两段母线电压频率均正常，则需要两段母线同时满足高频条件才判为系统高频故障；如果其中一段母线电压消失或者频率出现异常，则自动取电压频率正常的一段母线进行判断，当其满足高频条件时则判为系统高频故障。高频故障共分独立的 4 轮判断，每轮有独立的高频频率定值和延时定值，每轮高频切除一台机组，切机顺序按允切机组中出力由大到小排列。

(3) 收远方命令切机功能：瀑布沟电站与洪沟变电站和东坡变电站有通道联系，装置可同时接收洪沟变、东坡变电站发来的切机容量命令。在收到远方命令后，将可以切除机组的功率进行全排列，找出与需切容量最接近且超过需切容量的那一种组合予以切除。

(4) 失步解列功能：瀑布沟水电站还配置了两套不同原理的失步解列装置，其主要功能是监测电厂送出线路的运行状况，当其出现失步故障时，解列电厂出线。

(5) 切机原则：事故前装置对本站的发电机组按照出力大小、带厂用电的情况及人为设定的要求的切机排序，根据判断出的切机台数或切机容量、选择被切对象，执行切机控制。同时需将瀑布沟电站机组运行工况发送到洪沟变电站。

2. 东坡变电站　东坡变电站稳控装置采用双套配置并列方式运行，主要监测布坡 4 回线、坡山双线、资阳双线、天坡双线及 3 台主变的运行状态，当判出线路或主变压器发生跳闸时，根据系统的运行方式及故障前的断面潮流大小和方向，查策略表采取相应的控制措施按容量切瀑布沟机组。

(四) 结语

瀑布沟水电站地理位置适中，靠近负荷中心，输电距离距成都 200km、重庆 360km、自贡 180km、乐山 100km，是四川省继二滩电站之后又一具有战略性的骨干电源，该电站的建成发电对缓解系统供电紧张状况及改善系统运行条件起到了重大作用。瀑布沟水电站稳定控制系统的投运可以保障该送出电网的安全稳定运行，提高电站出力的送出，产生巨大的经济和社会效益。

(南京南瑞集团公司　李德胜)

新型数据采集装置在宜兴抽水蓄能电站成功试用

宜兴抽水蓄能电站位于江苏省宜兴市西南郊风景秀美的铜官山区，距宜兴市区约 7km。电站总装机容量为 1000MW，电站枢纽有：上水库、下水库、输水系统、地下厂房及地面开关站。上水库位于铜官山主峰附近沟源谷地，有效库容 507 万 m^3，采用全库盆防渗。主坝为面板堆石坝，坝顶高程 474.2m，坝顶长 516m，最大坝高 75m。下水库位于铜官山东北山麓，有效库容 522 万 m^3，大坝采用黏土心墙堆石坝，坝顶高程 83.4m，坝顶长 483m，最大坝高 50.4m。输水隧洞两条，单长 2800m，引水道设闸门井兼调压井，尾水道设有调压室。地下厂房洞室群位于输水系统中部，主要洞室有主副厂房、主变压器洞、进厂交通洞、出线洞等。水轮机最大、最小水头为 410.8m、336.4m。

根据宜兴抽水蓄能电站工程的规模和特点，水工建筑物监测自动化系统可分为 3 个基本采集子系统：上库子系统、引水发电子系统和下库子系统，所有系统共配置数据采集单元 DAU76 台、各类采集模块 133 块，共接入仪器 1409 支。为方便对各个测点进行人工比测，在该工程中全面使用了新型带电子式人工比测接口的数据采集模块。工程于 2009 年开始实施，新型数据采集装置试用成功。

在工程安全监测中，普遍使用带机械人工比测接口传感器自动数据采集装置，成本较高，可靠性低。机械人工比测接口由接口端子与多道多位旋钮机械开关组成，加接于传感器与数据采集模块之间，人工比测时，采用人工旋转机械开关切换传感器至人工比测接口，再连接到人工读数仪表。带电子式人工比测接口的数据采集装置由数据采集模块、通道选择器及电源模块组成，其中数据采集模块可同时接入多只传感器，按计算机软件设定的时间及周期对接入传感器进行测量，测量数据存储于装置内，并可通过计算机软件由通信电路传送至计算机存储、处理、输出。通道选择器与电源模块、数据采集模块相连。人工操作通过置数键、数字显示选择接入传感器编号，将编号通过通信电路传送至数据采集模块，由数据采集模块通过开关电路将相应的传感器信号切换至人工比测接口，以供传感器读数仪表进行人工读数。电源模块内含稳压电子线路，输入采用外部交直流供电或内部电池供电，以保障数据采集模块、通道选择器的电源供给。装置可完成对多只传感器的自动化测量及人工比测，有效降低生产成本，提高测量可靠性。

经过在宜兴抽水蓄能电站的试用，充分体现了带电子式人工比测接口的新型数据采集装置的优点，今后必将在大坝自动化监测行业得到广泛应用。

(南京南瑞集团公司　李桂平　蓝　彦　刘　果)

瑞丽江一级水电站跨国联网电气主接线设计

（一）电站概况

瑞丽江（Shweli）水电站位于缅甸北部掸邦境内紧邻中缅边境的瑞丽江干流上。电站距缅甸南坎、曼德勒的公路距离分别约为 63km、539km。电站所在地至中国及南坎已有公路相通，至中国境内的瑞丽、昆明的公路里程分别为 94km、893km。

工程采用引水式开发，坝高 47m，引水隧洞长约 5km，地面厂房，安装 6 台单机容量 100MW 的混流式水轮发电机组，总容量 600MW，保证出力 174. 8 MW，多年平均发电量 40. 33 亿 kW・h，年利小时数 6722 h。

（二）接入系统方式

瑞丽江一级电站的接入系统方式为：

(1) 在瑞丽江一级水电站第 1 台机组投产后 5 年，电站 50%电能分别送入缅甸国家电网和云南电网消纳；从第 6 年开始至电站 BOT 运营方式期限止的 35 年中，15%电能送入缅甸国家电网消纳，85%电能送入云南电网消纳，具体方案由中缅双方将来确认。

(2) 双方电网在任何情况下不通过该电站联网运行，电站送出主接线必须考虑分网运行措施。

(3) 电站分别以 220kV 和 230kV 电压接入云南电网和缅甸国家电网，并以 1 台 45MVA 变压器向缅甸当地供电。

(4) 电站通过 2 回 220kV 线路送入云南 500kV 德宏变电站，1 回 220kV 线路送入缅甸达贡山镍矿厂，并预留 1 回出线间隔。

(5) 电站通过 2 回 230kV 线路送入缅甸国家电网，并预留 1 回出线间隔。

（三）发电机与变压器的组合方式

瑞丽江一级电站单机容量为 100MW，电站初期设 2 回 220kV 线路接入云南电网 500kV 德宏变电站，不论瑞丽江一级电站发电机—变压器组接线方式采用单元还是扩大单元接线时，单元回路故障均不会影响到云南电网运行的稳定。

由于缺乏缅甸国家电网相关的电力系统资料，只能参照已投产的缅甸邦朗水电站进行分析。邦朗水电站总装机容量 3×85MW，当时约占缅甸电力系统装机容量的 26%。瑞丽江水电站 600MW，投产后在缅甸电力系统中会起到非常重要的地位。因此，发电机—变压器组接线方式采用扩大单元接线时，单元回路故障将会影响到缅甸国家电网的稳定运行。

考虑发电机—变压器组采用单独单元接线，并配合升高电压侧接线方式，易于满足向缅甸电力系统输送 0%～50%电量的要求，电站的运行方式最为灵活，可靠性高，单元回路故障对缅甸电力系统影响较小。因此，该电站发电机—变压器组接线采用单元接线。

为适应电站调峰运行的要求，有效地保护发电机组及变压器，延长高压开关寿命，确保厂用电可靠性，提高继电保护的选择性以及减少停电损失，该电站在发电机出口装设发电机断路器。

（四）220kV 侧接线方案

根据中缅双方签署的该电站电能分配方案，该电站将出现以下接机方案：①中方 3 台机组，缅方 3 台机组；②中方 4 台机组，缅方 2 台机组；③中方 5 台机组，缅方 1 台机组。

根据接入系统设计方案，该电站主接线必须按照“一厂两站”进行设计，而且还要满足以上电站运行的特殊要求。经对双母线四分段、双母线六分段和双母线八分段三种电气主接线方案分析，三个方案均可实现对中缅双方签署的该电站电能分配方案，但配电装置庞大复杂，采用分段断路器、母联断路器作为电气隔离，将电站分成两座电气独立的升压站，均要经过复杂的断路器及隔离开关的倒闸操作，事故几率较高，还需要装设复杂的母线保护，未能实现真正意义上的“一厂两站”，不能完全满足要求。

为有明显可见的断开点，考虑将以上接线方案的分段断路器取消，但这样又不能实现以上各种接机方案的要求。经与 GIS 制造厂咨询和共同深入研究，提出了“可拆卸式分段母线”的方案，以替代分段断路器。可拆卸式分段母线结构型式如图 1 所示。其拆卸、安装、试验时间需要 2～3 天。

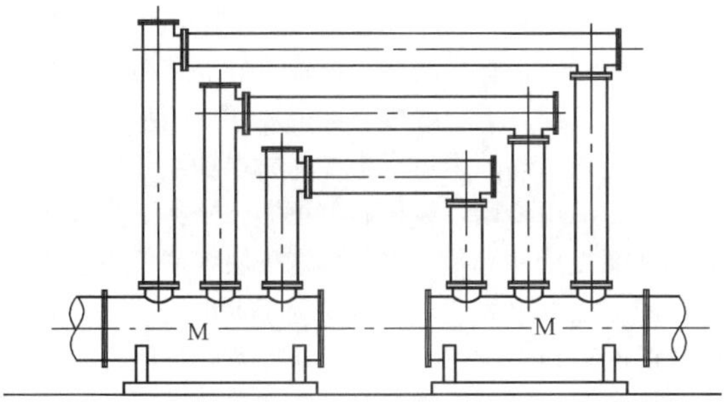

图 1　可拆卸式分段母线

最终，提出了图 2 所示的接线方案作为该电站的接线方案。此方案以方案三为基础，取消 6 台分段断路器，采用可拆卸式分段母线，从“硬件”上彻底将升压站分成两个独立的系统，大大减少了误操作的可能性，简化了继电保护，便于两个升压站分别运行和调度管理。

（五）结语

根据以上的比较和论证，瑞丽江一级电站主接线方案选择结论如下：

（1）推荐发电机—变压器组接线采用单元接线。该接线方式具有供电可靠性高，运行方式灵活，完全满足电站安全、可靠运行的要求；

（2）发电机出口装设发电机断路器在技术经济上均较为合理，推荐在发电机出口装设发电机断路器；

（3）根据电站的具体情况，结合目前国内大中型水电项目的发展趋势，在进行技术经济比较的基础上推荐 220kV 配电装置采用可靠性高、长期经济效益显著的 GIS 设备；

（4）双母线，“可拆卸式分段母线”分段接线方案可靠性高、与电站发电机—变压器组接线采用单元接线相配合时，电站调度运行灵活、且故障影响范围小、停电损失小，在备选方案中优势明显。同时，亦可满足电网对电站运行的特殊要求。

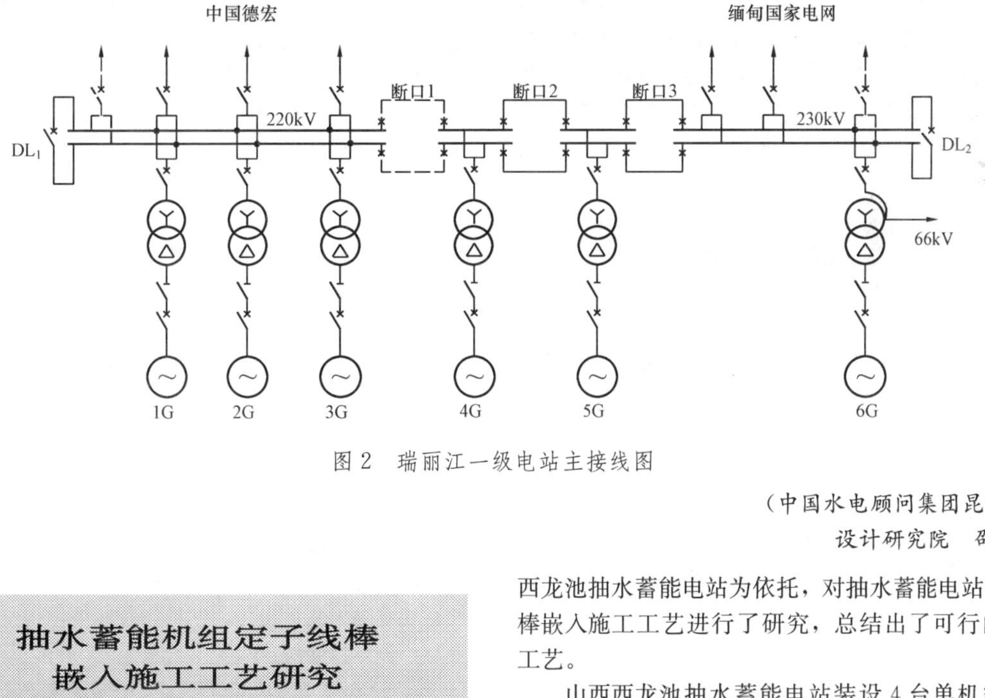

图 2　瑞丽江一级电站主接线图

（中国水电顾问集团昆明勘测设计研究院　邵光明）

抽水蓄能机组定子线棒嵌入施工工艺研究

大型机组定子线棒装配工艺的好坏很大程度上决定着机组的使用寿命。槽楔装配过松，在机组运行过程中易产生振动，长期振动导致线棒绝缘磨损，易产生放电，缩短使用寿命。槽楔装配过紧，施工过程易直接造成绝缘层损坏，也会缩短机组使用寿命。中国水利水电第三工程局有限公司的施工科研人员以山西西龙池抽水蓄能电站为依托，对抽水蓄能电站定子线棒嵌入施工工艺进行了研究，总结出了可行的施工工艺。

山西西龙池抽水蓄能电站装设 4 台单机容量为 300MW 的可逆式发电电动机组，定子部分由日方公司散装供货。发电工况单机额定容量 333.3MVA，额定电流 10691A，电动工况额定输出功率 319.6MW，额定电压 18kV，定子采用 3 相 6 叠 36 拍波形绕组，每 4 组并联共 12 极 216 槽，星形连接，绝缘等级 F 级。每台机组安装嵌入定子线棒 432 根，单根线棒宽度 90.28mm，线棒厚度 21.37mm，线棒高度4516mm，线棒嵌入铁心部分长度为2800mm。定子线棒嵌入过程中采用的新材料、新工艺值得推广。

（一）定子线棒嵌入工艺流程

定子线棒嵌入工艺流程如下：现场准备→铁心槽检查编号→支持环安装→下层线棒嵌入、耐压→绕组测温电阻安装→上层线棒嵌入、打槽楔、耐压→绕组端头焊接→汇流铜排安装→绝缘盒安装、绝缘包扎→定子绕组清扫、整体试验→定子整体喷漆→交接验收。

（二）定子下线施工工艺

1. 铁心槽检查编号　仔细检查铁心槽、通风沟、槽内凸凹点，将毛刺修磨平整，并检测槽形。用干燥的压缩空气吹扫铁心及线槽。按定子绕组接线展开图，确定第一槽位置，用胶布编写槽号并粘贴于线槽的上下端部。每隔5槽编一槽号。明确标示出绕组上、下层普通线棒、引出线，以及铁心上、下层线棒层间安装有测温电阻装置的铁心槽。

2. 绝缘支撑板及上端测温线夹安装　按图纸要求在定子上齿压板上表面焊接上部绝缘支撑板的固定角钢和上端测温线夹、汇流排支撑。在定子下齿压板下表面焊接下部绝缘支撑板的固定角钢后，将焊渣及毛刺用磨光机等清除打磨掉，并用吸尘器将焊渣及灰尘清除干净。然后，安装绝缘支撑板，配全绝缘支撑板固定螺栓的弹簧垫圈及螺母，用扭力扳手按规定扭矩拧紧螺母。

3. 支持环安装　绝缘支持环安装前，按定子槽数等分，在线槽槽底放置半导体垫条，均匀嵌入三根几何尺寸理想的下层线棒，线棒中心与铁心中心对齐，并用临时压线工具压舌片将线棒压靠至槽底。检查支持环外形、弯曲度、长度符合图纸要求。将支持环支架与绝缘支撑板临时固定，按图纸设计尺寸将其摆放在安装位置，抬起支持环，找正位置调整支持环段间接头使之落在支持环支架之间，并让支持环落入绝缘支撑板的槽口中。调整支持环与下层线棒之间的间隙，使其与下层线棒间预留1～2mm间隙，在间隙中塞入与设计间隙配套的用环氧树脂浸泡过的绝缘毡垫，然后将支持环与下层线棒用PG定向玻璃丝带临时绑扎牢固；调整支持环支架。支持环调整好后，用力矩扳手把紧支持环支架的螺栓，锁紧支持环支架螺母。锯除支持环闭合接头处多余部分，调整不锈钢接头位置，包扎接头处绝缘。先用PG定向玻璃丝带缠三层，再用云母带缠包四层，最外层用玻璃丝带缠一层，每层缠包时涂抹环氧树脂。待绝缘毡垫及不锈钢接头绝缘干透后，将绑扎支持环与下层线棒的PG定向玻璃丝带剪掉。

4. 下层线棒嵌入　检查线槽清洁无杂物，用干燥的压缩空气对铁心进行清扫。将线棒的端头打磨光亮，线棒清洁、无灰尘。检查线棒表面防晕层无损伤。按图纸要求在线槽槽底放置半导体垫条，垫条上下端露出的长度为0～10mm。将检查合格的线棒平行推入槽内，用橡皮锤均匀地将线棒逐步打入槽内，打入过程中不得损伤线棒外表面的防晕层，打入侧面压舌片临时固定。线棒侧面间隙用半导体垫片插入塞实。线棒端部绑扎前，用记号笔在端部标示出绑绳、槽口垫块、斜边垫块的安装位置，确保绑绳、垫块安装整齐、美观。下层线棒与支持环间用毡垫填充，线棒斜边之间的间隙用适形半导体材料和毡垫填充。在填充前，毡垫要用环氧树脂胶浸透。先将下层线棒与上、下端支持环绑扎牢固；再将下层线棒斜边垫块绑扎牢固，注意浸胶适形材料在湿态下进行绑扎，并将浸胶后的材料一次用完。端部绑扎完毕，环氧胶固化后再拆除压线工具。绑扎时，用塑料薄膜保护好线棒端部、铁心和上齿压板，以防环氧胶污染线棒及铁心，用纸片塞好上端槽口，以防环氧胶流入线槽内。

5. 下层线棒耐压试验　线棒试验时，线棒分支绝缘间做好防护，测试时分别将另一分支及其余线棒接地，并且已安装的铁心测温电阻线必须全部可靠接地，试验后要对测温电阻的完好性进行检查。交流耐压试验电压47kV，试验耐压过程无异常放电现象。

6. 测温电阻及中间垫片安装与上层线棒嵌装　检查线槽内清洁无杂物，用干燥的压缩空气对铁芯进行吹扫。按装配图在线槽层间放置测温电阻及半导体垫条。定子线圈测温电阻为通槽薄片型，厚度3mm，将线棒的端头打磨光亮，线棒清洁、无灰尘。检查线棒表面防晕层无损伤。上层线棒嵌入后，每槽线棒均采用压舌片及临时压线工具压紧在槽内，检查线棒和铁心槽的侧面间隙，塞好侧面半导体垫条。按图纸要求高度，安装层间假端箍，涤纶玻璃丝束先浸渍环氧树脂胶，浸透后压出多余汁液，扭绞不得使涤纶玻璃丝束直径变小，使用时涤纶玻璃丝束保持湿态。将上层线棒与下层线棒及上、下端支持环进行绑扎，上层线棒与槽口垫块、斜边垫块绑扎牢固，绑扎工艺与下层线棒绑扎相同。绑扎时，用塑料薄膜保护好线棒端部、铁心和上齿压板，以防树脂胶污染，用纸片塞好上端槽口，以防树脂胶流入线槽内。

7. 槽楔安装　打槽楔时，在里层斜楔底部垫半导体保护垫条及波形弹簧，垫条的厚度、层数选用应合适。槽楔插入到线槽表面，将楔下垫条在半导体垫条与槽楔间试配，紧度合适后将楔下垫条向下打紧，打入后的槽楔与线棒及铁心齿配合紧密，槽楔通风口和铁心通风沟中心一致，方向正确。槽楔由上端用专用打槽楔工具打入，上、下两端的各一根槽楔分别从上下两端最后打入。槽楔打好后，用百分表通过测量孔测量，槽楔压紧度在0.2～0.8mm范围内符合要求，用检查小锤敲打其余部位槽楔进行槽楔紧度检查。

8. 上层线棒耐压试验　因上层线棒、下层线棒到货时均焊好了相应一部分的连接铜排，上下层线棒全部嵌入后，上层线棒与下层线棒层间及相邻端头间很难做到完全绝缘，因此交流耐压试验很难再进行，上层线棒在工地施工现场仅作直流耐压试验，试验电压直流66.3kV，持续时间1min。线棒试验时，已安装的测温电阻线圈必须全部可靠接地，线棒试验后，对测温电阻的完好性进行检查。

9. 绕组端头焊接　焊前对银焊焊工进行培训，焊工经培训并考试合格后方可上岗操作。用制造厂提供的银焊机和自制试件，在现场进行焊接试验，以确定焊接工艺参数。线棒上、下端部用湿陶瓷带做好绝缘隔热防护，防止焊接中高温烧伤线棒绝缘，防止上端头焊接中焊料及焊后接头清理中的金属粉末进入铁心及绕组中。用专用接头整形工具对上、下层线棒端头进行整形。焊接按照先进行定子下端头焊接，依次进行定子上端头焊接、最后进行引出线焊接的顺序进行施工。按照银焊操作工艺要求，装配银焊片，用鲤鱼钳将端头夹紧，接头焊接过程中维持较小的间隙，以防止银焊料大量流失，严重影响焊接质量。焊前用制造厂提供的专用冷却焊接钳夹紧待焊接头部位，操作银焊机，按照试焊时确定的焊接工艺参数，通电对接头施焊，通电加热时间按厂家的规定进行控制。在接头焊接过程中，使用制造厂提供的焊条向焊缝处填补焊料，直至填满无间隙，然后停止焊接。焊接结束后，检查焊缝外观有无气孔、裂缝、夹渣、未焊满及未焊透现象。用扁铲、锉刀、砂布清除接头表面的残余焊料、焊瘤、毛刺及表面氧化物，使接头光亮，再使用蘸过酒精的白布擦洗干净接头。焊接接头检查合格后，全面清扫定子，拆除陶瓷带等防护设施，用干燥压缩空气彻底吹扫干净定子铁心及绕组。

10. 汇流铜排安装　按图纸要求安装汇流铜排基础支架，焊接及清除焊渣时作好防护，防止焊渣掉进线槽。在定子上齿压板安装汇流铜排，调整对正汇流铜排与出线线棒的接头，调整对准主引出线和中性点引出线的位置。将绝缘垫块按照图纸进行装配。按图用绝缘螺栓将汇流铜环绝缘支架安装在基础板上，固定牢固。从下往上逐层安装汇流铜排，调整对正汇流铜排与出线线棒的接头，按图纸设计调整对准主引出线和中性点引出线的位置，调整汇流铜排接头位置尽量错开绝缘支架。出线线棒与汇流铜排间连接采用银焊机焊接，其焊接工艺与线棒间接头焊接工艺基本相同；汇流铜排段与段之间接头焊接，采用手工气焊焊接连接，在汇流铜排接口处上下两侧加碳精块，使铜排受热均匀，避免出现铜排烧流或焊料不熔化现象。焊接时要用湿陶瓷布、陶瓷带遮盖好绕组端部及汇流铜排间焊接接头部位附近的绝缘，防止高温烧伤绝缘层。接头焊好后按规定检查焊接质量。用板锉等清理干净焊接接头表面的残余焊料，用砂布、钢丝刷等清理干净焊缝表面的氧化物。

定子绕组、汇流铜排焊接结束后，对定子绕组各相、各分支回路的直流电阻进行测量，测得的各相、各分支的直流电阻，在校正由于引线长度不同引起的误差后，相互间差别不大于最小值的2%。

11. 绝缘盒安装及绝缘包扎　彻底清扫定子铁心、绕组端头，逐个检查绝缘盒无裂纹、气孔、破损，并用白布蘸酒精将绝缘盒檫拭干净。按照制造厂的绕组绝缘工艺规范及绝缘盒安装工艺要求，在绕组端部套装绝缘盒，调整绝缘盒的高度及绝缘盒之间的间隙和圆度以符合图纸要求。绝缘盒套装好后，用环氧小心灌注绝缘盒，使环氧胶充满整个绝缘盒和接头四周空隙。灌注前用塑料薄膜保护好铁心上齿压板、槽口、绕组端部等部位，作好防护，防止环氧溢出及滴落污染线棒。清理干净绝缘盒表面、绕组端部、上齿压板上等处多余的环氧胶。按照制造厂的绕组端部绝缘工艺规范，包扎汇流排绝缘。包扎绝缘及绑扎后抹光滑表面，无毛刺。主引出线、中性点引出线接头绝缘包扎时，按图纸要求削好接头新旧绝缘搭接坡口，用酒精擦洗干净，再按工艺规范要求包扎绝缘，包扎绝缘时新旧绝缘的搭接长度满足要求，层间刷胶全面，薄且均匀。绝缘包扎好后，清理干净表面毛刺及多余环氧胶，抹光滑表面。清理干净绝缘包扎处附近及其他部位的环氧胶。

（三）整体直流泄漏试验及交流耐压试验

定子绕组清理结束后，进行整体直流泄漏试验及交流耐压试验。交流耐压试验前，分相分阶段进行54kV直流耐压试验，直流耐压试验持续时间1min，各相泄漏电流不随时间的延长而增大；各相泄漏电流的差别不大于最小值的50%。定子绕组整体39kV交流耐压试验，持续时间1min，交流耐压试验时起晕电压29.5～31kV，起晕电压情况良好。

试验结束后，拆除试验设备，进行喷漆。油漆干透后，将定子吊入机坑。

（四）结语

该施工工艺中波形弹簧衬垫的成功应用，使线棒的松紧程度在一定范围内可以通过波形弹簧衬垫进行自我调节；槽楔测量孔百分表测量法的应用，使槽楔装配松紧度可以量化测量，保证了线棒嵌入后槽楔松紧度在允许范围内，避免了机组运行过程中线棒过松产生振动，或线棒嵌入太紧造成线棒绝缘损伤，保证了机组稳定运行，延长了机组的使用寿命。

施工过程中一些新材料如陶瓷带、碳精块的成功应用，改善了焊接隔热传热条件，缩短了施工时间，保证了施工质量。大量使用陶瓷布（或陶瓷带）代替原来大量使用的石棉布，避免了石棉、玻璃丝对施工人员的职业伤害。

（中国水利水电第三工程局有限公司　李　楠）

亭子口水利枢纽左岸供水系统工程自控设计

（一）工程概况

亭子口水利枢纽位于四川省广元市苍溪县境内的嘉陵江干流中游河段上段，具有防洪、灌溉及城乡供水、发电、航运及其他综合利用效益。根据施工总体布置，施工供水系统左右岸分别设置，自成独立系统。其中，左岸供水系统由生产水系统和生活水系统组成。左岸生产供水系统主要承担大坝浇筑养护、砂石混凝土系统、土石方开挖、小型施工企业、公用设施等生产用水及消防用水，供水规模 5.5 万 t/d。生活供水系统主要承担施工营地用水，供水规模为 0.3 万 t/d。

（二）监控点范围

供水系统包括原水泵站、水厂及输配水工程。为满足施工期生产和生活用水的水质、水压及水量的要求，系统需要检测、监视和控制有关参数。根据水处理工艺及设备布置，在控制室设置两套计算机操作控制站和一个工程师站。计算机系统为一用一备。具体分布见表 1。

表 1　系统各部位监控点统计

序号	测量类型	测试介质	测量位置	测量范围	数量
1	液位监测	水	取水泵站、水厂、送水泵站	0～30m	9
2	压力监测	水	水厂	2MPa	2
3	流量监测	水	水厂、高位水池	0～4000T/H	3
4	pH 在线监测	水	水厂	0～14	2
5	浊度在线监测	水	絮凝搅拌池	0～100mg	2
6	余氯在线监测	水	加矾间检测余氯		1
7	水泵	水	取水泵站、水厂	0～440kW	26
8	电接点压力	水	取水泵站、水厂	0～1MPa	10

（三）系统设计

该工程主要为水利枢纽施工期生产和生活供水，根据 SL 303—2004《水利水电工程施工组织设计规范》中生产企业对水质的要求，以及《水利水电工程施工组织设计手册》中生产企业对水质的要求，生产水水质的浑浊度小于 20mg/l。生活水水质应满足 GB 3020—1993《生活饮用水卫生标准》的要求。设计方案应稳定、可靠、安全，并不落后于时代。

（1）该系统中每个 PLC 控制站都连在厂 Ether CAT 高速实时以太网上，不仅可以控制各自分站的运行，而且可在经由网络访问其他 PLC 控制站。中控室配有 2 台上位监控机，同时控制 3 个现地 PLC 控制站，向它们发送命令。这两个上位监控计算机互为功能备用。所有设备的电源均由 UPS 提供，每个控制回路的电源都由各回路开关控制，能独立操作。保证了系统安全性，和调试的方便性。整个系统采用 EtherNet 以太网网络，运行 TCP/IP 协议。EtherNet 是当今世界上技术成熟、应用最前端的开放型网络通信方式。

（2）系统采用在 WINDOWS 环境下运行的 MCGS6.2 软件包，它把实时动态的各种信息量以图形、文字、画面的方式有机地结合在一起，立体感强，操作简便，直观舒适。操作者可用鼠标完成对软件的全部操作，包括菜单选择、画面切换、实时数据显示、历史数据前/后翻页、报表生成及打印、故障查询及复位、文件管理、参数设定等，每页图形均固定有即时报警信息栏、向上翻页、回到主菜单、打开报警显示屏，操作人员姓名注册显示、故障/维修/模拟报警实时显示等功能。该软件包采用的是全中文界面更有利于操作者进行操作。

（3）工程师站/操作站（HMI），主要用于应用 PLC 软件和上位机软件开发、下装、水处理系统各参数的动态显示，包括：液位、流量、压力、pH、余氯、浊度等参数进行检测和控制。电气设备的状态（合/分闸、就绪/故障、运行/停止等）、PLC 系统的工作状态和故障诊断等。

（4）系统结构分为三层，底层为现场仪表和传感器单元，中间层为仪表数据显示单元，上层为数据采集和监控单元。所有现场一次仪表均安置在现场，根据现场的环境，配置现场仪表保护箱，保护仪表，延长仪表使用寿命。显示仪表采用单通道数显仪表，并配置有现场通信协议，该系统众多的监控量，液位、压力、流量等均可以通过通信传送到上位机，进行实时显示。上层监控采用服务器，选用 DELL Server 系列。配置不低于 DELL Server 1024M 内存、80G、19 寸液晶显示器、DELL 键盘、鼠标。系统通过 Ether CAT 以太网把数据送入服务器，在计算机上对整个生产工艺进行组态，实现整个工艺流程的实时监控。

（四）水处理工艺

1. 生产水处理工艺

（1）采用运行简单、效果较好的管式混合器进行混合。

（2）絮凝池与沉淀池合建。絮凝池分两组水处理池，每组处理水量29 000m^3/d，絮凝时间为12～20min。沉淀池表面负荷5～9m^3/(m^2·h)，采用虹吸式刮泥桁车排泥，刮泥桁车行走速度1.0m/min；排泥周期、时间根据需要设手动或自动，自动采用可编程控制器设定。

（3）设4500m^3矩形清水池2座，可独立放空检修。池内设液位变送器，液位控制信号传送至值班室。

2. 生活水处理工艺

（1）在生产调节水池内装两台潜水泵，加压后送至重力式净水器。潜水泵的单机流量65m^3/h，扬程12m。重力式净水器设2套，每套处理水量1500m^3/d，设计滤速6～8m/h。

（2）设200m^3矩形清水池2座，可独立放空检修。池内设液位变送器，液位控制信号传送至值班室。

3. 送水泵房 设有配电房兼值班室，装有生产水泵4台，3用1备，单机流量1150m^3/h，扬程73m；生活水泵2台，1用1备，单机流量185m^3/h，扬程73m；为便于安装及维修，装有电动单梁悬挂式起重机1台。

4. 加矾间和消毒间设计

（1）加矾间由加矾、矾库、消毒间及值班室组成。加矾选用常用的高效絮凝剂，平均投药量15mg/l，最大平均投药量30mg/l。消毒选用二氧化氯，采用化学法现场制备，二氧化氯与水应充分混合，有效接触时间不应少于30min。

（2）加矾间设计量泵，利用计量泵投加絮凝剂，计量泵根据投药量的大小进行调速控制药量，矾库按一个月储矾量设计。

（3）消毒间内应设有每小时换气8～12次的通风设施，并配备二氧化氯泄漏的检测仪和报警设施及稀释泄漏溶液的快速水冲洗设施。设备间应与储存库房比邻。二氧化氯系统的设计应执行有关规范的防毒、防火、防爆要求。二氧化氯的原材料库房储存量按最大用量10d计算。

（五）结语

该供水自动监控及调度系统设计，采用了分布式控制结构，以供水水厂的生产过程为背景，提出了一套基于PC机的自动供水计算机监控系统设计方案。现场调试证明，该方案切实可行，既保证了水厂的不间断生产又提高了水厂的管理水平。系统的开发时间短，成本低，节能效益明显。

（中国水利水电第五工程局有限公司 梁 涛）

金 属 结 构

景洪升船机承船厢对接系统设计

（一）工程概况

景洪水电站为澜沧江干流中下游河段水电开发梯级规划8级电站中的第6级，位于云南省西双版纳傣族自治州首府景洪市北郊约5km处，总装机容量为1750MW。电站坝址位于澜沧江通航河段上，电站枢纽按Ⅴ级航道、300t级船型的标准设计航运过坝建筑物。远期考虑500t船只通航过坝。根据云南省航务局提供的澜沧江水系最新的300t级机驳船型资料设计，船型总长46.2m，型宽7.6m，型深2.3m，满载吃水深度1.75m。

景洪升船机经过研究比较后，其型式确定为水力式升船机。该型式升船机的基本原理是将平衡重做成重量和体积合适的浮筒，浮筒井（简称竖井）布置在升船机塔楼中，承船厢布置在两侧塔楼中间的船厢室中，悬吊承船厢的钢丝绳布置在船厢两侧，钢丝绳绕过升船机塔楼顶部的卷筒、动滑轮后固定在钢丝绳固定端均衡梁上。平衡重浮筒的结构重量及配重重量分别大于承船厢结构重量和承船厢水体重量，利用充泄水工作阀门实现竖井内水位的升降，改变平衡重浮筒的入水深度实现浮筒的浮力变化，利用此浮力变化在船厢重与浮筒重之间产生的差值来驱动承船厢升降运行。承船厢在升降过程中由于漏水等原因造成的载荷变化，可以通过竖井内平衡重浮筒淹没水深的自动改变予以适应，保证在任意位置船厢侧的载荷与平衡重的载荷保持相对的平衡，通过控制竖井水位的升降来控制船厢的运行。船厢的运行速度由竖井中充、泄水的流速来控制。

（二）升船机船厢对接系统

船厢对接装置是升船机承船厢与工作大门对接时用于止水的一种设备。升船机对接装置是湿运升船机与航道实施连接和封水的重要设施，用于承船厢停靠在闸首时与挡水闸门之间的封水，使上、下游航道水域与承船厢水域连通，提供船只进、出承船厢的通道。因此，对接装置的性能及其工作的可靠性直接关系到升船机能否安全、可靠的运行。

通过对承船厢与上下游工作闸门对接时的运行工况进行分析研究，本着结构简单、功能可靠、投资节省的原则，设计了一种承船厢与上下游工作闸门的对接充压密封装置。

（三）船厢对接系统结构及技术特性

景洪水电站垂直升船机承船厢对接密封装置，在设计中采用充压伸缩止水。充压水封装置断面形成全封闭的空腔，当承船厢与上下游挡水工作闸门对接时，充压密封装置投入使用，适应挡水工作闸门受压后的变形，并封堵承船厢与挡水工作闸门间的间隙，防止对接过程中承船厢和挡水工作闸门间漏水。在承船厢升降过程中泄掉背压不投入使用，使止水元件回退，脱离与上下游挡水工作闸门止水座板的接触，以避免承船厢升降过程的干涉和对止水元件的磨损。

充压控制系统与承船厢升降系统互为闭锁，即升降系统操作承船厢运动时，充压控制系统无法充压，只能处于泄压状态。反之，充压控制系统在充压保压过程中，升降系统无法操作承船厢上下升降运行，必须在操作承船厢前将充压腔内的压力介质释放，使止水元件在止水橡皮弹力作用下回退而与上下游挡水工作闸门面板间形成间隙。确保不会发生误操作，对充压密封装置和承船厢升降系统都起到很好的保护作用。

止水元件的伸缩变形主要是由几何变形和少量弹性变形而获得。充压主止水布置在承船厢端部，充压水封端部设计带锯齿的形状，同时充压水封座和充压水封压板设计成与充压水封相匹配的断面。充压水封座与充压水封压板通过螺栓连接，紧密固定充压水封，为充压水封形成密闭腔。

充压密封装置的非工作状态、工作状态如图1所示。

主要技术特性：封水宽度14.51m；封水高度4.285m；止水间隙55mm；充气压力0.3MPa；空压机额定流量2.41m^3/min。

（四）工程进展

该充压密封装置于2008年3月取得实用新型专利，专利号：ZL 2007 2 0105052.0。

目前景洪升船机正处于制造、安装阶段，船厢对接系统也处于生产、制造阶段。

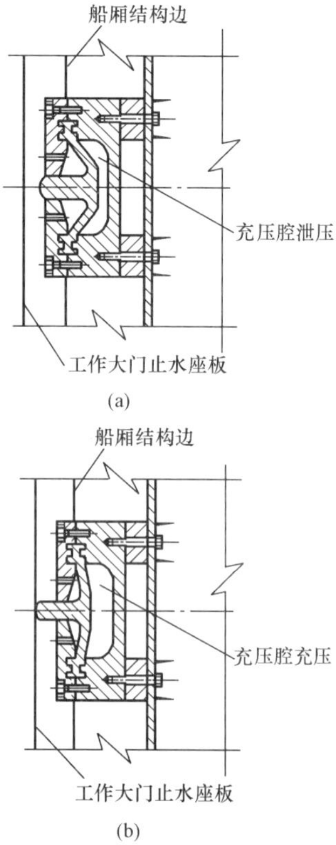

图1　充压密封装置

（a）非工作状态；（b）工作状态

（中国水电顾问集团昆明勘测设计研究院
李自冲　马仁超　崔　稚）

小湾放空底孔平面链轮闸门制造关键技术研究

（一）概况

小湾水电站工程属大（1）型一等工程，永久性主要水工建筑物为一级建筑物。工程以发电为主，兼有防洪、灌溉、养殖和旅游等综合利用效益，水库具有不完全多年调节能力，系澜沧江中下游河段的“龙头水库”。

放空底孔事故检修闸门为平面链轮闸门，2扇，孔口净尺寸为5m×12m，设计挡水水头160m，总水压力106 100kN，单扇门叶重297.071t，单套门槽重622.48t。闸门门叶分4节制造，在工地现场用螺栓连接成整体。门槽倾斜度为1∶6，断面为“Ω”形整体门槽，每段约5.5m，节间采用螺栓连接。闸门可在106m水头下动水关闭，启门时，先用设于坝体廊道中的充水阀充水，平压后，再启门。启闭设备为

6000kN 坝顶门机，门机通过拉杆与闸门连接。

（二）设备特点

（1）链轮门均衡座、链轮及门槽轨道材料为强度高、抗锈蚀性能好的 0Cr17Ni4Cu4Nb 沉淀硬化马氏体不锈钢，为水工金属结构设备制造首次采用，但该材料加工难度大，热处理工艺要求严格。

（2）闸门门叶采用两道止水，一道为山形自充压水封，一道为实心“P”形水封，闸门与门槽要求在制造厂内整体联合预装入槽试验。

（3）闸门门叶及整体门槽要求热处理退火消应，退火后残余应力小于材料屈服应力的 25%。

（4）设计水头为 160m，综合参数目前居世界首位，闸门门叶及门槽制造精度高于行业标准要求，难度大。

（三）制造产品关键技术措施

1. 闸门下料工艺余量控制及坡口备制

（1）根据门叶结构特点及制作经验，合理确定门叶下料工艺余量。边梁、主梁腹板宽度按单边 4mm 坡口加工余量、整体 2mm 焊接收缩余量控制，边梁、主梁长度按 30mm 收缩余量及二次修整余量控制；门叶各节高度按 10mm 加工余量、3mm 收缩余量控制，门叶宽度按 5mm 焊接收缩余量、单边 15mm 二次修整余量控制。

（2）门叶结构中主梁、边梁、纵梁隔板等与翼板及面板的组合焊缝均为坡口焊。经多次试验，最后确定采用特制 U 形坡口。经实践证明，减少了焊接工作量及焊接变形，同时焊接质量得到保证。

2. 拼装过程中的工艺控制　制作时先将两件节间连接板（两件分别留 5mm 的加工余量）进行配钻，两边梁连接板由于为公母止扣形式，采取预加工后再两两配对成整体，配钻完成后将筋板和隔板拼焊成整体并调校合格后参与门叶的组拼，这样既减少了门叶最后焊接时的填充量，同时又保证了单件的尺寸的合格率。

3. 闸门焊接工艺措施　门叶主梁、边梁、隔板等均采取单件制作、焊接完成。闸门在平台上整体组装后，面板朝下，整体焊接，焊接时对门叶变形进行监测。

4. 闸门应力热处理工艺措施

（1）整体门槽退火前对主、反轨间开口进行内支撑加固，整体门槽按槽口朝上水平位置摆放入炉；门叶按 4 节一炉、单节门叶在炉内立放形式摆放；门槽及门叶在退火炉内摆放后要求调平、支垫牢固；对构件退火热处理的升温速度、保温温度及时间、降温速度、空冷温度等工艺参数进行明确规定。

（2）在闸门门叶及整体门槽退火过程中，24h 派专人对退火热处理时的升温速度、保温温度及时间、降温速度、空冷温度等进行实时监控。

（3）门叶及整体门槽退火热处理后，经电力工业金属结构设备质量检测中心用盲孔法对各对接焊缝及组合焊缝进行应力测试，数据证明闸门残余应力小于 Q345B 材料屈服应力的 20%，完全满足设计要求。

5. 闸门加工工艺措施　整体门槽全长30 414mm，由 6 节组成，副轨全长126 000mm，由 21 节组成，其中所有主轨面、反轨止水面、副轨工作面、各节间连接面均为加工面。门叶由 4 节组成，除整套链轮装置全为高精度加工件外，门叶止水、节间连接面、门叶上各走道承载面及装配面、门叶底止水、吊轴装置等均须要加工。

（1）整体门槽的加工：①轨道先预加工，在工作表面及长度方面留有一定二次加工余量，待整体门槽上的止水座面及轨道承压槽加工完成后，将轨道压入槽内，根据实际检测情况再加工轨道表面及轨道端部与整体门槽节间连接面错位处。②轨道座承压槽及止水座面安排在同一个工位加工，以保证两者的平面平行度及距离。③为了保证轨道与整体门槽轨道座螺栓装配良好，设计了一套两块配加工的钻模板，一块用于轨道上装配孔的加工，别一块用于整体门槽轨道座上装配孔的加工。

（2）门叶加工：①门叶各节间连接面连接螺栓孔采取两两先配对加工好再参与门叶拼焊，顶底节与端部走道装配连接面上的螺孔则采取与端部走道配定位后，利用加工好的样冲按端部走道螺孔位置冲出门叶上连接螺孔的圆心样点，然后拆下端部走道再利用钻床对着圆心样点加工。②门叶退火后将各节门叶面板朝上重新组拼起来调平（面板水平在 3mm 之内，节间连接板共面度要求在 4mm 之内）后，画出加工线，并在边梁腹板上用水准仪做出用于机床调整的水平基准线。节间连接面的加工采用 W200 镗床进行。

6. 辊轮、轨道、均衡座的加工　所用不锈钢在切屑过程中硬化严重，切屑力大，切屑温度高，切屑不易折断、易黏结，刀具易磨损，线膨胀系数大。为此，除以最佳的化学成分配比来控制铁索体含量，保证良好性能，并在热处理工艺分别增加一个固熔、时效预处理过程，解决其产生裂纹问题外，采用了具有耐热性好、耐磨性高、与不锈钢的亲和作用小的高速钢和硬质合金刀具加工。

7. 闸门门叶与整体门槽预装入槽联动试验方案

（1）入槽联动试验方案的制定。小湾放空底孔事故检修闸门是在门槽 1∶6 的倾斜度状态上下运行工作，但由于整体门槽较长（30.414m）、较重（约 492t），门叶整体重量也达 297t，厂内无法模拟闸门工作状态进行门叶与整体门槽联合组装、滑动试验。

经研究，采取在水平状态下进行。在同一场地搭设联合试验平台，闸门及门槽分别组拼时两者中心线在同一直线上，而且整体门槽轨道工作面与门叶平面临时导轨工作面在同一水平面。在二者分别验收合格后，利用门叶下面铺设的两根加工好的导轨通过卷扬机等牵引装置将门叶拉入整体门槽，使门叶在整体门槽内进行滚动运行。

（2）门叶与整体门槽的联动试验及检测。闸门门叶的滚动及在整体门槽内运行通过在平台一端设置的5t卷扬机和滑轮组牵引进行。为了检测闸门滚动时牵引力计算出闸门链轮的滚动摩擦系数，准备一台10t的测力器用来测量门叶牵引力的大小。同时在整体门槽的轨道工作面涂一层红丹以检查试验时链轮与轨道的接触情况。闸门门叶在门槽内来回进行了多次滚动运行，链轮与链条均运行自如，无卡阻现象。对链轮与轨道工作面及均衡座接触面用塞尺进行了检测，结果表明链轮与轨道及均衡座接触面接触良好，85%以上链轮处于受力状态。同时通过电子秤显示牵引力在2.6～3.1t之间。门叶上止水座面与门槽上水封工作面的间距尺寸满足图纸及规范要求，小湾放空底孔1号链轮门联合试验主要技术标准比较及实际制造成果如表1所示。

表1　小湾放空底孔1号链轮门联合试验主要技术标准比较及实际制造成果表

序号	检测项目	设计值（mm）	DL/T 5018—2004	小湾标准（HNXW-J112-2007）	实测值
1	门槽孔口净宽	5000	±10.0	±3.0	上：−2.5 中：+3.0 下：+1.0
2	止水宽（侧止水间距）	5544	±6.0	±1.5	上：−1.0 中：+1.5 下：−0.5
3	左右槽主轨中心线距离	6950	±6.0	±1.5	上：−0.5 中：+0.5 下：0
4	左右槽副轨中心线距离	6950	±6.0	±3.0	上：+0.5 中：+1.0 下：−1.0
5	左右侧轮承压板面距离	8190	±6.0	±3.0	上：−1.5 中：+2.0 下：−2.0
6	主轮承压板到止水座面的距离	2105	−2.0～+4.0	−0.5～+1.0	左：−0.5～+0.9 右：−0.5～+0.92
7	构件组合处主轨工作面间隙			≤0.1	左：0.1　右：0.1
8	构件组合处水封工作面间隙			≤0.1	左：0.1　右：0.1
9	构件组合处非工作面错位		2.0	≤1.0	左：1.0　右：0.9
10	主轨工作面直线度			每5m范围内≤0.12	左：0.1/m 右：0.08/m
11	水封、副轨工作面直线度		1.0	0.5	左：0.5　右：0.5

（中国水利水电第八工程局有限公司　冯黎明　刘运华　曾　辉）

滩坑水电站泄洪洞工作弧门设计

（一）概况

滩坑水电站位于浙江省青田县境内的瓯江支流小溪中游河段，电站金属结构由引水发电系统、泄洪系统、施工导流系统三部分组成，其中泄洪系统设有6孔表孔溢洪道和1条泄洪洞。泄洪洞布置在左岸溢洪道与左坝肩之间，是一个三结合综合利用的建筑物，全长为815.58m，其主要功能是在500年一遇洪水时与溢洪道联合泄洪，水库检修时放空水库，及施工前期用于度汛泄洪，泄洪洞最大泄洪流量为1764m^3/s。在泄洪洞的进口布置有事故闸门，工作闸门布置在洞中部，工作闸门孔口尺寸（宽×高）为7.0m×7.0m，底槛高程65.0m，施工期工作闸门在115.0m设计水位下可局部开启调节水位，即操作水头50m；正常运行后165.87m（设计洪水位）挡水位，并在此水位下全开全闭操作运行，设计水头102.0m，总水压力89 000kN。工作闸门采用弧形闸门，液压启闭机操作，液压启闭机操作室设有一台桥机，用于启闭机的安装及检修。

（二）闸门止水型式的选择

1. 主止水　泄洪洞工作闸门正式投运后的水头高达102.0m，属高水头。国内外高水头弧门常用的止水型式有三种：预压式（即常规式，无突扩门槽）、偏心铰压紧式止水（需突扩门槽）和充压式止水（需突扩门槽）。考虑该工程正式投运后，泄洪洞工作弧门长期关闭挡水，500年一遇的洪水时才全开全闭运行，故封水是其重要功能。预压式由于可能存在的漏水并振动的风险，首先予以排除。剩余两种止水型式理论上均可用于该工程，但由于该弧门孔口尺寸7m×7m，要保证7m宽两偏心铰轴的同步转动，操作系统较复杂，而造价相对较低的充压式止水已能满足弧门全开全闭及长期封水的要求，故该工程最终选用了充压式止水作为主止水。

2. 辅助止水　无论是偏心铰压紧式止水还是充压式止水，闸门启闭过程中，门叶面板需脱离主止水，此时门叶面板与主止水间形成的缝隙会出现高压水流喷射现象，易引起空蚀并诱发闸门振动，同时，主止水内外侧的压差，会使主止水头部发生歪斜，影响闸门关闭时的封水效果。故在主止水外侧增设一套常规的预压式止水作为辅助止水，以改善主止水的受载状况，并避免大的射水。辅助止水侧止水采用方头P形止水，顶止水采用转铰式止水。辅助止水在施工期，还可满足弧门局部开启的要求，即在施工期工作水头约50m，仅投运常规水封足以满足运行要求，进入正常运行后，主水封再投入运行，以满足高水头止水的要求。

（三）弧门结构设计

门槽突扩后，弧门的实际尺寸为宽8604mm，高（弧长，未包括吊头）10 390mm，弧面曲率半径14.0m，总水压力89 000kN，其规模已达国内领先水平。

1. 水流流激振动研究　该弧门尺寸大、工作水头超过100m，闸下流速高达35m/s，运行时弧门在水中的自振频率若与水流脉动频率耦合将产生共振。为避免有害振动的产生，委托南京水利科学研究院进行了流激振动试验。结构弹性模型比尺1∶20，水工模型和水弹模型比尺1∶25。水工模型动水压力试验表明，脉动压力随着弧门开度的增大而逐渐增大，脉动强度均在15%左右，脉动压力主频在0～5Hz左右；结构弹性模型实验发现，虽然原设计的弧门结构主横梁与支臂的单位刚度比取了规范的下限5.5，其结构强度和刚度也均满足规范要求，但弧门的一阶模态频率为8.42Hz，实际运行工况下按80%考虑约6.73Hz，没有完全脱离动水激振的主频区0～5Hz。因此，对弧门结构进行了优化，在上支臂与门叶结合处增加了两块加筋板，上下左右支臂间增加了两层“十字”交叉的空间联接槽钢。优化后闸门的一阶模态频率提高到11.04Hz，基本脱离动水激振的主频区；水弹试验研究表明，弧门相对较大振动发生在0.2～0.3开度和0.8～0.9开度范围，三个方向的振动以侧向最大、切向次之、径向最小，但在规范操作、止水良好的情况下不至于产生有害振动。

2. 分节方式及面板加工　弧形闸门的设计除了要保证结构具有足够的强度和刚度外，还应便于制造加工、运输和安装。尤其是本深孔弧门要求面板外表面进行机加工，以保证启闭过程的顶止水封水的可靠性，面板加工的可行性显得尤为重要。设计过程就主横梁和主纵梁两种常用的结构型式进行了比较。由于孔口尺寸接近方形，从结构布置的角度两种型式均是合理可行的，主横梁结构弧门采用双主梁结构，可沿高度方向分成三节制造，每节重量不超过45t，水平次梁和主横梁均为直梁，加工方便，但面板加工需分三次进行，且门叶的装夹找正工艺相对复杂；主纵梁结构弧门门叶由面板、垂直次梁、横梁和主纵梁组成，沿宽度方向分两节制造，单节重量约65t，垂直次梁和主纵梁需弯成弧形，梁系制造相对复杂，但面板加工时，可将单节门叶横卧进行机加工，相对方便，易于保证精度。受中标制造厂吊装容量的限制，此弧门选用了主横梁布置，分三节制造，门叶节间设有连接板，节间由普通螺栓连接，连接板间的贴角焊缝承受剪力，连接板同时还为面板加工时的定位找正提供了方便。弧门采用4轴数控的落地镗铣床加工，横向分节弧门面板加工的方法与纵向分节弧门有所不同，主要程序如下：①单节门叶横向放置，弧门面板正对机床主轴，门叶弧度角平分线与水平面平行，先加工出门叶左右两侧弧面和节间连接面的轮廓线，轮廓面宽度约50mm；②以加工好的轮廓面为基准，以多面形加工原理加工面板弧面；③多边形的棱角用抛光片打磨去除。弧门整体拼装后的曲率半径偏差达到0～1mm。

（四）主止水设计

主止水设计主要需确定三方面的内容：一是门叶面板与止水头部的间隙的确定；二是止水的断面结构和材质；三是充泄水系统的设计。

为了解决第二方面的问题，在调查了国内工程运用状况的基础上，设计了三种不同型式的止水断面，其中断面1分别采用南京金三力橡塑有限公司的Ld-19和成都蜀都水利水电工程配件总厂的橡塑复合水封橡胶两种不同材料，断面2和断面3采用Ld-19，委托南京水利科学研究院进行了水封的试验研究，试验成果见表1。

表 1 水封试验成果列表

	断面 1(Ld-19)	断面 1(橡塑复合)	断面 2	断面 3	备注
水封外伸量	>40mm	>50mm	>40mm	>20mm	背压 1～1.25MPa
残余变形	无	无	无	1mm	
静水水密性试验	背压<库压	背压=库压	背压≤库压	背压≤库压	面板与水封头间隙 5～25mm
动水试验	头部偏向无压侧，封水效果较好	头部未偏向无压侧，封水效果较好	头部偏向无压侧，封水效果较断面 1 差	头部偏向无压侧，封水效果较好	

从表 1 可以看出，无论是外伸量还是封水性，断面 1 均相对较好，故确定断面 1 作为该工程的主止水断面；动水试验显示橡塑复合材料的头部偏斜较少，但两种材料均能满足工程要求，最终由制造厂确定选用了金三力的 Ld-19。试验还提示了如下成果：①止水两翼的预压缩量 10mm 可保证不漏水及止水端部不被拉出；②止水断面在安装后，头部会有所外伸，模型中平直段外伸 2mm，转弯段外伸 7～8mm。

影响门叶面板与止水头部间隙的因素较多，具体包括闸门受水压后变形量、止水的制造、安装误差、压板装配后止水头部外伸变形量、止水残余变形、闸门的制造、安装误差、门槽的制造、安装误差、温度影响等。门叶面板与止水的初始安装间隙的确定既要保证主止水在闸门受载压缩等各种不利因素组合产生最大间隙时能安全封水，又要确保此间隙大于 0mm，以避免启闭时发生门叶刮擦主止水压板，甚至切割主止水的现象。经反复测算，将此间隙定在 7mm，假定泄洪洞安装时和实际运行时的最大温差是 20℃，可保证运行过程中，实际出现的间隙在 4～24mm 之间。

为了尽量减少安装误差，借鉴类似工程的施工经验，要求泄洪洞弧门的安装顺序是先装门叶，再装门槽。水封实际安装时间在 2006 年 10 月到次年的 2 月，是一年中气温最低段，预计实际间隙会更理想，估计在 7～21mm 之间，可很好地保证主止水的封水效果。

充泄水系统主要应满足充水增压、保压、排水泄压、充排水过程的自动充排气等主要操作功能。弧门完全关闭后，水泵从库区取水往止水背部空腔内充水加压，使止水橡皮变形外突，并压紧在弧门面板上封水，该弧门的充水增压采用了两套增压泵互为备用，直接从水库取水，设计充水压力（即背压）为 1.2MPa。考虑弧门长期关闭，系统需要设置保压回路，尽管试验在 25mm 的间隙时利用库压均能保压，但出于安全考虑，系统仍设置了蓄能器保压和库压保压两条并联管路，实际需要的保压压力需要现场调试确定。排水泄压阀设在主止水下部，以确保止水背部的水完全排光，启门前，打开泄水阀，主止水背部放水卸压，主止水头部自动完全缩回。由于泄水阀位置较低，防护等级采用 IP57，并用密闭金属盒包裹保护。在充压系统出口还设有一只安全泄压阀和两只压力控制器，分别作为系统的高低压保护，当系统压力低于设定值时，水泵启动，往蓄能器和水封背部增压，当系统压力高于设定值时，安全泄压阀自动泄压保护，若自动泄压阀故障，压力继续上升，则高压保护的压力继电器自动跳闸保护。系统还分别在主止水的上部和操作系统的最高点设置了自动充排气阀。为避免误操作，闸门的启闭与主止水的充泄水操作相互闭锁。

（五）结语

泄洪洞弧形闸门及其液压启闭机 2006 年 9 月开始安装，2007 年 4 月 30 日完工并通过单体验收，工程 2008 年 4 月下闸蓄水，目前水库水位 135.6m，弧门挡水水头约 70m，主止水尚未投入运行，弧门止水的封水效果尚有待考验。

（中国水电顾问集团华东勘测设计研究院
金晓华　齐尔鸣　胡坚柯）

红花水电站金属结构设计

（一）工程概况

红花水电站位于广西柳江县，在柳州市下游约 30km 处，是《珠江流域西江水系柳江综合利用规划报告》确定的柳江干流最下游一个梯级，总库容 30 亿 m^3，装机 220MW；是一座以发电、航运为主，兼顾灌溉、旅游、养殖等综合利用的低水头径流式大型水利水电工程。工程等级为一等，规模为大(1)型，设计洪水标准：100 年一遇设计，1000 年一遇校核。

（二）金属结构总体设置

红花水电站金属结构包括泄水闸、厂房和船闸三部分。泄水闸共 18 孔，孔口宽度 16m，设上游检修闸门2扇，闸门为露顶平面滑动闸门，启闭设备为坝顶门机；工作闸门18扇，闸门为露顶平面滚轮闸门，启闭设备为固定式卷扬机；下游检修闸门1扇，闸门为浮式叠梁门，启闭设备为手拉葫芦。厂房部分有机组6台，设进水口前沿浮式拦污排一条，拦污排为升降式；进水口拦污栅共18扇，每台机组3扇，为倾斜露顶滑动式，启闭设备为耙斗式清污机；进口检修闸门6扇，每孔1扇，以满足施工期机组安装挡水的需要，闸门为潜孔平面滑动闸门，启闭设备为坝顶门机；尾水事故检修闸门6扇，每孔1扇，以满足施工期机组安装挡水的需要，闸门为潜孔平面滚轮闸门，启闭设备为台车。船闸1孔，为单线一级1000t级船闸，闸室净宽18m，设有上闸首工作闸门和下闸首工作闸门，闸门型式均为人字闸门，启闭设备为液压启闭机；上闸首平面式挡洪检修闸门，启闭设备为坝顶门机；下闸首浮式叠梁检修闸门，启闭设备为电动葫芦；输水廊道2条，左右各1条，上下闸首共设工作闸门和检修闸门各4扇，工作闸门为潜孔平面滚轮式，启闭设备为液压启闭机，检修闸门为平面滑动式，启闭设备为电动葫芦等。

整个电站共计有各种闸门49扇，倾斜式滑动拦污栅18扇，浮式拦污排1条，各种启闭设备共有26台。总工程量为12 320t。

（三）金属结构优化设计

1. 坝顶双向门机

（1）按常规设计，泄水闸、进水口和船闸部位坝顶应分别选用不同的启闭设备。该工程设计中，经与土建各专业协调配合，将这些部位的闸门门槽和吊物孔上下游位置尽量靠近一条线布置，用1～2台双向坝顶门机即可完成任务。门机轨道贯通于厂房、泄水闸、船闸以及左右岸门库段，使用方便，大大节省了工程量，且提高了机械设备的利用率。

（2）该门机最大容量为2×1600kN，最大扬程53.5m，轨上扬程15.5m，轨距7m。为了保证门机行走运行的安全以及稳定性，通过优化设计，降低门机重心，减少倾翻力矩；行走机构采用先进的变频技术，以保证门机的起、制动过程缓慢平稳加速；并严格控制门机大、小车启升速度和行走速度。

（3）泄水闸、厂房进水口和船闸闸首各闸门宽度相差较大，为了统一使用该门机，设计了三根规格不同的自动抓梁与主钩相配；另外还设计了一根带推力轴承的单钩平衡梁，专门用于厂房机电设备的吊运。

（4）初步设计阶段门机重量为440t，施工图设计阶段进一步进行优化，使门机重量减轻到394t，比原来减少了46t。

2. 泄水闸工作闸门　该闸门孔口尺寸（宽×高）为16m×18m，设计水头17.598m，属于超大型闸门。其优化设计情况如下：

（1）由于水库流量调度比较复杂，局部开启控泄频繁，曾考虑采用弧门方案。但根据设计规范规定，弧门支铰宜布置在过流时不受水流及漂浮物冲击的高程上。由于该工程上、下游泄洪水位高出正常蓄水位较多，若要满足规范推荐方式布置，需增大支臂长度，金属结构和土建工程量都比平面门方案高。通过采用新技术、新材料，解决了平板闸门的弊端，最终选定了平面定轮钢闸门，大大节省了工程量。

（2）大孔口闸门主支承以前多采用台车式结构，但台车式支承结构非常复杂，制作不便，而且需要较大的门槽深度，要求更宽的闸墩宽度，增加工程布置的难度。在方案比较时，也考虑过采用金属调心滚动轴承，但这种轴承需要经常加注润滑脂，且密封要求很严。通过调研，决定采用自润滑关节轴承。该轴承可以自动调心，能适应闸门的变形，避免了侧向力对门槽的破坏，滚轮不会因闸门的变形受卡阻，又不需要日常的维护保养。为方便布置，该闸门主轮采用后置式带轮架线接触筒支轮，使用自润滑关节轴承，以适应因闸门变形而在梁端形成的偏角，确保滚轮的线接触特性，解决了大跨度、高轮压主支承轮的设置难题。主轮支座处采用偏心轴套，克服了传统偏心轴带来的密封偏心问题。

（3）根据工程调度需要，洪水期泄水闸工作闸门需经常作局部开启，以宣泄洪水，保护柳州城。为进一步论证该门型及门槽的可行性，保证闸门运行的安全可靠性，在施工图设计阶段，委托南京水利科学研究院对该闸门做了水力学及激流震动模型试验。通过常压模型试验，考查闸室段水力学特性，分析门槽水流空化特性，把握作用于门体的水动力特性；分析闸门结构的模态特征、揭示闸门水弹性震动状态，寻找闸门结构动态薄弱环节，提出抗震优化方案，制定合理运行操作规程。

3. 船闸输水廊道工作闸门门槽　该闸门是潜孔式平面定轮闸门，孔口尺寸2.6m×3.2m，工作水头17.71m，处于空化的临界状态。船闸整体模型试验表明，廊道工作闸门门楣体形若设计不妥，不但对廊道产生气蚀，对闸门和门槽本身也会产生气蚀。为寻找合适的门槽型式，委托南京水利科学研究院做廊道工作闸门门楣1∶1的切片试验。经过多种水位组合的试验，结果表明：若采用适当的补气方案，对消除廊道工作闸门开启过程的空化现象很有效。通过比选，门槽除按Ⅱ形错距门槽设计外，在门楣沿宽度方向设置了许多进气管，利用开门瞬间产生的高速水流进行补气，消除空化现象。

4. 拦污排设置　红花水电站属低水头径流式电站，采用灯泡贯流式机组。该机型对水头损失十分敏感，根据以往的经验，在进水口前沿设置一道拦污排。该拦污排型式为浮筒自动升降式，最大跨度（直线距离）275m，按悬链线设计，最大矢高14m，设计最大拉力1400kN。拦污排由上下游锚头装置、中间拦污浮箱装置以及安全牵引装置等组成。中间拦污浮箱装置由分节浮箱铰轴连接而成，每节浮箱挂有拦污栅，为拦污排的主体部分。上、下游锚头装置均设计为活动浮式钢结构台车支承型式，滚轮支承在锚固槽里，各由一台PCL控制的QPQ400kN的固定卷扬机启吊，可随水位自动升降。

（中水珠江规划勘测设计有限公司　黎子球）

韩国潮汐电站钢闸门防腐蚀方案研究

韩国GAROLIM（贾洛林）潮汐电站工程位于韩国西部海岸，距韩国首都首尔120km，为单库单向退潮发电模式。电站总装机容量520MW（20×26MW）。工程建成后，其总装机容量、单机容量均将成为世界上潮汐电站之最。贾洛林潮汐电站由发电系统、水闸系统和船闸系统等组成，设机组进水口20孔、水闸12孔、船闸1道。金属结构设备包括门槽87套（含5套门库），闸门28扇、门机5台、台车式启闭机1台、液压启闭机12套。总工程量为11 672t，其中闸门（含门库）埋件2368t、闸门6720t、各类启闭机设备2584t。可以看出，贾洛林潮汐电站金属结构工程量很大，防腐蚀任务很严峻，必须予以高度重视。

（一）海洋钢结构的腐蚀特点

钢闸门是潮汐电站的重要组成部分，长期处于大气、海水干湿交替及海水环境中，受到不同水质、日光、温度等环境影响和泥沙、冰凌、漂浮物和船舶的撞击等物理、化学和电化学作用，其腐蚀速度与在淡水中比较明显加快。对沿海水工建筑物调查表明，有的钢闸门运行15年，构件因严重腐蚀，承载能力降低1/3～2/3；有的钢闸门甚至仅使用10年，就因闸门腐蚀穿孔而造成门叶失稳破坏。江苏省善后挡潮闸门面板厚度为10mm，使用不到20年发现普遍锈蚀穿孔现象，平均点蚀速度达到每年0.5mm。据统计，沿海水利和航道工程每年用于钢闸门防腐蚀保护维护的经费约占全年维修经费的60％。

（二）常用防腐蚀方法

1. 涂料保护　涂料保护是将涂料涂装在金属表面形成保护层，将金属基体与电解质或空气隔离，抑制发生腐蚀的条件产生，以达到防腐蚀目的。防腐蚀涂层一般由与基体金属附着良好的底漆和具有耐候、耐水性的面漆组成，而中间漆宜选用能增加与底、面漆结合力且有一定耐蚀性能的涂料。金属防腐涂料的品种很多，常用的主要有富锌底漆、环氧类或聚氨酯（聚脲）类涂料等。根据使用环境及运行工况选用不同的涂料，配合正确的施工工艺，才能使性能优良的涂料达到预期的保护作用。经常处于水下或潮湿状态的水工钢结构，宜选用具有良好的耐水性和耐蚀性的涂料；有海生物附着可能的结构，应使用防污涂料；水上部位宜选用耐候性和耐蚀性良好的涂料；受高速水流冲刷的结构或部位，宜选用耐水性和耐磨性良好的防腐涂料。涂料保护的特点是施工方便、造价相对低廉。但常规涂料在海洋工程上使用时，其保护效果不好，主要是防腐涂层寿命短、易脱落、不能有效防止海生物附着。

2. 热喷涂金属保护　热喷金属保护是将金属丝熔融喷射到钢铁表面上，形成涂层，以防止钢铁腐蚀的方法。热喷金属涂层对钢铁具有双重的保护作用：首先是物理覆盖作用，将钢铁基体与环境隔离；其次，当涂层有孔隙或局部损坏时，金属涂层与基体构成腐蚀电池，金属涂层成为阳极，钢铁基体成为阴极，由于电化学作用使得金属涂层溶解，而达到保护钢铁目的。在淡水环境中，一般选用的热喷涂金属材料以锌为主；海水环境中，则首选铝、锌铝合金等材料。热喷涂金属层与钢铁基体之间具有良好的附着力，韧性较强，也能适应结构受力而产生的变形、热胀冷缩及振动等情况，因此不易发生翘皮、脱壳等破坏现象。热喷金属保护与常规涂料保护相比，防腐蚀效果大大提高，保护年限也较长。但在海水环境中喷金属层消耗较快，其保护寿命大大低于淡水环境中的使用寿命，一般为10年左右，特别是主轨踏面、止水座板采用不锈钢材料时，喷涂金属层及钢闸门与不锈钢形成腐蚀电池，腐蚀速度明显加快。

3. 阴极保护　将金属进行阴极极化以减少或防止金属腐蚀的方法称为阴极保护法，是一种从根本上抑制金属电化学腐蚀的方法。阴极保护技术发明至今已有一百多年的历史，在土壤和海水等介质中已得到广泛应用，世界上很多国家已制订了阴极保护设计标准和规范。阴极保护可以通过外加电流或采用牺牲阳极两种途径实现。外加电流法由于结构复杂，管理要求高，其广泛使用受到一定限制。牺牲阳极法，是通过在被保护的金属上连接一种电极电位比被保护金属更负的金属（称为牺牲阳极，主要材料有锌合金、铝合金、镁合金），以牺牲（消耗）阳极为代价而达到防腐目的。牺牲阳极法由于安全性高、无需管理而受到广泛的应用。阴极保护不仅可以防止钢结构的均匀腐蚀，而且还能有效防止各种局部腐蚀，如点蚀、晶间腐蚀、应力腐蚀、电偶腐蚀等，从而使被保护钢闸门的使用寿命成倍延长。但是此方法对缺乏电解质的空气和浪溅区钢结构的保护效果并不理想。

（三）推荐方案

通过对3种防腐蚀方法的分析，得知喷金属保护可以有效防止闸门在空气中的腐蚀，而牺牲阳极保护可以延长水下热喷涂层的使用寿命，防止闸门腐蚀。若将两种防腐蚀方法结合起来，就能够有效地防止潮汐电站钢闸门在空气和海水中发生腐蚀破坏，据了解，这种方法已在部分工程上应用，并已取得良好的效果。

牺牲阳极保护法的实施较简单，只需将牺牲阳极进行合理的设计并焊接在被保护的钢结构上即可，在运行中不需要专门维护和管理，费用低，保护期一般可达15～20年。保护期内，钢闸门水下部位不会出现任何锈蚀状况；空气—海水交替变化部位也得到有效保护。

按照业主要求，针对韩国贾洛林潮汐电站特点，提出了如下两个推荐方案：

方案一：电弧热喷涂铝加牺牲阳极保护　具体施工方法：①金属表面喷砂除锈Sa3级；②热喷涂铝涂层最小局部厚度大于200μm，铝线材中铝的含量大于或等于99.5%；③铝涂层表面采用环氧锌铬黄封孔剂封孔处理（黏度小，厚度不计）；④金属涂层表面采用两道环氧云母中间漆涂装，每道涂层的干膜厚度为100μm，共200μm；⑤设计高潮位（校核高水位）以上采用两道可覆涂聚氨酯面漆涂装，每道涂层的干膜厚度为50μm，共100μm；设计高潮位（或校核高水位）以下采用两道防污涂料涂装，每道涂层的干膜厚度为50μm，共100μm；⑥采用牺牲阳极阴极保护措施。

方案二：热喷涂锌加牺牲阳极保护　具体施工方法：①金属表面喷砂除锈Sa2.5级；②热喷涂锌（可采用电弧喷涂或火焰喷涂），涂层最小局部厚度大于300μm，锌线材中锌的含量大于或等于99.99%；③锌涂层表面采用环氧磷酸锌封孔剂封孔处理（黏度小，厚度不计）；④金属涂层表面采用两道环氧云母中间漆涂装，每道涂层的干膜厚度为100μm，共200μm；⑤设计高潮位（或校核高水位）以上采用两道可覆涂聚氨酯面漆涂装，每道涂层的干膜厚度为50μm，共100μm；设计高潮位（校核高水位）以下采用两道防污涂料涂装，每道涂层的干膜厚度为50μm，共100μm；⑥采用牺牲阳极阴极保护措施。

上述两个方案中，应首选方案一，即：采用电弧热喷涂铝方式喷涂。只有当不具备电弧热喷涂施工条件的情况下，才可采用方案二火焰热喷涂锌。

（四）类似工程

我国已有多个工程已采用热喷涂金属结合牺牲阳极方法对海水中运行钢闸门进行防腐蚀保护，效果均比较理想。表1是钢闸门采用热喷涂金属加牺牲阳极保护的工程不完全统计表（表中施工时间统计于2006年末，仅供参考）。

表1　海水中热喷涂金属加牺牲阳极保护钢闸门

序号	工程名称	规　模	施工时间
1	镇江谏壁节制闸钢闸门牺牲阳极保护	15扇钢闸门（污染淡水）	2002年
2	淮河入海水道海口闸闸门牺牲阳极保护	16扇钢闸门（海水）	2004年
3	江苏大丰闸钢闸门牺牲阳极保护	7扇钢闸门（淡海水）	2004年
4	盐城射阳河闸钢闸门牺牲阳极保护	35扇钢闸门（淡海水）	2005年
5	江苏滨海新闸钢闸门牺牲阳极保护	8扇钢闸门（海水）	2006年
6	盐城翻身河闸钢闸门牺牲阳极保护	11扇钢闸门（海水）	2006年
7	南京武定门节制闸	18扇钢闸门（污染淡水）	设计中
8	江苏连云港新生节制闸	19扇钢闸门（海水）	设计中

（五）结语

综上所述，钢闸门防腐蚀技术直接关系到闸门的使用寿命，虽然，所述3种常用防腐蚀技术在特定运行条件下对闸门保护是有效的，但是针对韩国潮汐电站运行条件的特殊性，其中任何一种方案都存在局限性。经过对各种防腐蚀方案分析及对现有类似工程调查研究，综合考虑各种因素，提出了采用热喷涂金属加牺牲阳极保护的组合方案及相应具体施工方法。

推荐的钢闸门防腐蚀方案已经以“韩国贾洛林潮汐电站金属结构防腐蚀方案建议书”的形式提交业主。目前该建议书已经得到了业主和咨询工程师的批准。

（中国水电顾问集团西北勘测设计研究院　杨　凡）

超声波衍射时差法技术在瀑布沟水电站蜗壳焊缝质量检测中的应用

超声波衍射时差法作为一种新型的焊接检测技术，在国外众多行业的管道及压力容器焊缝质量检测中已得到广泛运用，国内核电、石油等行业的大型压力容器及管道焊接检测也正逐渐推广，但在水电行业，该技术尚处于探索引入阶段。通过瀑布沟水电站蜗壳焊接质量检测的具体运用和实践证明，该技术不仅具有良好的安全性、准确性和可追溯性，而且解决了传统射线检测方法的环境污染、施工干扰和辐射源对人体的伤害等一系列问题，保障了施工安全，提高了检测效率，在水电站大型金属结构设备的焊缝质量检测中具有广阔应用前景。

（一）超声波衍射时差法技术简介

超声波衍射时差法英文全称是：TIME-OF-FLIGHT DIFFRACTION，简称 TOFD。该检测技术是在 1977 年由 Silk 根据超声波衍射现象提出。检测时使用一对或多对宽声束探头，每对探头分置在焊缝两侧，声束覆盖检测区域，遇到缺陷时产生反射波和衍射波。探头同时接收反射波和衍射波，通过测量衍射波传播时间和利用三角方程，来确定出缺陷的尺寸和位置。图 1 所示为 TOFD 技术的整体设计。检测时，波传播路径如图 2 所示。

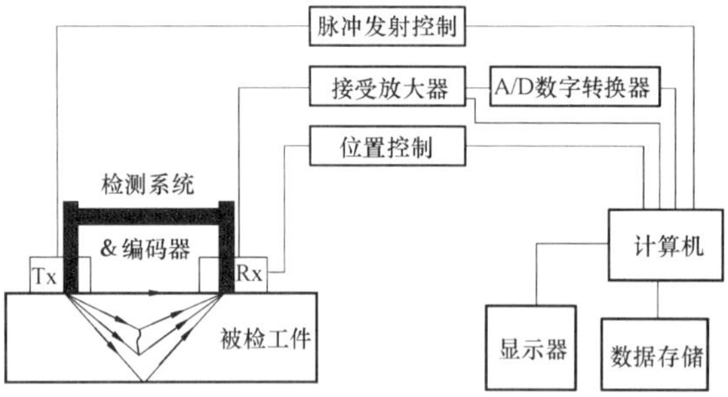

图 1 TOFD 技术的整体设计图

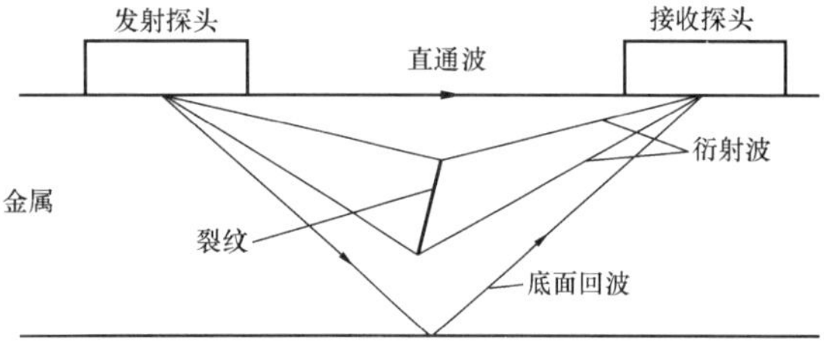

图 2 TOFD 技术的波传播路径

（二）在瀑布沟水电站运用情况

瀑布沟水电站安装 6 台单机容量 550MW 水轮发电机组。蜗壳材质为 ADB610，最大板厚 120mm，最小板厚 25mm，最大内径 8m；2、4、6 号机组为 35 节，单台蜗壳焊缝长度约为 750m；1、3、5 号机组为 23 节，单台蜗壳焊缝长度约为 600m。

在经过多次咨询、论证、研究并借鉴其他行业和单位经验的基础上，征得设备制造厂家同意后，瀑布沟水电站率先在 6 号机蜗壳焊接检测中试验运用该技术。由安装单位委托有丰富经验和实力的公司作为蜗壳探伤外委单位，并由业主公司委托的第三方检测单位代表业主对探伤单位的技术方案、检测质量、标准进行审核及过程监督，确保检测质量。在验证成功运用 TOFD 技术后，编制企业标准，规模推广应用。

由于 TOFD 技术国家标准及水电行业标准尚未建立，作为国内率先采用 TOFD 技术的水电站之一，针对 TOFD 技术的特点，瀑布沟水电站采取了以下检测方案，以确保蜗壳制造工期及焊缝质量。

（1）制造、安装单位的检测范围及检测方法为：全部焊缝的内外表面进行磁粉探伤；全部焊缝进行 100%的超声波探伤；全部纵缝、上下碟形边焊缝和舌板焊缝进行 100%的 TOFD 检测。

（2）第三方检测的检测范围及检测方法为：对全部环焊缝按 20%的比例进行超声波探伤（UT）；对蜗壳凑合节纵焊缝按 100%的比例进行 TOFD 检测，其他纵焊缝按 30%的比例进行 TOFD 检测；对蜗壳凑合节合拢环焊缝按 100%的探伤比例进行 TOFD 检测；对蜗壳与座环过渡板、舌板连接焊缝按 100%进行 TOFD 检测。

按照《瀑布沟水电站焊缝质量检测方案》，蜗壳焊缝检测按照先磁粉探伤，再超声波探伤，最后 TOFD 检测的顺序进行。已完成 4 台蜗壳的焊缝检测，经过磁粉和超声波探伤合格后，再进行 TOFD 检测，发现异常并进行解剖、处理的缺陷数量统计数据见表 1。

表 1 UT 检测合格后 TOFD 检测出的不合格缺陷数量统计表

蜗壳编号	缺陷性质				缺陷总数
	裂纹	未熔合	气孔	夹渣	
1 号机蜗壳	30	14	42	11	97
4 号机蜗壳	5	5	—	2	12
5 号机蜗壳	2	—	—	—	2
6 号机蜗壳	3	5	1	—	9

TOFD 检测技术具有对人体无伤害、可交叉作业、无需采取特殊防护措施等特点，瀑布沟水电站每台蜗壳采用该技术较合同约定的射线检测方法带来如下效益：①蜗壳焊缝本身探伤速度加快 20d 左右（第一台机组的焊缝焊接检验工作提前 29d 完成）；②避免因射线探伤导致厂房内其他工作面 20d 左右停工损失；③提高了对裂纹及未熔合等危险性缺陷检测的准确性，减少后续质量事故处理的经济损失及工期损失；④避免了射线探伤的环境污染并节省了额外的射线探伤环保措施费用。

（三）TOFD 与射线检测方法的比较

通过瀑布沟水电站的运用总结及实证对比分析，

TOFD检测与合同约定射线检测方法比较情况见表2。

（四）结语

在实践运用的基础上，参考国内外的一些行业应用成果及相关标准，国电大渡河流域水电开发有限公司制订了企业标准Q/DDR001－2008《水力发电设备焊接接头超声波衍射时差法检测》，并获得国家有关部门备案许可。为大渡河流域水电站应用TOFD检测技术提供了技术依据，同时也极大促进了水电站焊接检测技术的进步。

TOFD技术在瀑布沟水电站蜗壳焊缝质量检测中的成功应用，不仅改善了电站施工的工作条件、提高了设备的焊接质量，而且缩短了关键工期、减少了潜在环保风险、充分体现了现代水电建设中“以人为本”的科学发展观理念。该技术在水电工程的焊缝质量检测中必将具有广阔的应用前景。

表2　TOFD与射线探伤检测的优缺点比较表

内容＼方法	TOFD检测＋超声波	射线＋超声波（合同约定）
优点	1. 对比验证中，TOFD检测技术的缺陷检出准确率远大于常规检测技术； 2. 可以识别向表面延伸的缺陷，采用TOFD和脉冲回波相结合，可以实现100%焊缝覆盖； 3. 沿焊缝作一维扫查，具有较高的检测速度； 4. 定量、定位精度高；根据TOFD检测结果可对工件进行安全性评估； 5. 工期短、效率高，对人体无害等； 6. 经济效益显著	1. 能较直观地显示工件内部缺陷的大小和形状，易于判定缺陷的性质； 2. 射线底片可作为检验的原始记录供多方研究并作长期保存
缺点	1. 由于超声波的局限性，TOFD难以检查焊缝近表面的缺陷； 2. 由于TOFD检测的灵敏度很高，因而对一些粗晶材料，晶界的反射会类似缺陷的反射，不易区别； 3. 要求表面光滑、须打磨	1. 检测缺陷厚度有限，不能确定缺陷所在的深度位置，给焊缝的返修带来很大困难； 2. 检测速度较慢； 3. 缺陷检测准确度、精度有限（不易发现间隙很小的裂纹和未熔合等缺陷以及锻件和管、棒等型材的内部分层性缺陷）； 4. 射线对人体有害，需要采取额外的防护措施

（国电大渡河流域水电开发有限公司　黄张豪　李　林）

中國水力發電年鑒

8

科学研究与技术创新

水 电 科 学 研 究

水利水电工程风险及其应对技术的研究

一、水利水电工程风险问题

水利水电工程风险表现为发展性和累积性。在工程规划、设计和施工阶段存在的风险因素，若没有充分被识别，没有规避、控制或者转移，在运行阶段一定会因某种外因诱发而显现和发展，并具有放大效应，甚至可能导致无法控制的事故和重大的损失。

水利水电工程风险具有自然和社会两重属性。自然属性的风险因素包括地质、洪水、结构和抗力的不确定性，在一定程度上取决于人们认识自然的水平，其概率可以通过工程技术和措施加以控制和降低。社会属性的风险因素包括个人社会意识、企业管理、国家甚至国际政治、经济、文化、宗教和风俗习惯等，风险水平是发展变化的，非技术手段能够控制或降低，需要国家的经济基础和上层建筑共同作用，才能够加以控制、降低和转移。

二、我国水利水电工程安全状况

我国是世界上筑坝数量最多的国家之一，现有各类大坝超过 8.6 万座。这些水库大坝在防洪、发电、灌溉、供水及促进生态环境保护等方面发挥着重要作用，是我国防洪保安工程体系的重要组成部分，也是保障国民经济可持续发展的重要基础设施。

但是必须清醒地看到，我国大坝，尤其是修建于 20 世纪 50～70 年代的水利大坝，建设标准偏低，施工质量较差，其中一些病险水坝，不仅难以发挥应有的工程效益，而且极易酿成溃坝灾难，严重威胁下游人民生命财产、基础设施及生态安全。从 20 世纪 80 年代起，水利部和能源部（现国家电力监管委员会）就相继成立了水利部大坝安全管理中心和水电站大坝安全监察中心，分别负责水利大坝和水电大坝的安全管理，定期开展安全检查和安全评价，及时发现和治理大坝安全隐患，大大降低了大坝风险事故和溃坝率。

截至 2008 年底，国家电监会大坝安全监察中心共注册大坝 193 座。1991 年首次定检 96 座大坝，查出 7 座病坝、2 座险坝。2001 年第二次定检 130 座大坝，查出病坝 8 座。二次定检确定的问题大坝，除丰满大坝研究采用重建方案外，其余病、险坝维修加固均已完成或正在实施，已经有 9 座病坝、1 座险坝经过补强加固后恢复为正常坝。

水利部大坝安全管理中心管理 343 座大型水库、2683 座中型水库和所有的小型水库。从 1995 年开始，水利部大坝安全管理中心对大型水库开展安全鉴定。对首批鉴定的 43 座重点病险大坝进行加固，37 座恢复正常运用。此后，又对 1992 年确定的第二批 38 座重点病险大坝进行加固，其中 9 座恢复正常运用，其他正在除险加固中。据水利部统计资料，全国病险水库尚有近 3 万座，病险水库大坝的维修加固任务十分紧迫，加强水库大坝的风险管理是非常必要的。

总结水利水电工程事故的发生，有两条教训值得吸取：①事故的发生既有偶然性和突发性，又有累进性和规律性；②工程的缺陷加上管理不善，总会以事故或灾难的形式毫不留情地表现出来。因此，在水利水电工程安全的问题上，规划、勘察、设计、施工以及运行管理的各方都不应对客观存在的风险麻痹大意、熟视无睹或存有侥幸心理，而应缜密设计、精心施工、留有余地，做好预案，严格监管。

三、水利水电工程风险因素及处理措施

水利水电工程在规划、设计、施工和运行阶段，风险设计的内容各有所侧重，风险处理措施也应有所针对。在工程规划阶段的主要任务是风险识别，重在避让；在可研阶段主要是风险分析，重在防范；施工阶段主要是风险监测，重在控制；而运行阶段是风险管理，重在应急预案，旨在减少风险损失。

（一）在规划选址阶段，识别风险，采取避让措施

规划选址阶段，最大的风险来自活动断裂和巨型滑坡体。规划选址错误，尤其是在活断层上建坝，后期建设采取一切措施都将于事无补。规划修建于美国加利福尼亚州阿美利坚河支流北福克河上的奥本坝就是由于对坝区及其附近多条活断层认识不足而彻底停建的。

在规划选址阶段，采取避让措施可以最大限度地降低或避免风险损失。位于汶川地震灾区的大中型水电工程，虽然遭受了超过其设防烈度的强震，但由于工程选址均避开了活动断层，例如紫坪铺和沙牌水电站分别距离地表破裂带为 8km、32km，建筑物没有

发生同震错断破坏，整体震损轻微。

在选址过程中，还应识别库岸滑坡引起的超标准洪水、库内大型或者巨型滑坡可能造成库中坝的风险。位于意大利东部阿尔卑斯山区派夫河支流的瓦依昂河的瓦依昂拱坝，就是由于与大坝仅“一沟之隔”的托克山滑坡高速骤然下滑，导致大坝及水库报废。

存在巨大地质风险的河段，不适宜作为规划坝址。正确的坝址选择是远离活动断裂，避开滑坡体。在难以避开的情况下，至少不应在这些河段设置高坝大库，避免显著改变山体水文地质条件，降低触发地质灾害的概率和风险损失。汶川地震造成唐家山堰塞坝，使得下游2座小型水电站完全损毁。在如此巨大的地震灾害面前，2座小水电损毁而并未造成次生灾害，与工程规模的正确选择是分不开的。潜在地质风险河段，首先采取避让措施，其次是控制工程规模。

（二）在可研设计阶段，分析风险，采取防范措施

在可行性研究设计阶段，要对可能存在的各种风险进行分析、对风险级别进行评估，选择合适的坝型和合理的枢纽布置格局以防范风险，优化建筑物设计以降低风险，提出可靠的设计指标以控制风险，编制科学的运行调度方式以管理风险，综合提高枢纽工程的抗风险能力。

从防范地质风险角度，布置挡水建筑物时应首先考虑地形、地质条件的适应性。混凝土拱坝坝肩抗滑稳定问题是主要风险；混凝土重力坝应充分重视深层抗滑稳定问题；深厚覆盖层上当地材料坝坝基不均匀变形和渗透稳定问题是主要风险，要加强坝基防渗设计。从防范洪水风险角度，应优先选择混凝土坝，利用坝身泄洪，可降低枢纽布置风险；若覆盖层深厚，必须选取当地材料坝，则应考虑增大泄水建筑物的泄流能力，枢纽布置中应重视泄洪消能区的冲刷对挡水建筑物基础的影响。从防范地震及地震地质灾害风险的角度，在高山峡谷地区要优先选择地下厂房布置方案，上坝和进厂交通尽量采用隧洞方案；要加强对地面建筑物上部边坡工程地质条件的勘探分析，采取措施防范危岩体和变形岩体对建筑物造成的危害。位于吉尔吉斯斯坦共和国纳伦河下游的托克托古尔水电站，由于未认识到两岸坝肩岩体强烈卸荷对拱坝建设的风险，在施工过程中，原枢纽总体布置方案和施工方案被全盘或基本全盘否定，致使工程建设耗时17年。漫湾水电站左岸边坡塌滑，主要原因是缺乏对滑移机制的深入认识。

对一些由于有限的地质资料引起的不确定风险，可通过提高建筑物或地基处理的设计指标或设计标准来控制风险。根据国外资料分析，坝基失稳在重力坝事故中占34%，在拱坝中占37%，在当地材料坝中占30%。在我国水利水电工程中，坝基失稳所占比例也较高。坝基处理质量引起的风险具有隐蔽性，后期补强困难，除了提出与建筑物相同的可靠度指标外，更要提出耐久性要求。丰满水电站大坝受当时技术水平的限制，大坝混凝土只有强度设计指标，无抗冻、抗渗等耐久性指标，大坝运行60余年间不断补强加固，但大坝渗漏、溶蚀及冻胀等问题依然严重，未能彻底解决，被迫采用重建方案。

对于主要建筑物和设施设备的风险需要专门评估。坝工设计所采用的分析计算和模型试验成果都是在诸多人为假定和理想条件下求得的，计算参数、模型、判断准则选取不同，计算结果差异甚大，不可盲目信赖或直接引用，必须借鉴类似工程加以分析判断，合理采用。

主要建筑物不仅要求整体安全可靠，更要重视局部风险可控。例如挡水建筑物孔、洞和闸墩等关键部位，既要安全设计，更要局部应力、变形控制设计，降低应力超标开裂的风险和变形过大运行的风险；既要重视预应力锚索、钢筋等应力设计，更要关注锚索和钢筋引起的应力转移风险。

临时建筑物改建成永久建筑物的风险也要予以充分论证。改建方案、措施保证、施工方法和施工时间等均需要提出明确的技术要求。美国胡佛水电站和我国二滩水电站导流洞改建成永久泄洪洞，在初次泄洪期间均出现空蚀破坏。双沟水电站导流洞改建成生态流量泄放洞，在首次蓄水期间，因气爆致使生态引水竖井坍塌、钢管爆裂。

要高度重视采用新技术、新材料、新工艺或新设备引起的风险。对于未经实践的新事物，可积极采用，但更需稳妥。高抗冲磨材料聚脲在航空母舰的跑道上使用效果很好，但用在高速水流部位效果很差，如小浪底工程泄洪冲沙孔、景洪工程消力池底板、溪洛渡工程导流洞等部位采用的聚脲材料均全部损坏或彻底损坏，无法发挥其应有的作用。新技术可在风险小的工程或者部位积极采用，经充分实践后推广使用。例如碾压混凝土技术首先在低坝、纵向导流围堰等次要部位成功应用后，逐渐应用于高坝，目前已经成功建成高216.5m的龙滩碾压混凝土重力坝。

此外，还应分析单一梯级的超标准洪水、梯级水库洪水与区间洪水的组合、梯级水库防洪标准不协调可能引起的连环溃坝，以及地震引起的库岸滑坡。以上风险发生的概率较低，可以通过制订应急预案的方式加以防备。

（三）在工程施工阶段，监测风险，采取保障措施

施工期的主要任务是风险控制，其目标是安全保证、质量优秀、工期相对提前和造价相对节约。在施

工阶段，主要落实设计提出的各项风险防范措施，进行风险控制。施工安全和质量控制是水利水电工程施工期间面临的两大风险，各单位往往重进度，轻安全和质量，从而产生客观存在和主观意识引起的风险。

工程开挖时期，存在实际揭示的地质条件可能与可研勘测预测成果不一致引起的客观风险和参建单位重开挖轻支护的主观风险。因此，在工程开挖时期，要遵循动态设计原则，根据施工开挖揭示新的地质条件，或者根据安全监测资料，动态调整设计。

混凝土浇筑或大坝填筑期间，工程风险由安全风险转向质量风险，由表观转向内部，由显像转向隐蔽，具有不可逆性。大坝填筑尤其是混凝土浇筑期间，施工质量风险若得不到有效控制，后期补强困难，运行期处理难度更大。丹江口大坝和葛洲坝 1 号船闸下右 2 块均有这方面的教训。

（四）在工程运行阶段，管理风险，制订应急预案

建设期未彻底控制和避免的风险因素，在水库大坝运行阶段，尤其在运行初期会集中出现。从 56 个国家的 1609 个溃坝案例分析，在已知运行年数的 629 个溃坝案例中，238 个溃坝案例发生在运行初期的 5 年内，其中 124 个溃坝案例发生在投入运行后的第一年内，施工期和投入运行后第二年的溃坝数量也较多。即使规划合理、设计完美、施工质量优良的水利水电工程，后天的健康运行仍然需要维护和保养。因此，大坝的风险管理应贯穿于工程运行的全过程。

大坝的风险管理要明确责任主体，在组织上全面建立风险责任制。大坝风险不仅威胁工程安全，更涉及公共安全。大坝风险责任制要以地方政府行政首长负责制为核心，按照隶属关系，逐库落实同级政府、水库主管部门和水库管理单位的各级责任人，明确责任，并建立责任追究制度。

大坝的风险管理要制定应急预案、建立风险等级报告制度，为降低和避免风险损失提供制度保证。应急预案应包括组织体系、运行机制、应急保障和监督管理等内容。应急预案要注重实用性和基本要素的完整性、预防措施的针对性、组织体系的科学性、响应程序的操作性、保障措施的可行性。报告制度中要明确各类事故的报告主体、程序和时限，说明水库基本情况，事故发生的时间、地点和原因，事故的发展趋势、危害程度、威胁对象，以及拟来取的措施与落实情况。

四、对安全、质量和进度的讨论

规划选址阶段的风险识别和可行性研究设计阶段的风险分析，主要取决于技术、认识和实践水平。迄今我国科研、设计技术水平已有很大的提高，只要按照基本建设程序进行规划、设计，保证合理的勘测设计周期，开展必要的咨询，严格审查，保证勘察设计质量，该阶段的风险基本是可控的。施工阶段的风险，除了受技术因素限制外，还存在领导意识、行政干预和考核目标等非技术因素，这可以说是当前最大的风险因素。对此，国家七部委联合发出《关于加强重大工程安全质量保证措施的通知》，要求各级政府、企业强化安全质量意识，加强各环节风险管理，为排除非技术风险因素的干扰提供了行政保障。但施工期安全、质量与进度之间的矛盾，尤其是开发企业施工进度考核制度仍然是工程最大的主观风险因素。因此，需要从国家层面加强对安全与质量的监督，更需要各企业制定科学的进度目标奖励和安全、质量的奖惩制度，尤其需要制定对称的安全、质量奖惩制度。事后惩治的威慑作用固然重要，但事前的防范和奖励更为重要。

五、结束语

水利水电工程的风险是客观的、普遍存在的，但采取适当措施，也是完全可以防范的。在一定条件下，能够避免风险的发生或最大限度地降低风险损失。

水利水电工程的风险因素包括自然风险和社会风险。自然属性的风险水平在一定程度上是不变的，决定于工程技术水平和工程措施的有效性；社会属性的风险水平是发展变化的，非技术手段能够控制或降低，只有国家主管部门、大坝建设管理者制订并执行更加科学严格的管理措施，才能控制、降低和转移大坝所带来的风险，维护国家安全和社会稳定。

水利水电工程的风险管理是集自然因素与社会因素于一体的复杂的系统工程，是贯穿于风险识别、分析、评估、决策和控制各个环节的动态管理过程，其目的是最大限度地降低风险水平。

（中国水电工程顾问集团公司　杜效鹄　周建平）

丹江口重力坝加高裂缝处理研究

（一）概况

受水利部长江水利委员会长江勘测设计研究院的委托，根据已知资料，对丹江口大坝加高工程中的裂缝问题进行了研究，分析了具有代表性的 4 号坝段、右联 1 号坝段和 12 号坝段，主要完成了以下工作：

(1) 采用数值方法模拟加高之前坝体在各种水位运用条件下的裂缝开展情况，分析裂缝形成原因。对影响裂缝形成和发展的各种因素进行计算条件和计算参数的敏感性分析，并与坝体裂缝现状作对比，以调整计算参数，为大坝加高之后裂缝扩展分析及大坝安全度评价打下基础。

（2）对加高部分坝体进行温度徐变应力场仿真模拟，考虑新老混凝土的非线性接触过程，模拟大坝加高之后的各种运用工况下纵向裂缝的扩展情况，明确坝体各部位的应力变形情况，对加高前后的坝体应力和位移、纵向裂缝开展深度和宽度、坝体稳定等各个方面作出比较分析，对加高之后的大坝安全性作出合理评价。

（3）考虑坝体在位移、应力、纵缝张开度等各个因素的情况下，对拟定的裂缝处理方案进行方案比较，提出合理的建议。

（4）以12号坝段为代表，对水平缝、纵缝和劈头缝作适当概化，在较不利情况下，对新老坝体沿水平裂缝层面抗滑稳定安全性的分析。

项目于2007年4月开始，2008年12月结束。

（二）4号坝段的研究成果

（1）坝体纵缝在高温季节闭合，在低温季节时张开，坝体纵缝的形成主要是由于温降造成。特殊的施工、运行条件使得坝体部分起裂成为诱导缝后，水平裂缝在温降荷载作用下向下开展。裂缝开展深度的计算结果受水位、起算时间、弹性模量、抗拉强度、线胀系数、断裂能等不同因素的影响。

（2）在低水位运行工况下，大坝坝踵始终处于受压状态。而考虑纵缝张开后，坝踵仍然保持受压状态。

（3）大坝加高之后，坝体纵向裂缝的开展没有发现明显恶化现象。一方面由于新浇筑混凝土对于老坝体下游面起到保护作用，原暴露在空气中的老坝体下游面成为内部边界，温度变化幅度明显减小，导致坝体出现纵向裂缝的温降荷载也相应减少很多。另一方面是坝体下游贴坡混凝土对老坝体的压紧作用。高水位运行工况时，坝体纵向裂缝基本处于闭合状态。受到下游新坝面温降作用，新老混凝土结合面在冬季会出现部分张开现象。

（4）大坝加高之后坝踵应力没有发现明显的恶化现象。相对于新混凝土开始浇筑之前，加高完成之后同样是145m水位运行工况下，坝踵压应力水平有所提高，第二主应力及竖直向正应力水平提高了约1.7MPa，至2010年7月1日大坝坝前水位抬高至170m高程，由于水压力的作用，坝踵处竖直向压应力水平随时间变化的幅值明显减小了，变化范围由原来的－5.2～－15.98MPa减小到了－2.0～－9.27MPa。从整个计算过程来看，在计算时间段内坝体各个应力指标均随四季温度的变化而发生周期性变化，但坝踵一直是处于受压状态。

（5）从坝体踵及坝体应力水平的角度来看，三种纵向裂缝处理方案基本相当，而从限制纵裂缝进一步发展的角度来看，局部拆除和廊道顶部拆除方案缝面的张开度明显优于补强方案，前两者相差不大。三种处理方案对新老混凝土交界面的张开度影响比较小，三种情况下计算出的新老混凝土交界面的张开情况基本相同。

（三）右联1号坝段的研究成果

（1）坝体在自重、水压力及渗透压力作用下，位移分布连续，水平裂缝不会张开，坝体作为一个整体在外荷载作用下发生变形，由于坝前水位较低，坝体顶部有微小的向上游变形。坝体下部向下游变形，最大顺河向位移为0.81mm。坝踵处第一主应力为－0.633MPa，处于受压状态。坝体其他部位也基本处于受压状态。

（2）在变化的温度荷载作用下，水平裂缝会发生张开与闭合现象。夏季气温升高时，坝体表面处于受压状态，而坝体内部处于受拉状态，坝体内部水平缝就有可能会张开。反之，冬季温度降低，坝体表面处于受拉状态，坝体内部处于受压状态。外部水平缝有可能张开，而内部水平缝则会进一步压紧。

（3）水平缝的存在与否对坝踵应力没有太大的影响，而由于水平缝的张开对温度应力有释放作用，对坝体上部拉应力有一定减小作用。

（4）与水平缝存在与否类似，新老混凝土结合面的结合状况，对坝踵应力没有太大的影响，而对坝体上部拉应力水平有一定影响。从计算结果看，按照接触问题计算求解新老混凝土结合面工作状况的结果与假定直立段脱开、斜坡段闭合的结果基本相同。从新老混凝土之间布置接触点，在按照接触问题用有限元混合法求解的计算工况中，求解得出的新老混凝土结合面最大张开度沿高度方向的分布也可以印证这一点。

（5）大坝加高前后相比，大坝加高之后坝踵应力没有明显的恶化现象发现。相对于新混凝土开始浇筑之前（2006年3月18日，距离起算时刻351天），加高完成之后（2008年1月20日，距离起算时刻1024天），同样是145m水位运行工况下，坝踵压应力水平有所提高，第二主应力及竖直向正应力水平提高了约2.4MPa，至2010年7月1日（距离起算时刻1912天）大坝坝前水位抬高至170m高程，由于水压力的作用，坝踵处竖直向压应力水平随时间变化的幅值明显减小了，变化范围由原来的－6.04～－20.02MPa减小到了－1.53～－11.2MPa。从整个计算过程来看，在计算时间段内，坝体各个应力指标均随温度的四季变化而发生周期性变化，但坝踵一直是处于受压状态。

（四）12号坝段的研究成果

（1）坝体的纵向裂缝张开度随气温发生周期性变化，冬天有张开的趋势，夏天有闭合的趋势。当坝体贴坡和加高部分完成后，纵向裂缝的开裂深度没有变化，但张开度却略有增大，并随气温发生周期性变化。水位抬高到 170m 水位时，对缝的张开度起到了一定的限制作用，但是由于裂缝位置处于坝体上部，限制作用不是很明显。

(2) 大坝加高完成且由于水化热等产生的非稳定温度场稳定一段时间后，随着外界气温的变化，在低温季节坝顶新加高混凝土出现了部分开裂现象。这是由于温度降低时，坝体表面因温降而收缩，上游坝面向上游变形，下游坝面向下游变形，在坝体中形成上下游方向的拉应力，当超过混凝土的抗拉强度时，缝面被拉开。

(3) 受到下游新坝面温降作用，新老混凝土结合面在冬季会出现部分张开现象。坝体的新老混凝土结合面在浇筑完成的第一个温降过程中发生开裂。缝的开度随气温发生周期性变化。坝前水位抬高到 170m 水位时，新老混凝土结合面上的最大开度也未发现明显减小。

(4) 坝体拉应力分布主要受温度荷载控制。夏季气温升高时，坝体表层一定深度的热膨胀受到坝体内部混凝土的约束，坝体表面处于受压状态，而坝体内部处于受拉状态，拉应力主向为竖直方向。反之，冬季温度降低，坝体表面处于受拉状态，但是由于温降荷载的影响深度有限，表层受拉区域深度并不深。而水下部分坝面则由于水温变化幅度较之气温变幅要小，温度荷载引起的坝体应力没有那么显著。由于存在施工间歇，贴坡部分新浇筑混凝土在 141m 高程层面上存在相对较大的拉应力。

(5) 在本次计算所采用的条件下，大坝加高水位抬高到 170m 水位之后坝踵应力有一定恶化现象。相对于新混凝土开始浇筑之前，加高完成之后同样是 145m 水位运行工况下，坝踵压应力水平有所提高，第二主应力及竖直向正应力水平提高了约 1.1MPa，坝前水位抬高至 170m 高程时，由于水压力的作用，坝踵处竖直向压应力水平随时间变化的幅值明显减小了，变化范围由原来的－3.1～－6.4MPa 减小到了－1.5～－4.4MPa。从整个计算过程来看，在计算时间段内，坝体各个应力指标均随温度的四季变化而发生周期性变化，但坝踵竖直向正应力一直是压应力。而从坝踵 A 点第一主应力的变化情况来看，蓄水之后坝体应力状况出现了恶化。由加高之前－0.35MPa 的压应力转变为 0.6MPa 的拉应力。

(6) 为了对比裂缝的存在对加高前后坝体应力变化的影响，本报告还计算了坝体为完全弹性体的情况，即不考虑坝体的水平裂缝、两条竖向裂缝和新老混凝土结合面的张开，其他计算条件和前面的计算完全相同，两种情况下的坝踵应力几乎没有差别。也就是说，裂缝的存在对坝踵点应力没有太大影响，大坝加高后水位抬高至 170m 水位时坝踵应力的恶化现象主要是由于水荷载的变化以及水位的变化导致坝体边界温度的变化引起。

(7) 大坝加高前沿 150m 高程水平裂缝层面的抗滑稳定安全系数为 4.62，加高后安全系数有所减小，变为 3.65，都满足设计规范的要求。

(河海大学)

溪洛渡大坝孔口和预应力闸墩应力分析与配筋设计研究

本项目根据已知资料，对溪洛渡大坝孔口配筋问题进行了研究。项目于 2007 年 8 月开始，2008 年 12 月结束。主要完成了以下工作：

(1) 建立大坝、地基静力计算模型，根据孔口和闸墩应力分析的计算要求，进行单元剖分，模拟坝身表孔、深孔、导流底孔和闸墩结构，反映闸墩预应力锚索的施加作用，进行计算模型的建模工作。

(2) 分析在坝体自重、水压力、坝前淤沙压力、温度等荷载作用下已建坝体的应力和变形，其中坝体自重分析时近似考虑施工过程的影响。

(3) 分析大坝建成后运行阶段坝体自重、水压力、坝前淤沙压力、温度、预应力锚索等荷载作用下的结构应力和位移，坝体自重分析时近似考虑施工过程的影响。

(4) 根据结构整体应力分析成果，取每种工况下拉应力较大的典型孔口作为脱离体进行加密计算，精细分析孔口周边的应力和位移。对每个加密脱离体截取适量的典型剖面，根据应力分布图形计算配筋量。

(5) 选择控制工况，对深孔周边和深孔闸墩应力进行正常使用极限状态裂缝宽度复核，从而确定预应力锚索的布置方案及设计参数。

(6) 在空间线弹性计算的基础上，通过适当转化，将空间问题变为平面问题，按平面问题计算。采用非线性钢筋混凝土有限单元法，研究正常使用时钢筋用量及布置形式对裂缝分布与宽度的影响，根据裂缝控制标准调整钢筋用量与布置，进一步完善的配筋方案。

(一) 线弹性应力图形法配筋研究成果

应力计算采用局部加密的静力子模型方法，单元尺寸较小，有效地提高了静力计算精度，同时也提高了应力图形面积的计算精度。

1. 整体计算

(1) 导流底孔模型中坝体 x 方向最大位移为 25.0mm，y 方向最大位移为 106.0mm，z 方向最大位移为32.3mm；对温度荷载产生的应力进行折减后与其他荷载产生的应力进行叠加，坝体最大拉应力为3.9MPa，位于下游坝面277.8m高程；最大压应力为－14.9MPa，位于下游350.0m左右高程的拱端处。

（2）深孔模型中坝体 x 方向最大位移为24.4mm，y 方向最大位移为124.0mm，z 方向最大位移为28.2mm；坝体最大拉应力为3.6MPa，位于4号孔下游闸墩；最大压应力为－13.4MPa，位于1号孔内上壁。

（3）表孔模型中坝体 x 方向最大位移为27.6mm，y 方向最大位移为122.6mm，z 方向最大位移为29.9mm；坝体最大拉应力为3.0MPa，位于1号孔边墩（577.9m高程）；最大压应力为－11.9MPa，位于1号孔闸门支铰处（597.5m高程）。

2. 典型孔口局部加密计算

（1）7号导流底孔在不同工况下，最大拉应力为13.499MPa，最大压应力为－38.535MPa，都位于7号孔下游大梁处。这主要是由于将闸门荷载作为点荷载施加而产生的局部应力集中。从整体看来，拉应力主要集中在下游闸墩与坝体连接处，下游牛腿和大梁处，不考虑应力集中点的应力状况，拉应力最大值在2.5MPa。

（2）4号深孔在不同工况下，最大拉应力为6.596MPa，最大压应力为－21.003MPa，都位于4号深孔下游大梁处。从整体看来，拉应力主要集中在大梁中部、下游闸墩与坝体连接处和出口处孔身两侧，不考虑应力集中点的应力状况，拉应力最大值在4.0MPa。

（3）1号表孔在不同工况下，最大拉应力为5.424MPa，位于边墩右侧；最大压应力为－17.636MPa，位于墩与坝体上游面交界处。从整体看来，表孔拉应力主要集中在表孔孔身部位的边墩和下游侧边墩处，不考虑应力集中点的应力状况，拉应力最大值在3.8MPa。

3. 应力图形配筋

（1）导流底孔配筋计算所得钢筋用量比较少，按照构造配筋基本上就可以满足需求。究其原因：①对于环向钢筋，一方面由于导流底孔位于坝身的底部，承受的压应力较大，另一方面由于在水荷载的作用下拱坝径向剖面的拱推力是很大的，这样孔口在内水压力的作用下周围产生的拉应力也不是很大，环向钢筋用量不大；②对于径向钢筋，由于选取的特征孔口所在位置的坝身明显向上游倾并且坝身厚度较大，预应力锚索也有效的分散了闸门水荷载产生的拉应力，所以径向钢筋用量也不大。

（2）深孔的用筋量计算中，环向钢筋用量也较小，设计钢筋量可以满足抗拉需求，原因同上。径向钢筋用量计算结果较大，深孔孔身段和近出口处孔身段径向钢筋需求量很大，分别为13 980.415mm²/m和23 552.262mm²/m。但是，这些部位钢筋用量较大主要是由温度荷载引起的，由于坝体分缝，温度应力会得到一定程度的释放，考虑温度荷载作用计算所得的钢筋量是保守的。此外，在水荷载作用下，计算所得钢筋用量不大，设计钢筋完全可以满足需求。大梁处梁向钢筋需筋量很大，为14 806.208mm²/m，其环向需筋量不大。其他部位设计用筋量均能满足需求。

（3）表孔的孔口结构与深孔和导流底孔明显不同，其布筋方式也有区别。表孔孔口处径向钢筋需求量较大，为13 586.069mm²；进口段边墩两侧的径向钢筋和垂向钢筋需求量较大，分别为24 518.121mm²/m和15 736.513mm²/m；中墩用筋需求量比边墩要小，中墩左侧径向钢筋需求量为9506.464mm²/m；出口段边墩下游侧垂向钢筋需求量为23 097.926mm²/m，中墩左下游面垂向钢筋需筋量为40 289.438mm²/m。钢筋需求量大的地方其计算所得配筋量远大于实际配筋量。由于我们的计算是保守的，在切取应力图形的时候，控制范围往往选择比较大，即使距离钢筋较远位置的拉应力也认为由钢筋来承担，因此出现钢筋计算用量过于保守的情况。表孔其他部位设计钢筋用量均能满足需求。

（4）深孔设置预应力锚索后，典型剖面上的最大拉应力不超过2.086MPa，导流底孔设置预应力锚索后，典型剖面上的最大拉应力不超过1.616MPa。由预应力锚索配筋计算可知，按照设计情况施加预应力锚索之后，深孔和导流底孔出口段闸墩、牛腿、大梁处拉应力明显减小，某些部位甚至转化为压应力，表明设计的预应力锚索张拉吨位和布置位置是有效的。

上述成果是按弹性力学法计算出来的拉应力图形进行配筋，实际上是假设超过混凝土抗拉强度区域的混凝土完全开裂，不承担拉应力，而由钢筋来承担拉应力，从而力图达到提供一个最终的强度保证，这种设计一般来说是保守的。

（二）非线性钢筋混凝土有限单元法研究成果

利用空间计算结果，采用平面有限单元法，在4号深孔右边闸墩及4号深孔靠上游、中游和靠下游等部位截取4个剖面，进行承载能力按应力图形面积配筋及正常使用时钢筋混凝土有限元裂缝宽度计算。

1. 预应力闸墩

（1）闸墩施加预应力后，预应力钢筋经过部位的水平正应力已受压，主拉应力虽大于零，但应力值已很小；最大拉应力出现于闸墩顶面与大坝交界处附近，主拉应力最大值大于混凝土抗拉强度标准值，该部位有开裂的可能。因而，在闸墩顶部附近应多配置一些钢筋。

（2）从控制裂缝的角度出发，采用Ⅱ级钢筋比Ⅲ级钢筋有利，将一部分钢筋集中布置于闸墩顶部比沿高程均匀布置钢筋有利。

（3）当配5层36@300＋5层36@600＋20层32@600＋10层25@600时，闸墩顶部的裂缝宽度、垂直裂缝长度和钢筋应力最大值分别只有0.31mm、6.2m和114MPa，裂缝宽度已能满足设计要求。

2. 深孔环向

（1）设计水位与校核水位产生的应力与温度应力叠加后，应力值增大（以受拉为正）；温升产生的应力大于温降产生的应力。

（2）靠上游剖面和中游剖面的所有工况均未出现拉应力，即在设计水位、校核水位及设计水位加一倍的温升与温降、校核水位加一倍的温升均未出现拉应力。因而，靠上游面剖面与中游剖面的孔口环向只需按构造配筋。

（3）靠下游剖面的孔顶与孔底受压，孔左右两侧除靠近孔角处受压外其余受拉，拉应力最大值出现于孔左右两侧的中部。当设计水位加0.6倍温升时，最大拉应力已小于混凝土强度标准值，即在正常使用时孔口不出现裂缝，故温度作用参与系数最小取为0.6。

（4）当下游剖面采用Ⅱ级钢筋，孔顶与孔底为1层28@200，左侧与右侧为2层32@200时，表面裂缝宽度最大值只有0.06mm，裂缝长度最大值为1.4m，钢筋应力最大值只有55MPa，能满足设计要求。

（5）非线性计算表明，随混凝土强度等级降低，裂缝条数与长度增加，裂缝宽度有所减小，钢筋应力降低；随温度荷载参与系数的增大，裂缝条数增多，但钢筋应力与裂缝宽度变化不大。

（河海大学）

核安全级（1E级）GFD系列固定型铅酸蓄电池组支架抗震计算分析

在建和拟建的方家山、福清、桃花江核电站是我国能源战略中的重要部署，为国家重点工程。拟使用于上述核电站核岛的GFD系列固定型铅酸蓄电池组，作为紧急情况下的应急电源，对地震极端条件下的核安全至关重要。过去此类产品都依赖于进口，选用国产GFD（OPzS）系列蓄电池对于核电站设备国产化有重要战略意义。

本项目的目的是，对应用于方家山、福清、桃花江核电站核岛部分的GFD（OPzS）系列蓄电池组支架结构在极端地震环境下（S2，安全停堆地震）的内力场进行分析，确定结构特定部位内力，为该产品的生产设计和在核电厂使用提供依据。具体是按方家山、福清、桃花江核电站的1、2号机组范围的地震环境要求，对代号为LAA、LBA、LBB、LNA～LND、9LBG、LBJ、LBP、LCA、LCB、9LCD的GFD电池组支架进行基础反力分析。

项目内容包括以下几点：

（1）建立适合与上述特定环境和特定结构的地震动力分析模型。

（2）依照甲方提供的楼层反应谱对上述结构的多组合、多工况进行地震响应计算和内力分析。

（3）给出各工况下的支架结构与基础结合部位的内力值，供实际工程使用。

通过计算分析，报告在给定的SSE反应谱地震条件下，给出LAA(54只)、LBA(53只)、LBB(53只)、LNA-LND(27只)、9LBG(16只)、9LBG(24只)、LBJ(27只)、LBP(53只)、LCA(23只)、LCB(23只)和9LCD(23只)蓄电池组支架与基础连接处的立柱最大内力值、地震响应分布、自振频率等成果，供方家山、福清、桃花江核电工程参考使用。

本项目于2009年2月开始，2009年4月结束。

（河海大学）

白鹤滩水电站和桐柏抽水蓄能电站建设运行对经济社会拉动效应研究

水电站建设运行可以为项目建设当地和供电区域带来巨大的社会效率和经济效益。白鹤滩水电站位于金沙江下游，建成后将成为“西电东送”中部通道的骨干电站。桐柏抽水蓄能电站位于浙江省天台县，是一座日调节纯抽水蓄能电站，总装机容量1200MW（4×300MW），于2001年12月31日正式开工，1号机组于2006年5月25日投产，2号机组于2006年10月26日投产，3号机组于2006年12月5日投产，4号机组于2006年12月27日投产。针对水电站建设运行对经济社会拉动效应的测算主要还停留在定性研究层面的现实，为客观地得到经济社会效应的测算结果，中国水电顾问集团华东勘测设计研究院作为白鹤滩水电站、桐柏抽水蓄能电站的设计单位，委托河海大学针对这两座水电站建设运行对国民经济的拉动效应及发挥的提供就业等社会效应展开定量研究。

课题组通过方案的比选，选用投入产出模型对水电站建设投资在生产环节的经济拉动效应进行测算分析；采用边际消费倾向计算在消费环节由于水电站建设投资使居民收入增加导致消费需求增加而产生的乘数效应。在测算提供就业的社会效应时，按照水电站建设的首轮社会总产出乘数，计算出水电站建设带动本身及其他部门的产出，根据各部门劳动力的平均工资水平，分别计算在生产环节为本行业以及社会其他部门提供的就业岗位个数。预测运行期的经济效应时，在对区域全社会用电量与经济增长之间关系分析的基础上，采用回归模型计算长期弹性等指标，预测分析水电站运行对供电区域经济的拉动效应。定量研究表明，白鹤滩水电站建设、运行将为四川、云南两省及主要供电的华中、华东区域带来巨大的经济社会效应；桐柏抽水蓄能电站建设、运行将为浙江省带来较大的经济社会效应。研究成果可为有关部门制定水电站建设、运行的相关政策提供重要的依据。

本项目于2008年1月开始，2009年5月结束。

（河海大学）

区域水资源系统供水短缺风险分析及经济损失评估研究

该项目针对区域水资源短缺风险提出了包括风险识别、风险分析、风险评价、风险处理到风险决策的理论体系和具有可操作性的模型及方法。主要内容及技术要点为：

（1）在系统描述风险来源和对水资源短缺风险识别的基础上，利用水资源供需平衡分析模拟模型建立了区域水资源短缺风险分析模型，利用水资源投入产出宏观经济模型计算水资源短缺的经济损失及其概率分布。

（2）分别采用模糊综合评判方法、支持向量机方法、集对分析方法和基于最大熵原理的区域水资源短缺风险评价模型对水资源短缺风险分别进行了综合评价，同时提出了基于地理信息系统的水资源短缺风险的综合评价方法。

（3）从需水管理和供水管理两方面探讨了采取各种风险处理和调控的技术手段，对水资源系统风险性能指标的影响程度。利用系统理论中风险决策的理论与方法，将水资源短缺风险决策分为两个层次，即单目标风险决策和多目标风险决策，详细研究了水资源短缺风险的决策过程。

（4）基于供给与需求均衡原理，从两个方面建立了水资源短缺风险的最优控制标准理论，一是针对整个区域水资源保障系统，二是在区域发生水资源短缺风险后的调控准则。

（华北水利水电学院）

吉沙水电站厂房后山坡三维有限元分析研究

该项目研究采用的方法为：综合分析整理已有的地质研究成果，确定各高边坡的基本工程地质条件等；确立边坡岩体变形破坏模式和边界条件；建立边坡变形破坏地质模型，并判断边坡变形与稳定性现状；采用三维有限元数值模拟方法，对边坡稳定性进行模拟分析，评价边坡的稳定性。主要研究内容为：

（1）根据现场调查与分析，确立边坡岩体变形破坏模式和边界条件，建立边坡变形破坏地质模型，确定计算边界范围；确定计算模型。

（2）根据周边地形地质条件和厂区布置型式，建立包括厂房和后山坡的整体三维非线性有限元模型，分析计算厂房后山坡计算模型的初始应力场。

（3）运用三维有限元模拟方法，对崩塌堆积体在原始状态、施工期和运行期等多种工况下进行模拟，研究其应力应变分布规律和在不同工况下应力与位移的变化，进而研究它们的稳定性。

（4）根据有限元数值模拟和极限平衡方法综合分析在给出的支护参数、地质参数和地下水位下，后山坡从天然状态到不同的开挖坡度时在天然、饱和状态和有无地震状态下的稳定性。

（5）根据前述分析的结果，对厂房后边坡的开挖和治理方案进行初步论证。分析抗滑桩加固效果，研究了不同桩长、桩径和桩间距时的加固效果，计算结果表明抗滑桩处理效果是可行的、有效的，抗滑桩加固方案可满足崩塌堆积类边坡工程安全需要。

该项目针对吉沙水电站工程建设中存在的工程区厂房后山坡稳定性问题，运用三维有限元分析方法，模拟边坡开挖过程及崩塌堆积类边坡在原始状态、施工期和运行期等多种工况的应力应变分布规律和应力与位移的变化情况，对工程边坡稳定性和加固理论与方法进行了综合研究。突破以往极限平衡理论指导设计施工的方法，填补了以三维有限元计算成果验证边坡稳定性、指导边坡设计施工的空白。研究成果极大地简化了边坡开挖量的确定及支护方案的优化设计工作，丰富了针对崩塌堆积类边坡加固的理论研究方法和手段。通过对抗滑桩加固效果的研究和分析，验证了抗滑桩加固对崩塌堆积类边坡加固的可行性和有效性，为崩塌堆积类边坡的加固设计提供了理论依据。

本项研究为厂房边坡的稳定性分析提供了理论支

持，可以广泛应用于类似边坡工程的研究和计算工作。与初始方案相比，本项目研究方案减少坡体的开挖深度，大大减少开挖量，减少工程投资，加快工程进度；优化支护方案，减少抗滑桩的长度。在安全方面，采用此方案施工后减少坡体开挖，加快工程进度，增大厂房开挖的安全性；在社会效益方面，新的开挖和支护方案减少坡体开挖的坡度，加快工程建设进度。

（华北水利水电学院）

高陡崩塌边坡稳定性分析及BQD置入式中空锚杆加固治理技术研究

该项目通过大量的数值模拟分析和现场加固效果检测验证，全面分析BQD中空注浆锚杆、岩体和砂浆的应力特征，同时研究锚杆和岩体的变形，揭示中空注浆锚杆在碎裂结构岩体边坡加固的变形规律。应用刚体极限平衡分析方法、离散单元法（DEM）及大规模三维拉格朗日元（FLAC 3d）仿真数值分析等方法，对边坡的稳定性、不同类型锚杆的加固技术、滑坡影响范围和危害进行了全面分析研究，提出了工程加固措施。

通过对锚杆加固后边坡的现场检测（锚杆的抗拉、抗拔、锚杆及锚固体应力应变测试）结果分析，对比数值计算结果，全面分析中空注浆锚杆、岩体和砂浆的应力特征，以及锚杆和岩体的变形规律，提出了中空锚杆加固高陡崩塌边坡的技术方案。

该项目对边坡工程中中空锚杆的加固机理及效果的理论研究和技术分析部分属岩土工程加固理论研究的创新。成果已应用于工程实践，获得了较好的工程效果。

（华北水利水电学院）

混凝土高拱坝震害预警与对策系统研究

本项目依托小湾工程，对混凝土高拱坝的震害预警与决策系统关键技术进行研究，包括场址区域信息化、强震监测系统的硬件开发、强震记录数据库建设和大坝结构的抗震分析等。本项目将结构抗震理论、工程地震理论、地震和地质理论与电子技术、遥测传输通信技术相结合，研究了重要坝址地区震源机制和传播途径；建立了大坝抗震数学和力学模型库；开发了我国重要水工大坝震害监测远程自动化管理数据库、强震记录数据库和分析资料库；研制了大坝数字自动化固态存储强震仪。

本项目的混凝土高拱坝震害预警与决策系统对大坝强震监测、数据分析、地震信息管理与查询、结构安全评价、震害预警等进行了研究和改进，经进一步完善可成为混凝土重力坝或土石坝等的强震监测和地震分析与预警系统。

关于大坝的抗震安全关键技术问题，本项目对地震动输入、大坝的结构动力反应、大坝震害预警反应等进行了系统集成，提高了对大坝抗震安全的分析评估水平。

在吸收国内外有关强震安全监测技术最新成果的基础上，研制开发出24位固态存储多通道强震仪，具有实际推广应用价值。

本项目的混凝土高拱坝震害预警与决策系统在三峡、二滩等实际工程中得到了较好的应用。

（中国水利水电科学研究院）

300m级高混凝土面板堆石坝可行性研究

本研究时间为2007～2009年，在系统总结200m级高面板堆石坝建设经验与教训的基础上，针对澜沧江上的古水、怒江上的马吉、西藏的如美和黄河上游的茨哈峡等水电站大坝的综合特点，采用室内试验和数值计算分析的方法，研究了坝高250～300m左右的高混凝土面板堆石坝对这些坝址的适应性问题及其相关对策措施，明确进一步开展可行性研究的重点，为300m级高面板堆石坝方案研究提供技术支撑。项目研究主要包括以下几方面的内容：

（1）国际高混凝土面板堆石坝筑坝技术调研。调研了国外20世纪末至21世纪初修建的主要高混凝土面板堆石坝的建设情况，系统总结了国外高混凝土面板堆石坝筑坝技术的最新进展和经验教训。通过对近期国际上高混凝土面板堆石坝工程建设经验的回顾与总结，研究了近代高混凝土面板堆石坝建设中设计理念和施工方法上存在的技术问题。基于对300m级超高混凝土面板堆石坝建设中面临技术挑战的系统分析，提出了建设超高混凝土面板堆石坝所需解决的关键技术问题。

（2）国内高混凝土面板堆石坝技术总结和反馈分析。采用数值计算分析方法，对洪家渡和三板溪混凝土面板堆石坝进行了应力变形反演计算分析。总结、考察了土石坝反演分析的原理、方法和步骤，对200m级及较低混凝土面板堆石坝已有的计算模型进行了分析和评价。采用邓肯—张E-B非线性模型和沈珠江三参数流变模型，对洪家渡混凝土面板堆石坝的应力变形进行了反馈分析。采用邓肯—张 E-B 非线性模型，对三板溪混凝土面板堆石坝的应力变形进行了仿真分析。计算分析较好的对混凝土面板堆石坝的施工、蓄水过程进行了仿真或反演，较全面的考察了典型的 200m 级高混凝土面板堆石坝的应力变形特性。在反演计算分析的基础上，研究、改进了现有分析模型和计算方法。建立了适用于 300m 级高混凝土面板堆石坝的计算分析方法。

(3) 300m 级高混凝土面板堆石坝稳定性评价与变形控制标准研究。在总结国内外已建 200m 级高混凝土面板堆石坝建设经验和教训的基础上，从坝体应力、变形控制的角度，探讨了 300m 级高混凝土面板堆石坝建设的可能性，研究确定了需进一步开展研究的主要技术方向。研究工作从 300m 级高混凝土面板堆石坝的坝坡稳定分析、堆石材料的渗透稳定分析和坝体的应力变形分析三个方面展开，重点研究特高混凝土面板堆石坝的变形规律与特征，在此基础上，分析、研究了控制与适应特高混凝土面板堆石坝变形、改善混凝土面板应力状态、控制接缝位移的相关工程处理措施。

由于目前各相关工程均处于前期准备阶段，因此本专题的研究主要结合一些潜在工程项目的前期论证和预可研阶段的工作。探讨 300m 级高面板堆石坝建设的可能性和需进一步开展研究的主要技术方向，将为高山峡谷地区、交通运输不便、经济不发达地区选择 300m 级高面板堆石坝奠定理论基础。研究可以大大降低这些地区建坝的投资成本，有着巨大的经济效益和推广应用价值。本项目的研究成果可以为工程设计方案的选取和优化提供强有力的技术支撑。

（中国水利水电科学研究院）

近海风电场海上测风与试验研究

中国水利水电科学研究院于 2007 年 6 月～2009 年 10 月进行了该项目研究。本项目在以下几个方面进行了研究：

(1) 海上施工向陆上转化。与国内已有的海上测风塔采用高桩现浇混凝土承台的设计理念不同，响水海上测风塔采用了钢承台的结构型式。与常规的混凝土承台相比，可以不进行海上立模、绑钢筋、混凝土浇筑和养护等工序，钢承台可以在陆地加工完成，可节省施工时间和减少大型船舶（海上混凝土搅拌船、大型起重船等）的使用，大大减少海上作业的工程量、减少海上施工的时间和节省施工成本，具有明显的优势。

(2) 桩体与承台利用高强灌浆料连接技术。钢承台结构型式对连接段要求很高，通过室内试验和大量计算，连接型式采用了高强灌浆材料灌注为主的连接方式。经规范方法计算和有限元方法校核以及现场运行考验，连接段整体受力较好，能满足不同环境荷载的受力要求。研究的灌浆连接结构获得了国家实用新型专利。

(3) 海上桩基承载力检测的可行方法。与陆地桩基相比，海上桩基检测存在两大问题：①海上条件恶劣，受风浪影响很大，进行静载试验难度大、成本高。②进行高应变锤击时需要大型船舶，进行复打成本高、组织困难。在海上测风塔建设过程中，充分利用滩涂风电场类似地层条件，采用静载试验、埋设渗压计和不同时段的高应变检测，初步推断出：在该地质条件下，初打时的高应变检测承载力是桩基最终承载力的 60%左右，可以利用打桩时进行高应变检测，以此承载力计算桩基最终承载力。

(4) 海上风资源评估方法研究手段。①实验手段上，采用一塔两套测风设备，设置海洋观测设备；②资料丰富度方面，布置了 2 座海上测风塔、1 座滩涂测风塔，加上滩涂的 5 座测风塔和气象站近 30 年的气象资料，该区域内的测风塔密度高，测风数据及环境数据齐全、完整；③研究方法上，采用数理统计、比较研究和数值模拟等多种手段，并根据计算模型独立开发了计算程序。本项目利用这些实测数据开展了环境因素对测风数据的影响、风速与潮位的对应关系、海面粗糙程度与浪高之间的对应关系及海陆风对比等项目的研究，其研究方法、技术路线和研究内容均为国内首次采用。研究成果可信度高，并已用于海上示范风机的设计中。

(5) 测风手段的拓展性研究。根据风资源评估的特点和海上施工的难度，提出了可移动式测风塔的概念，并完成了移动式测风塔的结构设计、就位固定技术、浮运移动等关键技术的研究，为海上测风塔提供了一种新的结构型式，可进一步减少测风成本，具有较好的推广前景。

本项目于 2007 年 4 月完成测风塔选址、初设，5 月完成海上勘探，6 月完成施工图设计，8 月进行海上桩基施工、塔架吊装和仪器安装，2008 年 3 月测风数据传回，2008 年 7 月海洋观测数据传回，截止到 2009 年 10 月，已完成 1.5 年的测风数据收集和评估、1 年的海洋观测数据收集和评估，以及 2 年的运行维护工作。

该项目研究成果为海上风电场建设提供了翔实的风资源数据、海洋数据、地质数据和可供借鉴的施工经验。目前长江新能源公司已在该区域建设了 1 台 2MW 近海试验风机，三峡集团公司正在进行容量为

200MW的近海风电场的可研设计。

（中国水利水电科学研究院）

2009～2015年全国小水电代燃料工程规划调研与编制

中国水利水电科学研究院与水利部农村水电及电气化发展局于2007年12月～2008年12月进行2009～2015年全国小水电代燃料工程规划调研与编制工作。

小水电代燃料是水利部的重点项目，为了保质保量地完成《2009～2015年全国小水电代燃料工程规划》编制，首先对全国24个省（区、市）和新疆生产建设兵团进行了调研，组织各省水利厅和新疆生产建设兵团的相关人员进行规划编制的培训，协助他们先完成各省和新疆生产建设兵团的规划编制，然后在各省编制的规划的基础上，完成了《2009～2015年全国小水电代燃料工程规划》。

（1）规划范围。2009～2015年期间，在24个省（区、市）和新疆生产建设兵团的534个县实施小水电代燃料工程。

（2）规划总体布局。选择退耕还林区和天然林保护区，特别是退耕还林面积相对集中、生态脆弱、农民生活用能以薪柴为主的地区。重点选择中西部地区，优先选择贫困地区、少数民族地区和革命老区。适当考虑东部地区的少数民族地区、革命老区和经济欠发达地区。优先选择农村水电供电地区，尽量避开沼气建设重点地区。

（3）规划建设规模。在2009～2015年期间，在24个省（区、市）和新疆生产建设兵团实施小水电代燃料项目1022个，代燃料装机容量170.56万kW，代燃料年用电量24.38亿kW·h，长期稳定解决170.78万户、677.71万农村居民的生活燃料和农村能源问题，保护森林面积2390亩，每年减少和吸收二氧化碳3400多万吨。

（4）规划投资。小水电代燃料项目总投资141.3亿元，其中代燃料电站建设投资122.87亿元，占86.96%，项目区建设投资18.43亿元，占13.04%。西部、中部、东部中央补助投资占总投资比例为45%（不含西藏）、38%和15%，省级配套资本金占总投资的比例分别为10%、15%和25%，西藏地区小水电代燃料总投资全部由中央给予补助。中央补助资金为56.99亿元，占总投资的40.33%，平均每年8.14亿元。省级配套资金为18.47亿元，占总投资的13.07%，银行贷款为65.84亿元，占总投资的46.6%。

通过建设1022个小水电站，解决农村部分地区的能源问题，改善农民生活条件，提高农民生活水平，保护和改善生态环境。

建立政策支持体系，配套服务体系，提高小水电在农村能源消费中的比重，建立了保障代燃料工程健康发展和良性运行的长效机制。

建立"所有权、经营权、使用权"三权分设的管理体制和"国家补助、企业运作、农民参与、协会监督"的运行机制。

应用联合国的清洁发展机制（CDM），通过碳排放交易，从发达国家获得无偿的资金和先进的技术。

小水电代燃料是非营利公益性项目，从2003年起开始的小水电代燃料试点建设，取得圆满成功，成效显著。

（中国水利水电科学研究院）

黄河水利科学研究院科研项目进展情况

（一）黄河口物理模型关键技术研究

黄河口物理模型关键技术研究是"模型黄河"工程建设的重要工作，已取得较大进展，完成了模型沙选择、模型沙基本特性、河口模型相似律、生潮技术及进口含沙量自动控制技术等专项研究工作，为黄河河口模型试验的开展奠定了较好的前期工作基础。积极开展模型"两技术"研究与应用，完成了非接触免维护式水位计制作工作，并进行了室内及模型的试验工作；完成了激光式水下地形仪制作工作，并进行了室内及模型的试验工作；基本完成了浅滩式超声在线含沙量量测系统研制工作。黄河下游河道模型试验研究开展了运用方式二（15年系列）的工作，30年系列的试验研究工作也已经开始；黄河小浪底库区模型试验研究开展了运用方式二（20年系列）的工作及推荐方案的试验研究工作。

（二）黄河下游"驼峰"河段形成机理及治理措施综合研究

通过总结、调研，完成并向黄河水利委员会提交了黄河下游"驼峰"河段形成机理及治理措施综合研究任务书和工作大纲。并配合有关单位开展了黄河下游"驼峰"河段及"二级悬河"治理试验工程治理必要性、可行性、治理规模、治理效果等关键技术论证工作。

（三）黄河调水调沙关键技术研究

2009年黄河调水调沙生产运行中，黄河水利科学研究院（以下简称黄科院）承担了异重流人工塑造设计、下游河道边界条件分析、下游二维水沙数学模型预测计算、洪峰增值模拟等专项，完成了调控指标确定、预案编制、实时调度、运行效果评估等环节的相关内容，完成了年度调水调沙运行效果后评估报告。

（四）利用并优化桃汛洪水过程冲刷降低潼关高程试验

黄科院承担了利用并优化桃汛洪水过程冲刷降低潼关高程试验指标的优化研究、试验预案设计、实施预案的编制、试验实施和跟踪试验会商决策等任务，编制完成了《2009年利用并优化桃汛洪水过程冲刷降低潼关高程试验调度预案》，并开展了试验效果后评估。对2006～2008年期间“利用并优化桃汛洪水过程冲刷降低潼关高程试验”进行总结评估，并提出评估报告。

（五）“十一五”国家科技支撑计划项目

黄科院承担的“十一五”国家科技支撑计划项目包括“黄河流域水沙变化情势评价研究”、“维持黄河主槽不萎缩的水沙条件研究”、“黄河中下游水沙调控关键技术研究”、“基于GIS的黄河水沙输移模拟系统研发”、“黄河健康修复目标及对策研究”、“黄河流域水沙变化情势评价研究”5个课题和“大坝监测及隐患探测技术研究”专题，在2009年初提交初步成果的基础上，通过归纳、总结、咨询等环节，进一步提升了研究成果水平，项目已完成课题研究报告的撰写及结题相关准备工作。

2009年4月9日，由黄科院、黄河水利委员会水文局联合承担的“十一五”国家科技支撑计划重点项目“黄河健康修复关键技术研究”第一课题“黄河流域水沙变化情势评价研究”课题初步成果专家咨询会议在郑州召开。

课题组通过近2年的攻关研究，评价了黄河中游1997～2006年水沙变化程度，剖析了其变化原因，预测了未来水沙变化情势。同时，分析了诸如开矿、灌溉引水等典型人类活动对黄河水沙变化的作用程度，初步分析了水利水保措施对洪水的影响程度、探讨了水沙变化评价方法。专家组听取汇报后首先对课题的研究成果作了充分肯定，认为课题取得的研究成果对治黄具有一定参考价值。同时，专家们也对研究进展中存在的问题进行了认真分析和指导并对成果的推广应用等问题提出了建议和意见。

（六）黄河中游泥沙输移规律与二维数学模型研究

2009年4月1日，国家自然科学基金委在武汉组织召开了“2008年度国家自然科学基金重点项目验收会”。由黄科院和中国水利水电科学研究院联合承担的重点项目“黄河中游泥沙输移规律与二维数学模型研究”顺利通过了验收，项目评价为A级。本项目重点围绕扩散方程底部边界条件、恢复饱和系数的特性和不平衡输沙时含沙量分布与平衡/不平衡条件的恢复饱和系数计算方法、床面泥沙输移概率与状态概率、水量百分数性质及其作用、挟沙能力级配及有效床沙级配计算方法、非均匀沙挟沙能力、粗细泥沙交换机制、黄河揭底冲刷理论、非均匀推移质输沙规律、高精度数值格式、河势变化模拟、网格自动剖分和基于RS和GIS的三维地形生成、可视化和虚拟现实技术、基于MPI的并行化技术等方面开展了原始创新和集成性创新，在泥沙输移基本理论和模型核心技术等诸多方面均取得了突破性进展。

（七）2009年度国家自然科学基金重点项目申报

7月19～21日，2009年度国家自然科学基金重点项目评审会在长春隆重召开，来自全国各地的评审专家与重点项目申请人员近300人参加了会议。会议期间，国内几十所知名高校与科研院所展开了2009年度国家自然科学基金重点项目申请的角逐。21日下午，由杭州电子科技大学、四川大学、黄科院联合申请的国家自然科学基金重点项目“面向大型工程安全预测与评估的信息融合方法”项目组在会上进行了汇报与答疑。经评审专家现场表决，本项目高票通过审查。

（八）堤坝安全监测信息分析评价系统开发研究

2009年7月29日，黄河水利委员会在郑州组织召开“堤坝安全监测信息分析评价系统开发研究”成果评审会。

项目组汇报了项目研究成果、主要创新点、系统应用等情况，经评审委员会讨论，一致认为成果达到国际先进水平。成果取得的主要创新点有：在常规逐步回归模型中引入门限因子和门限值，采用最佳拟合相关分析法确定门限因子和门限值，提出了一种门限回归分析模型，并成功应用于堤坝安全监测；以界面优化为目标，利用可视化语言将各功能模块以菜单、图标、快捷键等方式嵌入界面，对功能模块进行了优化装配，实现了堤坝监测信息的快速建模与便捷分析。

（九）黄河泥沙重点实验室和工程技术研究中心

2009年9月3～4日，水利部国际合作与科技司会同规划计划司与财务司在郑州主持召开了“黄河水利科学研究院科研能力建设、重点实验室与工程技术研究中心评估会”。评估专家组认真听取了黄科院的汇报，察看了有关项目现场，查阅了相关项目资料，并就有关问题进行了质疑，同时还对水利部黄河泥沙重点实验室和水利部堤防安全与病害防治工程技术研究中心在服务水利行业发展、科学研究和技术开发、人才培养和学术交流、创新机制建设、科研能力建设等方面工作进行了综合考核评估。11月5日，水利部以水国科［2009］538号文发布了对水利部重点实验室和工程技术研究中心评估的结果。依托黄科院建设的水利部黄河泥沙重点实验室、水利部堤防全与病害防治工程技术研究中心评估结果为良好，并得到表彰。

（十）“人造大块石抢险材料研制技术”推广项目

2009年9月20日，水利部科技推广中心在黄科院组织召开“人造大块石抢险材料研制技术”推广项目验收会。该项目在总结利用黄河泥沙制作防汛石料技术的基础上，开展了人造大块石抢险材料研制技术的推广应用，取得了一批技术改进与创新成果：完善并优化了专用固化剂的配方；基于就地取材的原则，以河道泥沙为主要原料，现场生产，自然养护，制造的人造大块石抢险材料代替天然石材，减少了大量天然石料的开采，降低了运输成本；研发出专用切割机具，可根据抢险需要将大块石切割成不同的规格尺寸；研究及试验表明，人造大块石重量达300kg以上，可有效减少根石走失；生产大块石600m³，并应用于实际工程中；编制了《人造大块石制作工艺手册》，培训了一批熟练的操作人员和管理人员。经评审委员会讨论，该项目全面完成了合同规定的任务，达到了合同规定的考核指标，验收组一致同意通过验收，项目综合评价为A级。

（十一）黄河流域（片）山西省病险水库除险加固工程专项检查

根据《关于开展黄河流域（片）病险水库除险加固工作专项检查通知》文件精神，黄科院作为黄河流域（片）山西病险水库除险加固工程专项检查的责任单位，重点执行2009年度黄河流域（片）山西省病险水库除险加固工程专项检查工作。主要检查：病险水库除险加固责任制落实情况；项目前期工作、建设管理、资金筹措及使用管理、已下达投资项目的建设进度、工程质量与安全、工程验收和水库管理与体制改革等情况；历次检查、稽查督导中发现问题的整改落实情况等。黄科院组织专家检查组于2009年7～11月间两次分别对山西省晋城市申庄水库、临汾市巨河水库、运城市吕庄水库等3个中型水库及山西省晋中市田家湾水库、吕梁市瓦窑河、太平、阳坡水库等4个中小型水库进行了全面检查，圆满地完成了预定的检查工作目标。

（黄河水利科学研究院）

泄洪洞内气泡运动的图像测量方法研究

水利水电工程中，空蚀已成为高坝泄水建筑物的关键问题之一。向水流进行人工掺气是解决该问题的常用工程措施，但一些工程在采用掺气减蚀措施后仍有空蚀发生。因此，进一步研究高速水流中气泡运动规律，科学判定掺气保护范围，很有必要。

本项目研究泄洪洞气泡运动参数的图像测量方法，受到国家自然科学基金委员会、二滩水电开发有限责任公司雅砻江水电开发联合研究基金项目资助。通过自制的高速相机实验导轨、发光二极管面光源照明等设备，提高了图像质量，保证了测量精度，解决了不同机位测量数据的融合问题。在此基础上应用MATLAB语言进行数字图像处理，从而得出泄洪洞反弧段流场气泡数量、形状、尺寸及空隙率等参数，并得到了气泡的运动轨迹。该方法可在较大流场的图像测量中使用，测量结果正确，是一种可行的多相流检测技术，对于深入认识掺气水流流场中的气泡运动机理具有重要的科学意义和应用价值。

（一）试验设备与试验方法

试验装置主要包括两个部分，即流体系统和图像采集系统。

流体系统主要由潜水泵、水箱、泄洪洞反弧段、量水堰及空气压缩机组成。整个系统为一自循环系统，实验所用的液相为自来水，其流量通过矩形量水堰来控制；气相为压缩空气，经调节阀门经由进气口（即锐孔）通入反弧水体中，进气口为反弧段底板起始位置的中心，锐孔直径大小可以通过更换不同型号的针头来改变。

图像采集系统主要包括照明系统、记录系统以及图像采集软件。照明系统光源采用发光二极管，是体光源。图像记录系统采用美国Fastec Imaging公司生产的TroubleShoote高速摄像仪，其分辨率为640×480像素，帧频1000FPS，灰度256级；图像采集卡采用TroubleShoote高速摄像仪配置的1GB内存卡，将高速摄像机摄取的视频文件（AVI文件）存放于计算机中，并在MATLAB环境下，通过函数aviread将avi格式文件转化为bmp格式的图像；采用SAN-NI SAN—70云台镜头控制器，可方便地进行镜头焦距和光圈大小等参数的控制；同时，TroubleShoote高速摄像仪具有实时监测、回放等功能。

为获取满意的图像质量，采取了以下措施：

（1）采用由发光二极管组成的冷光源。考虑到高速摄像仪对光源亮度要求比较高，试验段用有机玻璃制作，光源发热会引起试验段的变形，因此本次试验光源采用发光二极管（LED）组成的冷光源。

（2）选用恒压电源。发光二极管的电源装置，电源频率对光的均匀度影响较大。若采用交流电源，用高速摄像机连续拍摄一组185幅静止物体图像，对这185幅图像分别求平均灰度值，其最大灰度平均值与最小值相差约10%，图像处理难度大。若选用恒压电源，同样拍摄185幅图像，其最大灰度平均值与最小值相差不到1%，可视为均匀光源。考虑到电源成本及其安全性，最终选用36V、4A恒压电源。

(3) 设计制造了便于拍摄整个流场的相机机架。图像摄取中，分辨率与拍摄范围始终存在着矛盾，即相机距离越远，拍摄流场的范围越大，拍摄得到的气泡图像分辨率越小。如果分辨率太小，势必导致得到的数字图像中小气泡太模糊甚至看不到。由于试验段比较大，必须在多个机位对试验段流场进行拍摄。采用传统的三脚架来固定相机无法保证不同机位相机与泄洪洞的距离保持相等，且均能垂直指向仪器。为解决此问题，设计制造了便于拍摄整个流场的相机机架。该装置在水平与垂直方向上分别安装带有刻度的直线导轨，相机可在水平与垂直两个方向上精确移动，同时记录相机具体位置。

（二）气泡的识别

图像的二值化处理是指通过某种方法，使得画面场景中被分为“目标物”及“非目标物”两类，分类所依据的特性可以是像素的灰度值、颜色或多普特性、空间特性和纹理特性等。本研究依据像素的灰度值，通过取阈值的方法进行分类，即将灰度值大于阈值的像素认为是物体（气泡），而灰度值小于阈值的像素认为是背景。

本次试验图像处理程序为：①对采集到的图像求反；②减去背景；③采用传统的阈值分割方法进行分割，分割阈值选用最大类间方差取阈法确定；④采用无方向的交叉微分算法（即Roberts算法）进行锐化处理，加强图像中景物的细节边缘和轮廓。为检验分割效果，将原始图像与提取出的气泡边缘图像叠加，叠加后的结果图几乎是不能发现两者之间的差别。

（三）反弧段单个气泡运动轨迹的求解

由于在拍摄过程中，反弧段流场速度较大（断面平均速度在3.5m/s左右），而相机移动速度是由人工控制，要跟踪气泡在反弧运动的整个过程几乎不可能，因此本研究只能给出反弧段流场单个气泡运动的部分轨迹。从拍摄到的大量图像中，选取一些典型的气泡（这些气泡肉眼看起来接近圆形，而且在运动的过程中不会发生粘连、分离等现象），然后求解这些气泡的运动轨迹。方法如下：

(1) 气泡区域的标记。首先对目标图像进行标记，即对不同的连通域对象用不同的整数值来标记，以示区别。本研究采用MATLAB7.0数字图像处理工具箱（IPT）函数bwlabel计算。每个不同的连通域的像素被分配给一个唯一的整数，该整数的范围是从1到连通域的总数，换言之，标记为1的像素属于第一个连通域，标记为2的像素属于第二个连通域，依此类推，连通域是按从上往下，从左往右的顺序标记的。

(2) 计算各连通域的质心。首先，调用函数find，找出各连通域所有像素的行索引r和列索引c。然后，利用r和c作为输入的mean函数来计算该对象的质心坐标（x，y）。

(3) 计算各连通域的大小。采用IPT函数length计算气泡大小S。在两相流中，气泡或颗粒等分散相的粒径一般情况下并非为绝对的球形，习惯上将具有等体积的球体的直径定义为该粒子的标准直径。由于图像测量获得的是粒子的投影面积，所以本研究定义具有相同面积的圆形的直径为粒子的标准直径。

(4) 求取单个气泡的运动轨迹。针对反弧段流场稀疏气泡的特点，根据PTV算法，首先在第一幅图像中标记出所要求取轨迹的气泡，然后在第二幅图像中标记出与目标气泡相匹配的气泡，依此类推，可以获取n幅连续图像中与目标气泡相匹配的气泡。为便于人眼观察，将所有匹配到的气泡叠加在一副图像中，并且剔除其他不必要的气泡信息，叠加结果即单个气泡的运动轨迹。

（四）反弧段流场空隙率的测量及其计算

为简化计算，气泡面积定义为连通域中像素的总数。对气液两相流，气相的空隙率（又称截面含气率、真实含气率或真实相含率）定义为：断面内气相面积除以总面积。气相的空隙率与掺气浓度不同，后者为水流中气体的体积占水气混合体的体积的比值。

本研究采用的图像是连续拍摄778幅两相流流场图像，时间间隔均为1ms，总历时0.78s。在这么短的时间内，空气压缩机气罐内气体压力可视为恒定，因此可假设这778幅照片中气泡的容积相等。断面的空隙率是按照以下步骤计算：

(1) 将图像二值化。

(2) 求出反弧底部某一点对应的断面线，然后确定以断面线为中心的计算区域，其宽度为16像素（即8.32mm）。

(3) 沿计算区域自反弧底部到水面依次取大小为16×16像素（即8.32mm×8.32mm）的计算窗口，窗口每次向上移动8像素（4.16mm），然后分别统计出每幅图像各个窗口内的气泡面积（本研究统计的气泡形心在窗口范围内，若形心不在窗口范围内，则不予统计）。

(4) 计算各个窗口的空隙率。

(5) 计算区域（即断面）的空隙率。

按照上述方法，某计算区域的空隙率沿水深方向的分布情况如下：沿反弧断面所取的7个计算窗口内存在气泡，相对水深0.37以下的断面内不存在气泡；相对水深0.37～0.67，空隙率是递增的；当相对水深为0.67时，空隙率为最大值；相对水深在0.67～0.82，空隙率是递减的；当相对水深在0.82以上时，空隙率为零。

（中国水电顾问集团西北勘测设计研究院
王化恒　薛　瑞
西安理工大学水利水电学院　邵建斌　陈　刚）

南京水利科学研究院 2009科研工作情况

南京水利科学研究院原全称为“水利部 交通部 电力工业部南京水利科学研究院”，2009年9月21日中央机构编制委员会办公室批复更名为“水利部 交通运输部 国家能源局南京水利科学研究院”。

2009年，全院承担各类科研项目1129项，同比增长16.51%，新签科研项目721项，同比增长34.26%。全院科研合同额达3.27亿元，比2008年增长5%。获得国家和省部级科技进步奖19项，其中国家科技进步一等奖1项、国家科技进步二等奖4项、省部级科技一等奖6项；全院提交科研报告1000余篇，科研成果288篇；公开发表论文394篇，出版专著11部；获得国家发明专利2项、国家实用新型专利11项。

（一）专著出版与标准编制

《暴雨洪涝》、《橡胶坝技术及应用》、《松辽流域生态需水研究》、《河口治理与大风骤淤》、《海岸泥沙运动研究及应用》、《唐山港京唐港区粉沙质海岸泥沙研究与整治》、《福建省海湾数模与环境研究》、《工程力学》、《Rural Hydropower and Electrification in China（第二版）》、《长江流域水沙生态综合管理》、《黄河水科学前沿》等一批专著相继出版。

2009年，全院承担了《小水电水能设计规程》、《中小河流水能开发规划编制规范》、《节水型社会评价指标体系》、《土工试验规程》（修订）、《水运工程数学模型研究参考定额》、《小型水库安全管理办法》、《水工混凝土耐久性技术规范》等数十项国家和行业规范的编制工作。

（二）“十一五”国家科技支撑计划项目

（1）主持的“水库大坝安全保障技术研究”取得重要成果。2009年在滁州基地进行了第六次现场溃坝实验研究，在大坝漫顶溃坝机理研究的基础上，开展了管涌导致溃坝破坏研究，分析了管涌渗透破坏的过程，取得了完整的原型坝体管涌溃坝数据资料，为揭示管涌溃坝机理提供了宝贵的原型实测资料；完成了“病险水库除险加固及溃坝案例信息系统”的开发并投入运行，制定了《水库大坝信息采集指南》；建立了水库大坝突发事件应急预案可行性和预见性评价指标体系，完成了《水库大坝突发事件应急预案编制导则》的编制；研究了快速准确地确定致灾因子及实时分析大坝安全性状与控制水位的关系；建立了应急调度方案评价指标体系，提出了水库降等与报废后的善后处理措施与标准；编制了《大坝风险标准指南》；出版专著2部，发表论文84篇。整个项目已完成工作大纲要求的研究任务，正在进行各课题验收和总报告的编写。

（2）主持的“雨洪资源利用技术研究及应用”，着重解决了雨洪资源可利用量及其分布、雨洪资源利用方式和制约风险等若干关键问题；构建了雨洪资源利用的完整技术体系，解决了一批关键技术难题；提出了《流域雨洪资源利用技术指南》，进行了研究成果的凝练；项目各课题在核心期刊发表学术论文177篇，其中在国外期刊发表34篇；申请专利5项，制订地方技术标准2项。

（3）承担的“中国国际河流水资源开发与安全保障关键技术研究”10个课题中的5个课题，各课题阶段成果均已通过中期检查。

（4）“南水北调运行风险管理关键技术问题研究”课题，完成了南水北调风险控制理论、技术和调水工程运行风险对策技术研究，提出了南水北调工程运行风险控制原则。

（5）“三峡工程运用后对长江中下游防洪的影响评价研究”课题，建立了长江中下游水沙数学模型，模拟了长江中下游水沙演进和河道冲淤变化过程，预测了长江中下游主要控制站的水位流量关系变化和江湖蓄泄关系的变化，为长江防洪调度方案的研究和长江流域综合规划的修订提供了技术支撑。

（6）“南水北调超大口径PCCP管道结构安全与质量控制研究”课题，首次开展了直径4m的PCCP中裂缝与预应力松弛对结构安全的影响评价、数值建模、阴极保护技术、PCCP管道接头灌浆砂浆等研究，成果已在南水北调北京段施工中应用。

（7）“防洪工程体系洪水调控模拟关键技术研究”课题等其他“十一五”支撑项目的课题也都进展顺利，取得预期成果。

（三）国家“973”、“863”和自然科学基金项目

（1）国家“973”项目。“土石坝－水库耦合系统动力学机理”课题，根据现场溃坝调查资料和大型溃坝试验结果，研究分析了土石坝的溃决机理和溃决过程，提出模拟土石坝主要坝型渗透破坏和漫顶破坏溃口发展过程的系列数值模型，在项目中期评估中被评为优秀；“973”专题“土石坝溃决实例研究及其反演分析”，提出了中国小型水库溃坝规律与对策、病险水库除险加固项目溃坝机理调查分析。

(2) 国家"863"项目。专题"混凝土箱梁桥用高强混凝土长期时变特性的理论与试验研究",采用标准试件和构件进行了多种工况下的试验,取得了重要成果;"重大环境污染事件风场预警技术"项目取得了阶段成果,研究工作得到专家好评。

(3) 国家自然科学基金重点项目。"突出骨料因素和温湿度历史的高性能大坝混凝土"、"高土石坝筑坝材料特性试验研究"、"高土石坝地震灾变模拟及安全控制方法研究"等均按计划开展研究并取得创新成果,已公开发表论文 34 篇,依托项目培养了多名博士、硕士研究生。

(四) 公益性科研项目

主持的水利部公益性行业重大科研专项"气候变化对我国水安全影响及对策研究",9 个课题研究全面开展,进展顺利,项目的研究不仅注重对科学规律的认识,而且提出了我国水利应对气候变化常态和非常态事件的工程措施与非工程措施,该项目的研究成果已应用到国家第二次评估报告的编写和"十二五"水利应对气候变化和低碳经济发展规划中。

承担的国家社会公益研究项目"水电风能互补蓄能关键技术研究"进展顺利。

(五) 工程建设技术研究项目

(1) 承担了国家重大基础建设项目"港珠澳大桥建设工程"的多项科研项目。围绕该重大工程的关键技术问题,全院集中河流海岸、岩土工程等多个研究所的科研力量,先后承担并完成了"港珠澳大桥对珠江口港口、航道影响物理模型研究"、"港珠澳大桥人工岛地基加固关键技术研究"、"港珠澳大桥沉管隧道试挖基槽容重观测与潮流泥沙数值模型试验"、"港珠澳大桥设计波要素和水流分析计算、波浪模型试验、冲刷及防护技术专题研究"等多个研究项目。大桥工程水动力环境影响的方案比选数学模型研究成果已作为大桥深化设计的依据。大桥设计波要素和水流分析计算、波浪模型试验、冲刷及防护技术专题研究通过了专家评审,提交了中英文报告。开展了典型断面应力变形与稳定性、地基流变特性与人工岛长期变形、施工过程中的渗流与渗透稳定性和软基处理离心模型试验等专项研究。

(2) 继续承担国家重大工程曹妃甸工业基地建设的科研工作。开展了"曹妃甸老龙沟航道治理数学物理模型及滩槽稳定性开发研究"、"唐山市滨海大道曹妃甸国际生态域段外线工程潮汐水流物理模型试验研究"、"曹妃甸西区港口开发潮流泥沙数学模型与滩槽稳定性研究"、"曹妃甸工业区仓储区围海造地工程和滨海新城围海造地工程设计波浪推算"等多项科研工作,研究成果为工程设计提供了科学的依据。

(3) 继续做好长江黄金水道建设关键技术研究工作。先后开展了"长江深水航道上延南京至浏河口段河势控制工程总体技术方案研究"、"长江下游福姜沙、通州沙及白茆沙水道深水航道整治工程河工模型试验研究"、"长江福姜沙河段海轮深水航道整治,双涧沙护滩工程模型试验"、"长江澄通河段综合整治模型试验研究"等多项针对性的工程研究,对长江航道碍航险滩的治理提出了多种优化方案。

(4) 清洁能源科研。在海上风能研究方向上实现突破,承担了"东海大桥 10 万 kW 海上风电场建设关键技术应用研究"项目,针对水、电、机、气四种因素耦合的海上风力场动力稳定安全问题开展研究,对推动我国海上风能发电建设具有重要意义。

(南京水利科学研究院)

黄河水利科学研究院 2009 年科研工作情况

2009 年,黄河水利科学研究院(以下简称黄科院)各项研究工作如下:

(1) 治黄重大实践科学试验与评估工作。完成了 2009 年调水调沙生产运行中异重流人工塑造设计、下游河道边界条件分析、下游二维水沙数学模型预测计算、洪峰增值模拟等专项任务,完成了调控指标确定、预案编制、实时调度、运行效果评估等环节的相关内容,完成了年度调水调沙运行效果后评估报告;完成了利用并优化桃汛洪水过程冲刷降低潼关高程试验指标的优化研究、试验预案设计、实施预案的编制、试验实施和跟踪试验会商决策等任务,编制完成了《2009 年利用并优化桃汛洪水过程冲刷降低潼关高程试验调度预案》,并开展了试验效果后评估。对 2006~2008 年期间"利用并优化桃汛洪水过程冲刷降低潼关高程试验"进行总结评估,并提出评估报告;完成了黄河下游"驼峰"河段形成机理及治理措施综合研究任务书和工作大纲。并配合有关单位开展了黄河下游"驼峰"河段及"二级悬河"治理试验工程治理必要性、可行性、治理规模、治理效果等关键技术论证工作;启动了《小浪底水库异重流调度关键技术研究》工作,在系统总结国内外水库异重流研究成果的基础上,结合原型观测、水槽试验和模型专题试验,初步提出小浪底水库异重流调度指标及塑造措施;完成了 2009 年小北干流放淤试验的前期准备工作,基本完成了小北干流放淤试验效果评价。

(2) 完成"十一五"国家科技支撑计划项目"黄河流域水沙变化情势评价研究"、"维持黄河主槽不萎缩的水沙条件研究"、"黄河中下游水沙调控关键技术研究"、"基于 GIS 的黄河水沙输移模拟系统研发"、

"黄河健康修复目标及对策研究"、"黄河流域水沙变化情势评价研究"5个课题和"大坝监测及隐患探测技术研究"专题的各项研究工作，正在等待结题验收。

(3) 完成流域综合规划修编项目"模型黄河"工程规划、"数学模拟"系统建设规划、"宽河固堤"与"窄河固堤"方案比较等项目的研究和修编工作，并做好干流河道排沙分析、流域综合管理规划等配合修编工作。

(4) 数学模型研发。①完成了黄土高原水土流失模型（第一期）阶段研究任务。初步研发了中等流域年产沙经验模型，为水土保持措施减沙效益评价提供了科学手段；研发了小流域次暴雨作业预报系统，实现了洪水泥沙过程实时预报，为今后黄河调水调沙提供参数打下了基础；初步研发了小流域分布式机理模型，为小流域水土保持规划，水土保持措施空间布设提供科学的依据。②黄河数学模拟系统1.0版本研究。先后完成了四站以下"三门峡库区一维模型"、"小浪底水库一维模型"、"黄河下游一维/二维模型耦合集成"等数学模型研发工作，建立了模拟系统的帮助文件，初步具备发布黄河数学模拟系统1.0版本的条件。

(5) "模型黄河"工程建设。完成了非接触免维护式水位计制作工作，并进行了室内及模型的试验工作；完成了激光式水下地形仪制作工作，并进行了室内及模型的试验工作；基本完成了浅滩式超声在线含沙量量测系统研制工作。黄河口物理模型关键技术研究工作取得了较大进展，完成了模型沙选择、模型沙基本特性、河口模型相似律、生潮技术及进口含沙量自动控制技术等专项研究工作，为黄河河口模型试验的开展奠定了较好的前期工作基础。黄河下游河道模型试验研究开展了运用方式二（15年系列）的工作，目前正在开展30年系列的试验研究工作；黄河小浪底库区模型试验研究开展了运用方式二（20年系列）的工作，目前正在开展推荐方案的试验研究工作。

(6) 国家自然基金和国家"973"专题等项目研究。国家自然基金重点项目"黄河中下游泥沙输移规律及二维数学模型研究"于2009年6月通过了国家自然基金委组织的验收，评审结果为优秀。"黄河下游冲泻质含量对水流输沙能力的影响"项目开展了多组次的水槽试验研究，完成了年度工作计划。"农业非点源污染物在排水沟渠中迁移机理及输出模型研究"项目系统归纳总结了国内外研究现状和发展趋势，选取青铜峡灌区为外业典型试验区进行了现场综合考察，完成取样和分析工作。联合申请的国家自然科学基金重点项目"面向大型工程安全预测与评估的信息融合方法"已立项并启动研究。"973"专题"黄河下游堤防溃口力学机理模拟研究"项目完成了不同流速、不同土质、不同密实度状态下的土体冲刷试验研究任务，探索土体冲刷变形过程与水流流场发展变化的规律。

(7) 完成了国家农业科技成果转化项目"黄河下游农业用水信息交换平台示范"项目调研报告的编写，初步确定了平台涵盖的信息和功能需求，目前研究进展顺利。

(8) 完成了行业标准研究项目"水利工程安全评价与鉴定标准关键技术研究"专题"水利工程施工质量检验与评定标准研究"的立项及启动工作，目前各项工作有序开展。

(9) 完成了科技部科研院所开发专项"移动式堤防全断面安全监测与预警系统开发"项目的国内外相关技术调研、历史数据分析及采集站设备、信息处理设备的初选工作。

(10) 组织、承办第四届黄河国际论坛"多沙河流泥沙处理及水库泥沙处理重大技术"专题会；成立黄科院青年科技工作委员会并成功举办了"首届黄河博士论坛暨黄科院第七届青年学术讨论会"和"黄河下游治理方向辩论赛"，有效促进了良好科研氛围的建立。

2009年，黄科院实现经济总收入10 733万元，其中财政补助收入3425万元，科研收入6022万元，经营及其他收入1286万元；科研收入得到了较大幅度增加。

编制完成了《黄河流域科技创新中心学科发展规划》、《黄河水利科学研究院学科建设与科研能力发展规划》、《黄科院科研能力建设规划》、《黄河水利科学研究院科研试验基地建设土地征用项目可行性研究报告》。黄河泥沙重点实验室、水利部堤防安全与病害防治工程技术研究中心顺利通过水利部验收，黄委质检中心完成了计量认证扩项复查评审工作。有针对性地做好各级各类的人才培养、储备和引进。制定了《黄河水利科学研究院博士后科研工作站管理办法》，为进站博士后提供住房等保障条件。分别与天津大学、清华大学和中国科技大学签订了联合培养博士后协议，共4位博士后先后进站工作。

组织参加各种学术交流活动。承办了"黄河论坛"、"多沙河流泥沙处理及水库泥沙处理重大技术"专题会；成立黄科院青年科技工作委员会，成功举办了"首届黄河博士论坛暨黄科院第七届青年学术讨论会"和"黄河下游治理方向辩论赛"。2009年全院已公开发表的科研论文约213篇，出版专著8部。主编的《堤防隐患探测规程》正式实施。

2009年，自主安排的科研项目经费近500万元。2009年组织院属各单位创新成果申报，向黄委会推荐2008～2009年创新成果9项，其中获得黄委会创新成果一等奖2项、二等奖1项、三等奖4项，同时荣获创新组织奖。

（黄河水利科学研究院）

中国水利水电建设集团公司科技工作情况

2009年，中国水利水电建设集团公司（以下简称中国水电建设集团）继续实施建设“国际行业科技领先型企业”的科技发展战略，科技创新体系不断完善，科技创新能力持续提高，科技工作取得了新的进步。

（一）科技工作基本情况

2009年，中国水电建设集团国家级企业技术中心通过两年一度的复审工作，子公司共有10个省级技术中心。初步形成了“集团公司统筹领导，充分发挥两级法人企业的积极性，以企业技术中心为主导力量，依靠科学技术委员会专家智力支持，走‘产、学、研’相结合的道路，调动全体科技人员共同参与科技研发与创新”的企业科技创新体系。

2009年，中国水电建设集团在北京召开了第二届科技大会暨科技委2009年年会，全面总结三年来中国水电建设集团科技工作，认真分析企业科技工作的新形势、新任务，总体部署今后的科技工作。会议审查了企业科技发展规划（2010—2015）的编制工作。发布了《中国水利水电建设集团公司重点推广新技术（2009版）》和《中国水利水电建设集团公司工法汇编》。

（二）科技攻关项目与科技奖励

2009年，中国水电建设集团立项的在研科技攻关项目105项，新批准立项项目44项，批准经费2858万元。全年累计结题并完成鉴定科技项目28项，被专家鉴定为国际领先3项；国际先进13项；国内领先8项；国内先进4项。从这些科技成果来看，攻克了一批高难度世界级技术难题，新设备、新材料、新技术、新工艺在工程项目上得到了较好的应用，进一步提高了生产效率，降低了施工成本，促进了质量安全环保管理水平，体现了较高的技术水平，社会经济效益显著，继续保持了中国水电建设集团水电施工建设国际领先水平。

2009年，中国水电建设集团共评审集团公司科技进步奖42项，其中特等奖1项，一等奖7项，二等奖15项。在2009年度中国电力科学技术奖评选中，获一等奖1项，三等奖5项；获得中国施工企业管理协会科学技术奖技术创新成果一等奖1项，二等奖2项。

（三）工法、专利与技术标准

2009年，中国水电建设集团发布企业工法113项，获得国家级工法10项，并完成了集团公司工法（2007～2008年度）汇编工作；共获得64项国家专利，其中发明专利9项，正在接受国家受理审查的专利50项。

2009年，中国水电建设集团在编行业技术标准28部，完成9部。集团公司牵头的近200万字的水电施工和水轮发电机技术国家及行业英文标准译审工作已圆满完成，共译审标准42部，出版28部。

（中国水利水电建设集团公司）

中国水电顾问集团贵阳勘测设计研究院2009年科技工作简况

2009年，中国水电顾问集团贵阳勘测设计研究院，制定、修订与科技管理、知识产权等相关制度和办法18项，基本建立了涵盖全院的科技、知识产权、信息、档案、保密等方面的管理制度并适应了机构调整的需要。

2009年度，完成中国水电工程顾问集团公司科研项目立项书和研究大纲编制、合同签订；超前策划拟报集团公司科研项目并通过院技术委员会评审；申报16项、审批11项院《电力科学技术发展基金》项目（含1项专著）。全年共组织了20项成果申报，获得9项奖励。在院有关人员共同努力下，洪家渡水电站工程设计获得2008年度全国优秀工程设计金奖。作为第五申报单位，依托新疆塔西河石门子水库碾压混凝土拱坝开展的《碾压混凝土拱坝的新设计理论与实践》科技成果获2009年度国家科技进步奖二等奖。2009年度，获得全国优秀工程咨询成果三等奖1项、贵州科技进步三等奖和贵州省优秀工程咨询成果奖一等奖各2项、贵州省优秀工程咨询成果奖二等奖和三等奖各1项。

（中国水电顾问集团贵阳勘测设计研究院
李月杰　王　芳）

太阳能电源点的合理开发

太阳能具有资源充足、长寿、分布广泛、安全、清洁和技术可靠等优点。若将地球表面每年接受太阳的辐射量（5.4×10^{24}J）的0.1%按转换率5%转换为电能，每年发电量可达5600TW·h，相当于目前全世界能耗的40倍。目前，我国太阳能利用产品已形成千亿元规模的产业。

太阳能利用形式主要有太阳能热水器和太阳能发电，其太阳能发电方式主要有太阳光伏发电和太阳能热发电两种基本方式。太阳能热水器和光伏电目前在实际中已得到广泛应用，其类型主要表现为屋顶散户供热与发电，或边远地区集中示范性供电。全球太阳能光伏发电主要集中在日本、欧盟和美国，其发电量约占世界光伏发电量的 80% 。目前，屋顶发电已成为一种新型的散户供热供电模式。集中联网太阳能发电亦将成为全球太阳能供电的另一种主要形式。太阳能热发电技术目前多处于研究状态，其发电系统目前主要有塔式、槽式和蝶式热发电系统 3 种类型；目前只有槽式发电系统实现了商业化，但近年来因部分技术问题没有扩大和推广。

（一）光伏发电

城市规模型或储能式发电方式目前正处于研发阶段。中国太阳能发电技术产业的三个阶段有：技术研发示范阶段——发电设备产品与开发技术研发；技术成熟期——太阳能发电与其他能发电互补阶段即太阳能发电技术成熟期；普及阶段——即太阳能发电走进千家万户。我国太阳能发电技术仍处于第一阶段，即技术研发示范阶段，其中不但包括发电设备产品（如单晶硅、多晶硅、无晶硅产品）发电技术的研发与推广，也隐含了开发模式（集中或是散户供电及有关问题研究）与类型（混合能源互补储能类型）的研究。

在我国西部无电和严重缺电地区，目前已建成 10～100kW 光伏电站 40 多座。山东的中国太阳谷日月坛——“微排”大厦，将于 2010 年 6 月将建成（其电站装机为 2MW），是一座集太阳能光热、光伏、建筑节能于一体的高层公共建筑。2008 年 12 月在上海建成的“上海鲜花港太阳能电站”，装机容量为 0.4MW，为我国首个利用绿色能源发展现代花卉产业的 3 倍聚光太阳能光伏模板系统。

（二）太阳热能

太阳热能使用目前技术水平处于半成熟阶段，一方面是民用热水器的技术与产品处于成熟期，另一方面为太阳热能规模性开发技术水平处于摸索性研究阶段。

(1) 太阳能热水器的应用范围目前几乎已走进城乡千家万户随处可见。工业性或规模性太阳热联产技术水平，规模型使用太阳热为工业服务，目前却仍处于研究前期工作阶段。即太阳热与城市基础建设、或与工业生产联合开发，根据太阳热设备产品行情，目前仍处于摸索探寻性研发阶段。

(2) 太阳能热发电目前正处在商业化前夕。我国太阳能热发电技术的研究开发工作始于 20 世纪 70 年代末，但由于种种原因太阳能热发电项目先后停止。与国外相比，差距很大，2005 年 10 月 29 日，国内首座 70kW 太阳能塔式热发电示范工程在南京江宁成功并网发电，揭开了我国太阳能热发电技术研究全新的一页。

（三）太阳能资源

就全球而言，美国西南部、非洲、澳大利亚、中国西藏、中东等地区的全年总辐射量或日照总时数最大，为世界太阳能资源最丰富地区。

我国陆地表面每年接受的太阳辐射能约为 50×10^{18} kJ，各地太阳年辐射总量达 335～837kJ/(cm^2·年)。我国青藏高原是高值中心，其平均海拔在 4000m 以上，拉萨市年平均晴天 108.5 天。四川盆地是低值中心，尤以成都市年平均晴天 24.7 天为最少。总体来说，西部地区高于东部地区，而且除西藏和新疆两个自治区外，基本上是东南低、西北高。

全国太阳能资源分布概况按接受太阳能辐射量的大小，见表 1。

表 1 中国太阳能资源分布表

地区类型	年日照时数 (h)	年辐射总量 (MJ/m^2)	包括的主要地区	备注
一类	3200～3300	6680～8400	宁夏北部，甘肃北部，新疆南部，青海西部，西藏西部	最丰富地区
二类	3000～3200	5852～6680	河北西北部，山西北部，内蒙古南部，宁夏南部，甘肃中部，青海东部，西藏东南部，新疆南部	较丰富地区
三类	2200～3000	5016～5852	山东，河南，河北东南部，山西南部，新疆北部，吉林，辽宁，云南，陕西北部，甘肃东南部，广东南部	中等地区
四类	1400～2000	4180～5016	湖南，广西，江西，浙江，湖北，福建北部，广东北部，陕西南部，安徽南部	较差地区
五类	1000～1400	3344～4180	四川大部分地区，贵州	最差地区

全国按接受太阳能辐射量的大小大致上可分为五类地区：一、二、三类地区，年日照时数大于 2000h，年辐射总量高于 586kJ/cm^2，是我国太阳能资源丰富或较丰富的地区，面积约占全国总面积的 2/3 以上；四、五类地区虽然太阳能资源条件较差，

但仍有一定的利用价值。

（四）资源开发形式

当前，许多国家和国际公司看好我国西北的太阳能利用市场，各种援助计划、示范应用项目纷至沓来。这对我国的太阳能产业来说是个大好机遇，但对我国太阳能电站研发技术也是一个挑战，因为我国目前在该方面的技术力量和水平，与国外先进相比，尚有一定的差距，仍需大力加强。资源开发形式如下：

（1）集中供发电。无论资金来自何处，无论发电设备产品的价格如何，目前流行的集中式太阳能电池板及电站建筑物布置形式、多数常见是采用平面式、立体式和光电建筑一体化几种布置形式，对于光电建筑一体化的形式多建于城市的集中供发电的太阳能电站，虽有更多的电站布置形式正在研发之中，但到底哪一种布置形式和结构更经济合理，这仍是一个有待进一步研究考证的问题。

（2）太阳能光伏电站。

（3）与其他能源结合发展。我国太阳能资源丰富的一类地区年辐射量为6680～8400MJ/m^2，同时这些地区的水电资源也非常丰富。

（五）开发趋势

在目前流行于市场的和未来可能的太阳能电源点开发模式中，最有可能发展普及的有以下三种模式：

（1）小型太阳能光伏电站及分散电源点的建设主要以工业民用建筑基础建设为主进行分散式建设，多以房屋或其他园林建设为载体建造。

（2）光电建筑一体化多建于城市，立体式、平面式更适于空旷地带，例如也可与中小型水电站、风电等其他野外建筑联合布置。

（3）大中型项目。模式一，为独立开发，这种开发模式主要用于太阳热电；模式二，可以混合火电或其他核电等同类大型项目为依托载体开发建造，这种开发模式主要用于太阳热电站，但也不排除光伏太阳能电站的研发；模式三，与其他大型基础建设联合建设的开发模式，例如与大型水电站或其他大型工程联合建设开发，这种开发模式主要用于太阳能光伏发电站的研发。

（中国水电顾问集团西北勘测设计研究院
杨爱菊　李红星　贾　宝　黄军辉
杨丽洁　乔飞义
西安市热力公司　肖松权）

水电技术创新

三峡右岸电站计算机监控系统研制开发

中国水利水电科学研究院、中国长江三峡集团公司和长江水利委员会设计院于2005年6月～2009年1月进行了三峡右岸电站计算机监控系统研制开发。完成了三峡右岸电站计算机监控系统的设计、有关设备的选型、制造、采购、软件开发、工厂试验、现场指导调试、现场试验、用户培训等，实现三峡右岸电站12台700MW机组的实时监控。设备包括厂站层系统各服务器、操作员站和大屏幕投影系统，2套开关站LCU、2套厂用电LCU、1套公用系统LCU、模拟屏驱动LCU、12台机组LCU及有关网络设备等。

主要突出成果如下：

（1）三峡右岸及右岸地下电站共18台70万kW机组（其中地下电站6台），计算机监控系统采用统一设计分步实施的方案，目前已实现了右岸全部12台70万kW机组、500kV开关站及全厂辅助设备的实时监控和生产管理。

（2）三峡右岸电站计算机监控系统是我国自主研发的监控系统，成功实现国产70万kW机组的自动化控制并投入商业化稳定运行。

（3）提出并成功研制了面向电站三网四层结构的分层分布开放式系统，采用电站控制网与信息网分离的模式，合理分布系统负荷。满足了电站对控制系统实时性、安全性、可靠性及可扩展性的要求。成功开发了多服务器负荷平衡管理与互备冗余技术，实现了数据采集的高可靠性。

（4）采用多链路、多线程处理技术，数据采集与传输性能提高了6～8倍，完全满足了电站海量数据（全系统超过60 000点）高速采集的实时性要求。

（5）面向服务的跨平台分布式系统架构，独特的高可控性的无主设计，各硬件节点之间并不存在相互依赖的逻辑上的主机，使系统具有很好的可控性。

（6）采用数据包编号、双网冗余传输技术，实现了完全的双网冗余。

（7）通过采用数据组包技术、数据压缩和数据插值技术实现了15 000点历史库数据秒级存取。

(8) 采用自适应、自学习算法确定电站在电网中的频率综合调差系数，解决了无法确定电站AGC频差系数的难题。

(9) 采用GTK图形技术，实现了异构操作系统环境下的用户外部界面、功能和性能及软件源代码的全兼容。

(10) 卫星时钟同步管理系统采用一、二级时钟系统的方案。采用一级时钟双机热备冗余配置与二级时钟冗余双光纤通道连接，保证全厂智能设备的时钟一致和时钟源的可靠。

(11) 水电站监控系统LCU总线通信应用多现场总线、分布式光纤通信技术。三峡右岸电站计算机监控系统，LCU盘柜布置分散，距离远，不同的智能设备和现场总线接口，实时性和可靠性要求高，采用此技术，使分散的远程单元、不同的职能设备和不同的现场总线的通信达到了高实时性、高抗干扰性。

(12) 水电站监控系统LCU远程I/O单元应用双环网光纤通信技术，使LCU的可靠性满足机组的高要求。三峡右岸电站计算机监控系统，所有LCU机箱中采用双光纤环网技术，进一步提高了LCU的可靠性。

(13) LCU在设备电源、采集控制电源、CPU、网络、远程单元机箱连接等方面采用多重冗余技术，进一步提高了LCU的可靠性。

(14) 在LCU中，采用NTP网络对时技术与串行同步时钟脉冲技术相结合使LCU控制器的时钟同步精度达到了微秒级，充分保证了SOE事件分辨率1ms的技术要求。

(15) 成功开发符合IEC 60870-6-TASE.2的先进可靠的通信技术。

(16) 无需制作网页，监控系统的画面可直接转换为SVG格式在WEB站点上展示，提供有多种动态效果展示生产过程和趋势分析曲线。

2009年11月6日，“三峡右岸电站计算机监控系统”项目顺利通过水利部组织的科技成果鉴定。与会专家一致认为：该系统首次研制成功了面向水电站计算机监控系统的三网四层的分层分布开放系统结构，突破了水电站计算机监控系统的传统结构模式，显著提高了水电站计算机监控系统的可靠性与实时性；在LCU首次采用多链路、多线程处理技术；并成功开发了多数据采集服务器负荷平衡管理与互备技术，提高了数据采集系统的可靠性和效率；首次采用自适应、自学习算法确定电站在电网中的频率综合调差系数，有效地保证了机组的安全平稳调节；首次采用分层分布的卫星时钟系统，实现了水电厂众多智能设备的时钟统一；首次采用GTK图形技术，实现了异构操作系统下的用户界面、功能和性能及软件源代码的全兼容。该系统成功实现了自主研发和集成创新，开发了具有自主知识产权的系统总体结构和应用软件系统，操作维护方便，实时性好，可靠性高，人机界面友好，推动了我国水电站计算机监控应用技术的发展，其成功运用，打破了国外公司在机组监控系统方面的垄断，推动了我国计算机监控技术的发展。系统的总体技术水平达到了国际先进水平，在三网四层总体结构设计、自适应AGC频差系数控制技术、系统可靠性设计等方面居国际领先水平，代表了当今国际水电站计算机监控技术和应用的最高水平。

该系统已被直接推广应用到四川瀑布沟等国内外30多个大型水电站，创造了良好的经济效益和社会效益，具有广阔的推广应用前景。

(中国水利水电科学研究院
中国长江电力股份有限公司　谢兴发)

小湾拱坝极限承载力及变形稳定分析与评价

该项目于2006年11月开始，2008年11月结束，主要研究情况如下：

(一) 小湾拱坝三维非线性变形稳定安全性分析

鉴于拱坝的结构形式、受力特点和复杂基础特性，为更合理地反映小湾拱坝的实际受力和变形、稳定安全度，采用三维非线性数值模拟分析小湾拱坝的应力变形特征，综合评价小湾拱坝的安全性。为了保证三维非线性模拟分析最大限度地反映工程实际，所建的三维模型以现有设计方案为基础，在模型中重点考虑了小湾拱坝特殊的地质条件，采取了多种方法进行模拟。

(1) 在三维模型中特别重视建基面附近卸荷松弛岩体地质条件的模拟，尤其在河床及低高程建基面附近的卸荷松弛带岩体加密网格到2m×2m。

(2) 对两岸坝肩岩体内的抗力体处理措施进行了细致的模拟。

(3) 为充分反映NS、EW长大节理的影响，重要部位通过各向异性模型进行模拟。

(4) 对坝体诱导缝及附近坝体单元进行细致的模拟。

(5) 由河海大学提供渗流场分析成果，对渗流场和应力场采用叠加的方式进行研究。

(6) 基本计算荷载包括水压力、泥沙压力、自重和温度荷载。拱坝承载能力研究以超载方式为主，研究不同情况下的超载安全度，适当辅以降强分析。

(7) 对于较难确定的岩体力学参数和开挖因素进

行了适当的敏感性分析。

（二）国内外典型工程类比与安全度研究

由于小湾工程的规模和难度举世瞩目，主要问题如坝基浅层抗滑稳定问题目前尚没有公认的标准和规范可循，因此通过对国内外相关工程进行工程类比研究，有助于解决小湾拱坝安全度的评价标准问题。本子题并行计算分析了国外两个、国内三个工程的情况。

(1) 收集类比工程的地形、地质、大坝结构的设计、施工、运行期资料，大坝及基础变形等多项观测资料，同时收集国际国内学者的分析研究成果。

(2) 对收集到的资料进行全面、综合分析，正确确定数值模拟分析的边界条件、荷载条件、地质结构条件（尤其是构造面）、运行条件等，在此基础上建立能反映大坝实际情况的分析模型。

(3) 用非线性有限元通过对大坝运行过程的模拟分析，利用收集到的实际观测资料，反演分析影响大坝基础、大坝受力和变形的重要热学力学参数。

(4) 在参数反演的基础上，在与小湾工程同样的计算条件下，用非线性计算通过超载的方法分析类比工程的安全度。

（三）小湾拱坝整体安全度综合分析研究

在以上分析的基础上，考虑类比工程的实际运行情况，通过工程类比的方法对小湾拱坝整体和局部的安全度进行评价。

小湾拱坝坝高 294.5m，在拱坝建基面浅表部位岩体开挖卸荷松弛现象严重，存在拱坝底部浅层抗滑稳定问题。此问题非常复杂，国内经验很少，对国外的情况也掌握不多，设计规范中也无明确说明，只能根据工程实际情况研究确定。

中国水利水电科学研究院承担的“小湾拱坝极限承载力及变形稳定安全评价”项目通过对小湾拱坝坝基浅层卸荷松弛岩体全面系统的分析研究，建立了较切合实际的数学模型，通过与国内外萨扬舒申思克、Kolnbrein、李家峡、石门、藤子沟等完建拱坝的工程类比，阐明了坝基浅层卸荷松弛岩体对小湾拱坝局部稳定安全性的影响和小湾拱坝的整体安全度状况，并进一步证明了采取具有针对性综合工程处理措施的必要性，为小湾拱坝的顺利建设和安全运行提供了强有力的技术支持，具有重大的社会效益。

（中国水利水电科学研究院）

景洪水电站水力浮动式升船机整体模型试验研究

中国水利水电科学研究院受委托于 2005 年 2 月～2009 年 10 月进行了该试验研究。

水力浮动式升船机是一个由水力系统、传动系统、机械系统和控制系统为一体的复杂结构体系，涉及流体、机械、自动控制、结构安全等学科领域。本项研究针对景洪水电站水力浮动式升船机，采用数学模型和物理模型结合的方法，对影响水力浮动式升船机稳定运行的众多关键因素及水力浮动式升船机整体运行过程进行了深入研究。

(1) 本项研究建立了水力浮动式升船机整体系统的物理模型，通过模型试验的方法，全面系统地研究了水力浮动式升船机在正常工况和事故工况下输水系统的水力学特性和承船厢的运行特性，为水力浮动式升船机的设计提供了关键的技术支撑。

(2) 本项研究根据水力浮动式升船机的工作原理，建立了一个能够描述其整体系统运行过程的数学仿真模型，全面考虑了众多的影响因素，包括钢丝绳重量的转移、系统的阻力、因施工误差引起的竖井水位不同步和充泄水阀门处的气蚀系数等，比较真实地反映了水力浮动式升船机运行过程中的输水系统水力学特性、承船厢运行特性和钢丝绳受力特性等。水力浮动式升船机整体系统数学仿真模型的建立为研究这种新型通航建筑物型式提供了一个重要手段，对于深入认识其在运行过程中的水力特性和运行特性等提供了理论基础。

(3) 本项研究对水力浮动式升船机等惯性输水系统的水力同步性进行了系统深入的研究，针对由于施工误差等原因造成的各竖井间水位不同步现象，提出了有效合理的措施，完善了水力浮动式升船机的等惯性输水系统，明显改善了机械同步轴的受力条件，更加有利于水力浮动式升船机的安全可靠运行。

(4) 本项研究系统研究了竖井与平衡重浮筒之间的间隙大小、承船厢和平衡重浮筒的底缘外形轮廓及充泄水阀门的启闭方式等问题对水力浮动式升船机运行特性的影响规律，为水力浮动式升船机的设计和运行提供了科学依据。

景洪水电站位于云南省西双版纳傣族自治州首府景洪市北郊约 5km 处，为澜沧江干流中下游河段规划梯级中第六级，是兼顾发电、航运的综合性水利枢纽工程。景洪水电站通航建筑物型式为水力浮动式升船机，作为快速过坝建筑，其重要性不言而喻。而水力浮动式升船机是一种新型的通航建筑物型式，国内外均无应用实例。中国水电顾问集团昆明勘测设计研究院委托中国水利水电科学研究院对景洪水电站水力浮动式升船机开展研究，全面论证了水力浮动式升船机的可行性，并且为景洪水电站水力浮动式升船机的设计提供了大量的科学依据，其主要研究成果均在景洪水电站水力浮动式升船机的设计中得到了应用和实施。本项研究结果还为水力浮动式升船机这种新型升船机型式的设计提供了理论依据和经验。

（中国水利水电科学研究院）

三峡梯调监控系统升级完善

2008年6～12月，中国水利水电科学研究院对三峡梯调监控系统进行了升级完善。

梯调完善项目是大型的监控系统改造、完善项目，难度大，要求高。该项目具有典型代表性，积累的技术经验可以用于众多待改造升级的各大监控系统。具体如下：

（1）获取ABB SPIDER系统实时数据。要在SPIDER系统上增加新的应用，获取实时数据是前提也是最大的难点，通过对SPIDER系统的深入研究，在SPIDER实时数据库服务器上嵌入进程，通过ABB实时数据库内部接口获取实时数据及事件信息；并且，该进程运行在主、备两台实时数据库服务器上，利用SPIDER系统的任务队列管理实现了双机、双网的切换，进程自我守护等功能。实现了SPIDER数据库与H9000历史库的无缝连接。

（2）建立了H9000历史数据库，把原SPIDER系统最高5s分辨率提高到1s。为其他高级应用提供了接口。

（3）采用H9000系列产品中的趋势分析软件SMA2000，部分功能按梯级调度需求定制开发。SMA2000以其友好的人机交互视图，符合用户个性化的定制曲线，方便的事故回放、故障诊断功能，以及多种方式的事故报警获得用户的好评，对有效地提高生产计划性，监测设备运行趋势，发挥了显著作用。

（4）采用ABB SPL（Spider Programming Language）与HReport相结合的方式生成统计报表。

（5）实现了发电计划自动流转。发电计划的自动流转使原来依赖人工完成的工作都有计算机自动完成，大大降低了人为因素造成错误的可能性。

（6）对SPIDER的历史数据库系统在线备份，更换故障率高的模块，增加历史数据库容量为实现SPIDER历史数据库系统的平稳升级。

（中国水利水电科学研究院）

湖南凤滩水电厂扩机工程计算机监控系统研制开发

凤滩水电厂原物理RTU，设备复杂、维护费用高，且需要专人维护，新监控系统取消物理RTU，扩机工程直接通过仿真RTU实现与调度通信，老厂改造中根据改造进度，分次逐步取消物理RTU，实现仿真RTU通信。

AGC/AVC根据省调通过仿真RTU下发的全厂总有功和高压母线电压目标值，计算电厂需要调节的有功值和无功值，优化分配到各机组自动调节有功和无功，调节全厂总有功和母线电压到目标值。在与省调握手信号中，充分考虑系统特点，制定了可靠的策略，保证系统安全，采用给定值步长限制来防止省调给定值可能出现的错误，保护电厂运行安全。

AGC优化算法采用修正等容量比例分配算法，并采用步长修正策略，在保证满足省调目标负荷的情况下减少了机组调节次数，减少了机组磨损。AVC优化算法采用修正等功率因数分配算法，类似AGC采用步长修正策略，减少无功调节次数。为了避免机组频繁跨越振动区，AGC制订了合适的跨越振动区策略，即在下列情况下跨越振动区：①机组不跨越振动区造成功率缺额比跨越振动区后造成的功率缺额大于跨越振动区死区；②当机组间负荷严重不平衡时，即实发功率与容量比值差距太大时。另外，水头值对于AGC非常重要，为了得到可靠的水头值，程序采用滤波并多次取平均方式得到电厂水头值。通过上述措施，有效保证了AGC运行安全，并有效减少机组调节次数，减少机组磨损。

2008年12月，该项目通过湖南省电力公司组织，东江水电厂、柘溪水电厂、湖南省电力试验研究院、湖南省电力调度通信中心参加的验收。新监控系统投运，取得了显著的经济与社会效益。

（中国水利水电科学研究院）

葛洲坝水电厂二次设备GPS统一对时系统改造

2008年10月～2009年6月，中国水利水电科学研究院和葛洲坝水力发电厂对葛洲坝水电厂二次设备GPS统一对时系统进行改造，采用GPS信号集中接收、分层、分布开放式网络结构。系统共分三层：大江一级主站层、二级从站及现地扩展单元层、三级现地扩展单元层。各层之间采用双光纤网总线连接，构成高可靠冗余的网络结构。系统具有较高的传输速率和良好的抗电磁干扰能力。

（1）在大江电厂中控室辅助盘室安装GPS主站屏1面，配置BSS-3型GPS同步主钟和北斗同步主钟各1台。每台装置均配天线、热备交直流双电源，高精度恒温守时时钟。2台主钟之间采用光纤互备，每台主钟均配有20路光纤输出接口。其中14路多模光纤输出接口用来连接大江电厂14台机组二级时钟扩展装置，2路单模光纤二级输出接口用来连接二江电厂辅助盘室GPS从站，2路单模光纤二级输出接口用来连接500kV开关站GIS室GPS从站。

(2) 在500kV开关站GIS室安装GPS从站屏1面，新屏上安装2台4U BSS-3型GPS时钟扩展装置构成GPS从站。每台扩展装置均配两路光纤输入接口，热备交直流双电源。2路卫星时钟信号分别取自大江主站的GPS信号和自大江主站的北斗信号，2套时钟信号互为热备用，当有一路收不到信号时自动切换到另一路备用通道，保证从站时钟正常工作。

(3) 在二江电厂辅助盘室安装GPS从站屏1面，新屏上安装2台4U BSS-3型GPS时钟扩展装置构成GPS从站。每台装置均配2路光纤输入接口、12路多模光纤输出接口、热备交直流双电源。2路卫星时钟信号分别取自大江主站的GPS信号和大江主站的北斗信号，2套时钟信号互为热备用，当有一路收不到信号时自动切换到另一路备用通道，保证从站时钟正常工作。10路光纤输出接口分别用来连接二江电厂7台机组、0F发电机组、葛茶线保护、闸门泵站集控时钟扩展装置。二江电厂GPS从站上还插有串行口输出模板、脉冲输出模板、NTP网络输出模板，用来为二江电厂各种线路保护等自动装置提供对时信号。

(4) 二江电厂区域厂房共有7台机组，按发电机组每台机组配置1套时钟扩展装置，故配置7台时钟扩展装置。每台扩展装置就地安装在所对应的机旁控制屏上。根据发电机组保护对时要求，扩展装置配置串行口模板、PPS/PPM脉冲模板。

(5) 二江电厂区域0F厂房配置1台时钟扩展装置。扩展装置就地安装在机旁控制屏上。根据发电机组保护对时要求，扩展装置配置串行口模板、PPS/PPM脉冲模板。

(6) 在葛茶线保护室配置1台时钟扩展装置。扩展装置安装在可控制屏上。根据保护对时要求，配置串行口模板、PPS/PPM脉冲模板。

(7) 在闸门泵站集控室配置1台时钟扩展装置(三级)。扩展装置安装在可控制屏上。根据对时要求，配置NTP网络模板、PPS/PPM脉冲模板。

该工程顺利通过葛洲坝水电厂二次设备GPS统一对时系统改造工程竣工验收，最终认为该项目质量、安全、进度、造价均符合合同要求，已取得了显著的经济与社会效益。

(中国水利水电科学研究院)

三峡左岸电站WEB生产实时信息发布系统升级

2008年10～12月，中国水利水电科学研究院与三峡水力发电厂对三峡左岸电站WEB生产实时信息发布系统进行了升级改造。

(1) 自适应变速数据写入功能，兼顾数据时效性、信息量与服务器性能。升级项目采用变速写入数据的方式，在数据量大时，快速写入，确保网站数据的实效性，在数据量小时，慢速写入保证服务器的性能，完成15 000条数据全部进入历史库，有效提高了服务器的工作效率，并且扩大了信息量。

(2) 利用缓存，进一步降低服务器工作量，提升使用效果。改造后的三峡左岸电站WEB生产实时信息发布系统采用的页面及数据双缓存，一方面降低了网站服务器端的工作，减少了访问数据库服务器的次数；另一方面，也提高了数据的查取效率，进一步降低了服务器的工作量，确保了服务器的性能，也提升了使用效果。

(3) 数据异步传输，画面刷新无闪烁。改造后的三峡左岸电站WEB生产实时信息发布系统采用Ajax网络技术，数据异步传输，由客户端进行画面局部刷新，画面刷新无闪烁。

(4) 提供调试页面，方便查询修改数据点。手工绘制网页的WEB发布系统一般都存在修改数据点链接困难的问题，本系统在此方面也作了一定的改进，提供调试页面。在此页面中，可看到每个动态图元所链接的数据点及所有数据点的原始数据信息，不但方便了后期的维护工作，也为用户提供了更多的数据信息。

(5) 跨监控系统平台，实现数据源完全解析。本系统所用的数据源是三峡左岸ABB公司的计算机监控系统，通过解析原数据源，实现了跨监控系统平台的WEB发布系统，可进一步在其他监控系统平台上推广应用，具有广泛的推广意义。

(中国水利水电科学研究院)

车载式液压驱动泵装置研制

天津水利电力机电研究所于2001年12月～2009年9月研制了车载式液压驱动泵装置。

该车载式液压驱动泵装置是一个集泵、动力机、进出水管、起吊、运输等设备为一体、经高度集成的装置。本课题研制的车载式泵装置是将系统所有设备全部集成在一个汽车底盘上或集装箱内，其功能与常规固定式泵站相同，但解决了流动和快速作业问题。由汽车拖至需要的地方以实现移动，系统自带柴油机作为动力机，通过液压传动、液压马达驱动水泵，机组可自动升降安装。

本项目设计采用液压马达驱动水泵，驱动源与水泵间靠柔性橡胶液压管连接，液压马达设在泵的导叶体内且与转轮直联。这样，液压软管根据水泵机组升降的位置不同可任意调整，同时采用柴油机为原动机而不需要电力设施，把泵系统集成在汽车底盘上或装入集装箱内，并借助于汽车，以实现泵装置的移动。

装置构成包括轴流泵、液压马达、液压泵、柴油机、液压输送管、泵的升降机构、液压站、控制箱、汽车底盘或集装箱等。

工作流程：控制箱→柴油机→液压泵→液压站→泵的升降安装→液压马达→水泵抽水。

产品应用情况：①2003 年应用在小汤山非典医院的防洪排水；②在北京市水利局河湖处“元大都遗址修复工程”小月亮河清淤排污工程中，运行 27 天，排污水 150 多万立方米；③在北京玉渊潭八一湖北湖清淤排水 10 万 m^3；④在南水北调中线工程北京段西三环路下涵洞排水中，3 天排水 30 万 m^3；⑤2008 年奥运会排水预案，备战在北辰立交桥下。

（天津水利电力机电研究所）

碧口大坝震后补强加固处理

“5.12” 汶川大地震使碧口大坝在水平和垂直方向均发生了明显变形。变形量最大点发生在坝顶河床部位，坝顶最大沉降量 27.5cm，向上游最大水平位移量 16.4cm，心墙最大沉降量接近 20cm。大坝背水面 691m 高程以下向下游位移，大坝护面开裂，坝面排水沟扭曲、变形，大坝渗流量也有所增大，受损情况严重。震后，水库采取低水位运行方式。为了消除大坝的安全隐患，保证大坝和下游人民生命财产安全，确保安全发供电，提高电站水能利用率，决定对大坝进行补强加固处理。

该项目由大唐碧口水力发电厂、中国水电顾问集团西北勘测设计研究院、四川明星水电公司共同完成。

碧口壤土心墙土石混合坝的防渗心墙与 L 型防浪墙接缝部位防渗问题，直接关系到高水位时大坝的安全稳定，大坝竣工后，对防渗心墙与 L 型防浪墙接缝部位分别于 1979 年、1983 年、1995 年及 2006 年进行了四次大规模水泥和化学水泥回填灌浆。解决“5.12” 汶川大地震后碧口大坝坝面出现的变形等问题，其中震后土石坝裂缝、渗漏、不均匀沉陷等技术是主要技术创新点。

壤土心墙坝坝顶混凝土防浪墙与防渗心墙顶部，只允许将混凝土层钻穿并入心墙 30cm 。防渗心墙与两岸接触部位钻孔时穿过心墙至基岩，为了防止心墙在灌浆过程中因灌浆压力过大而变形，对壤土心墙造成施工损伤，产生新的裂缝和渗漏点，采用下保护套管的方法保护心墙，并在套管底部半米内梅花型布设 6mm 孔，便于浆液顺利流出套管进入坝体缝隙。具体措施为：

（1）采用分排分序钻孔灌浆方式，钻孔穿过防浪墙与防渗心墙结合面 0.3m，防渗心墙与两岸的结合面，钻孔打到齿墙混凝土或基岩终孔，不入岩。

（2）水泥灌浆采用 42.5 号普通硅酸盐水泥，灌浆最大压力为 0.2MPa，控制抬动观测变形值不大于 0.2mm。

（3）水泥灌浆结束 14 天后进行“LW”化学灌浆。

（4）采用在检查孔内注入水泥浆液的形式，通过观察检查孔的注入率及压力变化情况，检验大坝灌浆效果，避免了采用注水检测对坝体的损害。

碧口大坝震后经补强加固处理，水库蓄水位超过正常高水位 704m，最高蓄至 704.98m，超蓄水 0.98m。根据“5.12”汶川大地震后大坝监测方案，对大坝水平垂直位移、浸润线、绕坝渗流等项目进行了加密测量，从监测数据来看，无突变、无异常，说明大坝补强加固效果良好，大坝又恢复到一个新的稳定状态。这使碧口水电站在发电、防洪等方面又能发挥出巨大的作用，同时，有效地保证了下游麒麟寺水电站的正常运行及下游人民生命财产安全，有良好的社会效益。

（中国大唐集团公司）

不吊转子对 45MW 水轮发电机定子槽内进行探查的方法研究与实践

大唐石泉水电厂 3 号 45MW 发电机，投运至今已 30 多年。在 2005 年 7 月 25 日机组定检时，发现定子内膛上下端部周圈约 300mm 内的铁芯、铁芯与槽楔接缝处有不同程度焦黑色略带红色附着物（红色粉末状锈斑），而且随着时间的推移附着物有增多的趋势，另外还有少量槽楔、环氧玻璃布板平垫条、半导体平垫条下移，且下移程度超过《水轮发电机基本技术条件》的规定。为此，大唐石泉水力发电厂研究了不吊转子的情况下对定子线棒上下端部槽内绝缘进行探查的施工工艺，对线棒、铁芯绝缘层的探查和试验，找出导致产生附着物的原因，提出解决办法；并且在不吊转子的情况下对发电机定子松动下移的槽楔、环氧玻璃布板平垫条、半导体平垫条进行紧固处理。在机组B级检修时完成了只有A级检修才能完成的项目。

该项目主要创新点如下：

（1）不吊转子对45MW水轮发电机定子槽内进行的绝缘探查的施工工艺，改变了传统的作业方式，施工方法上有所创新。

（2）在不吊转子的情况下用磁极键自制的“Z”字形和“I”形专用工具，对定子线棒端部槽楔取出和恢复紧固的施工工艺，以及对运行年限超过35年的机组绝缘状况分析及采取的应对措施。

（3）不吊转子对发电机定子松动下移的槽楔、环氧玻璃布板平垫条、半导体平垫条进行紧固处理，而且不损伤线棒的绝缘。

该方法可节约材料和人工费用，并明显缩短了检修工期，已在大唐石泉水电厂同型号同年代的1、2号发电机上和陕西省略阳县葫芦头水电站推广应用，对推动水电机组检修技术进步有积极作用。

（中国大唐集团公司）

百龙滩水电厂重锤下坠防护方案研究

百龙滩水电厂装有6台灯泡贯流式水轮发电机组，单机容量32MW。机组在导叶控制环上设有一个28.6t的重锤，以保证在调速器发生故障时能将导叶关闭。

该重锤的悬挂是通过一根直径为100mm、两端螺纹为M80的连杆与控制环连接，重锤离地最低2.9m。机组运行时，重锤随控制环实时上下运动，行程约1.3m，同时还小幅摆动。在重锤的下方装置有两根引自流道直径300mm的排水管，水管所处高程94m，低于上游正常水位126m达32m。虽然对一个28.6t的重物，其连接方式和受力分析都经过了设计、核算和监造，理论上是符合要求的，多年的运行考验也未出现异常，但是，如果重锤坠落，会导致两根排水管破坏造成大量漏水，估算的漏水量为5615m^3/h，厂房内水位上涨速度为10.2 cm/min，10min内就可使94m高程的设备瘫痪，造成全厂事故停机。该位置漏水无法短时间内控制，会造成水淹整个厂房的重大事故。

针对这一重大的危险因素，百龙滩水电厂在2005年9月开始组织厂家和设计单位研讨了重锤下坠防护方案。曾拟出了在水管上方用枕木等材料增设缓冲平台、用钢材焊制固定平台、在重锤上更换或加大连杆等方案，但都因为平台影响水管阀门日常操作检修、结构复杂、改造程序繁琐、周期长和投资大而未能采纳。后经电厂技术人员的调研和分析，最终采用了增设钢丝绳防坠的方案。该方案利用了重锤上4个吊耳，在控制环伸出的吊杆上焊定位吊耳，用2条直径28mm的钢丝绳在5个吊耳间穿挂成8股吊绳，整套钢丝绳的许用拉力为780kN，破断力不少于4000kN，即满足了承受重锤自身的重量和下坠所产生的动能，又大大节省了项目费用和制作周期。

该防护方案的主要创新点：

（1）在导叶控制环上焊接定位吊耳。对控制环吊锤位置的焊接可行性进行了分析研究，对定位吊耳的材质、规格进行了反复的推敲，并制定了焊接工艺和施工方案，避免影响控制环原有的刚度和操作灵活性。

（2）采用钢丝绳吊挂的方式，安全、经济、实用。临时和固定式缓冲平台难免影响到排水管阀门的日常操作和检修，而且制作复杂，投资大，周期长。采用钢丝绳吊挂的方式对重锤下坠进行防护是安全、经济、快捷、简便的创意。效果非常好。

（3）利用重锤本身吊运安装时用的吊耳，因地制宜，大大节省开支和施工时间。

（4）钢丝绳和卡环的选型恰当，安全、经济。

百龙滩水电厂于2006年4月底完成了全厂6台机组重锤下坠防护项目的工作，在2005年冬机组检修期间，曾用桥机通过防护钢丝绳起吊重锤，检验了防护钢丝绳对重锤下坠的防护能力。3年多来，作为辅助安全措施的防护钢丝绳虽然没有真正意义上的“动作”过，但它每时每刻都在担负着安全保驾护航的重要作用。

目前，我国灯泡贯流式水电机组的数量逐年增加，普遍采用重锤在调速器发生故障实现关机的方式，采用增设钢丝绳防坠的方案值得借鉴。

（中国大唐集团公司）

大化水电厂2号机协联曲线分析与校验

广西桂冠电力股份有限公司大化水力发电总厂，为了降低机组运行振动和噪声，减轻空蚀，提高水轮机工作效率，对大化水电厂首台增容改造的水轮发电机组2号机水轮机的协联曲线进行分析、校验。

项目选择大化水电厂具有代表性的高、中、低工作水头和不同导叶开度工况下，通过纯手动操作轮叶角度，按照机组运行振动、噪声相对较小，机组出力相对较大、负荷摆动幅度小，且水导轴承摆度值较小等要求，选择一一对应的最好协联轮叶角度，并与厂家提供的协联轮叶角度进行比较。

2002年3月，结合2号机组年度检修，对该机协联曲线进行修正，并结合大化水电厂洪水期低水头机组运行方式，收到了很好的效果，机组运行振动、噪声得以减轻，水轮机的工作效率得以提高，年尾机组检修检查，叶片正面进水边外沿的空蚀问题得到了有效控制。厂部决定在2003春季机组检修时，将修正后的协联曲线推广应用于大化电厂的其他3台机组（1、3、4号机）。

4台机组按照修正后的协联曲线运行，洪水期期间又结合大化水电厂洪水期低水头机组运行方式，机组、厂房、大坝安全运行得到很大改善，在此之后的机组检修当中，叶片正面进水边外沿的空蚀问题得到了有效控制，在前面增容改造的2、3、1号机组叶片空蚀的深度和范围都没有变化迹象，最后面增容改造的4号机组至今尚没有出现空蚀问题。

开展协联曲线校验，确保机组在各种水头和工况下按最优工况协联运行，对提高机组水能利用率和发电效率，减轻水轮机桨叶正面进水边外沿空蚀很有意义，值得推广。

（中国大唐集团公司）

乐滩水电厂汛期水位动态控制研究

水电厂水库一般在汛期降低水位运行，对水电厂的效益有一定的影响。乐滩水电厂在上游龙滩水库（多年调节）建成蓄水后，水情情况有了较大的改变，枯水径流会有所增加，而洪水将得到削减，入库泥沙将大为减少，实施汛期水位动态控制成为可能。为此，广西桂冠开发投资电力有限责任公司联合广西电力试验勘察研究院进行了汛期水位动态控制研究。通过对红水河流域水情的分析与研究，综合考虑安全与效益，从径流与洪水、大坝安全、动态控制范围确定、动态控制使用范围确定、效益、调度运行操作原则、实施条件、现状、风险分析及对策等方面进行了研究，在不影响大坝安全、不增加库区土地淹没损失、对电站下游不造成人为洪水的原则下，提出了乐滩水电厂汛限水位动态控制调度线。

根据研究成果，经广西区防汛办同意，广西桂冠开发投资电力有限责任公司乐滩水电厂于2007年、2008年进行了研究成果的试运应用，在确保水库安全的前提下，取得了显著的经济效益与社会效益。

该项目的主要创新点：

（1）按照不影响大坝安全、不增加库区土地淹没损失、不造成电站下游人为洪水的原则，所提出的乐滩水电厂汛限水位动态控制调度线合理。

（2）掌握好实施汛限水位动态控制调度线的条件。

（3）采取相应对策，使实施汛限水位动态控制调度运行的风险得到进一步的减小。

乐滩水电厂实施汛限水位动态控制调度线运行的经济效益显著。按汛期水位动态控制调度运行，枯、平、丰三代表年的平均有效电量较汛期按汛期水位110m运行增加1.375 2亿 kW·h，可增加售电收入3056万元；当扣除对百龙滩水电厂的电量损失后，代表年平均增加有效电量1.165 9亿 kW·h，售电收入增加2624万元。

乐滩水电厂实施汛限水位动态控制调度线运行的容量效益意义重大。实施汛限水位动态控制调度运行较汛期限制水位110m运行，6～9月枯、平、丰代表年预想出力增加的最大值分别为2.23、4.12、4.85万kW，这对汛期缺少调峰电源、水电机组出力严重受阻的广西电网来说具有特别重要的意义。

乐滩水电厂实施汛限水位动态控制调度线运行后，年平均实获有效电量1.165 9亿 kW·h，可替代火电发电量1.224 2亿 kW·h，每年可节省标煤约4.04万t，减少二氧化硫排放量约404t，有利于节煤减排保护环境。

（中国大唐集团公司）

可调式密封盖在水轮发电机油槽上的应用

广西平班水电开发有限公司推广应用了可调式密封盖，在防止水轮发电机组轴承油雾外逸和甩油，以及方便检修等方面取得了明显效果。

新应用的油槽可调式密封盖，采用两道与转轴直接接触的多等分内环瓣，每道内环瓣在密封槽内可以径向调节滑动，并采取一定方式控制内环瓣的跟踪量和退让量，而内环瓣之间的间隙由间隙补偿器来控制，形成一整套力学链相互控制对转轴的压力，使轴承运行时油槽内产生的油雾无法外逸。

可调式密封盖能保证机组运行5年不需更换零件。即便在检修中发现某处间隙略大，只需拆下2个M5的限位螺栓，将新的内环瓣再安装回去，就完全可以解决，工作量极小。且新密封盖外环采用特种轻质铝合金结构，其重量仅为旧密封盖的三分之一左右，开盖检修较为方便。

目前已有岩滩、天生桥一、二级、五强溪等多座水电厂使用，在防止油雾和甩油现象及方便检修等方面均有效果明显。

采用该项新技术，防止机组运行过程中形成的油雾外逸，可避免对环境、下游河道造成油污染。

（中国大唐集团公司）

微功耗无线网在线防误操作系统在那兰水电厂的应用

云南大唐国际电力有限公司在那兰水电厂成功应用了微功耗无线网在线防误操作系统，有效防止了该厂电气误操作的发生，并为其他水电厂应用此系统积累了宝贵的经验，对提高电力安全生产水平有积极意义。

实时在线防误综合操作系统是当今最先进的电气防误操作系统。它对硬件设备进行系统管理，以先进的“五层防线”为设计理念，在人和设备之间，依靠科学的技术措施构筑五层防线，这一理念是对传统五防概念的重大跨越。在涵盖传统五防概念的基础上，从设备操作过程全程防误的角度出发，采用不同的技术措施，从根本上杜绝电气误操作的发生。

该系统采用较低的成本，就将传统的离线式的微机防误操作系统提升为在线的实时的微机防误操作系统，无论是装置的性能方面还是装置的功能方面都有了很大的提高，为水电厂的安全生产特别是电气专业的安全操作构建了一道坚固的防线。其特点如下：

（1）引入了微功耗无线网络、移动操作终端等创新概念及先进技术。

（2）实时在线电脑钥匙的使用，使主系统与电脑钥匙能够实时进行信息交换。

（3）实现了电动设备远动操作的强制性闭锁。

（4）有线网络与无线网络能够双网互备，使用更加灵活，工作更加可靠。

该系统自 2008 年 1 月投入运行以来，工作可靠，运行稳定，有效防止了电气误操作的发生，为那兰水电厂安全生产提供了可靠保证。

实时在线防误综合操作系统将在云南中小水电厂推广。

（中国大唐集团公司）

黑启动试验方案首次在云南中型水电厂成功应用

云南大唐国际电力有限公司按照云南电网黑启动调度实施方案要求，研究制订了所属土卡河、那兰、崖羊山、龙马四个水电厂黑启动试验方案，并进行了黑启动试验，达到了预期的目的。

云南电力公司那兰水电厂位于云南省红河州金平县藤条江河段上，装机容量 50MW×3，为混流式机组，于 2005 年 12 月全部投产发电。崖羊山水电厂属李仙江流域开发中的第一级，装机容量 60MW×2，为混流式机组，于 2006 年 9 月全部投产发电。土卡河水电厂共装设 3 台水轮发电机组，河床式大坝，机组总出力为 3×55MW，于 2007 年 12 月全部投产发电。龙马水电厂属李仙江流域开发中的第四级，装机容量 95MW×3，为混流式机组，于 2007 年 12 月全部投产发电。

2007 年 1 月，云南大唐国际电力有限公司开始黑启动试验的准备工作，并根据自身设备的特点编写了土卡河、龙马、崖羊山、那兰水电厂的黑启动方案。黑启动试验方案确定后，开始对土卡河、那兰、崖羊山、龙马水电厂的技术供水、渗漏排水系统、调速器、蝶阀（快速闸门）、励磁系统、直流系统、不停电电源（UPS）、监控系统进行仔细的排查，及时消除了影响黑启动试验的隐患及人为因数。比如土卡河水电厂监控系统网络柜电源接至 400V 厂用电，在黑启动试验前改接至电厂 UPS。

2008 年 4 月 21 日，进行并完成土卡河电厂黑启动试验，5 月 14 日相继完成了龙马、崖羊山、那兰电厂黑启动试验。试验验证了 4 座水电厂全部具备黑启动能力。

为满足云南电网在系统崩溃时李仙江流域各电厂实现黑动能力，恢复电网安全稳定运行，2009 年黑启动试验推广到居甫渡电厂和戈兰滩电厂。这一系列的黑启动试验，为电网的安全稳定运行夯实了基础，使电网的安全水平得到极大提高。

云南大唐国际电力有限公司在云南中型水电厂率先进行了黑启动，并取得了成功。其中，在完全失去外来电源，仅靠直流系统蓄电池储存的电能量和油液压系统储存的液压能量下完成黑启动试验，推广价值大。

（中国大唐集团公司）

梨园水电站可能最大洪水研究

（一）工程概况及立项背景

梨园水电站位于金沙江中游河段，是金沙江中游水电规划的第三个梯级电站。坝址控制流域面积220 053km^2。

梨园水电站工程规模为大Ⅰ型、且采用当地材料坝型，根据国家有关标准和规范，应采用可能最大洪水作为大坝校核标准。因此，研究该电站的可能最大降水和可能最大洪水是必要的。

（二）课题研究的主要内容

本课题采用水文气象学与水文学方法结合进行梨园水电站可能最大洪水研究。内容包括：

（1）确定可能最大洪水研究的控制断面。石鼓水文站，其流域面积214 184km^2占梨园坝址的97.3%，与坝址洪水特性一致。因此推求石鼓站可能最大洪水，并由此推算得到坝址可能最大洪水。

（2）确定可能最大洪水推求的计算方案：一为直接推算石鼓站可能最大洪水，二为巴塘～石鼓区间可能最大洪水与巴塘以上流域相应洪水用水文学方法叠加。

（3）流域暴雨洪水普查及流域内天气气候与洪水特征关系分析。

（4）流域暴雨天气成因分析包含流域水汽输送规律、流域暴雨主要天气形势分析总结，包括1953～2005年共计53年317个流域强降水过程天气成因逐例分析。

（5）采用等雨量线法进行面雨量计算。其中针对地形复杂程度和站点分布差异采用了Cressman插值优化和等雨量线分析客观化对面雨量计算进行了改进，面雨量成果可用性得以提高。

（6）推求长、短历时可能最大降水。其中短历时可能最大降水采用当地暴雨放大方法推求，长历时可能最大降水采用典型暴雨组合替换法推求。

（7）依据推荐的可能最大降水推求可能最大洪水。根据流域特性，推求可能最大洪水时，产流采用扣损法和降雨径流相关法，汇流采用净雨同倍比方法。

（三）研究背景及技术难点

金沙江自然地理条件特殊，梨园水电站控制流域面积较大，在20万km^2以上。因此本专题属于特大面积(50 000km^2以上）可能最大降水和可能最大洪水的研究，难点主要表现在：

（1）洪水历时较长，暴雨组合序列的合理性论证存在较大困难。

（2）坝址控制流域跨越经纬度较大，地形地貌变化明显，该区为东亚地形起伏变化最大的地区，北纬30°上下的地理条件、气候条件、降雨径流特性、洪水特性、资料条件等差异较大，在可能最大降水和可能最大洪水推求时难以反映这种差异。总体而言，影响流域暴雨的天气系统多而复杂，雨量站点稀少且分布不均匀，可能最大降水和可能最大洪水分析工作的技术难度较大。就国内外目前的研究状况而言，类似于本项目的针对地形起伏变化大、涉及青藏高原区及横断山脉区、影响流域暴雨的天气系统多而复杂的流域的可能最大降水和可能最大洪水研究，在工程应用上尚属空白。

（3）本课题研究可能最大降水推求采用典型暴雨组合替换法。科学合理的暴雨天气形势分型是可能最大降水成果组合替换的理论基础。坝址控制流域空间跨度大，造就了流域天气气候空间差异大的特征，流域内具备除海洋性气候以外的我国各种气候区。针对流域的暴雨天气形势分型基础性工作难度大。目前国内外尚无适用于大空间跨度且复杂天气气候背景下流域可能最大降水成果组合替换的天气形势分型支撑技术。

（4）水汽输送直接制约强降水的发生发展。水汽输送分析也是降水组合替换的天气学分析基础。而目前对于青藏高原水汽来源多向、输送机制复杂的青藏高原地区降水尚无定量分析技术。

（四）关键技术与创新点

针对上述技术难点，本专题在推求可能最大降水和可能最大洪水时，在前人研究的基础上采用了创新的计算方案及分析方法，关键技术及创新点分述如下：

（1）首创按巴塘至石鼓区间可能最大洪水与巴塘（北纬30°）以上流域相应洪水用水文学方法叠加的计算方案，即以北纬30°为界，将青藏高原少雨区和巴塘以下横断山脉多雨区分开考虑，基本考虑到了本流域不同的天气成因和暴雨特性。本课题针对地形起伏变化大、涉及青藏高原区及横断山脉区；且影响流域暴雨的天气系统多而复杂、暴雨历时长、降雨时空分布极不均匀的流域的可能最大降水和可能最大洪水研究，填补了目前国内外在工程应用上的空白。

（2）项目相应研究建立了大尺度环流、区域环流两个空间尺度的客观聚类天气形势分型与强降水预报员概念主观模型结合的流域强降水主要天气形势分析技术。首先利用聚类分析、相关分析对强降水个例的北半球和流域关键区500hPa环流进行客观分型；然后引入预报员概念模型修正和动力解释。新方法确保了降水主要天气系统分型在大面积、复杂天气气候背景下的客观性和科学性。

（3）项目将国际上目前最先进且公认的HYSPLITM4（第4代气质点拉格朗日混杂后向轨迹分析模式）应用于青藏高原，对流域水汽运动轨迹进行了后向追踪并分析了水汽来源路径，克服了特大流域水汽来源多向的特有复杂性和水汽输送机制方面的研究困难。

（4）在面雨量计算中针对地形复杂程度和站点分布差异采用了Cressman插值优化和等雨量线分析客观化对面雨量计算进行了改进，面雨量成果可用性得以提高。同时开展了流域内不同观测站点密度条件下面雨量计算误差评估，分析了由于站点密度导致的面雨量计算出现振荡的原因。在提高计算精度的同时对流域不同时期站点雨量资料的可靠性进行了科学论证，提高了专题研究的科学性和实用性。

（5）由可能最大降水推求可能最大洪水采用传统的产汇流方法，其中汇流计算采用净雨同倍比放大法。该方法充分利用实测特大洪水典型流量过程，认为可能最大洪水发生条件下的净雨与典型洪水的净雨呈线性关系。特大流域产汇流机制复杂，且本流域资料条件不足以支撑单位线法和模型法的采用，而净雨同倍比放大法以典型洪水过程为基础，避免了模型法、单位线法中率定参数的主观任意性，且计算简便、可行性强，实践证明，该方法适用于特大流域的可能最大洪水推求，值得推广。

（五）课题研究效益及推广应用情况

本专题研究成果已于2008年5月在由水电水利规划设计总院主持召开的《金沙江中游河段梨园水电站可能最大洪水专题研究报告》审查会上通过了评审。成果已应用于梨园水电站可研设计中，为梨园水电站的防洪安全设计提供有效、合理的科学依据。

本专题是金沙江中游以上流域通过正式审查的第一个可能最大降水和可能最大洪水项目。水电水利规划设计总院已明确提出金沙江虎跳峡河段龙头水库比选专题的可能最大洪水成果均依据本专题提出的石鼓水文站可能最大洪水成果得到。这将显著地节省上述电站前期工作费用。

梨园水电站以上控制流域面积大，自然地理条件复杂，上游大部分为青藏高原区，地形相对平坦，气候寒冷，冰川融雪较多，暴雨量级小且发生次数少，且上游站点稀少；下游为横断山区，地形崎岖，暴雨是洪水的主要成因，雨量站点相对较多，但雨量随地形高程变化又十分明显。总体而言，流域地理条件、气候条件、降雨径流特性、洪水特性等差异较大、极为复杂，可能最大降水和可能最大洪水分析工作难度较大，澜沧江、怒江的上游也存在类似的问题，本专题研究中所采用的工作方法、研究思路、技术路线、分析成果等，可为金沙江其他电站、澜沧江、怒江各水电站可能最大降水和可能最大洪水研究工作提供参考、借鉴。

本项目中建立的主要天气形势聚类分析和强降水预报员概念模型结合的流域强降水主要天气形势分析技术，可推广应用于具有相似特点的流域。

项目引入的HYSPLITM4（第4代空气质点拉格朗日混杂后向轨迹分析模式）对流域水汽运动轨迹进行后向追踪并分析了水汽来源路径，提供了新的定量水汽分析技术。该技术可在其他流域水汽分析中推广应用。

项目中可能最大降水分析技术、典型年替换组合分析方法、面雨量分析方法、可能最大洪水产汇流计算方法均可在其他流域可能最大洪水推求中推广应用。

（中国水电顾问集团昆明勘测设计研究院　林　芸）

云南省低热微膨胀水泥研发及其在水电工程中的应用

（一）项目简述

2008年以前，云南省内没有能够供应低热微膨胀水泥的企业，省外周边地区供应低热微膨胀水泥的厂家也仅1～2家，且距离水电工程较集中的西南部三江流域在建的水电站较远。因此，中国水电顾问集团昆明勘测设计研究院（以下简称昆明院）结合小湾水电站需要开展了低热微膨胀水泥的相关工作。

小湾水电站拱坝坝肩抗力体洞井塞置换混凝土浇筑后不进行接缝灌浆，要求一期、二期混凝土之间的收缩缝张开度不大于0.3mm。曾考虑采用中热水泥外掺轻烧MgO的混凝土进行回填，并调查和检测了多个厂家生产的轻烧MgO，结果表明品质及稳定性均不理想，未达到相应要求。为解决工程实际困难，昆明院与云南红塔滇西水泥股份有限公司（以下简称滇西厂）采取院厂联合的方式，进行新型干法窑生产低热微膨胀水泥的开发研究，随即该项目得到云南省科技厅的扶持。

（二）主要研究内容

昆明院对实施方案进行总体策划，提出工作思路和技术路线，滇西厂积极组织跟进，双方共同检查控制、总结评估，主要研究工作如下：

（1）昆明院提出技术指标要求，滇西厂制定工业化生产参数进行试生产，初步掌握水泥的生产配方和工艺控制。

（2）在试生产的水泥指标达到国标要求后，通过研究水泥比表面积与线膨胀率的相关性、水泥比表面积与强度及水化热相关性、水泥组分与强度及水化热相关性，掌握水泥水化热、水泥强度及膨胀性能的变化规律，进行水泥优化研究。与此同时，通过工业性规模生产，探索煅烧工艺和粉磨工艺参数，确定低热微膨胀水泥的水化热、强度、线膨胀率等指标的最优控制范围。

（3）通过混凝土配合比及性能试验，研究低热微膨胀水泥用于工程的可行性，以满足混凝土性能指标作为水泥选择的标准，进一步开展水泥优化改性工作。最终成果表明：采用上述水泥配制的混凝土，其强度等级、抗渗及抗冻性能均满足小湾抗力体二期回填混凝土的要求，且水化热较低，混凝土的自生体积变形性能较好。

（4）在上述研究的基础上，昆明院利用三维有限元分析方法进行了抗力体混凝土温度场、温度应力及结构变形情况的计算工作，结果表明小湾抗力体二期回填混凝土采用低热微膨胀水泥的方案可行。

（三）技术创新点

（1）采用新型干法窑生产低热微膨胀水泥，填补了云南省空白。

（2）低热微膨胀水泥用于高拱坝坝肩抗力体洞井塞置换混凝土属国内首创。

（3）低热微膨胀水泥水化热较低，配制的混凝土自生体积变形具有微膨胀性能，变形形态较好、膨胀量较大、后期稳定不收缩，技术性能指标优越。

（4）采用院厂联合攻关模式，水电设计单位参与到水泥的整个生产过程中，与水电工程结合紧密，制定的技术路线正确、技术指标合理，研究工作效率高。

（四）成果应用及市场前景

小湾水电站采用红塔滇西低热微膨胀水泥浇筑坝肩抗力体二期回填混凝土3万多立方米，预埋测缝计检测：抗力体二期回填混凝土边墙及前后两段间施工缝的张开度绝大部分在0.3mm以内，约50%的缝处于挤压状态，满足设计要求。与采用其他厂家的低热微膨胀水泥相比，小湾坝肩抗力体混凝土仅运费就节省500万元以上，经济效益明显。

红塔滇西低热微膨胀水泥在小湾工程成功应用后，其他水电站（如阿海、金安桥、马鹿塘二期、威远江、苏家河口等）也相继在导流隧洞堵头及填塘混凝土中应用，其结果均满足要求，至今已应用近2万t。

云南省低热微膨胀水泥的研发，其研究成果和研究方式对其他工程具有一定的指导和参考价值；体现了昆明院坚持技术创新，节约自然资源，积极推进新材料、新工艺发展的工程设计理念。该项目在满足水电工程需要的同时，还部分解决了矿渣堆存的问题，符合国家环保政策。随着三江流域水电建设的发展，云南省以及缅甸、老挝等东南亚国家对该品种水泥的需求量逐渐增大，红塔滇西低热微膨胀水泥具有广阔的应用前景。

（中国水电顾问集团昆明勘测设计研究院　解　敏）

工程地球物理层析成像技术的研究和应用

（一）项目背景

工程地球物理层析成像技术是近十年来开发和运用的高新技术方法之一。主要推广应用于工程地基基础勘察和工程施工质量检测领域。

层析成像技术最早应用于医学，工程勘察领域的层析成像原理与医学CT扫描原理一致，即采用仪器系统地测量人为激发的某种射线（声波、地震波、电磁波等）从各个不同角度穿过探测区域的走时或衰减量，根据走时或衰减量精确计算与探测区域物质组成相关的某种特性的分布，从而达到探测其内部异常的一种地球物理反演技术。

对层析成像的研究，欧美20世纪80年代中期就已开始。20世纪80年代末，国内部分研究单位开始进行地震层析成像研究，直到90年代层析成像技术才逐渐应用于生产；到目前为止，尽管层析成像的精度较常规物探方法有较大提高，但由于诸多因素的影响，实际应用效果仍不尽如人意，成果精度的误差一直徘徊在2～3m，甚至更大。

中国水电顾问集团中南勘测设计研究院物探测试研究中心自20世纪90年代初期在向家坝水电站、广州市轨道交通2号线北延段工程和湖南金竹山火电厂扩建工程等基础勘察中，结合工程实际，对层析成像技术进行了大量的研究，主要在仪器设备选择、观测技术措施、数据处理和资料解释方法上进行了创新和规范，取得了可靠的、高精度成果资料（成果的误差不大于1m）和较好的社会效益，具有实用性和推广价值。

（二）项目研究的内容及成果指标

为了达到高精度层析成像，项目研究中重点对影响成果精度的四个环节（问题）进行了深入的研究并达到相应的成果指标：

（1）观测系统设计。在对射线密度和射线正交性进行充分讨论的基础上，提出了尽可能优化观测系统的方法和措施，即设计层析成像观测系统时，首先应考虑到射线有限视角对成像质量的影响，尽量增大最大排列长度（如各激发、发射点处均进行全测段测试）以增大投影角度；其次，不局限于探测段测试，尽可能向上下两端延长，如将孔深设计超出探测段一定深度，使探测段内射线密度和射线正交性均较好；同时，当地面距探测段较近时，应充分予以利用，尽可能达到三侧透射的观测系统。

（2）数据采集系统的选择。根据现阶段仪器生产技术水平和勘察精度，对用于层析成像数据采集的仪器性能指标和参数设置进行了研究，研究认为：①发射器或震源、接收器和数据采集器之间必须保持良好的频率响应，才能够获得高保真的原始记录；②能量越大，弹性波（或电磁波）的传播距离就越大；③频率越高，层析图像的分辨率越高。并据此提出了多种条件下井中发射器或震源、井中接收器和数据采集器等数据采集三部分的技术要求。

（3）测试技术措施。结合工程实际，针对层析成像现场测试环节，制订了一系列技术措施（如提高记录品质、成果精度）。

（4）数据处理和资料解释。理论结合实践，在分析、研究打靶法和弯曲射线搜索法各自优缺点的基础上，采用了弯曲射线快速搜索法进行射线追踪；在比较多种重建算法（平均值法 BPT、代数重建法 ART、联合迭代法 SIRT）的成像效果后，选取了对投影数据误差的敏感度小、迭代收敛性好的 SIRT 法进行重建迭代，并对资料解释进行了具体规定。

结合向家坝水电站$Ⅲ_2$类岩体固结灌浆工程和广州地铁 2 号线北延段三元里至远景段工程两个工程层析成像法探测实例，并经工程验证，层析成像成果精度误差达到 0.5～1m。

（三）项目研究成果的经济效益和社会效益

（1）与常规地球物理勘探方法相比较，由于解释成果精度高，所提供的资料（包括物理力学指标、地质异常体位置、形态）可直接作为精细化设计的科学依据，极大地减少了保守设计、盲目设计的可能性，使地基的施工处理方案、工艺、措施更具有针对性，在保证工程质量的前提下，节省了建设投资。

（2）高精度层析成像的成果精度误差一般不大于 1.0m，条件具备时，可达到 0.5m，甚至更小，这就为工程地基勘察提供了一种精度更高的地球物理勘探方法，使详细勘察工作布置能做到有的放矢，减少了勘察工作的盲目性。

（3）高精度层析成像的应用，能较大地减少勘探工作量的布置，在地质条件、场地和环境条件复杂区，不但可节约较大量的勘察成本，而且在保证勘察工作精度的情况下，节省勘探工期，加快了工程勘察周期，使工程更快发挥作用。

（4）近年来在十数个大、中型国家重点工程的各个勘察阶段成功地应用了高精度层析成像技术，解决了复杂情况下的地基详细勘察难题和隐蔽工程施工质量详检新课题，经济效益显著，意义深远。

（四）下一步研究发展目标

在下一步研究中，还需结合工程实际，逐步完善射线层析成像的技术措施，同时开展建立在波动方程理论基础上的图像重建层析方法研究，进一步提高地球物理勘探成果的可信性和可靠性。

（中国水电顾问集团中南勘测设计研究院　卢小林）

特大型深水软弱地基群桩基础施工成套技术研究

（一）研究背景和内容

苏通大桥是国家确定的“十一五”重点建设项目，是《国家高速公路网规划》中沈阳至海口高速公路跨越长江的重要节点工程。大桥位于长江河口地区，存在水文条件差、气象条件复杂、基岩埋藏深、通航标准高等建设条件，同时大桥具有高、大、长、柔等结构方面的特点。因此，为了确保大桥的长治久安，以苏通大桥为代表的大型群桩基础局部冲刷及冲刷防护技术的研究，已经成为提高桥墩基础安全度、确保工程安全可靠的关键技术问题。

苏通大桥的桥基冲刷兼有多项不利因素，即水深流急、底质抗冲性差、冲刷深度大且不均匀。鉴于现有深水大型群桩桥基的设计技术难度大、风险高，为提高桥基安全，必须对复杂水域的桥基进行工程防护。同时在主塔墩基础冲刷防护工程建设过程中实施了永久防护与施工期预防护相结合，冲刷预防护的实施有效控制了河床冲刷对钻孔平台的影响，降低了施工过程中的风险，并对永久结构的安全提供了保障。

本课题是针对国内首次实施的冲刷防护工程全过程中，所面临的科研、设计、监测、施工和维护技术难点和关键技术进行的攻关研究。目的是通过技术攻关，首先是解决好大桥基础建设中一系列技术难题和关键技术，为苏通大桥建设提供技术支撑，确保大桥建设的长治久安。同时，对大型群桩基础局部冲刷及冲刷防护的关键技术进行研究和突破，形成一批核心技术，填补我国有关桥梁基础建设的技术空白，补充和完善行业规范，提升我国大型桥梁建设整体技术水平。

（二）主要创新点

（1）在局部冲刷特性研究方面，建立了稳定流作用下的复杂布设群桩桥基的局部冲刷特性和最大冲刷深度预测公式和潮流作用下群桩桥基局部冲刷机理和最大冲刷深度的预测公式。

（2）在设计方面，一是提出在群桩基础施工前采用袋装沙预防护，有效解决了群桩基础施工引起的局部冲刷，实现了永久防护和施工期预防护相结合，变被动防护为主动防护，保证了基础施工的顺利进行；二是在冲刷防护设计中下沉护坦原理的运用。针对苏通大桥河床主深槽的演变可能引起防护工程外侧边坡坍塌的特点，运用护坦与防护床面柔性接触和重新分布特性，在防护区外形成较有效的护坦。

（3）在监测技术方面，通过多波束测深系统在潮汐水流中对冲刷防护材料水抛成型的微地形测量与数据处理技术的应用，以及对该系统精度分析的确认及其检测技术的完善，解决了工程施工中一系列关键技术问题，为冲刷防护材料在不同水文条件下的群体抛投规律和漂距的确定提供监测依据；为抛投冲刷防护材料的成型规律和周边冲刷工程效应提供准确的水下微地形监测；水下抛石厚度的确定等，其研究成果为监测研究、施工技术研究和验收技术研究提供了良好服务和有力的技术支撑。

（4）在总体施工方案方面，国内首次对大型桥梁基础在钻孔施工前提前进行砂袋预防护技术，实现了永久防护与施工期预防护相结合；在施工工艺和施工技术方面，国内首次对大型桥梁基础冲刷防护工程进行有序可控的抛投施工技术；冲刷防护工程的验收理念和验收技术也有创新。

（5）在维护技术方面，进行了冲刷防护工程稳定性分析，制定了维护标准；并进行了冲刷防护工程功效的监测分析。

该科研成果有效地指导了现场监测和科学合理的工程施工及验收，成为设计、监测技术、施工技术、验收技术和维护技术的理论基础和主要技术依据。

（南京水利科学研究院）

国产化计算机监控系统在龙滩水电站的研制应用

"国产化计算机监控系统在龙滩水电站的研制应用"项目由龙滩水电开发有限公司、国网电力科学研究院、中国水电顾问集团中南勘测设计研究院完成。

（一）研究内容

项目采用 NC2000 计算机监控系统软件平台和 SJ-500现地微机监控装置，全厂共 22 个 LCU 单元、监控测点43 902个，监视控制对象为 9 台单机容量 700MW 水轮机组及辅助设备、500kV GIS 设备等，电站上位机包括服务器、工作站共 22 台（套），通过双环网构成监控系统，满足电站"无人值班"（少人值守）的要求。

（二）主要创新成果

（1）龙滩水电站计算机监控系统被控对象全部为国产化设备，系统成功实施。

（2）为提高网络交换和数据处理速度，龙滩水电站计算机监控系统采用内存交换数据库、实时消息队列等关键技术，实现了单机容量 700MW 水电站监控系统海量数据的分析和处理，每节点支持 10 万测点数的数据交换。

（3）具有自主知识产权的 SJ-12C 自动准同期装置、DOP-1 型开出重漏选保护装置、SJ-30 通信管理装置在龙滩水电站的使用，是上述装置在单机容量 700MW 水电站机组的首次应用。

（4）为保证大量测温点数据处理，采用独立测温 LCU 配置的设计模式，降低主 PLC CPU 的负荷率，提高机组运行的安全性。该模式在单机容量 700MW 水电站还属于首次应用。

（5）采用新的监控系统调试方案，提高电厂和电网运行的安全性，该方法在单机容量 700MW 水电站复杂调试中保证电网安全具有原创性。

（龙滩水电开发有限公司　戴金芬）

电气主接线可靠性定量分析研究及完全 4/3 断路器接线在龙滩水电站的应用

龙滩水电开发有限公司、中南勘测设计研究院、清华大学针对大型水电站电气主接线设计需要研究的主要问题，以龙滩水电站工程为依托，提出了一套行之有效的计算与分析方法，并开发了相应的计算软件。主要创新成果如下：

（1）本研究成果 500kV 侧采用完全 4/3 接线的方案是在国内大型水电站电气主接线中首次采用，对国内大型水电站电气主接线的设计具有借鉴意义。

（2）本课题的研究成果具有普遍的实用性，为大型水电站电气主接线的设计、研究及应用提供了经验和技术支持，可推广应用。

（3）本项目深入研究了电气主接线系统中各元件的可靠性模型和影响因素（尤其是断路器元件），根据其将要出现的运行状况对不同位置的断路器元件故障率进行修正可以更客观地反映主接线的可靠性指标，使得到的指标结果更精确，更贴近工程实际。

（4）本项目研究提出了基于邻接终点矩阵的新型最小割集搜索算法，突破了传统算法的局限性，能够对多电源多负荷结构进行分析，同时处理普通支路和母线这类单节点元件，并适用于含有单向支路和双向支路的混合有向网络，可用于各种主接线形式的可靠性评估。同时，引入稀疏矩阵技术和特定的矩阵降维技术，计算速度大为提高。

（5）本研究成果计入了水电站水能特性的影响，使可靠性计算结果更符合水电站的实际情况。

（龙滩水电开发有限公司　戴金芬）

中国水利水电第三工程局有限公司 2009 年科技工作情况

2009 年，中国水利水电第三工程局有限公司（以下简称水电三局）加大了科研经费投入，增强了对科研项目的管控力度，取得了丰硕的科研成果。

（一）科研工作

2009 年，投入科技经费 1738.78 万元，占营业额 33.81 亿元的 5.14‰。

（1）水电三局组织集团公司牵头的《水电水利工程场内施工道路技术规范》、《门座式起重机安全操作规程》等4部电力行业标准的编写工作和《水电水利工程金属结构与机电设备安装安全技术规程》的翻译工作，还参与了其他单位牵头组织的4个行业标准的协编工作。反馈行业标准征求意见稿11份。参加了《水电水利工程施工技术全书》的编写工作。

（2）2009年，应各学会、政府监控部门的邀请，参加了交流、验收、咨询、评审会共计13次；参加集团公司、设计院和业主组织的各类科学技术交流、评审、鉴定、咨询会共计9次。

（3）2009年水电三局与西安理工大学和陕西省技术服务中心签订了科技战略合作框架协议，建立了工作领导小组；与西安理工大学和西北勘测设计研究院联合申报了国家级试验室；与中国技术进出口公司和湖南勘测设计院签订了战略合作框架协议，组建了联合专家组，对共同建设伊朗中部160亿元人民币的供水工程进行技术合作；与西安理工大学一道进行大坝温控研究，已完成一项科研课题；与河海大学、上海勘测设计研究院一起研究的《碾压混凝土单掺火山灰试验研究及应用》科研项目获集团公司科技进步二等奖。2009年，水电三局立项的科研项目12个，其中在集团公司立项4个，公司立项8个；验收2008年立项的科研项目12个，其中集团公司立项的1个，公司立项上档次到集团公司验收的1个，公司立项的10个。

（4）参加了2009年陕西省电焊工技能大赛和陕西省机械工技能大赛，获陕西省职工技术状元2名，技术能手6名；晋升技师14名，高级技师4名。同时，被评为2009年陕西省重点工程建设先进集体和陕西省技术创新优胜单位。2009年，水电三局获得陕西省技术创新优秀科技成果奖2项，其中一等奖二等奖各1项；获陕西省技术创新标兵2个，技术创新先进个人2个，工人先锋号2个。

（二）主要科技成果

（1）获得了国家和省部级优质工程奖2项。

（2）经典暨精品工程奖3项。

（3）获得行业和省级科技进步奖1项，集团公司科技进步奖4项，其中二等奖5项、三等奖4项；获得集团公司重点推广新技术5项，国家级重点推广新技术2项。

（4）创企业施工新纪录7项。

（5）完成了4个行业规范的主编任务，2个行业规范的协编任务，1个行业规范的翻译任务。

（6）编制了14个工法，其中5个获集团公司工法，1个获国家级工法。

（7）公司科技人员在各种杂志上发表论文150余篇，其中10篇被《中国水力发电年鉴》收录，9篇在各级学会和网站上进行了交流。

（8）申报专利20项，其中9项被受理或公告，11项被授权发证。

（9）获得行业聘任的专家3名，集团公司首批技术带头人2名，陕西省青年创新技术带头人1名。

（中国水利水电第三工程局有限公司）

中国水利水电第八工程局有限公司2009年科技工作情况

2009年，中国水利水电第八工程局有限公司（以下简称水电八局）的各项科技工作如下：

（一）科技创新体系

2008年12月15日，经湖南省经济委员会、湖南省建设厅考核，中国水利水电第八工程局有限公司技术中心被认定为首批“湖南省认定建筑业企业技术中心”。2009年10月，湖南省科技厅、财政厅、国家税务局和地方税务局四部门向我公司联合颁发了“高新技术企业”奖牌和证书。

（二）科研项目和标准化工作

水电八局申报的“溪洛渡水电站混凝土高拱坝抗裂材料性能研究”、“高水头作用下遇岩溶系统特大涌水情况的导流洞封堵技术“、“预应力FRP锚杆成套技术研发”3个项目获集团公司2009年科研立项，并获中国水利水电建设集团公司资助130万元。2009年，科研立项44项，投入科研经费7376万元。

水电八局承担的中国水利水电建设集团公司“特大型人工砂石系统研究与应用”、“平面链轮门高精度制作加工技术”、“大坝安全实时监测和预警系统”、“水工自密实混凝土研究及应用”等科研项目2009年顺利通过了中国水利水电建设集团公司验收鉴定，其中2项获国际领先水平，1项获国际先进水平，1项获国内领先水平。取得国家级工法2项，中国水利水电建设集团公司（省部级）工法17项。

（1）特大型人工砂石系统研究与应用。针对我国大型水利水电工程规模巨大，人工砂石料需求量大、质量要求高的特点，水电八局结合工程实际，从料场开采、工艺流程、设备选型、系统布置、骨料运输、质量控制、环境保护等方面进行系统研究，开发了针对不同地形地质条件、岩性、生产规模的大型人工砂石生产成套技术。

（2）平面链轮门高精度制作加工技术。小湾水电站放空底孔事故检修闸门为平面链轮门，共两扇，孔口净尺寸为5m×12m，设计挡水水头160m，总水压力106 100kN，单扇门叶重297t，单套门槽重622t，综合参数目前居世界首位。闸门制造精度要求高、难度大。闸门均衡座、链轮及门槽轨道材料为强度高、抗锈蚀性能好的0Cr17ni4Cu4Nb沉淀硬化马氏体不锈钢，为水工金属结构设备制造首次采用。该材料加工难度大、热处理工艺要求严格，通过优化加工工艺，制定、实施合理的热处理规范，解决了该材料强化和易裂的矛盾，保证了其力学性能、抗锈蚀性能，制作精度高于行业标准，满足合同与设计要求，提升了国内特大型水利水电工程高水头、高精度平面链轮门制造技术水平为水利水电工程大流量、高水头泄水建筑物设计应用创造了条件。

（3）大坝安全实时监测和预警系统。研究开发了大坝安全实时监控和预警系统，利用结构、渗流和非连续变形分析模块以及监控模型，对采集的变形、渗流和应力应变等监测数据进行分析计算，设定预警值，实现大坝安全实时监控和预警。该系统已在三峡工程、平班水电站、株溪口水电站、藤子沟水电站应用，首次实现了大坝施工期、初期蓄水、运行期安全监测资料的连续管理。

（4）水工自密实混凝土研究及应用。根据部分特殊水工钢筋混凝土结构特点及服役环境条件，研究开发了工作性好、耐久性优良的水工自密实混凝土，经工程实践应用，效果良好。课题研究的主要成果如下：提出了水工自密实混凝土材料设计与配制方法，试验研究了原材料对水工自密实混凝土性能的影响规律；系统研究了盐溶液浸蚀、磨蚀等对自密实混凝土的影响机理，配制了抗裂性能良好、低渗透性和耐磨性能优良的水工自密实混凝土；通过工程实践，提出了水工自密实混凝土应用的质量控制指标；进行了采用电通量作为水工自密实混凝土耐久性评定指标的试验研究，为水电工程推广应用自密实混凝土提供了技术支持。

（5）高速铁路施工技术。水电八局承建京沪高速铁路JHTJ-3标段六工区工程，总长35.67km，其中桥梁18.841km，路基16.834km。成功设计了邹城制梁场，掌握了900t大型简支箱梁预制技术、CFG桩施工和无砟轨道板的制作技术。邹城制梁场已为京沪客运专线铁路的后张法预应力混凝土铁路桥简支箱梁产品进行规模化生产；承建的辽河1号特大桥墩台身被评为质量样板工程，其桥梁墩台身施工技术成熟稳定、墩台身内实外美，在中国水利水电建设集团公司京沪高铁三标段全线推广应用。

（三）科技成果及推广应用

（1）双聚能预裂与光面爆破综合技术在龙开口、锅厂、泸定等水电站开挖中进行了推广应用，效果良好。该技术是水电八局2007年研发的新技术，将爆破能量聚集在预裂（光面）爆破面集中释放，使造孔工作量降低50%～65%、能耗降低50%～65%，面装药密度减少50%～65%、成本降低50%～55%，可广泛应有于水利水电工程轮廓控制爆破开挖和矿山等其他行业轮廓控制爆破施工，拥有两项专利和一项国家一级工法。

（2）BLJ600-40移动式混凝土布料机是由水电八局开发的一种新型混凝土浇筑设备，输入布料强度大于100m³/h，最大布料半径为40m，适应于输送各种级配的混凝土和各类颗粒性物料；具有运输转移拆装方便、操作简单可靠、生产效率高、混凝土浇筑质量好等特点，已推广应用于国内外众多水利水电工程建设中。

（3）真空溜管是碾压混凝土入仓的一种新型输送工具，采用碾压混凝土缓降垂直运输装置，解决了陡倾角、高落差碾压混凝土入仓难题，具有投资少、运行简便、输送效率高等特点。目前，真空溜管使用范围已突破50m的限值而达100m级，解决了高坝快速施工及混凝土垂直运输问题。这项技术已在思林、大花水水电站成功推广应用。其中思林水电站大坝利用100m级真空溜管垂直运输混凝土系统入仓技术，减缓混凝土下降速度，防止混凝土骨料离析，从而成功解决了碾压混凝土高达100m的垂直运输技术难题。该条供料线单台班（12h）实际输送强度达2000m³。无论从节省成本、提高生产效率、降低施工难度、保证混凝土的施工质量等方面，都取得了很好的效果。

（4）京沪高铁施工局在900T箱梁制运架施工、大跨连续梁现浇施工、路基高填方的施工质量控制、CRTSⅡ型轨道施工等高速铁路重点领域，进行了大量的技术攻关研究和现场实践，积累了宝贵的施工经验和技术总结。先后创造了单机单日架设5榀箱梁，月架设箱梁82榀的记录。

（5）构皮滩水电站1号导流洞涌水流量约30m³/s，水深8.5m，洞内涌浪达70～80cm。被众多专家誉为“具备世界级施工技术难度”。面对这一难题，在公司技术精英的指导下，联营体反复论证修订施工方案，终于成功地处理了1号导流洞突然涌水事故。

（6）梨园水电站项目针对料源玄武岩的特性，结合实际生产情况，优化设计方案，对系统工艺进行改造。通过采取干法生产工艺、大规模改造筛网、改造骨料入仓工艺等措施，解决了小石逊径和砂细度模数超标、混凝土坍落度损失过快等问题；征对生产过程中产生的灰尘大的问题，在系统的第五筛分车间设置了四台除尘器，在粗碎车间，安装了自制的防尘罩和喷雾降尘装置，在系统的其他扬尘部位也装上了喷雾降尘装置。征对系统在生产过程中产生的大量废水，投入200万元修建了一个废水处理车间，将系统产生的废水集中送到这里进行处理，处理后的废水再进行循环使用，取得了良好的效益。

（7）针对城镇污水治理的新材料新工艺——生物改性竹炭流床施工技术进行研究，并在凤凰河综合整治工程进行试点，为生物改性竹炭流床的大范围推广提供了成功经验；在广东省内首次采用充砂膜袋填海工艺，用作修筑防波堤和围海造陆的围堤。

（四）科技进步取得丰硕成果

2009年，水电八局获中国水利水电建设集团公司科学技术进步奖特等奖1项、一等奖2项、二等奖1项。

（1）《特大型人工砂石系统研究与应用》获中国水利水电建设集团公司科技进步特等奖，《大坝安全实时监控和预警系统》、《超高压高精度平面链轮门制造技术研究与应用》获中国水利水电建设集团公司科技进步一等奖，《水工自密实混凝土研究与应用》获中国水利水电建设集团公司科技进步二等奖。

（2）2009年1月，2008年度中国电力科学技术奖揭晓，《溪洛渡水电站截流设计与施工关键技术研究》获一等奖；《复杂地层围堰快速防渗施工技术研究与应用》获三等奖；《溪洛渡水电站拱肩槽开挖关键技术研究与实践》获2008年度中国岩石力学与工程学会科学技术一等奖；《溪落渡水电站大坝拱肩槽开挖精细爆破技术研究与应用》、《双聚能预裂与光面爆破综合技术》分别获2008年度中国工程爆破协会科学技术特等奖和二等奖；《双聚能预裂与光面爆破综合技术》和《带式混凝土布料机》分别获2008年度中国施工企业管理协会技术创新成果一等奖；《索风营水电站大坝碾压混凝土综合施工技术》获2008年度中国电力建设科学技术成果二等奖。

（3）2009年10月，中国水利水电建设集团公司授予水电八局"2008年度科技进步先进企业"称号。

（中国水利水电第八工程局有限公司）

获奖项目简介

中华人民共和国水力资源复查成果（2003年）

"中华人民共和国水力资源复查成果（2003年）"获2009年度中国电力科学技术奖一等奖。

为了进一步查清我国的水力资源量，填补水力资源经济可开发量的空白，原国家发展计划委员会决定从2001年开始用3年左右的时间对全国水力资源进行复查。

这次全国水力资源复查工作是利用已有的水电工程查勘、规划和设计成果，对重点复查范围的水力资源组织必要的野外查勘、测量和规划设计工作，对全国水力资源量进行复核和补充。复查范围包括我国大陆各省、自治区、直辖市及我国台湾省和香港、澳门特别行政区。台湾的水力资源尽量收集有关资料和有关最新数据，尽可能按本次水力资源复查有关技术标准进行统计分析。以复查成果为基础，建立了全国水力资源数据库。

参加本次复查工作的有国家有关部委、流域机构及各级水电和水利相关部门，参加的主要工作人员达千余人，历时3年多完成报告。水力资源复查成果按照分省（自治区、直辖市）、分流域分别进行了汇编。全套报告共计40卷，约1500万字；其中总报告1卷，京、津、冀等省（自治区、直辖市）卷29卷，长江等流域卷10卷。

（一）主要技术创新点

（1）国内首次提出经济可开发量评价标准，研究、评价了我国的水力资源，填补了我国水力资源经济可开发量的空白。以贵州省和四川省水电站为例，进行了大量的案例测算，并经多次会议讨论和修改，提出了水力资源经济可开发量评价标准。依据水力资源经济可开发量评价标准，对我国大陆各水电站进行了研究和判别，统计出我国水力资源经济可开发量。

（2）首次细化了分阶段分类统计成果，并首次对装机容量0.5～10MW的水电站进行了统计。分别按照规划、预可行性研究、可行性研究、已建、在建等前期勘察设计和建设情况进行统计；按照省（自治区、直辖市）进行统计，按照东部、中部、西部进行经济大区域统计，按照北部、中部、南部进行"西电东送"大区域统计；按照大型、中型、小型水电站进行统计；按照河流、流域进行统计。本次水力资源复查较1980年水力资源普查扩大了统计范围，各类统计数据翔实可靠，查清了我国水力资源量及其分布情况。

（3）首次系统、完整地建立了我国水力资源数据库。全国水力资源数据库是本次复查工作的重要成果之一，收录了此次复查的全部数据。本数据库是以本次水力资源复查成果为基础，通过各种标准表格和图形将有关数据进行分类录入，运用数据库技术组织管理录入的表格和图形，并根据用户需求，实现有关表格和图形的查询、统计，同时还运用电子地图技术实现图上数据的查询和统计。首次收录了港、澳、台水力资源量。通过收集内地已掌握的资料，并到台湾进行技术交流，收集了台湾水力资源及其已建和在建水电站资料，对香港、澳门特别行政区和台湾省的资源量进行了分类和统计。首次取得了我国完整的水力资源调查成果。

（4）综合采用各种技术手段开展水力资源调查。充分利用已有的查勘、规划、设计成果，并采用多种技术手段对重点复查范围的资源进行野外查勘、测量和规划设计。

（二）应用领域与推广前景

本成果在国家、各流域机构、各省（自治区、直辖市）等不同层面的能源、电力发展规划制定中得到广泛运用，如国家能源战略、国家能源发展规划、可再生能源发展规划、各省（自治区、直辖市）能源、电力5年发展规划等。这次复查成果查清了我国的水力资源量，将对我国水力资源的科学和合理开发起到重要的促进作用，将对研究制订国家、各流域机构、各省（自治区、直辖市）的能源政策和电力发展规划，以及做好水电规划设计工作发挥重要作用。

（三）获奖单位

水电水利规划设计总院、水利部水利水电规划设计总院、中国水电顾问集团成都勘测设计研究院、长江水利委员会长江勘测规划设计研究院、中国水电顾问集团昆明勘测设计研究院、黄河勘测规划设计有限公司、中国水电顾问集团西北勘测设计研究院、中国水电顾问集团贵阳勘测设计研究院、中水珠江规划勘测设计有限公司、水利部太湖流域管理局、中国水电顾问集团北京勘测设计研究院、中水东北勘测设计研究有限责任公司、湖北省水利水电勘测设计院、中国水电顾问集团中南勘测设计研究院、青海省水利水电勘测设计研究院、中国水电顾问集团华东勘测设计研究院、陕西省水利电力勘测设计研究院。

（四）获奖人

晏志勇、史立山、李菊根、曾肇京、彭程、袁定远、钱钢粮、高敏凤、李世东、蒋肖、严碧波、刘一兵、赵太平、李小燕、唐荣斌、邹幼汉、张平、宋红霞、王化中。

（摘自《中国电力科学技术奖获奖项目汇编》）

特大型人工砂石系统研究与应用

“特大型人工砂石系统研究与应用”获2009年度中国电力科学技术奖一等奖。

我国大型水利水电工程规模巨大，人工砂石料需求量大、质量要求高。项目结合工程实际情况，从料场开采、工艺流程、设备选型、系统布置、骨料运输、质量控制、环境保护等方面进行系统研究，开发了针对不同地形地质条件、岩性、生产规模的大型人工砂石生产成套技术。

（一）主要技术创新点

（1）研究采用控制爆破技术，有效地将毛料大块率控制在1.5%左右，提高了毛料开采质量；首次研究应用双聚能预裂与光面爆破技术，节能降耗效果显著，推动了水利水电工程预裂爆破技术的进步。

（2）首次研究采用深溜渣竖井垂直运输与大型地下洞室破碎厂组合的粗碎加工、地下竖井式成品料仓群方案，成功解决了高陡边坡、狭窄场地砂石系统布置的难题，在大型人工砂石料加工系统总体规划与布置上有所突破。

（3）首次研究采用了立轴冲击破碎机与棒磨机联合制砂工艺，并首创了立轴破碎机制砂与粗砂整形工艺，有效地控制了细度模数，提高了人工砂品质，解决了大规模人工制砂关键技术。

（4）通过耐磨件技术攻关，改进加工设备，优化生产工艺，解决了石英砂、流纹岩、玄武岩等强磨蚀性岩石制砂技术难题，拓宽了人工砂石料的料源范围。

（5）首次采用分级、脱水一体化新工艺；自行研制成品砂专用脱水筛，脱水效果良好。

（6）率先采用刮砂机、旋流器、压滤机的联合回收细纱、石粉工艺，采用废渣分级处理、固液机械分离技术，实现了废水处理达标和废渣零排放；采用尾渣库方案实现了废水循环利用和零排放。

（7）为防止粉尘污染，在干法生产工艺上，首次采用风选、除尘成套设备进行粉尘控制，生产环境显著改善，并实现了成品砂石粉含量的动态控制。

（8）开发了大型破碎加工设备锌合金填充材料的现场浇灌技术，有效地缩短了设备维修时间，提高了设备利用率，降低了运行成本。

（二）应用领域与推广前景

研究成果已成功应用于三峡、小湾、光照、构皮滩等水电工程的特大型人工砂石系统，并在其他工程推广。成果获得多项国家专利，并形成国家级工法，经济、社会和环境效益显著，可广泛应用于大型尤其是特大型水电工程、核电工程、建筑工程、公路工程、铁路工程等，具有广泛的推广应用前景。

（三）获奖单位

中国水利水电第八工程局有限公司。

（四）获奖人

刘志和、林修建、熊明华、涂怀健、刘金明、连普选、蹇尚友、杨建安、肖光彩、汪建军、罗艳、李兵、黄岳、唐瑞、蒋海军。

（摘自《中国电力科学技术奖获奖项目汇编》）

唐家山堰塞湖应急除险工程技术研究及实践

"唐家山堰塞湖应急除险工程技术研究及实践"获2009年度中国电力科学技术奖二等奖。

"5·12"汶川大地震形成的唐家山堰塞湖规模巨大，总库容3.16亿m^3，直接威胁下游绵阳、遂宁两市130多万人民生命和财产的安全，一旦整体溃决后果不堪设想。本项目即在此紧要关头展开。

（一）项目主要内容

（1）水文特性及处置紧迫性分析，包括堰塞湖区水位特性、险情和处置紧迫性分析等。

（2）堰塞坝的形成机制与地质特性，包括区域构造、地形地貌、形成过程推演、地质结构特征分析、过流前稳定性数值计算与评价、堰塞坝稳定性综合评价及溃坝破坏方式分析等。

（3）溃坝分析及风险评估，包括溃决方案的拟订、洪水演进计算、计算模型、计算成果和成果分析等。

（4）堰塞湖应急除险工程措施设计，包括设计思路和原则、引冲槽布置与结构设计、施工组织与施工技术、动态优化与调整设计和暂态泄流能力分析等。

（5）方案实施效果及泄流后稳定性评价，包括方案实施效果、复演验证、过流后稳定性评价、效益分析和下游河道冲淤演变分析等。

（二）主要技术创新点

（1）首次提出了堰塞湖处置的系统分析方法，包括快速判断、风险评估、计算分析和应急除险的系统分析方法等。

（2）首次提出了地震触发的近源高速岩质滑坡形成极高危大型堰塞坝的成因机制、坝体结构和整体稳定性判断的快速分析方法。

（3）结合分析计算成果分析，快速得出了唐家山堰塞坝不存在整体快速溃坝风险的结论，并提出了堰塞坝溃决方式和部位，为除险方案的制定提供了科学依据。

（4）提出了可控的引冲槽泄流应急处置工程方案，实现了控制泄流、溯源引流冲刷的目标，避免了堰塞坝的快速溃决，排除了险情。

（5）提出改进后的美国溃坝洪水预报模型（DAMBRK模型），成功应用于唐家山堰塞坝的溃坝分析，准确预测了唐家山堰塞坝的溃坝洪水演进过程，为下游避险方案的确定提供了决策依据。

（6）通过对大型堰塞坝溃决后下游淤积新河床冲刷演变趋势分析，首次提出了堰塞坝溯源冲刷后剩余堰塞体稳定的终极比降分析方法，为后续整治工程提供了有力依据。

本研究成果为今后堰塞湖及类似工程险情的处置提供了依据和借鉴。

（三）获奖单位

中国水电顾问集团成都勘测设计研究院、中国水电工程顾问集团公司。

（四）获奖人

晏志勇、郑声安、黄河、周建平、陈五一、王仁坤、彭土标、巩满福、谭建、施裕兵、唐朝阳、郑家样。

（摘自《中国电力科学技术奖获奖项目汇编》）

水布垭高面板堆石坝施工关键技术研究与实践

"水布垭高面板堆石坝施工关键技术研究与实践"获2009年度中国电力科学技术奖二等奖。

本项目依托水布娅水电站建设工程。水布垭混凝土面板堆石坝设计坝高233m，是世界最高混凝土面板堆石坝。该工程地质条件复杂、工程量大、质量要求高。在国内外尚无坝高超过200m面板堆石坝可资借鉴的施工经验与技术准则的条件下，项目通过研究、试验、创新和应用一系列施工新技术、新方法、新工艺、新机具，解决了多项高面板堆石坝施工技术难题，成功建成了里程碑式的世界最高混凝土面板堆石坝。

（一）主要技术创新点

（1）研究并首次实施了高混凝土面板堆石坝填筑时空预沉降变形控制技术，通过间隔分期填筑、反台填筑、高密实度碾压填筑和连续高强度填筑等施工方法与技术的创新和应用，从时间和空间角度有效地控制了堆石体的沉降和变形，提高了坝体密实度，保证了坝体填筑质量，为高堆石坝的安全运行奠定了基础。

（2）自主研究了高强度坝料动态优化调配技术，开发了高强度坝料填筑动态优化调配与管理软件系统（EOAMS），通过对料源、设备、道路、填筑等多因素的综合优化，实现了高强度坝料填筑的动态优化调配与信息化管理，提高了开挖料直接上坝率和利用率，减低了中转率和弃料量以及料场开挖量，有效地提高了施工效率。

（3）首次将强夯技术应用于水电工程坝基覆盖层

加固施工，有效减少基础开挖量和回填量，有效削减了坝体填筑强度，加快了工程进度，节约了工程投资，开辟了面板堆石坝同类坝基处理的新途径。

（4）采用智能传感原理，研制了灌浆抬动自动化报警技术，实现了趾板基础高压力灌浆抬动变形的实时精确监测，有效地保证了灌浆效果。

（二）应用领域与推广前景

本项目属水利水电工程土石坝施工技术领域，系列研究成果可广泛应用于面板堆石坝、土石坝等类工程的施工。同时，项目成果的高堆石坝时空预沉降变形控制填筑技术、高密实度坝体的施工技术、高强度坝料动态优化调配技术、灌浆抬动自动化报警装置、长铜止水片连续滚压成型机等可在具有灌浆施工、土石方调配施工、混凝土防裂施工、止水铜片施工的工程中广泛应用。

（三）获奖单位

中国葛洲坝集团股份有限公司、葛洲坝建设工程有限公司、葛洲坝集团第五工程有限公司、武汉大学。

（四）获奖人

周厚贵、邓银启、王亚文、廖光荣、王章忠、桂云峰、柳同祥、王欣、褚恩杰、曹生荣。

（摘自《中国电力科学技术奖获奖项目汇编》）

糯扎渡水电站截流和高土石围堰快速施工技术研究和应用

“糯扎渡水电站截流和高土石围堰快速施工技术研究和应用”获2009年度中国电力科学技术奖二等奖。

项目依托糯扎渡水电站工程，其主要成果为高流速、大落差截流及深覆盖层防渗墙和围堰快速施工技术研究与应用。项目从糯扎渡工程实际出发，对高流速、大落差截流及深覆盖层防渗墙和围堰施工技术进行全面分析研究。

（一）主要技术创新点

（1）截流施工：①截流戗堤进占过程中，采用柔软性、适应性强的钢筋石笼串（6个、8个或12个一组），不仅能有效控制堤头垮塌，而且能保证堤头安全、稳定进占，成功实现了单戗双向进占、立堵截流；②龙口抛投钢筋石笼串技术替代了传统的抛投大块石串、混凝土四面体技术，成功解决堤头垮塌的难题。

（2）围堰防渗墙施工：①“钻劈法”和“钻抓法”成槽施工技术和工艺代替了传统的冲钻工艺；②黏土和膨润土混合泥浆护壁技术代替了传统的单一膨润土护壁技术；③“气举法”结合“抽筒法”清孔换浆工艺代替了传统的“抽筒法”清孔工艺；④“接头管法”实施墙段连接先进工艺解决了墙段连接质量问题；⑤先预灌后成槽施工工艺确保槽体稳定，有利于加快槽体施工进度；⑥倒悬岩体采用可控性水泥灌浆工艺，解决了防渗墙体在复杂地质条件下与基岩结合成整体的局限性的问题。

（3）高围堰施工：①研究高土石围堰快速填筑施工技术，在一个枯水期内建成84m高的围堰，创造了高土石围堰施工平均每天上升1.16m、最高日填筑量3万m^3的国内纪录；②研究多料源品种填筑土工膜斜墙施工工艺，编写工法，确保围堰施工质量和进度。

（二）应用领域与推广前景

糯扎渡大江截流创造了近10年国内施工难度之最，其成功截流，为水电建设行业在大流量、高流速、高落差、大单宽功率工况下如何确保截流成功提供了宝贵施工经验。

围堰防渗墙施工工期短，工程量大，地质条件复杂，施工难度在行业中罕见，该防渗墙施工能按时、保质、保量地完成，为类似工程提供了可供借鉴的施工经验；高围堰填筑也为同类工程施工提供了依据和经验。

（三）获奖单位

中国人民武装警察部队水电第一总队。

（四）获奖人

吴桂耀、黄宗营、赵方兴、王洪源、唐先奇、贺博文、崔文光、叶晓培、吴国如、张礼宁。

（摘自《中国电力科学技术奖获奖项目汇编》）

水电站厂房和机电系统三维可视化协同设计研究与工程应用

“水电站厂房和机电系统三维可视化协同设计研究与工程应用”获2009年度中国电力科学技术奖二等奖。

国内外的水电工程设计单位一直采用传统的二维设计方式，制约了整个水电行业的设计效率和设计质量。

中国水电顾问集团华东勘测设计研究院在水电行业率先开展水电站厂房和机电系统三维可视化协同设计，大大提高了设计效率和设计质量，节约工程设计和建设成本，也为工程项目的全生命周期管理创造了条件。

（一）主要技术创新点

（1）在国内首次提出了水电站厂房和机电三维可

视化协同设计流程，有效地解决了水电站三维协同设计环境下的设计文件版本、权限及专业协作问题，可大大提高设计计划的协调性和产品标准的一致性。

（2）在国内首次通过二次开发建成参数化的“水电站工厂系统元件库和设备库”，共包括130个国家标准元件、72个行业标准元件，132种非标元件和167种常用参数化设备，规模近10万条，使水电站厂房设计质量和效率得到质的提升。

（3）实现了从三维水电站厂房模型中直接抽取施工需要的平面图纸，完全满足建设及施工方的要求。

（4）开发出国内第1个水电站厂房虚拟系统。

（二）应用领域与推广前景

本项研究的成果经过河南宝泉抽水蓄能电站（总投资43.27亿元）、安徽响水涧抽水蓄能电站（总投资38亿元）、四川锦屏二级水电站（装机容量4800MW，总投资297亿元）、云南金沙江龙开口水电站（总投资16亿元）、仙游抽水蓄能电站（总投资44.5亿元）、越南Sisan4水电站（总投资68 725 290美元）等多个国内外工程的应用检验，产生的直接和间接效益达数亿元。

该成果用于国际水电设计招标，得到业主的高度评价，被国外业主誉为他们遇到的最好设计单位。

该技术成果对加快水电站设计周期、提高设计质量、提高中国水电行业在国际市场上的竞争力有着非常重要的意义，可在全行业广泛推广，创造更大的经济和社会效益。

（三）获奖单位

中国水电顾问集团华东勘测设计研究院。

（四）获奖人

张春生、陈健、蒋海峰、姜忠见、陈宏钧、陈顺义、王金锋、冯硕、李成军、邓新星。

（摘自《中国电力科学技术奖获奖项目汇编》）

巨型水轮机转轮工地制造

“巨型水轮机转轮工地制造”获2009年度中国电力科学技术奖二等奖。

大型和特大型水电站多处于高山峡谷地区，交通运输困难，而巨型水电机组的关键部件水轮机转轮，因均为超重、超大件，运输尤其困难。转轮整体运输风险大、费用高；如果采用分半运输，到工地组装焊接又存在很多弊端，质量难以保证。因此，巨型水轮机转轮的工地制造技术已成为制约水电机组发展的瓶颈。

本项目依托龙滩水电站7台700MW机组的水轮机转轮制造。该项目水轮机转轮最大直径8051mm，总高度4250mm，加工后重量259t。课题的研究实践成功解决了巨型水轮机转轮的运输难题，并取得多项创新成果。《水轮机转轮现场焊接残余应力测试方法》已申报专利并被受理（专利申请号：200910009184.7）。通过龙滩水电站投产以来2年多的运行，证明水轮机转轮质量优良。

（一）主要技术创新点

（1）转轮工地制造工艺流程设计合理，使工地制造的转轮完全达到了在制造厂内制造的质量标准，并满足了工程进度对转轮交货工期的要求；

（2）选择合理的焊接方式和焊接工艺，采用先进的热处理工装和热处理工艺，使转轮最终的残余应力降低至材料屈服强度的三分之一以下，达到了同类产品焊接与热处理的世界领先水平；

（3）首次对转轮工地制造全过程各阶段的残余应力进行了对比测试，并在3个技术难点上有所突破，包括焊接熔合线的确定、退火前后测点的布置，以及针对被测表面复杂的空间曲面，对钻孔工装的优化，从而实现了精确钻孔，保证了测量精度；

（4）采用3支点压力传感器换位平衡新技术进行转轮静平衡试验，精度高、速度快，成果优于国际标准的规定；

（5）转轮加工首次采用标准立式车床，加工精度满足设计要求。

（二）应用领域与推广前景

本项目研究成果对巨型、大型水轮机转轮工地制造技术的发展起着决定的推动和示范作用，对交通运输困难的高山峡谷地区水电开发有着重大的技术经济意义，为今后水电机组进一步向大容量、大尺寸发展奠定了基础。自龙滩水电站转轮工地整体制造取得成功后，云南小湾等一大批水电站的转轮都已陆续在工地制作。巨型水轮机转轮工地制造的成果已被大力推广应用，具有很好的应用前景。

（三）获奖单位

龙滩水电开发有限公司、上海福伊特西门子水电设备有限公司。

（四）获奖人

初曰亭、杨振先、陈国庆、王怀茂、孙鸿秉、戴金芬、王宪平、于纪幸、任绍成、王鹏宇。

（摘自《中国电力科学技术奖获奖项目汇编》）

双曲薄拱坝快速施工技术研究与实践

“双曲薄拱坝快速施工技术研究与实践”获2009年度中国电力科学技术奖二等奖。

本项目属水利水电工程科学技术领域。由于拱坝结构比较单薄，单块独立坝块不能承受过大的上游水位压力，必须通过接缝灌浆将大坝形成一个整体后才能承受较大的水平推力。而施工进度对拱坝建设极为重要，如错过了灌浆的低温季节（一般不宜迟于4月底），整个工程就会推迟一个汛期，造成较大的经济损失。因此，简化拱坝的施工工艺、优化拱坝施工方案、加快拱坝的施工速度对拱坝技术发展有着重大意义。

本项目依托洞坪工程双曲拱坝开展研究。

（一）主要技术创新点

（1）大坝泄洪孔牛腿施工中设计开发了一种悬臂牛腿翻转模施工工艺，加快了施工速度，解决了施工难题。

（2）经过充分论证，采取合理总体布置、先进的施工工艺和配置，加快施工速度，取消导流底孔。

（3）坝后桥采用二期浇筑，为解决拱坝的结构布置和采用先进的DOKA模板提供了可能。

（4）采用球面键槽，简化横缝接缝灌浆系统，施工质量和速度得到了提高。

（二）应用领域与推广前景

本项目研究成果已成功应用于洞坪大坝中，其关键技术简化了拱坝的施工工艺，加快了施工速度，使该工程提前发电，取得了显著的经济效益和社会效益。其中一些技术成果在埃塞俄比亚的TEKEZE大坝中得到推广应用，部分成果获国家专利、国家级工法。该研究成果可广泛应用于拱坝及碾压混凝土筑坝技术领域，具有广泛的推广应用前景。

（三）获奖单位

葛洲坝集团第五工程有限公司、湖北省水利水电勘测设计院、湖北宣恩洞坪水电有限责任公司。

（四）获奖人

冷向阳、付俊雄、吕芝林、陈亚辉、郭光文、彭元平、杨正广、韩翔、薛伟、周山。

（摘自《中国电力科学技术奖获奖项目汇编》）

水利水电与电网气象综合监测系统

“水利水电与电网气象综合监测系统”获2009年度中国电力科学技术奖三等奖。

本项目采用平台化和模块化的设计方法，开发了新型数据采集器、多用途传感器适配器、高效和可靠的远程传输与控制协议、融合图像采集与数据采集的解决方案，以及中心站远程数据接收与管理软件等新技术和新产品。

本项目形成了以下科技成果：全国工业产品生产许可证1项、电信设备进网许可证1项、电力行业标准1项、发明专利1项、实用新型专利1项，通过中国电机工程学会组织的鉴定，鉴定意见认为，总体技术达到国际先进水平，其中微功耗和宽温度工作范围的性能指标优于国际同类产品的先进水平。

（一）主要技术创新点

（1）建立了一体化的硬件和软件通用平台。

（2）发明了多中心接收确认的单频无线组网方法。

（3）首次采用三处理器架构设计数据采集器，实现了系统微功耗和高性能。

（4）实现了宽工作温度范围特性。

（5）实现了低功耗视频和数据的综合传输控制。

（二）应用领域与推广前景

本系统适用于水情测报、防汛抗旱、污染源监测、输电线状态监测等领域，经过2年的研发于2007年投产。2007年的销售额为1855万元，形成利润278万元，为国家创税186万元；2008年销售额为3621万元，形成利润543万元，为国家创税362万元。在唐家山堰塞湖抗险救灾工程中，该系统提供了稳定可靠的自动监测数据，为指导堰塞湖最终安全泄洪发挥了关键作用，保证了下游100多万群众的生命和财产安全。

（三）获奖单位

国网电力科学研究院、南京南瑞集团公司。

（四）获奖人

曹年红、曹翊军、江海深、周海、熊光亚、程序、李震。

（摘自《中国电力科学技术奖获奖项目汇编》）

大荷载、高扬程固定卷扬式启闭机研制

“大荷载、高扬程固定卷扬式启闭机研制”获2009年度中国电力科学技术奖三等奖。

目前，长江上游干流及金沙江、大渡河上已建和即将建设的大型高水头水电站项目有33个，5000MW以上的水电站就有向家坝、溪洛渡、白鹤滩、乌东德、虎跳峡等，大容量启闭机的需求量越来越多。而随着抽水蓄能电站设计水头的增高，大容量卷扬式启闭机的需求量也越来越多。大容量卷扬式启闭机是近几年来随着我国高坝建筑的增多发展而来的新型非标准大型启闭机械，也是我国水工机械的一大特色。由于国外水工闸门的启闭机械液压化，几十米乃至上百米的高扬程卷扬式启闭机在国外是很难见到的。这种新型非标准大型启闭机械整机结构庞大，使

制造、运输、安装、水工布置难度大大增加，整机造价也十分昂贵。为适应市场发展需要，降低各方面难度及成本，中国葛洲坝集团机械船舶有限公司成立了大荷载、高扬程固定卷扬式启闭机研发小组，立项对设计和制造的关键技术进行研究。

通过分析研究，系统掌握了大荷载、高扬程固定卷扬式启闭机整体优化设计技术；通过实践，总结了大荷载、高扬程固定卷扬式启闭实现钢丝绳超多层缠绕双吊点同步技术，掌握了大荷载、高杨程固定卷扬式启闭机超多层折线缠绕方案的关键加工技术。

（一）主要技术创新点

（1）完成了大荷载、高扬程固定卷扬式启闭机整体布置要求紧凑、整机自重要求轻的优化设计。

（2）创新应用了钢丝绳在卷筒内壁上压绳设计技术。

（3）系统地研究并实践了启闭机设计新理论。

（4）创新地将电气同步、纠偏技术应用于双吊点启闭机。

（5）通过技术创新，解决了在普通车床上加工大型卷筒折线绳槽的技术问题。

（二）应用领域与推广前景

本成果主要应用于鱼跳电站 5000kN－50m，洪家渡电站 3600kN－90m，3200kN－90m，洞坪电站 6500kN－75m，6500kN－65m，2×2000kN－60m，董箐电站 2×4000kN－67m，溪洛渡电站 2×4000kN－50m，泸定水电站 2×6000kN－42m，滩坑电站 8000kN－100m、6300kN－70m，深溪沟电站 2×8000kN－47m，5000kN－40m 等大荷载高扬程启闭机。

本项目的研制完全依靠自主创新，成功地解决和掌握了大荷载、高扬程启闭机设计、制造的关键技术，攻克了多项技术难题，最终实现大荷载高扬程启闭机具有大容量、体积小、投资少、效率高、安全可靠的优良性能，满足高坝建设的需要。8000kN 启闭机为国际最大之水工起重机械，达到国际国内领先水平。

（三）获奖单位

中国葛洲坝集团机械船舶有限公司。

（四）获奖人

彭景亮、李丽丽、陈爱国、廖全勇、韩烈彪、张庆军、吴冰。

（摘自《中国电力科学技术奖获奖项目汇编》）

变顶高尾水隧洞施工技术研究

“变顶高尾水隧洞施工技术研究”获 2009 年度中国电力科学技术奖三等奖。

彭水水电站地下厂房建于地质条件复杂的岩溶地区，安装有 5×350MW 大型地下混流式发电机组，为中部式单机单洞布置方案。该电站在国内首次采用了“变顶高尾水隧洞”这一新型的尾水流道体形。隧洞轴线间距 35m，开挖后洞间岩柱厚 20m，隧洞最小开挖断面为 15.6m×26.1m，最大开挖断面为 16.6m×32.3m，长度为 359.86～481.61m。其开挖洞径大，区域挖空率高，特别是与施工支洞交汇处，隧洞之间的岩壁较薄。受岩溶影响，施工期洞室围岩稳定问题相当突出，同时施工工程量大，工期紧。彭水水电站其中变顶高尾水工程于 2003 年 10 月初开始施工，2007 年 5 月 30 日完工，是新建项目中第一个应用变顶高尾水隧洞得到成功实践的项目。电站于 2008 年 2～12 月 5 台机组相继并网发电，工程运行至今，工况良好。

课题成果经专家会议鉴定，总体上达到国际先进水平，填补了国内变顶高尾水隧洞施工技术领域的空白，解决了因修建尾水调压室导致的工程规模巨大、水工布置复杂、围岩稳定性差等问题，为今后类似工程的设计和施工提供了技术支持。

（一）主要技术创新点

（1）在国内专家对先拱后墙法施工存在较大争议的情况下，变顶高尾水隧洞施工首次采用了部分侧墙代替拱座的先拱后墙法施工变顶高尾水隧洞结构衬砌，并首次对下层开挖前实行边顶已衬砌部位的固结灌浆施工进行了技术研究，国内尚无此施工技术研究方面的报道。目前在我国乃至全世界范围关于变顶高尾水隧洞工程的施工经验，在整个水电工程施工方面还是空白。

（2）彭水水电站 W84 岩溶系统发育、规模巨大，岩溶系统的处理面临较大的安全威胁和技术挑战，国内已建电站中，能在短时间内处理这样大规模复杂岩溶系统的并不多见。

（二）应用领域与推广前景

本课题研究成果在彭水水电站工程中得到了成功应用，并为目前在建的锦屏、向家坝、三峡地下水电站工程提供了有益的借鉴和参考。课题研究成果主要通过工法、论文、学术交流会议等方式予以推广、应用，其中与课题相关的论文已发表 3 篇，省级工法认定 1 项。课题依托项目已荣获 2009 年度“中国电力优质工程奖”。

（三）获奖单位

中国水利水电第十四工程局有限公司。

（四）获奖人

范开平、刘文、徐华山、张国良、李强、路志利、冯建林。

（摘自《中国电力科学技术奖获奖项目汇编》）

沅水流域梯级水库调度系统开发与应用研究

“沅水流域梯级水库调度系统开发与应用研究”获2009年度中国电力科学技术奖三等奖。

该项目研究成果主要应用于五凌电力有限公司所辖的沅水流域梯级水电站群。主要研究内容包括沅水流域梯级水库调度自动化系统、沅水梯级水库洪水预报与调度子系统、沅水梯级水库经济调度子系统、五强溪水库汛期限制水位分期动态控制方案研究与应用。

（一）主要技术创新点

本项成果应用目前最先进的计算机及网络技术，开发建成适应五凌电力有限公司集中管理和流域梯级水库调度需要的自动化系统平台。该平台通过引入“数据服务”的概念，提出了厂站端多系统多数据源整合模型，有效解决了机组监控系统、闸门监控系统、大坝安全监测系统、电量计费系统等不同专业领域及不同厂家、不同数据特性、不同数据发生机制的大量数据集成问题。采用新安江模型，并结合数字高程模型（DEM）的建模技术开发了沅水流域三板溪、洪江、五强溪、凌津滩、碗米坡等水电站的水文预报模型；开发了水电站群短期发电收益最大化、短期发电水耗最小化和逐日滚动期望收益最大化等模型，取得了良好效果。作为首批试点单位，研究并制定了在五强溪水库汛期限制水位分期动态控制条件下凤滩、五强溪和凌津滩的洪水调度规则，分析了分期动态控制的风险与效益，成功研发了五强溪水库汛期限制水位分期动态控制方案，并在实践中不断完善，为国内同类水库汛期限制水位动态控制积累了经验。成果对提升五凌电力有限公司的生产管理决策水平、信息化水平具有非常重要的作用。

（二）应用领域与推广前景

研究成果应用于生产实践后，取得了显著的经济效益和社会效益。洪水洪峰、洪量的预报精度均高于85%，水文预报合格率为100%，达到规范规定的洪水预报甲等水平，洪水预报精度明显提高；2006～2008年五强溪的水量利用率均在85%以上，较以前历年最好的77%提高至少8%。据统计，2004～2008年五强溪水库应用汛限水位动态控制成果共减少弃水量37.55亿m^3，增加发电量5.624亿kW·h，流域电站群发电效益大幅提高。该项成果可在流域水电开发公司的梯级调度系统中推广应用。

（三）获奖单位

五凌电力有限公司、南京南瑞集团公司。

（四）获奖人

邓志华、谭文胜、汤煜明、吴作平、罗颖、魏志鹏、刘国全、李厚俊、王立、邝录章、伍昕、余有胜。

（摘自《中国电力科学技术奖获奖项目汇编》）

《碾压式土石坝设计规范》（DL/T 5395—2007）

“《碾压式土石坝设计规范》（DL/T 5395—2007）”获2009年度中国电力科学技术奖三等奖。

《碾压土石坝设计规范》（SD J 218—1984）自颁布以来，对我国土石坝的建设起到了巨大的推动作用。这期间修建了鲁布革、天生桥一级、小浪底等高土石坝工程。瀑布沟、水布娅、糯扎渡等世界一流土石坝工程的建设，积累了大量工程经验，同时，进行了“六五”、“七五”、“八五”、“九五”国家科技攻关，通过对上述工程和洪家渡、三板溪、公伯峡等项目的研究，土石坝筑坝新技术有了长足的发展，同时国外土石坝也有了新的发展。为反映这些新的建设经验，有必要对原规范进行修订，使土石坝的设计更加安全实用、经济合理、技术先进、确保质量。

本项目是水电水利工程碾压式土石坝设计标准，是对SD J 218—1984标准的修订。

本标准主要内容包括坝型选择和泄水、引水建筑物的布置，筑坝材料选择和填筑要求，坝体结构和坝基处理，坝体与坝基及其他建筑物的连接，坝的计算和分析，分期施工和扩建加高，安全监测等基本规定和要求。

（一）修订内容

本次修订与SD J 218—1984标准相比，主要做了如下内容的修订：

（1）增加了范围、规范性引用文件、主要术语3章内容。

（2）补充了重型击实试验压实度标准，规定了黏性土料新的压实度标准。

（3）增加了坝坡陡于1∶1.5的波浪爬高计算。

（4）取消了基岩灌浆帷幕厚度按渗透允许坡降计算的设计方法。

（5）增加了保护黏性土反滤层设计的方法。

（6）增加了土的渗透变形判别标准。

（7）大坝抗滑稳定计算，增加了采用概率极限状态设计原则，以分项系数设计表达式的设计方法（可靠度法），作为资料性附录。

（8）规定了抗剪强度指标均采用小值平均值的取值方法，并对防渗土料和粗粒料试验组数分别提出了要求。

（9）规定了面板堆石坝粗粒料抗剪强度应采用非线性指标，土质防渗体坝、沥青混凝土面板或心墙坝及土工膜斜墙或心墙坝粗粒料抗剪强度亦可采用非线性指标。

（10）抗滑稳定计算规定以计及条块间作用力的方法为主，并以有效应力法为基本方法。

（二）主要技术创新点

（1）粗粒料抗剪强度采用非线性指标，经论证写入规范，所有碾压式土石坝及有条件做抗剪强度试验的工程都可以采用，使土石坝设计上了一个台阶。

（2）规定了按重型击实试验的黏性土压实度标准。

（3）探索了坝坡稳定分析的可靠度设计法，并获得重大突破，编入规范附录。

（4）第一次规定了粗粒土抗剪强度采用小值平均值的最少试验组数。

《碾压式土石坝设计规范》（DL/T 5395—2007）已批准出版，从2008年6月1日起执行。本标准应用于水电工程中一级、二级、三级坝高200m以下的碾压土石坝的设计。本标准可在水电水利系统及其他领域土石坝设计中推广。

（三）获奖单位

中国水电顾问集团西北勘测设计研究院、武汉大学。

（四）获奖人

白俊光、张发中、陈洪天、侯建国、党振虎、苗喆、王伟、安旭文、陈树联。

（摘自《中国电力科学技术奖获奖项目汇编》）。

大花水狭窄河谷高碾压混凝土拱坝筑坝技术研究

“大花水狭窄河谷高碾压混凝土拱坝筑坝技术研究”获2009年度中国电力科学技术奖三等奖。

大花水水电站大坝采用河床拱坝和左岸重力坝的组合坝型，拱坝最大坝高134.5m，厚高比0.171，重力坝最大坝高73m。泄洪建筑物布置在拱坝坝身，为3个表孔和2个中孔，最大下泄流量近6000m^3/s。发电引水进水口布置在重力坝坝身。坝址地形不对称并存在地质缺陷，结构复杂，下泄流量大，技术含量高，在之前已建和在建的全碾压混凝土拱坝中还不多见。大花水水电站的成功建成，为在复杂地形、地质条件和复杂结构情况下修建高、薄碾压混凝土拱坝积累了成功的经验。

（一）主要技术创新点

（1）拦河大坝采用河床拱坝与左岸重力坝的组合坝型，充分考虑坝址区的地形地貌特征和地质特点，成功解决了左岸岸坡岩体强度偏低，煤层地层作为要求较高的拱坝坝肩带来的一系列处理问题。其布置形式，弥补了工程坝址区存在的地形地质缺陷。

（2）本工程最大下泄流量接近6000m^3/s，泄洪规模较大，采用3表孔与2中孔在拱坝坝身高低交错的布置形式，让泄洪中孔水流纵向拉伸，分散落点，达到不冲刷岸坡和消能的目的，解决了在狭窄河谷布置大泄量的泄洪建筑物的难题。

（3）将电站进水口布置在左岸重力坝上，避免了进水口布置在左岸岸坡带来的高边坡开挖和支护处理工程量大和进水塔基础地基处理等一系列问题。

（4）泄洪中孔弧形闸门闸墩的预应力锚索体系采用对穿锚的布置形式，避免了在拱坝坝身布置锚头孔洞带来的施工干扰，改善了闸墩和坝体的整体受力状况。

（5）大花水双曲拱坝采用拱坝坝体，设置2条诱导缝和横缝，重力坝不分缝。建筑物泄洪3表孔和2中孔布置在拱坝坝身，泄洪流量大，结构复杂。所采用的结构形式和措施，有效减少了施工中的干扰，全部碾压混凝土实际施工时间不到14个月，并实现了最大月碾压混凝土上升33.7m的纪录。

（二）应用领域与推广前景

大花水碾压混凝土拱坝的成功建成开创了我国狭窄河谷大泄量、高薄碾压混凝土双曲拱坝结构的新纪录，其结构设计研究与应用成果将有利于提高我国筑坝技术水平，为类似工程建设提供较为丰富的推广应用经验，将更好地推动我国碾压混凝土拱坝筑坝技术的进步和发展。

大花水碾压混凝土拱坝的高质量建成，为我国狭窄河谷大泄量、高薄碾压混凝土拱坝结构设计和建设提供了宝贵的经验和重要参考实例，也为我国向200m级高碾压混凝土拱坝发展提供了一个继续前进的平台，极有推广价值。

（三）获奖单位

中国水电顾问集团贵阳勘测设计研究院。

（四）获奖人

陈宏、罗洪波、崔进、范福平、杨家修、高永刚、费晶。

（摘自《中国电力科学技术奖获奖项目汇编》）

钢筋混凝土面板堆石坝坝身溢洪道关键技术研究及应用

“钢筋混凝土面板堆石坝坝身溢洪道关键技术研究及应用”获2009年度中国电力科学技术奖三等奖。

钢筋混凝土面板堆石坝通常采用岸边式溢洪道，布置在坝体一侧或两侧岸坡上，经开挖而成。但这需设置引水渠，可能引起下游水流归槽流态差，或因岸边地形地质条件较差，开挖造成的高边坡出现稳定问题，增加造价等。将溢洪道直接布置在面板堆石坝的坝顶和下游坡面上，可避免上述问题，且具有简化枢纽布置、顺畅水流、节约土地资源、降低工程造价、有利环境保护等一系列优点。

本项目以桐柏下水库面板堆石坝坝身溢洪道为依托，进行了水力学模型试验、坝体与溢洪道结构动力分析、现场锚固筋拉拔力试验，并对结构缝形式、冲刷问题等进行了研究。2008 年 6 月顺利实现了工程过流泄洪。从原型观测、数据分析看，溢洪道运行良好，与研究成果相吻合。

（一）主要技术创新点

（1）控制堆石体沉降变形。坝身溢洪道建造在堆石体上，基础的不均匀变形，会使底板伸缩缝错开及底板开裂，引起高速脉动水流通过伸缩缝或底板断裂缝进入底板下部，造成底板破坏。选好筑坝材料，严格控制填筑密实度，以提高堆石体的变形模量，最大限度地减少基础的绝对变形量。

（2）坝身溢洪道结构的柔性化处理。为吸收基础变形，防止底板断裂，该结构应具有足够的柔性以适应坝体变形。合理设计底板接缝、边墙接缝及底板与边墙间的接缝形式，使溢洪道结构可以适应基础变形和高速水流的冲击。

（3）坝身溢洪道结构稳定及与坝体间的锚固。溢洪道泄槽布置在坝体下游坡面上，由于下游坝坡较陡，底板在各种荷载组合作用下，抗滑稳定难以满足要求。为保证斜坡面上的泄槽稳定，泄槽与堆石体之间应采取特殊工程措施。另外，加强基础排水，增强基础层的透水性，提高溢洪道的稳定。

（4）抗冲及坝脚保护。选择合适的混凝土标号，严格控制泄槽混凝土表面不平整度，提高泄槽自身抗空蚀破坏能力；为防止下游涌浪及回流对坝脚的冲刷，溢洪道两侧坝脚采用超径块石或设置混凝土挡墙保护。

（二）应用领域与推广前景

本项目已成功应用于桐柏抽水蓄能电站，该电站装机容量 1200MW，年发电量 21.18 亿 kW·h，在华东电网中承担调峰、填谷、调频、调相以及事故备用等任务。下水库面板堆石坝坝身溢洪道最大泄量 496m^3/s，溢流落差 60 余米，是坝身溢洪道在大型水电工程中的首次应用，也是世界上规模最大者。

该设计与原岸边溢洪道方案相比，单项投资节省约 600 万元，且减少岸边溢洪道的征地、弃渣场及其水土保持与环境保护费等，合计节约直接经济效益约 1000 万元。

该研究技术成果不仅解决了桐柏抽水蓄能电站下水库因岸边地质条件较差、溢洪道布置难等技术问题，同时拓宽了堆石坝的适用条件，为类似工程泄洪设施和枢纽布置提供了一种经济合理、安全可靠的解决方案，进一步推动了堆石坝工程的技术发展。

目前该技术已在泰安抽水蓄能电站二期等多个工程方案设计中采用。

（三）获奖单位

中国水电顾问集团华东勘测设计研究院。

（四）获奖人

姜忠见、肖建宝、郑齐峰、张春生、丁连春、郎玲芳、李金荣。

（摘自《中国电力科学技术奖获奖项目汇编》）

大坝安全实时监测和预警系统

“大坝安全实时监测和预警系统”获 2009 年度中国电力科学技术奖三等奖。

为有效监控大坝的安全，多数大坝布置了较完整的监测系统。监测仪器种类多，数据量大，资料处理及分析工作复杂，单靠人工完成这些工作费时费力，更不易发现监测过程中出现的疑点。为适应“无人值班”（少人值守）的现代化管理要求，大坝安全实时监控和预警系统充分运用现代计算机科学、网络技术、数据库技术、人工智能等多学科理论和技术，实现对监测系统采集的数据进行科学有序的管理，迅速有效地分析评价工程的安全状况，及时发现影响建筑物安全的前兆信息，确保能在发生灾害性事故之前及时预警，以便将灾害损失降低到最小。本系统实现了以下主要功能：①对人工采集和自动化监测系统采集的监测资料，以及与安全有关的设计、施工资料进行科学有序的管理；②动态管理监测系统及其监测资料数据库，可根据需要增加或删除测点信息，而不影响系统运行；③对监测资料进行及时（人工）或实时（自动化）整编和初分析，而且用户可根据需要对监测资料的整编和归档进行调整；④依据监测资料及其分析成果，对大坝等水工建筑物的安全状况作出及时或实时的评价，实现及时或在线实时监控；⑤对及时或实时监控发现的异常测值进行在线实时反馈分析，首先对异常测值进行综合分析和监测检查，区分监测因素和建筑物异常或险情，然后对建筑物的异常或险情进行物理成因分析，并发出报警信息。

（一）主要技术创新点

（1）预警值确定。预警指标是评价和诊断大坝安全的重要指标，对于监控大坝等水工建筑物的安全运行非常重要。

(2) 本系统利用先进的PSO和GA-APSOR算法为分析方法库建立监控模型，对变形、渗流和应力应变等相关监测量进行分析计算，快速找出异常值，并对异常测值拟订报警级别。

(3) 本系统利用结构分析程序、渗流分析程序和非连续变形分析程序等对坝体、坝基和岸坡进行计算分析，及时了解大坝的安全性态，实现分析预警。

(4) 实时监控。通过数据自动采集系统或人工采集系统，将各监测点的监测信息及日常巡查信息实时或及时输入本系统。

(5) 系统对人工或自动采集的数据，自动选用相关计算方法或专业程序进行计算并将计算结果入库，最后对监测成果进行实时分析判断，对超出预警值的监控项予以报警提示。

(6) 根据监测点的重要性不同，系统可以实现对指定的重要测点进行实时显示，在数据库中数据变化后，可以实时显示在监控界面上。

(二) 应用领域与推广前景

现场应用情况证明，该项研究成果可为每个中型水利水电工程安全监测项目带来每年近20万元的经济效益，具有较大的商业价值和发展前景。

该项研究成果大大提高了数据分析的可靠性和大坝安全预警能力，确保能在发生灾害性事故之前及时预警，为业主或管理层决策提供支持，将灾害损失降低到最小，实现较大的社会效益。

本成果可应用于水利水电、矿山、公路、市政等建筑行业的安全监测工作中，应用前景广阔。现已在中国水利水电第八工程局有限公司承担的安全监测项目中推广应用，同时正准备进行商品化，完成后将进入市场进行销售推广。

(三) 获奖单位

中国水利水电第八工程局有限公司、河海大学。

(四) 获奖人

李桃凡、沈振中、李泽源、江世勇、毛春梅、丁长青、张峰、田承宇、温志萍、易伟、徐力群。

(摘自《中国电力科学技术奖获奖项目汇编》)

陡倾角薄层灰岩及大规模蚀变岩支护技术在地下洞室群中的研究应用

“陡倾角薄层灰岩及大规模蚀变岩支护技术在地下洞室群中的研究应用”获2009年度中国电力科学技术奖三等奖。

本项目依托琅琊山抽水蓄能电站，针对不良地质条件下（层间夹有碳质膜的陡倾角薄层Ⅲ类灰岩和大规模蚀变的Ⅳ～Ⅴ类围岩）地下洞室开挖支护问题，开展了工程地质特性、厂房“两机一变”布置、洞室位移反分析及稳定预报、洞室围岩支护、岩壁吊车梁应用及厂房不均一基础处理等方面的技术研究，通过采用新方法、新技术、新工艺，有效解决了工程技术难题。

(一) 主要技术创新点

(1) 创新采用倒悬直立混凝土边墙支护技术，突破了从稳定基础向上浇筑地下厂房混凝土边墙的常规方法，成功解决大范围（宽20m，高30m）Ⅳ～Ⅴ类围岩高边墙稳定问题，在国内外同类工程中处于领先水平。

(2) 在陡立薄层灰岩（Ⅲ类为主）和大规模蚀变岩带（Ⅳ～Ⅴ类）基础上，创新采用“L”型悬吊刚性基础垫座、悬空混凝土墙辅助支撑吊车梁等措施，在破碎岩体上成功建成了岩壁吊车梁，在国内外同类工程中处于领先水平。

(3) 创新利用蚀变岩原位特性（不开挖置换、不固结灌浆）和整体箱型结构处理地下厂房不均一岩性基础技术，在国内外同类工程中处于领先水平。

(4) 在国内抽水蓄能电站首次采用2台机组共用1台变压器的厂房布置形式，减少交叉洞室，有效解决了不良地质条件下电站大型地下洞室群因围岩稳定性差而布置困难的问题，领先于国内同类工程。

(5) 根据围岩稳定监测信息，通过位移反分析跟踪预报大型地下洞室围岩开挖的稳定和变形，指导洞室支护设计与施工，在国内外同类工程中处于领先水平。

(二) 应用领域与推广前景

本课题研究成果已成功运用于琅琊山抽水蓄能电站，解决了琅琊山抽水蓄能电站的关键技术问题，保证了工程安全、工期与投资，并经过工程运行检验取得了成功，产生的直接经济效益达1100万元。该工程于2008年通过了中国水电工程顾问集团公司组织的竣工安全鉴定。琅琊山抽水蓄能电站自2006年9月第1台机组投入运行以来，一直安全运行，各项监测结果表明，洞室围岩稳定，支护措施得当，结构安全，证明了科研成果正确、可靠。

本科研成果适用于复杂地质条件下地下洞室勘察、设计、施工等领域，对符合修建大型地下洞室群的围岩类别标准有了突破性的认识，为破碎岩体修建大型地下厂房提供了新思路，对于推动地下洞室支护技术的发展有深远意义。

(三) 获奖单位

中国水电顾问集团北京勘测设计研究院。

(四) 获奖人

郝荣国、吴奎、王敬武、王阳雪、宫海灵、储小钊、许文龙。

（摘自《中国电力科学技术奖获奖项目汇编》）

水轮发电机组励磁大功率整流自冷散热系统

“水轮发电机组励磁大功率整流自冷散热系统”获2009年度中国电力科学技术奖三等奖。

一直以来，发电机励磁整流柜的散热主要依靠强迫风冷方式。对整流柜而言，风机只是散热的辅助设备，但风机的故障却常常影响到整个励磁系统。尽管现在有一些解决措施，如采用双路供电、双风机备用、选择低噪声风机、采用密闭循环等，也取得了比较明显的效果，但始终未从根本上解决问题。葛洲坝湖北南河水电开发有限公司开发的发电机励磁大功率整流自冷散热系统将利用先进的热管散热技术，改变传统的散热观念，实现励磁大功率整流柜无风自冷运行，摆脱对风机这个辅助设备的依赖。

（一）主要技术创新点

（1）热管技术。大功率整流柜采用进口晶闸管组成三相全控整流桥，晶闸管触发回路采用高频脉冲列强触发技术，结合电压嵌位，避免晶闸管的误触发，提高了触发的可靠性和抗干扰能力。晶闸管散热采用汽液分离式环形热管散热器，利用热管很高的导热性、优良的等温性和环境的适应性等特点，与型材散热器完美结合，提高了散热器的散热效率。运行过程中不需要风机进行强迫风冷，从根本上解决功率柜内灰尘的积累，减少维护工作量，实现装置的免维护。

（2）自适应微机励磁控制技术。自适应微机励磁控制系统是同步发电机的重要组成部分，直接控制同步发电机磁场电流，从而控制同步发电机的电势，还间接控制发电机的端电压、无功功率、功率因数和电流等参量。它也控制着系统的运行状态，特别是系统的稳定与励磁控制方式密该相关，由励磁控制器、晶闸管整流单元、灭磁及过电压保护单元、起励单元和励磁变压器五部分组成。

（3）自适应微机励磁反馈控制器技术。自适应微机励磁控制系统是一个闭环控制系统，其反馈控制通过以下过程来实现：首先励磁控制器的测量单元检测电压互感器输入信号从而获得发电机的机端电压U_t，然后将U_t与给定电压U_r相比较获得电压差值$\Delta U=U_r-U_t$，该电压差ΔU经综合放大环节后得到控制电压U_c。

（二）应用领域与推广前景

过渡湾电站励磁系统改造应用了本成果。改造前，因励磁柜风机故障而被迫停机共计15次，因屏柜环境温度超标（超过75℃）而停机11次，累计停机26次（统计时间段为2001年10月～2007年4月）；改造后2008年4月30日～2009年1月15日期间，1～3号机励磁屏未发生一次因风机故障和屏柜环境温度超标而停机的事件，从停机电站发电量损失、电风对电站非计划停运而扣减发电量的损失及发生的相关管理费用三个方面测算，此次励磁系统改造对电站仅此期间就产生直接经济效益1540余万元。目前三个屏柜环境温度均控制在45℃以下，设备运行情况稳定。

该项目成果符合我国电力市场发展需要，可广泛应用于大、中型电厂发电机组励磁系统的功率转换装置，具有较明显的经济效益和社会效益。

（三）获奖单位

葛洲坝湖北南河水电开发有限公司。

（四）获奖人

冯新生、祝祖生、付军、汪涛、何浩、刘建华、蔡志强。

（摘自《中国电力科学技术奖获奖项目汇编》）

瀑布沟水电站砾石土心墙料筛分输送系统的应用研究

“瀑布沟水电站砾石土心墙料筛分输送系统的应用研究”获2009年度中国电力科学技术奖三等奖。

瀑布沟水电站大坝砾石土料筛分及输送系统的应用属于新技术应用型科技项目。砾石土筛分及输送技术的应用为国内首创。瀑布沟水电站大坝砾石土料筛分及输送系统是瀑布沟水电站大坝填筑的重要设备。

瀑布沟电站大坝心墙砾石土筛分和输送系统由一次条筛、振动筛给料皮带机、振动筛、出料皮带机、长距离皮带机系统、堆料机、电器控制系统、工业监控系统等组成。

以发包方提供的工程合同文件为基础，以行业规范和国家标准为依据，结合地形条件和民俗习性，以满足砾石土粒径、砾石土含水率、大坝最大月填筑强度、优化的性价比为设计原则。

该项目从2004年7月开始现场地形勘测、方案设计、方案审核、技术设计、试验研究和现场复勘，2006年2月开始本项目的加工、制造、安装和调试，2007年3月开始对输送系统的所有部位进行调试和优化，于4月中旬系统开始投入正常运行。

瀑布沟水电站砾石土输送系统累计输送方量280万m^3（压实方），日平均产量10 400m^3，最高产量13 000m^3，充分满足了大坝填筑用料和施工进度的要求。

（一）主要技术创新点

大方量的砾石土筛分及长距离皮带机输送系统在我国是首次设计和应用。通过科学计算、试验研究及模拟现场试验，掌握了用于砾石土筛分的条筛孔径、长度、倾角、断面形式及振动筛的孔径、振幅、振动频率、振动倾角等参数。砾石土料的筛分技术系国内空白，处于国内领先水平。下行多折点皮带输送机设计及输送机钢架设计技术处于同行业先进水平。

（二）应用领域与推广前景

砾石土心墙坝属于土石坝的一种，由于筑坝材料取自当地，可节省水泥、钢材和木材，并因对坝基工程地质条件要求比其他坝型低、抗震性能较好等优点得以推广。瀑布沟水电站大坝砾石土料筛分及输送系统的成功研制解决了国内砾石土料筛分和长距离连续输送这一难题，有利于砾石土心墙坝这一坝型在国内的推广。

该应用成果在砾石土料的筛分和连续输送领域填补了国内空白，对加快进度和节省工程投资、提高经济效益有着十分重要的意义，具有较高的推广应用价值。

（三）获奖单位

葛洲坝集团项目管理有限公司。

（四）获奖人

蒋涛、魏文俊、张安平、彭国勇、田英、马作兴、何永忠。

（摘自《中国电力科学技术奖获奖项目汇编》）

龙滩水电站大法坪砂石系统关键技术研究与应用

“龙滩水电站大法坪砂石系统关键技术研究与应用”获2009年度中国电力科学技术奖三等奖。

随着筑坝技术的发展，水电砂石系统无论在规模还是质量指标上，近年来都得到了大幅度提高。但由于起步晚，我国在砂石加工系统技术方面与大坝施工和设计所要达到的质量和技术指标还存在明显差距。本项目围绕龙滩水电站大法坪砂石系统施工难点和关键点展开专题研究。龙滩水电站大法坪砂石加工系统主要担负龙滩水电站Ⅲ标共计约641.63万m^3混凝土所需骨料的生产任务，共需生产成品砂石料1412万t，其中粗骨料939万t、细骨料473万t。具有供料总量大、强度高、料场与系统高差大、成品料品种多、废水处理量大等特点。

（一）主要技术创新点

（1）突破了传统料场破碎和场内运输技术。采用移动破碎和移动胶带机技术，布置灵活，石料通过胶带机运输可靠性高，解决了破碎、料场降段、石料运输等多项难题，为国内首次成功应用。

（2）垂直运输技术。转料仓之间及转料仓、半成品之间采用胶带机输送，避免了采用溜井可能出现的问题，具有明显的技术和经济优势，开创了国内先例。

（3）细骨料石粉回收工艺。在国内首次采用水力旋流分级工艺，利用高效脱水装置对冲洗水中的石粉进行回收利用，通过调整旋流器的数量确定石粉回收量，通过控制水量稳定浆液浓度，通过湿掺法保持石粉含量均匀，具有运行可靠、回收率较高、占地面积小等特点。

（4）新型的废水处理工艺。采用意大利劲马气动清淤泵及管道系统，把回收石粉后的泥渣以96%的浓度，长距离输送到堆渣库堆存、过滤，做到了废水零排放。

（二）应用领域与推广前景

本成果在龙滩水电站大法坪砂石系统得到了成功应用。截至2008年4月20日，大法坪砂石系统共向大坝供应合格的砂石骨料1682.5万t，系统的生产能力、产品质量完全满足设计技术规范及业主要求，实践证明采用以上先进技术创造了良好的经济效益和社会效益。

当前水电开发条件越来越艰难，该项目采用的移动破碎和移动胶带机为复杂地形条件下料场开采和运输提供了新思路。采用采场破碎、半成品胶带机转运的料场开采运输方式，适用于大面积料场开采，值得在国内水电和矿山、长距离隧洞开挖等领域借鉴。本项目总结了一套用于砂石系统生产各重点环节的施工工艺和技术，可广泛应用于类似砂石加工系统的设计与施工中，具有很好的应用推广前景。

（三）获奖单位

葛洲坝集团第五工程有限公司。

（四）获奖人

朱显山、赵小青、齐涛、付俊雄、吕芝林、郭光文、杨军。

（摘自《中国电力科学技术奖获奖项目汇编》）

新老混凝土结合界面密合剂

“新老混凝土结合界面密合剂”获2009年度中国电力科学技术奖三等奖。

在人为和自然环境的作用下，每年都有大量建筑物发生劣化和损伤，需要修补和加固，还有许多建筑物由于环境条件和使用功能的改变或使用龄期的延长也面临加固和改造问题。在混凝土结构的修补、加固、改造中，新老混凝土的黏结状态是关系到修补、加固、改造后混凝土结构质量的重要问题。采用合适的界面材料是提高新老混凝土黏结强度、改善新老混凝土黏结状态的重要措施之一。

目前工程中常用的新老混凝土界面材料包括水泥浆、膨胀水泥浆、环氧胶等均存在各种不足之处，例如，使用、施工不方便，对工程环境、气候条件的适应性差，对人和环境有毒害性，价格昂贵，新老混凝土的黏结强度低，抗侵蚀能力差，耐久性差等，因此，研制性能更优异的界面材料以提高新老混凝土界面黏结强度是较为迫切的任务。

本项目研制的密合剂具有使用方便、性能优异的特点，为提高新老混凝土界面黏结性能提供了一种好的界面材料，解决了长期以来新老混凝土界面黏结性能不佳的难题。

(一) 主要技术创新点

(1) 材料为水泥基的无机粉体，不燃、不爆，对人和环境无毒害。

(2) 使用、施工方便，按规定的比例加水，搅拌成均匀的浆体后即可使用。

(3) 操作时间可调。拌制好的浆体可以放置较长时间（3h之内）而不会影响其流动性、黏附性及黏结质量。

(4) 对基底混凝土状态的适应性强。在基底混凝土为垂直、倒立、潮湿、干燥状态时，材料涂刷的黏附性及新老混凝土的黏结效果都很好。

(5) 对现场施工环境及天气条件适宜性强。施工现场存在有水、雾、少量降雨及日照、风吹等不利因素时，可以照常进行本材料施工涂刷及后续的混凝土浇筑，新老混凝土的黏结强度不会受到影响。

(6) 各类气候条件下均可允许有较长的开放时间而不影响新老混凝土的黏结质量。

(7) 新老混凝土的黏结强度高。使用本密合剂后，新老混凝土界面的黏结强度可以大于混凝土本体的强度。

(8) 抗侵蚀性好、耐久性高。

(二) 应用领域与推广前景

在丹江口大坝加高工程中，本密合剂因效果最佳、成本最低而获得国内专家和业主的一致好评，现本密合剂已在该工程中使用约6000m^2，材料约30t，预计整个丹江口加高工程将使用本密合剂近1万m^2以上。

本密合剂已成功在景洪水电站消力池底板修复工程中使用约12 000m^2，材料约62t。

大量的混凝土工程即将进入维修期或即将逐步加固改造，在建的混凝土工程前期、后期混凝土的龄期差异较大时，将需要大量使用界面密合剂以提高新老混凝土界面黏结性能，因而本界面密合剂将会得到更广泛的应用，为解决了业界难题、提高工程质量、降低工程造价作出贡献。

(三) 获奖单位

葛洲坝集团试验检测有限公司。

(四) 获奖人

程润喜、宋拥军、谭恺炎、周厚贵、陈志远、程雪军。

(摘自《中国电力科学技术奖获奖项目汇编》)

高黏结高渗进在役混凝土复合增强材料的研究

“高黏结高渗进在役混凝土复合增强材料的研究”获2009年度中国电力科学技术奖三等奖。

渗漏是水工混凝土结构中普遍存在的一种现象，一旦发生渗漏，将严重影响混凝土结构的耐久性，降低建筑物的使用寿命，且维修费用也比较巨大。因此，混凝土结构工程对防水防渗的要求越来越高，混凝土破损结构修复对防水材料的需求量也越来越大。为满足工程需要，中国水利水电第十一工程局有限公司在反复实践中，研究出一种新型产品——高黏结高渗进在役混凝土复合增强材料。

(一) 主要创新点

(1) 主要力学性能优良，抗渗压力不小于1.2MPa，渗进深度不小于50mm。

(2) 含有能够反应生成钙矾石晶体以及使混凝土中不稳定晶体产生晶型转换，形成稳定型晶体的有效成分，可以提高混凝土的综合性能。

(3) 施工简便，综合单价较低，是国外同类产品的2/3。

(二) 应用领域与推广前景

2008年，在“5·12”汶川大地震后的紫平铺水电站面板混凝土上处理裂缝施工应用800多平方米，使用效果很好，在水位不断变化的考验下至今运行良好，无异常情况出现。

该产品既能够应用于混凝土的防渗补强，同时对混凝土表面的细微裂缝也有很好的修复效果。目前在国内处于技术领先水平，与国外同类产品相比性价比较高，具有很好的市场应用前景。

(三) 获奖单位

中国水利水电第十一工程局有限公司。

(四) 获奖人

张涛、高富龙、张汉平、黄俊玮、丁清杰、殷德文。

(摘自《中国电力科学技术奖获奖项目汇编》)

碾压式沥青混凝土面板防渗技术研究

“碾压式沥青混凝土面板防渗技术研究”获2009年度中国电力科学技术奖三等奖。

本项成果为原国家电力公司科研项目“沥青混凝土防渗及其施工技术研究”（项目编号SPKJ006－06）的部分内容。

沥青混凝土面板用于土石坝表面防渗已有多年。由于是一种黏弹性材料，其力学性质和温度与加荷速率密切相关，应力应变关系复杂，国内外对水工沥青混凝土的力学特性均缺少系统的研究，特别是不同温度条件下的应力应变特性、蠕变特性和低温抗裂性能等。以往的工程设计主要以经验为主，对水工沥青混凝土材料的力学特性和面板结构的受力变形规律缺少系统全面的了解。

本项目依托河北张河湾抽水蓄能电站上水库防渗工程，对沥青混凝土面板防渗技术进行了系统全面的研究，形成一套较系统完整的碾压式沥青混凝土面板防渗技术。

（一）主要技术创新点

（1）较系统全面地掌握了面板沥青混凝土在常温和低温（13.4～35℃）条件下的应力应变特性和规律。

（2）较全面地掌握了面板沥青混凝土在常温和低温（13.4～25℃）条件下的蠕变特性和规律。

（3）深入研究了面板沥青混凝土的低温抗裂和冻断性能。

（4）较全面地掌握了沥青混凝土面板结构的受力和变形规律，提出面板结构设计应主要以应变作为控制指标。

（5）研究提出了一种沥青混凝土面板防渗的简化复式断面结构形式。

（6）系统地提出了沥青混凝土面板设计的使用要求性能，即防渗性能、高温抗斜坡流淌、低温抗裂、适应地基变形、水稳定性、抗老化等，并提出了相应试验评价方法和各结构层的设计控制指标体系等，形成一套较系统完整的碾压式沥青混凝土面板防渗设计技术，并在张河湾抽水蓄能电站上水库防渗工程中成功应用。

（二）应用领域与推广前景

本成果主要应用于水利水电工程的沥青混凝土面板防渗设计领域，也可用于其他蓄水池和渠道防渗工程的设计。

本项目取得的有关面板沥青混凝土的基本力学特性规律、面板结构的受力和变形特性规律等成果，可作为今后类似防渗工程设计的依据和指导。提出的沥青混凝土面板各结构层的使用性能要求和相应的试验评价方法、设计控制指标体系等，可直接应用于类似工程的设计。

（三）获奖单位

中国水电顾问集团北京勘测设计研究院、河北张河湾蓄能发电有限责任公司。

（四）获奖人

吕明治、吴立新、李冰、张亚丽、张向前、郭清、李瑜霞。

（摘自《中国电力科学技术奖获奖项目汇编》）

岩石与水耦合理论及其应用

“岩石与水耦合理论及其应用”获2009年度中国电力科学技术奖三等奖。

岩石与水耦合理论及其应用是岩土工程领域的前沿课题之一。水在整个岩土体演变过程中起着非常重要的作用，而人类的营建建筑物建立在岩土体之上，研究水与岩土体相互作用的规律及效应，对岩土体稳定性、地质灾害的发生和营建建筑物的安全等具有重要作用。

（一）主要技术创新点

（1）基于岩石与水相互作用过程的损伤机理，首次建立了岩石与水塑性损伤耦合模型的分析方法。

（2）提出了各向同性及各向异性材料Biot系数、Skempton系数的实验及确定方法，以及基于偏应力与水压力关系确定岩体屈服应力极限的新方法。研究证明对于胶结较好的地质体，水的压缩性必须加以考虑。

（3）针对传统真假三轴物理力学试验方法和试件特点，首次提出假三轴试件应为长方体的观点及相应的材料物理力学参数的确定方法。对室内三轴试件在干燥及饱和水压力作用下的试验结果进行了成功模拟，如水压力能降低岩石峰值强度，增加岩石变形，改变试件破坏的各向异性等。

（4）基于均匀化理论，推导了含裂纹孔隙介质的能量方程，建立了岩石与水相互作用的耦合方程，首次提出了一种等效刚度矩阵的求解方法、一种新的裂纹扩展标准和弹塑性屈服标准，解决了损伤扩展和塑性的统一性和协调性。

（二）应用领域与推广前景

水岩耦合理论研究成果可广泛应用于工程建设、灾害防治和环境治理等广阔的工程领域，保证了营建建筑物的正常运营，从而保障了人民生命财产安全，节省了大量工程建设开支。在国内外大兴土木、水电开发的契机下，应用前景广阔。

（三）获奖单位

三峡大学。

（四）获奖人

卢应发、李建林、郑宏、田斌、黄悦华、王乐华、程圣国。

（摘自《中国电力科学技术奖获奖项目汇编》）

57MW超大型灯泡贯流式水轮发电机组安装技术研究

“57MW超大型灯泡贯流式水轮发电机组安装技术研究”获2009年度中国电力科学技术奖三等奖。

我国低水头水力资源丰富，在珠江流域、黄河上游龙羊峡至青铜峡河段，有大批低水头水电站尚待开发，灯泡贯流式水电站将成为未来我国水力资源开发的主要类型。广西桥巩水电站灯泡贯流式水轮发电机组单机容量57MW，转轮直径7.45m，为我国目前单机容量最大（亚洲第二）的灯泡贯流式水轮发电机组。

系统研究了灯泡贯流式水轮发电机组安装技术工艺，并对施工过程中采用的新工艺进行详细的阐述，如管型座安装、导水机构安装、双支点双悬臂轴系轴承间隙调整、转轮安装、定子安装新工艺。

（一）主要技术创新点

（1）导水机构下游侧内外环安装定位架设计。

（2）安装间桨叶组装后转轮吊装工具设计。

（3）定子套装滑轨技术。

（4）控制大型部件吊装时引起的塑性变形工艺。

（5）控制尾水管里衬、座环及导水机构的焊接变形工艺。

（6）组合轴承和水轮机径向轴承间隙调整工艺。

（二）应用领域与推广前景

桥巩水电站57MW的灯泡贯流式水轮发电机组的安装技术代表着世界先进水平，通过对桥巩水电站57MW的灯泡贯流式水轮发电机组安装技术进行研究和总结，直接运用在电站后续机组的安装施工中，保证了安装质量和工期；同时，为超大型灯泡贯流式水轮发电机组的设计、制造和安装提供了实践经验，并将为其他同类型机组的安装施工提供借鉴。

灯泡贯流式水电站主要应用于低水头水力资源开发的流域，在对灯泡贯流式水轮发电机组的设计、制造、安装及运行技术进行研究的同时，对相关技术形成的施工工法和技术论文进行推广。

（三）获奖单位

中国水利水电第七工程局有限公司、河海大学。

（四）获奖人

赵显忠、程云山、韩强、黄中良、谢学伦、曾洪福、潘勇。

（摘自《中国电力科学技术奖获奖项目汇编》）

大型渠道混凝土快速衬砌施工技术研究

“大型渠道混凝土快速衬砌施工技术研究”获2009年度中国电力科学技术奖三等奖。

南水北调中线工程是改善我国水资源配置的重大基础性战略工程，总干渠全长1275km，以明渠渠道施工为主。由于国内在大型渠道混凝土机械化衬砌施工方面暂无成型设备和成熟经验，中国水利水电第十一工程局有限公司作为最先进入南水北调中线工程的施工单位，在其依托承建的京石段小滹沱河倒虹吸出口及S6标渠道工程，率先开展了大型渠道混凝土快速衬砌施工技术研究，为更好地服务于南水北调工程打下了坚实基础。

（一）主要技术内容

（1）针对依托工程特点（渠道底宽20～21m，坡面斜长22m，坡比1：3，衬砌混凝土板厚8～15cm，属大面积薄壁素混凝土结构），自行研制了可连续浇筑、操作安全简便的大型渠道混凝土浇筑设备。

（2）通过对大型渠道结构断面的分析，分别从渠道建基面清理，保温板铺设，复合土工膜防渗层铺设，渠道混凝土衬砌、切缝、填缝等施工过程着手，总结大型渠道混凝土快速衬砌施工技术和工艺。

（3）通过各工序质量控制、混凝土配合比研究及在混凝土拌和料中引入超纤维植物纤维等方法，研究如何提高混凝土衬砌板的抗裂、抗渗及耐久性能。

（二）主要技术创新点

（1）研制的大型振碾式渠道混凝土浇筑机集混凝土布料、摊铺、振捣和整平功能于一体，可实现渠坡和渠底互用，适应渠道坡长和坡比的变化，结构新颖、轻便，操作维护简便安全，提高了渠道混凝土衬砌施工质量，加快了施工进度。

（2）通过研究实践，形成了基面整平压实，保温防渗结构层铺设，渠道混凝土衬砌、切缝、填缝等一整套大型混凝土渠道的快速施工技术和工艺。

（三）应用领域与推广前景

该研究成果解决了大断面渠道混凝土快速衬砌施工的技术难题，在南水北调中线总干渠一期工程中成功推广应用，采用同类型浇筑机及施工工艺进行渠道衬砌的标段近20个，对南水北调京石段应急供水工程的顺利通水起到了积极的推动作用。该项成果研究过程中获得国家8项实用新型专利，中国水利水电第十一工程局有限公司以专利为基础，使大型振碾式渠道混凝土浇筑机产品及配套工艺标准化，在南水北调后续渠道工程中大力推广应用。

（四）获奖单位

中国水利水电第十一工程局有限公司。

（五）获奖人

高海成、钟彦祥、任学文、余良碧、肖明方、李卫东、徐广建、张智宏、徐其阳。

（摘自《中国电力科学技术奖获奖项目汇编》）

基于节能的水电厂监控软件

“基于节能的水电厂监控软件”获2009年度中国电力科学技术奖三等奖。

该项目通过总结国网电力科学研究院实施的400多套水电厂监控系统的经验，根据新形势下水电厂管理与技术需求的变化，采用最新的计算机和通信技术，研制成功了新一代计算机监控软件。它可对全厂生产设备进行有效监视和控制，帮助厂站更加安全、可靠、经济地运行，实现“无人值班”（少人值守）的目标。

该项目通过了中国电机工程学会组织的鉴定，达到了国际先进水平，已获得1项软件著作权，发表论文10余篇，已申请1项发明专利，正在申请第2项发明专利。

（一）主要技术创新点

（1）采用面向服务的设计技术，提供全组态工具，支持C语言脚本编程，提供二次开发包，实现全数据监视、智能化报警、可视化控制、综合信息处理与分析等功能，满足用户的全面需求。

（2）独创可视化顺控流程图的方式实现顺序控制，并支持流程的执行、回放及异常陷阱处理。

（3）提供面向对象的报警系统综合服务功能，包括报警分类查询、屏蔽、基于优先级的语音报警、ONCALL系统和多媒体专家事故处理指导，其整体功能的设计与实现，在业界属于独创。

（4）建立基于节能的AGC/AVC多目标数学模型，首次实现可组态满足不同水电厂控制策略的AGC/AVC软件。

（二）应用领域与推广前景

该项目适用于中小型水电站、梯级电站、抽水蓄能电站、水利综合自动化等监控领域，已应用300多套系统，其中出口南美、中东、东南亚等国十几套，为公司赢得合同额4亿多元。该系统安全可靠、功能完善、运行稳定、使用方便、各项功能和技术指标均满足用户要求，人机接口友善，提高了电站的自动化和安全经济运行水平，为实现电站“无人值班”（少人值守）打下了良好的基础，具有很好的应用前景。

（三）获奖单位

国网电力科学研究院、南京南瑞集团公司。

（四）获奖人

徐洁、朱辰、王亦宁、纪菁、徐青、马杰、霍宁。

（摘自《中国电力科学技术奖获奖项目汇编》）

《水电水利工程环境保护设计规范》（DL/T 5402—2007）

“《水电水利工程环境保护设计规范》（DL/T 5402—2007）”获2009年度中国电力科学技术奖三等奖。

《水电水利工程环境保护设计规范》（DL/T 5402—2007）是国家发展和改革委员会批准立项的水电水利行业环境保护类标准。该标准是我国水电水利行业首次编制的环境保护类标准，其颁布实施填补了国内空白。

该标准适用于大、中型水电水利工程可行性研究阶段的环境保护设计，小型水电水利工程可参考本标准执行。

该标准的颁布实施提高了我国水电水利行业环境保护管理、设计、实施水平，促进了水电工程环境保护设计工作的规范化。

（一）主要技术创新点

（1）首次将环境保护设计作为独立的专业规范。

（2）首次明确规定了施工砂石料加工废水中悬浮物设计参数。

（3）首次明确规定了施工修配系统污水中石油类、COD_{cr}和悬浮物设计参数。

（4）首次明确规定了施工混凝土拌和冲洗废水中悬浮物设计参数。

（5）首次明确规定了移民安置区生活污水处理设计。

（6）首次在水电水利工程陆生生态保护中提出了迁地保护和就地保护设计。

（7）首次在水电水利工程水生生态保护中提出了过鱼设施设计、鱼类增殖站设计、人工建造鱼类产卵基地设计。

（8）首次明确规定了生态流量泄放和分层取水等水环境保护措施。

(9) 首次明确规定了环境管理和监理技术要求。

(10) 首次明确规定了工程施工期和运行期的环境监测设计要求。

(二) 应用领域

该标准已于2007年12月3日由国家发展改革委第81号公告颁布，于2008年6月1日起实施，可广泛应用于在建和新建的大、中型水电水利工程可行性研究阶段的环境保护设计工作，提高了水电工程环境保护管理、设计、实施水平，促进了水电工程环境保护设计工作的规范化。

(三) 获奖单位

中国水电顾问集团成都勘测设计研究院。

(四) 获奖人

李亚农、卢红伟、顾洪宾、谢光武、魏凡、孙大东、杨玖贤。

(摘自《中国电力科学技术奖获奖项目汇编》)

大掺量磨细矿渣混凝土关键技术研究与应用

"大掺量磨细矿渣混凝土关键技术研究与应用"获得2009年度大禹水利科学技术奖二等奖。

曹娥江大闸枢纽工程是国家重大水利基础设施项目，必须对其耐久性予以高度重视。为提高曹娥江大闸枢纽工程结构耐久性，延长工程使用寿命，特开展本项目研究。项目研究以耐久性与抗裂性为主要技术指标，对四种大掺量矿物掺合料混凝土方案进行了对比优选，推荐大掺量磨细矿渣混凝土用于曹娥江大闸主体工程。研究结果表明，大掺量磨细矿渣混凝土耐久性能优良。该混凝土中，使用活化剂明显减小了早期塑性收缩和干缩；复合使用强纶纤维，提高了闸墩混凝土抗裂能力；基于DuraCrete方法的寿命预测分析表明，保护层为40mm和60mm时，工程预测寿命分别在180年和1300年以上。

该成果的主要创新点：①研发的大掺量磨细矿渣活化剂可明显减小大掺量磨细矿渣混凝土的早期塑性收缩和干缩，并有利于改善施工工艺条件；②首次将强纶纤维和防裂网片等措施复合用于体型复杂的薄壁混凝土结构中，有效地解决了开裂问题；③结合大掺量磨细矿渣混凝土的特点，形成了大钢模和贝雷架龙门吊快速浇筑大体积混凝土的施工新工艺。

该成果于2008年12月26日通过水利部国际合作与科技司科技成果鉴定，鉴定意见认为：该成果总体上达到国际先进水平，其中在大掺量磨细矿渣与纤维复合技术解决海洋环境大体积混凝土的耐久性与抗裂性研究与应用方面达到国际领先水平。建议进一步总结项目成果，在工程中大力推广应用。

该成果在曹娥江大闸枢纽工程中得到应用，成功浇筑混凝土20万m^3。应用结果表明，该成果对处在腐蚀环境较为严重的沿海或近海工程以及容易开裂的薄壁异型结构工程有很好的借鉴作用，推广意义重大。

主要完成单位：南京水利科学研究院、绍兴市曹娥江大闸投资开发有限公司、南京瑞迪高新技术公司。

主要完成人：黄国泓、徐青松、林军、李克亮、邵全卯、唐修生、傅森彪、陈健、祝烨然、王毅。

(南京水利科学研究院)

碾压混凝土外掺MgO筑坝技术研究与应用

"碾压混凝土外掺MgO筑坝技术研究与应用"获得2009年度广西壮族自治区科学技术进步奖三等奖。

水利水电工程以往是采用轻烧MgO，产品质量稳定性差，不能很好地满足水工混凝土的要求，大坝易产生温度裂缝，且存在大体积混凝土工程与冶金工业争抢稀有的矿产原材料问题。为此，课题组进行碾压混凝土外掺MgO筑坝技术研究与应用。特性MgO混凝土筑坝技术是利用特性MgO所具有的独特延迟性微膨胀性能，补偿混凝土的温度变形及收缩变形，防止温度裂缝，简化温控，实现长坝块通仓、连续浇筑及夏天全天候施工，加快工程进度，减少或防止混凝土坝产生温度裂缝问题。

课题组经大量系统的科学研究，取得了如下成果：

(1) 研发特性MgO、制定特性MgO产品标准和性能检测标准。

(2) 确定外掺特性MgO混凝土安定性试验方法和评价指标。

(3) 外掺特性MgO混凝土配合比及物理力学性能试验成果。

(4) 外掺特性MgO混凝土热学性能试验成果。

(5) 外掺特性MgO混凝土膨胀变形试验成果。

(6) 基于Biot理论的外掺特性MgO微膨胀混凝土温度有效应力计算方法。

(7) 龙滩工程碾压混凝土围堰中间试验应用成果。

研发的特性MgO与产品标准、性能检测标准，已在南京海特曼工程新材料有限责任公司生产应用，效果良好。碾压混凝土外掺MgO筑坝技术研究与应用中多项技术正在进行专利申报和保护，本课题研究成果具有完全的自主知识产权。验收评审会上，评审专家提出应加大宣传力度，大力推广应用 MgO 混凝土筑坝技术，并制定与修改相应的规程规范。项目所提出的研究成果，经鉴定综合技术水平达到国内领先。

主要完成单位：龙滩水电开发有限公司、中国水电顾问集团中南勘测设计研究院、南京水利科学研究院、南京工业大学、中国水利水电科学研究院。

获奖人：冯树荣、龙件开、李善忠、程纲为、肖锋、陆采荣、钟志军、邓敏、梅明荣、张国新、朱岳明、李守义、金双全、成方。

（南京水利科学研究院）

河谷边坡稳定性演化机理与调控方法

“河谷边坡稳定性演化机理与调控方法”获 2009 年度教育部高等学校科技进步奖一等奖。

该项目系统地研究了河谷边坡演化与地应力场特征、河谷边坡变形破坏机理、边坡岩体力学参数时空演化、河谷边坡的爆破开挖效应、河谷边坡稳定性的锚固支护效应、河谷边坡稳定性的渗流作用效应、边坡变形与稳定性分析方法、维护边坡稳定性的设计与施工控制、边坡稳定性状态监测与反馈分析、边坡稳定性状态预测与预警及边坡稳定可靠度与风险分析等。取得了如下主要研究成果：①提出了河谷边坡“自然—工程”耦合的稳定性演化模式，建立了集自然演化、工程作用、动态调控、监测反馈、预测预报及风险评估为一体的河谷边坡变形和稳定性系统分析方法，构建了数值模拟与分析平台；②提出了边坡渗流 Signorini 边界条件及边坡渗控结构渗流模拟的子结构—变分不等式—自适应（SVA）方法，建立了岩土体非饱和多相流传输与 HM 全耦合模型及数值分析方法；③提出三维边坡稳定性整体分析法，实现了考虑侧向摩擦边界的三维滑动体严格极限平衡分析；④阐明了高应力强卸荷条件下边坡岩体大变形成因机制，发展了边坡应力变形分析的 DDA 方法；⑤提出了边坡安全监测模型与岩土体力学参数多源信息反演方法；⑥建立了基于变形破坏模式的边坡安全度与监测位移的关系，提出了工程类比、监测反馈、数值模拟相结合的边坡稳定性预测预警方法；⑦提出了边坡时变可靠度计算方法和动态风险评估方法、多失效模式下边坡稳定可靠度计算的 N 维等效方法及可靠度敏感性多层次分析法；⑧建立了基于设计优化、施工和运行控制的河谷边坡稳定性动态调控模式；⑨提出了考虑爆破损伤、动态卸荷和振动效应的边坡开挖与锚固施工优化程序及爆破开挖安全控制措施。

该研究成果已在三峡、锦屏、向家坝、大岗山等二十多个水电工程中得到成功应用，取得了显著的社会效益和经济效益。

主要承担单位：武汉大学、三峡大学等。

主要完成人员：周创兵、陈益峰、李典庆等。

（武汉大学　黄介生　韩春玲）

高混凝土坝结构安全与优化理论及工程应用

“高混凝土坝结构安全与优化理论及工程应用”获 2009 年度湖北省科技进步奖一等奖。

我国混凝土坝高度已达 200～300m 级，已超出现行规范适用范围，复杂坝基稳定和加固问题突出，体形优化及温控、施工要求更高，带来一系列世界性技术难题。高混凝土坝结构安全与优化是工程安全、投资和工期的关键，具有重要理论意义和工程应用价值。

本项目以构建理论和方法体系为目标，依托国家自然科学基金重点、国家重点科技攻关等 50 余项纵横向科研项目和龙滩、向家坝、金安桥、小湾、溪洛渡等 30 多个水电工程，采用理论研究与工程实践紧密结合的技术路线，通过力学、材料学、热学、水工结构、岩土工程及优化理论多学科交叉，对一系列热点科学问题和共性关键技术进行了较为系统的研究，建立了较完整的高混凝土坝结构安全与优化的科学理论、方法与技术平台体系。

（1）在理论和方法层面，提出了高混凝土坝材料宏观强度理论模型和计算方法、复杂坝基失稳机理及稳定临界准则、温控防裂非线性徐变模型、适用于多滑面的广义等 K 法、深层抗滑稳定新设计表达式及分项系数、稳定分析的分项系数有限元法、基于全有限元法和 SQP（序列二次规划法）的拱坝多目标体形优化方法、高混凝土坝的塑性极限分析方法、非概率可靠度分析方法等。

（2）在技术层面，丰富和发展了高混凝土坝结构安全数值模拟技术、大体积混凝土非线性温控防裂仿真技术、高拱坝横缝开度仿真技术、随机有限元分析模拟技术等。

（3）在仿真分析平台层面，集成上述理论、方法和技术，构建了高混凝土坝结构安全的多层次仿真分析平台（包括基于刚体极限平衡法、基于非线性有限元法以及塑性极限分析法三个分析层次）、施工期至运行期大型非线性温控仿真平台（包括高混凝土坝大型温度及弹性徐变温度应力仿真分析程序、高混凝土坝非线性有限元温控防裂仿真分析程序、基于无网格法的大体积混凝土温度开裂实时仿真分析程序以及考虑施工期瞬时温度荷载作用的高拱坝横缝开度仿真分析程序）和结构体形优化分析平台（包括基于不同材料分区的碾压混凝土重力坝整体体形优化程序、基于全有限元方法的碾压混凝土重力坝坝体整体优化程序、基于全有限元法和序列二次规划法的拱坝多目标体形优化程序）。

主要承担单位：武汉大学。

主要完成人员：常晓林、周伟、赖国伟等。

（武汉大学　黄介生　韩春玲）

南京水利科学研究院 2009 年度科研项目获奖情况

南京水利科学研究院 2009 年度科研项目获奖情况见表 1。

表 1　南京水利科学研究院 2009 年度获奖情况表

序号	项目名称	获奖情况
1	膨胀土地区公路建设成套技术	国家科技进步奖一等奖
2	海河流域洪水资源安全利用关键技术及应用	国家科技进步奖二等奖
3	沙漠、严寒地区长距离供水工程关键技术	国家科技进步奖二等奖
4	平原河流防洪安全水动力关键技术及工程应用	国家科技进步奖二等奖
5	中国分区域生态需水	国家科技进步奖二等奖
6	海河口防洪与综合利用开发关键技术研究	大禹水利科技奖一等奖
7	苏通大桥深水群桩基础施工关键技术研究与应用	航海科技奖一等奖
8	高水头船闸阀门防空化创意技术与实践	航海科技奖一等奖
9	波浪对地基土的软化作用及工程措施的研究	水运建设行业协会科技奖一等奖
10	三峡工程围堰发电期及通航初期提高船闸通过能力措施研究与实践	水运建设行业协会科技奖一等奖
11	特大型深水软弱地基群桩基础施工成套技术研究	陕西省科技奖一等奖
12	大掺量磨细矿渣混凝土关键技术研究与应用	大禹水利科技奖二等奖
13	在役海港码头钢筋混凝土电化学脱盐技术的研究应用	水运建设行业协会科技奖二等奖
14	珠江三角洲磨刀门水流泥沙运动规律及整治技术研究	水运建设行业协会科技奖二等奖
15	混凝土芯砂石桩复合地基处理深圳河河口防洪堤深厚软基试验研究	大禹水利科技奖三等奖
16	已建堤坝工程风险分析和应急对策的研究	大禹水利科技奖三等奖
17	高水头单级船闸水工结构关键技术研究及在红水河乐滩水电站的应用	水运建设行业协会科技奖三等奖
18	碾压混凝土外掺 MgO 筑坝技术研究与应用	广西壮族自治区科技进步奖三等奖
19	冀东南堡油田滩海工程环境与结构物相互作用影响分析研究	河北省科技奖三等奖

（南京水利科学研究院）

黄河水利科学研究院 2009 年度科技成果获奖情况

黄河水利科学研究院 2009 年度科技成果获奖情况见表 1。

表 1　黄河水利科学研究院 2009 年度科技成果获奖情况表

序号	项目名称	获奖情况
1	多沙河流洪水演进与冲淤演变数学模型研究及应用	大禹科学技术奖一等奖
2	黑河调水与近期治理后评价综合研究	大禹科学技术奖二等奖
3	黄河堤防工程放淤固堤设计的合理宽度研究	大禹科学技术奖三等奖
4	利用河沙制作防汛石料关键技术研究	黄委会科技进步奖一等奖

续表

序号	项目名称	获奖情况
5	黄河河道整治工程根石探测技术研究与应用	黄委会科技进步奖一等奖
6	堤坝安全监测信息分析评价系统开发研究	黄委会科技进步奖二等奖

（黄河水利科学研究院）

中国水电顾问集团华东勘测设计研究院2008、2009年科技成果获奖情况

中国水电顾问集团华东勘测设计研究院2008、2009年科技成果获奖情况见表1。

表1 中国水电顾问集团华东勘测设计研究院2008、2009年科技成果获奖情况表

序号	项目名称	获奖情况
1	桐柏抽水蓄能电站工程设计	全国优秀工程设计奖银奖
2	桐柏抽水蓄能电站工程勘察	全国优秀工程勘察奖铜奖
3	泰安抽水蓄能电站工程	2009年中国建设工程鲁班奖
4	江苏龙源如东风电场	新中国成立六十周年百项经典暨精品工程
5	混凝土坝运行期安全评价方法的初步研究	全国优秀工程咨询成果奖二等奖
6	江苏响水风电场可行性研究报告	全国优秀工程咨询成果奖二等奖
7	江西省洪屏抽水蓄能电站水资源论证报告书	全国优秀工程咨询成果奖三等奖
8	高地应力、高外水压力条件下地下洞室JPF围岩分类体系研究	全国优秀工程咨询成果奖三等奖
9	天荒坪抽水蓄能电站关键技术研究及实践	浙江省科学技术奖一等奖
10	水布垭面板堆石坝筑坝技术	湖北省科学技术进步奖特等奖
11	大型竖井泄洪洞的研究与应用	教育部科学技术进步奖一等奖
12	大跨度底轴驱动翻板闸门技术研究和应用	2008年度中国电力科学技术奖二等奖
13	特大跨度底轴驱动翻板闸门技术研究和应用	大禹科学技术奖二等奖
14	雅砻江锦屏深埋长隧洞岩溶水文地质研究及应用	2008年度中国电力科学技术奖三等奖
15	高地应力、高外水压力条件下地下洞室JPF围岩分类体系研究及应用	2008年度中国电力科学技术奖三等奖
16	山东泰安抽水蓄能电站工程	2009年度中国电力优质工程奖优秀奖
17	浙江慈溪风电场土建及安装工程	2009年度中国电力优质工程奖优秀奖
18	山东泰安抽水蓄能电站工程设计	2009年度钱江杯工程设计奖一等奖
19	杭州印象西湖工程设计	2009年度钱江杯工程设计奖三等奖
20	江苏如东第二风电场详勘	2009年度钱江杯工程勘察奖三等奖

（中国水电顾问集团华东勘测设计研究院 李良琪）

中国水电顾问集团昆明勘测设计研究院2009年获奖情况

中国水电顾问集团昆明勘测设计研究院2009年度获奖情况见表1。

表1 中国水电顾问集团昆明勘测设计研究院2009年获奖情况表

序号	项目名称	获奖情况
1	乌江洪家渡水电站	建设工程鲁班奖
2	乌江洪家渡水电站	第八届中国土木工程詹天佑奖
3	云南澜沧江糯扎渡水电站防震抗震研究设计专题报告	全国优秀工程咨询成果奖二等奖
4	云南省普渡河甲岩水电站可行性研究报告	全国优秀工程咨询成果奖三等奖

续表

序号	项目名称	获奖情况
5	云南弥勒雷打滩水电站工程安全监测	全国工程勘察设计行业优秀工程勘察设计行业奖三等奖
6	小湾水电站专一级监测控制网建网	全国工程勘察设计行业优秀工程勘察设计行业奖三等奖
7	中华人民共和国水力资源复查成果（2003年）	中国电力科学技术奖一等奖
8	坚持管理创新，构建集团型企业智能化财务分析系统	全国电力行业企业管理创新成果奖二等奖
9	智能化自动识别工程电子图档——快速收集、建立工程图文资源库计算机网络管理系统	全国电力行业企业管理创新成果奖三等奖
10	糯扎渡水电站导截流工程关键技术研究及应用	云南省科技进步奖一等奖
11	高水头闸门水封试验技术研究	云南省科技进步奖二等奖
12	水电工程建设征地实物指标调查规范	云南省科技进步奖三等奖
13	堆积体的综合物探方法研究与应用	云南省科技进步奖三等奖

（中国水电顾问集团昆明勘测设计研究院　刘一萍）

中水珠江规划勘测设计有限公司2009年度获奖成果

序号	项目名称	获奖情况
1	海南省宁远河大隆水利枢纽工程	中国建筑工程鲁班奖(国家优质工程)
2	广西柳江红花水电站工程地质勘察	全国优秀工程勘察设计行业工程勘察奖二等奖
3	柬埔寨王国湄公河淞博水电站工程测量	中国测绘学会优秀测绘工程奖铜奖
4	广州大学城堤防工程可行性研究报告	全国优秀工程咨询成果奖三等奖
5	海南省宁远河大隆水利枢纽工程设计	广东省优秀工程设计奖一等奖
6	广州地区高校新校区(广州大学城)堤防工程	广东省优秀工程设计奖二等奖
7	广东省英德市锦潭水电站工程地质勘察	广东省优秀工程勘察奖二等奖
8	云南红河南沙水电站工程地质勘察	广东省优秀工程勘察奖三等奖
9	珠江流域综合规划修编测量	广东省优秀工程勘察奖三等奖
10	基于GIS的水库淹没处理系统	广东省优秀工程勘察设计计算机软件三等奖
11	中水珠江规划勘测设计有限公司信息集成应用系统	广东省优秀工程勘察设计计算机软件三等奖

（中水珠江规划勘测设计有限公司　沈清华）

专利项目简介

无源零开断的自动灭磁装置及方法

2009年7月，中国长江电力股份有限公司葛洲坝水电厂收到国家知识产权局正式颁发的“无源零开断的自动灭磁装置及方法”发明专利证书，证书号为第522467号，专利号为ZL200510019636.1，专利有效期自2005年10月19日始，期限20年。该发明专利包括八项专利权利，属于国内外电机灭磁技术领域首创的先进的技术方法和电路结构，具有创造性、新颖性和实用性。

发明专利“无源零开断的自动灭磁装置及方法”的授权公告，标志着这项新技术的自主创新能力和水平达到了国内外领先，是长江电力葛洲坝水电厂获得的完全自主知识产权，也是该技术成功应用三年多来、通过鉴定和获得专利博览会双金奖之后的又一实质性成果。新技术突破了多半个世纪以来电机灭磁技术的落后和被动局面，是主要发明人黄大可积30年现场工作经验，结合现代大电机和电力电子技术的发展要求，集巧妙构思和先进技术于一体，同时融合多专业技术技巧，多年坚持不懈孜孜以求，终于在灭磁技术的技术方法、结构配置和极限参数等关键技术上取得全面性突破。该方法实现了全新的主动换流、自动建压和理想灭磁功能，极大地提高了安全可靠性，能满足任何容量规格的发电机事故保护要求。掌握了该方法的原创和核心技术，彻底摆脱了长期以来发电企业只能被动应用别人技术产品、无力有效保护大型电机内部故障的落后局面，使现行灭磁配置的性能提升，功能更完善，对发电机的保护更有效。

（中国长江电力股份有限公司　谢兴发）

无伸缩节坝后式引水压力钢管的结构

（一）相关背景技术

为适应大坝由于库水压力、气温变化引起相对变位，坝后式引水压力钢管通常设置伸缩节。

伸缩节在压力管道中作用：

（1）钢管能够沿着管轴线方向自由伸长或缩短。

（2）钢管产生轴向位移时，伸缩节处的摩擦阻力很小。

（3）伸缩节不但对轴向位移起到伸缩作用，还能适应管段产生的横向位移。

设置伸缩节使钢管受力明确，但造价高，制造、安装及运行期止水、日常维护等技术问题突出。

（二）本专利技术方案（专利号ZL200720065532.9）

本专利为实用新型专利，旨在通过设置曲线明管段、下端支座处设置弹性垫层适应大坝由于库水压力、气温变化引起的相对变位（0～30mm），辅以三维有限元应力分析取消坝后引水压力钢管伸缩节。

取消伸缩节可降低造价，制造、安装简单，运行期止水、日常维护方便。给工程带来了很大的社会效益和经济效益。

（三）实施实例

海南省大广坝水电站取消坝后引水压力钢管伸缩节等。新技术的采用给工程带来了很大的社会效益和经济效益。

（中国水电顾问集团中南勘测设计研究院　罗金生　陆文忠）

水电站尾水管检修闸门翻板式锁定装置

龙滩水电站尾水管检修闸门翻板式锁定装置于2008年10月获得实用新型专利，专利名称“水电站尾水管检修闸门翻板式锁定装置”（专利号ZL200720065366.2）。该装置主要特点是操作人员可在启闭机驾驶室对其进行遥控操作，不仅免去操作人员远赴现场进行人工操作的劳累，特别对于操作现场存在水位突然壅高被淹风险的特殊场合，更可避免操作人员承担安全风险；在装置本身的安全监控方面，设有开闭到位信号和系统超压保护，在操作到位和操作过程中系统超压时，启闭机驾驶室内均会有声光信号警示。

（一）技术背景

受条件所限，龙滩水电站尾水管检修闸门翻板式锁定装置安装位置相对较低，操作人员要到达现场相对艰难，且现场存在因水位突然壅高被淹风险。因此，现实条件对该翻板式锁定装置提出了自动化要求。

人工操作的翻板式锁定装置的工作情况如图1所示。基本结构包括翻板1、摇臂3、锁定座2、铰轴5和地脚螺栓4。摇臂与翻板通过焊接联结为整体，然后通过铰轴安装在锁定座上。操作者通过扳动摇臂上端的手柄使翻板—摇臂绕铰轴转动。图1所示翻板所处位置，为工作状态。工作时，闸门门体上的锁定耳坐在翻板的支承工作面上，有如双杠运动员通过双臂

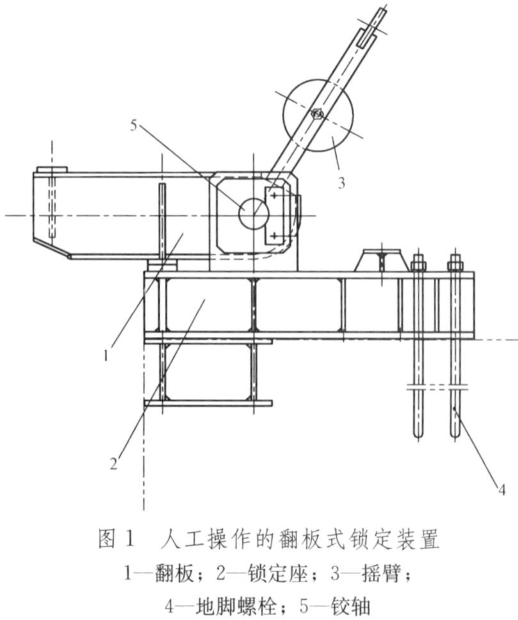

图1　人工操作的翻板式锁定装置

1—翻板；2—锁定座；3—摇臂；4—地脚螺栓；5—铰轴

支承在双杠上。当闸门通过启闭设施向上提起适当高度，操作者扳动摇臂手柄使翻板绕铰轴转动到达一定位置时，为翻板锁定装置非工作状态。闸门可以在启闭设施控制下沿门槽轨道向下移动进入工作位置。

（二）实用新型内容

该实用新型的技术方案是：除翻板、摇臂、锁定座外，还设有油缸支座、一端铰接在油缸支座上另一端铰接在摇臂上的油缸，控制油缸动作的液压控制系统和翻板开闭位置传感通信系统；翻板开闭位置传感通信系统的信号输入到液压控制系统中。

液压驱动的翻板锁定装置的工作过程是：翻板锁定装置的操作者按动起动按钮，液压泵站空载起动，然后按动开（闭）钮，液压系统通过油缸驱动翻板摇臂绕铰轴转动。当翻板摇臂转动到达设计开（闭）位置，翻板开闭位置传感通信系统触发，液压泵站自动停止。

在液压控制系统中还设有超压保护装置。当翻板锁定装置遇异常卡阻时，液压系统油压升高，触发超压保护装置，操作控制室会有声光报警信号。这些液压控制系统及其附属的超压保护装置都是现有技术。

（三）具体实施方式

为龙滩水电站尾水管检修闸门提供的翻板式锁定装置如图2所示，包括翻板1、摇臂3、锁定座2，还设有油缸支座6、一端铰接在油缸支座6上另一端铰接在摇臂3上的油缸7，控制油缸7动作的液压控制系统和翻板开闭位置传感通信系统；翻板开闭位置传感通信系统的信号输入到液压控制系统中。

液压系统原理图如图3所示。当系统得到“锁定”指令时，泵站电动机空载启动，液压油自油泵出油口经电控三位四通阀中位、低压回油单向阀流回油箱；电控三位四通阀DT1得电，线圈推动阀芯左移，液压油经三位四通阀进入油缸7有杆腔，使油缸拉动摇臂3使翻板1自释放位绕铰轴向锁定位转动；翻板1到达设计锁定位置，触动到位信号装置，系统自动停机。当系统得到“释放”指令时，泵站电动机空载启动，液压油自油泵出油口经电控三位四通阀中位、低压回油单向阀流回油箱；电控三位四通阀DT2得电，线圈推动阀芯右移，液压油经三位四通阀进入油缸无杆腔，使油缸推动摇臂使翻板自锁定位绕铰轴向释放位转动；翻板到达设计释放位置，触动到位信号装置，系统自动停机。

液压系统设有超压保护装置，当翻板锁定装置遇异常卡阻时，液压系统油压升高，触发超压保护装置，即压力继电器，操作控制室会有声光报警信号。

该翻板式锁定装置，机、电选材、配置均充分考虑防水设计。

（中国水电顾问集团中南勘测设计研究院　左长新）

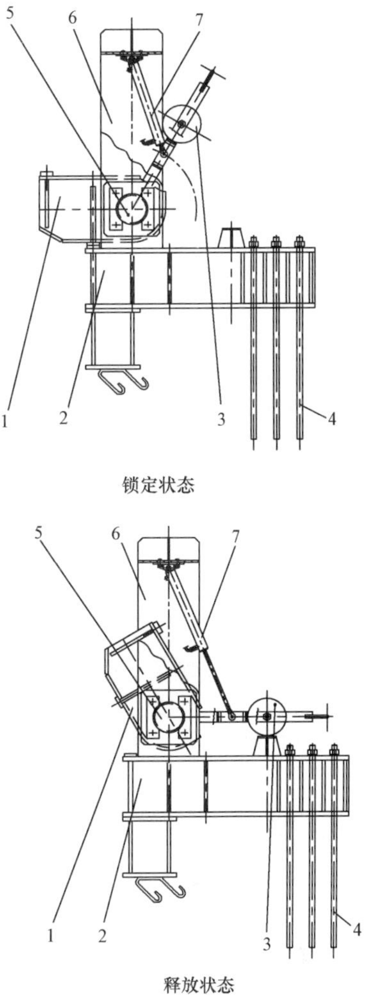

图2　龙滩水电站应用实用新型专利的翻板式锁定装置

1—翻板；2—锁定座；3—摇臂；4—地脚螺栓；5—铰轴；6—油缸支座；7—油缸

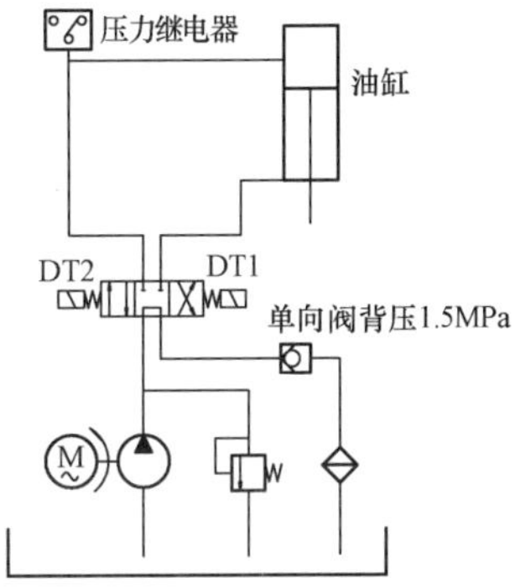

图3　液压系统原理图

水力浮动式升船机运行对接控制装置

“水力浮动式升船机运行对接控制装置”获国家实用新型专利，专利号为200820237773.1；专利权人为南京水利科学研究院；发明人为胡亚安、李中华、宣国祥、严俊秀。

（一）技术领域

本实用新型涉及一种升船机运行控制装置，具体地说是水力浮动式升船机运行对接控制装置。

（二）背景技术

水力浮动式升船机是一种以水能为驱动力的升船机型式，它主要通过调整输水主管路中的流量大小来控制升船机的承船厢出入水、船厢精确对接、船厢解锁前平衡调整等运行问题。

（三）发明内容

（1）该实用新型专利所要解决的技术问题是：针对现有技术存在的缺点，提出一种可以简单、安全、可靠的进行精确控制的水力浮动式升船机运行对接控制装置。

（2）解决以上技术问题的技术方案是：水力浮动式升船机运行对接控制装置，包括主充水阀门和主泄水阀门，在主充水阀门上并联至少一只辅助充水阀门，在主泄水阀门上并联至少一只辅助泄水阀门，通过小尺寸的辅充（泄）水阀门来解决升船机承船厢精确对接及承船厢运行控制问题。

大尺寸的主充水阀门和主泄水阀门仅在承船厢开始入水前（承船厢完全出水后）开启，以提高船厢在空气中运行速度。升船机船厢上升运行是承船厢完全出水前，大尺寸的主泄水阀门完全关闭，通过调整辅泄水阀门的开度控制承船厢出水速度，承船厢完全出水后开启主泄水阀门提高承船厢运行速度，承船厢准备与上游对接前完全关闭主泄水阀门，通过调整辅泄水阀门开度控制承船厢与上游精确对接。

（四）优点

能克服现有的水力浮动式升船机采用单个大尺寸阀门控制升船机运行及承船厢精确对接方面的不足，通过小尺寸的辅充（泄）水阀门来解决升船机承船厢精确对接及承船厢运行控制问题，能简单、安全、可靠地对水力浮动式升船机运行及对接进行精确控制。

（南京水利科学研究院）

高性能混凝土抗裂性能组合式评价装置

“高性能混凝土抗裂性能组合式评价装置”获国家实用新型专利，专利号为ZL200920037619.4；专利权人为南京水利科学研究院；发明人为胡智农、陈建国。

（一）技术领域

本实用新型涉及混凝土抗裂性能评价及测试领域，具体地说是涉及高性能混凝土抗裂性能组合式评价装置。

（二）背景技术

随着混凝土技术的发展，高性能混凝土以其高工作性、高强度、高耐久性得以广泛应用于建设工程。高性能混凝土由于大多采用低水胶比和高胶凝材料用量，因此混凝土容易产生裂缝。混凝土材料抗裂性研究是混凝土领域的重要研究内容之一。

目前，混凝土开裂性能的测试方法主要有无约束条件下混凝土收缩测试方法及约束条件下混凝土开裂性能测试方法。测试混凝土在约束条件下的变形性能，更能反映混凝土在实际工程中的使用状况。目前国家标准中尚无评价混凝土材料在约束条件下开裂性能的统一测试方法。因此对混凝土在约束条件下开裂性能测试方法的研究是十分必要的。

混凝土在约束条件下开裂性能的测试方法主要有平板法。平板法由Kraai发明，其主要问题是裂缝产生无规律性，无法精确对混凝土开裂性能进行评价，从而使其在裂缝的量化与后期数据处理方面存在不足。

国内同济大学采用多道应力诱导平板式方法，诱导产生的裂缝有一定的规律性，但是平板边缘没有诱导装置，因而平板边缘产生的裂缝规律性不强。所以目前迫切需要一个科学合理的评判混凝土裂缝的平板装置。

（三）实用新型内容

本实用新型专利目的在于提供一种高性能混凝土抗裂性能组合式评价装置。既适合实验室使用，又适合施工工地上使用。

本实用新型专利是几种模具的组合，组成一种高性能混凝土抗裂性能组合式评价装置。

一种高性能混凝土抗裂性能组合式评价装置，其特征在于该装置由水平底座、回字形下面板、回字形上面板、内侧板、短钢柱、人字顶屋形盒构成，其中将四块内侧板夹在回字形上面板和回字形下面板之间，置于上、下两块面板内口的四个边相焊接，连成一个贯穿的正方形盒体，再将此盒固定连接在水平底座上，在四块内侧板的内侧面上分别焊接有上、下两排短钢柱，在回字形下面板内口的中间设置有五排人字顶屋形盒，并将此盒固定焊接在水平底座上。

组合式评价装置所用的材料为轻质钢材。短钢柱的长度为50mm，直径为5mm，间距为50mm。回字形下面板的四个边框上各有3个螺栓孔。水平底座上布置有12个螺栓孔，并与回字形下面板的螺栓孔相匹配。贯穿正方形盒体是通过回字形下面板上的12个螺栓孔用螺栓与水平底座上的12个螺栓孔连接。人字顶屋形盒的长度为480mm，盒宽为50mm，顶部尖角为75°，从顶尖到底部高为55mm。

（四）装置的使用方法

（1）将“贯穿的正方形盒体”通过下面板四边每边三个贯穿螺纹插孔用螺栓固定在水平底座上，并确保“贯穿的正方形盒体”和水平底座之间没有间隙。

（2）将“贯穿的正方形盒体”中装满混凝土，将整个装置抬上震动台，震动30s，抹平混凝土表面。

（3）将装有混凝土的平板抗裂评价装置放在温度为30℃，湿度为60%的养护室，通过电风扇控制混凝土表面的风速为4.2m/s。

（4）养护24h后，观察表面的裂缝分布情况，包括裂缝的条数，裂缝的长度，裂缝的宽度。

（五）优点

（1）以往相似模具很难清洗，本实用新型专利通过螺孔将“贯穿的正方形盒体”固定在水平底座上，便于拆除清洗。

（2）内侧板的内侧面四周各焊有两排短钢柱和底板上焊有的“人字顶屋形盒”组成多方位诱导裂缝装置，使得混凝土试验块易于产生有规律的裂缝，有利于比较不同混凝土的抗裂性能，从而克服了现有装置诱导裂缝的无规律性和抗裂性能难以精确评价的问题。

（南京水利科学研究院）

地震波CT成像压电陶瓷串状检波器

地震波检波器是用于地质勘探和工程测量的专用传感器，是将机械能转化为电能的能量转换装置。

地震波数据采集系统主要由检波器和数字地震仪组成。检波器把地震波引起的震动转换成电讯号并通过电缆将电讯号送入地震仪；数字地震仪将接受到电讯号放大、经过模/数转换器转换成二进制数据、存储数据。

跨孔地震波CT成像是利用地震波对地质体的透射投影，来重建构成地质体内部地震波速度的分布形态，根据地震波速度与地质体的对应关系，通过数据处理，得到探测体的物性图像，从而判断地质异常体的构造形态和空间位置。

中国水电顾问集团北京勘测设计研究院研制的“地震波CT成像压电陶瓷串状检波器”获国家实用新型专利，专利号为ZL200820180227.9；授权公告日为2009年8月26日。

（一）发明内容

本实用新型专利“地震波CT成像压电陶瓷串状检波器”是由传输电缆将单个的检波器按一定的间隔距离串接在一起而形成的，单个的检波器是由环氧树脂浇筑而成的柱体，柱体内部包括压电陶瓷环、放大器和阻抗匹配器，同时，在由环氧树脂浇筑而成的柱体的中心，留有电缆孔。单个检波器的有益效果在于充分发挥了压电陶瓷环径向灵敏度高的特性，在垂直孔中水平方向灵敏度非常高，防水性能优良。地震波CT成像压电陶瓷串状检波器一次可以获得孔内不同深度的多道震动信号，从而提高了野外作业的工作效率。

（二）专利应用情况

本实用新型专利是国内首例使用压电陶瓷环制作的串状检波器，已在泰安抽水蓄能电站、西龙池抽水蓄能电站、板桥峪抽水蓄能电站、琅琊山抽水蓄能电站、十三陵抽水蓄能电站、马吉水电站、大华桥水电站应用，取得了良好的效果。此设备已在其他单位推广使用，中国海洋大学，长江水利委员会，黄河水利委员会，中国水电顾问集团成都、华东、中南、贵阳勘测设计研究院，以及铁路、核工业等单位都使用此设备。该专利推动了地震波CT成像技术的发展，提高了行业水平，解决了工程中重大技术问题，取得了一定的社会效益和经济效益。

（中国水电顾问集团北京勘测设计研究院　艾宝利）

黄河水利科学研究院获四项国家专利

由黄河水利科学研究院工程力学研究所完成的“聚束直流电阻率探测方法”获得国家发明专利证书，“水库自吸式排沙管道吸泥头吸泥浓度控制装置”、“悬沙模型进口清浑水控制装置”、“细颗粒模型沙水下休止角测量仪”等三项成果获得国家实用新型专利证书。

（一）聚束直流电阻率探测方法

专利号为ZL200610017562.2；授权日期为2009年4月29日。

本发明专利公开了一种聚束直流电阻率探测方法，它是采用1个负电极、1个测量参考电极、1个主电极、2个供电极性与主电极相同的屏蔽电极、4个监督电极相互作用组成的电极系对地面下一定范围和厚度进行探测，主电极、屏蔽电极用导线连接、与负电极共为供电回路，监督电极两两对称短路连接、均与测量参考电极构成测量回路。测得的视电阻率 ρ_s 按下式计算

$$\rho_s = \rho_i - \rho_{i-1}$$

$$\rho = K(U_{M1}/I_0)$$

式中 U_{M1}——监督电极 M_1 的电位；

I_0——主电极的电流；

K——聚束电极系装置系数，取值为1；

i——自然数。

该方法利用同性电场在地下的排斥效应，使电流在较深的地方有较大的电流密度分布，使得地下异常体在地表引起较大的电场变化，大大提高了探测深度，探测精度较高。

（二）水库自吸式排沙管道吸泥头吸泥浓度控制装置

专利号为 ZL200820148244.4；授权日期为 2009年5月6日。

本实用新型专利涉及一种在库区淤泥清除管道系统上使用的水库自吸式排沙管道吸泥头吸泥浓度控制装置，包括通过调节整体重量而悬浮在水库淤泥上的密封箱体，在密封箱体上面安装有浮箱平台，在浮箱平台中心安装有管道升降仪，在管道升降仪上安装有上下升降的排沙管道，在排沙管道中安装有含沙测量仪，可以通过控制管道入口与浆体液面位置关系，实现在管道吸泥及移动过程中可以更准确、更稳定控制管道泥沙浓度，达到管道系统高效、安全、稳定输沙目的的功能要求。

（三）细颗粒模型沙水下休止角测量仪

专利号为 ZL200820148245.9；授权日期为 2009年5月6日。

本实用新型专利涉及一种在水利行业模型中对泥沙水下休止角进行测定的细颗粒模型沙水下休止角测量仪，包括底板、放置在底板上的玻璃水箱、固定在底板上的支撑架和固定架，在固定架上通过旋钮活动安装有带刻度的测杆，在支撑架上固定有盛装试验浆液的盛沙筒，在盛沙筒下面接通有试样软管，试样软管的出口固定在测杆的底端，在玻璃水箱中设置有测试圆盘，试样软管的出口圆心的垂直投影与测试圆盘的圆心重叠，具有测量快速且较精确，测量重现性好，结构简洁，制作方便的优点。

（四）悬沙模型进口清浑水控制装置

专利号为 ZL200820070550.0；授权日期为 2009年5月6日。

本实用新型专利涉及一种对悬沙模型进口沙进行精确控制的悬沙模型进口清浑水控制装置，包括清水池、浑水搅拌池和清浑水混合前池，清水池中设有清水水泵，清水水泵通过清水管道与清浑水混合前池接通，清水管道上设有清水电磁流量计，清水水泵与清水水泵用变频器连接，计算机与清水水泵用变频器和清水电磁流量计连接；在浑水搅拌池中设有浑水水泵，浑水水泵通过浑水管道与清浑水混合前池接通，在浑水管道上设有浑水电磁流量计，浑水水泵与浑水水泵用变频器相连接，计算机与浑水水泵用变频器和浑水电磁流量计连接，在清浑水混合前池中设有清浑水混合器，具有结构简单，清浑水流量控制精确的优点。

（黄河水利科学研究院）

中国水电顾问集团华东勘测设计研究院 2009年获得专利情况

中国水电顾问集团华东勘测设计研究院2009年获得专利授权情况见表1。

表1 中国水电顾问集团华东勘测设计研究院2009年获得专利授权情况表

序号	专利名称	类 别	专 利 号
1	用于封堵高压地下水的混合灌浆装置及其混合法灌浆工艺	发明专利	ZL200610053050.1
2	混凝土流道渐变圆角段顶板施工的预制模板及其施工工艺	发明专利	ZL200710069301.X
3	一种用高密度少浆量少段量注浆加固的地基及其注浆方法	发明专利	ZL200510061030.4
4	一种悬挂于跨线桥下的轻型人行天桥	发明专利	ZL200710068075.3
5	一种库底填埋废渣结构	发明专利	ZL200610050097.2
6	一种地下厂房各洞室的连接结构及其施工方法	发明专利	ZL200810059698.9

续表

序号	专利名称	类 别	专 利 号
7	一种用单孔或对比电阻率法测量桩长的方法	发明专利	ZL200610155691.8
8	双重差动效应调压室	实用新型	ZL200820163810.9
9	施工交通和排洪通道共用的隧道结构	实用新型	ZL200820163867.9
10	用于接缝表面止水的止水带	实用新型	ZL200820086646.6
11	用于浅海钻孔的可伸缩护孔套管装置	实用新型	ZL200820167602.6
12	富水地带水电站地下厂房洞室分层排水结构	实用新型	ZL200820208828.6
13	大流量高水头叠梁门型通仓流道分层取水进水口结构	实用新型	ZL200920113798.5

（中国水电顾问集团华东勘测设计研究院　周才全）

中国水利水电第五工程局有限公司 2009 年度获得专利情况

中国水利水电第五工程局有限公司 2009 年获得专利授权情况见表 1。

表 1　　中国水利水电第五工程局有限公司 2009 年获得专利授权情况表

序号	专利类别	专利名称	专利号	授权公告日
1	发明	可方便拆卸的对拉螺栓配套装置	ZL200710050701.6	2009 年 9 月 23 日
2	实用新型	用于模板连接及固定的组合连接件	ZL200820064067.1	2009 年 4 月 1 日
3	实用新型	一种施工现场大型氨制冷设备集中控制系统	ZL200820064596.1	2009 年 6 月 3 日
4	实用新型	管口封孔盖装置	ZL200820140933.0	2009 年 8 月 5 日
5	实用新型	混凝土垂直运输缓冲装置	ZL200920079107.4	2009 年 12 月 23 日

（中国水利水电第五工程局有限公司）

中国水利水电第八工程局有限公司 2009 年获得专利情况

中国水利水电第八工程局有限公司 2009 年获得专利授权情况见表 1。

表 1　　中国水利水电第八工程局有限公司 2009 年获得专利授权情况表

序号	专利类别	专利名称	专利号
1	发明	双聚能槽管乳化炸药装药设备	ZL200910010084311.X
2	发明	混凝土复合引气剂及其制备方法	ZL200910043385.9
3	实用新型	应用于套管灌浆法中的灌浆装置	ZL200820054239.7
4	实用新型	可旋转式孔口封闭器	ZL200820158495.0
5	实用新型	棒磨机装棒台车	ZL200920064351.3
6	实用新型	用于电铲铲斗的斗门	ZL200920064398.X
7	实用新型	用于人工砂石的直线振动脱水筛分机	ZL200920064399.4
8	实用新型	双聚能槽管乳化炸药装药设备	ZL200920107039.8
9	实用新型	胶状物料输送机	ZL200920107036.4
10	实用新型	胶状物料输送的加压装置	ZL200920107038.3

（中国水利水电第八工程局有限公司）

中国水力發電年鉴

9

国际合作与技术交流

国 际 技 术 交 流

国际大坝委员会第 77 届年会和第 23 届大会简况

国际大坝委员会第 77 届年会和第 23 届大会于 2009 年 5 月 21～29 日在巴西首都巴西利亚召开，会议由巴西大坝委员会具体承办，除安排了第 77 届执行会议和各专业委员会会议外，还安排了“多功能水库与大坝”专题研讨会等活动。来自 60 多个国家的 1470 多名专家、学者参加了本届会议。

中国大坝协会组织了以水利部副部长（中国大坝协会副理事长）矫勇为代表团团长、以中国水利水电科学研究院副院长（中国大坝协会副理事长）贾金生为专家团团长的 42 人代表团参加了此次会议。

国际大坝委员会第 77 届执行会议于 2009 年 5 月 23 日在巴西首都巴西利亚 Alvorada 酒店召开，来自 63 个国家的代表参加了国际大坝委员会主席选举。中国水利水电科学研究院副院长、中国大坝协会副理事长兼秘书长贾金生高票当选为国际大坝委员会新一届主席。贾金生成为国际大坝委员会第 22 位主席，任期为 2009～2012 年，这是中国的第一位国际大坝委员会主席。参加主席竞选的还有美国前大坝协会主席 Walz 先生和英国前大坝协会主席 Hughes 先生。执行会议确定 2011 年国际大坝委员会第 79 届年会在瑞士卢塞恩（Luzern）召开，2012 年第 24 届大坝会议在日本京都召开。

多功能水库大坝国际研讨会于 2009 年 5 月 24 日在巴西利亚会议中心召开，重点强调水库大坝在防洪、灌溉、供水、发电、生态环境保护和应对气候变化中的作用。会议由巴西大坝委员会主办，应巴西大坝委员会主席邀请，矫勇副部长在大会上作了题为《大坝水库与和谐发展——中国的探索与实践》的主旨演讲。矫勇副部长向与会代表介绍了三峡工程、小浪底水库等大型水库大坝在中国经济社会可持续发展中的重要作用，紫坪铺水利枢纽工程在“5·12”汶川地震后对保障下游安全和供水供电保障的作用，以及珠江流域水库联合调度、保障珠江三角洲供水安全的成功经验，全方位地介绍了中国的水库大坝建设在防洪、灌溉、供水、发电、生态保护和促进人水和谐等方面为经济社会发展所发挥的作用，并提出中国愿与世界各国在大坝领域开展更加广泛的合作。矫勇副部长的主旨发言得到与会代表的高度赞同。在本次研讨会上，中国代表团共发表了 7 篇文章。来自中国水利水电科学研究院、中国长江三峡集团公司、南京水利科学研究院等单位的多位专家也在会上作了学术报告，报告准备充分，内容精彩，赢得了与会代表的一致赞誉，在与各国同行专家进行学术交流的同时，也积极向外宣传和推广我国的经验和成果。

2009 年 5 月 25 日，国际大坝委员会第 23 届大会在巴西利亚会议中心举行。新当选的国际大坝委员会主席、中国水利水电科学研究院贾金生副院长出席了开幕式。本次会议在全球金融危机的背景下召开，同时还面临着 H1N1 流感的威胁，在这种情况下，大会仍取得了注册代表 1470 人、实际到会 1170 人的成绩。参加会议人数较多的国家包括：巴西 417 人、伊朗 102 人、法国 61 人、日本 48 人、中国 46 人、阿根廷 26 人、韩国 21 人、印度 18 人。

本次国际大坝会议共进行 4 个技术专题的讨论：

（1）第 88 专题大坝和水电，主要讨论大坝和水库在可再生能源体系中的作用，水电开发的可持续发展，水电对减少温室气体排放的作用，水电开发和大坝建设中的技术、经济、社会和环境因素，以及多功能水库大坝（特别是 RCC 和 CFRD 两种坝型）的水电调度运行等。中国水利水电科学研究院岩土所教授级高工徐泽平应邀在大会上宣读论文，题目为《高混凝土面板堆石坝设计施工中关键技术问题的讨论》。论文从高混凝土面板堆石坝变形控制、面板应力控制和坝体渗流控制方面讨论了工程设计、施工中面临的问题，并提出了建议的方法。针对代表提出关于控制碾压质量的技术问题，徐泽平教授给出了中国在这方面取得的经验。

（2）第 89 专题已建和新建水库中的泥沙管理，主要讨论水库泥沙的管理、水库泥沙清淤技术、大坝上游库尾建拦沙坝控制泥沙入库、水库泥沙的可持续管理等。中国水利水电科学研究院教授级高工郭庆超等提交的论文《水库泥沙和控制》应邀在大会上交流，中国水利水电科学研究院副总工郭军代为宣读了论文并回答了会议代表的提问。交流讨论中，代表特别关注中国水库泥沙管理方面所采取的“蓄清排浑”的理念。

（3）第 90 专题已建大坝现代化，主要讨论对已建水工结构性能的提升，配合法规、环境、运用等要求的大坝改建，大坝升级、改建中的技术、经济等问题。南京水利科学研究院教授级高工郦能惠的论文《采用混凝土面板堆石坝加高横山黏土心墙堆石坝》应邀在大会上交流，中国水利水电科学研究院岩土所教授级高工徐泽平代为宣读了论文，并回答了专家提问。

（4）第91专题大坝安全管理，主要讨论大坝安全评价方法，大坝安全监控，水库运用、应急管理等方面的问题。中国水利水电科学研究院教授级高工徐泽平、副总工郭军及南京水利科学研究院教授级高工王士军等参加了大会的交流与讨论。

2009年5月26日晚，中国大坝协会和国际大坝委员会联合在巴西利亚国家酒店召开了联合国开发计划署（UNDP）“支持汶川地震灾后重建与早期恢复援助方案”之“加强水电安全项目”的工作会议，来自世界各国的坝工专家共60余人参加了工作会议。中国水利水电科学研究院教授级高工徐泽平首先介绍了“5·12”汶川特大地震及地震灾区水电工程震损的概况，并对联合国开发计划署“加强水电安全”项目的背景、目标及研究工作的内容进行了说明。随后，国际大坝委员会抗震专委会主席Martin Wieland博士、国际大坝委员会混凝土坝专委会主席Robin Charlwood博士和美国Donald Babbitt博士分别从各自不同的角度就汶川地震中大坝和水工结构的震损情况进行发言，并对汶川地震对大坝的影响进行初步的分析。会议最后，中国水利水电科学研究院陈厚群院士全面介绍了中国水利水电科学研究院在大坝和水工结构抗震研究方面的进展和成就，展现了中国水利水电科学研究院在大坝工程抗震领域所取得的先进成果。

2009年5月28日晚，中国大坝协会再次邀请了国际大坝委员会十余位专家就联合国开发计划署“加强水电安全”项目召开了第二次工作会议。国际大坝委员会荣誉主席Hoeg先生、国际大坝委员会副主席松本德久先生、国际大坝委员会抗震专委会主席Wieland先生等出席了会议。会议就UNDP项目的工作内容和研究重点进行了讨论，并对项目的实施方案进行了细化。

2009年5月29日，国际大坝委员会第23届大会闭幕仪式在巴西利亚会议中心举行。国际大坝委员会授予任期已满的国际大坝委员会副主席Maurer先生（巴西）、李舜铎先生（韩国）、Huges先生（英国）、Walz先生（美国）、Nombre先生（布基纳法索）等人国际大坝委员会荣誉证书。国际大坝委员会主席Luis Bergar先生在闭幕式上致辞，他回顾了3年任期的工作，对中国贾金生先生当选新任国际大坝委员会主席表示祝贺，认为这是国际大坝委员会的一个新的开端，坚信贾金生先生能够带领国际大坝委员会取得伟大的成就。国际大坝委员会新任主席、中国水利水电科学研究院贾金生副院长在闭幕式上致辞，高度赞扬了第23届大坝委员会的工作，表示今后将领导ICOLD增加与各国政府、公司、机构和科研单位的联系，促进发达国家和发展中国家的技术交流，为发展中国家的可持续发展作出更多贡献。

伴随着第23届国际大坝会议在巴西利亚会议中心的隆重开幕，第23届大坝会议的技术展览会也于2009年5月25日上午10时30分开展。尽管遍及全球的金融危及对本次大坝会议的技术展览造成了一定的影响，但仍有70余家企业参展，参展企业涵盖了水利水电工程的设备制造、工程施工、材料供应、仪器仪表、工程咨询等，巴西的Intertechne公司、法国的ALSTOM公司、瑞士的Walo公司等世界知名企业均参加了技术展览。各参展单位精心布展，展览形式丰富多彩，展台设计新颖独特，参观人员摩肩接踵，兴趣盎然，技术展览会的现场火爆。此次技术展览达到了扩大影响、增进交流、拓展商机的目的。

（摘自中国大坝协会网）

第一届堆石坝国际研讨会在成都召开

由中国大坝协会、巴西大坝委员会、中国长江三峡集团公司、中国水电工程顾问集团公司、中国水利水电建设集团公司和中国葛洲坝集团公司联合主办，由中国水利水电科学研究院承办的第一届堆石坝国际研讨会于2009年10月18～20日在四川成都隆重召开。来自中国、伊朗、日本、泰国、瑞典等30个国家的400多名代表参加了会议。出席会议的国内外领导和专家有：全国人大财经委副主任委员、原水利部部长、中国大坝协会理事长汪恕诚，中国工程院院士、中国大坝协会荣誉理事长陆佑楣，水利部副部长、中国大坝协会副理事长矫勇，中国水力发电工程学会理事长、中国大坝协会副理事长周大兵，国务院南水北调办公室副主任、中国大坝协会副理事长张野，中国大唐集团公司副总经理、中国大坝协会副理事长钟俊，中国水电工程顾问集团公司总经理、中国大坝协会副理事长晏志勇，中国水利水电科学研究院副院长、国际大坝委员会主席、中国大坝协会副理事长贾金生，中国水利水电建设集团公司总经理范集湘，中国葛洲坝集团公司副总经理丁焰章，中国长江三峡集团公司副总工胡斌，四川省省委副秘书长敖玉明，水利水电规划设计总院副院长、中国大坝协会副理事长刘志明，国际大坝委员会副主席 Ekpo（尼日利亚）、Matsumoto（日本），巴西大坝委员会主席 Maurer 等。

大会开幕式由中国水电工程顾问集团公司总经理、中国大坝协会副理事长晏志勇主持，中国大坝协会理事长汪恕诚，水利部副部长、中国大坝协会副理事长矫勇，中国大坝协会副理事长周大兵，国际大坝委员会主席贾金生，四川省省委副秘书长敖玉明等为大会致辞。

为了总结堆石坝在技术上取得的巨大成就，明确在国际坝工界具有里程碑意义和影响的工程，经过推荐、初评、复评等程序，国际大坝委员会同中国大坝协会和巴西大坝委员会在会上评选出国际堆石坝里程碑工程奖，颁发了由国际大坝委员会主席、中国大坝协会理事长和巴西大坝委员会主席联合签名的荣誉证书和纪念奖牌。获奖的工程有：

（1）国际里程碑面板堆石坝（按国家英文名称排名）为：①Foz DoAreia，坝高 160m，巴西；②Santa Juana，坝高 103m，智利；③水布垭，坝高 233m，中国；④Karahn jukar，坝高 196m，冰岛；⑤El CAJON，坝高 188m，墨西哥。

（2）国际里程碑心墙堆石坝（按国家英文名称排名）为：①Irape，坝高 208m，巴西；②小浪底，坝高 156m＋80m（防渗帷幕），中国；③Tehri，坝高 261m，印度；④Chicoasen，坝高 261m，墨西哥；⑤努列克（Nurek），坝高 300m，塔吉克斯坦。

（3）国际里程碑沥青心墙坝（按国家英文名称排名）为：①Finsterta，坝高 150m，奥地利；②Yashio，坝高 90.5m，日本。

紫坪铺面板堆石坝（坝高 156m）在 2008 年 5 月 12 日经受住了八级强震的考验，在堆石坝抗震史上具有里程碑意义，被评为特别工程奖。

本次研讨会是根据中国大坝协会与巴西大坝委员会合作协议召开的，该协议签订于 2008 年国际大坝委员会 80 周年庆典期间，双方确定轮流主办堆石坝国际研讨会，目的在于通过广泛深入的学术交流、实际工程考察等活动，增进各国坝工专家之间的友谊与合作，不断推进世界各国在堆石坝建设和管理方面的健康发展。

会议收录了国内外 140 篇学术论文，正式出版了中文论文集和英文论文集，印刷了中文摘要文集和全文光盘文集。2009 年 10 月 19 日是全体大会，10 月 20 日设 3 个分会场，分别围绕“堆石坝的历史和发展趋势，设计和分析，筑坝材料”、“堆石坝的施工、运行、维护和安全监测”、“堆石坝特别分会——加强水电安全”几个议题进行交流。参会代表报告精彩，交流深入，会场气氛十分热烈。

本次会议受到了媒体的广泛关注，中国水利报、中国水利杂志、科技日报、科学时报、中国能源报、21 世纪经济报道、科学新闻等国内众多媒体单位予以报道，起到了良好的舆论宣传效果。

第一届堆石坝国际研讨会于 2008 年 12 月开始筹备，得到了各位领导的关心、指导以及各有关单位的大力支持，是一次高水平、高品质、学术气氛浓厚和成果丰厚的会议。会后还安排了对三峡、水布垭、冶勒、向家坝、溪洛渡等工程的考察。

（摘自中国大坝协会网）

“气候变化对大坝的挑战”国际研讨会暨中日韩大坝委员会第六次学术交流会

“气候变化对大坝的挑战”国际研讨会暨中、日、韩大坝委员会第六次学术交流会于 2009 年 10 月25～27 日在韩国首尔召开。本次会议有 3 个主题：“气候变化对大坝的影响”、“大坝建设、运行和管理的新模式”和“抽水蓄能电站的设计和运行”。为了加强东亚地区大坝技术方面的经验交流与合作，在各单位的大力支持和配合下，中国大坝协会组织了以张国新副秘书长为团长的 25 人代表团参加了此次会议。参会代表分别来自水利部、中国长江三峡集团公司、中国水利水电科学研究院、中水淮河规划设计研究有限公司、中国华能集团有限公司、国电大渡河公司、长江委长江勘测规划设计院、华东宜兴抽水蓄能有限公司、中国科学院研究生院等单位。

中国长江三峡集团公司张曙光局长代表中国在开幕式上致辞，中国大坝协会张国新副秘书长、日本大坝工程中心主席 Tatsuo Hamaguchi 先生、韩国水资源集团董事 Kyung-Taekyum 先生分别代表中、日、韩三国大坝委员会报告了过去一年的工作情况以及大坝建设方面的新进展。

来自中国、韩国、日本和土耳其的 19 位专家分别就气候变化对水资源分布、水库调度的影响、河流修复与重建、大坝运行管理和抽水蓄能电站建设新技术等方面在大会上作了技术报告。中国长江三峡集团公司李勇泉工程师和居志刚高工分别作了题为“基于风险理论的大坝水文安全风险研究”和“溪洛渡水电站坝址区局部气象特点分析”的报告；中国水利水电科学研究院崔炜博士作了题为“呼和浩特抽水蓄能电站区域三维渗流场分析”的报告。华能四川水电有限公司陈其伟副总经理、中国水利水电科学研究院刘毅博士、中水淮河规划设计研究有限公司马东亮副总工作为中国代表团的代表分别主持了 3 个主题的报告会。另有张志会、常清睿等5人撰写的论文录入会议论文集。

参会代表会后分两组进行了技术考察，主要参观工程有：Pyeounghwa坝，坝高125m，混凝土面板堆石坝；Hwacheon坝，坝高123m，混凝土心墙堆石坝；Gunnam防洪闸和Hantangang碾压混凝土坝，坝高73m；在建的Sihwa潮汐电站；Yonggwang核电站；Buan水源工程；在建的Saemangeum围海开发工程等。参会代表对韩国在大坝设计与建设中对生态环境的保护、水库管理的设施和制度、水电的宣传等方面印象深刻，在会后写了收获体会。

中、日、韩大坝委员会第七次学术交流会将于2011年10月在中国召开，张国新副秘书长代表中国大坝协会向与会专家发出了热情的邀请。

（摘自中国大坝协会网）

农村水电国际交流与合作

（一）第五届“今日水电论坛”在杭州成功举办

2009年5月11～12日，由水利部和联合国工业发展组织主办，国际小水电中心承办的第五届“今日水电论坛”在杭州举行。本次论坛以小水电与民生改善为主题，水利部部长陈雷出席论坛并作了“大力发展水电　着力改善民生　促进经济社会可持续发展”的主旨讲话，水利部副部长胡四一主持会议，浙江省葛惠君副省长到会致辞，水利部水电局田中兴局长作了“小水电点亮中国农村”的专题报告。本次论坛探讨了小水电在改善民生方面的重要作用，展示了我国农村水电及电气化发展成果，交流了国际小水电发展方向和趋势，推动了全球小水电领域的合作与发展。来自瑞士、挪威等26个国家和联合国工业发展组织、国际水电协会等国际组织的50多名国外代表，以及来自全国各地水利部门、小水电行业企事业单位的120多名国内代表参加了论坛。

（二）国际小水电组织协调委员会成功换届

2009年5月12日，国际小水电组织协调委员会2009年年会在杭州召开，成功进行了国际小水电协调委员会换届选举。国际小水电组织荣誉主席、水利部副部长胡四一出席本次年会并在开幕式上致辞。本次年会选举产生了新一届国际小水电组织协调委员会，水利部水电局局长田中兴当选为协调委员会主席、斯里兰卡电力和能源部常务秘书费迪南多先生当选为协调委员会副主席，国际小水电中心主任刘恒当选为协调委员会总干事。会议还通过了国际小水电组织2009/2010年工作计划和《国际小水电组织章程》修改意见，并对国际小水电组织今后发展战略进行了深入讨论。

（三）小水电援外培训稳步开展

2009年，国际中心承办了“小水电与农村社区可持续发展官员研修班”，来自非洲、亚洲13个国家的20名学员参加了本次研修班。杭州农村电气化研究所成功举办了“小水电技术培训班”、“非洲小水电培训班”和“小水电研修班”等3期小水电援外培训班，来自46个国家的91名学员参加了培训。

（四）“点亮非洲”项目继续推进

“点亮非洲”项目由中国商务部和联合国工业发展组织共同支持，国际小水电中心提供技术支撑。目前，已在肯尼亚、尼日利亚和坦桑尼亚投产了14个100kW以下的微型水电项目。2009年9月，在联合国工业发展组织的见证下，国际小水电中心与赞比亚能源部、赞比亚国家电力公司签署了在赞比亚北方省合作建设1MW小水电站的协议；2009年11月，该项目举行奠基仪式，项目全面启动，预计2010年底建成投产。2009年11月，国际小水电中心派遣专家组对塞拉利昂及利比里亚的初选站址进行了实地查勘，为下一阶段实施“点亮非洲”项目开展前期工作。

（水利部农村水电及电气化发展局　付自龙）

武汉大学2009年水利水电国际合作与交流情况

2009年，武汉大学水利水电学院与瑞士、法国、美国、澳大利亚、新西兰、越南、伊朗、日本等国的学者进行了学术交流活动，国外专家、学者125人·次来院进行了参观访问和学术交流，有43人·次作了专题报告，30余人·次出国参加学术会议或进行合作研究。

2009年9月22～24日，由水资源与水电工程科学国家重点实验室和水利水电学院具体组织承办了中国工程院水利工程科学领域第三次院士论坛暨国际学术会议“2009水资源与可持续发展高层论坛”。本次论坛由中国工程院和水利部共同主办，中国工程院土木、水利与建筑工程学部，武汉大学，中国水利学会、长江水利委员会等单位承办，国际水资源协会（IWRA）、国际水利工程与研究协会（IAHR）、国际灌排委员会（ICID）等多个国际组织协办。

全国政协原副主席、中国工程院院士、论坛指导委员会主席钱正英出席会议。水利部部长陈雷，湖北省省委书记罗清泉，湖北省省委副书记、武汉市委书记杨松，湖北省副省长郭生练，中国工程院原副院长沈国舫，中国水利学会理事长敬正书，国际水资源协会主席 Cecilia Tortajada，长江水利委员会主任蔡其华，武汉大学党委书记李健，武汉大学校长顾海良等出席会议。共有300余名代表参加本次会议，其中国内相关领域院士20余名，国外代表50多人，包括来自美国、英国、俄罗斯、澳大利亚的8名水利界科学院和工程院院士。大会秘书长、武汉大学水利水电学院教授周创兵副校长主持了大会开幕式。

本次会议通过院士专家论坛这一高层平台，汇集世界各国顶级专家、学者和广大水利科技工作者，交流各国在水资源开发利用和保护方面的经验，深化对水资源与社会经济可持续发展之间关系的理解；探讨水资源与可持续发展方面的学术、工程技术、管理以及政策等问题。会议设置了水资源时空变异及其配置、农业水资源高效可持续利用、流域管理与河流健康、水能资源开发与环境保护等4个议题。

（武汉大学　黄介生　韩春玲）

黄河水利科学研究院2009年国际学术交流情况

（一）承办黄河国际论坛重大技术专题会

2009年10月20～23日，第四届黄河国际论坛在河南郑州召开，来自国内外800多位专家、学者参加了此次盛会。黄河水利科学研究院承办了“多沙河流泥沙处理及水库泥沙处理重大技术”专题会。在专题会上，来自美国、荷兰等国家及中国台湾地区的专家、学者与国内清华大学、武汉大学、华北水利水电学院、黄河水利科学研究院、河南黄河河务局、山东黄河河务局、黄河勘测设计有限公司、三门峡枢纽局等单位的专家、学者分别针对流域水沙变化、多沙河流水沙管理、泥沙输移理论与基本规律、水库调度与泥沙淤积、河道整治与工程冲刷、河道及水库疏浚与清淤、河流模拟、原型监测等问题进行了广泛深入的交流和探讨。

（二）与荷兰专家进行技术交流

2009年10月19日，荷兰DHV国际咨询公司高级顾问 Paul Van Meel（原黄委中欧流域管理项目组组长）带领DHV公司有关专家和荷兰交通公共工程水管理部相关官员一行4人，到黄河水利科学研究院进行了技术交流和考察。双方就泥沙管理、洪水管理理念、河道整治、丁坝设计、堤防安全等作了相关的专题报告，并对感兴趣的问题进行了深入交流。黄河水利科学研究院相关科研人员还陪同荷兰专家参观考察了“模型黄河”沙门基地和黄河花园口标准化堤防，并就双方的未来技术交流合作进行了初步探讨。

（黄河水利科学研究院）

对外经营与国外工程

中国水利水电建设集团公司2009年国际经营情况

（一）概况

2009年，中国水利水电建设集团公司（以下简称水电建设集团）在国家“走出去”战略的支持下，深入贯彻落实科学发展观，继续大力实施国际业务优先发展战略，实现了高风险期的稳步快速增长：国际业务营业收入比2008年同期增长31.79%，占水电建设集团总营业收入的24.81%；实现利润比2008年同期增长25.49%，占水电建设集团利润总额的62.5%；新签约国际项目46个，新签约合同额占水电建设集团新签约合同总额的40.49%。

从2009年水电建设集团的国际业务的发展态势分析，呈现如下特点：

（1）国际市场空间不断扩大。2009年，水电建设集团继续加大竞争性投标力度，巩固国际竞争性水利水电工程承包市场的领先地位，深度开发已进入的成熟的国别市场，并充分抓住国家利用工程承包和海外投资扩大出口以拉动内需的机遇，将营销重点放在双边合作项目、中国资金一揽子项目、中国政府双优项目、国际金融机构投资项目等项目可靠、支付能力有保障、安全环境较好的工程项目上，不断拓展国际市场空间。截至2009年底，水电建设集团在46个国家设立了59个驻外机构，在48个国家有在建项目211个，合同总额近160亿美元。其中5000万～1亿美元的项目35个，1亿美元以上的项目39个；形成了东南亚、北非、东非、中东等区域化的相对稳定市场，以及包括安哥拉、卡塔尔、利比亚、苏丹、老挝和印尼等9个以项目群为特点的大型国别市场，成功开辟了马里、科威特、厄瓜多尔等十国市场，在拉丁美洲市场取得了质的突破。

（2）产业结构呈现多元化格局。2009年，水电建设集团国际业务基本形成了以水电建设为核心的“大土木、大建筑”格局，业务领域已拓展到火电、机场、路桥、市政基础设施、房建与房地产基础设施、疏浚吹填与港航、矿业、咨询服务、建材等方面，国际业务产业结构呈现多元化态势。其中水电站项目、水处理和灌溉项目等水利水电工程形成的营业收入约占海外总营业收入的30%～40%，如路桥项目、矿产项目、房建及市政项目等非水利水电类工程形成的营业收入约占60%～70%。

（3）海外投资取得新突破。2009年，水电建设集团进一步开拓EPC总承包、出口信贷融资承包领域，并在海外投资方面取得新突破。目前，水电建设集团在海外投资建设的电站装机容量31万kW，已签订电源占有协议的项目计划装机容量约1000万kW。老挝甘蒙塔克水泥厂运行顺利，2009年销售水泥46万t，比2008年同期增长30%，营业收入超过2650万美元。老挝万象平原首采矿区的年产12万t钾盐建设项目的可行性研究报告已完成并获通过，老挝政府已正式批准水电建设集团开始建设首期年产12万t钾盐项目；建设工作计划在2010年全面启动，预计2012年建成投产。刚果（金）铜钴矿项目的资本金注入和中国进出口银行的贷款工作已完成，目前该项目可行性研究编制工作已经完成，正在完善和批复中。

（4）行业的影响力与市场地位进一步提升。凭借良好的经营业绩，水电建设集团在2009年美国新闻实录（ENR）全球最大225家国际工程承包商排名中位列第55位，在所有上榜的中国企业中排名第五。此外，在2009年ENR/建筑时报评选的“中国承包商和工程设计企业双60强”榜单上，中国水利水电建设股份有限公司位列承包商60强第六位、2009年最具国际拓展力承包商排行榜第5位、2009年“中国承包商60强”利润总额排行榜第6位、2009年承包商工程设计营业收入排行榜第九位。通过与有关国家政府、国际组织广泛的沟通联络，参与多边和双边合作，水电建设集团与之形成了良好的合作伙伴关系。水电建设集团已成为中国涉外金融机构优质大型客户，与多家银行建立了良好的业务关系，拥有足额银行授信和强有力的金融支持，是中国对外承包工程商会副会长单位、国际水电协会会员，2009年又成为了中国机电产品进出口商会副会长单位，并荣获中国对外承包工程企业社会责任奖。

随着水电建设集团承建国外项目的不断增多，也带动了大量劳务走出国门，为国内行业产能过剩的消化、转移以及解决境内劳动力就业困难作出了贡献。目前，水电建设集团有20 000多名员工奋战在海外工程现场。根据2009年6月外交部公布的2008年度签证数量统计结果，水电建设集团以17 015人·次的签证量居全国签证自办单位的第五位，位居中央企业签证自办单位第一名。

（二）海外主要电力工程承包项目进展情况

1. 埃塞俄比亚泰可泽水电站项目

泰可泽电站是埃塞俄比亚最重要的水电站之一，得到两国政府的高度关注，电站合同额约2.8亿美元，总装机容量30万kW，坝高188m，是非洲最高的混凝土双曲拱坝。2002年8月，水电建设集团作为牵头方与中国葛洲坝集团公司组成联营体承建该项目。虽然在工程建设的7年零3个月中，不断遇到前所未有的困难和挑战，但是在水电建设集团总部的大力支持以及项目部全体成员的共同努力下，电站最终于2009年9月18日在合同期内成功并网发电，2009年11月14日上午10时，埃塞俄比亚泰可泽水电站发电仪式在左岸坝顶成功举行。

2. 马来西亚巴贡水电站项目

巴贡水电站是马来西亚迄今规模最大的水电项目，项目合同额约4.7亿美元，水库设计容量高达440亿m^3，设计总装机容量240万kW。项目于2002年10月开工，截至2009年底，项目主体工程已完成约98%，电站蓄水计划在2010年3月进行。

3. 加纳布维水电站项目

布维水电站是加纳共和国的第二大水电站，合同额约6亿美元，设计装机容量40万kW。2007年8月24日，加纳布维水电站举行开工仪式。2008年12月2日，电站提前合同工期一年实现截流。2009年12月18日，加纳布维水电站大坝首仓碾压混凝土开盘浇筑，正式进入混凝土“大浇筑”施工阶段。

4. 苏丹麦洛维大坝项目

麦洛维大坝工程是一项用于发电与灌溉的枢纽工程，是继埃及阿斯旺大坝后在尼罗河干流上兴建的第二座大型水电站，也是苏丹乃至非洲目前在建的最大水电项目。麦洛维大坝全长9.65km，最大坝高67m，水库总库容量达140亿m^3，电站总合同额约7亿美元，总装机容量125万kW。2003年6月，项目开工；2009年3月3日，麦洛维电站首批两台机组正式投产发电；2009年5月15日，麦洛维大坝主体工程胜利完工；2009年12月30日，麦洛维电站1～8号机组全部投产并入国家电网发电。

5. 厄瓜多尔科卡科多—辛克雷EPC项目

2009年10月5日，水电建设集团与科卡科多—辛克雷公司在厄瓜多尔总统府正式签署科卡科多—辛克雷水电站EPC总承包合同。科卡科多—辛克雷水电站项目，合同额约20亿美元，总装机容量150万kW，年发电量88亿kW·h，是厄瓜多尔历史上外资投入额最大、规模最大的水电站项目，同时也是目前中国对外承建的投资最大的水电站工程。目前，各项前期准备工作及项目融资工作正在有序进行。

（三）海外主要电力投资项目进展情况

1. 柬埔寨甘再水电站BOT项目

由水电建设集团投资建设的柬埔寨甘再水电站是中国在国外第一个使用项目融资方式开展的BOT水电工程。甘再水电站项目总投资2.805亿美元，总装机容量19.32万kW，建设期4年，特许经营期40年。2007年8月，主体工程开始施工。2009年12月7日，甘再水电站项目首台机组投产发电。

2. 老挝南俄5水电站BOT项目

老挝南俄5水电站项目由水电建设集团与老挝国家电力公司组成南俄5发电有限公司共同进行开发，其中水电建设集团国际公司持股85%，老挝国家电力公司持股15%。南俄5水电站项目总投资1.99亿美元，总装机容量12万kW，年发电量5.07亿kW·h，建设期4年，特许经营期25年。2008年10月1日，主体工程正式开工。2009年10月16日，南俄5水电站提前1个月圆满完成大坝截流。2009年12月7日，电站大坝基础开挖完工。目前，进场公路、引水系统施工支洞和主洞、大坝坝肩和坝基开挖等工程项目正在施工。

（四）驻外机构情况

2009年，中国水利水电建设股份有限公司驻外机构见表1。

表1 中国水利水电建设股份有限公司驻外机构表

序号	机构中文名称	国家
1	中国水电尼泊尔代表处	尼泊尔
2	中国水电马来西亚代表处	马来西亚
3	中国水电巴基斯坦代表处	巴基斯坦
4	中国水电孟加拉代表处	孟加拉
5	中国水电乌兹别克斯坦代表处	乌兹别克斯坦
6	中国水电津巴布韦代表处	津巴布韦
7	中国水电泰国代表处	泰国
8	中国水电印度尼西亚代表处	印度尼西亚
9	中国水电缅甸代表处	缅甸
10	中国水电伊朗代表处	伊朗
11	中国水电吉尔吉斯斯坦代表处	吉尔吉斯
12	中国水电老挝代表处	老挝
13	中国水电埃塞俄比亚代表处	埃塞俄比亚
14	中国水电伯里兹代表处	伯里兹
15	中国水电(马来西亚)有限公司	马来西亚

续表

序号	机构中文名称	国家
16	中国水电阿尔及利亚代表处	阿尔及利亚
17	中国水电苏丹代表处	苏丹
18	中国水电印度代表处	印度
19	中国水电利比亚代表处	利比亚
20	中国水电也门代表处	也门
21	中国水电约旦代表处	约旦
22	中国水电安哥拉代表处	安哥拉
23	中国水电坦桑尼亚代表处	坦桑尼亚
24	中国水电阿富汗代表处	阿富汗
25	中国水电斯里兰卡代表处	斯里兰卡
26	中国水电卡塔尔代表处	卡塔尔
27	老挝水泥工业有限责任公司	老挝
28	中国水电蒙古国代表处	蒙古国
29	中国水电柬埔寨代表处	柬埔寨
30	中国水电塔吉克斯坦代表处	塔吉克斯坦
31	中国水电菲律宾代表处	菲律宾
32	中国水电刚果民主共和国代表处	刚果(金)
33	中国水电刚果共和国代表处	刚果(布)
34	中国水电越南代表处	越南
35	中国水电赤道几内亚代表处	赤道几内亚
36	中国水电甘再项目公司	柬埔寨
37	中国水电南非有限责任公司	南非
38	中国水电(阿联酋)分公司	阿联酋
39	中国水电(利比亚)分公司	利比亚
40	中国水电(安哥拉)有限责任公司	安哥拉
41	中国水电(博茨瓦纳)有限责任公司	博茨瓦纳
42	中国水电矿业(老挝)钾盐有限公司	老挝
43	中国水电加纳代表处	加纳
44	中国水电(俄罗斯)有限责任公司	俄罗斯
45	南俄5发电有限公司	老挝
46	中国水电(泰国)有限公司	泰国
47	中国水电斐济代表处	斐济
48	华刚矿业股份有限公司	刚果(金)
49	中国水电(厄瓜多尔)分公司	厄瓜多尔
50	中国水电(赞比亚)有限公司	赞比亚
51	中国水电(阿布扎比)分公司	阿联酋
52	中国水电(乌干达)有限公司	乌干达
53	中国水电委内瑞拉代表处	委内瑞拉

续表

序号	机构中文名称	国　家
54	中国水电厄瓜多尔代表处	厄瓜多尔
55	中国水电哥伦比亚代表处	哥伦比亚
56	中国水电(卡塔尔)国际工程有限责任公司	卡塔尔
57	中国水电哥斯达黎加代表处	哥斯达黎加
58	中国水电马里代表处	马里
59	RISH 有限责任公司	卡塔尔

（中国水电建设集团国际工程有限公司　任　敏）

越南广治水电站机电设备成套项目

（一）越南市场和项目背景

越南是一个发展中的国家，人口 8070 万，面积 32.9 万 km^2，境内有红河、湄公河等大小河流 1000 多条。近十年来，经济发展较快，每年的电力增长需求约为 12%～16%，政府计划由现在的人均 337kW·h 提高到 2010 年的 800kW·h。现在每年从中国进口 11 亿～13 亿 kW·h 电量，其他还从老挝等地进口电力，但还有多个地区缺电严重，常常拉闸限电。所以，近年来越南水电开发很热。

中国水电顾问集团华东勘测设计研究院（以下简称华东院）于 2002 年通过设计、咨询服务为切入点，在越南国家电力公司等部门宣传中国水电设备，使越南电力公司逐步了解了中国水电技术的发展水平，进而引导越南国家电力公司认识中国水电制造能力与优势，逐步打破西方和日本等国家在越南水电市场一统天下的局面，推动后续中国企业将建设材料和水电站机电成套设备进入越南市场，成为越南水电市场的主要供应商。

广治水电站设备成套合同的获得，使华东院成为中国水电设计院中第一个做海外成套设备项目的设计院。由于广治水电站的成功执行，华东院在越南电力系统获得很高的评价和声誉。

（二）项目概况

广治水电站位于越南中部广治省，该省是以前南北战争的重灾区和现在的贫困省份。本电站在越南属于一个扶贫项目，政治工程。

广治水电站为多用途综合利用工程，包括灌溉工程、溢洪道、进水口、压力钢管、厂房和开关站等，安装 2 台单机容量 32MW 的机组，转速 750r/min，最大水头 376m，年平均发电量 2.17 亿 kW·h，是一个系统多、水头高、转速高、装机容量不大但比较复杂的枢纽工程。

广治水电站业主为越南国家电力公司，建设单位为越南水电第二管理局；资金来源为买方信贷（业主向法国某银行贷款），中信保作为担保方。项目的土建设计和施工、安装由越方承担。工程监理单位也是越方咨询公司。

合同工作范围包括厂内外的机电设计和设备成套供货、安装指导和培训。

（三）项目进展情况

广治水电站项目，2003 年开始跟踪，2004 年 9 月 10 日完成投标；2004 年 12 月 1 日应邀开始合同谈判，2004 年 12 月 28 日签署合同，2005 年 1 月 21 日合同正式生效；2005 年 7 月 25 日第一批货物交付，2007 年 9 月 20 日 1 号发电机组成功并网发电，2007 年 11 月 27 日 2 号机并网发电；2008 年 1 月 31 日越南国家电力公司颁发临时验收证书，2009 年 3 月 1 日越南国家电力公司颁发最终验收证书。

（中国水电顾问集团华东勘测设计研究院　严　丽）

越南 SeSan4 水电站机电设备成套项目简介

（一）项目概况

SeSan4 水电站位于越南 Gia Lai 省 Pleiku 市西 70km 处的 SeSan 河上，是一个兼灌溉、防洪、供水、发电的水电综合利用项目。电站总装机容量为 360MW，装设 3 台单机容量 120MW 的混流式水轮发电机组，电站以 2 回 220kV 出线接入 500kV Pleiku 变电站。电站枢纽建筑物由碾压混凝土拦河坝、坝后地面式厂房、220kV 开关站等组成。SeSan4 水电站是越南国家重点项目。

该电站的业主是越南国家电力公司（EVN）。项目资金源自越南国家电力公司投资以及由投标人提供的买方信贷融资，贷款担保方为越南财政部。项目具体由 EVN 下属的水电第四管理办（Hydropower Project Management Unit No. 4）负责执行。

项目业主在 2006 年通过国际公开招标采购本电站的机电成套设备，最终中国水电顾问集团华东勘测设计研究院与天津阿尔斯通组成的联营体（ECIDI-ALSTOM Consortium）赢得了该合同（Supply of Electro-mechanical Equipment, Control and Communication systems），中国水电顾问集团华东勘测设计研究院作为联营体领导方负责协调合同的执行。

（二）工作范围及内容

根据合同规定，该项目工作范围及内容为电站的机电设备供货及现场技术服务工作，负责水轮机、发电机、调速器装置、油气水系统、励磁装置、主变压器、计算机监控系统、保护装置、发电机电压设备、开关站设备、厂用电设备、通信系统、工业电视系统、火灾报警及消防系统、给排水及通风空调系统等设备及材料的供货，以及相关的设计、安装指导、培训、调试指导等技术服务。

（三）项目进展情况

2006年11月21日，该合同在Pleiku签署；2007年1月4日，合同正式生效；从2007年6月28日第一批设备开始交货到2009年6月最后一台机组交货，合同规定的所有设备全部完成交货，共完成了24批次的设备交货。该项目机电设备交货进度完全满足合同的规定，获得了业主的高度好评。

经过现场的紧张安装、试验和调试，1号机组于2009年9月28日并网发电，12月18日完成30天试运行后，业主签发了初步验收证书并进入质保期；2号机组于2009年12月10日并网发电；预计3号机组将于2010年3月并网发电。

（四）结语

本项目经过联营体双方的共同努力，认真细致地履行合同，以项目管理为主线，在设计、采购、运输、出口、交货、现场服务等各个环节精心组织，确保了设备按期交货、机组按期发电。该项目的顺利推进，获得了业主好评，为中国机电成套项目出口越南市场赢得了良好的声誉，也为中国水电走向国际打下了良好的基础。

（中国水电顾问集团华东勘测设计研究院　时雷鸣）

哈萨克斯坦玛依纳水电站设计简介

（一）概况

玛依纳综合水利枢纽建筑物位于哈萨克斯坦共和国阿拉木图州的拉依穆别克区的恰伦河上。恰伦河流域位于哈萨克斯坦共和国东南部阿拉木图州，是伊犁河左岸的一级支流，发源于肯特敏山脉南坡，在与奥尔塔梅尔克河汇合之后称恰伦河，控制集水面积为7720km^2。

玛依纳水电站装机容量为300MW，安装2台单机容量150MW的冲击式水轮发电机组，最大水头为521.7m，最小水头为458.2m，多年平均发电量为10.27亿kW·h，年利用小时数3423h，由首部枢纽、引水发电枢纽和反调节水库组成。

首部枢纽是恰伦河上的别斯秋宾水库，反调节水库位于玛依纳水电站厂房下游1.2km处，这两部分的设计和建设全部由哈方完成。

引水发电枢纽由引水系统和水电站厂房组成，作为中国政府与哈萨克斯坦签订经济技术协作项目，由中方联营体承担设计和施工，为“交钥匙”工程。由中国水利电力对外公司、中国地质集团公司、中国水电顾问集团成都勘测设计研究院3家单位组成的中方联营体进行工程总承包，内容包括水工建筑物的进水口、引水隧洞、调压井、压力管道、地面厂房和涉及引水发电的机电设备采购、安装。该工程于2007年6～9月进行勘测，2008年6月完成设计报告，2008年7月全面开工。按计划，2010年9月引水隧洞开挖贯通，2011年底首台机组发电。

（二）引水发电枢纽设计

1. 工程地质条件

据哈方《哈萨克斯坦玛依纳水电站技术经济论证报告和地震专题研究报告》，玛依纳水电站工程场地设计计算地震烈度为Ⅸ度，但在设计中须进行大坝Ⅹ度抗震的校核计算。隧洞沿线山体较雄厚，地形较陡，地势海拔高程1370～1920m，相对高差60～510m，河谷下部多为“V”型，上部为中高山、构造剥蚀单斜山地貌。隧洞垂直埋深一般100～120m，最小垂直埋深为65m，最大埋深260m。隧洞区的主要岩性有凝灰岩、斑岩、玢岩、凝灰角砾岩、粗面流纹岩等，岩性复杂；构造上位于库卢克套背斜南西翼，受外围区域断裂、褶皱发育影响，岩体中小断层、挤压破碎带及节理裂隙发育且局部密集成带。调压井位于玛依纳克山NE侧条形山梁上与EW向山梁交汇处鞍部附近，山梁顶部高程1795m，山体整体稳定；场地基岩裸露，调压井均位于石炭系下统克特缅（$C_{1t-v1kt}$）英安斑岩及凝灰岩等地层中，主要构造为节理裂隙。压力管道为地下埋藏式，垂直埋深50～310m；围岩以英安斑岩、凝灰岩、花岗岩为主；穿越区为沟槽相间的斜坡地形，岸坡总体稳定性较好，但沿线冲沟发育，沟、脊相间起伏较大，地形复杂。地面厂房位于一级阶地的缓坡平台上，冲积堆积层厚10～15m，下伏基岩为奥陶系上统花岗岩，主要构造为3条走向近EW、倾向北的陡倾角断层及4组节理裂隙。岩体强风化强卸荷垂直埋深10～20m，弱风化弱卸荷垂直埋深25～30m。厂区覆盖层强透水，基岩具弱～中等透水性。

2. 引水建筑物布置

引水建筑物由进水口（哈方设计和建设）、闸门井、有压引水隧洞、调压井、压力管道组成。

（1）闸门井位于苏尔坦别克萨依沟左岸平台，闸室开挖尺寸为7m×8m（长×宽），闸门孔口尺寸为4m×5m（宽×高），闸门井段前后各设10m长的渐变段。

（2）引水隧洞布置于恰伦河右岸，根据进水口和调压井位置，洞线在平面上设置1个转点，转弯半径均为 50m。隧洞全长 4912m，引用流量 74.0m^3/s，开挖断面型式为马蹄形（宽×高为 4.2m×6.3m、5.0m×7.0m）和圆形（内径 D=5.6m）；对Ⅲ、Ⅳ、Ⅴ类围岩洞段分别采用单筋、双筋混凝土或钢板衬砌，衬砌后的隧洞内径为 4.1m。

（3）调压井位于引水隧洞末端的条形山脊内，为露天水室式调压井，由竖井和上室构成。竖井内径 6.0m，高 175.00m，井筒采用钢筋混凝土衬砌。露天水池内径 24.0m，池高 9.0m，池身采用钢筋混凝土衬砌。

（4）压力管道由上平段、竖井段、下斜段组成。主管长 4301m，内径 4.1m，上平段直段长约 220m，竖井高 205m，下斜段长约 3854m。主管末端由一个“Y”型岔管分接两条支管，每条支管的末端与厂内球阀相连，1、2 号支管长约 68m。压力管道全长采用钢板衬砌。

3. 厂区枢纽建筑物设计

厂区枢纽建筑物由主厂房、副厂房、露天主变压器场、综合办公楼、尾水渠组成。

（1）主机间、安装间呈“一”字形布置，主厂房上游侧布置综合办公楼、副厂房、露天主变压器场，下游侧是尾水渠。

（2）主机间长 50.90m、宽 28.00m、高 41.30m，安装 2 台 150MW 的冲击式水轮发电机组，水轮机安装高程为 1248.00m。主厂房宽度受配水环管和球阀吊装控制，机组纵轴线距上游吊车柱内边 15.50m，距下游吊车柱内边 8.50m，机组间距为 21.50m。安装间布置在主机间下游端，长 28.06m，宽 28.00m，高 24.50m。

（3）副厂房长 50.9m，宽 12.92m，分 2 层布置。一层地面高程 1255.80m，与电气夹层相通，布置有发电机断路器；二层地面高程 1261.30m，与发电机层相通，布置有配电装置室。

（4）综合办公楼总建筑面积 2631.00m^2，主体建筑层数为地上 4 层，总高度 16.80m。

（5）尾水平高程为 1248.70m，设有行走式启闭机；每个机组设置一个尾水闸门，闸门净宽 5.90m。

（6）尾水渠紧接尾水平台，全长为 60.00m，渠宽为 28.90～10.00m，过水断面为梯形。

（中国水电顾问集团成都勘测设计研究院
尹晓林 刘吉祥 唐 兰）

几个中国投资或承包的国外水电工程建设情况

（一）刚果（布）英布鲁电站截流

2009 年 1 月 24 日，刚果（布）英布鲁电站上游二期围堰于当地时间顺利合龙，顺利实现截流目标。在 2009 年 1 月 26 日的截流庆典仪式上，刚果（布）共和国总统萨苏·恩格索率总理、参议长、部长等数十名政府高层官员，在我国驻刚果（布）大使李树立、参赞蔡方财及业主、咨询、CMEC、设计、监理等主要负责人的陪同下，亲临英布鲁截流庆典现场观礼，萨苏·恩格索总统对电站的成功截流给予了热情祝贺和高度评价。

（二）缅甸瑞丽江一级电站竣工

2009 年 5 月 16 日，我国对外水电开发最大的 BOT 项目——缅甸瑞丽江一级电站竣工仪式在缅甸境内电站厂房隆重举行。瑞丽江一级水电站位于缅甸北部紧邻中缅边界的瑞丽江干流，是瑞丽江上游河段规划的第一个梯级电站，总装机容量 60 万 kW，保证出力可达 17.4 万 kW，年利用小时数为 6722h，年发电量 40.33 亿 kW·h。该电站是缅甸目前建成投产的最大的水电站。工程由华能澜沧江水电有限公司、云南和兴投资开发股份有限公司和云南机械设备进出口有限公司三方共同出资成立的云南联合电力开发有限公司负责开发建设，华能澜沧江水电有限公司控股。项目总投资约 32 亿元人民币，其中中方总投资 29.6 亿元。

（三）印尼阿萨汉一级水电站两台机组首次启动成功

2009 年 12 月 30 日，印尼阿萨汉一级水电站两台机组首次启动成功。印尼阿萨汉一级水电站是中国华电集团公司在海外投资的第一个水电项目，由华电工程进行 EPC 总承包，电站装有 2 台 9 万 kW 水轮发电机组，总装机容量 18 万 kW。工程于 2006 年 12 月 18 日开工建设，合同工期 41 个月。2009 年 11 月 27 日，阿萨汉项目顺利通过专项质量验收。2009 年 12 月 10 日，引水隧洞充水成功。2009 年 12 月 30 日，两台机组首次启动成功，与合同进度安排相比提前 5 个月。

（本年鉴编辑部摘编）

中国水电工程顾问集团公司与缅甸联邦电力一部签署瑙帕与曼栋水电站开发谅解备忘录

2009 年 12 月 19～20 日（当地时间），中国国家副主席习近平率领中国政府代表团访缅甸联邦，并与缅甸联邦政府签署了一系列协议。中国水电工程顾问集团公司与缅甸联邦电力一部经过充分协商，形成了丹伦江及其支流楠马河瑙帕与曼栋水电站开发谅解备忘录。2009 年 12 月 20 日上午，在习近平副主席和缅甸联邦和平与发展委员会副主席貌埃见证下，中国水电工程顾问集团公司总经理晏志勇与缅甸联邦电力一部代表签署了丹伦江及其支流楠马河瑙帕与曼栋水电站开发谅解备忘录。

丹伦江（Thanlwin River）也称萨尔温江（在中国境内称怒江），是缅甸的第二大河流，瑙帕水电站（Nao Pha）位于其干流河段，曼栋水电站位于其左岸支流楠马河段，两电站紧邻中缅边界，开发条件较好，签署瑙帕与曼栋水电站开发谅解备忘录将使中国水电工程顾问集团公司国际发展进入新的、更高的阶段。

（摘自中国水电工程顾问集团网）

湄公河干流大坝战略环境评价（SEA）合作初步会议在昆明召开

2009年11月10日，中国水力发电工程学会国际河流水电开发生态环境研究工作委员会（ESCIR）与湄公河委员会秘书处（MRCS）的关于湄公河干流大坝战略环境评价（SEA）合作初步会议在云南昆明召开。会议由中国水力发电工程学会国际河流水电开发生态环境研究工作委员会承办，该工作委员会的环保、规划、水文、泥沙等相关领域的专家委员与来自湄公河委员会秘书处SEA项目组的专家代表共20余人出席了会议。

中国水力发电工程学会国际河流水电开发生态环境研究工作委员会主任王斌出席会议并致辞，秘书长顾洪宾主持了本次会议。在为期两天的会议中，双方共同探讨和交流了湄公河流域水电发展和环境保护的相关内容。湄委会SEA项目组专家首先对中国政府自2002年以来向湄公河委员会提供澜沧江—湄公河水文报汛服务表示十分感谢，随后向中方介绍了目前湄公河下游12个水坝的规划和工作进展相关情况，同时介绍了本次战略环境评价工作对湄公河干流水电开发的重要意义，简要说明了本次SEA项目的工作程序和技术方法，并与中方分享了SEA项目初步阶段工作报告的草案，希望中方专家能够对此草案提出相关建议，并邀请中方专家共同参与SEA项目下个阶段的工作。同时，湄公河委员会提出，十分希望双方能够在澜沧江—湄公河流域水电规划和建设方面进行数据共享。

国际河流水电开发生态环境研究工作委员会向湄公河委员会SEA项目专家组介绍了目前中国澜沧江水电开发和规划的相关情况，并重点介绍了中国在澜沧江水电开发环境保护方面所开展的相关工作和研究成果，同时表示将在我国法律框架下，从加强中国与湄公河流域国家及湄公河委员会的友好关系出发，积极参与湄公河干流水坝战略环评工作，为促进湄公河流域的社会经济发展和生态环境保护作出应有的贡献。最后，双方初步讨论了本次SEA项目的合作目标、合作原则、合作范围和具体内容，同时在具体的合作形式以及研究经费等方面交换了意见，并达成了初步共识。

（摘自中国水电工程顾问集团公司《水电风电信息汇编》）

10

技术标准和科技图书

标准化工作管理

2009年电力标准化管理情况

（一）电力标准计划立项

2009年，经有关部门批准，确定电力国家标准、行业标准制修订项目计划共218项，其中：住房和城乡建设部批准的工程建设国家标准计划15项；国家能源局批准的电力行业标准计划203项（其中中国电力企业联合会管理的196项，水电水利规划设计总院管理的7项）。

为保证电力标准制修订计划的按时保质完成，中国电力企业联合会组织召开了标准编写工作会议，对国家在标准化工作领域中的新要求向各标准项目承担单位进行了通报，并对标准编写、审查、报批等技术方面的要求进行了宣讲。

为继续支持电力企业“走出去”战略，满足中外企业对电力标准英文版的需求，中国电力企业联合会下达了2009年电力标准英文版翻译计划共13项。2009年内翻译出版水电标准共16项。至此，水电标准英文版体系已基本建立。

（二）电力标准发布

2009年，国家标准化管理委员会发布电力国家标准15项，国家能源局发布电力行业标准116项。这些标准涉及各个专业，包括技术进步、自主创新、节能减排等项目。

截至2009年底，电力标准共有1586项，其中电力国家标准251项，电力行业标准1335项。

（三）重点领域电力标准化工作及有关课题的研究

2009年，特高压交流标准化工作取得重要突破，先后完成特高压交流16项国家标准、8项行业标准的审查，其中15项国家标准已获批准。与国家标准化管理委员会和国家电网公司共同组织，同意将1000kV晋东南至荆门特高压交流试验示范工程列为国家重大工程标准化示范，并向国家标准化管理委员会提出31项国家标准的立项建议。

为推动智能电网标准化工作，促进该领域国际标准的交流与合作，开展了前期研究。中国电力企业联合会与美国电气制造商协会（NEMA）、中国电器工业协会（CEEIA）共同召开了智能电网标准与技术研讨会。中国电力企业联合会还组织召开了数字化变电站标准化工作讨论会，确定了数字化变电站标准体系框架，提出了开展数字化变电站标准化工作的整体要求以及近期重点开展的领域。

为进一步适应电力工业的快速发展和技术进步，规范电力行业标准的计划、编写与报批工作，中国电力企业联合会启动了《电力技术标准体系表》（2006版）和DL/T 600—2001《电力行业标准编写基本规定》的修订工作。

（四）电力标准化组织体系的完善

根据2008年电力行业标委会秘书长工作会议的决议，并结合国家标准化管理委员会、国家能源局有关要求，对《电力行业标准化技术委员会管理细则》、《电力行业归口有关国际电工委员会技术委员会（IEC/TC）工作管理办法》等部分管理文件适时进行了修订，并以中国电力企业联合会文件的形式进行了印发。

经国家能源局同意，组建了节能和技术经济2个电力行业标准化技术委员会。

电力行业节能标准化技术委员会的工作任务是：构建电力行业节能标准体系，组织制（修）订电力行业节能领域技术标准，包括发电、输电系统中节能领域的基础、分析、检测方法和节能技术指标、能耗限制标准、能效要求等标准，节能审核标准，节能经济评价及后评价标准等，并负责以上标准规范的跟踪管理、修订、宣贯、咨询工作。

电力行业技术经济标准化技术委员会的工作任务是：构建电力行业技术经济领域标准体系，编制经济消耗和价值成本标准，包括各类消耗标准、费用标准、占用标准、生产率标准、价值成本测算标准、各种利润标准、费率标准、经济评价及后评价标准等，并负责以上标准规范的跟踪管理、修订、宣贯、咨询工作。

2009年，对电力行业电站汽轮机、电站阀门、热工自动化和信息、气体绝缘金属封闭电器等4个标委会进行了换届。对电力行业电力变压器、电力行业电能质量及柔性输电、全国架空线路标委会线路运行分标委会等3个标委会进行了调整。

截至2009年底，共有电力国家标准化技术委员会12个，电力行业标准化技术委员会42个。

（五）电力企业标准化良好行为评价确认试点及标准宣贯工作

根据《电力企业标准化良好行为试点及确认工作实施细则》（国标委服务联［2008］76号）要求，中国电力企业联合会在国家电监会和国家标准化管理委员会的领导下，先后召开电监会派出机构系统的研讨会、培训会议等，研制了试点与确认信息系统，实现了试点单位与评审专家的网上申报，为开展电力企业“标准化良好行为”试点工作迈出了实质性的一步。

2009年开展了国家强制性标准GB 50227—2008《并联电容器装置设计规范》宣传贯彻活动，并应邀多次组织专家到电力企业进行企业标准化工作的宣讲和指导。

（六）国际合作与交流

唯一由我国担任秘书的IEC技术委员会——国际电工委员会高压直流输电技术委员会（IEC/TC115）成立后，2009年在国家标准化管理委员会的支持和领导下，由中国电力企业联合会协助在京举办了该委员会的首次会议。按照《参加国际标准化组织（ISO）和国际电工委员会（IEC）技术活动管理办法》的有关要求，在与多方电力企业进行协商后，中国电力企业联合会向国家标准化管理委员会提出由中国电力科学研究院作为IEC/TC115国内技术归口单位的申请获得批准。

（七）电力标准化工作获得表彰

在国家标准化管理委员会组织的2009年度“中国标准创新贡献奖”评选中，华东电力设计院等单位负责起草的GB/T 14285—2006《继电保护和安全自动装置技术规程》获得二等奖。

（中国电力企业联合会　许松林）

我国电力企业标准化工作开展情况

（一）企业技术标准库及标准体系

根据对20家电力企业的统计，截至2009年底，有7家公司建立了企业技术标准库，有2家公司正在建设当中。其中，国家电网公司、中国大唐集团公司、广东省粤电集团有限公司等公司建立了基于计算机网络的标准化平台或信息系统，收录法规和国家标准、行业标准，实现了公司系统标准文本的信息资源共享。有9家公司建立了企业技术标准体系，有3家公司正在建设当中。其中，中国南方电网有限责任公司、广东省粤电集团有限公司的技术标准体系均建立于2003年；国家电网公司2006年建立技术标准体系，并于2007年和2009年两次进行修订；中国广东核电集团有限公司吸收并转化法国相关核电规范和标准，建立健全了二代改进型CPR1000核电技术规范体系。

（二）企业标准编制与管理

截至2009年底，有12家公司根据企业标准体系，编制并发布了数量不等的企业标准或类似标准的技术要求文件。这些企业标准立足国家标准、行业标准，针对企业实际情况提出了更高、更具体的要求，有效地推动了企业技术进步。其中，国家电网公司发布企业标准278项，中国南方电网有限责任公司发布企业标准72项，中国华能集团公司发布了火电、水电监督技术系列标准，北京国华电力有限责任公司共制定基建、发电类技术标准118项。2009年，共有6家公司计划制修订企业标准或技术规范222项，其中国家电网公司确定了127个标准计划项目。

截至2009年底，有14家公司明确了技术标准（或标准化）归口管理部门和企业标准管理流程。部分公司还发布了专门规范标准管理活动的办法、规定、规则等文件，组建了专门的标准化管理委员会、技术委员会、办公室等组织机构。

（中国电力企业联合会　许松林）

2009年农村水电技术标准制修订情况

2009年，水利部农村水电及电气化发展局主持和主编的农村水电技术标准共有29项，其中，2009年新增财政专项2项、基建前期10项。根据《水利标准化工作管理办法》要求和2009年水利技术标准制修订计划安排，启动了《小型水电站施工安全规程》等12项新增标准项目的制修订工作，组织召开了《小型水电站技术改造规范》等8个标准的编制工作大纲审查会，发文对《小水电接入电力系统技术规定》等10个标准征求意见，组织召开了《农村水电站技术管理规程》等10个标准的送审稿审查会，完成《水电农村电气化标准》等7个标准的报批工作。截至2009年底，已发布标准3项：《漏电保护器农村安装运行规程》（SL 445—2009）、《小水电水能设计规程》（SL 76—2009）、《中小河流水能开发规划编制规程》（SL 221—2009）；其余在编标准26项详见表1。

表1 农村水电在编标准情况表

序号	标准名称	工作要求	主编单位	编制进度
1	小水电代燃料标准	制定 SL	水利部农村水电及电气化发展局	报批
2	小水电代燃料工程规划编制规程	制定 SL	水利部农村水电及电气化发展局	报批
3	水电农村电气化标准	修订 SL 30—2003	水利部农村水电及电气化发展局	报批
4	水电农村电气化规划编制规程	修订 SL 145—1995	水利部农村水电及电气化发展局	报批
5	小型水电站机组运行综合性能质量评定标准	制定 SL	中国水利水电科学研究院机电研究所	征求意见
6	小水电接入电力系统技术规定	制定 SL	中国水利水电科学研究院自动化研究所	征求意见
7	泵站和小型水电站现场效率试验规程	修订 SD 140—1985	中国水利水电科学研究院机电研究所	征求意见
8	小型水电站初步设计报告编制规程	修订 SL/T 179—1996	山西省水利水电科学研究院	征求意见
9	小水电电网节能改造工程技术规范	制定 GB	水利部农村水电及电气化发展局	大纲审查
10	小水电建设项目经济评价规程	修订 SL 16—1995	水利部农村电气化研究所	征求意见
11	小型水电站技术改造规范	制定 GB	水利部农村水电及电气化发展局	大纲审查
12	小型水电站施工技术规范	修订 SL 172—1996	水利部农村电气化研究所	大纲审查
13	农村水电供电区电力发展规划导则	修订 SL 22—1992	水利部农村电气化研究所	大纲审查
14	水能资源调查评价导则	制定 SL	水利部农村电气化研究所	立项
15	小型水电站运行维护技术规范	制定 GB	水利部农村水电及电气化发展局	征求意见
16	小型水电站机电设备报废条件	制定 GB	水利部农村水电及电气化发展局	大纲审查
17	农村水电站技术管理规程	制定 SL	吉林省地方水电有限公司	送审
18	农村水电变电站技术管理规程	制定 SL	吉林省地方水电有限公司	送审
19	农村水电配电线路、配电台区技术管理规程	制定 SL	吉林省地方水电有限公司	送审
20	农村水电送电线路技术管理规程	制定 SL	吉林省地方水电有限公司	送审
21	小型水电站施工安全规程	制定 SL	水利部农村电气化研究所	立项
22	小水电网安全运行规程	制定 SL	水利部农村电气化研究所	立项
23	小型水电站建设工程验收规程	修订 SL 168—1996	水利部农村电气化研究所	立项
24	小水电代燃料项目验收规程	修订 SL/Z 304—2004	水利部农村电气化研究所	立项
25	小型水电站安全测试与评价规范	制定 GB	水利部农村水电及电气化发展局	立项
26	小水电代燃料生态效益计算导则	制定 SL	水利部农村电气化研究所	立项

（水利部农村水电及电气化发展局　孙亚芹）

中国水电顾问集团贵阳勘测设计研究院标准化工作开展情况

（一）加强企业技术标准基础建设

中国水电顾问集团贵阳勘测设计研究院（以下简称贵阳院）根据战略西移，川、滇、藏等地域环境的变化，加强了西部地区事先指导和有关重大问题的超前预测，初步总结和编制了《西部地区（川、滇、藏）勘测设计技术要求及应重视的主要问题》，阐述了西部与贵州在自然条件、社会和人文环境方面的异同，提出了技术要求及应重视的主要问题，以指导西部勘测设计工作，提高勘测设计质量。

贵阳工程勘察分院制定并发布了《预可研及可研阶段勘察大纲范本（2009版）》、《施工组织设计范本（2009版）》等4项范本，规范了大纲和施工组织设计编制等工作。

2009年，贵阳院完成了《中小型水力发电工程地质勘察规范》编制并通过中国电力企业联合会组织的审查；参编《水工建筑物水泥灌浆施工技术规范》和《水利水电工程测量规范》并按时提交初稿。

（二）加大行业标准申报力度

根据国家能源局“关于征集2009年第二批能源领域行业标准计划项目的通知”，贵阳院组织有关部门和技术人员认真研究行业标准的规划和项目，起草了6项技术标准项目任务书，及时报送中国水电工程顾问集团公司。

（三）加强国外技术标准收集和技术标准的反馈

2009年度共收集56项工程建设标准（英文版）目录，完成《水利水电工程碾压式土石坝施工组织设计导则》英文版校核工作。及时组织国内25项技术标准的意见反馈、修编工作。

（四）继续完善有效技术标准和适用法律法规清单

全年实时、动态维护有效技术标准3039项、适用法律法规622项，采购并配发技术标准3042册。

（中国水电顾问集团贵阳勘测设计研究院
李月杰　周维娟）

泰山抽水蓄能电站2009年标准化建设工作情况

2009年，山东泰山抽水蓄能电站有限责任公司（以下简称泰山公司）标准化建设工作有序开展，基本形成了以技术标准为主题、管理标准为支撑、工作标准为基础的泰山公司标准化体系。主要工作情况如下：

第一阶段：项目启动与成立组织机构。2009年3月22日召开泰山公司全体人员参与的标准化建设项目启动大会；成立泰山公司标准化组织机构并明确其职责，确定泰山公司各部门标准化专责人员；5月11日召开标准化工作启动会议。

第二阶段：咨询公司调研和诊断。咨询公司对泰山公司领导及各职能部门进行详细调研；与公司领导、各部门负责人和骨干面谈；翻阅制度、标准和国际管理体系标准等文件；翻阅现场相关记录；现场勘察、测量与访问。

第三阶段：相关知识培训。由咨询公司进行理念导入培训、企业标准化相关知识培训、流程管理基础知识培训、风险管理知识培训、ISO 9001/ISO 14001/OHSAS18001国际标准培训、流程图绘制（VISIO软件）培训、标准编制培训、企业标准体系运行培训、企业标准体系自我评价培训、5S现场管理知识培训、NOSA标准知识培训等工作。

第四阶段：体系策划与设计。咨询公司依据调研结果进行策划，形成完整的《企业标准体系框架策划方案》、《技术标准目录》、《管理标准及对应流程目录》、《工作标准目录》；泰山公司组织各部门对咨询公司策划的《企业标准体系框架策划方案》等文件资料进行讨论，咨询公司根据讨论意见修改并完善策划方案；咨询公司指导泰山公司编制《企业标准化管理标准》、《标准编写指南》、《标准编号规定》、《流程绘制规范》等指导性工作文件。

第五阶段：制度识别、清理。建立《规章制度管理流程》，制定或修订《规章制度管理办法》，实现规章制度有标准文本格式、有规范流程图示、有涉及哪些流程的说明、有检查标准、有考核评价标准、有绩效奖罚标准、有标准记录模板的“七有”目标；清理已发布的制度，识别可用的、作废的、修改的制度；按照专业范围进行划分，建立规范合理的规章制度体系，提高制度的系统性，规章制度体系与管理标准体系保持一致，以便制度与管理标准的转换，避免制度与标准冲突；建立规章制度转化为标准的途径和方式。

第六阶段：流程梳理优化与风险分析。咨询公司指导泰山公司各级领导及骨干进行流程实战具体演练，内容包括流程图的绘制方法运用、绘制要求、绘制原则、流程优化方法和工具的使用等；咨询公司组织各部门按照目前实际管理情况对流程进行梳理与绘制；咨询公司指导泰山公司人员以问题为导向，以国际标准为要求，优化流程，提高流程的效率和效益；咨询公司指导泰山公司人员识别流程的关键过程、关键绩效指标、基础资料（信息流），建立流程指标体系，量化过程，实现量化管理，建立流程的约束机制，确保流程高效运作；由咨询公司和企业标准体系工作小组对各个流程提出优化意见，各流程责任部门根据优化意见，绘制并确定优化后流程；泰山公司领导审核《公司管理流程》文件；咨询公司指导泰山公司识别流程中存在的各类风险，评估风险程度，制定《公司风险一览表》。

第七阶段：企业标准体系文件编写审定。泰山公司各专业部室分别通过各种渠道收集国际、国家、行业、国家电网公司、国网新源控股有限公司相关技术标准，指导收集和完善泰山公司现有的规程与作业指导书等企业技术标准。各专业部室分别按照已经确定的管理标准目录和已确定的流程，编制相关的管理标准，咨询公司现场进行编写指导，并分期分批审核管理标准，确定、汇总和审核管理标准。咨询公司指导各部室编写部门工作标准及岗位工作标准，确定、汇总和审核全公司的工作标准。

截至2009年12月31日，历时8个月，泰山公司共编写完成管理流程235个、管理标准146个、工作标准63个，编制了技术标准体系框架、管理标准体系表、工作标准体系表。

（山东泰山抽水蓄能电站有限责任公司　陈小宾）

技术标准的制修订情况

2009年国家标准化管理委员会批准的电力国家标准计划项目

序号	标准名称	编写单位
1	1000kV系统监控系统技术规范	国家电力调度通信中心、国网南京自动化研究院
2	1000kV系统变电站监控系统验收规范	国家电力调度通信中心、中国电力科学研究院
3	1000kV交流架空输电线路金具技术规范	国网北京电力建设研究院
4	1000kV带电作业用屏蔽服装	国网武汉高压研究院
5	±800kV直流架空输电线路运行规程	国网运行有限公司、湖北省超高压输变电公司
6	±800kV直流换流站运行规程编制导则	国网运行有限公司
7	重要电力用户供电电源及自备应急电源配置导则	国家电网公司
8	输电网运营评价	国家电监会输电监管部、各区域电监局
9	供电服务规范	国家电监会供电监管部
10	发电机组并网安全性评价标准	国家电监会安全监管局、中国电机工程学会
11	电力市场监管信息系统功能及技术要求	国家电监会市场监管部、南方电监局
12	电力企业节能降耗主要指标监管评价	国家电监会市场监管部、中国电力企业联合会

（中国电力企业联合会　许松林）

2009年住房和城乡建设部批准的电力工程建设国家标准计划项目

序号	项目名称	制定/修订	主编、参编单位	代替标准
1	风力发电工程施工与验收规范	制定	主编单位：中国电力企业联合会、中国长江三峡工程开发总公司 参编单位：龙源电力集团公司、深圳大学、中国水电顾问集团华东勘测设计研究院、中国水电顾问集团北京勘测设计研究院、长江新能源开发有限公司、武汉大学	
2	火力发电厂岩土工程勘察规范	制定	主编单位：中国电力企业联合会、北京国电华北电力工程有限公司 参编单位：西南电力设计院、中国电力工程顾问集团公司华东电力设计院、中国电力工程顾问集团公司东北电力设计院、中国电力工程顾问集团公司中南电力设计院、中国电力工程顾问集团公司西北电力设计院	

续表

序号	项目名称	制定/修订	主编、参编单位	代替标准
3	光伏发电场设计规范	制定	主编单位：中国电力企业联合会、上海电力设计院有限公司 参编单位：中国电子工程设计院、福建钧石能源有限公司、中国科学院电工研究所、北京科诺伟业科技有限公司、上海绿色环保能源有限公司、中环（中国）工程有限公司	
4	1000kV 母线装置施工与验收规范	制定	主编单位：中国电力企业联合会、国网交流工程建设有限公司 参编单位：中国电力科学研究院、湖北省输变电工程公司、北京送变电公司、山东送变电工程公司、江苏省送变电公司、北京电力建设公司、华北电网有限公司北京超高压公司、河南送变电建设公司	
5	低、中水平放射性核废料处置场岩土工程勘测规范	制定	主编单位：中国电力企业联合会、广东省电力设计研究院 参编单位：深圳中广核工程设计有限公司、中国核电工程有限公司	
6	水电水利工程压力钢管安装与验收规范	制定	主编单位：中国电力企业联合会、中国水利水电第七工程局 参编单位：水电水利规划设计总院、电力工业金属结构设备质量检测中心	
7	电力调度中心通信工程设计规范	制定	主编单位：中国电力企业联合会、广东省电力设计研究院 参编单位：待定	
8	1000kV 输变电工程竣工验收规范	制定	主编单位：中国电力企业联合会、国网交流工程建设有限公司 参编单位：北京送变电公司、江苏省送变电公司、山东送变电工程公司、华北电网有限公司北京超高压公司、北京电力建设公司、河南送变电建设公司、国网直流工程建设有限公司	
9	电气装置安装工程　电气设备交接试验标准	修订	主编单位：中国电力企业联合会、中国电力科学研究院 参编单位：安徽省电力科学研究院、国网电力科学研究院、广东省电力试验研究院、山东电建一公司、天津电力建设公司	GB 50150—2006
10	电气装置安装工程　35kV 及以下架空电力线路施工及验收规范	修订	主编单位：中国电力企业联合会、中国电力科学研究院 参编单位：北京电力公司、上海电力公司、大连供电公司	GB 50173—1992
11	建设工程施工现场供电安全规范	修订	主编单位：中国电力企业联合会、中国电力科学研究院 参编单位：北京电力建设公司、天津电力建设公司、冶金部自动化研究院	GB 50194—1993
12	电气装置安装工程　低压电器施工及验收规范	修订	主编单位：中国电力企业联合会、中国电力科学研究院 参编单位：南通信达电器有限公司、国华电力公司、辽宁省电力有限公司	GB 50254—1996
13	电气装置安装工程　电力变流设备施工及验收规范	修订	主编单位：中国电力企业联合会、中国电力科学研究院 参编单位：国网电力科学研究院、山东送变电公司、江苏送变电公司	GB 50255—1996

续表

序号	项目名称	制定/修订	主编、参编单位	代替标准
14	电气装置安装工程　起重机电气装置施工及验收规范	修订	主编单位：中国电力企业联合会、中国电力科学研究院 参编单位：天津电力建设公司、浙江电力建设公司、广东火电建设工程公司	GB 50256—1996
15	电气装置安装工程　爆炸和火灾危险环境电气装置施工及验收规范	修订	主编单位：中国电力企业联合会、中国电力科学研究院 参编单位：南阳防爆电器研究所、北京送变电公司	GB 50257—1996

（中国电力企业联合会　许松林）

2009年国家能源局批准的电力行业标准计划项目（水电、电气部分）

序号	项目名称	制定/修订	起草单位	代替标准
1	电测量指示仪表检验规程	修订	湖北电力试验研究院	SD 110—1983
2	载波电能表通用技术要求	制定	黑龙江省电力有限公司	
3	隐极发电机在线监测装置配置导则	制定	华北电力科学研究院有限责任公司	
4	额定电压66kV～220kV交联聚乙烯绝缘电力电缆敷设规程　第1部分：直埋敷设	制定	北京电力工程公司	
5	额定电压66kV～220kV交联聚乙烯绝缘电力电缆敷设规程　第2部分：排管敷设	制定	南京供电公司	
6	额定电压66kV～220kV交联聚乙烯绝缘电力电缆敷设规程　第3部分：隧道敷设	制定	北京电力工程公司	
7	额定电压66kV～220kV交联聚乙烯绝缘电力电缆线路检修规程	制定	武汉供电公司	
8	电力系统谐波管理规定	修订	中国电力科学研究院	SD 126－1984
9	电源快速切换装置技术规范	制定	中国电力科学研究院、北京电力公司	
10	电气装置安装工程　电气设备交接试验记录报告统一格式	制定	中国电力科学研究院	
11	架空输电线路大跨越工程跨越塔组立施工工艺导则	制定	浙江省送变电工程公司	
12	电力系统电压和无功电力技术导则	修订	华北电网有限公司、国网电力科学研究院	SD 325—1989
13	高压并联电容器单台保护用熔断器使用技术条件	修订	浙江省电力试验研究院	DL/T 442—1991
14	焊工技术考核规程	修订	中国电力科学研究院	DL/T 679—1999

续表

序号	项目名称	制定/修订	起草单位	代替标准
15	电力工业无损检测人员资格考核规则	修订	华北电力科学研究院有限责任公司	DL/T 675—1999
16	电力设备用六氟化硫气体	制定	中国电力科学研究院、广东电网公司电力科学研究院	
17	六氟化硫密度继电器校验规程	制定	中国电力科学研究院、华北电力科学研究院有限公司	
18	12kV～40.5kV电缆分接箱技术条件	制定	中国电力科学研究院、国网电力科学研究院	
19	变压器有载分接开关现场试验导则	制定	吉林省电力有限公司电力科学研究院、沈阳变压器研究所、上海华明电力设备制造有限公司、贵州长征电器股份有限公司、保定市精艺电子仪器有限公司	
20	冲击接地电阻测试导则	制定	四川电力试验研究院	
21	气体绝缘金属封闭开关设备带电超声局部放电检测应用导则	制定	青海电力科学试验研究院	
22	高压直流接地极技术导则	修订	国网电力科学研究院	DL 437—1991
23	7.2kV～12kV预装式户外开关站安装与验收规程	制定	河南省电力公司、郑州供电公司	
24	工商业电力用户应急电源配置技术导则	制定	中国电力科学研究院	
25	绝缘子用常温固化硅橡胶防污闪涂料技术条件	修订	国网电力科学研究院、中国电力科学研究院	DL/T 627—2004
26	9FA联合循环机组性能验收试验规程	制定	江苏华电戚墅堰发电有限公司	
27	农村安全用电规程	修订	国家电网公司	DL 493—2001
28	农村电网建设与改造技术导则	修订	中国电力科学研究院	DL/T 5131—2001
29	县级电网调度自动化系统实用化要求及验收	修订	国网电力科学研究院	DL/T 789—2001
30	气体绝缘金属封闭开关设备现场交接试验规程	修订	中国电力科学研究院、广东电力科学研究院、广州供电局	DL/T 618—1997
31	水利水电工程技术术语标准	修订	武汉大学、中国长江三峡工程开发总公司、水电水利规划设计总院、北京国电水利电力工程有限公司、长江水利委员会	SL26—1992（原水利、能源两部共颁）
32	灌浆记录仪校定规程	制定	中国水利水电基础工程局有限公司	
33	核子密度仪	制定	中国葛洲坝集团股份有限公司	
34	水电水利工程模板施工规范	修订	中国水利水电第一工程局有限公司	DL/T 5110—2000

续表

序号	项目名称	制定/修订	起草单位	代替标准
35	水电水利工程施工测量规范	修订	中国葛洲坝集团股份有限公司、中国水利水电第四工程局有限公司	DL/T 5173—2003
36	水电水利工程施工机械安全操作规程 单斗挖掘机	制定	中国水利水电第四工程局有限公司	
37	水电水利工程施工机械安全操作规程 推土机	制定	中国水利水电第四工程局有限公司	
38	水电水利工程施工机械安全操作规程 装载机	制定	中国水利水电第四工程局有限公司	
39	水电水利工程施工机械安全操作规程 混凝土拌和楼	制定	中国水利水电第八工程局有限公司	
40	水电水利工程施工机械安全操作规程 缆式起重机	制定	中国水利水电第八工程局有限公司	
41	水电水利工程施工机械安全操作规程 履带式起重机	制定	中国水利水电第三工程局有限公司	
42	水电水利工程施工机械安全操作规程 门座式起重机	制定	中国水利水电第三工程局有限公司	
43	水电水利工程施工机械安全操作规程 汽车式起重机	制定	中国水利水电第三工程局有限公司	
44	水电水利工程施工监理规范	修订	中国建设监理协会水电建设监理分会、长江水利委员会监理中心、华东水电勘测设计研究院、四川二滩国际工程咨询有限责任公司、北京勘测设计研究院、中南勘测设计研究院	DL/T 5111—2000
45	水电水利基本建设工程 单元工程质量等级评定标准 第8部分：水工碾压混凝土工程	修订	武警水电指挥部，中国水利水电第七、第八、第十六工程局有限公司	DL/T 5113.8—2000
46	水工混凝土掺用轻烧氧化镁技术规范	制定	中国长江三峡工程开发总公司	
47	水工混凝土掺用天然火山灰技术规范	制定	长江水利委员会长江科学院	
48	水工混凝土钢筋施工规范	修订	中国水利水电第四工程局有限公司、武警水电指挥部	DL/T 5169—2002
49	水工混凝土砂石骨料试验规程	修订	南京水利科学研究院、中国水利水电科学研究院	DL/T 5151—2001
50	水工混凝土施工规范	修订	中国长江三峡工程开发总公司、中国葛洲坝水利水电工程集团公司	DL/T 5144—2001
51	水工混凝土外加剂技术规程	修订	南京水利科学研究院、中国水利水电科学研究院	DL/T 5100—1999
52	500kV交流紧凑型输电线路带电作业技术导则	制定	国网电力科学研究院	

续表

序号	项目名称	制定/修订	起草单位	代替标准
53	带电作业绝缘鞋（靴）通用技术条件	修订	国网电力科学研究院	DL/T 676—1999
54	750kV输变电工程电磁环境限值	制定	国网电力科学研究院	
55	无线电干扰测量系统校准方法	制定	国网电力科学研究院	
56	变电站通信网络和系统 第6部分：与智能电子设备有关的变电站内通信配置描述语言	修订	国网南京自动化研究院	根据IEC标准修订 DL/T 860.6—2008
57	电力线载波机接口	制定	四川灵通电子科技有限公司	
58	电网管理的系统接口 第13部分：配网CIMRDF模型交换格式	制定	国网电力科学研究院	
59	电网管理的系统接口 第9部分：抄表与控制接口	制定	国网电力科学研究院	
60	能量管理系统应用程序接口（EMS-API）第402部分：公共服务	制定	国网电力科学研究院、中国电力科学研究院	
61	六氟化硫电气设备分解产物试验方法	制定	福建电力试验研究院、厦门加华电力科技有限公司、湖南省电力公司	
62	电力系统电压稳定评价导则	制定	中国电力科学研究院	
63	T型线夹	修订	中国电力科学研究院	国家标准降为行业标准 GB/T 2340—1998
64	电力金具制造质量 钢铁件热镀锌层	修订	中国电力科学研究院	DL/T 768.7—2002
65	屏蔽环、均压环和均压屏蔽环	修订	中国电力科学研究院	DL/T 760.3—2001
66	设备线夹	修订	中国电力科学研究院	国家标准降为行业标准 GB/T 2341—1998
67	输电线路铁塔及电力金具紧固用冷镦热浸镀锌螺栓与螺母	修订	中国电力科学研究院	DL/T 764.4—2002
68	架空输电线路直升机航检作业引航标志制作安装标准	制定	云南电网公司、云南送变电工程公司	
69	架空输电线路直升机巡视技术导则	制定	国网电力科学研究院、华北电网公司、齐齐哈尔超高压公司	
70	低压电力线通信宽带接入系统技术要求	制定	国网信息通信有限公司、福建省亿力电力网络信息设备有限公司、北京中电飞华通信股份有限公司、深圳市国电科技通信有限公司	
71	电弧防护及防护装具	制定	苏州热工研究院有限公司	
72	电力工业焊工培训机构基本能力要求	制定	北京电力建设公司	
73	电力设备预防性试验规程	修订	中国电力企业联合会标准化中心	DL/T 596—1996
74	电力数字调度交换机测试方法	制定	国网信息通信有限公司、国网电力科学研究院、电力工业通信设备质量检验测试中心、河北省电力公司	

续表

序号	项目名称	制定/修订	起草单位	代替标准
75	电力行业标准编写基本规定	修订	中国电力企业联合会标准化中心	DL/T 600—2001
76	基于以太网方式的无源光网络配电网通信技术条件	制定	国网信息通信有限公司、中国电力科学研究院、华北电力大学、山西省电力公司、广东电网公司、北京格林威尔科技发展有限公司、杭州华三通信技术有限公司、杭州富顿科技有限公司	
77	架空输变电线路施工机具产品型号编制方法	修订	中国电力科学研究院	SD 232—1987
78	架空输电线路导线及避雷线液压施工工艺规程	修订	中国电力科学研究院	SDJ 226—1987
79	架空输电线路机载激光雷达测量技术规程	制定	中国南方电网有限责任公司、广西电力工业勘察设计研究院、广东省电力设计研究院	
80	架空输电线路施工抱杆通用技术条件与试验方法	制定	中国电力科学研究院	
81	电力企业标准编制规则	修订	中国电力企业联合会标准化中心、黑龙江省电力有限公司、吉林省电力有限公司	DL/T 800—2001
82	供电系统用户供电可靠性评价规程	修订	中国电力企业联合会电力可靠性管理中心	DL/T 836—2003
83	750kV 电力系统继电保护	修订	南京南瑞继保电气有限公司	DL/Z 886—2004
84	水力发电设备焊接接头超声波衍射时差法检测规程	制定	国电大渡河流域水电开发有限公司、国电郑州机械设计研究所、中国水利水电第十四工程有限公司	
85	热喷涂陶瓷涂层液压启闭机活塞杆	制定	江苏武进液压启闭机有限公司	
86	钢弦式监测仪器鉴定技术规范	制定	国网电力科学研究院北京基康科技有限公司	
87	大坝安全监测仪器电缆基本技术条件	制定	北京木联能工程科技有限公司	
88	多点变位计装置	制定	国网电力科学研究院	
89	电力企业能源管理体系实施指南	制定	中国电力企业联合会、中电联（北京）认证中心有限责任公司	
90	水电站设备状态检修管理实施标准	制定	中国长江电力股份有限公司葛洲坝水力发电厂、华能集团公司、国电集团公司、中国电力投资集团公司	
91	发电设备可靠性评价规程	修订	电力可靠性管理中心	DL/T 793—2001

续表

序号	项目名称	制定/修订	起草单位	代替标准
92	供电系统用户供电可靠性评价规程	修订	电力可靠性管理中心	DL/T 836—2003
93	输变电设施可靠性评价规程	修订	电力可靠性管理中心	DL/T 837—2003
94	气体绝缘金属封闭输电线路现场交接试验导则	制定	中国电力科学研究院、西北勘测设计院	
95	高压试验/检测车通用技术条件	制定	国网电力科学研究院	
96	电能信息采集与管理系统　第 2 部分：主站技术规范	修订	中国电力科学研究院	DL/T 698—1999
97	电能信息采集与管理系统　第 3-1 部分：电能信息采集终端技术规范—通用要求	修订	中国电力科学研究院	DL/T 698—1999
98	电能信息采集与管理系统　第 3-2 部分：电能信息采集终端技术规范—厂站采集终端特殊要求	修订	中国电力科学研究院	DL/T 698—1999
99	电能信息采集与管理系统　第 3-3 部分：电能信息采集终端技术规范—专变采集终端特殊要求	修订	中国电力科学研究院	DL/T 698—1999
100	电能信息采集与管理系统　第 3-4 部分：电能信息采集终端技术规范—公变采集终端特殊要求	修订	中国电力科学研究院	DL/T 698—1999
101	电能信息采集与管理系统　第 3-5 部分：电能信息采集终端技术规范—低压集中抄表终端特殊要求	修订	中国电力科学研究院	DL/T 698—1999
102	电能信息采集与管理系统　第 4-1 部分：通信协议—主站与电能信息采集终端通信	修订	中国电力科学研究院	DL/T 698—1999
103	低压无功补偿控制器使用技术条件	修订	浙江省电力试验研究院、中国电力科学研究院	DL/T 597—1996
104	高压并联电容器装置保护使用技术条件	制定	国网武汉高压研究院、北京电力公司、华北电力科学研究院、山东迪生电子电气有限公司	
105	直流换流站用支柱绝缘子　第 1 部分：技术条件	制定	国网电力科学研究院	
106	直流换流站用支柱绝缘子　第 2 部分：尺寸与特性	制定	国网电力科学研究院	
107	串联电容器补偿装置系统设计导则	制定	中国电力科学研究院、华北电力科学研究院有限责任公司	
108	配电网静止同步补偿装置技术规范	制定	江西省电力科学研究院、思源电气股份有限公司	

续表

序号	项目名称	制定/修订	起草单位	代替标准
109	动态电压恢复器技术规范	制定	中国电力科学研究院、北京电力公司	
110	微机变压器保护装置通用使用技术条件	修订	国电南京自动化股份有限公司	DL/T 770—2001
111	微机电动机保护装置使用技术条件	修订	南京南瑞继保电气有限公司	DL/T 744—2001
112	高压直流输电系统用换流变压器保护使用技术条件	制定	北京四方继保自动化股份有限公司	
113	可控型高压并联电抗器保护的使用技术条件	制定	北京四方继保自动化股份有限公司	
114	电力变压器用片式散热器选用导则	制定	国网电力科学研究院、吉林省电力科学研究院	
115	220kV～750kV 电力变压器使用技术条件	修订	国网武汉高压研究院、华东电网公司、西北电网公司	SD 326—1989
116	220kV～750kV 并联电抗器使用技术条件	修订	国网武汉高压研究院、广东电网公司	SD 327—1989
117	电流互感器和电压互感器使用技术条件	修订	国网武汉高压研究院、华中电网公司、西北电网公司	SD 333—1989
118	组合式变压器使用技术条件	制定	国网电力科学研究院、北京市电力公司、上海市电力公司	
119	三相组合式互感器使用技术条件	制定	国网电力科学研究院	
120	油浸式全密封卷铁心配电变压器使用技术条件	制定	国网电力科学研究院、北京华力通科园电网设备技术有限公司、北京供电公司	
121	电力系统通信超长站距光传输工程设计规定	制定	国网信息通信有限公司、北京国电通信工程设计院有限公司、北京中电飞华通信有限公司等	
122	水电水利工程泥沙设计规范	修订	中国水电顾问集团、成都勘测设计研究院	DL/T 5089—1999
123	水电工程征地移民综合监理技术导则	制定	中国水电顾问集团北京勘测设计院	
124	水电水利工程环境监理规范	制定	中国水电顾问集团、成都勘测设计研究院	
125	水力发电厂安全预评价报告编制规程	制定	中国水利水电建设工程咨询公司，北京木联能软件技术有限公司，西北、华东、中南、昆明勘测设计研究院	
126	金属结构及机电设备焊缝 TOFD 检验规程	制定	郑州机械研究所、国电大渡河公司	
127	热喷涂陶瓷涂层液压启闭机	制定	江苏武进液压启闭机有限公司	

（中国电力企业联合会　许松林）

2009年电力标准英文版翻译计划项目

序号	标准编号	标准名称	负责编译单位	备　注
1	DL/T 5400—2007	水工建筑物滑动模板施工规范	中国水利水电建设集团公司	
2		土坝灌浆规范	中国水利水电建设集团公司	与中文版标准同步进行
3	DL/T 5332—2005	水工混凝土断裂试验规程	中国水利水电建设集团公司	
4	DL/T 5102—1999	土工离心模型试验规程	中国水利水电建设集团公司	
5	DL/T 5372—2007	水电水利工程金属结构与机电设备安装安全技术规程	中国水利水电建设集团公司	
6	SD J 249.3—1988	水利水电基本建设工程　单元工程质量等级评定标准（三）水轮发电机组安装工程	中国水利水电建设集团公司	按新修订标准进行
7	DL/T 5313.11—2005	水电水利基本建设工程　单元工程质量等级评定标准　第11部分：灯泡贯流式水轮发电机组安装工程	中国水利水电建设集团公司	
8		水工建筑物化学灌浆施工规范	中国葛洲坝集团公司	与中文版标准同步进行
9	GB/T 8564—2003	水轮发电机组安装技术规范	中国葛洲坝集团公司	
10		混凝土面板堆石坝挤压边墙混凝土试验规程	中国葛洲坝集团公司	与中文版标准同步进行
11	GB 50287—2006	水力发电工程地质勘察规范	水电水利规划设计总院	
12	GB 50060—2008	3～110kV高压配电装置设计规范	中国电力工程顾问集团公司西北电力设计院	
13	GB 50227—2008	并联电容器装置设计规范	中国电力工程顾问集团公司西南电力设计院	

（中国电力企业联合会　许松林）

电力行业标准《水电水利工程预应力锚索施工规范》（送审稿）通过审查

2009年6月27～29日，中国电力行业水电施工标准化中心组织召开的《水电水利工程预应力锚索施工规范》（送审稿）审查会在成都召开。规范的主要起草单位——中国葛洲坝集团股份有限公司技术专家参加会议。此次审查的《水电水利工程预应力锚索施工规范》是在DL/T 5083—2004《水电水利工程预应力锚索施工规范》的基础上进行修订的。修订增加了缓黏结预应力钢绞线、压力分散型预应力锚固体系和钢制锚墩等内容，使规范的内容更加全面、准确，可操作性更强。审查会上，与会专家对规范的内容进行了深入细致的讨论和修改，最后由编写组整理形成报批稿，提交国家能源局审批。该规范将代替DL/T 5083—2004《水电水利工程预应力锚索施工规范》，对促进该项技术的进一步发展具有重要意义。

（摘自中国葛洲坝集团公司网站）

《水电站气垫式调压室设计规范》送审稿通过审查

2009年8月31日～9月1日，中国水电工程顾问集团公司在成都主持召开了《水电站气垫式调压室设计规范》送审稿审查会。参加会议的有：水电水利规划设计总院，河海大学，中国水电顾问集团华东、中南、昆明、北京、西北、成都勘测设计研究院等单位的专家和代表。《水电站气垫式调压室设计规范》的编制任务由中国水电顾问集团成都勘测设计研究院承担。编制组在收集了国外气垫式调压室相关资料，总结了已建成的自一里、小天都、金康等气垫式调压室勘察设计与运行控制的基本理论与实践经验，并结合在建的木座、阴坪等气垫式调压室的设计开展了长距离水气测量系统、平压管网水力特点等专题研究工作，于2009年7月完成了送审稿。会议听取了编制组关于《水电站气垫式调压室设计规范》编制工作情况的汇报，与会专家对《水电站气垫式调压室设计规范》送审稿进行了认真的讨论、审议，同意该规范的总体框架和主要内容。会议认为《水电站气垫式调压室设计规范》系统地反映了当前气垫式调压室的技术水平，具有科学性、实用性的特点，达到国际先进水平。会议要求修编组按照会议纪要和专家提出的意见进行修改补充，同时对条文说明进行相应的修改，尽快提出报批稿。

（摘自中国水电工程顾问集团公司网站）

新 颁 标 准

2009年国家标准化管理委员会发布的电力国家标准

序号	标准编号	标 准 名 称	实施日期（年.月.日）	代替标准
1	GB/T 24833—2009	1000kV 变电站监控系统技术规范	2009.11.30	
2	GB/T 24834—2009	1000kV 交流架空输电线路金具技术规范	2009.11.30	
3	GB/Z 24835—2009	1000kV 气体绝缘金属封闭开关设备运行及维护规程	2009.11.30	
4	GB/Z 24836—2009	1100kV 气体绝缘金属封闭开关设备技术规范	2009.11.30	
5	GB/Z 24837—2009	1100kV 高压交流隔离开关和接地开关技术规范	2009.11.30	
6	GB/Z 24838—2009	1100kV 高压交流断路器技术规范	2009.11.30	
7	GB/Z 24839—2009	1000kV 交流系统用支柱绝缘子技术规范	2009.11.30	
8	GB/Z 24840—2009	1000kV 交流系统用套管技术规范	2009.11.30	
9	GB/Z 24841—2009	1000kV 交流系统用电容式电压互感器技术规范	2009.11.30	
10	GB/Z 24842—2009	1000kV 特高压交流输变电工程过电压和绝缘配合	2009.11.30	
11	GB/Z 24843—2009	1000kV 单相油浸式自耦电力变压器技术规范	2009.11.30	
12	GB/Z 24844—2009	1000kV 交流系统用油浸式并联电抗器技术规范	2009.11.30	
13	GB/Z 24845—2009	1000kV 交流系统用无间隙金属氧化物避雷器技术规范	2009.11.30	
14	GB/Z 24846—2009	1000kV 交流电气设备预防性试验规程	2009.11.30	
15	GB/Z 24847—2009	1000kV 交流系统电压和无功电力技术导则	2009.11.30	

（中国电力企业联合会 许松林）

2009年国家能源局发布的电力行业标准（水电、电气部分）

序号	标准编号	标准名称	实施日期（年.月.日）	代替标准
1	DL/T 415—2009	带电作业用火花间隙检测装置	2009.12.1	DL 415—1991
2	DL/T 492—2009	发电机环氧云母定子绕组绝缘老化鉴定导则	2009.12.1	DL/T 492—1992
3	DL/T 500—2009	电压监测仪使用技术条件	2009.12.1	DL/T 500—1992
4	DL/T 503—2009	电力工程项目分类代码	2009.12.1	DL/T 503—1992
5	DL/T 535—2009	电力负荷管理系统数据传输规约	2009.12.1	DL/T 535—1993
6	DL/T 543—2009	电厂用水处理设备验收导则	2009.12.1	DL/T 543—1994
7	DL/T 604—2009	高压并联电容器装置使用技术条件	2009.12.1	DL/T 604—1996
8	DL/T 634.5104—2009	远动设备及系统　第5-104部分：传输规约采用标准传输协议集的IEC 60870-5-101网络访问	2009.12.1	DL/T 634.5104—2002
9	DL/T 653—2009	高压并联电容器用放电线圈使用技术条件	2009.12.1	DL/T 653—1998
10	DL/T 662—2009	六氟化硫气体回收装置技术条件	2009.12.1	DL/T 662—1999
11	DL/T 665—2009	水汽集中取样分析装置验收导则	2009.12.1	DL/T 665—1999
12	DL/T 698.1—2009	电能信息采集与管理系统　第1部分：总则	2009.12.1	DL/T 698—1999
13	DL/T 756—2009	悬垂线夹	2009.12.1	DL/T 756—2001
14	DL/T 757—2009	耐张线夹	2009.12.1	DL/T 757—2001
15	DL/T 758—2009	接续金具	2009.12.1	DL/T 758—2001
16	DL/T 759—2009	连接金具	2009.12.1	DL/T 759—2001
17	DL/T 890.404—2009	能量管理系统应用程序接口（EMS-API）第404部分：高速数据访问（HSDA）	2009.12.1	
18	DL/T 890.405—2009	能量管理系统应用程序接口（EMS—API）　第405部分：通用事件和订阅（GES）	2009.12.1	
19	DL/T 1098—2009	间隔棒技术条件和试验方法	2009.12.1	
20	DL/T 1099—2009	防振锤技术条件和试验方法	2009.12.1	
21	DL/T 1100—2009	电力系统的时间同步系统　第1部分：技术规范	2009.12.1	
22	DL/T 1101—2009	35kV～110kV变电站自动化系统验收规范	2009.12.1	
23	DL/T 1102—2009	配电变压器运行规程	2009.12.1	

续表

序号	标准编号	标准名称	实施日期（年．月．日）	代替标准
24	DL/T 1104—2009	电位器式仪器测量仪	2009.12.1	
25	DL/T 1107—2009	水电厂自动化元件基本技术条件	2009.12.1	
26	DL/T 1108—2009	电力工程项目编号及产品文件管理规定	2009.12.1	
27	DL/T 1109—2009	输电线路张力架线用张力机通用技术条件	2009.12.1	
28	DL/T 1110—2009	卧式蒸发冷却电机基本技术条件	2009.12.1	
29	DL/T 1114—2009	钢结构腐蚀防护热喷涂（锌、铝及合金涂层）及其试验方法	2009.12.1	
30	DL/T 1120—2009	水轮机调节系统自动测试及实时仿真装置技术条件	2009.12.1	
31	DL/T 1122—2009	架空输电线路外绝缘配置技术导则	2009.12.1	
32	DL/T 1124—2009	数字电力线载波机	2009.12.1	
33	DL/T 1125—2009	10kV 带电作业用绝缘服装	2009.12.1	
34	DL/T 1126—2009	同塔多回线路带电作业技术导则	2009.12.1	
35	DL/T 1128—2009	风冷式钢带输渣机	2009.12.1	
36	DL/T 1129—2009	直流换流站二次电气设备交接试验规程	2009.12.1	
37	DL/T 1130—2009	高压直流输电工程系统试验规程	2009.12.1	
38	DL/T 1131—2009	±800kV 高压直流输电工程系统试验规程	2009.12.1	
39	DL/T 1133—2009	钢弦式仪器测量仪表	2009.12.1	
40	DL/T 1134—2009	大坝安全监测数据自动采集装置	2009.12.1	
41	DL/T 1135—2009	电位器式位移计	2009.12.1	
42	DL/T 1136—2009	钢弦式钢筋应力计	2009.12.1	
43	DL/T 1137—2009	钢弦式土压力计	2009.12.1	
44	DL/T 1145—2009	绝缘工具柜	2009.12.1	
45	DL/T 1146—2009	DL/T 860 实施技术规范	2009.12.1	
46	DL/T 1147—2009	电力高处作业防坠器	2009.12.1	
47	DL/T 1148—2009	电力电缆线路巡检系统	2009.12.1	
48	DL/T 5230—2009	水轮发电机转子现场装配工艺导则	2009.12.1	
49	DL/T 5057—2009	水工混凝土结构设计规范	2009.12.1	DL/T 5057—1996
50	DL/T 5065—2009	水力发电厂计算机监控系统设计规范	2009.12.1	DL/T 5065—1996
51	DL/T 5112—2009	水工碾压混凝土施工规范	2009.12.1	
52	DL/T 5125—2009	水电水利岩土工程施工及岩体测试造孔规程	2009.12.1	DL/T 5112—2000
53	DL/T 5128—2009	混凝土面板堆石坝施工规范	2009.12.1	DL/T 5125—2001

续表

序号	标准编号	标准名称	实施日期（年．月．日）	代替标准
54	DL/T 5407—2009	水电水利工程斜井竖井施工规范	2009.12.1	
55	DL/T 5408—2009	发电厂、变电站电子信息系统220/380V电源电涌保护配置、安装及验收规程	2009.12.1	
56	DL/T 5410—2009	中小型水力发电工程地质勘察规范	2009.12.1	
57	DL/T 5411—2009	土石坝沥青混凝土面板和心墙设计规范	2009.12.1	
58	DL/T 5413—2009	水力发电厂测量装置配置设计规范	2009.12.1	
59	DL/T 5414—2009	水电水利工程坝址工程地质勘察技术规程	2009.12.1	
60	DL/T 5415—2009	水电水利工程地下建筑物工程地质勘察技术规程	2009.12.1	
61	DL/T 5416—2009	水工建筑物强震动安全监测技术规范	2009.12.1	
62	DL/T 5419—2009	水电建设项目水土保持方案技术规范	2009.12.1	
63	DL/T 5420—2009	水轮发电机定子现场装配工艺导则	2009.12.1	
64	DL/T 5422—2009	混凝土面板堆石坝挤压边墙混凝土试验规程	2009.12.1	SD 287—1988
65	DL/T 5424—2009	水电水利工程锚杆无损检测规程	2009.12.1	
66	DL/T 5425—2009	深层搅拌法技术规范	2009.12.1	
67	DL/T 5426—2009	±800kV高压直流输电系统成套设计规程	2009.12.1	
68	DL/T 5429—2009	电力系统设计技术规程	2009.12.1	
69	DL/T 5430—2009	无人值班变电站远方监控中心设计技术规程	2009.12.1	SDJ 161—1985
70	DL/T 5431—2009	水电水利工程水文计算规范	2009.12.1	
71	DL/T 5432—2009	水电水利工程项目建设管理规范	2009.12.1	SDJ 214—1983
72	DL/T 5433—2009	水工碾压混凝土试验规程	2009.12.1	
73	DL/T 5434—2009	电力建设工程监理规范	2009.12.1	
74	DL/T 5438—2009	输变电工程经济评价导则	2009.12.1	
75	DL/T 5439—2009	大型水、火电厂接入系统设计内容深度规定	2009.12.1	
76	DL/T 5440—2009	重覆冰架空输电线路设计技术规程	2009.12.1	SDJ 84—1988

（中国电力企业联合会　许松林）

2009年水利标准完成情况

序号	标准名称	编　号	实施日期（年．月．日）
	一、国家标准		
1	灌溉用塑料管材和管件基本参数及技术条件	GB/T 23241—2009	2009.5.1
2	水资源公报编制规程	GB/T 23598—2009	2009.9.1
3	岩土工程仪器　土压力计　第1部分：振弦式土压力计	GB/T 23872.1—2009	2009.10.1
4	大坝监测仪器　检测仪　第1部分：振弦式仪器检测仪	GB/T 3412.1—2009	2009.10.1
5	大坝监测仪器　孔隙水压力计　第1部分：振弦式孔隙水压力计	GB/T 3411.1—2009	2009.10.1
6	岩土工程仪器术语及符号	GB/T 24106—2009	2009.12.1
7	岩土工程仪器型号命名方法	GB/T 24104—2009	2009.12.1
8	岩土工程仪器基本环境试验条件及方法	GB/T 24105—2009	2009.12.1
9	岩土工程仪器可靠性技术要求	GB/T 24108—2009	2009.12.1
10	土工试验仪器　三轴仪　第1部分：应变控制式三轴仪	GB/T 24107.1—2009	2009.12.1
11	土工试验仪器　固结仪　第2部分：气压式固结仪	GB/T 4935.2—2009	2009.12.1
12	泵站更新改造技术规程	GB/T 50510—2009	2010.2.1
13	微灌工程技术规范	GB/T 50485—2009	2009.12.1
14	灌区规划规范	GB/T 50509—2009	2009.12.1
15	旱情等级标准	已报批	
16	水功能区划分技术导则	已报批	
17	水域纳污能力计算规程	已报批	
18	节水型产品技术条件与管理通则	已报批	
19	水位观测标准（GBJ 138—1990 修订）	已报批	
20	雨水集蓄利用工程技术规范（指标需调整）	已报批	
21	灌区改造技术规程（指标需调整）	已报批	
22	渠道防渗工程技术规范（指标需调整）	已报批	
	二、行业标准		
1	水利系统通信工程验收规程	SL 439—2009	2009.6.2

续表

序号	标准名称	编　号	实施日期（年．月．日）
2	水利水电工程建设征地移民安置规划设计规范	SL 290—2009 替代 SL 290—2003	2009.10.31
3	水利水电工程建设农村移民安置规划设计规范	SL 440—2009	2009.10.31
4	水利水电工程建设征地移民安置规划大纲编制导则	SL 441—2009	2009.10.31
5	水利水电工程建设征地移民实物调查规范	SL 442—2009	2009.10.31
6	水文缆道测验规范	SL 443—2009 替代 SD 121—1984	2009.6.2
7	水利信息网运行管理规程	SL 444—2009	2009.6.2
8	漏电保护器农村安装运行规程	SL 445—2009	2009.6.30
9	黑土区水土流失综合防治技术标准	SL 446—2009	2009.6.9
10	周期式混凝土搅拌楼（站）	SL 242—2009	2009.9.10
11	水土保持工程项目建议书编制规程	SL 447—2009	2009.8.21
12	水土保持工程可行性研究报告编制规程	SL 448—2009	2009.8.21
13	水土保持工程初步设计报告编制规程	SL 449—2009	2009.8.21
14	堰塞湖风险等级划分标准	SL 450—2009	2009.5.12
15	堰塞湖应急处置技术导则	SL 451—2009	2009.5.12
16	水土保持监测点代码	SL 452—2009	2009.9.5
17	转子式流速仪计量检定规程	JJG（水利）001—2009	
18	浮子式水位计计量检定规程	JJG（水利）002—2009	
19	超声波测深仪计量检定规程	JJG（水利）003—2009	
20	水文年鉴汇编刊印规范	SL 460—2009	2009.12.29
21	中小河流水能开发规划编制规范	SL 221—2009 替代 SL 221—1998	2010.3.21
22	小水电水能设计规程	SL 76—2009 替代 SL 76—1994	2010.3.21
23	人才管理数据库结构及标识符标准	SL 453—2009	2009.11.7

（水利部国际合作与科技司　刘咏峰）

科　技　图　书　出　版

中国电力出版社有限公司 2009 年出版的水电新书

序号	书　　名	出版日期	作　　者
1	三峡电站运行管理	2009 年 12 月	李永安　张诚
2	锚固与注浆技术手册（第二版）	2009 年 10 月	中国岩石力学与工程学会锚固与注浆分会编　杨晓东　主编

续表

序号	书　　名	出版日期	作　　者
3	中国南水北调工程建设年鉴 2009	2009 年 10 月	《中国南水北调工程建设年鉴》编纂委员会
4	中国水利水电建设集团公司年鉴 2009	2009 年 12 月	中国水利水电建设集团公司年鉴编辑委员会
5	水利水电施工 2009 年第 6 期	2009 年 12 月	全国水利水电施工技术信息网
6	水利水电施工 2009 年第 5 期	2009 年 11 月	全国水利水电施工技术信息网
7	水利水电施工 2009 年第 4 期	2009 年 9 月	全国水利水电施工技术信息网
8	水利水电施工 2009 年第 3 期	2009 年 7 月	全国水利水电施工技术信息网
9	水利水电施工 2009 年第 2 期	2009 年 5 月	全国水利水电施工技术信息网
10	水利水电施工 2009 年第 1 期	2009 年 2 月	全国水利水电施工技术信息网
11	中国水电 60 年——庆祝中华人民共和国成立 60 周年	2009 年 10 月	中国水力发电工程学会
12	中国电气工程大典　第 5 卷　水力发电工程	2009 年 9 月	中国电气工程大典编辑委员会　主编　梁维燕　邴凤山　饶芳权　王国海　贺建华
13	改革开放三十年的中国水电	2009 年 1 月	中国水力发电工程学会
14	水利水电工程项目管理理论与实践	2009 年 3 月	张基尧
15	第二届水力发电技术国际会议论文集	2009 年 4 月	本书编委会
16	中国水力发电年鉴（第十三卷）	2009 年 12 月	中国水力发电工程学会
17	高坝岩石力学	2009 年 5 月	杨强　杨若琼　林鹏　刘耀儒　编著
18	混凝土建筑物修补材料及应用	2009 年 2 月	黄国兴　纪国晋　编著
19	水电厂安全评价丛书　水电厂人员行为安全评价	2009 年 2 月	葛洲坝水力发电厂　程刚
20	水电企业电力营销风险管理	2009 年 3 月	涂扬举　马光文　等
21	风力发电技术丛书　风电机组防雷与接地	2009 年 7 月	张小青

（中国电力出版社有限公司　姜　萍）

《中国小水电 60 年》出版发行

为了保存我国小水电发展的珍贵史料，再现小水电发展的光辉历程，记录 60 年来小水电发展中的重大事件，经水利部领导批准，水利部农村水电及电气化发展局在新中国成立 60 周年之际，组织编写了《中国小水电 60 年》。该书由水利部部长陈雷作序，水利部副部长胡四一任编委会主任，主编为水利部农村水电及电气化发展局局长田中兴。2009 年 9 月 28 日上午，新书首发仪式在北京举行，水利部副部长胡四一出席首发式并讲话。

《中国小水电 60 年》全书 40 万字，共分 10 章，分别为：概述、波澜壮阔的发展历程、与时俱进的政策法规、改革创新的行业管理、实用可靠的小水电技术、中国特色的水电农村电气化、保护生态的小水电代燃料工程、日益壮大的小水电产业、走向世界的中国小水电和更加光明的发展前景。全书图文并茂，既记录了大量我国小水电 60 年发展历程中的重大事件、重要改革、重大政策和重要技术突破，也展示了我国各地通过小水电建设形成的成果和对比图片，具有很强的说服力。

（水利部农村水电及电气化发展局　岳梦华）

11

水电建设管理

工 程 管 理

中国大唐集团公司水电工程建设管理综述

中国大唐集团公司（以下简称大唐集团）是全国五大发电集团之一，主要从事电力、热力生产和供应及相关专业技术服务。截至2009年底，大唐集团发电装机规模突破了1亿kW大关，达到10 017.23万kW，成为世界亿千瓦级特大型发电公司。

大唐集团自组建以来一直坚持科学发展观，注重清洁能源建设，在总体发展战略规划中，明确提出了优化电源结构、大力发展水电的指导思想。几年来，水电机组投产容量逐年增加。截至2009年底，大唐集团水电装机容量达到1451.74万kW，核准在建水电项目49个，容量为455.769万kW。其中，大型项目有嘉陵江亭子口水利枢纽工程（4×27.5万kW）、乌江银盘水电站工程（4×15万kW），中小水电项目较多，主要分布在云南、四川等省、市、自治区以及缅甸、柬埔寨等东南亚国家。云南分公司万家口子水电站（2×9万kW）将建成世界上最高的碾压混凝土双曲拱坝，坝高为167.5m。

大唐集团实施以集团公司，分、子公司，基层企业三级责任主体为基础的集团化管理体制和运行模式。在三级责任主体的共同努力下，建立健全了水电工程建设体制机制，按照“四控制、两管理、一协调”的管理模式，紧抓现场组织、设备催交、外部协调三大主线，使机组投产进度得以确保或提前；狠抓安全管理和文明工地建设，提高大唐集团水电建设安全文明施工水平；强化质量管理，开展创一流工作，提高机组达标投产水平；强调设计优化，严格合同管理和招投标管理，工程投资得到了有效控制。总结大唐集团几年来水电工程建设管理经验，主要有以下几点：

（一）落实项目的组织管理

大唐集团系统上下坚持以“业主是主导，监理是中心，施工是主体”的管理模式。

1. 管理组织机构

在项目公司层面，建立一个高效协同、经验丰富、善于管理、勇担责任的经营班子和管理团队，在项目建设过程中起到主导作用。对于总监理工程师人选、承包商项目经理班子人选，要经过项目公司与中标人多次磋商和考核确定。在各种困难条件下，各种利益发生冲突时，能平衡大局，带领自己的团队，协调各方完成任务。

2. 管理目标

根据大唐集团的管理目标和要求，系统内各单位坚持以不断优化设计作为基础，以创建安全文明施工样板工地和开展达标投产工作为抓手，以经济效益为中心，使工程安全、质量、工期、造价得到良好的平衡和控制，最终实现水电开发建设最大的投资效益。

3. 管理模式

（1）大唐集团建立健全了项目建设目标体系和管理考核机制。瞄准国内工程建设的先进指标，建立以工程项目安全、质量、工期和造价四要素为目标体系的管理标准和考核制度，明确项目建设单位工程管理的权利、义务、责任和目标，有效界定三级责任主体的管理职责，充分调动了各级工程建设管理人员的积极性和主动性。在项目建设总目标的框架下，通过分解细化落实年度管理指标，加强过程检查和年终考核工作，有效地促进了管理工作的加强和目标责任的细化落实，为保证项目总目标的实现起到了重要作用。

（2）各项目公司按照法人负责制的要求，对工程设计、质量、安全、工期、造价实行全面管理，除建立健全了内部管理机构外，还成立了由项目公司为主任、参建各方参加的电站安全生产委员会、质量管理委员会，防洪度汛领导小组，达标投产领导小组等组织。制定和完善了各项规章制度，使工程建设有章可循，实现工程管理现代化、程序化和标准化。招标工作严格按照国家法律法规和集团公司的规定进行，从监理、施工、安装、制造到设备、材料采购，全部经过招标公平、公正确定。在工程建设过程中，一是充分发挥了项目业主的主导作用；二是实行“小业主、大监理”的管理模式，充分依靠和信任监理，使监理能独立地行使职权。

4. 管理理念

随着电力体制改革的不断深入和社会主义市场经济秩序的不断完善，根据工程建设的实际条件和环境，各水电工程建设已形成了“五位一体”的管理理念和文化，即工程建设过程中，设计、施工、监理、业主、政府五方结合为有机的整体，相互团结，密切合作，各负其责，齐心协力，为了一个共同的目标，形成一个极具向心力的集体，形成一股巨大的动力，使工程朝着最终的目标推进。

（1）业主是主导。各单位在工程建设管理过程中，始终坚持业主在建设项目管理中的主导地位，按照“精简、统一、高效”的原则，减少管理层次，提高工作效率，坚持以合同为基础，充分发挥建设各方作用；作为项目业主单位，同时也把搞好工程建设服务作为第一任务，为设计、监理努力创造良好的工作环境和生活环境，为施工单位创造良好的施工条件，及时、准确地保证工程款的拨付，正确对待和解决合同执行中的分歧和意见。协调好工程施工干扰，协调好设计、施工、监理之间以及施工单位之间的关系，紧紧把参建各方团结在一起，组织参建各方参加的各种文体活动和劳动竞赛，大大增强了凝聚力。树立业主良好的工作形象和作风，提高办事效率，想工程之所想，急工程之所急，牢固树立服务第一的思想，将工作真正落到实处。

（2）设计是龙头。工程设计是确保工程安全、质量、工期、投资效益的前提和基础，作为水电工程设计单位，从勘测、可行性研究、立项、工程招投标、施工设计等阶段，经过了长期的研究和细致的工作，积累了非常丰富的经验。因此，各项目公司充分发挥和利用设计的龙头作用，搞好工程设计，不断进行设计优化，并做好现场设代工作，为工程建设提供优质的设计成果。

（3）施工是主体。施工单位作为工程建设的实施者，是实现工程管理目标的具体保证，是工程建设的主力军，只有施工单位精心施工，才能创造出优质工程。作为项目业主管理单位，充分认识到施工单位的主体地位，创造和提供一切条件，充分发挥他们的积极性、主动性和创造性，充分理解和帮助解决施工单位的具体困难，使施工单位有更大的工作热情和主人翁态度投入到工程建设中去。

（4）监理是指挥。监理单位是工程“四控制、两管理、一协调”的具体管理控制单位，是设计、业主思想的贯彻者和指挥者。对工程施工的具体指挥由监理单位实施和完成，设计和业主单位一般情况下不直接指挥施工，以免造成多重指挥的混乱局面，在执行施工指挥的同时，监理也必须按公平、公正的原则，维护施工单位的合法权益。

（5）政府是保障。为了搞好工程建设，各单位把积极争取到地方政府的大力支持、密切与地方的关系、创造宽松的建设环境当做大事来抓，并注意和当地党委、政府的沟通和协调，依靠当地政府开展各项工作，最大限度地发挥政府监管的作用。在不损害或少损失企业利益的前提下，最大程度地满足地方利益。企业与政府共同打造水电工程，互惠互利，使工程建设顺利进行。

（二）标准化管理提升管理水平

水电项目的总体管控是大唐集团工程管理部门对项目进行有效管理的措施。为了实施项目的总体管控，大唐集团制定了完善的项目管理制度，对建设项目的招标实施重点监控，组织进行项目质量巡视，项目之间的安全、质量互检，开展项目达标投产活动，对项目进行审计。2009 年，大唐集团工程部研究制定了《工程管理标准》，对工程进度、设计、合同、设备、材料、质量等的管理标准进行了细化。这些措施强化了项目的总体管控，提升了大唐集团的标准化管理水平。

（三）达标投产强化过程控制

作为提高水电建设项目管理水平的综合性措施，大唐集团高度重视在项目建设过程中推行“达标投产”，在中国电力企业联合会达标投产管理办法的基础上制定了《中国大唐集团公司水电建设工程达标投产考核管理办法（2009 版）》。

达标投产除了对项目建设结果进行系统的考评外，更注重对过程的考核，达标投产对工程建设过程的考核细则更能体现项目管理水平的提高。大唐集团的水电项目从一开工就开始进行项目达标投产策划，并作为必备合同的条款，对设计、监理、施工、厂家、调试各单位提出具体要求，参建各方在全过程中落实达标投产的措施，对提升项目的管理水平，创建优质工程，取得了很好的效果。

达标投产一定要狠抓关键性的细节，由于水电工程的复杂性和风险性，干扰因素多，计划执行中的一些关键性细节往往会成为决定建设目标成败的瓶颈因素。善于主动抓住这些细节加以突破，这对于实现目标将起到事半功倍的作用。项目主管领导和中层主管人员在狠抓关键细节上下工夫，跟踪目标，主动发现问题；跟踪管理，突破瓶颈环节。

（四）有效激励创建一流工程

工程是由人建设的，对各参建单位的激励措施是必不可少的。作为激励的重要手段，项目公司对每个里程碑都悬挂奖励，奖励实现目标的项目经理部、监理和驻现场的设计代表。项目公司则由董事会给予奖励。奖励是在考核期开始时就明确的。为了调动设计人员开展设计优化、技术创新的积极性，在设计招标和签订设计合同时，业主和设计单位应就激励的原则和计算办法加以明确的规定，作为“秋后算账”的依据。对技术难度大，或不确定因素影响较大，或合同工期偏紧的施工项目，采取的激励措施最好在合同中予以规定。工程建设过程中发生的非承包商责任需要的赶工，双方应以合同为基础，协商激励方案，并签署补充文件以便执行。在奖励的运作上执行规范的考核和支付流程，突显激励作用，尽量减少负面影响。

在给予物质奖励的同时，还注重精神鼓励，如评选工程建设功臣、安全文明标兵、质量标兵等。

（中国大唐集团公司）

缅甸太平江一级水电站项目建设管理

（一）工程概况

缅甸太平江一级水电站位于缅甸东北克钦邦（Kachin）境内紧邻中缅边境的太平江上，电站坝址位于中缅边境37号界桩以下约2km河道处。工程区上游为中国云南省德宏傣族景颇族自治州盈江县。

水电站开发方式采用混合式开发。混凝土坝轴线长204m，最大坝高45.5m，总库容578万m^3；右岸布置2条直径8m的发电引水隧洞，长约3.5km；安装4台60MW的混流式水轮发电机组，额定水头68.5m，额定流量96.5m^3/s，多年平均发电量为10.6亿kW·h，年利用小时数为4415h。电站通过一回500kV输电线路送回国内南方电网。

该电站为三等中型工程，预计总投资为17.13亿元人民币，主体工程于2008年12月19日开工，计划2010年4台机组全部投产发电。

（二）投资开发方式

缅甸太平江一级水电站采用BOT投资开发方式，运营期满后无偿移交缅甸政府。

该项目是中国大唐集团公司响应国家“走出去”发展战略，第一个组织实施的境外水电建设项目。中国大唐集团海外投资有限公司（以下简称大唐海外公司）、华中电力国际经贸有限责任公司、江西省水利规划设计院按78.8%、16.2%、5%的股比组成大唐（云南）水电联合开发有限责任公司（以下简称项目公司），负责太平江一级水电站的建设和运营管理。

根据项目公司和缅甸政府签订的谅解备忘录（MOU），项目在缅甸注册成立太平江一期水电有限公司，作为项目法人，股东为项目公司和缅甸联邦水力发电执行司。

项目公司受太平江一期水电有限公司委托，负责项目建设总承包与运营期的运营维护工作。建设期，项目公司成立总经理工作部、工程建设部、机电物质部、计划合同部、财务管理部、缅甸办事处等6个部门，负责工程的建设管理和对缅甸方的联系工作。运营期，项目公司增设安全生产部，上述人员部分转入太平江一期水电有限公司，部分转为电厂生产管理人员。

（三）项目建设管理

1. 建设管理模式

采用中国大唐集团公司、大唐海外公司、项目公司三级责任主体分级管理模式。中国大唐集团公司负责项目重大投资决策、制定工程建设管理制度和检查落实；大唐海外公司负责落实中国大唐集团公司的投资决策、项目开发、指导和检查项目的建设和运行管理、制定项目建设管理目标并考核；项目公司为三级责任主体，负责项目融资、建设、运行管理的具体实施。项目公司受太平江一期水电有限公司委托，履行项目业主的职责。

工程建设原先采用施工总承包模式，实施过程中，将施工总承包改为平行发包模式，将主体工程划分为4个标段，通过国内公开招标择优选择施工队伍。

项目建设生产采用基建生产一体化原则。基建期，项目公司人员负责工程建设事宜，随工程建设进程，组织机构和人员配置逐渐向生产准备和运营过渡。

项目运营期采用运行维护承包原则。考虑BOT项目有特许运营期和国内项目运行维护资源较丰富的特点，项目公司将太平江水电站运营维护工作中的电厂运行维护检修工作外委给大唐陈村发电厂。

2. 建设管理指导思想

海外工程建设按照“满足标准、有序建设”，“全面协调、互惠共赢”，“全员参与、过程控制”，“目标管理、奖惩结合”，“和谐共处、持续发展”的原则开展工作。项目建设以满足BOT协议约定的规范和标准为目标，分步骤、有序开展各项建设工作；坚持以业主管理为主导，全面协调工程建设；坚持以合同管理为核心，实现相关各方互惠共赢；坚持项目建设全员参与，进行事前、事中、事后控制，使项目建设全过程均处于受控状态；以实现既定的工程建设安全、质量、进度和概算控制目标为目的，制定目标考核激励机制，有奖有罚；坚持创建和谐友好的工程建设环境，达到人与人、人与自然、工程与当地部族的和谐相融，彰显大唐文化理念和核心价值观。

建设过程中，设计工作按照“安全稳定、简单可靠、经济适用、符合国情”的原则开展工作，在充分考虑项目BOT或特许运营期限内综合成本和收益的基础上，严格设计原则、优化设备选型、控制建设标准，做好设计方案的技术经济论证和优化比选工作，实现项目投资的利益最大化。

建设过程中，强调设计和工程优化工作的重要性，优化工作贯穿整个工程建设过程。在安全、稳定的前提下，以项目所在国的工程建设水平为参照，开展优化工作，力求避免建设标准过高和质量过剩情况，以简单可靠、经济适用为目的，节省工程投资，提高工程效益。

3. 安全、质量、进度和造价的控制管理

安全管理的重点落在：安全组织体系、保障体系、监督体系的健全；分阶段、分区域、分项目重大安全风险因素的分析、防范对策以及措施的落实；进场队伍以及人员的安全教育培训和特殊资格取证；特种机械和车辆的检验和过程维护；危险源（放射、炸药、油库等）专项控制管理，同时建立严格的安全文明施工、职业卫生健康目标管理奖惩机制。针对海外项目的特点，重点关注非工程因素（当地居民冲突、宗教冲突、卫生饮食、恐怖暴力事件等）引起的安全风险管理。

质量管理的重点是：建立完善的质量保证体系和质量监督体系；清晰划分各级质量验收清单和计划；严格执行各项质量管理制度；对关键控制点（高边坡、隐蔽工程、大体积混凝土浇筑等）进行质量趋势分析。在质量巡视和阶段验收方面，按国内的良好行业惯例，由中国大唐集团公司组织专家履行第三方监督和验收。

进度管理的重点是：建立高效、简洁的进度管理决策协调机制，大唐海外公司控制里程碑进度，项目公司控制各承包商、供应商之间的接口进度，各承包商控制承包范围工作进度；重点关注施工组织设计和重大施工方案的策划；及时对施工资源（人员、机械、材料、设备、资金、图纸、施工条件等）进行周、月、季度、年度的动态管理协调。

工程造价管理工作贯穿于设计、招标、采购、建设、交付的每一阶段。项目公司造价管理在逐级分解责任的基础上，以成本管理和风险控制为出发点，以合同及执行概算管理为核心，及时对材料价格、工程量、设计变更进行动态跟踪，以统计管理为手段，以定期的经济活动分析为纽带，确保工程造价可控、在控。

（中国大唐集团海外投资有限公司　宋新峰）

江边水电站施工期的风险评估咨询

中国水电顾问集团西北勘测设计研究院于2008年1月与江边水电站业主签订江边水电站项目施工期风险评估咨询服务合同。按照合同要求进行的风险评估咨询，取得了良好效果，得到了业主等方面的肯定。

（一）咨询背景

1. 电站简况

江边水电站位于四川省甘孜州东南部九龙县，是九龙河“一库五级”开发方案的最末一级电站。主要由首部拦河闸坝（最大坝高32m，闸坝顶部长度181.9m）、引水系统（引水洞线长约8568m，开挖洞径8.4m，衬砌后洞径7.2m）、尾部地下厂房（长×宽×高为100m×17.5m×44.2m）三大部分组成，最大水头325m，电站装机容量为3×110MW，共计330MW。江边水电站工程规划总工期46个月，其中前期工程12个月，主体工程38个月，于2008年1月正式开工。

2. 内容和要求

合同要求对施工期可能的各种不安全因素带来的潜在风险进行分析（识别、评估），定期提出分析报告，制定消除或减小风险的措施建议，提出风险发生后的处理意见；在提交咨询文件后，每半年派人到现场检查、落实情况，并结合下阶段工作重点提出阶段性咨询报告，针对半年来未引起业主重视的地方和可能还会出现的风险提出补充评估意见，并提出改进建议。

（二）咨询实践

1. 风险评价方法

风险是指建筑物对作用于生命、健康、财产和环境负面影响的可能性和严重性的度量，是对不利事件后果的数学期望值的估算［不利事件发生的可能性（失效概率）与危害后果的乘积］，风险大小既与不利事件发生的可能性成正比，也与损失的严重性成正比。其评价方法如下：

（1）根据江边水电站的布置和施工期、运行期特点，采用风险定性评价法，将损失程度的评分法、危险指数评价法、失效概率与风险水平对照法等相互参照后，通过划分等级把对危险源的评价相对量化，得出所评价风险发生的可能性、损失后果及风险严重程度。

（2）对损失后果的大小，基于成本、工期、声誉、人身安全和环境等5项内容的损失情况进行综合评分，划分为灾难性的、极严重的、严重的、轻度的、轻微的。其评分范围自1（可忽略的影响：轻微的）至5（灾难性的影响），要求每一项风险都须进行这5个方面的损失的评估。

（3）对许多不可量化的风险因素进行定性描述，如将失效概率的大小分为不同程度的可能性：十分可能、很可能、可能的、极少、不可能。

（4）由危险性事件发生的可能性和危险性事件后果，按风险评价指数矩阵得到风险程度5个等级。确定最高风险指数为25，相对应的危害性事件是频繁发生的并有灾难性后果的事件；最低风险指数定为1，相对应的危害性事件是几乎不可能发生并且后果轻微的事件。将其进行划分：21～25为不可接受的风险；18～20为不希望有的风险；6～17为有条件接受的风险；1～5为完全可以接受的风险。

2. 划分风险识别单元与风险点

根据江边水电站的特点，结合危险因素的辨识与分析，将整个工程划分为水库库区、永久建筑物、临时建筑物、施工质量及安全管理 4 个方面。其中包括：场内外交通、水库库区、挡水泄洪排沙建筑、引水建筑、地下厂房、施工导流、施工工厂、施工质量及安全管理 8 个评价单元，每个评价单元里包括若干风险点，有些风险点又被分解出若干子风险点。具体按专业划分如下：

（1）工程地质方面，库区存在的主要工程地质风险点：①张家沟泥石流；……；③水库塌岸。闸坝区存在的工程地质风险点：①坝基砂土地震液化、压缩变形及不均匀沉降问题；……；⑤岱家沟洪水。引水发电系统存在的工程地质风险点：①进水口段地基不均匀沉降问题；……；⑧氡气及γ辐射指标超标问题。坝区左、右岸交通洞存在的工程地质风险点：①洞脸边坡稳定问题；②洞身围岩稳定性问题。施工临时建筑物区存在的工程地质风险点：①施工场地边坡稳定问题；②施工区冲沟泥石流和洪水对施工临时建筑物的影响。

（2）水工与施工方面，场内、外交通及边坡工程的风险点：①施工区 S215 省道边坡（场内、对外交通）；……；④闸坝区右岸交通洞上、下游洞口边坡。挡水建筑的风险点：闸坝区基础开挖时渗流对施工期排水及开挖边坡稳定的影响。引水建筑的风险点：①洞内施工的通风排烟；……；④引水洞高温地带。地下厂房的风险点：①高空意外掉块、掉物伤人及洞室顶拱、边墙的围岩稳定和支护；……；⑦引水岔管及岔管前高压管道。施工导流的风险点：①明渠基础开挖时渗流对施工期排水及开挖边坡稳定的影响；……；③厂房尾水洞围堰防洪问题。施工建筑区的风险点：①挖金沟渣场；②施工人员临时营地。施工质量及安全管理方面的风险点：①施工管理制度的建立与执行；……；⑤各标段的施工测量的联测。

3. 进行风险评估

根据江边水电站设计报告和图纸、当时的施工状况、现场了解的情况以及电站今后施工特点，对各评价单元进行风险评估，其评估分析步骤为：

（1）针对初步识别的风险，结合现场了解的情况，再次查询相应的设计报告和图纸资料。

（2）针对初步识别的风险，分析产生风险的原因并进行归纳分类。

（3）按照风险评估标准确定风险发生的可能性、损失后果及风险程度等级。

4. 提出降低风险度的对策及风险发生后的治理措施

考虑到业主、设计、监理、承包商在此前已经制定了大量相关的施工控制程序、标准、管理制度，咨询报告有针对性地对所识别、评估的风险点提出扼要的控制措施。

5. 风险注册登记

风险识别、评估并拟订降低风险度的对策以及风险发生后的治理措施后，编制了风险注册登记表。登记表里包括初始风险水平、措施落实情况、最终风险水平。每次专家到现场检查、落实情况时，首先按第一次及上一次向业主提供的咨询报告中风险注册登记表逐一了解情况，针对半年来未能引起业主重视的工程技术风险和施工安全问题以及可能将会出现的风险提出补充评估意见，并提出了风险更新的意见。

（三）施工期风险评估咨询的作用

（1）每隔半年一次到现场评估，保持了前后的一致性、连贯性，对重要风险更新的要求有利于在连续性基础上的动态性。

（2）识别风险是对设计的再认识，设计本身是考虑了风险因素的，但照图施工时容易淡化设计意图的“为什么”。识别风险就是分析产生风险的原因，多一个视角重新问一问“为什么”。

（3）按照风险评估标准确定风险发生的可能性、损失后果及风险程度等级，有利于分轻重缓急，抓主要矛盾。

（4）提出降低风险度的对策，即风险发生后的治理措施，针对性强，有利于施工单位完善施工组织设计，有利于纠正习以为常、熟视无睹的不正确方法，多了一个视角指出“怎么办”。

（5）风险注册登记后，有利于突出风险点，提醒各有关方跟踪、落实风险控制措施。

（中国水电顾问集团西北勘测设计研究院　冯兴中）

琅琊山抽水蓄能电站项目监理档案的质量审核

浙江华东工程咨询有限公司受华东琅琊山抽水蓄能有限责任公司委托，承担琅琊山抽水蓄能电站所有土建施工、金属结构制作安装、机电设备安装项目的监理工作。

监理单位在竣工归档资料管理工作中，根据有关规定和要求，按照“统一领导，统一管理，统一规格，统一标准”的原则，在认真整理、编制、提交监理单位负责的相关归档文件资料的同时，检查、督促施工单位做好竣工资料的整理、编制工作，对施工档案的质量进行了严格审查把关。

（一）归档文件质量要求

1. 基本要求

（1）项目应归档文件材料齐全，并制作光盘一套。向建设单位移交的项目档案，交接手续齐全、完备。项目监理归档文件资料齐全、完整。施工归档文件及竣工图齐全、完整，满足建设单位管理及运行的需要，工程质量评估报告及监理工作总结完整齐备。电子文件与纸质文件一一对应。

（2）有确保竣工归档文件资料真实、准确的有效措施和相关制度。各专业监理工程师依据《工程档案管理实施细则》收集、整理立卷后，总监理工程师进行全面审查，确认符合要求后，提交监理公司审核。经监理公司审核、确认后归档。

（3）归档文件材料真实、准确，反映施工、监理过程和竣工验收过程的实际情况；文件材料记载齐全，数据真实、准确；签章手续完备。

（4）竣工资料的档案号、编写卷内页号、卷内目录、卷内备考表和案卷封面等均按要求进行编制，字迹清楚、图样清晰、图表整洁、签章手续完备。竣工资料一式两份，其中一份为原件；竣工图一式三份。

2. 竣工图编制要求

（1）设计图纸有电子版的，以设计电子版为基础进行修改、审核和制作，同时作出如下规定：①原施工图上设计单位的图签全部删除，改为施工单位的竣工图图签，格式与竣工图编制要求一致；②图号仍采用施工图纸号码，但须在后面加注“（竣）”；③在竣工图说明中应将原施工图以外的编制依据全部罗列出来，具体包括设计修改通知、技术联系单、现场签证单、监理工程师现场指令和会议纪要等；④编制完成的竣工图纸打印出来后，施工单位的编制人、技术负责人对竣工图按规定审查并完成签字；⑤监理工程师对施工单位审查合格并签字的竣工图进行审查确认，满足要求的由审查人签字后向建设单位移交。

（2）设计图纸没有电子版且施工图没有变更修改的，在施工蓝图上加盖竣工图章，施工单位相关人员和监理审核人在图章处签字确认，蓝图即作为竣工图。

（3）设计图纸没有电子版，局部进行了修改变更但变更不大且在蓝图上可以补充修改的，在修改部位加盖红章并标注修改依据，并在图上盖上竣工图章，相关人员签字后作为竣工图。

（4）没有电子版且变更较大，如结构形式改变、平面布置改变等重大变更，不宜在原图上修改的，应重新绘制。

（二）质量审核情况

1. 竣工图

大部分设计图纸均有电子底版，故绝大部分竣工图是采用以电子版为基础进行修改、审查、制作的方式完成编制的。在竣工图审查过程中，以下问题比较突出并多次出现：①有设计通知、技术联系单等对原设计图纸进行修改，但竣工图中未予体现，即未完全修改完成；②根据设计通知、技术联系单等在原设计图纸上进行了修改，但案卷编制说明表和竣工图说明中未能体现；③在案卷编制说明表和竣工图说明中有修改依据，但竣工图细部未作修改；④案卷编制说明和竣工图说明不吻合；⑤竣工图中修改内容与变更的设计通知、技术联系单内容不一致。在监理的把关和检查督促下，以上问题得到了及时整改和有效解决，保证了竣工图的归档移交质量。

2. 项目监理归档文件

（1）工程项目监理过程的监理工程师通知单、监理工作联系单、监理工程师通知回执单齐全，整改项目均形成闭环，能客观反映项目监理的实际状态。

（2）施工图会审纪要、协调会议纪要齐全，能反映会议的真实情况，并有会议签到单。

（3）监理月报齐全。月报编写规范，能按监理公司贯标文件的要求编写，具有一定深度，真实反映施工监理过程的进度、质量、安全、投资和组织协调工作。

（4）监理日记齐全，能真实反映现场施工过程监理工作的情况。发现问题、解决问题，均有完整记录，具有备查的使用价值。

（5）质量控制文件材料齐全。主要是：质量控制措施；质量控制程序；质量控制制度，包括文件资料审查制度、材料构配件/设备实物检查制度以及现场巡视、见证、旁站等制度。

（6）进度控制文件材料齐全。主要有：单位工程进度控制一级网络图和二级网络图，季度计划进度、月度计划进度和工程施工形象进度，月报表、周报表。

（7）投资控制文件材料齐全。每月审查一次施工单位提交的工程支付报审表和统计月表。

3. 施工质量有关文件

（1）与质量有关的报审文件和材料，均有监理单位的审核签字。

（2）单元工程各道工序现场检查验收，均有现场监理签单记录和监理日志。

（3）组织中间验收，均有验收组织机构、验收方案、验收记录、验收报告。

（4）各分部工程监理过程提出的整改、中间验收提出的整改、竣工验收提出的整改等问题，均有施工单位提交的监理工程通知回执单监理复检意见。

（三）审核效果

监理工程师对审核合格的竣工资料及时签字确认，对过程中发现的问题详细记录，并将问题记录在需退回重做的不合格竣工资料中要求逐项整改，工作进展情况及时向建设单位汇报。同时，对施工单位竣工图编制过程中存在的问题和困难，积极与建设单位协商以尽可能帮助解决，并多次提出合理化建议，协助施工单位加快了编制进度，也保证了竣工资料的质量。经过多次反复修改和审查，施工单位编制的竣工资料最终达到归档文件质量要求。

监理单位对工程档案质量的审核结论：经审查，琅琊山抽水蓄能电站工程档案质量符合现行档案归档规范要求，工程归档资料规范、完整、真实、齐全，符合国家、地方、行业及主管部门关于竣工资料归档验收的有关规定，具备工程档案专项验收条件。

2009年6月10日，琅琊山抽水蓄能电站工程档案资料顺利通过国家档案局主持的工程档案专项验收，其中项目监理档案质量审核工作的做法和成效得到了与会有关领导和专家的肯定和好评。

（浙江华东水电工程咨询公司　王　伟）

思林水电站导流洞工程施工监理

思林水电站采用枯期围堰挡水、隧洞过流的导流方式。导流隧洞共布置有2条，左右岸各1条，过流断面尺寸13m×15m（宽×高）。左岸导流隧洞全长932m，进出口明渠混凝土段分别长41.16m、25.0m，进出口高程分别为370.0m、364.0m。右岸导流隧洞全长820.89m，进水塔高47.5m，内设平面闸门，进出口明洞分别长15.0m、70.0m，进出口明渠混凝土段分别长20m、35m，进出口高程分别为364.0m、362.0m。

（一）监理工作的难点

（1）前期三通一平准备不足。左、右岸导流隧洞分别于2004年11月5日和2004年10月26日开工，业主负责架设的10kV线路到12月26日才架通；受大雪及冰冻等恶劣天气影响，2005年1月10日～3月7日又停电，影响了施工工期约2个月。在上游面，1号公路2005年4月底才具备重车通车条件，到小溪沟渣场的4号公路2005年3月21日才基本可运渣；下游面，2号公路2005年3月底才具备重车通车条件，3号公路2005年10月路面混凝土才浇筑完成；上下索桥2005年2月才具备通车条件。

（2）工程地质条件复杂。工程建于石灰岩地区，导流洞进口位于吴家坪组 P_{2w}^{2}、P_{2w}^{4} 地层，为陡坡地形，局部为陡壁，斜至顺向坡（左岸导流洞进口岩层还向后及外侧倾倒），左右岸导流洞进口在开挖过程中均发生了不同程度的塌方。隧洞埋深5～130m，出口部分洞段上覆或侧向岩体厚度不足一倍洞径；由上游至下游，沿线穿越吴家坪组 $P_{2w}^{1\sim5}$、长兴组 P_{2c}、夜朗组 T_{1y}^{1-3}、永宁镇组 T_{1yn}^{1-2} 夹煤层砂岩、含燧石结核泥晶灰岩、硅质岩与硅质黏土岩互层夹黏土质灰岩、含燧石结核灰岩夹黏土岩、含石英黏土质灰岩夹黏土岩及炭质页岩、方解石化黏土岩夹极薄层泥质灰岩、泥晶灰岩、白云质灰岩、灰岩、泥质灰岩、黏土岩夹薄层灰岩及石膏层、粉晶灰岩、灰质白云岩、角砾状白云岩等地层，其中 P_{2w}^{5}、T_{1y}^{1}、T_{1y}^{3}、T_{1yn2}^{-1}，岩性复杂，岩层薄，岩质软弱，成洞条件差，一般属Ⅳ～Ⅴ类围岩；P_{2w}^{2}、P_{2w}^{4}、P_{2c}、T_{1y}^{2-1}、T_{1y}^{2-3} 中上部岩质较坚硬，但岩层较薄，裂隙发育，洞室围岩一般为Ⅳ～Ⅴ类。下游段岩层在地壳运动中发生了倒转，岩层薄及破碎，易发生掉块及塌方。左岸导流洞受K30及K31岩溶系统影响，在开挖至0＋196～0＋252洞段发生了较大的岩溶涌水及岩体塌方。出口地形亦为一陡斜坡，由 T_{1yn}^{2-1} 角砾状白云岩、T_{1yn}^{2-2} 底部薄层灰岩组成，斜至顺向坡（岩层倾角为30°～40°）；坡面局部有崩积碎块石及冲积砂砾石覆盖。左岸导流洞Ⅳ、Ⅴ类围岩占总长24％，Ⅲ类围岩占52％，Ⅱ类围岩占24％。右岸导流洞Ⅳ、Ⅴ类围岩占总长25％，Ⅲ类围岩占52％，Ⅱ类围岩占23％。

（3）工程进度与施工质量的矛盾突出。导流洞为大型临时工程，工期紧、任务重。左岸导流隧洞于2004年11月5日开工，2006年4月施工结束；右岸导流隧洞于2004年10月26日开工，2005年11月20日完工。由于前期道路不通、停电及溶洞涌水等原因造成了工期延误，右岸导流洞工程有效工期仅有10个月左右。施工方为了抢进度，容易忽视质量，工程进度与施工质量的矛盾突出。

（二）监理的对策

针对导流洞工程中存在的难点，采取的监理对策如下：

（1）配备经验丰富及责任心强的监理人员。监理工作的成效取决于监理人员的经验、素质和责任心。为确保导流洞工程监理工作更好地开展，监理部选派了具有丰富监理经验、工程经验和较强责任心的水工、施工、地质、试验、灌浆等专业监理工程师，组建了导流洞工程监理站，这从组织及人员配备方面确保了导流洞工程的顺利进行。

（2）要求施工单位建立健全管理体系。施工单位管理体系的有效运行是确保导流洞工程顺利进行的关键，包括组织管理体系、质量管理体系、安全管理体系等。监理部要求施工单位在导流洞工程开始实施前报送相应的管理体系，并认真检查其管理体系的有效性，严格检查落实现场人员、设备配备及到位情况，在保证导流洞施工强度和施工进度的前提下才允许开工。

（3）严格审查施工组织设计。要求施工布置、方法合理，资源配置恰当，对特殊地质洞段的开挖支护、岩溶涌水及防洪度汛措施等方面的合理性进行严格审查。

（4）搞好质量控制，以质量保进度。在工程建设监理工作中，监理部始终贯彻执行“在监理中服务、在服务中监理，精心组织、周密计划，按期保质地建好电站”的要求。监理部不仅依靠较为完善的制度规范监理人员的行为，而且不断提高监理理念，提高监理人员的综合素质，加强关键点的控制，以良好的工作质量确保施工质量和施工安全。同时在施工监理中，坚持实行施工现场不间断巡检、关键线路重点部位的旁站监理；坚持“事前、事中、事后”三控制，注重主动监理和超前监理；坚持本道工序不合格就不能转入下道工序施工的质量控制、行使质量问题一票否决权、行使安全问题一票否决权等制度。这些质量安全措施的执行对防止质量隐患、避免工程质量事故的发生起到重要的作用，保证了工程的顺利实施。在质量管理工作中结合工程实际，严格对项目施工质量进行监督控制，将质量责任层层落实到个人，做到全员、全方位、全过程的有效控制，将质量隐患消灭在萌芽状态，消灭质量事故，坚决杜绝由于质量事故引起的误工、返工、安全等造成的损失，确保工程质量合格率达100%，工程总体达到优良水平。

（5）制定控制性进度计划，确保关键结点的实现。监理部商业主、设计及施工制定控制性进度计划，组织参建四方讨论通过后实施，确保关键结点的实现，如右岸导流洞工程施工中紧抓以下关键结点进行控制：①隧洞中导洞，2005年4月30日贯通（实际于2005年4月27日完成）；②洞挖工程，2005年6月30日全部完成（实际完成日期为2005年7月20日）；③主洞混凝土施工，2005年7月初开始，10月底完成（实际2005年8月初开始，11月6日完成）。

（6）将目标分解到日，以日完成量保总目标。制定7天进度计划，每周组织召开例会，检查上周进度计划完成情况，若未按时完成，则找出原因，并采取必要的赶工措施。在施工的关键时段，采用了日控制计划，进行检查落实。

（7）加大工程协调力度。由于导流洞工程工期紧，为保证施工进度按计划进行，确保工程施工质量安全，监理部做了以下协调工作：①施工场地、交通、爆破作业、与相邻单位之间的沟通；②设备、施工材料调配；③施工中遇到技术问题，召开参建四方参加的技术专题会议；④施工方与业主之间的索赔。

（8）积极推进技术创新，提工程优化建议，采用新材料、新工艺。监理四控制工作中的首要任务是进度控制，积极推进技术创新，提工程优化建议，采用新材料、新工艺是进度控制的重要手段。监理通过协调，充分发挥了参建各方的技术优势，采用了洞口改明挖为洞挖减少开挖量及支护、优选2005年度汛方案、优化4条尾水洞与右岸导流洞相交段的施工、优选导流洞九级滩泥岩段的开挖及支护方案、优化导流洞混凝土衬砌、大量简易钢模台车运用于洞内混凝土衬砌、右岸导流洞进口岩塞拆除方案的优选等技术创新、工程优化、新材料及新工艺运用，确保了右岸导流洞按期完工。

（9）抓好分包商的资质审查，对技术力量薄弱的队伍坚决清退出场。右岸导流洞工程最初引进了4家分包商，其中施工进口工作面的两家由于资质较差，进度严重滞后。监理部要求主承包商采取果断措施，将其清退出场，重新引进信誉度好的分包商，扭转了被动局面。

（中国水电顾问集团昆明勘测设计研究院
宗宪全　刘富万　王国强）

缅甸瑞丽江一级水电站的开发建设模式

（一）工程建设概况

瑞丽江一级水电站位于缅甸北部掸邦境内紧邻中缅边界的瑞丽江干流上，至中国境内的瑞丽的公路里程为94km，开发任务以发电为单一开发目标。

2003年8月8日，中国云南省机械设备进出口公司和缅甸电力部水电局在仰光签署了由前者承建缅甸瑞丽江水电站的合同，即采用EPC模式开发。电站装机容量为400MW，年发电量30.22亿kW·h，占缅甸全国现有发电总装机容量的35%。

2004年2月15日，瑞丽江一级水电站工程开工，但工程开工后进展缓慢。2004～2005年，主要进行了电站进水口开挖、导流洞开挖、电站进水口高边坡加固、厂区一期开挖、施工支洞和1832m引水隧洞的上部开挖，2005年7月起，引水系统基本处于停工状况。

2006年5月，经中国云南省机械设备进出口公司与缅甸电力部水电局协商，将本工程运作改为BOT项目，并拟将该工程扩建为6台100MW机组电站。同年8月，由云南华能澜沧江水电有限公司、云南省电网公司和云南省机械设备进出口公司共同组建了云南联合电力开发有限公司，按照BOT方式进行该项目的投资建设和运行管理。中国水电顾问集团昆明勘测设计研究院于2006年8月完成《6×100MW可行性研究报告》，并通过了国内评审。

缅甸瑞丽江一级水电站在2006年8月由云南联合电力开发有限公司实行建设管理后，当年12月就实现大江截流；2007 年 9 月，引水隧洞、调压井、压力管道全线贯通；2008 年 9 月，首台机组发电；2009 年 4 月 29 日，最后一台机组如期投产发电。

（二）采用 BOT 模式后的变化

电站自 2006 年 8 月由 EPC 转为 BOT 模式后，作为云南联合电力开发有限公司第一个走向境外的大型项目，集成了国内水电开发企业的优势。以中国发电集团（华能澜沧江水电有限公司）为电站建设主体、云南省电网公司电网售电、云南省机械设备进出口公司为物资进出口的管理模式进行运作，翻开了该电站建设崭新的一页。由此，电站建设全面铺开，并以日新月异的速度进展。

该电站布置是典型的引水式电站，7.2km 的河道有 300m 落差，仅通过一个 47m 高的小坝、5km 裁弯取直的引水隧洞和 1.1km 的压力钢管道就获得了该落差，再加上充沛的径流，使得本电站电能量指标达到世界少有的资源条件。经中国水电顾问集团昆明勘测设计研究院扩机可行性研究，该电站装机 6×100MW，年发电量 40.33 亿 kW·h，达到了天生桥一级水电站（装机容量 1200MW）的发电量水平，接近缅甸 2004 年全年的发电量，并对电站首部枢纽布置、边坡加固、引水系统、厂区枢纽布置等都进行优化，使电站设计更加合理、经济和科学，而总投资还不到 30 亿元，其经济指标相当优越。

2006 年 8 月复工时，导流洞下部洞段还未开挖，近 120m 洞段还有大量欠挖，顶部还有大量回填木头，并有 30 多米的塌方洞段要处理。但只到 2006 年 12 月 10 日，4 个月时间，导流进出口闸室、引洞、洞身衬砌灌浆、出口明渠开挖、衬砌等全部完成，并实现了截流。近 13km 的地下洞室（导流洞、引水隧洞、调压井、压力管道、施工支洞、压力斜井和排水洞等），在短短的 2 年内，一年贯通，一年浇筑完成，在中国水电建设史上并不多见。工程地处龙陵、瑞丽大断裂边缘，其次生二级构造面安德鲁大断裂最近的只有 100～300m，在沿引水隧洞短短的 20～30m 以内地质条件就出现了突变，其地质条件可谓复杂。然而中国水利水电第十四工程局有限公司精心组织，克服重重困难，约 202m 的上斜井在 3 个月内攻克了，90m 高、内径 16.5m、开挖直径 18.5m 且有 40m 较差地质的调压井，如期完成了开挖、混凝土浇筑并封顶。近 7000t 的压力钢管，包括承担 400m 的水头的钢管，实现了完全由中国人设计、生产制作和现场安装。

在复工不到 2 年的时间内，完成了瑞丽江一级电站超过 90%的工程量，不得不说是个奇迹。

（三）BOT 开发模式的前景

国际水电开发的主要模式有 EPC 模式和 BOT 模式。如果该国国力好，这两种开发模式都适用。但如果该国国力较弱，而资源条件又非常丰富，通过 BOT 模式能充分发挥资源的优势，可以较快实现预期目标。对有资源但缺乏开发资金和技术的国家，EPC 开发模式不太适合，资金融合、项目运作、建设管理、原材料供应等都有不少困难。因此，对于像缅甸这种欠发展但富有资源的国家，采用 BOT 模式进行国际合作开发水电，有很好的前景。

缅甸近年来进行前期研究和调查的电站有伊洛瓦底江的密松、萨尔温江上的滚弄、瑙帕以及瑞丽江的二级、三级、曼栋等，它们距中国边境都很近。在不远的将来，依托中国水电开发的成功经验和“大湄公河次区域”（GMS）的广泛合作，这些电站开发将成为热点地区。

（中国水电顾问集团昆明勘测设计研究院　彭富平）

水利水电建设项目的后评价

按照工程项目建设程序的定义，后评价是基本建设程序的最后一个环节，是项目实施阶段管理的延伸，是对项目建设和运营是否达到投资决策时所确定目标的判断。水利水电建设项目作为国家基础性项目，由于建设周期长、投资额大、社会影响广泛、社会问题复杂等特点，项目的实际情况与项目前评价的预测数据发生偏离，需要后评价建立科学、合理的指标体系检验预测结论真实性与可靠性，通过综合评价评判效果，反映工程决策者的管理水平与投资效果，并给予修正指导。

水利水电建设项目后评价是在项目后评价时点，根据过程后评价、技术后评价、财务后评价、国民经济后评价、影响后评价的指标或结论，运用系统工程思想和多目标决策方法或模型，论证项目的综合效益水平，得出项目实施成功与否的结论，为改善项目的运营管理及提高项目的效益水平提出对策，为今后项目管理提供经验教训。

（一）水利水电建设项目后评价的内容及指标体系

水利水电项目后评价的内容应包含从项目提出到项目投产运行的全过程，也可以根据项目的具体情况和评价的侧重有所增删，主要包含以下几个方面：

1. 过程后评价

过程后评价是根据项目的结果和作用，对项目周期的各个环节进行回顾和检查，对项目的实施效率作出评价，水利水电项目过程后评价基本内容为前期工作评价、建设实施评价、运行与管理评价，评价指标有决策周期、建设周期、工程优良品率、投资总额、投资总额变化率、单位生产能力投资。

2. 技术后评价

技术后评价主要是对工艺技术流程、技术装备选择的可靠性、适用性、配套性、先进性的再分析。水利水电项目技术后评价反映的特征参数主要内容有项目生产能力、达产年限、项目生产成本、装机容量、设备利用率、年发电量、水库的总库容、防洪库容、兴利库容、水库各种特征水位高低、水库调节流量及水量利用率、保证出力、灌溉面积、通航能力（吨位及其通航长度）、供水及水产等情况。

3. 效益后评价

效益后评价包括项目的财务评价和国民经济评价。从项目投资者的角度考虑，需要对水利水电项目的盈利能力、偿债能力、生存能力进行财务评价，计算的特征参数包括财务内部收益率、财务净现值、投资回收期、投资利润率、投资利税率、借款偿还期、资产负债率、流动比率等。从国家宏观经济角度出发，分析水利水电项目对国家贡献以及需要国家为项目付出的代价，以影子价格为工具在财务评价的基础上进行国民经济评价，计算的主要参数为经济内部收益率、经济净现值、经济效益费用比。

4. 影响后评价

影响后评价包括社会影响评价、移民安置影响评价、环境影响评价、水土保持影响评价等。

（1）社会影响评价主要评价项目对所涉及的受益者和受损者群体的影响，分析水利水电项目对生产力布局、产业结构、土地利用及地区国民经济、人民生活水平等方面的影响。主要评价指标包含 GDP 增长率、地区社会总产值增长率、地区财政收入增长率、新增发电量、新增水量、灌溉面积增长率、水产增收效益、旅游交通程度、社会就业状况、人口素质变化、生活质量等。

（2）移民安置影响评价主要对移民安置工程实施和政策落实及后期移民扶持执行效果进行评价。主要评价指标包括生产资料指标（人均农用地面积、人均后备资源占有量、人均矿产资源占有量、工矿企业效益增量、人均粮食产量）、社会经济发展指标（移民人均安置费用及补偿费用、安置区人均纯收入及年增长率、安置区年社会生产总产值及增长率、移民投资效果系数、土地净效益增量物质投入水平、用电满足程度）、人文方面（安置移民总数及稳固率、人均经济收入差值比、地区劳动就业增长率、地区居民生产生活水平指数、涉及文化教育、医疗卫生、居住环境及配套设施的改善程度、涉及社会稳定、民族关系、宗教信仰、迁建对移民思想观念改变等影响）。

（3）环境影响评价和水土保持影响评价主要阐述建成后的水利水电项目已经发生和未来可能产生的相关影响，并对照前评估的结论进行对比评价，提出减免不利影响的措施。环境影响评价一般包括项目的污染控制、地区环境质量、自然资源利用和保护、区域生态平衡和环境管理；评价内容主要包括水环境评价、大气环境评价、声环境评价、固体废弃物环境评价、生态环境评价；评价指标有气候变化情况、水温及水质影响、环境地质影响程度、库区淤积及下游冲刷影响、生物物种变化、人体健康影响、自然景观文物古迹影响、移民及施工造成环境的影响等。水土保持影响评价一般包括水保工程执行情况、实施后水土流失的防治效果、水土保持效果、水土流失监测体系的运行、水保设施运行和管理；评价指标主要有扰动土地治理率、水土流失控制情况、拦渣率、林草覆盖率、植被恢复指数等。

5. 目标及可持续性评价

项目目标评价包括对项目原定目标的实现程度、适应性等进行分析。对照项目立项时确定的目标，从工程建成、技术建成、经济建成等方面分析项目的实施结果和作用，分析项目目标实现程度，评价与原定目标的偏离程度。目标评价的指标通常包含在技术参数和经济指标范畴之内。

可持续性评价是指项目的建设资金投入完成之后，既定目标是否还能持续，是否可以持续发展，接受投资的项目业主是否愿意并可能依靠自身的力量继续去实现既定目标，项目是否具有可重复性，是否可在未来以同样的方式建设同类项目。从影响水利水电项目外部、内在因素分析项目的可持续性运转条件，评价内容大致包含项目相关的持续性、经济增长的持续性、环境功能的持续性、管理体系的持续性。主要指标有投资环境改善程度、项目的外部效益、技术进步效益、生产技术清洁性、区域环境效益、相关群体的满意度、项目运行持续能力等。

（二）水利水电建设项目后评价的方法

目前，后评价的方法主要是对比法、逻辑框架法、综合评价法。

1. 对比法

对比法又称指标对比法，是水利水电建设项目后评价中最常用的方法，它通过项目运营时各指标的实际值与项目决策时的预测值的对比，对项目进行评价。对比法又可分为“前后对比法”和“有无对比法”。“前后对比”是将项目实施之前与项目完成之后的情况加以对比，找出差异原因，以确定项目效益的一种方法。这种对比用于揭示项目的计划、决策和实施质量，是项目效益评价应遵循的原则。“有无对比”是将项目实际发生的情况与没有运行投资项目可能发生的情况进行对比，以度量项目的真实效益、影响和作用。由于水利水电项目是大型社会经济项目，实施后的效果不仅仅是项目的效果和作用，还有项目以外多种因素的影响，运用有无对比法更好地分清项目本身的影响和非项目因素的影响。

2. 逻辑框架法

逻辑框架法用来总结一个项目的诸多因素（包括投入、产出、目的和宏观目标）之间的因果关系（如资源、活动、产出)、评价发展方向（如目的、宏观目标)，其核心是根据事物的因果逻辑关系，即“如果”提供了某些条件，“则”会产生某种结果，这些条件包括事物内在的因素和事物所需要的外部条件，结果分析包括项目的效率、效果、影响和可持续性等方面。此方法强调运用因果关系的思维模式提出主要问题（目标)，分析主要缺陷（风险)，为决策者提供更为客观、科学的信息；同时又能系统而符合逻辑地全面分析事物的各个方面有利于加强项目各个方面的沟通和管理，因此对于定性分析水利水电建设项目实施后的各种效益和影响非常适用。

3. 综合评价法

综合评价法是将评价内容分解成各子项目，对各子项目建立相应的评价指标体系，将各子项目后评价指标的实际值与相应的各级标准值进行比较，运用系统工程的思想和方法，定性分析与定量分析相结合，最终将各子项目的评价转化为一个能够客观、全面的整体性评价。目前综合评价的方法很多，大体可以分为两类：一类是偏向定性分析的方法，如主成分分析法、Delphi 法、层次分析法、成功度综合评价法等；另一类是采用定量分析的方法，如综合指数法、模糊综合评判法、灰色关联层次法、DEA 模型法等。

（三）基于模糊多层次综合评价的方法及理论

水利水电建设项目可以认为是一个系统工程，按照系统工程理论，当一个系统复杂性增大时，对它精确的能力将减低，在达到一定阈值时，复杂性和精确性将相互排斥，即复杂性和精确性成反比例关系。用传统数学方法难以解决这类问题，但是利用综合评价具有多方面性、多层次性、模糊性和同一层次各因素不同重要性的特点，将模糊数学与层次分析法相结合而产生的模糊多层次综合评判原理，常运用于目前很多水利水电项目综合后评价，可以较好地解决上述问题。

水利水电建设项目因涉及技术与经济、环境与管理以及社会经济效益和目标可持续性能力等诸多因素，评价内容又包含定量和定性分析，使得有些指标是无法直接进行量化的，只能通过专家打分进行间接的量化，具有不确定性或单一性，而专家打分只能给定一个大致区间，没有明确外延，具有一定的模糊性，故采用模糊多层次综合评价理论解决这一矛盾。模糊多层次综合评价方法的思路为：运用 Delphi 法匿名讨论及统计，优化绩效评价指标，拟定出绩效评价指标体系；建立评价指标递阶层次结构；运用 Delphi 法确定评价指标相对重要性程度，并运用模糊多层次分析法计算评价指标体系各层次的权重；根据多层次模糊综合评判法原理，运用隶属函数给出评价指标评估值矩阵；依据模糊数学理论形成评判矩阵；进行模糊运算，得出综合评价结果。

（四）水利水电建设项目后评价的应用

项目后评价的发展应用，经历了从单一的财务评价向过程评价、效益评价、影响评价、可持续评价发展的过程，从单目标内容评价向多目标内容综合评价发展的过程。后评价应用的范围也从不同的评价角度出发各有侧重，比如从项目投资的角度，可侧重于为未来投资决策服务；从银行贷款的角度，可侧重于提高贷款项目决策管理水平及信贷资产质量；从技术的角度，可侧重于项目的安全稳定及适用性和新技术的推广；从社会和环境的角度，可侧重项目对社会的贡献以及促进人与自然和谐统一。水利水电建设项目涉及的面比较广，进行项目后评价时，既要重视技术和经济方面的内容评价，还必须对项目的社会外部效果进行充分的论证和分析。因此，水利水电项目后评价应用除了对整体项目进行后评价外，逐渐将移民安置后评价、项目环境影响后评价、项目水土保持影响后评价等作为专项后评价进行研究。

随着水利水电行业的发展，决策者和使用者对后评价会有新的要求，后评价的内容也必须根据行业要求而有所增加，比如水利水电建设项目的生态环境影响具有流域性和区域性特征，许多影响之间具有相关性，影响的效应具有长期性和复杂性，进行流域内水电工程之间以及流域中其他开发项目环境影响后评价综合分析整个流域生态系统结构、功能环境的累积效应及累积影响；跨区域引调水工程的建成极大影响受水地区的用水效率和经济产业结构，以及水源区域的水资源的承载力和生态系统，则需要对水资源可持续性利用进行后评价，从而分析水资源合理配置对国民经济持续发展的影响。

目前水利水电项目后评价重视不够，即便是有的项目进行了后评价工作，但只注重形式，后评价成果的反馈和扩散效果未能发挥。同时调查表明，目前后评价并不是很成功，因为很多项目的投资者对评价结果缺少信心，评价的结果并没有有效地用于后继项目的决策和企业运营状况及投资环境的改善。因此，在这种形势下需要行业主管部门规范后评价的操作和应用的推广，使后评价成为一种“需求驱动型”的工作反馈机制，满足不同决策层的要求，以便使水利水电项目后评价的作用能更好地发挥出来。

（中国水电顾问集团西北勘测设计研究院
赵刚毅 陈军强 周 俊）

对铁川桥水电站工程总承包的初步认识

（一）工程建设概况

铁川桥水电站为云南大理州宾川县与楚雄州大姚县交界的金沙江一级支流渔泡江上第四级电站，正常蓄水位 1272m，相应库容 2529 万 m^3，装机容量 42MW，多年平均发电量 12 490 万 kW·h。

项目核准前业主为大理辉煌水电有限公司，勘察设计工作由中国水利水电第十四工程局科研设计院完成，2007 年 1 月通过预可行性研究审查，8 月通过可行性研究审查，11 月取得项目核准批复。2008 年 4 月，中国大唐集团公司云南分公司取得电站开发权，6 月进行总承包邀请招标，11 月大唐宾川水电有限责任公司与中国水电顾问集团中南勘测设计研究院签订了《云南渔泡江铁川桥水电站工程设计、采购和施工（EPC）总承包合同》。

（二）工程总承包优点

工程总承包是发包人将建设工程的勘察、设计、施工和采购等工程建设的全部任务一并发包给一个具备相应总承包资质条件的承包人，由该承包人对工程建设的全过程向发包人负责，直至工程竣工，向发包人交付经验收合格符合发包人要求的建设工程的发承包方式，其优点包括：①有利于理清工程建设中业主与承包商、勘察设计与业主、总包与分包、执法机构与市场主体间的各种复杂关系；②有利于优化资源配置；③有利于优化组织结构并形成规模经济；④有利于政府部门打破行业垄断，并集中力量解决建筑市场最突出的问题，也有利于实行风险保障制度；⑤有利于控制工程造价，提升招标层次；⑥有利于提高全面履约能力，并确保质量和工期；⑦有利于推动管理现代化。

（三）值得注意的问题

本工程采用的“业主、监理、总承包”工程建设管理模式，在中国五大发电集团公司中尚属首次，处于启蒙和探索水电工程建设总承包管理经验阶段。回顾一年多来铁川桥水电站工程建设情况，有如下问题值得注意：

（1）可行性研究问题多，项目核准草率。经中国水电顾问集团下属几家设计院的多次咨询，专家认为铁川桥水电站勘察设计工作深度尚未达到现行规程规范要求，特别是地质勘察工作不到位，主要工程地质问题未查明，报告中漏项、错项多，需对可行性研究报告进行必要的补充复核工作。总承包单位在电站规模和特征水位、枢纽布置总格局不变的条件下对工程进行了复核设计研究，其成果在以下几方面与可行性研究出入较大：①坝址多年平均流量 23.6m^3/s 较原可行性研究 28.45m^3/s 减少 21%，坝址洪峰流量较可行性研究成果大 4%～17%，正常蓄水位对应库容 2529 万 m^3、死库容 1294 万 m^3、调节库容 1235 万 m^3 较可行性研究的 7600 万 m^3、4640 万 m^3、2960 万 m^3 减幅近 60%；②经专门地震安全性评价，电站场地地震基本烈度为Ⅷ度，提高了一度；③在装机容量 42MW 不变情况下，多年平均发电量 12 490 万 kW·h、装机利用小时 2975h，较可行性研究提出的 19 328 万 kW·h、4602h 也有大的降幅。

（2）参建单位分散，工作效率较低。开工建设一年多来，业主住在大姚县城，总承包和监理住在大姚县三岔河乡，施工分包商住在铁川桥。大姚县城与三岔河乡相距 50km，有县道相连，三岔河乡与铁川桥相距 40km，2009 年 5 月才有简易公路连通。正常情况下，从县城到三岔河乡单程需 1h，从县城到工地单程需 2.5h。由于参建单位分散，战线长，路上耗时多，有效的工作时间大大减少，导致工作效率低。

（3）铁川桥电站工程建设监理合同金额 320 万元，按 12 人 35 个月计算，人均月费用不到 8000 元，按此价格，请不到素质高的监理人员。从过去一年多的实际工作来看，监理工作力度弱，监理效果较差，难以形成小业主、大监理的有利于管理的局面。

（4）铁川桥水电站小，施工分承包商企业大、项目多，对本项目的重视程度不够，投入的人员和设备不足，工程安全、质量、进度等的保证性较差。

（5）总承包方面对铁川桥这样一个先天不足、各种建设条件都很差的水电项目，尽管作出了很大努力，制定了管理办法，找出了现场存在的问题，提出了解决办法和措施，但仍旧难落实，难实现闭合管理，对施工分承包商控制效果和管理效果不佳。

（四）结语

虽然铁川桥水电站工程建设存在这样或那样的困难和问题，但随着参建各单位的共同努力和投入，各项措施正在逐步得到落实，困难和问题也正在逐步得到解决。目前大江已截流，大坝混凝土在上升，项目建设的安全、质量、进度、投资仍然处于可控在控范围。选择总承包的管理模式进行该电站建设的思路和方向是正确的，铁川桥水电站一定会保质、保量如期完成建设任务。

（大唐宾川水电有限责任公司　李孟德）

龙滩水电工程信息化管理体系

（一）概况

通过对外部环境的资源整合以及对龙滩水电工程

管理模式的深入分析，依托互联网、大型关系型数据库、面向对象、可视化等先进信息技术，龙滩水电工程成功建立以“资源共享、协同合作、高效迅捷”为特色的信息化管理体系。龙滩水电工程信息化管理体系由7类业务系统组成：

1. 龙滩工程信息管理系统

该系统是龙滩水电工程信息化管理体系中的核心系统，按功能分为7个子系统共36个功能模块。此系统在建设过程中体现以工程项目管理为基础，以投资控制为核心，以合同管理为纽带，以进度控制为主线的开发原则；在使用过程中，内部功能模块能够动态调整和优化配置，协调参建各方，为工程管理提供灵活的决策支持，达到全面控制施工进度、投资成本和质量安全，实现科学化、现代化管理的目的。

2. 物资设备实时调运指挥系统

该系统能采集散装水泥、粉煤灰等材料需、产、运、储、供、管等有关信息，实现散装水泥、粉煤灰从物资需求计划、资源综合平衡、采购计划制定、调运方案生成、方案执行监控、应急处理到信息查询、统计分析、报表编制和公共信息发布等各环节、全过程统一管理的实时动态调度管理。系统包括南丹转运站和调度中心两大子系统。此系统自投入运行以来，较好地满足了龙滩水电工程物资设备调运业务的特点和需要。

3. 办公自动化系统

该系统用于处理龙滩水电工程管理中的行政事务管理，由20个功能模块组成，涵盖公文流转、个人信息、公共信息、设备管理、党群工作、监察审计等多个方面。此系统的应用，对于加快公文流转，节约办公成本，传达公司政策具有良好效果。

4. 远光财务管理系统

该系统与新会计准则接轨，能够快捷处理工程复杂账务；能够高效管理工程固定资产；能够快速发放员工工资；能够自动生成各种报表。

5. 超越2000档案管理系统

在龙滩水电工程建设中，所有工程合同中均约定预留合同价款3%～5%的工程尾留价款，作为工程竣工资料、项目档案的保证金。该系统的应用，是对龙滩水电工程各类档案从处理到档案组卷、整理、编目、打印、编研、鉴定以及库房管理全过程的计算机管理，这对于实现管理要求，规范并完善工程档案起到关键作用。

6. 宏景世纪HRP人力资源管理信息系统

该系统具体包括组织管理、人事管理、招聘管理、薪酬管理、福利管理、时间管理、培训发展、绩效管理以及动态报表等多个业务模块。系统在功能上涵盖了人力资源管理的全部过程，从战略、管控、流程驱动、事务等4个层面全面支持龙滩水电工程人力资源管理建设。

7. 公司网站

龙滩公司网站用于发布龙滩水电工程的各类新闻动态、工程进展情况和招投标公告等重要信息。网站自投入使用以来，至今点击率已过36万人·次，成为龙滩公司对外宣传的重要窗口。

（二）主要创新点

1. 管理技术的创新

水电管理过程中，对于曾经很多需要手工统计核对的数据，现在由各业务应用系统自动归类汇总，而统一的数据库又确保了数据的完整性和唯一性，使员工从烦琐重复的事务性劳动中解放出来，能把更多时间投入到思考性的管理工作之中。

2. 管理模式的创新

改变传统管理模式下管理手段粗放和管理信息滞后的弊病，实现工程管理信息实时监控，实现工程管理目标和业务流程数字化、规范化，提升工程管理效率。

3. 管理组织的创新

一方面压缩工程管理层级，减少人员投入，使得各类信息的传递更加直接、迅速和准确，增加了工程管理的反应能力；另一方面打破参建各方的组织边界，把原本相互独立的各单位融合为一个整体，发挥出最佳的规模优势。

（三）效益

(1) 节省办公成本。各业务应用系统投入运行后，使大部分业务流程实现无纸化办公，办公耗材的消耗明显减少。

(2) 节约人力资源。龙滩水电工程业主单位管理人员定额180人，业务应用系统实施后，在工程建设高峰期只用74人即可满足工程管理需要，节约人力资源成本一半以上。

(3) 提高工作效率。龙滩水电工程信息化体系自构建并投入使用以来，各系统共处理各类业务合同1128份、行政文档4500多份。合同结算周期由传统的平均15天缩短至7天；公文处理由传统的平均7天缩短至1天，工作效率显著提高。

(4) 加快信息检索。龙滩水电工程信息化体系中的各类信息保存在数据库中，方便了数据填报和查询，减轻管理者日常重复的工作量；数据的自动汇总，方便了查询统计历史数据。

(5) 加强全局掌控。龙滩水电工程信息化体系涵盖工程管理各个方面，可以帮助管理者从不同的层次，方便、简捷、清楚地实施对项目的管理，得以把握建设过程全局性、综合性的信息。

(6) 助力提前发电。龙滩水电工程首批3台机组分别于2007年5月21日、7月20日、10月30日相继提前8个月、11个月、14个月投产发电，4号机组亦于2008年4月13日提前14个月投产发电。信息化管理体系提高了工作效率，对机组的提前投产起到助推器的作用。

（7）创建信息化模板。龙滩水电工程信息化建设是建立在龙滩水电工程管理模式上信息技术应用的成功实践，为以后新开工水电工程开展信息化建设积累了经验，提供了一个可以借鉴的信息化体系模板。

（8）重塑企业文化。龙滩水电工程信息化体系的推行，转变了管理人员的工作方式，提高了团队合作精神与协同工作意识。业务系统的应用，不仅仅实现了信息处理的自动化，而且是工作环境与工作方式的转变，信息交流与沟通的平等化，形成了强调协同合作的企业文化。

（龙滩水电开发有限公司　李晓勇）

企 业 管 理

中国长江电力股份有限公司 2009年经营情况

（一）概况

截至2009年底，中国长江电力股份有限公司（以下简称长江电力公司）装机容量达到2103.5万kW，外部权益装机容量267万kW（不含在建），实现总收入129.04亿元，利润总额58.86亿元，净利润44.87亿元，每股收益0.456元，电费全额回收，为股东、为社会创造了巨大的经济效益和社会效益。长江电力公司资产总额达到1616.35亿元，净资产616.57亿元，总股本达到110亿股。

长江电力公司在资本运营方面富有成效：截至2009年底，公司已投资16家企业，累计完成股权投资总额92.9亿元，实现现金收入50.95亿元，其中处置股权收入39.91亿元，累计分红11.04亿元；剩余股权投资79.59亿元，其中持有上市公司股权市值96.6亿元，非上市公司权益净资产60.2亿元，相应权益装机容量267万kW（不含在建权益容量56.9万kW）。

2009年，长江电力公司顺利完成了重大资产重组工作，拥有全国装机容量最大、技术最先进的水力发电资产，资产规模得到大幅提升，进入A股市场前20名。这更加有利于长江电力公司与中国长江三峡集团公司（以下简称三峡集团公司）的协调发展，更加有利于深化企业内部改革和提升管理水平，为长江电力公司未来发展奠定了坚实的基础。

这一年，长江电力公司先后被授予"全国电力行业首批AAA级信用企业"、"中央企业思想政治工作先进单位"、"中国文化管理十佳单位"、"2008年中国上市公司法律风险最小五佳上市公司奖"、"建国60周年中国企业文化建设十佳单位"、"中国电力信息化标杆企业"、"全国电力系统企业文化建设标杆企业"、"2008年度湖北省国税十强百佳纳税人"、"中国纳税百强企业"、"2008年度中国上市公司百强企业"、"2009中国上市公司最佳董事会"和"2009中国上市公司最佳市值管理董事会"等荣誉称号。

（二）成功完成重大资产重组工作

2009年5月15日，长江电力公司召开第二届董事会第二十九次会议，审议通过了关于《中国长江电力股份有限公司重大资产重组预案》的议案，长江电力公司拟以承接债务、向三峡集团公司非公开发行股份和支付现金的方式，收购控股股东中国长江三峡工程开发总公司（以下简称三峡总公司）持有的目标资产。

本次重大资产重组也即三峡集团公司主营业务整体上市的目标资产，包括三峡工程发电资产和辅助生产专业化公司股权，具体是：三峡电站9～26号共18台单机容量为70万kW、合计装机容量为1260万kW的发电机组及对应的大坝、发电厂房、共用发电设施（含装机容量为2×5万kW的电源电站）等发电资产，以及与发电业务直接相关的生产性设施；长江三峡实业有限公司、三峡设备物资公司、三峡水电工程公司、三峡国际招标公司、三峡高科公司等5家为水电工程建设和电力生产提供设备管理、招标、监理、供水、通信运行维护管理等服务的辅助生产专业化公司。此前，长江电力公司已完成对三峡电站1～8号发电机组及相关设施的收购，本次交易完成后，长江电力公司则拥有三峡工程全部发电资产。

本次重大资产重组的目标资产评估值约为1043亿元。长江电力公司支付的对价包括承接债务、非公开发行股份和支付现金，具体内容是：①承接与目标资产相关的债务约500亿元，包括三峡债、外汇借款和人民币借款；②2008年5月8日长江电力股票停牌前20个交易日股票均价并经过除息调整的价格12.89元/股，向三峡集团公司非公开发行股份约15.52亿股，三峡总公司以其持有的、评估价值约200亿元的部分目标资产认购发行的全部股份，若在定价基准日至发行日期间发生除权、除息，发行数量将相应调整，具体发行股份数量由三峡总公司和长江电力公司双方另行签署补充协议予以确定；③向三峡集团公司支付现金约375亿元，即期支付现金200亿元，剩余现金在交割日后一年内支付给三峡集团公司。

本次重大资产重组有利于提高长江电力公司的核心竞争力，进一步规范公司运作。通过本次交易，将有效规避与三峡总公司在电力生产领域的同业竞争，消除与三峡集团公司之间委托管理三峡发电资产的经常性关联交易，消除分次注入三峡工程发电资产而产生的持续关联交易。本次交易完成后，长江电力资产规模将成倍增长，盈利能力大幅提升，在水电行业的龙头优势地位更加巩固。资产重组即整体上市后，三峡集团公司主要履行三峡枢纽工程的统一管理和国有股权管理职能，集中精力开发长江上游的水电工程；长江电力公司主要负责三峡工程经营性职能，三峡总公司和长江电力公司的战略定位与职责边界将更加清晰，有利于三峡水利枢纽综合效益的充分发挥，为三峡集团公司和长江电力公司全面、协调、可持续发展奠定更加坚实的制度基础。

2009年9月27日，中国证监会出具了《关于核准中国长江电力股份有限公司重大资产重组暨向中国长江三峡工程开发总公司发行股份购买资产的批复》和《关于核准豁免中国长江三峡工程开发总公司要约收购中国长江电力股份有限公司股份义务的批复》，核准长江电力公司通过承接债务、非公开发行股份和支付现金的方式收购控股股东三峡总公司拥有的目标资产（评估值1073亿元），标志着本次重大资产重组交易的决策、审批程序全部完成，进入方案实施阶段。

2009年9月28日零时，三峡总公司和长江电力公司按照双方签署的协议完成了资产交割，长江电力公司收购控股股东三峡总公司拥有的目标资产。至此，历时一年多的长江电力重大资产重组的主要工作已经全部完成。

（三）长江电力股票复牌

为充分发挥三峡工程防洪、发电、航运等综合效益，加快金沙江下游开发，推进企业改革发展及集团化管控体系建设，三峡集团公司主营业务整体上市，对长江电力公司进行重大资产重组，长江电力股票（600900）于2008年5月8日开始停牌。由于国际金融危机蔓延的影响，资本市场系统性风险导致A股股价重心大幅下移，上证综指从长江电力停牌时的3656点最低跌至1664点，给资产重组方案设计带来压力。一年来，根据相关部门和投资者的意见，长江电力公司对方案及时进行调整，取得积极成果。整体上市方案公布后，得到了市场的高度认可。2009年5月18日，在投资者的热切关注中，长江电力股票复牌。尽管停盘期间资本市场重心大幅下移，但长江电力股票仍受到市场资金的追捧，逆势上扬，走势强劲，复牌当日收盘涨4.11%。复牌后股价走势平稳，长江电力仍然保持了大盘蓝筹股的形象。

（四）获“2008年度湖北省国税十强百佳纳税人”荣誉

长江电力公司成立以来一直坚持规范纳税行为，完善财务管理，自觉履行法律赋予的纳税义务，始终将依法纳税作为企业信用的核心内涵，大力弘扬纳税报国的崇高精神，为湖北省经济社会稳定、持续、健康发展作出了积极的贡献。湖北省国税局表彰“2008年度湖北省国税十强百佳纳税人”，长江电力公司以2008年度缴纳国税182 325万元排名全省国税荣誉十强纳税人第四位。

（五）加强内控管理

2009年9月15日，长江电力公司《内部控制管理手册（试行）》和《内部控制评价手册（试行）》正式发布实施，标志着长江电力公司内控管理和风险管控进入到规范化和系统化的新阶段。长江电力公司自改制上市以来，坚持“诚信经营、规范治理、信息透明、业绩优良”的经营理念，创造性地开展各项生产经营管理工作，内部控制管理具有较好的基础，但随着经营管理领域、范围的快速发展，需要更高的内部控制和风险管控能力。长江电力公司以贯彻落实财政部等五部委联合发布的《企业内部控制基本规范》、学习落实科学发展观为契机，于2008年启动内部控制体系优化项目，在多次学习、考察、调研的基础上，先后开展理论培训、专项调查、内控访谈、梳理评估、流程描述、风险点识别、专家评审、领导小组审查等工作，投入6000多工作日完成两个《手册》的编制工作。

《内部控制管理手册》围绕内部控制五要素，从公司层面、业务流程、关键控制点3个层次制定标准与要求，选取27个重要业务模块，制定48个二级子业务控制流程和800多个关键控制点的控制标准，形成了与现行规章制度的良性互动。《内部控制评价手册》明确了长江电力公司内部控制“自我评价、独立评价、第三方独立鉴证”的运行管理机制，制定了评价质量标准和计分标准。

（中国长江电力股份有限公司　谢兴发）

中国水利水电建设集团公司的企业经营管理

2009年，中国水利水电建设集团公司（以下简称水电建设集团）坚持以科学发展观为指导，积极应对国际金融危机影响，坚定不移地贯彻落实防控风险和促进发展的各项措施，及时把握发展机遇，大力开拓市场，着力调整优化上水平，各项工作取得新的成果，主要经营指标再创历史新高，取得了经营质量效益持续快速提高，实现了在高风险期的持续稳步发展。

（一）经营规模和效益同步大幅增长

一是营业收入大幅增长。实现营业收入778.61亿元，比2008年增长28.04%。二是市场营销总体保持良好势头。新签合同金额929.88亿元。合同存量1787.26亿元，比2008年增长15.5%。三是经济效益持续稳步提高。实现利润总额30.74亿元，比2008年增长90.23%。四是水电建设集团实力和竞争力进一步增强。总资产达到1022.63亿元，同比增长33.88%，净资产增加到156.05亿元，净资产收益率12.95%，国有资产保值增值率152.96%。在经营规模大幅增长的同时，资产负债率受控并相比于2008年降低1.91%。五是产业结构调整初见成效，投资业务板块已成为水电建设集团新的收入增长源，其中，2009年实现发电销售收入16.38亿元，占总收入的2.1%，而利润占16.03%。实现房地产销售收入9.97亿元。

（二）水利水电建筑业务板块得到巩固发展

(1) 水电建设集团在国内水利水电建筑市场营销取得好的成效，继续巩固保持行业主导地位，彰显了“中国水电建设第一品牌”的核心竞争力优势。在水电站招标项目减少，水电市场竞争更为激烈的情况下，水电建设集团采取积极有效的措施，实现了水电项目新签合同214.7亿元，水利项目新签合同132亿元，中标大型机组安装98台、装机容量3664万kW，确保了水电建设集团在国内水利水电建筑市场的主导地位。

(2) 水电建筑业务经营质量有了很大提高，经营利润水平继续好转。

(3) 水电在建项目进展顺利，国内国际大型水电建筑项目履约良好，质量、安全等总体受控。水电建设集团对在建的14个项目进行顾客（业主）调查，满意度全达到92.19%，较2008年有所提高。2009年完成国内水电机组安装119台，总装机容量1934万kW，累计完成水电装机容量1.3亿kW。

（三）国际经营业务板块持续快速健康发展

面对国际金融危机的严重冲击和国际市场大环境萧条的挑战，水电建设集团坚定实施国际业务优先发展战略，推动、引导各子公司继续大力开拓国际市场，国际市场空间不断拓展，市场份额不断扩大，国际业务经营管理水平进一步提升。水电建设集团新签约国际项目59个，成功开辟了贝宁、多哥、马里、科特迪瓦、科威特、厄瓜多尔等十国市场，并积极开发南部非洲市场及拉美市场，初步形成了9个以项目群为特点的大型国别市场。成立了卡塔尔、安哥拉、利比亚3个区域业务总部，推动了水电建设集团国际业务向区域化管理方式的转型。截至2009年底，水电建设集团在48个国家有在建项目211个，合同总额1029.49亿元。在46个国家设立了59个驻外机构。国际业务涵盖了水利水电、非水利水电和投资项目，形成了业务多元化格局。海外投资业务稳步推进，经营业务升级取得新突破。目前，在海外投资建设的电站装机容量31万kW，已签订占有电源项目协议计划装机容量约500万kW。水电建设集团参股的刚果（金）铜钴矿项目完成可行性研究编制等待批复。水电建设集团在国际经营项目中高度重视合同履约，持续打造“中国水电”国际知名品牌，国际声誉和影响力进一步彰显。

（四）非水电建筑业务板块持续增长

按照“大集团、大土木、大市场、大品牌”的战略思路，水电建设集团加快推进经营结构的战略性调整和优化转型，确立了基础设施业务在水电建设集团持续发展中的重要战略定位。加强了基础设施业务的经营管控，完善了基础设施业务发展战略、具体考核措施及支持政策，从制度和机制上促进各子公司在基础设施业务领域加快发展，使基础设施建筑业务成为水电建设集团重要的经济增长源。在铁路市场方面，京沪高铁等铁路项目的带动作用进一步彰显，铁路市场开发取得新的进展，以29.5亿元中标新建南宁至广州铁路5标段，以49.4亿元中标南京至杭州铁路客运专线2标段，实现了水电建设集团在铁路建设业务领域的进一步拓展。在公路市场方面，中标了广东惠深高速公路路面工程，实现了新的突破。在城市轨道交通市场方面，中标西安地铁一号线10标段工程，进一步巩固了水电建设集团在西北区域轨道交通领域的市场地位，也为水电建设集团纵深开拓轨道交通市场奠定了基础。

总之，集团公司改革发展的各项工作都取得了新进展、新成效。水电建设集团承建的山东泰安抽水蓄能电站、西安市黑河金盆水利枢纽工程、海南省大隆水利枢纽工程、伊朗塔里干水利枢纽工程获得“鲁班奖”；公伯峡水电站工程等3项工程荣获国家优质工程金奖和银奖；小浪底斜心墙堆石坝、紫坪铺面板堆石坝获得“国际堆石坝工程里程碑工程奖”；获得中国电力优质工程奖7项、中国水利工程优质（大禹）奖3项、“新中国成立60周年百项经典暨精品工程”12项；获得国家发明专利9项、实用新型专利55项。在杭州召开的2009中国企业500强发布暨中国大企业高峰会中，水电建设集团在“2009中国企业500强”中排名第89位，在“2009中国企业效益200佳”中排名第160位。

（中国水利水电建设集团公司）

黄河上游水电开发有限责任公司2009年经营管理情况

2009年，黄河上游水电开发有限责任公司（以下简称黄河水电公司）成功克服金融危机带来的不利因素影响，全面实现了年度经营目标任务；全年累计取得核准建设项目容量115.9万kW，其中积石峡水电项目是国家2009年唯一核准的百万级水电项目；实现了年度安全生产目标，保持了安全生产局面持续稳定；拉西瓦水电站成功实现“四投”目标，创造了多项中国水电建设新纪录；股权重组收购实现重要突破，解决了盐锅峡、八盘峡水电站长期存在的一厂多制问题；超额完成中国电力投资集团公司（以下简称中电投集团）下达的年度发展目标，在中电投集团单项考核中名列第一。

（一）主要指标

全年完成发电量272亿kW·h，较2008年增长28.66%；综合厂用电率0.85%，同比降低0.01个百分点；机组台均利用小时3855.83h，同比增加了186.78h；机组等效可用系数93.88%，高于计划值2.24个百分点，同比增加了3.01%，创黄河水电公司成立以来的最好水平；设备C、D类缺陷消除率完成99.54%，与2008年同比提高1.48个百分点；继电保护投入率等多项生产指标继续保持100%的完成率；各电站耗水率均在控制指标范围。

（二）基本建设

拉西瓦水电站实现“一年四投”目标，新增电力装机容量280万kW，完成2009年计划的133.33%，创造多项水电建设新纪录；6号机组和2号机组分别被授予“全国电力装机突破8亿千瓦”和“青海电力装机超千万千瓦的标志性机组”荣誉。公伯峡水电站喜获“新中国成立60年百项经典暨精品工程”称号和国家优质工程金奖。纳子峡、巨亭水电站正式开工建设。

（三）安全生产

（1）安全生产标准化工作整体推进。加强了对各电站技术规程的管理，全年修订各类技术规程325部，技术图册5册。安排在流域各电站移植公伯峡水电站生产管理信息系统，逐步统一各电站生产管理模式。修编印发了《应急管理工作手册》，进一步规范了应急管理工作。

（2）反违章工作逐步深化。发布《黄河水电公司反违章管理制度》和《黄河水电公司反违章学习手册》，印发到每位员工。组织开展“学制度，纠违章，查隐患”百日安全活动，将反违章工作进一步推向深入。活动期间，查处各类缺陷和隐患1121项，整改率达95%；查处违章行为12次，累计罚款达35万余元。

（3）加强设备日常维护管理。设备巡视检查到位，全年发现和消除设备缺陷3265项。公伯峡5号机组出口开关操作机构故障、李家峡水电站下导瓦调整螺杆断裂等一批缺陷得到及时处理，设备可靠性显著提高。2009年发生一般电力生产事故一次，发生机组非计划停运3次，同比减少3次。安全事件总量同比下降27.7%。

（4）优化设备检修管理。全年完成机组计划检修45台·次,其中:A级检修4台·次,B级检修4台·次，C级检修31台·次，D级检修6台·次，完成了年度机组检修计划，检修全优率达到100%。

积极开展安全生产效能监察和隐患排查治理，查处重大隐患16项，治理12项；一般隐患1995项，整改1779项，整改率达到89%。存量资产实现“零非停”目标，各水电站继续刷新长周期安全生产纪录，保持了国内领先水平。完成了中电投集团下达的安全生产目标，保证了安全生产的顺利进行。

（四）标准化管理

深入开展中电投集团“标准化管理推进年”活动，积极推行管理流程、指标体系、作业规程标准化管理，建立了战略、经营、安全生产、工程建设、人力资源、风险、监督七大管理体系流程，对296部规章制度进行全面梳理，对5000余部作业规范进行分类修订或补充完善，标准化管理水平进一步提高。

积极开展水电生产和成本对标，全年发电单位成本在中电投集团排名第一，其他各项成本指标大多处于中电投集团领先水平。

初步完成了黄河水电公司本部风险辨识、风险评估和流程梳理等工作，设置了黄河水电公司风险模型及风险评估标准，理清了黄河水电公司目前面临的重大风险，积极推进风险管理得到实质性落实，进一步提高了风险防范能力。

针对国际贸易合同、工资制度改革、辅业改制、征地移民等工作中存在的问题，确定了14项软科学课题，深入开展前瞻性研究，及时为黄河水电公司发展提供政策依据和研究意见。进一步加强企业法律风险防范机制建设，充分发挥法律顾问作用，积极参与企业重组、改制、合同谈判等重大决策和经营活动。

加强电费回收管理，实现当年电费回收100%、陈欠电费回收64.3%的工作目标。积极建立适应市场经济的营销模式和定价机制，加强综合产业原料采购、仓储保管、产品销售、铁路运输管理，初步形成了采供销存运管理体系。

（五）人才队伍建设

深入推进“四好”领导班子创建活动，进一步加强各级领导班子建设，黄河水电公司领导班子连续3年被中电投集团命名为“四好”领导班子，黄河水电公司系统基层单位“四好”领导班子创建优良率达到95%。不断完善企业领导人员选拔用人机制，首次采用谈话、问卷等形式，对122名二级单位领导班子成员进行了集中考察，对后备干部进行民主推荐，全面掌握了黄河水电公司系统干部队伍情况。按照适度超前、梯次储备的原则，加强急需和紧缺人才的储备，招聘引进各类人才430多名。加强内部人力资源的挖掘与调配，全年内部交流140多名，提高了人力资源的使用效率。首次对优秀大学毕业生进行表彰，积极营造崇尚先进、学习先进、争当先进的良好舆论氛围和环境。完成水力发电国家技能鉴定站的建站工作，积极开展职工技能培训与技术比武，提高了技能人才的数量和质量。全面实施年度各项专业培训计划，举办培训班65期，3074人·次参加了培训，形成了“培训就是福利”的共识。加强离退休及内退人员管理，妥善解决有关问题，确保了队伍稳定。

（黄河上游水电开发有限责任公司
胡耀斌　许为宁　张文俊）

龙滩水电开发有限公司2009年经营情况

2009年是龙滩水电开发有限公司（以下简称龙滩公司）由工程基建向生产经营重心转移关键的一年，也是生产经营面临巨大困难的一年。受国际金融危机影响，我国经济受到严重冲击，南方区域电力供需形势发生了重大的变化，电力供需形势从供应紧张转变为一时性的需求不足，全社会用电量出现了连续数个月的负增长。与此同时，2009年红水河流域龙滩库区为干旱偏枯年，上游来水量明显低于常年，降雨量低于多年平均水平2～3成，发电量受到较大影响。面对前所未有的困难和挑战，龙滩公司全体员工深入学习实践科学发展观，按照中国大唐集团公司“攻坚年”的总体部署和要求，紧紧围绕年初制定的工作目标，以安全生产为基础，以经济效益为中心，紧抓生产经营和工程建设两条主线，积极应对严峻的考验，团结一心，迎难而上，全面完成了2009年的各项工作任务。

（一）较好完成各项主要指标

2009年，龙滩电厂累计发电量为131.40亿kW·h，累计上网电量为130.50亿kW·h；龙滩公司实现营业收入34.28亿元，实现利润10.76亿元，完成年度目标利润的107.60%；完成投资13.65亿元，占年度调整投资计划的123.63%。截至2009年底，龙滩工程累计完成投资279.47亿元，占预计工程动态总投资327.87亿元的85.24%。

2009年度，龙滩水库累计总来水量359.68亿m^3，总弃水量0.015亿m^3，发电平均耗水率3.182m^3/(kW·h)，水量利用率99.98%。

2009年，龙滩公司没有发生电力生产人身死亡事故；没有发生人身重伤事故；没有发生重大及以上的设备事故；没有发生其他电力生产事故，安全生产形势稳定良好。全面实现龙滩公司本年度安全目标。

（二）电力生产安全稳定，管理跃上新台阶

深入贯彻落实国家“安全生产年”和电力安全生产“三项行动”各项工作，按照中国大唐集团公司新厂新制管理模式和点检定修管理要求，结合龙滩电厂自身特点，坚持管理创新，以创建“国际知名、国内一流水电厂”为标杆，夯实工作基础，努力创建本质安全型企业，实现了电厂自投产以来连续安全稳定运行，出色地完成了2009年春节、“两会”、国庆、澳门回归十周年、第六届东盟博览会等重大节日、重大会议的保电任务。

制度体系建设日趋完善。龙滩电厂已编制修订完成行政制度17部、生产规章制度61部、运行规程68部、检修规程95部、点检标准86部、管理标准90部、检修作业标准177部、生产岗位工作标准54部、应急预案40部，进一步夯实龙滩电厂运转工作基础。

标准化作业水平显著提升。一是“两票三制”基本实现了规范化、标准化管理，违章行为得到有效遏制。2009年共办理工作票3838份，合格率100%；共完成5711项操作任务，共164 785项操作，合格率100%。二是实行《运行管理部工作考评细则》等工作考评，规范运行管理。三是编制《危险点分析与预控手册》，严格按照危险点分析与预控的标准化执行，纠正习惯性违章行为。四是规范特种设备安全管理，定期检查，对问题及时整改，杜绝重大事故的发生。

设备健康水平较大提高，安全稳定运行。一是积极开展隐患排查治理和风险控制，2009年检查整改共346项，按时整改完成率为100%。二是对各种重大危险源进行评估、建档，评估一级、二级、三级重大危险源均为0个，四级14个，重大危险源均控制在四级以内。对问题制定整改计划，落实到自然人，限期完成。三是加大设备缺陷处理力度，确保设备健康运行。2009年共发现缺陷835项，处理814项，消缺率为97.5%。四是圆满完成1号、2号、5号、6号、7号机组的C级检修工作，共完成检修项目360项，技术改造40项。五是完善点检定修体系建设，优化点检路线、点检标准、点检周期以及点检人员，定期就设备的运行状况、缺陷的发生及处理、异常现象原因等进行分析和总结。六是完成1～7号机组并网安全性评价自查评工作。

抓好水库优化调度。一是对水情测报系统进行功能完善，并加强管理维护。二是对上游电站及库区水情进行调研，积极联系地方气象部门，尽可能全面掌握相关水情、气象数据。三是积极联系南网总调、珠江水利委员会等相关单位，开展动态汛限水位研究、流域梯级调度优化方案研究等工作，及时组织开展水情及影响电量分析，确保水库调度计划及发电计划实施，提高水能利用率。

（三）工程建设稳步推进

2009年，龙滩公司狠抓龙滩375m方案建设工程完工验收、竣工结算及尾工项目的组织协调与统筹安排，各项工作齐头并进，全面实现了年度工期目标。

积极配合广西、贵州两省（区）开展龙滩库区淹没耕地长期补偿相关工作，解决移民搬迁安置工作中的重大问题。截至2009年底，龙滩库区累计完成移民搬迁75 921人（含随迁人口），累计向两省（区）支付淹没处理及移民安置补偿费80.26亿元。

工程枢纽区环保水保专项验收顺利通过，库区水土保持主要项目已基本完成。

组织召开龙滩400方案建设专家咨询会议，加强协调，从多方面、多渠道推动400方案建设审批进程。

（四）营销管理工作成绩突出

一是配合完成电价核定工作，2009年11月18日国家发展改革委发布发改价格［2009］2926号文件，核定龙滩上网电价为每千瓦时0.307元。二是加强对区域电力市场的研究，及时作出电力供需形势分析，根据龙滩公司的实际情况做好应对，积极参与市场竞争。三是积极主动与中国南方电网有限责任公司等相关单位和部门进行沟通和联系，创造良好的营销工作外部环境。四是认真做好电量计划和电厂生产经济活动分析工作，实时跟踪分析电厂电量完成情况，不断完善电量完成预警机制。五是做好电量结算工作，加强对每月电费和陈欠电费的催收工作，电费回收情况良好。

（五）成本管理工作卓有成效

一是不断完善涵盖行政管理、工程建设、安全生产、市场营销等全过程的全面成本控制体系，强化对成本管理重点和主要环节的管理。二是优化融资结构，降低资金使用成本，2001年开工至2009年底，龙滩工程累计发生融资费用19.55亿元，与执行概算相比节约了18.97亿元。三是紧抓工程的成本费用控制，重点加强对大坝标和地下厂房标的变更审核。2009年共审批施工单位申报的变更（含索赔）项目256项，批复变更金额5.65亿元，共核减不合理金额4.88亿元，核减幅度达46.37%。四是组织做好工程造价审计以及对龙滩公司财务收支和有关经济活动的例行审计，促进项目管理，控制工程造价。

（六）项目前期工作顺利推进

积极推进松塔水电项目前期工作，目前该项目预可行性研究阶段工作基本完成，已着手开展可行性研究阶段工作。

（七）南宁基地建设工作稳步推进

龙滩大厦全面竣工并投入使用，较好地改善了龙滩公司南宁办公条件。努力推进电厂职工周转房建设，报建相关手续已基本完成，为项目的顺利开工创造了基础条件。

（八）公司党建、人才、思想政治工作全面加强

一是着力加强领导班子建设和人才队伍建设，优化人力资源结构，健全完善教育培训的配套制度和实施方案，培养造就高素质专业人才队伍。二是正确把握宣传导向，做好对外宣传，组织编写《龙滩水电工程志》，全面记录龙滩工程建设辉煌的历史；紧扣中国大唐集团公司同心文化主题，开展各类文化实践活动，培育和打造龙滩品牌；加强自身建设，党、工、团组织得到进一步健全和发展。三是加强对重点部位和环节的监督，开展专项效能监察和治理商业贿赂专项工作，推进教育、制度、监督并重的惩治和预防腐败体系建设。

（九）学习实践科学发展观活动取得明显实效

按照中国大唐集团公司党组统一部署和要求，龙滩公司党组高度重视，精心组织，周密部署，扎实推进，较好地完成了学习实践科学发展观活动学习调研、分析检查、整改落实3个阶段6个环节的各项规定内容。做到在求实效上下工夫，创造性的开展工作，真正实现了“党员干部受教育、科学发展上水平、人民群众得实惠”的总体目标，学习实践活动取得了显著实效，为龙滩公司各项工作的顺利开展提供了精神保障。

（龙滩水电开发有限公司 曾 浩 张峰玉）

华能澜沧江水电有限公司开展融资租赁

华能澜沧江水电有限公司（以下简称澜沧江公司）致力于澜沧江流域等水电资源开发，目前已投产运行机组容量 410 万 kW，但小湾、景洪、糯扎渡、功果桥、里底、黄登、苗尾等水电站还处于在建和筹建阶段，规模约 1800 万 kW。澜沧江公司发电收入尚不能实现自我滚动发展。虽然先后采用了资产证券化、信托、短期融资券等直接融资方式，但比重不高，对动辄上百亿的水电建设投资来说还远远不够。水电项目投资具有建设周期长、资金逐步投入、投资金额巨大、投资回收期长等特点，并且在项目建设期内资产负债率会随着工程的进度逐渐上升。因此，破解水电开发的资金瓶颈，拓宽融资渠道，就成了澜沧江公司加快水电业发展的重中之重。

租赁业是世界上仅次于银行信贷的第二大金融工具，是发达国家商品流通的主渠道。随着政策环境的改善，我国的融资租赁业在近几年取得较快发展，2008 年业务总量完成约 1550 亿元。

我国融资租赁业的发展，为水电开发提供了新的资金来源渠道。水电站是国家基础产业，有很高的信誉度和稳定的现金流量，其建设项目中有很多子项目如设备购买安装可以采用融资租赁方式。

澜沧江公司为进一步拓宽融资渠道、改善资金来源结构、降低资金成本、提高资产使用效率，充分挖掘自身潜力，以水电设备为载体，通过售后回租的方式，为流域后续项目建设融资。

（一）融资租赁的优势

（1）以较小的资金投入，得到较大的规模效应，是融资租赁的优势所在。在进行水电站建设时，如果采用融资租赁，用较小的资金就可以取得水轮机、发电机、变压器及 GIS 等重大设备的使用权。由于可以用电站投产后实现的收益支付租金。大大降低传统融资手段因一次性支付带来的资金压力。

（2）可将已拥有所有权的电站资产通过售后回租的方式转让资产所有权，使电站资产的所有权与使用权分离，将所有权资产变为租赁资产，将物化资本变为货币资本，在不影响正常使用的前提下达到资产变现、筹集建设资金的目的。因此。这种方式有助于充分挖掘现有资源的融资潜力，筹集尚不具备申请银行项目贷款条件的新项目所需的前期开发资金，从而减少公司对银行贷款的依赖。

（3）除股东投入资本金外，水电开发公司目前的融资渠道主要是银行贷款。这种融资结构导致了水电项目建设期不断上升的资产负债比率，限制了公司继续融入债券性资金，比如发行短期融资券等。水电站建设周期长，资金需要量大，但投产后会产生稳定的现金流，如果全部采用传统的融资模式，这种未来大额稳定现金流的优势就得不到利用。而融资租赁却可以采用售后回租的方式，将电站建设部分资产卖给租赁公司，从租赁公司获得建设资金，并且不丧失资产的使用权，项目建成后，以未来稳定的现金流支付租金。这种方式的好处就是可以有效降低水电项目建设期的资产负债比例，保持优良的债务结构，为其他融资方式提供更好的财务基础，保障其他融资渠道的融资能力。

（4）根据《企业所得税法实施条例》的规定，以融资租赁方式租入固定资产的折旧费，可以在税前提取扣除。另外，根据租赁期与租赁资产使用寿命孰短的原则确定折旧年限，尽量缩短租赁期，可在前期多提折旧，有利于获得延迟纳税的好处。

（二）识别融资需求，确定融资手段

澜沧江公司此次用于开展融资租赁项目的标的物均为水电设备，包括水轮机、发电机、GIS、变压器等大型专用设备，与其他飞机、轮船等通用设备有所不同。一般来说，这些水电设备都是为某个电站项目量身定做的，承租人对资产的型号、规格等方面有特殊的要求，而且水电设备一般不可拆卸使用，必须整体才能发挥作用，资产专用性强，在租赁期届满时，资产的所有权都会转移给承租人。

与银行贷款相比，融资租赁是以物为载体的融资，可根据客户的实际要求进行相应的变动，融资方式更为灵活。与风险投资相比，融资租赁是以物的方式给客户进行融资，通过租金回收的方式退出，不占企业股份，不影响现有股东的利益，企业有更大的自主权。澜沧江公司此次所采用的售后回租方式是将自制或外购的资产出售，然后向买方租回使用，按期支付租金。售后回租的实质在于，它使设备制造企业或资产所有人（承租人）在保留资产使用权的前提下获得所需的资金，可以改善承租人（即出售方）的财务状况，盘活其存量资产，同时又为出租人提供有利可图的投资机会。

（三）采取恰当的融资租赁方式

（1）分次起租、分次提款。大型水电设备制造周期长，资金为渐进式投入。就国内现状而言，在大型水电设备制造合同签订后的很短时间内，必须向厂商支付相应的预付款，在设备制造的各个阶段完成后，还需支付进度款。所以，有可能在融资租赁业务开展之时，以上款项已发生了支付，这给融资租赁业务在操作上出了很大的难题。为解决以上问题，经与相关租赁公司反复研究，创新性地提出了分次起租的概念，即将起租日与设备到货日相结合，按设备制造合同中约定的设备到货计划将同一设备进行分次起租，各笔融资起租日期随设备所有权转移日期而定。如此灵活的安排，切合了大型水电设备制造的实际情况，解决了融资租赁起租日的传统模式与大型水电设备到货周期之间不匹配的难题。

（2）采用售后回租。融资租赁有多种模式，澜沧江公司根据现实情况，在与租赁公司充分沟通的情况下，选择采用售后回租方式。该方式具有其明显的优势，隔离了出租人与设备制造厂商，在设备制造合同不发生变化的情况下即可完成融资租赁业务。由于大型水电设备制造专业性较强，如按融资租赁业务的通常做法，将制造合同的甲方由承租人转为出租人的话，存在诸多难以逾越的障碍。而采用售后回租模式，在不对设备制造合同进行任何变更的情况下，即可完成融资租赁业务。

（四）选择合作银行，提升融资租赁能力

澜沧江公司选择与有国内大型商业银行背景的建信租赁公司、工银租赁公司和招银租赁公司合作开展融资租赁业务。其中建信租赁公司是中国建设银行和美国银行共同筹建设立的从事金融租赁业务的合资股份有限公司，是目前中国国内同业中首家获得批准筹建的金融租赁公司，也是我国目前已开业和正在筹建的金融租赁公司中资金实力最强的一家；工银租赁公司和招银租赁公司是我国银行系首批挂牌营业的租赁公司，分别是中国工商银行、招商银行的全资子公司。澜沧江公司选择在融资租赁业务上与他们合作，既可以加深与中国建设银行、中国工商银行和招商银行的银企关系，又可以充分发挥澜沧江公司在这3家银行的优质信用资源，再加上这3家银行深厚的金融从业经验、良好规范的管理和人才优势，能使澜沧江公司融资租赁业务的成功运作得到充分保障。在实际操作中，各相关银行总行均将给澜沧江公司的授信额度作为租赁公司对澜沧江公司开展租赁业务的保证条件，间接将澜沧江公司银行授信额度转化为融资租赁。

2008年，我国为严控通货膨胀风险，实行信贷紧缩政策，澜沧江公司在保障水电项目建设资金供应上面临着更为巨大的压力。为强化资金保障，减轻资金压力，以及力争在创新型融资领域取得更多突破，以有效规避融资风险，澜沧江公司利用多年来在银行业界所树立的优良信誉，抓住金融租赁业刚刚在我国起步的难得机遇，积极与各正在筹备期的金融租赁公司联系，主动推介自己，并在各相关金融租赁公司主管上级总行的大力支持下，得到3家金融租赁公司的青睐，成为它们成立后的首批顾客。经多轮磋商，相关金融租赁公司同意与澜沧江公司合作进行融资租赁业务，并采用融资租赁模式中的售后回租方式，以小湾水电站水轮机发电机为载体与建信租赁公司签订了13.5亿元设备转让合同和融资租赁合同，利率为同期银行贷款利率基础上下浮5%；以小湾水电站电气设备为载体与招银租赁公司签订了4.6亿元设备转让合同和融资租赁合同，利率水平与建信租赁公司相同；以景洪水电站水轮机发电机为载体与工银租赁公司签订了5.9亿元的设备转让合同和融资租赁合同，利率为同期银行贷款利率基础上下浮11%。截至2009年12月底，澜沧江公司累计实际利用租赁公司资金31.51亿元，累计已节约了融资成本600万元左右。并且，随着合同的继续执行，今后将为澜沧江公司节约更多的融资成本。

（华能澜沧江水电有限公司　廖为民
邓炳超　张象瑾　孔令兵）

国网新源控股有限公司 2009年工作情况

国网新源控股有限公司（以下简称新源公司）是国家电网公司投资设立的国有独资公司，主要负责开发建设和经营管理国家电网公司经营区域抽水蓄能电站、新能源电站和可再生能源项目等业务。截至2009年底，新源公司所属全资、控股企业26家，抽水蓄能电站装机总容量1517万kW，其中已投入商业运行机组装机容量1027万kW，在建装机容量490万kW。

2009年，新源公司本部保持中央国家机关文明单位称号，北京十三陵抽水蓄能电厂、山东泰山抽水蓄能电站有限责任公司分别获得“全国文明单位”和“全国精神文明建设先进单位”称号，湖北白莲河抽水蓄能有限责任公司和华东宜兴抽水蓄能有限公司分别获得“省级文明单位”和省级“五一劳动奖状”荣誉。新源公司共有3个集体荣获省部级“工人先锋号”称号，3个基层工会荣获省级“模范职工之家”称号，2个职工被评为省部级劳动模范，展示了新源公司的良好形象。

（一）工程建设情况

2009年，新源公司实现投产装机容量209.95万kW，其中抽水蓄能投产205万kW，分别为河北张河湾4号机组、山西西龙池3号机组、河南宝泉1～3号机组、湖北白莲河3～4号机组。

2009年，新源公司基建工程单元工程质量验评6318个，合格率100%，平均优良率93.54%。

2009年，江西洪屏、浙江仙居项目通过国家发展改革委审查，吉林敦化、河南天池项目取得国家发展改革委"路条"，山东文登、河南天池、河北丰宁等项目可行性研究有序开展。快速推进坚强智能电网首批示范项目——风光储输示范项目，完成项目选址、可行性研究及专题报告编制等工作，2009年12月29日，项目一期工程获得河北省发展改革委核准批复，项目进入国家"金太阳"工程，被列为国家级示范项目。全年实现新开工项目3个，开工装机容量141.8万kW。

2009年，山东泰安抽水蓄能电站完成工程档案、劳安及竣工决算等全部专项验收；浙江桐柏抽水蓄能电站完成工程档案、库区移民专项验收工作；安徽琅琊山抽水蓄能电站完成工程档案及劳安专项验收；江苏宜兴抽水蓄能电站完成环保、水保、消防以及职业病防治等专项验收；河北张河湾抽水蓄能电站完成消防及职业病防治专项验收。

山东泰安抽水蓄能电站于2009年6月8日获得"2009年度中国电力行业优质工程奖"，同年10月26日荣获2009年中国建设工程"鲁班奖"（国家优质工程）。

（二）安全生产情况

2009年，新源公司系统没有发生人身、设备、电网事故，未发生恶性误操作事故。截至2009年12月31日，实现连续安全生产1737天。蓄能机组全年发电启动10 886次，成功率99.98%，同比上升0.06个百分点。抽水机组启动6435次，成功率99.85%，同比上升0.14个百分点。

安全生产机构逐步理顺，建立了管理清晰、执行和监督相对独立的"两部两分场"组织机构。安全生产专项活动扎实开展，安全性评价取得实效，自主编制完成了《抽水蓄能电站安全性评价查评标准》，开展了山东泰山抽水蓄能电站有限责任公司、华东宜兴抽水蓄能有限公司等8家生产单位安全性评价自查评和专家查评工作。严格落实发电厂重大反事故措施等制度要求，对影响安全生产的设备设施隐患优先实施检修技改工作，设备设施健康水平明显提升。组织开展《抽水蓄能电站设备事故案例汇编》编制工作，汇总抽水蓄能设备设施在安装、调试、运营等阶段曾发生过的各类典型故障案例，便于各单位吸取教训，开展针对性反措。

（三）经营管理情况

强化综合计划和预算管理。加强综合计划和专项计划执行情况的分析与监控，增强综合协调能力。建立以成本标准为基础的经营预算管理系统，增强预算刚性约束力。

认真抓好资金、资本、资产管理。通过采取融资结构置换、存量贷款利率下浮、筹集低成本资金等措施，节约财务费用。加强电量、电价、电费工作，提高新源公司盈利能力。认真研究落实电监会"两个细则"，积极协调电量电费，精心组织新机组转商运工作，保证经营成果。深入开展"三节约"活动，新源公司荣获国家电网公司"三节约"活动先进单位荣誉。

2009年2月，新源公司全面启动标准化建设工作。截至2009年底，确立本部四大管理体系，21个管理模块体系框架，基本完成本部管理流程、管理标准和工作标准编制工作。初步建立起以发展目标为统领，集团化运作、集约化管理为核心，业务流程为主线，安全生产为基础，基于风险有效控制的企业标准体系。

（四）科技工作情况

2009年，完成专利申请27项，取得授权专利13项；组织集中发表技术论文47篇；完成17项科技项目的验收和成果鉴定，其中"大型蓄能电站首机首次启动方式研究"和"宜兴电站上水库钢筋混凝土混合堆石坝设计与施工关键技术"研究成果达到国际先进水平。

建成了基本覆盖各业务部门的19个信息系统，构筑了纵向贯通、横向集成的一体化企业信息集成平台，初步形成了企业信息化的安全防范、标准规范、管理调控、人才队伍、评价考核及技术研究的保障体系。在生产管理系统中实现了9家生产单位的实时数据接入本部，2家生产单位生产管理信息系统上线试运行，3家基建单位和总部数据纵向贯通。基本实现了新源公司上下信息畅通和数据共享的目标，顺利通过国家电网公司信息化工程验收。

（国网新源控股有限公司　韩　冰）

黄河万家寨水利枢纽有限公司2009年经营管理情况

（一）概况

2009年，黄河万家寨水利枢纽有限公司（以下简称万家寨公司）牢固树立民生理念，全面推进民生水利，深入学习科学发展观，积极贯彻落实可持续发展治水思路，围绕电力安全生产和水利工程建设两条主线，锐意进取，较好地实现了年度各项工作目标。2009年，万家寨公司累计销售电量25.73亿kW·h，其中：万家寨水电站24.48亿kW·h；龙口水电站1.25亿kW·h。全年向山西和内蒙古供水1.58亿m^3，实现经营收入9.04亿元，利润总额1.86亿元，比2008年增加5174万元，缴纳各种税费1.76亿元。万家寨公司的净资产收益率、主营业务利润率、资本保值增值率等主要盈利状况指标、发展能力指标及偿债能力指标较2008年向好。龙口水利枢纽工程提前一年实现首台机组并网发电，取得了重要的阶段性成果。

万家寨公司顺利完成了领导班子的换届工作。2009年7月20日，黄河万家寨水利枢纽有限公司第四届董事会、监事会第一次会议于在山西五台山召开。根据股东方推荐，会议选举李兰奇为黄河万家寨水利枢纽有限公司第四届董事会董事长，选举营二拴、薛昇旗为副董事长，选举杨富锁为黄河万家寨水利枢纽有限公司第四届监事会主席。经组织考察，董事长提名，会议审议通过，聘任陈永志为黄河万家寨水利枢纽有限公司总经理。新一届领导班子带领全体员工围绕万家寨公司的总体部署和工作目标，努力克服和消除阻碍万家寨公司发展的消极因素，着力解决制约万家寨公司发展的突出问题。

万家寨公司成立“发展战略研究领导小组”，组织开展企业发展战略规划的研究。继续进行质量、环境、职业健康安全管理体系运作，通过了北京中安质环认证中心年度监督审核。创新干部管理制度，研究制定了《干部轮岗交流办法》、《非领导职务岗位设置及管理办法》等，提高公司管理人员的专业化和年轻化水平；以高效精简为原则，调整组织机构，强化公司的安全监督、防汛、宣传、信息管理、交通安全管理等职能；以德才兼备为用人导向，严格按照程序选拔任用了一批干部走上新的领导岗位；进行全员的岗位职责摸底调查，为薪酬改革做好前期准备；对中层干部的政治素质、工作能力等进行全面考核。为了弥补公司专业技术力量的不足，同时引导中青年员工重视专业技术的学习，万家寨公司实行专业技术首席专家聘任制度。

深入学习实践科学发展观，努力构建和谐企业，积极倡导以敬业、团结、利他精神为核心的道德规范，强化全体员工的服务意识、责任意识和协作意识。万家寨公司继续保持了“全国水利系统文明单位”、“山西省直和谐单位标兵”等荣誉称号，万家寨水电站管理局荣获“第四届全国精神文明建设工作先进单位”称号。

（二）水电开发工作

万家寨公司公司除了做好已建的万家寨水利枢纽的运行管理和负责在建的龙口水利枢纽的建设管理工作外，还努力做好其他水电开发工作。

1. 成立水电开发部

2009年3月，万家寨公司成立水电开发部，主要负责公司后续发展项目的信息搜集、调研等前期工作。按照公司安排，积极收集整理国家有关能源开发方面的法律法规，做好对外发展项目的调研工作。同年3月中旬赴陕西安康实地考察调研汉江流域白河和孤山等水电站项目，同时考察陕西新华水利水电投资有限公司在陕南区域的水电开发项目；11月下旬，赴新疆对区域水电开发项目进行考察调研，对尚未开工的乔巴特、葵花尼水电站项目及哈巴河县的风电项目进行深入了解；12月初，对乌海市海勃湾水利枢纽项目进行调研；按照公司统一安排，抽调人员参加了云南龙江水利枢纽开发有限公司合同管理专家咨询工作和公司发展战略规划的制定工作。

2. 新疆吉勒布拉克水电项目代建工作

2009年3月，万家寨公司成立吉勒布拉克项目部，主要负责新疆吉勒布拉克水电项目代建工作。作为万家寨公司对外承揽的第一个代建项目，龙口建管局抽调精干力量参加项目部工作，2009年4月项目部人员赶赴吉勒布拉克工程现场，各项工作正常开展。截至2009年底，主要情况如下：

（1）共完成投资约4200余万元，完成土石方明挖约50.94万m^3。

（2）深孔泄洪洞及导流洞工程开挖约47 489m^3，喷锚支护约8155m^2；场内施工道路已具备交通条件；料场、混凝土拌和站等附属设施已基本完成；35kV施工用电11km线路及变电所工程2009年10月已正式送电；管理区工程已完成部分场地平整工作。

（3）全年共签订工程项目合同10个。《液压启闭机设备制造采购项目》、《深孔泄洪洞暨导流洞工程闸门及启闭机设备采购项目》标书已发售并于2009年11月26日开标。

（4）完成库区、坝区征用土地的勘界工作，解决了工地生产的施工用地。完成20多项征地所需报批材料准备工作；完成水土保持原则、水土生态监测工作的合同签订工作；完成砂石料场的占地勘界和开发利用方案等工作。

（黄河万家寨水利枢纽有限公司 赵 欣）

国电陕西水电开发有限公司2009年经营管理情况

（一）基本情况

国电陕西水电开发有限公司（以下简称陕西公司）是中国国电集团公司设立的全资子公司，公司注册资本金1.191亿元人民币，负责中国国电集团在陕西、甘肃的水电项目及水电上下游产业开发、建设及生产运营工作。公司积极投资控股和建设区域内中小水电项目，推进陕西丹江流域、南江河等流域和甘肃白水江、白龙江流域的水电项目开发，并已成功收购了陕西丹江流域莲花台电站、南江河双河口电站和甘肃白水江流域柳园电站、白依坝电站及白龙江流域凉风壳电站、代古寺电站等水电项目。同时，还有一批陕甘水电项目的并购正在进行中，实现滚动发展。

目前，陕西公司下设综合管理部、财务产权部、经营计划部、工程建设部、安全生产部、项目开发部、甘肃项目办、丹江公司、柳园公司、凉风壳公司以及镇坪分公司等机构。

（二）2009 年主要事件

（1）1月14日，国电陕西水电开发有限公司经中国国电集团公司批准注册，完成了陕西商南宇泽电力开发有限公司的变更手续，国电陕西水电开发有限公司正式组建。

（2）2月16日，国电陕西水电开发有限公司揭牌暨丹江莲花台水电站项目开工仪式在陕西商南举行。

（3）2月17日，国电陕西水电开发有限公司成立甘肃项目办，具体负责公司在甘肃白水江、白龙江等水电项目的开发，抢占发展机遇。

（4）5月8日，在甘肃兰州举行“合作开发建设凉风壳水电站”和“文县柳园（白依坝）水电开发有限公司股权转让”签字仪式，标志着甘肃水电项目开发取得突破性进展。

（5）7月20日，与镇平县人民政府签署了南江河双河口水电站开发合同书，正式获得双河口35MW水电项目开发权，电站建设步入实质性阶段。

（6）8月1日，与兰州新盛电力有限公司在兰州签署了《关于柳园、白依坝水电站转让交接工作结束的确认书》；8月5日，与东城集团签订了《凉风壳发电有限公司股权转让协议补充协议》，标志着甘肃白水江流域梯级收购工作已进入实质性阶段。

（7）9月16日，国电丹江水电有限责任公司成立，作为国电陕西水电开发有限公司的全资子公司，全权负责商洛市境内丹江流域的梯级水电开发与建设工作。

（8）10月上旬，国电陕西水电开发有限公司正式迁址西安，办公场所移至西安市二环南路西段208号捷瑞智能大厦9层。

（三）取得成绩

（1）工程建设稳步推进，安全、质量、设计优化与造价管理可控、在控。在安全管理方面，各工程项目安全生产态势良好，未发生人身伤亡和设备损坏事故，安全管理达到“双零”目标，工程安全处于可控、在控状态。在质量管理方面，莲花台水电站、柳园水电站、凉风壳水电站作为先期开工建设的3个工程，均以树立“样板工程”的要求来严抓质量管理，全部实现旁站监理，开展质量检查工作，确保了工程的质量达到了设计要求。在建工程严格遵守“经济、科学、长远”的设计优化原则，通过确定合理目标、聘请水电专家现场勘测等手段，为工程造价控制工作奠定了良好基础。

（2）经营工作取得良好开端，风险管控能力逐步提升。结合实际情况，深入分析2009年陕甘区域中小水电市场形势，对经营管理工作提方案、定措施、细执行，初步完成了经营构架的建设。通过认真学习和借鉴兄弟水电、火电企业的经营管理经验，将公司总部集中管理与各项目部自主管理科学地衔接起来，经营指标逐级分解、层层落实。通过明确各级人员职责，严格监督，严肃考核，建立制度，规范流程，逐步向精细化管理迈进。全年资金使用按预算执行和资金管理相关规定进行，资本金足额到位，不存在投资资金不足、贷款资金积压等情况。为确保项目的并购成果，将财务管理置于项目管理的前沿，先后完成了并购莲花台、柳园、凉风壳电站财务资料接受、账务处理及日常核算工作，并顺利通过了国电西北分公司财务专项检查。

（3）抓住重点，统筹兼顾，基础管理日臻完善。陕西公司成立后，确定第一要务是发展和扩张，当务之急是规模融资，重中之重是项目建设，立企之策是建章立制。公司以规范化管理为纽带，根据中国国电集团公司和国电西北分公司的有关规定及本公司的实际需要，确定了发展目标、运作模式，建立和优化了“责任链、责任圈、责任体系”，在国有企业定位的基础上吸纳民企管理经验，在最短的时间内初步建立起符合现代企业制度、符合中国国电集团公司和国电西北分公司管理模式、符合中小型水电开发公司特征的法人治理结构和管理机制，初步建立了劳资和社保体系，完善了相关管理流程，开始走上规范化的公司运作模式。

（中国国电集团公司）

国电海南大广坝发电有限公司 2009 年经营管理情况

（一）基本情况

国电海南大广坝发电有限公司（以下简称大广坝公司）的前身是海南省大广坝水电厂，2004年12月30日经债转股改制成立，注册资本8.692 2亿元，中国国电集团公司控股66.1%，现有员工337人。大广坝工程位于海南省东方市境内昌化江流域，是一个具有发电、灌溉、供水和旅游等综合经济效益的大型综合性工程，作为海南省最大的水力发电厂，在海南电力系统中主要起调峰、调频和事故备用的作用，对改善海南电力电能质量，保证电网的稳定运行起着举足轻重的作用。

（二）安全生产管理

大广坝公司始终坚持“安全第一，预防为主”的方针，认真贯彻落实中国国电集团公司关于安全生产的规定要求，强化安全教育，重视发电、消防和交通的安全管理，严防电气误操作等人为责任事故的发生；认真落实重大节假日和重大会议期间的安全保电工作措施，积极开展春季安全生产大检查、防汛安全大检查和安全隐患治理专项活动。

2009 年，共排查治理生产隐患 568 项，已整改 557 项，整改率 98%；开展各项安全性评价整改治理工作，完成中国国电集团公司安评整改 178 项，整改率 95.2%；完成并网安全性评价整改 133 项，整改率 97.1 %。在工作中，加强运行、检修人员的安全培训和岗位技能培训，为稳定运行创造条件，为完成各项工作任务提供了安全保证。

2009 年，大广坝公司累计连续安全生产天数为 1825 天，创建厂以来的安全最高纪录。年内百日安全记录 3 个。主设备未发生损坏事故，未发生人为误操作或检修不当导致对外停电事故，未发生火灾事故，继电保护、自动装置等设备没有发生误动作引起对外停电事故，投入率、正确动作率均为 100%。工作票 1497 张，操作票 2980 张，合格率均为 100%。完成 2F 机组 A 级检修，1F、3F、4F 发变组 C 级检修，“三漏”整治 17 项，设备消缺 760 项，设备消缺处理率 94.86%，设备及时消缺率 98.3%，设备运行健康状态良好。

（三）生产经济指标

大广坝公司在生产经营中全面加强财务预算管理，严格生产、经营的绩效考核，坚持“年零基，季滚动，月分析，周监控”预算管理模式，积极开展“节能降耗减支”的生产成本费用降控活动，最大限度地调动各方面的积极性。

在经营管理中，充分利用有限的水资源，积极与调度沟通，减少机组在低负荷长时间运行，始终保持机组设备的完好和最佳出力，提高了机组效率与水能利用率。同时，大力加强电量营销，全年超额完成了计划发电任务。加强资金管理，加大电费回收的力度，确保新电费回收率为 100%，收回陈欠电费 1000 万元。同时，大广坝公司还积极与政府物价部门协调沟通，争取电价上调。自 2009 年 11 月 20 日起，单位电价上调了 1 分，电价的上调长期保证了大广坝公司能够增收，为进一步拓展利润空间作出巨大的贡献。

由于多项措施并举，2009 年全年生产经营考核目标完成情况较好：发电量、售电量、营业收入、主营业务（发电）收入、度电可控费用（含库区基金）、息税折旧摊销前利润、利润总额等项，均完成了中国国电集团公司下达的年度考核指标。

（四）实行绩效考核

大广坝公司在 2009 年进一步强化管理，落实责任指标，把公司内部经济责任制与目标成本管理有机结合起来，全面建立起量化考核体系，严格实行了绩效考核。

（1）各部门、辅业公司深化实施有效的绩效考核，鼓励并推进各部门、辅业公司对分配制度的改革，实行员工的收入与工效挂钩，严格考核制度，全年共考核 364 次数，考核金额 29 460 元。奖励 423 次数，奖励金额 59 575 元。通过奖勤罚懒，激发员工的积极性和主动性。

（2）根据中国国电集团公司下达的生产经营考核目标，分解细化，2009 年初就与各部门、辅业公司签订了目标考核责任书，量化各项考核指标，确定了目标评分规定，每月实行部门的自评分和考核员的初审分，由总经部企管人员规范过程控制，并在每个月的综合会议上汇报各单位的考核分数，年终再根据综合分数对各单位的经营指标完成情况进行奖惩。同时，对涉及企业生产经营关键环节的水位、电量、电价、电费回收等工作，实行公司领导主管的单项目标责任制管理，将责任落实到部门，落实到个人，年终与生产经营责任制同步考核兑现。

（3）在检修维护部继续实行“点值工资”，有效地调动职工工作的积极性和服从性，打破吃“大锅饭”的劳动薪酬分配制度，有效地改变了“干多干少都一样，干好干坏都一样”的现象，提高了检修维护部每一位员工的执行力，职工对待工作的积极性和责任心得到了提高。

（中国国电集团公司）

国电新疆艾比湖流域开发有限公司 2009 年经营管理情况

国电新疆艾比湖流域开发有限公司（以下简称艾比湖公司）于 2008 年 1 月 6 日成立。2009 年，艾比湖公司实现吉林台二级引水发电工程（以下简称吉林台二级电站）当年投产、当年创效，确保公司实现基建生产、经营管理、安全稳定各项目标，全面完成中国国电集团公司下达的目标责任书各项指标。

一、工程进度与质量

2009 年，艾比湖公司抢抓吉林台二级电站建设工期：8 月 1 日，大坝具备初期蓄水条件；9 月 20 日，第一台机组正式并网发电；9 月 27 日，第二台机组正式并网发电。

吉林台二级电站工程质量实行由业主统一领导、垂直分层指挥、横向联系的工程质量管理组织体系，施工质量控制以“保证每一项施工符合设计要求、实现设计意图，保证施工质量达到技术条款的规定，达到规定引用规范、标准”为原则，严格控制施工队伍素质、施工作业方法、施工机械设备和材料质量，确保每个单项工程质量。2009年，该工程实现了大坝混凝土浇筑合格率100%、优良率85.4%，厂房混凝土单元质量评定合格率100%、优良率86.26%，金属结构及机电安装工程单元质量评定合格率100%、优良率98.2%。

二、经营管理

艾比湖公司严格按国家法律法规及中国国电集团公司有关招投标规定，做好招标和合同管理工作，坚持按“同等质量比价格，同等价格比服务”的思想，控制工程造价，全年共签订合同241份。吉林台二级电站项目核准概算投资46 192万元（不考虑因政策调整增加的耕地占用税200万元），实际完成工程投资43 299万元，尽管建设期发生了发电洞进口开挖量及锚固量增加、引水隧洞围岩大部分恶化及多处大规模塌方、厂房后边坡不稳定岩体处理等较大的新增及变更项目，投资较核准概算仍减少2893万元（降低约6%），工程造价控制在中国国电集团公司核准的执行概算内。

吉林台二级电站2009年度发电量5127万kW·h，售电量5073万kW·h，实现收入1192万元。

三、安全生产管理

2009年，艾比湖公司健全了安全生产组织机构和管理规章制度，坚持“安全第一，预防为主”的方针，强化运行管理，严格“两票三制”，建立和落实以工程项目法人为核心的工程建设各级安全生产责任制，对工程现场安全文明生产工作进行系统、完整的策划，并通过一系列安全管理文件明确了工程项目安全文明生产目标、管理体系和各方职责，系统地建立了安全质量技术认证日志制度、安全施工措施审批制度、安全检查和重大事故隐患管理制度等，使安全管理工作制度化、规范化。同时，加强对运行学员的培训，及时消除机组在基建期遗留的缺陷，深入开展安全大检查并落实整改，使设备可靠性得到提高，等效可用系数达99.72%，主设备和辅机设备完好率100%，确保机组安全稳定运行。吉林台二级电站到2009年12月31日，已连续安全生产107天。

四、完善制度管理

2009年，艾比湖公司坚持与中国国电集团公司管理对标、制度接轨的工作原则，分类建立了本公司的标准体系文件，明晰了工作流程，规范并逐步完善了管理工作。随着工程进展由基建向生产过渡，于2009年11月制定、完善了3项管理标准：制定出台了生产管理类的安全生产管理标准、运行和检修规程；制定了计划管理类中的工程价款结算管理办法；修订完善了人力资源管理类中的员工请休假管理办法和绩效考核管理办法。

（中国国电集团公司）

新型水电厂培训仿真系统在二滩水电站成功应用

二滩水电开发有限责任公司位于四川省成都市，自1991年成立之日起，致力于雅砻江流域的水电开发，二滩水电站便是其实施雅砻江流域梯级滚动开发的第一个项目。二滩水电站位于雅砻江下游河段，距攀枝花市约40km，为混凝土双曲拱坝，最大坝高240m，水库总库容58亿m^3，水电站装机容量330万kW，多年平均发电量170亿kW·h。随着雅砻江流域滚动开发计划的深入，2012年起锦屏一级水电站、锦屏二级水电站、官地水电站将陆续投产。为了应对后续电站的运行维护工作，二滩水电开发有限责任公司招聘了大量应届毕业生，并建立了新型水电厂培训仿真系统。

2008年2月，水电厂培训仿真系统首次在二滩电厂培训中心进行试用，其仿真范围涵盖水电站几乎所有的一次和二次设备，主要包括发电机组、调速系统、励磁系统、主变压器、一次系统（母线、断路器等）、输电线路、油压装置、供气系统、直流系统、消防系统、厂用电系统、监控系统及自动装置等。经过二滩水电站工作人员及领导、各个电站参与调试的人员、国网电力科学研究院（南瑞公司）几方的共同努力，2008年5月水电厂培训仿真系统通过竣工验收。2009年3月，系统通过了四川省科技厅组织的科学技术鉴定。

水电厂培训仿真系统提出大型水电厂数字仿真和物理仿真相结合的仿真系统原型设计方法，支持大型水电厂AGC/AVC/EDC等水电行业高级应用技术的仿真，仿真系统收敛性和鲁棒性强、精度高。基于模糊辨识的分层状态估计智能算法，建立了逼真的水电厂运行在线初始仿真断面，实现水电厂监控系统与仿真系统的有机结合，以提供与实际生产设备一体化的操作运行环境、运行设备仿真分析、调节参数修正、控制策略研究平台。系统提供包括事故重演、操作指导、故障设置、考核系统、检修操作等培训功能，教学培训方式全面，实现了培训仿真系统的培训需求识别、智能教案生成、智能培训控制和智能培训评估等机制。

经过在二滩水电站的应用，充分体现了新型水电厂培训仿真系统的优点，今后必将在水电自动化监测行业得到广泛应用。

（国网电力科学研究院　蔡　杰）

中国水利水电第三工程局有限公司信息系统安全建设

随着企业信息化建设的发展，业务系统对信息系统的依赖程度越来越高，这也意味着信息安全问题越来越突出。为了有效防范和化解风险，保证企业信息系统平稳运行和业务持续开展，必须建立企业的信息安全保障体系，以增强企业对信息安全风险的防范能力。

企业的信息安全体系的建设，已成为企业加强内部控制和管理，降低运营风险，建立高效、统一、运转协调的管理体系的必要保证。

中国水利水电第三工程局有限公司（以下简称水电三局有限公司）信息系统网络结构分为3层：第一层为公司总部，第二层为二级单位，第三层为项目部；分成两级广域网：一级广域网连接公司总部与二级单位，二级广域网连接二级单位与项目部。通过安全风险分析，进行了相应的信息安全建设。

（一）建设原则

（1）实用性原则。安全体系建设将始终遵循“面向应用，注重实效”的指导思想，紧密结合企业现有网络和应用情况，充分保证原有系统和结构的可用性。

（2）完整性原则。企业网络安全建设必须保证整个防御体系的完整性。在安全体系建设中，通过采取多种安全防御的技术和措施并行，来保障企业的网络系统安全运行。

（3）整体均衡原则。要对信息系统进行全面均衡的保护，要提高整个信息系统的“安全最低点”的安全性能，保证各个层面防护的均衡。

（4）安全目标与效率、投入之间的平衡原则。要综合考虑安全目标与效率、投入之间的均衡关系，确定合适的平衡点，不能为了追求安全而牺牲效率，或投入过大。

（5）动态发展原则。安全防范体系的建设不是一个一劳永逸的工作，而是一个长期不断完善的过程，所以技术方案要能够随着安全技术的发展、外部环境的变化、安全目标的调整而不断升级发展。

（6）节省投资原则。在满足上述原则的基础上，应尽量做到节省设备采购投资，不要形成一种“用价值10元的设备来保护价值5元的资产”的局面。

（二）信息安全建设

围绕着“建设一个安全、高效、动态网络信息化安全系统”的指导思想，水电三局有限公司从以下几个方面对网络进行了安全建设：

1．出口边界防护建设

实现出口边界的访问控制、防病毒、入侵防御和审计等安全策略。根据对市场已有安全产品的分析，功能全面、维护简单且性价比较高的UTM类产品是比较好的选择。UTM产品提供了完整的边界安全保护能力，是对传统防护手段的整合和升华，它能在原有安全网关设备的基础上，又拥有防火墙、入侵防御（IPS）、防病毒（AV）、内容过滤、反垃圾邮件等多种功能。公司总部通过安装UTM产品，有效地实施访问控制、入侵检测与防护、防病毒、应用层信息过滤、流量管理、带宽管理等能力。同时，仅利用一台设备，即可实现完整的边界安全解决方案，大大降低了采购成本和维护成本。利用UTM设备，水电三局有限公司还把网络分为外网区、内网区、DMZ区，实现重要区域的重点防护。

2．内网安全建设

内网安全建设包括防病毒系统建设和终端管理系统建设。防病毒系统建设是在内网终端和网络出口均建立防病毒系统，两层立体的防病毒系统，能更好地进行病毒防护。终端管理系统建设是通过终端监控与审计系统，实现对终端的控制和管理，通过对终端的威胁主动防御和终端网络行为控制，保证内网安全、可靠。终端管理系统建设包括以下几个方面：

（1）软件管理：自动发现识别客户端安装的软件信息（名称、版本、安装时间），将相关数据入库，检测客户端运行软件信息。

（2）终端流量管理：对网络客户端流量进行监控报警，客户端输入或输出流量超过管理员设定阈值时报警，对可疑发包、可疑并发连接进行阻断，防止滥用网络资源。

（3）进程运行管理：远程查看客户端运行进程列表，支持进程强制终止，对需要控制或异常的进程进行强制管理。

（4）上网访问控制：对网络客户端访问的网站进行控制，可以禁止客户端非法访问策略中不允许访问的网站。

（5）终端杀毒软件管理：对客户端安装的杀毒软件进行识别，并能够对客户端未执行杀毒软件作出对应操作。

3．网络设备自身安全建设

面对网络设备自身面临的威胁，水电三局有限公司从以下几个方面提高网络设备的安全性：

(1) 对于支持Web访问配置的设备，使用https加密的方式进行控制。

(2) 使用SSH方式代替远程TELNET访问控制，并只允许特定的用户访问。

(3) 交换机、路由器、防火墙配置静态路由防止路由欺骗和路由攻击。

(4) 及时更新路由器、防火墙、交换机版本，提高网络设备产品自身的安全性。

(5) 交换机IP、MAC、端口的绑定。

4. VPN系统建设

水电三局有限公司总部与二级单位和三级机构进行业务数据传输是通过不安全的互联网进行的，为防止核心数据通过互联网被窃取，需要采用安全等级较强的VPN技术实现传输安全。通过比较成熟的IP-SEC协议，采用3DES算法进行数据加密，选用加速VPN产品，实现了快速、安全的广域网建设。水电三局有限公司的VPN建设，通过百兆光纤，上与中国水利水电建设集团公司，下与二级单位、三级项目部以及移动办公，均实现了广域网建设。水电三局有限公司的核心业务应用，利用安全的VPN通道，实现了数据交换和信息共享。

5. 安全管理建设

单一的安全产品部署并不能够解决全部问题，必须要配合管理手段。纵观整个安全体系建设，其中最为重要的环节就是管理。建设有针对性的安全策略和安全技术规范，建立有效的安全监控措施和评估检查制度，有效地发现和监控安全事件，并采取相应的措施；建立完善的灾难应急计划和制度，对突发的安全事件制定有效的应对措施，建立有效的对安全事件的处理流程和制度，是信息安全的最终保障。通过安全管理的建设，进一步保障了网络高效安全的运行。

总之，水电三局有限公司经过整体信息化安全建设，从出口防护、内网控制、技术防护和管理运行多方面并行建设，大大提高了信息系统的安全，从而保障了企业信息化系统的正常运行。

（中国水利水电第三工程局有限公司　石　露）

中國水力發電年鉴

12

水电站生产运行

电力生产及管理

中国长江电力股份有限公司 2009 年电力生产情况

2009 年，三峡—葛洲坝区段长江来水总量仅为 3881.29 亿 m^3，年平均流量为 12 300m^3/s，相应来水频率 90.3%，较多年均值（14 300m^3/s）偏枯 14.0%，与 2008 年（13 600m^3/s）相比偏枯 9.6%。

中国长江电力股份有限公司（以下简称长江电力）管辖的三峡—葛洲坝梯级电站全年完成发电量 960.96 亿 kW·h，完成本年度预算的 97.07%，同比减少 1.8%。其中，三峡电站 798.53 亿 kW·h（其中左岸电站 402.41 亿 kW·h，右岸电站 392.27 亿 kW·h，电源电站 3.86 亿 kW·h），较本年度计划 830 亿 kW·h 少发 35.321 5 亿 kW·h，比上年度 803.109 6 亿 kW·h 少发 8.431 1 亿 kW·h；葛洲坝电站 162.430 1 亿 kW·h（其中大江电站 97.653 8 亿 kW·h，二江电站 64.776 3 亿 kW·h，0 号机组 0.725 4 亿 kW·h），比本年度计划 153.8 亿 kW·h 多发 7.904 7 亿 kW·h，比上年度 169.413 9 亿 kW·h 少发 7.709 2 亿 kW·h。

2009 年度长江电力安全生产取得好成绩，连续安全生产天数达 285d，没有发生设备事故。长江电力下属的葛洲坝电厂实现“零设备事故、零人身伤害，零设备障碍”的“三零”目标，连续安全生产天数达 2451d，三峡电厂连续安全生产天数达 1233d，梯调通信中心连续安全生产天数达 2527d，检修厂连续安全生产天数达 285d。三峡电厂设备可用小时为 7978.55h，利用小时达 4372.92h，等效可用系数 93.34%；葛洲坝电厂设备可用小时为 8183.58h，利用小时达 5957.13h，等效可用系数 93.42%；设备运行状况良好，为安全生产奠定了基础。

三峡电站全年节水增发电量为 39.587 亿 kW·h，水能利用提高率为 5.23%，厂用电率 0.084%，发电耗水率 4.36m^3/(kW·h)，发电水量利用率 94.6%；葛洲坝电站节水增发电量为 10.975 亿 kW·h，水能利用提高率为 7.28%，厂用电率 0.166%，发电耗水率 19.54m^3/(kW·h)，发电水量利用率 87.0%；三峡—葛洲坝梯级电站累计节水增发电量 50.56 亿 kW·h，平均水能利用提高率为 5.57%。三峡—葛洲坝梯级电站 2009 年节水增发的电量相当于节约燃煤约 182 万 t，减少二氧化碳排放约 477 万 t，有力地助推了节能减排工作，创造了良好的经济效益和社会效益。

2009 年，三峡工程在汛期有效发挥了防洪作用，最大削减洪峰流量 15 000m^3/s，减轻了长江下游的防洪压力。在枯水季节，三峡水库对下游实施补水调度，累计补水 127.3 亿 m^3，保障了长江中下游通航水深和生产生活用水要求，为缓解旱情发挥了重要作用。

2009 年 8 月 6 日，长江上游出现五年以来最大洪峰，三峡大坝上游来水最大达到 55 000m^3/s，由于三峡大坝控制下泄流量不超过 40 000m^3/s，三峡大坝上游水位不断上升，8 月 8 日已达到 152.6m，机组运行水头达到 84m。2009 年 8 月 8 日凌晨 2 时 20 分，三峡电站的最大出力一度达到 1823.1 万 kW，首次达到全厂设计出力 1820 万 kW，三峡工程和电厂经受了考验。

2009 年 8 月，三峡—葛洲坝梯级电站单月发电达 145.63 亿 kW·h，完成月计划的 104.5%，其中三峡电站月发电量 127.16 亿 kW·h，三峡电站和三峡—葛洲坝梯级电站都创造了单月发电量历史新高。2009 年 7 月 1 日三峡电厂日发电量突破 4 亿 kW·h，达到 4.0199 亿 kW·h，再创历史新高。

2009 年 4 月 7 日凌晨 2 时 3 分，三峡电站累计发电量突破 3000 亿 kW·h。三峡电站是我国继葛洲坝电厂发电 24 年累计 3000 亿 kW·h 之后的第二个累计发电量突破 3000 亿 kW·h 的电站，但三峡电厂仅用了 7 年。对于这一成绩，国务院三峡工程建设委员会办公室专门致电祝贺。

2009 年，长江电力金沙江电力生产筹备工作全面展开。4 月 30 日，长江电力成立溪洛渡水力发电厂筹建处、向家坝水力发电厂筹建处和三峡水利枢纽梯级调度通信中心成都分中心筹建处。金沙江下游电站电力生产准备工作已从方案编制进入方案实施的新阶段。根据“强化电站责任、优化资源配置、深化精益管理、创建国际一流”的电力生产管理总体思路，溪洛渡水力发电厂筹建处、向家坝水力发电厂筹建处和三峡水利枢纽梯级调度通信中心成都分中心筹建处，积极参与溪洛渡、向家坝电站工程建设和相关设计方案审查，对《溪洛渡、向家坝电站电力生产管理方案》进行了分步细化，组织编制了接机发电倒计时工作计划，开展了“调控一体化”等重点管理项目的研究，努力探索符合溪洛渡、向家坝电站特点的生产管理方式，为顺利接管和运行管理好电站打下了良好基础。

（中国长江电力股份有限公司　谢兴发）

黄河上游水电开发有限责任公司所属大中型水电站2009年生产管理情况

一、龙羊峡水电站

2009年，龙羊峡水电站全年累计入库水量237.46亿m^3，较多年同期多蓄水73.61亿m^3，年末水库水位2591.47m，较上年同期高11.42m，相应水库蓄水量215.4亿m^3，较上年同期多蓄水39.17亿m^3；全年完成发电量58.48亿kW·h，完成年计划的101.7%；电压合格率100%，频率合格率100%；继电保护装置投入率100%，继电保护动作3次，正确动作率100%；故障录波器完好率100%，保护定检率100%，自动装置投入率100%，正确动作率100%；主设备一类率100%，辅助设备完好率100%；综合厂用电率为0.85%，比计划值减少了0.05%。

2009年，龙羊峡水库水位达到历史第二高水位2593.91m，组织力量进行了全方位监控，有效保证了水库的安全运行。截至2009年12月31日，年内安全生产实现365d，长周期安全运行4531d，创投产发电以来最高安全生产长周期纪录。

全年累计设备缺陷消缺数量379条，主设备消缺率100%，辅助设备消缺率99.21%；完成了机组A级检修1台·次，C级检修3台·次，D级检修1台·次，330kV线路春检预试2条·次，辅助设备检修完成了厂内6kV系统Ⅰ、Ⅱ、Ⅲ段和坝上6kV系统Ⅴ、Ⅵ段清扫预试工作，并对1号主变压器进行了更换；完成了2009年下达的第一批、第二批生产工程项目计划中的所有大修项目共计13项、技术改造项目10项。

2009年，共修订制度30部，制定制度12部，修订图纸52份，修编检修规程7份、试验规程5份、水工规程5份和运行规程23份，制度建设进一步加强。

二、拉西瓦水电站

2009年5月12日，拉西瓦发电分公司顺利完成了首批6、5号机组的接收工作，标志着生产准备工作全面完成。此前，共制定管理标准112部、工作标准36部、技术标准58部、应急预案14部，绘制完成系统图册168张，编制生产图表134种；先后安排107人次进行学习培训，9人参加工程监理培训；聘请专家开展技术讲座13次，参加人员239人次；53人次参加技术方案讨论会等各类技术活动，为生产工作的顺利开展打下良好基础。

2009年，拉西瓦水电站全年共完成发电量38.20亿kW·h，完成年计划105.51%；上网电量38.02亿kW·h，完成年计划105.64%；超发电量1.99亿kW·h。全年耗水率2.78m^3/（kW·h），比计划值降低了0.882.78m^3/（kW·h）；综合厂用电率0.49%，比计划值降低了0.11个百分点。

自投产发电以来，共查找缺陷507条，消除467条，消缺率达92.11%；设备等效可用系数93.71%，比计划值提高0.25个百分点。针对二次设备缺陷的隐蔽性特点，组织技术人员对二次监控系统进行了全面诊断，进一步完善了设备定值，提高了设备健康水平。认真分析机组经济运行区域，积极协调沟通，不断优化机组间的负荷分配，顺利完成年度发电任务。2号机投产发电以后，集中力量完成了5号机组的D级检修，消除了设备隐患，确保机组安全稳定运行。

三、李家峡水电站

2009年，李家峡水电站完成发电量57.39亿kW·h，为计划的102%，与上年同期相比增加7.57%，创历史新高。厂用电率0.3%，与计划指标持平，与上年同期相比减少0.025个百分点。电压、频率合格率为100%。全年入库水量192亿m^3，出库水量191亿m^3，水能利用率100%。发电耗水率3.33m^3/(kW·h)，低于计划值0.01m^3/（kW·h），与上年同比减少0.044m^3/（kW·h）。设备等效可用系数91.15%，高于计划值2.38%，与上年同期相比增加0.3个百分点。设备利用小时数3586.73h，与上年相比增加252.03h，完成年度计划指标的101.65%。

年内安全运行365d，连续安全生产3495d；发生设备二类障碍1次，设备异常1次，完成了安全责任目标。

加强电站设备管理，年内完成1号发电机变压器组的B级检修，1、2、3、4号发电机变压器组的C级检修，机组检修一次启动成功率100%。结合机组检修完成了1号机监控系统改造、集成保护换型、快速闸门检修及防腐处理、水轮机转轮叶片裂纹处理、3号机组调速器换型改造、330kV GIS四串大修、李吉Ⅰ线辅助保护屏换型、生产管理系统移植等一批影响电站安全运行的生产工程项目，全年未发生非计划检修。全年电站共发现设备缺陷488条，消除481

条，消缺率 98.5%；主要消除了 2～4 号发电机出口开关分合闸主控阀螺杆断裂、1802DL 冷却风机异音、205 液控阀控制管路破损以及 2 号和 4 号机组下导轴承调整螺栓断裂等较大设备缺陷，未发生由于设备缺陷而导致的非计划停运。

完成了 53 部规定、预案、制度的修编、发布、实施工作。严格执行 2009 年技术监督计划，全年 6.3kV 以上系统保护装置动作次数 19 次，正确动作次数 17 次，正确动作率 89.5%。

四、公伯峡水电站

2009 年，公伯峡水电站完成发电量 53.73 亿 kW·h，年完成率 102.03%，创历年最高值；综合厂用电率为 0.50%，比计划值低 0.11%；耗水率 3.65m^3/(kW·h)，比计划值降低 0.08m^3/(kW·h)；机组等效可用系数 94.85%，比计划值提高了 1.97%。

年内处理影响设备运行的重大缺陷有：1、2 号机组励磁变压器 TV 二次接线插头改进；1～5 号机组厂用高压变压器、励磁变压器跳闸线的恢复，加装了延时保护；对 1B～5B 主变压器冷却器散热片进行了冲洗，夏季主变压器温度明显下降；对接力器液压锁定闸板脱落隐患采取调整加固措施；利用 2 号机组 C 级检修的机会对 2B 进行了滤油，处理了主变压器气体含量超标问题；更换了 4、5 号发电机空气冷却器自动排气阀手阀；处理了 1805 断路器液压操动机构油泵不打压缺陷；处理了 5 号机组定子 520 号线棒绝缘击穿放电缺陷等。年内累计发现设备缺陷 377 项，累计消除缺陷 377 项，年消缺率 100%，一些影响设备安全稳定运行的缺陷得到及时根治处理。

截至 2009 年底，公伯峡水电站完成了机组 C 修 5 台·次、机组 D 修 5 台·次和三条线路的检修工作任务，检修后设备均一次启动成功，检修工作全部按计划完成，设备健康水平得到进一步提高。

2009 年 6 月，公伯峡发电分公司被中国能源化学工会授予“2009 年度全国大型水电厂(站)劳动竞赛先进单位”称号，这是该分公司连续五年获此殊荣。9 月，公伯峡发电分公司还荣获了“青海省模范集体”称号。

五、苏只水电站

2009 年，全年发电量 9.13 亿 kW·h，为年计划的 102.24%，创历史新高；上网电量 9.03 亿 kW·h；综合厂用电率 1.13%；耗水率 21.94m^3/(kW·h)，比计划控制值低 0.56m^3/(kW·h)。等效可用系数、水能利用提高率两项指标均在黄河上游水电开发有限责任公司对标管理指标中名列前茅。

圆满完成了 1、2、3 号机组 C 级检修任务；对大坝及水工建筑物、全厂排水设施、泄洪闸启闭机进行了全面检查和处理，分别利用厂用电和柴油发电机进行了提落门试验；对电站部分继电保护定值进行了详细的核查和计算；制订了特种设备的年检计划，对全厂的起重设备、压力容器、安全阀及承压阀门进行了全面的检查，建立了相应的技术台账；完成了苏只电站计量系统改造工程。

安全生产持续稳定，年内安全生产 365d，连续安全记录 1462d；实现了“零弃水”、“零非停”控制目标。

全年共发现设备 C、D 类缺陷 269 条，消除 268 条，消缺率为 99.6%。制定管理制度 23 部，制定工作流程 12 个、工作规程 4 部。

六、盐锅峡水电站

2009 年，完成年发电量 16.77 亿 kW·h，完成年计划的 101.39%；上网电量 16.45 亿 kW·h；综合厂用电率 1.92%；发电耗水率 10.87m^3/(kW·h)。

完成 110kV 乙母线、主变压器、线路、单元清扫预试工作；完成 8 条线路小修预试、保护校验工作；完成 5 台主变压器小修预试、保护校验工作；完成 1～10 号机组小修预试、保护校验工作；完成 7 号深井泵大修工作；完成厂用 11B、12B、13B、14B、17B、17B—1 小修预试、保护更换工作；完成 1 号机组 B 级检修工作。

完成 8 台 110kV 开关更换工作；完成 4 号机进水口闸门及启闭机大修工作；配合完成电能计量系统改造工作并已投入运行；完成生产管理系统移植工作，目前进入试运行及完善阶段。

全年未发生任何不安全事件，实现了安全生产责任目标。截至 2009 年 12 月 31 日，年内安全生产 365d，长周期安全生产记录 3180d。

年内共查出安全隐患 17 项，列入治理计划 3 项，已治理完成 2 项，申请立项 12 项，未完成项目已全部采取和落实了防范措施。发现设备缺陷 393 项，消除 392 项，待消缺陷 1 项，实际消缺率 99.75%。

七、八盘峡水电站

2009 年，全年发电量 8.25 亿 kW·h，完成年计划的 101.44%；上网电量 8.08 亿 kW·h；综合厂用电率 2.04%；耗水率 26.6m^3/ (kW·h)。

完成 110kV 母线、主变压器、线路、单元清扫预试；完成 5 号机组 A 级检修工作；完成 5 台机组 C 级检修工作；开展跨年度的 4 号机组 A 级检修工作。

完成 5 号机组出口开关更换、3 号和 5 号机组励磁系统改造、尾水门机大修技改、主厂房 2 号桥机大修技改、38B 更换、3501 断路器更换、5 台 110kV 断路器更换、7台断路器端子箱更换工作。

完成大坝观测自动化系统改造工作；配合完成电能计量改造工作。

全年未发生任何不安全事件，实现安全生产责任目标。截至2009年12月31日，年内安全生产365d，长周期安全记录3961d。

全年共排查出隐患17项，列入整改计划2项，已治理完成6项，需申请立项9项，未完成项目已全部采取和落实了防范措施。发现设备缺陷826项，消除825项，待消缺陷1项，实际消缺率为99.88%。

八、青铜峡水电站

发电量：1～8号机完成10.28亿kW·h，同比增加9.74%，完成年发电计划的102.3%；唐渠电站完成1.26亿kW·h，同比减少3.9%，完成年发电计划的100.58%。上网电量：1～8号机完成10.06亿kW·h发电量，同比增加9.8%；唐渠电站完成1.24亿kW·h发电量，同比减少3.9%。综合厂用电率：1～8号机2.19%，同比降低0.05个百分点；唐渠电站1.68%，同比增加0.1个百分点。入库水量：261.30亿m^3，同比增加9%。发电耗水率：1～8号机为21.50m^3/(kW·h)，同比增加0.65%；唐渠电站为25.93m^3/(kW·h)，同比增加2.73%。继电保护：全部继电保护装置共动作1次，正确动作1次，正确率100%；全部继电保护装置投入率100%。自动装置投入率100%。电气主设备预试率100%。

全年电站安全生产长周期记录3499d，创历史新高。

2009年，电站生产工程任务繁重，共下达生产工程项目25项。先后组织开展了5号机组的A级检修、6号机组跨年度A级检修、9号机组的B级检修和3台机的C级检修。完成了大修项目22项、防汛项目2项、零购项目5项、技改项目6项，生产工程项目完成率为88.36%，资金完成率为74.13%。主变压器更换、110kV开关站设备改造两个重点改造项目竣工，完成了遗留的生产工程项目。开关站二期设备改造正式完工，标志着为期三年总投资900万元的110kV开关站改造工程全部结束。

积极配合地方政府开展水库清障、防凌等工作，建设了库区泥沙观测站，圆满完成了水库汛末冲库拉沙任务。拉沙总历时67.5h，排出淤积泥沙1049.5万t，使坝前冲刷漏斗得到了有效恢复，初步解决了泄水建筑物和灌溉取水口闸门被泥沙淤死的问题。

为加快技术改造工作步伐，成立了技术改造工作办公室。4月，中国电力投资集团公司批复了技术改造可行性研究报告，电站全面技术改造工程进入实质性的实施阶段。按照中国电力投资集团公司“统一规划、分步实施”的指导方针，全力做好技术改造的各项工作；7月，青铜峡水电站技术改造工程启动仪式在银川隆重举行；8月，签订了第一期两台水轮发电机组采购合同，1、8号水轮发电机组及其辅助设备进入制造阶段。

（黄河上游水电开发有限责任公司
胡耀斌　许为宁　张文俊）

龙滩水电站2009年生产运行情况

（一）生产运行统计

2009年，龙滩水电站按照大唐集团公司新厂新制管理模式和点检定修管理要求，结合自身特点，坚持管理创新，以创建“国际知名、国内一流水电厂”为标杆，夯实基础，到位做实，加强隐患排查和风险防控，抓好水库优化调度，保证了生产运行工作顺利开展，实现投产发电连续安全稳定运行955d，累计发电量131.40亿kW·h，出色完成了2009年春节、“两会”、新中国成立60周年国庆、澳门回归十周年、第六届东盟博览会等重大节日、重大会议的保电任务。

2009年，计划发电量156亿kW·h，年累计发电量131.40亿kW·h，年度发电量完成率为84.23%；年累计上网电量为130.50万kW·h；厂用电量2588.83万kW·h，厂用电率0.197%；年累计综合厂用电量8460.43万kW·h，年综合厂用电率0.692%。

2009年内无非计划停运事件发生，1～7号主变压器共计停运5组次，进行了1、2、5、6、7号主变压器C级检修，计2612.04h；停运备用542.99h。2009年内机组共停机备用1487台·次，共计备用29 822.25h;年度发电设备台年平均运行小时为4058.05h，利用小时2681.61h；机组平均等效可用系数为94.91%。

2009年度入库水量为359.68亿m^3，发电用水量为418.16亿m^3，弃水水量为0.015亿m^3（弃水原因是11月19日溢流坝段底孔闸门动水试验）；最高水位370.35m（1月），汛期来水量较历年来水量偏少很多，汛期后库水位最高蓄至359.12m，年末水位349.60m；发电平均耗水率3.18m^3/(kW·h)。

（二）安全生产措施

龙滩水电站自2007年5月21日首台机组投产之日起，到2009年底已连续安全生产955d，创造了国内特大型水轮发电机组投运后的安全运行新纪录。

（1）深入开展“安全生产年”各项活动。为贯彻落实党中央、国务院关于“安全生产年”的重大部署，龙滩水电开发有限公司（以下简称龙滩公司）制定了“安全生产年”活动实施方案，组织开展了“安全生产月”、电力安全生产“三项行动”活动、春秋季安全大检查、“迎国庆、保安全”隐患排查专项治理、防洪度汛、防止自然灾害、重大危险源评估，以及工程建设和发电生产运行中使用的易燃易爆等危险化学品等专项隐患排查治理等一系列的重要活动，消除各种事故隐患。认真执行国家、行业有关电力生产的法律法规，确保企业生产经营合法规范。

（2）高度重视各种重大节假日及重要政治活动期间的安全保电工作。在春节、“两会”、国庆、中国东盟博览会期间，龙滩电厂都安排有专业技术人员和生产管理人员 24h 值班，并制定有相应的保电措施方案。协同大唐集团公司安全检查组和地方公安部门、武警消防支队，对龙滩电站生产区域的安全保卫情况进行了全面检查，认真落实安保防范措施，每天按时报送电力安全生产信息，确保国庆期间安全发供电。

（3）持续推进电力安全生产“三项行动”各项工作。龙滩公司制定和颁布了《龙滩水电开发有限公司深入开展“三项行动”活动实施方案》，全面部署了龙滩公司的“三项行动”计划。在执法行动检查中，严格遵守国家安全生产法律法规的有关规定，无论是在工程建设还是发电生产中均未发现有违法违规现象。在安全隐患治理行动中，累计检查出一般安全隐患 246 项，均已经全部进行整改，未发现影响发电生产安全运行的重大安全隐患项。在宣传教育行动中，龙滩公司委派安全管理人员及专业技术人员共计 44 人次，外出参加了国家安全生产监督管理总局和国家电力监管委员会举办的事故应急预案持续改进、安全生产长效机制建设、电力建设施工安全管理、电力二次系统安全防护及电力系统安全运行管理等培训班。同时企业内部还开展了多种形式的培训活动，外请专家、学者到企业内部授课培训等。全年参加安全监督专业培训人数为 140 人，培训人次为 161 人次，安全监督专业培训总学时数为 4008h。

（4）认真贯彻落实《突发事件应对法》，强化应急演练培训。龙滩公司成立以总经理为组长的应急领导小组，编制完善各种应急预案，建立健全应对突发事件的监测预警机制，强化应急队伍建设。2009 年间，龙滩公司共修订印发 40 部应急预案，共组织开展包括黑启动、电缆着火、特大暴雨洪水倒灌等以及厂用电全停等 40 余次突发事件应急预案演练，累计参加人数达 1168 人次。通过不断健全应急预案，采取形式多样、内容丰富的应急演练和培训，企业应急队伍应对各种突发事件的处置能力得到进一步的提高。

（5）完善安全生产管理体系，健全规章制度。龙滩公司不断加强安全保证体系建设，树立起“安全生产可控、能控、在控”的理念；树立起“事故是可以预防的、失误是可以避免的、异常是可以控制的”理念；树立起“确保人身安全是安排各项工作的前提，确保人身安全是现场安全管理的重点”的理念；树立起“违章就是事故，以零违章确保零事故”的理念，加强全面、全员、全方位的安全管理与监督。实施安全责任和目标的四级控制，即公司控制重伤和事故；车间控制轻伤和障碍；班组控制未遂和异常；个人控制违章。做到层层落实、层层控制、一级保一级、一级对一级负责。

（6）努力提高设备健康水平。龙滩公司新发布了《备品配件管理暂行规定》、《技术改造项目管理暂行规定》、《生产设备异动管理规定》等管理制度，确保了主辅设备安全、可靠、经济、环保目标的实现。2009 年，龙滩公司共投入检修资金 1328 万元，投入技术改造资金 723 万元，完成了龙滩水电站 1、2、5、6、7 号机组的 C 级检修工作，共完成检修项目 360 项，组织实施了计算机监控系统的流程改进、水导瓦托块支撑改造、机组顶盖平压管改造、机组水轮机端子箱改造、增压泵停泵卸载改造、机组空冷器供排水管路空气阀改造、直流系统绝缘测试仪检查和整改、柴油发电机带载试验、定子机座螺栓拉伸技术改造等技改项目 40 项，共发现缺陷 835 项，处理 814 项，消缺率为 97.5%，确保了机组长期安全稳定运行，首次实现了全年机组“零非停”。

（三）运行调度的新举措

2009 年龙滩水库流域为偏枯年，全年平均入库流量与多年平均同比减少约 60%。龙滩电厂采取了加强与气象部门、电网调度及水库调度部门的沟通等举措，优化水库调度。

（1）龙滩公司成立了防汛领导小组，制定了《红水河龙滩水电站 2009 年度汛要求》，明确了度汛标准，同时认真执行珠江防汛抗旱总指挥部来文，从而确保了大坝及移民安全，保证了机组安全稳定运行。

（2）对水情测报系统进行了功能完善，并加强巡检管理及维护，确保龙滩水情自动测报系统正常运行，为龙滩水电工程安全度汛打下了坚实的基础。

（3）编制完成《调度运用计划》、《洪水调度方案》及各月年发电计划方案，并根据实际来水情况和气象预报不断地对《发电计划》进行修订，调整调度方案，在保证防洪安全的同时也确保电站发电效益。

（4）积极联系中国南方电网电力调度通信中心（以下简称南网总调）、珠江水利委员会等相关单位，开展动态汛限水位研究、流域梯级调度优化方案研究等工作，提高水能利用率。

（5）编制了《龙滩流域区间来水分析报告》及《龙滩控制流域小水电调查情况》，摸清了流域区间来水情况和小水电分布情况；配合完成龙滩水情数据接入南网总调水调系统，之后根据总调要求不断进行完善；同时配合完成视频会商系统的调试，以及配合完善《南方电网水电经济运行评价指标体系》等一系列工作。确保了下游生产生活用水、防洪度汛和澳门、珠海等珠江三角洲地区的供水安全，创造了巨大的社会效益和经济效益。

2009年4月，龙滩水电厂荣获国家防汛抗旱总指挥部办公室及水利部水文局颁发的“全国先进报汛站”称号。

（四）质量、安全、环境职业健康管理体系认证与执行情况

2009年，按照既满足标准要求又有可操作性的原则，初步编写了龙滩水电厂质量、环境、职业健康安全管理体系文件。该文件包括环境、职业健康安全管理体系手册，程序文件和管理制度。以手册为核心，程序文件为基础，规程、规范为支持的具有龙滩水电厂特色的管理体系得到进一步完善，在作业指导书的编写中引入“W点”和“H点”的控制方法，使工作更规范、更有效。目前此项工作正在紧锣密鼓地进行，争取用最短的时间通过质量、安全、环境职业健康管理体系认证。

（五）标准化工作

2009年标准化工作显著提升。进一步规范设备资料整理，加强备品备件管理。根据现场各系统、设备改造及完善等变更情况，及时收集设备有关运行维护资料，不断更新整理设备台账，确保生产现场图纸、资料的正确、完善。特别是就技术改造工作的测试记录、分析报告等资料，做到及时收集并按类别存档，为日后设备运行指标提供基准资料。建立人员、网络、制度、现场和谐统一的闭环管理体系，通过信息网络逐步实现网络化、规范化、制度化。

2009年，龙滩水电厂“两票三制”已经基本实现规范化、标准化管理，违章现象得到有效遏制。2009年共办理工作票3838份，合格率100%。共完成5711项操作任务，共164 785项操作，合格率100%。同时充实标准操作票库，标准操作票由2008年的2000多份增加到2009年的6000多份，标准操作票使用率不断提高。“三制”实现标准化管理，运行交接班保持穿着整齐、列队交接的良好作风，交接内容做到清楚全面，不遗漏。做到严格按巡回检查项目定时定线路进行巡检。定期工作做到标准化，将定期工作表上墙，严格按规定开展定期工作；实行工作考评制度，规范运行管理。编制完成《标准操作指导书》、《标准措施指导书》及《运行技术教程》并印刷成册，使基础管理工作愈加扎实、完善；编制完成《危险点分析与预控手册》，全面分析作业过程中存在的危险点，要求检修人员严格按照危险点分析与预控的标准化执行，纠正习惯性违章行为。规范特种设备安全管理，对坝顶快速门机、清污机、尾水门机、电梯等设备进行定期检查，对问题及时整改，杜绝重大事故的发生。

（龙滩水电开发有限公司　张继承　张　娟　陆　军　赖亦农　林　前　徐　刚）

江苏宜兴抽水蓄能电站 2009年运行及管理情况

江苏宜兴抽水蓄能电站由华东宜兴抽水蓄能有限公司（以下简称宜兴公司）负责建设与运营管理，4台机组于2008年12月全部投入商业运营，2009年运行及管理情况如下：

（一）生产运行统计

2009年，电站4台机组共完成发电启动2010次、抽水启动1037次，启动成功率均为100%；完成发电电量11.143 2亿kW·h，抽水电量13.568 6亿kW·h，综合效率80.19%，等效可用系数83.88%。

（二）安全生产情况

2009年，电站机组消缺、生产并存，安全生产任务繁重。为确保实现年度安全生产目标，宜兴公司年初明确了全年安全工作要点，层层分解落实安全生产责任，及时调整完善安全保证和监督体系，不断健全各类安全生产管理制度；坚持行政正职到岗到位；深入开展“反违章”、“三项行动”、“三查一整改”、安全性评价等专项活动；定期召开各类安全例会，分析制定整改及防范措施；严格执行“两票三制”，落实“两措”；加强安全工器具、防误装置、特种设备的监督管理；认真落实新中国成立60周年国庆保电、迎峰度夏和防汛措施；加大隐患排查力度，全年共组织开展了12次安全生产大检查；深入开展各类安全教育培训、消防、应急演练；在国网新源控股有限公司组织的安全性评价活动中取得了良好成绩。

全年共完成3个百日安全生产，未发生负主要责任的重大电网事故、重大设备事故、恶性误操作事故、水淹厂房事故和全厂停电事故，全面实现了国网新源控股有限公司下发的安全10项、生产5项考核指标，全年发生非计划停运次数控制在考核指标以内。截至2009年底，实现了自1号机组商业运行以来，电站连续安全生产609d，保持了稳定良好的安全生产业绩。

（三）机组检修与消缺

设备检修维护是2009年宜兴公司工作的重点之

一，事关安全生产及经营指标的全面实现。为确保检修计划按期进行，宜兴公司早安排、早谋划、早沟通，动员一切可以利用的资源，全力保证检修工作的顺利开展。全年共完成1、2、3号机组B级检修，2号机组C级检修，1、3、4号机组D级检修各一次；完成500kV 1号电缆线电缆头的更换、1～4号主变压器的滤油处理、1～6号渗漏排水泵的检修工作。通过机组检修和预防性试验，彻底解决了机组导叶小开度振动问题，消除了部分设备缺陷，提高了设备的整体健康水平，保证了电站设备百分百完好率，为电站设备安全稳定运行打下坚实的基础。

（四）竣工专项验收及相关工作

2009年，宜兴公司加大电站尾工建设力度，全面完成了土建工程及部分机电设备的消缺处理工作，顺利完成了职业病防治、水土保持、环境保护3项专项竣工验收工作，完成了工程档案专项竣工预验收。开展了枢纽工程竣工安全鉴定活动，进行了电站工程达标投产自检及创建优质工程咨询活动，工程竣工结算工作全面铺开，为2010年工程整体竣工验收打下了坚实基础。

（五）科技发展方面

2009年，电站共承担9个科研项目，完成率100%。其中“上水库钢筋混凝土面板混合堆石坝设计施工”、“地下厂房开挖施工”和“大型钢岔管设计、制作与安装”三个项目分别完成国家电力科技进步奖和江苏省科技进步奖的申报工作；“上水库大坝渗流安全研究”和“抽水蓄能电站工程项目划分和科技档案分类研究”已完成专家评审。在群众性创新和专利申请方面，“抽水蓄能电站埋藏式钢岔管与围岩联合受力结构”收到国家知识产权局的专利证书；“下游位于倾斜山坡上的面板堆石坝”和“使用于弱围岩地下厂房支护的新型顶拱结构”取得了专利申请号。

（六）2009年取得的荣誉

宜兴公司2009年荣获了“江苏省五一劳动奖状”、“江苏省平安企业”、“国网新源控股有限公司先进集体”称号；宜兴公司总经理黄悦照荣获“江苏省五一劳动奖章”、“国家电网公司劳动模范”等光荣称号。

（华东宜兴抽水蓄能有限公司　郭惠民　尹　路）

山东泰山抽水蓄能电站 2009年运行及管理情况

山东泰山抽水蓄能电站总装机容量为1000MW，2007年6月4台机组全部投产。山东泰山抽水蓄能电站有限责任公司（以下简称泰山公司）连续6年保持了“省级文明单位”的荣誉称号，并被评为“全国精神文明建设工作先进单位”。

（一）2009年生产运行统计

2009年四台机组发电工况启动388次，发电启动成功率均为100%；抽水工况启动157次，抽水启动成功率均为100%。全年完成发电量为11 347.09万kW·h，抽水电量为14 356.9万kW·h，上网电量11 246.4万kW·h，受网电量15 393.67万kW·h，有效地满足了山东电网安全经济运行的要求。

（二）运行调度情况

2009年应山东电力调度中心要求，机组发电紧急启动76次。圆满完成了配合华北网调联合反事故演习、网上机组跳闸顶负荷、山东电网黑启动试验等任务，充分体现了抽水蓄能机组调峰调频、事故备用的作用，保证了山东电网安全稳定经济运行。

2009年3月30日，泰山抽水蓄能电站1号机组参与了山东电网黑启动试验。山东电网以泰山抽水蓄能电站1号机组为黑启动电源机组，经过500kV泰山站、220kV天平站、220kV桃园站和220kV高余站的101.66km线路，为国电石横发电厂300MW的5号机组提供厂用电，石横电厂5号机组黑启动并入主网成功，1号机组从黑启动开始到送电成功前后仅用了42min，山东电网大范围仿真状态黑启动试验圆满成功。

（三）安全生产情况

2009年，山东泰山抽水蓄能电站认真贯彻执行山东省安监局、泰安市安监局、济南电监办和国网新源控股有限公司有关安全生产的部署，紧紧围绕“稳定运行、服务电网、精雕细刻、提升自我”的目标，不断丰富管理手段，进一步提高精益化管理水平。修订完善制度、强化日常工作中的安全检查，扎实开展各项安全管理工作，顺利完成国网新源控股有限公司“风险评估”试点工作；完善“隐患排查治理”长效机制，建立须跟踪重点工作的管理台账，落实闭环管理；进一步推进长期外委项目、短期外包工程项目的规范管理；按要求开展“反违章”、安全生产三项行动、“三查一整改”等7项专项安全活动；组织开展并顺利通过工程“劳动安全与工业卫生”专项验收；配合国网新源控股有限公司信息化验收进行泰山公司安全监督与管理系统的应用；积极开展山东省“安全文化建设示范企业”申报活动。截至2009年12月31日，已实现连续安全生产1269d。

（四）技术改造情况

1. 全厂主要辅助系统设备信号增加进入监控系统　因部分重要辅助系统的主要参数未进入监控系统，运行操作人员无法监视该设备运行是否正常，不满足“无人值班，少人值守”的工作要求。为此，

2009年将1～4号机组球阀压力油罐的压力、油位，1～4号机组高压油顶起装置出口压力，1～4号渗漏排水泵电动机运行电流、泵出口压力，1～4号机组主轴密封冷却水流量、压力，励磁变压器三相温度等辅助系统的重要信号引入了CSCS系统，提高运行监测水平，适应无人值班要求。

2. 主轴密封磨损实时监测技术改造　在机组运行过程中，如出现主轴密封磨损3mm报警，通过现有的磨损监测装置很难判断该磨损是否为误报警。为从根本上解决这一问题，2009年4月1号机组C级检修期间，对该机组主轴密封磨损监测装置进行了改造。通过增加高精度水膜厚度测量仪（测量精度为0.01mm）和信号处理单元装置，将主轴密封磨损量通过信号处理单元后转换为1～20mA信号送至监控系统，以实现主轴密封磨损量的实时监测。

3. 2号机组水导油盆密封盖板改造　原水导油盆密封盖板改造与大轴采用密封环式的密封，在运行中常出现甩油现象，影响现场安全文明生产。为从根本上解决这一问题，2009年11月2号机组C级检修期间，对水导油盆密封盖板进行了改造，将其改造为接触式密封盖板，彻底解决了油及油雾的溢出，提高了设备安全文明运行水平。

（五）工程创优情况

泰山抽水蓄能电站在工程建设伊始，就提出了争创“鲁班奖”的总目标。目的在于通过建设成一个省内抽水蓄能电站建设施工现场的样板工程、标志性工程和窗口工程，提高工程基建管理水平。2009年，泰山抽水蓄能电站开展了工程创优活动，泰山公司先后荣获国家电网优质工程奖、中国电力优质工程奖、中国建设工程“鲁班奖”。泰山抽水蓄能电站是国网新源控股有限公司抽水蓄能电站建设工程中的第一个“鲁班奖”，也是全国抽水蓄能电站建设工程第一次荣获“鲁班奖”。

（六）标准化建设情况

根据国网新源控股有限公司标准化建设工作要求，2009年3月22日，泰山抽水蓄能电站成立标准化办公室；5月11日，泰山抽水蓄能电站标准化建设工作启动会议顺利召开。在国网新源控股有限公司的正确领导下，泰山抽水蓄能电站按照预定计划圆满完成了2009年标准化建设各项工作任务。2009年12月31日，泰山抽水蓄能电站企业标准正式发布，形成了标准化管理手册及标准化体系，共完成编制管理流程235个、管理标准146个、工作标准63个，并建立健全了泰山抽水蓄能电站标准化组织机构。

（山东泰山抽水蓄能电站有限责任公司　苏胜威）

万家寨水利枢纽2009年生产运行情况

（一）电力生产及供水情况

2009年，面对电网呈现的供大于求的严峻形势，万家寨电站坚持“电调服从水调，水调支持电调”的运行原则，按照来水情况及时调整机组检修计划，控制机组检修和改造进度，努力提高机组利用小时数和负荷率，力争发电效益的最大化。电站全年向内蒙古电网完成发电量11.439亿kW·h，售电量11.352亿kW·h；向山西电网完成发电量13.051亿kW·h，售电量12.979亿kW·h；向两网累计完成发电量24.490亿kW·h，比去年同期24.639亿kW·h同比减少了0.06%；向两网累计完成售电量24.331亿kW·h，比去年同期24.475亿kW·h同比减少了0.59%；完成全年22亿kW·h售电计划的110.59%。

电站全年共为晋蒙两网开机调峰794台·次，比去年同期1121台·次减少了327台·次，开机成功率100%。全年机组负荷率为54.98%，比去年同期机组负荷率61.33%降低了6.35个百分点。

2009年，万家寨电站全年库水位在951.86～978.01m之间运行，与2008年相比，水库蓄水增加0.02亿m^3，年最高库水位978.01m（4月10日），最低库水位951.86m（3月24日），平均库水位970.77m，比去年同期平均库水位969.51m提高了1.26m。

2009年水库累计来水166.99亿m^3，出库水量165.42亿m^3。年发电用水量161.75亿m^3，非发电用水量3.67亿m^3（3月配合冲刷降低潼关高程试验用水1.76亿m^3，4月补充出库流量0.46亿m^3，9月保证不超汛限水位泄水1.45亿m^3）。2009年准格尔煤田引水0.14亿m^3，山西引水1.26亿m^3，年度发电用水率97.78%。

截至2009年12月，全年厂用电量为594.51万kW·h，与去年同期578.88万kW·h比较增加了15.63万kW·h，年厂用电率为0.243%，与去年同期0.235%比较增加了0.008个百分点；年综合损耗电量为1585.43万kW·h（含厂用电量594.51万kW·h），年度综合厂用电率为0.649%，与公司下达的年度综合厂用电率0.7%的考核目标比较低了0.051个百分点；全年发电耗水率为6.62m^3/(kW·h)，比2008年同期6.51m^3/(kW·h)增加了0.11m^3/(kW·h)，同比增加了1.70%，与公司下达的年度发电耗水率6.73m^3/(kW·h)的考核目标比较低了

$0.15m^3/(kW \cdot h)$。

2009年内坝顶最大水平位移为13.05mm，坝顶最大垂直位移为7.21mm，坝基最大垂直位移4.69mm；坝体最大渗漏水量为$871.92m^3/d$，坝基最大渗漏水量为$23.69m^3/d$。通过观测资料分析，大坝变形符合一般规律，坝基、坝体渗漏无异常，坝基扬压力小于设计采用值，大坝运行状况安全。

截至12月31日，万家寨电站连续安全运行纪录达1726d。

（二）防凌防汛情况

2008～2009年度内蒙河段凌情比较严重，而万家寨库尾河段凌情相对较轻，主要是因为托县至鄂尔多斯运煤专线上游200m左右修建公路桥，施工围堰侵占河道近半，上游冰凌到此便形成卡冰封河，拦截了上游入库冰凌。在入库冰凌较少的情况下，库尾河段封河缓慢，基本全是平封状态，开河期基本没有大的冰坝壅水。

2009年开河历时较长，开河期间$1000m^3/s$以上达9d，合计入库水量18.38亿m^3。开河过程中，为保证安全度过凌汛，密切监视凌情变化，及时作出凌情、水情预报，并保持与黄河防汛抗旱总指挥部联系，及时调整库水位，减轻库尾防凌压力，保证了凌汛洪峰顺利入库。3月17～25日凌峰期间，电站发电1.38亿kW·h，发电泄水9.05亿m^3，平均发电耗水率$6.56m^3/(kW \cdot h)$，3月22日、23日连续两日发电量超过2000万kW·h。由于严格执行黄河防汛抗旱总指挥部的调度指令，顾全大局，为平稳封河、开河创造了条件，被黄河防汛抗旱总指挥部评为“2008～2009年度黄河防凌先进集体”。

根据2009年气象特征及枢纽运行状况，考虑龙口蓄水及首台机组发电计划，及时制订并上报《黄河万家寨水利枢纽2009年防洪预案》、《黄河龙口在建工程水利枢纽2009年度超标准洪水应急预案》，更新《黄河万家寨水利枢纽防洪抢险应急预案》、《水情自动测报系统崩溃应急预案》，制订2009年防汛调度计划。汛期，建立完善的防汛组织机构，密切关注水情，实行领导问责制，接受黄河防汛抗旱总指挥部的指挥，并与地方各级防汛机构及时保持联系。坚持24h值班，及时采取防护措施，顺利度过汛期。

（三）配合冲刷潼关高程试验和调水调沙

2009年黄河水利委员会第四次进行利用桃汛水量冲刷潼关高程试验。试验从3月20日开始，3月26日结束，库水位从970.81m降到951.87m的年最低水位；共向下游输水8.82亿m^3，其中非发电用水1.76亿m^3；期间，共进行闸门操作64门次，其中：底孔操作20门次，排沙孔操作34门次，排沙孔事故门操作10门次；出库沙量为634万m^3，最大含沙量为$63.3kg/m^3$。

为扩大下游主河槽过洪能力，黄河水利委员会2009年继续安排调水调沙工作。在6月25日12时至27日18时调水调沙期间，安排人员24h值班。根据黄河水利委员会防汛办公室指令，万家寨水库集中下泄，坚持6台机全日运行3d，平均出库流量为$1142m^3/s$，泄流误差4.83%，共向下游输水2.26亿m^3，其中释放库存水量1.90亿m^3，水库水位由975.15m降至966m以下，圆满完成了调水调沙任务。

（四）技术改造与科技创新情况

根据两网要求及2009年度计划安排，主要进行了机组C级检修及线路定检，并结合设备检修对影响机组安全运行的设备进行了更换，全年完成了6台机组C级检修、220kV 251～256六条线路及相关设备的定检、变电站设备及其外线的春检、预试；完成了全厂消防系统、压缩空气系统等辅助系统的维护；完成了全厂电梯的定检工作；完成了两台坝顶门机、尾水门机的防腐，4扇机组进水口拦污栅及盖板的大修、防腐及厂内1台渗漏排水泵的大修；组织完成了厂外防火、防爆库的整治；完成了220kV电压切换盘更换、事故照明电源盘的更换、6台机组保护装置的更换、山西侧3回220kV线路保护装置更换、监控机房不间断电源装置的更换、施工变电站主变压器保护、综合自动化及直流系统的更换、1号机组调速器压力油罐和气罐的更换；完成了内蒙古侧3台机组故障录波装置的加装和山西侧3台机组PMU装置的加装工作；完成了全厂直流馈电网络改造；2009年12月21～23日召开了电站2009年度已完成技术改造项目竣工验收会议，以上项目全部通过验收。

2009年8月，组织申报的电站管理局水工部“提高坝基真空激光系统监测数据可靠性QC小组”和防汛办公室“万家寨流量实测方法优化QC小组”及其活动成果，经中国水利电力质量管理协会评审，再次荣获“水利系统部级优秀质量管理小组”称号。

（黄河万家寨水利枢纽有限公司　赵　欣）

乐滩水电厂2009年生产运行情况

2009年，乐滩水电厂坚持以科学发展观统领全局，紧紧围绕“改变年”的工作思路，落实责任、强化管理、克服困难、扎实工作，在罕见的大旱之年发电量仍达电站设计多年平均值，安全生产形势稳定，经营管理效果良好。

（一）重点防控，安全生产继续保持平稳态势

（1）强化安全责任，总结经验教训，紧抓安全生

产基础管理工作。用“五确认，一兑现”的工作方法，做到“按系统、分层次、程序化、责任制”狠抓安全生产工作，积极开展安全生产宣传教育、设备整治和现场管理、安全生产治理等专项活动，进一步提高员工的安全意识与业务技能。加强基础管理，将“三讲一落实”活动与学习型班组建设、6S管理及星级考评工作相结合，逐步形成“日沟通、周走访、月交流、年总结”的机制，定期开展重大危险源评估、安全设施评估、两措管理等工作，有针对性地开展重大危险源应急预案演练，在实践中不断对标总结、闭环管理、持续改进，杜绝各类事故的发生。截至12月31日，安全生产天数达1527d。

（2）注重日常维护，加强机组检修，确保了设备的可靠性与稳定性。加大设备巡回检查力度，强化定期管理工作，加强责任意识，鼓励员工主动查找问题、发现问题、解决问题，全年共发现缺陷348项，可处理344项，已处理344项，消缺率100%，消缺完成率98.85%；合理安排检修计划，提前10d完成了4台机组的年度检修工作任务，特别是在2台机组重叠检修的情况下，合理安排工期，避免了弃水的发生。在2008～2009年度的机组检修中，4台机组共消除和处理了转轮、上导抗重螺栓裂纹等28项重大缺陷；更换了10组GIS电流互感器，11个间隔内的60个耐油橡胶板，消除了设备的重大隐患，增强了机组的可靠性，全年设备平均利用小时4764.17h，机组等效可用系数为88.2%，同比增加1.15%。

（二）精心筹划，尽最大努力确保电量增效益

2009年是红水河流域60多年以来最枯的年份，水库来水量仅为491.29亿m^3，较2008年减少155.94亿m^3。从4月份开始，下游桥巩水电站开始蓄水至84m，发电水头有1～2m的损失，使公司的发电形势更为严峻。为了增加发电量，公司对外加强营销力度，增强与电网的沟通，争取更多的上网电量；对内挖潜降耗，通过加强汛期水位动态控制，提高水能利用率，增发电量5923.30万kW·h；通过安装清污抓斗，及时清理坝前拦污排和拦污栅垃圾1600m^3，增发电量1000万kW·h；通过合理优化厂用电、机组辅助系统、通风空调及照明等设备的运行方式，节约厂用电近100万kW·h，为完成全年的发电任务尽最大努力。截至12月31日完成发电量28.59亿kW·h，上网电量28.23亿kW·h，综合厂用电率1.29%。

（三）以“6S”管理为载体，加强现场管理，厂容厂貌耳目一新

制定了整理（Seiri）、整顿（Seiton）、清扫（Seiso）、清洁（Seiketsu）、素（修）养（Shitsuke）和安全（Security）“6S”管理推行手册，在员工中树立“隐患可查找，违章可杜绝，事故可避免”的安全理念，搭建了违章行为“曝光台”等“6S”管理活动平台，结合机组检修工作的“双监”制度，及时掌控作业风险，进一步规范检修作业现场。同时，充分利用安全设施标准化的优势，进一步降低环境对安全生产的影响，加大对安全设施的投入，加强逃生标志等警示牌的标示、防护用品购置，制作并安装紧急疏散地域图、事故处理流程图、机组检修流程图共59块，有效地指导现场作业行为，塑造了一个整洁、有序、高效的工作环境，厂容厂貌耳目一新。

（广西桂冠开投电力有限责任公司乐滩水电厂
姚小斌　李　春）

国电万安水力发电厂 2009年生产运行情况

（一）生产运行统计

2009年，国电万安水力发电厂（以下简称万安电厂）发电7.51亿kW·h；全年安全生产无事故和障碍，未发生非计划停运现象，1～4号机组累计运行14 102.45h，备用17 682.26h，发生计划停运8次共3255.29h（包括2008年1号机组跨年度大修），机组等效可用系数达90.71%；直接厂用电率1.43%，综合厂用电率2.54%。其他生产运行指标如下：水能利用提高率5.24%，主设备完好率100%，辅助设备一类率99.77%，自动装置投入率99.99%，自动装置正确动作率100%，继电保护投入率和正确动作率均为100%；水情自动测报系统畅通率和可用度分别为96.4%和0.982，最大一次洪水预报准确率97.47%，洪水预报平均准确率96.87%；流域降雨量1271.4mm，水库来水量166.02亿m^3。

（二）万安水库汛限水位动态控制研究与应用

受“洪水资源化管理”的理念影响，国家防汛抗旱总指挥部、水利部对水库汛限水位设计与应用非常重视，并选择部分水库开展了第一批水库单位的试点工作。

江西省防汛抗旱总指挥部办公室（以下简称江西省防办）非常重视这项工作，拟在省内条件较好的水库开展试点工作，在中国国电集团公司的支持下，万安电厂向江西省防办提出申请并获准。项目由中国水利水电科学研究院、万安电厂等单位协作共同承担具体研究工作，期间邀请了长江水利委员会的原设计资深专家咨询指导。2006年12月，江西省防办在南昌主持召开了报告审查会。根据专家评审意见，课题组对报告又进行了补充和完善，形成最终报告，提交给江西省防办审批。

江西省防办本着安全、科学、积极、稳妥的原则，从2006年开始将万安水库汛期度汛方案作以下调整：

（1）4月1日～6月20日水库水位在85～87.5m之间实行动态控制调度。

（2）6月21日～9月30日按后汛期运行水位94～96m进行动态控制调度。

通过三年的运行，积累了丰富的实际操作经验，并为进一步挖掘动态控制潜力奠定了基础。2008年6月，万安水库被国家防汛抗旱总指挥部（以下简称国家防总）核准为第二批开展汛限水位动态控制试点水库，成立了由长江水利委员会防汛抗旱办公室、江西省防办、万安电厂组成的试点工作领导小组指导开展工作。万安电厂委托具有甲级资质的江西省水利规划设计院按照国家防总下发的《水库汛限水位动态控制试点工作意见》开展了补充研究论证工作。2009年2月，江西省水利规划设计院提交的《万安水库汛限水位动态控制研究报告》建议万安水库汛期水位采用分期动态控制，其具体方案为：

（1）4月1日～6月20日水库水位在85～88m之间实行动态控制调度。

（2）7月1日～9月30日水库水位按在93.5～96m之间实行动态控制调度。

（3）过渡期6月21日～6月30日视水情相机蓄水。

2009年2月24日在武汉召开了技术审查会并将成果上报到国家防总。

（三）左岸非溢流坝段裂缝的发现和分析

2008年底，万安电厂管理人员在对挡水建筑物进行例行检查时，发现左岸非溢流坝段（以下简称左非坝段）3～5号坝段临空面存在大量裂缝。万安电厂于12月5日致函长江勘测规划设计研究有限责任公司（以下简称长江设计公司），通报了左岸非溢流坝段裂缝情况。长江设计公司分两次派出专家和设计人员对现场进行考查调研后，于12月12日提出了《万安水电站左非坝段裂缝检查技术要求》。2008年12月25日，万安电厂委托湖北武大珞珈工程结构检测咨询有限公司（以下简称武大珞珈检测公司）对裂缝情况进行检测，2009年1月17日武大珞珈检测公司提交了检测报告。检测表明，左岸非溢流3～5号坝段共发现裂缝103条，总长度973.3m，裂缝宽度一般为0.2～0.4mm，最大深度为5.4m。

2009年9月，长江设计公司完成了对左岸非溢流坝段裂缝成因及其危害性计算分析，提交了《江西万安水利枢纽左非坝段混凝土裂缝研究与加固处理设计报告》。2009年10月17～18日，国电江西电力有限公司在万安电厂主持召开了审查会。会议认为：

（1）通过对左岸非溢流3～5号坝段裂缝的调查、检测，并结合典型坝段仿真计算分析，左岸非溢流3～5号坝段混凝土裂缝成因基本分析清楚。产生裂缝的主要因素是温度荷载和坝体混凝土施工存在薄弱环节。施工和运行期，受温度荷载的影响，坝体内部存在较大拉应力区，有些部位拉应力甚至接近混凝土的极限抗拉强度。气温的年变化作用，以及2008年初遭遇极寒天气持续时间较长作用，使得坝体表面一定深度范围内的拉应力明显加大，导致裂缝发展，甚至产生新的裂缝。

（2）计算分析表明，目前左岸非溢流坝段的裂缝在当前运行条件下，不影响大坝整体稳定，满足大坝安全运行的要求。敏感性分析表明，当混凝土抗拉强度降低，或遭遇极寒天气等情况，裂缝仍有进一步扩展的可能。

（3）对于上游面的裂缝、漏水横缝进行防渗处理，对于非迎水面的Ⅰ类裂缝可不作处理，对于Ⅱ类及以上裂缝进行灌浆和表面嵌缝处理，对于规模较大的坝轴向裂缝采取锚固措施。

（中国国电集团公司）

国电四川南桠河流域水电开发有限公司生产运行有关情况

（一）优化调度研究

2009年，国电四川南桠河流域水电开发有限公司主持开展了《南桠河流域梯级水电站联合优化调度研究》，对南桠河流域水文资料进行收集，结合电网调度管理和冶勒电站、姚河坝电站联合调度运行管理的实际，从南桠河流域梯级水电站调度管理模式、冶勒电站水库中长期径流预测、冶勒电站水库日径流预测、南桠河流域梯级水电站优化调度及发电量预计划编制、南桠河梯级水电站群联合优化调度决策支持等方面进行探索和研究。该研究通过了国电四川发电有限公司主持的专家组验收。这为南桠河流域梯级水电站生产调度运行和管理提供了有力的技术支持，有利于提高南桠河流域梯级水电站的水能利用率和发电效益。

（二）水轮机改造

南桠河发电厂机组水轮机由于设计、制造时间的历史局限性，采用的是20世纪60年代研制的A45转轮。其性能指标（如效率、空化和稳定性等参数）水平落后，水能利用率低，水轮机过流部件在泥沙磨损及空蚀作用下损坏严重，机组大修间隔时间短（1～2年），远远达不到SD 230—1987《发电厂检修规程》4年的要求，严重影响发电量和经济效益。

经可行性研究，2006年，南桠河发电厂完成2号水轮机改造。改造后，其直接和间接的效益主要体现在以下几个方面：

(1) 机组安全性、可靠性、稳定性提高，检修次数减少，机组的可用小时数增加。按南桠河电厂单机多年平均负荷率75%计算，一台机可减少无效运行时数约1000h，折合发电量约3000万kW·h，相应的减少了机组的磨损，降低了机组运行成本及枯期水耗。

(2) 由于增设技术供水由顶盖取水的方式，在河水水质好的情况下，机组技术供水由循环水泵供水切换为本机供水。这既降低了厂用电率，同时又节约了水泵的修理费用。

(3) 机组大修周期由2年一次延长到4年一次，每台机一年可增加可用小时数360h。4年内减少一次扩大性大修，即可节约大修费用上百万元。

(4) 机组效率提高，增加发电量。机组加权平均效率可由原来的88.08%提高到92.7%，提高率为4.62%。经计算，每年每台机可增发电量约1000万kW·h。

（中国国电集团公司）

龙羊峡电站开展推进无人值班运行专题调研

2009年，龙羊峡发电分公司明确提出加强设备综合治理，夯实安全生产基础，着力推进电站无人值班（少人值守）工作。通过现场调查、班组访谈、召开座谈会的形式，认真了解目前制约进一步推进无人值班（少人值守）工作的现实问题，形成专题调研报告。主要情况如下：

从20世纪90年代初开始，龙羊峡水电厂逐年进行技术改造，努力提高机电设备的安全运行水平，提高机组和全厂自动化程度，提高人员素质，基本实现了无人值班（少人值守）运行。然而目前随着社会的发展和企业发展的需要，无人值班（少人值守）工作需要进一步向前推进，即如何割掉（少人值守）这个“尾巴”，实现真正意义上的无人值班这一现场运行方式。

要实现这一目标，先要统一认识，还需要从设备、人员和管理三方面来认真分析现状，找出问题和差距，有计划分步骤地逐步完善。

（一）设备方面

稳定可靠的设备是实行无人值班的基础。龙羊峡水电站主辅机电设备和自动监控保护设备的情况如下：

1. 主设备　目前运行较稳定，4台机组中有3台水轮机转轮叶片发现了不同程度的裂纹，通过检修处理，暂不影响机组的稳定运行，但还需要通过进一步分析论证，找到彻底消除叶片发生裂纹的方法并加以解决。4台主变压器存在内部局部过热问题，目前已找到原因，通过检修、改造，可以逐步消除此隐患。330kV GIS开关运行较为稳定可靠，但需要通过定期检修，保持良好运行状态。

2. 计算机监控系统　采用全开放、分布式系统结构。采用最新的计算机硬件、软件及网络技术，模块化、结构化设计，留有硬件及功能软件的扩充接口和容量；网络采用双冗余光纤以太网，传输速率100Mbps。监控系统应为容错设计，不会因任何一台机器发生故障而引起系统误操作或降低系统性能，各LCU也不会因主控级发生故障而影响LCU各自的监控功能。采用成熟的、可靠的、标准化的硬件、软件、网络结构和汉化操作系统。LCU中各PLC既可协同工作又可独立完成各自承担的功能。目前具备的功能有：①控制功能：实现4台发电机组单元的现地和远方自动开停机、发电机出口开关和主变压器接地开关分合、闸门启闭、机组单机准同期并网、6kV和400V开关分合操作；②调节功能：4台发电机组有功、无功调节，AGC功能；③监视功能：4台发电机组、5条330kV输电线路出口开关，厂用系统、公用系统设备的运行工况监视（模拟量、开关量、事故量、温度量等），语音报警；④事故追忆：事故前后记录（断路器动作顺序和时间、电气量、非电气量和温度量的瞬时值记录等）；⑤报表打印：生产日报、月报、一览表的打印储存；⑥远程通信：与网调通信，与MIS通信；⑦远程监控：通过与黄河上游梯级调度的通信，实现在西宁梯级调度中心对龙羊峡水电站发电设备的远程监视和控制。

3. 励磁调速与继电保护系统　通过近年来的技术改造，目前电站的励磁系统、调速系统均已实现双重化、微机化配置，设备运行稳定，性能满足标准规定的要求。继电保护系统330kV出线、母线和机组的继电保护，目前均采用了双重配置的微机保护，在每一套微机配置中的主保护或后备保护又由单独的CPU控制。在设计和配置上保证了保护在任何情况下都能可靠动作。自投运以来电站主保护运行正常。

4. 基础自动化元件　通过历年的技术改造，已将机组单元的自动化元件进行了更新改造，目前基本满足现场安全生产的需要。

5. 厂用电系统　有完善可靠的备用电源自动投入装置，双电源应互为备用，保证电源消失及设备故障时可以自动投入备用电源。

6. 机组及公用辅助设备系统　机组压力油、技术供水、水轮机顶盖排水、全厂高低压压缩空气等具备必要的备用运行方式和容量，系统能自动运行，出现异常情况时有报警信号。

7. 直流电源系统　目前电站直流系统控制单元满足双重化配制，蓄电池容量满足事故放电 0.5～1h 的要求。浮充电设备可以自动稳压运行，并有系统工作异常时的报警信号。

8. 渗排水系统　厂房集水井具备足够的容积；深井泵和射流泵通过运行方式的调节，可以满足排水要求；厂、坝内排水系统均能按水位变动自动运行，水位信号器冗余配置。

9. 在线监测系统　电站目前在 1 台机组和 1 台变压器上安装了在线监测装置。机组在线检测装置可对机组的振动、摆动、压力及脉动、过机流量、定转子间气隙和机组有功、无功等工况参数进行实时监测。变压器在线监测可对变压器运行过程中油的色谱、微水和温度进行在线监测。

10. 工业电视监控系统　可以对生产区域内的环境和设备进行监控。

11. 通信系统　配置了光纤通信系统、载波通信系统、固定电话通信系统。光纤和载波通信系统主要用来与调度部门联系，水情、计算机监控信息传输以及调度部门实现遥控、遥调、遥信、遥测均通过光纤实现。

12. 消防系统　目前电站配备的是计算机集中控制灭火装置，它有报警系统和火灾联动系统两部分组成，在中控室与计算机室采用的是气体灭火装置，其他则安装了烟感式、温感式、气体采样、缆式报警装置和水消防装置。当发生火灾时火灾联动系统迅速关闭火灾现场的风道，在报警的同时并启动灭火系统灭火。

（二）人才方面

高素质的专业人才是实行无人值班的支撑。目前，通过不断的培训教育和现场实际工作的积累相结合，已经培养出了一批懂技术、会管理、善经营的管理人才；造就了一批业务强、肯奉献的运行人才；锻炼了一批技术精、能吃苦的检修维护人才；储备了一批负责任、肯钻研的技术监督人才。这些人才都是实现无人值班目标的有力支撑。

（三）管理方面

创新的管理是实行无人值班的保障。电站实现无人值班，必须建立必要严格的管理制度，明确工作责任、工作内容和范围，落实各级安全生产的责任，不断创新和完善管理模式，满足生产现场安全生产的需要。新的形势下调整安全生产管理体系，建立完善安全生产问责制和奖惩制，建立健全无人值班的相关制度体系，使得人员减少而安全生产的实效不减。要做到这些，还需要进行大量管理创新工作。

随着信息化技术的不断发展，电站的安全生产、经营管理均已逐步实现了网络化、信息化，远程办公已经成为现实。要利用这一有利工具，探索无人值班条件下的工作票、操作票的管理，交接班管理，缺陷管理，检修管理，技术监督管理等。

通过此次调研，发现有部分员工存在片面思想，认为无人值班就是减人，自己所承担的责任会越来越重，工作量也越来越大，而实惠却得不到。这需要加以引导，进一步转变观念。大部分员工认为，通过分阶段、抓实效的工作，改造、检修存在问题的设备，提高设备运行安全稳定可靠水平，不断学习提高自身业务技能水平，健全完善相关管理制度，一定能够按期实现无人值班的目标。

（龙羊峡发电分公司　吴亚星）

国电长源老渡口水电有限公司的生产管理

（一）概况

国电长源老渡口水电有限公司是长源电力的全资子公司，负责老渡口水电站的建设与营运。老渡口水电站位于湖北省恩施市清江左岸一级支流马水河河口以上 7.5km 处，坝址距恩施市约 50km，是一座以发电为主、兼顾航运等综合利用效益的大型水电工程；水库总库容 2.2 亿 m^3，电站安装 2 台机组，总容量 9 万 kW，设计年发电量 2.52 亿 kW·h。2009 年 7 月 10 日，1 号机组投入商业运行，12 月 24 日 2 号机组投入商业运行，国电长源老渡口水电有限公司（以下简称老渡口公司）实现了预期目标，为长源电力打赢“保卫战”作出了贡献。

（二）生产经营

老渡口电站生产机构的设置紧扣“无人值班，少人值守”的原则进行设置，生产管理以生产部为主，安全管理以安监部为主。为满足生产运行需要，在明确生产岗位标准的基础上，建立健全了 45 项有关生产管理的制度，编制完成了水库调度规程、运行和检修维护规程、安全规程，并开展制度规程和实际操作技能的学习培训。针对新机组、新工况、初运行的特点，老渡口公司高度关注机组消缺，全年完成维护消缺 102 项，其中处理重大缺陷 4 项、设备改造 3 项，电站生产运行逐步规范。此外，借助水情测报系统进行科学调度，有效提升水库调度准确率，确保老渡口电站优质、高效运转。

在测算老渡口临时结算电价为 0.34 元/(kW·h) 的基础上，通过各种渠道努力争取，省物价局批准电站临时结算电价为 0.35 元/(kW·h)；11 月 20 日，又提高至临时电价按0.36元/(kW·h)执行。2009年全年，老渡口电站全年完成发电量4574.36万kW·h，累计实现营业收入1207.00万元。

（三）安全生产

2009年，老渡口公司从制度建设入手，不断强化内部管理，规范公司运作，严格执行基建管理程序，全面落实基建管理制度。针对工程施工、设备安装任务重，场地狭窄，土建施工与机电设备安装交叉施工矛盾突出，现场施工队伍力量不足等情况，在选择合理时间、空间和优化设计方案、施工方法以及选择施工队伍上下工夫，从源头和大处着手，避免发生重大安全事故。此外，在电站1号机组转入运行以来，在继续抓好基建施工安全工作的基础上，注重基建施工在运行机组区的施工活动给安全运行带来的安全隐患及处理预案，尤其抓好落实“两票三制”制度，严格按照安全生产有关规定加强安全生产管理，实现了安全管理“双零”目标。

（中国国电集团公司）

技术改造

三峡发输电安全稳定控制系统改造工程

（一）系统概况

三峡发输电系统安全稳定控制系统（以下简称三峡安控系统）是国家电网公司为三峡发输电系统配套建设的重点工程之一。

随着电网和三峡电站的建设，三峡外送电网已逐步演变成为网、省间潮流汇集中枢：①三峡电力经龙政、宜华、葛南500kV直流线路向华东输电7200MW；②经江城500kV直流线路向南方电网输电3000MW；③经斗樊双回线、斗孝双回线、江兴双回线、江复双回线、龙万双回线、葛岗线等11回500kV交流线路实现湘鄂豫川电网的互联；④1000kV“晋东南－南阳－荆门”交流特高压试验示范工程接入三峡近区电网，三峡电网已经成为全国电网的中心和枢纽。

三峡电网安全约束复杂，局部故障均可能引发连锁反应而导致互联电网系统失稳，三峡安控系统为三峡电力的可靠送出以及全国大区互联电网的安全稳定运行发挥了极其重要的作用。2009年5月南京南瑞集团公司电网安全稳定控制技术分公司对三峡安控系统进行了全面的升级改造。

（二）系统配置

三峡安控系统涉及9个厂站，包括龙泉、江陵、宜都、葛洲坝等4个换流站、斗笠变电站及三峡左一、左二、右一、右二等4个厂站，实时监控电网在10种运行方式下8回500kV直流线路、30回500kV交流线路、5台主变压器及三峡26台水电机组的运行状态。

同时，在国家电力调度通信中心还配置了一套三峡安控集中管理系统（SCMS），通过电力调度数据网汇集各厂站安控装置决策数据，作为国家电力调度通信中心电网方式安排的依据。

随着电网结构的改变和三峡机组的陆续投产发电，三峡安控系统主要经历了三峡左岸、三峡右岸和我国第一条1000kV特高压试验示范工程投产三个阶段的建设和实施。整个工程于特高压线路投产前全面实施完成，历时6年。

（三）功能配置及技术创新点

为了解决系统的暂稳问题，三峡安控系统实时检测各主要输电断面，当系统发生故障时，装置及时查询内置策略表，采取切机及调制直流措施，保证电网的稳定；为了解决系统的热稳问题，三峡安控系统各站装置均配有过负荷功能模块，当判断出线路过载时，通过切机措施保证设备安全；为了解决系统的频率问题，三峡安控系统电厂装置配有高周功能模块，当判断出系统高频时，通过切除保证系统频率稳定；同时为了应对复杂故障下系统失稳的可能性，三峡安控系统还实时检测川渝—华中断面，当判断出该断面失步振荡时，华中和川渝电网解列运行；为了保证特高压电网的安全稳定，当德阳变安控装置判断出德宝直流闭锁时，通过光纤通道发生命令调制龙泉和宜都的直流功率，保证系统安全。

三峡电网是我国首个交直流、特高压混合电网，各种运行方式下系统均会有安全稳定问题。三峡安控系统为了解决这些问题，在功能配置方面进行了不少创新：

(1) 首次实现了交直流系统的联合控制。通过直流极的控制，将三峡电网交流元件故障影响范围控制到最小；通过机组的切除，保证了直流线路故障后三峡电网的稳定。

(2) 首次在一个安控系统工程中，同时考虑并实现电网的第二、三道防线的协调配合控制。不同厂站不同型号安控装置通过控制手段、控制延时、控制范围的相互配合，保证了电网在多重严重故障下依然保持稳定。

(3) 首次实现安控装置对直流极的直接控制。装置通过输出代表不同意义的触点组合，实现不同的调制类型、调制挡位及调制速度的调制直流命令。

(4) 首次实现了跨区域直流功率的联合调制，保证了特高压系统的安全稳定运行。

(5) 首次实现了安控系统在多电站、多机组间的切机措施的自适应性。安控系统通过判别4个电站的运行方式，实现不同电站间在出现各种特殊情况下切机命令的自动转切，避免措施不足导致电网失稳。

(四) 经济及社会效益

三峡安控系统于2003年10月正式投入运行至今，保持了既无误动也无拒动的纪录。

2003～2008年期间，三峡安控装置共正确动作14次，其中：龙政直流故障切机10次，江城直流故障切机2次，宜华直流故障切机2次，无交流系统故障切机。

三峡安控系统投运后，三峡电网每年向负荷中心多输送电力400亿kW·h。三峡安控系统改造后将为保证三峡电力送出和全国电网安全稳定运行发挥更重要的作用，创造更大的经济和社会效益。

(南京南瑞集团公司电网安全稳定控制技术分公司　曹一中)

二滩水电站送出安全稳定控制系统改造工程

一、系统概况

二滩水电站位于四川省、雅砻江干流下游河段上，距攀枝花市约40km，总装机容量为3300MW，以发电为主，兼有其他综合利用效益。二滩电力通过3回470km 500kV输电线路送往洪沟变电站，再分别通过180km和140km的2回500kV输电线路送往龙王变电站（成都）和板桥变电站（重庆）。由于沿途地理环境恶劣、输电通道紧张，普洪一线、普洪二线有4.1km线路为同塔架设，洪龙双回线也为同塔架设，加上500kV与220kV存在电磁环网，以上因素引发出功角稳定、电压稳定和频率稳定三大稳定问题，严重制约二滩电厂电量的送出，并严重威胁主网的稳定运行。因此，为确保二滩水电站电量能大量稳定送出，并且在500 kV系统发生故障后，不至于破坏主网稳定运行，在主网配置了二滩安全稳定控制系统，作为电网稳定运行的第二、三道防线。随着菩提500kV开关站加装串补装置、二滩输电系统加强方案的实施以及瀑布沟电站的建成，南京南瑞集团公司电网安全稳定控制技术分公司在2009年12月对二滩送出工程安全稳定控制系统进行了全面完善和升级改造，使其能更好地适应当前电源及电网的建设和系统运行方式的变化。经计算分析，本次二滩安控系统改造后投入运行，可以将二滩电厂的暂态稳定输送限额提高500～600MW，同时提高500kV洪龙线、洪南线和洪板双回线的输送能力。

二、系统配置

二滩电站送出工程安控系统是当时国内规模最大的区域型安控系统，2009年底改造后主要由500kV洪沟变电站控制主站、500kV普提变电站控制子站、500kV板桥变电站控制子站、500kV黄岩变电站控制子站、500kV陈家桥变电站控制子站，二滩电厂切机控制子站及220kV重庆7个切负荷执行站构成。其中二滩电站、洪沟变电站、菩提变电站、板桥变电站、陈家桥变电站、黄岩变电站采用南瑞稳定公司生产的FWK-300型分布式安全稳定控制装置，双套配置；重庆7个切负荷执行站采用南瑞稳定公司生产的UFV-200C型稳定控制装置，单套配置，以上各厂站通过2M通道联系为一个系统。本系统主要功能为：当二滩电站送出通道发生线路（或主变压器）故障时，及时切除二滩电站或菩提变电站及重庆侧负荷，从而确保该区域电网安全稳定运行。

系统电气接线图如图1所示。

三、功能配置

(一) 二滩电站

稳控装置采用双套配置主/辅方式运行，防止由于采样误差引起机组排序不一致而导致过切机组，主要检测500kV二普三回线及6台机组的运行工况，具有跳闸联切、高频切机和收远方命令切机等功能。

1. 跳闸联切功能　装置检测二普三回线的电气量，根据元件投停及特殊方式连接片投退情况判断系统的运行方式，当二普三回500kV线路故障时，根据事故前的电网运行方式、事故时判断出的故障元件及故障类型，查找控制策略表的对应措施，确定本站切机的总容量。

2. 高频切机功能　装置检测二普三回线路的电压，分独立的4轮判断系统高频，每轮高频动作按照出力由大到小的顺序切除一台投运且允许切除的机组。为保证高频切机功能的可靠，防止误动作，在有2回及以上的线路运行时，需要至少2回线路满足高

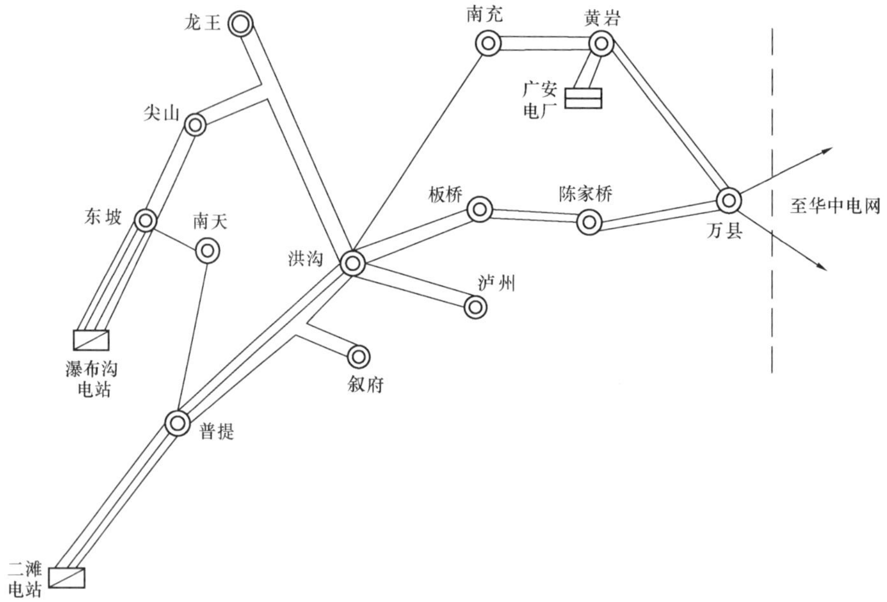

图1　二滩送出系统电气接线示意图

频判据才判断为系统高频；当仅有一回线路投运时，则只要该线路满足高频判据即判断为系统高频。

3. 接收远方切机命令的功能　二滩电厂和洪沟变电站、普提变电站、黄岩变电站、泸州变电站均有通信联系，可接收并执行以上各站的按容量切机命令，按照机组排序找出与需切容量最接近且超过需切容量的组合进行切除。

4. 机组排序　事故前装置对本站的发电机组按照出力大小、带厂用电的情况及人为设定的要求进行排序，根据判断出的切机台数或切机容量选择被切对象，执行切机控制。同时需将二滩电站机组运行工况发送到洪沟变电站。

（二）洪沟变电站

位于川渝500kV电网的枢纽位置，是二滩送出工程稳定控制系统的主站，其稳控装置采用双套配置并列方式运行，同时柜间进行信息交换以保证切机措施的一致性，主要检测本站出线和主变压器的运行工况，当线路或主变压器发生故障时，根据故障前的潮流断面及系统运行方式，及时查找对应控制策略表向二滩电站发送切机容量或向板桥发送切负荷命令。

（三）菩提变电站、黄岩变电站、板桥变电站、陈家桥变电站

这几个控制子站稳控装置采用双套配置并列方式运行，主要检测变电站出线及主变压器运行工况，当判出线路或主变压器发生跳闸或过负荷时，根据系统的运行方式，查策略表采取相应的控制措施切二滩机组及菩提或陈家桥变电站负荷。

（四）重庆7个切负荷执行站

稳控装置采用单套配置，主要采集本站220kV母线，判断系统低频低压切负荷，并接收陈家桥变电站发来的切负荷命令，分轮次切除本站负荷线。

四、经济及社会效益

以二滩电厂为主的四川水电的开发和外送，是实现中央西部大开发、电力结构调整战略决策的重要组成部分，有利于形成更大范围内的电力市场，更充分发挥市场机制，达到更好的电力资源优化配置，并将对全国联网的结构产生重大影响。二滩电力送出系统距离远、容量大、规模大，对川渝电网和华中主网的安全稳定都有较大影响。因此，做好二滩送出稳定控制系统的功能设计与工程实施是关系到二滩外送经济效益和保证电网安全稳定运行的关键。随着2009年底该稳控系统改造并投入运行，二滩送出及川电东送的系统稳定性得到进一步的提高，将更好地服务于我国飞速发展的经济建设。

（南京南瑞集团公司电网安全稳定控制技术分公司 尹旭阳）

二滩水电站川电东送安控装置技术改造

二滩水电站安全稳定控制系统（以下简称安控系统）是川电东送安控系统的重要子站，由两套完全独立的稳控装置和失步解列装置构成。原安控装置型号

为 GFWK 型，属国内第一代产品，可靠性较差，元件性能不稳定，维护不方便，自 2001 年 7 月投运以来，出现过几次误动，共进行过 14 次改进和升级，仍不能满足电网对安控系统可靠性的要求。为更好地发挥安控系统在电网中的安全防护作用，二滩水电厂根据四川省电力公司的要求，于 2009 年 12 月份开始对安控装置进行更新改造。

（一）主要改造内容

（1）更换新的安控装置，安控设备由 GFWK 升级为 FWK-300，失步解离装置由 UFV-2F 升级为 UFV-200F。

（2）停用以前的载波通道，改为全光纤通道，两套安控装置信号通道完全独立。

（3）增加二滩电站至省调度中心安控信息实时上送功能。

（4）增加至成都“二滩集控中心”信息上送通道。

（5）更新站内实时监视终端，便于二滩电站运行人员实时远程查看安控信息。

（6）新装置软件升级，全部按收到的切机容量切二滩机组。

（二）新设备的特点

1. FWK-300 及 UFV-200F 硬件特点　FWK-300 装置可用于区域性电网或大区互联电网的安全稳定控制，既可适应单个厂站的就地控制，又能构成大型的稳定控制系统，满足电力系统安全稳定控制的需要。该装置是一种分布式、模块化、拼装式结构的通用性很强的稳定控制装置，能适应电网暂态稳定控制、频率稳定与电压稳定控制、主变压器或线路过负荷控制等。FWK-300 装置结合了最新的微机和通信技术，属新一代分布式微机稳定控制设备，具有如下特点：

（1）装置的硬件由基本的功能模件拼装而成，功能模件都已定型批量生产，质量与可靠性得到保证。

（2）装置采用了免维护设计，结构上采用强弱电分开的设计方法，使得装置的结构更加合理，抗干扰能力更强。装置中所有的模件全部采用表贴工艺，使用了多层板设计方法，在电路设计时增加了一些抗干扰电路，使得装置的抗干扰能力更强。

（3）速度更快，精度更高，采用 32 位 CPU、DSP 处理器及 14 位 A/D 技术。

（4）输出轮次更多，能控制更多的对象，且灵活方便。

（5）具有多种通信接口，有常规的串行通信接口（RS-232/RS-422/RS-485）、调制解调器、E1 接口（2M）、64k 数字同向口（G.703）接口设备、符合 TCP/IP 协议的以太网接口、专用光纤通信接口或拨号通信方式，可让用户有多种选择。

2. FWK-300 及 UFV-200F 软件特点

（1）软件采用了模块化结构，各模块已规范化和标准化，模块之间连接方便、灵活，根据工程需要可以比较快地组装专用软件；模块经过反复试验和现场长期运行考验；使用了一些新的算法，装置在采集数据时更加准确可靠，对数据的分析能力更强。

（2）人机交互软件采用全汉字显示，使用 PC104 嵌入式工控机作为管理机，使用现在流行的实时多任务操作系统 VxWorks，因此其操作性得到较大提高。

（3）装置大量使用了智能化的调试软件，使得装置调试更加方便。

（4）可与在线预决策系统有机地集成，满足系统升级的需要，利于实现电力系统稳定的自适应实时控制。

3. 通信系统特点　原装置与站内通信设备采用音频通道连接，通道可靠性较差且其信息传输速率较低。二滩电站在本次改造中将其数据业务全部改为光纤连接，从而提高了通信的可靠性和通信速度。利用新装置丰富的通信接口，完成与不同设备之间的互联。

（1）站内通信实现光纤通信后具有以下优点：光纤抗干扰能力强，可解决由于误码及通道异常导致的误动作；通信容量大且扩容方便，从而满足装置升级的需求。

（2）通道实现了完全双重化，不仅通信线路实现了双重化，而且通道中相关信号转换装置也实现了双重化，从而确保通信通道的完全孤立。

（3）具有多种通信接口：常规的串行通信接口、调制解调器、数字同向口接口、以太网接口、专用光纤通信接口等。

（4）支持与厂站监控系统通信，支持与 SCMS 稳定控制集中管理系统通信，浏览装置运行情况、装置定值、策略表定值等数据。

（三）试运行效果及结论

二滩电站新安控装置投运以后，在系统发生的多次单瞬接地故障和单永接地故障中，都正确判断出系统故障的类型，执行正确的策略；对不同的运行方式也能自动正确判别；对数据通道的异常状态都实时报警，表现出很好的可靠性和稳定性。

（二滩水力发电厂　何能全）

泰山抽水蓄能电站 2 号机组水导油槽盖板改造

泰山抽水蓄能电站装有四台 250MW 可逆式水泵水轮机—发电电动机组，总装机容量为 1000MW，以二回 220kV 出线接入山东电网。水轮机设备由德国

Voith公司提供。原水导轴承油槽盖板，密封结构不合理，油雾易外逸，影响设备安全文明运行水平；且盖板为不锈钢材质，重量较大，不便于拆装维护。为从根本上解决这一问题，2009年11月，结合2号机组C级检修对其进行了改造。

（一）改造前水导油盆状况

长期以来，水导油槽存在多处渗油现象，主要有：

（1）密封处油雾易外逸。由于本机组转速较高，水导轴承油槽里易产生油气混合物，形成大量油雾。梳齿密封的疏齿环与轴有间隙，油雾易从该处逸出。

（2）呼吸器处渗油。呼吸器把油槽上腔与厂房大气连通，起平衡气压作用。由于所配呼吸器过滤能力不足，反而成为油雾外逸的通道而渗油。

（3）测温电缆穿线处因密封处理不好导致渗油。

（二）改造方案

1. 轴密封改造　将原有的铜质疏齿环密封改造为极限间隙密封。该密封为自润滑非金属复合材料，耐温性能好。在安装方式上，新型密封为镶嵌式密封，在密封件上开若干个槽，用以镶嵌密封齿，通过一圈压缩弹簧，使机组在运行状态时，保证密封能够与大轴径向随动，确保极限间隙密封，并且不会产生较大摩擦，如图1所示。

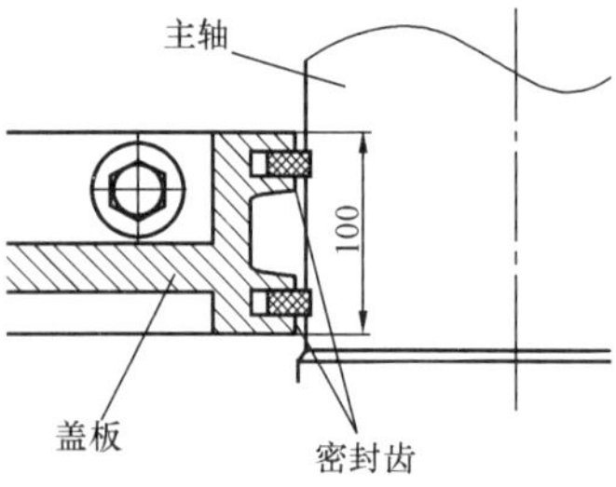

图1　改进后的密封结构示意图

2. 呼吸器改型　选用KF型油雾分离装置。该装置的优点是无动力，滤油雾效果优良，透平油无密封损失。KF型油雾分离装置由本体、折流板、集油分离器等组成。它可使油雾在通过折流板到集油分离器的过程中，由油雾凝结成油滴，返流回油槽内，经过过滤的空气被排出，使油槽内外气压保持一致。无压油雾则无法从密封间隙处挤出，实现无透平油损失密封。该油雾呼吸器结构如图2所示。

3. 穿线结构改造　将测温电缆穿线由油槽外壁改为布置于密封盖上部。首先将所有穿线集中于一接线板（材质采用绝缘垫木）上，并将接线板适当下沉，预留出线束打弯空间。在接线板上部同时配有铝合金电缆壳体（壳体为整体结构，详见图3），使其既不影响密封盖整体美观，又有利于线束密封。接线板采用绝缘垫木，并将电缆夹紧密封接头固定于接线板上，待电缆穿过后通过锁紧螺纹使电缆密封。

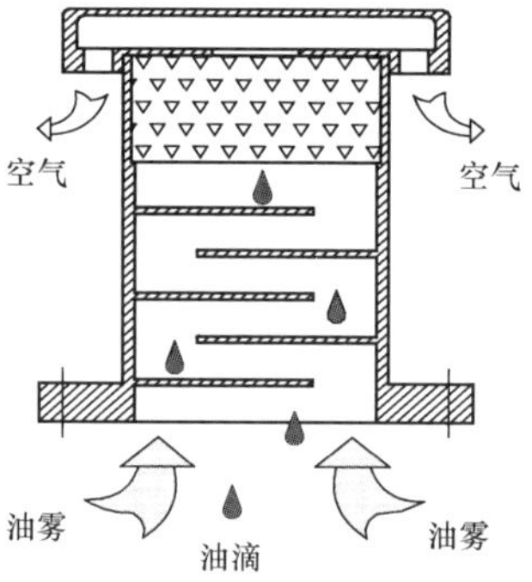

图2　改进后的呼吸器结构示意图

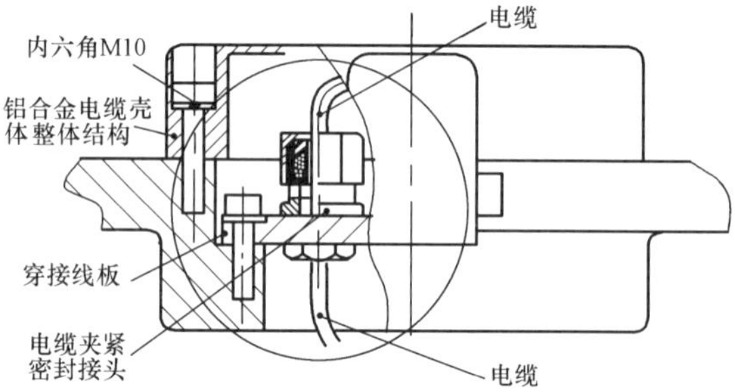

图3　改进后的测温电缆穿线

4. 密封盖材质和样式改造　将钢质材料的盖板改造为铝合金材料，并由两瓣对接改造为四瓣对接安装，重量减轻，便于检修；密封盖连接螺栓全部采用不锈钢材质，使其与铸铝合金密封盖浑然一体，不仅美观，螺栓不锈蚀也给设备检修带来很大方便。另外密封盖与油槽连接部分的连接孔采用沉孔式连接，使密封盖外部整体为平面结构，既美观又便于检修人员在其上进行其他操作。

（三）改造效果

（1）有效改善了水导油盆盖板与大轴间的密封状况和呼吸器正常工作，消除了水导渗漏油的现象。

（2）盖板总重量减少420kg，极大地方便了水导油盆及内部设备的检修工作。

（山东泰山抽水蓄能电站有限责任公司　苏胜威）

龚嘴水电站机组增容改造情况

（一）改造前机组状况

龚嘴水电站设计安装7台混流式机组，机组设计水头为48m，额定出力为100MW，首台机组于1971年12月26日投产发电。经30多年运行后，普遍存在着发电机定子线圈端部压指异常发热、线圈绝缘下降、水轮机过流部件磨蚀严重等重大隐患，甚至出现过转轮叶片断裂、转轮止漏环脱落、尾水管锥管段撕裂等重大缺陷。由于电站按高坝设计、低坝施工，机组引用流量较小，每年汛期均会产生大量弃水，造成宝贵的水能资源流失。汛期机组运行水头主要集中在42～46m，低于机组设计水头，最大出力只能达到额定出力的80%～90%，机组在额定工况点的效率也只有90%左右；再加上经过多年运行，过流部件空蚀磨损严重，流道型线偏离设计值，近年来实测机组额定工况点的效率仅为86%左右。总体来说，龚嘴电站长期以来一直存在着机组老化隐患较多、汛期弃水多并且机组不能满负荷运行、平枯期机组耗水率偏高、影响安全生产和经济效益等问题。

因此，经过科学分析论证，决定对龚嘴电站水轮发电机组进行技术改造和机组增容，即将机组额定出力由100MW增容至110MW，以提高机组安全性能和机组出力水平。

（二）机组增容改造情况

2003年和2004年先后完成了龚嘴电站1、5号机组增容改造。这两台机组改造后，主要性能参数均优于老机组，但运行中也暴露出一些问题。

（1）机组在空负荷或低于50MW负荷时，水车室及尾水人孔处有异常响声。在30MW时响声达到高于规范要求的95dB，明显大于相邻其他未改造机组；在50MW以上负荷运行时则声音正常。经分析，这种声音异常是由水轮机流道中叶道涡与尾水锥管的碰撞所致。经在机组顶盖真空破坏阀位置装设补气装置后，机组在空负荷和低负荷区运行时异响消除。

（2）顶盖异常磨蚀穿孔。水轮机转轮止漏环高度、间隙配合不合理，转轮上冠上平面与顶盖之间距离偏小，转轮上冠空腔大，转轮泄水孔排水面积与止漏环缝隙面积之比值偏大。通过加高顶盖止漏环，转轮上冠加设引水挡板并浇筑混凝土，减小转轮上冠空腔，改善转轮上冠水流流态等处理后趋于正常。

2号机组采用东方电机有限公司自主研发的D443A转轮，设计了大轴中心孔补气装置，增容改造于2008年4月30日完成，投运一年多来运行平稳。增容改造后的机组，设计水头由48m降低为44m，设计流量由241m^3/s提高为289m^3/s，额定出力由100MW增加为110MW。2009年主汛期单机增发电量0.71亿kW·h。

（中国国电集团公司）

风滩水电厂2号机组尾水锥管改造土建施工工艺

（一）概况

风滩水电站为混凝土空腹重力拱坝，坝内式厂房；安装6台机组，总装机容量800 MW。因机组运行近30年，2006年风滩电厂开始对老机组进行增容改造。首先启动了2号机组，更换了水轮机、发电机等主设备，机组容量由100MW增容到115MW，并根据机组效率及水力要求，对尾水锥管进行改造，钢衬更换为不锈钢材料。

（二）锥管改造土建施工工艺

2号机组尾水锥管根据机电设计的要求，其主要土建施工内容包括锚筋施工、灌浆系统制作与安装、排气系统制作与安装、新浇二期混凝土、基础环上部砂浆回填、接触面水泥灌浆、化学灌浆等。

1. 锚筋施工　在新老混凝土接合面布置2排ϕ20@400锚筋，上下排错位呈梅花形布置。将锚固剂浸水到适当程度，灌入孔内，再将锚筋杆体插入锚孔内，锤击到位，少量锚固剂由孔口流出，要确保注浆饱满、密实。内置混凝土段锚筋安装完成后，锚筋外露部分长度，以不影响锥管钢衬安装为原则。

2. 化学灌浆、排气系统制作与安装　灌浆系统共布置两套灌浆管，在锥管侧上部布置一套灌浆管，在混凝土侧上部布置一套灌浆管，管路上每间隔1.00m布置1个出浆接头。在基础环上开8个出气孔并焊接带球阀的排气镀锌管及两个ϕ30mm的进浆管孔。灌浆管采用ϕ20mm镀锌管，采用三通连接。混凝土壁侧灌浆管，必须在锥管钢衬下基坑安装前按设计图要求安装固定到混凝土壁侧相应位置上。出浆口用ϕ20mm直接头制作，一端用胶带密封，另一端用内丝与灌浆管的三通连接。老混凝土开挖凿除到位后，需对出浆直接头安装段位的凿除面进行修整凿平处理，使壁面形成一个直径约为35mm基本平整的圆面。

3. 混凝土浇筑　新浇二期混凝土设计强度等级为C30掺高效减水增强剂。在基础环上开设8个100mm×100mm左右的混凝土浇筑槽孔。

（1）混凝土拌和采用磨盘式搅拌机拌和，水泥砂石储料场及混凝土搅拌机布置在厂房门口空地。混凝土拌和投料配合比，按设计配合比参数值控制。混凝土搅拌均匀，出料口不夹带生料，混凝土坍落度按180～200mm控制。

（2）混凝土运输采用人力斗车、PVC管溜筒分段、分层运送法。先浇锥管钢衬振捣孔以下部分，之后浇筑以上部分。混凝土浇筑振捣工作在锥管施工平台进行，一个浇筑孔进料，采用两台振捣器同时在进料浇筑孔下方相邻的两个振捣孔进行振捣平仓，将混凝土料向两侧赶，使浇筑面尽量平缓、密实。下部浇筑完毕接着浇筑振捣孔以上部分，振捣工作在浇筑平台上进行，同样使用两台振捣器，一台振捣器在进料浇筑孔内作业，另一台振捣器在相邻浇筑孔内进行振捣平仓作业。

4. 混凝土壁侧回填接触灌浆　6套灌浆管路的进回浆口分别引出管头，浆液搅拌和灌注设备、水泥材料安放于右岸厂房安装间外空地。灌浆采用自下而上排气赶灌法。灌浆主要设备有灌浆泵、制浆机。采用华中42.5MPa普通硅酸盐水泥。拌浆用水采用2号机组就近水源接管取水。采用ZB-1A减水剂，以改善浆液流动特性，增强接缝灌浆填充密实的可靠性。灌浆水灰比采用1∶1、0.5∶1两个比级的浆液。开灌采用水灰比为1∶1的浆液，待排气管（孔）出浆后，其水灰比接近1∶1时即改用水灰比为0.5∶1的浆液灌注，直至结束。灌浆压力为0.15MPa，在灌浆过程中应设立专人负责监测和检查灌注与钢衬变形情况。在设计的压力下，缝面停止吸浆，持续10min即可结束。灌浆结束时，应先绑扎封闭管口后再停机，闭浆时间不宜少于8h。考虑新浇混凝土的收缩时效性，要求在混凝土浇筑完成60d后再进行回填接触灌浆。

5. 钢衬侧化学灌浆　为确保锥管钢衬与新浇二期混凝土间的微细收缩缝填充密实，在混凝土浇筑完成60d后，还必须对钢衬侧进行灌浆。

（1）化学灌浆工艺流程：施工准备与灌浆孔布置→钻孔→进浆管排气管焊接安装→浆液配制→灌浆→质量检查。主要材料：杭州国电三墩科研实验厂HKG-2型新型环氧树脂型灌浆材。主要设备：手动试压泵、IE-01型电动灌浆机、磁座钻、手电钻、配浆计量称重器具和容器。

（2）对锥管钢衬进行混凝土收缩后的脱空检查，在每一施工层内根据钢衬脱空检查情况分区布置灌浆孔，环周孔间距300～500mm，面积较小的单个灌浆区域至少应钻孔2个以上。造灌浆孔采用磁座钻钻孔，孔径15mm。灌浆孔的进浆管与排气管采用ϕ15mm镀锌管，长度150mm，要求与钢衬焊结牢固，对灌浆孔应进行编号。

（3）灌浆孔开通后焊接进浆、排气管前及焊接完毕后，均需对灌浆孔进行通畅性检查。检查时可在现场用压缩空气将灌浆孔吹洗干净，吹风同时需用铁榔头在灌浆孔周围及其相互连通区域间敲击，通过锤击振荡使其间的微细颗粒灰尘杂质随高压风排出。确认灌浆区域灌浆孔间畅通情况后应在现场按编号做好记录，同时在钢衬上标示。

（4）灌浆时要求根据灌浆孔通畅性的检查情况由下至上、由右岸至左岸分施工层依次进行，其下部设1～2个进浆管，上部设为1～2个排气管，数量应根据现场灌浆情况现场调节。灌浆时必须控制灌浆压力，以免造成钢板鼓包，灌浆压力要求控制在0.3MPa范围内。当灌浆泵压达到0.3 MPa且不吸浆时，停泵观察5min，泵压不下降则可结束该孔的灌浆。

（5）灌浆孔封孔可根据现场施工进度分期进行。封堵时先割除灌浆钢管，然后在灌浆孔内钻孔，钻孔深度约50mm；再将相同直径的钢筋（Ⅱ级）打入（应将钢筋顶端表面打入至钢衬内表面，钢筋长度应根据现场钻孔深度确定），检查钢筋打入情况，验收合格后再将打入的钢筋与钢衬焊接，焊接时要求在灌浆孔内用堆焊焊满至钢衬上表面。

（6）考虑新浇混凝土的收缩时效性，要求在混凝土浇筑完成60d后检查钢衬空鼓情况再进行灌浆处理。

（三）改造后情况

2号机组尾水锥管改造工作于2006年1月开始，2006年8月全部完成。2006年9月2号机组增容改造工作全部完成，投运后达到设计出力，尾水锥管运行正常，运行期锥管人孔门处无任何渗水。2008年9月在2号机组扩机增容安全运行近2年后进行机组扩大性检查，无空鼓、变形等任何异常情况，施工质量可靠。

（湖南省电力公司凤滩水力发电厂　蒋忠宪）

水情预报与调度

三峡水库洪水预报方案设计

长江三峡作为世界上最大的水利枢纽已有多个洪水预报系统投入运行，但原有系统的预报范围大都为三峡水库区间，面积约5.5万km²，预见期很短。为了提供长预见期的洪水预报，三峡梯级调度通信中心于2007年开始进行金沙江屏山—寸滩区间水情遥测系统的建设，同时接入金沙江中下游水情自动测报系统。本次长江三峡水库洪水预报方案编制即依据三峡目前所有已接入的遥测站网信息（共527站）进行，预报范围从金沙江龙街站至三峡坝址区间，预报区间总面积约39万km²。

（一）洪水预报方案概况

根据此次三峡预报的对象和范围，预报区域共分为7个大区间：金沙江流域、岷江流域、沱江流域、嘉陵江流域、乌江流域、长江上游干流区间和寸滩—三峡坝址区间。每个区间范围根据预见期要求和遥测站网覆盖区域确定。

此次三峡预报范围很大，且流域地形、水文气象特征复杂多样，因此洪水预报方案的制作需要考虑不同类型的地形地貌和下垫面条件、不均匀的降雨面分布和多汇入点的河网汇流，分区间、分块、分单元逐级进行预报方案的制作。

（二）预报模型、方法简介

每个大区间是三峡入库洪水的组成之一，但同时又是独立的水系/流域区间，可作为独立的预报区域；预报区域按水文站网布设再划分子区间，从而实现不同类型地形地貌和下垫面条件选择不同模型参数的目的；子区间内为考虑降雨面分布的不均匀性和不同地点河网汇流的影响，进一步细分为单元。

子区间是预报方案制作的基本单位，子区间的逐级预报形成大区间的预报方案，大区间根据水力联系的逐级演算最终形成三峡入库的预报方案。子区间由单元构成，单元划分、参数文件建立、资料整理等是预报的前期准备。在此基础上，各单元的产汇流计算、单元至子区间出口的河道汇流演算和上游子区间至该子区间的河道演算合成为子区间完整的预报过程。

针对每一个子区间进行细致的资料整理、单元划分、方案配置、模型应用、成果分析过程，按照水力联系串联至大区间，并对整个大区间进行全区间预报方案检验。而后依据水力联系将其大区间串联为整体，并对三峡总预报范围内的入库预报进行检验，如此层层把关，尽量减少三峡入库预报误差。

本次预报采用ARIGIS软件进行流域信息的提取，采用新安江三水源模型、马斯京根河道汇流模型进行产汇流计算；面雨量计算采用流域单元与泰森多边形叠置分析实现；实时校正的通用方法较多，通过比较分析选用了卡尔曼滤波技术。

（三）结语

三峡水库预报范围很大，每一个小区域的预报误差都会或多或少地影响三峡入库的预报精度，因此要对每一个小流域进行细致的方案制作、分析和检验，尤其是流域的暴雨中心地区，以确保高精度的入库洪水预报。

三峡水库的预报方案从大流域到小区间层层嵌套设计，并从小区间到大流域逐级预报、逐级检验，该方案从大处着眼、小处入手，对大、中、小流域的预报方案设计都有一定的借鉴意义。

（国网电力科学研究院　李春红　王建平　桑联秀
三峡梯级调度通信中心　王玉华）

南瑞通用实时洪水预报系统设计与开发

洪水预报是水文学的一个重要组成部分，是根据客观水文规律以及水、雨情信息对未来水文现象进行预测，在防汛减灾、水库调度等领域有着重要的作用。现代计算机及通信技术的发展，为洪水预报系统的建立提供了技术条件，使水情信息的采集、传输处理、洪水预报数学模型的计算分析、预报信息的发布服务等环节联为一体，构建实时洪水预报系统成为现实。目前洪水预报软件主要存在以下几个方面的问题：①洪水预报软件的通用化程度低；②预报软件中专业分析支持的功能偏弱；③系统对多预报方案的支持较差；④预报方案率定的复杂性和人为性。

南京南瑞集团公司水利水电技术分公司针对以上问题进行深入研究，掌握了通用型实时洪水预报系统实现的核心技术，主要包括数字流域拓扑关系构建技术、通用预报方案构建技术、模型库技术、预报方案参数人工及自动优选技术、实时校正技术等，并设计开发了通用性很好的实时洪水预报系统，实现了对大范围的水库水情测报系统的水、雨情信息的数据预处理、分析和预报应用，为大范围、跨流域和梯级水库对预报的高要求提供了完整、通用的解决方案，并在实践应用中取得了较好的效果。

（一）系统结构及组成

南瑞通用性实时洪水预报系统（NRTFFS），按功能分主要包括预报方案制作、实时人工交互预报、实时自动预报三大子系统，如图1所示；按软件设计模块分为预报引擎、预报驱动界面、数据库三部分，如图2所示。

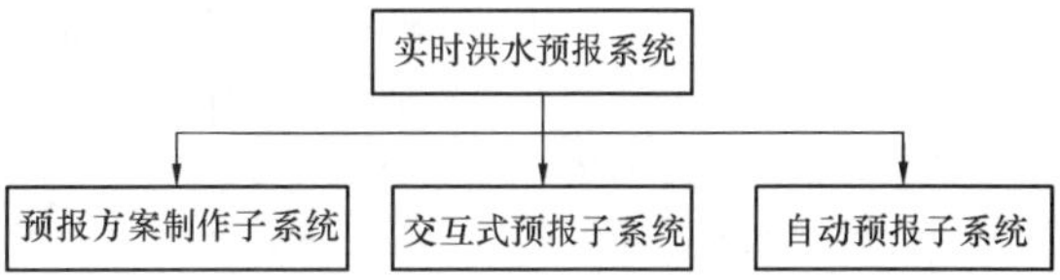

图1　系统组成图

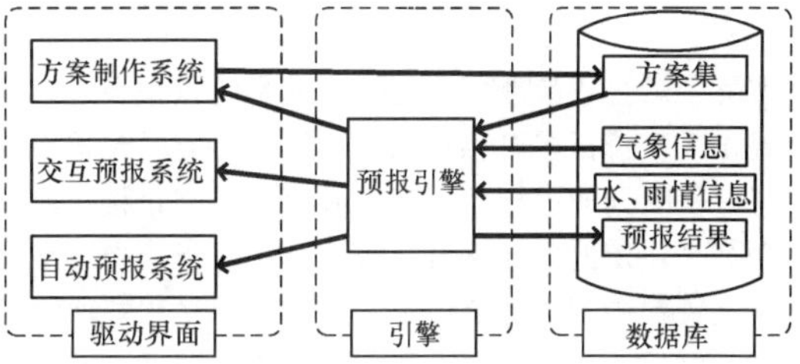

图2　模块结构图

预报方案制作子系统调用预报引擎完成预报方案构建及各方案参数率定工作，是实时洪水预报系统的核心模块。实时人工交互预报子系统针对预报方案集中各方案进行交互预报工作，是实时洪水预报系统中面向所有预报系统使用用户的模块，用户可对作业预报进行全程交互控制，以得到合理满意的预报结果。实时自动预报模块针对无人值守设计，在后台根据设置好的时间、特定方案或者方案集全部方案全天候在线运行，并将预报计算结果自动存库。

（二）关键技术

1. 数字流域拓扑关系构建技术　研究了 Martz 和 Garbrent 研制的数字高程流域水系模型（Digital Elevation Drainage Network Model，缩写为 DEDNM）、王加虎 Chanel Network Tool 等成果的基础上，采用数字高程模型和栅格化主干河网方法进行预报流域水文特征提取，构建相应流域拓扑关系。基于该拓扑关系和水文特征将预报流域抽象出八类最基本的对象并对其进行数字化定义和表示。

2. 模型库技术　本项目在吸取了国内外先进预报系统多模型库技术的基础上，采用系统分析方法，根据系统开发平台工具特点，从各种模型实现函数中抽象出统一的实现接口，用接口来定义水文模型以及相应的参数。在此基础上定义和实现各种水文模型。目前加入模型库的产流模型有新安江模型、API 降雨径流模型、陕北模型、水箱模型、混合产流模型、新安江改进融雪径流模型、经验拟合法等，加入模型库的河道汇流模型有：马斯京根河道汇流、滞时演算法、经验公式法等。通过这些模型的组合基本能满足绝大多数地区的水文预报需求。

3. 预报方案构建技术　本项目中预报方案构建技术设计中吸收了国内外先进经验并且考虑了它们的不足。工作实践中，在数字流域拓扑关系构建技术和多模型库技术的基础上，从通用性、移植性以及易用性上考虑，设计了一套完整的预报方案制作系统。该系统从方案创建、流域拓扑关系构建、拓扑关系上各元素节点属性配置、模型添加配置、参数配置全部采用可视化操作，界面友好直观，用户即使没有经过培训也可很快地掌握该系统。

4. 方案参数人工及自动优选技术　模型参数修正实际上就是将参数率定工作嵌入实时预报系统，系统提供人工修正接口和自动修正接口。实时预报系统经过一段时间的运行后，手工调用人工修正接口或者按照某个设定的条件下自动激活自动修正接口，从历史水文资料中基于规范要求，以大多数洪水能取得好的预报结果为优选准则，寻求最佳模型参数，并将修正后的模型参数用于后面的预报工作，可以理解成系统的自学习过程。本系统选择常规的 ROSENBROCK 方法和较新的微粒子群算法。

5. 实时校正技术　本系统采用基于马斯京根矩阵方程的实时校正技术、基于误差序列的自适应滤波算法和反馈模拟实时校正算法三种算法自适应，能够有效满足预报的实时性、精度和预见期要求，能在“新息”驱动下进行全流域的合理校正，提高预报精度，而又不损失预见期。

（三）应用实例

本预报系统成功地运用在三峡梯级流域、大渡河梯级流域、陕西省、黑龙江省、彭水等水调系统中，在实际运行中取得了较好的效果，为调度提供了决策依据。

（国网电力科学研究院　王建平　李春红　王文鹏）

2008 年三峡入库洪水特点与预报效果评价

三峡联机水文预报系统是一套完整的通用实时洪水预报系统，进行了包括新安江三水源模型、API 降雨径流模型在内的多模型、多方案配置，于 2008 年 5 月在三峡工程现场投入试运行。该系统基于三峡所有已建和已接入的遥测站网信息进行入库预报，包括 427 个遥测水文/水位/雨量站，预报范围从金沙江龙街站至三峡坝址区间，预报面积约 39 万 km^2。

三峡联机水文预报系统目前已运行一个汛期，本文对 2008 年三峡洪水特点进行分析，并针对场次洪水和连续自动预报两种方式对三峡入库洪水预报结果进行误差统计和分析。

（一）洪水特点

2008 年汛期三峡水库统计 7 场洪峰流量大于 30 000m^3/s 的洪水，分别为 20080705、20080723、20080812、20080829、20080912、20080929、20081103 号洪水，其中 20080812 号洪水的洪峰流量最大，达 41 500m^3/s。

7 场洪水既包括寸滩上游来水为主的洪水（嘉陵江、岷江等支流是洪水过程的重要组成部分），同时包括库区较大洪水和全流域降雨洪水，基本涵盖了三峡入库洪水的大部分地区组成方式。20080723、20080912、20080929 号洪水主要为寸滩上游来水；20081103 号洪水基本为全流域洪水，乌江来水较大；20080705、20080812、20080829 号洪水为上游来水与三峡区间叠加，区间来水相对较大，尤其 20080705 号洪水对应的库区洪峰达 16 000m^3/s。

（二）场次洪水预报

在不考虑未来降雨的情况下，对统计洪水进行

108h 预报，7 场洪水预报精度差别较大，部分场次洪水在较长预见期能获得较高的预报精度（20080912、20080929 号洪水），而有些洪水场次即使预见期较短，预报精度仍然不高（20080705、20080812、20080829 号洪水）。

结合场次洪水特点与预报误差分析，发现三峡 2008 年 7 场洪水预报精度差别较大的主要原因是由于形成入库洪水的暴雨分布不同，一般来讲，以上游来水为主的洪水预见期相对较长，暴雨中心越接近流域下游，预报的预见期越短。在不考虑未来降雨的情况下，库区来水所占比重较大的洪水无法预测未来较长时间的来水情况，预报精度必然较低。

为了分析未来降雨对三峡入库预报的影响程度，结合未来降雨重新进行预报计算，预报精度有了明显提高，达到 SL 250—2000《水文情报预报规范》规定的甲级标准，表明未来降雨对三峡部分场次洪水预报的预见期和精度影响很大。

（三）连续自动预报

为了更客观地反映预报方案的实时预报精度，本次采用三峡自动水文预报系统的实时运行结果（未来降雨采用三峡发布的降雨预报），针对 2008 年汛期（6 月 1 日～11 月 15 日）每日 8 时、20 时的滚动预报过程进行误差统计。

统计表明实时运行的 336 次入库预报中，随着预见期的增长，预报误差加大：12h 预见期，流量相对误差小于 5%的比例达 87.5%；而 48h 预见期只有 61.31%；流量相对误差小于 10%的比例，在 24h 预见期超过 95%，36h 预见期达 90%，48h 预见期只有 85%。随着预见期增长、涉及的预报区域增大，预报误差的影响因素增多，导致预报误差加大。譬如，以寸滩、武隆水文站至三峡水库的入库汇流时间为 12h 计，则三峡 12h 预见期的入库预报只涉及寸滩、武隆当前的实测流量过程和三峡库区的降雨径流过程；而 24h 预见期的入库预报涉及的因素除三峡库区的降雨径流外，还包括寸滩、武隆 12h 的预报过程，该预报过程又与其上游的降雨径流和河道汇流相关，因此存在自上游向下游的误差累积，导致随着预见期增长预报误差加大。

（四）结语

针对 2008 年多场三峡入库洪水，进行了场次洪水和实时预报误差统计、分析，结果表明：

(1) 针对 2008 年的 7 场洪水，三峡入库预报精度在一定预见期内都能够达到 SL 250—2000《水文情报预报规范》规定的甲级标准，预报合格率 100%。

(2) 针对 2008 年 6 月 1 日～11 月 15 日每日 8 时、20 时的实时自动预报结果进行了统计，336 次的预报结果统计表明：相对误差小于 10%的比例，在 12h、24h 预见期都超过 95%，36h 预见期超过 90%，48h 预见期为 85%；相对误差小于 20%的比例，在 48h 预见期内都超过 90%。

(3) 三峡入库预报的预见期与洪水组成密切相关，当三峡库区洪水较大时，三峡入库预报的预见期较短，主要为上游来水的入库洪水则预报的预见期相对较长，在实际作业预报中，结合未来降雨是获得长预见期、高精度预报的必要条件。

(4) 三峡联机水文预报系统经过 2008 年的实际运行检验，预报精度达到 SL 250—2000《水文情报预报规范》规定的甲级标准，为电站汛期安全运行和水库优化调度决策提供了科学依据，对于合理利用水力资源和减轻洪涝灾害损失具有重大意义。

（国网电力科学研究院　李春红　王建平
三峡梯级调度通信中心　王玉华
河海大学水资源高效利用与工程安全国家工程研究中心　任立良）

南瑞通用实时洪水预报系统在三峡 2009 年洪水预报中的应用情况

三峡洪水预报系统采用南瑞通用实时洪水预报系统对长江干流上金沙江龙街站至三峡坝址区间各目标断面进行预报。预报区间总面积约 39 万 km^2，其中岷江、沱江、嘉陵江、乌江四支流基本上包括其全部流域。预报对象为：屏山、高场、富顺、北碚、横江、寸滩、武隆、三峡坝址、葛洲坝共 9 个断面的流量。该通用实时洪水预报系统采用数字高程流域水系信息模型进行流域信息的提取，采用新安江三水源模型、马斯京根河道汇流模型进行产汇流计算，采用流域单元与泰森多边形叠加计算面雨量。2009 年汛期洪水预报取得了较好的效果。

该系统是在三峡梯级水库调度自动化系统屏寸区间水情遥测系统遥测站点水雨情信息、短期 48h 降雨预报和中期 7d 降雨预报信息的基础上，进行三峡坝址入库流量 96h 预见期的预报。由于三峡预报范围很大，且流域地形、水文气象特征复杂多样，因此洪水预报方案的制作需要考虑不同类型的地形地貌和下垫面条件，不均匀的降雨面分布和多汇入点的河网汇流，将整个预报区域划分为几个大的区间，大区间内根据水文站点分布划分为若干块，块内考虑降雨分布的不均匀，再划分为若干个单元，逐级进行预报方案的制作。

由于系统接入了短期48h和中期7d的预报降雨信息，预见期大大增长。经对三峡现场2009年汛期7月1日～9月1日每日10时自动预报精度进行统计，81次预报结果中，其中48h预见期预报合格78次，合格率96.3%；96h预见期预报合格73次，合格率达到90.12%，均达到了甲级标准。2009年8月上旬，受长江上游持续暴雨天气影响，三峡发生了自1998年大洪水后的第二大洪水，该系统8月2日8时进行96h预见期的预报，预报洪峰流量为56 800m^3/s，洪峰预报相对误差为3.3%，预报峰现时间提前5h；8月3日8时进行72h预见期的预报，预报洪峰流量为54 900m^3/s，洪峰预报相对误差为0.2%，预报峰现时间提前2h，准确地预报了这次大洪水，为防洪调度提供了决策支持。

鉴于提供和收集水文资料的限制，部分流域方案制作所采用的资料年限尚达不到规范的要求；有些遥测雨量站刚建立不久，积累的资料不多，在沿用历史水文资料时又有时段过粗、缺测等问题，导致个别流域拟合计算精度不够理想。

三峡以上流域地域广阔，随着经济建设开发的需要，人类活动日益增多和复杂，流域广、汇流条件也将不断改变，这将给预报工作带来很大难度。同时对于那些在建或规划兴建的大中型水库电站，其蓄放水将受人为干预，当前除了在实时系统中留有接口外，日后也将在统一规划、统一领导下建立起一个流域水资源开发利用、运行管理的完整系统。

（国网电力科学研究院　王建平　李春红　桑联秀）

基于洪水地区组成的梯级水库群防洪控制水位研究

（一）研究背景

在实际的防洪调度中，通常会面临以下两个问题：

（1）由于来水的不确定性，在汛期水库通常都是长期维持在汛限水位下运行，等待洪水到来。应该指出，水库规划设计中确定的各种防洪特征水位及其相应的防洪库容（或调洪库容）的依据，是考虑出现大坝安全标准相应的特大洪水及下游防洪标准相应的大洪水。实际运行中大量出现的是一般年份的常见洪水，对于这类洪水，显然不必预留设计中确定的那么大的防洪库容（或调洪库容）。

（2）近年来，随着各大流域的逐步开发，成立了诸多的流域管理机构统筹协调流域内各级水库的蓄放。如何协调水库工程特别是梯级水库群的防洪效益和洪水资源利用率成了一个新课题。而防洪效益和洪水资源利用率的关键技术是如何控制汛期各个时段的水库水位，在保证安全的前提下达到防洪效益与洪水资源利用双赢。

由此可见，洪水来临时的起调水位和洪水过后的拦蓄水位控制尤为重要。研究地区洪水组成的梯级水库群防洪控制水位计算方法具有重要的理论意义和实用价值。

（二）研究内容

研究针对以下三个问题进行：①在给定的调度期内，若水库群各水库都按照满发流量运行，在区间洪水来多大的情况下可以达到设定的期末水位，即调度期末拦蓄控制水位；②在给定的调度期内，若水库群各水库都按照满发流量运行，在区间来水频率给定的情况下可以计算出起初控制水位，也就是调度期初的起调控制水位；③在给定的调度期内，若水库群各水库的起调水位和拦蓄水位给定，在区间来水频率多大的情况下才不至于发生弃水。其中主要是区间来水的可能性分析问题，结合洪水地区组成方法提出了基于皮尔逊（P－Ⅲ）型频率曲线的区间来水分析。

（三）算例

乌江流域乌江渡水库以上控制面积27 790km^2，流域内洪水遭遇组成复杂，存在着区域型、全局型等多种致灾性洪水。出于防洪与兴利需要，该区域内逐渐形成了由洪家渡、东风、索风营、乌江渡等四座大型水库组成的防洪工程体系。虽然这些工程的防洪效果取决于其群体效应，但由于地理分布及水库特性的差别，在不同类型的洪水事件中，各个水库所预留的防洪库容、调洪库容也不相同。为使防洪工程效果达到最优，需要进行水库群补偿调度，确定各水库防洪调度中期控制水位。

按照汛期洪水特点，把整个汛期分为6～8月、9～10月两个阶段。利用1959～2007年汛期6～8月最大1日、3日平均流量进行分析，频率曲线计算结果见图1。

1. 起调控制水位计算　根据天气形势，指定各区间的来水频率、洪水天数和洪水过后的拦蓄目标水位，求解在没有弃水的情况下水库群各水库的起调控制水位的方法是：

（1）利用三天最大平均入库（区间）流量频率曲线确定对应频率下的来水，叠加上游来水得出水库的平均入库流量。

（2）在水电站满发的情况下，根据水量平衡方程，计算得出起调控制水位。

根据计算结果可以得出，当水库当前水位等于计算起调控制水位时，洪水调度期末水位能达到拦蓄水位。当水库当前水位高于计算起调控制水位时，会发

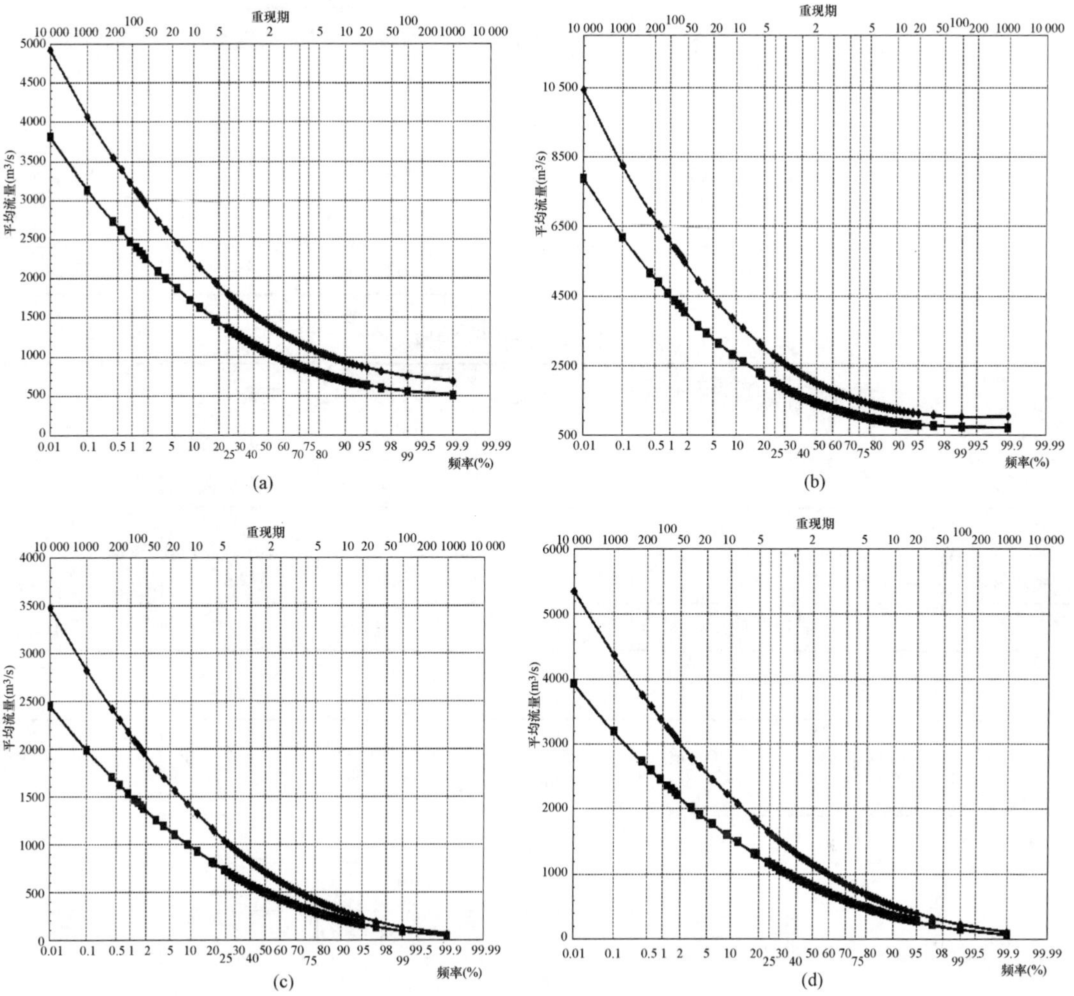

图 1　区间流量频率曲线图

(a) 洪家渡水库入库流量站平均流量综合频率曲线；(b) 洪家渡—东风区间平均流量综合频率曲线；(c) 东风—索风营区间平均流量综合频率曲线；(d) 索风营—乌江渡区间平均流量综合频率曲线

生弃水。当水库当前水位低于计算起调控制水位时，洪水调度期末水位不能达到拦蓄水位。计算成果见表 1。

2. 拦蓄控制水位计算　根据天气形势，指定各区间的来水频率、洪水天数和起调水位，求解在没有弃水的情况下水库群各水库的拦蓄控制水位的方法是：

(1) 利用三天最大平均入库（区间）流量频率曲线确定对应频率下的来水，叠加上游来水得出水库的平均入库流量。

(2) 在水电站满发的情况下，根据水量平衡方程，计算得出拦蓄控制水位。

根据计算结果可以得出，在起调水位给定的情况下，当来水频率大于给定的来水频率时，就会超过计算的拦蓄控制水位。当来水频率小于给定的来水频率时，就会达不到计算的拦蓄控制水位。计算成果见表 2。

3. 弃水风险的概率计算　给定控制目标水位，利用当前水位和水库满发流量计算出对应的平均入库流量，扣除上游水库出库查对应的来水频率曲线得到对应流量下的频率，如果来水频率小于计算值则有弃水风险，如果来水频率大于计算值则没有弃水风险。计算成果见表 3。

从表 3 可以看出，给定起调水位和拦蓄水位的情况下，对于洪家渡水库来说，当三日来水频率大于 56%时会发生弃水。

表1 起调控制水位计算成果表

水库	来水频率(%)	对应频率流量(m^3/s)	平均入库流量(m^3/s)	满发流量(m^3/s)	拦蓄水位(m)	起调控制水位(m)
洪家渡	5	1920	1920	395	1140	1134.92
东风	10	2720	3210	585	970	921.56
索风营	50	502	982	828	837	822.08
乌江渡	20	1260	2160	1030	760	753.91

表2 拦蓄控制水位计算成果表

水库	来水频率(%)	对应频率流量(m^3/s)	平均入库流量(m^3/s)	满发流量(m^3/s)	起调水位(m)	拦蓄水位(m)
洪家渡	5	1920	1920	395	1134.92	1140
东风	10	2720	3210	585	921.56	970
索风营	50	502	982	828	822.08	837
乌江渡	20	1260	2160	1030	753.91	760

表3 弃水风险计算成果表

水库	起调水位(m)	满发流量(m^3/s)	拦蓄水位(m)	平均入库流量(m^3/s)	区间来水流量(m^3/s)	来水频率(%)
洪家渡	1138	496	1140	997	997	56
东风	955	480	970	1260	865	89
索风营	832	900	837	928	343	73
乌江渡	756	1200	760	1740	912	41

(四)结语

在时间尺度上，设计院设计的汛期限制水位给的是长期调度。根据洪水预报进行防洪调度确定水库水位控制是个短期调度。本研究在长期调度和短期调度之间构建一个以日为单位的中期防洪调度水位控制方法，可以更好地衔接长期控制水位和短期控制水位，旨在更好地利用水库库容，发挥洪水资源化作用。

(国网电力科学研究院 江浩
贵州乌江水电开发有限责任公司 肖燕 唐玉兰
中国水电顾问集团贵阳勘测设计研究院 唐洪波)

碧口水库水情测报系统改造情况

(一)概况

碧口水电站位于甘肃省文县碧口镇上游3km的白龙江干流上，大坝为壤土心墙土石混合坝，最大坝高101.8m，控制流域面积26 000km^2，占全流域面积的80%。设计多年平均流量为275m^3/s，为一季调节水库。装机容量3×100MW。水库正常蓄水位704m，校核洪水位708.8m，总库容(708.8m以下)为5.21亿m^3。

碧口水情自动测报系统于1990～1993年首先进行了1∶3短波系统试验，1993年扩建为1∶10短波、超短波混合组网系统，设有1个中心站、5个水文站、3个雨量站，坝上(含雨量)、坝下站，是当时国内最先建成投运的以短波通信为主，短波、超短波混合组网的水情遥测系统。2001年对短波进行了升级改造。但随着系统投用时间的增长，系统总体性能逐步下降，系统的可靠性、稳定性降低，因此进行了系统改造。

(二)系统改造方案

短波系统由于未广泛应用已趋于淘汰，根据白龙江流域地形的特点，选择性能稳定的设备是系统改造成功的关键因素。为此，电厂组织人员对现有水情测报的应用情况进行了调研。通过考察，选定了采用北斗星卫星通信，以点对点组网。卫星接收机选用成都国星通讯公司生产的北斗一号通信卫星接收器（型号YDD-3-01)；超短波通信，电台选用日本日精889A电台，数传仪选用南京水文所YDH-1型遥测数传，所选关键设备均非常成熟且运行稳定。

碧口水电厂水情测报系统改造是在原短波、超短波混合组网的水情遥测系统功能基础上进行整体设备更换，同时考虑上游汉坪嘴电站的投运，迁移、增设了部分站点。对洪水预报调度软件改造升级，并充分考虑上游在建苗家坝电站和下游即将发电的麒麟寺电站建设，预留了系统的扩展功能。

这次改造选择：遥测站采用北斗星卫星、手机短信、超短波通信方式进行组网，建成总体规模1：15的水情遥测系统，系统有水文站7个、雨量站5个、水位站3个、中心站1个。主要测站增设GSM短信冗余通道，当卫星发送不成功时自动切换，启动GSM信道发送。改造方案总体达到综合、先进、实用化。

改造主要为4个部分：①对系统测站布设进行了站网论证，扩充测点；②对测报系统测站设备全部进行更新；③对各测站测井进行整修、改造，采取较好的防淤、防浪措施；④中心站组建水调局域网络，将机组实时信息、闸门实时信息接入水情实时监测系统，实现水务计算自动化。

（三）改造实施及主要功能

碧口水情测报系统由南京水文所负责水情测报硬件及测报软件的建设；水务计算、洪水预报软件、系统组网、水调网站由中国水利水电科学研究院承担建设。系统2006年4月中旬开始安装，5月初投入试运行阶段，系统主要功能有：

(1) 水情遥测站主要功能：①自动采集降雨量和水位，人工设定定时报数，报数间隔1、2、3、6、8h可选；②增量自报，雨量每变化2mm、水位每变化5cm则自报；③测站具有重发功能，即当中心站首次收不到数据时，可自动重发一次；④遥测终端机自动开关机。

(2) 中心站主要功能：①对接收的数据和格式进行合理性校验、纠错处理和自动分类并存入数据库；②对水情数据进行实时计算、处理；③用户人工修改、输入数据；④测站管理，对测站的参数能够远程修改，对测站进行故障判别；⑤雨量、水位、流量、电压越限报警；⑥显示输出流域水情实时数据。

(3) 水调自动化系统：①模块化设计，系统可扩充；②自动水务计算；③洪水预报及调度；④来水预报；⑤数据查询；⑥报表管理；⑦图形输出；⑧调洪演算功能；⑨短信群发报信功能；⑩水调信息网站。

（四）系统实施中发现的问题及改进措施

(1) 运行初期卫星畅通率不高。软件进行更改，增加了回执功能，提高了卫星测站畅通率。

(2) 接收天线故障。更换卫星接收天线后问题解决。

(3) 传输线路故障。更换数据线后恢复正常。

(4) 水位计故障。更换了超声波探头，水位计恢复正常。2007年7月发现超声波水位计晚上数据不正确，数据跳跃较大，11月更换超声波电路集成板后恢复正常。

(5) 通信终端故障。2006年5月3日，超短波系统收不到数据，发现中心站多信道通信终端故障，中心站通信卡串口烧坏，更换后恢复正常。卫星接收天线、数据线在运输过程中要加强保护，提高包装质量；超声波水位计性能不太稳定。

（五）系统应用情况

该系统于2006年4月底投入运行，系统功能逐步完善。2006年，系统畅通率93.3%，可用度91.7%；2007年，系统畅通率达97.3%，可用度93.2%，提高了工作人员的工作效率和管理水平，增长了洪水预报的预见期，提高了预报精度，取得了良好的经济运行效益。

但该水情测报系统与电厂自动化监控系统两网络还未进行可靠隔离后联网，不能自动采集机组电量，未达到自动进行水务计算的功能。

（大唐碧口水力发电厂　何录合）

乌江流域梯级水库远程集中调度与水电站群安全经济运行

贵州乌江水电开发有限责任公司（以下简称乌江公司）是我国成立的第一家按流域进行水电开发的公司，负责开发建设和经营管理乌江干流的洪家渡、东风、索风营、乌江渡、构皮滩、思林、沙沱和支流清水河的大花水、格里桥等9座水电站，总装机容量8655MW。乌江公司已建立水调自动化系统，对梯级水库群实施远程集中调度，以实现梯级水电站群安全经济运行。

乌江公司水调自动化系统充分利用短期洪水预报、防洪优化调度、发电优化调度、水调自动化系统、卫星气象云图等先进技术，研究了适合于乌江流域梯级水库群的调度规则和优化水能水量利用的方案，开发了相应的应用系统。建立了乌江流域梯级水库群短期调度预报模型，考虑了软件的通用性设计，是一套构皮滩水电站以上5级水库短期洪水联合预报模型。经过4年运行，洪水预报平均精度达到了92%以上。与高等院校联合研制了乌江流域梯级水库群防洪优化系统，采用均匀安全度法、削平头、预泄调度等多种优化调度方法，形成了完整的用于解决多级首尾相接的大型水电站群的联合优化调度模型和算法。建立的乌江流域梯级水库群包含大气环流因子影响的逐步回归模型和选点法的自回归中长期径流预报模型，方案确定性系数达到90%以上。乌江梯级水库群发电优化调度研究，提出了求解复杂梯级水库群蓄能最大模型的动态搜索法和快速分配法。

乌江公司建立健全规章制度，规范梯级水库远程集中调度管理；加强防汛应急预案的学习和演练，提高各级人员应急处理能力；实行流域水库集中调度，优化人力资源，实现减人增效；实行梯级水库联合调度，实现梯级水电站防洪度汛安全，取得了良好的效益。

水库采取均衡发电、动态控制梯级水库水位、汛末抬高梯级水库水位运行的调度思路，采取“上游先发、下游后发、均衡匹配”的优化调度原则，合理安排梯级电站发电运行方式。2007年乌江公司梯级综合耗水率比2006年同期降低了11.1%，同比节水增发电量11.5亿kW·h，全年因耗水率降低所节约的总水量达45.24亿m^3，接近于洪家渡和乌江渡两座水库的兴利库容之和。

乌江流域2007年7月中下旬出现了较大洪水，采取汛期动态控制梯级水库水位运行，汛末有效拦蓄洪水，既保证了梯级防汛及大坝安全，又充分利用了洪水资源，各水库洪水利用率达60%以上，提高了20%，获得了电量效益1.163 8亿kW·h。通过水库集中调度，充分利用上游水库削峰错峰调节，不但成功调度了乌江流域2007年7月下旬发生的10年一遇洪水，同时乌江渡水库最大入库流量6940m^3/s，最大出库流量5150m^3/s，削峰流量达1790m^3/s，削峰25.8%，为下游构皮滩、思林、沙沱电站等在建工程减轻了防汛压力，实现了乌江梯级水库大坝及在建电站的防洪度汛安全。

乌江流域已建成了目前国内投产最为复杂的水电站及水库群，除乌江公司所属的9座水电站外，还有属于黔源电力股份有限公司的乌江上游三岔河的普定、引子渡2座水电站和属于中国国电集团公司的乌江支流猫跳河的红枫梯级水电站，大中型水电站共计13座。乌江下游的构皮滩、思林、沙沱都是装机容量百万千瓦级以上水电站，占乌江流域总装机容量的56.3%，在贵州电网中具有举足轻重的作用。乌江流域梯级水电站只有实行统一调度、统筹兼顾，才能满足大坝防洪、航运调度、生态调度等综合调度要求。

（贵州乌江水电开发有限责任公司　聂明慧　田　毛）

华光潭梯级水电站的水库优化调度问题

华光潭梯级水电站位于浙江省临安市境内的钱塘江支流分水江上游的昌北溪，由一、二级水电站组成，总装机容量85MW，设计多年平均发电量1.85亿kW·h，在电网中主要承担调峰任务。由于容量在电网中占的比重较小，一般情况下机组均采用满负荷运行，水库调度的核心内容是尽最大可能提高水能利用率。设计正常蓄水位即水库发电运行的最高控制水位，故汛期水库控制水位须在留出适当的调节库容后选定。水库蓄水投运后至2007年9月的两年多时间里，一级水库按汛期435m水位控制运行，因连续几年降水偏枯，一直未能蓄至正常蓄水位；而二级水库的调节库容过小，虽已适当降低发电控制水位至226m，但遭遇区间暴雨时仍被迫多次弃水。

2007年10月的“麦莎”台风和2008年6月的梅雨是华光潭梯级水电站投产后至今仅有的两次流域性大暴雨过程。这两次大暴雨过程的一级水库调度情况如下：

（1）2007年10月7～8日，一级水库流域遭受“麦莎”台风袭击，普降大暴雨，平均降雨量达到216.2mm，而该流域10月多年平均降雨量为101.4mm。10月7日8时，雨前一级水库水位438.37m，台风带来的暴雨强度已远远超过了当前水库的调节能力；于8日3时开闸泄洪，最大下泄流量287m^3/s，泄洪历时39h。本次暴雨拦蓄洪水1505万m^3，弃水1489万m^3。

（2）2008年5月，梅汛期雨量偏多，降水集中。汛前，一级水库按425m控制水位，一度降至424m以下。6月8～10日，入梅后的第一场大暴雨，过程雨量达215.5mm，其中10日库区面雨量达到144.8mm。10日15时出现最大入库流量902m^3/s，雨前一级水库起涨水位424.87m，相应库容2470万m^3，至12日6时出现本次洪水最高库水位442.66m，相应库容6042万m^3。由于分水江流域汛情全线告急，防汛部门要求不开闸泄洪，本次洪水调度过程共拦蓄洪水3572万m^3，通过机组发电利用水量905万m^3。13～14日遭遇了入梅后的第二场暴雨，过程雨量达到45mm，单站最大过程雨量为57mm，由于调度合理，机组连续满负荷运行，水量得到充分利用，没有造成一级水库弃水。17～18日，第三场大暴雨来临，过程雨量达到111.7mm，远超出一级水库调节能力，于17日19时开闸泄洪，弃水量1310万m^3。

对于有年调节能力的一级水库，主汛期前水库水位控制在死水位414m以上运行即可，但为了提高水能利用率和电站的经济效益，应尽可能地抬高水头运行。相对于6月多年平均降雨量262.6mm，理论上控制水位430m运行是可行的，但对于2008年所遇到的极为典型的梅雨，降雨集中且量大，汛前的水位控制还是值得探讨的。

华光潭一级水库大坝为薄型高拱坝，对温度的变化极为敏感。浙西北山区冬季气温较低，极端最低气温可低于－15℃。从几年的大坝运行观测资料分析，大坝在低温期间向下游水平位移值较大，低温高水位是大坝最不利的运行工况。因此，水库调度必须要以为工程营造良好的运行工况为前提，每年年初至汛前的低温季节要控制一级水库水位在435m以下。

拦蓄洪水既是流域防洪的需要，也是收回水库建设投资的需要。几年来的运行实践表明，如来水偏枯或运行调度不当，一级水库不能有效地拦截几次较大的洪水，则水库的功能得不到有效的体现，往往不能完成年度的发电生产经营任务。为此，一要合理确定一级水库的汛期控制水位；二要进一步完善水情测报和洪水预报系统；三要在掌握天气趋势的前提下，尽量拦蓄洪尾；四要做好与电力部门的协调和联系工作。

二级水库水位尽量控制在227.0～227.7m之间。遇气象预报有较大降雨时，可通过减少一级电站出力或二级电站尽可能提前开机发电来降低库水位，减少弃水。由于库水位降至221m时，机组仍能安全稳定运行，二级水库实际死水位可按221m控制，相应库容126万m^3。这样，二级水库调节库容由原来的15.8万m^3增大到129万m^3，调节能力提高了7倍（相当于8个多小时的发电耗水量），可有效减少弃水。

华光潭梯级水电站单位电能投资较大，建成投产时间不长，还本付息任务较重，电站赢利水平较低，遇来水偏枯年份，容易出现经营亏损情况。因此，做好梯级水库优化调度有着重要的现实意义。

（浙江华光潭水力发电有限公司
方克宇　罗谊深　邱清华）

大 坝 安 全 管 理

2009年水电站大坝安全监管工作概况

水电站大坝安全监管是电力安全监管的重要组成部分，多年来一直得到国家电力监管委员会（以下简称电监会）领导的高度重视。2009年，国家电力监管委员会大坝安全监察中心（以下简称大坝中心）加强与电监会安监局和各派出机构的协调配合，在积极开展大坝安全常态工作的同时，为大坝安全监管提供技术支撑，保障了大坝安全监管工作的顺利进行。

大坝中心密切配合电监会安监局开展了以下各项安全监管活动：

（1）编制了《2008年电力安全监管报告》中有关大坝运行安全的章节。

（2）配合福州电监办召开了福建省水电站大坝安全监管工作会议。

（3）派员参与水电站大坝的隐患排查，如3月对昆明电监办开展的防汛安全检查意见建议进行了跟踪、督促和落实。7月初会同电监会安监局和成都电监办再次对汶川地震灾区的大中型水电站大坝进行了防汛和恢复重建安全检查。7月中，配合华中电监局对湖北、重庆、江西的6座水电站大坝进行抽查。8月参加了电监会电力安全生产抽查组对南方区域的检查。9月会同安监局和长沙电监办对东江一、二级放空洞存在的问题进行了核查，摸清了东江一、二级放空洞存在问题的详细情况，并向国家电网公司进行了通报，督促其整改。

（4）四季度，按照电监会领导的指示，开展了俄罗斯萨扬—舒申斯克水电站“8·17”事故的原因分析，并组织翻译了事故调查报告，提出了应对措施和建议。配合安监局召开了“水电站安全管理研讨会”，总结、分析了萨扬水电站安全事故的经验教训。

（5）配合成都电监办对四川省内水电站大坝安全管理办法进行了协调，修改完善四川省水利厅提出的有关通知，初步取得了共识。配合电监会法规部等部门对《洪水影响评价管理条例（修订稿）》、《风力发电场并网安全性评价管理办法（征求意见稿）》、《电监会行政复议办法》等8部法规或规范性文件反馈了修改意见。

（6）完成了国家抗震救灾志电力部分有关大坝安全的提纲编写，提供了翔实的材料。

这些活动，既配合开展了安全监管工作，更密切了大坝中心与派出机构的联系和工作交流，在行业内形成了良好的监管合力，有力地促进了大坝安全监管工作，也为新中国成立60周年国庆保电作出了贡献。

（国家电力监管委员会大坝安全监察中心　何海源　张秀丽）

2009年水电站大坝安全注册情况

2009年是大坝安全注册工作的高峰年。年初国家电力监管委员会大坝安全监察中心（以下简称大坝中心）根据电力企业的注册申请和注册证到期换证的情况，制订了年度大坝安全注册检查计划，严格按照《水电站大坝安全注册办法》的要求办理大坝安全初始注册和换证注册工作。

2009年，大坝中心开展了75座大坝的注册现场检查工作，评审了其中的50座大坝，同时对左江、浮石、雪山湖、羊湖进行了复评；最终同意46座大坝安全初始注册或换证注册，上报国家电力监管委员会批复。

在福州电监办的督促下，福建省有51座中型水电站陆续向大坝中心提交了大坝安全初始注册申请，大坝中心根据《水电站大坝运行安全管理规定》和《水电站大坝安全注册办法》的要求，认真审查了每座大坝的申请材料，对符合注册条件的西门、丰海、北津等大坝安排了现场检查，对于尚不具备条件或进行现场检查后发现尚不具备安全注册条件的大坝，大坝中心及时书面回复意见或在现场提出意见，指导其开展下一步工作。

2009年，大坝中心继续做好注册证书的发放工作，全年共发放注册证书54份。截至2009年底，在大坝中心注册的大坝达205座，其中甲级187座、乙级15座、丙级3座。注册水电站大坝的水库库容2387亿m^3，占全国水库总库容的35%，装机容量6351万kW，占电力系统水电装机总容量的65%。

随着经济社会发展的需要，一些地方政府对水电站功能和水资源综合利用提出了新的需求。大坝中心以科学发展观为指导，与时俱进，积极开展了富春江船闸扩建改建工程对大坝安全影响的评价工作，一方面以确保大坝安全为前提，另一方面兼顾地方经济发展对资源配置的新要求，提出合理调整的建议，为寻求“双赢”出谋划策，客观、公正、科学地提出了评价意见，得到了地方政府、电力企业、咨询公司等各方的普遍认可。

（国家电力监管委员会大坝安全监察中心　杜德进）

2009年水电站大坝安全定期检查工作进展情况

大坝安全定期检查是排查大坝安全隐患、评定大坝安全等级的技术活动，其结论是对水电站大坝实施监管的依据。通过定检促进了大坝安全隐患排查和补强加固治理，为确保大坝安全运行起到了关键的作用。

2009年3月下旬，国家电力监管委员会大坝安全监察中心（以下简称大坝中心）在杭州组织召开了年度大坝安全定检暨大坝安全信息化建设工作会议。通过宣传法规、剖析流程、讲解案例和问题研讨，使水电站大坝业主和运行单位提高对大坝定检和信息化建设工作重要性的认识，明确了工作内容、技术要求，为顺利启动年度大坝定检和信息化建设工作打下了良好的基础。

根据国家电力监管委员会关于第三轮大坝安全定期检查的规划，结合新注册大坝及时开展大坝安全定检的要求，2009年大坝中心安排了太平湾、新安江、水口等27座大坝定检工作。截至2009年底，已按计划启动了所有大坝的定检工作，加上原计划2008年启动定检的以礼河二～四级大坝及新增加的山秀、金鸡滩、京南、鱼跳大坝，2009年共启动了34座大坝的定检工作。对2009年以前启动的大坝定检工作，也按计划要求积极推进，完成了紧水滩、石塘、广蓄上库和下库大坝、流溪河、长湖、螺丝湾、麻石、拉浪等大坝定检的专家组工作。2009年7月，大坝中心完成了25座大坝安全定期检查报告审查意见的编制和审核，并上报国家电监会备案。

为了详细检查“5·12”汶川地震对水电站大坝安全的影响，2009年大坝中心完成了四川映秀湾、铜头，陕西碧口3座大坝的特种检查，正在开展四川太平驿大坝的特种检查。

截至2009年底，第三轮定检共启动了134座大坝的定检工作，其中111座为规划内大坝，23座为规划外大坝；同时，完成了63座规划内大坝的定检报告审查上报和下发工作。目前，在大坝中心注册的211座大坝中，被评为正常坝或通过安全鉴定（特种检查）的大坝有208座，被评为病坝的有3座（丰满、黄龙滩、浮石）。

（国家电力监管委员会大坝安全监察中心　谢宵易）

2009 年水电站大坝安全信息化建设进展情况

自2006年国家电力监管委员会发布《水电站大坝运行安全信息化建设规划》，正式启动水电站大坝安全信息化建设以来，在电监会领导的关心支持和各水电站主管单位、运行单位的共同努力下，国家电力监管委员会大坝安全监察中心（以下简称大坝中心）根据电监会大坝安全信息化建设规划的要求，扎实推进大坝安全信息化建设。2009年大坝中心根据电监会的部署，继续加强大坝安全信息系统的建设和完善，进一步完善了大坝安全信息系统及有关子系统的功能，为更好地开展水电站大坝安全信息化建设提供了技术保障。

2009年，大坝中心计划完成54座大坝的网络报送工作，任务十分艰巨。为此，大坝中心在3月召开了定检和信息化建设工作会议，通过宣传、交流和沟通，部署、制订了工作计划。经过一年的努力，已有40座大坝完成了网络报送。针对未按要求开展大坝安全信息化建设工作的大坝，大坝中心已正式发文给有关主管和运行单位，督促其尽快按要求开展工作。截至2009年底，有105座大坝完成了信息化建设，实现了大坝安全信息的网络报送。

按照电监会发布的《水电站大坝运行安全信息化建设规划》，截至2009年底，信息化建设规划中69座采用邮件报送方式的大坝中的红林、镜泊湖、六郎洞、以礼河三级、平地哨5座大坝因规模较小，无监测系统，不再要求接入；李官已经转地方水利系统监管，其余63座中已完成了50座大坝的信息化建设工作。其他13座大坝中，映秀湾、渔子溪、耿达、太平驿4座大坝监测系统因震损破坏，目前正在重建；古田溪二～四级、马迹塘4座大坝改为网络报送；百丈漈一级大坝因坝面整修停止监测，尚未开展邮件报送接入；白渔潭、峡阳、落坡岭、珠窝4座大坝仍未提供基本参数，未接入。规划外新增1座（过渡湾大坝）已经完成邮件报送。目前，共有51座大坝实现了监测信息的邮件报送。

2009年大坝中心还承担了汶川地震灾区水电站9座大坝2个监管机构大坝安全信息系统恢复重建项目。已完成了单一来源采购手续的审批和各子、分系统的委托定制，并按照政府采购程序完成了两个批次的设备采购，完成碧口、宝珠寺、太平驿、紫坪铺4座大坝的系统和设备的安装与运行，基本完成映秀总厂下辖的映秀湾、耿达、渔子溪3合1分系统的系统和设备的安装与试运行。其余2座大坝和2个监管机构的系统将于2010年1月进行第三批设备采购，项目可提前完成。

（国家电力监管委员会大坝安全监察中心　沈海尧）

2009 年水电站大坝安全监测管理简况

大坝安全监测是大坝安全的耳目，是监控大坝运行安全的重要手段。2009年国家电力监管委员会大坝安全监察中心（以下简称大坝中心）继续加强注册水电站大坝的安全监测管理工作，主要有：

（1）完成了浙江新安江、福建水口、广西岩滩、贵州天生桥一级、广州蓄能电站、云南大朝山等15座大坝的监测系统评价和资料分析。

（2）完成了浙江石塘、紧水滩，云南以礼河一级等大坝的监测系统综合评价，掌握了相关大坝监测系统的现状，并据此对监测系统更新改造提出了具体的意见。

（3）受理并批复了福建芹山、周宁，山东泰安，湖北葛洲坝，浙江天荒坪、桐柏，四川二滩等大坝的监测项目封存停测或改变监测频次的申请，同时提出了大坝监测系统在此后运行维护过程中应注意的问题。

（4）受理了福建棉花滩大坝安全监测系统的实用化验收申请，完成了云南大唐国际有限公司所属水电厂水工建筑物自动化规划设计的审查。

（5）为进一步掌握重要注册大坝的运行性态，指导具体大坝的运行管理和缺陷诊断，大坝中心还开展了贵州三板溪、江苏宜兴、河南宝泉、云南龙开口、四川锦屏二级等在建工程或即将竣工投运的水电站大坝安全监测系统评价和监测资料分析工作。

（国家电力监管委员会大坝安全监察中心　王玉洁）

2009 年水电站大坝缺陷消除和补强加固工作情况

2008年12月25日，丰满发电厂7号机大修期间，吊车行走在8号机附近时，发生与厂房天棚相刮，电厂检查发现，天棚局部存在一定程度的塌陷，随后进行的检查发现，厂房钢屋架有四处存在断裂和弯曲变形的安全隐患。针对这一影响电厂运行安全的隐患，国家电力监管委员会大坝安全监察中（以下简称大坝中心）及时派出专家参加丰满一期厂房钢屋架安全隐患应急处理方案效果评估和永久处理方案讨论。2009年7月，大坝中心参加了在北京召开的丰满水电站大坝全面治理方案论证会，会上，大坝中心阐明了对于丰满大坝全面治理问题的观点和立场；9月，大坝中心以专报的形式向电监会呈报了《关于丰满大坝有关情况的报告》，进一步阐明了大坝中心对类似丰满大坝这样运行时间较长大坝的补强加固治理意见。

针对定检中发现的东江一、二级放空洞存在的重大安全隐患，大坝中心本着科学负责的态度，会同电监会安监局和长沙电监办进行了核查，进一步查清了存在的问题，分析了原因，对处理措施提出了具体的意见。东江一、二级放空洞的问题正在加快处理中。

对定检中发现的广西拉浪大坝扩建改造项目，大坝中心严格把关，督促主管单位对扩建改造项目进行了总体布置、设计方案、施工方法等要素的复核和评价，提出了扩建改造过程中需重点关注的技术要求，为该项目的实施和保证大坝的安全奠定了基础。

根据大坝安全远程管理系统的监控资料，大坝中心发现浙江华光潭一级水电站大坝左岸基础扬压力持续升高的异常现象，及时通报运行单位，要求查清原因，并于7月、8月两次派技术人员去华光潭现场进行检查和商讨对策，目前正在对扬压力升高的原因和对大坝安全的影响进行分析。

2009年8月，在抗击“莫拉克”台风过程中，浙江百丈漈一级水电站发现大坝坝顶公路路面裂缝，大坝中心得到消息后及时联系运行单位核实情况，分析原因，并督促其采取临时应急措施，抗击台风结束后又派专家参与方案选择和论证，百丈漈一级大坝路面缺陷正在得到根治。

（国家电力监管委员会大坝安全监察中心　谢宵易）

强化大坝安全培训，夯实大坝安全管理的基础

水电站运行单位和大坝主管单位运行管理人员的业务素质是做好大坝安全工作的基础。国家电力监管委员会大坝安全监察中心（以下简称大坝中心），多年来一直将水电站运行单位大坝安全管理人员的培训作为一项公益性活动和基础性工作，积极组织、认真实施，以切实提高一线运行管理人员的大坝安全责任意识和业务能力，夯实大坝安全工作基础。2009年，大坝中心主要做了以下安全培训工作：

（1）3月，为中国华能集团公司在四川组织的大坝安全培训编写监测技术培训材料并授课。

（2）5月，会同中国水力发电工程学会大坝安全监测专业委员会、电力行业大坝安全监测标准化技术委员在杭州召开了大坝安全监测仪器应用培训班，并对神华集团有限责任公司进行了安全培训。

（3）6月，为国网新源控股有限公司在杭州召开的大坝安全和观测分析培训班进行授课，讲解了大坝安全管理法规、安全监测资料整编分析要点、监测技术最新发展、自动化监测技术及实用化要求。

（4）8月，为广西大唐广源水力发电有限公司进行了大坝安全法规及管理要求的培训；并分别在黑龙江牡丹江、山西太原配合电监会安监局举办的“2009全国电力应急管理培训班”进行了三次有关水电站应急管理的授课。

（5）9月，派专家参加东北电网公司在丰满举办的大坝安全培训班进行授课。

（6）10月，派专家参加华能技术监督水工技术标准专题会议。

（7）9月、11月，两次为二滩水电开发有限责任公司和二滩水力发电厂举办的大坝安全监测培训班授课。

（8）11月，继续与河海大学联合举办“大坝安全监测人员上岗培训”（第13期），水电站运行管理单位97人参加了培训。

所有这些培训，宣贯了新时期大坝安全管理的法规和要求，指导企业开展日常检查、维护等工作，对促进企业的大坝安全管理、提高运行管理人员的业务素质发挥了重要的作用。

（国家电力监管委员会大坝安全监察中心
杜德进　许传桂）

2009年水电工程安全鉴定情况

水电站工程安全鉴定是贯彻落实“安全第一、预防为主、综合治理”的重要手段，也是大坝安全管理关口前移的具体措施。通过安全鉴定，掌握了水电站工程建设期的工程质量和存在的问题，督促及时消缺，为大坝安全运行奠定了良好基础。

2009年度，国家电力监管委员会大坝安全监察中心、中国水电工程顾问集团公司、中国水利水电科学研究院完成的水电建设工程安全鉴定见表1。

表1　2009年完成的水电建设工程安全鉴定情况汇总表

序号	水电站名称	坝　型	鉴定阶段	鉴定单位
1	三峡三期工程	混凝土重力坝	蓄水至175m	中国水电工程顾问集团公司
2	云南小湾	混凝土双曲拱坝	蓄水（第二阶段）	中国水电工程顾问集团公司

续表

序号	水电站名称	坝　型	鉴定阶段	鉴定单位
3	四川瀑布沟	心墙堆石坝	蓄水	中国水电工程顾问集团公司
4	四川沙湾	混凝土重力坝	蓄水	中国水电工程顾问集团公司
5	青海拉西瓦	混凝土双曲拱坝	蓄水（第二阶段）	中国水电工程顾问集团公司
6	吉林双沟	混凝土面板堆石坝	蓄水	中国水电工程顾问集团公司
7	吉林石龙	混凝土重力坝	蓄水	中国水电工程顾问集团公司
8	陕西蜀河	混凝土重力坝	蓄水	中国水电工程顾问集团公司
9	四川龙头石	沥青混凝土心墙堆石坝	竣工	中国水电工程顾问集团公司
10	青海康扬	混凝土重力坝	竣工	中国水电工程顾问集团公司
11	江苏宜兴蓄能	混凝土面板堆石坝	竣工	中国水电工程顾问集团公司
12	重庆彭水	碾压混凝土重力坝	竣工	大坝安全监察中心
13	重庆酉酬	碾压混凝土重力坝	竣工	大坝安全监察中心
14	重庆巴山	混凝土面板堆石坝	蓄水	大坝安全监察中心
15	重庆马岩洞	碾压混凝土重力坝	蓄水	大坝安全监察中心
16	湖北红岩一级	混凝土面板堆石坝	竣工	大坝安全监察中心
17	湖北大峡	碾压混凝土重力坝	竣工	大坝安全监察中心
18	湖北庙子头	混凝土闸坝	竣工	大坝安全监察中心
19	湖南株溪口	混凝土闸坝	竣工	大坝安全监察中心
20	湖南木龙滩	混凝土闸坝	竣工	大坝安全监察中心
21	甘肃柴家峡	混凝土闸坝和土石坝	竣工	大坝安全监察中心
22	甘肃峡城	混凝土闸坝	蓄水	大坝安全监察中心
23	四川小姓	混凝土闸坝	蓄水	大坝安全监察中心
24	四川天龙滩	堰塞湖	竣工	大坝安全监察中心
25	四川城东	混凝土闸坝	竣工	大坝安全监察中心
26	贵州董箐	混凝土面板堆石坝	蓄水	大坝安全监察中心
27	云南云鹏	土石坝	竣工	大坝安全监察中心
28	云南吉沙	混凝土重力坝	竣工	大坝安全监察中心
29	云南南沙	碾压混凝土重力坝	竣工	大坝安全监察中心
30	缅甸瑞丽江一级	混凝土重力坝	竣工	大坝安全监察中心
31	云南大盈江一级	混凝土闸坝	竣工	大坝安全监察中心
32	云南马鹿塘二期	混凝土面板堆石坝	蓄水	大坝安全监察中心
33	水牛家水电站	碎石土心墙堆石坝	竣工	中国水利水电科学研究院
34	木座水电站	混凝土坝	竣工	中国水利水电科学研究院
35	立节水电站	混凝土坝	蓄水	中国水利水电科学研究院
36	戈枕水利枢纽	混凝土坝	蓄水	中国水利水电科学研究院
37	泗南江水电站	混凝土面板堆石坝	竣工	中国水利水电科学研究院
38	硗碛水电站	砾石土心墙堆石坝	竣工	中国水利水电科学研究院
39	吉林台二级	混凝土坝	蓄水	中国水利水电科学研究院
40	乌金峡水电站	混凝土坝	竣工	中国水利水电科学研究院
41	格里桥水电站	混凝土坝	蓄水	中国水利水电科学研究院
42	天王沟水电站	混凝土坝	竣工	中国水利水电科学研究院
43	朱岔峡水电站	混凝土坝	竣工	中国水利水电科学研究院
44	水泊峡水电站	混凝土坝	蓄水	中国水利水电科学研究院

（国家电力监管委员会大坝安全监察中心　聂广明
中国水电工程顾问集团公司　余　奎
中国水利水电科学研究院　朱耀泉）

大坝安全管理与对丰满病坝的处理意见

（一）运行水电站大坝的安全管理

大坝安全定期检查是对大坝的定期“体检”，主要任务是：①确定大坝的安全等级；② 提出存在的影响大坝安全的问题和处理意见，指导和督促大坝维修加固和更新改造。大坝安全定期检查，一般情况下每五年开展一次，动态管理大坝安全状态和评定大坝安全等级。具体工作包括：① 组织专家组开展定期检查工作，专家组形成检查报告；②国家电力监察委员会大坝安全监察中心（以下简称大坝中心）审查专家组的检查报告，评定大坝安全等级，提出存在问题和处理意见；③上报电监会备案；④向大坝主管单位转发电监会的批复意见及大坝中心对定检报告的审查意见。

电力系统将水电站大坝的安全等级分为正常坝、病坝和险坝三级，不同的大坝安全等级决定了对其不同的管理要求。

安全等级评定有以下五项内容：

(1) 设计标准符合性，包括工程等别、建筑物级别、防洪标准、抗震标准等与现行规范的符合程度。严重不符合、不符合、符合分别对应着险坝、病坝、正常坝的等级评定。

(2) 坝基是否存在影响大坝安全的隐患。

(3) 坝体稳定性与结构安全度是否符合现行规范的要求；泄洪消能设施是否满足规范要求。

(4) 大坝的运行状态如何。如有缺口、溃决等事故倾向是险坝的征兆，如有坝体结构破损、泄洪消能设施局部损坏，影响大坝安全储备但损坏程度尚不影响大坝起正常挡水作用和不影响挡水建筑物安全，是带病运行的状态。

(5) 近坝库岸稳定情况。近坝库区发现有危及大坝安全的严重塌方或滑坡的迹象是险坝的征兆；近坝库区塌方或滑坡，经过分析对大坝挡水结构安全不会造成威胁，为带病运行的状态。

“险坝”为有危险类型的坝，安全隐患最严重，管理上首先必须限期通过工程和非工程应急措施除险，确保公众安全，然后实施永久除险加固工程措施恢复正常。“病坝”为带病运行的坝，需要维修加固。正常坝也可能有缺陷需要消除，只是这些缺陷近期对安全的影响轻微。

大坝安全等级是有时效的，正常坝只代表在今后的五年内可以安全运行，不会发生大的安全问题；病坝代表在今后的三年内可以带病运行，但必须维修加固消除“病症”。险坝必须限期除险，然后采取工程措施维修加固。病坝、险坝经处理可以摘帽，成为正常坝。

水电站大坝定期检查工作开始于 1985 年，目前已进行到第三轮，首轮定检共检查了 96 座大坝，查出 7 座病坝、2 座险坝。二轮定检检查 130 座大坝，共查出病坝 8 座，无险坝。

（二）丰满大坝“病”在何处

丰满大坝到目前为止已经进行过两次大坝安全定期检查，首次定检始于 1995 年 5 月，1998 年底专家组工作结束，聘请了 14 位专家，历时三年半。二次定检始于 2003 年 9 月，结束于 2005 年底，聘请了 13 位专家，完成了 9 份专题报告、4 份补充报告，中国水利水电科学研究院、大连理工大学、中水东北勘测设计研究有限责任公司参加了专题工作。经过专家多年的分析论证，达成以下共识：丰满大坝坝顶加高后，已可以保证千年一遇设计洪水标准的防洪安全，考虑梯级水库联调和预泄等非工程措施，已基本具备抵御万年一遇校核洪水的能力。在坝体结构强度和整体性方面，经持续的历次维修加固，特别是 1986 年以后完成的系统、全面的加固补强工程，大坝整体性得到一定程度的改善，大坝整体稳定性及非地震工况下的坝体应力满足规范要求；坝体渗漏量明显减少，混凝土老化进程缓解，坝体变形符合一般规律。基础无异常位移，基础渗流控制基本有效；泄洪系统闸门及启闭机经改造能够满足正常使用要求；近坝库岸稳定。因此，丰满大坝在建基条件、坝体抗滑稳定、结构应力、近坝库岸稳定、设计洪水标准下的防洪能力方面都满足现行规范的要求。大坝已安全运行近 70 年，经历过多年累计 417d 正常蓄水位 263.5m 以上高水位的考验，最高运行水位达到 266.18m，运行实践证明对丰满大坝的认识是正确的。

但丰满大坝存在先天性缺陷，主要有四大先天性问题：①坝体上游和表面混凝土不满足抗渗、抗冻要求，特别是坝体的渗控缺陷致使溢流面混凝土冻害日益严重而影响泄洪安全性；②校核洪水工况下大坝防洪能力不足；③坝体纵缝的存在，造成设计地震工况坝体内部产生拉应力；④F_{67} 断层的存在使 34～36 号坝段整体抗滑稳定性安全裕度不高。进一步分析这四个问题，34～36 号坝段的问题是局部问题，且只是计算结果安全裕度不高，变形监测结果并未见异常。但渗漏冻胀问题是全坝段系统性和常遇的问题，特别是溢流面冻胀损坏在泄洪情况下，会造成像 1986 年那样溢流面的冲坏，如继续泄洪会使冲坏程度加剧直至坝段失去稳定，反之被迫关闭闸门，逼高库水位，后果会使经常性小洪水导致稀遇大洪水情况下的安全风险。因此，二次定检时，大坝中心经过大量复核分析，认为虽然丰满大坝的安全状况与首次定检相比，结构受力、稳定状态、运行性态、防洪能力等均无大的变化，但突出问题是大坝混凝土先天质量缺陷使坝体防渗体系存在缺陷，影响耐久性，坝体渗漏至今尚未有效遏制，坝身排水不畅，坝体扬压力高，大坝冻胀损害较严重，尤其是溢流面混凝土冻胀开裂，溢流坝面破损程度较首次定检时加剧，渗漏冻胀引起下游坝面渗水面积扩大，可能较首次定检时影响泄洪安全是更大的安全隐患。最终确定丰满病坝的主要“病症”就是坝体渗漏问题比首次定检时恶化，旨在督促开展维修加固工作。

（三）对丰满病坝的处理意见

丰满水电站是东北电网目前最大的水电站，装机百万千瓦，库容百亿立方米，坝高近百米，下游有大城市，社会影响巨大。在丰满大坝的安全等级定为病坝的问题上，大坝中心十分慎重，充分分析论证，聘请院士、设计大师等专家咨询，采取必要的措施防止引起不必要的社会恐慌，更为重要的是考虑加固补强措施，摘除“病坝”帽子，确保大坝安全运行。

2007年在确定丰满大坝为病坝时，大坝中心提出的要求是按照“综合治理，远近结合，尽快实施”的原则“三步走”。即：第一步开展丰满水电站大坝安全隐患排查，加强运行管理和现场巡查监测，修补溢流面破损部位；第二步开展灌浆试验和溢流坝段防渗降渗工程设计，抓紧实施构建溢流坝段防渗排水体系，降低渗水下游面出逸点，遏制溢流面冻胀损坏进程；第三步落实人力、物力、财力，抓紧开展丰满大坝全面综合治理的各项前期工作，充分论证，科学选择方案，彻底消除安全隐患。

将丰满大坝存在的四方面的“病症”通盘考虑，力争全面彻底治愈，不能“头痛医头，脚痛医脚”。“远近结合”的“远”是第三步工作，治理方案需要多方案研究论证科学选择，确定方案和实施需要相对较长的时间。“近”是第一步和第二步，是易于实施的事情。第二步和第三步的事情应尽可能有机结合起来。对于丰满病坝的处理，大坝中心要求是2008年底完成第二步防渗降渗工程，经过一年多的效果检验，于2010年启动大坝第三次定期检查，评价防渗降渗工程的效果和大坝安全状况，证明确已消除了确定病坝时的病症，运行状态正常，同时全面治理工程的各项工作有序开展，治理方案和施工时间确定后可重新评定大坝安全等级。

（国家电力监察委员会大坝安全监察中心　张秀丽）

参数查询在大坝安全信息系统中的应用

我国的大坝安全监测信息系统，随着自动化监测技术的发展和超大规模的坝群系统的导入，软件与数据库数据的交互变得越来越多，越来越频繁，同时软件的结构复杂性不断增加。国网电力科学研究院研究了在现有的基础上提高数据库的访问性能的方法，使数据库参数化查询在大坝安全监测信息系统中得到应用。

（一）存在问题

（1）存在SQL注入攻击。注入攻击是一种发生于应用程序与数据库层的安全漏洞，是在输入的字符串之中注入SQL指令，在设计不良的程序当中忽略了检查，这些注入进去的指令就会被数据库服务器误认为是正常的SQL指令而运行，系统因此遭到破坏。SQL注入攻击的存在，影响系统安全。

（2）数据执行缓冲低下。执行缓冲是数据库引擎对一些可以重复使用的过程、语句进行存储，减少相同过程、语句的重新编译。编译完成后将把该语句的执行计划等的分析保存在数据引擎缓冲中，等待下一次的使用。一旦数据库引擎发现有相同的存储过程或是SQL语句，它就可以直接运行，而不需要再进行语义、语法分析等。数据执行缓冲低下，影响数据库的访问性能。

（3）SQL语句组合困难及书写不规范。大坝信息安全系统，往往是由多名人员进行开发；复杂的SQL语句由多个函数生成的字符串进行拼接，组合困难；书写不规范，多了一个空格或是字母大小写不分屡屡出现，数据库缓冲中相同的SQL语句比比皆是，导致数据库引擎认为是无法复用，从而将会重新生成执行计划，消耗大量的内存和时间。

（二）解决方法

（1）数据库参数化。在撰写SQL指令时，利用参数来代表需要填入的数值。使用参数来给值，是目前被视为最有效预防SQL注入攻击的方法。

（2）判定语句相同。当系统执行SQL语句时，首先通过HashCode（哈希值）来判断，查询是否有缓存的相同语句。当哈希值相同，也就是说是同一个存储过程、SQL语句，这时数据库即按照已经分析好的执行计划进行执行，无需分析SQL语句，节约分析所花费的时间。

（3）查看数据库的缓冲表。通过对SQL缓冲计划表查询，可以看出执行效率，即SQL查询语句重复使用情况。

（三）设计结构

1. SQL语句分析　为了进行参数化设计，需对大坝安全信息系统所有常用的SQL语句进行结构分析。在大坝安全信息系统中，真正很复杂的SQL并不太多，此类的SQL查询仍然使用常规方法处理，参数化设计中暂时不考虑。最常用的SQL语句是Select（选择）、Insert（插入）、Update（更新）、Delete（删除）四大类语句。对这四类语句进行分析并分解，得到最基本的元素。

2. 参数化类设计

（1）首先设计参数管理类。此类可以对在SQL语句中使用的参数进行添加、删除、获取、更新等操作，并可以对加入的参数组进行合并操作，起到管理参数表的作用。

（2）然后通过先前准备好的SQL元素进行各种组合，实现SqlSelcol列元素类、SqlFrom表元素类、SqlCond条件元素类和SqlSelect选择元素类的设计。

（3）为方便开发者书写，特地创建了一个SqlSimp简单参数化类，可以简单对SQL语句进行分析并提取参数。

（4）在对参数进行添加时，应对所有的语句和变量统一进行大小写规范，以保证不出现因为一个字母不一样，数据库认为是两个不同的查询。

（四）结语

通过以上方法对大坝安全信息系统数据组件部分进行的改造，SQL查询语句的命中次数大幅度提高，数据库对于同一语句的响应也加快，系统使用明显感觉到速度提高。

目前，参数化已经在大坝安全信息系统中广泛使用，使软件的数据库交互、数据导入导出大大地提高了运行效率，为后期软件集成、云计算提供了良好的底层基础。

（国网电力科学研究院　张　轩　王卫列）

乐滩大坝安全管理

2009年，乐滩大坝安全管理的主要工作是完善规章制度、大坝安全监测、水工建筑物维护和防汛管理等。

（一）规章制度的完善

2009年通过制定、修订和完善有关规章制度，使大坝安全管理工作有法可依，有章可循。2009年新制定和修订的规章制度有：①广西桂冠开投电力有限责任公司工作票、操作票使用和管理标准；②重大危险源安全监督管理规定；③广西桂冠开投电力有限责任公司事故隐患排查治理制度；④乐滩水电厂周生产调度例会制度（修订）；⑤广西桂冠开投电力有限责任公司乐滩水电厂6S管理工作标准（试行）；⑥广西桂冠开投电力有限责任公司技术监控管理办法。

（二）大坝监测系统运行与管理情况

乐滩水电站主体工程埋设的观测仪器主要有：温度计、渗压计、测缝计、钢筋计、应变计、无应力计、基岩变位计、锚杆测力计、锚索测力计、多点变位计、测斜管等。其埋设部位在厂房1～4号机组段、安装间段，3～5号重力坝、6～12号溢流坝（10号坝除外），船闸上下闸首及闸室。监测项目有大坝变形、应力应变、坝基渗漏、扬压力、绕坝渗流等。该系统已于2008年安装并通过了初步验收后投入试运行，目前该系统运行正常；复检验收和实用化验收正在申报中。

2009年进行了信息化建设，增设了与国家电监会大坝安全监察中心的接口，使大坝安全监察中心对监测数据的采集和接收与乐滩水电站大坝安全监测自动化系统同步进行；分批进行监测仪器年度送检工作，所送检仪器校验结果全部合格；并做好监测仪器年检前后存在问题的定期检查和有关技术参数的详细记录和备案管理，建立台账，规范管理。加强专业培训，组织技能比武活动，提高员工安全监测专业理论、工作技能和管理能力。2009年5月，参加了由国家电力监管委员会大坝安全监察中心、中国水力发电工程学会大坝安全监测专业委员会、电力行业大坝安全监测标准化技术委员会在杭州联合举办的第一期大坝安全监测仪器应用培训班；8月，参加了国家安监总局在黑龙江牡丹江主办的电力应急管理培训和大坝安全监察中心与中国大唐集团广西分公司联合举办的大坝安全管理培训和专业技术研讨会；11月，水工观测班组织监测工进行了一次现场监测技能比武活动。

乐滩水电站于2008年4月完成大坝安全注册，有效期至2013年4月。

（三）水工建筑物运行情况

乐滩水电站工程，2006年11月通过了竣工安全鉴定，2008年6月通过了枢纽工程专项验收。2009年，根据验收意见和建议以及安全性评价的要求，结合年度机组检修，汛前、汛后专项检查的整改，对水工建筑物存在的缺陷进行了处理。工程经过四个完整洪水期的考验，监测数据表明，各水工建筑物变形小、渗漏量小，大坝运行正常。

（四）防汛管理工作

防洪度汛是大坝安全管理一项重要工作。汛前做好防汛物资库存的统计、采购和储备工作。汛期加强挡水水工建筑物、泄洪闸门与启闭设备、电气设备、通信设备、排水设备等设施设备的观测、试验、检查和维护，使之处于良好的技术状态，并根据水情，必要时增加观测和巡检频次。

按有关要求，编制“2009年度防汛工作计划”、“2009年度水库控制运用计划”、“2009年水库防洪抢险应急预案”和“2009年度洪水调度方案”，分别上报上级主管单位、省级防汛办和地方防汛办。同时加强与流域上下游水电站以及气象部门的联系，沟通水情汛情。此外，加强汛期库区和近坝库岸安全检查。

（广西桂冠开投电力有限责任公司乐滩水电厂 阮启业 韦爱华）

大坝安全监测与分析

南瑞大坝安全信息管理系统使用PocketPC实现人工观测数据的自动化处理

大坝安全信息管理系统一般包括自动化测量项目和人工观测项目。自动化测量项目数据采集处理和入库都是由信息管理系统完成的，通过网络连接，操作人员在计算机上就可以完成全部数据处理工作，信息传递和展示都方便、快捷。人工观测项目（如渗流量观测、引张线、垂直位移观测等）通常的处理方法是在信息管理系统中创建人工测点，然后去现场观测后记录在纸上，带回到办公室后将纸上记录的数据录入到信息系统中处理。这种处理方法，观测数据的差限控制只能由观测人员进行，观测成果在现场必须手工计算，观测人员的负担较重，工作效率降低；有时人工观测完成后，回到办公室才发现数据不合格，还要返回现场进行补测。大坝人工观测项目迫切需要现场自动化处理。

随着科技的发展，移动计算技术越来越成熟，以PocketPC为代表的新一代掌上电脑，可以担当这一角色。国网电力科学研究院开发了基于嵌入式电脑的大坝安全监测应用软件，在南瑞大坝安全信息管理系统中使用PocketPC来实现人工观测数据的记录、处理和入库工作。

南瑞大坝安全信息管理系统（以下简称南瑞系统）能够进行自动化测点数据采集，成果计算、数据整编和入库功能，还有报表输出、图形输出和Web平台数据展示功能。同时对于人工观测项目也可提供强有力的支持，如人工测点管理、人工观测数据录入和成果计算等，人工观测数据的输出显示功能与自动化观测项目一致。南瑞系统具有很强的信息交换能力，可以将测点和测值信息导入、导出，并能够支持多种常用的文件格式，如文本文件和Excel文件。

PocketPC是新一代的掌上电脑的简称，具有体积小、重量轻，功耗低、工作时间长、便于携带和使用的特点，使用嵌入式处理器，数据处理能力很强。它安装微软的Windows CE V4.2操作系统，该操作系统的操作和开发与微软台式电脑的Windows操作系统在界面风格和操作上是一致的，具有使用方便、交互能力强等优点，用户学习快、容易上手，用于现场数据录入和处理是很理想的工作平台。

PocketPC通过USB接口与PC通信，可以上传和下载文件，PocketPC上提供Pocket Excel和Pocket Word等应用软件，用户可以在移动的环境中创建和修改文档，回到办公室后与PC同步，非常方便。

由于PocketPC上无数据库系统，信息管理功能主要依靠南瑞系统进行。南瑞系统通过其数据导出功能将需要的测点信息和测值信息导出到文件中，然后传输到PocketPC中。PocketPC可以显示这些信息，但是不能修改；PocketPC获得测点数据以后就可以进行数据录入的工作，处理完成后将现场录入的数据保存在文件中，然后导入到南瑞系统的数据库实现最后处理。现场测值记录程序的主要功能是通过南瑞系统的导出功能获得必要的测点信息和数据信息，在现场进行人工测量录入观测数据后，进行差限检查，也可以进行一些成果计算和人工检验，返回办公室后将PocketPC数据导入到南瑞系统中进行处理，完成一次人工测量录入数据过程。此外为了方便用户，提供测点查询、测点信息浏览、测值浏览等功能。

PocketPC是新一代掌上电脑，具有掉电保护功能，保障记录数据的安全。将它配合南瑞大坝安全信息管理系统使用，能充分发挥它的优点，实现与PC数据库系统的无缝连接，加强人工观测数据现场处理能力，扩展南瑞大坝安全信息管理系统的应用范围。

（国网电力科学研究院 吴 骏）

新型大坝安全监测系统在八盘峡水电站成功试用

八盘峡水电站位于甘肃省兰州市黄河上游52km处，是“黄河综合利用规划技术经济报告”中拟定的第十一个梯级。电站上游有盐锅峡和刘家峡水电站，分别距本电站17km和50km。电站于1969年10月主体工程开工建设，1975年7月1日第一台机组发电，1980年2月24日全部建成投产。2001年8月1日六号机组竣工投产，目前总装机容量220MW。

2009年10月，新型大坝安全监测系统首次在甘肃八盘峡水电厂自动化改造工程中进行试用。共安装了5套监测设备，包括坝顶两条单向引张线（17个测点）、6条倒垂线、坝基静力水准（16个测点）、坝基渗压观测（29个测点）、环境温度观测（1个测点）、三向缝（3个测点）共6个项目的监测。整个系统从2009年8月6日开始安装、调试，于2009年9月30日顺利完成。2009年11月，八盘峡水电站自动化改造工程通过了竣工验收，整个安全监测系统性能满足合同要求，总体运行情况良好。

新型大坝安全监测系统采用嵌入式技术为系统平台。硬件方面，以ARM系列处理器为核心，其作为业界技术领先、有最成功的多行业广泛应用业绩及32位处理能力的RICS嵌入式计算机系统，为新一代自动化系统提供了稳定可靠的技术支撑，从综合技术特点来讲，最符合工程安全监测自动化系统的要求。在系统及应用软件方面，新系统以成熟的实时多任务操作系统（RTOS）作为软件基础平台。在RTOS技术支持下的多任务嵌入式系统中，重要性各不相同的任务将能得到统筹兼顾的合理调度，保证每个任务及时得到执行。

新型大坝安全监测系统在设计上按功能划分，采用模块化的设计方法进行设计，可分为主控制模块和数据采集子模块。通用的主控制模块与不同的数据采集子模块进行适当配置，即可完成现场各类传感器信号的采集。新系统全面支持网络通信，包括嵌入式Web访问功能，支持数据和程序的远程下载或更新功能。

新型大坝安全监测系统非常适应于工业现场分布式测量领域，尤其是在大规模、多层次的复杂网络领域。随着社会的发展进步，人们对大坝安全监测自动化系统性能要求不断提高，新型大坝安全监测系统将会得到更广泛的应用。

（国网电力科学研究院　孙　骏）

二滩大坝安全监测系统技术改造

（一）概况

二滩大坝安全监测的项目主要包括环境量、变形、渗流渗压、应力应变、强震和水力学等方面，总测点数达到1000个以上。随着国家对大坝安全监管工作的不断加强，以及监测仪器技术、自动化水平的不断进步，二滩大坝原有安全监测系统在投运十年后已无法完全满足日常工作的需要，主要表现在人工测读工作量较大、监测和采集等设备故障率增加、部分厂家的设备无法接入自动化系统、分析软件实用性差等方面。为此，在2008年对仪器设备、采集系统和分析系统进行了全面改造。系统改造后，大坝强震观测、泄洪振动观测采用独立的自动化系统，大坝外部变形测量网采用大地测量仪器观测，其余监测项目采用自动化或人工测读的方式进行数据采集并进入分析系统集中管理，在分析系统中完成监测数据整编、报表生成、信息报送和重要监测数据的分析工作。

（二）仪器及采集系统改造

1. 监测仪器设备

（1）二滩大坝变形观测在不同坝段布设了5个监测断面，分别安装了20台垂线坐标仪和人工读数盘进行自动化观测和人工比测。此次垂线坐标仪更换时保留部分原有观测情况良好的垂线坐标仪，更换并安装了10台南瑞NGDZ-50型垂线坐标仪，在个别部位同时采用2种不同型号的垂线坐标仪进行相互验证。

（2）原有8条倒垂线的浮体装置较小，不满足规范相应要求，改造中对其进行了全部更换。

（3）在下游左右岸抗力体边坡、水垫塘和二道坝共设置了43个绕坝渗流孔，部分需人工测读。本次改造进行了渗压计安装和引入自动化采集单元，走线考虑了泄洪影响和防雷措施。绕坝渗流孔渗压计采用与原型号一致的Rectest公司生产的PWS型渗压计，量程根据孔深和历史测量资料选用0.75MPa和0.35MPa两种。

（4）原在各部位安装的31个量水堰，此次改造全部安装流量计并接入自动化采集单元，在重点部位采用不同厂家的流量计进行对比观测，共安装了45台量水堰流量计。

（5）原采用的气象仪无法接入现有自动化采集单元，新采购了气温传感器和配套百叶箱、降雨量传感器，并安装独立的自动化采集单元后通过光纤接入采集计算机。

2. 自动化采集单元安装　二滩大坝采用了振弦式、电容式、电感式和数字等多种类型监测传感器。

为便于监测数据的统一采集和管理，此次改造采用南瑞公司生产的DAU2000自动化采集单元和相应采集模块对大坝所有自动化采集设备进行了更换，共使用28个DAU2000自动化采集单元和55块NDA模块。

3. 通信网络　本次改造仍保留原有的两种通信方式：一种为总线方式，采用2芯双绞线进行RS 485数据通信传输，通信线接入各自动化采集单元的通信端口；另一种为光纤通信方式，通过RS 232接口与光端机连接，采用双环路自愈光缆进行通信。经调试，两种通信方式可互为备用，满足大坝监测系统通信要求。

（三）分析系统改造

此次分析系统改造，结合二滩大坝监测工作的实际情况和监测重点，建立以基本资料、监测数据、巡视记录为基础的二滩大坝分析系统，实现大坝安全信息的集中式管理、监测数据整编、资料分析和信息报送。

1. 自动化数据采集和管理模块　建立了以二滩大坝工程基础资料、监测数据、巡视记录等大坝安全信息为基础的原始数据库，实现所有测点的分类、分项、分部位的图形化、可视化管理。利用INTERNET网络精确时钟，在数据库服务器上实现了对自动化采集单元时钟的定期自动校准。同时，新增了大坝强震与自动化采集系统的联动功能。

2. 成果输出模块　通过计算得到整编后的数据，并写入数据库，建立用户使用方便、快捷、易于操控的成果资料输出系统，如报表、数据、图表、备份等，并满足混凝土坝监测资料整编规程的有关规定。

3. 分析模块　依据混凝土坝监测资料整编规程，利用统计模型等方法，建立各监测项目的在线自动化安全监测分析模块，通过相同部位不同测点、不同部位相同测点、相同物理过程测点的趋势、极值、时效与残余量等评价方法，进行大坝安全的初步评判。

4. 信息发布子系统软件和广域网远程数据传输软件模块　实现了向大坝安全监察中心传送相关监测数据，并通过已有光纤通道实现后方远程管理，建立了重要监测信息的Web发布系统。

（四）结语

二滩大坝安全监测系统改造工作从2007年开始准备，2008年底开始施工，2009年底全部完工，通过设计、施工和运行管理人员等的共同努力，监测传感器、自动化采集单元和分析软件等各项技术和性能指标均满足规范要求，通过专家验收。

（二滩水力发电厂　宋明富）

乐滩水电站大坝安全自动化监测系统试运行自评价

乐滩水电厂大坝安全监测自动化系统采用南瑞集团公司的DAMS-Ⅳ采集装置，共安装静力水准仪49台、双金属管标6组、引张线仪48台、垂线坐标仪17台（其中倒垂14台、正垂3台）、量水堰6台、温度计1台、扬压力（新科渗压计）32支，安装采集模块84块，接入测点883个（含第三方共享数据三个，即上游水位、下游水位和降雨量），其中有效测点860个。控制中心设在办公楼的206房，通过光纤电缆与厂房大坝的采集装置连接。

系统于2008年3月25日施工，经过4个多月的施工与安装调试，于2008年8月4日投入试运行。为了方便计算，考核期选定在2008年9月1日～2009年8月31日，共计365天。考核情况如下：

（一）系统的稳定性

试运行期间，系统每天自动定时采集数据1次，每月自动定时交叉备份数据2次。考核期内，系统没有发生停测故障，在各种环境下，基本上能保持正常运行，所采集的数据与人工实测数据基本一致。

（二）系统的可靠性

根据《大坝安全监测自动化技术规范》（DL/T 5211—2005）的要求，系统的可靠性可用平均无故障工作时间（以下简称MTBF）以及数据缺失率（以下简称FR）来衡量。以此为据，乐滩大坝安全监测自动化系统采用测点作为考核单元，最终整个的MTBF是各考核单元MTBF的算术平均值；FR除了人为因素或者现场埋设仪器故障而引起的数据缺失外，其他按实际统计。

1. 平均无故障工作时间　统计数据显示，MTBF大于6300h的测点有773个，占总测点860个的90%，满足规范要求。其中：有54块采集模块共583个测点的MTBF为8760h，即为零故障，占系统模块的64.3%，占总测点的68%；MTBF小于6300h的模块有14块共87个测点，占系统模块的17%，占总测点的10%；发生故障次数最多、MTBF最低的为NDA84模块（正垂第一测点PL1），故障次数为17次，MTBF为440.47h。

2. 数据缺失率　FR小于3%的测点有818个，占总测点860个的95%，满足规范要求。其中：无数据缺失（采集率100%）的模块有54块，占系统总模块（84块）的64%；有30块模块277个测点存在不同程度的数据缺失；数据缺失最多的模块是NDA29（厂坝基础廊道倒垂测点），258次；单点数据缺失最多为98次（倒垂BIP-4测点）。

（三）人工比测

根据《大坝安全监测自动化技术规范》关于系统考核要求规定，人工比测一般采用过程线或方差分析进行对比。系统中除NDA1103、NDA1104用方差分析进行比对（内观比测）外，其余模块用过程线进行对比（外观比测）。

1. 内观比测　方差分析取了监测点试运行期（2008年9月～2009年7月）内自动化监测和人工比测相同时间、相同测次的测值，分别组成自动化测值序列和人工测值序列，计算其标准差σ，取2σ作为测值误差的限值，即$\delta\leqslant 2\sigma$。经统计，系统共有46块采集模块、584个测点参加方差分析对比。模块测量精度如下：

（1）电阻和满足$\delta\leqslant 2\sigma$的采集模块中，合格率达80%的有32块，占比对采集模块的70%；合格率不达80%的有14块，占比对采集模块的30%。

（2）电阻比满足$\delta\leqslant 2\sigma$的采集模块中，合格率达80%的采集模块有40块，占比对采集模块的87%；合格率不达80%的采集模块有6块，占比对采集模块的13%。

2. 外观比测

（1）水平位移，通过7条引张线48个测点采集，共接入自动化测点48个。从人工对比过程线看，差值最大的是3.13mm（BCEX-24的2009年7月28日）。影响比测偏大的原因为垂线仪2008年年检时维修过，坝顶引张线于2009年5月25日调整过初始值。另外，坝顶振动也是影响测值结果的另一因素。

（2）垂直位移，通过沉陷点（或静力水准点）采集，共62个测点，有效测点62个。因顶点静力水准点（自动化观测）与顶点沉陷点（人工观测）不在同一高程，故用过程图作比对。典型测点BCLS-10、BCLS-12（自动化观测）与坝顶对应沉陷点（人工观测）一年中的变化趋势基本一致，满足监测要求。

（3）坝基扬压力，共32个测点，接入自动化32个测点，最大的比测差值5.8m（B12UP-1的2008年9月22日），640次比测数据中，比测差值小于1m的有538个，占总比的84%。

（4）绕坝渗流，左右岸共12个测点，接入自动化12个测点，RUP-7、ZK504两测点仪器已坏，不列入分析，最大的比测差值为4.69m（RUP-3，2008年10月18日）。RUP-1、RUP-2、RUP-3在右岸灌浆平洞内，洞上方有一水池，水池溢水直接影响这三个绕坝渗流测值。

（四）系统评价

经过一年多的试运行，系统存在的问题已逐步完善；系统的硬件设备、数据采集处理系统、数据通信系统、人机界面（图形、报表、Web），以及数据库管理等功能均满足大坝监测要求。经现场实测，系统的平均无故障工作时间为7865.05h，数据缺失率为0.4%，单点采集时间为3～4s，全部测点采集时间为14min，各项技术指标满足规范要求。

（广西桂冠开投电力有限责任公司乐滩水电厂　韦爱华　蓝建芳　罗文高　石奇琴　韩素娟　邱美玲）

水电站高精度外部变形监测网

外部变形监测网一般包含平面位移监测网和垂直位移监测网，作为水电站变形监测的最重要组成部分之一，已受到越来越多的重视。中国水电顾问集团昆明勘测设计研究院在设计和实施各种大型水电站外部变形监测网中积累了一些经验，应用了一些新方法和新技术，逐步形成了一套较成熟的水电站高精度外部变形监测网的设计和实施方案。

（一）外部变形监测网主要设计或实施成果

表1列举了昆明勘测设计研究院设计或实施的部分大型水电站外部变形监测网的一些主要指标，从表中可看出，大型水电站外部变形监测网的精度都达到了一个较高的水平。目前在景洪水电站和小湾水电站已经多次实施的精度最高的外部变形监测网的测角精度优于0.5″，测距精度优于±（0.5mm+0.5ppm×D），最弱点位中误差优于±2mm。外部变形监测网精度的提高，为水电站变形监测提供了良好的基础和保障。

表1　昆明院设计或实施的部分大型水电站外部变形监测网主要指标表

电站名称	坝型	坝高（m）	测角精度	测距精度	水准网精度（mm/km）	最弱平面点位中误差（mm）	最弱高程点位中误差（mm）
漫湾	混凝土重力坝	132	0.7″/1.0″	±(1mm+1ppm×D)	±0.45	±3.5	±2
天生桥	混凝土面板堆石坝	178	0.7″/1.0″	±(1mm+1ppm×D)	±0.45	±4.0	±2
大朝山	碾压混凝土重力坝	118	0.5″	±(1mm+1ppm×D)	±0.45	±2	±1.4

续表

电站名称	坝型	坝高(m)	测角精度	测距精度	水准网精度(mm/km)	最弱平面点位中误差(mm)	最弱高程点位中误差(mm)
小湾	混凝土双曲拱坝	292	0.5″	±(0.5mm+0.5ppm×D)	±0.45	±2	±1.4
糯扎渡	黏土心墙堆石坝	261.5	0.5″	±(1mm+1ppm×D)	±0.45	±3.5	±2
景洪	碾压混凝土重力坝	110	0.5″	±(0.5mm+0.5ppm×D)	±0.45	±2	±1.4
阿海	碾压混凝土重力坝	138	0.5″	±(1mm+1ppm×D)	±0.45	±2	±1.4
观音岩	左岸河中碾压混凝土重力坝、右岸心墙堆石坝	158	0.5″	±(1mm+1ppm×D)	±0.45	±2	±1.4
金安桥	碾压混凝土重力坝	160	0.5″	±(1mm+1ppm×D)	±0.45	±2	±1.4
梨园	混凝土面板堆石坝	155	0.7″	±(1mm+1ppm×D)	±0.45	±3	±2

（二）设计时考虑的主要问题

1. 精度指标

(1) 对于混凝土重力坝、拱坝等，平面网点相对于平面基准点的最弱点位中误差小于±2.0mm，在主要位移方向的中误差小于±1.4mm；高程网点相对于高程基准的最弱高程点位中误差小于±1.4mm。

(2) 对于混凝土面板堆石坝、心墙堆石坝等，平面网点相对于平面基准点的最弱点位中误差小于±3.0mm，坝前可适当放宽，在主要位移方向的中误差小于±2.0mm；高程网点相对于高程基准的最弱高程点位中误差小于±2mm。

(3) 平面位移监测网各观测量的多余观测分量应在0.3以上；内部可靠性一般小于5，外部可靠性一般小于3。

(4) 监测网点的灵敏度椭圆尽量小，并可根据监测网图形、观测精度等确定一个最弱值。

2. 网形布置　外部变形监测网点从功能区分来说，由两部分组成：基准点组和工作基点组。基准点组一般布置在坝后，点位选择主要考虑稳定性、通视性和安全性，根据电站规模、地形、地质条件等，由3～6个点组成。工作基点组布置在大坝等主要水工建筑物周围，点位选择主要考虑能否有效对监测对象上的监测点按照符合要求的观测方法进行监测，即根据工作基点的布置采用边角交会法、极坐标差分法、边角网法等，按照一定观测精度是否能达到规范规定的监测精度要求。故主要考虑通视性，其次是稳定性和安全性。

网形设计应满足精度、可靠性和灵敏度要求等，留有一定富余，因为监测网在建网初期几年受各种因素影响，网形变化是不可避免的。平面位移监测网网形布置的总体原则是：基点稳定、控制关键、精干高效。垂直位移监测网网形布置的总体原则是：基点稳定、控制全面、连接紧密。

3. 基准点组布置　由于规范中对外部变形监测网点位精度的规定是相对于起算点的，故起算点的选择是非常重要的。因此，起算点都尽量布置在监测网中部，同时又作为基准点组的一部分，一般选择在坝下游400～700m范围内。其他基准点布置在起算点下游，一旦起算点坐标变化，可通过稳定的基准求得新的起算点坐标。

4. 平差基准　因为选择秩亏基准和拟稳基准都十分不可靠，故平面位移监测网的平差基准均为经典自由网基准。垂直位移监测网的平差基准为经典自由网基准或拟稳基准。

（三）在监测网实施中取得的研究成果

1. 基准点埋设　平面位移监测网基准点的埋设是一件比较困难的事情。基准点要稳定需要基准点所在的山体稳定，同时基准点埋设要牢固，而要同时满足以上两个条件又是比较困难的。因此，昆明勘测设计研究院在不同的工程中埋设过多种形式的基准点，如现浇钢筋混凝土桩、钢管标、附加倒垂线的钢筋混凝土桩等，基准点均不能全部稳定。垂直位移监测网基准点组埋设采用平洞标或双金属标，基准点都是稳定的，但平洞标可靠性更好。

2. 监测网的观测　平面位移监测网的观测仪器主要有：TCA2003全自动全站仪、干湿温度计、精密高原空盒气压计、棱镜和基座等。全站仪内置有昆明勘测设计研究院自主开发的观测程序，能实现自动观测、记录、限差检验和执行自动重测功能等。垂直位移监测网的观测仪器主要有：DNA03电子水准仪、因钢条码尺等。在0.5″级高精度平面网观测流程中应用了多测次边长观测、分组分时段方向观测等方法，均获得了满足设计要求的观测成果。

3. 监测网的数据处理　监测网的数据处理包含

外业数据预处理、外业数据检验、平差计算和变形分析等。外业数据预处理包含数据输入、边长化算、测站平差等；外业数据检验包含边长、方向和水准测量的各种闭合差和图形条件的检验，在这个过程中，关键是要找出所有的基本图形；平差计算功能应包含各种平差模型，以满足不同基准计算的要求；变形分析包含整体检验法、单点检验法、分块检验法和稳健迭代权法等。为克服传统稳健迭代权法基准易变化的特点，进行基准稳定性分析，假设一个点的权为无限大进行分析，获得了理想的分析成果。

实践表明，只有经过以上多种方法的相互印证，所得到的变形分析结果才是可靠的。昆明勘测设计研究院的“TCA2003测量机器人及变形监测数据处理软件的开发利用”曾获2004年中国水电工程顾问集团公司优秀计算机软件二等奖。经过多年的发展和不断完善，目前形成了多套独立开发的相互校核的软件，极大地提高了监测网的数据处理能力、灵活性和可靠性。

（中国水电顾问集团昆明勘测设计研究院　肖胜昌）

我国大型水电工程的安全监测有关情况

（一）监测仪器设备

大坝安全监测系统中，变形监测是监测系统中的主要监测设备。从国内外近二十余年来陆续推出基于不同工作原理的垂线坐标仪、引张线仪、静力水准仪、激光准直系统等各种变形监测设备就可以看出，变形监测仪器是监测系统中最不容易研制的监测设备。在大型、特大型水电工程安全监测中，既要能适应变形监测的大范围、大量程，又要满足测量精度，因此对变形监测设备提出了更严格的要求。为了满足这些大型工程的不同需求，国内科研院所、仪器厂家在总结多年仪器研发和推广应用的基础上，相继推出了性能更为优良的产品。世界上最长、监测距离达1625m的葛洲坝坝顶管道真空激光准直系统的成功建设以及稳定运行5年多，表明我国有能力为大型、超大型混凝土坝的变形监测设备提供充分的支持。

垂线、引张线是最简单可靠、维护方便、直观实用的大坝变形监测方法，基于电容式原理的垂线坐标仪和引张线仪在国内得到了广泛的应用。为了满足大型工程的更高要求，近年进行了重大改进，大大提高了仪器的稳定性和抗恶劣环境能力，并已应用于三峡工程中。

电感式仪器的最大特点是防潮性能和长期稳定性好。为适应大型水电工程的特殊需求，研制了新型的电感式垂线坐标仪。它是一种非接触式、开口的电感式坐标仪。该型坐标仪的精度高、量程大，防潮防尘和抗干扰性能好，具有仪器结构简单、安装维护简便的特点，已在新安江、青铜峡大坝中应用。从电感式坐标仪的工作原理和结构特点可以预计，这种类型的坐标仪将是长期运行于大坝恶劣环境的较为理想的变形监测仪器。

应用现代光电器件CCD构建的垂线坐标仪（引张线仪），是一类新型的变形监测仪器，它是完全非接触式的变形监测仪器，线体上不附设任何电器部件。因此，若采用高强质轻的碳纤维增强复合材料（CFRP）作为线体，可在适当的准直长度内构建无浮托的CCD引张线仪监测系统。葛洲坝和三板溪大坝无浮托引张线系统的成功应用，标志着一种维护更为简便的引张线系统为变形监测提供了一个新的选择。由于采用了CFRP作为引张线线体，该线体的挠度远小于常用的钢丝，仅为其1/5左右。因此，引张线测点的定位和仪器安装、运行均无难度。无浮托引张线的这些特点有助于将引张线系统延伸到坝基廊道的斜坡段，使重力坝斜坡段坝基水平位移的监测成为可能，这无疑将是一个非常有实用价值的功能拓展。

（二）仪器设备的安装埋设

大型、特大型水电工程的大坝通常体形高大，原有的一些大坝监测仪器安装埋设方法已不适用。例如，应力应变监测中的无应力计是监测大坝混凝土无应力变形的仪器，通过对混凝土无应力变形的监测，可以了解大坝混凝土随着龄期的增长，混凝土自身体积变形、湿度变形等随时间的变化过程。

实现无应力应变监测需要借助于一端开口的无应力计筒，将应变计置于无应力计筒中，以期获得混凝土的无应力应变。无应力计筒一般采用DL/T 5178《混凝土坝安全监测技术规范》中推荐的形式，以保证无应力计筒内的混凝土既同筒外混凝土完全一样，又处于无应力状态。

近年建设的青海拉西瓦（坝高250m）、云南小湾（坝高294m）等特高混凝土拱坝的监测资料分析显示，坝体应力较高部位的无应力计应变实测成果反映出与水位呈现出一定的相关，说明原来附着于无应力计中被忽略的应力应变部分在高应力混凝土坝体中显现了出来。因此，常规的、适用于低混凝土应力环境的无应力计筒的结构和尺寸已不能满足应力水平较高的特高拱坝，在大型、特大型工程中应采用新型结构的无应力计筒。

高土石坝分层沉降监测设备的安装是另一个较典型的例子。云南糯扎渡心墙堆石坝，由于坝高达261.5m，常规的垂直分层沉降人工监测设备已不可取，一般的连续布置的自动监测设备也不能满足大量程的需求，因此，必须考虑采用自动监测设备并按照分段接力的方法进行安装。工程实践表明，采用NHCJ型电位器式横梁式沉降仪进行分段式安装，较圆满地解决了糯扎渡大坝垂直分层沉降监测设备的安装埋设问题，实现了超高土石坝垂直分层沉降的自动化监测。

（三）施工期监测及资料分析

施工期安全监测，就是要利用施工过程（和首次蓄水过程）中监测的资料及时分析大坝与基础可能出现的问题，及时预警，以便采取必要的预防或改进措施，以避免大坝施工过程中的工程质量和安全隐患。

施工期的监测资料包含有丰富的信息，这些信息不仅客观地反映了监测对象的变化过程，同时也可能蕴含着因工程材料、施工方法、施工质量等问题造成对结构物的安全隐患。施工期安全监测对于改进施工、消除隐患、确保工程质量的作用，已得到建设单位和管理单位的认可和重视。四川瓦屋山水电站就是一例。瓦屋山混凝土面板堆石坝（坝高138.76m）坝体中设置了多种安全监测仪器设备。在施工期安全监测过程中，通过对实测资料实时、细致的分析，及时地反映了坝体填筑区内临时道路边坡压实密度偏低的问题，该工程填筑料的洒水量对碾压密度的影响问题，挤压边墙下土体存在脱空的问题，左岸坝肩结合处因碾压密度不均而产生裂缝的问题等。特别是通过实时综合分析渗压计和面板变形监测资料，及时、准确地预警了上游混凝土面板隆起，并提出建议立即停止上游基坑抽水，组织加强下游基坑抽水，以逆转上下游水头差。后经现场查看，证实了当时的应急措施是正确、及时的，避免了面板进一步隆起开裂的大事故。

首次蓄水是工程结构物首次承受设计荷载的过程，是检验设计施工质量的重要时区，也是评估大坝运行安全状况的敏感阶段。三板溪混凝土面板堆石坝（坝高185.5m）蓄水期资料分析是一个较典型的例子。

三板溪大坝为目前国内第二、世界第三高的面板堆石坝。在三板溪首次蓄水过程中，监测发现一、二期面板间部分仪器相继失灵，经现场分析判定该处面板可能因破损而致仪器损坏并报告了相关部门。经潜水检查，确认该处面板水平施工缝挤压破损，并立即采取工程措施，降低蓄水水位，进行面板修补，避免了事故的扩大，保障了大坝的安全。进一步分析表明，三板溪面板破损的直接原因是面板水平缝缝面压应力过大和结构上的缺陷；而首次蓄水水位上升过快是诱因，它引起大坝变形速率过大，致使面板偏心受压，最终导致面板水平缝挤压破损。

（四）区域性大坝安全监测管理系统

随着我国水利水电建设事业的蓬勃发展和现代科技的长足进步，在水利水电行业，集约化、扁平化的现代管理模式已逐步得到了工程管理单位的认同与接受。以大型、特大型工程为骨干的区域性（流域性）规模化管理的模式正在逐步形成，这就对大坝安全的管理水平提出了更高的要求。

信息技术的迅猛发展对实现大坝安全管理的集约化和扁平化起到了积极的推动作用，新建大坝在建成之初就基本实现了该大坝安全的数据采集和管理的自动化；已建大坝也在有计划有步骤地实现大坝安全的数据采集和管理的自动化系统改造，因此实现区域性大坝的坝群安全集中管理的条件已经成熟，并正在逐步推广应用。

五凌电力有限公司是我国首个建设区域性大坝安全监测管理系统的跨流域的集团公司，该公司现辖有沅水流域、湘江流域、资江流域的五强溪、凌津滩、洪江、碗米坡、三板溪、挂治、白市、托口、近尾洲、马迹塘、东坪、株溪口水电厂，以及黑麋峰抽水蓄能电厂共13座大坝，自2007年开始实施区域性大坝安全监测管理系统的建设。

五凌电力有限公司的大坝安全监测管理系统是一个由多个水电站工程安全监测系统作为支点组成的综合性系统。主要包括公司所辖水电站的工程安全监测、安全运行评估、决策支持、水电站大坝安全信息报送等现代大坝安全管理的功能和内容。

五凌电力有限公司区域性大坝安全管理信息系统由长沙监测信息中心和五强溪、三板溪等水电站监测信息分中心组成。

监测信息中心是工程安全监控管理中枢，能够接收并处理所有工程的监测、监控数据，对监测系统进行远程控制，并能对接收的数据进行分析处理，为工程安全运行决策提供依据，从而优化所属各水电厂的运行方案，确保工程的安全和提高经济效益。

水电站监测信息分中心能够及时、准确、可靠地完成对所辖大坝、电站、船闸、地下洞室、隧洞等水工建筑物及库岸等与工程安全相关的监测对象的数据采集、数据预处理、存储，并能迅速同步到监测信息中心。

五凌电力有限公司区域性大坝安全监测管理系统采用面向服务的分布式设计，易于扩充与维护，各分中心系统结构独立，在数据层上中心与分中心各自独立，确保了单个系统发生故障时其他系统不受其影响，同时可随意扩充新的分中心系统。系统建成后，经实际应用表明，系统运行效果良好，管理效能大为提高。

（国网电力科学研究院　彭　虹）

大坝安全实时监控和预警系统的开发及应用

中国水利水电第八工程局有限公司为满足大坝安全运行和科学管理的需要，针对大坝在施工期、初次蓄水期和正常运行期出现的问题，研制和开发了高水平的行业专业管理软件系统——大坝安全实时监控和预警系统。该系统可以充分发挥大坝安全监测系统的作用，及时掌握大坝的实际工作性态，实时分析、预警，确保工程安全运行。

（一）系统简介

该系统的研制和开发始于2007年4月，到2008年12月基本完成。在此期间完成了调研、系统设计（包括硬软件配置选择、系统功能设计、界面设计、数据库设计、子系统关联设计、程序调用接口设计等）、监测资料分析、相关渗流分析、相关结构分析、安全预警指标研究等大量的工作，编制和调试了各计算程序和功能模块，并经子系统调试、总装调试和安装测试等环节和步骤，最终完成本系统的研制开发。

系统主要由以下几个模块组成：①高度可自定义的工程部位及仪器管理模块；②功能强大的人工输入模块；③便捷的仪器数据管理模块；④高度可自定的报表制作模块；⑤可自定义的过程线生成模块；⑥实时监测模块；⑦预警分析模块。

（二）关键技术

1. 数据库及网络技术应用　为保证数据处理的高效性、安全性、稳定性，采用Microsoft的SQL Server商用数据库。系统的数据结构分为原始数据库、分析数据库、整编数据库、工程资料库以及分析方法库。管理中心的服务器通过网络与数据采集工作站连接，将数据采集工作站的数据分析判断后存入数据库。数据采集单元通过485或CAN-bus传输协议将从传感器采集到的数据上传到工作站。系统实现了C/S（Client/Server）和B/S（Browser/Server）两种构架，在管理中心设立服务器，对大坝实时监控，通过客户端程序或Web系统，可以对服务器进行局域网或远程访问。

2. 监测信息分析技术　本系统对监测信息的分析方法主要有逐步回归分析法、粒子群算法。

（1）本系统的逐步回归算法最后结果的拟合度非常高，为分析预警提供了有力保证。

（2）粒子群算法（PSO）是近几年备受关注的仿生优化算法。由于算法概念清晰、参数少、简单易行，已广泛用于参数反演、函数优化、优化组合等问题。基于粒子群算法的大坝安全预警方法主要是以优化理论为支撑。PSO算法用于优化模型的求解，比最小二乘法的误差小。而经改进的GA-APSOR算法，在提高PSO算法精度的基础上，进一步提高了算法的收敛速度。通过自适应调整函数调节学习因子，能够较为有效地提高粒子个体及粒子群整体的搜索能力，因此将该方法用于大坝安全监控领域是合理的和有效的。表1为对某大坝10号坝段监测数据的预测时各算法的三种误差统计指标比较。

表1　各算法的三种误差统计指标比较

误差＼算法	最小二乘算法	粒子群算法	GA-APSOR
平均绝对百分比误差（MAPE）（%）	12.137	7.925	6.404
均方误差（MSE）（mm）	1.847	1.286	0.939
平均绝对误差（MAE）（mm）	1.544	0.963	0.801

3. 专业分析软件的嵌入应用

（1）嵌入线弹性有限元分析、弹塑性有限元分析等专业结构分析软件，对岩质边坡结构采用弹塑性有限元计算分析。

（2）嵌入渗流分析程序，主要对坝基和两岸的渗流场进行分析。

（3）嵌入非连续变形分析程序。非连续变形法是以研究非连续块体系统不连续位移和变形的一种崭新的数值分析方法，不仅可以计算块体系统的小变形、小位移，而且可以计算块体系统的大变形、大位移，可以分析岩体从破坏前到破坏后的整个非连续变形的动态过程。

（三）主要创新点

（1）本系统利用先进的PSO和GA-APSOR算法为分析方法库建立监控模型，对变形、渗流和应力应变等监测资料的相关监测量进行分析计算，快速找出异常值，并对异常测值拟定报警级别。

（2）本系统利用结构分析程序、渗流分析程序和非连续变形分析程序等程序对坝体、坝基以及岸坡等进行计算分析，及时了解大坝的安全性态，实现分析预警。

（3）系统对人工或自动采集的数据，自动选用相关计算方法或专业程序进行计算并将计算成果入库，最后对监测成果进行实时分析判断，对超出预警值的监控项给以报警提示。

（4）根据监测测点的重要性不同，系统可以实现对指定的重要测点进行实时显示，数据库中数据变化后，可以实时地在监控界面上显示出来。

（四）结语

大坝安全实时监控和预警系统是监测大坝安全运行，指导设计、施工的一套软件，可提高大坝安全预警能力和数据分析可靠性，迅速有效地分析评价工程的安全状况，及时发现影响建筑物安全的前兆信息，确保能在发生灾害性事故之前及时预警，为业主或管理层决策提供支持，以便将灾害损失降低到最小，从而实现较大的社会效益。

该系统已应用于广西平班水电站（最大坝高62.2m，水库总库容2.78亿m^3，总装机容量405MW）、湖南株溪口水电站（4台灯泡式贯流机组）和重庆藤子沟水电站（最大坝高127m，库容0.186亿m^3，装机容量70MW）的大坝安全监测。

（中国水利水电第八工程局有限公司 田承宇）

三板溪混凝土面板坝面板破损原因分析

（一）工程概况

三板溪水电站位于沅水干流清水江中下游贵州省黔东南锦屏县境内，下距锦屏县城25km，总库容40.94亿m^3，总装机容量1000MW。工程于2002年7月1日开工，2006年1月7日下闸蓄水，2006年7月25日首台机组发电，同年12月24日4台机组全部建成投产。主坝为混凝土面板堆石坝，坝顶高程482.50m，最大坝高185.50m，坝顶长423.75m，坝顶宽10.0m，上、下游坝坡均为1∶1.4。

（二）面板破损情况

水库于2006年1月7日下闸蓄水，同年6月库水位升至429m后，一直在该高程附近运行，持续时间约一年。2007年6月初，水库再次蓄高。库水位快速上涨过程中，相继出现渗流量和幕后坝基部分渗透压力突增，总渗漏量最大达303L/s，部分监测仪器测值异常突变或失效，面板固定式测斜仪不能下放等。2008年1月10日，库水位降至426.25m，对面板进行水下检查，发现左MB3～右MB9等12块面板一、二期施工缝部位多处局部破损，外层钢筋向外弯曲，破损最大宽度达4m，最大深度达40cm。高面板坝面板水平缝破损比较少见，目前仅巴西202m高的Campos Novos坝出现明显挤压破损的情况。因此，有必要对面板的破损原因进行分析。

（三）面板破损原因分析

1. 河谷形状和面板结构　坝址区为稍不对称的V形横向河谷。基础开挖处理后，趾板周边连线为不规则的折线，尤其是右岸各折点连线转角较大，如折点X3～X4、X4～X5和X5～X6的连线存在较大的折角，容易造成应力分布不均，实测结果也证明了该部位应力较大。面板大部分区域受压，一期面板、二期面板中间压应力较大，其中顺坡向最大压应力集中在一期面板X5点附近。水平缝破损前最大值为26.2MPa，超过混凝土的抗压强度，但小于面板施工抽检强度。水平向最大压应力为22.8MPa，出现在一期面板的上部河谷中部，也已接近混凝土的抗压强度。尽管X5点附近应力略超出规范允许值，但该部位在底部较深水下，面板为三向受压状态，主应力方向大致为顺坡、水平向及垂直于面板的水压力，每向实际抗压强度随另二向压应力增加而增加，极限压应变可大大增加，且面板底部不易产生挠曲变形，结构上也没有明显缺陷，因此该处没有引起破坏。左侧MB3～右侧MB9等12块面板一、二期施工缝部位多处发生局部破损，可能与施工缝的结构有关。面板水平施工缝原设计从面板表面至约面板半厚为垂直于面板顶面，另一半接近水平，钢筋穿过截面，与混凝土面板一起整体受力。这种结构存在明显缺陷，其两个角点是面板的薄弱部位，必然引起应力集中，再加蓄水后堆石体沉降，面板与垫层之间的摩擦力造成面板小偏心受压，就在薄弱部位出现挤压破损情况。另外，由于面板上下层钢筋没有设置箍筋，面板底部有垫层约束，而面板上层没有约束，上层钢筋屈曲向外凸起加剧混凝土破损。

2. 蓄水后坝体不均匀沉降　2004年10月～2008年9月，三板溪大坝的最大沉降量为175.4cm，发生在坝右0+071.8m断面404m高程偏上游，其总沉降量与同类工程相比并不大。但蓄水初期及2007年7月水库再次蓄高期，各测点均出现明显的下沉，且沉降不均匀。坝顶沉降最大，其次是坝体内部404m高程上游侧。靠近面板的两个测点沉降量也不完全相等，基本为堆石处的测点沉降量大于垫层部位的沉降量。2007年6月21日～12月1日，库水位在450～472m间运行，坝顶沉降量约13cm。445m高程的沉降量与404m高程的沉降量基本接近，为7～8cm；379m、346m高程下沉较小，均在1～4cm之间。对应坝后马道向下游的水平位移也是404m高程最大，约3～4cm；其他高程的水平位移相对较小，为1～2cm。可见水库再次蓄高期间，404m高程靠上游侧的坝体变形速率较其余部位大，即379～404m高程间堆石压缩变形相对较大。面板在堆石沉降摩擦引起的顺坡向压力和侧胀挤压力共同作用下破损。

3. 水位上升速度过快　库水位蓄至429m后，因库区移民搬迁进度滞后，库水位在433m左右运行了约一年。期间坝体变形缓慢，面板内的压应力和钢筋应力也保持在较低水平，未见明显增大趋势。2007年6月5日开始再次蓄高，坝体变形、面板应力和渗流量也随之增大；2007年7月26日库区普降暴雨，入库洪峰流量7650m^3/s，一日之内库水位暴涨约5m，坝体沉降速率增大，面板压应力来不及调整出现破损迹象，表现为渗漏量由113.64L/s增大到255.42L/s，面板的压应力监测值也随库水位上升快速增大到接近抗压强度后，突然减小或变成拉应力或异常损坏。面板385m施工水平缝挤压破损发生在水位快速上升期间，施工水平缝挤压破损与再次蓄高水位期间水位上升速度过快、面板应力来不及调整有一定的关系。

（四）面板修复后的运行状况

2008年2～3月，经过认真研究提出了修复处理方案：凿除左MB3～右MB9等12块一、二期施工缝处有缺陷的面板表层翘起和剥落的混凝土，并对凿除后的混凝土进行周边修整平直。凿除部位部分钢筋整形、绑扎，但不破坏原结构钢筋，然后采用强度等级为C35、黏结剂附着力为1～2级、水下黏结强度大于2.5MPa的PBM混凝土进行水下填补修复，回填混凝土表面布置一层双向ϕ4@100钢筋网，保护层厚度3cm。

2008年3～6月，对9块面板进行了修复，剩余3块计划于2009年2～4月修复。截至2009年4月初，除右MB8面板约25m裂缝尚未修复外，其他部位均已修复。2008年6月，部分面板修复后，大坝渗流量明显减小，2008年8月20日达187.17L/s，对应库水位为462.31m；2008年汛期以后，渗流量最小为95.91L/s，对应库水位424.53m，发生在2009年2月25日。

（五）结语

该水平施工缝挤压破损直接原因是蓄水期间堆石体不均匀沉降变形使面板偏心受压，不对称折线趾板导致局部压应力集中，在变形量相对较大的385m高程，有缺陷的面板水平施工缝缝面出现挤压破损。诱因是2007年7月再次蓄水时水位上升过快，引起大坝变形速率过大，面板应力来不及调整。虽然面板修复取得了一定的效果，但面板坝体内部和外部变形尚未收敛，面板受力状况没有改变，一期面板顺坡向的压应力很大。截至2009年底，有2个测点压应变超过1000×10^{-6}，混凝土压应力超过20MPa，钢筋压应力超过200MPa，面板中部水平向的压应变也较大，水平向最大应变为-994×10^{-6}，对应压应力为22.8MPa，且仍有缓慢增大的趋势。为此，需密切关注各监测量的变化，及时进行系统分析。

（国家电力监管委员会大坝安全监察中心
王玉洁 朱锦杰 李 涛）

云鹏水电站大坝渗流安全监测资料分析

（一）工程概况

云鹏水电站位于云南省南盘江中下游河段干流，上游为雷打滩水电站，下游为天生桥一级水电站。挡水建筑物为土质心墙堆石坝，大坝为1级建筑物，校核洪水位902.45m，设计洪水位902.00m，正常蓄水位902.00m，防洪限制水位882.00m，死水位877.00m。坝顶高程904.0m，坝基开挖最低高程为807.5m，最大坝高96.5m，坝顶长456.8m，坝顶宽度10m，上游坝坡为1∶2.0，下游平均坝坡为1∶1.8，心墙顶高程903.0m，顶宽4m，上、下游坡比均为1∶0.25。心墙上游侧布置一道厚3m的反滤层，心墙下游侧布置两道各厚3m的反滤层及一道厚5m的过渡层，坝面上、下游侧均为干砌石护坡。

（二）渗流监测设计

为监测施工期、初蓄期的渗流情况，在心墙及下游坝壳区布置坝体渗透压力及渗流量等监测项目，共布置38支渗压计和1座坝后量水堰。本文选取河谷0+208.53m断面进行渗流监测资料分析，该断面有渗压计19支，沿高程880.0m、855.5m、831.0m、807.5m布置4层，在每层下游反滤料中布置1支渗压计，在心墙轴线及其两侧对称部位各布置1支渗压计，另外在心墙下游侧的坝壳与地基交接面上布置3支渗压计，在下游坝脚设置截水墙，布置1座量水堰，用以监测通过坝体和坝基的渗流量。

（三）渗流监测资料分析

1. 心墙及坝壳渗透压力　由于施工等因素导致部分渗压计失效，目前运行良好的渗压计在心墙区有7支，反滤料有1支，在下游坝壳区有1支。心墙区渗压计P01～P03、P08、P10、P14、P17水位受库水位影响明显，与库水位成正比，但同一高程上的渗压计水位靠近上游较高，变幅较大，靠近下游则较低，变幅较小，这表明心墙和坝基帷幕防渗效果良好。反滤料处P04及坝壳区处P05水位主要受坝下水位影响，变幅较小。从库水位和时效分量所占比例可知，库水位分量占总量的39%～69%，越靠近上游的测点，库水位分量所占比例越大，如靠近上游的P01测点，库水位分量为69%，时效分量仅占31%，而下游侧P03测点，库水位分量仅占39%，时效分量占到61%。根据2008年2月3日渗压计实测水位绘制坝体浸润线，此时库水位901.45m，坝下水位824.0m，心墙对水头的消减作用显著，心墙区平均水力坡降为1.88，一般认为黏土心墙的允许水力坡降可达到4.0以上，且在心墙下游布置有反滤层，因此认为不会出现渗透破坏情况。为验证设计阶段渗流计算采用的渗透系数的合理性，采用有限元方法进行渗流计算。心墙区实测浸润线与计算值较为接近，下游坝壳区实测浸润线略高于计算值，实测心墙溢出点高于计算溢出点约1m，表明坝壳填筑料灰岩渗透系数略小于计算参数。

2. 渗流量　为监测大坝渗流量，在大坝下游坝脚设置截水墙，布置梯形量水堰1座，堰底宽1.0m，堰高0.5m，编号为W1。根据现场检查，发现量水堰两侧边墙自上而下各有一条贯穿性裂缝，最大缝宽2～3cm，长达2m，裂缝是在大坝下闸蓄水后不久出现的，因此初蓄期的实测渗流量小于实际渗流量，2008年12月3日对量水堰裂缝进行封堵。2008年渗流量相比于2007年显示出整体性的左移，渗流量向有利的方向发展，说明随着坝体次固结的持续，心墙的防渗性能在不断改善。

（四）结语

目前云鹏大坝渗流状况正常，心墙区水位受库水位影响沿上下游方向逐渐减弱，渗压计时效水位分量趋于收敛，心墙区对水头消减作用明显，平均水力坡降为1.88，不会出现渗透变形破坏。渗流量受库水位和降雨的影响，最大实测渗流量达81.71L/s。随着坝体次固结的持续，心墙的防渗性能将不断改善，渗流量会逐步减小。

（国家电力监管委员会大坝安全监察中心
周建波　朱锦杰　杜雪珍）

陈村拱坝下游面105m高程水平向裂缝长期分析研究情况

（一）概况

陈村水电站大坝为混凝土重力拱坝，最大坝高76.3m，坝顶弧长419m，共分28个坝段（由左至右编号为3～30），坝顶高程126.30m，在坝顶左右1/4拱部位对称布置两个开敞式溢洪道，溢流堰顶高程113.00m，横缝封拱灌浆高程为111.50m，大坝上游面105.00m高程以下为10∶1倒坡。水库正常蓄水位119.00m，死水位101.00m。1971年冬至1972年春，下游面出现许多水平向裂缝。其中105.00m高程附近水平向裂缝规模最大（以下简称此缝为105裂缝），它不仅横跨5～28坝段，大部分坝段被水平向贯穿，且部分坝段有2～3条水平向裂缝，累计延伸总长约450m，裂缝缝口宽度多为0.1～0.5mm，个别缝段最大达7mm。自1972年以来，就105裂缝做过多方位的分析研究，对这一裂缝重大缺陷的认识逐步加深，为保证陈村拱坝安全运行提供了一些定量或定性的科学依据。

（二）裂缝深度和走向检测分析

1972年、1987年和2007年，曾采用钻孔方法检测105裂缝的缝深和走向。绝大多数测孔达设计深度时未见明显裂缝，只有1987年灌注环氧后，22号坝段一个孔在距坝面约1.5m处发现裂缝内有环氧胶结物。1987年，在11号坝段缝口用130mm钻具骑缝垂直坝面钻孔进行检测，裂缝在74cm深处偏出孔壁。1984年采用超声波钻孔对测法，对12～15、18～21号共计8个坝段的105裂缝进行检测。为尽量避免裂缝因走向摆动而偏出两个对测孔所框定的范围，根据裂缝位置周围条件，缝两侧的测孔实际间距为2.34～2.73m，测孔深约6.5m，检测结果显示，8个坝段垂直下游面方向的缝深都超过5m。2004年，采用表面波法对7、12～14、18～21号共计8个坝段的105裂缝进行检测。检测结果显示，7、12、13、21号坝段缝深为5.3～5.7m，14、18、19、20号坝段的缝深分别为4.2m、2.7m、3.9m和3.7m。相频特性曲线分析表明，18、19号坝段裂缝内有被充填而裂缝面闭合接触现象，对准确判断缝深有一定影响。105裂缝在缝口部位与坝面基本垂直，但沿缝深的走向不规则。超声波钻孔对测法大致框定裂缝摆动范围后，Ⅱ期断面垂直下游面方向的厚度约6m，105裂缝已将Ⅱ期断面混凝土贯穿，由于Ⅰ期断面具有限裂作用，估计裂缝深度终止在纵缝处。相隔20年后2004年表面波法检测结果，总体上与超声波钻孔对测法基本吻合，并表明因Ⅰ期断面的限裂作用，105裂缝未再向其内部扩展。Ⅰ期断面顶部是一个薄弱面，105裂缝有可能沿Ⅰ期断面顶部向上游方向扩展，这是需要密切关注的一个问题。

（三）缝宽骤变扩展期对拱坝刚度和整体性影响分析

拱坝的径、切向位移变形是坝体刚度和整体性的直接反映。坝顶向上游的最大径向位移量呈逐年增大趋势，1978年夏季和冬季与1975年同期相比，18号坝段向上游的最大位移量分别由5.28mm和1.91mm增大为9.07mm和6.47mm。该坝因左岸坝肩基岩弹模仅为右岸的1/2左右，蓄水初期拱坝整体出现的向左岸侧移不对称变形在这阶段明显增大，以105.00m高程为例，1978年拱坝整体都明显偏向左岸，拱冠18号坝段向左岸切向位移量大于7mm，超过向上游的径向位移量。为了定量分析这阶段105裂缝对拱冠坝段径、切向位移影响程度，将18号坝段1973年11月至1982年初的坝顶位移实测资料作为样本区间，并将裂缝缝宽与水位、温度和时效三个因素同时列为影响因子，进行回归统计分析。105裂缝对18

号坝段坝顶位移的影响程度，在径向超过时效分量，接近水位分量；在切向仅次于时效分量，为温度分量的2倍。虽然缝宽变化与温度及水位变化有着密切关系，将裂缝宽度变化作为独立因子进行回归统计分析，但裂缝分量所占比重如此之大，足以说明105裂缝缝宽骤变扩展使拱坝105.00m高程以上坝体的刚度和整体性受到比较明显的削弱。

（四）改性环氧灌浆处理利弊分析

1972年曾用水泥浆液对105裂缝进行灌浆和插筋处理，并采用环氧对21号坝段裂缝进行灌浆处理，但环氧浆液难以灌入缝内。1987年春天，采用改性环氧对105裂缝进行全面灌浆处理。现场和室内试验得知，改性环氧纯浆体1年期极限抗压强度达100MPa以上，“8”字形抗拉强度达10MPa左右，“8”字形环氧砂浆抗拉强度达5MPa以上，潮湿和干燥状态黏结抗拉强度相同，在气温为5～6℃、浆温30℃时，浆液绝对黏度，0.5h小于0.5×10^{-3}Pa·s，1h为0.65×10^{-3}Pa·s。采用骑缝和穿缝两种方式进行灌浆，灌前压水压气冲洗和干燥缝面，灌浆时在缝口装设百分表，严格控制灌浆压力，灌后对缝口用环氧砂浆填平封闭。总共耗用改性环氧浆液约1t，扣除穿缝钻孔孔内所占用的浆液，大部分已灌入缝中。浆液主要集中在距离缝口约1m的范围内，深部裂缝并未被充填密实，仍为薄弱裂缝界面。这次采用大规模改性环氧对105裂缝进行全面灌浆处理。

此次环氧灌浆，在缝口部位加进了一个强度较高的塞子，高气温缝口两侧混凝土膨胀时，因其阻塞作用裂缝不能自由闭合。灌浆当年105裂缝缝宽年变幅比灌前大幅度减小，以后随着最大缝宽的逐渐增大，年变幅也逐渐增大，表明这次灌浆可能带来了一定副作用。实测该坝105.00m高程距下游坝面6m处坝体内部混凝土温度，在夏季气温最高时仍处于低温向高温转变时段，约滞后气温变化50d，比气温低10℃左右，此时105裂缝缝端因温度变化引起的应力在缝口无塞时由两部分组成，一是缝端相对于缝口温降引起的张开作用；二是缝口混凝土温升膨胀带动缝端的压缩作用，两者有一定抵消效应，而缝口加塞后第二种作用力基本消失了，这就促使缝端应力趋于恶化而产生不利影响。

（五）遭遇设防地震时可能扩展深度研究

陈村拱坝设防地震烈度为Ⅶ度，105裂缝缝深可能扩展到什么程度，这是关系到非常运用条件下拱坝安全的重要课题。1993年，采用断裂力学方法对这一课题作了专题研究。计算裂缝扩展是非线性断裂力学问题，研究中采取逐段扩展法，用线弹性断裂力学方法分析裂缝扩展过程，解决非线性问题。

（六）对105.00m高程以上坝体应力和稳定影响的复核计算

由于该坝坝顶左右两侧设有开敞式溢洪道，溢流堰面以上坝体已无拱的整体作用，不考虑105.00m以上整体拱的作用，将105.00m以上坝体作为重力坝，复核计算坝体的应力和稳定。按缝深6m进行计算，采用材料力学方法复核计算结果，在自重＋正常高水位＋Ⅶ度地震时，18号坝段105.00m高程上游面将出现0.21MPa的拉应力，有可能出现水平向裂缝。采用刚体极限平衡法核算105.00m高程以上坝体地震时的稳定性时，假定105.00m高程上游面产生了水平裂缝，并与105裂缝已经贯穿，105.00m高程计算截面上的扬压力作用面积假定为100%，在自重＋正常高水位＋Ⅶ度地震时，105.00m高程以上坝体的抗滑和抗倾覆稳定安全度仍满足要求。按105裂缝缝深已扩展至10.4m，105.00m高程坝体上游侧尚保留7.6m，在校核洪水位时，对105.00m以上坝体的稳定进行核算，抗滑稳定安全度亦满足要求。复核计算结果表明，105裂缝对坝体局部应力影响较大，105.00m高程上游面是一个敏感部位，运行中应加强监测；在105裂缝缝深已扩展4.4m承受校核洪水时，以及105.00m高程坝体已被裂缝贯穿遭遇正常高水位＋Ⅶ度地震时，上部坝体仍然不会发生滑动和倾覆破坏。

（七）缝宽长系列变化趋势及增长速率分析

自1973年开始，陆续对各坝段105裂缝缝口宽度进行监测，大多数测点积累了长系列的资料。各测点监测数据具体量值有差异，但都呈现出一个共同的变化趋势，即缝宽在逐渐增大。15-Ⅰ和18-Ⅰ两个测点在1973～2005年的32年中，最大缝宽分别增大了3.15mm和2.95mm；19-Ⅰ、18-Ⅲ、21-Ⅰ和14-Ⅰ测点，在1980～2005年的25年中，最大缝宽分别增大了1.88mm、1.61mm、1.56mm和1.04mm；18-Ⅳ、13-Ⅰ、20-Ⅰ、16-Ⅰ和12-Ⅰ测点，在1990～2005年的15年中，最大缝宽分别增大了0.78mm、0.60mm、0.52mm、0.47mm和0.38mm。拱冠18号坝段18-Ⅰ测点测值连续性好。最大缝宽随时间的变化至今尚未趋于收敛稳定。20世纪70年代中后期是缝宽骤变扩展阶段，以后缝宽缓慢增大，但增长速率却有变化，1990～2000年的增长速率比1980～1990年全面减小，而2000～2005年的增长速率比1990～2000年又全面增大，半数测点已超过1980～1990年的增长速率。105裂缝最大缝宽仍在缓慢增大，近几年各测点增长速率均超过20世纪90年代，这样的变化趋势需引起重视。

（八）不利运行工况的反馈研究和控制

裂缝宽度的变化与长时段低水位运行密切相关。20世纪70年代，水库长期处于低水位运行，平均水位 99.52m，比设计死水位约低 1.5m，1976 年 7 月～1979 年 4 月的 980d 之内，有 720d 低于死水位，最低比死水位低 10m 左右，其中经历了 3 次低水位高温和 3 次低水位低温组合运行工况，这段时间内 105 裂缝缝宽骤变扩展。20 世纪 80 年代，平均水位为 107.96m，比前一时段高出 8m 多，105 裂缝缝宽转变为缓慢增大。20 世纪 90 年代，运行水位进一步提高，平均水位为 110.39m，比上一时段高约 2.4m，1996 年最高水位达 121.81m，接近洪水重现期 100 年设计水位，这一时段 105 裂缝缝宽增长速率进一步减小。21 世纪头 5 年中，运行水位有所降低，平均水位为 107.90m，与 20 世纪 80 年代相接近，105 裂缝在这几年内的缝宽增长速率比上一时段普遍增大。自 20 世纪 80 年代初开始，在水库调度时注意控制水位不低于死水位 101.00m，对于防止 105 裂缝缝宽再次骤变扩展，达到了预期目的。上述不同时段 105 裂缝缝宽增长速率变化规律分析结果表明，为了减小缝宽增长速率，尽可能抬高运行水位是一个切实可行的手段，若能在控制水位不低于死水位的基础上，进一步使年平均水位达到 110.00m 左右，预计将会取得较好效果。

（九）结语

陈村拱坝 105 裂缝产生至今已有 30 多年，对其展开的分析研究也持续了 30 多年，得出了一些定量或定性的成果，为指导该坝安全运行发挥了重要作用。多方位的分析研究表明，105 裂缝目前尚没有危及拱坝的整体安全。

（国家电力监管委员会大坝安全监察中心
邢林生　陈　铿）

上标水电站压力钢管的安全监控系统

（一）建设简况

上标水电站水轮机设计水头高达 448m，引水系统钢管总长 1031m，为高水头压力钢管明管，管线铺设条件复杂，距离长，坡度陡。钢管发生严重漏水或爆破事故时，其瞬时泄水流速将高达 40～90m/s。如此高速的水流可将所到之处夷为平地，严重威胁电站安全运行及下游人民的生命财产安全。为保证压力钢管的运行安全，上标水力发电厂决定建立压力钢管安全监控系统。2000 年 11 月，上标水力发电厂、河海大学水电学院及南京水利水文自动化所三家单位共同合作完成了《上标水力发电厂压力钢管安全监控系统水力分析及控制模型研究报告》；2001 年 4 月 3 日，该系统建成投入试运行；2001 年 12 月 13 日通过浙江省电力公司组织的科技项目验收，至今已投入运行近 8 年。

（二）系统构成

上标水电站压力钢管安全监控系统以流量、压力检测为基础，根据研制的压力钢管水力分析与预测模型，对钢管的各种异常运行状态进行预测，最终采用故障诊断系统判别各种故障和事故的发生，并发出相应的控制命令，从而实现钢管安全的长期在线安全监控。该系统分为监控中心站、现地监控单元、传感器测量单元、通信和执行机构五部分。

（三）系统原理及功能

1. 系统工作原理

（1）根据压力钢管的结构参数求出压力钢管沿线各节点的承载能力，并根据 DL/T 5141《水电站压力钢管设计规范》确定压力钢管沿线各节点的设计承载能力、校核能力和极限承载能力。

（2）对电站发电引水系统的各种正常运行情况和各种增、弃负荷过渡过程情况进行数值模拟计算分析，确定压力钢管沿线各节点的流量，内水压力瞬态变化过程及其最大、最小控制值在钢管沿线的分布规律。

（3）分析压力钢管沿线某节点可能发生过压爆破事故和已经发生破裂漏水事故时压力钢管首端、末端的流量、内水压力变化过程，确定其相应的控制值。

（4）输入在线监测数据的量测误差并考虑适当的控制裕量后，确定本系统发出“报警信号”和“重锤阀动作指令”的阈值，并据此建立本系统的控制模型。

2. 系统功能　采用故障诊断系统判别各种故障和事故的发生，并发出相应的控制命令，从而实现钢管长期在线安全监控。进水端流量超过正常运行范围时，中心站计算机发出光报警信号，超过事故动作门限时，经事故全面分析与识别，发出相应的控制指令，迅速进行事故处理。该系统可实时提供管道中发电用水的流量、发电用水量累计值和异常情况判别，供钢管保护、计算机组效率及监控系统经济运行之用。系统配备监测单元故障分析软件，可进行故障检测并发出信号。系统能有效判断钢管的各种异常运行状态，准确掌握压力钢管的状态和安全裕度，有解决由水锤和结构导致的压力钢管的运行故障和判断事故的能力和预见性。其具体功能有：参数实时监测、状态实时监视、保护功能、记录功能、事故数据查询、设备故障自检功能。

（四）基本资料及水力计算成果（略）

（五）压力钢管的事故模拟分析

1. 压力钢管过压事故预测分析　工况 1：水库水位为正常蓄水位 987.0m，每台机组的引用流量为最大流量 2.22m^3/s，两台机组同时全弃荷，针阀按一段直线规律快速关闭。工况 2：水库水位为正常蓄水位 987.0m，每台机组的引用流量 1.15m^3/s 为本电站机组实际情况出现的最小流量，两台机组同时全弃荷，针阀按一段直线规律快速关闭。对于工况 1，当压力钢管末端的最大内水压力为 1043.27m 时，压力钢管沿线上的第七节点的内水压力首先达到其极限承载能力 595.0m；对于工况 2，当压力钢管末端的最大内水压力为 919.85m 时，压力钢管沿线上的第七节点的内水压力首先达到 594.95m，接近其极限承载能力 595.0m。故本电站"安全监控系统"针对过压事故发出重锤蝶阀关闭"动作指令"的阈值设为：HEMD=920.0m，即当系统实时监测到压力钢管末端的内水压力大于等于 920.0m 时，发出重锤蝶阀关闭"动作指令"。

2. 压力钢管漏水情况模拟分析　在恒定漏水情况下，由于流量计的量测误差为±（1.0%～1.5%），而本电站两台机组额定运行时的总引用流量为 4.44m^3/s，求得"安全监控系统"所测得的压力钢管首、末端流量差的最大误差为 0.133m^3/s。另外，在各种正常的机组增、弃负荷过渡过程工况下，"安全监控系统所测得的压力钢管首、末端的总流量差小于等于 0.14m^3/s。拟定"安全监控系统"发出漏水量过大的"报警信号"的阈值为 0.16m^3/s；发出因漏水太大而关闭重锤蝶阀的"动作指令"的阈值为 0.35m^3/s，约为两台机组总额定流量的 8%。当压力钢管首端监测到的最小内水压力小于等于 0.0m 时，即发出钢管负压"报警信号"。

（六）水力控制模型（系统工作原则）

1. 压力钢管漏水检测　令 Q_{in}、Q_1、Q_2 代表压力钢管首端重锤阀、1 号、2 号机处流量计实测流量，则：①如果 $Q_{in}-(Q_1+Q_2)\geqslant 0.25m^3/s$，则"报警 1"；②如果 $Q_{in}-(Q_1+Q_2)\geqslant 0.50m^3/s$，则"动作 1"。

2. 压力钢管过压检测　本项目检测的目的是防止压力钢管过压爆裂，或发现爆裂后及时关闭蝶阀。令 P_{in}、P_1、P_2 分别代表蝶阀、1 号、2 号机处压力变送器的实测值，则：①当 $P_1\geqslant 660m$ 水柱压力或者 $P_2\geqslant 660m$ 水柱压力时，则"报警 2"；②当 $P_1\geqslant 920m$ 水柱压力或者 $P_2\geqslant 920m$ 水柱压力时，则"动作 2"。

3. 事故记录模型　本项目检测的目的是记录事故过程中的各种数据和信号，为事故原因分析和设备维修提供资料和依据。令 A、B 为两个数据记录缓冲区，监控系统依次在 A、B 区内动态记录水力系统中的各运行参数，每个缓冲区能容纳 60s 期间的上述参数值，后一次使用缓冲区时，前一次存储的数据自动被覆盖。一旦系统发出"动作 1"或"动作 2"信号，所用缓冲区存储存满后，监测数据转而计入其他存储区，直到蝶阀动作结束。

4. 系统故障自检模型　系统每隔 10s 执行一次系统自检。当系统出现"故障报警"时，系统的"报警信号"和"动作指令"不再执行，以故障报警优先。系统必须在各个在线监测数据均有效的情况下，才可发出相应的指令。

（1）Q_{in} 失效检验：当 $(Q_1+Q_2)\geqslant 1.0m^3/s$ 时，如果 $Q_{in}\leqslant 0.01m^3/s$，则发出"故障报警"信号。

（2）P_{in} 失效检验：当 $|Q_{in}-(Q_1+Q_2)|\leqslant 1.0m^3/s$ 时，如果 $P_{in}\leqslant 0.1m$ 水柱压力，则发出"故障报警"信号。

（3）Q_1 失效检验：当 $N_1\geqslant 0.01kW$ 时，如果 $Q_1\leqslant 0.0m^3/s$，则发出"故障报警"信号。

（4）Q_2 失效检验：当 $N_2\geqslant 0.01kW$ 时，如果 $Q_2\leqslant 0.0m^3/s$，则发出"故障报警"信号。

（5）P_1、P_2 失效检验：当 $Q_{in}-(Q_1+Q_2)\leqslant 0.24m^3/s$ 时，如果 $P_1\leqslant 20.0m$ 水柱压力或者 $P_2\leqslant 20.0m$ 水柱压力，则发出"故障报警"信号。

5. 压力钢管负压监测模型　如果 $P_{in}\leqslant 0.00m$ 水柱压力，则"报警 3"。此报警必须持续 30s 后发出。

6. 压力钢管过流监测模型　当重锤阀室压力钢管首端进口 $Q_{in}\geqslant 6.0m^3/s$，则发出"动作 3"。此模型在通信中断的情况下也能执行处理钢管的异常情况。

（七）结语

上标水电站的压力钢管安全监控系统建成投运已近 8 年的时间，未出现过误动作的情况。2007 年 6 月，发现 6 号伸缩节漏水较大的情况下，停机解列，远程关闭重锤阀动作正确。如增加测流装置，测量精度将会有大的提高。

压力钢管水力分析计算软件包和数学模型的开发是该系统的创新点。该系统通过对在线流量、压力数据和引水系统成因的计算分析，实现了对钢管爆裂、失稳的实时判断、预报和监控。由于国内目前还没有此类项目的应用，因此，该项目均经过了主管部门组织的多次专家论证才得以确认。此项目的建设成功对上标水电厂压力钢管的运行提供了安全保障，并填补了我国水电站压力钢管安全监控运行的空白，有着一定的推广意义。

（上标水力发电厂　赵慧荣）

大 坝 维 修

混凝土防渗灌浆技术及在丰满电站降渗工程的应用

一、概况

我国在20世纪60～70年代建设的大坝，由于当时历史条件等原因，不少工程出现坝基和坝体渗漏。近几十年来，对坝体的渗漏处理一直没有取得很好效果，成了一项技术难题。经研究，一般坝体渗漏的原因是大坝存在渗漏通道，水库蓄水后，在库水渗透压力的作用下，渗漏通道不断发展而不收敛，渗漏就会越来越严重。而采用一般灌浆技术处理坝体渗漏，存在两方面问题。一是使用的是普通水泥，其粒径较大，只适合灌注宽度为0.2mm以上的裂隙，对细微裂隙的充填度不够，处理的效果甚微。虽然目前可以使用超细水泥来解决这一问题，但超细水泥在包装和储存上都有很高的要求，成本较高。二是灌浆的压力选择和浆液的配比上缺乏依据，盲目沿用基岩灌浆的数据，对混凝土不合适，压力大了会使裂隙发育，给大坝造成二次危害。为了更好地解决对病坝处理的施工质量，提高经济效益，中国水利水电第一工程局有限公司对混凝土防渗灌浆在施工方法和用材方面进行了改进，形成了孔口封闭孔内循环磨细水泥灌浆技术，并在丰满降渗工程中应用。

该灌浆技术，首先选用了湿磨细水泥做灌浆材料。湿磨细水泥灌浆是在施工现场将普通水泥通过一种鼓形湿式碾磨机进行再加工使水泥颗粒进一步细化，满足微细裂缝灌浆需要，并且随磨随用，不需要专门包装和储存，成本较低。其次通过对比试验的反复验证，确定了合理的灌浆压力，优选了浆液水灰比，既保证不给大坝造成二次危害，又获得了较大的注入量，使细微裂隙得以充填。

二、在丰满电站降渗工程的应用情况

丰满水电站位于吉林省吉林市境内第二松花江干流上，总装机容量1004MW，始建于1937年日伪时期，并经20世纪50年代续建完成，至今已运行达68年。由于历史原因，大坝建成后就存在着一些质量缺陷。经1986～1997年的全面加固，大坝安全运行水平得到了提高，但坝体渗漏问题仍没有得到根本性解决。因此，2008年3月～2009年3月又启动了降渗工程。丰满电站降渗工程应用了本混凝土防渗灌浆技术，主要情况如下：

（一）主要施工工艺

1. 钻孔　灌浆孔双排布置，各排孔距均为1.0m，上、下排错孔布置，在堰顶垂直钻。孔位严格按施工图纸布置，与设计孔位的偏差不得大于5cm，孔深应符合设计规定。

2. 冲洗　每段灌浆孔钻完灌浆前要进行压力水冲洗。孔壁冲洗应冲至回水澄清后10min结束，且总的时间要求：单孔不少于30min，串孔不少于2h；对回水达不到澄清要求的孔段，应继续进行冲洗；孔内残存的沉积物厚度不得超过20cm。裂隙冲洗可结合简易压水试验进行，冲洗水压采用灌浆压力的80%但不大于1MPa，冲洗时间20min。

3. 压水试验　在钻孔冲洗结束后进行。基本孔和加强孔中的一序孔及灌后检查孔采用“五点法”压水试验；其他灌浆孔做简易压水试验。试验压力采用该段灌浆压力的80%，如压力大于1.0MPa时，则采用1.0MPa。“五点法”分5个压力阶段进行压水试验，在一定压力下，每5min测读一次压入流量，连续4次读数中最大值与最小值之差小于最终值的10%，或最大值与最小值之差小于1.0L/mim，则转入下一个压力阶段；取终值为计算值。简易压水试验，每5min测读一次压入流量，压水20min结束，取最终值为计算值。

4. 灌浆

（1）采用抚顺大坝硅酸盐水泥，强度等级不低于42.5，用3台湿磨机串联施工，浆液平均颗粒直径$d_{50}\leqslant 10\mu m$，同时在水泥浆液中掺加水泥重量0.5%的非引气型缓凝高效减水剂，以提高浆液的流动性与和易性。

（2）采用自上而下分段灌浆方式，堰顶以下第一、二、三段单独灌浆，第四段以下采用重复灌浆，灌浆塞均塞在堰顶以下10m处，射浆管距孔底距离小于50cm。

（3）各段灌浆压力根据灌浆试验成果确定，不论透水率大小均按技术要求进行，对特殊地层灌浆段采取相应的施工技术措施，有效控制灌浆量。

（4）尽快达到设计压力，但对于注入率较大或易于抬动的部位应分级升压。

（5）在设计压力下，灌浆段注入率不大于

0.1L/min,持续 30min，即达到标准，结束本段灌浆。

5. 灌浆孔封孔

（1）每个帷幕灌浆孔全孔灌浆结束后，监理工程师验收合格后，才能进行封孔。

（2）封孔应采用“分段压力灌浆封孔法”。

（3）封孔材料采用水泥砂浆，配合比采用水：水泥：砂的重量比为 1：1：0.6，并要求掺加水泥重量 1%的 EVA 膨胀剂。

（4）溢流面的表面封孔质量应满足监理工程师的要求。

（二）施工质量检查结果

共验收 47 个单元工程，除 WD-01 单元（生产性试验段）评定为“合格”以外，其余 46 个单元均评定为“优良”，单元优良率 98%；全部 7 个分部工程均评定为“优良”，分部工程优良率 100%。全部检查孔 628 段（203 孔）压水试验结果，试段合格率（$q \leqslant 0.15$Lu）为 95.5%、各坝段声波测试对比提高范围为 3%～10%，各分部工程检查孔孔内电视检测裂隙充填率在 91.1%以上。

三、成果鉴定情况

混凝土防渗灌浆技术在丰满电站降渗工程中的应用属国内首创。该项技术成果已于 2010 年 1 月通过鉴定，鉴定意见认为：

（1）研究使用湿磨机串联磨细工艺，水泥浆液颗粒可达到 $d_{50} \leqslant 10\mu m$，满足微细裂缝灌浆需要。

（2）通过对比试验，确定了合理的灌浆压力，既保证了大坝安全，又获得了较大的注入量。

（3）通过试验研究，优选了浆液水灰比。采用了 0.6：1 和 0.8：1 浓水泥浆液，效果较好。

（4）针对灌后透水率 $q \leqslant 0.15$Lu 的高标准要求，结合坝体混凝土灌浆的特点，采用孔口封闭法灌浆工艺，并确定了“在 2.0MPa 压力下，注入率不大于 0.1L/min，持续 30min”的灌浆结束标准。

（5）通过综合研究与应用，形成了系统的病害混凝土大坝防渗灌浆施工工艺。

（6）课题研究成果已获得 3 项实用新型专利，1 项发明专利获得受理，具有自主知识产权。

（7）课题研究成果在丰满水电站混凝土大坝降渗工程的成功应用，经济和社会效益明显，对类似工程具有借鉴意义。

（8）课题研究成果总体上达到了国际先进水平。

该施工技术和工艺，在国内类似混凝土大坝降渗工程中，具有良好的借鉴意义，也是一个成功的工程参考实例。

（中国水利水电第一工程局有限公司
张发林　卢洪彦　李　明　李志刚）

碧口水电站汶川地震受损修复情况

在 2008 年 5 月 12 日汶川地震中，大唐甘肃发电有限公司所属碧口水电厂震感强烈，经济损失惨重，人身安全和生产安全受到极大威胁。地震发生时，碧口电厂 4 号联络变压器高压侧避雷器三相断裂；一台 110kV 主变压器损坏；大坝背水面拱起、断裂；迎水面左侧混凝土护面层裂缝；大坝垂直沉降 24cm，水平位移 19cm；尾水平台贯穿性裂缝；主厂房与副厂房结合部错位；主厂房下游侧墙面裂纹；闸门启闭机室墙体破裂损坏严重，主体结构破坏；职工住宅也几乎全部损坏，无法居住。

灾情发生后，在中国大唐集团公司强有力的领导下，迅速启动了地震应急预案，卓有成效地开展了抗震救灾工作，确保了职工群众生命财产安全、碧口水库大坝安全和救灾保电安全。在最短的时间内第一个向电网供电，为震区的抗震救灾作出了积极贡献。随后立即开始了地震破坏设备、设施的加固和修复工作。至 2009 年初，已完成了大坝加固、厂房和启闭机室修复加固等工作。大坝在 2009 年汛期经受了历史最高水位的考验，运行正常。职工住宅的重建工作也将于 2010 年底前完成。

（甘肃大唐白龙江发电有限责任公司）

葛洲坝三江防淤堤护坡破损原因分析及加固措施研究

（一）概况

葛洲坝三江防淤是葛洲坝水利枢纽的重要导沙、护航建筑物。全长 3.8km，两边为 0.3～0.6m 厚混凝土护坡，坡度比为 1：3、1：4、1：5 三种。护坡坡脚以下由多种土质组成，其中底层为砂岩，砂岩以上有 2～10m 厚的覆盖层，坡脚以上有天然覆盖层和人工回填土。

2006 年发现左右岸护坡局部均出现护面不同程度断裂变形、淘空等状况，需要及时修复。2007 年，在对葛洲坝三江防淤堤护坡的破损情况进行分析的基础上，根据不同部位有针对性地制定加固措施。

（二）破损原因分析

葛洲坝三江防淤堤护坡运行多年才开始破损，破损机理较为复杂，水下部分破损原因归纳起来主要有：①三江防淤堤左岸是三江航道，航船过闸以及风浪产生的高速水流重复冲击，逐渐淘刷，导致坡脚以下产生空洞，从而引起坡脚混凝土面板的断裂变形；②混凝土护坡基础下天然覆盖层夹有松散土层，引起地基不均匀沉降，导致混凝土护坡的破裂；③护岸排水系统或反滤层有缺陷，导致砂石垫层从分缝处或破损处流失，面板下淘空后发生沉陷、坍塌，造成护坡架空；④原施工受技术水平限制，存在一定的质量缺陷，以及混凝土面板本身存在的耐久年限不足导致出现面板破裂；⑤三江航道水位在63.5～66.5m高程范围浮动，工作人员其他生产活动时对护坡造成损坏。

（三）加固措施

葛洲坝三江防淤堤左岸受三江面航运影响，坝前水位变化较大，右岸二江电站面相对水位变化小，因此，三江面护坡破损情况相对严重，二江面护坡情况较好。根据破损部位的不同，综合考虑其可能的破损原因，分为水上部分和水下部分两种情况制定有针对性的加固修复措施。

1. 水上部分　水位高程在63.5m以上的护坡作为水上部分，可采用传统的加固方法。具体可分为：①对原护板进行就地破碎；②重新处理地基；③每块护板预设2个泄水孔，安装ϕ75mmPVC排水管；④修复护坡，按5m×5m分格预留伸缩缝，缝宽为20mm，嵌入双层SBS沥青板；⑤采用C20混凝土浇筑；⑥养护。

2. 水下部分　水下部分修复一直是护坡修复中的难点，结构可靠性差，不易弄清水下混凝土面板的破损原因和破损程度。此次水下部分修复采用水下模袋混凝土这一新型水下加固技术。在三江防淤堤左岸护坡水下破损部位，直接采用模袋混凝土水下封堵破损缺口，右岸踏步台阶采用模袋混凝土水下封堵缺口和采用导管法浇筑水下不分散混凝土填充空穴。

（1）模袋混凝土技术利用强化纤维编织成上下两层并能控制一定间距的大面积连续袋状体做模板，通过混凝土泵将混凝土冲灌进模袋，凝固后形成一个刚性的板状防护块体，并能适应地形变化而紧贴在岸坡或河床上起到防护层作用，具有整体性和耐久性好、地形适应性强、施工速度快的特点。

（2）不分散混凝土设计。考虑到导管泄入混凝土的冲击压力不能过大，以免将混凝土护坡板拱起，理论限定混凝土护坡板水下所能承受最大压强计算为2.88×10^{-3}MPa。本工程混凝土设计强度应大于20MPa。陆上干地配置强度比设计强度标准值应提高40%～50%。导管施工坍扩度控制在36～45cm区间。水灰比不大于0.60。UWB-Ⅱ的掺入会使拌和物内部水的黏性提高，因此用水量较普通混凝土大。当坍扩度约45cm时，用水量为220～230kg/m^3；坍扩度约40mm时，用水量为215～225kg/m^3。水下不分散混凝土还应满足泵压式导管施工时水泥的最小用量限制（370kg/m^3），以满足混凝土的耐久性和有关施工方法的要求。水下不分散混凝土的砂率一般应在35%～40%之间。此次护坡水下模袋混凝土采用先铺后灌法施工，按照实验确定配合比组织现场使用，其中水泥强度等级为42.5MPa。UWB-Ⅱ为水下不分散混凝土中掺加的水下不分散外加剂，增加混凝土的黏聚力和充填能力，提高水下混凝土强度和保证水下混凝土工程质量。

（3）施工步骤为：①破损缺口清理及空穴探测钻孔；②水下模袋铺设及导管安装；③水下混凝土浇筑，直接采用商品混凝土运送到现场，由汽车泵加压直接送入模袋口和导管口进行填充；④待填堵缺口的模袋混凝土达到一定强度后即可开始水下空穴导管浇筑。

（四）结语

葛洲坝三江防淤堤护坡修复加固于2007年4月开始实施，5月底完成加固施工。模袋混凝土强度值均达到强度等级，平均值为25.3MPa，标准差为2.12MPa，概率度系数为2.5，强度保证率为98.8%，符合设计要求，满足护坡要求。经近两年的运行，三江防淤堤护坡修复部位完好，原淘空部位没有出现塌陷或破裂现象，说明加固方案切实有效。

（中国长江电力股份有限公司　张壮志　刘畅快
中国长江三峡集团公司　王　云
中国水利水电第十一工程局有限公司　赵　强）

安康水电站表孔消力池底板破坏原因分析及补强加固处理

（一）概况

安康水电站位于汉江上游陕西省安康市，总装机容量800MW，保证出力175MW，多年平均发电量28亿kW·h。

安康水电站表孔消力池长108m，宽91m，纵横缝将池底板分成36块，除最右侧11坝段6块宽9m，其余为19m×18m。池底板高程229.00m，尾坎高程243.00m，池深14m。消力池底板厚≥7m，最厚处达20m。底板表面为1m厚R_{28}300号抗冲混凝土，其内设一层抗冲防裂钢筋网，以下为R_{28}150号基础混凝土，深度大于7m，坑槽部位回填R_{28}100号混凝土。各块纵横缝在面层抗冲混凝土内设铜止水和塑料止水各一道，基础混凝土纵横缝内设键槽相嵌连接，对0+090.00m、0+108.00m两条纵缝进行了并缝灌浆。消力池底板下设抽排系统、纵横排水廊道，廊道底板高程 222.50m，横向廊道骑缝布置，纵向廊道在缝下 3.75m 处，廊道内设有基础排水孔，用以降低消力池底板的扬压力。廊道集水汇入小导墙的集水井，经布置在 252.5m 高程的深井泵抽排至尾水渠。池底板除 11 号坝段池 4～池 6 和 12 号坝段池 3～池 4 底板很厚，未进行灌浆外，其余底板均进行了固结灌浆。

安康水电站表孔消力池主要担负着 5 个表孔的消能任务，而 5 个表孔承担着总流量 52%～62%的下泄任务。宣泄大坝校核洪水 $P=0.01\%$时的表孔单孔泄量为 $3809m^3/s$，单宽下泄能量 126.7 万 kW/m。

（二）表孔消力池底板主要缺陷

（1）纵横伸缩缝局部止水破坏。

（2）消力池底板普遍出现上抬现象，比原设计高 50～130mm。

（3）底板出现大面积新裂缝，原修补过的裂缝环氧被冲掉或表面又出现裂缝。

（4）锚筋孔、灌浆孔及废孔表面的环氧砂浆护面被冲蚀掉。

（5）在底板内、反弧段和溢流面上有大小不一的冲蚀坑。

（6）下游表面抗冲层磨损严重。

（三）表孔消力池底板破坏原因分析

宽尾墩和消力池联合运行时，表孔射流区的下游出现一个时均压力下降区，因此，存在缺陷，动水压力传入底板面层混凝土下，易对池 2、池 3 区面层混凝土造成损坏。两层混凝土间结合不良是抗冲层混凝土脱开的重要原因。消力池面层混凝土与基础混凝土虽经过几次灌浆修复，但脱空处的缝隙很难充填密实。表层环氧保护层的破坏还与施工工艺有关，分析认为是因为基础处理不到位而造成黏结强度不够。

（四）表孔消力池底板历次补强加固处理的情况

1. 1996 年补强加固处理　消力池底板全范围布置锚筋，锚筋采用 ϕ28 钢筋，间、排距皆为 1.5m，锚筋孔向上游倾斜，倾角 75°，孔深 2.5m。锚筋孔用膨胀锚固剂锚固，全池共打锚筋 3952 根，锚筋孔表面采用环氧砂浆封堵。对消力池底板所有横缝及池 2 下游纵缝进行接缝灌浆，灌浆压力控制在 0.2MPa 以下。对消力池抗冲层与基础混凝土接触面裂缝进行回填灌浆。表面裂缝采用表面凿槽，环氧砂浆回填。12 号坝段池 3 表面剥落层全部凿除，回填抗冲混凝土。其他明显的表面缺陷按有关技术要求采用环氧砂浆处理。

2. 2000 年补强加固处理

（1）纵、横缝止水表面采用柔性接缝处理。

（2）表面裂缝采用柔性接缝方式。

（3）预应力锚筋加固，范围为消力池内脉动压力较大的部位，同时也是此次抽水检查锚筋出露的区域，分布在 11 号坝段池 2～池 4，12 号和 13 号坝段的池 1～池 4，15 号坝段的池 2～池 4，总加固面积约 $4800m^2$，共布置锚筋 1550 根。预应力加固采用预应力螺杆锚筋方式，锚筋型号为 JL540 型 ϕ32 精轧螺纹钢筋，锚孔直径 ϕ65mm，内锚头采用胶结式，并附加一节连接器以增加其安全储备，外锚头采用螺母锁定。锚筋设计吨位为 30t，张拉锁定吨位为 20t。锚筋长 4.2m，内锚固段长度 2.5m，锚固段浆体材料强度不得低于 C40，自由段浆体材料不低于 C30。

（4）对预应力锚筋加固区域的池底板面层混凝土与基础混凝土之间的水平层间缝进行回填灌浆。回填灌浆孔深 1.5m，灌浆压力不得超过 0.2MPa，回填灌浆应分块分序并在锚筋张拉后进行。

（5）对局部较深的磨蚀坑进行修补处理。

（6）对原已损坏的加固锚筋出露孔，在水平层间缝回填灌浆并在向孔内灌满水泥浆后，进行环氧砂浆封堵孔口保护处理。

（7）冲坑按常规修补方法处理，清除坑内石渣和凿除不密实或已松动的老混凝土，将原钢筋网剥离并距老混凝土面至少 20cm，加焊 ϕ19 钢筋，进行钢筋网补强修复，再在老混凝土面上回填 C40 聚合物砂浆。

3. 2002 年补强加固处理

（1）损坏的纵横缝止水，采用聚合物砂浆与老混凝土接合，U 形复合止水带、GB 止水板柔性材料接缝，表面用环氧砂浆抹面保护并预留伸缩缝的方法进行处理；其余破坏伸缩缝按 2000 年的方法处理。

（2）裂缝处理、冲蚀坑处理、出露锚筋孔及废孔处理与上次方法相同。

（3）在水流漩滚强烈且表面磨损严重的 13 号坝段池 2 板块，采用力学性能良好和抗磨性能较好的铁钢砂砂浆和弹性环氧砂浆进行抗磨试验处理。

4. 2004 年补强加固处理

（1）冲蚀坑采用环氧砂浆进行回填处理。

（2）伸缩缝采用化学灌浆与环氧砂浆护面结合进行处理。

（3）底板环氧护面被冲掉的裂缝封闭，原槽不再凿深凿宽，将原槽清理，松动块去除，槽面清理后回填环氧砂浆进行处理。底板新出现的裂缝封闭采用环氧胶泥沿缝薄层涂抹进行处理。

（4）出露锚筋孔及废孔表面的护面采用割除锚筋头，环氧砂浆回填进行处理。

（5）将 13 号坝段池 2 板块上抗磨试验层遗留部分清除，重新采用薄层环氧砂浆进行抗磨试验。

5. 2007 年补强加固处理

（1）底板冲蚀坑采用环氧砂浆进行回填的处理方法。

(2) 底板环氧护面被冲掉的纵横伸缩缝封闭，采用化学灌浆与环氧砂浆护面结合进行的处理方法。

(3) 底板环氧护面边缘出现裂缝的纵横伸缩缝封闭，采用凿除原环氧砂浆护面，再重新回填环氧砂浆进行处理。

(4) 底板环氧护面被冲掉的裂缝封闭，原槽不再凿深凿宽，将原槽清理，松动块去除，槽面清理后回填环氧砂浆进行处理。

(5) 底板新出现的裂缝封闭采用环氧胶泥沿缝薄层涂抹进行处理。

(6) 出露锚筋孔及废孔表面的护面采用割除锚筋头，环氧砂浆回填进行处理。

(7) 13号坝段池3原型观测仪器孔封堵采用回填环氧砂浆进行处理。

(8) 13号坝段池2板块采用薄层环氧砂浆进行抗磨处理。

(9) 底板表面聚脲喷涂抗冲磨试验。根据底板表面实际情况，选择100m^{2}进行聚脲喷涂抗冲磨试验。

（五）结语

消力池经过了5次不同规模的补强加固处理。由于每次补强加固处理都是应急措施，未对泄洪建筑物进行全面检查。目前经受过的最大下泄流量为19 000m^3/s，与原设计洪水下泄流量31 500m^3/s相比，仍有较大差距。设计单位提出对已损坏的面层混凝土进行彻底修复，应将已损坏的面层混凝土清除后重新浇注面层混凝土，并在下层混凝土中植入插筋，以及新浇面层混凝土纵横伸缩缝内设置两道止水，尽量避免在薄层水垫工况下运行。当短时段无法避免下游水垫深度较浅时，高流速和大脉动并存，此时应保证底板下抽排系统正常工作，防止导致底板不稳定的多种不利因素组合而造成底板失稳。汛前应先关闭消力池通小导墙的密封门。对表孔闸门的开启方式及运用组合也应进行进一步总结研究。

（陕西省安康水力发电厂　冯　超　周洪林　张云海）

鲁布革水电站发耐滑坡综合治理实施

一、概述

鲁布革水电站发耐滑坡为一古滑坡体，位于云南省与贵州省交界的黄泥河中下游鲁布革水电站库区，处于大坝上游1400～2200m的河流峡谷进口段左岸山坡。该滑坡前缘部分地段于1983年出现横向张开裂缝，并持续发展至1988年。1988年11月水库下闸蓄水引起两次较大的诱发地震后，裂缝连续贯通并进一步张开形成新的滑坡，1989年雨季出现加速蠕滑变形现象，后逐渐缓慢。1997年7月水库冲沙库水位骤降，引发了该地段失稳破坏整体下滑及前缘其他地段多处小规模的坍塌，同时在整个古滑坡体后缘产生环状拉张裂缝及坡体上居民建筑物拉裂等现象。

滑坡前缘宽约750m，中部宽690～820m，后缘宽380～520m，纵向长850m，平面上滑坡周界呈梨形，面积约0.58km^2，体积约4300万m^3。

二、滑坡体地勘结论及评审意见

（一）地勘结论

鲁布革水力发电厂和上级主管部门对发耐滑坡稳定极为重视，多次组织专项地质勘测，主要结论为：发耐滑坡为一古崩滑堆积体，是牵引—推落式滑坡，规模巨大，按稳定程度在平面上可将滑坡划分为四个区：A区为相对稳定区，B区为较稳定区，C区为较不稳定区，D区为不稳定区。滑坡体不会产生大范围的复活而发生大规模的失稳破坏，一般C区和D区以局部滑动破坏为主，对水库运行有一定影响，但不会危及大坝安全；地下水动态对滑坡稳定性有一定影响，库水位连续大幅度快速下降时对滑坡稳定性产生较明显的不利影响。

（二）评审意见

2004年1月，南方电网超高压输变电公司邀请以谭靖夷院士为首的专家组的主要评审意见为：结合水库实际运行条件，采用其他方法对滑坡稳定性进行复核。水库调度需严格控制库水位降幅和下降速度。建议建立规范的监测系统，监测其变化发展趋势。建议做好滑坡体坡面的系统排水、截水措施。封闭滑坡体地表裂缝，并进一步研究D区的处理措施。根据《中国地震动参数区划图》（2001版）按规范可不考虑地震因素的影响。关于滑坡整治方案及滑坡对冲沙和水库运行的影响，建议下一步专题研究。建议将滑坡区居民全部搬迁，并将滑坡区作为工程边坡进行封闭管理。

（三）滑坡体稳定复核计算

根据评审意见对滑坡稳定性进行复核计算。计算采用北京理正软件研究所编制的岩土工程计算程序，求出抗滑力与滑动力之比的抗滑稳定安全系数。结果与昆明岩土工程公司在《发耐滑坡稳定性分析报告》中所采用的边坡稳定极限分析能量法计算结果基本一致。

三、滑坡综合治理

（一）滑坡治理的前提和原则

滑坡体上有当地数十户居民和一所小学，为确保人民生命财产安全、保证电站工程安全，同时为了消除人为活动对滑坡体的不利影响，首先必须全部搬迁住在古滑坡区的居民，才能对滑坡区进行治理并把滑坡区作为工程范围进行封闭式管理。因此，将滑坡区居民全部搬迁是滑坡治理的前提，在保证工程安全前提下，不作为“加固性根治”，而是以投入不多的经费，采取综合治理措施为原则，目的是控制变形发展，保持边坡的动态平衡。

（二）综合治理实施主要措施

1. 居民搬迁　居民搬迁工作于2004年启动，至2007年9月9日，历经三年多的搬迁工作圆满完成，发耐滑坡体上原住村民共98户412人，全部完成了异地搬迁安置。

2. 削坡减载处理　滑坡体的C区、D区存在局部滑动破坏的可能，其前缘已于1997年7月13日水库放空冲沙时下滑于水库中。本区域的稳定性较差，其抗滑稳定性安全系数为1.031～1.294，部分小于规范规定值1.05，需局部采取削坡减载处理。经过削坡回填处理，该区的抗滑稳定安全系数为1.150，达到规范规定值。

3. 地表裂缝封堵、新建排水系统　对滑坡体后缘的地表裂缝进行详细检查并封堵。对于小的裂缝，可直接用黏土或黏土水泥浓浆填塞。在滑坡体后缘外侧设置截水沟，以拦截从山坡下来的地表水并排至滑坡体外两侧上、下游的水库岸边。截水沟从滑坡体后缘外侧沿着古滑坡道顺山坡至水库边布置，自上到下平面呈“∩”形。实际新建截水沟约1.4km，翻新和新建排水沟3.1km。

4. 观测系统布设　根据SL 52—1993《水利水电工程施工测量规范》的要求，滑坡体变形监测平面和高程位移量中误差为±3～±5mm。规定工作基点网的点位和高程中误差小于±4mm。选定最终观测方法为极坐标差分法。根据选定的观测方法，确定工作基点的布设。在观测站的山坡（即水库右岸）布置2个基点，在滑坡体两侧稳定的山体上设置2个基点，组成一个4点工作基点网。工作基点网按照三等边角网的精度观测。结合现场实际情况，从滑坡体的后缘至前缘布置了5排共计18个测点，高程分布在1319～1157m之间。

5. 控制库水位降幅和降落速度　堆积体局部滑动比沿古滑坡道整体滑动影响大，这与滑床的位置、滑动体在水下的厚度等有关；库水位降幅对滑坡的影响较大，库水位骤降30m时，稳定安全系数不能满足规范要求。所以，水库调度运行时要严格控制库水位的分段下降，一次降幅不应超过10m，每个降幅的水位需保持稳定12h以上，并且控制每段水位降落速度在每昼夜3m以内。

四、结语

通过先后多次对发耐滑坡的勘察和调查以及长期以来的监测，基本上查明了发耐滑坡的地质条件、滑坡范围、发展趋势及其对工程的影响。其失稳破坏主要为牵引式渐进破坏，塌滑后会增加水库的淤积，采取必要的防范措施和改善滑坡自身的稳定性是必要的。在搬迁滑坡区全部居民后，对影响稳定的陡坡进行适当削坡减载，并将削坡土石方填压在滑坡前缘；削除陡坎、凸壁回填洼地、封闭地表裂缝；新建排水系统及封山育林等，以改善滑坡体稳定性，维持滑坡体的动态平衡。在滑坡体上重新布置了监测网，定期观测滑坡体的变形，并控制库水位骤降综合处理。

（中国南方电网鲁布革水力发电厂　张正梅　王立福）

葛洲坝二江弧门工作模态测试

葛洲坝水利枢纽二江泄水闸共有27孔，已经运行了近30年。长江河势复杂，水流情况变幅很大，对需经常在局部开启状态下工作的闸门很不利。葛洲坝二江的泄水弧门已使用20多年，为了解其目前的闸门动力特性又不妨碍正常运行，对弧门进行了理论计算和工作模态测试。

（一）工作模态方法简介

传统的模态分析技术需要施加一个已知的激励并测量相应的系统响应。尽管理论上，对输入－输出的测量是可行的，但测试的复杂性和能够完成的数据质量常使这一方法受到了限制，即使是实物应用，也需要结构停止运行，可能还需要将结构放到特定的场所才能进行。

一个结构的模态与一个连续时间线性系统在某个激励驱动下的特征结构是一样的，这个连续时间线性系统的输出向量是加速度计的测量数据。关键问题是识别在未知输入的自然工作激励下的特征结构。这就需要使用仅对输出数据进行模态参数识别的方法即工作模态分析方法，仅从输出数据中提取模态参数。主要的模态识别方法有：多参考点最小二乘复指数（LSCE）方法以及随机子空间方法，这些方法适合于捕获系统的特征结构。

（二）动力学理论计算

实际测试常和有限元理论计算结合起来，测试前的理论计算可以为测试方案提供参考意见。本次计算模型采用了空气介质下的无阻尼理想模型，计算了弧门提门约束下的模态，闸门由系于门顶的钢丝绳悬吊，可用等效弹簧来模拟，支铰处绕坝轴转动自由，无其他约束。侧向计算结果可作实际测试参考之用。

从计算结果来看，低阶频率主要为支臂振型。

（三）工作模态测试

1. 测点布置　测量所关心的弧门低频振动主要表现在支臂上，其中径向刚度比切向和侧向刚度大，将上支臂的切向和侧向作为研究重点。侧向传感器移位，分析主要以切向为主。分析结果中下支臂振型随上支臂，动画中将面板处理成刚体，随支臂振型运动。

2. 现场测试　本次检测采用自然水流脉动法。实际测试时，闸门上游水位 65.23m，下游水位 52.66m，底槛高程为 37m，中孔区其他闸门开度均为 4.8m。

3. 测试结果　弧门一阶整体切振的频率为 4.73Hz，阻尼比为 4.43%，支臂一阶切振的频率为 19.46Hz，阻尼比为 1.56%，支臂二阶切振的频率为 34.00Hz，阻尼比为 0.29%。

（四）试验与计算比较

弧门理论计算和实测结果对比，两者在低阶频率上有出入，越高阶越接近。一阶计算值为 6.63Hz，实测值 4.73Hz，相差 29%；二阶计算值为 20.31Hz，实测值 19.46Hz，相差 4%；三阶计算值为 36.26Hz，17 号弧门实测值 34.00Hz，相差 6%。计算未考虑流固耦合，按理想情况假设，现场闸门的实际约束难免与假设有差异，结构刚度也与理想假设有差别。

根据统计闸门振动特性数据，结构在实际工作中的自振频率较空气中低，据资料介绍，一般要低 20%～40%，也有达 50%的，实测结果合理。

（五）结语

（1）空气介质下的理论计算为实际测量提供了测点布置、频率响应范围等方面的指导，让实验准备更充分，测量更精确。

（2）利用闸门正常工作时的出流水流来激励闸门，采用了工作模态测试方法，测得工作状态下闸门的动态特性。

（3）结合水流脉动压力的特性，其主要能量集中在 3Hz 以内，闸门工作模态的测试结果可判断闸门工作时候不会发生共振。

（水利部产品质量标准研究所　李　勤　关　磊）

13

环境保护与水库移民

环 境 保 护

三峡水库开县消落区综合治理与保护规划

三峡工程建成后，将在高程 145～175m 之间库区两岸，形成与天然河流涨落季节规律相反、涨落水位差高达 30m 的水库消落区。消落区夏季出露为陆、秋季由陆域迅速向水域转变、冬季全部成为水域、春季由水域渐次转变为陆域。

三峡水库消落区是三峡库区的重要组成部分，包括重庆市 22 个区县（市）和湖北省 4 个区县，据量测统计，三峡库区 145～175m 消落区总面积 348.93km²，175m 岸线长 5578.21km。位于重庆市范围内消落区面积 306.28km²、岸线长 4881.43km，涉及巫山、巫溪、奉节、云阳、开县等 22 个区县（市），其中开县范围内消落区面积 42.78km²，是三峡库区消落区面积最大且集中分布的县，占全库区消落区总面积的 12.3%，占重庆库区面积的 13.97%，主要集中分布于人口稠密的开县新城周围的河谷平坝区，连片面积达 24km²。三峡水库建成后形成大面积、高落差的消落区，带来一系列生态环境问题。其生态系统的稳定是水库安全运行的重要保障，关系到库区社会经济的持续稳定发展。三峡水库开县澎溪河（小江）流域消落区问题一直受到党中央、地方各级政府的重视，1993 年以来，从党中央到地方政府，各方面专家集思广益，深入研究，提出大量的关于消落区生态环境治理的方案和研究成果。

2001 年，国务院以国函［2001］147 号文件将澎溪河（小江）流域综合整治项目列入了《三峡库区及其上游水污染防治规划》。2003 年 12 月，国家环保总局环境规划院编制完成《三峡库区澎溪河流域生态环境综合整治规划》（以下简称《规划》），提出综合治理三峡水库开县消落区的规划方案是：建设水位调节坝，形成三峡水库的“前置库”，调控消落区面积与落差；岸边设立生态功能区，进行生态防护；上游拦沙；调整排污方式等 4 项治理措施。2004 年 3 月，重庆市发展改革委以渝发改农［2004］272 号文件对该规划予以批复。2006 年 7 月，国家发展改革委以发改经［2006］1406 号文件对《三峡水库开县消落区生态环境综合治理水位调节坝工程可行性研究报告》予以批复。根据可行性研究报告及其批复，开县消落区生态环境综合治理工程包括水位调节坝工程和库区生态环境建设工程两大部分。2007 年初，生态调节库水位调节坝工程正式开工建设，预计 2010 年完工。

调节坝工程建成后，使库内水位长期稳定在 170.28m 以上，最大消落水深由 30m 减少至 5m 左右，坝址以上消落区面积由 24km² 缩小至 9.52km²。同时，通过开县新县城建设，可进一步缩小消落区范围，根据开县新城总体规划，消落区面积可进一步减少至 5.20km²，大幅度减少了消落区面积和水位消落变幅的高度。在水位调节坝工程可行性研究和初步设计成果中，明确提出了调节库库区生态环境保护和建设的要求，并提出了初步方案，但由于设计中提出的消落区治理技术尚欠成熟，国家相关部委均提出另需专题研究。

在此背景下，中国水电顾问集团华东勘测设计研究院编制完成《三峡水库开县生态调节库生态保护与建设规划》（以下简称《规划》）。《规划》编制工作自 2006 年 10 月开始，于 2008 年 8 月完成。通过资料收集、整理、现场查勘和技术研究策划，对制约三峡库岸区可持续发展的各种因素进行分析。同时，根据消落区的现状条件，开展土地适宜性分析评价，对各种类型的消落区有针对性地采用湿地重构、生态堤防、环库防护林构建和生态景观建设等技术手段进行综合治理，形成了消落区生态保护与建设体系。形成规划方案后，广泛听取各方意见，于 2007 年底上报规划方案，2008 年 4 月由国务院三峡工程建设委员会办公室、重庆市发展改革委在开县联合召开“重庆市开县生态环境综合治理战略咨询研讨会”，对规划成果进行了咨询审查，最终修订、编制完成规划成果。该《规划》被评为 2009 年度全国优秀咨询成果二等奖。水库消落区治理是一项国际性的技术难题，本《规划》具有较强的前瞻性、创新性和先进性，主要体现在以下几个方面：

（1）《规划》研究方法先进、治理思路明确，前瞻性较强。《规划》提出了 5 种湿地形式、2 类防护林和多种生态堤防结构等消落区治理技术方案，根据土地适宜性分析，将消落区分为 4 大类，采用保护、治理与建设相结合的方法，进行分区分类治理。《规划》采用的关键技术主要有湿地重构、生态堤防、环库防护林构建和生态景观建设等，采用生态建设优先、工程治理与生态治理相结合的技术理念，能较好地解决三峡库区消落区生态保护和建设的复杂要求，可为国内其他水库消落区生态环境综合治理提供思路和方法。《规划》在生态修复的基础上，融入景观建设等技术要求，在生态治理的同时，恢复和建设库周生态景观，提高区域人居环境质量，并为破解库区产业空心化、改善投资环境、旅游环境、促进城乡一体化建设等提供条件。结合相关规划，规划建设内容分近期和远期两部分实施，合理、有序地进行项目推进。总之，该规划采取了保护与治理结合、分区分类治理的方法，具有生态建设优先理念，系统规划了建设内容和分期实施方案。

（2）《规划》为消落区治理的难题提供了较为系统的解决方案。水库消落区的水文、土壤、地质等生境条件复杂，消落区内水位周期性的涨落，使其在天然情况下，既不能形成有效的陆生动植物群落，也不能形成水生动植物群落，对生态系统的稳定产生了极为不利的影响，从而引发环境、水利、景观、土地资源等问题，必须采取人工干预加以治理。三峡水库年水位消落差高达30m，消落区治理涉及生态学、水力学、环境学、岩土力学、流体力学、植物学、景观学等多个学科，在复杂的水文、地质等条件下进行生态修复和建设，是国内外的一个难题，目前尚无成熟的技术成果和案例。《规划》在开县生态调节库工程的基础上，将消落区划分为0～25m、25～30m两部分进行治理，并集中对靠近库周的25～30m区域，结合库周陆域生态保护和建设，因地制宜，广泛吸收了国内外的研究成果，采用多种生态化治理手段，提出了系统的治理规划方案，预计可取得较好的综合治理效益，为三峡水库消落区综合治理提供技术依据。

（3）《规划》对三峡水库消落区治理的决策影响较大。国务院三峡工程建设委员会办公室、重庆市发展改革委于2008年4月15～16日在重庆市开县联合召开“重庆市开县生态环境综合治理战略咨询研讨会”，以本次规划成果为基础，对开县消落区生态环境综合治理方案展开研讨。与会专家对《规划》提出的消落区治理思路给予了充分肯定，原全国政协副主席钱正英认为该《规划》符合开县消落区实际，是目前最具有可实施性的技术方案，建议有关部门将开县消落区治理作为示范地，进一步在三峡库区推广；国务院三峡工程建设委员会副主任汪啸风认为该《规划》具有战略性和普遍性；甘宇平等三峡水库技术专家认为该《规划》具有探索性、适用性、阶段性、理想性。重庆市发展改革委、国务院三峡工程建设委员会等部门基本达成一致意见，同意将规划工程作为三峡水库消落区治理试点项目，纳入三峡工程后续建设试点。本《规划》在一定程度上推进了三峡水库消落区综合治理的步伐，加快了国家和国务院三峡工程建设委员会对消落区治理的决策进程。

（4）规划项目规模较大，社会反响强烈。三峡水库由于位于人口稠密区，消落区的保护和建设工作在国内外得到了广泛的关注。开县是三峡水库消落区中面积最大的县，本规划治理消落区面积9.52km^2，并涉及周边20余平方千米的延伸区域，涉及现状人口30万人，规划人口50万人。规划总投资达10亿元，一期工程投资3.4亿元，在社会和行业内反响较大。规划成果得到各方的一致认可。

（5）规划成果可操作性较强。目前，《规划》所涉及的各治理项目已逐步列入各级政府的实施计划，部分项目已进入可行性研究阶段、初步设计、技施设计等阶段。

规划项目实施成功后，由于开县消落区在三峡库区具有较强的代表性，规划提出的技术思路可为三峡库区消落带生态系统恢复、水库生态屏障建设提供技术参考，在三峡库区及其他同类水库消落区治理工作中有较好的推广价值。

（中国水电顾问集团华东勘测设计研究院　杜运领）

澜沧江水电开发与生态环境保护

澜沧江—湄公河发源于青海省玉树州杂多县的唐古拉山，经西藏流入云南，于云南南部的西双版纳州流出国界。经缅甸、老挝、泰国、柬埔寨、越南后注入南海。该河在中国境内称澜沧江，出境后称湄公河。

澜沧江—湄公河全长4880km，其中中国境内长2153km。全流域总面积74.4万km^2，中国境内17.4万km^2。湄公河出海口年径流量4750亿m^3，中国境内汇入640亿m^3，占总径流量的13.5%。

澜沧江中下游河段水电开发规划为“两库八级”方案，依次为功果桥、小湾、漫湾、大朝山、糯扎渡、景洪、橄榄坝、勐松，总装机容量1660万kW，除大朝山外均由华能澜沧江水电有限公司负责开发运行。

（一）澜沧江水电开发环境影响研究工作

根据国家有关环境保护法规要求，澜沧江中下游各电站在动工之前均开展了环境影响研究，编制了工程环境影响报告书，并上报国家环境保护主管部门审批。目前，除已建成的漫湾、大朝山电站外，景洪、小湾、糯扎渡、功果桥电站已通过了环保专项审批，橄榄坝电站正在报批过程中。

为做好澜沧江水电开发的环境保护工作，华能澜沧江水电有限公司在项目环评的基础上，又委托有关单位开展了多项流域环境影响研究工作。目前已完成或正在开展的工作有：

(1) 2002 年，委托中国水电工程顾问集团公司等单位开展“澜沧江中下游水电梯级开发环境影响评价”工作。研究成果于 2006 年 6 月通过国家环保总局的审查和批复。

(2) 2004 年，委托云南大学亚洲国际河流中心开展“澜沧江梯级开发的跨境影响和对策研究”。研究成果通过专家的鉴定验收。

(3) 2005 年，委托中国水电顾问集团公司和中国水利水电科学研究院开展“澜沧江水电梯级开发对生态环境及下游地区影响分析工作”，现已完成第一和第二阶段工作，并提交了相应成果。

(4) 2007 年，委托加拿大迪龙科技咨询公司开展“澜沧江水电开发对下游湄公河影响研究”，现已完成研究初步成果。

(5) 2008 年 5 月，成立了中国水力发电工程学会国际河流水电开生态环境研究工作委员会，由澜沧江水电有限公司资助，长期和系统地开展澜沧江—湄公河等国际河流水电开发生态环境影响。目前主要开展网站建设、澜沧江—湄公河基础数据整理、景洪电站运行对下游水文情势变化调查与分析、小湾蓄水对澜沧江—湄公河水文情势影响研究、跨境河流开发国际公约分析研究等工作。

(二) 澜沧江水电开发对下游影响研究结论

1. 下游水资源利用

(1) 澜沧江占湄公河流域总面积的 22.2%，径流量仅占 13.5%，湄公河径流量主要集中在中、下游地区，占 86.5%。

(2) 澜沧江水电梯级开发，不存在水量消耗和跨流域引水，梯级水电开发不会对境外水资源利用产生影响。

2. 出境流量及下游航运

(1) 澜沧江水电开发不会改变出境处的总水量，但会在一定程度上改变流量的时空分布。小湾和糯扎渡电站建成后，可以把汛期部分水量拦截在库内，以减少下泄洪水流量，到枯期下泄，以增大枯期下泄流量。这对湄公河的枯季航运、灌溉、防止海水入侵以及汛期防洪等具有积极意义。但因澜沧江占湄公河水量很小（仅占 13.5%），这种作用仅局限在出境河段。

(2) 2000 年 4 月，中、老、缅、泰四国签订了澜沧江—湄公河通航协议。2001 年 6 月 26 日，澜沧江—湄公河国际航道正式通航。目前，由于现天然河流水深较浅，枯水季节航运受到较大影响，只能季节性通行 300t 以下的小型船只。小湾、糯扎渡电站建成后，将增加河流枯水季节的流量，对澜沧江—湄公河的航运发展、改善航运条件是十分有利的。同时，为减少景洪等电站调峰运行造成的水位波动，已考虑景洪电站运行时设置一定的航运基荷，并决定投资 60 多亿元兴建橄榄坝电站。通过橄榄坝水库的反调节，使澜沧江下游的流量均匀下泄，满足航运对水位、流量及流速变化等要求。在橄榄坝电站建成投产前，通过对景洪电站的运行限制和设置航运基荷来解决上述问题。

(3) 为进一步避免和减少电站蓄水和调度运行可能对下游产生的影响，在澜沧江出境口建成了水文监测站，积极推进橄榄坝反调节水库建设，配合有关部门制定澜沧江流域调度管理规定。

3. 出境泥沙

根据流域泥沙监测资料，湄公河流域的主要产沙区是清盛至琅勃拉邦河段区域，该区域位于老挝北部。澜沧江梯级电站建成后，出境泥沙将有较大减少，但澜沧江出境后近 200km 河段是典型的山区性河流，河床基岩出露，抗冲刷性好。研究表明，在近坝河段，河床的冲刷深度在 1m 左右，随着时间的增加，河床逐渐形成粗颗粒的抗冲保护层，达到新的冲淤平衡。

出境泥沙变化对洞里萨湖和湄公河三角洲地区渔业的影响，因其距离有 2000 多千米，且湄公河的主要产沙区位于老挝北部，梯级水电开发出境泥沙变化对下游的影响很小。

4. 下游水质

水电属清洁能源，在生产过程中不产生污染物质，河流水质主要取决于污染物的排放量和排放浓度。根据近年来的水质监测资料，出境断面水质满足《地表水环境质量标准》（GB 3838—2002）Ⅲ类标准，符合《云南省地表水功能区划》要求。

5. 下游鱼类

(1) 根据调查，澜沧江—湄公河流域绝大部分鱼类分布在湄公河中下游。澜沧江上有鱼类 130 种，占湄公河流域鱼类总数的 10%，现已发现的芒科洄游鱼类 4 种，主要分布在下游地区，偶尔上溯到上游支流补远江产卵。

(2) 一般来讲，电站建设对鱼类的影响因素有大坝阻隔、水流形态变化、下泄低温水等，这些因素影响鱼类的迁途、饵料来源、产卵、栖息地及生存生境。影响范围主要是开发河段及下游一定区间，对出境后的湄公河无影响。

6. 洞里萨湖

洞里萨湖是湄公河流域重要的汛期与枯期水量自然调节区，也是东南亚最大的淡水湖。湖区渔业和湖周农业是柬埔寨的经济基础。要维护湖区渔业，最重要的是要求湄公河上游有相当的洪水来量，使汛期有一定的洪泛面积。研究表明，老挝是下湄公河主要的径流补给区，且多暴雨，其汛期巨大的区间洪水补给量，远远超过澜沧江梯级电站的调洪能力，是洞里萨湖洪水的主要来源。

虽然小湾和糯扎渡水库在汛期会削减部分洪峰流量，但出境水量仍然是汛期大、枯期小，且澜沧江出境处的年平均径流量仅占湄公河入海口处的13.5%，影响的河段范围也十分有限。澜沧江出境处距离洞里萨湖还有2000多千米的天然河道，湄公河流域的降雨量远大于上游澜沧江，流域内天然洪水本身也有较长的错峰时段，因此澜沧江水电不会改变洞里萨湖的洪水现状，不影响湖区渔业生产。

（三）澜沧江水电开发采取的环境保护措施

（1）调整开发规划及开发目标，减少对下游的影响。根据洄游鱼类调查研究成果及澜沧江水电开发环境影响评价，重新研究澜沧江下游最后一个梯级——勐松电站的开发建设问题。在景洪电站下游设置反调节水库，将原规划的以发电为主的橄榄坝电站，建成以反调节为主的电站，以保护下游水生生态环境，确保河道通航要求。

（2）采取分层取水措施，降低下泄低温水影响。糯扎渡电站水库总库容237.03亿m^3，具有多年调节能力。水库水温属稳定分层型，下泄低温水对鱼类的生长繁殖有不利影响。为了减缓工程建设对鱼类的影响，在工程设计中，将发电取水采用分层取水方式，提高下泄水水温。目前采用叠梁门取水方式，增加工程投资2.4亿元。

（3）采取鱼类增殖、栖息地保护、网捕过坝等措施，保护鱼类资源。为保护澜沧江珍稀濒危鱼种和土著鱼类，在糯扎渡和功果桥电站业主营地内，分别建设人工鱼类增殖放流站，用于鱼类增殖放流和技术研究。下一步还将在橄榄坝电站建设一座鱼类增殖放流站。建立包括南腊河和补远江两支流在内的澜沧江橄榄坝至南腊河的鱼类自然保护区，保护鱼类栖息地和鱼类资源。在糯扎渡和功果桥电站采取人工网捕过坝，加强大坝上下游鱼类的基因交流。

（4）采取移栽、建立珍稀植物园和动物拯救站等措施，保护陆生动植物。对工程建设涉及的珍稀濒危植物，采取移栽、采种育苗、种质资源等方式进行保护。在景洪、糯扎渡电站，建立了占地30亩和100亩的珍稀植物园，将库区保护植物移栽入园。针对糯扎渡电站周边野生动物较多的情况，在业主营地建立珍稀动物拯救站，对受伤和幼小动物进行救护。同时加强管理，严禁施工人员乱捕滥猎。在小湾电站，将永平金光寺自然保护区设为野生动物避难所，建立巍山绿孔雀保护点和猕猴保护区。在景洪电站涉及西双版纳自然保护区和纳板河自然保护区设立水上管理站，并建立野生动物饲料基地。

（5）采取水土保持、废水处理等措施，减少施工期间的环境影响。对施工弃渣规划专门的堆放地点，采取挡护、排水、护坡、绿化等措施进行治理，严禁乱倒弃渣和沿江弃渣。对场内外公路、土石料场、施工场地等区域，施工结束后，进行清理平整，植树种草，恢复植被。对砂石料加工系统废水进行沉淀处理，对混凝土拌和系统废水进行中和沉淀处理，生活污水采用成套一体化污水处理设备，机械维修废水采用隔油池处理，医疗废水进行消毒处理。对施工人员产生的生活垃圾，在糯扎渡和功果桥电站建设专门的卫生填埋场，景洪电站运至景洪市垃圾填埋场处理。

（6）为了从法律角度规范和控制电站的调度运行，国家有关部门正在制订《澜沧江流域调度管理条例》。

（7）在澜沧江出境处设立水文环境监测网站，全面监测河流的水文状况和水质情况，为分析对下游的影响研究，优化梯级电站的调度运行提供科学依据。目前，澜沧江出境处的关累综合监测站已于2006年底建成，正在全面开展各项环境监测工作。

（华能澜沧江水电有限公司　黄光明
王烈恩　彭　新　王海龙）

向家坝水电站工程环境保护实施情况

向家坝水电站装机容量6400MW，工程下游左岸为四川省宜宾县安边镇，右岸为云南省水富县县城。坝址距云天化生活区直线距离700m，地下厂房尾水渠距云天化小学约100m，距云天化厂区直线距离1700m，距长江上游珍稀、特有鱼类国家级自然保护区的河道距离1.8km。工程建设十分重视环境保护工作。

截至2009年底，向家坝水电站施工区已建成并投入运行的环境保护工程如下：

（1）金沙江溪洛渡向家坝水电站珍稀特有鱼类增殖放流站于2007年12月正式开工建设，占地面积2.67hm^2，2008年7月底正式建成，随后引进鱼苗进行了养殖繁育，取得了良好的效果，并分别于2008年和2009年成功举行放流仪式，放流鱼苗共计5万多尾。

（2）截至2009年底，施工区已绿化面积92.2hm^2，网格梁植草护坡面积16.63hm^2，TBS和CBS液压喷播植草护坡面积7.97hm^2，绿化美化工程使施工区生态景观焕然一新。

（3）马延坡砂石加工系统废水处理工程 2007 年 10 月与工程建设同步实施，并与工程运行同步投入运行，使向家坝工程施工区近 70%的生产废水都得到了很好的处理，实现了废水零排放，马延坡砂石加工系统废水处理工程是向家坝环保工程的亮点。

（4）田坝生产废水处理工程（$200m^3/h$）首次在水电行业采用“DH 高效旋流净化器＋真空带式过滤机”处理方案处理混凝土生产系统废水，2008 年 9 月底建成并投产使用，相关设备运行基本正常，废水经过处理后出水悬浮物≤70mg/L。扩建工程 2009 年 11 月底开工，工程按 $450m^3/h$ 处理能力进行安装建设。

（5）莲花池生活污水处理厂 2007 年 8 月投入运行，采用 DAT-IAT 工艺，处理规模为 $5000m^3/d$，向家坝工程 94%的生活污水在此得到集中处理后排放，各项指标均符合《城镇污水处理厂污染物排放标准》（GB 18918—2002）一级标准中的 B 标准。

（6）施工区各生产系统累积配备的 38 套除尘设施运行状况良好，施工现场无明显扬尘产生；开挖爆破过程中制定合理的施工方案，对大型钻机安装收尘装置，采用湿法爆破方案等有效地控制了粉尘的产生和飘移；道路除尘保洁使施工区主要交通干道近 30km 路面始终保持干净、通畅、无扬尘，有效地保护了施工区空气质量。

（7）田坝区 200m 声屏障试验工程 2009 年 1 月建成，根据监测值对比分析，施工噪声控制效果显著。540m 声屏障扩建工程于 2009 年 12 月建设完成，总长度达 740m 的隔声屏障将有效地降低施工噪声对水富县城的影响。

（8）金沙江干流施工区江段水质监测，施工区两岸大气、噪声、生产废（污）监测，施工区爆破控制安全监测，施工区疫情（左岸）监测，水土保持监测都依据环评报告书监测工作内容、监测频率开展了相关的工作，监测数据为向家坝水电站环境污染的控制，工程环境管理、环保工程竣工验收提供可靠的资料。

向家坝水电站在环境保护管理中所开展的工作，得到了相关政府部门的广泛认可。2008 年 10 月 30 日，由长江水利委员会水土保持局、云南省水利厅和水保处、四川省水土保持局等多家单位组成的专家组对向家坝工程截流前水土保持执行情况进行了检查。检查组对工程建设中已建成的水土保持设施和向家坝工程建设中水土保持工程建设、管理、监理、监测等工作给予了高度评价。

2008 年 12 月 6 日，环境保护部环境评价管理司组织了金沙江向家坝水电站工程截流前环境保护执行情况专项检查，环境保护部、西南环保督察中心、水电水利规划设计总院、四川省环境保护局、云南省环境保护局等多家单位参与了此次检查。检查组认为：向家坝水电站在有序开展工程建设的同时，高度重视环境保护工作，环境管理体系健全且运行有效，严格执行了“三同时”制度，在工程截流前完成了《金沙江向家坝水电站环境影响报告书》及其批复意见要求的各项环保工作。

2009 年向家坝工程在做好环保水保工程建设外，同时加强对已建环保工程的运行管理，并坚持作好了信息报送、月例会、环保工作考核、环保合同项目完工验收等工作，得到了云南省昭通市人民政府的充分肯定。

（中国水电顾问集团中南勘测设计研究院 冯云海）

金沙江白鹤滩水电站“三通一平”水土保持工作

（一）工程概况

白鹤滩水电站是我国继三峡、溪洛渡之后的又一座千万千瓦级的巨型水电站，坝址位于四川省宁南县白鹤滩镇与云南省巧家县大寨乡交界处，是金沙江下游河段规划的 4 个梯级电站中的第二级，上接乌东德，下邻溪洛渡。库区涉及四川省宁南县、会东县和云南省巧家县、会泽县、禄劝县、昆明市东川区等 6 个县（区）。白鹤滩水电站以发电为主，兼有防洪、拦沙、发展库区航运和改善下游通航条件等综合利用效益，是西电东送骨干电源点之一，具有装机容量大、工程量少、水库淹没损失小、技术经济指标优越、效益十分明显等特点，是“世界上不可多得的极其优越的能源点”。

白鹤滩水电站工程等级为一等，属大（1）型工程，电站装机容量 14 000MW，多年平均发电量 602.4 亿 kW·h，正常蓄水位 825m，死水位 765m，水库为年调节水库，正常蓄水位对应库容 190.06 亿 m^3，死库容 85.70 亿 m^3，调节库容 104.36 亿 m^3，防洪库容为 75.00 亿 m^3。工程投资 682.06 亿元，计划 2020 年首批机组发电。

白鹤滩水电站枢纽包括挡水坝、泄洪消能设施、引水发电系统等主要建筑物。挡水坝坝型采用混凝土双曲拱坝，最大坝高 277m；枢纽采用分散泄洪、分区消能的布置方式；引水发电采用全地下首部开发方式，左右岸各布置 8 台机组。

（二）“三通一平”工程

白鹤滩水电站“三通一平”工程涉及四川省宁南县和云南省巧家县，项目组成包括 6 部分，即主体准备工程（三通一平工程施工所涉及的坝肩区域的边坡整治等工程)、场内交通工程、弃渣场、表土堆存场、施工临时设施、移民安置等;土石方开挖总量为2942.24万m^3,填筑总量为1192.45万m^3,弃渣总量为1749.79万m^3。采用封闭施工管理方式,封闭区面积14.12km^2, “三通一平”工程占用面积为861.57hm^2。至规划水平年2010年,“三通一平”工程生产安置人口为2572人,搬迁(生活)安置人口为2929人,移民安置区占地596.66hm^2。“三通一平”工程投资为50.94亿元,计划2010年开工,2013年完工。

(三)前期工作水土保持

金沙江流域开发规划源于20世纪50年代,水利部长江水利委员会、中国水电顾问集团昆明勘测设计研究院、中国水电顾问集团成都勘测设计研究院及中国科学院等单位做了大量的勘测、规划和设计工作。1990年7月,国务院批准了水利部长江水利委员会《长江流域综合利用规划简要报告》,报告提出了将金沙江下游河段分为乌东德、白鹤滩、溪洛渡、向家坝4级开发的梯级规划,明确了金沙江中下游河段的开发任务。从2000年开始,中国水电顾问集团华东勘测设计研究院(以下简称华东院),自筹资金启动了预可行性研究工作,作为项目支持全面开展水文、水能和地质勘测等基础性工作。2002年1月,水电水利规划设计总院开展白鹤滩水电站预可行性研究勘察设计招标,确定华东院承担白鹤滩预可行性研究勘察设计任务。2002年11月30日,国家计划委员会在金沙江溪洛渡和向家坝水电站建设第一次协调会议上,明确白鹤滩水电站的项目业主为中国长江三峡集团公司,同时与华东院签订了《金沙江白鹤滩水电站预可行性研究合同协议书》。2005年,受业主委托,华东院全面开展白鹤滩水电站可行性研究工作。同年8月,《金沙江白鹤滩水电站水土保持方案大纲》通过咨询。2006年5月,《金沙江白鹤滩水电站预可行性研究报告》通过水电水利规划设计总院会同四川、云南两省发展改革委的审查。2007年3月和11月,完成了《金沙江白鹤滩水电站可行性研究正常蓄水位选择专题报告》、《金沙江白鹤滩水电站可行性研究回水计算分析专题报告》,水电水利规划设计总院会同四川、云南两省发展改革委对报告进行了审查。2007年8月,《金沙江白鹤滩水电站可行性研究阶段选坝报告》通过审查。2007年11月,《白鹤滩水电站可行性研究阶段施工总布置规划专题研究报告》通过审查。2008年1月,为了满足白鹤滩水电站开工建设要求,完成《金沙江白鹤滩水电站可行性研究阶段筹建期工程初步规划报告》。2008年10月,根据水利部《关于加强水电建设项目“三通一平”工程水土保持工作的通知》(水保[2007]86号)的要求,华东院编制完成《金沙江白鹤滩水电站“三通一平”工程水土保持方案报告书(咨询本)》,随后通过中国水利水电建设工程咨询公司组织的咨询。根据咨询意见,华东院修编完成《金沙江白鹤滩水电站“三通一平”工程水土保持方案报告书(送审稿)》。2009年5月22日,水电水利规划设计总院在北京主持召开《金沙江白鹤滩水电站“三通一平”工程水土保持方案报告书(送审稿)》技术评审会议,会后于2009年9月编制完成《金沙江白鹤滩水电站“三通一平”工程水土保持方案报告书(报批稿)》。2009年底,《金沙江白鹤滩水电站“三通一平”工程水土保持方案报告书(报批稿)》已上报水利部批复。

(四)水土流失防治方案

工程区属国家级和省级水土流失重点治理区,水土流失类型以水力侵蚀和重力侵蚀为主。左岸宁南县水土流失以中度、强烈侵蚀为主,并伴有滑坡、泥石流等极强烈和剧烈侵蚀;右岸巧家县境内水土流失以轻度和强烈侵蚀为主。工程水土流失防治标准执行建设类项目一级标准。“三通一平”工程水土流失防治责任范围面积2016.01hm^2,扰动原地貌面积1458.23hm^2,损坏水土保持设施面积1353.67hm^2(其中宁南县975.94hm^2,巧家县377.73hm^2);可能造成的水土流失总量约190.48万t,新增水土流失总量178.94万t;产生水土流失的重点时段为施工期,主要部位为弃渣场、场内交通等区域。

工程水土流失防治分为6个防治分区,分别为Ⅰ区主体准备工程防治区、Ⅱ区场内交通工程防治区、Ⅲ区弃渣场防治区、Ⅳ区施工临时设施防治区、Ⅴ区移民安置防治区、Ⅵ区其他封闭区防治区。水土保持措施主要包括:主体准备工程防治区的边坡防护、大寨沟泥石流治理、各开挖边坡的截排水设施及植物措施;场内交通工程防治区的拦挡、排水、护坡等防护措施以及植物措施、临时措施和散落浮渣清除;弃渣场防治区的沟水处理、坡面水处理及拦挡防护、场地排水、堆渣要求以及后期迹地恢复;施工临时设施防治区的边坡防护、场地防护、排水、沉沙、绿化以及表土堆存场防护措施;移民安置防治区的拦挡、排水、沉沙、绿化以及临时措施;其他封闭区防治区的退耕还林、移民搬迁之后的建设用地以及原有未利用地和疏林地进行生态修复、原有林地的封禁治理等。水土保持总投资119 439.70万元,其中主体已列水土保持投资16 794.16万元,水土保持工程专项投资102 645.54万元。

预期在方案各项措施实施后,扰动土地整治率为100%,水土流失总治理度100%,土壤流失控制比1.07,拦渣率达99%以上,林草植被恢复率100%,林草覆盖率34.86%,各项水土流失防治指标均能达到方案防治目标要求，工程区水土流失及其危害得到有效治理，生态环境得到恢复，并同时具有一定的生态效益、社会效益和经济效益。

（中国水电顾问集团华东勘测设计研究院 杜运领）

锦屏二级水电站弃渣场防护

锦屏二级水电站工程设计，在各阶段方案分析、比较、拟定中都将水土保持、环境保护内容纳入工程主体设计中。弃渣场作为水土保持工作的重点，在工程前期勘察、规划、预可行性研究阶段作为主体工程方案比选的重要分项内容开展了大量的选址分析、比较工作。可行性研究阶段，对弃渣场选址、防护措施设计等内容进行了进一步加深、细化。经多阶段分析比较后，锦屏二级水电站工程最终拟定了4处弃渣场，分别是东端的模萨沟弃渣场、海腊沟弃渣场、楠木沟弃渣场，以及西端的磨子沟弃渣场，规划弃渣量分别为920.00万m^3、443.00万m^3、7.00万m^3和203.00万m^3，总占地面积43.76hm^2。锦屏二级水电站招标、技施阶段，随着工程设计的深入，工程根据实际情况对弃渣场防护进行了专项设计。

（一）弃渣场选址

经多次分析，最终选定的模萨沟弃渣场位于大水沟厂址下游右岸约6km模萨沟内，选定的海蜡沟弃渣场大水沟厂址上游左岸约6km的海蜡沟内，选定的楠木沟弃渣场位于大水沟厂址上游雅砻江右岸楠木沟内，选定的磨子沟弃渣场位于西段闸址下游左岸约5km的磨子沟内。工程弃渣场选址相对合理、科学。

（1）选址考虑合规性，符合相关法律法规、规程规范要求。工程选定的弃渣场均未设置于河道、湖泊、建成水库内，下游无重要建筑物、居民点及学校、厂矿等敏感设施。经地质勘察，各弃渣区未发现滑坡、泥石流等不良地质现象。

（2）考虑了与工程施工组织衔接要求。工程弃渣场设置时主要从地形、堆渣条件、渣料来源和渣量等方面综合选择弃渣位置，同时为提高土石方综合利用率、减少工程占地，部分弃渣场兼为中转料场，堆渣平台设置骨料加工系统、混凝土拌和系统等施工场地，如模萨沟弃渣场1430.00m、1496.60m平台设置中转堆料区、混凝土骨料加工系统，加工利用土石料。4个弃渣场皆为沟道型弃渣场，沟口狭窄。沟道内堆渣区开阔，沟道坡降小，容渣量较大，堆渣条件优越。各出渣点距渣场较近，弃渣运距在0.5～5km之间，运距合理，且弃渣运输均有较好的道路条件，交通便利。

（3）考虑了环保生态要求。4个弃渣场弃渣区现有土地利用类型以灌草地为主，耕地仅占15%，且单位面积平均堆渣高度较大，避免分散零星堆放，减少了占地特别是耕地占用。4个弃渣场选择荒沟，堆渣条件较好，堆渣区“口小肚大”，容渣量大，堆渣有一定的裕度，拦挡防护工程量及投资小。

（二）防护措施设计

（1）工程防护措施安全到位。由于4个弃渣场均为沟道型弃渣场，为保证渣场排水顺畅、渣体稳定，堆渣前首先进行沟水处理，渣场上游侧设置挡水坝和排水洞，排导沟水。堆渣坡面设置马道，堆渣区两侧设置排水沟，渣体底部按原有沟道设置盲沟，排导渣体渗水。弃渣场坡脚设置挡渣墙，挡渣墙下游侧抛填块石。模萨沟、海腊沟和磨子沟3个弃渣场弃渣规模皆百万立方米以上，弃渣规模大，根据《水电枢纽工程等级划分及设计安全标准》（DL 5180—2003）、《水电建设项目水土保持方案技术规范》（DL/T 5419—2009）等规程规范要求，结合主体工程等级和弃渣规模，确定挡渣水坝（挡渣墙）、排水隧洞按为4级次要永久性建筑物标准设计，防洪设计标准采用50年一遇，并按100年一遇防洪标准校核。楠木沟弃渣场弃渣量相对较小，周边和下游无重要防护设施，挡渣墙和排水涵洞按5级次要永久性建筑物标准设计，防洪设计标准采用20年一遇，按50年一遇防洪标准校核。工程拦挡排水措施安排在前期进行，保证弃渣时弃渣场能够满足各项防护要求，以达到水土保持先拦（排）后弃的施工时序要求。

（2）渣面防护及时跟进，以生态恢复为主。弃渣场按1∶1.7～1∶1.8的堆渣坡比进行堆渣，分层压实，要求其相对密实度不小于0.6，每隔15～20m高程设置4～5m宽马道。渣场按规划堆渣完成后，及时进行渣面绿化，恢复植被，以减少弃渣裸露时间和水土流失。结合堆渣实际情况分阶段实施绿化，做到堆完一级，绿化一级。绿化前渣面表层下部设置碎石土垫层、上部覆耕植土，以提高渣面保土保水性。绿化方式根据现场实际情况采用撒播灌草＋鱼鳞坑整地、穴植乔灌木、培育生态林或浆砌石框格植草护坡等多种形式，努力营造生态型渣场。同时，工程根据弃渣场不同情况进行渣面防护，模萨沟弃渣场为沟道临河型弃渣场（其余渣场为一般沟道型渣场），堆渣起坡高程为1336.00m，渣场临河侧100年一遇洪水位为1342.85m，工程对1345.00m高程以下渣面采取2m厚混凝土护坡，1355.00m高程以下渣面设置土工格栅护坡，加筋固土，加强渣面防护效果。1355.00m高程以上渣面，以生态恢复为主。

（3）防护措施考虑地域特殊性。锦屏二级水电站项目区属干热河谷气候，降雨较为集中，年蒸发量大，且弃渣场立地条件较差，为提高渣场植物措施后期效果，渣场排水与蓄水相结合，在渣场合适的平台位置、渣场两侧排水沟内侧设置蓄水池，为渣场后期灌溉、植物养护提供条件。

（中国水电顾问集团华东勘测设计研究院　应　丰）

光照水电站进水口分层取水工程

为减轻北盘江光照水电站工程建设对其下游河段水生生物的不利影响，原国家环保总局提出应采用分层取水的要求。依据此要求，光照水电站于2007年9月建成进水口六孔叠梁门后置分层取水工程。

（一）工程简况

六孔叠梁门后置分层取水工程的结构布置为：在原单层进水口的基础上向上游延长11.5m，主要由直立式拦污栅、叠梁闸门、喇叭口段、检修闸门段等组成。进水口底板高程670m，顶部平台高程750.5m，与右岸上坝公路连接。进水口前缘总宽度75.5m，顺水流向长度34m。进水口设1道直立式拦污栅，拦污栅共14块，每块宽度3.5m，拦污栅顶高程746m，高76m。在拦污栅与检修闸门之间设置4个钢筋混凝土隔墩，隔墩底部高程670m、顶部高程750.5m，垂直水流向宽度为4.95m、顺水流向长度为6.5m；隔墩之间设置横向钢筋混凝土联系梁，隔墩与拦污栅墩净距3m、与进水室胸墙净距8m；隔墩水流向设钢筋混凝土支撑梁与拦污栅墩及喇叭口胸墙连接。沿进水口中心线设钢筋混凝土隔墙，隔墙底部高程670m，顶部高程750.5m，将进水口分为2个相对独立的对称的进水室。4个隔墩与进水口两侧的边墙及中间的隔墙形成6个高程670～750.5m的取水口，每个取水口宽度为7.5m，取水口内布置叠梁钢闸门，叠梁门分为20节，每节门高3m，最高门顶高程730m，底槛高程670m，水库表层水通过取水口叠梁门顶部进入取水道，门顶最低运行水深15m。在进水口紧贴大坝处设1个叠梁门库，门库底板高程685m，顺水流向长15.58m，垂直水流向宽10.8m。引水隧洞进水口喇叭口段长12m，上缘采用1/4椭圆曲线，两侧采用1/4圆曲线，喇叭口中后段设1道检修闸门，闸门尺寸8m×10.4m（宽×高）。

（二）工程运行说明

六孔叠梁门后置分层取水工程的运行原理是：叠梁门和钢筋混凝土墙挡住水库中下层低温水，水库表层水通过取水孔叠梁门顶部进入引水道，根据水库运行水位变化提起或放下相应数量的叠梁门，从而达到引用水库表层水，提高下泄水体水温的目的。叠梁门操作采用2×320kN门机启闭，根据水库水位的涨落情况控制叠梁门的启闭，工程主要运行方式分为以下几个程序阶段：

（1）当光照水电站水库水位下降，水位低于745m（正常蓄水位）高程时，打开第一节叠梁门，使库水位在745～742m运行。

当水库水位低于742m时，打开第二节叠梁门，使库水位在742～739m运行。

（2）按水库水位每降低3m打开1节叠梁门，依次打开第三节、第四节、第五节……，以满足分层取水发电的水位高于叠梁门顶15～18m的要求。

（3）当水库水位上涨时，根据叠梁门顶的水深情况进行控制，当叠梁门门顶水深超过15m时，依次放下1节叠梁门，保证门顶水深控制在15～18m运行，其操作方式与水库水位下降时相反。

（三）工程运行效果预测

根据水温预测，光照水电站进水口六孔叠梁门后置分层取水工程运行后，水库全年平均下泄水体水温14.6℃，比原方案提高了3.1℃。水库下泄水体水温1月略高于天然水温，2月在10km内恢复到天然水温，3月、10月、11月、12月下泄水体水温分别在120km、110km、90km、30km处恢复到天然水温，其余各月下泄水体水温在60km处恢复到16～19℃，120km处恢复到18～22℃。

（四）维护与管理

六孔叠梁门后置分层取水工程可实现单元独立供水，检修时只需部分停机，进水室水流对称平稳，水头损失较小，产生的年电量损失相对较少，运行操作灵活，能根据水库水位变化情况控制从水库表层取水发电，有效减小水库运行时下泄低温水对下游生态的影响。

（五）结语

为对光照水电站进水口六孔叠梁门后置分层取水工程的实际运行效果进行深入研究，为其他水温分层型水库工程的下泄低温水不利影响减缓措施的设计提供参考，目前，光照水电站已展开其水库库区水体水温分布及水库下泄水体水温的科研工作，为类似工程的进一步推广应用积累资料和工程技术经验。

（中国水电顾问集团贵阳勘测设计研究院　陈　凡）

贵州北盘江水电开发两生态保护项目简介

北盘江属珠江流域西江水系，为红水河上游左岸的最大支流，发源于云南省曲靖市马雄山西北坡，流经云南、贵州两省，于贵州省望谟县蔗香与西来的南盘江会合，会合后称为红水河。1988年12月编制的《北盘江干流（茅口以下）规划报告》，明确了该河段的规划方案为：光照(745m)＋马马崖(580m)＋董箐(490m)方案。光照水电站位于北盘江中游，是北盘江上最大的一个梯级水电站，也是北盘江干流茅口以下的龙头梯级水电站，水库正常蓄水位745m，相应库容31.35亿m^3，水库淹没面积为51.54km^2。马马崖水电站位于光照水电站下游，两级开发方式均为坝后，其中一级水库正常蓄水位585m，相应库容1.365亿m^3，水库淹没面积为6.45km^2；二级水库与一级相衔接，正处于规划阶段。董箐水电站位于光照水电站下游，主要任务是发电，其次是航运，开发方式为坝后式，水库正常蓄水位490m，相应库容8.82亿m^3，水库淹没面积为24.14km^2。

为减轻北盘江光照水电站工程建设对生态环境的不利影响，环境影响报告书及批复意见要求光照、马马崖、董箐梯级水电站联合修建鱼类增殖放流站与采取珍稀古大树移栽措施。为此，光照水电站于2007年8月组织相关人员进行了珍稀古大树移栽，而光照、马马崖、董箐鱼类增殖放流站也于2008年4月在光照水电站正式开工。

（一）鱼类增殖站

1. 场地选择

由于光照水电站已经基本完工，部分营地和施工场地开始撤离现场，同时考虑管理的方便和梯级电站的衔接，因此将鱼类增殖站选择在光照水电站营地范围内。

2. 总体布局

增殖站建设分办公区、孵化培苗车间区、亲鱼及大规格苗种饲养区。主要设施包括蓄水池、孵化培苗车间、孵化设施、供电设施、增氧设施、办公用房、道路、捕捞设施、亲鱼培育池、苗种培育池、排灌系统、滚水坝等，增殖站建成后，具有从亲鱼饲养到大规格鱼种培育的一整套人工繁育系统。在设计规划上，一方面考虑增殖站功能的需要；另一方面兼顾环境的美化。整个增殖站用铸铁花栏杆进行封闭，对外形成透视。站内种植四季常青的树木和草皮，绿化面积不少于40%。

3. 放流对象

从技术角度考虑，增殖放流按先易后难的原则进行，同时根据鱼类资源监测结果及水库鱼类资源状况，逐步调整增殖放流对象。近期，优先选择人工繁殖已获成功，不存在增殖放流技术瓶颈的鱼类。

4. 放流点位

根据鱼类对生境的要求，放流地点的选择需避开坝址下泄水所造成的气体过饱和及下泄低温水影响河段。同时，应根据放流鱼类对生境的要求，将放流点设置于库区干支流交汇处，以保证放流鱼类的成活率。

5. 放流数量

从经济合理性角度出发，综合考虑养殖场地、苗种成本、成活率及放流最低需求等多种因素，初步确定放流数量为60万尾/年，苗种规格控制在全长5～12cm。

6. 科研及监测

为保证增殖放流任务顺利完成，并达到放流苗种在自然环境中的存活、繁衍，需进行相应技术的科技攻关研究。为满足日后放流效果评价监测的需要，放流前还需进行放流苗种标志技术的研究。该方面的研究可为建立标准化放流程序奠定基础。

（二）珍稀古大树移栽

1. 移栽保护措施

天然生长的树木大部分生长在森林生态环境中，移植后不适应小气候生态环境，成活率较低。移植大树，要遵循植物生长的自然规律进行，才可收到较好的成活效果。大树移植必须做好：

(1) 掌握大树生物特性、生态习性及大树来源地、种植地的土壤等环境因素。

(2) 准备好必须的机械设施、人力及辅助材料，并实地勘测行走路线，制定出详细的起运栽植方案。

(3) 预先进行疏枝、短截及树干伤口处理，以及栽植地树穴的处理。

(4) 挖掘大树时，首先保证根系少受损伤。

2. 成活保障措施

(1) 选择合适的水电站营地为移栽的地点，以便于移栽后的管护；营地海拔高度和环境须与需移栽植物生长地的环境相近，保证成活的条件。

(2) 选择有实力、有大树移栽经验的单位承担移栽工作。

(3) 移栽后必须进行一年的管理抚育，包括浇灌、遮盖、防止病虫害及其他自然的不利因素，防止人为破坏等。

（中国水电顾问集团贵阳勘测设计研究院　陈　凡）

滩坑水电站工程水土保持设计、监理和监测工作

（一）水土保持设计

滩坑水电站位于浙江省丽水市青田县。2002年6月，滩坑水力发电厂建设筹备处委托中国水电顾问集团华东勘测设计研究院（以下简称华东院）承担《浙江省瓯江滩坑水电站工程水土保持方案报告书》（以下简称《报告书》）的编制工作。2003年3月华东院编制完成了《报告书》送审稿，并于2003年8月2日通过了水电水利规划设计总院主持召开的技术审查会；根据技术评审意见，编制完成了《报告书》报批稿，2004年3月水利部予以批复。工程开工建设后，

建设单位于2006年12月委托华东院进行滩坑水电站水土保持专项设计工作。水土保持设计人员进场后，结合滩坑水电站施工实际情况，在水利部批复的水土保持方案报告书的基础上，对滩坑水电站的水土流失防治措施体系进行了相应的调整，对主要的变更进行了招标、技施后续阶段的水土保持设计，并提供了相应的设代服务。水土保持方案报告书为可行性研究阶段编制的成果，电站开工建设以后，部分主体工程根据实际情况发生了一些设计变更，相应的水土保持工程也随之变更，且变更设计的设计标准不低于批复的水土保持方案报告书的设计标准。与批复的《报告书》相比，滩坑水电站工程在实际施工过程中，水土保持工程变更的原因可以归纳为两种：①因为主体工程设计发生变更而引发的水土保持工程设计变更；②根据主体工程施工的实际情况，对方案报告书中的水土保持设计进行补充、完善和优化的水土保持工程设计。根据相关法律法规的规定，水土保持工程设计与水保方案差别较大时，相应的变更应按规定报水行政主管部门备案。为此，华东院于2009年9月编制完成了《浙江省瓯江滩坑水电站工程水土保持工程设计变更方案》；同月，浙江省水利厅组织召开变更方案审查会，并形成了会议纪要。华东院根据会议纪要，修改完善了《浙江省瓯江滩坑水电站工程水土保持工程设计变更》，并上报浙江省水利厅备案。

（二）水土保持专项设计内容

水土保持专项设计主要内容为坝址下游河道岸坡水土保持工程。根据《浙江省滩坑水电站下游河道防洪影响评价》分析结果，确定坝址下游河道岸坡的堤线。在满足河道防洪、电站泄洪、岸坡冲刷的前提下，采用生态河道的理念，构建河道生态系统。各段岸坡防护设计如下：

（1）左右岸交通桥下游左岸至电站永久办公区段岸坡。护坡型式选择斜坡式堤，坡比为1∶1.3，断面设计分为护坡和护脚。护坡采用两种类型，分界线高程根据20年一遇防洪水位计算得出，此高程以上采用浆砌石拱形骨架植草护坡，以下采用干砌石护坡。护脚相应采用C15细骨料混凝土挡墙和混凝土脚槽两种型式。

（2）左右岸交通桥上游左岸至溢洪道出口段岸坡。护坡型式选择斜坡式堤，堤身分为两部分，分别为护坡和护脚。护坡采用干砌石护坡和浆砌片石拱形骨架植草护坡两种类型相结合的方式，坡比为1∶1.3，护脚采用重力式挡墙＋抛石护脚方式。

（3）泄洪洞至溢洪道左岸边坡。护坡根据地质情况划分为两个部分进行防护，上游段边坡坡脚基岩外露，坡脚采用混凝土挡墙拦挡防护，坡面和坡顶采用乔灌草绿化；下游段边坡坡脚基础为松散的堆积料或为砂砾石层，地基承载力低，坡脚拟采用植生铅丝石笼沉排防护，坡面和坡顶采用三维网植草护坡和乔灌草绿化方式进行防护。

（4）左右岸交通桥下游右岸岸坡。根据现场地形特点并结合生态护坡设计理念，岸坡坡比为1∶2.0，与河床水面相接处设置休闲平台，平台可采用鹅卵石或水泥砂浆嵌砌鹅卵石铺设道路，路边种植亲水性小乔木，上下通行采用条石踏步，坡脚和坡面采用植生铅丝石笼护底＋三维网植草护坡，20年一遇防洪水位以上采用草皮护坡，在局部坡脚可适当堆置一些大块石以模拟自然河道和防止洪水冲刷。

（三）水土保持监理工作

2006年10月，浙江北海水力发电有限公司委托华东院承担该工程水土保持监理工作。接到任务后，华东院组织专业技术人员进驻工程现场，并设立水土保持监理部（以下简称监理部），实行总监理工程师负责制。

1. 监理部主要工作情况

（1）依据有关法规、规范与水土保持方案报告书及相关批复要求，结合工程实际编写了《水土保持监理实施细则》，作为开展监理工作的指导。同时制定了《监理人员工作职责》、《现场监理工作纪律》、《监理报告制度》、《监理往来函件管理制度》等一系列监理部管理制度，规范了监理工作。

（2）发文要求工程水土保持相关参建单位设置分管领导和专职管理人员，并召集专题会议，建立联系人机制，协助业主建立健全水土保持组织机构。

（3）提交监理部总结的《水土保持法律、法规汇编》，协助业主完善项目水土保持管理制度。

（4）组织、开展水土保持知识宣讲，举办了滩坑水电站工程水土保持知识讲座。走访主要施工单位，宣传水土保持法规和理念，交流建设中存在的水土保持主要问题，听取施工单位对水土保持工作的建议。

（5）定期组织召开水土保持专项监理例会，对水土保持工程建设中存在的问题进行专项协调解决。同时，定期参加由建设单位、工程建设监理单位定期召开的工程建设进度协调会、防汛会及其他有关会议，沟通、协调并解决工程施工过程中存在的水土保持问题，确保工程施工安全和防治水土流失。

（6）及时巡查现场，对施工中存在的水土流失问题下发通知单要求责任单位立即予以整改、完善；对重大问题及时以联系单上报建设单位，与参建各方及时沟通，协调、解决水土流失问题。

（7）协助建设单位对尚不能满足验收要求的水土保持设施召开专项整改会议，审查施工单位上报整改实施方案，督促施工单位进行整改完善，保证水土保持设施尽早落实到位，发挥防治效益。

（8）通过现场详查，对工程水土保持设施进行了分析、评估，补充编制《工程开工后至监理部进场前水土保持阶段性补充调查报告》。提交水土保持监报告，共计提交阶段性补充报告1期、监理季报13期、监理年度报告4期，为工程水土保持专项设施竣工验收积累了充分的过程资料。

（9）对具备验收条件的水土保持设施，依据《开发建设项目水土保持设施验收技术规程》（GB/T 22490—2008）开展水土保持专项自查初验。在验收前指导施工单位进一步完善水土保持实施、整理汇编专项验收资料。协助建设单位组织召开水土保持专项验收会议，对验收材料进行审查、验收，并形成水土保持设施验收鉴定书。完成“滩坑水电站范村埠营地场地平整工程、左岸公路护坡和挡墙工程”等单位工程的水土保持专项验收。

（10）协助业主和设计单位对工程实施过程中发生的重大变更编制变更报告上报浙江省水利厅备案。协助建设单位迎检，协助建设单位编制迎检汇报材料，参加了2008年1月28日、2009年12月29日等两次由浙江省、丽水市、青田县三级水利部门对工程监督检查的迎检，均顺利地完成配合工作。

2. 水土保持设施竣工验收准备

2009年5月，为满足项目水土保持竣工验收要求，对工程现场进行详查、整理水土保持资料、组织技术人员召开专题会议研讨，从项目水土保持工作程序闭合情况、工程现场符合验收要求情况和水土保持档案资料完备情况等方面，对现状、尚存问题方面进行了分析，并提出了解决对策，形成《浙江省瓯江滩坑水电站工程水土保持设施竣工验收前需落实的补充完善措施意见》，并提交建设单位，促进了水土保持专项设施验收工作的开展。

3. 水土保持工程质量及防治效果

枢纽防治区所采取的各项防护措施，在稳定边坡、保证主体工程安全的同时，也起到了有效的水土保持作用。未产生滑坡、崩塌等水土流失现象，无重大水土流失问题发生。临时设施防治区的水土保持设施正常运行。交通道路防治区水土保持措施在工程准备期已修建并投入使用。场内公路已完成的防护工程运行状况良好。周转料场、弃渣场防治区设置挡渣墙、排水系统，起到了防治水土流失的作用。移民安置防治区已实施的措施，不仅起到了排水、拦挡、固土等水土保持作用，而且美化了居住区环境。已实施的各项水土保持措施在水土保持监理的配合下，一并由主体工程监理单位（中国水利水电建设工程咨询西北公司滩坑监理中心）验收合格。

（四）水土保持监测工作

2006年，浙江北海水力发电有限公司委托华东院承担本工程的水土保持监测工作。

1. 监测内容

（1）水土流失影响因子：地形地貌，降水，防治责任范围，扰动地表面积，项目挖填方、弃渣量等。

（2）水土流失状况：水土流失面积变化情况，水土流失量变化情况，对下游和周边地区造成的危害及趋势等。

（3）水土流失防治效果：防治措施的数量、质量、完好程度和运行情况，林草措施生长及覆盖情况，防治措施的拦渣保土效果等。

2. 监测方法

（1）地形地貌：根据地貌类型区和小地形地貌部位划分指标确定监测区类型，采用现场调查和相关资料收集的方法确定。

（2）降水：主要包括年降水量、年内分布及暴雨情况，通过向设置在坝址下游约2km处的巨浦水文站收集的方法获取。

（3）水土保持设施：通过现场调查及查阅相关资料的方法，对工程区范围内的各项水土保持设施数量、面积等进行量测。

（4）侵蚀形式：各个部位采用现场调查的方法确定，动态适时监测，定期或不定期对各个侵蚀部位的侵蚀形式情况进行调查。

（5）流失量：对于水力侵蚀，在上述侵蚀模数测定的基础上，实地量测各个部位的侵蚀面积，从而计算水土流失量。对于侵蚀沟流失量推测，也可根据现场侵蚀沟形状、尺寸等指标现场测定，直接计算土壤流失体积，然后利用土壤容重换算土壤流失量。对于重力侵蚀，则根据实际调查量测侵蚀的方量，根据测定的土壤容重换算土壤流失量。

（6）水土保持设施及其防护效果：水土保持设施的规格、数量、破损情况、保护维修等，依据设计方案和相关技术规范要求，采用实地调查量测和查阅施工、监理等相关记录的方法进行确定。防护效果则根据上述侵蚀模数、流失量等指标测定反映。根据上述监测内容相关监测方法设计，其中地形地貌、降水、水土保持设施数量、侵蚀形式、防护效果等指标以调查监测为主，流失量等指标以地面观测为主。同时，在地面观测和调查监测的基础上，采取定期或不定期场地巡查的监测方法。

3. 监测结果

截至2009年底，项目实际防治责任范围共计7982.99hm^2，较方案报告书及批复所列的8026.81hm^2减少43.82hm^2。各监测分区皆已扰动，累计扰动原地貌面积约为7655.13hm^2。工程产生弃渣、周转料共计约167.67万m^3，分别堆放在范村、堰前与郎回坑弃渣场、周转料场以及角湾、滩坑沟周转料场。实施的水土流失防治措施有：锚杆支护、边坡喷混凝土、干砌石护坡、挡墙、截、排水沟、挡水堰、挡渣墙、钢筋石笼防护、种树植草绿化等。已完成的水土保持设施基本运行正常，发挥了水土保持作用。随着防治措施的实施，水土流失面积及水土流失量减少。根据现场调查和水土保持监测的结果，项目区采取的各项水土流失防护措施基本运行正常，基本控制了项目防治责任范围内的水土流失，有效地发挥了水土保持作用，未对下游及周边地区的生态环境造成危害或不良影响。

（中国水电顾问集团华东勘测设计研究院
苏　展　康致远）

桐柏抽水蓄能电站水土保持设施验收

桐柏抽水蓄能电站位于浙江省台州市天台县，为日调节纯抽水蓄能电站，装机容量4×300MW，平均年发电量21.18亿kW·h，年抽水用电量28.13亿kW·h，属一等大（1）型工程。工程于2000年12月开工，2006年12月建成并投入运行。该工程按照水利部《开发建设项目水土保持设施验收管理办法》及《开发建设项目水土保持设施验收技术规程》（GB/T 22490—2008）规定，于2007年12月～2008年12月开展并完成了水土保持设施专项验收工作。主要情况如下：

1. 水土保持方案编报审批

2000年6月，建设单位华东桐柏抽水蓄能发电有限责任公司委托中国水电顾问集团华东勘测设计研究院承担桐柏抽水蓄能电站工程水土保持方案编制工作。2001年12月，水利部以水保监便字［2001］第64号批复《浙江桐柏抽水蓄能电站工程水土保持方案大纲》；2002年12月，水利部以水函［2002］136号批复《浙江桐柏抽水蓄能电站工程水土保持方案报告书》。

2. 水土保持监测与监理

2003年5月，建设单位华东桐柏抽水蓄能发电有限责任公司委托杭州华辰生态工程咨询有限公司开展桐柏抽水蓄能电站工程水土保持监测工作。这是华东地区首个开展开发建设项目水土保持监测工作的项目。监测单位定期向各级水行政主管部门报送水土保持监测月报和年报，并于水土保持设施验收前提交了水土保持监测总结报告。在工程施工初期，建设单位委托主体工程施工监理单位浙江华东工程咨询有限公司一并承担水土保持监理工作。监理单位于水土保持设施验收前提交了水土保持监理总结报告。

3. 水土保持工程设计与落实

工程建设期间，建设单位严格按照水土保持方案、法律法规及规程、规范要求，与主体工程同步开展了水土保持工程的专项设计工作。并在施工过程中，按水土保持要求落实了水土保持设计内容及要求，确保了水土保持设施的如期建设。同时，针对弃渣场、料场等重大设计变更，向浙江省水利厅及时进行汇报，并报送《关于上报〈浙江桐柏抽水蓄能电站水土保持变更报告〉备案的请示》（桐电字［2008］46号），对水土保持设计变更进行了备案。

4. 水土保持设施自查初验

工程于2007年初投入试运行后，建设单位随即组织设计、施工、监测、监理等单位开展了水土保持设施自查初验工作；2008年3月，编制完成《浙江桐柏抽水蓄能电站水土保持方案实施工作总结报告》和《浙江桐柏抽水蓄能电站水土保持设施验收技术报告》，为后续水土保持设施验收技术评估工作的开展奠定了基础。

5. 水土保持设施验收技术评估

（1）2007年12月，建设单位委托中国水利水电建设工程咨询公司开展工程水土保持设施验收技术评估工作。

（2）2008年1月，评估单位经全面查阅相关资料和工程现场首次核查后，按照验收要求提出了《浙江桐柏抽水蓄能电站水土保持设施验收补充措施意见》。

（3）2008年3月，建设单位完善了相关水土保持措施，评估单位随即对照批复的水土保持方案报告书，从设计和实际两方面，对水土流失防治责任范围、水土保持措施工程量、水土保持投资等方面进行了对比评价。同时，通过查阅工程质量检验评定资料和现场核查，对水土保持工程质量进行了评定；通过现场调查，对水土保持措施布局进行了调查评价；通过查阅资料和调查询问，对水土保持监理、水土保持监测工作的开展情况，水土保持效果等进行了评价；开展了公众满意度调查。2008年4月，编制完成了《浙江桐柏抽水蓄能电站水土保持设施验收技术评估报告》，作为水利部进行行政验收的技术支撑文件。

（4）2008年4月，评估单位完成了向水利部太湖流域管理局和浙江省水利厅对工程水土保持设施验收的征求意见工作。

6. 水土保持工程质量评价

（1）根据《开发建设项目水土保持设施验收技术规程》（GB/T 22490—2008）规定，技术评估工作中水土保持工作质量评价内容主要包括施工工艺的先进性，水土保持措施布局的合理性，施工原材料、隐蔽工程、分部、单位工程质量的合格率及外观质量，以及水土流失防治效果等方面。

(2) 评价方法采用内业和外业、抽查和详查相结合的方法进行。内业通过查阅工程施工记录、原材料试验报告、监理质量检验评定资料进行核实。外业在全面普查的基础上，先确定重点评估范围和其他评估范围、重要单位工程等，确定核查对象、核查内容及核查比例后，全面调查各项水土保持措施的外观质量和关键部位的几何尺寸。其中，工程弃渣场区和临时设施区作为重点评估范围；其他区域作为其他评估范围；弃渣场防护，下水库开关站区、业主营地、上库进出水口区、中转料场、施工布置区、上库环库公路区等绿化工程作为重要单位工程。重点评估范围单位工程全部查勘、分部工程抽查核实比例达到50%，其他评估范围单位工程查勘比例达到50%，分部工程抽查核实比例达到30%，重要单位工程全部查勘，其分部工程抽查核实比例达到50%。

(3) 评估组核查了工程包含的22个水土保持单位工程及其所属的36个分部工程，单位、分部工程核查率100%，单位、分部工程质量全部合格，工程质量评定为合格，满足水土保持设施竣工验收条件。

7. 水土保持监测工作评价

(1) 工程水土保持现场监测时段为2003年6月～2007年12月，监测方法采用地面观测和调查监测相结合。地面观测采用在下库弃渣场坡面监测小区、弃渣场沉沙池、简易观测场、上水库排水渠出口和下水库排水渠出口等进行监测采样，调查监测以现场巡查和内业资料查阅为主。

(2) 监测结果显示：工程实际水土流失防治责任范围面积161.94hm^2，监测期累计造成土壤流失量为6.40万t，上、下库区排洪渠出口累计输沙量为0.52万t，占流失总量的8.1%。监测期内，各年度平均土壤侵蚀强度均大于项目区容许土壤流失量500t/(km^2·年)，但总体呈逐年下降趋势。至运行初期，土壤侵蚀强度降至215t/(km^2·年)。

8. 水土流失防治指标

扰动土地整治率为95%，水土流失总治理度为90%，土壤流失控制比为2.3，拦渣率达99%，林草植被恢复率为96%，林草覆盖率20%。

9. 行政验收

2008年12月28日，水利部在天台县召开了工程水土保持设施竣工验收会议。会议认为：桐柏抽水蓄能电站水土保持方案审批及设计变更备案手续完备，开展了水土保持后续专项设计、监测和监理等工作，资料齐全；在工程建设和试运营阶段，积极开展了水土流失防治工作，水土保持设施已按批准的水土保持方案报告书和设计文件的要求建成，质量合格；扰动土地整治率、水土流失总治理度、土壤流失控制比、拦渣率、林草植被恢复率和林草覆盖率等指标达到了设计要求；水土保持设施具备正常运行条件；运营期管理维护责任已得到落实，同意水土保持设施通过竣工验收。

(中国水电顾问集团华东勘测设计研究院
李　健　江　涛)

周公宅水库水土保持工程设计

一、概况

周公宅水库位于浙江省东部沿海宁波市鄞县章水镇周公宅村，距宁波市区51km。工程以供水为主，结合防洪、发电等综合利用。总库容11 180万m^3，属大(2)型水利工程。

周公宅水库建设开发有限公司于2001年5月委托浙江省水利水电勘测设计院编制工程水土保持方案。2001年10月，浙江省水利水电勘测设计院最终完成了本工程水土保持方案报批稿，并得到了水利部的批复。

在工程建设过程中，主体设计单位中国水电顾问集团华东勘测设计研究院受建设单位委托，先后编制完成《宁波市周公宅水库水土保持工程设计报告书》、《宁波市周公宅水库工程枢纽防治区、临时设施防治区水土保持工程补充设计报告》及《宁波市周公宅水库进石料场道路上下边坡治理工程设计报告》等相关设计报告。周公宅水库水土保持专项工程于2007年5月2日正式开工，2008年10月底完工，并于2009年通过水利部竣工验收。

根据水利部批复的水土保持方案，水土流失防治责任范围包括项目建设区和直接影响区，共计88.43hm^2。其中，项目建设区63.81hm^2，包括坝址区、厂址区、施工道路、辅助企业及施工生产生活区等；直接影响区24.62hm^2，包括水库库岸区、移民安置区、专项工程改建区、管理区(宁波)。结合周公宅水库工程的施工总布置、建设时序及可能造成水土流失的部位特点，周公宅水库水土流失防治责任范围划分为枢纽防治区、石料场及弃渣场防治区、道路防治区和临时施工设施防治区，并对各防治分区进行防护、治理工程措施设计。

二、防治措施设计

(一) 枢纽区

1. 大坝区域

大坝基础开挖完成后对建基面上下游两侧边坡进

行锚杆、素喷混凝土、挂网喷混凝土等方式进行支护。

2. 进水口洞脸及上游右边坡

引水洞进口开挖边坡为1∶0.25，洞口削坡自上而下进行，及时处理洞脸危石，采用钢筋网，随机锚杆和喷射混凝土等坡面加固措施，并对洞脸两侧和坡顶设置排水孔。进水口上游边坡形状为V形冲沟，坡比为约30°，在施工期间为了保证施工安全和边坡稳定性，临时采取干砌石护坡措施，并在两侧设置排水沟，在施工期间起到一定安全效果措施。由于水库蓄水后长期位于水位以下，为了满足大坝下闸蓄水后的长期稳定，后经过设计变更对该施工部位要进行浆砌石护坡，要求边坡两侧排水沟加固加宽，并在岩石表面布置埋设排水管，呈梅花形。

3. 大坝左右岸238.17m高程以上边坡

按永久边坡进行支护，及时采用锚杆、素喷及挂钢筋网喷混凝土支护措施。配电房上游冲沟边坡采取浆砌石护坡永久支护，坡面埋设排水孔，坡角设排水沟。

4. 水垫塘及坝后雾化区

143.13m高程以上根据清理后的边坡地质条件稳定性进行支护，主要采取锚杆及喷混凝土，局部进行C15混凝土护坡；先清理边坡岩石表面石渣，并且要清洗边坡岩石表面，然后进行挂网、钻排水孔。

5. 二道坝

开挖分为左、右岸2个区进行施工。各区开挖施工时，按自上而下分层开挖的方式进行。分层高度为3m左右。边坡开挖后，将边坡上的浮石撬除，并将岩石清理干净，对局部不稳定的岩石进行锚杆支护。

6. 厂房后边坡

发电厂房后边坡及两侧边坡为Ⅹ级砂质岩，开挖坡度1∶0.3，顶高程118.13m，底高程为107.83～106.13m，开挖形成后，用C20混凝土浇筑挡墙护坡，并在挡墙底部增设200mm×400mm的排水沟。在高程118.13m设一道宽2.5m宽的马道，高程118.13～135.13m开挖边坡采用M10浆砌石护坡处理。在浆砌石护坡以上至上坝公路段边坡坡积层较厚，采用砌M10浆砌石花格防护，花格内回填种植土栽种植物。

（二）石料场及弃渣场区

1. 厂区弃渣场

总面积约6700m^2，弃渣堆放量5.7万m^{3}左右。为了防止弃渣流失影响河道，对该段河道设置浆砌石挡墙防护，挡墙顶宽40cm，底宽300cm，M10浆砌石二层挡墙，挡墙基础为360cm宽、50cm厚C20混凝土。为了满足水保和绿化作用，采用挖掘机平整堆渣上部，平整完毕后覆盖种植土，以满足种树要求，根据实际地形分块、分区进行种植。

2. 库区弃渣场

位于库区上游右岸楼梯弄采石场下游，与采石场下方弃渣相连，蓄水后位于水位线以下。为了保证岸场的长期稳定，在蓄水前进行整治，主要对边坡进行修整，坡脚用干砌石挡墙进行防护。

3. 楼梯弄石料场

距坝址0.8km，开采高程在240～330m，开挖面积6.67hm^2，在水库正常蓄水位以上，北部和南部山坡各有一条小溪沟。由于石料开采现场形成3个平台，防治实际面积28 388m^2。用挖掘机对防治范围进行挖填平整，对渣体坡面进行修坡至1∶1.75～1∶2.0,加强其稳定性能，并在边坡上部修筑干砌石挡墙防止耕土流失。共设干砌石挡墙10道，总长1537m，干砌石排水沟5道，总长417m。后边坡坡角底部也增设干砌石排水沟，并连接北侧排水沟，防止了雨水对耕土冲刷。在北部小溪进行浆砌石排水沟砌筑，顺延至水库。石料场在耕植回填完后经检验收合格进行植物种植，分别在5个台阶种植乔木，铺设马尼拉草皮，对边坡部位进行撒播草籽，并在后边坡坡角处种植爬山虎。

（三）道路区

工程开挖前，清除地表杂草、碎石及表土层，对道路两侧边坡的松散土体进行拍实处理，松动的块石及时清除。施工开挖过程中，控制爆破范围和强度，避免因爆破导致坡面松动失稳，引起滑坡。路堑开挖边坡根据开挖面地质条件，形成合适的坡度，土质边坡要求1∶1以上，强风化岩面坡度1∶0.75，弱风化岩石边坡1∶0.5～1∶0.3。同时，加强路堤、路堑坡面的防护，按照设计、施工与养护相结合的原则，采取综合防护措施，如喷浆、抹面、挡土墙、砌石护坡等措施，确保路基、坡面的稳定。做好排水设施，在道路路堑边坡的坡脚设置临时排水设施，从而避免坡面形成的水流对路基及其边坡的冲蚀。对施工后继续利用的部分道路，路肩栽植行道树，以乔木为主，树种选用香樟。采用护坡绿化技术，对采取路堑裸露面全程进行垂直绿化，绿化植物选用攀缘植物爬山虎，沿公路内侧路堑坡脚单行种植，株距1m。具有一定土层的路堤、路堑边坡采用喷播草种进行绿化，草种选用狗牙根。施工结束后不再利用的施工便道，以乔灌草相结合恢复植被，乔木选用湿地松和枫香，灌草采用胡枝子、狗牙根和白三叶进行混播，既防止水土流失，又起到恢复植被、改善生态环境和美化景观的作用。

（四）临时施工设施区

治理范围共分为9个地块（分别为3～9号、11号、13号），主要范围有：位于右坝头公路右侧，原缆机平台下方，沿通往轧石场道路路边区域；右坝头、缆机平台两侧，原拌和楼平台以南区域；原为砂石料堆场、轧石场平台、库内右岸等主要防治区域。工程措施主要进行地面平整清理，砌干砌石挡墙，按设计要求内容进行回填耕植土。植物措施主要在耕植土回填完成后结合地块区域，乔灌木结合进行绿化，靠山侧附近珊瑚树与爬山虎结合进行种植绿化。沿库岸侧种植垂柳，间距5m，局部地表铺植马尼拉草皮，其他地块结合区域进行乔灌木结合方式绿化。

三、投资与成效

根据周公宅水库工程水土保持专项设计及水土保持竣工验收相关资料，本工程实际完成的水土保持投资1768.86元，包括主体工程中具有水土保持功能的投资244.81万元（其中工程措施124.18万元，植物措施120.63万元），新增的水土保持措施实际投入1523.05万元（其中工程措施1235.82万元，植物措施84.42万元，临时防护工程25.22万元，独立费用77.43万元，水土保持设施补偿费100.16万元）。

根据水土保持监测结果，工程建设区域采取了边坡防护、拦挡、排水、土地整治和绿化等防护措施，分区水土保持措施适宜，水土保持工程的总体布局合理，各项水土保持设施运行情况良好，起到了较好的水土保持作用。水土流失防治6项指标——扰动土地整治率、水土流失总治理度、土壤流失控制比、拦渣率、林草植被恢复率、林草覆盖率均达到了相应的防治目标要求。

（中国水电顾问集团华东勘测设计研究院 丰 瞻）

龙开口水电站开展施工期环境保护与水土保持监理工作

（一）概况

龙开口水电站位于金沙江中游河段，属云南省鹤庆县朵美乡中江办事处辖区，是规划的金沙江中游河段8个梯级电站中的第六级，上接金安桥电站，下邻鲁地拉电站，坝址以上流域面积约24万km^2。电站距鹤庆县公路里程约100km。

电站工程开发任务主要为发电，兼顾灌溉、供水等综合利用，主要由枢纽工程、施工辅助工程、水库淹没及移民安置等项目组成。枢纽工程主要有挡水建筑物、泄洪冲沙建筑物、右岸坝后式引水发电系统及左、右岸灌溉取水口、电站办公生活区及配套设施等。施工辅助工程包括导流工程、场内道路、料场、弃渣场、施工临时设施等。

水库正常蓄水位1298m，相应库容5.07亿m^3，调节库容1.13亿m^3，库容系数0.21%，装机容量1800MW，保证出力710.6MW，在龙盘电站投入后年均发电量为82.7亿kW·h。工程为一等大（1）型工程，永久性主要水工建筑物挡水建筑物、泄洪及冲沙建筑物、引水发电建筑物为1级建筑物。永久性次要水工建筑物为3级建筑物。工程计划总工期为88个月。

工程2007年下半年开展筹建期“三通一平”工程施工，包括建设场内道路、交通桥、砂石料加工系统、炸药库、油库、业主营地、承包商营地、机电设备库、供水、供电及通信工程、枢纽区征地及移民安置等工程，2009年1月完成了大江截流。

建设单位重视工程环境保护与水土保持工作，在主体工程可行性研究阶段同步委托中国水电顾问集团华东勘测设计研究院承担龙开口水电站工程环境影响评价与水土保持方案的编制工作。2007～2009年，陆续编报完成了《云南省金沙江龙开口水电站工程水土保持方案报告书》、《金沙江龙开口水电站环境影响报告书补充报告》及各专题报告。

建设单位依据《金沙江龙开口水电站工程环境影响报告书（报批稿）》及相关许可、《云南省金沙江龙开口水电站工程水土保持方案报告书（报批稿）》及其批复（水利部水保函［2008］354号）等要求，组织了项目环境保护与水土保持工程的实施，并委托云南省大理州鹤庆县环境监测站承担工程的环境保护监测工作、云南省水利科学研究院承担工程水土保持监测工作、中国水电顾问集团华东勘测设计研究院承担工程环境保护与水土保持监理工作，保证了项目环境保护与水土保持工程的正常实施。

（二）环境保护现状调查

环境保护现场调查主要对现场的水环境、大气环境、声环境和固体废物等设施进行调查。水环境调查包括砂石料加工系统废水处理设施、二次筛分系统废水处理设施、混凝土系统废水处理设施、左右岸施工工厂区废水处理设施和生活污水处理设施等；大气环境调查包括砂石料加工系统粉尘削减与控制措施、交通粉尘削减与控制措施、施工现场扬尘控制等；环境噪声调查包括砂石料系统噪声控制措施、交通噪声控制措施等；固体废物处置调查包括生活垃圾处置和建筑垃圾处置。水土保持现场调查分区进行，按枢纽工程、场内道路、弃渣场、料场、施工临时设施进行调查。枢纽工程区调查包括水土保持工程实施情况，开挖边坡稳定、防护效果及危害，弃渣清运及临时措施实施等；场内道路区调查包括道路边坡开挖、防护情况，临时挡墙实施，坡面清渣和坡面防护，耕植土剥离防护及道路绿化等；弃渣场调查包括弃渣场启用，弃渣堆放，弃渣场拦挡、排水等防护措施实施，弃渣场绿化等；料场调查包括料场扰动原地表，开采边坡，挡墙、护坡、排水等防护措施实施，土石渣清运，临时堆土的防护、开采迹地的绿化情况等；施工临时设施调查包括挡墙、护坡、排水等防护措施的实施情况，临时办公区、堆存场地绿化，耕植土剥离及防护等。

（三）环境保护设施

筹建期砂石料加工系统废水处理设施，布置在上游右岸岸坡，系统由粗、细两部分加工系统构成，工作时间两班制，利用废水处理能力为 300m^3/h 的回用系统设施使工程产生的废水 190m^3/h 回用，不外排。燕子崖砂石料加工系统废水处理设施，布置于坝址下游中江河右岸燕子崖，已设置废水处理 1 套，主要设施包括沉淀池、斜管沉淀池、石粉回收车间、污泥干化池和清水回用装置，系统废水计划处理后回用于本系统，不外排。C2 标二次筛分系统废水处理设施，布置在右岸，主要废水处理设施包括初沉池、二沉池和清水回用装置，C3 标二次筛分系统废水处理设施布置在右岸，包括沉淀池和清水回用装置，利用废水处理能力为 100m^3/h 的回用系统设施使工程实际产生的废水 100m^3/h 回用，不外排。混凝土系统废水处理设施，共有 3 处，包括左岸公用混凝土系统、C2 标混凝土系统和 C3 标混凝土系统废水独立处理设施，3 个混凝土系统均为 3 班制，冲洗废水在时间、水量上有很大的相似性，因此在废水处理方案上采用同一种处理方案，即废水经沉淀池沉淀后，用清水回用装置重新回用。3 处废水回用处理设施处理能力为 410m^3/天的系统设施，使其实际产生的废水 850m^3/天回用，不外排。生活污水处理设施，完成业主营地生活污水处理设施、1 号和 2 号承包商营地生活污水处理设施、燕子崖承包商营地生活污水处理设施、加油站生活污水处理等。采用单套设施处理能力为 2m^3/h 地埋式污水成套设施、单套废水处理量为 20m^3/h 成套污水处理系统等，处理后的水主要用于周围绿化灌溉。大气污染防治措施，砂石料加工系统粉尘削减与控制措施、施工区道路非雨日经常性进行洒水降尘等。环境噪声污染防治措施，选用了低噪声的设备和工艺，对振动大的设备如砂石料系统中的振动筛等通过使用减振机座或减振垫，从源头上降低了噪声；在施工时间上也作了合理安排，避免了在夜间（22：00～6：00）进行生产活动；在交通沿线部分敏感区段设置了限速标志。固体废弃物处置措施，各参建单位都设置了垃圾池（桶），统一收集后，运送至垃圾临时堆放场进行处理；建筑垃圾主要采取了能回用的基本回用，不能回用的由各施工单位自行整理堆放。垃圾填埋面积约 4 万 m^2 的垃圾填埋场已建成投入运行，鱼类增殖站在建。

（四）水土保持设施

枢纽工程区，实施了挡墙、截排水沟、左右岸开挖边坡喷锚支护、框格植草护坡等水土保持措施。场内道路区，实施了地表硬化、截排水沟、边坡防护及道路绿化，并对临时道路实施了钢筋石笼、干砌石挡墙等临时拦挡措施。弃渣场区，工程规划布置有 1～7 号弃渣场和燕子崖弃渣场共 8 个弃渣、倒运场。本阶段，1、2 号弃渣场取消；3～5、7 号弃渣场位于水库淹没区内，其中 3～5 号弃渣场现已开始弃渣，弃渣沿江侧坡脚实施了钢筋石笼拦挡防护，7 号弃渣场暂未开始堆渣；6 号弃渣场位于淹没区外，堆渣完成并实施了护坡、挡墙、排水及绿化等措施；燕子崖弃渣场位于石料场开挖区，共设置两处，拦挡防护措施随主体工程分阶段实施。料场区，工程设置燕子崖石料场 1 处，开挖料现在燕子崖砂石料场进行筛分处理，砂石加工系统场地部分边坡已采取框格梁护坡或喷混凝土护坡，坡脚设置了钢筋石笼拦挡并设置沉砂池对泥沙进行沉淀。施工临时设施区，左岸布置的 1、2 号承包商营地已实施护坡、拦挡、排水和绿化等防护措施，现已投入使用中；右岸布置的砂石料筛分系统、设备堆场、混凝土搅拌系统等均已建成投入使用，结合场地情况实施了护坡、挡墙、排水等措施。

（五）监理工作情况

龙开口水电工程筹建处在筹建期施工建设过程中，认真贯彻和落实有关法律法规，按环境保护与水土保持相关设计积极开展工作，相关设计和审批手续基本完备，通过施工合同及工程监理手段，指导承包商按照环境保护和水土保持“三同时”制度的要求，实施相关环境保护与水土保持措施；委托开展了环境保护与水土保持监理和监测等工作；环境保护与水土保持管理机构、制度和人员落实，资料登记建档与使用流程较规范；环境保护与水土保持监理进场后在委托合同与《工程环境保护监理与水土保持监理规划》框架开展工作；建立健全了监理内部制度；开展技术培训，组织编印《工程环境保护与水土保持监理指南》、《环境保护与水土保持法律法规汇编》，并向相关参建方宣贯；通过现场旁站、巡视监理和工程监理例会、专项监理例会的协调管理完成实现监理目标；采用工程师指令、监理联系单、通知单处理解决现场监理事务，使环境保护与水土保持专项工程质量、进度和投资得到有效控制；经现场调查完成《云南金沙江龙开口水电站工程施工期环境保护与水土保持工程监理阶段调查报告》，以指导后期的相关工作；按月（季、年）提交《工程环境保护与水土保持工作月（季、年）报》。目前，建设单位在已进行的筹建期工程建设中，积极开展环境保护和水土流失防治工作，建成的相关设施达到了设计文件和有关技术规范、标准的要求。建成的设施已运行可具备正常运行条件，运行管理维护责任落实。多数已完成的实体工程正在发挥效益。相信在未来的工作中将继续做好工作，完善环境保护与水土保持工程措施，使工程建设与环境保护相协调。

（中国水电顾问集团华东勘测设计研究院 尉全恩）

多自然型河流建设措施的初探

从20世纪的70年代起，一些城市化程度很高的发达国家，如欧美、日本一些国家，开始重视对城市河流湿地的保护，并着手对部分已被破坏的城市河流湿地进行恢复。这些国家在河流环境综合整治中，广泛地采用了“多自然型河流”的建设方法。这种方法是把水边作为多种生物生息空间的核心，并把河流建设成尽量接近于自然的形态，即把自然河流的状况作为样本，在确保防洪安全的基础上，努力创造出具有丰富自然的水边环境，恢复城市河流湿地的自然生态和环境功能。

在我国，河道建设正在经历一个艰难转型。水利河道治理工程如何在满足工程要求的基础上，保持河流的原有的自然生态环境是我们现在面临的问题。

（一）水利工程对河流生态环境的影响

（1）河流形态的均一化和非连续化改变了河流生境多样性。所谓河流形态的均一化主要是指自然河流的渠道化或人工河网化，具体表现为：①平面布置上，河流形态直线化。即将蜿蜒曲折的天然河流改造成直线或折线型的人工河流或人工河网。②渠道横断面几何规则化。把自然河流的复杂形状变成梯形、矩形及弧形等规则几何断面。③河床材料的硬质化。渠道的边坡及河床采用混凝土、砌石等硬质材料。防洪工程的河流堤防和边坡护岸的迎水面也采用这些硬质材料。④河流的裁弯取直。

所谓河流形态的不连续化是指有些工程在河流筑坝形成水库后，导致下游或局部河段的水流在时空上形成的不连续性。有的河流进行梯级开发，更形成河流多级非连续化的格局。水体在水库中形成相对静水，其流速、水深、水温及水流边界条件都发生了重大变化。河流形态的均一化和不连续化导致水库的生态系统比河流的生物生产量低，相对要脆弱，自我修复能力弱。有的水库蓄水后，淹没了原有的河流两岸的陆生植被，使得丘陵和平地岛屿化和片断化，陆生动物被迫迁徙，被搬迁的城镇及废弃的农田沉入库底，这样就改变了生态环境多样性。

（2）河流形态多样性降低，其结果将导致水域生物群落多样性的降低，河流生态系统的退化，使生态系统的健康和稳定性都受到不同程度的影响。水利工程入河流的渠道化和裁弯取直工程彻底改变了河流蜿蜒型的基本形态，急流、缓流、弯道及浅滩相间的格局消失，而横断面上的几何规则化，也改变了深潭、浅滩交错的形式，生态环境的异质性降低，水域生态系统的结构与功能随之发生变化，特别是生物群落多样性将随之降低，可能引起淡水生态系统退化。另外，河床材料的硬质化切断或减少了地表水与地下水的有机联系通道，本来在沙土、砾石或黏土中辛勤工作的数目巨大的微生物再也找不到生存环境，水生植物和湿生植物无法生长，使得植食两栖动物、鸟类及昆虫失去生存条件。本来复杂的食物链在某些关键物种和重要环节上断裂，这对于生物群落多样性的影响是全局性的。

（二）建立多自然型河流的基本原则

（1）恢复河道的原有结构，尽可能地保护河流形态的多样性。在河道整治中，恢复原有区域的结构形态与自然特征是改善水质、回迁原有生物群，特别是重新建立水生生物生态系统等方面取得成功的基础。如果把河道搞成像人工水渠那样单一的断面形状，那么河道内的水也将以单一的形态流动，环境条件就变得十分单一，只能形成贫瘠、不稳定的生态系统。保持河流的蜿蜒性是保护河流形态多样性的重点。在河道整治工程中，尊重天然河道形态，保持河流断面形状的多样性，尊重河流原有的自然断面形态，避免直线和折线型的河道设计。河道整治工程中应尽可能避免采用几何规则断面，疏浚工程施工中避免河道断面的均一化。

（2）使用各种材料，恢复原有自然环境。为了保全河流原有的生态环境，多自然型河道建设要求尽量采用当地已有的植被、石材等自然材料，使建成的河道形态尽量接近于自然的河流。河道防护工程的岸坡采用有利于植物生长的透水材料，特别注意采用当地天然材料，尽可能减少材料之间的不良影响，也要注意整理、发掘和发展传统治河方法和材料。

（3）以人为本，建设生态河堤。生态河堤是以“保护、创造生物良好的生存环境和自然景观”为前提，在考虑具有一定强度、安全性和耐久性的同时，充分考虑生态效果，把河堤由过去的混凝土人工建筑改造成为水体和土体、水体和植物或生物相互涵养，适合生物生长的仿自然状态的护坡。目前世界上一些发达国家都在进行河流回归自然的改造。瑞士、德国等于20世纪80年代末提出了全新的“亲近自然河流”概念和“自然型护岸”技术。所谓“自然型护岸”技术，就是放弃单纯的钢筋混凝土结构，改用无混凝土护岸或钢筋混凝土外覆土植被的非可视性护岸。这些国家普遍认为，保持河道的自然环境对保护动植物资源、保护水质、防止水资源流失都有极为重要的作用。修建生态河堤，恢复河岸植物群落与河畔林，已成为国际上河堤建设的总趋势。

（4）扩大水面和绿地，为生物提供更多的生存区域。对于具有多种多样的、丰富环境条件的河道来讲，如果具备这种条件的区段过短，而且是孤立的话，那么该处的生态系统将十分贫瘠，同样也会威胁物种的生存。但是，如果将这一区段向上、下游延伸，并扩大到支流，增加绿化通道，与岸边绿地、树林之间形成水、绿网络，增强岸边动物栖息地的连续性，那样，生物就可能在该范围内移动，丰富了物种，使整个生态系统变得更加稳定。

（5）确保水的良好循环。水是生命之源，其循环的天然动力是太阳提供的能量。水在大气圈（云、雨）—岩石圈（土壤）—生物圈（动物、植物、微生物）—水圈（地表水、地下水）之间循环，达成动态平衡。水只有能充分良好地循环，自然生态环境才能得以可持续的发展。河道中地表水的来源主要是降水，从地下水渗出进入地表水系的水基本上也来自降水，降水只有在良性的循环条件下才能良性供给河道需要。

（三）多自然型河流建设的基本方法

建立多自然型河流，针对不同的河流，各地有不同的方法。在制定河道规划的时候，在确保防洪治理的安全性的同时，尽量不改变或者少改变已有的良好的生物生息、繁衍环境。

1. 河道形态修复

修复河道形态，即采用工程措施把经过人工裁弯取直的河道修复成保留一定自然弯曲形态的河道，重新营造出接近自然的流路和有着不同流速带的水流，恢复河流低水河槽（在平水期、枯水期时水流经过）的蜿蜒形态，使河流既有浅滩，又有深潭，造就水体流动多样性，以有利于生物的多样性。河道恢复的措施已经比较成熟，可从以下几个方面着手：

（1）拆除废旧拦河坝、堰，将直立的跌水改为缓坡，设置辅助水道，并在落差大的断面设置专门的各种类型鱼道，恢复河道的连续性。

（2）采用植石治理法，即在河底埋入自然石，造成深沟及浅滩，形成鱼礁，有利于形成水的紊流，重现水体流动多样性。

（3）降低滩地的高程，修改堤线，撤去河岸护坡，重现水际线的自然变化，以扩大河道的泄洪和调蓄能力，给河流更多的空间。

其步骤一般是：利用河流地貌学的基本原理，采取各种非结构化或结构化手段让诸如深潭、浅滩、自然形状的河床以及混合的可渗性河底基面等自然河道特征重新形成，或通过保育、恢复措施促进其自我恢复，在此基础之上再进行生物和美学方面的恢复工作。

2. 河床的修复

对于河床的治理可以采取工程措施，主要的方法有：

（1）拆除河床铺设的硬质材料及废旧拦河坝，恢复河底的自然泥沙状态，恢复河道的连续性以利于河底水生生物的生存及河水下渗回补地下水，并可根据情况用植石法设置鱼巢。

（2）部分河段采用复式断面，将不同保证率的河道径流分成数个等级，分级逐步扩宽河道开度，河道的上部平台和上部护坡过流频率较低，裸露时间长，可以种草或栽植低矮乔木，平时作为河道立体绿化的一部分，洪水时期作为临时洪水通道。

3. 河岸护坡的修复

河岸护坡的生态修复方法主要通过改造原有的河道护坡护岸，拆除原有的石块、混凝土结构，将其改造成适合生物生长的仿自然状态的护坡，护岸材料采用具有耐久性、抗侵蚀性、抗冲击性，同时具有渗透性和亲水性材料，最好为天然材料如木桩、竹笼、卵石等。对于坡度缓或腹地大的河段，可以考虑保持自然状态，配合植物的种植，达到稳定河岸的目的，如种植柳树、水杨、白杨、芦苇以及菖蒲等具有喜水特性的植物。对于较陡的坡岸或冲蚀较严重的地段，不仅种植植被，还采用天然石材、木材护底，以增强堤岸抗洪能力。对于防洪要求较高且腹地较小的河段，在必须建造重力式挡土墙时，也要采取台阶式的分层处理，在自然型护堤的基础上，再用钢筋混凝土的材料确保大的防洪能力。

4. 水体的修复

工农业和生活污染是造成水环境污染的主要原因，是对河流健康的最大威胁。现阶段维持城市河流健康的首要任务是水污染治理与控制，改善水质：一是要减少污染物排放，增加水量，稀释水体，输移污染物，提高水体纳污能力，从而提高水环境容量和水环境承载能力；二是要采取工程措施，在河床及护坡种植适量的水生植物（如芦苇、香蒲等）。另外，通过河道河底及坡面表层泥面生长的大量微生物、藻类、水生动植物形成的自然生物膜净化水体，提高河道本身的自净能力，全面提高水环境质量，达到修复与改善水环境的根本目的。

5. 河堤的修复

河堤是河流的组成部分之一，具有廊道、缓冲带和植被护岸等功能。目前，复合式河堤断面越来越得到广泛的运用，即在常年水位以下用现代材料砌筑直立式河堤，以节约用地并保证堤防强度，而在常年水位之上则保留斜坡式土堤并进行绿化，保持河堤及城市的生态性。在河岸带生物恢复与重建的基础上在两岸建立起一定宽度的植被带，发挥河岸带植被护岸功能，是河岸带生态重建的标志，也是河流生态修复的目的所在。在城市河滨地带的生态修复过程中不能简单地加以“绿化”和“美化”，而要从整体上保护和恢复原有的自然生态结构和天然景观，避免过多的人工化。

（中国水电顾问集团西北勘测设计研究院
余晓华 乔 白）

黄河上游已建梯级电站的水环境累积效应

龙羊峡至刘家峡河段开发自1956年刘家峡开工建设至今已有半个世纪，开发的力度随国家经济实力增加而加快，1978～1992年建成了黄河上最大库容的龙羊峡水电站，1988～1998年建成李家峡水电站，2000年以来，相继开工或建成了公伯峡、拉西瓦等大型电站和尼那、苏只等中型电站，河段水电开发格局已基本形成。梯级中具有多年调节能力和年调节能力的龙羊峡、刘家峡水电站已建成并运行多年，对水环境产生的累积影响已逐渐显现。

（一）水文累积效应

龙羊峡至刘家峡河段水文情势变化的内在原因是河段控制性水库的调节作用。龙羊峡是龙—刘河段第一个梯级，1986年10月下闸蓄水，正常蓄水位以下库容247亿m^3，是黄河干流唯一具有多年调节能力的水库。刘家峡是龙—刘河段最后一个梯级，1968年10月蓄水，正常蓄水位以下库容42亿m^3，具有年调节能力。因此，河段水文格局以两个控制性水库的蓄水时间可以划分为3个阶段，即天然状态、刘家峡单库运行状态、龙羊峡建成后龙刘联合调度运行状态。

1. 水库的调节性能特征

水库的调节过程是河段径流、泥沙发生变化的内因。根据对不同时期刘家峡、龙羊峡历年进、出库水量及年内平均各月入出库水量、蓄水位变化的分析，可以得出：在刘家峡单库运行期，其调节方式是蓄丰补枯，按年调节运行；龙羊峡投入运行后，其调节方式与刘家峡单库时基本相同；龙羊峡、刘家峡采取联合调度，刘家峡的调节方式发生改变，与龙羊峡调节方式相比，刘家峡是反调节。

2. 径流变化分析

（1）年际变化。根据对河段各水文站1956～2000年年径流量的分析，除大型水库初期蓄水年份外，龙—刘水库蓄水运用对年径流影响较小，变化趋势主要与来水有关。从3个时期水文站的年平均流量分析，刘家峡单库运行期与天然状态相比，各站流量均增加，增幅相差不大；龙刘联合运行期与刘家峡单库运行期相比，各站流量均减小，并随沿程减少幅度增加（15.6%～21.6%）。

（2）年内变化。刘家峡单库运用时期，出库（小川站）流量发生明显变化。汛期流量减少，由天然情况下占全年的57%减少到48%；非汛期流量增加，由天然情况下占全年的43%增加到52%。龙羊峡水库投入运行后，恰逢黄河上游汛期来水偏枯，以及防凌期和灌溉期向下游大量补水，径流年内分配变化较大。以小川站分析，汛期流量减小，由天然情况下占全年的57%降为39%，非汛期流量增加，由天然情况下占全年的43%增加到61%。

3. 泥沙变化分析

（1）年际变化。根据对河段各水文站1956～2000年年输沙量的分析，大型水库蓄水运用的拦沙作用是非常明显的。从3个时期水文站的平均含沙量分析，刘家峡单库运行期与天然状态相比，含沙量明显降低，下降幅度达81.67%；龙刘联合运行期与刘家峡单库运行期相比，龙羊峡以下贵德、循化站含沙量分别下降86.6%、48.26%。

（2）年内变化。刘家峡水库单库运用期，出库水含沙量较天然明显降低，小川站汛期含沙量为天然情况时的1/4，非汛期为1/10。龙羊峡水库投入运行后，贵德站汛期沙量仅为天然情况下的1/3，小川站为1/2；非汛期贵德站含沙量是天然情况下的1/100，小川站为天然情况下的1/6。

4. 河道形态

梯级水库群后，天然河道段显著缩短，河段长度由天然情况的417km降为已在建梯级形成后的54.2km，河段水面面积显著增加，由天然情况下的60km^2增加为梯级形成后的610km^2，为天然情况下的10倍。对各水库而言，随着运用年限的增加，库区泥沙淤积床面逐步抬高，库区水面较宽段将淤积逐步发展形成滩地，水流趋于天然河道状态。

根据以上分析，龙—刘河段形成梯级水库后，由于大型水库对水沙的调节作用，汛期水量减少，非汛期水量增加，水量年内分配较天然趋于均匀。梯级水库的拦沙作用更加明显，无论汛期、非汛期，含沙量都出现明显减少的情况。河道形态已由天然河流改变为11个首尾几乎相接的人工湖。

（二）水温累积效应

流域梯级开发在改变河道径流的年内分配和年际分配的同时，也改变了水体热量的年内分布，引起水温在沿程和纵向深度上的时空变化，因此，可以从水库及下游河道两个方面水温的变化。

1. 水库水温

（1）龙羊峡水库。根据龙羊峡水库2006年3～10月的水温监测，水温垂向分布的特点是：从3月开始，随气候升高，表层水温日趋升高，表层较高温水层的厚度也日渐增厚，到7～8月表温达到最高（20℃），表层较高温水层的厚度从达到20～30m；随后进入降温期，到10月中旬，表面温度降至15℃，厚度达40m，这期间，库底温度从4.9℃升高到6.8℃，变化很小。水温纵向分布的特点是：龙羊峡坝前呈典型分层现象；大坝至51.37km那让水域，水温呈现分层分布；那让至库尾水域，受来水控制，水库出现温度混合分布，两种水温分布类型转变区域大概在从水库中部。

（2）刘家峡水库。根据刘家峡水库1985年4月～1986年3月的水温监测资料分析，刘家峡水库是混合型水库。水温垂向分布特点是：坝前峡谷段大多月份水温呈混合分布，仅在5、9月呈现一定的分层现象，可能与洮河水体以异重流潜没入水库底层，并向干流库区返流有关；湖泊段水温正分层只在5月比较典型，7、8月水温分布呈现出混合性；各断面库底水温年内变化大（在13.7～18.4℃之间），使垂直温度梯度小，这在大型水库是少见的；库尾峡谷段各月水温呈混合分布。

2. 下游河道水温

水库对水量调节的热量调蓄作用使期对下游河段水温产生了一定的影响，梯级水库联合作用还存在水温的累积效应。

（1）以公伯峡水库下游的循化水温站长系列资料分析天然状态、龙羊峡、公伯峡、刘家峡运行期间的水温变化规律。龙羊峡运行后河道月平均最低水温从0℃升到2.1℃，月平均最高水温从18.1℃降到17.6℃，年平均水温从9.1℃上升到9.9℃，简谐波位向后推迟30天；李家峡水库运行后月平均最低水温升到3.6℃，月平均最高水温降到15.2℃，年平均水温从9.9℃降到9.5℃，谐波位仍与龙羊峡蓄水后一致。可以看出，龙羊峡运行后下游河道水温年较差减小，平均水温有所升高，而李家峡运行后的累积影响，主要是进一步降低了暖季月平均水温，谐波推后现象已不明显。公伯峡水库运行后，河道月平均最低水温较李家峡运行后有所下降，为2℃；最高水温较李家峡投入运行后有所上升，为16.1℃，年平均水温从9.5℃升到9.6℃。根据资料初步判断，公伯峡水库起到了使下游河道水温向天然河道水温回归的作用。

（2）以刘家峡下游小川站水温监测分析天然状态、刘家峡运行后及近年的水温变化规律，刘家峡运行后河道月平均最低气温从0.4℃上升到3.2℃，月平均最高水温由19.2℃降到19.1℃，年平均水温由9.0℃上升到9.9℃。水温最大降幅在4～8月，差值为3～4℃；8月～次年2月，水温明显升高，差值在3.2～5.8℃之间。水温简谐波向后推迟一个月。近年来，受水库运行和洮河来水影响，刘家峡水库泄放水体的温度混合较均匀，使得龙羊峡、刘家峡、公伯峡建成后的累积影响，无论是谐波推后现象，还是月平均水温的升、降幅度，均不如循化断面突出。

（三）水质累积效应

黄河龙羊峡至刘家峡干流河段没有经过大型城市和大面积农业灌溉区，点、面污染源较轻，水质良好，为Ⅰ～Ⅱ类。区间汇入3条较大支流，其中大夏河、洮河污染较重，水质较差。

1. 水库水质

由于水量大、污染少，已建成的各水库水质良好，而刘家峡水库由于库容大、自净能力强，即使汇入大夏河及洮河两条污染较重的支流，水质仍能达到Ⅱ类标准。根据监测，还没有水库发生富营养现象。

2. 河道水质

根据对河段内水质监测长系列资料，分析刘家峡、龙羊峡、李家峡、公伯峡等几座大型水库蓄水后的各水质指标的时间和空间变化规律。

（1）时间变化。由于龙—刘梯级水量调节作用，河段枯水期、丰水期水质变化不很明显。各时期水质单项和综合指标都反映出随着梯级电站建设，即使是在水量偏枯和污染源有所加重的趋势下，河段沿程水质指标变化也趋于平缓并且整体有下降趋势。

（2）空间变化。河段沿程水质变化规律是：龙羊峡断面的水质综合污染指数最低，说明上游段水质良好；经循化断面后，由于沿途接纳了贵德县、循化县生活污水，污染指数略有上升，但循化断面历期综合污染指数下降，说明该时期河段尼那、李家峡、直岗拉卡、公伯峡、苏只等梯级水库的建成对河段污染物起到了拦截作用；在循化断面以下，沿途接纳了零散的生活污水和灌溉退水，同时汇入污染较重的支流大夏河、洮河，但由于刘家峡水库水体的稀释净化以及拦截作用，在刘家峡坝下断面污染指数反而有所下降，说明大型水库对污染物的稀释作用是非常明显的；刘家峡以下干流沿途接纳了污染较重的湟水及几座化工厂的废水，到达新城桥断面时各污染指数上升，但该断面历期综合污染指数下降也说明了梯级水库枯水期下泄水量增多对下游水质的改善起到了一定作用。

（四）结语

通过对黄河干流龙羊峡至刘家峡河段已建梯级电站开发对河段水环境中水文、水温、水质要素的长系列实测资料分析，可以总结出如下的结论和规律：

（1）梯级布局对水环境的影响较大。河段控制性水库的布局和调节方式决定了梯级电站对水文情势的影响作用、范围和程度。龙羊峡作为“龙头”水库，它对整个龙—刘河段，甚至刘家峡以下更长河段的作用和影响都是巨大的。

（2）梯级开发对水文要素（包括径流、泥沙和河道形态）的影响最大，其规律也是普遍的，不同河段（流）仅是变化程度上有所不同。主要的表现是：径流年内分配更趋均化、水库下游含沙量明显减小、天然河流湖泊化、库区淤积有所增加。

（3）水温和水质的影响是基于水文要素影响而产生的。水库水温的性质与水库特性和布局有关，河道水温的变化不一定是同向叠加。

（4）黄河上游污染轻、水量大、自净能力强，水电梯级建设对河段及下游水质呈改善趋势。

（中国水电顾问集团西北勘测设计研究院 寇晓梅 牛天祥 黄玉胜 潘文光 杨忠敏）

龙滩水电工程库区水土保持治理

2009年1月，龙滩水电站库区水土保持治理项目全面启动。为确保项目措施顺利推进，尽快发挥其水保功能，保证2010年顺利通过国家水土保持专项验收，龙滩水电开发有限公司（以下简称龙滩公司）积极与广西、贵州两省（区）水利厅协商，由两省（区）水行政主管部门推荐，分别委托广西壮族自治区水利科学研究院、贵州省水土保持监测站承担龙滩水电站移民安置工程的水土保持治理项目的实施工作（包括项目设计、工程招标、工程监理委托及施工组织管理）。龙滩公司负责项目资金筹措和项目实施协调以及项目综合监理委托；综合监理为中国水利水电建设工程咨询公司；广西、贵州两省（区）水利厅负责项目实施监督。

2009年2月底，贵州省水土保持监测站成立“龙滩水电站贵州库区移民安置工程水土保持治理项目管理部”。将项目按行政管理区域分成了两个标段，通过招标的方式，确定了施工单位。2009年3月底，除部分未整平场地外，贵州项目部完成了全部植物措施的建设，工程措施建设也于2009年底基本完成。贵州库区水土保持项目已完成投资1941.8万元，完成土石方52 641.69m^3；种植水保林、行道树等270 884株，植草绿化365 100m^2。

2009年4月，广西水利科学研究院通过公开招标的方式，确定了广西库区移民安置工程水土保持治理项目4个标段的施工单位。各施工单位与2009年5月进场。截至2009年底，Ⅰ标完成报告设计工程措施的95.9%、植物措施的45%；Ⅱ标完成设计工程措施的79.4%、植物措施的50%；Ⅲ标完成设计工程措施的81%、植物措施的97.24%；Ⅳ标完成设计工程措施的71.4%、植物措施的76%。广西库区水土保持项目累计完成投资1216.4万元，种植行道树、蟛蜞菊等1 025 843株（丛），植草绿化625 079m^2。

由项目业主与省级行政主管部门协商，委托相关水保单位负责库区水土保持项目的组织实施在全国水电行业尚属首次。

龙滩公司在工程建设过程中高度重视环保水保工作，紧紧围绕创建“绿色龙滩”的目标，不断加大环保水保工作的宣传力度，明确参建各方的环保水保职责，健全工程的环保水保管理体系，不断完善和强化环保水保管理工作措施，认真组织环保水保规划设计，严格按国家环保水保要求落实各项环保水保设施，做到了环保水保设施与主体工程建设“三同时”，并率先在国内水电工程建设中开展了环保水保综合监理制度，结合龙滩工程建设实际，不断探索环保水保工作管理新模式，创建了以实现“绿色龙滩”为目标的环保水保“六到位”管理新模式，即加强领导，业主主导，积极协调，强化管理，在环保水保管理工作中努力做到“思想认识、机构人员、管理措施、建设投资、规划设计、综合监理”六到位，实现“绿色龙滩”的目标。

经过7年多的管理工作实践，这一管理新模式对龙滩工程的环保水保建设与管理工作发挥了巨大的推动与促进作用，不但龙滩公司全体干部职工的环保水保思想认识明显提高，环保水保管理工作的成效也显著提高，而且取得巨大的经济效益和环境效益。管理成果的主要内容为：

（1）思想认识到位。其关键点是：在思想上做到了“四个充分认识”，在管理工作中做到了“四个坚持”。“四个充分认识”：一是充分认识到加强环保水保管理工作领导的重要性，即加强领导；二是充分认识到项目业主在环保水保管理工作中的主导作用，即业主主导；三是充分认识到积极、主动地协调好国家、地方各级环保水保行政主管部门、环保水保综合监理、工程监理、施工单位之间的工作关系是做好环保水保管理工作的基本条件，即加强协调；四是充分认识到不断加强对所有龙滩工程参建职工的环保、水保思想教育，强化环保水保观念，是做好环保水保工作的基本保证。“四个坚持”：一是坚持坚决贯彻执行国家的环保水保法律法规，依法建设，依法施工；二是坚持环境影响评价制度，并严格按照国家有关规定认真履行各项环保水保报批手续；三是坚持项目环保水保设施与主体工程同时设计、同时施工、同时投产使用的“三同时”制度，防止环境污染和水土流失；四是坚持将环保水保工作贯彻到施工过程中的各个管理环节，全面实现文明施工目标。

(2) 机构人员到位。其要点是：设立环保水保管理机构，配备专职管理人员，建立健全工程环保水保管理工作体系。

(3) 管理措施到位。管理措施到位就是不断强化管理，通过制定强有力的管理措施，切实加强施工现场的环境监督，防止环境污染和水土流失事故的发生。

(4) 建设投资到位。其要点是：一是规范环保水保专项设施建设程序；二是落实环保水保建设投资。

(5) 规划设计到位。规划设计到位即统筹环保水保总体设计规划，工程措施与生态植物措施紧密结合，做到投资省效果好。

(6) 综合监理到位。其特点是：充分授权环保水保综合监理部代表业主在现场行使环保水保监督职责，对工作中出现的问题进行及时、有效地协调与纠正，实时监控环保水保项目的质量、进度、投资，切实保护生态环境，防止和减轻水土流失。

这一管理新模式，紧紧与龙滩公司创建“绿色龙滩”的目标相结合，有力地推进了“绿色龙滩”目标的提前实现，切实尽到了一个特大型国有企业落实环境保护工作的社会责任。“绿色龙滩”作为龙滩水电工程的一个响亮品牌，已得到社会各界的广泛认同，全面提升了龙滩公司良好的企业形象。

这一管理新模式，创造性地把环保水保建设与管理工作从思想到行动，从宏观到微观，从管理到设计，从实施到监督，集合成一套科学、行之有效的管理体系，进而把企业的环保意识快速转化为环保成果，在工程发挥巨大发电经济效益的同时，同步发挥出显著的社会环境效益，成效显著。

经测算，龙滩公司通过推行“绿色龙滩”环保水保“六到位”管理新模式，将各项环保水保措施落到实处，产生直接经济效益 4201 万元，回收重复利用水量 456 万 m^3；环境效益方面，龙滩工程施工区各种生产废水处理设施共处理沉淀废渣 236 万 m^3，极大地减少了水土流失，保护了江河水环境；提前发电增发电量 79 亿 kW·h，为此节省电煤用量 560 万 t，减少 CO_2 排放量 1463 万 t。另外，龙滩水电站提前下闸蓄水发电，对抵御珠江口海水咸潮回溯，确保澳门、珠海生活饮用水安全发挥了极大作用，为抵抗贵州省黔南、黔东南 2008 年冰冻自然灾害作出了重大贡献。

该管理新成果主题突出，内容全面，体系科学，目标明确，可操作性强，对龙滩工程的环保、水保工作具有指导意义和重大促进作用，为水电工程的环保水保管理工作探索出一条新路子，得到国家环保部、水利部及地方各级主管部门、专家的高度认可，一致认为在全国水电工程建设环保水保管理工作中具有很高的推广价值和示范作用，管理成果水平国内领先。

2009 年 9 月，“绿色龙滩”环保水保“六到位”管理新模式荣获全国电力企业管理创新成果一等奖。

（龙滩水电开发有限公司　齐彦斌　黄海雁）

移　民　工　程

龙滩水电站库区移民实行淹没耕地长期补偿

（一）龙滩移民安置状况

根据国家批复的龙滩水电站库区移民安置规划，采用土地生产开发进行移民生产安置。至规划水平年 2008 年，全库需生产安置人口为 80 472 人（贵州省 47 122 人、广西壮族自治区 33 350 人）。2007 年秋冬，贵州库区移民综合监理部在贵州省移民主管机构的支持下，会同贵州库区各州（市）、县、设计部门共同对已迁移民耕地落实情况进行了调查，结果表明：贵州库区已完成对接落实耕地的移民仅有 2 万人，人均对接耕地 0.73 亩，为淹没前人均 1.02 亩的 71.5%，占已迁需有土安置移民人数 3 万人的 65.5%；未对接耕地和长远生计无保障的移民达 1 万余人，占 35%。而广西库区河池市的天峨县移民对接土地平均为水田 0.3 亩/人，或旱地 0.6 亩/人，均未达到设计规划标准，南丹县移民已达到安置标准；百色市的乐业、田林县移民耕地开发困难，需生产安置 9224 人口中仅完成新造水田 506 亩。龙滩库区的客观现状是人多地少、人地矛盾突出，而根据农村移民安置规划主要是采取有土安置，故只能在有限的耕地资源中采取降低耕地安置标准的办法，因此在对水库移民实施“有土安置”时，移民所能得到的耕地，无论数量、质量均比淹没前减少和降低。现行的移民安置方式是前期补偿补助与后期扶持相结合的办法，不能很好地满足部分移民搬迁后的生产安置问题。

（二）龙滩水电站开展移民长期补偿的工作进程

2008年2月，在贵州省移民工作会议期间，贵州省移民办与库区各州（市）、县对龙滩库区移民生产安置形势进行了专题分析研究，并针对无法落实移民生产安置的突出问题提出拟采取淹没耕地实施长期补偿的解决思路。经组织各有关单位到库区进行广泛调研和协调论证，编写了《龙滩水电站贵州库区水库淹没耕地长期补偿方案（征求意见稿）》，发各有关单位征求意见。

龙滩水电开发有限公司（以下简称龙滩公司）将库区各级政府陆续要求实行淹没耕地实行长期补偿等有关问题上报中国大唐集团公司，2008年7月17日，中国大唐集团公司在《关于龙滩水电站贵州库区淹没耕地实行长期补偿问题的批复》中明确："为切实有效地解决龙滩水电站贵州库区生产安置不落实移民的长远生计问题，确保库区社会长期稳定和龙滩项目建设的顺利进行，龙滩水电站贵州库区实施淹没耕地长期补偿方案是比较现实的，应配合地方政府稳步推进"。龙滩公司为确保库区移民补偿政策"一库一策"，于2008年9月1～2日组织广西、贵州两省（区）政府办公厅、发展改革委、移民主管部门和有关单位，在贵阳市召开龙滩水电站库区移民安置工作研讨咨询会。在这次会议上，龙滩库区各级政府主管部门表示库区移民补偿必须坚持"一库一策"，地方各级政府和移民主管部门对长期补偿均表示大力支持。

2009年5月4日，广西、贵州两省（区）人民政府及移民主管部门在贵阳召开了龙滩库区移民安置问题座谈会议，会议对龙滩库区淹没耕地实行长期补偿议定了两项重大问题：一是明确解决龙滩水电站移民安置问题的原则为"一库一策"；二是明确对龙滩无法落实生产安置的移民实施耕地长期补偿办法，统一了长期补偿的对象、范围、标准、时限、程序、保障措施、工作费用等。

2009年8月18～20日，应广西、贵州两省（区）政府及移民主管部门要求，龙滩公司再次组织广西、贵州两省（区）政府办公厅、发展改革委、移民主管部门和有关单位在广西桂林市召开龙滩库区移民工作研讨会。会上，各方就长期补偿的重大原则问题进行了重点讨论并达成基本一致的意见。会后，经反复协调，广西、贵州两省（区）移民主管部门和龙滩公司共同会签形成了《龙滩水电站库区水库淹没耕地长期补偿方案》。

2009年10月14日，贵州省人民政府办公厅以黔府办函［2009］122号《省人民政府办公厅关于龙滩水电站贵州库区移民安置补偿有关问题的复函》原则同意了《贵州库区长补方案》，并要求抓紧组织实施。贵州省水利水电工程移民局、黔南布依族苗族自治州人民政府、黔西南布依族苗族自治州人民政府、安顺市人民政府联合印发了《龙滩水电站贵州库区无法落实生产安置移民耕地长期补偿实施细则》，明确2010年8月31日为耕地长期补偿手续办理截止日期，自2011年起每年的4月、10月各兑现一次长期补偿资金。贵州库区无法落实生产安置移民耕地长期补偿工作正式进入实施阶段。

广西壮族自治区水库移民工作管理局也已将广西库区的长期补偿方案上报自治区人民政府，一经批准，立即组织实施。

（三）龙滩库区长期补偿基本内容

1. 长期补偿的概念

耕地长期补偿是指在一定时期内，以淹没耕地的地类、面积和审定的年产值，对其所有权人（集体经济组织）或法定承包人进行长期逐年补偿。对无法落实生产安置的移民和涉淹农户实行耕地长期补偿，是对原移民安置规划的补充和完善，目的是保证水库淹没后移民和涉淹农户生活水平不降低，长远生计有保障。

2. 龙滩长期补偿范围和对象

（1）补偿范围为电站枢纽建设和水库淹没征占用的水田和旱地。对由水田和旱地演变而来，补偿标准高于水田和旱地的城郊菜地、菜稻田、甘蔗田、菜旱地等，对应水田和旱地地类部分纳入长期补偿；高出水田和旱地的补偿费部分，兑现给所有权人或法定承包人。国有土地（耕地）、集体未承包的耕地，陡坡地、鱼塘、林地、园地和荒山草坡地等不在长期补偿范围，仍按照国家审定的标准一次补偿。

（2）补偿对象为龙滩库区和枢纽区无法落实生产安置的移民，以及自愿退回已领取的耕地补偿费后，要求参加长期补偿的移民和涉淹农户。对无法对接耕地或开垦耕地的移民，按其被淹耕地面积、地类实行长期补偿；对已对接耕地或开垦了耕地的移民，在移民群众自愿的情况下，可按淹没耕地与对接耕地的面积之差实行长期补偿，或一次性退、扣回已领取的土地补偿费后参加长期补偿。

3. 补偿标准及时限

（1）补偿标准：2009年及以前，以耕地年产值水田1247.50元/亩、常年旱地850.50元/亩兑现补偿。2009年以后，按照两省（区）谷物、玉米价格变化因素，依据省级部门公布的价格指数，原则上每3年由两省（区）商龙滩公司对长期补偿标准进行一次调整。

（2）补偿时限：长期补偿自2007年1月1日起实施，到电站报废年止。

（四）实施长期补偿的利弊分析和存在问题

1. 有利因素

（1）实施长期逐年补偿后，农民的长远生计问题得到妥善解决。被征占地群众不需对土地进行投入和管理，每年便有稳定的土地收益，实质上达到了有土安置的目的。按照现行移民政策，一次性补偿方案等同相当于按目前审定的年产值标准补偿16年就永久买断移民户及后代后续的生存之本，而长补方案是按照被征占用耕地、旱地面积计算其补偿费，按时间进行补偿，不再占用之时进行复垦恢复其耕种功能，充分考虑了被征地移民户长远生计问题。广大库区移民可发展其他生产项目，改善生产生活环境，有利于调整和改善产业结构。

（2）实行长期补偿政策，建设业主减少一次性投资额度，有利于解决融资难题和市场风险。水电站建设具有前期投资额度大、需要通过从金融部门贷款解决融资问题的特点。实施长期补偿政策，可使有限的资金集中投入基础设施建设，产生更大的经济效益。

（3）实施长期补偿，库区各级政府积极支持长期补偿政策的实施，可有效解决移民安置过程中无地可调（可垦）的困惑和压力，不必再为解决土地调补等问题而发愁，有利于库区当地政府引导失地农民调整产业结构致富奔小康，可大大避免和减少因移民安置问题引发的群体性事件的发生。

2. 不利因素及存在问题

（1）龙滩水电工程375m方案水库移民已于2008年5月全面完成移民搬迁，而龙滩库区长期补偿在2010年才正式启动，参加长期补偿的对象原则为生产开发不落实的移民，需要充分考虑处理好以下的问题：一是已经兑现耕地补偿补助费又未落实或无法落实生产安置的移民，如要参加长期补偿的话，应退还补偿补助费；二是已对接了耕地，又要参加长期补偿，要予以明确规定不能参加长期补偿，并做好解释疏导工作，正确处理好面对的长期补偿问题。

（2）在龙滩的《长期补偿方案》中明确：对已领取了耕地补偿补助费的移民，但生产安置不落实的，在一次性退回所领款项后（抵扣2007～2010年4年的长期补偿金），方可参加长期补偿。有部分移民的耕地补偿补助款已挪用建设房屋或发展其他生产使用，移民能否退回相应的数额来参加长期补偿，在实施过程中需以退回领款作为一个硬性指标，同时需合理控制好参加长期补偿移民和有土安置移民的比例问题，避免原先已生产开发好的地无人耕种，合理引导移民开展长期补偿工作。

（3）市场风险问题。长期补偿的实物量标准保持不变，每年的补偿费则根据当年省级有关部门调查统计的稻谷市场价折算成现金逐年兑现。若谷物价格不断上涨也就意味着龙滩长期补偿的标准在不断提高。采取长期补偿方式，由于向移民支付补偿的年限无限期延长，项目业主建设征地补偿费支出将增加，而且随着市场粮食价格的不断提高，增加的幅度会不断加大，在目前全球金融危机的影响下，存、贷款利率在同步降低，建设期一次性补偿贷款成本在降低，而实行长期补偿后因补偿费用的增大，反过来又进一步加大了电站的建设运行成本。

（4）影响库区稳定问题。一是实行有土安置与长期补偿移民之间的矛盾，处理不好这一矛盾将会产生移民群体上访事件；二是若大多数移民要求退回甚至无法退回已对接耕地补偿费，又要求参与长期补偿，则有可能造成龙滩库区移民生产安置工作的翻盘，全面否定国家已批准的移民生产安置规划方案，对移民工作产生重大影响。

（5）在贵州库区实行的长期补偿方案中，没有明确长期补偿费的资金来源，而长期补偿费用是否能计入发电成本，目前国家也无政策规定。近期的移民长期补偿资金先从国家2006年审定的耕地补偿费由参加长期补偿的移民退回的一次性补偿资金中逐年支付，目前可先从工程建设资金中解决。但移民退回的一次性补偿资金支付完后，如何将长期补偿资金计入生产成本，并通过调整电价来解决，这是一个能否确保龙滩长期补偿方案长期顺利实施的关键。

（龙滩水电开发有限公司 梁冰凌）

现行水电工程移民人口界定方法的合理性

（一）问题的提出

2006年《国务院关于完善大中型水库移民后期扶持政策的意见》（国发［2006］17号）出台以后，开始实行新的水库移民后期扶持政策。特别是2007年以云南省为代表的部分省（区）制定并开始实行移民长效补偿政策，使当前的水电工程移民（主要是农村移民）在安置思路、安置方式、补偿标准、移民资金兑现方式以及移民后扶待遇等方面与传统移民安置方式及补偿政策相比，均发生了较大的变化。这种以政策为主导的变化在一定程度上改变了水电工程建设征地区移民的生产生活方式，改变了移民群体经济利益量的变化，造成了工程建设区域的非移民以及安置区原住居民心理上的严重失衡，从而加剧了已经完成并经审批（审核）的移民安置规划的实施难度。问题的主要原因是水电工程水库移民政策与建设征地移民人口界定方法相互影响。这种矛盾无疑使水电工程建设业主、移民安置规划设计单位，尤其是负责移民安置规划实施的地方政府面临着一个新的复杂敏感问题。

（二）传统生产安置人口计算方法简介

水电工程建设征地范围按地域不同主要分为5个区域：一是水库淹没影响区（简称一区，以下类推）；二是枢纽工程建设区；三是受淹城（集）镇新址建设区；四是农村移民安置区（包括搬迁安置区和生产安置区）；五是专项设施迁（改）建区。

长期以来，在国家原移民条例、移民专业技术规范的主导下，水电工程建设征地区农村移民生产安置人口数量只包括一区和二区。2007年由国家发展改革委发布的《水电工程建设征地移民安置规划设计规范》（DL/T 5064—2007）明确规定："水电工程建设征地处理范围是指水电工程建设涉及的水库淹没影响区和枢纽工程建设区。"这一规定明确地将建设征地的三至五区排除在建设征地处理范围之外，也是目前各水电工程主体设计单位在进行移民安置规划设计工作中必须遵循的一个重要法规依据。其计算方法是根据水库淹没影响区和枢纽工程建设区的永久征收耕地数量及人均耕地测算，移民安置补偿费用则按照建设征地实物指标数量和移民安置规划进行计算。其他三、四、五区的永久征地则依据建设征地实物指标数量，并参照水库淹没影响区的补偿标准进行一次性补偿，这部分征地涉及的生产安置人口和搬迁人口通常不纳入移民的范畴。

传统的移民安置方式相对单一，主要采取"以农为主，以土为本"的大农业安置方式，而且工程建设永久征收的农用地（耕地、园地、林地、草地）的补偿费和安置补助费原则上由当地政府掌握和支配，主要用于移民生产安置规划项目的实施，包括资源开发、土地整治、土地流转、农业生产设施配置等，一般不直接兑现给移民个人。另外，在2006年以前国家实行的库区建设基金、库区维护基金、库区后期扶持基金等后期扶持政策规定后扶资金主要用于解决移民安置实施后的遗留问题，用于移民工程的维护以及移民安置区基础设施建设，没有采取直接发放货币给移民的形式。

这种传统的前期补偿和后期扶持政策使水电工程建设征地区涉及的生产安置人口和搬迁安置人口在安置前后的生产生活方式、经济利益和社会福利等方面没有实质性差别，而且这种政策兼顾了建设征地涉及区域（包括上述5个区、库区和移民安置区非移民）相关各方利益的相对均衡，使大家共同享受着水电建设带来经济效益和社会效益，并已被地方政府、移民群体以及当地居民所接受。

（三）现行处理方法及存在的问题

2006年以来，国家和有关省新出台的水库移民政策对水库移民提供了较为优厚的待遇，主要体现在以下几个方面：

一是2006年出台的《国务院关于完善大中型水库移民后期扶持的政策的意见》（国发［2006］17号），重新调整了水库移民后期扶持政策，根据移民安置规划成果核定的移民数量有针对性地进行后期扶持。并明确规定："扶持方式，后期扶持资金能够直接发放给移民个人的尽量发放到移民个人，用于移民生产生活补助……"，"扶持标准，对纳入扶持范围的移民每人每年补助600元"，"扶持期限，从其完成搬迁之日起扶持20年"。

二是2007年以云南省为代表的部分省（区）对农村移民实行长效补偿安置政策，将水电工程建设征地区（包括一区、二区）涉及的生产安置人口作为长效补偿人口对待，长效补偿费用按照"淹多少、补多少"的原则，根据测算的土地补偿补助标准，以货币形式对移民实行逐年长效补偿。移民长效补偿费用实行逐年定量递增，电站建设期，从原审定的投资概算中列支；电站运行期，水电项目法人从发电收益中提取资金补充移民长效补偿费用，交由当地人民政府负责兑付。长效补偿期限与电站运行期限相同。移民死亡后，其农村家庭主要成员可以继续享受。

受以上国家和各省（区）现行移民政策法规的主导，被界定（认定）为水电工程建设征地的移民群体，将享受长效补偿和后期扶持政策。另外，由于移民问题日益引起国家和地方政府的高度重视，新的政策法规已经在一定程度上向移民群体倾斜。仅从云南省的云政办发［2007］157、159号文件和国发［2006］17号文件足以看出，移民群体在生产生活方式、经济利益和社会福利等方面享受了比非移民比较优厚的待遇。新政策出台以前库区移民不愿当移民，而新政策出台以后，出现了非淹没区群众争当移民现象。这同时也造成了一、二区移民群体与三、四、五区建设征地区域涉及的非移民以及安置区原住居民的不平衡。

（四）案例分析（以鲁地拉水库为例）

金沙江流域水力资源丰富，但由于土地资源匮乏，民族问题特殊，移民安置环境容量极其有限，该流域水电梯级开发面临的最大问题主要是移民安置问题。在这一背景下，2007年云南省政府办公厅下发了云政办发［2007］159号文件，提出了新的移民补偿安置方式，主要内容是："立足一个长效补偿机制、实行六种安置方式并举、建立一项库区发展资金、享受统一后期扶持政策、采取八条移民安置措施"，简称移民安置"16118工程"。金沙江鲁地拉水电站是云南省最早实行移民长效补偿政策的水电工程之一。

鲁地拉水电站工程位于云南省丽江市永胜县和大理白族自治州宾川县交界的金沙江干流上，是金沙江中游水电开发河段水电开发一库八级水电开发方案的第七个梯级电站。水库正常蓄水位1223m，水库长度约100km，总库容17.18亿m^3，调节库容3.76亿m^3，电站装机容量2160MW。

工程建设征地涉及云南省大理州和丽江市的3个县（永胜、鹤庆、宾川）5个乡镇29个村民委员会。该水电站工程规模较大，建设征地数量大，移民人口数量多，专业项目齐全。

根据《金沙江鲁地拉水电站工程建设征地移民安置规划总报告》（审定本，2009年1月），鲁地拉水电站工程建设征地主要实物指标如下：建设征地总面积为65.34km^2（包括水库淹没影响区和枢纽工程建设区），其中陆地面积43.27km^2，水域面积22.07km^2。征收（用）耕地33 449亩，基准年（2007年）直接搬迁人口22 783人，淹没等级公路71.8km；10kV以上等级输电线路93.2km；通信线路光缆55.2km，电缆68.0km；广播电视网络线缆152.1km。

1. 移民人口分析

依据本文第二部分提出的5个分区，鲁地拉水电站建设征地一区征收耕（园）地30 846亩，生产安置人口23 274人；二区征收耕（园）地2259亩，生产安置人口1561人；三区征收耕（园）地2635亩，生产安置人口967人；四区占地面积4935亩，生产安置人口1771人；五区（主要是库周等级公路改建）征收耕（园）地1035亩，生产安置人口544人。

按照传统的生产安置人口计算方法，即仅计算一、二区，鲁地拉水电站生产安置人口为24 835人，如果计算全部的一至五区，生产安置人口为28 117人，两者相差3282人，详见表1。

表1　　鲁地拉水电站生产安置人口计算分析比较表

序号	项目		单位	一区	二区	三区	四区	五区	合计	人口比重（%）	后扶资金（万元）	备注
1	征收耕（园）地		亩	30 846	2259	2635	4935	1035	41 709			
2	搬迁安置人口		人	23 356	1406	49		24	24 835			一至五区
3	生产安置人口	方法一	人	23 274	1561				24 835	88	29 802	一、二区
		方法二	人	23 274	1561	967	1771	544	28 117	100	33 740	一至五区

从表1看出，鲁地拉水电站具有与一般大中型水电工程的共同点，即水库淹没影响区和枢纽工程建设区是建设征地移民安置的主体区域，而其他几个区域所占比重很小。

2. 补偿政策分析

根据审定的《金沙江鲁地拉水电站工程建设征地移民安置规划总报告》，鲁地拉水电站计算长效补偿耕地总面积为永胜县和鹤庆县建设征地涉及耕（园）地总面积为31 047.2亩（其中水田25 364.7亩，旱地3910.3亩，可调整园地1772.2亩）。

根据云政办发［2007］159号文件的规定，长效补偿支付期限与电站运行期限相同。从移民搬迁之月起，由县移民主管部门按月以货币形式发放到移民户。长效补偿资金按《移民条例》规定的补偿补助标准，以货币形式对移民实施逐年长效补偿，根据《移民条例》规定的补偿倍数16倍计算，列入概算的建设征用耕地补偿费用为110 529.23万元，其中长效补偿部分补偿费用108 307.10万元。

根据当前正在开展筹建工作的金沙江中游有关电站地方政府的实际操作情况，移民生产生活补助标准（也是长效补偿标准的基础）暂按人均每月280～300元发放（这一标准还有提高的趋势），如果再加上后期扶持补助，人均每月可以拿到330～350元，年纯收入为3960～4200元。而非淹没区群众的农业年收入远远低于享受长效政策移民的收入，据统计，2008年鲁地拉水电站建设征地区涉及各县农业人均年纯收入为1548～2838元，涉及各乡农业人均年纯收入仅为628～1716元。即使根据库区淹没耕地年产值测算，农业人均年纯收入也只有2000元左右。

移民实际补偿标准与非淹没区群众农业年收入产生差距的主要原因：一是长效补偿费用没有扣除生产成本；二是政策过分地向移民倾斜，制定标准偏高，这种做法导致的结果将是"好心办坏事"。

一、二区移民享受的优厚待遇，导致三、四、五区的非移民以及安置区原住居民心理失衡并竞相攀比，从而加剧了三、四、五区征地拆迁工作的难度。目前，鲁地拉库区正在开展移民安置点土地流转工作，安置区原住居民强烈要求按移民身份对待。

（五）影响实质及其利弊分析

新的水库移民政策与传统的移民人口界定方法已经产生激烈碰撞，问题主要出在两个方面：一是在新的移民政策环境下，被界定的移民人口享受着优厚的长效补偿政策和后期扶持政策，导致移民与非移民产生不平衡；二是在新的移民政策环境下，传统的移民人口界定方法也存在一定局限性。

以鲁地拉水库为例，表面问题是不同的移民人口界定方法产生的移民人口数量的差异，但实质问题是建设征地涉及各区域以及当地居民享受的待遇不同以及经济利益分配不公，造成了他们之间的心理失衡，从而产生社会矛盾。加之水电工程建设征地区大多属于少数民族聚居区，经济发展和文化教育比较落后，这种社会矛盾出现在特殊的民族地区，最终将危及社会的和谐与稳定。目前，金沙江鲁地拉水电站主要建设征地区在移民安置规划实施一开始这种矛盾就已经凸显出来，给地方政府和移民实施机构提出了一道无论是从理论上还是从实践中都难以解决的技术难题。

传统水电工程移民人口界定方法的有利之处主要是：降低了农村移民生产安置人口数量，从而在一定程度上提高了工程的社会形象（因为移民问题已上升为水电建设发展瓶颈的高度），减轻了实行长效补偿政策的工作量和传统的大农业安置移民的难度（是否能降低经济成本很难说）。同时，这种界定方法因认定的移民数量较小，必然减少了国家后期扶持的资金投入。

在新的移民政策主导下，传统的水电工程移民人口界定方法的弊端主要体现在经济利益和社会效益分配失衡，而这种失衡必然会产生各相关利益群体之间的矛盾，主要包括：

（1）一、二区移民与三、四、五区被征地居民之间的矛盾。

（2）接安区原居民与移民之间的矛盾。

（3）搬迁人口与生产安置人口之间的矛盾。

（4）同一地区实行长效补偿政策与传统农业安置移民之间的矛盾。

而这些矛盾的产生，近期可能影响移民安置规划的实施，影响水电工程的顺利建设和运行，远期可能危及建设征地区的社会和谐以及长治久安。

（六）移民人口界定方法的合理性分析

现行国家移民政策法规不论是国发［2006］17号文件，还是国务院令第471号，对水电工程建设征地移民人口的计算方法都没有明确规定和限制，国家行业主管部门对此也无权威性的解释，规划设计单位主要依据《水电工程建设征地移民安置规划设计规范》（DL/T 5064—2007）规定的建设征地处理范围，将所计算的生产安置人口作为移民人口和长效补偿人口。这种处理方式虽然符合传统的水库淹没处理理念，而且也被地方政府和被征地区居民所接受，但与新时期移民安置理念以及后期扶持政策难以衔接，同时也缺乏可操作性。

上述建设征地的5个区域虽然征地数量不同、用途不同、建设用地性质也不完全一样，但对地方政府尤其是被征耕（园）地承包者和经营者而言，不管是哪一个区域，或被征土地做何用途，都属于水电工程建设用地，理应执行相同的补偿政策和安置政策，特别在安置方式和经济利益等方面应该享受同等待遇。因此，从工程建设、移民安置以及社会和谐的角度，研究并调整水电工程移民人口界定方法，也是今后水库移民工作顺利开展的前提。

从国家和建设单位投资效益考虑，对大型水电工程而言，建设征地主要集中在水库淹没影响区，其他几个区域征地数量有限，而且即使生产安置人口按全部建设征地区域计算，所增加的移民人口也是有限的。鉴于移民安置长效补偿资金来源按照建设征地数量计算和支付，而长效补偿所兑现的资金主要来自移民自身前期补偿费用，这部分资金如果进行有效运作，可以不突破前期补偿费用的额度。另外，现行移民人口界定方法反映在移民后扶资金上确实存在差异，初步计算，鲁地拉水库即使将所有建设征地区统一纳入移民人口的界定范畴，移民人口将会增加3282人，后扶资金增加不足4000万元，这种多区域计算方法所增加的投资与移民安置的实施、对水电工程顺利建设所产生的经济效益以及对当地社会的稳定所带来的社会效益相比，应该是显而易见的。因此，从建设征地的角度，除第五区可以按专业部门的规定处理外（目前还没有规定），将建设征地的一至四区统一纳入移民人口计算范畴可能更趋合理。而且，由于长效补偿和后期扶持政策施行时间不长，移民人口界定方法的调整和变更，基本不存在历史遗留问题，不会带来更大的社会风险。

（中国水电顾问集团西北勘测设计研究院
王枧安　辛乾龙）

水电工程移民综合监理工作程序与方法研究

（一）项目研究背景

水电工程建设征地移民安置综合监理（以下简称移民综合监理）作为社会性的综合技术经济监督管理模式，对贯彻国家的开发性移民方针，监督移民安置规划的执行，规范移民工程建设管理，发挥移民资金最大效益，提高移民安置效果，保障移民生产生活规划目标实现等诸多方面将发挥重要作用。然而，我国水电工程移民综合监理工作起步很晚，各省（自治区、直辖市）移民管理机构和项目法人基于所在区域的实际情况与实践上的差异，对移民综合监理工作的认识与要求存在较大的不同。因此，在移民监理的工作程序和方法存在较大的差异，这对移民综合监理工作的全面开展产生了一定影响，也不利于移民综合监理作用的发挥。

中国水电顾问集团北京勘测设计研究院编制完成了《水电工程移民综合监理工作程序与方法研究报告》（以下简称《研究报告》），并于2009年6月通过了中国水电工程顾问集团公司组织的验收。

（二）研究成果概述

《研究报告》在充分调研各主要水电工程建设地区移民安置工作管理模式的基础上，根据国家、地方的水电工程建设征地移民安置管理政策法规，围绕着移民综合监理的中心任务和目标，结合项目法人、省级移民管理机构、县级移民实施机构以及移民对移民综合监理的期望，提出了较为统一的移民综合监理工作内容、工作程序、工作方法。

（1）移民综合监理的主要工作内容包括质量、费用、进度控制，环境安全、合同、信息管理，相关方协调。

（2）针对综合监理任务委托方式、综合监理进场、征地移民综合监理组织及工作流程、设计变更监理、资金拨付与使用监理、征地移民进度控制的监理、征地移民质量控制的监理、征地移民综合监理例会制度、信息管理等进行程序研究。

（3）移民综合监理工作方法主要包括目标规划法、报告审核法、对比分析法、调查法、巡视检查法、专家法、经验法、综合法、会议法、财务审计法、网络图法、横道图法、进度曲线法、图表法、计量法、试验检验法，共16种方法。

（三）主要创新点

（1）《研究报告》首次在国内提出了“三控三管一协调”的移民综合监理工作内容。研究成果对移民综合监理工作内容高度而系统的概括，不仅符合国家现行法律法规及相关规范的要求，也非常符合移民综合监理工作的实际情况，得到了移民主管部门、水电建设项目法人等相关方面的高度认可。

（2）根据水电工程移民安置实施的特点，研究成果首次在国内提出了移民安置进度包括移民安置工作综合进度及移民项目进度，并就移民综合监理开展“综合进度”控制和“项目进度”控制分别提出控制程序和方法。

（3）根据水电工程移民安置实施的特点，研究成果首次在国内提出了移民安置的质量分为综合质量、功能质量与建设质量3类，针对“综合质量”、“功能质量”与“建设质量”分别提出控制程序和方法，并明确提出，在建设质量控制过程中，移民综合监理对移民工程建设监理的技术监管职责。

（4）根据水电工程移民安置资金的特点，研究成果首次在国内提出了移民综合监理重点是对移民安置协议内的资金进行监管，其中尤以工程项目资金、补偿补助资金、移民工作资金为重点监督对象。此外，还应对地方移民实施机构申请使用预备费提出意见和建议。

（5）针对目前水电工程移民综合监理的工作现状和发展形势，研究成果首次在国内提出了将环境安全管理工作纳入到监理工作范围内，但其工作重点仅是涉及电站建设征地区和移民安置区的环境安全管理，不同于水电工程的环境保护与水土保持专项监理。

（6）在移民综合监理工作方法方面，研究成果首次在国内系统地提出了目标规划法、报告审核法、对比分析法、巡视检查法、财务审计法、横道图法、进度曲线法、图表法、计量法、试验检验法等16种监理工作方法，并针对不同监理工作内容适用于不同的监理工作方法进行了归纳和分类。

（四）对移民综合监理发展的影响

《研究报告》首次在水电行业内建立了一套完整的移民综合监理工作程序和工作方法，既理顺了移民综合监理各项工作的工作程序，又建立了可行的移民综合监理工作方法。研究成果提出的移民综合监理工作内容、工作程序和工作方法，不仅可以有效统一各移民综合监理单位的工作内容和职责，规范各水电工程移民综合监理的工作程序和工作方法，同时还为编制《水电工程建设征地移民安置综合监理技术导则》、制定管理文件提供了宝贵的实践经验和参考资料。目前，中国水电顾问集团北京勘测设计研究院受中国水电工程顾问集团公司委托，正在编制《水电工程建设征地移民安置综合监理技术导则》。

（中国水电顾问集团北京勘测设计研究院　敬大捷）

乐滩水电站2009年移民安置工作简况

乐滩水电站的移民安置工程，截至2009年末，除都安县拉烈集镇迁建项目开始进行移民建房外，原实施规划设计的项目已基本实施完毕。

2009年，主要的工作是编制本工程的移民安置实施规划调整报告。鉴于近几年来国家的移民安置政策和土地政策有所调整，广西在建和新建的大型水电站移民补偿政策也相应有所调整。因此，从2008年以来，为了解决电站库区移民稳定问题，广西地方各级政府相继要求乐滩水电站抓紧进行建设征地移民安置补偿投资概算调整工作。之后，有关各方即积极开展和推进此项工作。为了较好地完成此项设计工作，项目业主广西桂冠开投电力有限责任公司和广西壮族自治区移民局共同委托中国水利水电建设工程咨询公司对设计报告的编制进行咨询。

经咨询，专家认为：设计报告的编制若以调高电价为目的，可以给设计报告定性为“调概报告”，报告完成后报项目原审批单位即国家发展改革委审批；如此次调整后的移民投资加上项目其他的总投资，仍未突破项目原审定的总投资，那就不具备申请调高电价的条件，根据国家发展计划委员会计基础［2002］2623号文件，关于“建设征地移民工作实行省级人民政府全面负责”，省级人民政府负有“审批建设征地移民安置实施规划”职责的规定，只需将实施阶段的实施变化和自治区人民政府要求进行的政策调整编入“实施规划调整报告”，由自治区人民政府审批即可。而且，即使要“调概”，也必须先完成这一步。

据此，乐滩水电站建设征地移民安置工作此阶段的设计规划，由编制“实施规划报告”和“调概报告”，改变为编制“实施规划报告”，目前此项工作正在推进中。

（广西桂冠开投电力有限责任公司　李晓峰）

中國水力發電年鉴

14

水电工程综合效益

我国水电的经济效益和社会效益显著

（一）促进经济社会的可持续发展

水电是我国重要的可再生能源，开发水力资源对满足电力增长需求、保证国家能源安全、提高清洁能源利用比重、改善能源结构和减少温室气体排放、保护环境等都具有重要意义。水电的经济效益显著，据原电力工业部财务口径统计，1980～1996年，全国总发电量62 660亿kW·h，水电占15.3%；总售电利润1037亿元，水电约占64%。不少水电工程除发电效益外，还具有防洪、灌溉、供水、航运、旅游等综合利用效益。我国水力资源主要在西部，开发水电是西部大开发的重要组成部分，实施“西电东送”就是将西部的水电向东部发达地区输送，实现我国能源资源的优化配置。因此，水电对于我国经济社会的可持续发展具有重要的作用。

（1）满足电力需求，优化能源结构，促进节能环保。电力是当今社会最重要的能源，现代社会一刻都离不开电力。我国生产电力的一次能源资源主要靠煤电（2008年装机容量占76%，年发电量81%），水电在电力结构中仅次于煤电，位居第二位。多年来，我国水电装机容量占全国电力总装机容量的比重一直维持在20%～30%，最高时达到过31.7%。2008年，我国水电装机容量达到1.72亿kW，年发电量5655亿kW·h，分别占全国电力总装机容量和年发电量的21.8%和16.4%。与2007年相比，水电的装机容量和年发电量分别增长18.6%和20%，发展很快。但近年来火电站大量投产，增长过快，比重持续上升，电源结构不合理的趋势突显。在采用措施使有害气体排放得到控制减少以后，煤电和其他化石能源消耗排放的CO_2、SO_2和粉尘，依然是引发气候变暖、环境变差的主要污染，是我国应对气候变化、实现节能减排目标中的主要任务。

水电与风电、太阳能等可再生能源以及核电相比，具有资源明确、技术成熟、队伍强大、设备配套的优势。大力发展水电符合我国能源发展及可持续发展战略，是我国电力发展的重要组成部分。预计到2020年，我国电力装机容量约达到15亿kW，其中水电装机容量达3亿kW，占20%，西部主要水电省份四川和云南东送的电力将达到80 000MW。届时除西藏外，西南地区大部分水电将得到开发。通过实施“西电东送”可有效缓解我国中东部地区能源短缺状况，优化我国能源结构，满足中东部地区电力需求，为中东部地区经济发展提供重要的能源保证，从而促进地区经济协调发展。

我国中东部地区经济发达，人口稠密，但能源资源较为贫乏，由于煤电装机规模大，环境容量有限，环保压力大，将西部地区丰富的水能资源开发后实施水电“西电东送”，在满足中东部电力需求的同时，可缓解该地区的环保压力。水电建设在环境保护和节能减排、实现经济和社会的可持续发展方面可起到重要的保证和支撑作用。

（2）具有防洪、灌溉、供水、航运、旅游等综合利用效益。水电站特别是具有调节能力的水库电站建成后，除发电外，一般还具有较好的防洪、灌溉、供水、航运、旅游等综合利用效益。20世纪50年代建设的新安江水电站、20世纪90年代建设的龙羊峡水电站、21世纪初期建成的长江三峡水电站和龙滩水电站等，都发挥了巨大的综合利用效益。

1998年，长江流域发生了自1954年以来最大一次洪水。三峡工程处在建设初期，位于干支流的葛洲坝、隔河岩、丹江口、凤滩、五强溪等水电站拦蓄洪水250多亿立方米，削峰60余次，减少洪灾损失上百亿元。

新安江水电站1959年蓄水发电，带动了我国第一条220kV高压输电线的开通，它作为华东电网骨干电厂和第一调峰调频电厂，为杭州、上海和华东地区这片工业发达、钱粮满仓的鱼米之乡输送了清洁稳定和强大的电力。新安江水库拦洪削峰显著，是当地供水和灌溉的主要水源，它形成的千岛湖旅游风景区早已闻名遐迩。

龙滩水电站375m一期工程于2008年提前一年投产发电，综合效益显著。在2008年初的南方雨雪冰冻灾害中，龙滩水电站已投产的3台机组承担了广西电网40%的负荷，成为抗击冰冻灾害的中流砥柱；2008年6月，广西普降暴雨，梧州遭遇洪水，由于龙滩水库控制调节，使梧州洪峰削减，洪水由50年一遇降至10年一遇；龙滩下闸蓄水后，梧州断面的流量始终保持在1800m^3/s（供水安全最低流量）以上，有效地保证了珠海、澳门地区的供水安全；龙滩水电站建成后，把红水河天然情况不通航的干流形成深水航道，实测最小流量为天然情况下最枯流量的5倍多，红水河成为全面通航河段，为该地区煤炭和矿产品外运提供了一条廉价的水上运输线和重要出海通道。

水电站一般位于交通闭塞、经济较为落后的地区，水电建设可使当地的交通条件得到有效改善，有利于当地城市化进程。水电站建设需要的大量建筑材料和劳务，为当地相关行业的发展提供了机遇。建设期和运行期电站所交纳的税金，对地方经济实力的增强也将产生重要的拉动作用。

(3) 带动我国民族工业的发展。新中国成立以来，我国水电建设从小到大、从弱到强，不断发展壮大。二滩、三峡、小湾、龙滩、锦屏一级、锦屏二级、溪洛渡、向家坝等水电站的建设，标志着我国水电建设已经逐步迈向世界先进水平。水电规划、勘测、设计、施工和机电制造等各方面的技术水平获得了明显的提高，水电建设整体实力不断增强。通过大型水电站的建设，引进消化国外先进技术，我国水电机组制造技术不断突破。继刘家峡、龙羊峡、岩滩等一批单机容量30万kW以上的大型水轮发电机组相继投产发电，李家峡单机容量40万kW、二滩单机容量55万kW机组已先后建成，三峡单机容量70万kW机组也已投产，我国机电制造水平得到快速提升。

由于水电一般离负荷中心较远，伴随着大型水电站的投入，我国的长距离输电技术水平也不断提高。回顾中国电网发展历史，从电厂直配地区负荷开始，由小到大，由低电压到高电压，都是随着大型水电站的建设而扩展的。新中国成立初期对丰满水电站的复建改造，形成了110kV高压输电线路；20世纪50年代建设的新安江水电站向上海送电，促成了第一条220kV高压输电线的开通和浙江省与上海市电网的联网，为华东电网奠定了基础；20世纪60年代建设的丹江口水电站，实现了湖北省与河南省电网互联；20世纪70年代初，配合刘家峡水电站的投运，于1972年建成了刘家峡至关中的首条330kV输电线路工程，形成陕甘青宁电网；1989年葛洲坝至上海南桥±500kV直流输电工程建成投运，实现了华中与华东两大区电网互联；20世纪90年代初，随着天生桥水电站的建设和天生桥至广东500kV输电工程的投产，促成了南方联营电网的产生；三峡工程的建设，将使华中、川渝、华东电网互联，形成中部电网，并使中部电网与南方电网互联；黄河上游公伯峡水电站的电压提高到750kV，促进了西北电网与华北电网互联，形成北部电网。最终，南方电网、中部电网、北部电网将互联，形成全国联网。

水电机组制造及长距离输电技术水平的突破，极大地推动了我国民族制造业的发展，充分体现了水电站建设对我国电力工业发展的推动作用。

(二) 拉动地方经济和社会的发展

拉动地方经济和社会的发展，是指大中型水电站建设和运行对促进枢纽建设和水库淹没地区的发展所产生的带动或联动影响。

(1) 增加地方固定资产投资。水电站开工建设直接导致地方电力行业固定资本投资大幅上升，加快了当地的固定资本形成，促进了电力行业以及相关上下游产业的发展，增强了对外来投资的吸引力，继而引发整个社会各行业固定资产投资的普遍增长，为加速当地经济发展带来重要契机，加快固定资本形成，推动地方经济社会发展。

(2) 拉动地方GDP的增长。水电站在建设期间，需要投入大量的水泥、钢材等建筑材料和施工机械、发输变电设备等物资，其中部分是当地采购；需要投入大量劳动力，就地采购大量的施工辅助加工服务，就地消费大量食品和日用品等，因此也相应带动地方相关产业、服务加工等第三产业的发展，对地方GDP增长起直接和间接的促进作用，通过投资和消费两个环节拉动地方的GDP增长。水电站建成投入运行后，在为电力系统提供电力电量的同时，拉动了电力系统覆盖区域的GDP增长。另外，水电站具有的防洪、灌溉、供水、航运、养殖、旅游开发等综合利用效益，也对地方GDP增长也起到了直接和间接的拉动作用。根据水电水利规划设计总院对有关水电站的调研和测算，电站建设对GDP的拉动效应见表1。

表1　部分水电站建设期对所在省（区）GDP拉动测算表

水电站	所在省（区）	总投资（亿元）	拉动地方GDP（亿元）
龙　滩	广西	243	800
大朝山	云南	41.39	112
瀑布沟	四川	199.33	690
桐　柏	浙江	35.3	133

(3) 增加地方税费收入。水电站在建设期间和运行期间，直接为国家和地方贡献了巨额税费，同时还能通过带动地方相关产业贡献税费。根据现行财税政策，水电站建设中产生的建筑工程费和安装工程费用，须向劳务的发生地交纳营业税、城市建设维护税和教育费附加等3项税金。营业税税率为3%；城市维护建设税在市区的税率为7%，在县城、镇的税率为5%，不在市区、县城或镇的税率为1%；教育费附加税率为3%。水电站建成后的经营期税费主要有增值税、企业所得税、城市维护建设税、教育费附加、水资源费、大中型水库库区基金等。其中：增值税税率为17%，为中央与地方共享税金，中央为75%，地方为25%；企业所得税税率为25%，为中央与地方共享税金，中央为60%，地方为40%；城市维护建设税及教育费附加均为地方税；水资源费以发电量为基础按一定标准提取，为地方税；库区基金，从有发电收入的大中型水库发电收入中筹集，根据水库实际上网销售电量，按不高于0.008元/(kW·h)的标准征收，由地方政府管理。

（4）改善地方基础公共设施。通过水电站建设，水电工程区对外交通条件得到改善。水电站水库淹没影响的交通、邮电、广播等绝大部分专项工程结合库周村镇布局统筹复建或改建，基础设施大多有所改善。改革开放以来，依托大中型水电站建设，对移民生活基础设施及文教卫设施的建设起到了较大的促进作用，提高了地方群众的生活质量，取得了较好的社会效益。

（5）提高地方城镇化水平。水电站建设从3个方面提高了城镇化率：一是山区移民直接迁入城镇安置；二是移民规模化集中安置，新建移民集镇；三是随着库周城镇基础设施、生产生活条件及环境的大幅改善，吸引了非移民的周边农村群众自发迁入城镇发展。交通网络等基础设施的改善、水电建设本身提供的就业机会、旅游业的开发等，都推动了城镇化进程。

（6）优化群众燃料结构，有利于生态环境保护。水电站建设所在地生活基础设施改善后，当地群众增加了煤气、电力和沼气等燃料的使用，减少砍伐树木作燃料。解决了燃料问题，有效地保护了植被和生态环境，减少了温室气体的排放。据测算，建一座沼气池，可解决3～5口人之家的燃料问题，节约柴木10t，保护约6亩活立林地，节电约100kW·h。

（7）促进地方就业。水电站在建设和运行的过程中，可通过生产和消费两个环节拉动相关产业的发展，发挥提供就业岗位等社会效益。水库有防洪、灌溉、供水、航运、养殖、旅游开发等社会服务功能，为库区群众拓宽就业门路、增加收入。

（8）促进地方产业结构调整。水电站建设形成的具有一定规模水域面积的水库，为发展淡水养鱼创造了良好条件。环境优美的水库，借助复建的周边地区交通、电力、通信等基础设施，可以大力发展旅游产业。随着养殖、旅游等库区经济的发展，地方群众收入渠道单一的状况逐步改变，促进地方产业结构逐步调整和优化。

（摘自中国水力发电工程学会主编的《中国水电60年》）

沅水梯级开发综合效益显著

沅水自西南向东北流经黔、湘、渝、鄂四省，从湖南常德注入洞庭湖，流域总面积90 000km²。根据规划，沅水干流按12个梯级开发，自上而下有革东（5万kW）、三板溪（100万kW）、挂治（15万kW）、白市（42万kW）、托口（83万kW）、洪江（27万kW）、安江（17万kW）、铜湾（18万kW）、清水塘（12.8万kW）、大伏潭（24万kW）、五强溪（120万kW）、凌津滩（27万kW）水电站。其中，上游三板溪、挂治、白市3个电站位于贵州省境内，其余8个梯级位于湖南省境内。三板溪、托口、五强溪3座水电站为一等大（1）型工程。

目前，由五凌电力有限公司开发的五强溪、凌津滩、洪江、碗米坡、三板溪、挂治等6座电站已相继建成投产，装机容量313万kW，白市、托口两个电站在建，装机容量125万kW，预计2013年将全面完成沅水流域梯级开发任务。另外，沅水干流由地方投资建设的铜湾、清水塘电站已建成，安江、大伏潭电站在建；酉水支流最大的凤滩电站20世纪80年代建成投产，2000年后进行了扩机改造，目前装机容量已达80万kW，资产属湖南省电力公司管理。

沅水流域的水电开发，实现了发电、防洪、航运等协调发展，不仅产生了巨大的经济效益，而且产生了广泛的社会效益。

（一）发电效益

在五凌电力有限公司从事沅水开发前，沅水仅有凤滩电站40万kW，年发电量仅20亿kW·h。五凌电力有限公司经过近20年的开发建设，已建成投产容量313万kW，年发电量112.22亿kW·h，占湖南全省水电发电量的35%。截至2009年底，五凌电力有限公司沅水各梯级电站累计发电量930亿kW·h，相当于节约标准煤3700万t，减少二氧化硫排放量279万t，减少二氧化碳排放量9270万t，按每度电0.3元计算，直接经济效益279亿元。

（二）防洪效益

沅水自古多水患，洪灾严重且很频繁，流域开发前，洪水缺乏水利调节，仅能依靠河道天然调蓄，洪水肆虐，给沅水流域人民生命财产带来了巨大损失。仅1991年沅水洪峰洗劫常德等地，造成直接损失就达28亿元。同时，沅水汛期流量占洞庭湖入湖流量的40%左右，沅水的汛情严重威胁到洞庭湖区的防汛安全。沅水流域开发后，沅水流域的防洪标准大幅提高，洪灾损失大幅减少，防洪效益十分显著。

1. 提高防洪标准

三板溪水库是沅水龙头水库，总库容40.94亿m³，调节库容26.16亿m³，具有多年调节性能。水库建成后，下游地区的防洪标准由建库前的10年一遇提高到20年一遇。五强溪水库是沅水流域防洪控制性工程，控制流域面积83 800km²，占全流域总面积的93%，水库总库容43.50亿m³，调节库容20.2亿m³，具有季调节性能。汛期预留防洪库容13.6亿m³，与上游凤滩水库进行联合调度，下游尾闾桃源、常德、汉寿等地区的防洪标准由建库前的5年一遇提高到20年一遇。上述地区地势低洼，河势宽广，汛期河道洪水水位可高出地面数米，经常遭受洪水威胁，全靠堤防保护。现有14个堤垸，总面积2476km²，保护耕地191.64万亩，人口近170万人，是五强溪水库下游主要防护对象。

2. 五强溪的实际防洪作用

五强溪水库自1994年下闸蓄水以来，连续经历了1995年、1996年、1998年、1999年的大洪水，为下游拦洪、削峰、错峰，削峰率均在30%以上，为减轻下游防洪压力，减少洪灾损失发挥了巨大的作用，防洪效益十分显著，详见表1。

表1 五强溪水库在历年大洪水中发挥的作用

年份	最大入库流量（m^3/s）	时间	最大出库流量（m^3/s）	时间	削峰流量（m^3/s）	最高水位（m）	滞洪时间（h）	拦蓄水量（亿 m^3）
1995	34000	070114	24600	070202	9400	106.69	12	14.330
1996	40000	071611	26400	071614	13600	113.26	3	20.563
1998	35000	072305	23000	072320	12000	109.86	15	13.150
1999	37000	062911	24100	063020	12900	107.77	33	14.320

（1）1996年超蓄调洪，确保常德“三个100”的安全，防洪效益数百亿。1996年7月，沅水流域发生了自1834年以来最大的一次洪水，流域内先后有十几个城镇被洪水淹没。五强溪水库最大入库流量达到40 000m³/s，相当于设计频率100年一遇。这次洪水峰高量大，3天洪量75.88亿m³，洪水总量达到173.3亿m³，相当于整个洞庭湖的蓄水量。五强溪水库对这场特大洪水进行了超常规调度，最大出库流量控制在26 400m³/s，削减洪峰13 600m³/s，占洪峰流量的34%，拦蓄洪量近21亿m³，水库最高调蓄水位达到113.26m，相当于5000年一遇的洪水位。对这场百年不遇的洪水，五强溪水库及时进行了拦蓄、削峰和超蓄调洪。湖南省省委、省政府统筹兼顾，科学调度，以“牺牲局部，顾全大局，保大中城市，保交通干线，保生命安全”为指导原则，在确保大坝安全的前提下，取得了巨大的防洪效益，保住了常德、桃源、汉寿等城镇以及尾闾地区重点堤垸的安全，保护了100多万人口、100万亩粮田、100亿元资产免遭洪灾损失，直接经济效益数百亿元。

（2）1998年为洞庭湖蓄洪，确保洞庭湖防洪大堤的安全，减灾70多亿元。1998年6～8月，长江流域发生了1954年型特大洪水，洪水持续时间之长、水位之高，历史罕见。五强溪水库1998年超过15 000m³/s的洪水有5次，最大一次洪峰流量为35 000m³/s。为了减轻洞庭湖区的防洪压力，五强溪水库承担了艰巨的蓄洪任务。五强溪水库共调蓄洪水9次，拦蓄洪水总量46亿m³，降低洞庭湖水位0.7m左右，为城陵矶水位未超36m起了重要作用，避免了洞庭湖区大面积溃垸的发生，发挥了巨大的经济效益和社会效益，减少直接经济损失70多亿元。

（三）航运效益

沅水干流全长1050km，是联系湘黔的重要黄金水道。但是沅水滩多水急，素有九滩十八湾之称。在自然通航条件下，受地形和水文特性影响，一般情况下，每年有1/3的时间不能通航，严重影响和制约了黄金水道的作用和效益的发挥。随着沅水梯级电站的开发，三板溪、洪江、五强溪、凌津滩、碗米坡水电站相继建成，彻底改变了沅水自然通航条件，昔日的险滩急流成为平湖。沅水梯级电站全部开发完成后，可改善航道1000km，将大大提高沅水的通航能力，实现沅水干流贵州锦屏以下河道全年通航，250t的船只可经洞庭湖直接进入长江水运。

五强溪船闸自1995年2月通航以来至2009年底，累计过船77 000多艘，货运量达657万t，为湖南湘西地区经济崛起和航运事业的发展发挥了重要作用。

三板溪水库正常水位475m时，水库面积85km²，回水长度120km，水库蓄水后，使剑河至三板溪80多千米的急流、险滩变成平湖。当地百姓抓住机遇，纷纷购买船只从事水上运输和旅游观光。现在，三板溪库区的水上运输业已发展成为当地支柱产业之一。

（四）促进地方经济发展

五凌电力有限公司开发的8个水电项目共搬迁安置移民近30万人，移民投资107亿元。通过专项投资，库区新建了大量的移民城镇，一栋栋漂亮的楼房，一条条宽阔的街道，大大改善了当地移民的居住环境。新建、改建公路400多千米，1000km河道基本渠化，极大地改善了当地交通和航运条件，为村民开辟出一条条脱贫致富的康庄大道。

根据测算，水电工程每投资1元钱，将带动3元钱的相关投资。沅水流域处于我国中西部边远山区，社会经济发展缓慢。五凌公司水电开发累计投资近400亿元，以水电开发为龙头，流域内养殖、旅游、运输、建材等相关产业迅速兴起，加快了贫困山区脱贫致富的步伐，做到了建一个电站、富一方民众、带动一方经济，项目所在地的沅陵、保靖、锦屏等国家级贫困县的GDP一跃进入当地市州前列。

（五）旅游效益

梯级电站建成后，形成一个个人工湖泊，湿地面积大幅增加，大大改善了当地生态环境，加上道路交通和水上交通的改善，目前各梯级电站水库已成为当地居民休闲、度假的最佳选择，地方政府已把旅游作为当地主要经济增长点之一。

（1）五强溪库区将建国家级湿地公园。根据沅陵县政府规划，从2010年到2025年，沅陵县将在五强溪库区建设湖南五强溪国家湿地公园。该湿地公园地处沅陵县境内，包括五强溪水库、酉水、沅水五强溪水库下游段及周边区域。湿地公园由西南向东北呈狭长形廊道走向，最南端至五强溪水库沅陵县与泸溪县交界处，最北端至五强溪镇，湿地规划总面积20 613.9hm²。该项目将以“重在保护，生态优先，合理开发，永续利用”为理念，立足湿地自然资源的保护，坚持可持续发展观，以五强溪库区和森林生态环境的自然优势为依托，融入自然质朴的田园风光，以民俗文化资源为特色，致力打造出湿地休闲旅游为主体的精品工程，把湿地公园建设成为湿地—森林复合生态系统保护和恢复的示范点，具有浓郁湘楚文化特色的湖南湿地生态旅游目的地，以及湿地资源“保护—利用—提高”的国家示范点和湖南湿地科普宣教基地。

（2）三板溪水库成当地旅游胜地。三板溪电站大坝为混凝土面板堆石坝，高185.5m，为国内第二、世界第三高坝。湖区森林覆盖率高，空气综合指数等级为优，航道达120km，湖面面积85km²，风光旖旎，水质无污染，两岸民族文化古朴神奇，可开发为避暑、探险、水上运动、航渡、生态观光等为一体的综合休闲娱乐旅游目的地。项目总投资500万美元，项目建成后可实现年销售收入380万美元，利润150万美元。该项目已完成景区总体规划，目前处于招商引资阶段。

（六）保证流量提高

流域梯级水库形成后，明显改善了河流自然径流条件，保证流量明显增加，提高了河流沿岸居民生产生活用水的可靠性。沅水干流的挂治、白市、托口、洪江、五强溪、凌津滩水电站独立运行时保证流量分别为 54m³/s、73m³/s、81m³/s、120m³/s、590m³/s、600m³/s，三板溪水库建成后保证流量为176m³/s，为下游各电站增加保证流量126m³/s。当沅水干流电站全部投运并联合调度运行时，挂治、白市、托口、洪江、五强溪、凌津滩水电站的保证流量分别提升为180m³/s、209m³/s、234m³/s、280m³/s、770m³/s、780m³/s。

（五凌电力有限公司　王　立）

清江梯级枢纽工程的综合效益

清江干流中下游河段分三级开发，龙头为水布垭水电站，中间为隔河岩水电站，最下游一个梯级为高坝洲水电站。水布垭工程是一座以发电为主，兼顾防洪、航运效益的大型水利枢纽；于1999年开工，2008年主体工程完工；坝型为混凝土面板堆石坝，坝顶高程409.0m，最大坝高233m；库容系数0.25，水库具有多年调节能力；安装4台单机容量460MW的混流式水力发电机组，装机容量1840MW，保证出力312MW，多年平均电量39.2亿kW·h。电站建成后，对下游隔河岩、高坝州两电站的梯级补偿效益也比较显著。隔河岩工程1999年竣工，枢纽建筑物由混凝土重力坝、泄水建筑物、右岸岸边式厂房、左岸垂直升船机组成；大坝坝顶高程206m，大坝全长653.5m，最大坝高151m；电站装机容量1212MW，保证出力241MW，多年平均电量29.4亿kW·h；汛限水位193.6m；具有发电、防洪、航运和旅游等巨大综合效益，其中防洪发电是隔河岩水库最主要的功能。高坝洲水电站以发电为主，兼有航运、水产效益的中型水利枢纽；工程于2001年竣工，水库具有日调节能力，电站装机270MW，保证出力7.7万kW，年发电量9.01亿kW·h。水库正常蓄水位80m，死水位78m，总库容4.86亿m³，是隔河岩电站调峰和航运的反调节水库。

（一）发电效益

清江干流3个梯级电站分别于2008年（水布垭）、1994年（隔河岩）、2001年（高坝洲）完成主体工程建设。从开始发电算起，至今为止建成年份最长的隔河岩电厂已有17年发电历史，总发电量已达391.20亿kW·h。加上后来建设的高坝洲、水布垭水电厂，干流各梯级截至2010年5月底，总计发电量达到568.56亿kW·h，发挥了巨大的发电效益。

（二）防洪效益

清江梯级通过利用防洪库容进行拦蓄，将最大限度地避免或减少长江荆江段相应的洪灾损失。据计算，清江每增加1000m³/s流量注入荆江段，沙市站水位将抬高8～10cm。但是，清江对荆江河段的防洪作用，与清江、荆江洪水的遭遇有关，与清江洪水占荆江洪水的比重有关：①长江发生洪水，而清江未发生洪水，此时清江水库起不到防洪作用；②长江洪水自身已超过荆江河段行洪能力，清江也发生相应洪水时，清江水库的防洪作用为推迟荆江分洪时间，减少荆江河段分洪流量；③长江洪水尚未超过荆江河段行洪能力，清江发生相应洪水，两江汇合后超过荆江河段行洪能力时，清江水库对荆江防洪作用为对其削峰、错峰，降低荆江河段洪峰水位，使之避免分洪。

1. 隔河岩水库的防洪作用

隔河岩水库建成后，连续遇到了1997年、1998年、1999年大洪水，在实际运用中发挥了较好的防洪效益，多次避免了荆江河段的分洪。

(1) 在1997年洪水中的作用。1997年7月，清江发生超百年一遇的大洪水，是有实测记录以来的第一大洪水，坝址洪峰流量高达18 400m^3/s。经隔河岩水库拦蓄，最大下泄流量10 550m^3/s，最大削峰约8000m^3/s，使清江下游免遭与1969年相近洪水带来的巨大灾害。这次清江发生大洪水时，长江宜昌站同期流量为32 000m^3/s左右，汇入清江10 000m^3/s左右流量后，未对荆江河段构成威胁。因此，本次隔河岩水库防洪对象主要为隔河岩下游清江沿岸地区，尤以长阳县城。应当指出的是，经过1969年以来近30年的发展建设，清江沿岸的经济有了较大的发展，如果没有隔河岩水库的拦蓄，1997年洪水造成的经济损失将至少是1969年洪灾损失的1～2倍。

(2) 在1998年长江洪水中的作用。1998年6月中旬至9月上旬，长江流域发生了继1954年以来全流域长时间、高频度的特大洪水。尤其是7月初以来，长江上游地区暴雨洪水频发，宜昌站从7月3日至8月31日60天之内连续出现8次洪峰，洪峰出现频度之高，超过了1954年，为历史罕见。而长江中游（宜昌—城陵矶段）素称"九曲回肠"，河道疏洪能力小，频繁的洪水导致荆江河段水位长时期居高不下。而清江流域自5月中旬以来，也连续发生了8次洪峰，其中第4、5、7、8次洪峰与长江第1、3、4、6次洪峰不同程度地遭遇。隔河岩多次运用水库的防洪库容与宜昌洪峰进行了错峰调度，降低了沙市最高洪水位，延缓了最高洪水位出现的时间，有效地减轻了沙市河段的防汛压力。其中，宜昌站发生的第六次洪峰（流量为63 600m^3/s）形势最为危急，遭遇了隔河岩8200m^3/s的入库洪峰，当时水库及时进行了拦蓄，峰现时刻控制下泄4000m^3/s，削减洪峰4200m^3/s，削减洪峰比例51%。从8月16日8时至17时共拦蓄9h，拦蓄洪水1.36亿m^3，库水位从201.98m涨至203.85m。随后，为确保大坝本身的安全，加大了泄量。由于隔河岩水库的超标准拦蓄，峰现时刻控制下泄4000m^3/s，延迟了沙市最高洪水位出现时间约5h，降低了沙市最高洪水位0.3～0.4m，为长江荆江河段防洪发挥了重要的作用，最终避免了荆江分洪区的使用，为国家和人们挽回了巨大的损失。

(3) 在1999年洪水中的作用。1999年7月长江流域发生大洪水，宜昌站洪峰流量52 000m^3/s，与此同时，清江受流域内强降雨影响，形成入库洪峰流量6300m^3/s，两洪峰恰好遭遇。由于在清江洪水到来之前，隔河岩水库水位预先已降至181.07m，离水库汛限水位近12m，尚留库容6.96亿m^3。根据洪水预报，清江此次洪峰入库洪量9.9亿m^3，水库维持满负荷发电，库水位将超过193.60m，但不会超过195m，离200m的正常高水位尚欠5m。根据这一情况，最终实施了保持满负荷发电、暂不开闸泄洪、与长江洪水错峰、以减轻荆江河段防洪压力的调度方式。这次调度实际效益十分明显，水库削减清江洪峰流量5100m^3/s，削减洪峰比例85%，拦蓄洪水7.41亿m^3，占总来水量的74.8%。由于水库及时拦洪削峰，荆江沙市实际出现洪峰水位43.55m，超警戒线0.55m。如果没有隔河岩水库的及时拦蓄，沙市洪峰水位将达到44.10m左右。通过这次合理的错峰调度，降低了沙市水位0.55m，大大地减轻了荆江防洪压力，也使隔河岩水库及时拦蓄水量，创造了良好的直接经济效益。

2. 水布垭建成后清江梯级水库对长江防洪作用

清江干流梯级在水布垭建成以后总库容87亿m^3，调节库容46亿m^3，为长江预留10亿m^3防洪库容（6月1日～7月31日，水布垭、隔河岩各5亿m^3），可配合三峡水库对长江中下游起防洪作用。

(1) 可提高荆江地区防洪标准。三峡工程建成后，荆江地区的防洪标准为100年一遇，清江梯级预留防洪库容控制宜沙区间大部分来水（约85%），可使荆江地区的防洪标准得到进一步提高。经计算，清江梯级预留10亿m^3防洪库容，可使荆江地区的防洪标准提高到124年一遇。

(2) 荆江地区遇100年一遇以上洪水，可减少荆江地区分洪量及推迟分洪时间。如荆江遇1000年一遇洪水，清江梯级预留10亿m^3，可减少荆江地区分洪量约10亿m^3，可推迟荆江地区分洪时间18.8h。

(3) 减少城陵矶地区分洪量。三峡建库后，荆江地区的防洪问题得到一定程度的解决，但城陵矶地区的防洪问题依然严峻，清江梯级预留10亿m^3防洪库容，如遇类似1954年洪水，可减少城陵矶地区分洪量约7.1亿m^3。

(4) 清江梯级预留防洪库容，控制了宜沙区间大部分来水，有利于三峡水库调度，增加了三峡水库调度的灵活性。

（湖北清江水电开发有限责任公司）

新安江水电站建成50年来对钱塘江水量调节的贡献

钱塘江流域属典型的季风气候区，雨季旱季十分明显。新安江是钱塘江两条主要支流之一，地处安徽省南部和浙江省西北部，多年平均降水量1658.4mm，但3～7月降水量为全年64.5%，来水量占74.2%，尤以梅汛期来水量更为集中。新安江水电站未建成前，当地民谣"走遍天下路，难过白沙渡，二点毛毛雨，洪水窜上屋"是对该地区无雨即旱，有雨成灾的生动描述。水电站建成后，洪涝灾害得到控制和调节，50年间共拦蓄洪峰流量大于4000m³/s的洪水135次、大于10 000m³/s的洪水31次，平均年拦蓄洪水30.6亿m³。50年间仅有5年正式开闸弃水，且洪水通过削峰后，下泄流量最大也仅6710m³/s，防洪效益显著。杭州湾特殊的地理环境为钱塘江带来了壮观的海潮，但同时也给杭州市洁净用水带来严峻挑战，水电站未建成前杭州市受咸潮侵袭几乎是年年发生。水库建成后，通过合理调节，大大减少了受咸潮影响的天数。50年来，新安江电站月平均出库流量为200～400m³/s，通过丰蓄枯补，明显改变了原来河流骤涨陡落的规律，钱塘江河道径流量更加均匀，也为改善钱塘江的生态环境起到重要作用。

（一）新安江水电站重视洪水资源化利用，为钱塘江成功防洪作出重要贡献

新安江和兰江是钱塘江上的两大支流，也是造成建德、桐庐、富阳、萧山等县市洪灾的主要河流。新安江属山溪性河流，春夏季多暴雨，常因暴雨引发山洪而泛滥成灾，历史上1935、1942、1954、1955等年均造成很大洪灾。如1955年6月，新安江、兰江洪水同时泛滥，建德市梅城镇水位猛涨，达29.46m，超警戒水位11.46m，沿江房屋大部分被冲毁，全市49个乡镇遭灾，毁房21 968间，死21人，伤49人，桐庐、富阳二城市水深3m，3个县市受灾农田计330余平方千米。

新安江水电站建成后，下泄流量得到有效控制，千年设计或万年＋安全保障校核洪水时，水库最大出库流量仅11 300m³/s、14 200m³/s，洪峰流量削减69.0%、70.7%。通过50年的运行，水库实际的泄洪次数、泄洪总量及削峰率远优于设计标准。如1999年6月下旬出现的7日洪量超100年一遇特大洪水时，最大下泄流量仅仅为6710m³/s，比设计下泄流量小1090m³/s，拦蓄了66%的洪水量。

50年来，水库平均每年拦蓄洪水30亿m³以上，水库水量利用系数达到98%，比原设计高出3.5%，提高了洪水的资源化利用。如1998年，成功利用水文气象预报，于1997年11月加大发电量，一直持续到1998年5月，用大发电来消落水库水位，腾出库容，流域于1998年6月16日入梅后，接连发生两次洪水，为与兰江错峰调节，1998年6月19日12时至20日8时，新安江水电站停止发电。两次洪水（合计35.1亿m³）均被拦蓄于库内，有效缓解了下游建德、桐庐、富阳、萧山、杭州等地的防洪压力，当年4次总量达46.37亿m³的洪水全部拦蓄在水库中，为多发电创造了条件。

通过洪水资源化利用，不但增加了丰水年的发电量，同时减少了泄洪次数和下泄总量。而在枯水年通过合理降低电站出力，保障枯水年钱塘江的生态环境不受大的影响。

（二）新安江水电站优化了钱塘江的径流分配，改善了生态环境

水库蓄水前的1951～1958年，下游罗桐埠水文站实测4～7月径流量最丰，占全年总量的65.2%，其他8个月仅占34.8%。水库蓄水后，明显改善了电站下游河道的径流分配，年际间、年内的丰枯悬殊程度大大缩小。由于下游河道流量调节均匀，促进了良好的生态环境，创造了生态财富。

首先变化的是水温。电站下游罗桐埠、芦茨埠、闸口三站的年平均水温明显降低5.5℃、2.5℃、1.4℃，而平均年最高水温下降，平均年最低水温升高，终年维持在14～18℃，影响直达杭州闸口以下，详见表1。

表1 新安江水库建库前后各主要站水温变化

各站名称	平均水温（℃）			平均最高水温（℃）			平均最低水温（℃）		
	建库前	建库后	降低	建库前	建库后	降低	建库前	建库后	降低
罗桐埠	19.0	13.5	5.5	34.8	23.5	11.3	3.4	6.3	2.9
芦茨埠	19.0	16.5	2.5	34.1	27.1	7.0	3.0	5.3	2.3
闸　口	19.5	18.1	1.4	34.3	28.6	9.7	3.4	5.1	1.7

1988年1月，建德市开始利用下泄的低温库水降低电影院温度，使两小时放映期间室内温度保持在26℃左右，成功地开创了低温库水降低室温的先例。其农业局还在梅城、千鹤等地利用江水低温灌溉农田，防止早稻高温逼熟和晚稻青枯死苗。通过1982年、1984年两年样板田对比，每亩提高单产15～25kg。建德市水产局还利用水电站大坝以下河段的低温水，养殖虹鳟鱼，1981年11月成功后，1982年供应市场1.5t。1984年投资建设年产商品虹鳟鱼160～200t的基地，一直坚持到现在。由于江水温度低，在江面上易形成薄雾，不但美化了沿江两岸环境，而且为新安江旅游业发展提供了独特的条件。

（三）新安江水电站为杭州市顶潮拒咸、改善饮用水质量起了关键作用

新安江水库建成之前，钱塘江江水含氯度大于300ppm的大数年年有发生，影响生活与生产。新安江修建水库前1955～1959年的10月至翌年2月，年均受咸潮影响56.3天，最多达121天。

当钱塘江流量呈天然状况时，即便遇到丰水年，由于降水径流年内分配不均匀，杭州市自来水厂取水口氯离子浓度仍会超标，遇枯水年更甚。

随着经济社会的不断发展，一方面用水量急剧增加，另一方面对水的质量也提出了更高要求。1960年新安江水库建成时，日供水量为3万t，至2009年已达到330万t，期间增加了110倍。可以想象，如果没有新安江水库的调节作用，杭州市连解决饮用水安全都成问题，更不用说发展工、农业生产了。

研究资料表明：在大潮汛时，一般要求钱塘江河口流量大于500m³/s，最好为700m³/s，才能达到顶潮冲淡的目的；当潮水小时，要求流量在300m³/s以上，才能保障杭州市饮用水质量。有时，虽年来水量偏多或特多，但时空分布不均，仍需新安江放水冲淡。如1990年7月，兰江、新安江天然流量之和达1700m³/s，但上旬大，旬均流量为4820m³/s，中下旬很小，分别为57.9m³/s和5.8m³/s，该月22～25日正是阴历六月朔潮，8月5日又遇望汛大潮，新安江水电站加大发电流量到580m³/s，最大的8月9日达746m³/s，超过天然入流量的18倍，使杭州市区和郊区避免了自来水供应中断。近几年，杭州市供水量每年都有10%以上的幅度增长，加重了对钱塘江顶潮拒咸的任务。2003年后，浙江省成立了杭州抗咸工作联席会议办公室，加强了对顶潮最小流量的预测和新安江水库的补偿调度工作，使最近7年杭州市饮用水质量得到极大提高。总之，50年来，新安江水库为杭州市顶潮拒咸工作起到了不可替代的作用。

（新安江水力发电厂　李福钢　粟运华）

棉花滩水电站的综合效益

棉花滩水电站位于福建省永定县境内，坝址位于汀江干流棉花滩峡谷河段中部、永定河汇入口以上700m处。坝址控制流域面积7907km²，坝址处多年平均径流量73.2亿m³，多年平均流量232m³/s，流域内多年年降雨量1657.1mm。工程以发电为主，兼有防洪、航运、水产养殖等综合效益。调节库容11.22亿m³，属不完全年调节水库，总库容20.35亿m³。工程属一等枢纽工程，主要建筑物大坝及泄水建筑物按500年一遇洪水设计，5000年一遇洪水校核，设计洪水流量12 000m³/s，校核洪水流量15 500m³/s。电站枢纽由拦河主坝、湖洋里副坝、泄水建筑物、左岸地下厂房发电系统、开关站、右岸过坝设施等建筑物组成。电站装机4台，单机容量150MW，共计600MW，年发电量15.2亿kW·h，保证出力88MW，年利用小时数2533h。工程于1998年4月正式开工，2001年12月全部建成投产。

在汀江流域中，福建棉花滩水电站的工程规模和水库库容最大，其余的电站规模均较小，棉花滩水电站是该流域的控制性工程，在防洪、发电、水运及库区建设等方面均发挥了重要作用。

（一）防洪

棉花滩水库对下游广东省韩江三角洲（潮汕经济特区）防洪有相当大的作用。韩江三角洲面积1035km²，区内建有防洪围区13个，防洪堤线总长314km，总保护人口405.7万人、耕地面积158万亩。其中最大堤围为南北堤，位于韩江右岸，由北堤、城墙堤和南堤组成，防护区人口298.7万人，耕地106万亩。南北堤由于其堤身较单薄，堤基防渗能力较差，其防洪能力相当于20年一遇，相应潮安河道安全泄量13 700m³/s。为提高韩江三角洲的防洪能力，每年5、6月主汛期，棉花滩水库正常蓄水位以下须预留防洪库容2.59亿m³，当洪水（$P=2\%$）主要来自汀江时，水库控制泄流5210m³/s，能使下游潮安50年一遇洪水（洪峰流量16 000m³/s）削减为相当于25～27年一遇（洪峰流量14 300～14 400m³/s）；次汛期（7月上旬～8月中旬），棉花滩水库须预留库容1.07亿m³，当遇主要洪水来自汀江（$P=2\%$），水库控泄4400m³/s，可使潮安流量削减到13 700m³/s，防洪标准提高到50年一遇。

（二）发电

棉花滩水电站总装机容量600MW，年发电量15.2亿kW·h，主要供电对象为福建省网的龙岩、漳州及厦门等地区。福建省煤炭资源不足，水力资源

较丰富，但大多属调节性能差的径流式水电站，丰水期大量弃水，而枯水期电力电量不足。棉花滩水电站是福建省为数不多的具有不完全年调节能力的大型水电站，是闽西南最大的水电电源，也是福建省网主力电源之一，可以担任福建省网调峰、调频任务，同时，对增加网内有调节能力的水电比重发挥补偿效益，减少水电弃水，改善福建省网电源北重南轻的布局，效益均较显著。另外，经棉花滩水库调节后可使下游13.0km处的广东青溪水电站年发电量增加1.04亿kW·h，保证出力增加20.1MW，大大提高了青溪水电站的发电效益。

（三）水运

整个汀江水系由于干支流河道滩多水浅，航道条件一直未能得到较为有效的整治。汀江河道最险段为福建省峰市至广东省石市间约5.5km的河段，因该段河道江面狭窄，滩多水急、礁石密布，历史上一直不通航，通过该段的运输方式是水路运至峰市后上岸，改成陆路运输。20世纪80年代后，随着公路交通的发展，水上运输已逐渐被公路运输所取代，至棉花滩工程开工前，据当时峰市乡的运输情况调查表明，那时汀江棉花滩水电站坝址实际上已无货物通过，每年只有少量原本漂运。棉花滩水电站工程建成后，水库回水至上杭城郊，距坝址38～46km的上游河道为水库区，原来滩多水急、礁石密布的峡谷河段都成为了深水航道，大大改善了通航条件。棉花滩库区形成以来，库区已兴建了等级码头5座、小型交通码头1处、简易码头3处、生产生活渡口77岸，为库区群众的生产生活提供了很大的交通便利。

（四）库区建设

棉花滩水库正常蓄水位高程的水库面积为60.56km^2，库区淹没涉及福建省永定县及上杭县，共搬迁人口3.54万人，淹没耕地3万亩、各类结构房屋168.78万m^2。移民安置采取了后靠安置、外迁安置、自行择地安置3种形式，在移民生产就业安置方面采取了耕地资源开发利用、耕地防护工程、山地经济作物开发、养殖业生产开发、扶持非农产业项目等措施。通过移民前与移民后的统计数据对比，库区群众的生活水平及库区经济有较快的提高和发展。

（1）在移民居住条件方面，永定县移民的人均住房面积由搬迁前的35.17m^2/人增长为搬迁后的56.30m^2/人，增加了21.13m^2/人，是搬迁前的1.60倍；上杭县移民的人均住房面积由搬迁前的35.88m^2/人增长为搬迁后的51.16m^2/人，增加了15.73m^2/人，是搬迁前的1.44倍。比照迁移前原居住条件，移民群众居住的房屋质量明显提高，居住安全性也有相当提高；与同期全县农村平均水平相比，移民目前的居住条件明显高于当地农村平均水平。

（2）在移民收入水平方面，永定县移民搬迁后的3年平均人均总收入为5084元/人，比移民搬迁前的3179元/人增长了1905元/人，增长幅度为59.92%；上杭县移民搬迁后的3年平均人均总收入为4548元/人，比移民搬迁前的3763元/人增长了785元/人，增长幅度为20.86%。从上述移民搬迁前后人均收入水平看，移民搬迁后的收入水平已经达到搬迁前的收入水平，并比搬迁前有一定幅度的增长。

（3）在移民生活环境方面，以前大部分移民的房屋都是土木结构，水、电、通信、文化等设施比较简陋，村内、村外道路泥泞，就医、就学困难。搬迁后移民新村的水、电设施都比较完备，对外交通较为便捷，电话、有线电视等配套设施基本齐全，新建的房屋基本都是砖混结构，宽敞明亮，居民基本都已实现自来水入户，卫生条件明显改善，有的安置区（点）还建设了相应的公建设施和绿化场所等公益性设施。通过移民集中安置，移民搬迁建设与农村小城镇建设基本框架结合后，安置点的公用设施、卫生设施、集市交易、相关文娱场所得到了较好的恢复建设，有些已初具社区式的居委会雏形。部分移民安置点位于县城辐射范围内，移民在较高层次的起点上享受了文化教育、医疗卫生等公益事业设施服务。

（4）在交通设施方面，规划复建了各类道路250km、桥梁32座、各类码头8座，改善了库区乡村的交通条件。

（5）在教育设施复建方面，永定县共完成新建、扩建学校28所，并对安置点周边的原有13所学校进行了补助，上杭县共复建扩建学校11所，改善了库区的教育条件。

总体上讲，通过工程移民安置，移民的居住条件、收入水平、生活设施条件、社区建设、教育及交通条件等，均较移民前有了较大的改善和提高，并优于当地农民的平均水平。

（上海勘测设计研究院）

贵州农村水电惠及山区百姓

新中国成立60年来，贵州省认真贯彻党和国家有关发展小水电的一系列方针政策，因地制宜积极开发小水电，全省87个县（区、市）中有80个建有小水电站，共建设了21个农村水电初级电气化县，13个水电农村电气化县，11个小水电代燃料试点项目区。通过开发利用小水电，解决了广大农村人民生活和工农业生产用电，为促进贫困山区，特别是少数民族地区的经济发展和社会进步发挥了积极作用。小水电作为清洁可再生能源，并以其淹没土地少、移民搬迁少、就地发电、就地利用、输电距离短、变电环节少、电能损耗少、电价低的优势，为全省农业、农民和农村经济的发展作出了显著的贡献：

（1）改善了农民群众、特别是边远贫困山区少数民族群众的物质文化生活。“七五”以来，小水电解决了1200万农村人口的用电问题，乡通电率由73.3%提高到100%，村通电率由55%提高到99.82%，户通电率由45%提高到97.84%。小水电给全省农村近1/3的县和1/2的农村人口提供用电需要。水电农村电气化县的户通电率达到98.88%。

（2）带动了扶贫开发以及农村经济、县域经济的发展，促进了区域经济结构的调整和优化。各地通过开发当地农村水能资源，为地方经济发展提供廉价的电力支撑，为拉动地方经济发展、促进农村劳动率转移、增加农民收入发挥了积极的作用。“七五”以来，贵州省达标验收的初级电气化县和个水电农村电气化县的国内生产总值、农民人均纯收入、财政收入年均增长率均高于全省平均水平。

（3）促进了自然生态环境的保护和建设。水能资源是可再生的清洁能源。把近年来小水电的发电量折算为燃煤发电，相当于每年少消耗458.4万t标准煤，减少1375万m^3二氧化碳和其他有害气体的排放，相应减少治理二氧化碳和其他有害气体排放所需的大量投入，有效保护了环境。同时，小水电资源的开发利用使全省约43万户144万人实现了丰水期以电代燃料，水电农村电气化建设县的森林覆盖率年均增长1.74%，有效地巩固了退耕还林的成果。

（4）加快了中小河流治理步伐，提高了水资源综合利用效益。贵州省建成的农村水电形成的总库容达近30亿m^3，这些水库在提高下游防洪标准、增加灌溉和供水水源、发展旅游、水土保持等方面均发挥了较大的效益，为解决贵州省工程性缺水发挥了积极的作用。据估算，农村水电平均年增加灌溉面积5万亩以上，治理水土流失面积200km^2，解决15万人的饮水难问题。一些小水电的建成使下游一些城镇良田的防洪能力一下提高了很多。一些地区还利用小水电建设形成的水面发展旅游业、养殖业。贵州省的许多闻名遐迩的国家级风景名胜区都是在开发水电资源的过程中开发出来的。

（5）在涵养水源、净化水质改善环境方面发挥了积极的作用。贵州省修建的一些小型水电站，很多都是中型以下的小水库，对于调节能力较小的水库，库内水体交换很快，不容易发生水质富营养化的现象。而调节能力稍大的水库，通过加强管理、合理调度，采取蓄清排浊等措施，水质不仅没有变坏，而且因水库水体的降解作用，水质大大改善。许多小水电的入库水质都是四、五类水，但出库水质就变为了二、三类水，如三岔河、清水江、舞阳河、油菜河等都有修建电站水库后对下游水质明显改善的现象。同时，一些小河流，修建梯级水电站形成一些小水库后，枯水期也有一定的水流下泄，基本上没有再出现过长距离断流现象，小水电起到了涵养水源的积极作用。

（6）为“西电东送”提供了有力的支撑。小水电是电力工业的重要组成部分，是大电站的有益补充。“十五”期间，贵州省“黔电送粤”总电量为335亿kW·h，而同时期全省小水电总的发电量为225亿kW·h，占“黔电送粤”电量的67%。“十五”期农村水电为满足“黔电送粤”的任务、保障省内地方经济社会发展用电发挥了积极的作用。

农村水电的建设成就，是新中国建设成就的一部分，贵州农村水电的发展壮大史，也是贵州省发展的一个缩影，几代水电人为之付出的努力没有白费。随着水能资源开发利用更加科学有序，小水电代燃料将得到更广泛的实施，水电农村电气化水平将大幅提高。农村水电的发展，将为贵州省的经济建设、江河治理、生态保护、扶贫开发和社会进步作出新的、更大的贡献。

（贵州省农村水电及电气化发展局　吴新黔　谭剑虹）

猫跳河梯级建设对贵州经济社会发展的促进作用

猫跳河是乌江南岸的一条支流，1958～1981年，为满足贵州省电力负荷急剧增长的需要，对猫跳河进行了以发电为主，结合灌溉、工业供水和水产养殖等综合利用的梯级开发。全流域为6级开发，分别命名为红枫（一级）、百花（二级）、修文（三级）、窄巷口（四级）、红林（五级）、红岩（六级）水电站，总库容8亿m^3、总装机容量23.9万kW（1992年猫跳河梯级在一级及二级之间增加二级半李官水电站，加之梯级电站增容改造，目前总装机容量为27.7万kW）。

随着经济社会的发展，水库功能逐渐转变，目前实际功能是以城市供水、发电、旅游为主，兼有防洪、灌溉、养殖、调节生态等多项功能。猫跳河梯级水库成为我国开发最早且功能最为齐全的梯级开发的成功典型，它为贵州省经济社会的发展起到了很大的促进作用，也为我国梯级水电开发提供了积极的借鉴作用。

（一）电站建设曾为贵州省提供了2/3的电力

猫跳河梯级首台机组（红枫水电站1号机组）于1960年6月并网发电，投产初期所发电量占贵州电网的17.7%；修文水电站和百花水电站相继投产后，发电量随之增大，1966年发电量占贵州电网的77.6%。截至1988年，共发电量108.31亿kW·h，以不变电价计创产值6.74亿元，同时拥有固定资产原值3.23亿元，29年平均全员劳动生产率为4.33万元/(人·年)，1965年最高达17.26万元/(人·年)，1988年人均产值32 681元，为清镇市1988年人均生产总值1095元的近30倍。

1965年贵阳地区的发电设备容量为9.9万kW，其中水电5万kW，猫跳河一、三级占4万kW。在“文化大革命”期间，由于交通阻塞，原煤运输困难，火电被迫停产，贵阳地区的工业和照明用电全靠猫跳河一、三级电站供电。

红枫水电站建成40多年来累计发电258.3亿kW·h，拉动了周边工业、农业、旅游业的发展，为贵州省电力工业发展壮大、贵州工农业生产和人民生活水平提高作出了重大贡献。

（二）电站建设对地方的防洪效益

猫跳河属山溪性河流，山洪猛烈，洪峰时间短，洪水陡涨陡落。据调查，1954年洪水为近百年的特大洪水，流域内受灾面积约6万亩，受灾人口4万余人，损失粮食420万斤，死人20名，死牲畜12头，冲毁房屋300间，冲毁水利工程35处。红枫坝址以上流域面积1596km^2，正常蓄水位1240.00m时库容5.896亿m^3，总库容7.529亿m^3，为不完全多年调节水库。百花坝址以上流域面积1895km^2，正常蓄水位1195.00m时库容1.82亿m^3，总库容2.208亿m^3，为年调节水库。两电站分别于1960年和1966年建成发电，自水库兴建以来，曾发生的最大历史洪水为“91.7”洪水，所形成的洪水达到了100年一遇的量级。在此次洪水过程中，红枫、百花水库充分发挥了拦洪错峰作用，使洪水顺利通过，保证了下游水库的安全，同时大大提高了周边及下游的防洪能力，减少了洪水的灾害。

（三）红枫、百花水库为周边工业、农业、城市用水提供了水源

猫跳河红枫湖位于清镇和平坝境内，清镇市人口和工业主要集中在红枫湖周边，有清镇火电厂、省有机化工厂、省化肥厂、中国七砂集团、省铁合金厂、贵阳煤气气源厂、清镇铁合金厂和红湖、黎阳、环宇、高峰等20多家大中型企业，以及中八、夏云、平坝和红枫畜禽水产等国营农场，是贵州省能源、化工、纺织、机械、冶金、农副业发展重要基地。据统计，周边工农业每年在红枫湖取水4.57亿m^3，红枫水库为周边工业、农业用水提供了足够的水源。从百花水库取水的工厂主要有贵州铝厂、贵阳耐火材料厂、清镇纺织印染厂等。百花水库对贵州的铝工业发展起着较大的积极作用。

2005年，贵州省政府将红枫湖的功能调整为以城市供水为主，贵阳市西郊水厂（设计规模80万m^3/天）从红枫水库取水，白云水厂（设计规模10万m^3/天）从百花水库取水。在水库调度管理上优先服从城市供水，再协调猫跳河流域梯级电站的发电和防洪调度，红枫、百花水库作为贵阳市城市供水水源，极大地缓解了贵阳市供水压力。

（四）电站建设对周边工业的拉动作用

红枫湖和百花湖两个水库为黔中地区工农业发展奠定了良好的物质基础。红枫湖回水28km，形成水面面积57.2km^2，蓄水6.01亿m^3，跨越清镇、平坝两县。百花湖回水13km，形成水面面积14.5km^2，蓄水1.82亿m^3，连接清镇和贵阳市。两湖分别距贵阳市31.5km和28km，处于全省经济中心，其浩瀚明净的水体成为工业生产必须的优质水源，对贵州省工业布局产生了深远的影响。在猫跳河建设之前，猫跳河流域的工业生产几乎空白，紧随红枫水电站的兴建，清镇发电厂、贵州化肥厂、清镇棉纺厂、贵州有机化工厂、贵州铝业公司等十多家大、中型国有企业在红枫湖畔拔地而起，成为贵州省中部主要的工业区。湖畔众多企业的建立，远远超过猫跳河自身经济效益，1989年工业总产值7.07亿元，占全省工业总产值201.45亿元的3.5%，在全省经济发展中具有重要的地位，仅1970年建成投产的清镇发电厂，到1988年创造的11.35亿元产值，就超过猫跳河经济效益本身。同时，由于红枫湖区域具有资源、能源、交通和技术的有利条件，地方工业和乡镇企业如雨后春笋般发展起来，在清镇县建有水泥厂、印刷厂、粮油加工厂、饲料加工厂、铝矿厂、酒厂、农机修造厂、磨具厂、砂轮厂、玻璃厂、服装厂、皮鞋厂等，据1988年统计，各类企业的产值达25 229万元，占全年该区域大中型国企产值的1/3强，是红枫湖地区经济结构中的重要组成部分，是改善和提高当地人民生活水平的重要途径。

（五）电站建设对周边农业的拉动作用

红枫湖、百花湖区域内的农业结构以种植业为主，约占农业总产值的60%，畜牧业（包括水产养殖业）次之，约占农业总产值的30%，林业比重最小，不足农业总产值的5%。

红枫湖、百花湖将猫跳河枯水期流量从2.0m^3/s提高到20.0m^3/s，提高近10倍，解决了河源地区枯水季节流量偏小的问题，为沿湖农业生产提供了可靠的灌溉用水。自1960年以来，清镇县在两湖沿岸修建了大小电力提灌工程数百处，有效灌溉面积达4万多亩，占全县有效灌溉面积的74%强，灌溉粮食增产近两倍。1962年于红枫湖建成的贵州省当时最大

的电力提灌工程——红枫电力提灌站，装机 10 台，总装机容量 3111kW，设计灌溉面积 15 000 多亩。这为促进当地以粮食作物为核心的农业经济的发展起到了显著的作用。

随着红枫水电站的建成，红枫湖区域内的国营农场如八果树园艺场、平坝果树园艺场、清镇农牧场、夏云农场、红枫湖畜禽水产公司等也相继建成，其农副产品具有一定的规模，对城市、工矿人民的生活供应，对市场供应和丰富人们的"菜篮子"作出了重要贡献。

（六）电站建设对当地旅游业的拉动作用

由于红枫水电站、百花水电站大坝建成形成了贵州省最大的人工水库——红枫湖及百花湖。红枫湖和百花湖山峦叠嶂，景致独特，风光互补，被誉为贵州高原上的姊妹明珠，吸引着成千上万的中外游客，成为著名的游览胜地，构成贵州省西线旅游的第一站。

红枫湖在正常高水位时水域面积为 57.2km²，群山环抱的红枫湖，有大小 190 多个岛屿星罗棋布，使红枫湖除具有喀斯特作用形成的风景地貌、溶洞峭壁、石林等外，尚有各种湖湾港汊、孤岛独石及各川飞禽水鸟，加上少数民族风情和历史遗留下来的文物古迹，以及茂密的植被和宜人的气候，使红枫湖旅游资源丰富而独特，山中有湖、湖中有岛、岛中有洞、洞中有水的"四绝"奇观令人叹为观止。1981 年 8 月，贵州省省委和省政府综合开发红枫湖，开辟了旅游业，1988 年红枫湖被列为国家 AAAA 级旅游区。清镇县也被列为国家甲级对外开放县。

百花湖在正常高水位时水域面积为 14.8km²，山峦倒映的百花湖，以临江预度的"八仙过海"和雄奇险峻、绮丽清幽的"小三峡"等游览景点及"烟云浩瀚白鸥闲"的景观引人入胜。1988 年，百花湖被列为省级风景名胜区。

随着旅游业的发展，也拉动了相关的饮食、交通客运等产业的发展。

（七）电站建设对当地教育事业的贡献

猫跳河电站建设初期正值我国三年困难时期，全国经济落后，社会发育度很低，教育软硬件均很差，贵州省又是我国贫困省份，受教育人口比例和受教育程度明显低于全国平均水平。电站建设后，陆续修建了小学、中学，随着办学规模的不断扩大和师资力量的不断强化，电站的自办学校在清镇县具有一定的知名度，近几年的大学升学率达到 60%以上，2005 年已被清镇市收编，成为清镇市的正式编号学校，为当地的教育发展作出了较大的贡献。

（八）电站建设对环境影响

从水资源的利用方式看，猫跳河水电站用水是非消耗性用水，所引水量回归至下游，运营过程中利用的主要是优质、清洁的可再生水能。猫跳河水电站利用水能发电，可替代、节约化石燃料能源，可减排温室气体量和其他污染物。

从节能效益和减排效益上分析，猫跳河水电站建成发电以来共发电 258.3 亿 kW·h，与发电规模相当的火电相比，按发电标准煤煤耗 330g/(kW·h)计，可为国家节约标准煤 853 万 t。

水电作为一种清洁能源，除了可节约化石燃料外，与相同发电量的燃煤发电相比，相应每年可减少多种有害气体的排放。自发电以来与系统发电量的燃煤发电相比共减排 CO_2 2000 万 t，同时可减排 CO、NO_2、碳氢化合物（C_nH_m）、灰渣，节约淡水，并减少相应的水力排灰废水和温排水等对水域的污染，还减少大量烟尘的排放。除此以外，燃煤火电站主要产生 SO_2 排放物，形成酸雨污染。按西南地 SO_2 排放绩效指标值 2.2g/(kW·h)计算，猫跳河水电站已减排 SO_2 5.7 万 t。

（九）电站建设对我国水电事业的积极影响

猫跳河梯级电站的建设为国内水电事业提供了建设和管理方面的经验。6 座风姿各异的拦河大坝引起了国内外水电、地质专家学者的浓厚兴趣，猫跳河梯级成为我国最早、最全的"电站博物馆"，引来众多的水电同行前来参观学习，为我国水电建设事业作出了贡献，特别为贵州省"西电东送"工程在建设和管理上积累了许多宝贵经验。

猫跳河梯级率先实行集中管理，将各电站职工集中到厂部，统一布置生活和生产管理基地，运行实行轮班制。这种管理方式解决了边远职工生活上存在的多种困难，从人为环境的优化上保证了生产和安全，为全国同类企业所借鉴。

猫跳河水电设计、建设、运行，为贵州省的水电建设培养了大批科技设计、建设、运行、管理等方面的队伍和人才，对国家西部大开发及贵州省水利水电快速发展起到积极作用。

（十）水电工程对移民生产生活的积极影响

1958～1974 年，猫跳河梯级水库库区共搬迁移民 34 848 人，其中非农业移民 381 人。到 1985 年后期扶持前，库区移民增长到 59 384 人，增加了24 536人。由于移民安置存在着较多的问题，存在"十大难"，即吃饭难、住房难、饮水难、用电难、行路难、上学难、看病难、生活燃料难、生存难、脱贫难。从 1986 年开始，国家对猫跳河梯级水库库区进行移民遗留问题处理。先后分为 4 个阶段：第一阶段为 1986～1989 年；第二阶段为 1990～1995 年；第三阶段为 1996～2001 年；第四阶段为 2002～2015 年。根据水利部水库移民局制定的 2002～2015 年的目标要求，为移民建成能满足粮食自给的旱涝保收基本农田、户均有一亩以上农业园地（菜园、果园）或经济作物、户均一项养殖业或其他家庭副业。按国家规定的人畜饮水标准，基本解决移民人畜饮水困难，移民乡（镇）通低等级公路，移民村组通机耕道，移民村建有医疗点或卫生室，移民村通电，户均有一名劳动力从事非农产业。

经过长达20年的遗留问题处理和后期扶持，猫跳河梯级水库移民的“十大难”遗留问题得到了较好的处理，移民的生活条件较大的改善，库区经济得到了一定的发展。到2007年，155个村已通公路，公路覆盖率为93.37%；移民的人均住房面积已达13.9m^2，其中，砖混结构房屋面积为9.34m^2；人均旱涝保收耕地面积达到0.32亩；移民村组已全部通电；适龄儿童就学率已达100%。扶持后的2006年与扶持前的1985年相比，移民人均纯收入从1985年的138元增加到2006年的1937元；年人均自产粮食从1985年的100kg增加到2006年的314kg；初步越过温饱线的移民达到64 268人，移民贫困面从扶持前的79.5%下降为2006年的5.45%。

（中国水电顾问集团贵阳勘测设计研究院 陈文春）

我国2009年批准的清洁发展机制水电项目为世界每年减排温室气体723万余吨

清洁发展机制（Clean Development Mechanism，CDM），是2005年2月正式生效的《京都议定书》中建立起的国际合作机制。发达国家通过提供资金和技术的方式，与发展中国家开展项目合作，通过项目所实现的“经核证的减排量”，用于发达国家缔约方完成在议定书第三条下关于减少本国温室气体排放的承诺的规定。项目所产生的额外的、可核实的CO_2减排量称为“核证减排量”，由发展中国家的项目企业所拥有，并可出售。

2009年，国家发展改革委批准了我国企业所拥有的58个水电项目作为清洁发展机制项目，这些项目的预计总年减排量为7 232 459t二氧化碳当量。所核证减排量出售给国外合作方，为世界减少温室气体排放作出贡献。2009年国家发展改革委批准作为清洁发展机制的58个水电项目情况，详见表1。

表1 2009年国家发展改革委批准作为清洁发展机制的58个水电项目情况表

序号	水电项目名称	装机容量（MW）	国外合作方	预计年减排CO_2量（t）
1	新疆宁家河山口		ECO ASSET Incorporated	33 335
2	陕西灯芯桥	5	Shell Trading International Limited	14 491
3	四川省越西县响水河一级	10	Carbon Alliance Holding AG	32 883
4	重庆市城口县蹇家湾	26	AES Carbon Exchange Ltd	67 560
5	四川省德昌县新马		Vitol S. A.	497 880
6	四川省木里县宁郎		Vitol S. A.	376 585
7	四川省平武县三岔		Vitol S. A.	167 042
8	云南省武定县永厂河	9.6	Carbon Asset Management Sweden AB	39 282
9	云南省乡城县玛依河一级		Shell Trading International Limited	60 221
10	湖南省双牌县永江流域梯级		CCAN Consulting GmbH	52 250
11	湖南省双牌县社江流域梯级		CCAN Consulting GmbH	58 838
12	广西南丹县更偶		荷兰安智银行股份有限公司	15 211
13	湖南省桃寮梯级	10.49	Standard Bank Plc	40 936
14	湖南省资水一级		韩国大宇集团（德国）	71 641
15	大关县飚水岩和新街	8	Climate Corporation Emissions Trading GmbH	30 493
16	湖北省来凤县金龙滩		赫尔克里斯绿色交易有限公司	71 533
17	云南省盈江县支那河一级		意大利国家电力公司	62 050
18	云南省盈江县支那河二级一期二期		意大利国家电力公司	160 947
19	甘肃省临洮润狄		Climate Corporation Emissions Trading GmbH	49 029

续表

序号	水电项目名称	装机容量（MW）	国外合作方	预计年减排 CO_2 量（t）
20	云南省沧源芒回		Vitol S. A	67 201
21	云南省彝良县龙府	12	瑞典碳资产管理有限公司	37 336
22	湖南省安化县小水电打捆项目		Climate Corporation Emissions Trading GmbH	24 972
23	四川省昭觉县打捆水电站项目		维多石油集团	42 184
24	四川省泸定县磨河沟下松		维多石油集团	48 061
25	四川省泸定县磨河沟打捆水电站项目		维多石油集团	67 573
26	云南省岗曲河二级		MGM 碳资产投资组合	531 727
27	青海省俄博图		伊藤忠商事株式会社	45 850
28	江西省洋田		Eneco Energy Trade B. V.	6503
29	湖南省溆浦县小山阳		ecolutions Trading GmbH	20 900
30	四川省马边县鱼孔		维多石油集团	36 590
31	浙江省唐村	32	瑞典能源署、亚洲开发银行亚太碳基金	25 633
32	云南省尼汝河金汉拉扎	58	Austrian CCAN Consulting GmbH	228 417
33	湖南省小河		Eneco Energy Trade B. V.	13 079
34	贵州省楼下河		Eneco Energy Trade B. V.	25 909
35	湖南省金桥梯级	7	Eneco Energy Trade B. V.	22 725
36	湖南省梧桐小水电		Eneco Energy Trade B. V.	17 072
37	重庆市城口县巴山		AES Carbon Exchange Limited	382 861
38	江西省会昌县白鹅	21	碳资产管理株式会社	61 619
39	云南省禄劝县江边		复兴碳投资有限公司	134 239
40	四川省美姑河坪头	180	ECO 资产管理公司	541 389
41	湖南省瑶人坪		环保桥有限公司	25 801
42	青海省加定		英国喜来碳资产管理公司	44 013
43	甘肃省舟曲县巴藏	51	环保桥有限公司	166 583
44	云南省耿马铁厂河	12.6	日本三菱 UFJ 证券株式会社	39 421
45	四川省越西县团结		维多石油集团	101 834
46	湖南省溆浦县朱溪江	10	环保桥有限公司	28 263
47	四川省黑水河毛尔盖		英国排放贸易有限公司	1 661 705
48	湖南省泸溪县能滩	6.4	Carbon Asset Management Sweden AB	17 783
49	四川省松潘县木瓜墩		EcoSecurities 国际有限公司	77 000
50	云南省红河马堵山		CF 碳基金Ⅱ有限公司	906 657
51	甘肃省齐家坪		Carbon Asset Management Sweden Pte Ltd.	64 968
52	云南省潞西市南马河二级	4	环保桥有限公司	13 961
53	重庆市綦江县珠滩		Fine Carbon Fund Ky 和 Nordic Carbon Fund KY	25 826
54	云南省高河四级		日本碳基金	68 241
55	甘肃省张掖石庙二级	8.0	环保桥有限公司	19 159
56	甘肃省龙王台		第一气候变化投资Ⅱ	70 230
57	青海省宝库河三级		伊藤忠商事株式会社	50 034
58	湖北省房县三里坪	70	住友商事株式会社	152 598
总计				7 232 459

（本年鉴编辑部摘编）

15

农村水电及电气化

农村水电建设

小水电点亮中国农村

编者按：本文是水利部农村水电及电气化发展局局长田中兴2009年5月11日在第五届“今日水电论坛”上的发言。

中国是一个农业大国，农村人口占相当大的比例。解决好农业、农村、农民问题，始终是中国政府工作的重中之重。中国水能资源技术可开发量5.42亿kW，居世界首位。其中小水电技术可开发量1.28亿kW，主要分布在经济发展相对落后、农村人口较多的中西部地区和少数民族地区。长期以来，在中国政府支持下，广大山区群众通过开发小水电，建设配套电网，使中国1/2的地域、1/3的县市、3亿多农村人口用上了电。中国通过开发小水电实现农村电气化的做法受到了联合国和世界各国的关注，中国开发小水电的技术和经验得到许多发展中国家的借鉴。

一、中国小水电的发展历程

中国的水力发电是从小水电开始的。20世纪初建成的首座水电站——云南昆明石龙坝水电站就是小水电。目前，中国已经建成了包括三峡等特大型电站在内的数万座水电站，装机容量达1.71亿kW，年发电量5600亿kW·h；其中小水电装机容量5100万kW，年发电量1600多亿kW·h，约占中国水电装机和发电量的30%。中国小水电发展可以大致划分为三个阶段。

（一）第一阶段

从新中国成立到20世纪70年代末的30年。因资金、技术和体制等原因，小水电发展速度慢、规模小，以分散独立供电为主，总装机容量还不到700万kW，年均投产装机仅21万kW。由于国家电力紧缺，输变电设施也跟不上，有数亿农村人口处于无电状态。

（二）第二阶段

从中国实行改革开放到20世纪末的20年。改革开放极大地解放了生产力，国家的工作重点转向以经济建设为中心，电力基础设施薄弱问题越来越突出。当时国家的财力还不能满足日益增长的用电需求，亟须调动各方面办电的积极性，加快电力发展和普及。在邓小平倡导下，国家通过政策支持、财政补助、技术培训等措施，鼓励地方政府和当地农民自力更生兴办小水电，开创了有中国特色的农村电气化道路。经过20年的努力，到1999年底，小水电总装机容量达到2350万kW，增加了1650万kW，年均投产装机达82万kW，基本解决了当地用电问题，小水电点亮了中国农村。

（三）第三阶段

进入新世纪以来的10年。中国政府更加重视小水电在农村经济社会发展中的作用，强调要大力发展小水电，建设农村电气化，实施小水电代燃料工程。随着国家经济体制改革的不断深化，社会资本大量进入小水电开发领域，促进了小水电的快速发展，小水电总装机容量达到5100万kW，增加了2750万kW，年均投产装机容量达306万kW。小水电在解决山区农村用电问题的同时，也极大地促进了农村经济社会的全面发展。

二、中国小水电的巨大作用

小水电没有大量水体集中和移民，规模适宜，技术成熟，可就地开发、就近供电，适宜解决分散、边远、贫困山区的用电问题，在促进中国农村经济社会发展中发挥了巨大作用。

（一）实现了农村电气化

从1983年起，中国政府启动了农村水电电气化县建设。依靠开发小水电，建设配套电网，“七五”至“九五”期间建成了653个农村水电初级电气化县，“十五”期间建成了409个水电农村电气化县。“十一五”期间400个水电农村电气化县建设正在实施中。目前1600多个县（市）建有小水电，近600个县以小水电供电为主，200多个县拥有完整的小水电供电网，3000多个乡村有小水电自供区。农村水电地区户通电率从1980年的不足40%提高到2008年的99.6%，供电质量和可靠性大大提高，基本解决了山区农村的用电问题。

（二）带动了农村经济社会发展

各地政府都把开发水能资源、建设小水电作为带动当地经济社会发展、增加地方财政收入的支柱产业来抓。许多县小水电提供的利税在县财政收入中占了很大比重，有的县财政收入的一半以上来自小水电。通过小水电的开发建设，初步治理了上万条中小河流，增加了水库库容，扩大了灌溉面积，提高了防洪抗旱能力。

（三）改善了农民生产生活条件

不少地方通过发展小水电改善了当地基础设施，壮大了集体经济，促进了公益事业的发展，使封闭的山村有了电、供了水、通了路、改了厨，农村科学技术不断普及，山区农民的精神面貌发生了很大的变化。湖南桂东是一个贫困县，通过开发小水电，3万多农民摆脱了贫困，农民人均收入比1999年增长了5倍多。许多办电的乡村，办电收入还为全村文化、教育、通信、医疗、社会保障和其他公益事业提供了资金渠道，年满60岁的老人都能领到一份“养老补助”。

（四）保障了应急供电

在2008年初中国南方发生的雨雪冰冻灾害中，小水电在为部分大电厂提供启动电源的同时，还保障了200多个县城、2000多个乡镇春节和电力主网恢复重建期间的供电，并为京九、鹰厦、渝怀、湘黔等铁路畅通发挥了关键作用。“5·12”汶川地震后，重灾区电力主网因灾失电，灾区人民通过修复当地的小水电及其配电网，短时间内恢复了不少县城和片区的供电。距汶川县城8km的下庄水电站（装机容量1.275万kW）在地震中严重受损，当地政府紧急组织抢修，作为当时汶川唯一的电源点，有效保障了县城的应急供电。重灾区理县的红叶二级等水电站，紧急抢修后第一时间向县城供电。重灾区茂县在地震后不到20天，紧急抢修出12座小水电站临时为全县16个乡镇供电。小水电有力地支援了抗震救灾。

（五）促进了节能减排

小水电替代化石能源，减少污染物排放效果明显。2008年小水电发电量1600多亿千瓦时，相当于节约了5600万t标准煤，减少二氧化硫排放70多万吨、二氧化碳排放1.4亿t。小水电代燃料试点工程，使得80多万农民实现了小水电代燃料，保护森林面积350多万亩，改变了山区农民依靠砍伐树木作为生活用能的传统生活方式，保护了山区植被，巩固了退耕还林，避免了水土流失，恢复了青山绿水。

（六）推动了世界小水电发展

中国小水电资源和装机容量都占到世界一半以上。中国开发小水电，在消除贫困、改善民生、保护生态等方面的成效，得到了国际社会特别是发展中国家的高度评价。20多个省（区、市）开展了小水电对外合作与交流，向50多个国家的数百个项目提供了技术咨询、对外劳务和工程承包。总部设在中国杭州的国际小水电中心和亚太地区小水电培训中心，先后举办了66期技术培训班，为60多个国家培训了数千名工程技术人员；开展了小水电清洁发展机制（CDM）合作项目；组织召开了全球小水电会议、国际小水电高级进程会议和国际三方合作会议等，特别是“今日水电论坛”已成为具有一定影响力和号召力的国际性会议。由联合国工业发展组织和国际小水电中心共同倡导的“点亮非洲”项目，得到了联合国有关组织和非洲国家的充分肯定和热烈欢迎。

三、中国发展小水电的主要经验

中国小水电的发展道路是尊重人民首创精神，并将人民群众和地方政府的经验和做法上升为国家政策的具体实践。

（一）尊重人民群众的首创精神

开发小水电解决当地用电问题，建设农村电气化是群众的首创。为鼓励群众自主办电的积极性，国家先后提出了电力建设必须坚持大、中、小并举和国家办电与地方办电相结合；小水电要坚持“自建、自管、自用”的方针，贯彻“以电养电”、“小水电要有自已的供电区”和小水电“优先调度”、“全额上网、同网同价”等一系列政策。在国家政策引导和资金支持下，充分调动了地方和群众办电的积极性，小水电得到快速发展，有效解决了农村用电问题。

（二）坚持为农业、农村、农民服务的宗旨

小水电发展于农村，服务于农业、农村和农民，是农村经济社会发展的重要支柱。中国政府始终把农业、农村、农民问题放在各项工作的重中之重，把发展小水电作为加强农村工作、提高农业综合生产能力的重要举措。新时期，我们将继续坚持小水电为农业、农村、农民服务的宗旨，使其在农业增产、农村繁荣和农民致富中发挥更大的作用。

（三）探索出了小水电开发与生态建设有效结合的新路子

为保护山区生态环境和退耕还林成果，中国政府启动了小水电代燃料生态保护工程。通过政府扶持开发小水电，就近低价供给农民，解决农民的生活燃料，使农民不再上山砍柴，保护山区植被。小水电代燃料工程的实施，解放了农村劳动力，增加了农民收入，有效保护了生态环境。山区农民告别了祖祖辈辈上山砍柴、烟熏火燎的日子，过上了现代、文明、健康的新生活，精神面貌焕然一新。温家宝总理批示，小水电代燃料“经验宝贵”。

（四）建立了完善的小水电技术服务体系

中国始终坚持科学规划，使小水电开发、电气化建设和小水电代燃料与河流综合利用、区域电源电网发展及农村经济社会发展相协调。逐步建立了小水电规划、设计、施工、安装、试验、运行、设备制造等完整的技术标准体系，为小水电发展提供了完善的技术支撑与服务。目前，中国有100多家科研院所、

1000多家设计和施工单位、500多家小水电设备企业为小水电的发展提供产品和服务。中国小水电产品和服务也得到了国际上的广泛认可。

中国小水电在取得了巨大成就、积累了宝贵经验的同时，新的发展时期也面临着新的情况：①法规体系的完善和政策的落实；②资源的有序开发；③生态与环境的保护；④投资主体多元化形势下的安全监管。这些都对小水电的健康发展形成了挑战，需要引起我们的高度重视。

四、中国小水电的发展前景

中国小水电资源区位分布与相对贫困人口分布基本一致，主要分布在中西部地区和少数民族地区。这些地区小水电可开发量占全国总量的82%，目前开发率仅为32%。《中华人民共和国可再生能源法》把水能列为能源发展的优先领域。2007年国务院通过的《可再生能源中长期发展规划》提出，在水能资源丰富地区，结合水电农村电气化县建设和实施小水电代燃料工程需要，加快开发小水电资源，到2020年全国小水电装机容量达到7500万kW。按照规划，中国政府将以提高农村用电水平和农民致富为目标，持续推进水电农村电气化建设，解决有水无电地区用电问题。全面实施小水电代燃料工程，基本解决退耕还林区、天然林保护区、自然保护区和水土保持重点治理地区1000万户农民的生活燃料问题。继续完善小水电技术服务体系，全面推进小水电技术进步和现代化管理，无人值班、少人值守的农村水电站及其配套电网达到90%以上。进一步优化农村能源结构，实现小水电资源有序开发、可持续利用。

我们将继续坚持有中国特色的小水电发展之路，学习借鉴世界各国小水电发展的经验和做法，促进中国小水电又好又快发展。进一步加强国际交流，深化南南合作，推进小水电“点亮非洲”项目的实施，为世界小水电的繁荣发展作出我们应有的贡献。

（水利部农村水电及电气化发展局 田中兴）

2009年农村水电发展综述

一、农村水电发展综述

（一）农村水电基本建设情况

1. 农村水电站 2009年，全国农村水电继续保持平稳发展。全年完成投资456亿元，新增装机380.7万kW，新增装机主要集中在西南、华中和华东地区。在建项目装机容量保持在2000万kW左右，截至2009年底，全国共建成农村水电站44 804座，装机容量5512万kW，形成水库总库容2118亿m^3。全国部直属水电站15座，装机容量609.4万kW，其中部直属大中型水电站12座，装机容量598.9万kW。2009年，全国农村水电发电量1567亿kW·h。农村水电供电区通电率进一步提高，用电量进一步增加，解决了80万无电人口的用电问题，为促进社会主义新农村建设发挥了重要作用。

2. 农村水电网 截至2009年底，全国农村水电电网共建成110kV及以上变电站538座，变电容量2564万kVA；35（63）kV变电站2748座，变电容量1682万kVA；配电变压器36.4万台，容量3463万kVA；10kV及以上高压线路52万km，低压线路112万km。受国民经济平稳快速增长的强劲拉动，农村水电网内全年用电量达541亿kW·h。县城居民平均到户电价0.502元/(kW·h)；农村居民平均到户电价0.521元/(kW·h)。

3. 农村水电投资及资产 2009年，全国水电建设共完成投资456亿元。其中，中央和地方财政配套资金占3.8%，银行贷款占39.9%，自筹资金占56.3%。水电站建设投资410亿元，电网建设投资46.2亿元。农村水电全年发售电总收入684.8亿元，上缴税金65.4亿元。截至2009年底，全国农村水电站资产3416亿元，电网资产355亿元。全国农村水电拥有独立核算单位共24 802个，其中有78%的企业为非国有企业；从业人数64.4万人，其中技术人员17.7万人。

（二）农村水电管理情况

1. 水能资源管理 2009年，各级水行政主管部门继续加强水能资源管理。圆满完成新中国成立以来首次全国农村水能资源调查评价，完成中小河流水能开发规划的技术标准制定。全国14个省（自治区、直辖市）开展了水能资源使用权有偿出让，9个省（自治区、直辖市）制定了出让实施办法。11个省（自治区、直辖市）出台了水能资源开发利用的规范性文件。12个省明确了由水行政主管部门负责水能资源统一管理。

2. 安全监管 各级水行政主管部门以强化农村水电安全监管为重点，组织开展了汛前安全生产大检查和事故督查，加强了违规水电站整改工作力度，已有95%的违规水电站完成整改任务，福建、湖北、重庆、贵州等9个省（市）的整改率达到100%，清查整改工作进展顺利。与国家安监总局、工商总局、电监会等部门联合出台了《关于加强小水电安全监管工作的通知》，进一步理顺农村水电安全监管体制，对农村水电安全生产发挥重要作用。

3. 法规和标准化建设 在广泛开展立法调研的基础上，编制完成了《农村水能资源管理办法（送审稿）》，通过了专家审查。逐步完善农村水电技术标准体系，目前，已有58项标准纳入水利部技术标准体系，2009年编制、修订了29项。

（三）涉及民生的农村水电工作进展情况

1. 小水电代燃料　2009年，小水电代燃料工程全面启动。在水利部部长陈雷和副部长胡四一的关怀下，《2009～2015年全国小水电代燃料工程规划》正式批复实施。当年安排的中央年投资由1亿元增加到3亿元，用于19个省（自治区、直辖市）和新疆生产建设兵团的108个项目。8月在吉林省长白县召开的小水电代燃料现场会有力促进和规范了小水电代燃料项目建设与管理，加快小水电代燃料工程技术进步和标准化管理步伐，把小水电代燃料工程逐步建设成农村水能资源开发的示范和样板工程。

2. 水电农村电气化　2009年水电农村电气化建设持续推进，当年安排中央投资3亿元用于25个省（自治区、直辖市）和新疆生产建设兵团的424个水电农村电气化建设项目。在扎实做好“十一五”水电农村电气化县建设的同时，提前谋划“十二五”电气化工作，制定了水电新农村电气化标准和规划编制规程，召开规划工作研讨会，8月正式启动了规划编制工作。农村水电信贷支持力度明显加强，7月中国农业发展银行下发《关于做好信贷支持小水电代燃料和农村电气化加建设工作的通知》，要求对代燃料和电气化项目降低贷款门槛限制，实行信贷优惠政策。

3. 增效扩容　农村水电增效扩容改造工程前期工作正式开展。会同水利部有关司局，积极与财政部沟通协调，努力开辟农村水电建设资金新渠道。进行了大量调研，完成了农村水电增效扩容工程规划大纲等起草工作。

二、全国农村水电工作会议概述

2009年5月16日，全国农村水电工作会议在浙江省杭州市隆重召开。这次会议是继2001年全国农村水电暨“十五”水电农村电气化县建设会议后召开的又一次重要会议。水利部部长陈雷出席会议并讲话，浙江省副省长茅临生到会致辞，水利部副部长胡四一主持会议并作总结讲话。国家发展和改革委员会农村经济司副司长胡恒洋、财政部农业司副司长曹广生到会并讲话，水利部农村水电及电气化发展局局长田中兴作工作报告。

这次会议的主要任务是：认真贯彻党的十七大、十七届三中全会和中央一系列重要会议精神，深入贯彻落实科学发展观，总结工作，交流经验，分析形势，理清思路，部署当前和今后一个时期的农村水电工作，努力开创农村水电工作新局面。

大会通报表扬了全国农村水电及电气化建设先进集体和先进个人，发布了全国农村水能资源调查评价成果，浙江省、吉林省、湖南省等18家单位作交流发言。

陈雷部长在会上做了《加强农村水能资源开发和管理　促进经济社会可持续发展》的重要讲话，讲话共分五个部分：①认真总结近年来的农村水电工作；②充分认识农村水电发展面临的形势；③准确把握农村水电发展的目标和任务；④扎实做好农村水电发展的重点工作；⑤切实加强对农村水电工作的领导。

陈雷部长充分肯定了农村水电工作取得的成绩，总结了近年农村水电工作的突出特点：①坚持服务“三农”，治水办电结合，水电农村电气化建设迈上新台阶；②坚持面向山区，统筹农民利益与生态建设，小水电代燃料试点成效显著；③坚持开拓创新，理顺体制机制，水能资源管理初见成效；④坚持多管齐下，强化整改落实，农村水电安全监管逐步到位；⑤坚持深入实际，科学编制规划，农村水电基础工作得到加强；⑥坚持对外开放，增进国际合作，小水电国际影响不断扩大。

陈雷部长深入分析了当前农村水电发展面临的形势。他指出从实施可持续发展战略看，农村水电肩负着重要使命；从加强“三农”工作看，农村水电发挥着突出作用；从扩大国内需求看，农村水电承担着新的任务；从促进行业健康发展看，农村水电面临着新的挑战。他强调，必须从战略和全局高度，充分认识加强农村水电工作的重要性和紧迫性，准确把握农村水电工作面临的新形势，顺应全面建设小康社会新要求，努力开创农村水电工作新局面。

陈雷部长进一步明确了农村水电发展的目标和任务。当前和今后一个时期农村水电工作总体要求是：全面贯彻党的十七大、十七届三中全会精神，深入贯彻落实科学发展观，积极践行可持续发展治水思路，按照全面建设小康社会和推进城乡经济社会发展一体化的要求，统筹流域水资源综合利用，严格资源管理，强化安全监管，创新体制机制，完善政策法规，推动技术进步，加快小水电代燃料和水电农村电气化建设，提高贫困山区农民用电水平，增加农民收入，改善农村生产生活条件，保护生态环境，促进经济社会可持续发展。到2020年，要实现农村水能资源开发科学有序，小水电代燃料广泛实施，水电农村电气化水平大幅提高，农村水电技术进步全面推进的目标。

陈雷部长指出，做好农村水电工作，要坚持四项原则：①坚持把保障和改善民生放在农村水电发展的首要位置；②坚持把促进人与自然和谐作为农村水电发展的核心理念；③坚持把政府调控和市场配置相结合作为农村水能资源开发的重要手段；④坚持把加强工程质量和安全监管作为农村水电工作的重要任务。

陈雷部长要求，要扎实做好农村水电发展的重点工作：①突出抓好水能资源管理；②突出抓好小水电代燃料工程建设；③突出抓好水电农村电气化建设；④突出抓好农村水电供电区建设；⑤突出抓好农村水电行业管理；⑥突出抓好农村水电国际交流与合作。他强调，当前和今后一个时期，农村水电工作任务重、要求高、难度大，要切实加强对农村水电工作的领导：①进一步强化责任；②进一步增加投入；③进一步完善法规；④进一步深化改革；⑤进一步加强宣传；⑥进一步抓好队伍。

国家发展改革委、财政部、国家能源局、国家电监会、国家安监总局、中国农业发展银行、国家开发银行的有关负责同志和代表，水利部机关各司局和有关事业单位、各流域机构负责人，各省、自治区、直辖市、新疆生产建设兵团水利（水务）厅（局）的负责人和水电处（局）长出席会议。广西水电集团公司，吉林省地电公司，浙江丽水市水利局，四川天全县、甘肃临泽县、江西铜鼓县政府有关负责人参加会议。

（水利部水电及农村电气化发展局　曲　鹏）

水电农村电气化建设

一、“十一五”水电农村电气化建设

“十一五”期间，我国水电农村电气化建设取得了较好的成效。据统计，2006～2009年底，全国共完成水电农村电气化县建设投资143亿元。其中中央投资12亿元，涉及459个县的1024个项目，占完成投资的8.4%；电站工程中央投资11.24亿元，线路工程中央投资0.76亿元。

2009年，电气化建设计划投资25亿元。其中中央投资3亿元，地方投资22亿元，涉及383个县、426个项目。截至2009年底，共完成投资18亿元。其中中央投资3亿元，占2009年完成投资的16.7%；省级配套资金0.82亿元，占2009年完成投资的4.6%；其他资金14.18亿元，占2009年完成投资的78.7%。

二、“十二五”水电新农村电气化规划全面启动

2009年6月，水利部农村水电及电气化发展局在云南召开了2011～2020年水电新农村电气化建设规划编制工作座谈会。同年8月，水利部办公厅印发了《关于做好“十二五”水电新农村电气化规划编制工作的通知》，标志着“十二五”水电新农村电气化规划编制工作在全国正式启动。截至2009年底，全国已有26个省（区、市）和新疆生产建设兵团的689个县、5134个乡向水利部报送了规划材料。

2009年上半年，农村水电及电气化发展局在河北、湖南召开了两次水电新农村电气化标准和规划编制规程编写组会议，初步提出了“十二五”水电新农村电气化建设思路，修改完善了《水电新农村电气化标准》（初稿）和《水电新农村电气化规划编制规程》（初稿）。目前，这两项标准的修订工作已基本完成，并已正式报水利部审批。

（水利部农村水电及电气化发展局　程　骏）

小水电代燃料工程建设

党中央、国务院从保护生态环境、解决农民燃料和长远致富的战略高度，作出实施小水电代燃料工程的决策，温家宝总理亲自命名“小水电代燃料工程”，通过建设代燃料电站，让农民用低价电做饭、取暖，替代砍树烧柴、烧煤，保护森林植被和生态环境，提高农村居民生活质量，改善生产生活条件。2003年开始在全国开展了小水电代燃料试点建设，到2009年底，新增代燃料装机容量20多万千瓦，实现代燃料人口80多万人，保护森林面积350多万亩。小水电代燃料建设受到广大农民的一致欢迎和支持，也得到国务院领导的充分肯定。2009年初，国家正式批复《2009～2015年全国小水电代燃料工程规划》，小水电代燃料工程全面启动。根据规划，小水电代燃料工程将在7年内解决170.78万户、677.71万农村居民的生活燃料和农村能源，新增代燃料装机容量170.56万kW，保护森林面积2390万亩，总投资141.3亿元，其中中央投资56.99亿元。

一、工程建设

2009年，国家共下达小水电代燃料投资11.6亿元，其中，中央投资3亿元，地方配套0.9亿元，贷款7.7亿元。涉及全国19个省（区、市）和新疆生产建设兵团的108个项目，新增代燃料装机容量22.5万kW，解决21万户、78.6万农民生活燃料，保护退耕还林85万亩，天然林保护面积242万亩，其他森林植被318万亩。

2009年安排的108个项目中，西部地区和中部六省比照实施西部大开发有关政策的项目73个，中央投资22 325万元，占74.4%；中部地区33个，中央投资7025万元，占23.4%；东部地区2个，中央投资650万元，占2.2%。

二、工程管理

为做好2009～2015年小水电代燃料工程建设工作，2009年7月，国家发展改革委和水利部联合印发了《关于加强小水电代燃料和水电农村电气化建设与管理的通知》（发改农经［2009］1937号），对小水电代燃料项目前期工作、项目建设、管理体制机制、监督检查和验收等提出了具体要求，明确了就近直接供电、按成本核定过网费、将代燃料电价列入电价目录等政策。

根据国家发展改革委、水利部《关于加强小水电代燃料和水电农村电气化建设与管理的通知》（发改农经［2009］1937号）要求，凡申请中央补助投资的小水电代燃料项目都必须编制项目实施方案。为做好小水电代燃料项目实施方案的编制工作，2009年8月，水利部下发了《关于做好小水电代燃料项目实施方案编制工作的通知》（水电［2009］409号），明确了小水电代燃料项目实施方案编制的内容和要求，批复后的实施方案作为项目验收的依据。

2009年，水利部对小水电代燃料建设项目加强了日常督促检查，由专人负责督促小水电代燃料建设进度，每季度报送进度表，及时掌握项目进展情况，分析存在的问题，进行分类指导，加快建设进度。在初步排查摸底的基础上，11月由水利部农村水电及电气化发展局局长、总工带队开展了现场专项检查。分4个检查组到12个省（区、市）对小水电代燃料项目进行督促检查，对2010年小水电代燃料新上报项目进行审核。

三、工程建设现场会

为贯彻落实2009年全国农村水电工作会议精神，加强和规范小水电代燃料项目建设与管理，加快小水电代燃料工程技术进步和标准化管理步伐，扎实做好小水电代燃料工作，2009年8月，水利部在吉林省长白县召开了全国小水电代燃料工程建设现场会。会议由水利部农村水电及电气化发展局局长田中兴主持，水利部副部长胡四一出席会议并作了题为《总结经验　真抓实干扎实做好小水电代燃料工作》的讲话，吉林省人民政府副秘书长刘延春到会致辞，国家发展和改革委员会农村经济司副司长胡恒洋到会讲话。会议还邀请国家发展改革委农村经济司，水利部办公厅、规划计划司等有关领导出席，部分省（区、市）水利厅（局）的分管领导，各有关省（区、市）和新疆生产建设兵团水利（水务）厅（局）水电局（处）长，部分项目所在县领导和项目单位代表参加会议，11家单位代表进行了大会交流发言。

胡四一副部长在讲话中充分肯定了小水电代燃料扩大试点建设的成效，指出各地在小水电代燃料扩大试点建设中进行了大量的实践探索，积累了许多好的经验和做法，各地领导高度重视，群众积极拥护，出台了一些扶持政策，在扩大试点实践中探索建立了“国家所有、企业经营、农民使用”的管理体制和“国家补助、企业运作、农民受益、协会监督”的运行机制，保证了代燃料工程长期发挥效益。小水电代燃料从根本上解决了农民的燃料问题，有效保护了生态环境；解除了农民砍树烧柴的艰辛，提高了生活质量；显著改善了农民生活条件，美化了人居环境；解放了受砍树烧柴束缚的农村劳动力，增加了农民收入；增加了清洁可再生能源，促进了节能减排。

胡四一副部长同时指出，小水电代燃料是民生水利的重要内容，利在当代、功在千秋。2009年中央1号文件要求“扩大小水电代燃料建设规模”。陈雷部长在全国农村水电工作会上要求，高标准高质量搞好项目建设，把小水电代燃料项目建成农村水能资源开发利用的示范工程，到2015年基本解决200万户农民的生活燃料问题，到2020年基本解决1000万户农民的生活燃料问题。为落实党中央、国务院关于实施小水电代燃料工程的战略决策，按照陈雷部长的讲话精神，当前和今后一段时期，要着力抓好小水电代燃料工程建设：①要做好项目前期工作，夯实代燃料工程建设基础；②要搞好工程建设，打造农村水电示范工程；③要加强供用电管理，切实降低代燃料电价；④要建立管理体制机制，确保工程长期发挥效益。同时要切实加强小水电代燃料工作的领导，落实责任、搞好协调、强化监督、广泛宣传，在水利部党组和地方党委政府的正确领导下，在国家发展改革委和有关部门的大力支持下，积极践行可持续发展治水思路，总结经验，开拓进取，真抓实干，扎实做好小水电代燃料工作，全面开创农村水电事业新局面。

水利部农村水电及电气化发展局局长田中兴在总结讲话中要求：①尽早开工建设2009年小水电代燃料项目，抓紧审批项目实施方案，抓紧落实中央投资；②规范项目建设与管理。严格实行项目法人责任制、招标投标制、建设监理制和合同管理制，尽快组建项目法人，高质量地搞好项目建设，实施标准化管理，提高管理水平；③做好会议精神的贯彻落实；④切实做好农村水电安全生产工作。增强责任感、使命感、紧迫感，强化安全意识，加强监督检查，采取有效措施，杜绝安全隐患，确保安全生产。

四、标准化建设与管理

为进一步规范小水电代燃料项目建设和管理，促进小水电代燃料快速健康发展，2009年，水利部编制完成了《小水电代燃料标准》和《小水电代燃料规划编制规程》。

《小水电代燃料标准》适用于国家组织实施的小水电代燃料建设项目，共分 8 章 45 条和 1 个附录，主要技术内容有：总则；术语；小水电代燃料基本条件；小水电代燃料电站；小水电代燃料项目区；小水电代燃料供用电；小水电代燃料项目管理；小水电代燃料效益。

《小水电代燃料工程规划编制规程》适用于县级小水电代燃料工程规划的编制，共分 10 章 51 条和 2 个附录，主要技术内容有：总则；术语；基本资料；代燃料项目区规划；代燃料电源规划；代燃料供用电规划；环境影响分析；项目管理；投资估算及资金筹措；效益分析。《小水电代燃料工程规划编制规程》在《小水电代燃料标准》的基础上，进一步明确了规划编制的原则、目标、主要内容和技术要求，目的是规范小水电代燃料工程规划的编制，保证规划工作质量，从而保证小水电代燃料工程项目建设的质量。

为落实陈雷部长关于"高标准搞好项目建设，强化工程建设管理，大力推进技术进步，统一标准标识，统一管理制度，把小水电代燃料项目建成农村水能资源开发利用的示范工程"的要求，根据相关政策文件和技术标准的要求，在充分调查、研究、座谈、讨论和征询各地意见的基础上，2009 年 7 月水利部下发了《小水电代燃料技术进步和标准化管理指导意见》，明确了今后一段时间小水电代燃料技术进步和标准化管理发展的方向及要求，并统一了标准标识和管理制度。《小水电代燃料技术进步和标准化管理指导意见》较好地反映了小水电代燃料的特点，既要求有一定的技术先进性，又要求安全可靠和经济实用，具有较强的可操作性，对大力推进小水电代燃料项目技术进步、统一标准标识、统一管理制度具有重要作用。

小水电代燃料标识见图 1。

图 1　小水电代燃料标识

标识释义：

标识的主题颜色为蓝色，取水利部 LOGO 蓝色为标准，寓意是水利事业的重要组成部分。

标识造型为圆形，有两层含义：①小水电代燃料项目目的是保护生态环境，使生态链不断循环；②代表地球，小水电代燃料能减少二氧化碳排放，保护我们的地球家园。

中间三条曲线同样有两层含义：①代表众多的中小河流，其水能资源可以永续利用；②曲线形似正弦曲线，寓意小水电发出的三相交流电力。

三棵象形的树代表森林，夸张的象形树又似屋顶状，又象征着代燃料项目区的代燃料户。小水电代替木柴为燃料，从而保护生态环境。

图形被中、英文环绕，上部文字为"国家小水电代燃料工程"，下部文字为"NATIONAL SMALL HYDROPOWER ECOLOGICAL PROTECTION PROJECT"。

（水利部农村水电及电气化发展局　赵　虹）

农 村 水 电 管 理

水能资源管理

一、水能资源管理职能得到加强

2008 年国务院办公厅印发的水利部新"三定"规定，明确了水利部水能资源管理和农村水能资源开发利用的有关职能。在 2009 年机构改革中，湖南、湖北、吉林、新疆等省（区）明确水行政主管部门负责全省水能资源开发利用管理工作，其他省也比照水利部"三定"规定明确了相关职能。总体上农村水电职能普遍得到加强，机构不断健全，体制基本理顺。2009 年，河南省正式成立了农村水电及电气化发展中心，落实了人员编制和工作经费，结束了多年来政企不分的状况。

二、水利部发布了全国农村水能资源调查评价成果

2009年5月8日，水利部以《关于发布全国农村水能资源调查评价成果的通知》（水电［2009］257号）发布了全国农村水能资源调查评价成果，填补了我国水资源调查和水能资源普查工作的空白。本次农村水能资源调查评价涉及大陆地区河流16 572条，其中单河水能资源理论蕴藏量10MW及以上河流5095条；单河水能资源理论蕴藏量10MW以下河流11 472条。全国单站技术可开发装机容量0.1（含）～50MW（含）农村水电装机容量128 032MW，年发电量5350亿kW·h。截至2005年底，全国已、正开发农村水电装机容量69 086MW，年发电量2875亿kW·h，分别占技术可开发总装机容量和总发电量的54%和53.7%。

三、中小河流水能开发规划进一步规范

2009年12月21日，水利部以2009年32号公告批准发布了《中小河流水能开发规划编制规程》（SL 221—2009）以及《小水电水能设计规程》（SL 76—2009），这两项标准考虑了河流生态需水量，提出了跨流域引水限制条件，以及尽量少占用耕地、减少社会矛盾等近年来对中小河流水能开发规划以及小水电水能设计的新要求、新理念，为各地开展中小河流水能开发规划以及小水电设计提供了统一规范。

四、积极推动水能资源管理立法

继湖南、吉林省人大常委会颁布水能资源管理条例，贵州省颁布了水能资源开发使用权有偿出让政府规章后，2009年3月吉林省人民政府发布了《吉林省水能资源开发利用权有偿出让若干规定》；2009年6月，经湖南省人民政府同意，湖南省人民政府办公厅出台了《关于加强水能资源开发利用管理工作的意见》；贵州省出台了《关于水能资源使用权有偿出让工作有关问题的通知》（黔水电［2009］9号）以及《关于对水能资源使用权出让金征收工作进行检查的通知》（黔水法［2009］33号）。这几部水能资源管理配套措施明确了水能资源开发利用权有偿出让细则，详细规定了水能资源开发利用规划和技术审查程序，并对贯彻落实水能资源管理地方性法规提出了具体要求。

（水利部农村水电及电气化发展局　张学进）

农村水电行业安全监管

2009年，水利部农村水电及电气发展局深入贯彻落实科学发展观，牢固树立以人为本、安全发展的理念，根据水利部安全生产领导小组的统一部署，围绕农村水电中心工作，继续深入开展“安全生产年”活动。在加强安全生产监督管理“三项行动”和“三项建设”中，突出预防为主，着力做好强化监管、健全制度、落实责任、协作联动、培育队伍、加强宣传等各项工作。完善各项措施，加大工作力度，坚决杜绝重特大安全事故，减少较大和一般安全事故，保持农村水电安全生产形势持续向好。

一、初步理顺安全生产监管体制

各级水行政主管部门把理顺农村水电安全监管体制作为工作重点，在新的一轮机构改革中，主动向政府汇报情况，明确安全生产管理职责和范围，积极承担起农村水能资源开发利用中的安全监管责任。2009年水利部、国家工商总局、国家安监总局和国家电监会联合发布的《关于加强小水电站安全监管工作的通知》（水电［2009］585号），进一步明确水利部门与相关部门和机构的职责分工，形成中央与地方政府相衔接、综合监管与专业监管相结合的农村水电安全监管体制。

目前，除少数地区外，大部分省区市的农村水电安全管理体制已较为健全。省、地、县农村水电主管部门均成立了安全监察管理机构，配备了专兼职管理人员。各农电企业均设立了安全管理部门，并配备了专兼职安全监察员、安全管理员岗位，基本形成三级安全生产管理网络。

二、全面落实安全生产责任制

农村水电行业普遍建立起以一把手为安全生产第一责任人、分管领导为直接责任人的农村水电安全管理责任制度。各地农村水电主管部门和农电企业基本做到了层层落实岗位责任制，签订安全生产管理目标责任书，制定安全生产管理目标考核办法并实施考核，实行安全生产目标管理。福建省水利厅在落实安全生产行业监管主体和企业安全生产责任主体的“两个主体”责任中不断创新工作机制，强化主体责任落实。河北省农村水电行业各级主管部门大力加强安全生产的行业监管和行业指导，层层签订《安全生产责任书》，做到了逐级落实、层层把关、齐抓共管、立体防控，为安全生产提供了保障。

三、组织开展安全生产大检查

1. 安全生产大检查工作部署执行情况　安全生产大检查的范围包括四川、湖南、重庆、广西等27个省市区（未含上海、天津、江苏、宁夏）和新疆生产建设兵团。各单位均对水利部布置的2009年度安全生产大检查工作高度重视，通过转发文件的方式，将有关精神传达贯彻到各市县水利（水务）局。各市县局迅速组织辖区内农村水电在建工程业主单位和农村水电站及电网供电单位开展了自查自纠工作。

各单位按照通知要求，结合本单位实际情况确定了安全生产大检查的范围、内容、重点和步骤，采用了自查、互查和抽查等多种检查形式。检查中基本做到了认真严格、求真务实、不留死角，对检查出的安全隐患，限期监督整改，达到了安全大检查的预期目的。各单位对安全生产大检查工作进行了总结，并按时向水利部报送了安全大检查工作报告。

2. 各单位安全度汛措施落实检查情况　各地水行政主管部门认真抓好农村水电工程防洪度汛工作，健全了防汛责任制，制定了防洪度汛预案并报相应防汛抗旱指挥部门审批或备案，积极落实防洪度汛的物资，建立健全防汛抢险应急机制，做到机构、责任、队伍、方案、物料和报警六落实。如：广东省水利厅要求全省各地按照“属地管理、分级负责”的原则，逐级落实各项防汛责任制。湖北省实行以防汛行政首长负责制和项目法人责任制为核心的防汛责任制。各地按照有关规定，对辖区内的全部水电工程项目都明确了防汛行政责任人和水库水电站六大责任人，统一指挥防汛工作。

3. 安全生产管理制度建立和执行检查情况

（1）各地水行政部门结合水利部及相关部门发布的政策法规，相应制定了安全管理规章制度。吉林省经过多年的努力，在安全生产责任制、安全生产监察管理体系方面形成了稳定的管理模式。湖南省发布了《湖南省水利系统电站、电网安全生产管理考核办法》，在安全管理工作中做到有规可依，有章可循。

（2）各地农村水电企业已形成一整套以“二票”（工作票、操作票）、“三制”（交接班制度、巡回检查制度、设备缺陷管理制度）为核心内容的安全管理规章制度体系。此外，各地农电企业还制定了许多相关配套安全管理制度。如黑龙江、甘肃、河北、陕西、重庆等省市农电企业制定了年度定期检查制度、安全累进记录制度、安全例会制度、安全事故分析制度、安全监督奖惩制度、持证上岗制度、设备定期检修制度、设备评级制度和安全培训考核制度等多种规章制度。这些制度的建立和执行，使企业安全管理工作目标明确、职责清楚、奖惩分明，提高了职工安全生产和事故防范意识，为水电企业安全生产、消除事故隐患起到了非常重要的作用。

四、违规水电站清查整改取得明显成效

各地水利部门高度重视违规水电站的清查整改工作，进一步加强领导，违规水电站清查整改取得明显成效。2009年初，水利部办公厅印发了《关于全面加快违规水电站清查整改工作的通知》（办水电［2009］88号）。各地各级水行政主管部门与有关部门联合执法，加大了对违规水电站的清查整改力度。截至2009年底，全国已有95%的违规水电站完成了整改任务。其中，广东、福建、湖北、重庆、贵州等19个省区市已100%完成了违规水电站清查整改任务。

五、安全教育培训进一步规范

各地通过定期组织各类安全生产培训、举办安规考试、举办知识竞赛等各种形式，加强对职工的安全生产教育培训，提高职工的安全生产意识。如：广西壮族自治区农村水电系统组织开展了安全管理、安监员和安全员岗位培训，特种作业人员做到了持证上岗。贵州省水利厅多次组织全省农村水电系统干部职工参加水利部举办的农村水电安全生产监察员培训和贵阳电监办举办的电工证培训，要求企业主要负责人、安监员、特种作业人员必须经培训后持证上岗。

（水利部农村水电及电气化发展局　刘京和）

中國水力發電年鉴

16

人物、机构与学术团体

人　　物

中国科学院院士王光谦

王光谦，男，1962年4月生，河南南阳人，中国民主同盟盟员；现任清华大学水沙科学与水利水电工程国家重点实验室主任、教授、博士生导师；2009年当选中国科学院院士。

王光谦1982年毕业于武汉水利电力学院治河工程专业，1985年获清华大学水利工程硕士学位，1989年获清华大学水利工程博士学位。1990～1992年在中国科学院力学研究所博士后流动站工作。1992年后历任清华大学水利系副教授、教授、博士生导师，清华大学责任教授、水沙科学教育部重点实验室主任、国土矿产资源与利用研究中心主任、水电工程系河流海洋研究所所长。2000年起任教育部“长江奖励计划”特聘教授。王光谦为第九届全国政协委员，第十、十一届全国政协常委、全国政协人口资源环境委员会委员，民盟中央委员、常委、北京市副主任委员。现还兼任国务院学位办水利学科评议组召集人、国家自然科学基金委员会材料与工程学部咨询专家、《应用基础与工程科学学报》编委会副主任、国际水利工程与研究协会亚太地区分会《J Hydro-environment Research》副主编。

王光谦致力于江河治理事业，从事水力学与河流动力学教学与科研工作，其研究领域为泥沙学科与江河治理，开展了水沙两相流基本理论、流域水沙过程模拟及工程应用等方面研究。建立了水沙两相流的动力学模型，得出泥沙颗粒浓度分布及速度分布公式，揭示了泥沙颗粒运动与清水湍流的不同特性。建立了流域泥沙动力学模型，实现了河道与流域过程的耦合，将泥沙研究从河流拓展到流域尺度。研究成果为解决黄河治理及长江三峡工程泥沙问题发挥了作用。承担“复杂条件下坝堤溃决机理与风险调控理论”973项目，研究成果应用于汶川地震堰塞湖除险中。他对固液两相流尤其是泥沙运动和泥石流进行了较深入的研究，解决了泥沙运动中的一些重要课题，如悬移质浓度垂向分布的类型，并探讨其成因，得到泥沙浓度的统一公式。他所进行的快速颗粒流研究，在高含沙流、泥石流以及固料输运等方面有广泛的应用。同时他还发展了固液两相流的新的双流体模型，对固液两相流基本理论及其应用加以总结。他不仅在学术上有所成就，而且在承担重点工程课题中，解决生产问题表现突出。

王光谦共发表论文150余篇，出版专著3部，获得国家科技进步一等奖及省部级奖励10项。

（本年鉴编辑部摘编）

中国工程院院士张建云

张建云，男，1957年8月生，江苏沛县人，汉族，中共党员；现任南京水利科学研究院院长，兼水利部大坝安全管理中心主任，水利部应对气候变化研究中心主任、首席科学家，教授级高工，博士生导师；2009年当选中国工程院院士。

张建云1982年7月于华东水利学院陆地水文专业大学毕业；1987年5月于河海大学水文水资源专业研究生毕业，获工学硕士学位；1992年12月获爱尔兰国立大学一等荣誉理学硕士学位，1996年6月于爱尔兰国立大学土木及环境工程专业毕业，获博士学位。

张建云长期从事水文、防汛抗旱、气候变化影响、水利水电信息化等科研工作。曾长期从事和负责全国水文情报预报工作，研究并主持开发了“全国洪水预报系统”、“国家防汛会商系统”和“防汛抗旱水文气象综合信息系统”等一系列业务系统，为国家防洪抗旱调度决策和指挥提供科学依据和技术支撑。主持国家防汛抗旱指挥系统工程设计和一期工程建设的技术工作，构建了国家防汛抗旱减灾决策平台，提升了全国防汛抗旱决策指挥水平，推动了全国水利信息化，已在近年的防汛抗旱工作中发挥了重要作用。在洪水预报理论研究及应用、气候变化对水文水资源影响评估和适应研究、设计暴雨和设计洪水应用研究等方面取得重要研究成果。主持编写了《水文情报预报规范》、《水文自动测报系统规范》等国家、行业技术标准和国家防汛抗旱指挥系统工程一系列标准规范和技术规程，推动了行业技术进步，培养了一大批专业人才。

张建云主持完成国家科技攻关（科技支撑计划）、“863”、省部级重大科研项目20余项。获国家科技进步一等奖1项、二等奖3项，省部级一等奖2项、二等奖3项。出版专著4部、译著1部、主编著作5部，发表论文百余篇。指导培养博士后2名、博士12名和硕士6名。

张建云曾任水利部水文局总工程师、副局长兼总工程师，国家防汛指挥系统工程副总设计师、总设计师，国家防汛指挥系统工程建设办公室副主任等职。荣获国家有突出贡献的中青年专家、全国留学回国人员先进个人、全国杰出专业技术人才、江苏省首批中青年首席科学家等称号。享受国务院政府特殊津贴。

（本年鉴编辑部摘编）

中国工程院院士钟登华

钟登华，男，1963年11月20日生，江西赣县人，中共党员；现任天津大学副校长、天津大学研究生院院长、教授、博士生导师；2009年当选中国工程院院士。

钟登华1985年毕业于江西工业大学土建系，同年进入天津大学水利系攻读硕士学位，1988年获得水工结构工程硕士学位，1992年获得天津大学系统工程博士学位，1994年破格晋升为教授。

钟登华是天津大学水利工程国家重点学科学术带头人。二十多年来，长期致力于水利水电工程领域的科技攻关、技术开发、推广应用和人才培养工作，先后承担并出色完成了10多项重大工程的科技攻关与技术开发任务。围绕重大工程设计与工程建设，探索并发展了水利水电工程施工仿真与实时控制分析技术、水利水电工程地质三维精细建模与分析技术，提出并实施了面向心墙堆石坝施工过程的质量监控与系统集成技术，研究成果先后在我国30多项水利水电工程（如黄河拉西瓦、澜沧江糯扎渡、红水河龙滩、雅砻江锦屏一级和金沙江向家坝等）中得到了应用。作为第一完成人获国家科技进步二等奖2项，省部级一等奖1项，省部级二等奖4项；出版专著5部，发表论文116篇（SCI/EI收录56篇），被引用653次。在重大水利水电工程技术创新与推广应用方面取得了突出成果，为水利水电工程新技术的发展作出了重要贡献。

钟登华重视团队建设，作为学术带头人组建了一支长期稳定的致力于水利水电工程科技攻关、技术研发的科研队伍。曾获国家或省部级学术荣誉10余次，入选“新世纪百千万人才工程”国家级人选，获国家杰出青年基金资助，享受国务院政府特殊津贴，获教育部“优秀骨干教师”称号，获第八届“中国青年科技奖”和第七届“光华工程科技奖青年奖”。

（本年鉴编辑部摘编）

机　　构

水电建设单位情况一览表

单位名称	地址	电话	邮政编码
国家电网公司	北京市西长安街86号	010-66597721	100031
国网新源控股有限公司	北京市白广路二条1号		100761
中国南方电网有限责任公司	广东省广州市珠江新城华穗路6号	020-38122222	510623
南方电网调峰调频发电公司	广东省广州市龙口东路32号		510630
中国华能集团公司	北京市西城区复兴门内大街4号	010-62291666	100031
中国大唐集团公司	北京市西城区广宁伯街1号	010-66586666	100033
中国华电集团公司	北京市西城区宣武门内大街2号		100031
中国国电集团公司	北京市西城区阜成门北大街6-8号	010-58682000	100034
中国电力投资集团公司	北京市西城区金融大街28号院3号楼	010-66216666	100032
中国长江三峡集团公司	湖北宜昌市西坝建设路1号	0717-6738068	443002

续表

单位名称	地址	电话	邮政编码
国家开发投资公司	北京市阜成门外大街7号	010-68095101	100037
新华水利水电投资公司	北京市丰台区海鹰路1号院7号楼	010-83681365	100070
二滩水电开发有限责任公司	四川省成都市双林路288号	028-82907333	610051
大唐国际发电股份有限公司	北京市西城区广宁伯街1号		100032
国投云南大朝山水电开发公司	云南省昆明市护国路2号广业大厦	0871-5168729	650011
云南华能澜沧江水电有限公司	云南省昆明市官渡区世纪城中路1号	0871-7216597	650214
金沙江中游水电开发有限公司	云南省昆明市人民东路115号水电科技大厦		650051
云南华电怒江水电开发公司	云南省昆明市东风东路48号金泰大厦		650051
华能四川水电有限公司	四川省成都市人民南路四段47号华能大厦		610041
龙滩水电开发有限公司	广西南宁市民族大道126号	0771-5644008	530028
中国大唐集团广西分公司	广西南宁市民族大道126号		530028
广西桂冠电力股份有限公司	广西南宁市民族大道126号	0771-5640938	530028
贵州乌江水电开发有限责任公司	贵州省贵阳市新华路9号	0851-5784588	550002
贵州黔源电力股份有限公司	贵州省贵阳市市南路48号	0851-5592190	550002
国电大渡河流域水电开发有限公司	四川省成都市高新区天韵路7号	028-86896600	610041
四川华电杂谷脑水电开发有限责任公司	四川省成都市羊西线蜀汉路530号	028-87575412	610036
四川南桠河流域水电开发公司	四川省成都市一环东四段8号江源大厦6楼B座	028-84457992	610066
五凌电力有限公司	湖南省长沙市天心区五凌路188号	0731-5893188	410004
湖北清江水电开发有限责任公司	湖北宜昌市东山大道95号清江大厦	0717-6318830	443000
黄河上游水电开发有限责任公司	青海省西宁市五四西路43号	0971-6322201	810003
国电新疆吉林台梯级水电开发有限公司	新疆尼勒克县	0999-4859956	835716
国电新疆开都河流域水电开发有限公司	新疆库尔勒市人民东路华誉商务大厦14楼	0996-5396288	841000
国投甘肃小三峡发电有限责任公司	甘肃省兰州市敦煌路157号	0931-2954701	730050
陕西汉江投资开发有限公司	陕西省西安市沣惠南路32号		710065
吉林松江河水力发电有限责任公司	吉林省抚松县抚松镇南新区	0439-6228011	134500
汉能控股有限公司	北京市西长安街88号首都时代广场11层		100031
湖北省能源集团有限公司	湖北省武汉市武昌武珞路586号江厦大厦20层		430070
汉江水利水电集团有限责任公司	湖北省丹江口市		442700
福建省尤溪流域水电开发有限公司	福建省尤溪县城关镇解放路63号	0598-6208088	365100
中国水电建设集团四川电力开发有限公司	四川省成都市玉沙路161号	028-86918102	610017

（本年鉴编辑部）

水电设计单位情况一览表

序号	单位名称	主要领导及总工程师	在职职工人数	地址	邮编	电话	传真	网址
1	中国水电工程顾问集团公司	总经理：晏志勇 总工程师：彭程 周建平	270	北京市西城区六铺炕北小街2号	100011	010-51973399	010-82084665	http://www.checc.cn

续表

序号	单位名称	主要领导及总工程师	在职职工人数	地址	邮编	电话	传真	网址
2	中国水利水电建设工程咨询公司	总经理：晏志勇 总工程师：彭程 周建平		北京市西城区六铺炕北小街2号	100011	010-51973399	010-82084665	http://www.checc.cn/ZX
3	中国水电顾问集团北京勘测设计研究院	院长：李志谦 总工程师：吕明治	830	北京市定福庄	100024	010-51977001	010-65766934	
4	中国水电顾问集团华东勘测设计研究院	院长：张为民 总工程师：张春生	1222	浙江省杭州市上塘路	310014	0571-88076606	0571-56738301	http://www.ecidi.com
5	中国水电顾问集团西北勘测设计研究院	院长：马海晨 总工程师：白俊光	2026	陕西省西安市丈八东路18号	710065	029-88290000	029-88290006	http://www.chidi.com.cn
6	中国水电顾问集团中南勘测设计研究院	院长：李玲龙 总工程师：冯树荣	1860	湖南省长沙市圭塘	410014	0731-5584080	0731-5075441	http://www.msdi.cn
7	中国水电顾问集团成都勘测设计研究院	院长：郑声安 总工程师：王仁坤	1660	四川省成都市浣花北路1号	610072	028-87329997	028-87399557	http://www.chidi.com.cn
8	中国水电顾问集团贵阳勘测设计研究院	院长：潘继录 总工程师：范福平	1014	贵州省贵阳市金阳新区兴黔路16号	550081	0851-5565974	0851-5560914	http://www.ghidri.com.cn
9	中国水电顾问集团昆明勘测设计研究院	院长：蔡绍宽 总工程师：张宗亮	1485	云南省昆明市人民东路115号	650051	0871-3138701	0871-3135723	http://www.khidi.com

（中国水电工程顾问集团公司 张 建）

水利设计单位情况一览表

序号	单位名称	主要领导及总工程师	在职职工人数	地址	邮编	电话	传真	网址
1	水利部水利水电规划设计总院	院长：刘伟平 总工程师：刘志明	186	北京市西城区六铺炕北小街2-1号	100120	010-62033377	010-62070508	http://www.giwp.org.cn
2	水利部长江水利委员会长江勘测规划设计研究院	院长：钮新强 总工程师：杨启贵	3130	湖北省武汉市解放大道1863号	430010	027-82829200 027-82827793	027-82829202	http://www.cjwsjy.com.cn

续表

序号	单位名称	主要领导及总工程师	在职职工人数	地址	邮编	电　话	传　真	网　址
3	黄河勘测规划设计有限公司（原黄委设计院）	董事长：李文学 总工程师：景来红	1853	河南省郑州市金水河路109号	450003	0371-66026449 0371-66023520	0371-65959236	http://www.yrec.cn
4	中水淮河规划设计研究院	董事长：万　隆 总工程师：何华松	209	安徽省蚌埠市凤阳西路41号	233001	0552-3092542 0552-3092539	0552-3092509	http://www.cwhh.com.cn
5	中水珠江规划勘测设计有限公司（原珠委设计院）	总经理：游赞培 总工程师：林少明	550	广东省广州市天河区天寿路105号天寿大厦1102房	510610	020-87117779	020-87117050	http://www.prpsdc.com
6	中水东北勘测设计研究有限责任公司（原东北院）	总经理：金正浩 总工程师：苏加林	1600	吉林省长春市朝阳区工农大路800号	130021	0431-85092001 0431-85607262	0431-85092000	http://www.neidri.com
7	中水北方勘测设计研究有限责任公司（原天津院）	总经理：何志华 总工程师：杜雷功	1129	天津市河西区洞庭路60号	300222	022-28702818 022-28702222	022-28343991	http://www.tidi.ac.cn

（中国水利水电勘测设计协会）

水利水电施工单位情况一览表

序号	单位名称	主要领导及总工程师	地　址	邮编	电　话	传　真	网　址
一	中国水利水电建设集团公司	总经理：范集湘 总工程师：宗敦峰	北京市海淀区车公庄西路22号	100044	010-58382678	010-58382888	http://www.sinohydro.com
1	中国水利水电第一工程局有限公司	执行董事、总经理：茹彩江	吉林省长春市绿园区锦西路933号	130062	0431-87987316	0431-87991536	http://www.zsyj.com
2	中国水利水电第二工程局有限公司	执行董事、总经理：刘国栋 总工程师：常满祥	北京市西城区六铺炕南小街1号	100120	010-58689270	010-62018014	http://www.sdej.com
3	中国水利水电第三工程局有限公司	执行董事、总经理：章运礼 总工程师：王鹏禹	陕西省西安市二环北路东段609号	710016	029-86178686	029-86178686-8511	http://www.cteb.com
4	中国水利水电第四工程局有限公司	执行董事、总经理：王维斌 总工程师：席　浩	青海省西宁市互助西路7号	810006	0971-8140656	0971-8149160	http://www.csdsj.com.cn

续表

序号	单位名称	主要领导及总工程师	地　址	邮编	电　话	传　真	网　址
5	中国水利水电第五工程局有限公司	执行董事、总经理：郑久存 总工程师：吴高见	四川省成都市一环路东四段8号	610066	028-84461307	028-84422633	http://www.zswj.com
6	中国水利水电第六工程局有限公司	执行董事、总经理：厉建平 总工程师：杨成文	辽宁省丹东市锦山大街324号	118002	0415-6191612	0415-6191600	http://www.zgsdjl.com
7	中国水利水电第七工程局有限公司	执行董事、总经理：张建文 总工程师：向　建	四川成都市解放路二段329号	610081	028-87912035	028-87912515	http://7j.sinohydro.com
8	中国水利水电第八工程局有限公司	执行董事、总经理：林修建 总工程师：涂怀健	湖南省长沙市城南中路2号	410007	0731-82822169	0731-85563353	http://www.baju.com.cn
9	中国水利水电第九工程局有限公司	执行董事、总经理：陈学云	贵州省贵阳市金阳新区观山路3号	550081	0851-7980581	0851-7980582	http://www.zgsdjj.com
10	中国水利水电第十工程局有限公司	执行董事、总经理：杜学泽 总工程师：陈　茂	四川省成都市十二桥路七号	610072	028-87772278	028-87716129	http://www.cwet.com.cn
11	中国水利水电第十一工程局有限公司	执行董事、总经理：孙玉民 总工程师：钟彦祥	河南省郑州市高新技术开发区莲花街9号	450001	0371-86019001	0371-86019003	http://www.cwbll.com
12	中国水利水电第十二工程局有限公司	执行董事、总经理：孙　阳 总工程师：李秋生	浙江省杭州市环城北路141号	310004	0571-28906018	0571-28906018	http://www.water12.com
13	中国水利水电第十三工程局有限公司	执行董事、总经理：何占颂 总工程师：杨　涛	天津市华苑产业区榕苑路2号	300384	022-58569000	022-58569002	http://www.sdssj.com
14	中国水利水电第十四工程局有限公司	执行董事、总经理：周　宇 总工程师：和孙文	云南省昆明市环城东路192号	650041	0871-3335216	0871-3333460	http://www.fcbmis.com
15	中国水电建设集团十五工程局有限公司	董 事 长：王增发 总工程师：何小雄	陕西省西安市高新科技路16号	710065	029-88758206	029-88758100	http://www.sinohydro15.com
16	中国水利水电第十六工程局有限公司	执行董事、总经理：李良顺 总工程师：吴秀荣	福建省福州市湖东路82号	350003	0591-87821294	0591-87853663	http://www.mjgcj.com
17	中国水利水电基础局有限公司	董 事 长：张源智 总工程师：肖恩尚	天津市武清区雍阳西路86号	301700	022-29341551	022-29345523	http://www.chinafec.com
18	中国水电建设集团夹江水工机械有限公司	执行董事、总经理：雷建容 总工程师：曾　文	四川省夹江县西河路40号	614100	0833-5672462	0833-5672451	http://www.jhmw.com

续表

序号	单位名称	主要领导及总工程师	地　址	邮编	电　话	传　真	网　址
二	中国葛洲坝集团公司	总 经 理：杨继学 总工程师：周厚贵 江小兵	湖北省宜昌市清波路1号	443002	0717-6713010	0717-6718330	http://www.cggc.cn
三	中国人民武装警察部队水电指挥部（中国安能建设总公司）	主任（总经理）：李光强 政委（党委书记）：贾方亮（1～9月） 韦秀锁（10～12月）	北京市丰台区莲花池南里13号	100055	010-83999999	010-83999951	http://www.anneng.cn
1	中国人民武装警察部队水电第一总队（江南水利水电工程公司）	总队长（总经理）：马青春 政委（党委书记）：王　军	广西区南宁市	530028	0771-5751000	0771-5751000	
2	中国人民武装警察部队水电第二总队（江夏水电工程公司）	总队长（总经理）：邹永明 政委（党委书记）：刘跃龙	江西省南昌市	330096	0791-7662000	0791-7662000	
3	中国人民武装警察部队水电第三总队（安蓉建设总公司）	总队长（总经理）：林友汉 政委（党委书记）：翟从福	四川省成都市	610036	028-82863000	028-82863000	
4	中国人民武装警察部队水电三峡工程指挥部（湖北安联建设工程有限公司）	主任（总经理）：赵方兴 政委（党委书记）：剧军志	湖北省武汉市	430223	027-81995000	027-81995000	

（中国水利水电建设集团公司　中国葛洲坝集团公司　中国人民武装警察部队水电指挥部）

华北水利水电学院简况

华北水利水电学院现有水利学院、资源与环境学院、土木与交通学院、机械学院、电力学院、环境与市政工程学院、建筑学院、管理与经济学院、数学与信息科学学院、信息工程学院、外国语学院、法学院、社科部、体育部、研究生处、人文艺术教育中心、国际教育学院、继续教育学院等18个教学单位；设有49个本科专业，全日制在校本科生、研究生15 000余人。学校1981年获得国家首批硕士学位授予权，目前共有水利水电工程、水工结构工程、水力学及河流动力学、地质工程、水文学及水资源、农业水土工程、岩土工程、结构工程、管理科学与工程、计算机应用技术、机械设计与理论、流体机械与工程、应用数学等28个硕士点，其中3个硕士学位一级学科。学校有3个省部级一级重点学科，21个省部级二级重点学科。学校具有硕士研究生单考权资格，具有推荐并接受免试研究生资格、开展同等学力申请硕士学位资格和工程硕士招生培养资格。学校与中国科学院地质研究所、中国农业科学院农田灌溉研究所、清华大学、同济大学等20余所高等院校和科研院所联合培养博士研究生。

学校拥有教职工1300余人。两院院士潘家铮为学校高级顾问，中国工程院院士顾金才、王浩、倪维斗、周丰峻为学校教授、双聘院士，学校还聘请了刘光鼎、王思敬、林皋、赵国藩、厉以宁等国内外知名学者、科学院院士或工程院院士担任兼职教授。学校设有6个省级特聘教授岗位。近年来，先后有100余人次获得全国模范教师、教育部优秀骨干教师、国家“百千万人才工程”人选、省级教学名师、省管优秀专家、省级学术技术带头人等荣誉称号。经过多年的建设，一支数量充足、结构合理、教学水平高、发展趋势好的教师队伍已经形成。

学校与90多个科研院所和企业建立了长期稳定的合作研究或联合培养研究生的协作关系。现有3个省部级重点实验室，1个院士工作站，1个院士实验室，11个研究（院）所。近年来，先后承担了30多项国家级科研项目。

学校是水利部、建设部监理工程师定点培训基地，培训点遍布全国，每年为国家培养监理工程师和监理员2000余名。学校工程监理中心是甲级建设监理资质单位，承担了东江—深圳供水改造、珠江河口整治、山西万家寨引黄工程等多项大型工程的监理任务。学校参与科研和参加监理的“东江—深圳”供水改造工程荣获中国建筑工程“鲁班奖”、广东省科学技术进步特等奖，被中纪委誉为“廉洁工程”。学校注重产、学、研相结合，主动参与地方经济建设和国家大型水利工程，先后参与了三门峡、万家寨、葛洲坝、小浪底、长江三峡、南水北调、东深港（东莞—深圳—香港）供水、珠江入海口疏浚等国家重大水电建设项目的科研、设计、监理、模型试验等工作。学院勘察设计研究院具有乙级资质，曾成功承接设计了海南国际会展中心“美丽之冠”、郑州市杂技馆等省市重点、亮点工程，获得了国内外同行的高度评价。

（华北水利水电学院）

学 术 团 体

中国水力发电工程学会2009年工作情况

2009年是新中国成立60周年，是国家应对金融危机冲击，保持国民经济平稳较快发展，推进“十一五”规划顺利实施，谋划“十二五”规划的关键年。在中国科协和挂靠单位中国水电工程顾问集团公司的关心指导下，中国水力发电工程学会（以下简称水电学会）根据年初制定和六届三次理事会部署的重点工作，积极开展各项工作和任务，取得了一定的成果，较好地完成了全年工作计划。

（一）紧跟形势，积极学习和努力提高政治理论水平

水电学会支部参加了由挂靠单位中国水电工程顾问集团公司党委组织的深入学习实践科学发展观活动。按照活动小组的学习部署，分阶段进行了系统学习，平时根据工作实际按照学习要求和提供的学习书目灵活安排自学，做好学习笔记，副处级以上干部还提交了学习科学发展观的体会文章。多次参加了科学发展观的辅导报告会。通过本次深入学习，每位党员深感受益匪浅，一致表示要把学习和体会到的理论知识运用到工作实践中，努力开拓学会工作新气象、新局面，为政府、行业、各会员单位和广大会员提供更加优质的服务。

水电学会秘书处组织学习了胡锦涛总书记《在纪念中国科协成立50周年大会上的讲话》、中国科协韩启德主席的总结讲话等文件，结合学会工作进行了广泛讨论和交流，并一致达成共识：学会工作要认真落实科学发展观，同心同德，富有朝气，严谨务实，开拓创新，进一步提高工作能力，快速高效完成各项任务，努力搭建好学会的全国水电工程师平台和全心全意为电力工业服务的平台。

（二）加强组织建设，在学会工作的新起点迎接新挑战

以一年一度的中国水电新春联谊会为纽带，水电学会始终努力搭建全国各水电有关单位和新老水电工作者最重要的联系交流平台。2009年中国水电新春联谊会由水电学会与中国大唐集团公司联合举办，国家电力行业的领导和嘉宾以及来自全国各地的新老水电界同仁200余人出席了会议。国家发展和改革委员会副主任、国家能源局局长张国宝出席大会并发表了重要讲话，强调水电开发建设对我国能源工业的重要性。作为中国水电界一年一次的重要盛会，水电新春联谊会已经连续召开了15年。

组织召开了六届三次理事会和六届四次常务理事会，审议并通过了《深入学习实践科学发展观　积极推进水电开发　促进经济社会可持续发展》的工作报告；通报了2008年度学会财务报告；通过投票表决的方式调整和变更了理事会常务理事和理事。

认真落实中国科协关于专业委员会有关工作要求，全面推进专委会的换届工作，完成了16个分支机构变更报批材料和换证工作。获准设立风险管理专业委员会并组织召开了“电力企业风险管理研讨会及风险管理专业委员会成立大会”。成立风险管理专业委员会的宗旨，就是要充分发挥学会的行业地位、技术力量和专家群体等优势，积极推行国家相关政策，

把脉行业最新发展动向，为电力企业风险管理搭建广泛的学术交流和技术服务平台，并通过归纳、总结和借鉴国内外电力企业的风险管理经验，努力打造有中国电力行业特色的风险管控体系，帮助电力企业从根本上提高风险管理水平，使风险管理成为企业防范风险和实现经济增长的新亮点，为整个电力行业的健康、稳定和可持续发展作出新的贡献。

根据上级主管部门的文件通知要求，完成了中国科协直属的期刊年检工作和民政部一年一度的学会年检工作。

进一步加强了对地方学会的协助和指导，加强相互之间的沟通联络和联合开展学术交流、科普宣传等行业服务工作。协助北京水力发电工程学会完成了换届工作，并在北京召开了成立大会。

（三）积极开展国内、国际学术交流，增进海峡两岸友好往来

水电学会始终积极履行学术交流主平台的服务职能，多层次、多边组织举办各种学术交流和研讨活动，并不断拓宽行业各专业领域的广度和纵深度，做到目的明确，务实办会，注重实效，切切实实为推动水电事业和广大水电企业又好又快发展做好服务。

组织召开了第二届水力发电技术国际会议。经过一年多的紧张准备，大会于 2009 年 4 月在北京胜利召开，来自国内外水力发电技术领域的专家、学者、工程技术人员和国内外各大制造企业的高层管理人员近 400 人参加了会议。这次会议就世界最新的水力发电技术和管理经验进行了广泛的交流探讨，为世界各国相互学习和吸收水力发电技术搭建了国际平台。会议共收到论文近 300 篇，并精选了大部分优秀论文出版了中、英文两册论文集。

应印度方面邀请，水电学会在 2009 年协办了 11 月于新德里举办的“第六届国际绿色电力会议和展览”，增进了中印水电方面的交流，并对我国西藏的水电开发提出了一些建议。

为纪念汶川地震一周年，水电学会与抗震防灾专委会联合组织召开了“全国水工抗震防灾学术交流会”。共有来自全国各地高校、科研机构以及水利水电设计、施工和管理单位的专家、学者 150 余人参加，对社会各界极为关心的水坝、水电站在地震中的安全问题，进行了广泛深入的学术交流讨论，盘点中国水电在地震中的表现，总结水坝、水电抗击特大地震的经验。通过交流，代表们确信，本次会议的交流成果将会对我国未来的工程抗震起到重要的支持和推动作用。

组织参加了 2009 年第十一届中国科协年会学术分会场的宣传，与中国长江三峡集团公司共同举办了“三峡工程社会生态环境效应研讨会”。会议主要是讨论分析介绍三峡工程的生态环境效益，回答社会各界的疑问，并对我国水电未来的发展方向进行探讨。会议得到了水电学会各会员单位和与会专家的积极响应，取得了预期效果。

成功举办了“中国水电可持续发展座谈会”，来自全国水电开发、设计、施工、科研、高等院校等各有关方面的 29 个单位近 60 名代表出席了会议。与会代表围绕如何更好发挥可再生能源水电在社会经济发展中的重要作用和巨大综合效益；如何实现各大流域的科学合理规划和有序开发；如何保护好生态环境，把水电建设成为环境友好型工程；如何做好移民安置工作和落实移民后扶持政策，把水电建设成为民生工程；如何更好更有力地做好水电宣传工作；如何推动抽水蓄能电站加快建设等几大方面，从不同角度深入探讨了中国水电可持续发展这一重大问题，发表了个人的看法，介绍了经验，分析了问题，提出了建议。

应台湾有关方面的邀请，水电学会于 2009 年 4 月和 11 月共组织了两次专家交流考察团，赴台参加“海峡两岸水利水电行业合作研讨会”和开展水利水电科技学术交流考察活动，期间双方互赠水利水电发展与技术成就方面的资料书籍，更进一步加深了海峡两岸水电同行互访往来的频度，增进了海峡两岸水电同行的友谊，促进了对海峡两岸水电建设、水电技术和水电发展的相互了解，为今后海峡两岸水电行业开展实质性的互助合作进一步夯实了基础。

（四）发挥学会优势，积极开展科研咨询活动

水电学会充分利用行业影响力和专家群体优势，积极履行服务社会、行业、会员企事业单位和广大会员的办会宗旨，进一步加强与各大电力集团、流域开发公司和水电企业的交流与合作，围绕水电开发中的热点和难点问题，大力开展科研课题、技术咨询服务。分别与中国水利水电科学研究院和河海大学签订了“全面合作框架协议”，就水电科技研究、学术交流、课题合作、人才培养等多方面达成了共识。组织开展了龙滩水电工程正常蓄水位 400m 建设方案专家咨询课题，编写了《龙滩水电站正常蓄水位 400m 建设方案咨询报告》，为“龙滩 400 方案”能尽快建成出谋划策，提交有关部门决策参考。组织开展红水河流域梯级水电站优化调度研究课题，贯彻落实国家节能调度政策，充分利用红水河水资源，协调流域发电、防洪及综合利用关系，保障电网安全经济运行和澳门地区供水安全。组织 20 余位中国工程院院士和专家，开展国家“十一五”科技支撑重点项目“特大型梯级水利水电工程安全及高效运行若干关键技术问题研究”咨询课题，通过对该项目完成的质量、进度等进行技术咨询，对完成科技合同的阶段及终结成果进行阶段咨询及评估，对科技合同的技术报告及成果进行评审，为项目甲方提供技术支撑和决策支持。组织开展“乌江梯级水电站优化调度效益评价体系研究及软件开发”课题，完成了雅砻江下游梯级水电站投产并网若干重大问题研究课题，继续履行好新疆吉林台一级水电站技术咨询服务课题。

为了深入了解 MgO 筑坝技术的应用，受中国大唐集团公司委托组织召开了 MgO 筑坝技术专题讲座。组织了《MgO 膨胀材料的制备与性能》、《龙滩下游碾压混凝土围堰外掺 MgO 试验及监测成果》和《溪洛渡水电站 MgO 混凝土技术研究》专题报告，并进行了 MgO 筑坝技术的讨论和探讨。

（五）潘家铮水电科技基金进入良性运作，推荐院士等工作取得良好成效

由水电学会和挂靠单位中国水电工程顾问集团公司共同发起设立的潘家铮水电科技基金于 2008 年 5 月成立，2009 年分别召开了基金一届一次理事会和基金秘书长工作会议，审议通过了理事会名单、基金章程和实施办法、奖励办法等，明确了基金相关运作事宜。经过多方努力，水电学会申请的“水力发电科学技术进步奖”已经国家科技奖励办批复设立，将于 2010 年开始开展奖励评选工作，相关奖励由潘家铮水电科技基金作支撑。2009 年 12 月，首届潘家铮水电奖学金颁奖典礼在河海大学隆重举行，已届 82 岁高龄的中国科学院、中国工程院院士潘家铮亲临大会，为首批 39 位获奖学生颁奖，并为 400 余名师生作学术报告。通过设立“潘家铮水电奖学金”，用以奖励和激励水电水利学科专业品学兼优、勇于创新的本科生和硕博研究生，为国家培养水电水利科技领域的优秀人才。

根据中国科协有关推荐、提名两院院士的通知要求，组织成立了推荐工作小组，制定了工作办法，完成了为中国工程院推荐、提名院士候选人的工作。2009 年水电学会推荐的 3 名候选人中有 2 名成功当选（钟登华、张建云）。根据中组部、人事部和中国科协的通知精神，学会组织了第十届中国青年科技候选人推荐评审与上报工作，其中水电学会推荐的候选人有 1 名获奖。组织申报了全国优秀工程咨询成果奖工作，组织专家初评并编写报告，在电力组评审时答疑，经过水电学会的努力，2009 年共获得 3 项一等奖、6 项二等奖、9 项三等奖。根据国家发展和改革委员会价格司的要求，水电学会组织开展了调整工程咨询服务收费调研、修订工程项目建设前期收费等工作，并参与了《工程咨询业 2009～2015 年发展计划纲要》、《工程咨询管理条例》、《工程咨询服务价格管理办法》、《投资建设项目咨询服务收费规定》等修订工作。根据尚未正式颁布的《注册咨询工程师（投资）继续教育暂行办法》规定，水电学会组织开展了注册咨询工程师（投资）专业课继续教育前期准备工作。

（六）做好学会刊物的编辑出版及网站建设

为纪念新中国成立 60 周年，总结我国水力发电 60 周年的发展历程、突出成就和宝贵经验，水电学会编撰出版了《中国水电 60 年》一书，向祖国生日献礼，向中国水电人致敬。在年鉴编委会全体专家的努力下，顺利完成了《中国水力发电年鉴》第十三卷的编纂出版工作。

为了进一步拓宽水电宣传的力度，提升宣传的广度和深度，水电学会对老网站进行了全面的更新改版，于 2009 年 4 月启用了新网站，新购置的独立服务器保证了网站的顺畅运行。改版后的网站不但由专人每天对行业热点新闻、水电建设、水电环保、水电移民、领导专家话水电、论文资源库等栏目进行及时更新，而且还实现了对重要会议和活动的实时网络直播，在行业内产生了深远的影响，大大丰富了网站内容，提高了宣传时效，进一步提升了水电学会的知名度和认知度。水电学会网站正一步步实现由简单的新闻宣传向集热点新闻、行业动态、专家观点、技术资源等内容的全面丰富的行业宣传平台的质的转变。

（中国水力发电工程学会　雷定演）

中国水力发电工程学会分支机构情况表

专委会名称	主任委员	秘书长	专业内容	挂靠单位
水能规划及动能经济专业委员会	晏志勇	钱钢粮	水能规划及动能经济	水电水利规划设计总院
水库经济专业委员会	董述春	李明传	水库移民安置、水电工程征地、区域经济发展规划等	水电水利规划设计总院
环境保护专业委员会	彭　程	顾洪宾	环境影响评价、咨询，环境保护设计，水土保持方案设计	水电水利规划设计总院

续表

专委会名称	主任委员	秘书长	专业内容	挂靠单位
水文泥沙专业委员会	何根寿	朱鉴远	水文、泥沙专业的学术交流和技术总结	水电水利规划设计总院
地质及勘探专业委员会	郭义华	袁建新	水电水利工程地质、测绘、物探、钻探、岩土试验专业的学术交流	水电水利规划设计总院
水工及水电站建筑物专业委员会	王柏乐	党林才	水工	水电水利规划设计总院
水工水力学专业委员会	刘之平	吴一红	水工水力学	中国水利水电科学研究院
高坝通航工程专业委员会	张瑞凯	李　云	通航技术交流、通航科技发展战略及政策咨询、委托项目论证	南京水利科学研究院
碾压混凝土筑坝专业委员会	梅锦煜	郑桂斌	碾压混凝土筑坝技术（坝工、材料、运行、建设管理等）	武警水电指挥部
混凝土面板堆石坝专业委员会	周建平	孙永娟	混凝土面板堆石坝设计、施工、材料、变形观测、运行管理等技术交流、咨询	水电水利规划设计总院
工程造价专业委员会	王民浩	郭建欣	工程造价、工程经济技术管理	水电水利规划设计总院
电气专业委员会	李定中	于庆贵	电气一次专业	水电水利规划设计总院
自动化专业委员会	闫华锋	施　冲	水电电气二次技术及相关内容	国网电力科学研究院
水力机械专业委员会	赵　琨	戴康俊	水力机械设计、试验、安装、运行、改造	水电水利规划设计总院
水工金属结构专业委员会	龚建欣	林朝晖	闸门及启闭设备、通航设备的设计、安装、调试	水电水利规划设计总院
水电站运行管理专业委员会	赵玉柱	裴哲义	水电站运行管理、水库经济运行	国家电力调度通信中心
水电建设管理专业委员会	石成梁	毛亚杰	水电建设管理经验与技术交流	中国水力发电工程学会
信息化专业委员会	汪小刚	王桂平	计算机及自动化技术在水电工程规划、设计、施工及电站运行中的应用	中国水利水电科学研究院
大坝安全监测专业委员会	何海源	许传桂	水库、大坝的安全监测技术与安全管理	国家电力监管委员会大坝安全监察中心
机械疏浚专业委员会	王杨群	王　究	机械疏浚与吹填学术交流，推广先进经验，介绍新的技术、材料、设备、产品	水利部综合事业局
电网调峰与抽水蓄能专业委员会	崔继纯	郝荣国	开展抽水蓄能电站建设必要性、经济合理性及优化布局的研讨，介绍先进技术，组织学术交流，承接站点规划和技术咨询服务	中国水电顾问集团北京勘测设计研究院
水电监理专业委员会	陈东平	王平稳	水电监理经验与技术交流，监理技术与理论研究	华北电力大学
建设合同专业委员会	李跃平		编制水电工程涉及的各类合同范本，起草管理文件，组织有关软件课题研究，开展学术交流	中国水利水电建设集团公司
水电控制设备专业委员会	杨晓东	田忠禄	水轮机调速、励磁装置，自动化元件，智能仪表	中国水利水电科学研究院
施工专业委员会	孙洪水	阮光华	大坝浇筑填筑、混凝土生产、砂石料开采加工三大系统及设备	中国水利水电建设集团公司
抗震防灾专业委员会	李同春	张燎军	大型水利水电工程、大电网的抗震、防灾技术、预案、对策研究	河海大学

续表

专委会名称	主任委员	秘书长	专业内容	挂靠单位
电力系统自动化专业委员会	毕亚雄	陈国庆	水电厂自动化系统，自动调压、调频装置，水电长距离输电稳定装置	中国长江电力股份有限公司
梯级调度控制专业委员会	袁　杰	侯保民	流域梯级调度控制、流域水资源运用	三峡水利枢纽梯级调度通信中心
小水电专业委员会	刘晓田	程夏蕾	小水电方面学术交流、技术咨询、继续教育	水利部农村电气化研究所
继电保护专业委员会	许可达	文伯瑜	发电机、变压器和高压线路的继电保护	国务院三峡工程建设委员会办公室
风险管理专业委员会	孙家康	时　斌	风险管理理论研究，水电施工单位实施风险管理规划，组织专业培训，开展行评行检	江泰保险经纪有限公司
国际河流水电开发生态环境研究工作委员会	王　斌	顾洪宾	澜沧江开发的研究、监测、收集信息，建立监测站，对其水情进行分析评价	中国水电工程顾问集团公司

（中国水力发电工程学会秘书处　王　玉）

各省、市、自治区水力发电工程学会组织情况表

地方学会名称	会员总数	会员分类					办事机构设置地点	学术专业设置	会刊学报
		教授级高级工程师	高级工程师	工程师	助理工程师	其他			
北京市水力发电工程学会	1200						北京市定福庄 中国水电顾问集团北京勘测设计研究院		
天津市水力发电工程学会	1297	102	655	357	23	160	天津市河西区洞庭路60号 中水北方勘测设计研究有限责任公司	施工及基础处理专委会 水电成套设备专委会 水工专委会 机电专委会 大坝安全监测与管理专委会 动能经济及抽水蓄能专委会 勘测专委会	《水利水电工程设计》
河北省水力发电工程学会	175	18	87	38	22	10	石家庄市富强大街3号		
山西省水力发电工程学会	629	56	192	264	95	22	太原市南肖墙12号	水电电气自动化专委会 水工建筑及水力机械专委会 水电站运行管理专委会 农村水电电气化专委会 抽水蓄能电站专委会	《电力学报》（双月刊）、《山西省水力发电工程学会简报》

续表

地方学会名称	会员总数	会员分类					办事机构设置地点	学术专业设置	会刊学报
		教授级高级工程师	高级工程师	工程师	助理工程师	其他			
江苏省水力发电工程学会	782	113	259	317	51	42	南京市西康路1号 河海大学水电馆306室	水工结构专委会 水工水力学专委会 水电站电气及自动化专委会 仪器仪表专委会 小水电专委会 泵站及流体机械专委会 水资源及环境专委会	
上海市水力发电工程学会	244	40	138	46	20		上海市逸仙路388号 上海勘测设计研究院		《上海水利水电技术》、《上海市水力发电工程学会会讯》
浙江省水力发电工程学会	1317	155	516	547	99		杭州市梅花碑7号	水能规划及动能经济专委会 水工及水电站建筑专委会 水电站运行管理专委会 中小水电开发与管理专委会 施工专委会 机电设备专委会 地质勘测及技术处理专委会 计算机运行及信息专委会 大坝安全监测专委会	《浙江水利水电》（内刊、学会通讯）
安徽省水力发电工程学会	764	31	213	321	142	57	合肥市芜湖路415号 安徽省电力公司	水工专委会 小水电专委会 水电站运行专委会	
福建省水力发电工程学会	2326	204	765	974	211	172	福州市五四路252号金百合大酒店15楼1509房	水能规划及动能经济专委会 工程勘查专委会 水工及水电站建筑物专委会 水力机械及金属结构专委会 水电站电气及自动化专委会 施工机械及施工管理专委会 水电建设管理专委会 水电站运行管理专委会 农村电气化专委会 水库经济专委会 水电站经济及水库调度专委会	《福建水力发电》
河南省水力发电工程学会	733	84	375	260	9	5	郑州市金水路11号 黄河水利委员会国际合作与科技局	水能规划及动能经济专委会 水工及水电站建筑物专委会 水电站电气及自动化专委会 施工机械及施工管理专委会 水电站运行管理专委会 水工金属结构专委会 中小型水电专委会 地质专委会	《河南省水力发电工程学会简报》

续表

地方学会名称	会员总数	会员分类					办事机构设置地点	学术专业设置	会刊学报
		教授级高级工程师	高级工程师	工程师	助理工程师	其他			
湖北省水力发电工程学会	4354	391	857	1820	1072	214	武汉市 武昌武汉大学工学部行政楼	水能规划及动能经济专委会 水工及水电站建筑物专委会 水工水力学专委会 水利水电工程施工专委会 水电站运行管理专委会 水力机械专委会 中小水电专委会 电气与自动化专委会	《湖北水力发电》
湖南省水力发电工程学会	3010	292	1453	1059	147	59	长沙市圭塘 中国水电顾问集团中南勘测设计研究院	勘测专委会 环境保护专委会 施工专委会 库区经济专委会 水电站设备专委会 水电站运行管理专委会 小水电与农村电气化专委会 计算机应用专委会 水工结构与水电站建筑物专委会 水能规划与动能经济专委会	《中南水力发电》
广东省水力发电工程学会	1566	58	669	606	206	27	广州市五羊新城寺右南二街四巷3号 广东电网公司	水能利用专委会 水工及水电站建筑专委会 水电建设管理及施工专委会 水电站运行与自动化专委会 风电及新能源专委会	
广西水力发电工程学会	3428	126	1121	1458	553	170	南宁市民主路6号 广西电网公司	水能规划及动能经济专委会 地质勘测专委会 水工及水电站建筑物专委会 水力机械专委会 金属结构专委会 水电站电气及自动化专委会 施工机械及施工管理专委会 水电建设管理专委会 水电站运行管理专委会 小水电及农村电气化专委会 水库经济专委会 水电厂防汛及水库调度专委会 计算机应用专委会 工程造价专委会 电气及自动化专委会	《红水河》

续表

地方学会名称	会员总数	会员分类					办事机构设置地点	学术专业设置	会刊学报
		教授级高级工程师	高级工程师	工程师	助理工程师	其他			
四川省水力发电工程学会	3168	213	1342	1500	81	32	成都市东风路21号	地质勘探专委会 运行专委会 工程造价专委会 施工专委会 水工专委会 规划专委会 水机专委会	《四川水力发电》
贵州省水力发电工程学会	1926	56	553	852	392	73	贵阳市新华路9号 乌江水电开发有限责任公司	水资源及水能规划专委会 地质与勘探专委会 水工及水电站建筑物专委会 水电站建设及工程经济专委会 金属结构及水力机械专委会 施工管理专委会 水库经济专委会 水电站运行管理专委会 小水电技术专委会 环境与资源专委会	《贵州水力发电》
云南省水力发电工程学会	1988	127	650	873	264	74	昆明市拓东路49号 云南电网公司3号楼203室	水工及水电站建筑物专委会 水能规划及动能经济专委会 水电站电气及自动化专委会 水力机械及金属结构专委会 施工机械及施工管理专委会 水电站运行管理专委会 工程经济定额预算专委会 地质及勘测专委会	《云南水力发电》
陕西省水力发电工程学会	4018	1088	1309	833		学生会员788	西安市丈八东路18号 中国水电顾问集团西北勘测设计研究院	水工专委会 规划动能经济专委会 工程地质勘测专委会 小水电专委会 机电运行专委会 水电站施工专委会 工程造价专委会 通航专委会 水电站自动化专委会 水库及环保专委会 风电与新能源专委会	《西北水力发电》［西北五省（区）联合办刊］
甘肃省水力发电工程学会	1207	23	396	430	111	247	兰州市七里河西津东路628号 甘肃省电力公司	水能规划与动能经济专委会 地质与勘探专委会 水力机械专委会 水电站运行管理专委会 小水电专委会 水工与施工专委会	《甘肃电力技术》、《西北水力发电》

续表

地方学会名称	会员总数	会员分类					办事机构设置地点	学术专业设置	会刊学报
		教授级高级工程师	高级工程师	工程师	助理工程师	其他			
宁夏水力发电工程学会	481	39	197	161	56	28	银川市贺兰山西路539号 宁夏大学土木与水利工程学院	水电站运行专委会 水力机械气蚀磨损专委会 电气自动化专委会 水工专委会 水电施工专委会	《西北水力发电》［西北五省（区）联合办刊］
青海省水力发电工程学会	1018	24	292	524	120	58	西宁市五四西路43号 黄河上游水电开发公司	水电工程经济定额预算专委会 小水电专委会 水工专委会 水能经济专委会	《青海水力发电》
新疆水力发电工程学会	217	39	86	92			乌鲁木齐市黑龙江路19号 水利部新疆水利水电勘测设计研究院	水利水电工程大坝专委会 水电站机电及自动化技术专委会 岩石力学与工程专委会 水利水电工程招标投标专委会 水能规划与动能经济专委会 水电工程经济专委会 水工与施工专委会 水库与环保专委会 金属结构水工机械专委会 水库经济专委会	《新疆水利水电》

（中国水力发电工程学会秘书处 王 玉）

中国大坝协会2009年工作情况

2009年，中国大坝协会成功召开了成立大会；积极推荐中国水利水电科学研究院副院长贾金生参加国际大坝委员会主席竞选并成功当选；主办了“地震与大坝安全国际研讨会”，组织国内专家参加了国际大坝委员会第23届国际大坝会议和中日韩第六次学术交流会，编印了《中国大坝协会成立专刊》和旨在宣传中国大坝建设成就的《Current Activities—Dam Construction in China》，主办了第一届堆石坝国际研讨会，加强了秘书处能力建设，各项工作取得了良好的进展。

一、中国大坝协会成立及注册登记工作

2009年5月11日，中国大坝协会成立筹备会议在中国水利水电科学研究院召开。会议就成立会议文件进行了讨论，对会员单位的发展提出了指导意见，并推荐贾金生代表中国大坝协会参加国际大坝委员会主席竞选。

2009年6月8日，中国大坝协会成立大会暨第一次会员代表大会在北京隆重召开。本次大会得到了各级领导的高度重视，全国政协原副主席、中国工程院院士钱正英，水利部党组书记、部长陈雷，全国人大财经委员会副主任委员、水利部原部长汪恕诚，中国工程院院士陆佑楣，中国科学院、中国工程院院士潘家铮，水利部副部长矫勇，中国国电集团公司原总经理、中国水力发电工程学会理事长周大兵，民政部民间组织管理巡视员廖鸿出席大会开幕式。出席成立大会的还有水利部、国家电力监管委员会、国家能源局等各部门的领导，中国大坝协会的老领导，水利界知名专家，兄弟学会的嘉宾，以及流域机构、各水利水电企事业单位及有关院校的主要领导和代表，参会代表共280余人。

成立大会之后召开了中国大坝协会第一次会员代表大会和中国大坝协会第一届理事会第一次全体会议，会议审议并通过《中国大坝协会第一次全国会员

代表大会工作报告》、《中国大坝协会章程》、《中国大坝协会会费管理办法》，选举产生中国大坝协会第一届理事会、常务理事会，通过了第一批会员名单，选举了理事长、副理事长、秘书长和常务理事。全国人大财经委员会副主任委员、水利部原部长汪恕诚当选中国大坝协会理事长。

经审核，民政部于2009年12月23日正式批复同意中国大坝协会成立登记，颁发了社会团体登记证书。

二、组团参加国际大坝委员会学术活动

（一）矫勇率团参加第23届国际大坝会议

国际大坝委员会第77届年会和第23届大会于2009年5月21～29日在巴西首都巴西利亚召开，会议由巴西大坝委员会具体承办，除安排了第77届执行会议和各专业委员会会议外，会议组委会还安排了“多功能水库与大坝”专题研讨会等活动。来自60多个国家的1470多名专家、学者参加了本届会议。

为了积极参与国际大坝委员会的活动，广泛进行学术交流，在水利部的领导下，在各流域委员会、流域水电开发公司、高校、设计和科研等单位的大力支持下，中国大坝协会组织了以水利部副部长矫勇（中国大坝协会副理事长）为代表团团长、以中国水利水电科学研究院副院长贾金生（中国大坝协会副理事长）为专家团团长的42人代表团参加了此次会议。

应巴西大坝委员会主席邀请，矫勇副部长在“多功能水库大坝”国际研讨会上作了题为《大坝水库与和谐发展——中国的探索与实践》的主旨报告，来自中国水利水电科学研究院、中国长江三峡集团公司、南京水利科学研究院等单位的多位专家也在会上作了学术报告，报告准备充分、内容精彩，赢得了与会代表的一致赞誉，在与各国同行专家进行学术交流的同时，也把我国的经验和成果积极向外宣传和推广。

（二）贾金生当选国际大坝委员会新一届主席

国际大坝委员会第77届执行会议于2009年5月23日在巴西首都巴西利亚召开，63个国家的代表参加了选举，贾金生以高票成功当选为国际大坝委员会新一届主席（任期从2009年至2012年），是国际大坝委员会第22位主席，是我国历史上的第一位国际大坝委员会主席。参加主席竞选的还有美国前大坝协会主席Walz先生和英国前大坝协会主席Hughes先生。

（三）张国新副秘书长率团参加中日韩大坝会第六次学术交流会

“气候变化对大坝的挑战”国际研讨会暨中日韩大坝委员会第六次学术交流会于2009年10月25～27日在韩国首尔召开。本次会议有三个主题：“气候变化对大坝的影响”、“大坝建设、运行和管理的新模式”和“抽水蓄能电站的设计和运行”。为了加强东亚地区大坝技术方面的经验交流与合作，在各单位的大力支持和配合下，中国大坝协会组织了以副秘书长张国新为团长的25人代表团参加了此次会议。

来自中国、韩国、日本和土耳其的19位专家分别就气候变化对水资源分布、水库调度的影响、河流修复与重建、大坝运行管理和抽水蓄能电站建设新技术等方面在大会上作技术报告。中国长江三峡集团公司的李勇泉工程师和居志刚高工分别作了题为《基于风险理论的大坝水文安全风险研究》和《溪洛渡水电站坝址区局部气象特点分析》的报告；中国水利水电科学研究院崔炜博士作了题为《呼和浩特抽水蓄能电站区域三维渗流场分析》的报告。

参会代表会后分两组进行了技术考察。

三、主办第一届堆石坝国际研讨会

由中国大坝协会、巴西大坝委员会、中国长江三峡集团公司、中国水电工程顾问集团公司、中国水利水电建设集团公司和中国葛洲坝集团公司联合主办，由中国水利水电科学研究院承办的第一届堆石坝国际研讨会于2009年10月18～20日在四川成都隆重召开。来自中国、伊朗、日本、泰国、瑞典等30个国家的400多名代表参加了会议。

为了总结堆石坝在技术上取得的巨大成就，明确在国际坝工界具有里程碑意义和影响的工程，经过推荐、初评、复评等程序，国际大坝委员会同中国大坝协会和巴西大坝委员会，在会评选出12个国际堆石坝里程碑工程奖（面板堆石坝5个，其中有中国的水布垭，坝高233m；心墙堆石坝5个，其中有中国的小浪底，坝高156m；沥青心墙坝2个）。紫坪铺面板堆石坝（坝高156m）在2008年5月12日经受住了里氏8.0级强震的考验，在堆石坝抗震史上具有里程碑的意义，被评为特别工程奖。

会议收录了国内外140篇学术论文。参会代表报告精彩，交流深入，会场气氛十分热烈。会后还安排了三峡、水布垭、冶勒、向家坝、溪洛渡等工程考察。

四、联合国开发计划署（UNDP）“加强水电安全项目”系列专题研讨会

中国“5·12”汶川地震后，为了更好地总结大坝抗震方面的成果和经验，积极回应社会上关于大坝抗震安全、水库触发地震等问题的关注，从而进一步推动科学建坝、科学管理大坝等工作，中国商务部与联合国开发计划署（UNDP）签署了《支持汶川地震灾后重建与早期恢复援助方案》的“加强水电安全项

目”，旨在通过对汶川地震灾区的各种水利水电设施开展针对性的调研、试验、分析以及标准制定，提高中国地震灾害地区的水利水电设施的抗震安全水平；加强政府部门间在水利水电抗震安全方面的协调；促进国际间在相关领域的交流与合作，中国大坝协会参与组织和承办了系列专题研讨会，以促进项目成果在国内外的推广和应用。

（一）地震与大坝安全国际研讨会

经水利部国际合作与科技司批准，地震与大坝安全专题研讨会于2009年3月30日～4月3日在北京和成都召开，会前中国大坝协会理事长汪恕诚亲切会见了各国专家。来自中国、美国、加拿大、瑞士等8个国家的大坝抗震专家近60人参加了专题研讨会。国内外专家针对混凝土大坝抗震实例与安全评估、大坝抗震监测与结果评价、国内外大坝抗震设计规程规范比较研究和水库触发地震问题等议题展开了广泛的交流，形成了三份书面报告。3月31日～4月3日，代表们参观考察了紫坪铺面板堆石坝、沙牌碾压混凝土拱坝、福堂闸坝、太平驿闸坝和映秀湾闸坝。

（二）大坝安全与地震学术研讨会

围绕UNDP“加强水电安全项目”，中国大坝协会于5月26日即国际大坝委员会第77届年会和第23届大会期间，在巴西首都巴西利亚举办了大坝安全与地震学术研讨会。会议由项目主任、新任国际大坝委员会主席、中国大坝协会副理事长贾金生博士和项目首席国际专家、挪威岩土工程技术学院教授、国际大坝委员会荣誉主席Hoeg教授主持，来自挪威、美国、瑞士、日本、法国等24个国家的60多名坝工专家参加了会议。各位专家分别从各自不同的角度就汶川地震中紫坪铺混凝土面板堆石坝、沙牌碾压混凝土拱坝及岷江上游几座重力式混凝土闸坝水工结构的震损情况进行初步的分析，就汶川地震对大坝安全的影响、未来大坝抗震安全研究的课题等提出了看法，并对项目涉及的大坝工程的数值分析、仿真计算、大坝抗震安全监测，以及未来在大坝抗震研究领域的国际合作提出了相关的建议。与会专家对汶川特大地震对大坝安全影响的相关分析、研究成果开展了广泛交流。会议促进了大坝抗震研究成果在发达国家同行间的交流，以及在发展中国家的推广应用。

（三）UNDP“加强水电安全项目”协调推进会

中国大坝协会于2009年7月24～27日在四川成都组织召开了UNDP“加强水电安全项目”协调推进会。会议重点围绕项目预期的产出成果，针对既定初步研究方案的落实情况、前期工作成果的共享、后续工作过程中的深度合作，以及项目涉及工程在灾害应急管理和环境保护方面的延伸研究等议题进行讨论，并对10月的项目会议进行筹备。参会单位有：联合国开发计划署驻华代表处、中国国际经济技术交流中心、水利部水利水电规划设计总院、四川大学、中国水利水电科学研究院和中国大坝协会，共40余名专家代表参加了会议交流和讨论。

（四）UNDP“加强水电安全项目”国际专题研讨会

作为第一届堆石坝国际研讨会的重要分会之一，UNDP“加强水电安全项目”国际专题研讨会于10月20日召开。来自联合国开发计划署，中国国际经济技术交流中心、水利部，以及日本、巴西、瑞士、塔吉克斯坦、台湾等10个国家和地区的70余位代表和专家参加了会议。受项目执行单位中国水利水电科学研究院的委托，中国大坝协会组织召开了本次研讨会。通过研讨，国内、国际专家和项目各方代表充分交流了项目取得的成果，交换了对项目成果的认识和建议，提出了进一步合作的想法，为推进大坝抗震安全经验交流和项目成果应用提供了平台，受到了与会专家的一致好评。会后安排有关专家赴紫坪铺、沙牌等项目相关工程进行了考察，进一步加深对项目成果的了解。

五、协助国际大坝委员会主席做相关工作

中国大坝协会副理事长、中国水利水电科学研究院副院长贾金生当选国际大坝委员会主席以后，应各方的邀请，参加了以下活动：

（1）2009年6月17～24日，参加了世界水理事会董事会会议和国际大坝委员会官员会议。

（2）2009年9月2～4日出席了在塔吉克斯坦努列克电站召开的“萨雷兹湖现状、安全问题及水资源合理利用”国际研讨会，并作了题为《国际对大坝和大坝安全的新要求》的大会报告。

（3）2009年10月11～18日，参加了在奥地利召开的召开第二届大坝长效运行国际研讨会并作大会报告，之后，出席法国马赛召开的世界水理事会董事局会议，当选为世界水理事会董事。

（4）出席2009年10月25～29日在法国里昂召开的水电2009国际研讨会并致辞。

就以上活动，中国大坝协会秘书处承担了与境外联络、安排行程、草拟致辞稿、准备相关学术报告初稿等工作。

六、推选工程参与中国土木工程詹天佑奖评选

2009年12月23日，由中国大坝协会推荐申报的湖北清江水布垭工程获得了第九届中国土木工程詹天佑奖。

七、组织对萨扬—舒申斯克水电站事故、巴西停电事故等突发事件进行调研

2008年8月17日，俄罗斯西伯利亚地区萨扬—舒申斯克水电站发生严重事故，造成75人死亡、13人失踪。萨扬—舒申斯克水电站事故受到世界广泛关注，影响重大。

事故发生后，中国大坝协会秘书处陆续收到了来自各方的质疑和不同的信息。为澄清事实，以正视听，秘书处积极联系俄罗斯大坝委员会和全俄各水利工程研究院等单位，收集事故发生原因的相关资料。经多方联络，秘书处已收到俄罗斯方面发来的关于事故原因的俄文官方报告，并组织精通俄语的专家进行了翻译，印刷了《萨扬—舒申斯克水电站事故原因技术报告书（摘译）》，供我国水利水电工作者参考。

2009年11月10日晚，巴西发生大面积停电。事情发生以后，秘书处和巴西大坝委员会进行了联系，询问事故发生的原因，并跟踪巴方调查分析的进展情况。

八、组织翻译国际大坝委员会公报《遥感在水库水质管理中的应用》

国际大坝委员会每年都不定期出版技术公报，这些公报反映了国际坝工领域的技术进步和新成果、新经验、新理念。翻译这些公报，有助于国内专家了解国外的动态。

《遥感在水库水质管理中的应用》公报汇总了历时三年的研究成果，评估新的遥感技术在水工程规划和运行中的适用性，以及以遥感技术作为工具来标定水库及相关水域水质参数的能力。中国大坝协会组织翻译本公报，旨在有助于关注水库水质的领导和专家以及相关部门了解国际上水库水质管理的新技术，以期在我国水库和下游河道水质管理中予以借鉴。

九、中国大坝统计

补充和校核中国大坝协会坝高30m以上大坝统计数据库，并将符合要求的抽水蓄能电站纳入统计范畴。开展世界大坝统计和分析，将中国和世界大坝建设及水电开发情况整理成文发表。

（摘自中国大坝协会网《中国大坝协会秘书处2009年工作总结》）

中国水利学会2009年工作情况

（一）组织建设

1. 召开第九次全国会员代表大会　中国水利学会于2009年5月25～26日在北京召开了第九次全国会员代表大会。水利部部长陈雷出席开幕式并作重要讲话，中国科协书记处书记冯长根到会祝贺并讲话。大会听取审议了八届理事会工作报告和财务报告，审议了《中国水利学会章程》修改报告，选举产生了中国水利学会第九届理事会，聘任了九届名誉理事长和名誉理事，并通过中国水利学会会费标准等文件。大会期间还召开了九届理事会第一次全体会议及九届一次常务理事会。

2. 加强自身建设　学会秘书处于2009年3月新设立了“事业发展部”，主要负责技术咨询与培训、会议服务与展览、奖励等相关工作。调整后学会秘书处内设机构由4个部门组成：综合组织部、学术交流部、标准化部和事业发展部。

3. 加强对专业委员会的管理　河口治理与保护专委会、水利统计专委会、地基与基础专委会等召开了换届会议，选举产生了新一届委员会。

4. 指导省级水利学会工作　2009年8月21～22日在北戴河召开了省级水利学会秘书长工作座谈会。贵州、山东和福建等省水利学会召开了全省会员代表大会。

（二）国内学术活动

据不完全统计，2009年中国水利学会秘书处及各分支机构共召开各类学术会议60余次，参会人数逾6000人，出版论文集10余种。主要活动如下：

9月22～24日，在湖北省武汉市举办“2009水资源与可持续发展高层论坛”，全国政协原副主席、中国工程院院士钱正英出席会议，水利部部长陈雷出席会议并作重要讲话，中国水利学会理事长敬正书在开幕式上致辞。共有200余名代表参加，其中国内相关领域院士20余名，国外代表50余名，包括来自美国、英国、俄罗斯、澳大利亚的8名水利界的科学院和工程院院士。

10月10～12日，水力学专委会在西安主办“第四届全国水力学与水利信息学学术大会”，主题为“生态水利与环境的可持续发展”，设有环境与生态水力学、工程水力学、河口岸边生态与环境、灾害水力学、信息技术在水利工程与研究中的应用5个专题，同时组织了英语分会场和经理论坛。大会共收到论文218篇。

10月17～19日，岩土力学专委会与工程管理专委会共同主办的“第六届全国水利工程渗流学术研讨会”在武汉召开，近百名代表与会，收到论文107篇。

10月18～19日，陕西省水利学会、全球水伙伴（中国陕西）等单位在西安共同举办“第三届渭河论坛”，论坛主题为“渭河水与环境”，来自社会各界的

100余名专家学者就渭河水环境管理体制与机制、水污染、水生态、渭河健康生命等内容进行了探讨，达成了基本共识，并对渭河水环境问题提出了具体建议。

11月3～4日，湖北省水利学会等单位承办中国科协“2009年促进中部崛起专家论坛暨第五届湖北科技论坛”水利分会场，主题为“发展民生水利，保障安全饮水”，160余名代表与会，中国工程院院士王浩等在会上作了特邀学术报告。该分会场被中国科协评为本次论坛优秀分会场。

（三）国际民间科技交流

（1）由中国水利学会牵头的科技部国际合作专项“石羊河流域生态环境修复研究与示范”进入实施第二年，进展顺利。项目组成员于11月赴加拿大进行了为期9天的技术考察和交流。

（2）中国水利学会成功申请加入世界水理事会(World Water Council)，成为首批加入世界水理事会的8个中国水利机构之一，并派人参加了世界水理事会第五次会员代表大会。

（3）完成2009年中国科协“赴欧洲社团组织管理”出访任务，团组成员访问了位于西班牙马德里的国际水利环境工程与研究协会（IAHR）总部，双方对未来合作进行了深入探讨。

（四）学术期刊管理和专著出版

中国水利学会主办的期刊有《水利学报》、《水科学进展》、《岩土工程学报》、《泥沙研究》、《灌溉排水学报》及《中国防汛抗旱》。根据中国科技期刊统计结果，中国水利学会主办的《水利学报》参与中国科技信息所2009年期刊综合指标评价，在全国1868种统计源期刊中排名第7。同时《水利学报》还荣获“新中国60年有影响力的期刊”称号，主编陈炳新荣获“新中国60年有影响力的期刊人”称号。《中国防汛抗旱》出版了庆祝中华人民共和国成立60周年纪念增刊。

水资源专委会继《水知识读本（小学低年级适用)》分册于2008年出版后，《水知识读本（小学高年级适用)》分册于2009年出版发行。

（五）科学普及

中国水利学会及各分支机构结合世界水日、中国水周、全国科普日等主题活动开展了形式多样的科普活动。完成了对中国水利学会推荐、中国科协命名的第一批全国科普教育基地“水利部节水灌溉示范基地”和“水文水资源与水利工程科学国家重点实验室”的评估报告，通过中国科协评估认定。

中国水利学会于2009年着手开展了水利科普教育基地建设前期准备工作，起草了《全国水利科普教育基地管理办法》。

（六）科技奖励与人才举荐

1. 科技奖励　完成了第三届大禹水利科技奖奖励委员会的换届，并在新一届奖励委员会的领导下，完成了大禹奖的评审工作，共38项成果获2009年度大禹奖，其中一等奖8项、二等奖14项。

2. 人才举荐　学会推荐的王光谦教授当选中国科学院院士，学会提名的张建云教授当选中国工程院院士。中国水利水电科学研究院王建华经中国水利学会推荐荣获第11届中国青年科技奖。

（七）政府委托任务

1. 标准化　积极完成水利部标准化工作主管部门委托的水利标准化规划、计划、项目管理、宣贯等任务，提高了中国水利学会在行业标准化工作中的地位。组织召开了水利科技标准新项目启动会议，对180个项目进行了项目启动，完成了39项标准的发布工作。完成了中国科协“学会承接标准化工作改革创新试点”和水利部“《水利技术标准体系表》修订”等多个项目的验收。

2. 职称考试　中国水利学会承担了2009年度水利部直属单位职称考试工作。召开了“职称考试大纲和试题库修订专题研讨会”，修订了职称考试大纲和试题库。

3. 工程教育专业认证　中国水利学会参加中国科协、教育部组织的工程教育专业认证工作，认证了西北农林科技大学、内蒙古农业大学的水文与水资源工程专业；申报了中国科协《水利工程教育专业认证》课题并获得批准。

（八）第四届中国水博览会

2009年11月18～20日，第四届中国水博览会暨“辉煌历程——中国水利60年”成就展在北京展览馆隆重召开，全国人大副委员长蒋树声出席了开幕式，水利部部长陈雷等领导参观了展览。本届水博览会参展国家和地区共18个，参展企业200余家，与会专业观众近万人。

水博览会期间同期举办了以“中国水资源可持续利用”为主题的第四届“中国（国际）水务高峰论坛”，内容涉及水价、农村饮水安全、节水灌溉、水利信息化与应急管理、水务投融资等，得到政府部门、中介组织、企业的广泛欢迎和参与。

（中国水利学会秘书处）

中國水力發電年鑒

17

统 计 资 料

2009 年全国水电增长情况表

全国及各省、自治区、直辖市	装机容量（万 kW）			发电量（亿 kW·h）		
	总 量	水 电	水电增长率（%）	总 量	水 电	水电增长率（%）
全 国	87 410	19 629	13.7	36 812	5717	1.1
北 京	622	105		247	4	−2.5
天 津	1004	1		413	0.1	
河 北	3829	179	16.1	1764	7	5.4
山 西	4088	161	103.2	1873	22	−6.5
内蒙古	5556	83	0.1	2250	18	56.5
辽 宁	2577	146	2.5	1194	32	−24.0
吉 林	1593	390	0.1	547	52	7.3
黑龙江	1886	94	0.3	732	18	29.3
上 海	1658			783		
江 苏	5662	114	0.1	2984	3	−18.4
浙 江	5610	956	6.7	2251	152	3.6
安 徽	2841	162	3.9	1329	29	3.6
福 建	3036	1098	3.8	1171	276	−16.8
江 西	1533	377	1.4	524	78	−11.9
山 东	6079	106	0.4	2871	1	−67.8
河 南	4680	365	20.9	2068	82	0.9
湖 北	4569	3001	3.3	1798	1167	−2.7
湖 南	2736	1146	7.6	952	319	2.0
广 东	6407	1126	9.5	2666	197	−22.9
广 西	2552	1475	5.6	905	477	−7.1
海 南	385	70	70.7	135	21	89.0
重 庆	1134	453	11.4	430	125	7.0
四 川	3808	2581	16.1	1449	945	13.1
贵 州	3091	1361	43.7	1345	367	0.1
云 南	3169	2090	32.8	1174	624	0.3
西 藏	57	44	1.5	18	15	5.7
陕 西	2181	192	5.6	840	65	20.0
甘 肃	1767	594	9.1	704	251	15.8
青 海	1067	874	47.8	380	273	26.6
宁 夏	952	43		468	17	7.0
新 疆	1280	243	11.0	548	81	9.4

（中国电力企业联合会）

2009年全国电源工程建设项目投资完成情况表

全国及各省、自治区、直辖市	总投资额（万元）	水电投资额（万元）	全国及各省、自治区、直辖市	总投资额（万元）	水电投资额（万元）
全　国	38 033 127	8 671 860	河　南	822 467	51 726
北　京	78 635		湖　北	1 768 193	1 315 583
天　津	717 456		湖　南	408 658	112 784
河　北	1 672 991	13 892	广　东	3 044 714	174 228
山　西	764 916	56 189	广　西	414 842	240 234
内蒙古	4 353 947	21 778	海　南	313 434	25 896
辽　宁	2 909 483	79 063	重　庆	302 964	291 148
吉　林	1 258 105	6794	四　川	3 449 146	3 231 975
黑龙江	735 181		贵　州	914 614	817 711
上　海	1 140 237		云　南	1 620 709	1 322 968
江　苏	1 856 235	42 863	西　藏	39 132	39 132
浙　江	1 667 426	27 765	陕　西	382 223	88 622
安　徽	566 688	46 021	甘　肃	1 334 368	323 215
福　建	1 437 893	28 810	青　海	173 311	173 237
江　西	695 852		宁　夏	1 042 491	
山　东	1 477 105		新　疆	669 707	140 226

（中国电力企业联合会）

2009年水电施工企业完成产值及工程量表

单位名称	企业总产值（亿元）	企业建筑业总产值（亿元）	实物工程量					
			土方（万 m^3）	石方（万 m^3）	混凝土（万 m^3）	金属结构安装（t）	水电机组投产	
							台	万kW
中国水利水电建设集团公司	751.7	519.6	21 553.4	17 388.2	3511.1	296 696.0	178	1850.4
中国葛洲坝集团公司	260.6	210.5	6820.2	4546.8	1736.0	532 800.0	15	189.5
中国人民武装警察部队水电指挥部（中国安能建设总公司）	73.2	73.2	5392.0(挖) 1072.0(填)	260.0	301.0	9745.0	6	112.0

（中国水利水电建设集团公司
中国葛洲坝集团公司
中国人民武装警察部队水电指挥部）

2009年全国农村水电年末装机及发电量情况表

行政区划	农村水电年末装机容量		农村水电发电量	
	kW	%	万 kW·h	%
全　国	55 121 211	100.00	15 672 470	100.00
北　京	42 920	0.08	1393	0.01
天　津	5000	0.01	1400	0.01
河　北	370 178	0.67	29 127	0.19
山　西	172 600	0.31	17 470	0.11
内蒙古	53 460	0.10	8375	0.05
辽　宁	307 333	0.56	69 624	0.44
吉　林	390 980	0.71	102 322	0.65
黑龙江	241 605	0.44	61 922	0.40
江　苏	52 656	0.10	8888	0.06
浙　江	3 610 103	6.55	745 235	4.76
安　徽	828 404	1.50	178 884	1.14
福　建	6 846 790	12.42	1 718 042	10.96
江　西	2 588 517	4.70	632 077	4.03
山　东	69 733	0.13	9156	0.06
河　南	354 291	0.64	73 964	0.47
湖　北	2 697 835	4.89	687 834	4.39
湖　南	4 883 357	8.86	1 348 895	8.61
广　东	6 526 256	11.84	1 450 533	9.26
广　西	3 453 354	6.27	887 357	5.66
海　南	297 036	0.54	109 395	0.70
重　庆	1 381 190	2.51	452 907	2.89
四　川	6 571 132	11.92	2 424 496	15.47
贵　州	1 954 274	3.55	655 963	4.19
云　南	7 218 555	13.10	2 447 550	15.62
西　藏	183 996	0.33	37 425	0.24
陕　西	827 345	1.50	255 989	1.63
甘　肃	1 553 481	2.82	613 312	3.91
青　海	593 830	1.08	272 987	1.74
宁　夏	3200	0.01	800	0.01
新　疆	690 015	1.25	227 978	1.45
新疆兵团	246 485	0.45	91 402	0.58
部直属	105 300	0.19	49 769	0.32

（水利部农村水电及电气化发展局　曲　鹏）

2009年全国大中型水电厂生产运行情况表

一、抽水蓄能电厂

电厂名称		总装机容量	机组台数	年发电量	年抽水电量	等效可用系数	各类工况运行总时间	各工况启动次数	启动成功率
		万kW	台	亿kW·h	亿kW·h	%	h	次	%
1	十三陵蓄能电厂	80.00	4	4.05	5.54	95.35	1479.99	1848	99.95
2	潘家口蓄能电厂	27.00	3	0.60	0.92	97.69	802.53	688	100
3	张河湾蓄能电厂	100.00	4	1.72	2.26	93.39	345.67	463	100
4	白山抽水蓄能电站	30.00	2	0.44	1.45	86.31	1193	303	100
5	宜兴抽水蓄能电厂	100.00	4	11.14	13.57	83.89	2606.22	3047	100
6	天荒坪抽水蓄能电厂	180.00	6	18.07	22.59	92.60	2300.95	3233	100
7	桐柏抽水蓄能电厂	120.00	4	10.24	12.30	94.71	1925.96	1945	99.95
8	瑚琊山抽水蓄能厂	60.00	4	6.64	8.26	96.81	2372.83	2483	100
9	响洪甸抽水蓄能电厂	8.00	2	1.28	1.69	92.90	3101.42	1502	99.73
10	泰安抽水蓄能电厂	100.00	4	1.13	1.44	93.45	310.66	545	100
11	回龙抽水蓄能电站	12.00	2	1.22	1.69	79.48	2417.08	1151	99.39
12	广州蓄能水电厂	240.00	8	33.81	44.38	90.94	29 368.00	12 099	99.74
13	河北华电混合蓄能水电公司	5.70	4	0.50	0.00	96.39	33.50	10	100.00

二、常规水电厂

水电厂名称		发电运行情况				水库运行情况			
		总装机容量	年发电量	平均耗水率	等效可用系数	年入库总水量	发电用水量	年末水位	年末库容
		万kW	亿kW·h	$m^3/(kW\cdot h)$	%	亿m^3	亿m^3	m	亿m^3
14	北京华电水电有限公司	5.20	0.08	11.20	99.08	1.89	0.90	135.86	10.40
15	万家寨水电厂	108.00	11.44	6.62		166.99	161.75		
16	太平湾发电厂	34.00	13.11		98.13				
	其中：太平湾	19.00	6.45	30.11	96.80	335.17	200.01	29.18	1.63
	长甸	13.50	6.66	5.87	100.00	386.40	36.10	115.10	88.78
17	辽宁和禹发电公司	45.50	8.30	3.40	93.95	30.60	28.10	296.23	18.50
	其中：太平哨发电厂	16.10							
	桓仁水电厂	29.45							
18	白山发电厂	170.00	19.66						
	其中：白山	150.00	16.03	3.64	89.07	48.92	58.50	405.85	41.43
	红石	20.00	3.63	17.09	81.64	62.04	62.03	290.14	1.65

续表

水电厂名称		发电运行情况				水库运行情况			
		总装机容量	年发电量	平均耗水率	等效可用系数	年入库总水量	发电用水量	年末水位	年末库容
		万 kW	亿 kW·h	$m^3/(kW \cdot h)$	%	亿 m^3	亿 m^3	m	亿 m^3
19	丰满发电厂	100.25	9.05	8.96	85.94	83.42	86.26	249.86	42.74
20	云峰发电厂	40.00	11.02	5.13	92.59	56.12	53.87	301.16	21.76
21	新安江水力发电厂	85.00	16.98	5.32	93.29	88.30	90.79	100.31	135.83
22	富春江水力发电厂	35.72	7.89	28.51	85.93	226.22	225.08	23.00	4.41
23	乌溪江水力发电厂	34.45	5.18	3.49	94.61	18.62	18.06	205.90	7.83
24	石塘水电站	8.58	1.35	19.5	92.27	26.62	26.36	102.28	0.71
25	沙溪口水力发电厂	30.00	7.41	18.51	92.27	154.02	141.23	87.17	1.40
26	古田溪水力发电厂	27.60	6.83	1.33	94.50	10.29	9.07	365.96	1.44
27	华安水力发电厂	6.00	3.10	9.11	95.56	36.64	28.23	93.02	0.04
28	安砂水力发电厂	11.50	3.57	6.83	96.26	33.59	24.41	260.08	4.92
29	池潭水力发电厂	10.00	3.04	8.87	94.19	29.03	26.94	251.49	1.43
30	闽东水电开发公司	32.00	6.69	0.66	97.18	4.35	4.43	730.20	0.96
31	棉花滩水电厂	60.00	10.27	4.62	90.50	45.41	47.44	156.33	8.89
32	白沙水电厂	7.00	1.09	7.06	93.30	7.94	7.72	261.84	1.53
33	高砂水电公司	5.00	1.54	39.57	91.37	67.57	60.91	103.01	0.25
34	照口水电厂	6.00	1.78	42.63	89.00	86.82	75.87	97.59	0.26
35	水口水电厂	140.00	42.50	7.69	93.10	342.50	326.75	59.60	18.36
36	街面电站	30.00	2.55	4.05	91.03	9.67	10.28	275.55	12.29
37	水东电站	8.00	2.06	11.10	93.37	23.14	22.78	142.26	0.95
38	雍口电站	5.00	1.44	19.81	94.91	29.89	28.48	86.13	0.23
39	万安水力发电厂	40.00	7.50	21.00	90.71	166.00	158.20	94.97	10.00
40	小浪底水力发电厂								
	其中：1～6 号机组	180.00	50.45	3.92	91.60	199.75	193.93	240.14	32.25
	7～10 号机组（西霞院）	14.00	4.46	43.68	91.15	215.55	186.08	130.82	0.73
41	三峡水力发电厂	1830.00	798.53	4.60	93.35	3881.29	3667.10	169.44	338.78
42	葛洲坝水力发电厂	271.50	161.71	20.60	93.42	3852.30	3336.85	65.42	6.93
43	水布垭水力发电厂	184.00	29.60	2.34	91.87	64.45	69.18	382.88	33.24
44	隔河岩水力发电厂	121.20	23.87	4.02	91.96	92.58	95.99	186.15	21.81
45	高坝洲水力发电厂	27.00	8.88	11.46	95.01	106.47	101.74	79.06	3.77
46	五强溪水电厂	120.00	49.73	8.66	95.40	507.30	430.56	106.39	27.95
47	凌津滩水电厂	27.00	10.68	42.42	95.94	525.54	452.85	51.01	1.48
48	碗米坡水电厂	24.00	5.67	10.99	95.44	63.72	62.37	239.62	1.46
49	近尾洲水电站	6.32	2.54	57.40	96.79	175.12	145.93	66.00	1.54
50	洪江水力发电厂	27.00	10.91	17.29	94.80	212.42	188.60	189.30	1.84

续表

水电厂名称		发电运行情况				水库运行情况			
		总装机容量	年发电量	平均耗水率	等效可用系数	年入库总水量	发电用水量	年末水位	年末库容
		万 kW	亿 kW·h	m³/(kW·h)	%	亿 m³	亿 m³	m	亿 m³
51	三板溪水电厂	100.00	20.76	3.39	93.40	62.74	70.29	434.67	14.68
52	挂治水电厂	15.00	3.74	18.91	96.58	70.70	70.63	320.45	0.36
53	马迹塘水电厂	5.55	2.23	67.42	95.32	205.74	150.10	55.79	0.13
54	东坪水电站	7.20	2.08	62.83	96.72	144.01	130.54	93.84	0.14
55	株溪口水力发电厂	7.40	2.10	63.87	95.38	143.42	133.86	87.34	0.32
56	白石窑水电厂	9.20	2.20	39.30		89.82	86.43	36.50	1.08
57	飞来峡水电厂	14.00	5.21	33.60		208.80	175.10	22.89	3.46
58	南水水电厂	7.90	1.79	3.56	95.45	7.07	6.38	203.85	5.19
59	流溪河水电厂	4.80	0.72	4.45	93.48	3.88	3.19	229.45	2.45
60	长湖水电厂	7.60	1.85	13.02	94.68	24.54	24.15	58.81	1.06
61	新丰江水电厂	33.50	5.58	7.40	96.78	28.98	41.40	98.60	55.60
62	枫树坝水电厂	17.60	3.41	8.08	94.04	25.43	27.58	146.65	7.37
63	长潭水电厂	6.00	0.85	10.80	96.04	10.61	9.21	147.82	1.14
64	青溪水电厂	14.40	2.50	21.01	94.20	52.69	52.61	69.28	0.43
65	平班水电厂	40.50	12.78	11.89	92.97	151.97	151.95	438.85	1.99
66	龙滩水电厂	490.00	131.39	3.18	94.91	359.63	418.15	349.60	87.60
67	岩滩水电厂	121.00	66.17	6.58	90.60	436.30	435.68	221.66	24.71
68	大化水电厂	56.60	25.15	16.86	86.02	437.8	424.06	154.74	3.88
69	百龙滩水电厂	19.20	8.65	42.63	84.22	470.01	368.79	125.27	0.67
70	乐滩水电厂	60.00	28.58	17.08	88.20	491.20	488.19	111.10	3.81
71	西津水力发电厂	24.22	9.80	27.17	61.65	283.21	266.27	60.80	10.29
72	大广坝水电厂	24.00	5.60	6.10	95.79	34.20	34.20	137.96	13.00
73	华能戈枕水电厂	8.20	0.64	16.96	217.48	39.26	10.79	52.24	0.91
74	二滩水电厂	330.00	150.52	2.33	95.07	483.54	350.45	1197.57	55.47
75	龚嘴水力发电总厂	133.00	61.00	4.80	92.00	410.00	294.10	526.28	0.70
76	南桠河水电公司	62.40	18.50	0.20	96.09	3.50	3.70	2643.89	2.40
77	太平驿水电站	26.00	7.67	3.41	93.45	79.90	26.12	1078.50	0.01
78	东西关水电站	18.00	9.17	18.89	90.00	285.25	173.19	247.00	2.01
79	青居水电站	13.60	4.84	36.01	88.78	274.01	174.15	261.86	0.66
80	雨城水电站	6.00	2.33	27.00	91.83	95.00	62.81	598.00	0.08
81	铜头水电站	8.00	4.80	5.40	92.94	31.00	25.92	760.00	0.08
82	小关子水电站	16.00	7.69	2.80	90.54	28.00	21.53	990.00	
83	硗碛水电站	24.00	8.19	0.85	87.20	7.00	7.00	2126.23	1.49
84	宝兴水电站	19.50	1.02	1.30	100.00	28.10	1.32	1352.00	0.01

续表

水电厂名称		发电运行情况				水库运行情况			
		总装机容量	年发电量	平均耗水率	等效可用系数	年入库总水量	发电用水量	年末水位	年末库容
		万 kW	亿 kW·h	m^3/(kW·h)	%	亿 m^3	亿 m^3	m	亿 m^3
85	冷竹关水电站	18.00	8.79	1.10	93.27	10.19	8.89	1760.20	
86	小天都水电站	24.00	9.26	1.00	91.98	10.19	9.37	2152.23	
87	水牛家水电站	7.00	2.21	2.10	94.40	4.37	4.65	2263.81	
88	自一里水电站	13.00	5.97	0.95	95.92	5.75	5.68	2030.47	
89	木座水电站	10.00	4.31	1.61	98.00	7.26	6.94	1542.41	
90	阴坪水电站	10.00	2.18	2.08	100.00	4.91	4.53	1240.50	
91	明台水电站	4.50	1.95	33.68	94.13	83.15	65.68	380.80	0.36
92	宝珠寺水力发电厂	70.00	16.87	4.86	92.43	81.91	81.88	587.06	20.07
93	紫兰坝水电开发公司	10.20	3.38	24.60	96.91	86.63	83.21	486.00	0.25
94	红叶二级水电站	9.00	3.52	2.57	98.62	14.27	9.04	2085.63	
95	薛城水电站	13.80	5.40	2.79	97.36	19.76	15.06	1707.11	0.01
96	联补水电站	13.00	3.27	0.97	93.38	6.76	3.16	1671.41	0.01
97	久铁水电站	11.00	2.99	1.22		6.58	3.64	2035.68	0.16
98	地洛水电站	10.00	0.06	1.37		0.31	0.09	1216.74	0.03
99	沙湾水电站	36.00	7.70	20.07	97.64	335.45	154.50	427.29	0.23
100	大金坪水电站	12.90	4.48	2.21	81.00	13.86	9.91	1208.00	0.50
101	洪一水电站	8.00	2.71	1.27	81.00	4.72	3.53	1529.00	0.20
102	五一桥水电站	13.20	4.45	2.01	96.60	15.17	8.94	2422.35	0.004
103	柳坪水电站	12.00	4.87	6.30	88.56	43.51	30.68	1779.3	0.01
104	色尔古水电站	15.00	3.87	6.10	87.67	39.40	23.61	1872.5	0.04
105	乌江渡发电厂	125.00	36.16	3.51	93.16	130.94	126.94	753.01	18.30
106	东风发电厂	69.50	27.69	3.70	95.58	100.31	102.40	945.35	4.85
107	洪家渡电站	60.00	17.71	3.14	95.83	51.01	55.64	1086.06	14.72
108	索风营电站	60.00	20.73	4.16		86.13	86.19	834.86	1.56
109	构皮滩水电站	180.00	16.81	0.79		18.42	13.32	588.88	26.06
110	思林水电站	78.75	13.03	6.07	97.39	244.31	79.05	431.76	9.11
111	大花水水电站	20.00	6.72	3.19	86.76	22.52	21.40	865.67	2.34
112	光照发电厂	104.00	20.42	3.02	97.33	62.32	61.64	717.49	19.28
113	普定发电公司	8.40	2.64	8.58	87.69	26.62	22.68	1135.88	2.02
114	引子渡水电站	36.00	7.57	4.46	90.10	31.27	33.75	1058.16	1.72
115	贵州鱼塘电站	7.50	1.94	8.16	96.67	22.31	15.86	455.70	0.61
116	董箐发电厂	44.00	2.18	2.88		6.27	6.28	484.57	7.68
117	生桥水力发电总厂（二级）	132.00	64.95	2.23	90.05	144.78	144.79	640.77	0.09
118	红枫水力发电总厂	26.70	5.40	0.70	89.14	2.10	4.00	1235.24	3.70

续表

	水电厂名称	发电运行情况				水库运行情况			
		总装机容量	年发电量	平均耗水率	等效可用系数	年入库总水量	发电用水量	年末水位	年末库容
		万 kW	亿 kW·h	$m^3/(kW·h)$	%	亿 m^3	亿 m^3	m	亿 m^3
119	大朝山水电厂	135.00	53.78	5.30	93.87	306.41	285.18	896.50	6.48
120	漫湾水电厂	167.00	56.54	4.64	92.49	277.67	278.31	990.79	1.83
121	景洪水电厂	175.00	54.80	7.14	85.72	416.83	389.25	595.63	1.19
122	小湾水电厂	210.00	16.66	2.25	100.00	316.06	37.93	1164.16	45.20
123	瑞丽江一级水电站	60.00	29.97	1.20	90.19	80.63	36.04	718.15	0.05
124	华能大理水电有限责任公司	8.58	3.32	8.04	93.33	30.44	26.68	1305.35	0.67
125	香格里拉水电公司	25.03	8.50	0.30	93.65	4.80	3.00	3124.78	0.02
126	鲁布革水力发电厂	60.00	16.90	1.29	94.48	26.04	21.75	1126.55	0.74
127	以礼河发电厂	32.15	14.02	0.35	90.59	2.60	4.88	2206.37	1.46
128	绿水河发电厂	6.55	3.35	1.37	92.43	5.35	4.58	476.75	
129	青铜峡（含唐渠）水电厂	30.20	11.54	21.99	93.71	261.30	253.68	1155.88	0.34
130	龙羊峡水电厂	128.00	58.48	3.39	95.84	237.47	198.30	2591.47	215.40
131	拉西瓦水电厂	280.00	38.20	2.78	93.71	178.16	106.34	2419.50	6.21
132	李家峡水电厂	160.00	57.39	3.33	91.15	192.49	191.08	2179.17	16.22
133	公伯峡水电厂	150.00	53.73	3.65	94.85	197.24	196.35	2004.23	5.35
134	苏只水电厂	22.50	9.13	21.94	96.86	201.61	200.36	1899.16	0.41
135	盐锅峡水电厂	35.20	16.77	10.87	95.42	243.95	243.93	1619.27	0.29
136	八盘峡水电厂	18.00	8.25	26.60	90.85	277.17	277.18	1577.29	0.17
137	吉林台水电公司	46.00	10.20	3.60	92.66	33.80	37.10	1398.47	14.70
138	开都河水电公司	30.90	11.10	3.00	93.78	34.20	33.90	1630.55	0.63

（各发电公司、各省水力发电工程学会、各水电厂提供资料）

2009 年全国电力统计基本数据一览表

	单 位	2009 年	2008 年	比上年增长（±、%）
一、发电装机容量	万 kW	87 409.72	79 273.13	10.26
水 电	万 kW	19 629.02	17 260.39	13.72
火 电	万 kW	65 107.63	60 285.84	8.00
核 电	万 kW	907.82	907.82	
风 电	万 kW	1759.94	838.77	109.82
二、关停机组	万 kW	1812.79	1892.64	−4.22
水 电	万 kW		42.05	

续表

	单　位	2009年	2008年	比上年增长（±、%）
火　　电	万kW	1812.79	1850.50	−2.04
三、基建新增发电设备能力	万kW	9667.35	9201.88	5.06
水　　电	万kW	2105.70	2148.27	−1.52
火　　电	万kW	6585.76	6554.54	0.48
核　　电	万kW			
风　　电	万kW	973.00	499.07	94.96
四、年底电源在建规模	万kW	17 407.56	16 053.00	8.44
水　　电	万kW	6724.80	7343.61	−8.43
火　　电	万kW	7749.10	6911.70	12.12
核　　电	万kW	2192.00	1210.00	81.16
风　　电	万kW	720.75	586.97	22.79
五、基建新增110kV及以上输电线路长度	km	69 217	67 592	2.40
其中：1000kV	km	640		
±800kV	km	1375		
750kV	km	2021	651	210.35
500kV	km	12 959	15 436	−16.05
其中：±500kV	km	574		
330kV	km	1766	1796	−1.63
220kV	km	22 697	23 994	−5.41
110kV	km	27 760	25 716	7.95
六、基建新增110kV及以上变电设备容量	万kVA	37 105	31 878	16.40
其中：1000kV	万kVA	600		
±800kV	万kVA	593		
750kV	万kVA	1080	360	
500kV	万kVA	11 902	10 095	17.90
其中：±500kV	万kVA	357		
330kV	万kVA	780	654	19.27
220kV	万kVA	12 801	12 359	3.57
110kV	万kVA	9349	8410	11.17
七、单机6000kW及以上机组	台	9081	8890	191台
	万kW	79 901.58	72 047.19	7854万kW
水　　电	台	2860	2653	207台
	万kW	15 768.11	13 357.96	2410万kW
火　　电	台	6221	6237	−16台
	万kW	64 133.47	58 689.23	5444万kW
平均单机容量	万kW/台	8.80	8.10	0.70万kW/台
其中：水电	万kW/台	5.51	5.04	0.47万kW/台

续表

	单 位	2009年	2008年	比上年增长（±、%）
火 电	万kW/台	10.31	9.41	0.9万kW/台
八、35kV及以上输电线路长度	km	1 229 370	1 168 857	5.18
其中：1000kV	km	640		
±800kV	km	1375		
750kV	km	2747	630	336.03
500kV	km	121 935	107 993	12.91
其中：±500kV	km	13 298		
330kV	km	19 156	16 717	14.59
220kV	km	253 573	233 558	8.57
110kV	km	422 863	401 310	5.37
35kV	km	407 077	408 649	−0.38
九、35kV及以上变电设备容量	万kVA	324 771	279 861	16.05
其中：1000kV	万kVA	600		
±800kV	万kVA	593		
750kV	万kVA	1740	660	163.64
500kV	万kVA	64 145	52 588	21.98
其中：±500kV	万kVA	4031		
330kV	万kVA	5656	4665	21.24
220kV	万kVA	103 498	89 685	15.40
110kV	万kVA	112 965	99 130	13.96
35kV	万kVA	35 574	33 133	7.37
十、电力投资	亿元	7701.61	6302.40	22.20
1. 电源工程投资	亿元	3803.31	3407.39	11.62
其中：水电	亿元	867.19	848.86	2.16
火 电	亿元	1543.56	1678.50	−8.04
核 电	亿元	584.01	329.49	77.25
风 电	亿元	781.78	527.27	48.27
2. 电网工程投资	亿元	3898.30	2895.01	34.66
十一、发电量	亿kW·h	36 811.86	34 510.13	6.67
水 电	亿kW·h	5716.82	5655.48	1.08
火 电	亿kW·h	30 116.87	28 029.97	7.45
核 电	亿kW·h	700.50	692.19	1.20
风 电	亿kW·h	276.15	130.79	111.14
十二、6000kW及以上电厂供热量	万GJ	258 198.07	249 701.62	3.40
十三、6000kW及以上电厂供电煤耗	g/(kW·h)	340	345	−5
十四、6000kW及以上电厂发电煤耗	g/(kW·h)	320	322	−2
十五、6000kW及以上电厂厂用电率	%	5.76	5.90	−0.14

续表

	单　位	2009年	2008年	比上年增长（±、%）
水　　电	%	0.4	0.36	0.04
火　　电	%	6.62	6.79	−0.17
十六、6000kW及以上电厂利用小时	h	4546	4648	−102h
水　　电	h	3328	3589	−261h
火　　电	h	7716	4885	37h
风　　电	h	2077	2046	31h
十七、供、售电量及线损				
供电量	亿kW·h	32 613.74	30 617.02	6.52
售电量	亿kW·h	30 423.09	28 537.22	6.61
线损电量	亿kW·h	2190.65	2079.80	5.33
线路损失率	%	6.72	6.79	−0.07
十八、全社会用电量	亿kW·h	36 595.15	34 379.69	6.44
A. 全行业用电合计	亿kW·h	32 019.99	30 297.56	5.69
第一产业	亿kW·h	939.90	879.25	6.90
第二产业	亿kW·h	27 136.40	25 920.16	4.69
其中：工业	亿kW·h	26 754.49	25 577.80	4.60
1. 轻工业	亿kW·h	4535.55	4572.24	1.38
2. 重工业	亿kW·h	22 118.94	21 005.56	5.30
第三产业	亿kW·h	3943.70	3498.15	12.74
B. 城乡居民生活用电合计	亿kW·h	4575.16	4082.13	12.08
其中：城镇居民	亿kW·h	2670.00	2407.04	10.92
乡村居民	亿kW·h	1905.16	1675.09	13.73
十九、6000kW及以上电厂燃料消耗				
发电消耗标准煤量	万t	91 478.17	86 857.72	5.32
发电消耗原煤量	万t	139 669.62	131 902.75	5.89
供热消耗标准煤量	万t	10 199.06	10 022.73	1.76
供热消耗原煤量	万t	14 959.97	14 732.18	1.55
二十、6000kW及以上电厂热效率				
电厂热效率	%	40.44	39.57	0.87
电厂供热效率	%	86.38	85.01	1.37
能源转换总效率	%	43.89	43.19	0.70
二十一、发电设备比				
发电设备容量：用电设备容量		1∶3.16	1∶3.12	
二十二、电力弹性系数				
电力生产弹性系数		0.73	0.60	
电力消费弹性系数		0.71	0.57	
二十三、电力消费能源占一次能源消费的比重	%	40.96	40.94	

注　国家能源局于2009年将核电设备在运容量调整为908万kW，故计算当年及上年设备利用小时是按国家能源局2009年核定后设备容量计算的。

（中国电力企业联合会）

中國水力發電年鉴

18

大 事 记

一 月

1月6日 我国自主研发、设计和建设的，具有自主知识产权的1000kV交流输变电工程——晋东南—南阳—荆门特高压交流试验示范工程，顺利通过168h试运行考核，正式投入运行。这标志着我国在特高压输变电核心技术和设备国产化上取得重大突破，对优化能源资源配置，保障国家能源安全和电力可靠供应具有重要意义。

1月6～9日 水电水利规划设计总院会同云南省发展改革委，在昆明主持召开了《金沙江中游河段龙开口水电站可行性研究报告》审查会议。审查认为：报告满足本阶段设计工作内容和深度的要求，基本同意该报告。龙开口水电站位于云南省大理州鹤庆县境内，是金沙江中游河段规划“一库八级”开发方案的第六个梯级，电站总装机容量1800MW，为一等大(1)型工程；工程以发电为主，兼顾灌溉和供水。枢纽工程主要由碾压混凝土重力坝、泄洪冲沙及坝后式厂房等建筑物组成，最大坝高119.00m，坝顶长768.00m。

1月9日 由中国大唐集团公司、中国水力发电工程学会联合主办的2009年中国水电新春联谊会在北京希尔顿逸林酒店隆重举行。国家有关部委领导，从事水电建设的老同志、老专家以及在京的近30家有关单位的领导共100多人出席了联谊会，互祝新春，共谋水电发展大计。国家发展改革委副主任、国家能源局局长张国宝作重要讲话。

1月9日 中国华电集团公司2009年工作会议在北京召开。会议总结了2008年的主要工作，部署了2009年任务，提出把中国华电集团公司建设成为以电为主具有综合竞争力的现代化能源集团的发展思路。2008年，中国华电集团公司投产发电装机容量737万kW，关停小火电机组16台144.8万kW；完成发电量同比增长13.1%；供电煤耗同比下降6.1g/(kW·h)；平均二氧化硫排放绩效同比降低0.2g/(kW·h)。

1月11日 青藏直流联网工程通过了由中国国际工程咨询公司组织的专家评估，这是该项目前期工作的又一重大进展，为项目取得核准奠定了重要基础。±500kV格尔木—拉萨直流联网工程，本期直流输电规模为75万kW，最终为150万kW；线路总长约1038km，其中青海段长约616km，西藏段长约422km，本期双极一次建成，计划2010年投运。

1月12日 仙游抽水蓄能电站工程举行开工仪式。仙游抽水蓄能电站位于福建省莆田市仙游县西苑乡，北距福州市95km，南距厦门市125km，为周调节抽水蓄能电站。电站装机容量120万kW，安装4台单机容量30万kW的混流可逆式水泵水轮发动机组，设计年发电量18.96亿kW·h，年发电利用小时数1580h，综合效率75%。

1月14日 中国华能集团公司在北京召开2009年工作会议。会议总结了2008年的主要工作，研究部署了2009年任务，动员公司全体干部职工奋发有为，不断超越，为推进公司又好又快发展而努力。2008年，中国华能集团公司装机规模突破8500万kW，约占全国装机容量的10.5%；完成发电量3645亿kW·h，同比增长11.5%；销售收入1513亿元，同比增长30.9%；完成煤炭产量2188万t，形成煤炭产能2724万t/年；供电煤耗333.59g/(kW·h)，同比下降3.71g/(kW·h)。

1月15日 中国大唐集团公司2009年工作会议在北京召开。截至2008年底，中国大唐集团公司发电装机容量达到8242万kW，清洁和可再生能源比重达到19.22%；全年发电量达到3529.56亿kW·h，同比增长15.82%；实现营业收入1016亿元，同比增长18.34%；供电煤耗335.15g/(kW·h)，同比下降7.79g/(kW·h)。会议确定2009年为中国大唐集团公司“攻坚年”，实现装机规模“翻两番”，提前一年完成“十一五”节能减排任务和冲刺世界500强三大目标。

1月15日 中国电力投资集团公司2009年工作会议在北京隆重召开。会议总结了2008年的主要工作，部署了2009年任务。2008年，中国电力投资集团公司增加控股装机容量628万kW；完成发电量2051亿kW·h，同比增长15%；煤炭产量3705万t，同比增长36%；电解铝产量46万t，同比增长26%；营业收入715亿元，同比增长21%；供电煤耗同比下降8.15g/(kW·h)；关停小火电机组24台245.5万kW，提前两完成“十一五”小火电关停任务。

1月16～17日 中国南方电网有限责任公司在广东召开2009年工作会议暨一届二次职工代表大会。会议总结了2008年的主要工作，部署了2009年任务，提出全面深入推进南方电网科学发展、力争售电量增长5%的目标。2008年，中国南方电网公司主要生产指标优于上年，完成售电量4826亿kW·h，增长4.5%；西电东送电量1056亿kW·h，增长22%；完成固定资产投资647亿元，其中电网建设投资481亿元。

1月17日 国家电网公司一届四次职工代表大会暨2009年工作会议在北京召开。国家电网公司党组书记、总经理刘振亚在大会上作了题为《积极进取 努力超越 深入推进“一强三优”现代公司建设》的工作报告。2008年，国家电网公司完成固定资产投资2579亿元，同比增长14.2%；投产110(66)kV及以上输电线路5.7万km，变电容量2.7亿kVA；特高压工程建设实现重大突破；完成售电量21 235亿kW·h，增长7.5%。

1月22日 太平驿水电站震后修复首台机组成功启动。由于“5·12”汶川大地震，四川华能太平驿水电站全厂机组受损，大坝、厂房、输电线路等遭受了严重破坏和重创，尾水出水口被彻底封堵，水淹到发电机层以上60cm，导致电站4台水轮机组被水淹没。大地震后，中国水利水电第七工程局有限公司机电安装分局受命承担检修任务，发扬抗震救灾精神，做到了人员安全并保质保量完成首台机组修复。

1月26日 国家发展改革委以发改办能源［2009］201号文件，出具了同意黄河班多水电站开展项目前期工作的批复。

二 月

2月3日 全国能源大会在北京举行。这是自1992年能源部撤销后，我国17年来首次举行的全国性能源工作会议。国家能源局宣布，2009年国家对于电力的总投资将达到5800亿元，核电、风电等新能源的建设将明显提速。

2月11～12日 中国水利水电建设集团公司2009年工作会议在北京隆重召开。会议总结了2008年工作，部署了2009年和今后一段时期内的主要任务。2008年，中国水利水电建设集团公司实现营业收入601.31亿元，同比增长19.3%；总资产达到733.72亿元，同比增长44.93%；新签合同同比增长56.5%；实现利润总额16.1亿元，在受到地震灾害损失影响的情况下基本与2008年持平。

2月12日 滩坑水电站2号机组顺利完成72h试运行并投入商业运行。滩坑水电站设计装机容量为3台20万kW机组，年发电量约为10.23亿kW·h；拦江大坝为钢筋混凝土面板堆石坝，坝高160m，是华东目前第一高坝，水库总库容41.5亿m^3。

2月13日 中国三峡工程报报道：由武警水电二支队承建的贵州洪家渡水电站大坝工程日前荣获中华人民共和国住房和城乡建设部、中国建筑业协会联合颁发的“鲁班奖”。洪家渡大坝为高181m的钢筋混凝土面板堆石坝。

2月18～19日 中国长江三峡工程开发总公司2009年工作会议在宜昌召开。会议总结了2008年工作，分析了当前形势，部署了2009年工作。2008年，三峡工程建设取得了具有里程碑意义的重大进展。三峡枢纽主体工程提前一年基本完工，顺利进行了试验性蓄水，26台机组全部投产，升船机续建工程和地下电站工程施工进展顺利。

2月22日 国家电网公司特高压直流试验基地和西藏高海拔试验基地在北京顺利通过总体验收。评审委员会认为，特高压直流试验基地的设备参数和性能指标取得了15项世界第一，且在方案论证、科研设计、施工调试等方面申请专利55项，取得了重大技术创新成果，综合试验能力达到国际同类试验基地的领先水平，可满足我国超/特高压直流输电发展的需要；西藏高海拔试验基地在设计和建设过程中实现了多项技术创新，其整体试验研究能力可满足高海拔地区超/特高压输变电工程建设及发展的需要，高海拔高压试验能力达到国际领先水平。

2月23～24日 中国国电集团公司一届一次职工代表大会暨2009年工作会议在北京召开。会议总结了2008年工作，部署了2009年任务，加快建设综合性能源集团。2008年，中国国电集团可控装机容量达到7023.5万kW，同比增长16.9%；完成发电量同比增长12.3%，供热量同比增长19.7%；供电煤耗340.5g/(kW·h)，同比下降7.5g/(kW·h)；实现销售收入增长27.4%。

2月 国家发展改革委核准贵州北盘江董箐水电站项目，建设4台22万kW的混流式水轮发电机组，该项目总装机容量88万kW。

三 月

3月1～2日 西藏自治区发展改革委会同西藏自治区电力工业局在西安共同主持召开了《西藏尼洋河巴河口以下河段水电规划报告》审查会议。尼洋河发源于西藏自治区米拉山东侧，属雅鲁藏布江一级支流。规划河段长110km，海拔高程3210～2920m之间，装机容量735MW，年发电量33.69亿kW·h，约占尼洋河干流水力资源理论蕴藏量的35.3%。会议听取了中国水电顾问集团西北勘测设计研究院关于规划成果的汇报，并进行了认真的讨论和审议。会议认为：《西藏尼洋河巴河口以下河段水电规划报告》满足河流水电规划工作内容和深度的要求，规划思路正确，主要结论基本合理，同意该报告。

3月3日 四川福堂水电站首台机组恢复发电。福堂水电站在2008年“5·12”汶川特大地震中受损严重，2008年7月启动了恢复重建工作。在施工、监理、设计各方的全力支持和配合下，克服了重重困难，完成阶段性目标——2009年2月26日完成大坝恢复蓄水，3月3日实现首台机组恢复发电。但由于送出工程还未完全恢复，预计4月底可正式恢复向电网供电。

3月3日 由中国公司承建的海外最大单项水电工程——苏丹麦洛维大坝正式落成并向苏丹电网发电，苏丹总统巴希尔、阿拉伯国家投资方代表、中国承建方代表及当地民众万余人出席仪式。麦洛维大坝长9.7km，高65m，库容达124亿m^3，是尼罗河干流第二大水电项目，装机容量达125万kW，相当于苏丹全国现有装机容量的2倍以上，水库灌溉面积达

100多万亩，惠及400多万苏丹人民。大坝主体工程由中国水利水电建设集团公司和中国水利电力对外公司组成的联营体承建，2003年6月正式开工。

3月5日　我国首批国产2MW直驱式风力发电机组，在大唐漳州六鳌风电场成功并网运行。专家组在严格审核试验数据后当场宣布，各项技术指标均达到或超过国家风机稳定性运行试验标准。大唐漳州六鳌风电场总装机容量101.6MW，分三期开发。第一、第二期分别采用西班牙GAMESA公司和印度SUZLON公司的发电机组，第三期则选用了湖南省湘电风能公司的XE72-2000直驱式风电机组。湘电生产的这种直驱式设计的风电机组具有效率高、系统可靠、维护简单、噪声小及上网电源质量好等明显优势。

3月6日　国家发改委以发改办能源［2009］641号文核准积石峡水电站项目，建设3台34万kW混流式水轮发电机组，该项目总装机容量102万kW。

3月13日　大渡河龙头石电站2号机组顺利结束72h试运行，正式并网发电。龙头石水电站位于四川省石棉县安顺场上游10km处，是大渡河干流规划22级方案的第十五级电站，装设4台单机容量17.5万kW的混流式水轮发电机组，总装机容量70万kW，多年平均发电量31.21亿kW·h。该电站1号机组于2008年9月30日投产发电。

3月13日　500kV输电线路可移动直流融冰技术方案及装置研制项目在湖北省武汉市顺利通过了专家验收，成为国家电网公司首个通过验收的直流融冰装置科技项目。验收专家组认为，这一装置在国内外首次采用了二极管整流桥单元级联直流融冰技术，实用性强，处于国际先进水平，具备推广应用价值。

3月14日　云南凤凰谷水电站首台机组顺利完成72h试运行，投入商业运行。凤凰谷水电站位于南盘江中游河段师宗县境内，为单一发电功能的河床式电站，装设两台5万kW水轮发电机组。

3月19日　中国水利水电建设集团公司成功向社会公开发行2009年中国水利水电建设集团公司企业债券。本期债券共募集资金13亿元，期限5年。这是中国水利水电建设集团公司第二次通过企业债券市场融资。前次债券于2006年发行，期限为10年期。

3月19日　三峡地下电站30号机组座环通过业主验收，并正式交付使用。该座环重达310t，直径16m，是世界上第一台在水电站施工现场制造的大型座环，为大型水电设备现场制造开启了新篇章。

3月20日　国家海上风电示范项目东海大桥海上风电场首台3000kW风机整体安装取得成功。东海风电场位于上海东海大桥以东、南汇岸线以南海域，由34台国内最大单机容量的风电机组组成，总装机容量10.2万kW，设计年发电利用小时数2600h，年上网电量2.67亿kW·h，项目总投资23.65亿元，计划于2010年上半年世博会前完成安装、调试，投入运行。

3月22日　1000kV特高压交流试验示范工程科研成果在北京通过专家总验收。专家们一致认为，特高压交流试验示范工程技术研究项目已完成合同规定的全部内容，整体满足工程需要，标志着我国掌握了特高压交流输变电工程和设备制造的核心技术，为设计和建设特高压交流工程、设备国产化提供了技术支撑，提升了我国输变电工程自主创新能力。项目研究成果整体处于国际领先水平。

3月26日　乌江洪家渡水电站工程荣获第八届中国土木工程"詹天佑奖"。这是该工程继荣获国家优质工程奖（鲁班奖）、国家电力工程优质奖、贵州省"黄果树杯"优质施工工程奖等荣誉之后获得的又一殊荣。

3月27日　中国第二大水电站——溪洛渡水电站大坝首仓基础混凝土开始浇筑。这标志着溪洛渡水电站拱坝正式开始混凝土施工，工程建设进入到任务更加艰巨的时期。

3月30日～4月4日　中国大坝委员会分别在北京和成都组织召开了地震与大坝安全专题研讨会，来自美国、英国、加拿大、日本、瑞士、奥地利、英国、中国的30余名大坝专家参加了会议。3月31日～4月2日，代表们先后考察了"5·12"大地震中心的紫坪铺、沙牌、福堂、太平驿、映秀湾等水电站工程和中国水电顾问集团成都勘测设计研究院。4月3日，中国水电顾问集团成都勘测设计研究院总工程师王仁坤在研讨会上作了"沙牌拱坝经受了强震的考验"专题报告，受到会议高度评价。

3月31日　全球最大的水电站CDM项目——炳灵水电站CDM项目在甘肃揭牌，中国和意大利合作机构的代表联合举行揭牌仪式。炳灵水电站总装机容量为240MW，是甘肃电投炳灵水电开发有限责任公司在黄河甘肃段开发的第一座水电站，2005年6月开始CDM项目开发；2008年5月，与意大利国家电力公司签署了核证减排量购买协议；2005年8月，提交《联合国气候变化框架公约》清洁发展机制项目执行理事会注册，2009年2月注册成功。

3月　国家发展改革委核准四川大渡河泸定水电站项目，建设4台23万kW的混流式水轮发电机组，该项目总装机容量92万kW。

四　月

4月7日　小浪底水利枢纽工程顺利通过国家竣

工验收。小浪底最大坝高160m，水库正常运用水位275m，总库容126.5亿m^3，其中淤沙库容75.5亿m^3，长期有效库容51亿m^3，电站装机容量1800MW。

4月14日 大盈江四级水电站4号机组顺利并网发电。该电站位于云南省盈江县，是大盈江干流中国境内规划的最后一个梯级电站，电站装机容量4×17.5万kW。

4月15日 沙湾水电站首台机组正式并网发电。沙湾电站位于四川省乐山市沙湾区境内，是大渡河下游河段的一个梯级电站，为一级混合式（河床式厂房加长尾水渠）开发，以发电为主，兼顾灌溉；总装机容量48万kW，年发电量24.07亿kW·h；总投资约50亿元，由中国水利水电建设集团公司投资建设；计划于2010年全部投产发电。

4月20～22日 由中国水力发电工程学会和中国长江三峡工程开发总公司联合主办的第二届水力发电技术国际会议在北京举行。国家发展改革委、国家能源局、水利部、国家电力监管委员会、国务院三峡工程建设委员会办公室、国家电网公司及国内众多知名水电企业，国内以及来自法国、德国、英国、加拿大、日本等60多个国家和地区的专家、学者共300余人参加了会议。

4月23日 拉西瓦水电站首台机组（6号机组）顺利通过72h试运行并投产发电。拉西瓦水电站为黄河流域装机容量最大、单机容量最大，工程位于青海省贵德县与贵南县交界的黄河干流上，是黄河上游龙羊峡至青铜峡河段规划的第二个梯级电站。电站装有单机容量70万kW的水轮发电机组6台，总装机容量420万kW，多年平均发电量102亿kW·h。工程于2001年正式启动，计划于2011年竣工。

4月25日 中国能源研究会第六届全国会员代表大会在北京人民大会堂隆重举行。大会通过投票选举产生了中国能源研究会第六届理事会理事长、副理事长和秘书长，全国政协常委、国家电监会原主席柴松岳当选为理事长，中国长江三峡工程开发总公司副总经理毕亚雄等当选为副理事长，国家发展改革委能源研究所原所长、国家能源专家咨询委员会副主任周大地任秘书长。

4月25日 由中国电力科学研究院承担的国家电网公司重大科技项目——国家电网仿真中心顺利通过验收。验收专家组认为，该中心综合试验能力已达到国际同类实验室的领先水平，将为我国特高压电网建设及大电网安全稳定运行提供强有力的技术支撑。项目在建设过程中，已开展了一系列特高压及跨区电网等方面的技术研究，共取得技术创新27项，获专利授权8项，申请专利12项，获软件著作权8项。

五 月

5月12～13日 在"5·12"汶川地震一周年纪念日，由中国水力发电工程学会、中国长江三峡工程开发总公司等单位主办的全国水工抗震防灾学术交流会在成都举行。来自全国高校、科研院所和水利水电设计、施工、管理单位的150余名专家、学者参加了会议。本届会议对当前社会各界极为关心的水坝在地震中的安全问题进行学术交流讨论，盘点中国水坝在地震中的表现，谋划中国水坝未来抗震安全课题。专家表示，有信心、有能力设计抗强震的超高大坝。

5月12日 国际小水电组织协调委员会2009年年会在杭州召开，选举产生了新一届国际小水电组织领导成员。中国水利部部长陈雷、副部长胡四一继续担任该组织的名誉主席，水利部农村水电及电气化发展局局长田中兴当选为主席，斯里兰卡电力和能源部常务秘书费迪南多（Ferdinando）先生当选为副主席。国际小水电中心主任刘恒当选国际小水电组织秘书处总干事。国际小水电组织成立于1994年12月，是第一家总部设在中国的国际组织，由联合国开发计划署、联合国工业发展组织、中华人民共和国水利部、中华人民共和国商务部共同发起成立，是一个由各区域、各政府、各有关公用事业单位及企业按自愿原则建立起来的以社会效益为主的国际小水电促进机构。会议还授予前国际小水电中心主任童建栋"国际小水电组织杰出贡献奖"。

5月16日 我国对外水电开发最大的BOT项目——缅甸瑞丽江一级电站竣工仪式在缅甸境内电站厂房隆重举行。瑞丽江一级水电站位于缅甸北部紧邻中缅边界的瑞丽江干流之上，是瑞丽江上游河段规划的第一个梯级电站，总装机容量60万kW，是缅甸建成投产的最大的水电站。电站设计平均发电量为40.33亿kW·h，年利用小时为6722h，保证出力可达17.4万kW。工程由华能澜沧江水电有限公司、云南和兴投资开发股份有限公司和云南机械设备进出口有限公司三方共同出资成立的云南联合电力开发有限公司负责开发建设，华能澜沧江水电有限公司控股。项目总投资约32亿元人民币，其中中方总投资29.6亿元人民币。

5月18日 黄河上游水电开发有限责任公司拉西瓦水电站首批机组投产发电庆典仪式在拉西瓦隆重举行。会上，6号机组被国家发展改革委、中国电力企业联合会授予"我国电力装机容量突破8亿kW标志性机组"荣誉。

5月19日 广东惠州抽水蓄能电站首台机组投产发电。广东惠州抽水蓄能电站位于广东省惠州市博罗县城郊，装机8台，总装机容量240万kW，分A、

B两厂布置，同期建设。

5月21日　2009特高压输电技术国际会议(UHV2009)在北京隆重开幕。本次会议的主题是“特高压输电技术·创新与可持续发展”。来自21个国家和地区的400余人，包括26家电力企业、11家研究咨询机构、9家协会组织、11所大学、27家制造企业的代表和40余家中外新闻媒体应邀出席会议。

5月21日　国家电网公司正式宣布启动智能电网的建设。按照国家电网公司设想，2020年我国将全面建成统一的“坚强智能电网”。届时，国家电网优化配置资源能力将大幅提升，清洁能源装机比例达到35%，分布式电源实现即插即用，智能电表得到普及。

5月23日　中国大坝委员会秘书长、中国水利水电科学研究院副院长贾金生博士，在第23届国际大坝会议上正式当选为国际大坝委员会主席。这是我国科学家首次在这一组织中当选主席。此前，我国著名的水电科学家，原中国水利电力部副部长、总工程师李鹗鼎，原中国水利水电科学研究院副院长沈崇刚，原中国长江三峡工程开发总公司技术委员会副主任张津生和贾金生博士分别在该组织担任过副主席职务。这次贾金生博士的当选是国际社会对中国水电建设的认可和重视。

5月26日　国家发展改革委以发改能源［2009］1352号文件核准批复华能云南澜沧江功果桥水电站项目。功果桥水电站是澜沧江中下游河段梯级开发的最上游一级电站，下游为在建的小湾电站，上游为规划的苗尾水电站，安装4台22.5万kW混流式水轮发电机组，总装机容量90万kW，年均发电量40.4亿kW·h。

5月26日　国家能源局发布《中国能源发展报告2009》。报告指出：要积极推进水电开发利用，转变水电移民观念，由“重工程、轻移民”转为“先移民、后工程”，把水电开发与帮助移民脱贫致富、促进地方经济发展很好地结合起来。

5月26～27日　中国长江三峡工程开发总公司召开《长江三峡水利枢纽梯级水库调度自动化系统屏山—寸滩区间水情遥测系统》完工验收会，会议同意该系统通过完工验收。至此，三峡水情遥测系统一、二期工程全部通过完工验收。三峡水情遥测系统分两期建设：一期工程在寸滩—宜昌区间5.5万km^2的流域范围内布设了128个水、雨情遥测站，2004年6月1日投入正式运行；屏山—寸滩区间水情遥测系统建设属于三峡水情遥测系统建设的二期工程。该工程在一期工程的基础上新增299个水情遥测站点，集水面积约37万km^2。系统建设于2006年9月启动，2008年5月完成系统联合调试验收，投入为期一年的试运行。

5月27日　华能景洪水电站最后一台水轮发电机组顺利完成72h试运行，正式投产发电。至此，电站5台机组全部投产。景洪水电站是我国西部大开发和“西电东送”的重点工程，位于云南省西双版纳州景洪市，澜沧江下游，坝高108m，装机5台，总装机容量175万kW，年均发电量79.3亿kW·h。

5月28日　贵州乌江思林水电站首台机组顺利结束72h试运行后，直接转入商业运行。思林水电站位于贵州省思南县境内的乌江上，是乌江干流梯级电站的第八级。枢纽工程以发电为主，其次为航运，兼顾防洪、灌溉等。思林水电站安装4台单机容量26.25万kW水轮发电机组，总装机容量105万kW，设计年发电量为40.64亿kW·h，水库总库容为12.05亿m^3。工程于2006年11月8日开工建设。

六　月

6月4日　黑麋峰抽水蓄能电站1号机组通过SFC拖动水泵工况空载运行达到额定转速，成功启动。运行期间，机组各主要部位的温度、压力、振动、摆度等各项指标均处于正常范围。

6月8日　中国大坝协会成立大会暨第一次全国会员代表大会在北京隆重召开。本次会议有127家会员单位、280余名代表参加。会议审议并通过《中国大坝协会第一次全国会员代表大会工作报告》、《中国大坝协会章程》及《中国大坝协会会费管理办法》，选举产生中国大坝协会第一届理事会、常务理事会。著名的水利水电专家、原水利部部长汪恕诚将担任首届中国大坝协会理事长。中国大坝协会组织的成立，一定会有力地推进我国坝工技术的提高，进一步促进我国水利水电建设事业的繁荣和发展。

6月11日　国家电网公司支援地方电网重建工程竣工总结会在成都召开，标志着历时近一年的国家电网公司支援四川省6个重灾区地方电网恢复重建工作全部完成。国家电网公司对口援建工作总投资3亿多元，经过近一年的努力，恢复110kV线路1.1km，35kV变电站6座、线路94km，10kV配电台区45个、线路210km，低压线路377km。对口援建工作在灾区抢险救灾、恢复民生、促进经济社会重建等方面起到了积极的作用。

6月11日　环境保护部认定“云南华电鲁地拉水电有限公司建设的鲁地拉水电站和华能龙开口水电有限公司建设的龙开口水电站，未经环评审批于2009年1月截流，对金沙江中游生态影响较大。”决定：“责令两违法项目停止主坝建设，采取有效措施确保上下游围堰安全度汛；对金沙江中游已批和未批的水电开发建设项目环境影响进行补充论证，并根据论证结论进一步完善环境影响评价。在上述工作完成前，暂停审批金沙江中游水电开发建设项目。”

6月20日 为晋东南（长治）特高压变电站研制的世界首台单相单柱式1100kV、320Mvar特高压交流并联电抗器，在湖南衡阳一次成功通过试验考核。据悉，该产品的容量达到国际最高水平，并在国际上首次采用了单柱结构设计，在无局放绝缘结构设计、局部过热控制、降低振动及噪声、铁芯饼制作等方面采用了多项国际领先技术，具有容量大、体积小、噪声低等突出特点，性能指标达到国际同类产品最高水平。

6月24～29日 国际水电协会主办的第二届世界水电大会（IHA 2009 World Congress）在冰岛首都雷克雅未克举行。来自50多个国家的政府代表、水电界代表以及联合国、国际金融机构、非政府组织等270余名代表参加了本次大会。大会就能源政策、水资源政策、水电与气候变化、水电项目投资与融资模式、碳汇交易、温室气体排放及水电可持续发展等多个热点议题展开了讨论。中国长江三峡工程开发总公司副总经理林初学应邀向大会代表介绍了三峡工程的投融资管理情况，中国水利水电科学研究院陈厚群院士应大会组委会邀请作了“汶川地震下的大坝安全与中国水库诱发地震研究”的演讲。

6月30日 甘肃黄河炳灵水电站3号机组并网发电，标志着该电站5台机组全部投产，正式进入全面运行阶段，投产日期比计划提前了3个月。炳灵水电站位于甘肃省永靖县与积石县交界处黄河干流寺沟峡峡谷，下距刘家峡电站44.5km；2004年11月开工，2008年7月实现首台机组投产发电。该电站装有5台单机容量4.8万kW的灯泡贯流机组，总装机容量为24万kW，年均发电量9.74亿kW·h，也是全球最大的水电站CDM（清洁发展机制）项目。

6月30日 针对大用户直购电试点的规定出台。在当日发布的《国家电监会、国家发展改革委、国家能源局关于完善电力用户与发电企业直接交易试点工作有关问题的通知》中，直接确定了直购电价的构成要素，并明确了输配电价的确定方式。

6月30日 国家发展改革委正式批准了嘉陵江亭子口水利枢纽项目，标志着该项目具备了正式开工条件。嘉陵江亭子口水利枢纽工程位于四川省广元市苍溪县境内的嘉陵江干流中游，是以防洪、灌溉及城乡供水为主，兼顾发电、航运，并具有拦沙减淤等作用的综合利用工程。枢纽正常蓄水位458m，相应库容34.68亿m^3，总库容41.16亿m^3，灌溉农田316.85万亩，电站装机容量110万kW，年发电量31亿kW·h。

七　月

7月5日 广西桂冠大化水力发电总厂大化水电站二期工程11万kW发电机组成功并网投入商业运行，预计年增发电量1.53亿kW·h。大化水电站地处红水河中游河段，是红水河综合利用规划的第六级梯级电站。该电站分两期建设，其中一期工程装机容量为45.6万kW，于1986年6月建成投产；二期扩建工程装机容量为11万kW，于2007年7月开展工程前期工作。

7月6日 国家发展改革委会同财政部、水利部共同下发《关于中央直属和跨省水利工程水资源费征收标准及有关问题的通知》，规定了中央直属和跨省、自治区、直辖市水利工程的水资源费征收标准。其中，水力发电用水征收水资源费每千瓦时0.3～0.8分钱，抽水蓄能发电用水暂免征收水资源费。

7月10日 滩坑水电站工程3号机组通过72h连续试运行后投入商业运行。至此，滩坑水电站3台20万kW机组全部投产发电，成为位居新安江水电站之后浙江省第二大常规水电站。滩坑水电站建设项目集发电、生态、灌溉、防洪、供水、旅游为一体，建成后将形成一个水域面积达70.93km^2的人工湖，是西湖面积的10倍，水库总容量达41.5亿m^3。电站大坝高162m，为华东第一高坝，总装机容量60万kW。

7月15日 西藏目前最大的水利枢纽工程——旁多水利枢纽工程开工仪式在拉萨河畔隆重举行。旁多水利枢纽工程地处拉萨河流域中游河段，坝址位于林周县旁多乡下游1.5km处，距拉萨市直线距离约63km，以灌溉、发电为主，兼顾防洪和供水等综合利用，是拉萨河流域的骨干性控制工程，也是拉萨河干流水电梯级开发的龙头水库。水库总库容11.74亿m^3，灌溉面积75.26万亩，电站装机4台，单机容量3万kW，总装机容量12万kW。工程施工总工期为69个月，总投资约50亿元。

7月20日 龙头石水电站最后一台机组投入商业运行，比原计划提前36天实现了发电目标。龙头石水电站位于四川省石棉县境内，是大渡河上设计开发22级中的第十五级，上接在建的大岗山水电站，下连待建的老鹰岩水电站，装机容量4×17.5万kW。该电站2005年开工，2008年10月3日实现了首台机组并网发电，2009年3月13日、5月26日分别完成了2号、3号机组发电的任务。

7月20日 青铜峡水电站技术改造工程全面启动。改造后，电站灌溉、防汛防凌、设备自动化水平等都将大大提高。青铜峡水电站是一座以灌溉、发电为主，兼有防洪、防凌功能的综合性水利枢纽工程，

1960年2月工程建成投运。经过近50年的运行，电站主设备基本达到了运行寿命极限。工程总投资6.7亿元。

7月27日　国家发展改革委发布了《关于完善风力发电上网电价政策的通知》。该通知规定：按风能资源状况和工程建设条件，将全国分为4类风能资源区，相应制定风电标杆上网电价。4类资源区风电标杆电价水平分别为每千瓦时0.51元、0.54元、0.58元和0.61元。

7月28日　2009年中国能源蓝皮书正式发布。蓝皮书认为，中国能源供应前景堪忧，寻找替代能源、发展新能源和可再生能源成为中国的必然选择。蓝皮书显示，中国能源资源总量约为世界的一成，人均资源量为世界平均水平的40%，然而优质资源少，保证程度低。蓝皮书指出，中国煤炭剩余储量的保证程度不足100年，石油剩余储量的保证程度不足15年，天然气剩余储量的保证程度不足30年，而世界平均水平分别为230年、45年和61年。

7月31日　贵州构皮滩水电站首台机组（5号机组）顺利完成72h试运行，正式并网发电投入商业运行。构皮滩水电站是国家“十五”期间开工建设的大型水电工程项目及贵州西电东送的标志性工程，也是乌江流域水电开发规划中最大的水电站。

八　月

8月2日　巴山水电站第二台机组（1号机组）顺利投产发电。此前，2009年6月20日，电站首台机组（2号机组）投产发电。至此，电站两台机组已全部实现投产。巴山水电站位于重庆市城口县巴山镇境内任河干流，为引水式电站。电站拦河坝为我国首座高折线型钢筋混凝土面板堆石坝，最大坝高155m，坝顶长477m，其中折线段170.4m，水库正常蓄水位680m，总库容3.154亿m^3，总装机容量为2×7万kW，年平均发电量4.498亿kW·h。

8月5日　随着贵州乌江干流最大水电站——构皮滩水电站首台60万kW机组投产，中国华电集团公司的水电装机规模突破1000万kW。这标志着包括水电在内的清洁能源发电占到中国华电集团公司总装机容量的20%，电源结构进一步优化。

8月8日　我国第一座千万千瓦级风电示范基地——甘肃酒泉风电基地开工建设，标志着我国风电开始进入过渡化发展的新阶段。

8月10日　中国水力发电工程学会申报设立的“水力发电科学技术奖”通过中华人民共和国科学技术部审批，正式由国家科学技术奖励工作办公室颁发了相关登记证书。设立该奖项，是基于“潘家铮水电科技基金”成立后进一步提出的。“水力发电科学技术奖”从2010年起正式启动，实行一年一评。奖励范围及对象，面向全国水力发电行业。

8月15日　“福建电网新一代大规模跨流域水电站群智能调度系统”项目在福建省电力有限公司通过鉴定。专家认为，项目成果总体达到国际先进水平，其中的混合自适应智能模型算法、短期与实时调度的实用化建模技术达到国际领先水平。

8月21日　贵州构皮滩水电站第二台机组（4号机组）顺利完成72h试运行，正式投入商业运行。构皮滩水电站位于贵州省余庆县境内乌江干流河段，是乌江梯级水电开发的第七级电站，装机容量300万kW（5×60万kW），设计多年平均发电量96.67亿kW·h。

8月29日　长江三峡三期枢纽工程最后一次验收——正常蓄水175m水位验收获得通过，标志着三峡枢纽工程建设任务已按批准的初步设计全部完成，三峡工程可以全面发挥其巨大的综合效益。本次验收范围内的检查项目满足2009年汛后蓄水至175m水位的要求。

8月31日　海南戈枕枢纽工程2号机组正式并网发电，比合同工期提前7个月，标志着戈枕枢纽工程正式发挥供水、发电、防汛等综合效益。海南戈枕水利枢纽工程位于海南西部东方县和昌江县境内，是海南岛第二大河流昌化江干流3个梯级规划电站的最下游电站，总装机容量8万kW，2007年2月正式开工建设。

九　月

9月3日　三峡地下电站31号机组水轮机转轮到达三峡工地，并在三峡重件码头顺利下船。31号机转轮是三峡地下电站首台到货的水轮机转轮，由哈尔滨电机厂有限责任公司制造，最大外径10 600mm，总高5245mm，总质量约450t。

9月4日　中共中央政治局委员、全国政协副主席王刚率全国政协代表团到西藏电力有限公司林芝老虎嘴水电站建设工地考察、指导工作，西藏自治区党委常委、自治区政协副主席巴桑顿珠陪同考察。

9月9日　以“三峡工程社会生态环境效应”为主要内容的中国科学技术学会第十一届年会第八分会在重庆市举行。与会院士、专家和代表讨论并分析了三峡工程的生态环境效应，解答了社会各界的有关疑问。会议认为，三峡工程生态效益显著，相关区域生态环境总体良好。

9月11～12日　大自然保护协会（TNC）亚太理事会2009年年会在北京召开。来自亚太地区的商界以及中国国家发展改革委、外交部、环境保护部官员等约30人出席会议。大自然保护协会是世界上具有影响力的环保组织之一，在中国已有多个项目启动。其中，长江保护项目是其集全球资源重点实施的长期项目。

9月12日 国务院三峡工程建设委员会办公室副主任卢纯在重庆举行的三峡工程移民培训工作会上表示，截至目前三峡工程已累计搬迁移民127万人，移民搬迁安置任务基本完成，三峡移民工作正由大规模搬迁安置阶段转入“稳得住、能致富”新时期。经过17年的搬迁、建设，三峡工程已进入扫尾阶段，截至2009年6月底，已累计搬迁移民127万人，复建房屋4967万m^2，其中规划建房人口122万人，还建房屋4303万m^2，分别占规划的97%和98%。关破、迁建工矿企业1632家，其中关破1102家，工矿企业迁建任务全面完成。文物保护任务完成99%。工程淹没涉及的12座城市、县城和114座集镇已完成整体搬迁。库区基础设施有较大改善，库区面貌焕然一新。

9月15日 经国务院批准，按照国家防汛抗旱总指挥部和长江防汛抗旱总指挥部批复意见，三峡工程2009年175m试验性蓄水于9月15日凌晨启动。蓄水期间，每天水位涨幅不超过3m。2008年，根据国务院三峡工程建设委员会第十六次会议决定，三峡工程进行了首次试验性蓄水，最高水位达到172.8m。按设计规定，三峡工程最终蓄水位为175m。

9月15～18日 三峡枢纽工程质量检查专家组工作组成员到三峡工地进行调研，对三峡地下电站土建施工、金属结构埋件和升船机续建工程进行质量检查，同时了解三峡工程2009年试验性蓄水和度汛情况。工作组还将通过查阅相关资料、与参建各方展开专题座谈讨论，形成初步意见，供质量检查专家组参考。

9月18日 山西黄河龙口水利枢纽首台机组提前一年并网发电。黄河龙口水利枢纽位于山西省和内蒙古自治区的交界地带，总装机容量42万kW。

9月19日 国家水电可持续发展研究中心成立大会暨高层论坛在北京隆重召开。水利部部长陈雷出席大会开幕式并发表重要讲话，国家发展改革委副主任、国家能源局局长张国宝出席并讲话。为了推动水电可持续发展理论研究，提高环境友好型水电建设技术水平，加强水电建设的生态环境保护研究工作，实现在保持生态基础上有序开发水电的目标。国家能源局于2009年1月26日正式批复中国水利水电科学研究院成立国家水电可持续发展研究中心（国能局新能［2009］33号）。国家水电可持续发展研究中心的主要职责是：负责组织开展我国水电可持续发展的政策、法规及重大战略问题研究；组织开展水电可持续发展支撑理论和关键技术研究；组织开展水电可持续发展管理研究、技术推广、人才培养和宣传工作；为有关部门提供国内外水电发展最新资讯；完成主管部门下达的其他日常性工作。

9月22日 国家主席胡锦涛在联合国气候变化峰会上郑重表示，中国将进一步把应对气候变化纳入经济社会发展规划，并继续采取强有力的措施。他特别提出，大力发展可再生能源和核能，争取到2020年非化石能源占一次能源消费比重达到15%左右。

9月23日 国家发展改革委以发改办能源［2009］2012号文件复函河南省发展改革委、国家电网公司，同意河南天池抽水蓄能电站开展前期工作。河南天池抽水蓄能电站初拟装机容量120万kW，由国家电网公司全资建设。

9月24日 国家能源局新能源和可再生能源司在北京主持召开了俄罗斯水电站事故分析座谈会。俄罗斯萨彦—舒申斯克水电站安装10台单机容量640MW的混流式机组。据报道，2009年8月17日莫斯科时间4时13分，电站发生了严重灾难性事故。事故造成电站发电机层以下厂房淹没，至少74人死亡，1人失踪，电站2号、7号、9号机组完全损毁，主厂房部分机组的基础和风罩、桥机轨道大梁、厂房排柱、边墙、屋顶和地板等被摧毁，短期内难以恢复发电，停电损失难以估量。

9月25日 小湾水电站首台机组投产发电。小湾水电站位于云南省南涧县与凤庆县交界处，为澜沧江中下游河段规划梯级中的第二级，以发电为主，兼有防洪、灌溉、拦沙及航运等综合利用效益，电站坝高294.5m，库容150亿m^3，最大水头251m，边坡高700m，装机容量420万kW，单机容量70万kW，年发电量190亿kW·h，是国家重点工程和实施西部大开发、云南“云电外送”和“西电东送”的标志性工程。

9月27日 经国务院同意、国务院国资委和国家工商总局批准，中国长江三峡工程开发总公司正式更名为“中国长江三峡集团公司”。这标志着中国长江三峡工程开发总公司初步完成战略转型，迈入发展新阶段。

9月30日 在三峡坝区研究基地，中国长江三峡集团公司中华鲟研究所养殖的子一代中华鲟个体成功催产并授精。该研究由中华鲟研究所和水利部中国科学院水工程生态研究所研究人员联合攻关，历时4年，突破了人工驯养、性腺诱导和人工催产等一系列技术难关，取得了中华鲟全人工繁殖首次成功。该成果对中华鲟物种保护具有里程碑式的重要意义。

十　月

10月19～20日 由中国大坝协会、巴西大坝委员会联合举办的第一届堆石坝国际研讨会在成都召开。来自巴西、伊朗、日本、泰国、瑞典等 30 多个国家的 100 多名代表和 300 多位国内代表，围绕堆石坝的历史和发展趋势、案例和经验介绍、设计和分析、筑坝材料、施工、运行维护和安全监测以及抗震安全等议题进行了广泛研讨。国内外 12 座不同类型的堆石坝工程获得国际堆石坝里程碑工程奖。其中，中国的清江水布垭面板堆石坝、小浪底斜心墙堆石坝获“国际里程碑堆石坝工程”荣誉称号；都江堰的紫坪铺大坝因在 2008 年的汶川特大地震中经受住了 8 级强震的考验，在堆石坝抗震史上具有里程碑意义，获得国际堆石坝里程碑特别工程奖，这标志中国已经走在世界堆石坝建设前列。

10 月 21 日　宝泉抽水蓄能电站 2 号机组正式投入商业运行，该电站装设 4 台单机容量 30 万 kW 的立轴单级混流可逆式水泵水轮机发电机组。

10 月 23 日　金沙江溪洛渡、向家坝水电站机电设备安装与调试工程举行合同签字仪式。由此，金沙江溪洛渡、向家坝水电站进入机电设备安装阶段。标的为 6.7 亿元的溪洛渡、向家坝水电站机电设备安装与调试工程共分为溪洛渡水电站左岸电站机电设备安装与调试工程、溪洛渡水电站右岸电站机电设备安装与调试工程和向家坝水电站机电设备安装与调试工程，经过公开招标，分别由中国水利水电第八工程局有限公司、葛洲坝集团机电建设有限公司和中国水利水电第四工程局有限公司中标。

10 月 25 日　国网能源研究院成立，标志着国家电网公司在深化能源领域重大问题研究、促进电网与能源协调发展方面，迈出战略性一步。国网能源研究院是国家电网公司从事软科学研究及咨询服务的直属科研单位，定位为服务国家电网公司与行业发展的综合性能源研究智库和交流平台。该院在国网经济研究院已有的软科学研究力量的基础上组建而成，研究领域包括能源战略与规划研究、能源与电力供需研究、清洁能源发展研究、智能电网研究等。

10 月 27 日　中国水利工程协会印发了《关于颁发 2009 年中国水利工程优质（大禹）奖的决定》，小浪底工程名列其中，并排在十大获奖工程第一位。中国水利工程优质（大禹）奖是全国水利工程行业优质工程的最高奖项，旨在表彰工程质量优良、建设管理规范、效益发挥显著、社会影响较大的优秀工程。小浪底工程荣获中国水利工程优质（大禹）奖，充分体现了水利界同仁对小浪底工程建设质量和综合效益的高度肯定，也是工程建设者的巨大荣誉。

10 月 28 日　广西长洲水利枢纽内江 15 号机组顺利结束 72h 试运行，成功并网发电。至此，该电站 15 台机组全部投产发电。长洲水利枢纽位于广西壮族自治区梧州浔江下游河段与珠江西江交汇处，是一座以发电为主，兼有航运、灌溉和养殖为一体的低水头径流式大型水利枢纽工程，电站安装 15 台单机容量 4.2 万 kW 的贯流式水轮机组，总装机容量 63 万 kW，是我国装机总容量最大的贯流式机组群电站。

十　一　月

11 月 6 日　由中国水利水电科学研究院、中国长江三峡集团公司、长江委设计院共同承担完成的“三峡工程右岸电站计算机监控系统”项目，顺利通过水利部组织的科技成果鉴定。与会专家认为，该系统的总体技术水平达到了国际先进水平，在三网四层总体结构设计、自适应 AGC 频差系数控制技术、系统可靠性设计等方面居国际领先水平，代表了当今国际水电站计算机监控技术和应用的最高水平。

11 月 11～12 日　第三届中国工程管理论坛在成都召开。我国学术界、产业界和管理部门的 17 位院士和近 200 位代表参会。本次论坛以“西部大开发与工程管理”为主题，分别围绕“西部开发与灾后重建”、“工程哲学与重大工程管理”、“工程管理教育与工程管理信息化”等专题进行了深入探讨和交流。陆佑楣院士主持了论坛演讲，中国长江三峡集团公司副总经理樊启祥在论坛上作了题为《西部水电开发的项目管理》的演讲。

11 月 12～15 日　“中国水电可持续发展座谈会”在苏州召开。大会由中国水力发电工程学会主办，中国水电顾问集团华东勘测设计研究院和上海勘测设计研究院协办。会上一共有 20 余位领导和专家分别发表了专题发言，从不同的角度探讨了中国水电可持续发展这一重大问题，发表了看法，介绍了经验，分析了问题，提出了建议。

11 月 13 日　国家电监会印发了《跨省（区）电能交易监管办法（试行）》。该《办法》要求各电力企业开展跨省（区）电能交易时，要以市场为导向，坚持公开、透明和市场主体自愿的原则。

11 月 13 日　国家电监会印发了《电力用户与发电企业直接交易试点基本规则（试行）》。该《规则》从操作层面上对三部门联合印发的《关于完善电力用户与发电企业直接交易试点工作有关问题的通知》（以下简称 20 号文件）进行了细化，强调在 20 号文件规定的准入条件的基础上，直接交易双方在合同期内原则上不得退出直接交易，如需退出直接交易，由有关部门审核批准。

11 月 15 日　云南小湾水电站 2 号机组顺利完成 72h 试运行，顺利并网发电，提前实现 2009 年两台机组投产的目标。小湾水电站安装 6 台 70 万 kW 水轮发电机组。该机组于 2009 年 10 月 22 日进入充水试验，10月25日一次启动成功后进入动态调试，11月12日零点进入72h试运行。多项试验表明，其整机的安装质量达到了优良水平。

11月18日 四川华能宝兴水电站2号机组顺利完成72h试运行，正式投入商业运行，至此，该电站3台机组全部发电建成投产。宝兴水电站位于四川省宝兴县境内，属宝兴河流域水电站梯级开发的第三级，共安装3台6.5万kW混流式发电机组，总装机容量19.5万kW，年平均发电量8.74亿kW·h。截至2009年9月，电站3台机组同时进行调试，11月初均完成所有试验项目，具备72h试运行条件，并分别于2009年11月10日、15日、18日顺利完成1号、3号、2号机组72h试运行，机组各项参数优于规范要求，运行稳定。

11月18日 内蒙古呼和浩特抽水蓄能发电有限责任公司股东会第一次会议暨第一届董事会第一次会议和第一届监事会第一次会议在呼和浩特召开。这标志着由中国长江三峡集团公司投资控股的内蒙古呼和浩特抽水蓄能发电有限责任公司正式成立，呼和浩特抽水蓄能电站项目由此驶入规范运作轨道。

11月18～21日 国家电监会大坝安全监察中心、兰州监管办、大唐甘肃发电公司和西北勘测设计研究院组成检查组，对大唐碧口水力发电厂大坝开展安全特种检查，最终评定该水电站大坝为正常坝，具备安全注册换证条件。受“5·12”汶川大地震影响，碧口水电站大坝泄水建筑物启闭机室墙体出现裂缝或破坏，部分监测设施损坏，但坝坡稳定、渗流正常，坝址区边坡和近坝库岸基本稳定。震后，碧口水电厂全力开展恢复工作，投入大量资金和人力、物力，对震损建筑物分别采取了加固、拆除重建和修复等措施。

11月19日 国家发展改革委宣布，自2009年11月20日起全国非居民电价每千瓦时平均提高2.8分钱，暂不调整居民电价，未来居民用电将逐步推行阶梯式递增电价，用电越多电价越高。同时将可再生能源电价附加标准提高到每千瓦时0.4分钱，弥补了可再生能源电价补贴资金缺口。

11月19日 人民日报报道：国务院三峡工程建设委员会办公室目前正在组织编制、完善《三峡工程后续工作总体规划》，11月底有望报国务院审批。受国务院三峡工程建设委员会办公室委托，由水利部长江水利委员会牵头制定《三峡工程后续工作总体规划》。2009年10月，完成了各专项规划编制，并接受了中国国际工程咨询公司的评估，目前正在进一步修改。

11月25～26日 全国人大常委、环资委主任汪光焘率全国人大环境与资源保护委员会考察团调研三峡生态环境。考察团听取了湖北省和中国长江三峡集团公司有关三峡工程生态建设与环境保护的情况汇报。随后，与会人员围绕三峡工程对地方经济社会的影响、三峡工程生态建设与环境保护工作实施进展和存在的问题、对今后生态建设与环境保护工作有哪些建议等问题进行了讨论。

11月26日 哥本哈根国际气候峰会之前，中国正式对外宣布控制温室气体排放的行动目标，决定到2020年单位国内生产总值二氧化碳排放比2005年下降40%～45%。国务院总理温家宝在2009年11月25日主持召开的国务院常务会议还决定，这将作为约束性指标纳入国民经济和社会发展中长期规划，并制定相应的国内统计、监测、考核办法。

11月26日 国家电监会颁布《供电监管办法》。该办法将自2010年1月日起施行，2005年6月21日发布的《供电服务监管办法（试行）》同时废止。该办法旨在规范供电行为，维护供电市场秩序，保护电力使用者的合法权益和社会公共利益。《供电监管办法》共5章40条，对供电服务监管的目的、对象和原则，监管内容、监管措施以及罚则等作了明确规定。

十 二 月

12月1日 北盘江董箐水电站首台机组在成功完成72h试运行后，正式投入商业运行。董箐水电站位于贵州省镇宁县与贞丰县交界的北盘江上，为北盘江干流（茅口以下）梯级规划的第三个水电站，下游接龙滩水库库区。电站装机容量880MW（4×220MW），工程核准总投资69.63亿元，由贵州黔源电力股份有限公司控股开发。

12月4日 由《英才》杂志、北京青年报社、新浪网、中央电视台经济频道、北京电视台财经频道联合举办的2009（第九届）中国年度管理大会暨双十管理盛典在北京隆重举行。中国长江三峡集团公司在本次大会上荣获“双十具价值管理榜样”称号。大会授予中国长江三峡集团公司的获奖理由是：她是全球最大的水电公司，也是国际一流的清洁能源集团；中国长江三峡集团公司不断书写人类水利工程的伟大纪录。全国政协副主席张榕明为中国长江三峡集团公司颁奖。

12月7日 国家工程建设质量奖审定委员会发布2009年度国家优质工程表彰决定，5项金奖工程、146项银奖工程受到表彰。由黄河上游水电开发有限责任公司开发建设的公伯峡水电站再获殊荣，荣获“2009年度国家优质工程金质奖”。

12月8日 中国林业科学院湿地研究所所长、研究员崔丽娟在重庆市奉节县召开的“重庆三峡库区湿地生态系统定位研究站专家咨询会”上宣布：“三峡库区湿地生态系统定位研究站定在重庆市奉节县!”据介绍，在重庆建立三峡库区湿地生态系统定位研究站的意义重大，将为库区气候、水文水质、水生动植物、鸟类迁徙、土壤性状、消落带植物群变化、湿地沉积物等进行长期的科学研究，对推进库区生态体系建设具有重大的意义。

12月11日　贵州乌江思林水电站最后一台机组（1号机组）成功结束72h试运行，在不停机、不消缺的情况下直接投入商业运行。至此，思林水电站一年4台机组发电目标顺利实现。思林水电站是乌江干流的第六个梯级水电站，总装机容量为4×26.5万kW。2009年是思林水电站机电安装工程的冲刺年，分别于2009年5月28日、7月25日、9月19日如期实现前3台机组发电目标。

12月11日　溪洛渡水电站右岸电站首台机组（18号机组）基础环顺利吊装就位，标志着该工程已全面进入机组安装阶段。首台机组基础环分为两瓣，每瓣质量约为48.7t，总质量97.4t，组装后最大外径10 420mm，最小内径6320.2mm，总高度1799.5mm。

12月11日　国家发展改革委以发改能源［2009］3168号文件，核准安徽佛子岭抽水蓄能电站项目。佛子岭抽水蓄能电站位于安徽省霍山县境内，安装2台8万kW的混流可逆式机组，总装机容量16万kW，电站枢纽由已建的上、下水库以及新建的过渡性下库、输水系统、地下厂房和开关站等组成。

12月13日　瀑布沟水电站首台机组（6号机组）顺利通过72h试运行，成功投产发电，正式进入商业运行。瀑布沟水电站作为国家“十五”重点建设项目，也是四川省灾后重建中的最大水电工程。电站坝址位于大渡河中游四川省汉源县和甘洛县境内，水库总库容53.9亿m^3，具有不完全年调节能力，装机容量经优化调整后为360万kW，共6台机组，单机容量60万kW，多年平均发电量145.85亿kW·h，是一座以发电为主，兼有防洪、拦沙等综合效益的大型水电工程。该工程于2004年开工。

12月14日　《中国三峡工程报》报道：800kV气体绝缘输电线路（GIL）工程设计专题研究项目近日通过了由青海省科技厅组织的科技成果评价，从而在国内首次实现了水力发电工程领域高电压和高落差垂直竖井敷设。这项研究中采用的额定电压和传输容量均走在国际前列，在国内率先解决了207m高落差竖井气体绝缘输电线路的安装方式，成果达到了国际领先水平。

12月16日　广西桥巩水电站最后一台机组，在顺利完成72h试运行后投入商业运营。至此，该电站8台全国单机容量最大的灯泡贯流式水轮发电机组全部实现投产发电。桥巩水电站是红水河流域梯级开发规划建设的第九级电站，总装机容量45.6万kW，安装8台单机容量5.7万kW的灯泡贯流式水轮发电机组，单机容量为同类型机组中国第一、亚洲第二。

12月17日　广东清远抽水蓄能电站主体工程开工仪式隆重举行。该电站位于珠江三角洲西北部清远市清新县太平镇境内，距广州市直线距离为75km。电站设计安装4台32万kW立轴单级可逆混流式机组，总装机容量128万kW，设计年发电量23.316亿kW·h。工程概算动态投资49.9亿元，由中国南方电网有限责任公司全额投资，南方电网调峰调频发电公司负责建设。计划2015年第一季度第一台机组发电，2015年电站建设完工。

12月18日　国家电网计量中心在北京举行揭牌仪式，标志着国家电网计量中心正式投运，国家电网公司集团化运作的一项重要内容——“四基地两中心”建设全面完成。国家电网计量中心的正式投运，为国家电网公司电力计量技术的发展奠定了基础，并大大提升了国家电网公司在量值传递、计量检定等计量技术领域的试验研究能力。

12月18日　华能戈枕水利枢纽工程4号机组正式并网发电。至此，华能戈枕水利枢纽工程提前10个月全面投产。华能戈枕枢纽工程由华能海南公司投资9亿多元建设，是海南省“十一五”期间重点工程——大广坝水利水电二期（灌区）工程的核心工程，包括高32m、长1092m的大坝，装机容量8.2万kW的水电厂及水库等核心部分。工程于2007年初开工。

12月21日　由潘家铮水电科技基金管理委员会主办、河海大学承办的“首届潘家铮水电奖学金颁奖典礼”在河海大学隆重举行。39位热爱祖国水利水电事业、品学兼优、勇于创新的本科生和研究生获奖。潘家铮水电科技基金以著名水电水利专家、中国科学院和中国工程院两院院士潘家铮先生名字命名，是一项由中国水力发电工程学会和中国水电工程顾问集团公司联合倡议发起，全国水电水利系统42家企事业单位捐赠成立的旨在促进水电科技创新和人才培养的公益性专项基金。潘家铮基金的宗旨是：贯彻落实科学发展观，弘扬新中国水电科技工作者的创新精神，支持水电科研创新，奖励水电创新人才，建设创新型国家。

12月22日　金沙江中游流域环保监测管理中心成立揭牌仪式在昆明隆重举行。这是国内成立的首个流域开发环保监测管理机构，是云南金沙江中游水电开发有限公司站在国家生态安全和流域开发可持续发展的高度，积极创建环保文化，为流域环保工作搭建的多层次、全方位的工作平台，对加强流域生态环境保护，促进流域开发与滇西北生物多样性保护的和谐发展具有重要意义。

12月24日 世界第一个±800kV特高压直流输电工程——云南—广东特高压直流输电工程单极800kV成功送电，树立起世界直流输电领域新的里程碑。

12月24～27日 中国工程院“中国能源中长期发展战略研究咨询项目组”在三峡工地召开研讨会议。有关专家在讨论中提出，水电是清洁、低碳和经济性好的绿色能源，是我国最具有资源优势的优质能源，在我国能源中长期发展战略中，要坚定不移地优先发展水电，使水电进一步成为绿色能源支柱。

12月25日 中国电力企业联合会第五次全国会员代表大会暨第五届理事会第一次会议在北京召开。会议听取并审议通过了由第四届理事会常务副理事长谢振华所作的工作报告，审议通过了修订后的《中国电力企业联合会章程》等，进一步完善了工作制度。会议通过民主选举产生了中国电力企业联合会第五届理事会。国家电网公司总经理刘振亚任理事会理事长，孙玉才任常务副理事长，魏昭峰任专职副理事长，袁懋振、曹培玺、翟若愚、云公民、朱永芃、陆启洲、孙勤、李永安、张喜武、王炳华、钱智民、潘力、吴国潮任副理事长，王志轩任秘书长。

12月26日 由我国自主设计、自主建设的向—上线奉贤换流站极Ⅰ直流系统和直流线路成功升压至800kV。这标志着由国家电网公司负责建设的世界上输送容量最大、送电距离最远、技术水平最先进、电压等级最高的向家坝—上海±800kV特高压直流输电线路全线带电成功。

12月26日 十一届全国人大常委会第十二次会议表决通过关于修改可再生能源法的决定，新的可再生能源法将自2010年4月1日起施行。

12月27日 全国能源工作会议在北京召开。国家能源局局长张国宝在开幕式上再次强调，2010年我国将大力发展可再生能源和核能，争取非化石能源占一次能源消费比重比2008年提高0.5个百分点左右。2010年国家将合理开发水电，继续抓好溪洛渡、向家坝、锦屏一二级、瀑布沟等在建大型水电站的建设工作，处理好金沙江中游、澜沧江流域水电站的前期及项目核准工作。

12月28日 构皮滩水电站最后一台机组顺利完成72h试运行，正式投产发电。该电站是乌江水电梯级开发规划中最大的水电站，总装机容量300万kW，由5台60万kW水轮发电机组组成，年均发电量97亿kW·h，2003年11月正式开工。2009年7月31日、8月21日、11月22日、12月22日，电站其他4台机组相继投产发电。在一年的时间里，成功实现了5台大型机组全部投产发电目标。

12月28日 宝鸡—德阳±500kV直流输电工程投产仪式在四川德阳举行。该工程的投运，增强了西北和华中两大电网的电力交换能力，提高了区域电网的安全运行水平，增强了抵御重大电网事故的能力，对促进资源节约型和环境友好型社会建设具有重要意义。

12月29日 蜀河水电站首台机组顺利完成72h试运行后，正式投产发电。该电站位于旬阳县境内的汉江干流上，是汉江上游梯级开发规划中的第六个梯级电站，是陕西省“十一五”重点建设项目。该电站以发电为主，兼顾防洪、航运，总装机容量27.6万kW，年平均发电量9.53亿kW·h。

12月29日 由中国长江三峡集团公司主办的水库温室气体研究进展研讨会在湖北宜昌召开。中国科学院、中国水电科学研究院、长江科学院等科研院所和北京师范大学、重庆大学、上海大学、三峡大学等院校的十余位专家汇报了三峡水库和其他西南水库温室气体研究课题的最新进展，并进行了深入的交流和讨论。这些平行、交叉的实证研究，不仅可以加深对三峡水库干支流、大坝及下游河道温室气体汇源问题的科学认知，也能够从温室气体排放的机理上更进一步向社会公众客观地解答为什么水电是绿色能源，澄清反坝宣传对水电清洁性的质疑。

12月29日 日新（无锡）机电公司研制的特高压交流气体绝缘全封闭组合电器（GIS）用电磁式电压互感器在湖北武汉通过了全部型式试验。此前两周，国网电力科学研究院研制的1000kV电容式电压互感器已通过型式试验。这两种产品均为世界首次研制，代表了国际高压电压互感器技术的最高水平。1000kV晋东南—南阳—荆门特高压交流试验示范工程，采用了敞开式的电压互感器。为进一步压缩特高压交流GIS变电站的占地面积，实现紧凑型设计，国家电网公司在2009年启动了特高压交流GIS用电压互感器（简称罐式电压互感器）的研制工作，以满足后续特高压交流工程的迫切需要。

（本年鉴编辑部）